CLIMBERS ON *FREEDOM*:

"It is fair to say that *Freedom* is the definitive guide to mountains and climbing."
—Conrad Anker

"Not long after I learned to read, I would grip the flashlight in my teeth and stay awake late into the night scouring my parent's copy of the 3rd edition of *Freedom of the Hills*. . . . What this book captured, what it meant, what it hinted at that was so crucial to my fascination with mountaineering was this: Freedom, itself, was the most important thing. Freedom to explore who I am. Freedom afforded by learned skills to explore any mountain wilderness. Freedom to move, to climb. It's what still drives me today."
—Steve House

"*Freedom* is truly the Everest of mountaineering texts and a great preparation for a life wandering among high hills, including the big one itself."
—Tom Hornbein

"Growing up in Southern California in the 1960s, I couldn't find anyone who shared my passion to learn how to climb. So I bought an ice axe, crampons, and *Freedom of the Hills* and still remember being on a snow slope with axe in one hand, book in the other, trying to teach myself how to self-arrest. It worked: I'm still around and still climbing."
—Rick Ridgeway

"For many generations of climbers, *The Freedom of the Hills* is more than just a book. It's a passport to a rare and wild place."
—Andrew Bisharat

"I have never felt more alive than when adventuring in remote mountains, dependent on a rope, a rack, and the partner that's got my back. . . . *Freedom of the Hills*, risk's best friend, is that partner."
—Timmy O'Neill

"In my early years of heading into the mountains I used *Freedom of the Hills* to learn how to calculate fuel needs for the backcountry, to study crevasse rescue, and in general to just muse about the alpine craft. Everyone should have a copy of this standard tome."
—Kit DesLauriers

"There is no substitute for learning to climb from a skilled and tested mentor. . . . But sometimes it's nice to learn key skills at your own pace from the comfort of your own kitchen table. . . . For those times, there is no better book than the Mountaineers' *Freedom of the Hills*."
—Bree Loewen

"The lessons I learned in the Mountaineers climbing course in 1945 stood me on the summit of Mount Everest in 1963. To see that knowledge put into a book was wonderful. That it has evolved into the best book on climbing, updated by active climbers, is remarkable. I have told many people, including my sons, 'If you want to climb mountains, read *Mountaineering: The Freedom of the Hills*. Then read it again so you know, for sure, how to get down.'"
—Jim Whittaker

"As chief guide for Rainier Mountaineering for over 30 years, I have trained hundreds of new guides. And *Freedom of the Hills* is the required textbook for their basic training on Mount Rainier."
—Lou Whittaker

"The 2nd edition of *Freedom of the Hills* jump-started my climbing education. The manual's content has kept pace with the evolution of the sport and should be considered mandatory reading for every mountain climber. This truly remarkable resource has no equal in any language."
—Mark Twight

"A notorious reference for climbers and outdoor enthusiasts!"
—Lynn Hill

"*Freedom* does a remarkable job of staying not just current, but on the cutting edge. Turning on new climbers to this resource is one of the best things I can do to prepare them for life in the big hills."
—Dave Hahn

"If the mountains are my church, then *Freedom* is my bible. . . . As a very young climber I read it cover to cover, then dug through it again and again for nuggets of wisdom. I still do."
—Will Gadd

"A 'must have' for any aspiring mountaineer's library."
—Ed Viesturs

MOUNTAINEERING

The Freedom of the Hills

MOUNTAINEERING

The Freedom of the Hills

**EDITED BY ERIC LINXWEILER
AND MIKE MAUDE**

**MOUNTAINEERS
BOOKS**

MOUNTAINEERS BOOKS is the publishing division of The Mountaineers, an organization founded in 1906 and dedicated to the exploration, preservation, and enjoyment of outdoor and wilderness areas.

1001 SW Klickitat Way, Suite 201, Seattle, WA 98134
800.553.4453, www.mountaineersbooks.org

Printed in Canada
Distributed in the United Kingdom by Cordee,
www.cordee.co.uk

First edition, 1960. Second edition, 1967. Third edition, 1974. Fourth edition, 1982. Fifth edition, 1992. Sixth edition, 1997. Seventh edition, 2003. Eighth edition, 2010. Ninth edition, 2017.

Project editor: Laura Shauger
Developmental editor: Kris Fulsaas
Copyeditor: Erin Moore
Design and layout: Jennifer Shontz
Illustrator: John McMullen
Cover design: Jen Grable
Chapter opener illustrations: Heidi Smets
Index: Rich Carlson

Cover photographs: front: Conrad Anker climbs across a ridgetop near Ama Dablam, Khumbu Valley, Nepal. (*Photo © Jimmy Chin*); spine: A climber works her way up a route in Joshua Tree National Park. (*Photo by Aurora Photos/Kyle Sparks*); back: Climbers balance on a narrow moutain ridge in Switzerland. (*Photo by iStock/dominikmichalek*)

Interior photographs: p. 4: A group of mountaineers head up Aiguille du Midi, Mont Blanc. (*Photo by iStock/glogowski*); p. 8: A climber concentrates on a frozen waterfall. (*Photo by iStock/AlexSava*); p. 13: Basecamp with a view (*Photo by iStock/Lysogor*); p. 149: A few quickdraws and a rope—some of the equipment rock climbers use (*Photo by iStock/abstudio annaburek*); p. 223: A lead climber focuses on her next move in a crack. (*Photo by iStock/ericfoltz*); p. 329: A climbing party ascends a snow-covered slope. (*Photo by iStock/Georgijevic*); p. 479: A leader breaks trail on a snowy ridge. (*Photo by iStock/rcaucino*); p. 539: View from the summit of Mont Blanc (*Photo by iStock/MaRabelo*)

Library of Congress Cataloging-in-Publication Data
Names: Mountaineers (Society)
Title: Mountaineering: the freedom of the hills / the Mountaineers.
Description: Ninth edition. | Seattle, Washington: Mountaineers Books, [2017] | "Eighth edition, 2010"==T.p. verso. | Includes bibliographical references and index.
Identifiers: LCCN 2017018860 (print) | LCCN 2017022769 (ebook) | ISBN 9781680510058 () | ISBN 9781680510034 (hardcover) | ISBN 9781680510041 (paperback) | ISBN 9781680510058 (ebook)
Subjects: LCSH: Mountaineering. | Rock climbing. | Snow and ice climbing.
Classification: LCC GV200 (ebook) | LCC GV200 .M688 2017 (print) | DDC 796.522—dc23
LC record available at *https://lccn.loc.gov/2017018860*

Mountaineers Books titles may be purchased for corporate, educational, or other promotional sales, and our authors are available for a wide range of events. For information on special discounts or booking an author, contact our customer service at 800-553-4453 or mbooks@mountaineersbooks.org.

♻ Printed on 100% recycled paper

ISBN (hardcover): 978-1-68051-003-4
ISBN (paperback): 978-1-68051-004-1
ISBN (ebook): 978-1-68051-005-8

MIX
Paper from
responsible sources
FSC
www.fsc.org   FSC® C016245

CONTENTS

PREFACE

"The quest of the mountaineer, in simplest terms, is for the freedom of the hills. . . ."

—The first line of the first edition

Mountaineering: The Freedom of the Hills is much more than a book—it is a gateway to experiencing the joy of the outdoors. Whether you want to learn to camp and cook outdoors, hike in your local forest, climb hills, cross glaciers, scale rock walls, or summit the world's highest peaks, *Freedom* is for you. Welcome to the community of climbers and mountaineers who count on *Freedom* as a critical part of their outdoor education.

For this ninth edition in *Freedom*'s seven-decade history, each chapter has been critically reviewed, revised, and—where necessary—expanded. All illustrations have been updated, and most have been completely redrawn, allowing for fantastic detail in both printed and electronic media. These revisions reflect the ongoing rapid changes in mountaineering, including the development of safer techniques and improved equipment. In this edition, we continue to emphasize the responsibility we assume as climbers to practice good stewardship and to minimize our impact on the lands we pass through in order to leave no trace of our passage. In addition to leveraging the collective knowledge of The Mountaineers, this edition had unprecedented access to and input from experienced guides, organizations that teach climbing and avalanche safety, elite climbers, and outdoor equipment manufacturers.

Whether this is your first copy of *Freedom* or you own every edition, this book offers the skills, confidence, and knowledge you need to be a safe, competent mountaineer.

SCOPE OF THE BOOK

As did previous editions, the ninth edition of *Freedom* soundly covers the current concepts, techniques, and problems involved in the pursuit of mountaineering, and helps climbers grasp a fundamental understanding of each topic covered. In addition to informing the novice, this book can help experienced climbers review and improve their skills. Coverage of some topics, such as rock climbing, ice climbing, and aid climbing, is detailed enough to be useful to readers interested in those specific topics.

This book is not intended, however, to be exhaustive. Some climbing disciplines are not comprehensively addressed in these pages. Gym and sport climbing (making use of artificial climbing walls or fixed-protection routes at developed climbing areas), for example, have become increasingly popular. Although many techniques related to both disciplines are interchangeable with those of mountain and rock climbing, there are differences—not all of which are discussed in these pages.

Mountaineering cannot be learned simply by studying a book. However, books can be an important source of information and can complement solid instruction. *Freedom* was originally written as a textbook for students and instructors participating in organized climbing courses. The learning environment in a climbing course taught by competent instructors is essential for beginning climbers.

Climbing requires continual situational and environmental awareness. Conditions, routes, and individual abilities and skills vary, and the individual climber and climbing team must apply their knowledge, skills, and experience to the circumstances before them and then decide how they will proceed. To reflect this process, *Freedom* presents a variety of widely used techniques and practices, and then outlines both their advantages and limitations. Material is presented not as dogma or the definitive word but as the basis for making sound decisions. To adventure safely, climbers must realize that mountaineering is about problem-solving, not merely applying techniques.

The type of climbing described in this tome is frequently experienced—and many people would say, best experienced—in the wilderness. Wilderness mountaineers take responsibility for helping to preserve the wilderness environment for present and future generations. Preserving wilderness is crucial to protecting the health of our ecosystem.

ORIGINS OF THE BOOK

A synopsis of *Freedom*'s evolution presents a capsule history of The Mountaineers. From its beginnings, *Freedom* has been the product of the concerted effort of a team of volunteer leaders. For each edition, the team of contributors has sprung forth from across the organization's membership, representing the best the organization has to offer. It has always been an honor to work on this project.

When The Mountaineers was founded in 1906, one of its major purposes was to explore and study the mountains, forests, and waterways of the Pacific Northwest. *Freedom*'s direction and emphasis originated from the nature of climbing in this region. The wild, complex character of these particular mountains, with their abundance of snow and glaciers throughout the year, furthered the mountaineering challenge. Access was inherently difficult. There were few roads, the terrain was rugged, and initial explorations of them were essentially expeditions, often requiring the assistance of Native American guides.

As interest in mountaineering grew in the region, so did a tradition of, and commitment to, education. Increasingly, experienced climbers took novices under their wings to pass on their knowledge and skills. The Mountaineers formalized that exchange by developing a series of climbing courses.

Prior to the publication of the first edition of *Freedom* in 1960, The Mountaineers climbing courses had used a number of European textbooks, particularly Geoffrey Winthrop Young's classic *Mountain Craft*. These books, however, did not cover the various subjects unique and important to American and Pacific Northwest mountaineering. To fill the gaps, course lecturers prepared outlines, which they distributed to students. First fleshed out and compiled as the *Climber's Notebook*, these outlines were subsequently published as the *Mountaineers Handbook*. By 1955, the tools and techniques had changed so drastically, and the climbing courses had become so much more complex, that a new, more comprehensive textbook was needed.

The first edition of *Freedom* was published in 1960 (work on it had begun in 1955), with an eight-person editorial committee coordinating the efforts of more than seventy-five contributors. Chief editor Harvey Manning was the primary individual responsible for establishing the scope of the book. It was his idea to add the distinctive subtitle "The Freedom of the Hills." An outgrowth of more than a century of teaching mountaineering, the first edition of *Freedom* included 430 pages, 134 illustrations, and 16 black-and-white plates organized into 22 chapters. In comparison, this ninth edition features 608 pages, more than 400 illustrations, and more than a half dozen black-and-white photos organized into 27 chapters.

LEGACY OF THE PRECEDING EDITIONS

This book embodies the collective wisdom and experience of thousands of climbers and mountaineers. The previous editions of *Freedom* represent a tradition of compiling, sorting, and integrating the knowledge, techniques, opinions, and advice of many practicing climbers. Both in training sessions and on climbs, students have always been a pivotal sounding board and testing ground for advancements in techniques, equipment, and methods. Each new edition has been carefully built on the foundation of the preceding editions.

The first edition editorial committee included Harvey Manning (chair), John R. Hazle, Carl Henrikson, Nancy Bickford Miller, Thomas Miller, Franz Mohling, Rowland Tabor, and Lesley Stark Tabor. A substantial portion of the then relatively small Puget Sound climbing community participated (including such mountaineering icons as Dee Molenaar, Jim and Lou Whittaker, and Wolf Bauer)—some seventy-five were writers of the preliminary, revised, advanced, semifinal, and final chapter drafts, and an additional one hundred to two hundred were reviewers, planners, illustrators, typists, proofreaders, financiers, promoters, retailers, warehouse workers, and shipping clerks. In fact, most Mountaineers climbers were involved somehow with the book. Those members donating their time and effort were rewarded by how well the book was received, and those donating their money were repaid from the success of the book. *Freedom* became the first title published by the now very productive Mountaineers Books.

The second edition revision committee included John M. Davis (chair), Tom Hallstaff, Max Hollenbeck, Jim Mitchell, Roger Neubauer, and Howard Stansbury. Work on the second edition began in 1964. Even though much of the first edition was retained, the task force was, again, of impressive proportions, numbering several dozen writers and uncounted reviewers and helpers. Members of the first committee, notably John R. Hazle, Thomas Miller, and Harvey Manning, provided continuity to the effort. As with the first edition, Harvey Manning once again edited the entire text and supervised production. The second edition was published in 1967.

The third edition revision committee, which was formed in 1971, included Sam Fry (chair), Fred Hart, Sean Rice, Jim Sanford, and Howard Stansbury. Initially, the planning committee analyzed the previous edition and set guidelines for its revision. Once again, many climbers contributed to individual chapters; the reviewing, revising, editing, and collation of chapters and sections were a true community effort. Peggy Ferber edited the entire book, which was published in 1974.

The fourth edition revision committee included Ed Peters (chair), Roger Andersen, Dave Anthony, Dave Enfield, Lee Helser, Robert Swanson, and John Young. Published in 1982, this edition of *Freedom* involved a major revision and included complete rewrites of many chapters, most notably the entire section on ice and snow. A team of hundreds was guided by the revision committee: numerous climbers submitted comments to the committee, and small teams of writers prepared a series of drafts for review by the technical editors. In addition to the substantial contribution such writers made, many others provided valuable help through critiques of subsequent and final drafts, not only for technical accuracy and consistency, but also for readability and comprehension.

The fifth edition revision committee, which was chaired first by Paul Gauthier and later by Myrna Plum, included section coordinators Marty Lentz, Margaret Miller, Judy Ramberg, and Craig Rowley, and editorial coordinator Ben Arp. Work on the fifth edition began in late 1987, involved another major revision, and was published in 1992. Content was brought up to date, and the layout and illustrations were made more contemporary and readable. Professional editor and writer Don Graydon blended the volunteers' efforts into a consistent, approachable style.

The sixth edition revision committee included Kurt Hanson (chair), Jo Backus, Marcia Hanson, Tom Hodgman, Myrna Plum, and Myron Young. Don Heck coordinated the illustrations, while Don Graydon again edited the text. The committee began work in the autumn of 1994 and the sixth edition was published in 1997. Three new chapters were added: "Mountain Geology," "The Cycle of Snow," and "Mountain Weather."

The seventh edition revision committee included Steven M. Cox (chair), Ron Eng, Jeremy Larson, Myrna Plum, Cebe Wallace, John Wick, and John Wickham. Jeff Bowman and Debra Wick oversaw the preparation of the illustration materials. Kris Fulsaas edited the text. Planning for the seventh edition began in autumn of 2000, and the book was published in 2003. It included a new chapter, "Waterfall Ice and Mixed Climbing," and many new illustrations.

The eighth edition celebrated 50 years of *Freedom*. Its revision committee included Ron Eng (chair), Peter Clitherow, Dale Flynn, Mindy Roberts, Mike Maude, John Wick, and Gretchen Lentz. Jeff Bowman oversaw the preparation of the illustration materials. The staff of Mountaineers Books, particularly project editor Mary Metz, freelance editors Julie Van Pelt and Kris Fulsaas, and illustrators Marge Mueller and Dennis Arneson, also contributed their time and talents.

CONTRIBUTORS TO THE NINTH EDITION

Over the course of its 110-year history, The Mountaineers has taken pride in its volunteer spirit of getting people outside through both exploration and education. Through the organization's efforts, countless people have been introduced to the outdoors and then, as volunteers, have found ways to give back to our collective community. The contributors to this ninth edition, listed below, are a special group of our volunteers, who selflessly gave of their time, intellect, and expertise to help make this new edition possible. What you hold in your hands represents more than simply what one or two (or twenty) people could put down on paper. It is, rather, the collective knowledge of an organization that, for more than a century, has been dedicated to celebrating and sharing the freedom of the hills.

PREFACE

Cochairs, 9th Edition: Eric Linxweiler, Mike Maude

Part I: Outdoor Fundamentals: John Ohlson (Chair)

Chapter 1: First Steps: John Ohlson

Chapter 2: Clothing and Equipment: Steve McClure

Chapter 3: Camping, Food, and Water: Steve McClure

Chapter 4: Physical Conditioning: Courtenay Schurman

Chapter 5: Navigation: Bob Burns, Mike Burns, John Bell, Steve McClure

Chapter 6: Wilderness Travel: Helen Arntson

Chapter 7: Leave No Trace: Katherine Hollis and Peter Dunau

Chapter 8: Access and Stewardship: Katherine Hollis and Tania Lown-Hecht

Part II: Climbing Fundamentals: Cebe Wallace (Chair)

Chapter 9: Basic Safety System: Erica Cline

Chapter 10: Belaying: Deling Ren, Yinan Zhao

Chapter 11: Rappelling: Alex Byrne

Part III: Rock Climbing: Loni Uchytil (Chair)

Chapter 12: Alpine Rock Climbing: Loni Uchytil

Chapter 13: Rock Protection: Loni Uchytil

Chapter 14: Leading on Rock: Loni Uchytil

Chapter 15: Aid and Big Wall Climbing: Holly Webb and Jeff Bowman

Part IV: Snow, Ice, and Expedition Climbing: Anita Wilkins (Chair)

Chapter 16: Snow Travel and Climbing: Tab Wilkins

Chapter 17: Avalanche Safety: Nick Lyle

Chapter 18: Glacier Travel and Crevasse Rescue: Anita Wilkins, Gregg Gagliardi, Steve Swenson, and Mike Maude

Chapter 19: Alpine Ice Climbing: Anita Wilkins, Gregg Gagliardi, Steve Swenson, and Mike Maude

Chapter 20: Waterfall Ice and Mixed Climbing: Anita Wilkins, Gregg Gagliardi, Steve Swenson, and Mike Maude

Chapter 21: Expedition Climbing: Jenn Carter

Part V: Leadership, Safety, and Rescue: Doug Sanders (Chair)

Chapter 22: Leadership: Doug Sanders

Chapter 23: Safety: Doug Sanders

Chapter 24: First Aid: Doug Sanders, Eric Linxweiler

Chapter 25: Alpine Rescue: Doug Sanders

Part VI: The Mountain Environment: Eric Linxweiler (Chair)

Chapter 26: Mountain Geology: Scott Babcock

Chapter 27: The Cycle of Snow: Sue Ferguson

Chapter 28: Mountain Weather: Jeff Renner

Several other professionals played noteworthy roles in the book's development and production process, particularly staff and contractors affiliated with Mountaineers Books. Managing editor Margaret Sullivan laid the groundwork for the revisions. Jeff Bowman played a crucial role in the early stages of illustration evaluation and notes. Kris Fulsaas deftly performed a developmental edit, and Erin Moore skillfully copyedited the materials.

Production manager Jen Grable designed the covers and managed the book design and illustration process. Jennifer Shontz refined the book design and pieced together the puzzle that is text and illustrations. John McMullen expertly tackled the monumental task of vectorizing all the existing figures and of drawing many illustrations from scratch, as well as editing much of the existing artwork; his deep climbing knowledge informed his work. Editor Laura Shauger kept the project moving forward from rough draft on, despite the inevitable hurdles.

For help with the significant updates to the clothing and equipment and camping and food chapters, contributors wish to thank individuals at several companies for their technical assistance: Owen Mesdag and Zac Gleason at MSR; Jim Boswell, Jim Giblin, and Brandon Bowers at Therm-a-Rest; the crew at Outdoor Research; and Brant Broome at REI.

Thank you to the following individuals for their contributions to this project: Dale Remsberg, Ronnie Parker, Ron Funderburke, Matt Schonwald, Jim Nelson, Wayne Wallace, and Mike Libecki.

This tome will introduce you to the skills and knowledge you need to embark on adventures for a lifetime. Absorb these instructions and wise tips, study the technical illustrations, and then go out into the hills to practice and see where it all can take you.

PART I

OUTDOOR FUNDAMENTALS

CHAPTER 1

FIRST STEPS

Mountaineering is many things: climbing, breathtaking views, and wilderness experience. It can be the fulfillment of childhood dreams or an opportunity to grow in the face of difficulty. Mountains harbor adventure and mystery. The challenge of mountaineering offers you a chance to learn about yourself by venturing beyond the confines of the modern world and to forge lifetime bonds with climbing partners.

In the words of British climber George Leigh Mallory, "What we get from this adventure is just sheer joy." To be sure, you will also find risk and hardship, but despite the difficulties climbers sometimes face—or maybe because of them—mountaineering can provide a sense of tranquility and spiritual communion found nowhere else. But before you find joy or freedom in the hills, you must prepare for the mountains by learning technical, physical, mental, and emotional skills. Just as you must take a first step in order to climb a mountain, you must also take first steps to become a mountaineer. And though becoming skilled in the mountains is a process that continues as long as you spend time there, you have to begin somewhere. This book can serve as your guide and reference in acquiring those skills and, as such, your passport to the freedom of the hills.

TECHNICAL KNOWLEDGE AND SKILLS

To travel safely and enjoyably in the mountains, you need skills. You need to know what clothing, basic equipment, and food to bring into the backcountry and how to spend the night outside safely. You need to know how to cover long distances while relying on only what you carry in your pack, navigating without trails or signs. You need technical climbing skills, including belaying (the technique of securing your rope partner in case of a fall) and rappelling (using the rope to descend), to competently scale and descend the mountains you reach. And you must have the specific skills for the terrain you choose—whether it is rock, snow, ice, or glacier. Mountaineers strive to minimize risks, but mountain travel can never be completely predictable. Thus, every mountaineer should be trained in safety, wilderness first aid, and rescue with the goal of becoming truly self-reliant.

PHYSICAL PREPARATION

Mountaineering is a physically demanding activity. Nearly every type of climbing has become increasingly athletic, especially at the higher levels of difficulty. Climbers today accomplish feats that were once considered impossible. In rock, ice, and high-altitude climbing, new standards are set regularly. Limits are being pushed not only on the way up peaks but also on the way down. Steep routes once considered difficult or impossible to ascend are now also descended on skis and snowboards. Among the changes to the landscape of climbing, notable are the advances in and increasing popularity of steep ice climbing and "mixed" climbs, those that include a combination of rock and frozen water. Although most people appreciate such extreme achievements from the sidelines, higher standards at these maximal performance levels of climbing often result in increased standards at all levels.

Whatever your skill level and aspiration, good physical conditioning is critically important. The stronger you are, the better prepared you will be to face the challenges of climbing mountains, whether your outing goes as planned or includes unexpected difficulties. You will have a wider choice of mountains to climb, and you will be more likely to enjoy trips rather than to simply endure them. More important, the safety of the whole party may hinge on the strength—or weakness—of one member.

MENTAL PREPARATION

Just as important as physical conditioning is mental attitude, which often determines success or failure in mountaineering. The ability to keep a clear, calm mind helps in everything from deciding whether to stay home because of a weather forecast to pushing through a difficult technical climbing move or rescuing a climbing partner after a crevasse fall. Mountaineers need to be positive, realistic, and honest with themselves. A can-do attitude may turn into dangerous overconfidence if it is not tempered with a judicious appraisal of the circumstances and environment.

Many a veteran mountaineer says the greatest challenges are mental. Perhaps this is one of mountaineering's biggest appeals: while seeking the freedom of the hills, we come face-to-face with ourselves.

JUDGMENT AND EXPERIENCE

Essential to mountaineering is the ability to solve problems and make good decisions. Sound judgment, perhaps a mountaineer's most valued and prized skill, develops from integrating knowledge with experience. This book outlines equipment and techniques ranging from the basic to the advanced, but the goal of every mountaineer is to determine how best to use that learning to answer the sometimes unpredictable challenges faced in the mountains.

Much of what mountaineers need are coping skills and problem-solving skills—the ability to deal with external factors such as adverse weather, long hikes, and mountain accidents, as well as internal factors including fear, exhaustion, and desire. As climbers experience challenging situations, they become better decision makers, gaining judgment and experience that can help them in the future.

Mountaineering, however, tends to provide many new situations that require careful judgment rather than automatic responses. Although you may use past experience to make decisions in the mountains, you will never face the same exact situation twice. To be sure, this uncertainty can be scary, but it also creates the allure and challenge of mountaineering.

Many situations similarly involve risk, challenge, and accomplishment. As Helen Keller observed in 1957 in *The Open Door*, "Security is mostly a superstition. It does not exist in nature, nor do the children of men as a whole experience it. Avoiding danger is no safer in the long run than outright exposure. Life is either a daring adventure, or nothing."

CARING FOR THE WILDERNESS

The mountaineering skills in this book are tools that allow you to visit and enjoy remote areas of the world. But remember that the beauty of wilderness often becomes its undoing by attracting visitors—leaving the landscape touched by human hands and eventually less than wild.

People are consuming wilderness at an alarming rate—using it, managing it, and changing it irreparably. For this reason, The Mountaineers and many other outdoor enthusiasts have adopted a set of principles and ethics referred to as Leave No Trace.

Mountains owe climbers nothing, and they ask nothing of climbers. Hudson Stuck, a member of the first team to ascend Denali (formerly Mount McKinley), fervently described this attitude in *The Ascent of Denali*: the summit party felt they had been granted "a privileged communion with the high places of the earth." All mountaineers who travel in the wilderness can consider their minimum charge for this privilege to be leaving the hills as they found them, with no sign of their passing.

PRESERVING WILDERNESS

The privileges climbers enjoy in the mountains bring the responsibility not only to leave no trace but also to help preserve these environments they love. The facts of mountaineering life today include permit systems that limit access to the backcountry, environmental restoration projects, legislative alerts, clashes among competing interest groups, and closures of roads, trails, and entire climbing areas. In addition to being vigilant in treading softly in the mountains, mountaineers must now speak loudly in support of wilderness preservation, access, and sensitive use of public wildlands. Climbers can no longer assume that they will have access to explore the vertical realms of Planet Earth. In addition to being mountaineers, climbers, and adventurers, everyone must be active wilderness advocates if they want to continue to enjoy what was once taken for granted.

A CLIMBING CODE

The Mountaineers have devised a set of guidelines to help people conduct themselves safely in the mountains. Based on careful observation of the habits of skilled climbers and a thoughtful analysis of accidents, these guidelines have served well not only for climbers but, with slight adaptation, for all wilderness travelers. (See the "Climbing Code" sidebar.)

This Climbing Code is not a step-by-step formula for reaching summits or avoiding danger, but rather it is a set of guidelines for encouraging safe mountaineering. It is recommended especially for beginners, who have not

CLIMBING CODE

- Leave the trip itinerary with a responsible person.
- Carry the necessary clothing, food, and equipment.
- A climbing party of three is the minimum, unless adequate prearranged support is available. On glaciers, a minimum of two rope teams is recommended.
- Rope up on all exposed places and for all glacier travel. Anchor all belays.
- Keep the party together, and obey the leader or majority rule.
- Never climb beyond your ability and knowledge.
- Never let judgment be overruled by desire when choosing the route or deciding whether to turn back.
- Follow the precepts of sound mountaineering as set forth in books of recognized merit.
- Behave at all times in a manner that reflects favorably upon mountaineering, including adherence to Leave No Trace principles.

yet developed the necessary judgment that comes from years of experience. Seasoned mountaineers often modify these guidelines in practice, making judgments based on an understanding of the risk as well as the skill to help control that risk.

Climbers sometimes question the need for such standards in a sport notable for the absence of formal rules. However, many serious accidents could have been avoided or minimized if these simple principles had been followed. This Climbing Code is built on the premise that mountaineers want a high probability of safety and success, even in risk-filled or doubtful situations, and they want an adequate margin of safety in case they have misjudged their circumstances.

GAINING THE FREEDOM OF THE HILLS

"Freedom of the hills" is a concept that combines the simple joy of being in the mountains with the skill, equipment, and strength to travel without harm to yourself, others, or the environment. The hills do not offer this freedom freely—but only in trade for your training, preparation, and desire.

This is an age that requires a conscious choice to avoid civilization with all of its technologies and conveniences. In the modern digital world, many people are accessible by phone or email every minute of every day. With the right equipment, this can be true anywhere on the planet. Although you do not have to leave these things behind to go to the mountains, for those who want to step out of—if only briefly—this mechanized, digitized world, the mountains beckon. They offer a place of richness and communion with the natural world that is now the exception rather than the rule.

Mountaineering takes place in an environment indifferent to human needs, and not everyone is willing to pay the price for its intense physical and spiritual rewards. But those who dream of climbing mountains can use this book to follow that dream. And if you learn to climb safely and skillfully, body and spirit in tune with the wilderness, you too can heed the inspiration of John Muir. "Climb the mountains," he wrote in *Our National Parks*, "and get their good tidings. Nature's peace will flow into you as sunshine flows into trees." Like Muir, you too can "walk away quietly in any direction and taste the freedom of the mountaineer."

CHAPTER 2
CLOTHING AND EQUIPMENT

Packing everything you might need to keep you safe, dry, and comfortable on a wilderness trip can paradoxically lead to danger, chill, and misery. The challenge is to limit the load enough to allow for fast and light travel while still having the gear essential for success and survival. Each onerous ounce limits how far, fast, or high you can climb and how speedily you can retreat to safety.

To strike a balance between too much and too little, monitor what you take on a trip. After each trip, determine what was used, what was genuinely needed to achieve a reasonable margin of safety, and what items were unnecessary. When buying equipment, go for lightweight, low-bulk alternatives that offer sufficient performance and durability.

If you are new to mountaineering, wait until you have experience before spending too much money on clothes, boots, or packs. Rent, borrow, or improvise during early outings, gaining hands-on experience before you invest. Get advice from seasoned climbers, window-shop at outdoor stores, and scout mountaineering magazines and online sources. The latest and greatest products or most expensive items are not always best overall. Neither is the cheapest gear necessarily the most economical since certain gear features justify a higher cost.

This chapter provides information on basic and essential wilderness gear, including guidelines on what constitutes good equipment, and though it does not recommend brands, it will help you select high-quality items that work flexibly together. Additional gear for eating and sleeping in the great outdoors is covered in Chapter 3, Camping, Food, and Water.

CLOTHING

Clothing helps a person stay comfortable by creating a thin insulating layer of air next to the skin. The enemies of comfort—precipitation, wind, heat, and cold—work against this protective air layer. The right clothes protect that layer. "Comfort" is a relative term for mountaineers. Inclement weather often forces climbers to endure conditions that deteriorate far below most people's definition of comfort. Still, in climbing, the key to maintaining relative comfort is to stay dry—or, after getting wet, to stay warm and dry out quickly. Safety is the primary concern. When venturing into remote territory, climbers need layers of clothes and a layering system that helps them deal with difficult conditions for however long those conditions last.

Prolonged periods of dampness, even in moderately cool temperatures, can cause your body's core temperature to fall, possibly triggering hypothermia, a frequent cause of death in the mountains. Failure to protect yourself from wind exposes you to windchill and can contribute to hypothermia or lead to frostnip or frostbite. (See "Cold-Related Conditions" in Chapter 24, First Aid.) Carefully select the clothes you will layer to ensure that you can survive sustained exposure to cold and wet conditions.

17

CHOOSING A STARTER ENSEMBLE

Get started by purchasing a few high-quality, well-fitting pieces to serve as the core of your layering system for most trips:

- Boots and socks
- Light- or medium-weight base layer—two tops and one bottom
- One or two synthetic or wool (knit) tops of varying weights—one with a zip collar or full-length zip and one with a lightweight hood
- Synthetic pants and shorts
- Insulated ("puffy") coat
- Hardshell jacket and pants
- Warm hat and gloves
- Sunglasses

Outdoor clothing must also protect climbers from overheating on hot days and prevent excessive sweating, which can dampen clothes from within and lead to severe dehydration. Ventilation, breathability, and sun protection are additional key considerations. Because an overwhelming variety of garments, high-tech fabrics, features, and brands all proclaim superior performance, assembling a layering system for the first time can be daunting. When shopping, ask questions and read tags. Evaluate garments for their functionality and versatility: Will this work when wet? Does it have a wide comfort range? Be skeptical; clothing is an area of strong marketing claims and weak data. In addition to cost, consider durability, fit, and versatility. Clothes designed for other sports may also be suitable for climbing.

Keep in mind that one climber may select a clothing system markedly different from that chosen by another with a different body structure, metabolism, or preference. A solid core of garments lets you adapt to season and activity to meet the demands of many conditions. (See "Layering," below.) Thoughtful additions can expand your clothing quiver to meet the challenge of upcoming adventures. Eventually, you will pare down your packed layers, but if you are new to wilderness travel, start out carrying more than enough to stay warm and dry. Leave items at home only when you are certain that it is possible to survive and thrive without them. Try to minimize the weight of your clothes but not at the expense of safety. Before heading out, get a weather forecast and think ahead about the temperature and weather extremes you may encounter, and then pack accordingly.

FABRICS

Clothing suitable for the outdoors is made from a great variety of fabrics, each with its particular advantages and drawbacks.

SYNTHETIC FABRICS

Synthetic fibers—polyester, nylon, spandex, and acrylic—have largely replaced natural fibers in mountaineering fabrics. Synthetic fibers are hydrophobic, meaning they tend not to absorb moisture. Synthetic fabric garments will absorb some moisture but only in the spaces between the fibers and between the filaments making up each thread. (Bacteria thrive in these spaces, setting up a factory of funk, turning your sweat into stink. See "Clothing Care" below for solutions.) Most of the moisture in a wet synthetic garment can be wrung out; the rest evaporates quickly. Synthetic fabrics are slicker than natural fibers, a disadvantage to the climber in a fall on steep snow or ice. Table 2-1 compares wind resistance, breathability, waterproofness, and stretchiness of outdoor clothing fabrics.

Polyester. High-quality polyester threads can each contain more than 100 filaments, giving the final fabric a soft, cotton-like feel. Fabrics made of them are often chemically treated or shaped to help wick away moisture. In today's garments, polyester has largely replaced polypropylene, offering a softer feel against the skin and somewhat less odor retention.

Nylon. Fabrics made of nylon, technically known as "polyamide," are very strong, resulting in somewhat better abrasion resistance than polyester. These characteristics lead to nylon's use in ropes and in outerwear, including the outer layer of waterproof-breathable laminated fabric. Nylon fabrics also have a soft "hand," leading to their use in many garments. Nylon retains twice as much water as polyester but still only one-fourth as much as cotton or wool. Water-repellent finishes reduce this further.

Spandex. This stretchy fiber, also known as Lycra or elastane, is added to fabrics to give a tight fit yet allow freedom

WARM WHEN WET?

Wool used to carry the banner of "warm when wet," a badge now heralded by synthetic fabrics and fills. But a wet fabric is a cold fabric, and there's no getting past the physics: it takes a lot of energy (warmth) to convert the liquid sweat in damp clothes into vapor. If you want to stay warm, *stay dry*.

2

TABLE 2-1. FABRIC FEATURES				
FABRIC	**WIND RESISTANCE**	**BREATHABILITY**	**WATERPROOFNESS**	**STRETCHINESS**
Fleece	Poor	Excellent	Poor	Excellent
Double-weave softshell	Fair	Excellent	Poor	Excellent
Laminated softshell	Good	Good	Fair	Good
Waterproof-breathable laminated softshell	Excellent	Fair	Good to excellent	Fair
Waterproof-breathable hardshell	Excellent	Fair	Excellent	Poor

of movement. Base layers stay close to the skin to help the body's heat move moisture to the next layer (although some non-spandex knit fabrics can do this too). In other layers, spandex can keep the fabric close to the body to minimize the "bellows effect" that blows away some of your hard-earned warm air layer as you move. Spandex adds significantly to the weight of a garment and increases drying time. Look for blends containing 10 percent or less spandex to optimize the benefits of fit, stretch, and warmth with minimal additional weight and drying time.

Synthetic fleece. Also known as "polar fleece," "fleece," or "pile," this warm and lightweight polyester fabric replaced most wool in garments for climbing starting in the 1980s. Clothes made of it absorb little moisture and retain loft and reasonable insulating properties when wet. Fleece has a good warmth-to-weight ratio but very little ability to block the wind, and it can be bulky.

Dyneema (or Spectra). These lightweight fibers, the strongest in the world, are commonly used in climbing runners and utility cord. More recently, Dyneema is being woven into extremely lightweight abrasion-resistant fabrics for backpacks and sandwiched into ultralight-weight, waterproof-nonbreathable Dyneema Composite fabric (formerly Cuben Fiber) for tents and raingear.

Softshell fabrics. Made up of a dense flexible cloth woven with two interconnected layers, softshells typically have a fleecy interior for warmth and a smooth exterior treated with durable water repellent (DWR) that sheds and deflects some snow and wind. Newer softshell materials are laminated with an abrasion-resistant, stretchable nylon face. Some types include a full or perforated waterproof-breathable membrane for additional wind and weather resistance. Softshell materials generally fall into three categories:

1. **Double-weave softshell.** The original "ski pant" material, this softshell fabric is ideal for high levels of activity and modestly cold conditions. Its stretch allows freedom of movement, and a relatively hard finish resists wind, snow, and abrasion.

2. **Laminated softshell.** A stretchy woven nylon fabric added ("laminated") to the exterior of this fabric significantly blocks wind, sheds snow, and adds some rain protection.

3. **Waterproof-breathable laminated softshell.** This material sandwiches a waterproof-breathable membrane between a layer of fleece on the inside and woven nylon on the outside. The result is a soft-to-the-touch, slightly stretchy fabric with most of the weather resistance of a waterproof-breathable (hardshell) fabric, described below.

WATERPROOF FABRICS

Hardshells—rain parkas and rain pants—are generally made of nylon or nylon blends. Since nylon itself is not waterproof, rain garments derive their waterproofing from either different fabrication methods and/or fabric treatments.

Waterproof-nonbreathable. The simplest way to create a waterproof fabric is to coat or impregnate nylon with waterproof but nonbreathable polyurethane or silicone (silnylon). Such coatings are lightweight and relatively inexpensive, but they often are not very resistant to abrasion or mildew. Although such coatings keep rain out, they also seal sweat and water vapor in. If your sweat does not have a way to escape through your clothes, you will get wet.

Waterproof-breathable (hardshell) fabrics. Created to repel rain and snow while allowing some liquid in vapor form—perspiration—to escape, these fabrics have billions of microscopic pores per square inch. Because moisture vapor from the skin is emitted as individual water molecules (much smaller than droplets of rain), the holes in the waterproof-breathable coating are large enough to let vapor escape but too small for raindrops to get in.

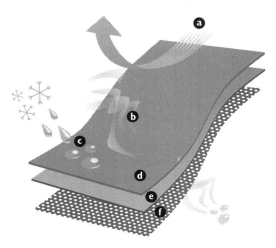

Fig. 2-1. Waterproof-breathable fabric system: a, wind is repelled; b, sweat as water vapor transpires through fabric; c, snow and water bead up due to thin molecular coating of a durable water repellent (DWR) finish; d, outer nylon fabric; e, waterproof-breathable film or coating; f, inner liner (optional).

Coatings or lamination provide the waterproofing and breathability of waterproof-breathable fabrics (fig. 2-1). Coated fabrics are less expensive and less durable than laminated fabrics. Waterproof-breathable laminated fabric—Gore-Tex is the best known—is more expensive to make; it consists of an interior fabric, or membrane-protective coating (to help spread out any condensed perspiration), an inner membrane, and an outer nylon shell that protects the membrane. These laminated fabrics tend to last longer since the waterproof-breathable membrane is protected between two other layers of fabric.

Waterproof-breathable fabrics are a marked improvement over nonbreathable coated nylons, but they are not perfect. A person who is working hard will exceed the garment's ability to pass water vapor, and sweat will condense inside the shell. In liquid form, sweat can no longer escape and the original problem is back again. All waterproof-breathable fabrics have a factory-applied DWR finish added to make rainwater bead up on the surface. DWR treatments are not permanent but are critical to these fabrics' functioning. If rain does not bead up, it coats the exterior, physically blocking the micropores and greatly reducing the fabric's ability to breathe. In cool weather, the "wetted out" shell fabric becomes cold, increasing condensation inside the garment. (See the "Care and Feeding of Waterproof-Breathable Fabrics" sidebar, below.)

Construction techniques and features such as zippered vents under the arms or along the torso can significantly improve a garment's ventilation, but extra ventilation features often command a higher purchase price. Plus zippers and extra material add to the garment's weight. A base layer can help, too, by absorbing liquid sweat, spreading it out, and allowing it to vaporize from body heat and then escape directly through the fabric or via a vent. Minimize perspiration by wearing the smallest amount of clothing possible on top of the base layer—start out a bit cold and assume you'll warm up as you climb.

NATURAL FIBERS

In the early days of mountaineering, natural-fiber clothes were all that was available. Cotton, with the possible exception of a t-shirt on a hot day or in base camp, now has no place in the climber's pack. The rise of synthetic fleece has allowed climbers to dismiss "ragg wool" as a coarse and itchy fabric, but base layers, knit shirts, and socks made from merino wool and blends have had a resurgence in popularity.

Cotton. Comfortable to wear when dry, cotton loses its insulating qualities when wet, absorbs many times its weight in water, and generally takes a long time to dry—it is dangerous to rely on cotton for warmth. Cotton plays a common role in many hypothermia tragedies, leading to the adage "cotton kills." Wet cotton also chafes the skin, a particularly annoying characteristic in underwear and socks or in sweat-soaked shoulder areas under pack straps. Yet in hot, dry weather, cotton can provide good sun protection and ventilates well. The sweat evaporating from a wet cotton t-shirt on a hot day will cool you off.

Modal, rayon, and viscose. These yarns are essentially "synthetic" cotton fibers chemically extruded from wood pulp. They exhibit all the downsides of cotton. Avoid them in the outdoors.

Merino wool. Under such brands as SmartWool, Ibex, and Icebreaker, modern wool fabrics use small-diameter silky fleece, primarily of merino sheep. Chemical descaling removes most of the fabric's itchiness and tendency to shrink. The downsides are that this luxurious fabric is expensive and delicate, and lightweight versions are especially prone to holes. Wool, in general, can become heavy with absorbed moisture and is slower to dry than synthetics.

Nevertheless, merino wool gets high marks for comfort and warmth next to the skin. One hundred percent wool has amazing natural anti-stink qualities currently unrivaled by synthetics and especially appreciated by tent mates on longer trips.

INSULATING FILLS

Insulation for outdoor clothing and gear, such as sleeping bags, is made of either down or synthetic materials.

Down. High-quality goose or duck down is the warmest, lightest, most compressible insulating fill available. Down compresses well yet quickly regains its loft—and therefore its warmth—when unpacked. High-quality goose down has 650 to 900-plus fill power, which means that each ounce, uncompressed, expands to fill 650 to 900-plus cubic inches (or 376 to 520-plus cubic centimeters per gram). Down's low weight-to-warmth ratio makes it popular for cold-weather jackets and especially for sleeping bags. Good down is expensive yet has a much longer useful life than other insulating fills. Unfortunately, down loses all its insulating value when wet and is almost impossible to dry in damp conditions. DWR-treated down ("water-resistant" down) can give a false sense of security, providing only a brief delay until a down coat becomes sodden (although such treatment may shorten the drying time).

Synthetic fill. Unlike down, synthetic fills do not collapse when wet, providing more reliable insulation in damp climates. Heavier and less compressible than down, they are also less expensive and easier to clean. Compared with down, synthetic fills may not withstand as many compression cycles (stuffing and unstuffing), which means they lose their loft and insulation properties more quickly.

Typically, the fabrics needed to hold down or synthetic fill in place need to be robust, so puffies tend not to be very breathable. Some newer insulation can be stabilized by thinner fabric allowing for better breathability, packability, and stretch. Garments using Polartec Alpha or Patagonia's FullRange insulation fall into this category of "active insulation."

LAYERING

Dressing in layers makes it easier to adapt to fluctuating temperatures and conditions in the mountains. The goal is to minimize clothing weight and bulk while efficiently maintaining a comfortable body temperature by removing or adding layers as needed. Experienced mountaineers develop a basic strategy of layering consisting of a few select garments of high functionality, which they use in combination—depending on conditions and personal preference—for most of their activities. They may swap in a new base layer, carry more or fewer midlayers or a different outer garment, or try something new—but the layering system has withstood the test of time and the elements. An outdoor clothing layering system consists of four types of layers:

1. **Base layer.** The base layer, immediately next to your skin, allows perspiration to evaporate, keeping your skin warm and dry.
2. **Midlayer.** Midlayers trap warm air close to your body. The thicker the layer of trapped air, the warmer you will be. Although less efficient than a single, monolithic block of "dead" air (as in a down parka, for example), several light, loosely fitting layers can trap a lot of insulating air, and such an arrangement is very adjustable.
3. **Shell layer.** Shells protect midlayers from wind and precipitation. These could be waterproof-breathable hardshells, softshells, or wind shells, depending on conditions.
4. **Belay jacket.** Donned quickly when you stop moving in cold conditions, an insulated jacket sized to fit over everything can preserve hard-won warmth.

Think of layers as a system intended to maintain comfort in a wide variety of mountain weather, or worn all at once to survive an unplanned bivouac. Try the layers on together before you commit to the complete system for a climb to make sure the shell layer fits comfortably over all the midlayers without compressing insulation or restricting movement.

PUTTING TOGETHER A LAYERING SYSTEM— FROM THE SKIN-SIDE OUT

Armed with knowledge of outdoor fabric characteristics and the strategy of layering, you can assemble an effective mountaineering clothing layering system. Figure 2-2 shows how various articles in a complete clothing system are mixed and matched to function throughout a spectrum of weather conditions and different levels of physical exertion. The exact garments chosen will vary significantly from climber to climber. The goal is to create a flexible system that keeps you safe. Following are some specific guidelines for particular mountaineering conditions.

Cool conditions with rain or wet snow are the most difficult to prepare for. Waterproof-breathable garments are the best available, but condensation will still form under them during exertion. Dress minimally underneath to avoid overheating, vent as much as possible, and assume the clothes you are wearing underneath are going to get wet. Wear gaiters under rain pants. A rain kilt or poncho is an option for the approach hike. Colder conditions and precipitation in the form of snow is a bit simpler to dress

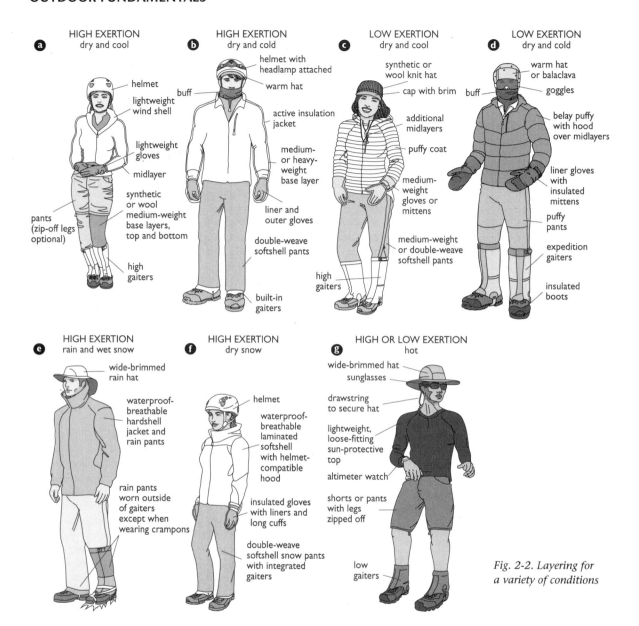

ⓐ HIGH EXERTION dry and cool
- helmet
- lightweight wind shell
- lightweight gloves
- midlayer
- synthetic or wool medium-weight base layers, top and bottom
- pants (zip-off legs optional)
- high gaiters

ⓑ HIGH EXERTION dry and cold
- helmet with headlamp attached
- warm hat
- buff
- active insulation jacket
- medium- or heavy-weight base layer
- liner and outer gloves
- double-weave softshell pants
- built-in gaiters

ⓒ LOW EXERTION dry and cool
- synthetic or wool knit hat
- cap with brim
- additional midlayers
- puffy coat
- medium-weight gloves or mittens
- medium-weight or double-weave softshell pants
- high gaiters

ⓓ LOW EXERTION dry and cold
- warm hat or balaclava
- buff
- goggles
- belay puffy with hood over midlayers
- liner gloves with insulated mittens
- puffy pants
- expedition gaiters
- insulated boots

ⓔ HIGH EXERTION rain and wet snow
- wide-brimmed rain hat
- waterproof-breathable hardshell jacket and rain pants
- rain pants worn outside of gaiters except when wearing crampons

ⓕ HIGH EXERTION dry snow
- helmet
- waterproof-breathable laminated softshell with helmet-compatible hood
- insulated gloves with liners and long cuffs
- double-weave softshell snow pants with integrated gaiters

ⓖ HIGH OR LOW EXERTION hot
- wide-brimmed hat
- sunglasses
- drawstring to secure hat
- lightweight, loose-fitting sun-protective top
- altimeter watch
- shorts or pants with legs zipped off
- low gaiters

Fig. 2-2. Layering for a variety of conditions

for than rain. Cold snow will sluff off garments before it has a chance to melt. Waterproof-breathable garments do not breathe as well as other outer layers; more-breathable softshells (either laminated or waterproof-breathable laminated) may be sufficient.

Closely monitor your personal temperature levels. To avoid overheating, vent as much as possible and adjust layers as needed. Try to start off feeling a bit cool to avoid overheating as you exert more energy and warm up. Remove waterproof-breathable garments as soon as possible. For resting, belaying, or in camp, waterproof-breathable garments are at their best, when both exertion and perspiration are low. Increase midlayers under the shell layer while at rest.

MANAGING MOISTURE: THE KEY TO STAYING WARM

To protect your midlayers from precipitation and perspiration and keep your clothing system functioning at its best:

- Start up the trail feeling a bit cool. Readjust layers 10 to 20 minutes after starting and whenever needed and practical during the day.
- Avoid waterproof-breathable fabrics until necessary—and then wear minimal clothes underneath.
- Use zippers and vents to shed excess heat.
- Dry damp clothes when possible.
- Just say "no" to cotton.

BASE LAYER

Protection from cold begins with an appropriate base layer, formerly known as long johns or thermal long underwear. Wicking fabrics made of polyester (and perhaps a bit of spandex) or merino wool are very popular for this purpose. A good base layer will also sop up liquid sweat, disperse it, and allow the body's heat to vaporize it. Dark-colored base layers dry quicker in sunlight than light-colored layers do, but light colors absorb less heat in the sun and are better on hot days, when a base layer may be worn alone as protection from sunburn or insects.

For rock climbing, spandex-blended polyester tights are sometimes worn as a base layer that allows a full range of motion. Versatile lightweight nylon or double-weave softshell pants can be worn alone against the skin.

T-shirts and shorts. In hot weather, a cotton t-shirt or tank top may suffice as a base layer, although long sleeves provide more sun and insect protection. But even on a moderately cool day, a cotton t-shirt can become soaked with sweat during a steep ascent, and you can get a deep chill when stopping for a break. Non-cotton fabrics are nearly always the better choice. Warm-weather shirts should be light-colored for coolness and moderately baggy for good ventilation. Clothes offer more sun protection than sunscreen (see "Sun Protection" in the Ten Essentials, later in this chapter). Ventilation and durability are key requirements for shorts. A loose-fitting pair of nylon shorts, perhaps with an integral mesh brief, can work well. A popular combination for mild conditions is a lightweight base layer under a pair of synthetic shorts (fig. 2-2a). Lightweight nylon pants with zip-off legs that convert to shorts are also very popular and versatile.

Underwear and sports bras. Although underwear and sports bras do not constitute an adjustable "layer" (they are inconvenient to put on and take off), they add additional warmth and insulation and need to perform as part of the total system. Cotton chafes when damp and so is a poor choice for tight-fitting garments like underwear and socks. Sports bras, of course, can do double duty as a top.

MIDLAYERS

The workhorse of any layering system, the midlayer slows the inevitable escape of warmth and allows perspiration to evaporate while providing light protection from the elements. Climbers carry and wear a variety of midlayers, mixing and matching fleece, down or synthetic jackets or sweaters (puffies), and double-weave softshell depending on the challenge (see Table 2-2).

Synthetic shirt and pants. Simple nylon or polyester shirts and pants are lightweight pieces that provide sun and insect protection while being adaptable to cold weather. Shirts and fleece tops should be long in the torso so they can be tucked into or pulled below the hips to prevent gaps that let valuable heat escape.

Synthetic fleece. Core elements of the midlayer are synthetic fleeces and non-cotton hoodies. Climbers usually combine thin to medium fleece shirts with other midlayer options. Having one fleece layer with a hood and one or two with zip-up collars can provide significant warmth or sun protection with little added weight. For pants, fleece is a virtual snow magnet and so has mostly been replaced by more formfitting, smooth-finished, double-weave softshell pants. The venting allowed by full-length zippers increases the temperature range and flexibility of such pieces.

TABLE 2-2. MIDLAYER OPTIONS

TYPE OF MIDLAYER	WARMTH-TO-WEIGHT RATIO	BREATHABILITY
Synthetic shirts and pants	Good	Good
Synthetic fleece	Good	Excellent
Wool knit shirts	Fair	Good
Synthetic puffy	Good	Fair
Down puffy	Excellent	Fair
"Active insulation" puffy	Good	Excellent
Double-weave softshell	Good	Excellent

CHOOSING A COLD-WEATHER STRATEGY

In addition to layering, these tactics can also help with your cold-weather defense:

- Manage moisture carefully.
- Add additional midlayers that can function with the rest of the system.
- Add a belay jacket and puffy pants.
- Eat more, starting with a big breakfast. Fat and calories correlate directly with warmth, so keep high-calorie snacks at the ready in a pocket where they won't freeze and can be eaten gradually.
- Drink more water, even when urinating may be inconvenient. Dehydration results in low blood volume that will make you extra cold.
- Manage cold feet and hands. Rotate wet gloves or mittens and socks with dry ones as needed. Try chemical hand and foot warmers, but to prevent burns, avoid direct skin contact especially while asleep. Monitor for frostbite and have a contingency plan.
- On a day trip bring hot water and a stove.
- From base layers to one-piece climbing suits, consider one-piece options for extreme cold.
- Accept being a little cold, but be vigilant of the line between discomfort and injury.

Merino wool knit shirt. The allure of this luxurious fabric comes from its warm-to-the-touch feel and organic renewable source—a welcome contrast to a pack full of petroleum-derived yardage.

Puffy jacket. Modern insulated jackets (typically referred to as a "puffy")—compressible, lightweight, trim-cut garments insulated with down or synthetic fiber—have largely replaced bulky and heavy synthetic fleece jackets. Down is ideal for cool, dry conditions or where the climber can protect the garment from precipitation with a hardshell. Synthetic-filled puffies are better in damp conditions. Puffies have become the indispensable pillar of most layering systems—light enough to wear during activity, thin and trim enough to work well with other layers. For most trips in cool to cold weather, a thinner, highly breathable synthetic fabric that is less affected by sweat absorption is best while on the move. Keep a second, heavier insulating layer, such as a puffy, ready to put on as soon as your activity level drops when resting, belaying, or camping.

Double-weave softshell. A garment made of this fabric is a good outer midlayer to provide reasonable wind and weather resistance for most conditions. The spandex content makes for trim-fitting garments, and the fabric works particularly well as warm, flexible pants for skiing or climbing in cool or snowy conditions. (Softshell laminates offer even more waterproofing and are used in outer shells; see "Shell Strategies," below.)

Puffy pants or skirt. For colder conditions, insulated ("puffy") pants, typically filled with synthetic insulation, help your legs retain heat. Look for full-length side zippers that make it possible to put the pants on while you are wearing boots, crampons, or snowshoes. While less useful, a puffy skirt can help you avoid deeply chilled thighs.

SHELL STRATEGIES

The ideal shell would be fully waterproof, windproof, and breathable. No single garment achieves all these objectives, but various strategies come close. Many mountaineers carry two shell layers: a lighter, wind-resistant, breathable jacket and a somewhat heavier, waterproof-breathable set of jacket and pants. They wear the more breathable wind-resistant gear in cool, windy, and even lightly drizzling conditions and for periods of heavy exertion and reserve the more weatherproof hardshell for periods of lighter exertion or heavier rain.

Wind shells. Compressible to the size of an apple and as light as 2 ounces (60 grams), a wind shell helps the body retain the warmth captured by the midlayers. It packs more warmth per gram than any other garment. Wind shells are highly breathable, yet their DWR coating can shed light precipitation.

Softshells. Laminated softshells feature an outer layer that is stretchy and more breathable than a hardshell while still offering some resistance to wind and dry snow. Waterproof-breathable laminated softshells are another step up, offering about the same breathability of a hardshell, but with a bit of stretch and good to very good weatherproofness. Yet when there is a risk of extended exposure to precipitation, skip this category entirely and pair the midlayers of your choice with a hardshell.

Hardshells. Stormy weather requires serious protection in the form of a hardshell. Made of either two- or three-layer waterproof-breathable fabric, hardshells sacrifice breathability for complete weatherproofness. A quality hardshell jacket may be the most expensive garment in your arsenal. For ventilation, hardshells have full front zippers plus a variety of tricks to improve their mediocre breathability, including adjustable openings at the front, waist, underarms, sides, and cuffs. Hardshell pants (rain pants) should have full-length zippers so you can don or remove them over boots, crampons, or snow-shoes. Because rain pants tend to be worn less often than parkas—and because they can be ruined by bushwhacking or glissading—choosing a nonbreathable pair can save money. In cold conditions, as a lower-body shell layer, some climbers use waterproof-breathable bib pants held up by suspenders.

Insulated bibs are considerably warmer than rain pants because they cover much of the torso and keep snow from entering around your waistline. They are a good option for backcountry skiing, waterfall ice, and mixed climbing. Some climbers use one-piece ("8,000 meter") suits, the warmest, but least versatile, option.

BELAY JACKET

In cold weather one final layer, a thickly insulated jacket commonly referred to as a belay parka or belay puffy, helps keep the stationary belayer warm and therefore attentive. Good features include an integral hood, thick but very compressible insulation, and lightweight, water-resistant shell material. If large enough to fit either member of the rope team (on top of all their other layers), one belay jacket could suffice. But one jacket for each climber can be a lifesaver.

HEADWEAR

The adage says, "If your feet are cold, put on a hat." Your body, when cold, reduces blood flow to the arms and legs to warm other more vital areas. Putting on a hat helps to reduce heat loss. Climbers often carry several different types of hats to quickly adapt to changing temperatures. To prevent the misfortune of having a hat blow off and sail over a cliff, some choose headgear with a strap or leash. Consider carrying two insulating hats: an extra hat provides almost as much warmth as an extra sweater while weighing much less. Thin hats can be worn beneath a climbing helmet in cold weather.

Insulating caps come in wool, acrylic, or polyester fleece. Balaclavas are versatile insulators because they can cover both your face and neck or can be rolled up to allow ventilation of the collar area. Stretchy knitted cylinders known as Buffs (also called neck tubes or neck gaiters), worn around the neck, help seal the jacket neck opening that continually bellows warm air. Buffs can be used as a hat to cover the head and ears and are thin enough to wear under a helmet. On a very cold day, they can be pulled up from the neck to cover the mouth, helping with conditions such as the trek to Everest Base Camp where yak-dung dust can bring on the "Khumbu cough."

CHOOSING A SHELL JACKET

Fabric makes a difference:
- Uninsulated shells are lighter and more versatile.
- Two-layer waterproof-breathable fabric costs less and weighs less than three-layer, and two-layer shells are good for moderate weather.
- Three-layer waterproof-breathable fabric creates a shell that performs better in severe weather.
- Laminated or waterproof-breathable laminated softshell fabric is a good alternative for cold, dry conditions where precipitation would likely be dry snow.

Features are important:
- Large enough to fit over all midlayers and a climbing harness
- A hood with a brim that fits over a helmet
- Neck construction that covers the chin comfortably and allows the head to move freely
- Good ventilation
- Waterproof zippers
- Pockets that are easily accessible even while wearing gloves and carrying a pack
- A length sufficient to seal the waistline and sleeves that cover the wrists

---

A rain hat made of waterproof-breathable fabric is useful because it provides more ventilation (for exertion) and frequently is more comfortable than a hood. Sun-protective hats, with wide brims or protective shades that drape over your neck and ears, are popular for glacier climbs, as is a baseball cap with a bandanna pinned on or worn under it. A brim shades your eyes and keeps rain and snow off glasses. Remember to confirm each hat's helmet compatibility.

HANDWEAR

Fingers are perhaps the most difficult part of the body to keep warm because of the body's tendency to sacrifice blood flow to the extremities when cold. Unfortunately, this altered blood flow can inhibit tasks that require dexterity—such as pulling zippers and tying knots—which may slow a climbing party's progress at the very time when they need to move fast to find shelter from the cold.

Mitten and glove selection usually entails a compromise between dexterity and warmth. In general, bulk means increased warmth and reduced dexterity. The more technical a climb, the more significant the compromise. As with other insulating garments, mittens and gloves must be made of fabrics that retain some warmth when wet and then dry quickly. Suitable gloves and mittens come in synthetics, wool-synthetic blends, or sometimes wool. Double-weave softshell fabric is common in alpine gloves. The layering concept for clothing also applies to hands. The first layer may be a light pair of gloves; additional layers are usually heavier gloves or mittens. Mittens are warmer as a layer because they allow fingers to share warmth.

Climbers need hand protection from cracks, ropes, and cold. Some handwear allows inner gloves or mittens to be removed to add versatility and speed drying. Some provide a nonslip coating on the palm to improve grip for snow and ice tools. To combat cold, handwear cuffs should overlap the parka sleeve about 4 to 6 inches (10 to 15 centimeters), and Velcro closures should cinch around the forearm. Security cords can prevent loss when mittens must be removed to climb rock or apply sunscreen. Heated gloves aid ice climbers. Touch screen compatibility helps navigators in cold weather.

In camp, wearing glove liners or fingerless gloves inside mittens can permit good dexterity for delicate chores without exposing bare skin. Be aware that many synthetics can melt in high heat (from a stove, for instance). Even so, in freezing temperatures it is important to keep fingers from freezing to metal: glove liners are better for this than fingerless gloves. But when you are rock climbing in cold weather, fingerless gloves are often best. Handling wet rope or scrambling over wet rock can saturate gloves or mittens, even in dry weather. Some climbers carry several pairs of gloves or liners, rotating them to inside pockets when they become wet and cold to start each pitch with dry gloves and warm hands.

Often worn for rope handling such as rappelling or belaying, leather gloves provide a better grip and prevent rope burns. While most leather gloves do not insulate when wet, and dry slowly, some climbing versions have waterproof-breathable liners and water-resistant leather. Mechanics' work gloves with leather palms can be an inexpensive alternative for scrambling, belaying, and rappelling.

SLEEPWEAR

Many climbers carry a dry set of base layers and socks for camp and sleeping. Changing into this dry set at the end of the day helps thwart the chill of long shadows from a setting sun. At times, however, a climber may have to dry out damp clothes by spreading them out within the sleeping bag or wearing them to bed.

CLOTHING CARE

The key to laundering most outdoor fabrics is simply to follow the garment's washing instructions. For outdoor clothing: close all zippers and fasteners; wash in cold or warm water with a liquid sports wash or mild, powdered laundry soap; and then line dry or tumble dry on a low setting. Avoid fabric softeners (ruins water repellency), scented detergent (attracts bears and bugs), chlorine bleach (ruins colors, except polyester), hot irons (synthetics have low melting points), and dry cleaning down garments (strips essential oils). Launder double-weave softshell fabric like most garments, but pay attention to their DWR treatment (see more about DWR and hardshells, below). Launder both laminated and waterproof-breathable laminated softshells the same as waterproof-breathable hardshells. Clean gently, rinse thoroughly, dry carefully, and touch up or reapply the DWR coatings to help your gear live long and prosper.

Funk. Bacteria thrive in the interstitial spaces of synthetic thread and even survive the gentle laundering recommended above. On each outing this microbiome generates its factory of funk, turning your sweat into stink. Fabric labels to the contrary, most polyester fabrics (but not nylon or other synthetics) can be safely laundered with chlorine bleach. For other stinky souvenirs, try a presoak using a nonchlorine bleach followed by normal cleaning.

Waterproof-breathable garments. Whether they have a coating or a laminated membrane, waterproof-breathable shells depend on relatively delicate components to function. Dirt and oils, such as sunscreen or insect repellent, can clog and contaminate fabric pores, reducing breathability. Keeping waterproof-breathable fabric clean helps keep it in optimal working condition. It's best to use a sports wash detergent. Do not use fabric softener. Understand that detergent is hydrophilic; it is critical to rinse the garment a second time. Then dry it on a line or in a tumble dryer on medium (140 degrees Fahrenheit or 60 degrees Celsius), and then test the DWR as explained below.

DWR on hardshells and softshells. The durable water-repellent finish on waterproof-breathable fabric is a critical component. DWR may be "durable," but it will not last the life of a garment. Eventually rainwater "wets out" the outer shell surface, making the fabric appear dark; water vapor is blocked and can no longer pass through the fabric. The fabric also becomes heavy and the surface, cold, compounding the issue by causing vaporized sweat to condense on the inside.

At home, test the garment with a spray bottle. When water no longer beads up on the surface, the DWR can

CARE AND FEEDING OF WATERPROOF-BREATHABLE FABRICS

The DWR feature of waterproof-breathable fabrics fails over time. Following these steps will help keep these fabrics functioning well for as long as possible.

- **Keep it clean.** Wash the garment regularly using a liquid sports wash and do not use fabric softener.
- **Rinse it well.** After washing, put the garment through a second rinse.
- **Dry it.** Drip-dry or use a dryer set on medium (140°F or 60°C).
- **Revive it.** Once the garment is completely dry, tumble dry for an additional 20 minutes on medium heat to revive the DWR.
- **Conduct a spray test.** Water should bead up.
- **Reapply DWR.** If the garment fails the test, reapply the DWR coating.

be restored somewhat by heat. The chemistry of DWR works like a microscopic version of the fine hairs found on plant leaves that repel water. Abrasion tends to bend these molecular structures, but heat helps straighten them out and somewhat restores water repellency. To revive the DWR finish, after your shell is clean and completely dry, tumble it dry for an additional 20 minutes on medium heat. If you are unable to tumble dry, you can try ironing the dry garment on a gentle setting (warm, no steam), placing a towel or cloth between the garment and the iron.

When the fabric no longer responds to this method, try applying a spray-on or wash-in DWR. Always treat clean garments, following the manufacturer's instructions. These procedures may or may not work to revive an expensive hardshell or softshell—but it's your only chance.

Home-applied products are either fluorinated or not. Nonfluorinated DWRs repel water but are currently more susceptible to contamination from oils—sunscreens, insect repellents, and body oils. Fluorinated DWRs, while environmentally dubious, are currently the most effective and durable at repelling both oil and water. Unfortunately, labels can be vague. Products with labels that say "PFC-free," "contains no fluorocarbons," or simply "fluorine-free" do not contain fluorine. Products with labels that say "PFOA & PFOS free" are likely fluorinated.

Spray-applying these textile home remedies to clean, wet garments allows the DWR to penetrate the surface of the fabric slightly better, displacing the water as it evaporates. For a more uniform application, you can also use a wash-in

DWR product. Wash-ins are particularly helpful to softshells. Hand washing can ensure that more of the chemistry ends up on the garment. Read the instructions carefully as there are some incompatibilities when using wash-in DWR on coated (nonlaminated) waterproof-breathable fabrics.

After applying the DWR, dry the garment according to the reviving directions noted above. Some newer home-applied fluorinated chemistries do not require the second drying step, though doing so may help revive the garment's original factory DWR. Reapply the DWR coating when you start to see signs of "wetting out" on the surface of the garment. Or simply touch up high abrasion areas after every trip or two. It is quite satisfying after spray-testing to see the water bead up on the surface like it would on a well-waxed car.

DWR is factory-applied to many other garments such as fleece jackets, wind shells, pants, hats, and gloves. These treatments are also not permanent and can be revived and reapplied, although they are less critical to these garments' functionality.

FOOTWEAR

A climber's feet are the means for reaching the objective, so they need especially good gear including boots, socks, gaiters, and sometimes specialized footwear.

CHOOSING SPECIALIZED FOOTWEAR

Depending on the trip, a climber may wear one kind of boot for the approach hike, another type of footwear in camp, and yet another when climbing. If footwear other than boots is desired and you are willing to carry the extra weight, consider these options:

- **Lightweight, sticky rubber approach shoes** are less likely to cause blisters and less fatiguing to wear than climbing boots on some easy approaches; however, they may not provide the support needed for carrying a heavy pack, especially on rough ground or descents.
- **Lightweight athletic shoes, sandals, or neoprene socks or booties** offer comfort in camp, give boots and feet a chance to dry, and can be used for stream crossings.
- **Insulated booties or fleece socks** provide warmer lounging and sleeping.
- **Rock shoes,** for climbing technical rock, are lightweight and compact.

BOOTS

A good alpine climbing boot is a compromise between performance and suitability for the likely range of conditions. No single boot type or design will do everything well. The rigidity of the boot's sole, the stiffness and support provided by the upper, and how the sole and upper interact in use are the key design features, while proper fit is key to happy feet. A full mountaineering boot (fig. 2-3) must strike a balance between being tough enough to withstand being scraped on rocks and rigid enough for kicking steps in hard snow and wearing crampons, yet comfortable enough for the approach hike. In a single day of climbing, boots may have to contend with trails, mud, streams, gravel, brush, scree, steep rock, hard snow, and ice.

The "classic" all-leather-upper boot, while respected for its versatility, has been supplanted by new designs: boots with plastic-composite shells, pieces of leather, fabric panels, synthetic leather, waterproof linings, integrated gaiters, and overall lighter construction. Boot designs are evolving, but the many jobs they need to do are not.

Lightweight Mountaineering or Scrambling Boots

Some boots that incorporate synthetic fabric panels to reduce weight and increase breathability are suitable for climbing. These lightweight mountaineering or scrambling boots (fig. 2-4) are basically a rigid hiking boot and provide several advantages over more robust boots:

- Reduced weight
- Improved comfort hiking long approaches; shorter break-in time
- More flexible sole allows for better friction climbing
- Faster drying time
- Lower cost

However, lightweight boots may have significant drawbacks from full mountaineering boots:

- Less stability when edging and toe holding
- Less waterproofness and durability
- Insufficient weight or stiffness for step-kicking in firm snow or for wearing crampons

If you are considering lightweight mountaineering or scrambling boots for climbing, check that the uppers are high and rigid enough for good ankle support, that stiff counters wrap the heel and toe, and that abrasion areas are reinforced. If the boot is too flexible, your body will waste energy when moving across difficult ground as your feet flex unnecessarily with each step. The boot may not edge well or be suitable for some crampons. A more rigid boot acts as a tiny platform wherever you step so that bigger muscle groups perform simpler movements and save energy.

Full Mountaineering Boots

Full mountaineering boots include fabrics and features making them more robust, durable, and expensive than lightweight climbing boots. Typically lined with neoprene-like padding, they are also warmer and more waterproof. The best choice for a full mountaineering boot depends on how it will be used and is generally a compromise between the boot's walking comfort and its technical capability. For trails and easy snow or rock routes, boots with moderately stiff soles and uppers provide enough support while being acceptably flexible and comfortable.

For technical alpine rock climbing, a more rigid boot is desirable for its edging capabilities. Flexible boots (fig. 2-5a, c, e, and g), while sometimes used on technical rock, are usually a poor substitute for rock shoes. (To learn more about rock shoes, see Chapter 12, Alpine Rock Climbing.) Stiffer boots can make walking less comfortable, but

cuff

crampon lip

crampon lip

lug sole

Fig. 2-3. Full mountaineering boot.

Fig. 2-4. Lightweight mountaineering or scrambling boot.

2

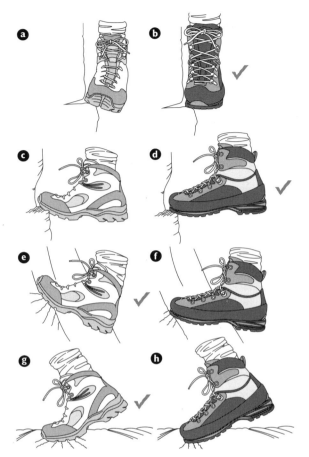

Fig. 2-5. Performance of flexible boots versus stiffer boots in various situations: a and b, edging; c and d, toe holding; e and f, friction climbing or smearing; g and h, hiking.

they greatly reduce leg fatigue when a climber is standing on small rock nubbins. Look for boots stiff enough to permit edging on narrow rock ledges with either side of the boot (fig. 2-5b) or with the toe (fig. 2-5d).

For traveling on hard snow, a highly flexible boot is a disadvantage. It takes a stout boot to kick good steps or plunge-step with confidence. Snowshoes and (especially) crampons may not stay on if boots are too flexible for the bindings.

Ice climbing demands an even higher level of boot support and very stiff soles and uppers. Plastic-composite boots or extremely stiff leather boots are generally best (see Chapter 19, Alpine Ice Climbing).

Plastic Mountaineering Boots

Plastic mountaineering boots consist of hard synthetic outer shells with inner insulating boots. The synthetic shells of these boots are usually quite stiff, which makes them good for use with crampons or snowshoes. They permit straps and bindings to be cinched tightly without impairing circulation in the feet. They provide solid support for edging and kicking steps. Being truly waterproof, plastic mountaineering boots are great in wet conditions. The inner insulating boot remains free of snowmelt and keeps feet warm. In camp, the inner boot can be removed and warmed, which helps in drying out perspiration. Unfortunately, the factors that make plastic boots ideal for snow and ice (rigidity, waterproofness, and warmth) make them a poor choice for general trail use.

BOOT CARE

With proper care, well-made boots can last many years. Keep them clean and dry when not in use. With plastic composite boots, remove the inner boots after use and allow them to dry. Shake or wipe out any debris in the shells to prevent abrasion and excessive wear. Avoid exposing boots to high temperatures, because heat can damage leather, linings, and adhesives. During an outing, water can seep into boots through the uppers and seams. Waterproofing agents help limit the entry of water. Waterproofing needs to be repeated regularly.

Before waterproofing, clean boots with a mild or special purpose soap and a stiff brush. Apply waterproofing appropriate to the boots' construction according to product instructions. Most mountaineering boots feature a Gore-Tex seam-sealed waterproof bootie, which keeps feet drier in wet conditions. Functioning like DWR on a hardshell, a Gore-Tex-approved waterproofing should be applied a year after purchase and then once or twice a year after that. Waterproofing should be applied to boots that have been cleaned and are still very damp. Gore-Tex is no panacea; boots that include a Gore-Tex bootie are usually more expensive, they may make feet uncomfortable during hot weather, and the membrane can degrade from dirt and sweat.

PROPER FOOTWEAR FIT

The key to happy feet is proper fit, and the key to proper fit is to consider boots, socks, and insoles as the three pieces of a footwear system. Purchase insoles and socks at the same time as your boots; try on not only different boot types and sizes but a variety of insoles and socks.

Boots

No matter what the boot's design or materials, fit is critical. The shape of a boot is defined by the unique "last" on which it is built. The complex dimensions of the boot are not completely captured by length and width, so try on several makes and styles. Some brands are available in multiple widths; others offer both men's and women's models. Some men do better in women's models and vice versa.

After lacing up the boots firmly, stand on a narrow edge or rock side to side to test their stability. Walk in the boots, with a heavy pack on if possible, to allow the boots and your feet to get used to each other. Note whether the boots have any uncomfortable seams or creases or whether they pinch anywhere. In boots that fit properly, the back two-thirds of your foot will feel firmly anchored in place while your toes will have plenty of room to wiggle. Try standing on a downward incline for a critical test of toe space. Kick something solid—your toes should not jam against the toe box.

Boots that are too tight will constrict circulation, leading to cold feet and increasing the chance of frostbite. Overly tight or excessively loose boots can cause blisters. Be especially careful that boots intended for use in extreme cold and/or at high altitudes do not constrict your feet and impede circulation. Because fit is critical for comfort and performance, climbers with impossible-to-fit feet may need custom-made leather boots.

Socks

Socks cushion and insulate the feet and reduce friction between the boot and the foot. Socks made of nylon or merino wool help reduce friction; those made of cotton do not. Cotton socks become abrasive when wet, leading to blisters. Socks need to fit closely; too-large socks lead to wrinkled fabric and irritated skin. Discard old socks: threadbare, worn sections can cause blisters. Because boots do not breathe appreciably, sweat generated by the feet collects and builds up until the boots are removed. In dry conditions, some climbers will change their socks once or twice per day, donning a dry pair while drying out the other. Synthetic socks dry faster than wool.

Many climbers wear two pairs of socks. Next to the skin, thin, smooth liner socks help resist blisters by transporting perspiration away from the foot while staying somewhat dry in the process. Liner socks also allow a climber to fine-tune the fit of the footwear system. The outer sock is thicker to absorb the moisture passing through the inner sock and to cushion against the boot lining. Others prefer a single medium- or heavy-weight blended sock. There are

exceptions. Rock climbers want flexible rock shoes to fit like skin, and so they wear no socks or one thin pair. Hikers using trail shoes on a warm day may wear a single pair of socks; winter climbers on very cold days may wear three pairs of socks inside oversized boots. Whatever the strategy, keep your toes free enough to wiggle; an additional pair of socks will not improve warmth if they constrict circulation.

Before donning socks, consider protecting your feet at places prone to blisters, especially the back of the heel, with specialized tape or Moleskin. For more information, see "Blisters" in Chapter 24, First Aid. Foot powder and lubricants, such as petroleum jelly, are commonly recommended blister fighters; yet studies show no benefit and perhaps even a detrimental effect.

Waterproof-breathable Gore-Tex socks can improve comfort in wet conditions. Worn over an inner pair of standard socks, these socks function much like Gore-Tex liners in boots, while providing a higher, snugger cuff. In extremely cold weather, a vapor-barrier sock worn between the two main sock layers can reduce the danger of frostbite. Because vapor-barrier socks do not breathe, your feet get damp; but they retain more heat and so your feet stay warmer. However, if feet stay moist for too long, you risk developing the serious condition of immersion foot (see Chapter 24, First Aid). Dry your feet thoroughly at least once each day if you use vapor-barrier socks.

Insoles

Most climbers toss out the cheap, stock insoles that come with boots. Aftermarket insoles come in an array of arch sizes and thicknesses ("high volume" means very thick). They provide additional comfort, insulation, and support—and affect the final fit considerably.

GAITERS

During an outing, water, snow, and debris can get into boots over the cuff. Gaiters seal the boundary between pant legs and boot tops. Climbers often carry gaiters in both summer and winter, because rain, dew, mud, and snow provide year-round opportunities to saturate pant legs, socks, and boots. Wet socks and boots can, in turn, prove very uncomfortable and even lead to serious foot problems.

Short trail gaiters (fig. 2-6a), extending a bit above the tops of the boots, are adequate for keeping corn snow and debris out of boots in summer. The deep snows of winter, however, usually call for standard alpine gaiters (fig. 2-6b) that extend up to the knee. Expedition gaiters (fig. 2-6c) are made from beefier material and sized to accommodate

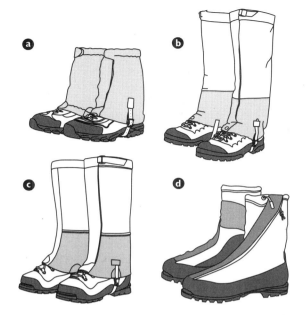

Fig. 2-6. Gaiters: a, trail; b, alpine; c, expedition; d, integrated.

the top of the gaiter keeps it from sliding down. A snug fit around the calf helps prevent crampon points from catching on the gaiters, leading to a fall.

A close fit all around the boot is essential to prevent snow from entering under the gaiter, especially when you are plunge-stepping during descents. A cord, lace, strap, or shock cord runs under the foot to help the gaiter hug the boot. The parts underfoot will wear out during the life of the gaiter, so look for designs allowing easy replacement. Neoprene straps work well in snow but wear quickly on rock, whereas cord survives rock better but can ball up with snow. Women's gaiters are typically shorter in height and a bit wider at the top.

PACKS

Climbers usually own at least two packs: a day pack to hold enough for a single-day climb, and a full-size backpack to carry gear for camping in the backcountry. All packs should allow climbers to carry the weight close to their body and centered over their hips and legs (see Figure 2-9).

BUYING AN OVERNIGHT OR EXPEDITION BACKPACK

First, determine the needed pack capacity depending on the demands of the climb (see Table 2-3). Then, find a pack that fits your body. The backpack's adjustment range must be compatible with the length of your back. Some backpacks adjust to a wide range of body sizes; others do not. Try on various packs and make your own decision (see "Choosing a Pack" sidebar). Figure 2-7 shows a typical 50-liter climbing pack with a streamlined design.

Don't be in a hurry when fitting a backpack. Load it up, as you would on an actual climb; bring personal gear to the store. Without a typical load, you cannot tell how the pack rides or if the adjustments provide a good fit.

large-sized plastic boots; insulation built into some expedition gaiters covers the boots for added warmth. Boots with nonremovable (integrated) gaiters are a growing trend in winter mountaineering boots (fig. 2-6d). Snow pants often have built-in gaiters, eliminating the need for a separate piece in some conditions.

Gaiters are usually held closed with snaps, zippers, or Velcro; Velcro offers the easiest fastening in cold weather. If you select gaiters with zippers, be sure the teeth are heavy-duty. A flap that closes over the zipper with snaps or Velcro protects it from damage and can keep the gaiter closed and functional even if the zipper fails. Elastic or a strap at

TABLE 2-3. TYPES OF PACKS

TYPE	CAPACITY	NOTES
Day pack	30–50 liters; 20–30 lb (9–14 kg)	Best for single-day climbs. Efficient packers facing good weather can overnight with a pack this size.
Overnight pack	50–80 liters; 30–55 lb (14–25 kg)	Most popular size for overnight trips, winter day trips, or backcountry skiing. Compression straps minimize size for day trips. Careful packing may accommodate longer trips.
Expedition or winter pack	70-plus liters	Extended trips of 5 days or more or winter treks usually call for packs of 70 liters or larger to accommodate extra food and clothes, warmer sleeping bag, and four-season tent.

To test for fit, first follow the steps in the next section "Properly Fitting and Adjusting a Backpack." Check the fit in a mirror to see if the frame follows the curve of your back. If it does not, check whether the stays or frame can be bent to improve the fit; some frames of composite materials cannot. The shoulder straps should attach to the backpack between your shoulder blades and leave little or no gap behind your back.

Once the backpack is adjusted, check your head clearance while wearing a helmet. Is it possible to look up without hitting the back of your head? Next, check for adequate padding wherever the pack touches your body. Pay particular attention to the comfort of the shoulder straps and hip belt; note the quality of the padding while realizing that thicker and softer is not necessarily more comfortable. The hip belt should be substantial; its padding should cover your hip bones by good margins. For proper load transfer to your hips, ensure that the hip belt wraps directly onto the top, not the sides, of your hips and not around your waist.

Women's backpacks. Most women prefer a women's-specific design with shorter back length, narrower shoulder width, shorter, narrower shoulder straps, and a slightly larger belt flare angle at the hips. Although a larger hip belt flare angle can be somewhat accommodated by adjusting the angle of the belt's webbing, a women's-specific hip belt is often best. Women's hip belts are also generally narrower and more padded than men's to avoid the possibility of putting pressure on the lower ribcage. Some women find that men's or unisex packs fit better.

PROPERLY FITTING AND ADJUSTING A BACKPACK

First, loosen all the straps. Then shoulder a full pack and follow these steps (fig. 2-8).

Step 1. Position the middle of the hip belt over the top of the iliac crest (hip bones). Raise your shoulders and *firmly tighten* the waist belt. Virtually all the weight should be on the hips since the shoulder straps are slack at this point.

Step 2. Tighten the shoulder straps—but not too tight—so they form a smooth arc over your shoulders. Note that the shoulder stabilizer straps are slack at this point. The main weight should be on the hip belt, with minimal load carried by the shoulders.

Step 3. Gently tension the shoulder stabilizer straps (day packs generally don't have these) to bring the pack close to the body. Ideally, they should end up at around a 45-degree angle. Excess tension interferes with the smooth arc of the shoulder pad over the shoulder. Tension any hip belt stabilizers and (optionally) any sternum straps.

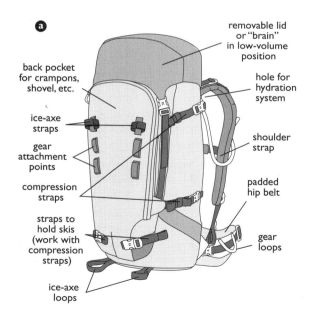

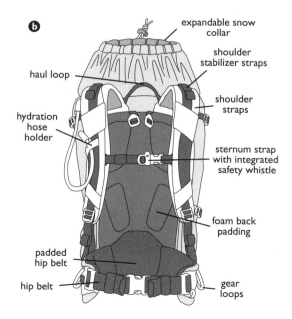

Fig. 2-7. Typical climbing pack: a, view of back and side; b, view of back pad and straps, with lid removed

Fig. 2-8. Fitting and adjusting a backpack.

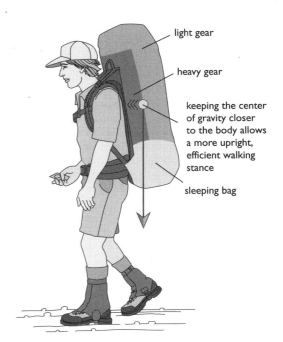

light gear

heavy gear

keeping the center of gravity closer to the body allows a more upright, efficient walking stance

sleeping bag

Fig. 2-9. Loading heavier items closer to the center of the back improves balance, efficiency, and endurance.

Each time you put on your backpack, adjust the straps in the same sequence, from bottom to top: position the waist belt and firmly tighten while raising the shoulders, tighten the shoulder straps, and then tension the stabilizer straps.

BUYING A DAY PACK

Day packs for climbing usually have volumes of between 30 and 50 liters, enough to carry 20 to 30 pounds (9 to 14 kilograms). The large selection of day packs on the market covers a wide spectrum of sturdiness. Some are designed without rigid frames or padded hip belts and may be too flimsy for carrying the heavy tools of climbing: rope, rack, crampons, and ice axe. Seek a pack with a sturdy internal frame and a hip belt that is at least 2 inches (5 centimeters) wide at the buckle and 4 inches (10 centimeters) wide where it covers the hips. Insist on ice-axe loops, a haul loop, and compression straps. Most of the features you would consider in choosing a full-size pack apply to day packs. Try on and compare day packs as thoroughly as you would a full-size backpack.

TIPS ON PACKING

Strategically loading items in a pack can dramatically influence a climber's speed, endurance, and enjoyment of an outing. Generally, climbers will feel best if they can concentrate the load on their hips. Pack heavy items as close to your back as possible to bring in and lower your center

CHOOSING A PACK

First, you must decide on capacity: day, overnight, or expedition. Consider the weight and volume of what you will need to carry, and then factor in the length of your trip. Your back length matters more than your height. Beyond those factors, consider each pack's features and details:

- Does the pack have a smooth profile, or will it get tangled up in heavy brush or when hauled up a steep rock face?
- How sturdy and durable are the suspension system, stitching, and zippers?
- How convenient is it to store, arrange, and access gear?
- Can it carry special items such as crampons, skis, snowshoes, and a snow shovel?
- Does the pack have a haul loop, ice-axe loops, and compression straps (to reduce volume and prevent the load from shifting)?
- Can the pack's capacity be increased for extended trips (for example, expandable snow collar, side-pocket accessories)?

33

of gravity; center them in the pack to allow you to more easily keep your balance (fig. 2-9). Heavy items such as ropes placed high in the pack create top-heavy instability.

Along with arranging items for optimum weight distribution, organize them for quick access. Carry the gear that you will need most often close at hand. Articles such as gloves, hats, sunglasses, maps, and insect repellent are often most convenient in side and top pockets, jacket pockets, or a fanny pack worn in combination with the main pack. Keep snacks and water close at hand for easy and frequent refueling. In cool weather, keep a puffy coat at the ready. Readjusting the backpack during use will help reduce soreness and fatigue.

Determine a strategy to keep pack contents dry in rainy weather. Even packs constructed from waterproof materials are rarely waterproof; water can leak through seams, zippers, pockets, the top opening, and places where waterproofing has worn off. Individual plastic bags or waterproof stuff sacks can help protect pack contents, while a waterproof pack cover can keep the entire pack dry. Some climbers prefer to line their pack with a large plastic trash bag.

ESSENTIAL EQUIPMENT

Certain equipment deserves space in every pack. A climber will not need every item on every trip, but essential equipment can be a lifesaver in an emergency. Exactly how much equipment "insurance" should be carried is a matter of healthy debate (see the "Ultralight Travel" sidebar). Some respected minimalists argue that weighing down a pack causes people to climb slower, making it more likely they will get caught by a storm or nightfall. "Go fast and light. Carry bivy gear, and you will bivy," they argue. The other side of this debate is that, even without the extra weight of bivy gear, climbers still may be forced to bivouac. Each party must determine what will keep them safe.

Most climbers take along carefully selected items to survive the unexpected. Whatever your approach to equipment, a checklist (Table 2-5) will help you remember what to bring in the rush to get ready for a trip. Adapt this list to suit your needs, and get in the habit of checking it before each trip. The best-known list, first developed by The Mountaineers in the 1930s, has become known as the "Ten Essentials."

THE MOUNTAINEERS' TEN ESSENTIALS

The point of the Ten Essentials (Table 2-4) has always been to help answer two basic questions: First, can you prevent emergencies and respond positively should one occur?

Second, can you safely spend a night—or more—outside? The Ten Essentials is a guide that should be tailored to the nature of the climb. Weather, remoteness from help, and complexity should be factored into the selected essentials. The first seven essentials tend to be compact and vary little from climb to climb, and so they can be grouped together to facilitate packing. Add the proper extra food, water, and clothes, and you're ready to go. This brief list is intended to be easy to remember and serve as a mental pretrip checklist. Each essential is discussed in more detail below.

1. Navigation

Modern tools have revolutionized backcountry navigation. Today's mountaineer carries five essential tools while navigating the backcountry: map, altimeter, compass, Global Positioning System (GPS) device, and a personal locator beacon ("PLB") or other device to contact emergency first responders. Wilderness navigators need to carry these tools and know how to use them—if life is threatened, they need to be able to communicate with emergency responders. Using multiple tools increases confidence in location and route, provides backup when tools fail,

ULTRALIGHT TRAVEL

The ultralight concept is as much a philosophy of mountain travel as it is a specific set of gear recommendations. It is the antithesis of the style used by the huge Himalayan expeditions of the mid-twentieth century, which typically involved hundreds of porters and tons of equipment.

In contrast, the ultralight concept espouses two principal considerations: first, consider each item of gear and select the lightest version, and second, take the minimum amount of gear consistent with your chosen degree of commitment. Circumstances may limit what can be accomplished, and ultralighters, with their minimal gear, have less margin for error.

There have been ultralight devotees for as long as there have been mountaineers. But the modern movement toward ultralight was first popularized by Yosemite climber Ray Jardine in the 1990s. The idea is to use multipurpose, lightweight gear and clothes in place of technically sophisticated equipment.

For mountain travel, less weight may mean a more enjoyable trip. For many technical routes, climbing light means climbing faster and, consequently, more safely (see Chapter 12, Alpine Rock Climbing, for further discussion).

TABLE 2-4. THE MOUNTAINEERS' TEN ESSENTIALS

To prevent emergencies and respond positively should one occur:
1. Navigation
2. Headlamp
3. Sun protection
4. First aid
5. Knife

To safely spend a night—or more—outside:
6. Fire
7. Shelter
8. Extra food
9. Extra water
10. Extra clothes

and increases situational awareness. Refer to Chapter 5, Navigation, for in-depth information on navigation tools and techniques.

Map. Maps synthesize a vast amount of information about a region that cannot be replicated by written descriptions or memory. Each climber should carry a physical topographic map protected in a case or resealable plastic bag—it is not fragile, needs no electricity, and provides both backup and the "big picture" about a region that cannot be replicated by written descriptions or a tiny screen. If your primary map is a fragile battery-driven electronic device, carry at least one redundant device and backup power, and always carry a printed topographic map as a backup.

Altimeter. Mountaineers have long understood the importance of knowing elevation for navigation. Referring to a topographic map and knowing your elevation solve half of the navigation equation, day or night, clear skies or foggy. With just one more scrap of data—a trail, a stream, a ridge, or a bearing to a known peak—climbers can often determine where they are. Today's altimeter is a sliver of silicon that can measure air pressure or use GPS satellite signals or a combination of the two. The modern mountaineer tends to use an altimeter more frequently than a compass.

Compass. Robust and easy to use, this essential tool allows wilderness travelers to orient the map and themselves to the landscape. A compass with a baseplate is essential for taking, measuring, and following field bearings and matching them up with the map. Many smartphones, GPS devices, and wristwatches also contain an electronic compass.

GPS device. GPS has revolutionized navigation and accurately gives climbers their location on a digital map. Modern phones, combined with a reliable GPS app, rival the best dedicated GPS units for accuracy and are easier to use (see Chapter 5, Navigation). Devices often have extensive libraries of maps, many available free; download the ones you need before your trip. Together with downloaded digital maps, phones (or tablets) can guide climbers in the wilderness far from any cell towers. The caveats? Phones are fragile and they need electricity. Climbers should take steps to armor these delicate devices, keep them dry in the rain, and extend their battery life. Bringing a fully charged external battery pack is an important precaution. Dedicated GPS devices are often more rugged and weatherproof than phones, making them a good choice for extreme environments.

PLBs and satellite communicators. Historically, the mountaineer has needed to be completely self-reliant, and climbers should still have that mindset when entering the wilderness today. But when an emergency unfolds despite good tools, preparation, and training, most climbers welcome help. PLBs and satellite communicators determine your position using GPS and then send a message using government or commercial satellite networks. These devices have saved many lives; all backcountry travelers should strongly consider carrying one. Satellite phones are reliable in wilderness, but regular phones, which rely on proximity to cell towers, are not. Unless you are certain you will have a signal, assume that your phone will not function to make calls from the backcountry.

CHOOSING A GPS DEVICE

Modern mountaineers have several options available to them when it comes to GPS technology:

- **A phone combined with a good app** has become the most popular way for climbers to navigate by GPS. The extensive libraries of free digital worldwide maps made available by these apps, if downloaded before entering wilderness areas, allow freedom to travel hills near and far.
- **Dedicated GPS units** are more difficult to use and have fewer maps available, but they are more rugged and weatherproof than phones.
- **Digital wristwatches** can now provide GPS coordinates and altitude, to be used in conjunction with a physical map. Some now show tiny maps.

2. Headlamp

For climbers, headlamps are the flashlight of choice, freeing the hands for anything from cooking to climbing. Even if the climbing party plans to return before dark, each climber must carry a headlamp and consider carrying a backup. The efficient, bright LED bulb has completely replaced the inefficient incandescent bulb of a few years ago. An LED bulb lasts virtually forever but batteries do not, so carry spares. If you are using a rechargeable headlamp or batteries, start with a full charge. Any headlamp carried by an outdoor shop will be weatherproof, and a few models can survive submersion. All models allow the beam to be tilted down for close-up work, such as cooking, and pointed up for looking in the distance. Some headlamps feature a low-power red LED to preserve night vision and help climbers avoid disturbing tent mates during nocturnal excursions.

3. Sun Protection

Carry and wear sunglasses, sun-protective clothes, and broad-spectrum sunscreen rated at least SPF 30. Not doing so in the short run can lead to sunburn or snow blindness; long-term unpleasantness includes cataracts and skin cancer.

Sunglasses. In alpine country, high-quality sunglasses are critical. The eyes are particularly vulnerable to radiation, and the corneas of unprotected eyes can easily burn before any discomfort is felt, resulting in the excruciatingly painful condition known as snow blindness. Ultraviolet rays penetrate cloud layers, so do not let cloudy conditions fool you into leaving your eyes unprotected. It is advisable to wear sunglasses whenever you are outside and it is bright. This becomes critical on snow, ice, and water and at high altitudes.

Sunglasses should filter at least 99 percent of UV (ultraviolet) light, including both UVA and UVB. (Most opticians can test an old pair if you are unsure.) The tint in sunglasses allows only a fraction of the visible light through the lens to the eyes. Sunglasses, when rated, are usually scored by VLT (visible light transmission), or occasionally by percentage of light blocked. For glacier glasses, a lens should have a VLT rating of 5 to 10 percent. For conditions that don't involve snow or water, "sports sunglasses" with a VLT rating of 5 to 20 percent are sufficient. Many sunglasses have no VLT rating and should be treated as cornea-scorching fashion accessories. Look in a mirror when trying on sunglasses: if your eyes can easily be seen, the lenses are too light. Lens tints should be gray or brown for the truest color; yellow provides better contrast in overcast or foggy conditions.

Sunglass lenses should be made of polycarbonate or Trivex (a form of polyurethane). Glass, while more scratch-resistant, is heavy and can shatter. High-quality sunglasses can have a variety of helpful coatings including ones that repel water or minimize scratches or fogging. While polarized lenses can decrease glare, they annoyingly black out camera and phone LCD screens in certain orientations. Photochromic lenses automatically adjust to changing light intensity, but most lack a sufficient VLT rating

---

CHOOSING A HEADLAMP

- **Beam type, output, and distance.** Choose a headlamp that has both a wide beam and a spot beam. Each headlamp has a source output rated in lumens, a beam distance measured in meters, and a runtime measured in hours. For general-purpose mountaineering, look for a lamp rated at least 50 lumens that casts a beam at least 160 feet (50 meters) and has a runtime of at least 24 hours. Keep in mind that the amount of daylight varies significantly depending on the time of year and latitude. If you anticipate significant nighttime operations (for example, search and rescue), choose a brighter beam with a top strap and larger battery pack positioned at the back of the head. Brighter illumination consumes more battery power.
- **Weight.** The typical headlamp weighs 3 to 4 ounces (85 to 115 grams), and all are about the same size. High-powered models are bulkier and heavier (up to 11 ounces, 300 grams). Ultralight models can weigh less than an ounce (28 grams). Choose according to need.
- **Brightness modes.** Most headlamps offer varying brightness. Use low for around camp to conserve battery life and not annoy your belay partners. A high beam is useful for moving through terrain at night.
- **Battery type.** Choose a headlamp powered by AA or AAA batteries, a battery type shared by other electronics you may be taking such as a SPOT Messenger or dedicated GPS device (for more on batteries see "Batteries" later in this chapter).
- **Additional features** include a blinking mode for use as a beacon, a red lamp to preserve nighttime vision, and regulated output to keep the beam brightness constant until the batteries are exhausted.

2

for snow and adjust slowly in cold conditions. Sunglass frames should be a wraparound style or have side shields to reduce the light reaching your eyes, yet allow adequate ventilation to prevent fogging. Problems with fogging can be reduced by using an antifog lens cleaning product.

Groups should carry at least one pair of spare sunglasses in case a party member loses or forgets a pair. Eye protection can be improvised by cutting a bit of mylar from an emergency blanket or making small slits in a piece of cardboard or cloth.

Sun-protective clothes. Clothes offer more sun protection than sunscreen. Long underwear or wind garments are frequently worn on sunny glacier climbs. The discomfort of long underwear, even under blazing conditions, is often considered a minor nuisance compared with the hassle of smearing on sunscreen. Some garments are given a UPF (ultraviolet protection factor) rating, a system that is calibrated the same as the SPF rating. A UPF 50–rated garment allows $1/50$th of the UV radiation falling on its surface to pass through it. Most clothes do an admirable job blocking UV rays, but don't expect a thin white t-shirt to protect you on a long glacier climb. For the most part, UPF ratings are not critical except to those with sensitive skin. And whenever possible, wear a hat—preferably one with a full brim.

Sunscreen. Sunscreen is vital to climbers' well-being in the mountains. Although individuals vary widely in natural pigmentation and the amount of screening their skin requires, the penalty for underestimating the protection needed is severe, including the possibility of skin cancer. Certain diseases, such as lupus, and some medications, such as antibiotics and antihistamines, can cause extra sensitivity to the sun's rays.

While climbing, use a broad-spectrum sunscreen that blocks both ultraviolet A (UVA) and ultraviolet B (UVB) rays. UVA rays are the primary preventable cause of skin cancer; UVB rays primarily cause sunburn. To protect skin from UVB rays, use a sunscreen with a sunburn protection factor (SPF) of at least 30. If you are near snow or water, use SPF 50 on thin-skinned areas such as the nose and ears.

The EPA highly recommends using sunscreens that carry the regulated term "broad spectrum." While there is no standard rating for UVA such as SPF, the term "broad spectrum" means "that the product provides UVA protection that is proportional to its UVB protection." Most sunscreen ingredients absorb UV light through a chemical reaction—although titanium dioxide and zinc oxide physically block UV and cause the fewest skin reactions. Of all the chemicals used in sunscreen, these four are most likely to

CHOOSING A SUN PROTECTION STRATEGY

- First, wear appropriate sunglasses.
- Then, wear sun-protective clothes: hat, long sleeves, and pants.
- "Slop on" minimum SPF 30 broad-spectrum sunscreen to all exposed skin.
- Protect lips with sunscreen or an SPF-rated lip balm.
- Reapply sunscreen frequently.
- When using both sunscreen and insect repellent, first apply sunscreen and allow it to dry. After it has bonded to your skin, apply the repellent.

cause adverse skin reactions: aminobenzoic acid (PABA), dioxybenzone, oxybenzone, and sulisobenzone.

All sunscreens are limited by their ability to remain on the skin while you are sweating. US manufacturers can no longer claim that sunscreens are "waterproof" or "sweatproof" or identify their products as "sunblock." It is feasible for a sunscreen to be water resistant for up to 80 minutes; but regardless of the claims on the label, reapply it frequently. Frequent reapplication is often impractical on a climb, so put on a heavy coating in the morning, wear sun-protective clothes, and reapply when you can.

Generously apply sunscreen to all exposed skin, including the undersides of your chin and nose and the insides of nostrils and ears. Few climbers apply enough—follow the Australian adage "Slop it on!" Even if you are wearing a hat, apply sunscreen to all exposed parts of your face and neck to protect against reflection from snow or water. Apply sunscreen 20 minutes before exposure to the sun, because it usually takes time to start working. Sunscreen that migrates into the eyes from sweat stings relentlessly. Kids' "no-tear" sunscreen is pH balanced to help prevent this problem and so some climbers only use these products. Lips burn, too, and require protection to prevent peeling and blisters. Reapply lip protection frequently, especially after eating or drinking. When your sunscreen is past the expiration date or more than three years old, replace it. (See Chapter 24, First Aid, for information on sunburn and snow blindness.)

4. First Aid

Carry and know how to use a first-aid kit, but do not let the fact that you have one give you a false sense of security. The best course of action is to always take the steps necessary to avoid injury or sickness in the first place. Chapter 24,

First Aid, covers much more about first aid for climbers. Training in wilderness first aid or wilderness first responder skills is worthwhile. Most first-aid training is aimed at situations in urban or industrial settings where trained personnel will respond quickly. In the mountains, trained response may be hours—even days—away.

The first-aid kit should be compact and sturdy, with the contents wrapped in waterproof packaging. Commercial first-aid kits are widely available, though most are inadequate. A basic first-aid kit (see Table 24-1 in Chapter 24, First Aid) should include bandages, skin closures, gauze pads and dressings, roller bandage or wrap, tape, antiseptic, blister prevention and treatment supplies, nitrile gloves, tweezers, a needle, nonprescription painkillers and anti-inflammatory, antidiarrheal, and antihistamine tablets, a topical antibiotic, and any important personal prescriptions, including an EpiPen if you are allergic to bee or hornet venom.

Consider the length and nature of each trip in deciding what to add to the basics of the first-aid kit. For a climbing expedition, consider bringing appropriate prescription medicines.

5. Knife

Knives are so useful in first aid, food preparation, repairs, and climbing that every party member needs to carry one, preferably with a leash to prevent loss. In addition, a small repair kit can be indispensable. On a short trip, many climbers carry a small multitool, as well as strong tape and a bit of cordage. The list lengthens for more remote trips, and climbers carry an imaginative variety of supplies depending on previously experienced—or imagined—calamities. Supplies include other tools (pliers, screwdriver, awl, scissors) that can be part of a knife or pocket tool or can be carried separately—perhaps even as part of a group kit. Other useful repair items are safety pins, needle and thread, wire, duct tape, nylon fabric repair tape, cable ties, plastic buckles, cordage, webbing, and replacement parts for equipment such as a water filter, tent poles, the stove, crampons, snowshoes, and skis.

6. Fire

Carry the means to start and sustain an emergency fire. Most climbers carry a disposable butane lighter or two instead of matches. Either must be absolutely reliable. Firestarters are indispensable for igniting wet wood quickly to make an emergency campfire. Common useful firestarters include chemical heat tabs, cotton balls soaked in petroleum jelly, and commercially prepared wood soaked in wax or chemicals. Alternatively, on a high-altitude snow or glacier climb where firewood is nonexistent, it is advisable to carry a stove as an additional emergency heat and water source. (For more information on stoves, see Chapter 3, Camping, Food, and Water.)

7. Shelter

Carry some sort of emergency shelter (in addition to a rain shell) from rain and wind, such as a plastic tube tent or a jumbo plastic trash bag. Single-use bivy sacks made of heat-reflective polyethylene are an excellent option at less than 4 ounces. "Emergency space blankets," while cheap and lightweight, are inadequate to the task of keeping out wind, rain, or snow while retaining body heat. A tent can serve as the essential extra shelter only if it stays with the climbing party at all times. A tent left behind in base camp is not enough. Carry an insulated sleeping pad to reduce heat loss while sitting or lying on snow or wet terrain.

Even on day trips, some climbers carry a regular bivy sack as part of their survival gear. A bivy sack at about 1 pound (0.5 kilogram) protects insulating clothing layers from the weather, minimizes the effects of wind, and traps much of the heat escaping from your body inside its cocoon. (See "Shelter" in Chapter 3, Camping, Food, and Water, for details on tents, insulated pads, and bivy sacks.)

8. Extra Food

For shorter trips, a one-day supply of extra food is a reasonable emergency stockpile in case foul weather, faulty navigation, injury, or other reasons delay a climbing party. An expedition or long trek may require more, and on a cold trip remember that food equals warmth. The food should require no cooking, be easily digestible, and store well for long periods. A combination of jerky, nuts, candy, granola, and dried fruit works well. If a stove is carried, cocoa, dried soup, instant coffee, and tea can be added. Some climbers only half-jokingly point out that exotic flavors of energy bars and US Army meals ready to eat (MREs) serve well as emergency rations because no one is tempted to eat them except in an emergency. And a few packets of instant coffee can help a dedicated coffee drinker keep a clear head. (See more on food in Chapter 3, Camping, Food, and Water.)

9. Extra Water

Carry sufficient water and have the skills and tools required to obtain and purify additional water. Always carry at least one water bottle or hydration bag or bladder. Wide-mouth containers are easier to refill. While hydration bladders are designed to be stored in the pack and feature a plastic hose

TABLE 2-5. SAMPLE EQUIPMENT LIST

2

All your gear does not go in your pack. Some you wear, some you leave in the car (out of plain sight, of course), and some you leave at home, depending on the adventure. Items with an asterisk (*) are optional, depending on personal preference and the nature of the trip. Items within brackets [ ] can be shared by a group. See various other chapters for details on some of the gear on this list. *Note:* Because Essentials 1–7 are typically small and change little from trip to trip, keep them grouped together and ready to go.

ITEMS LEFT IN OR NEAR THE TRAILHEAD VEHICLE

- Map, directions to trailhead, and weather forecast
- *Refreshing drinks
- *Spare key (hidden on the outside of the car or near the car)
- *Pack scale (for checking pack weight at the start of the trip)
- Extra water
- *Fresh clothes for the drive home

ITEMS WORN OR CARRIED (assuming a cool morning to start, dressed as in Figure 2-2a)

- Day pack (day trips), or
- Backpack (overnight)
- Boots and *gaiters
- Socks (synthetic or wool) and *liners
- Brimmed hat
- Base layer top
- Long-sleeved shirt
- *Base layer bottoms
- *Underwear
- *Shorts
- Lightweight nylon pants (*zip-off legs)
- Wristwatch altimeter
- Trekking poles
- Keys to trailhead vehicle

PACKED GEAR FOR ALL TRIPS

THE TEN ESSENTIALS

1. **Navigation:** map, altimeter, compass, [GPS device: phone with GPS app or dedicated GPS device], [PLB, satellite communicator, or satellite phone], [extra batteries], [battery pack]
2. **Headlamp:** plus extra batteries
3. **Sun protection:** sunglasses, sun-protective clothes, and sunscreen
4. **First aid:** including foot care and insect repellent (if required)
5. **Knife:** plus repair kit
6. **Fire:** matches, lighter and tinder, or stove as appropriate
7. **Shelter:** carried at all times (can be lightweight emergency bivy)
8. **Extra food:** beyond minimum expectation
9. **Extra water:** beyond minimum expectation, or the means to purify
10. **Extra clothes:** beyond minimum expectation, as detailed below

CLOTHING

Garments that may be worn during the active portion of a climb as well as "extra clothes" that could be needed to survive the long, inactive hours of an unplanned bivouac. Choices depend on probable worst-case weather, thus none are marked as optional:

Base layer:
- Top and bottoms to wear while active
- Extra dry set for camp and to wear while sleeping

Midlayers:
- Synthetic shirts and pants
- Synthetic fleece
- Wool knit shirts
- Double-weave softshell jacket
- Double-weave softshell pants
- Puffy jacket (synthetic, down, or "active insulation")

Shell layers and belay jacket:
- Wind shell jacket
- Wind shell pants
- Laminated softshell jacket
- Waterproof-breathable laminated softshell jacket
- Hardshell jacket
- Hardshell pants (rain pants)
- Belay jacket

Head, hands, and feet:
- Warm hat (synthetic or wool)
- Warm hat (under-helmet)

- Rain hat
- Balaclava
- Buff or neck tube (extra)
- Leather gloves for belaying and rappelling
- Gloves or mittens (extra)
- Glove or mitten liners
- Socks (extra)
- Waterproof-breathable socks
- Stream-crossing footwear
- Gaiters: short, long, or expedition

continued

OTHER (NONCLIMBING) GEAR
- Lunch and/or snacks sufficient for the climb
- Water (minimum 2 liters)
- Toilet kit (toilet paper and blue bags), *trowel
- *Insect repellent
- *Local communication devices: whistle, walkie-talkie
- *Spare eyeglasses
- *Cup
- *Nylon cord
- *Camera
- Battery backups for electronic gear
- *Binoculars
- *Bandanna
- *Protective phone cover

BASIC CLIMBING GEAR FOR ALL CLIMBS
- Helmet
- Climbing harness
- Personal anchor with locking carabiner
- Carabiners (including a large HMS locking carabiner or pearabiner)
- Runners
- Belay-rappel device
- *Leather gloves for belaying and rappelling
- Prusik slings
- [Climbing rope]
- *Approach shoes

ADDITIONAL ITEMS FOR AN OVERNIGHT TRIP
- Sleeping bag and stuff sack
- Sleeping pad
- [Tent], [tarp], or *bivy sack
- *[Ground cloth]
- [Food]
- [Water container(s)]
- [Group first-aid kit]
- [Group repair kit]
- [Stove, fuel, and accessories]
- [Pot(s) (and cleaning pad)]
- Spoon
- *Fork
- *Bowl
- *Toiletries
- *Alarm clock or alarm watch
- *Clothes to wear in camp and while sleeping
- *Camp footwear
- *Pack cover

ADDITIONAL GEAR FOR ROCK CLIMBS
- [Rack: chocks, cams, etc.]
- [Nut tool]
- *Rock climbing shoes
- *Chalk
- *Athletic tape

ADDITIONAL GEAR FOR SNOW, GLACIER, OR WINTER CLIMBS

CLIMBING
- Ice axe
- Chest sling or harness
- Waist and foot prusik slings
- Rescue pulley
- [Pickets and ice screws]
- Crampons adjusted to boots
- *MICROspikes
- *Powder baskets for trekking poles

ADDITIONAL WARM CLOTHES
- Base layer: Consider heavier-weight top and bottom.
- Midlayers: Consider additional and heavier-weight layers for insulation.

- Shell layer: Consider sturdier or additional shell layers.
- Belay jacket: increasingly important as the temperature drops. Consider one for each climber (rather than shared).
- Head, hands, and feet: consider taking more items that can work as a system as well as backups.
- Boots: Consider more-robust mountaineering boots.

OTHER GEAR
- [Dedicated GPS device (extreme environments)]
- [Spare sunglasses]
- [Snow shovel]
- *Snowshoes or *skis
- *Avalanche transceiver
- *Avalanche probes
- *[Wands]
- *[Snow saw]
- *Hand and foot warmers
- *Thermos bottle

and valve that allow drinking without slowing your pace, they are prone to leaking and freezing, are notoriously hard to keep clean, and often lead climbers to carry more water than they need to.

Before starting on the trail, fill water containers from a reliable source. In most environments, you need to have the ability to treat water—by filtering, using purification chemicals, or boiling—from rivers, streams, lakes, and other sources. In cold environments, you will need a stove, fuel, pot, and lighter to melt snow. Daily water consumption varies greatly. For most people, 1.5 to 3 quarts (approximately the same in liters) of water per day is enough; in hot weather or at high altitudes, 6 quarts may not be enough. Plan for enough water to accommodate additional requirements due to heat, cold, altitude, exertion, or emergency. See "Water" in Chapter 3, Camping, Food, and Water, for details on water sources and purification.

10. Extra Clothes

What extra clothes are necessary for an emergency beyond the basic climbing garments used during the active portion of a climb? The term "extra clothes" refers to additional layers that would be needed to survive the long, inactive hours of an unplanned bivouac. Ask this question: *What extra clothes are needed to survive the night in my emergency shelter in the worst conditions that could realistically be encountered on this trip?*

An extra layer of long underwear can add warmth without adding much weight. An extra hat or balaclava will provide more warmth for its weight than any other article of clothing. For your feet, bring an extra pair of heavy socks; for your hands, an extra pair of mittens. For winter and expedition climbing in severe conditions, bring more insulation for your torso as well as your legs. (See "Choosing a Cold-Weather Strategy" sidebar, earlier in this chapter.)

OTHER IMPORTANT ITEMS

Many items in addition to the Ten Essentials are, of course, useful for climbing. Every climber has an opinion and with experience all climbers develop their own preferences. Think ahead. Take time periodically to envision scenarios of possible accidents and unexpected circumstances, including being separated from your party, lost and alone. What would you do in those situations? What equipment would be necessary to be prepared? What risks are you willing to accept?

Ice Axe

Indispensable for preventing or arresting falls on steep snow and glaciers, an ice axe is very useful on snow-covered alpine trails and for traveling in steep heather, scree, or brush; for crossing streams; and for digging sanitation holes. (For details on ice axes and their uses, see Chapter 6, Wilderness Travel, and Chapter 16, Snow Travel and Climbing.)

Crampons and MICROspikes

While an ice axe is indispensable, especially for arresting a fall on steep snow or ice, crampons help prevent a fall from occurring. On icy alpine trails, MICROspikes—essentially "tire chains" for your boots—can prevent an unintended triple axel into a tree. (See "Crampons" in Chapter 16, Snow Travel and Climbing to learn more.)

Trekking Poles

Trekking poles help propel climbers uphill and brake on the way down. They offer stability to cross streams and travel on snow or scree. They redistribute effort across arms and legs, minimizing the peak loads on leg muscles to increase overall endurance.

Some climbers shorten adjustable trekking poles slightly when traveling uphill (fig. 2-10a) and lengthen them slightly when traveling downhill (fig. 2-10b). If you need to change their length quickly, for example, when traversing uneven terrain, slide your uphill hand as far as necessary

CHOOSING TREKKING POLES

Take these features into consideration when choosing trekking poles:

- **Grips.** Foam or cork grips are designed for bare hands. Rubber grips are for use with gloves but tend to cause blisters on bare hands.
- **Shafts.** Aluminum poles tend to bend before they break. Carbon fiber poles are lighter but more expensive and may fracture unexpectedly.
- **Shock absorbers.** They add weight and cost, but some people prefer them.
- **Baskets.** Most poles come with small snow baskets, helpful also on ground or rock where it's easy to catch a pole tip. Larger baskets are useful when the snow is soft.
- **Tips.** Carbide steel withstands abrasion.
- **Length.** Most poles are adjustable using a locking mechanism; they should be long enough to allow a 90-degree angle at the elbow when standing on level ground. Poles should telescope or fold for easy stowing inside the pack. Women's trekking poles are shorter and have smaller grips.
- **Locking mechanisms.** Older designs primarily used twist-locks, which were prone to slipping when weighted. External lever and push-button locks are more secure and quicker to adjust in the field. Folding poles use an internal cord to keep sections together and tightly aligned.

Fig. 2-10. Using trekking poles while traveling: a, shorten poles to go uphill; b, lengthen poles to go downhill; and c, slide hand down the uphill pole for quick changes as needed when scrambling in uneven terrain.

down the shaft of the pole below the handle (fig. 2-10c). Using the wrist strap is a bit counterintuitive. First, put your hand up through the strap and then grab both the strap and pole grip so that the strap comfortably supports the wrist. To scramble a short, steep section, let the poles dangle by the wrist straps. For a longer stretch, collapse the poles and stow them in the pack. Some ultralight tents use trekking poles in lieu of tent poles to save weight (see Chapter 3, Camping, Food, and Water).

Toilet Kit

A toilet kit might consist of paper, sanitary wipes, a small digging trowel, "blue bags," and hand sanitizer. Location and regulations will dictate actions, but each climber needs to act responsibly to not allow human waste to foul the wild spaces we all love. Typically, alpine areas lack toilet facilities and so climbers must transfer all feces and toilet paper into blue bags, and store them at the bottom of their packs. Alpine areas have no soil to decompose feces or toilet paper, which if left behind foul the area for decades. Lower-elevation sites may have sufficient soil to aid the decomposition of feces, but few areas have sufficient capacity to decompose toilet paper. Wipes are primarily made from polyester and do not decompose. Climbers should always plan to remove toilet paper and wipes for disposal at the end of the trip. (See "Managing Human Waste in the Mountains" in Chapter 7, Leave No Trace, for proper disposal procedures.)

Insect Repellent

Some insects—mosquitoes, ticks, chiggers, biting flies, no-see-um gnats—feast on the human body. In the United States in the past 20 years we have seen a substantial increase in reported cases of mosquito-borne and tick-borne diseases. For winter trips or for snow climbs any time of year, insect repellent may be unnecessary; for a low-elevation summer approach, however, thwarting these pests may be essential. When traveling in areas in the United States with disease-carrying mosquitoes (think Zika virus and West Nile virus) or disease-carrying ticks (think Lyme disease and Rocky Mountain spotted fever), take extra precautions to avoid being bitten and infected. Internationally, the situation is more complicated and the risk of malaria, Zika, and dengue loom large. In tropical areas, antimalaria medications and bed-netting may be warranted.

CHOOSING A BUG DEFENSE STRATEGY

- First, wear pants, long sleeves, et cetera, as a physical barrier.
- Wear factory- or home-applied permethrin-treated clothes.
- Apply insect repellent to clothes in the field.
- Lastly, carefully apply the minimum needed insect repellent to skin.

TABLE 2-6. CHOOSING INSECT REPELLENTS

If insects are expected to be a potential health hazard and not just an annoyance, use multiple lines of defense: protective clothes, clothes treated with permethrin, and insect repellents applied in the field.

ACTIVE INGREDIENT (available concentrations)	APPLICATION	EFFECTIVENESS AGAINST		
		Mosquitoes	Ticks & Chiggers	Biting Flies & Blackflies
Field Application				
DEET (5%–100%)	Clothes and skin	2–12 hours	2–10 hours	Poor
Picaridin (5%–20%)	Clothes and skin	4–14 hours	6–14 hours	Good
IR3535 (7.5%–20%)	Clothes and skin	2–10 hours	2–8 hours	Yes
Oil of lemon eucalyptus (30%–40%)	Clothes and skin	6 hours	6 hours	Yes
Home or Factory Application				
Permethrin (0.5%–10%)	Clothes only	Yes	Yes	Yes
Avoid				
Citronella and other natural ingredients	Not applicable	No	No	No

Notes: "Yes" means the repellent's effectiveness in number of hours has not been quantified; "No" means it did not meet the benchmark of more than 2 hours' proven repellency. Permethrin applied at home is good through several launderings; factory applications claim effectiveness for the life of the garment. Catnip oil sold as "refined oil of nepeta cataria 7% lotion" is a new, natural ingredient, registered effective against mosquitoes but not ticks.

The first line of defense against voracious insects is covering up with clothes heavy enough to provide a physical barrier, including gloves and head nets in really buggy areas. In hot weather, long shirts and pants made of netting may prove worthwhile.

The next defensive measure is wearing factory- or home-applied permethrin-treated clothes as a chemical barrier and applying a spritz of (non-permethrin) repellent (for example, picaridin) as needed in the field to the outer layer of clothing—whether permethrin treated or not. A solid application to hat and scarf helps protect the face. Pay particular attention to socks as mosquitoes have an uncanny ability to target ankles. Finally, carefully apply an appropriate insect repellent to exposed skin being especially careful around the face. And know that sometimes the bugs win the battle; retreating to a tent with a full bug screen may be the only way to preserve sanity.

In the United States, insect repellents must be registered with the Environmental Protection Agency (EPA) and have solid evidence for all safety and effectiveness claims (Table 2-6). There are currently only five active ingredients with EPA registrations that claim to repel mosquitoes and ticks for more than two hours: DEET, picaridin, permethrin, IR3535, and oil of lemon eucalyptus. Botanical oils (citronella, soybean, lemongrass, cedar, et cetera) are no

better than minimally effective. Insect repellents come in spray, liquid, cream, stick, and wipe forms and in various concentrations, with sprays the only easy option for clothes. Treated wristbands, vitamin supplements, garlic, and ultrasonic repellents are all equally ineffective.

Be extra bug-vigilant between dawn and dusk when bugs bite most. Mosquitoes have trouble tracking targets in windy conditions so camp and take breaks accordingly. When using sunscreen and repellent, first apply sunscreen and allow it to dry. After it has dried, apply the repellent. To minimize your attractiveness to insects (and bears!), avoid wearing fragrances. In tick country—especially on days when you have been thrashing through brush—check your clothes, body, and hair thoroughly at night.

DEET. Developed in 1944 for the US Army, DEET entered civilian use in 1957 and it is still the gold standard against mosquitoes, although permethrin and picaridin are solid competitors. One application of a repellent with a high concentration or a controlled-release formula of DEET will keep mosquitoes from biting for several hours, though they may still hover about annoyingly. Be aware that DEET is a powerful chemical that can dissolve plastics and synthetic fabrics. While products can be purchased in varying concentrations up to 100 percent, a 30 percent concentration is safer and likely sufficient. For multihour protection use a 30 percent concentration in a time-release formula. DEET is not very effective at repelling biting flies. Permethrin-treated clothes and picaridin repellents are better against blackflies, deer flies, and gnats.

Permethrin. *For long-lasting use on clothes only,* never on skin, permethrin is the synthetic chemical analog to the naturally occurring chemical found in chrysanthemum flowers. It is the only insect repellent registered for factory treatment of clothes. The amount of permethrin allowed in clothes is very low and is poorly absorbed through the skin, so is not a safety concern. The more members of the party that use permethrin-treated clothes, the more effective it will be. Permethrin-treated clothes are odorless and compatible with being sprayed with the other four repellents listed here.

Picaridin (also known as Icaridin, KBR 3023, Bayrepel, and Saltidin). Available in Europe since 2001 and first registered with the US EPA in 2005, this odorless, nongreasy, non-plastic-melting repellent is preferred by many to DEET. Picaridin is recommended to repel disease-carrying mosquitoes by both the World Health Organization and the US Centers for Disease Control and Prevention. The EPA allows claims for up to 14 hours for the 20 percent concentration.

IR3535. According to the EPA, "IR3535 has been used as an insect repellent in Europe for 20 years with no substantial adverse effects."

Oil of lemon eucalyptus (also known as OLE and PMD). Commercially available oil of lemon eucalyptus is chemically synthesized to mimic a naturally occurring molecule similar to menthol. This ingredient is effective against mosquitoes, ticks, biting flies, and gnats.

LOCAL COMMUNICATION DEVICES

The climbing party may need tools for communicating locally. Whistles, avalanche transceivers, and walkie-talkies may facilitate communication among a climbing party that finds itself spread out along the route or to locate a lost or incapacitated member.

Whistle. A whistle's shrill, penetrating blast greatly exceeds the range of the human voice and can serve as a crude means of communication in situations in which shouts for help cannot be heard—such as being trapped in a crevasse or becoming separated from the party in fog, darkness, or thick forest. Whistles prove much more useful if a climbing party designates specific signals before the trip for "Where are you?," "I'm here and OK," and "Help!" Three signals from any signaling device, repeated several times in sequence, is universal for "SOS."

Avalanche transceiver. Conditions may call for mountaineers to carry avalanche transceivers, used to locate victims of a snowslide. See Chapter 16, Snow Travel and Climbing, for detailed instructions on using avalanche transceivers.

Walkie-talkie or handheld two-way radio. The sounds of wind and water and physical obstacles between the two ends of a climbing rope can make communication difficult. Walkie-talkies can greatly ease communication between climbing partners or between a climbing party and base camp. Walkie-talkies include both family radio service (FRS) two-way radios and handheld amateur "ham" radios. FRS radios are commonly used by climbing parties for short-range communications (up to a few miles or kilometers). Modern handheld amateur "ham" radios are inexpensive, lightweight, and in some areas, can communicate worldwide through "repeaters." They are more complex than FRS radios. To be useful, all walkie-talkies in the party must be set to operate at the same frequency. Bring sufficient batteries. For summoning help in remote mountain areas, walkie-talkies are generally not reliable. Carry a PLB, satellite communicator, or satellite phone instead.

More tools. In the field, route markers can aid the return trip where the party lacks redundant GPS capability, or otherwise mark dangers such as crevasses. Remove route markers (such as glacier wands) after use to leave no trace.

BATTERIES

An expanding list of backcountry electronics—including GPS devices, satellite communicators, headlamps, walkie-talkies, and avalanche beacons—run on batteries so battery type and size are part of the equipment checklist. The standard batteries for most devices are 1.5 volt AA and AAA. AA cells contain roughly twice the capacity of the smaller AAA at a similar price. Batteries operate through chemical processes adversely affected by cold temperatures; Table 2-7 compares overall performance of batteries at low temperatures.

TIPS FOR USING ELECTRONIC DEVICES IN COLD WEATHER

- Use disposable lithium batteries where possible; bring extras.
- Use your pockets and sleeping bag to keep electronics as warm as possible.
- Cycle batteries and backups through warm pockets.

TABLE 2-7. BATTERY PERFORMANCE AT COLD TEMPERATURES				
TEMPERATURE IN DEGREES	DISPOSABLE ALKALINE	LITHIUM	RECHARGEABLE NiMH	Li-ION
Overall	Poor	Excellent	Poor	Excellent
32°F (0°C)	70%	100%	75%	90%
-4°F (-20°C)	25%	80%	25%	80%
-40°F (-40°C)	0%	50%	0%	50%

Note: The minimum recommended operating temperature for each type of battery (in order from left to right) is -4° (-20°), -40° (-40°), 32° (0°), -40° (-40°).

Alkaline batteries. Alkaline batteries are the most commonly available general-purpose batteries. Their major problem is that voltage (hence, brightness) drops significantly as they discharge. Cold temperatures drastically accelerate this voltage drop, resulting in much shorter battery life.

Lithium batteries. Much longer lasting and lighter than alkaline, lithium batteries also cost more. Voltage remains almost constant over their charge, and efficiency at 0 degrees Fahrenheit (minus 18 degrees Celsius) is nearly the same as at room temperature. The more powerful the electronic device, the bigger the advantage lithium batteries have over alkalines. Cold temperatures compound this advantage. For cold-weather trips, lithium batteries are the clear choice for high-powered headlamps and other critical devices such as the SPOT Messengers.

Rechargeable batteries. One popular strategy is to use rechargeables for main batteries and disposable batteries as spares. Nickel–metal hydride (NiMH) rechargeables have replaced the once common nickel-cadmium (NiCd) in standard AA and AAA sizes, while lithium-ion (Li-ion) batteries are usually found in higher-voltage consumer electronics such as phones. Caution: NiMH batteries tend to self-discharge rapidly in storage at approximately 30 percent per month. Always start with a full charge.

Lithium-ion batteries. Li-ion batteries (not to be confused with disposable lithium batteries) are the power plants inside phones, cameras, and most battery packs (see below). Li-ion batteries are not yet available in standard 1.5 volt AA and AAA sizes. Li-ion batteries perform well in cold temperatures.

Portable battery packs. Based on Li-ion technology, battery packs are a handy way to store additional power to recharge Li-ion-powered devices such as phones and cameras. Their capacity is rated in milliamp hours (mAh), with about 3000 mAh currently needed to recharge a cell phone. Make sure they are fully charged at the start of each trip.

Solar panels. Affected by weather, length of day, and sun exposure, the use of portable solar panels requires planning and attention. The higher a panel's wattage, the faster it charges. While panels can charge devices directly, each passing cloud might interrupt the process. A more reliable alternative is to charge an intermediate portable battery pack.

Regardless of your choice, make sure you start each trip with batteries compatible with your headlamp and navigation tools, all with more than sufficient charge to handle any reasonable emergency.

PREPARING FOR THE FREEDOM OF THE HILLS

When you go into the wilderness, you should carry essential gear and leave the rest at home. Achieving that balance takes knowledge and good judgment. Understanding the basics of clothing and equipment will help you decide on those essentials needed to be safe, dry, and comfortable in the mountains. This is only the beginning of your discovery of the freedom of the hills. The next chapter on camping, food, and water will further expand your horizons.

CHAPTER 3

CAMPING, FOOD, AND WATER

The art of alpine camping under the "starry firmament" allows us to pass through primeval mountain locations. Camp offers the restoration of warm food, shelter, and sleep, and the best campers go stealthily through wild spaces, leaving no trace of their passing. In the words of John Muir, founder of the Sierra Club, ". . . standing alone on the mountain-top it is easy to realize that whatever special nests we make . . . we all dwell in a house of one room—the world with the firmament for its roof—and are sailing the celestial spaces without leaving any track."

THE SLEEPING SYSTEM

The sleeping system is what gets you through the night in the wilderness in safety and comfort. The system has four components: sleeping clothes, a sleeping bag, ground insulation, and shelter.

SLEEPING CLOTHES AND ACCESSORIES

Experienced climbers carefully guard a dry set of clothes to wear at camp and in their sleeping bags, typically a spare base layer, warm hat, gloves, and dry socks. Upon arriving at the evening's camp, they'll ditch the damp clothes from the climb and don the dry, warding off the evening chill. Sleeping clothes, a puffy coat, camp shoes, and a hot drink boost the revitalization process. In addition, this reduces the moisture introduced into the sleeping bag and keeps the bag clean. Since climbers cannot afford the weight of multiple sets of clothes, while wearing their dry evening set they use any final sunshine to attempt to dry out what will be tomorrow's climbing clothes. Precipitation, of course, complicates the evening procedure.

A few accessories can help climbers get a good night's sleep. A small inflatable pillow is especially useful for side sleepers. A conveniently placed (and well-marked!) pee bottle can minimize the chill and hazard of nocturnal excursions.

SLEEPING BAGS

A good sleeping bag fits your body, retains body heat, and is light and compressible. For cold conditions, nothing beats the efficient mummy bag (fig. 3-1). A sleeping bag's fill material traps an insulating layer of air between the climber's warm body and the external cooler air. A bag's thermal efficiency depends on each climber's unique physiology; fit of the bag to the body; and the type, amount, and loft (thickness) of the insulation.

Physiological factors. A sleeping bag only slows body heat's inevitable escape. Individuals vary considerably in their ability to generate heat and tolerate cold, depending on muscle mass, age, and gender. Young, fit men typically produce more body heat than older men and much more heat than women. Experienced mountaineers and people who work outside may feel more comfortable in cold environments than people who work in offices. Heavier people often run warmer than slim people.

Fit. A sleeping bag that is too long or wide creates excess interior volume that needs heating and adds unnecessary

46

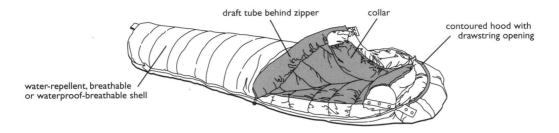

Fig. 3-1. Mountaineering mummy bag features and components.

weight. Being too tight in any dimension forces your body to compress the insulation, making the bag colder. Choose a design that fits you well. Size the bag a little larger for winter camping or expedition use; the extra room together with your convective body heat helps dry small items such as wet gloves, socks, and boot liners. Use caution, however, when trying to use your sleeping bag as a dryer: the excess moisture can collect in the insulation, particularly on longer trips.

THIEVES IN THE NIGHT

A sleeping bag and mattress or pad are used to prevent excessive heat loss. As the night gets progressively colder, insulation is needed to balance heat generation against thermal theft, which happens in all of the following ways:

- **Warm air (convection).** The body continually warms the air around it. Clothes and sleeping bags trap this warm air, slowing its escape to the atmosphere.
- **Breathing and sweat (respiration and evaporation).** People lose about a liter of water through breath and sweat every night. In colder environments, the warm, moist air you breathe out can be a significant form of heat loss.
- **Cold ground (conduction).** Direct contact with cold ground also sucks heat away from the body. Rock and snow are the most conductive surfaces encountered in the wilderness; grass, dry dirt, and forest duff are the least. Camping mattresses or pads help to insulate you from cold ground; look for higher R-values for colder surfaces.
- **Radiant heat (infrared radiation).** The night vision goggles of the movies remind us that every living body has a heat signature from the direct loss of heat through infrared radiation. Radiant heat represents up to 10 percent of our heat loss, and recent innovations that use reflective materials in insulating air mattresses and clothes capture and return some of this heat.

Bag Rating Systems

Historically, a sleeping bag rating gave only rough guidance of the coldest temperature at which an average person would stay warm through the night, assuming use of long underwear, a hat, and an insulated pad. Now, many sleeping bags—though not all, including some high-quality bags—are independently rated under international standard ISO 23537 or EN13537. These new standards do not apply to use by children or military personnel or in extremely cold conditions.

Under the standard, each bag is assigned four temperature ratings:

1. **Upper Limit:** The highest temperature for a "standard man" to sleep without sweating.
2. **Comfort:** The lowest temperature for a "standard woman" to have a comfortable night's sleep.
3. **Lower Limit:** The lowest temperature for a standard man to have a comfortable night's sleep.
4. **Extreme:** The survival rating for a standard woman.

Women and men should use the Comfort and Lower Limit ratings, respectively, for choosing a sleeping bag. Table 3-1 offers rough seasonal guidelines. For a three-season camping example, Table 3-1 gives a rough low temperature of 15 degrees Fahrenheit; the average woman would want a bag with a Comfort rating of 15 degrees Fahrenheit, and the average man would want a bag with a Lower Limit rating of 15 degrees Fahrenheit.

Most of us are not "standard"; climbers must consider their personal metabolism, body composition, and particularly any additional insulation that they may wear in the sleeping bag. Other factors that affect warmth are the level of hydration or fatigue, and the quality of shelter

TABLE 3-1. SEASONAL GUIDELINES FOR SLEEPING BAGS	
SEASON	TEMPERATURE RANGE
Summer	Above 40°F (above 4°C)
Three-season (spring, fall, and high altitudes in summer)	15° to 40°F (-9° to 4°C)
Winter camping	-10° to 15°F (-23° to -9°C)
Polar and extreme alpine	Below -10°F (below -23°C)

and ground insulation (see the "Tips on Staying Warm in a Sleeping Bag" sidebar).

Insulation, Fabric, and Environmental Factors

The two types of insulation for mountaineering sleeping bags are natural down (goose or duck) and polyester fibers, each with advantages and disadvantages. Both types can now be treated with durable water repellent (DWR) chemicals to increase their hydrophobic properties. (See Chapter 2, Clothing and Equipment, for a discussion of insulating fills and DWR.)

The nylon or polyester fabrics used in mountaineering sleeping bags are tightly woven to keep the insulation in place. Waterproof-breathable fabrics are expensive but advantageous in damp environments such as a snow cave or wet tent; they are especially desirable with a down bag. Shell materials are treated with DWR, giving the same advantages and limitations as when used in clothing (see "Waterproof Fabrics" in Chapter 2 for details).

Any attempts to waterproof a sleeping bag, including using waterproof-breathable materials, will decrease the bag's ability to pass body moisture through to the atmosphere. The trade-off is between the risk of external water—rain, snow, tent condensation, dew—and the risk of significant perspiration and damp clothing. In wet environments most climbers will want to use a bag with synthetic insulation or waterproof-breathable fabrics.

Condensation dampness or dew is particularly insidious. As the evening's air cools, it releases moisture, condensing as dew, especially on cold objects. In humid environments, avoiding dew in the evening as the temperature falls toward the dew point is critical for sleeping bags and clothes. As the night air cools, keep tents zipped (and thus slightly warmer), sleeping bags stuffed, and clothes stowed away until bedtime to minimize dampness.

Features and Components

The features and components of a sleeping bag affect efficiency and ventilation (see Figure 3-1). A close-fitting hood surrounds your head, retaining precious heat while leaving your face uncovered for respiration. Collars that seal around the neck and draft tubes along the length of the zipper further retain heat inside the main body of the bag. Long zippers make it easy to get in and out of the bag and help ventilate excess heat if the bag gets too warm. Some designs offer complementary left- and right-hand zippers so that two bags can be zipped together. Using a half- or three-quarter-length zipper saves weight and bulk but sacrifices flexibility in ventilation.

Accessories

Washable sleeping bag liners add a few degrees of warmth and keep body oils from soiling the bag's interior and insulation. But bag liners add weight and bulk, and the same objective can be accomplished with a clean, dry set of multipurpose sleeping clothes.

Vapor-barrier liners (VBLs) are either a sleeping bag liner or a full multipiece suit constructed of a waterproof-nonbreathable material. In frigid conditions and especially on longer trips, VBLs can be used to protect clothing and

TIPS ON STAYING WARM IN A SLEEPING BAG

- **Eat well and stay hydrated.** If you wake up cold, increase your metabolism by drinking and eating.
- **Use proper ground insulation.** A fully inflated pad or insulating air mattress will maximize the insulation potential.
- **Wear dry clothes,** including a base layer, hat or balaclava, gloves, and dry socks.
- **Augment loft** by wearing insulated clothes inside, or placing an insulated jacket on top of the sleeping bag.
- **Place a leakproof bottle of hot liquid in the bag.**
- **Use a pee bottle** when nature calls to avoid getting cooled down from stepping outside.
- **Change clothes inside the sleeping bag.**

sleeping bag insulation from the degradation caused by per-spiration condensing *inside* the insulation. You sleep inside the VBL (typically wearing a base layer), inside the sleeping bag. These liners reduce evaporative heat loss and the amount of moisture (in arctic environments: ice) buildup within the sleeping bag's insulation. Clothing insulation, especially that worn on the hands and feet, can be similarly protected. Test out a VBL before using it on an expedition; many climbers find them awkward and clammy.

Most sleeping bags come with a semi-waterproof stuff sack for storage during trips and a larger, breathable storage sack for storage between trips. In possibly wet conditions, use a waterproof stuff sack or plastic bag. Use a compression stuff sack to save pack space, especially with typically hard-to-compress synthetic bags. Fleece-lined stuff sacks double as a pillow.

Specialty Bags

Some climbers prefer to go as light as possible, sacrificing a little comfort for less weight. Used in conjunction with an insulating jacket, half- or three-quarter-length bags can be adequate to just below freezing. Some ultralight enthusiasts prefer a simple zipperless, hoodless quilt with down or polyester insulation.

Care and Cleaning

With a little care, a sleeping bag will last for many years.

Storage. Always store the bag fully lofted. Only keep the bag in a compression stuff sack for short periods of time, for instance, while traveling or when carrying it in a backpack.

Cleaning down and synthetic bags. Spot-clean soiled areas with soap specified by the manufacturer, then wash in full, when needed. Never dry-clean a down sleeping bag. Before washing, secure all zippers and snaps, and remove detachable pieces. Bags with waterproof-breathable shells should be washed inside out. Wash the bag with mild non-detergent (preferably down-specific) soap on the gentle cycle in a large front-loading washing machine. Run the bag through the rinse cycle several times to remove all soap. Re-treat the DWR finish as required (see "Clothing Care" in Chapter 2, Clothing and Equipment) while still wet, and dry the bag in a large clothes dryer using medium heat. Remove the bag occasionally and break up clumps of down, or throw a few tennis balls into the dryer. Squeeze the insulation to check for moisture. Washing and drying a bag takes several hours. Some outdoor repair shops specialize in laundering sleeping bags.

GROUND INSULATION

The foundation of a comfortable night in the outdoors is good insulation under the sleeping bag. A sleeping pad reduces the amount of heat you lose to cold ground or snow. If you are forced to sleep without a pad, use extra clothing, your pack, climbing rope, or boots for padding and insulation.

Type

There are four common types of pads; for a comparison, see Table 3-2.

Closed-cell foam. Bulkier than pneumatic options, a thin pad of closed-cell foam provides good lightweight insulation that cannot fail from a puncture. Textured designs lend a softer sleeping surface, lower weight, and increased ability to trap air, resulting in greater thermal efficiency. Some molded patterns make for simple and compact storage.

Self-inflating pad. The bulky, water-absorbing open-cell foam pad of long ago evolved into the self-inflating pad, with Therm-a-Rest being the best-known brand. The open-cell foam is enclosed in an airtight, waterproof chamber that compresses well.

TABLE 3-2. CHOOSING GROUND INSULATION		
GROUND INSULATION	**TYPICAL R-VALUES**	**TYPICAL USES**
Closed-cell foam: 0.38 in., 0.63 in., 0.75 in. (1 cm, 1.5 cm, 2 cm)	R1.5, 2.7, 3.5	Inexpensive and puncture-proof. Multipurpose pads for sitting, dressing, cooking. Frequently combined with three-quarter-length self-inflating pad or insulating air mattress.
Self-inflating pad: 1.5 in.–2 in. (3.8–5 cm)	R2–5	General-purpose insulating pad.
Non-insulating air mattress	R1	Not appropriate for mountaineering except in mild weather.
Insulating air mattress	R2–5	General-purpose insulating mattress.

Non-insulating air mattress. A basic inflatable mattress provides plenty of cushion to cover bumps, rocks, and roots. Non-insulating air mattresses are typically compact, but the air in the mattress convects heat away from the body by internal air circulation. Coupling non-insulating air and closed-cell foam mattresses is an effective and inexpensive solution for colder weather.

Insulating air mattress. Modern versions of the air mattress employ complex internal chambers and insulation to minimize air convection currents, and they use radiant-heat-reflective materials to reflect infrared radiation back to the sleeper. Once inflated, these lightweight, extremely small sleeping pads have high warmth ratings, very useful on snow and ice. However, these mattresses offer no insulation if punctured.

Size and Warmth

Self-inflating pads and insulating air mattresses come in various lengths, but a shorter (4 feet, or 120 centimeters) size is usually adequate for general mountaineering; you can use a smaller closed-cell foam sit pad (or items of gear) to pad and insulate feet and legs. For greater insulation when camping on snow or in winter or arctic environments, use a short, self-inflating pad on top of a full-length closed-cell foam pad.

Pads are rated for warmth by R-value, a measure of thermal resistance. For example, pads with a rating of R2.5 protect well down to about freezing; R4, to about 15 degrees Fahrenheit (minus 10 degrees Celsius); and R5-plus, for colder temperatures. Lower R-values are needed for sleeping on grass or dry forest duff than for sleeping on wet ground, rock, and snow, which have relatively high conductivity. Table 3-2 shows typical R-values and uses of ground insulation.

SHELTER

The seventh of the Ten Essentials, shelter is key to surviving a night in the wilderness and usually means a tent, tarp, or bivy. If you are not carrying shelter on a day trip, or will be away from shelter on the summit attempt, carry emergency shelter that is sufficient for the entire party.

The most common and versatile mountain shelter, tents are relatively easy to set up and provide rainproof privacy and refuge from wind or sun. They are usable in almost any terrain, and are often roomy enough for people and their gear. Tents usually are the first choice above timberline, on glaciers, in winter, and in bear or mosquito country.

A lightweight alternative to tents, tarps can be used in conjunction with bivy sacks to provide effective shelter

from rain and sun. Bivy sacks also make great lightweight emergency shelters.

When selecting a tent or tarp, climbers must weigh protection (sturdiness and coverage), weight, and space (fig. 3-2). There are trade-offs. Consider how and where you will use the shelter as well as your personal preferences (see the "Choosing a Tent" sidebar). Shelters come in many shapes and sizes (fig. 3-3).

Moisture Strategies

Tents serve two competing functions in managing moisture: keeping out as much moisture as possible from the external environment while venting as much moisture as possible from the interior. A single person exhales and perspires a substantial amount of water overnight. If the tent were waterproof, this water vapor would dampen sleeping bags and clothing. Therefore, the tent must "breathe."

Double-wall tents. Double-wall construction consists of an inner wall, which is breathable, separated from an outer, detachable, waterproof rain fly. Exhaled moisture and perspiration escape from the vented space between these two layers. The fly of a mountaineering tent should come fairly

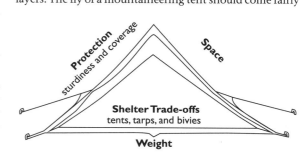

Fig. 3-2. When choosing a shelter, climbers consider weight, space, and protection (sturdiness and coverage).

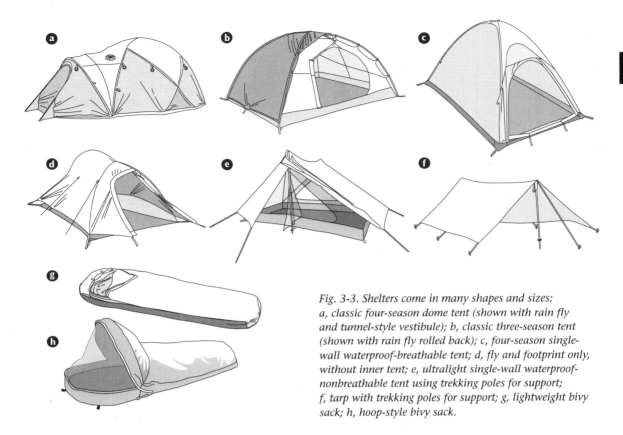

Fig. 3-3. Shelters come in many shapes and sizes: a, classic four-season dome tent (shown with rain fly and tunnel-style vestibule); b, classic three-season tent (shown with rain fly rolled back); c, four-season single-wall waterproof-breathable tent; d, fly and footprint only, without inner tent; e, ultralight single-wall waterproof-nonbreathable tent using trekking poles for support; f, tarp with trekking poles for support; g, lightweight bivy sack; h, hoop-style bivy sack.

close to the ground, covering the tent and entryway and shedding wind-driven rain. Tent floors are typically coated nylon with a sill, which extends up the sides. A higher sill offers more protection from rain blown in under the fly; yet it also reduces the amount of breathable fabric and can gather condensation. To avoid unnecessary seams, the floor and sill are typically one continuous piece of fabric, commonly known as a bathtub floor. All seams in the rain fly and floor should be factory-taped to keep water out.

Single-wall waterproof-breathable tents. Lightweight, rugged, and expensive, these tents use just one layer of waterproof-breathable fabric (see Chapter 2, Clothing and Equipment). The inside is a fuzzy, blotter-like facing that holds and distributes excess moisture to assist its passage through the fabric.

The great advantage of a single-wall tent is its light weight. The lightest two-person version currently weighs 3.3 pounds (1.5 kilograms), and typical versions, about 5 pounds (2.3 kilograms). They are also quieter in high winds because there is no outer fly to flap against the tent walls. Their major disadvantages are their price tags and tendency to collect moisture during warm, wet weather.

Ultralight single-wall waterproof-nonbreathable tents. These tents trade efficient breathability for lighter weights. Moisture management is accomplished through vents.

Tarps. Having no walls, tarps easily vent moisture. They are usually paired with ground sheets. Tarp campers in marginal weather will often use an all-weather "splash bivy" for additional protection. (See "Bivy Sacks," below.)

Three- and Four-Season Tents

Tents for mountaineering are either three-season tents (for nonwinter use) or four-season tents (for all situations, including snow camping). All-season climbers often own both types and perhaps a tarp and bivy sack as well.

Three-season tents. The side or top panels of many three-season tents are made with transparent netting, providing ventilation, bug protection, and lower weight.

CHOOSING A TENT

Before purchasing a tent, try it out at the store to check space, protection, and weight:

- **Space:** Tents are rated for the number of sleepers, usually assuming no gear inside and smaller, rather friendly climbers. Is there sufficient head and foot room? How vertical are the walls? The steeper the walls, the greater the interior usable space. Is it easy to go in and out of the door(s)? Does each side have a door? How easy is the tent to set up?
- **Protection:** Summer in the Sierra, autumn in the Alps, or winter in the Cascades? Will the shelter need to withstand above-timberline wind or heavy snowfall? A four-season tent implies more protection.
- **Weight:** What does it really weigh? Break out the scale since manufacturers are notoriously optimistic. With two-person, four-season tents weighing from 3.3 to almost 10 pounds (1.5 to 4.5 kilograms), a tent can be the heaviest piece of gear in the pack. Ultralight two-person tents can weigh as little as 1.3 pounds (600 grams), and tarps, much less. Tents often list a "minimum weight" (excluding stakes, stuff sacks, instructions, et cetera), and a "packaged weight," which includes everything. Use "minimum weight" for comparisons.

However, blowing snow and condensation can come in through the netting. Adequate for mountaineering in a wide variety of conditions from late spring to early fall, they can be ideal for longer trips where weight is more of a concern.

Four-season tents. Usually heavier, more expensive, and built to withstand winter conditions of high winds and snow loading, four-season tents have higher-strength aluminum or carbon fiber poles and more-durable reinforcing. The doors, windows, and vents have solid panels that zip, and the fly extends close to the ground. Four-season tents often have more than two poles and a greater emphasis on guylines. Usually, the tent shape is some variation on the dome.

Ultralight tents. Often associated with long-distance hikers and moderate weather, ultralight tents can be used by climbers in moderate conditions. They are made of Dyneema Composite fabric (formerly known as Cuben Fiber) or silnylon and may use trekking poles as tent poles to save weight. These designs are not freestanding and so are less well suited to windy, wet alpine environments.

Tent Design

Designers shape tents to maximize usable interior space, load-bearing strength, and ability to withstand high winds, while at the same time minimizing a tent's weight. A great tent must be easy to pitch and disassemble but tenacious when storms attempt to take it down. Mountaineering tents use a variety of clever crisscrossing pole architectures to form various dome or tunnel shapes. Some are freestanding and need no stakes to hold their shape. These can be picked up and moved but must be secured with stakes and perhaps guylines to prevent being blown away—a real danger in a storm, especially when unoccupied.

The two-person tent is the most popular tent size for mountaineering, offering the greatest flexibility in weight and choice of campsite. For a group, it is generally more versatile to bring two two-person tents rather than one larger tent. Many two-person tents can handle three people in a pinch, yet are light enough to be used by one person. The tent will be warmer, however, with more than one occupant.

Some three- and four-person tents are light enough to be carried by two people who crave luxurious living (or two large people who crave adequate space). Larger tents, especially those high enough to stand in, are big morale boosters during an expedition or long storm but are burdens to carry. Before you set out, distribute the tent parts (tent, fly, poles, and stakes) among the party to share the weight.

Tent Features

A good mountaineering tent keeps out most of the rain and snow as climbers get in and out. Manufacturers offer many different features, such as extra doors, interior pockets, gear loops, tunnels, alcoves, vestibules, and hoods. Of course, most extra features add both weight and cost.

Vestibules. Four-season tents, and some three-season models, commonly include a protruding floorless protected area known as a vestibule. Some expedition rain flies come with their own poles for extending the vestibule area (see Figure 3-3a). Vestibules help shelter the entrance and provide more room for storing gear and boots, dressing, and cooking. In foul weather, cooking in the tent vestibule is an art to be appreciated—carefully (see "Stove Safety" later in this chapter). Some four-season tents provide two vestibules, allowing for specialization (for example, cooking in one, boot storage in the other).

Vents. Vents near the ceiling that allow warm, moist air (which rises) to escape are useful. Mosquito netting allows air to flow freely when the doors are unzipped and will keep out rodents, reptiles, and bugs (see Figure 3-3b and e).

Color. Tent color is a matter of personal taste. Warm tent colors such as yellow, orange, and red are cheerier if the party is stuck inside, and they make it easier to spot camp from afar. On the other hand, subdued hues blend into the landscape.

Go out a few times with a rented or borrowed tent and establish some preferences before you buy.

Anchoring the Tent

Bring stakes designed to handle the terrain. In forest duff, short plastic or wire stakes, such as those that come with most tents, are just fine. In rocky alpine terrain, metal skewer-type stakes (fig. 3-4a) or sturdier plastic T-shaped stakes (fig. 3-4b) may be required. In sand or snow, a broader surface area on the stake will help (fig. 3-4c).

Stakes simply driven into snow in the normal fashion will pull out in heavy wind and melt out during the day. Ice axes, skis, and trekking poles can make solid anchors but cannot be used for anything else while they are securing the tent. For extra security, tie the tent to an available rock or tree.

In snow, the best anchors are deadman anchors (fig. 3-5). These can be stakes, stuff sacks packed with snow, metal plates called flukes made specifically for this purpose, or even rocks or sticks, which you do not have to dig up when breaking camp if the knots for the cords attached to them are above the snow. First, tie the deadman to the tent guyline, or form a loop in the line and slip the deadman into it. Dig a T-shaped trench at least 12 inches (30 centimeters) deep, with the long leg of the T facing the tent. Put the deadman into the trench in the crossbar of

the T, then pull the line taut, backfill the trench, and stamp down the snow.

Guylines can be kept taut with small plastic or metal tensioners (fig. 3-6a and b) or with a simple taut-line hitch (fig. 3-6c).

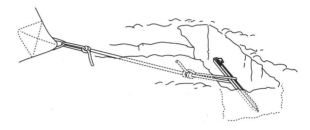

Fig. 3-5. Deadman anchor: Dig a T-shaped trench about 12 inches (30 centimeters) deep, fasten the tent's guylines around the anchor, and place it in the trench's crossbar. Pull the line taut to tension the tent. Backfill the trench and stomp the snow to compact it over the anchor.

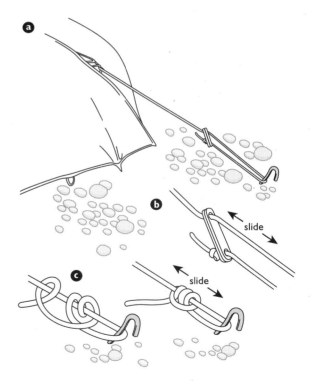

Fig. 3-6. Tensioning guylines: a, guyline with a tensioner device; b, close-up view of a tensioner; c, taut-line hitch.

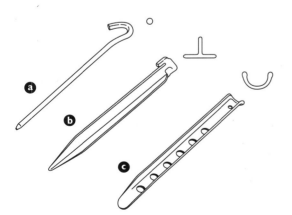

Fig. 3-4. Tent stakes (note profile cross sections at upper right): a, skewer; b, T-shaped; c, snow or sand stake.

Tent Setup, Care, and Cleaning

When setting up or taking down a tent, push poles through the tent sleeves rather than pulling them. Pulling can separate the pole sections and risk breakage at the joints. A tent goes up quickly if members of the party are familiar with the tent design.

To protect the tent floor from water, dirt, and abrasion, discourage people from wearing boots inside the tent. Before packing up, turn the tent inside out and shake it to clear out debris and remove condensation or rain. When not on an ultralightweight trip, bring a tarp or ground cloth to protect the tent floor from abrasion (tuck any excess underneath the tarp or cloth to avoid channeling rainwater). Footprints—ground cloths shaped for a specific tent—can be purchased from manufacturers or made from polyethylene fiber fabrics (such as Tyvek) or another lightweight, durable material. Fabric repair tape is a good idea for the repair kit.

Tents last longer when carefully cleaned and air-dried after each trip. To clean a tent, hose it off or hand wash it with mild soap and water. Scrub stains with a sponge. Spot-clean any tree sap. Hang to dry.

High temperatures and prolonged exposure to sun damage tent material, so do not leave the tent set up for unnecessary periods of time. The damage from ultraviolet light can ruin a rain fly in a single season of prolonged exposure. Do not touch tent fabric just after applying DEET-based insect repellent to yourself; the chemical can ruin fabric coatings.

TARPS

A tarp—lightweight and low cost—may offer adequate shelter from all but extreme weather in lowland forests and among subalpine trees. Compared with a tent, a tarp offers less protection from heat loss and wind and none at all from insects or rodents. A tarp also requires ingenuity and some cooperation from the landscape to set up (fig. 3-7). It may be a poor choice as the main shelter above timberline unless you bring ice axes or trekking poles. A tarp shelter, however, can be very helpful as a cooking and eating area in camp during inclement weather. Avoid wrapping yourself in a tarp as if it were a blanket because perspiration will condense inside the waterproof material.

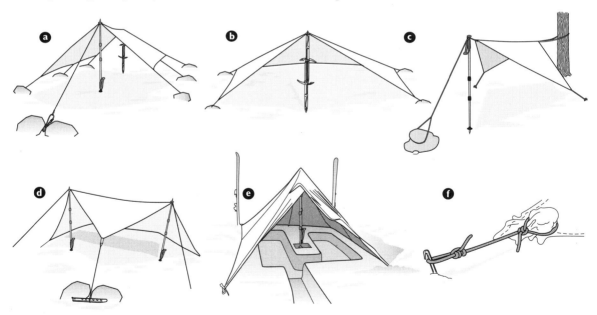

Fig. 3-7. Improvised tarp shelters: a, A-frame using trekking pole and ice axes secured by a chock; b, arrowhead using two lashed ice axes; c, dining fly with tree and trekking pole; d, using two trekking poles and secured by a stake wedged between rocks; e, dining fly for kitchen in snow using skis, a stake, and a trekking pole; f, tying off corners of a tarp that has no grommets or tie-off loops.

Plastic tarps are inexpensive but unsuitable for mountaineering. Coated nylon or silnylon tarps are stronger and usually very lightweight. Tarps made of Dyneema Composite fabric are the lightest available. Many tarps come with reinforced grommets or tie-off loops for easy rigging. Alternatively, create corner tie-in points using a bit of the tarp's fabric wrapped around a small cone or pebble from the campsite (fig. 3-7f). Bring lightweight cord, a few light stakes, and use taut-line hitches (see Figure 3-6c) to string the tarp up.

Some manufacturers offer lightweight, floorless nylon tents and usually at least one pole. Similarly, the rain fly of some double-wall tents can be set up without the tent, serving as a freestanding lightweight shelter.

BIVY SACKS

A lightweight alternative to a tent, a bivy sack is a large fabric envelope with a zipper entrance, typically with zippered mosquito netting. Bivy sacks provide some insulative value and the moisture-management functions of a tent—keeping out external moisture while venting internal water vapor. The bottom is usually waterproof-coated nylon; the upper is either a waterproof-breathable or weather-resistant material. Bivies come in three main types:

1. **All-weather bivies** are able to fully function as a shelter weighing from about 1 to 2.5 pounds (about 0.5 to 1.1 kilograms).
2. **Splash bivies** are weather-resistant on the top, allowing them to be extremely lightweight (as light as 6 ounces/180 grams) and breathable. Intended for mild weather, they protect from splashing rain and snow drift when used with tarps.

WHEN YOU GOTTA GO

Each climber needs to drink plenty of water during the climb to stay hydrated and avoid fatigue. Finding a safe and private place to pee is more difficult for women. Some are comfortable just undoing the quick-release elastic leg loops at the back of their climbing harness and pulling down their pants. Alternatively, commercially developed pee funnels allow women to urinate through their pants fly while standing. Climbing parties should allow climbers the time and opportunity to urinate on a regular basis to avoid dehydration, embarrassment, and dangerous situations. As a reminder for all climbers: do not remove your climbing harness and do not untie from the rope unless you are in a safe situation.

THREE CARDINAL RULES FOR LEAVE NO TRACE CAMPING

1. **Camp gently.** Camp in established campsites or on durable surfaces whenever possible. Research regulations and special issues for the areas you intend to climb. Use a camp stove instead of building a fire. Wash people and dishes well away from campsites and water sources.
2. **Do not disturb.** Leave flowers, rocks, and wildlife undisturbed by "taking only pictures and leaving only footprints." Keeping human food from wildlife minimizes the chance of future unwanted human-animal encounters.
3. **Dispose of waste.** Dispose of human waste properly, at least 200 feet (75 steps) away from water, trails, and campsites. In forest, dig a hole to fully bury your poop. In the alpine, human waste must be packed out in "blue bags" or WAG BAG waste bags (see Chapter 7, Leave No Trace). Go stealthily and pack out all garbage and scraps of food.

3. **Emergency bivies** weigh so little, about 4 to 9 ounces (113 to 255 grams), that each member of the climbing party can always carry one as an emergency shelter.

Styles vary from spartan sacks (see Figure 3-3g) to mini-tents that may be staked out and have a hoop to keep the fabric off the sleeper's face (see Figure 3-3h). Bivies are typically designed for one person, two in an emergency.

A bivy can be used as primary shelter or carried only as an emergency shelter. Test that the length and circumference can accommodate the sleeper, a fully lofted sleeping bag, and ground insulation inside the bivy, as this is common practice. In mild conditions, a bivy sack, with a tarp set up over it, offers good protection at less weight than most tents. In wet conditions, a bivy sack inside a tent will keep the sleeping bag dry no matter how damp the tent.

SELECTING A CAMPSITE

The ideal campsite has great views, a nearby water source, protection from the elements, and flat space for tents and cooking. Some places have it all, but selecting a campsite usually involves trade-offs. Climbers may deliberately walk past an idyllic spot in the forest in favor of a cramped mountain ledge that puts them closer to the summit.

Wind. Wind is a big consideration in choosing a campsite. In most areas, prevailing winds tend to come from a particular direction. A ridge-top camp is very exposed, and a notch or low point on a ridge is the windiest of all. Alpine breezes can be capricious. An afternoon breeze blowing upslope may reverse at night as heavy, chilled air rolls downslope from snowfields. Cold air flows downward during settled weather, following valleys and collecting in depressions. Thus, there is often a chilly breeze down a creek or dry wash and a pool of cold air in a basin. Night air is often several degrees cooler near a river or lake than on the knolls above.

Consider wind direction when pitching a tent. Pitching camp on the lee (downwind) side of a clump of trees or rocks is often best. Facing the door into the wind in good weather will distend the tent and minimize flapping. In stormy conditions, pitch the tent door away from wind so rain and snow will not be blown inside.

Location. Consider how changes in temperature or weather may affect the campsite. For example, avoid camping in gullies or creek beds, which are susceptible to flash floods during a thunderstorm. Consider that a river or stream may rise if conditions change. The braided rivers in the Alaskan interior, for example, often rise considerably due to increased glacial runoff as the day warms up. In winter or in the high country, make sure the tent is clear of any potential avalanche path or rockfall. If you camp under trees, look up to assess the health of the branches.

Leave No Trace. After safety considerations, environmental impact is critical in campsite selection. The more human traffic there is and the more fragile the setting, the more careful climbers need to be (see "Three Cardinal Rules for Leave No Trace Camping" sidebar). The detailed campsite discussion of Chapter 7, Leave No Trace, can be summarized as follows:

- **Best choices:** Established, fully impacted site; snow; or rock slab
- **Good choices:** Sandy, gravelly, or dirt flat; or duff in deep forest
- **Poor choices:** Grass-covered meadow, or plant-covered meadow above timberline
- **Worst choice:** Waterfront along lakes and streams

Bear country. Many wild areas visited by climbers are also home to bears, and camping in bear country means thinking about how to avoid potential conflict. Bears have powerful noses and can smell food from up to a mile away. Consider this as you are setting up camp and choosing a campsite. In treeless bear country, the target is to set up camp in a triangle configuration (fig. 3-8) that is at least

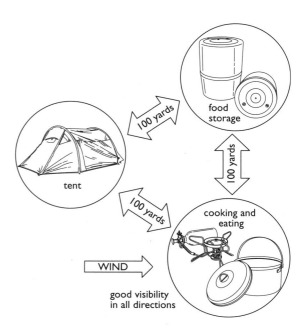

Fig. 3-8. Optimal campsite triangle for camping in bear habitat.

100 yards (or meters) on each side. That distance is usually impractical, but set the configuration points as far apart as feasible: one point of the triangle that has good visibility in all directions is the cooking and eating area; at another point, put storage of food, camp kitchen items (stove, pots, scrubber, et cetera), and any other items with an aroma (such as toothpaste, deodorant, lotions, and human waste); at the third, upwind point, establish the tent site. Know that large animals such as bears and cougars are not known to attack parties of four or more persons, so this may be a useful minimum group size for extended trips in wilder areas—if everyone stays together. Make sure to sleep in a tent rather than out in the open. Keep in mind that bear and cougar attacks are extremely rare and fatalities much less frequent than fatalities from snakes, lightning, or bees.

PROTECTING FOOD FROM ANIMALS

Do not leave food inside the tent. Bears, rodents, skunks, raccoons, birds, and other animals can smell food and will tear or gnaw through plastic bags, stuff sacks, and even packs. Ravens, crows, and jays can peck through mesh tent windows; weasels can skillfully fiddle with zippers; other animals simply rip or chew through the fabric, taking food,

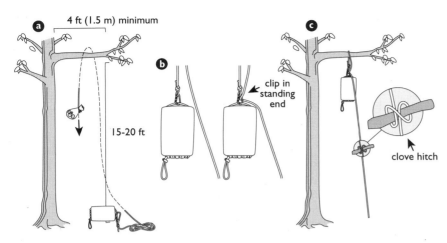

Fig. 3-9. The PCT method for hanging food: a, toss a line over a high, sturdy tree limb; b, attach food bag, clipping the standing end of the rope back through the attachment carabiner; c, hoist the bag all the way up, then, as high as you can reach, clove-hitch a stick to the lower line. Then lower the food bag, which will move the stick upward until it jams against the carabiner.

making a mess, and ruining your shelter. The traditional solution was to suspend a stuff sack or pack from a line strung between two trees. But stout, high branches are in short supply in the alpine, and clever critters, ever fond of a free lunch, can thwart the cleverest of contraptions. If a tree is your only option, try the Pacific Crest Trail (PCT) method (fig. 3-9). Today's land managers may provide steel-wire high lines, poles, or metal food storage cabinets in popular backcountry camping areas, so use them when available.

Bear-resistant canisters and bags. Managers of numerous wilderness areas in the western United States find that special bear-resistant, unbreakable plastic food can-

isters (fig. 3-10a) are more effective than the traditional hanging food bag. Canisters are bulky, however, and are heavier than nylon or plastic sacks. In places with significant bear populations, land managers often loan or rent these containers. Some areas require them and may assess significant fines on the containerless. Lightweight collapsible bear bags such as the Ursack (fig. 3-10b) are allowed in many areas as an alternative to rigid bear canisters. These are made of "bulletproof" Spectra fabric advertised as being impervious to bears; optional aluminum inserts help keep the food from being mashed.

Hiding a food cache in the wilderness is generally a poor practice that is prohibited in some areas. Where allowed, use a bear-resistant container. When animals get into an improperly protected cache they get in the habit of seeking out people for food. If a bear or cougar becomes habituated to people's campsites as a food source, the animal may become a "problem animal" that must be relocated or killed. Remember, a fed bear is a dead bear.

PREPARING A MEAL IN BEAR COUNTRY

When you prepare a meal, remove only the items for that meal, and bring them to the cooking and eating site. Maintain a lookout during cooking and eating. If a bear is ambling toward the group, quickly pack up the food.

At the end of the meal, wash up well with unscented soap to remove food odors from people, clothes, and equipment. Dispose of cleaning water downwind from the campsite and well away from water sources (see Chapter 7, Leave No Trace). Return all the cooking equipment and leftover food to the food storage site. Do not keep any food in the tent, and avoid bringing clothes with food stains or

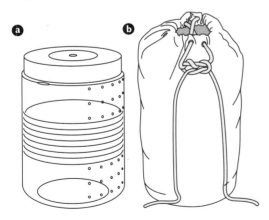

Fig. 3-10. Bear-resistant containers: a, bear canister; b, Ursack. For the latter, cinch the bag tight, leaving no gaps, and secure the cord with a surgeon's knot (shown loose here for clarity).

cooking odors into the tent. When storing food to protect it from animals, include such odorous objects as toothbrushes, toothpaste, lotions, used feminine-hygiene products, the garbage bag, and even Esbit fuel.

SNOW AND WINTER CAMPING

For successful winter camping, a good shelter, proper insulation, and the skills to stay dry are essential. Tents are the preferred choice when weather conditions are changing, with temperatures near the freezing point, as well as in terrain with little snow, on short trips, or when camp must be set up quickly. If the sun is out at midday, the inside of a tent can be 40 degrees Fahrenheit (20 degrees Celsius) warmer than the outside air, allowing climbers to dry clothes or sleeping bags. More exotic snow shelters such as snow caves and igloos require more time, effort, and skill but may be stronger, more spacious, and even warmer in very cold weather.

TOOLS

A mountaineering snow shovel is essential for preparing tent platforms, building wind-blocking walls, digging emergency shelters, excavating climbers from avalanche

blade guard

Fig. 3-11. Snow tools: a, scoop-style shovel with T-shaped handle; b, scoop-style with L-shaped handle; c, straight-bladed shovel with D-shaped handle; d, snow saw with blade guard.

debris, and sometimes even for clearing climbing routes. In winter, each party member should carry a shovel. For summer snow camping, take one shovel per tent or rope team, with a minimum of two shovels per party.

Look for a lightweight shovel with a compact sectional or telescoping handle and a sturdy aluminum blade for chopping into icy snow. The blade may be scoop-shaped (fig. 3-11a and b), which makes it easier to move large volumes of snow, or relatively straight-bladed (fig. 3-11c), which makes cutting snow blocks easier. A D-shaped handle (see Figure 3-11c) or L- or T-shaped handles (see Figure 3-11a and b) can provide leverage and a firm grip.

A snow saw (fig. 3-11d) is the best tool for cutting blocks to make an igloo, a snow trench, or a wind-blocking snow wall around your tent (see Figure 3-12).

TENTS IN WINTER

Locate a winter camp away from hazards such as crevasses, avalanche paths, and cornices. Observe the local wind patterns: A rock-hard or sculpted snow surface indicates frequent wind, whereas an area with loose, powdery snow indicates a lee slope where wind-transported snow is deposited. An area deep in powdery snow may be protected from wind, but the tent may frequently have to be cleared of snow. (For more, see Chapters 17, Avalanche Safety; 18, Glacier Travel and Crevasse Rescue; and 27, The Cycle of Snow.)

Select a flat spot. Establish a tent platform by compacting an area large enough to hold the tent and to allow for movement around it to check guylines or clear snow. A straight-bladed shovel works well to flatten the tent site. Tromping around on it with snowshoes will compact the surface. A ski does a great job of grading it. Flatten and smooth the tent platform thoroughly to keep occupants from sliding downslope and to avoid uncomfortable bumps that will be cast in ice during the night. If the site is unlevel, sleep with your head toward the high side. See "Anchoring the Tent" above for securing a tent in snow.

After pitching the tent, dig a pit about 1 foot (30 centimeters) deep in front of the tent door (fig. 3-12). Climbers can then sit comfortably in the doorway to put on boots and gaiters. In bad weather, the vestibule-protected pit is a convenient, wind-protected location for the stove.

Stormy weather may require a snow wall around most mountaineering tents to protect them from the wind and to avoid tent collapse (see Figure 3-12). Don't dig the floor of the tent down but stake it at snow level; a tent in a pit will be buried faster by falling snow. Unless necessary, avoid fully surrounding the tent or tents as this tends to

vestibule-protected
pit as a kitchen area

WIND | snow wall

snow piled
against windward
side of snow wall

Fig. 3-12. Typical winter camp: snow walls and a tent placed with its door downwind, with a vestibule-protected pit as a kitchen area.

trap drifting and falling snow. Build the wall in an arc on the windward side with walls 3 to 6 feet (1 to 2 meters) high. Blocks cut by a snow saw or straight-bladed snow shovel make the easiest, quickest walls and cut the wind more effectively than a rounded pile. Keep snow walls at least as far from the tent as they are high: for example, a 3-foot-high wall should be at least 3 feet away from the tent, because wind will quickly deposit snow on the wall's leeward side. Piling snow against the windward side of the wall strengthens the blocks and helps minimize drifting on the leeward sides.

During a storm, party members will periodically have to clear snow away from the tops and sides of the tent. In most storms, the problem is drifting snow not falling snow. Snow deposits develop on the leeward side of tents and snow walls. Even a partially buried tent poses a risk of asphyxiation, especially if stoves are used inside. Snow can load the tent enough to break poles and collapse the tent. Shake the walls regularly and shovel out around the tent, taking care to remove snow from below the lower edge of the fly so air can flow. Be careful not to cut the tent with the shovel; nylon slices easily when tensioned. In a severe or prolonged storm, a tent may begin to disappear between neighboring snowdrifts, making it necessary to reestablish the tent on top of the drifted snow.

Useful items for winter camping. These include a small whisk broom to sweep snow from boots, packs, clothing, and the tent; a sponge for cleaning up food and water spills, and removing interior condensation; an LED lantern for cheer during long winter nights. For a larger community tent, a gas lantern can repay its price in weight and bother by adding tremendous brightness and warmth.

House rules for tent-bound hours. Having a few house rules in place makes time spent tent-bound more pleasant.

It often helps to have one person enter the tent first to lay out sleeping pads and organize gear. Packs may have to be stored outside a small tent; if your tent has vestibules, brush off all snow before bringing packs inside. House rules may also dictate that boots be taken off outside, brushed free of snow, and placed in a waterproof boot bag inside the tent. Boots can tear holes in the tent floor. Mountaineering boots with removable liners are a real advantage— leave the shells outside or in the vestibule and bring the liners inside. Use stuff sacks to reduce clutter and protect personal gear. Put dry clothing inside your sleeping bag or a waterproof sack so it does not get wet from condensation.

Sleeping bags also offer an opportunity to dry out gear. Add small items, such as boot liners, gloves, and socks, to your bag before you go to sleep, and they will be dry and warm in the morning. Do not attempt to dry large items of clothing by wearing them to bed; they will just make you and the bag wet and cold. In extreme cold, put boots inside an oversized stuff sack and place them inside or next to the sleeping bag to keep them from freezing. To prevent a water bottle from freezing or a compressed gas fuel canister from getting chilled (and performing poorly at breakfast), place them inside the sleeping bag overnight.

SNOW SHELTERS

When the temperature drops or winter storms bring strong winds and heavy snowfall, seasoned mountaineers may prefer to sleep in a snow shelter rather than a tent. A snow cave or an igloo takes more time to build, but either is more secure than a tent and warmer in cold weather.

Construction time, effort, and the near certainty of getting wet during construction are the major drawbacks of snow shelters. Among the different types of snow shelters, snow trenches are relatively quick to complete, snow caves take more time to build, and igloos are typically too complex and time intensive to construct. Snow shelters require no special equipment other than a snow shovel and perhaps a snow saw to cut blocks—but they do require skill. Practice before committing to a trip that may need to rely on them.

Dripping water is a potential problem in any snow shelter. Body heat warms the air, which rises to the ceiling, resulting in some melting. If the ceiling is smooth, most of the meltwater will absorb into the snow. But little spikes and bumps will become dripping points, so take the time to smooth the inner walls. Finally, do not cook inside the snow shelter; inadequate ventilation may lead to carbon monoxide poisoning.

3

IMPROVISE WITH NATURAL FEATURES

The best shelter in a snow environment is a four-season tent, and setting one up is certainly quicker and easier than building a snow shelter. However, knowing how to construct a snow shelter could prevent an unplanned bivouac from becoming fatal. With a little improvisation, natural features can convert into snow hideaways. Such shelters occur under logs, along riverbanks, or in the pits or wells formed when the limbs of large conifer trees deflect snow from the tree trunks. For a tree-well shelter, enlarge the natural hole around the trunk and make a roof from any available covering, such as ice blocks, tree limbs, an emergency space blanket, or a tarp.

Blocking the wind is often essential for survival. Boughs and bark can insulate and support, but only cut live trees in an emergency. Make sure your chosen location is not in the path of a potential avalanche (see Chapter 17, Avalanche Safety).

Snow Trench

A snow trench can take only a half hour to build, making it suitable for bivouac use as well as for spartan one- or two-person quarters. It is the simplest structure to build out of snow blocks. Unlike a snow cave, a trench does not require particular terrain features; it is appropriate for the flats or on an avalanche-safe slope. However, the snow must be deep enough that the completed trench floor still sits in snow.

To build a snow trench, establish an initial cut line 6 to 7 feet (about 2 meters) long with either a straight-bladed shovel or a snow saw (fig. 3-13a). Dig a narrow trench along this cut line by using the snow saw or shovel to quarry snow blocks about 1 to 1.5 feet (40 centimeters) wide by 2 feet (60 centimeters) long by 3 feet (90 centimeters) tall (fig. 3-13b). The blocks can be created as part of the process of removing snow for the trench, or they can be quarried nearby. Set each snow block aside carefully when it is removed from the quarry—they will form the roof of the trench.

Once the trench area is large enough—2 feet (60 centimeters) wide by 6.5 feet (2 meters) long by 3 feet (90 centimeters) deep for one person—roof the trench, A-frame style, with the snow blocks (fig. 3-13c). Close off the back with another snow block. When the A-frame roof is in place, crawl underneath it into the trench and enlarge the interior down and out to accommodate the intended

number of occupants. Build steps leading down into the trench. Provide a ventilation hole in the roof. Use loose snow to caulk any gaps between roof blocks and around the back. Smooth out any bumps or irregularities in the ceiling so meltwater will run down the blocks to the sides rather than dripping on the occupants. Cover most of the entrance with a pack wrapped inside a plastic bag, but leave some space for ventilation. Cook outside of the trench.

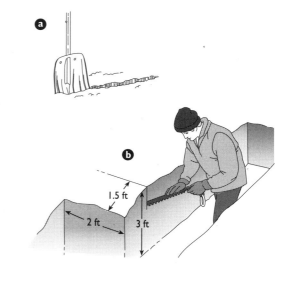

Fig. 3-13. Building a snow trench: a, establish an initial cut line with straight-bladed shovel; b, quarry snow blocks 1.5 feet wide by 2 feet long by 3 feet tall (40 by 60 by 90 centimeters); c, build an A-frame roof with snow blocks, enlarge interior, provide ventilation hole in roof, and shield the door opening with a large backpack.

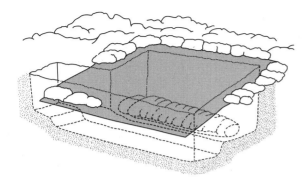

Fig. 3-14. Basic snow trench roofed with a tarp.

A more basic, emergency snow trench shelter can be built by digging a trench some 4 to 6 feet (1.2 to 2 meters) deep and large enough for the party to sleep in. Stretch a tarp over the top and weigh the edges down with snow (fig. 3-14). On a flat site, provide some slope to the tarp by building up the snow on one side of the trench. This quick shelter works moderately well in wind or rain, but a heavy snowfall can collapse the roof. As with all snow shelters, the smaller the trench, the easier it is to keep warm.

Snow Cave

Snow caves are most suitable in locations where climbers can burrow into a substantially snow-covered hillside. The snow must be deep enough to leave about 2 feet (60 centimeters) of ceiling thickness. A strong and stable cave also requires somewhat firm (consolidated) snow. Several people can shelter in one snow cave. A well-built cave dug in firm snow is a very secure structure. However, if the outside temperature is warming toward freezing, a tent or tree well shelter may be a better choice. The collapse of a snow cave roof can cause serious injury.

Find a short—7 feet (2 meters) tall at minimum—snowdrift or 30- to 40-degree slope that is clear of any potential avalanche hazard (fig. 3-15a). It is easier to dig the cave into a steep slope than a gentle slope. The snow must be deep enough that you will not hit ground before you finish excavating the entire cave. Dig an entry that is 1.5 feet (0.5 meter) wide and 5 feet (1.5 meters) high (fig. 3-15b), and dig it into the slope about 3 feet (1 meter) deep. Then create a temporary construction-debris exit slot by digging a waist-high platform centered on the entryway, forming a T that is 4 feet (1.2 meters) wide by 1.5 feet (0.5 meter) high (fig. 3-15c). Develop this platform so that it forms a horizontal slot extending into the slope, allowing for easy snow

removal. Shovel snow out through the horizontal slot; a second person, working outside, can clear the snow away.

Create the main room by digging inward and expanding the room to the front, sides, and upward—all directions except down (fig. 3-15d). Keep digging until all the snow within easy reach has been excavated. Extend the original entry hallway another 2 feet (60 centimeters) into the slope, permitting the person excavating to get farther into the cave to continue excavating outward and upward (fig. 3-15e). Now it should be nearly possible to stand inside. Continue to excavate, now out of the wind; when enough snow has been cleared to allow the excavator to sit up on the floor, another person can enter and help continue to expand the cave in all directions except downward.

Excavate until the inside dimensions are about 5 feet (1.5 meters) from front to back by 7 feet (2 meters) wide and 3.5 feet (1 meter) high, a comfortable minimum for two people. Make the cave larger for more occupants, but remember that a small cave is warmer than a large one. Keep a minimum of 2 feet (60 centimeters) of firm snow on the slope above the cave ceiling (see Figure 3-15g) to provide enough strength to keep the roof from collapsing. Avoid building a flat ceiling. The more dome-shaped the contour, the stronger the ceiling.

Fill in the temporary horizontal slot with snow blocks (fig. 3-15f); one large block or two smaller blocks leaning against each other may be sufficient. Caulk any spaces around the blocks with snow. The top of the completed entrance tunnel should be at least 6 inches (15 centimeters) lower than the cave floor, keeping warm air in the cave and cold drafts out (fig. 3-15g). Use snow blocks to build a wind-screening wall on either side of the entry path.

Poke a pair of ski-pole-basket-sized ventilation holes through the cave ceiling from the inside out (fig. 3-15h) to prevent asphyxiation. If it gets too warm inside, enlarge these holes. Do not use a camp stove inside the cave—cook outside in open air.

Smooth the domed ceiling so that it is free of any bumps or protrusions (fig. 3-15i); this way, melting water will flow down the walls of the cave instead of dripping from bumps onto the occupants. Scratch a small ditch all around the base of the wall to channel meltwater away from the floor. Place a ground sheet on the floor—clear of the meltwater ditch—to help keep things dry and to prevent equipment loss. Keep stormy weather out by putting a small tarp or a pack (inside a plastic bag) over the entrance, but leave an opening for ventilation. Mark the outside area around the cave with bamboo wands (fig. 3-15j), so that someone does not inadvertently walk onto the roof.

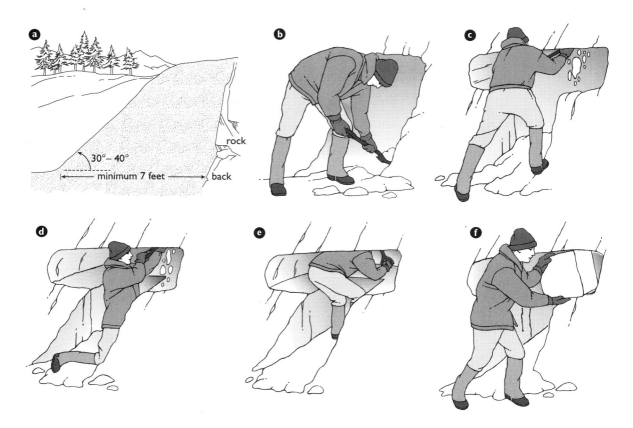

Customize the inside by digging small alcoves into the walls to store boots, stoves, and cooking utensils or to hold candles for illuminating the cave at night (fig. 3-15k). Digging the entrance tunnel deeper under the wind-screening snow blocks will make entry easier. Entrance area seats, a cooking platform, and other personal touches make the cave a snow home. Collapse the snow cave when you leave the area so that it is not hazardous for others.

Igloo

If conditions are right, igloos are undeniably fun to build and use, but their complex and time-intensive construction makes them impractical on most mountaineering trips or in an emergency. A possible exception might be a long-term base camp in a flat, remote area.

STOVES

Fire is the sixth Ten Essential, and for fire, mountaineers rely on stoves. Stoves are faster, cleaner, and more convenient than campfires for backcountry travel. They will operate under almost any conditions with minimal environmental impact. Whatever stove and fuel you choose, practice using your stove at home first. When choosing the right stove (fig. 3-16) for the next trip, consider four key questions:

Petrol preference. Choose a fuel and then a stove for each adventure. Canister fuel dominates today's outdoor industry, but in some countries liquid or alternative fuels (see Table 3-3) are sometimes easier to find or more suitable for cold weather, high altitudes, or ultra lightweight travel.

Boil or simmer. Some stoves are tiny infernos optimized to boil water and melt snow, while others are appropriate for more complex cooking. Consider your cooking preferences when choosing your stove.

Windy weather. A wind of merely 5 miles per hour (8 kilometers per hour) can double to triple the fuel consumption of an unprotected stove-on-top canister stove. On all but short trips, there is little excess fuel. If you anticipate windy conditions, consider a windproof canister stove system or a remote-fuel stove. Remote-fuel stoves

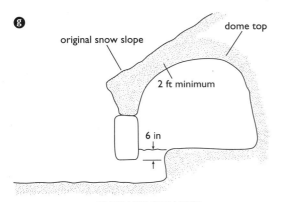

CUTAWAY SIDE VIEW

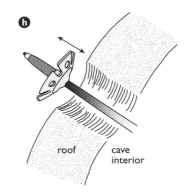

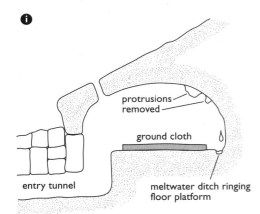

CUTAWAY SIDE VIEW
meltwater management

CUTAWAY TOP VIEW

Fig. 3-15. Building a snow cave:
a, choose location;
b, dig entry;
c, dig T-shaped slot;
d, dig inward, expanding up, left, and right;
e, expand to desired size;
f, fill in T-shaped slot;
g, consider the snow cave cross section;
h, create ventilation holes;
i, smooth ceiling and dig meltwater ditch;
j, mark cave perimeter and erect wind blocks;
k, create storage alcoves and deepen entryway.

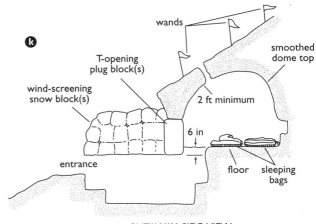

CUTAWAY SIDE VIEW

allow a full windscreen to protect the burner from the heat-stealing wind while keeping the fuel reservoir safely away from the inferno. If you are using a stove-on-top canister stove or personal cooking canister system stove, shield the windward side with rocks or gear, but *do not* encircle the stove with a windscreen or the trapped heat will have you serving a Molotov cocktail.

Cooking for a crowd. For one or two climbers sharing a pot up to about 1.5 liters, stove-on-top and canister system stoves are best. Groups of four or more, or those with substantial snow to melt, need a 2- to 5-liter pot paired with a remote-fuel stove. These are low profile and therefore sufficiently stable for larger pots. Canister system stoves currently can accommodate their specially designed pots of up to 2.5 liters.

STOVE FUELS

Because the type of fuel drives the design and functionality of the stove, it is helpful to learn about fuels before diving fully into stoves. Fuel for camp stoves comes in several varieties, each with advantages and disadvantages. See Table 3-3 for a full comparison of fuel type advantages and disadvantages.

Canister fuel. These convenient canisters of liquefied petroleum gas (LPG) are blends of isobutane, propane, and butane. As the self-sealing valve opens, the pressure in the canister forces fuel out, eliminating both priming and pumping. This makes the stoves they power popular and convenient—easy to light, good flame control, immediate maximum heat output, and no chance of fuel spills. But because the fuel is liquefied, cold and high altitude often hinder stove performance. Butane canisters are the cheapest and work best in warm weather. Purchase blends of isobutane and propane for reasonable performance at high altitude and cold temperatures. Virtually all brands of threaded LPG canisters are interchangeable but contain different gas blends.

Liquid fuels. White gas and kerosene used to be the most popular mountaineering stove fuels in North America and Europe, respectively. These fuels pack about the same heat output per ounce or gram as LPG and so are still favored for expeditions due to their low cost, availability, ability to refill fuel bottles, and performance in cold, high-altitude locations. Some stoves run only a single type of liquid fuel. Multifuel stoves, with their ability to burn white gas, kerosene, diesel, and others, are a good choice for international trips where fuel availability is uncertain. Unleaded automobile gas can be used, but fuel additives are prone to clogging stoves.

Alternative fuels. Suitable for ultralightweight cooking, solid fuels (Esbit or hexamine fuel tablets) and alcohol are options when their slow heat output is not hindered by bad weather or a need to melt snow or ice. These fuels' lower heat output makes for slow boil times but can be a good trade-off for the weight savings in fuel and stove. Bio-fuel (used in small woodstoves) is a new category that can make sense in places where it is responsible to burn small amounts of available dry wood.

STOVE TYPES

Once climbers have chosen their preferred petroleum, they can choose from among canister, liquid fuel, and alternative-fuel stove types.

Canister stoves. Simple LPG canister stoves come in two types. *Stove-on-top canister stoves* (fig. 3-16a) simply screw onto the canister, which forms the base. The Snow Peak GigaPower stove is an example. Very lightweight and compact, they are susceptible to wind and prone to tipping over. Do not use a full windscreen since that risks an explosion from superheating the canister. *Remote-fuel canister stoves* are low-profile stoves that attach the canister to the burner via a flexible hose (fig. 3-16b). They accommodate larger pots and are compatible with full windscreens. Some remote-fuel canister stoves permit the canister to be inverted to supply liquid fuel to the burner, improving performance in cold weather.

Canister system stoves. These stoves also use compressed gas canisters, but they up the ante with specially integrated pots with built-in heat exchangers to capture as much of the stove's heat as possible. These stoves are medium-weight and compact, with the stove and fuel stowable within the pot. System stoves come in two types. *Windproof systems* (fig. 3-16c) are extremely efficient in calm air and

---

CALCULATING CANISTER CONTENTS

To calculate the fuel remaining in a canister, do one of the following:

- Shake and guess.
- Float the canister in water (first burping the bottom concavity) and compare the float line against a full canister (some have an index).
- At home, weigh the canister on a kitchen scale and subtract the weight of an empty canister to determine the remaining fuel. Write the percent of fuel remaining on the side.

TABLE 3-3. COMPARISON OF STOVE FUELS

FUEL	ADVANTAGES	DISADVANTAGES	BEST FOR
CANISTER FUELS			
Blends of isobutane, propane, and butane	No priming or pumping required. Near zero maintenance. Immediate maximum heat output. Ability to simmer on some models. Readily available in North America, Patagonia, the Himalaya, Pakistan, Europe, and South Africa.	Spent canisters must be carried out. Not available everywhere. Tricky to judge fuel level. Less efficient in cold temperatures.	Short, light trips under any conditions. Good at high altitudes if temperatures are above freezing or somewhat colder (with a pressure-regulated stove).
LIQUID (PETROLEUM) FUELS			
White gas or naphtha (for example, Coleman fuel, MSR fuel), kerosene, diesel, jet fuel, aviation gas, unleaded automobile gas	Widely available and inexpensive. Stable stove designs. Simple to judge fuel level and pack exact amounts. No spent canisters.	Stoves require priming and are a bit heavier. Require separate fuel bottle. Fuel spills possible. Stoves require periodic maintenance, tinkering (for example, matching jets to fuel).	Winter (very cold) or high-elevation use. International expeditions where fuel availability is unknown. Large groups.
ALTERNATIVE FUELS			
Esbit or hexamine fuel tablets	Simple, ultralight, inexpensive stoves. Fuel output not affected by altitude. Titanium versions are compatible with burning wood.	Leaves a sticky residue on the bottom of pots. Smelly, expensive fuel. Lower heat output.	Ultralightweight cooking on long trips where melting snow or ice is not required.
Alcohol (grain alcohol 95%, pure or denatured alcohol, marine stove fuel, liquid fondue or chafing dish fuel, methyl alcohol [for example, HEET gas-line antifreeze in yellow bottle])	Simple ultralight, inexpensive stoves. Widely available inexpensive fuel.	Lowest heat output.	Ultralightweight cooking on long trips where melting snow or ice is not required.
Biofuel (used in small woodstoves)	Free fuel that does not have to be carried. Uses minimal fuel.	Dry wood is often not available in alpine environments. Burning wood is prohibited in many areas.	Woodland approaches in dry weather.

remain almost as efficient in windy conditions. They do not need a windscreen. If you can see the flame, the stove is not windproof. *Personal cooking systems* (fig. 3-16d) are designed to allow cooking and eating from a single pot but are susceptible to wind and incompatible with windscreens.

Liquid fuel stoves. The classic Primus and Svea 123 stoves had refillable liquid fuel reservoirs under the burner, but they have been replaced by a *remote-fuel* design featuring a refillable fuel bottle connected to the burner by a flexible hose (fig. 3-16e). The liquid fuel bottle must

Fig. 3-16. Types of mountaineering stoves: a, stove-on-top canister stove; b, remote-fuel canister stove; c, windproof canister system stove; d, personal cooking canister system stove; e, multifuel liquid fuel stove; f, ultralight Esbit (solid fuel) stove; g, two alcohol stoves; h, biofuel stove.

be pumped up to operating pressure by hand each time the stove is lit, and periodically during use for full heat output. Consequently, hand pumping a liquid fuel stove to full operating pressure allows the user to compensate for cold and elevation, the curse of canister-based stoves. Liquid fuel stoves are currently less efficient than canister system stoves even though the two fuels pack about the same BTUs (kilojoules).

Since liquid fuel bottles are refillable, there is no spent canister waste to take back down the mountain. Some models run only on one type of fuel, white gas (naphtha). *Multifuel* models, however, burn a wide variety of "petrol" found around the world including white gas, kerosene, diesel, and even, in a pinch, unleaded auto gas. Note that automobile gas has additives that can clog jets and destroy rubber seals, and diesel fuels generally only work well in stoves specifically engineered to run on diesel and fitted with the proper jets.

Hybrid-fuel stoves run off either liquid fuel or compressed gas canisters, delivering the ease of canister fuels but switching easily over to liquid fuels for longer trips, cold weather, and international use.

Alternative-fuel stoves. For ultralightweight cooking, Esbit (solid fuel) stoves and alcohol stoves (fig. 3-16f and g), often constructed from bits of aluminum, titanium, and beer cans, barely register on the weight scale. These featherweights are sufficient for heating water for drinks and freeze-dried meals; they are the standard for long-distance hikers, for example, on the Pacific Crest Trail. They are not, however, powerful enough to efficiently melt snow and ice. In their own category are the *biofuel stoves* (fig. 3-16h) that efficiently burn available dry forest litter and small pieces of dead wood. Freedom from buying or carrying fuel, combined with the ambience of a flickering flame, gives these stoves a unique appeal. Some create electricity from the heat to recharge electronics and run a fan on the flames.

Accessories

A few stove accessories can be quite helpful.

Windscreens. A full wraparound aluminum windscreen (fig. 3-17a) is necessary for many stoves to be efficient. Never wrap a windscreen around any canister stove unless you can exclude the canister from the windscreen, such as

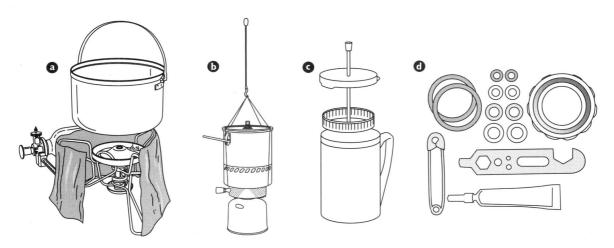

Fig. 3-17. Stove accessories: a, windscreen; b, hanging kit; c, coffee press; d, liquid fuel stove maintenance kit.

with a remote-fuel stove. Using a windscreen incorrectly may superheat the canister and cause it to explode.

Hanging kits. Stove-on-top canister stoves and canister system stoves are somewhat prone to tipping. Hanging kits allow the entire stove and pot to hang as an integral unit from a chain or wire (fig. 3-17b). They are primarily used for big wall climbing and at high camp on expeditions.

Coffee press. Climbers who enjoy caffeine may consider a coffee press (fig. 3-7c), which is offered as an accesssory for some canister stoves.

STOVE OPERATION

A stove ignites when a spark or flame is applied to vaporized fuel at the burner. While some stoves have integrated piezo ignitors, they are notoriously unreliable. With most stoves, you must use matches or a lighter. In stormy conditions, you may need waterproof or stormproof matches and/or several disposable lighters. Keep matches and lighters dry; they may be the only path to ignition.

Stoves can fail, often at inconvenient times. With more than two climbers, bring a backup stove. Modern stoves are compact and lightweight, making the added burden a reasonable trade-off and integral to having the eighth and ninth Ten Essentials, "extra food" and "extra water." In windy, dusty conditions, debris can clog the jet and cause a stove to fail. Liquid fuel stoves are finicky. Clean them regularly and rebuild them periodically, replacing seals and pump cups and using a maintenance kit as necessary (fig. 3-17d). Read the manufacturer's instructions to learn what tools are needed and practice repairing the stove at home.

With canister stoves running in upright mode, the fuel is already vaporized, so starting the stove is a simple matter of turning the regulating valve and lighting the released fuel. In contrast, a liquid fuel stove must be "primed" by preheating the generator tube. Using the stove's valve, release a small amount of fuel (or alcohol carried for the purpose) into the priming cup and light it, with the stove

TIPS FOR IMPROVING THE PERFORMANCE OF CANISTER STOVES

- Use a windproof stove system.
- Alternatively, use a remote-fuel stove that allows a liquid feed (upside-down cartridge) mode. Wrap the windscreen around the pot, allowing about a 1/2-inch (1- to 2-centimeter) gap.
- Use a pressure-regulated stove.
- Use isobutane fuel mixes and keep them warm in a sleeping bag or puffy coat prior to use.
- Insulate canisters from cold ground.
- Keep a lid on the cook pot and don't bother boiling unless necessary.
- During use, the evaporating liquid chills the canister exterior, even causing frost to form. To minimize a loss of pressure and performance, swap out cold canisters for warm ones or sit the canister in a bowl of tepid (even warm) water during use.
- Run the stove a bit below maximum for increased efficiency.

off, thus preheating the generator tube. When the flame from the priming process wanes, open the fuel regulator valve. The liquid fuel vaporizes as it passes through the now hot generator tube toward the jet, and ignites from the residual priming cup flame. Be aware of these pitfalls: Using too much fuel prolongs the process and wastes fuel. Opening the regulator valve too soon may cause a dangerous flare-up. Wait for the flame to subside but not go out. Opening the regulator valve after the priming fuel has extinguished requires quick, careful action with a match or lighter.

HOW MUCH FUEL?

To compute how much fuel is needed for a wilderness trip, consider the needs of the party, type of stove, and type of fuel to compute the baseline. Fuel, like water, is heavy, so it might be tempting to go light. Yet running short when an open fire is not an option means cold food, and running short when snow is the only source for drinking water puts the climb and climbers at risk. Taking sufficient fuel is key to the success of any wilderness trip. Longer trips require careful computation tempered by experience, as well as factoring in a cushion for the unexpected.

For amounts of water needed per person, a good estimate is between 0.75 and 1 liter of hot water per meal and 3 liters of drinking water per day per climber. Dividing the liters that need to be boiled by your type of stove's

TIPS FOR MELTING SNOW

Increasing the temperature of snow or ice from the frozen state at 32 degrees Fahrenheit (0 degrees Celsius) requires a surprising amount of energy (fuel) to cause a "phase change" from solid to liquid. In fact, it takes almost the same amount of energy to melt ice as it does to increase the temperature from there all the way to boiling. Always start with some liquid water in the pot to prevent overheating and improve heat transfer. To save fuel, use liquid water for your boil whenever possible.

efficiency factor (Table 3-4) gives the baseline number of ounces of fuel required. Remember that where snow and ice are the only sources of water, additional fuel will be needed to melt water for normal drinking needs. This water will not need to be brought to boiling unless boiling is needed for purification. However, if it is not boiled, and the snow is anything other than newly fallen, it is prudent to purify the water as you would using any other source (see "Water Treatment," later in this chapter).

Adverse factors. Preparing for the trip, it's critical to do the math, adding into the equation adverse environmental factors. Baseline calculations assume that you are starting with room temperature water (70 degrees Fahrenheit,

TABLE 3-4. BASELINE STOVE PERFORMANCE, NO WIND, 70°F (21°C)

TYPE	WEIGHT	TIME TO BOIL 1 LITER OF WATER	EFFICIENCY FACTOR (liters boiled per ounce of fuel)	WIND PROTECTION OPTIONS
CANISTER STOVES				
Stove-on-top	Light	3–4 minutes	1.8	None
Remote-fuel	Medium	3–4 minutes	1.8	Windscreen
CANISTER SYSTEM STOVES				
Windproof	Medium	3–4 minutes	2.5	Built-in
Personal cooking	Medium	3–4 minutes	2.5	None
LIQUID FUEL STOVE				
Single-fuel or multifuel	Medium	3–4 minutes	1.6	Windscreen
ALTERNATIVE-FUEL STOVES				
Esbit (solid fuel)	Very light	10 minutes or longer	1.0	Built-in or windscreen
Alcohol	Very light	10 minutes or longer	0.7	Built-in or windscreen
Biofuel	Heavy	10 minutes or longer	NA	Built-in

Note: Under efficiency factor: for canisters, 1 ounce (28 grams) is by fuel weight; for liquid fuels, 1 ounce is a fluid ounce, which weighs 0.66 to 0.8 ounce depending on the specific gravity of the fuel used.

TABLE 3-5. CALCULATING FUEL FOR A SAMPLE TRIP

WATER REQUIREMENTS FOR FOUR CLIMBERS FOR FIVE DAYS

A = Cooking water: boiling 2 liters per day = **40 liters**
B = Drinking water: warming 3 liters per day to 70°F (21°C) = **60 liters**
C = Total water = 100 liters
D = Stove efficiency factors: For each of the three stoves below, this figure is **1.8, 2.5,** and **1.6,** respectively (as in Table 3-4).

FUEL NEEDED TO HEAT WATER	CANISTER STOVE-ON-TOP	WINDPROOF CANISTER SYSTEM	LIQUID FUEL (white gas and a windscreen)
Baseline: Calculate as A ÷ D	22 oz.	16 oz.	25 fl. oz.
Cold water: Calculate as C ÷ D x 25%	14 oz.	10 oz.	16 fl. oz.
Snow or ice: Calculate as C ÷ D x 100%	56 oz.	40 oz.	63 fl. oz.
Subtotal	**92 oz.**	**66 oz.**	**104 fl. oz.**
Windy conditions: Add 100%, 10%, 20%	92 oz.	7 oz.	21 fl. oz.
TOTAL	**184 oz. (5.2 kg)**	**73 oz. (2.1 kg)**	**125 fl. oz. (2.6 kg)**

FUEL SHORTCUT
To calculate one climber's fuel needs per day, divide the baseline and adverse conditions by 20 person-days (four climbers for five days).

Baseline conditions	1.1 oz./day	0.8 oz./day	1.3 fl. oz./day
Adverse conditions above	9.2 oz./day	3.7 oz./day	6.3 fl. oz./day

Notes: Totals exclude the weight of canisters or fuel bottles. Example assumes conditions are just below freezing. Conditions significantly below freezing would require additional fuel to heat the ice or snow up to freezing before it can be melted. To convert ounces to grams, multiply by 28.3. To convert fluid ounces to milliliters, multiply by 29.6. To convert milliliters to grams, multiply by 66%–80% depending on the specific gravity of the type of fuel used (fuels are lighter than water). The specific gravity of white gas (70%) is used in this example. The fuel shortcut assumes a single climber is starting with room temperature water for the baseline conditions, and snow and wind as in the example above for adverse conditions.

21 degrees Celsius) and heating that water to boiling in still air. Yet real-world climbing conditions typically require heating cold water, or perhaps even snow, at high elevations and often in windy weather. These adverse factors can increase fuel consumption by many times the baseline For details, see Table 3-5, Calculating Fuel for a Sample Trip.

The impact of wind on fuel consumption is highly stove dependent. Breezy conditions can double or triple the fuel consumption of an unprotected stove-on-top canister stove or a personal cooking system, and additional wind can prevent boiling altogether. Stoves that allow a windscreen do much better, and windproof stoves are almost unaffected. Temperatures substantially below freezing require additional fuel to heat the snow or ice up to freezing.

Example fuel calculation. Table 3-5 details a step-by-step example calculation for fuel needs for four climbers on a five-day trip. First, they will be melting snow or ice and then boiling it to create 2 liters of cooking water each per day (two meals at 0.75 to 1 liter per meal). "Cooking" is assumed to require simply boiling water without simmering. They will also be melting snow or ice for an additional 3 liters of drinking water each per day to "room temperature" 70 degrees Fahrenheit (21 degrees Celsius). These water requirements may be insufficient, depending on conditions (see "Hydration" in Chapter 21, Expedition Climbing).

The baseline calculation assumes "room temperature" water is heated to boiling in windless conditions. Next, "adverse factors" will require additional fuel on our example trip: snow or ice will be the water source and the stoves will be exposed to an 8 mile-per-hour (13 kilometer-per-hour) wind. Heating cold water (33 degrees Fahrenheit, 1 degree Celsius) to room temperature requires an additional 25 percent fuel beyond the baseline. Melting snow or ice to liquid, but still cold, requires an additional 100 percent fuel beyond the baseline. The effect of wind on stoves can be dramatic but is highly stove dependent. Following along with the math in Table 3-5 demonstrates that, depending on stove type, this sample wilderness trip will require from 2.1 to 5.2 kilograms of fuel to sustain our climbers, before factoring in a cushion for the unexpected.

LIQUID FUEL STORAGE

Carry extra white gas or kerosene in a metal bottle designed specifically for fuel storage, with a screw top and rubber gasket. Plainly mark the fuel container to distinguish it from other containers, such as water bottles, and stow it in a place where any leaks will not contaminate food.

Leave about 1 inch (2–3 centimeters) of air space in the stove's fuel reservoir, rather than filling it to the brim, to prevent excessive pressure buildup. At the end of the season, empty stoves of any fuel. Date any leftover fuel to be sure to use it by the end of the next season. Aging fuel becomes gummy and prone to clogging.

CONTAINER RECYCLING

Canister stove fuel containers are not refillable. But because they are made of steel, when empty they are recyclable in many places after first punching obvious holes in and flattening the container walls.

STOVE SAFETY

Tents have been blown up, equipment burned, and people injured by careless stove use. Before lighting a stove, check fuel lines, valves, and connections for leaks. Let stove cool completely before changing canisters or adding liquid fuel. Change pressurized fuel canisters, and fill and start liquid fuel stoves, outside the tent and away from other open flames.

Do not cook inside the tent unless it is so windy that the stove will not operate outside or so cold that the cook risks hypothermia. The risks range from the relatively minor one of spilling pots onto sleeping bags to the deadly dangers of tent fires or carbon monoxide poisoning.

If it is absolutely necessary to cook inside a tent, follow these safety rules:

1. Light a liquid gas stove outside or near a tent opening so you can toss it away if it flares; wait until it is running smoothly before putting a pot on top.
2. Cook near the tent door or in the vestibule, for better ventilation and so you can throw the stove outside quickly in an emergency.
3. Run stoves at a high setting to make sure as much of the fuel combusts as possible. Colorless and odorless carbon monoxide is undetectable by humans and is absorbed into the blood faster at high altitudes—provide plenty of ventilation.
4. In subfreezing weather liquid petroleum fuel or alcohol can quickly freeze skin. Avoid spilling fuel on yourself.
5. Never use a full wraparound windscreen with any canister stove unless you can exclude the canister from the windscreen, such as with a remote-fuel stove. An incorrectly used windscreen risks an explosion from superheating the canister.

WATER

Replenishing your water supply from wild sources requires tools and knowledge. With the sustained exertion of mountaineering, dehydration can cause fatigue, disorientation, and headaches. It becomes debilitating more quickly than you might expect. Dehydration is a factor in several mountain maladies, including acute mountain sickness (see "Hydration" in Chapter 21, Expedition Climbing and "Dehydration" in Chapter 24, First Aid). Always make plans so there is more than sufficient water on mountaineering adventures. "Extra water" is ninth in the list of Ten Essentials.

To combat dehydration, drink more water than usual, perhaps 1 to 2 extra liters, during the 24-hour period before a climb. Additionally, it is wise to drink a cup or two of water immediately before beginning a climb. Skin and lungs release large amounts of moisture into cold, dry, high-altitude mountain air. Don't ignore thirst, the body's fine-tuned notification system. Monitor the color of your urine: darker-than-normal color means dehydration. At high elevations, dehydration can contribute to nausea that, ironically, reduces the desire to take in fluids.

Keep water handy. Have a bottle within easy reach inside your pack or in a pouch on the hip belt. Some climbers use a hydration bladder carried in their pack, with a tube

TABLE 3-6. WATER TREATMENT SUMMARY

METHOD	PURIFIES	ADVANTAGES	DISADVANTAGES
BOIL			
Boiling	Yes	Simple method.	Slow and inconvenient. Requires additional fuel, which adds weight to pack.
FILTER			
Purifier-Filter	Yes	Same advantages as microfilter, plus effective against viruses	Same advantages as microfilter, except with regard to viruses. Possible cross-contamination from hoses.
Microfilter	No	Quick. Clarifies water making it more palatable. Very effective against parasites, protozoa, and bacteria.	May be bulky or heavy. May clog or break. River water carrying dirt and sediment will clog filter. Filter must be protected from freezing. Ineffective against viruses but may be combined with any chemical or UV method to purify. Possible cross-contamination from hoses.
CHEMICAL			
Chlorine Dioxide Drops or Tablets	Yes	Taste of water not altered significantly. Lightweight and compact. Inexpensive.	Waiting time: drops require letting the two chemicals mix for 5 minutes plus 15 to 30 minutes in the water; killing cryptosporidium in worst-case water takes 4 hours. Tablets may be difficult to dissolve in cold water.
Electro-chlorinators	Yes	Taste of water not altered significantly. Lightweight and compact.	Requires device, batteries, and salt. Waiting time: 15 to 30 minutes in the water; killing cryptosporidium in worst-case water takes 4 hours.
Chlorine or Iodine (halogens)	No	Effective against all bacteria and viruses. Lightweight and compact. Inexpensive.	Ineffective against cryptosporidium and only somewhat effective against giardia. Slow (1 hour for cold or cloudy water). Disagreeable taste unless cleared afterward with vitamin C. Persons with active thyroid disease should not use iodine.
ULTRAVIOLET (UV) LIGHT			
UV Light and Microfilter	Yes	Taste of water not altered.	Requires clear water from a microfilter with pores no larger than 0.2 microns. Users cannot reliably assess if water is sufficiently clear that a microfilter is not needed (see "Water Treatment," below). Battery-operated, fragile UV lamp. The microfilter also prevents some bottle-thread and stirring contamination risks that may otherwise exist.

Notes: None of the above treatment methods are effective against chemicals, heavy metals, or toxins. "Yes" in the "Purifies" column means effective against all three classes of pathogens: parasites (including protozoa), bacteria, and viruses.

clipped to the shoulder strap for convenient sipping. Purify drinking water to stay healthy and hydrated. Table 3-6 compares the advantages and disadvantages of various water treatment methods.

SOURCES OF EXTRA WATER

Some climbs have abundant streams and snowfields to replenish water supplies, but often the high peaks are bone dry or frozen solid, and the only water available is what

PURIFICATION METHOD	PATHOGENS TREATED			
	Parasites & Protozoa (large)	Bacteria (medium)	Viruses (small)	Purifies?
Boiling	Yes	Yes	Yes	YES
Purifier-Filter	Yes	Yes	Yes	YES
Microfilter	Yes	Yes	No	NO
Chlorine Dioxide Drops or Tablets	Yes	Yes	Yes	YES
Electrochlorinators	Yes	Yes	Yes	YES
Chlorine or Iodine (halogens)	Unreliable	Yes	Yes	NO
UV Light and Microfilter	Yes	Yes	Yes	YES

TABLE 3-7. WATER PATHOGEN SUMMARY

climbers carry with them or obtain by melting snow or ice. On one-day climbs, the usual source is simply the tap at home. For most people, 1.5 to 3 liters of water per day is enough. Take more than you think is necessary. During a tough three-day climb, each person might drink 6 quarts while hiking and climbing, plus another 5 quarts in camp. At 2 pounds per US quart (or 1 kilogram per liter) that is too much to carry, so supplies must be replenished from lakes, streams, and snow. Melt enough snow in the evening to fill all water bottles and cooking pots.

When the only water source along the trail is snow, pack it inside a water bottle and place the bottle on the outside of your pack to melt the snow and prevent any condensation from getting your pack's contents wet. Start with a bit of water in the bottle to hasten the melting time.

Try catching the drips from overhanging eaves of melting snow. Or find a tongue of snow that is slowly melting into a trickle, dredge a depression below, let the silt settle, and channel the resulting puddle into a container.

If you have sufficient sun and time, set out pots of snow to melt. Otherwise, use the stove. Either way, get the snow from a "drinking snow" pit, well away from the designated toilet and cleaning areas. The snow need not be boiled if it will be otherwise purified, and with care, can be filtered directly from the pot as it melts. A pot can burn if it contains only dry snow—add a little water to it. If you are cooking in the tent vestibule, collect snow in a stuff sack before bringing it inside.

PATHOGENS IN WATER

In the old days, there were few joys as supreme as naïvely drinking refreshing alpine water right from the source. We still lack much data on water quality in remote areas and although most of it may be pure, we purify it anyway. Animal and human waste can contaminate water and older snow, and microscopic organisms can survive freezing temperatures. Tainted snow melts, trickling and percolating its way to cross-contaminate other snow a long distance away. Purify melted snow just as if it were any other water source. Treat water to guard against the three types of waterborne pathogens: parasites, bacteria, and viruses.

Parasites. Larger parasites include amoebas, tapeworms, and flatworms. Smaller parasites include single-cell protozoa such as *Giardia lamblia* ("giardia") and *Cryptosporidium parvum* ("crypto"), which are between 1 and 20 microns in size. (The period at the end of this sentence is roughly 500 microns.) Exposure to giardia and crypto are major health concerns for alpine travelers. Both are found in backcountry waters worldwide, including all of North America, but there is insufficient data to accurately assess frequency and risk. The illnesses giardiasis and cryptosporidiosis take 2 to 20 days to manifest themselves, with symptoms that include intense nausea, diarrhea, stomach cramps, fever, headaches, flatulence, and belches that reek like rotten eggs. Some parasites have tough cell walls that are resistant to chemical treatment. But because of their larger size, they are easily filtered, and boiling kills them.

Another protozoa, cyclospora, which commonly contaminates water in Nepal during spring and summer, is increasingly found in other areas, including North America. About the same size as crypto and susceptible to the same chemicals, it can be treated in the same way.

Bacteria. Mountain waters contain a wide range of bacteria, tiny living organisms between 0.1 and 10 microns in size. Common harmful waterborne bacteria include *salmonella* (incubation period 12–36 hours), *Campylobacter* *jejuni* (incubation 3–5 days), and *Escherichia coli*, or *E. coli*, (incubation, 24–72 hours). In some parts of the world, water may contain bacteria that cause severe illnesses such as cholera, dysentery, and typhoid. Like viruses, most bacteria can be effectively killed with chemicals. Bacteria are larger than viruses, and so they can be removed more easily with the proper filters. Boiling kills all bacteria.

Viruses. Viruses such as hepatitis A, rotavirus, enterovirus, and norovirus are exceptionally tiny specks of DNA that cause diseases that can be contracted by drinking contaminated water. Viruses are narrowly species-specific, and therefore human viruses are spread by human waste. Although wilderness waters in North America are usually free of human viruses, the risk comes from human traffic and waste handling, so it never hurts to treat against them. Every year people get sick from viruses in heavily used lakes. Viruses are easily killed with chemical treatment but are too tiny to be removed by most filters. Boiling kills viruses.

Table 3-7 summarizes the ability of the major water purification methods to eliminate human pathogens from water sources in the wilderness.

WATER TREATMENT

The principal methods of backcountry water treatment are boiling, filtering, and chemical treatment. No single method is best for every situation. Before using any of these treatment methods, strain water containing sediment or debris through a cloth, paper coffee filter, or paper towel to remove the bulk of the organics. Filtering, chemical disinfecting, and even UV light work more efficiently if the water source has been prefiltered in this way. (See "Additional Water Treatment Considerations," below.)

Boiling

Boiling, the surefire method of water purification, kills all waterborne pathogens. The US Centers for Disease Control and Prevention (CDC) recommends bringing water to a rolling boil and maintaining the boil for 1 minute, or 3 minutes above 6,500 feet (2,000 meters). Other reliable sources state that simply bringing water to a boil is sufficient, even at elevations as high as Everest Base Camp.

Filtering

Water filters (fig. 3-18) are relatively quick and easy to use and create clear, palatable water. Look for a model that is compact and lightweight and is easy to use, clean, and maintain in the field. Filters come in many gravity-fed and pump formats. Water passes through a hollow-fiber membrane or porous ceramic filter to separate parasites, bacteria,

and sometimes viruses. This microscopic strainer collects the pathogens, still alive, on its surface. There is a risk of cross-contamination from the two hoses; be careful handling them. Follow the manufacturer's instructions to periodically clean the filter by backflushing, scrubbing, boiling, and/or chemical disinfection.

Microfilters. The effectiveness of microfilters to remove parasites and bacteria depends on the filter's pore size. Manufacturers describe filter pore size in various ways, so look for an "absolute" pore size that is 0.2 microns or less. However, even at the smallest pore size, *microfilters do not remove viruses*. To guard against viruses, use a purifier-filter instead, or post-treat the water with UV light or any of the chemical disinfectants below. Tannins, dissolved sticky tea-colored solids, clog filters and can be impossible to remove so backflush often.

Purifier-filters. Purifier-filters are also effective against the exceedingly tiny virus. Purifier-filters work either by physical filtration or by the process of "adsorption." Physical filtration is the method currently used by only a few filters on the market, which use hollow-fiber membrane technology. This filter needs to be replaced when it becomes difficult to pump, a sign that the filter is clogged. Adsorption-based purifier-filters force viruses to cleave to a special material. However, they are difficult to monitor for ongoing effectiveness. Depending on how much water and how dirty the water passing through is, the useful life of this material is often very short, silently ending when the cleaving sites are full, with no indication to the consumer.

Chemical Disinfecting

After adding chemical disinfectants to water, loosen the bottle lid and slosh a bit of the treated water onto the threads around the bottle's top and the cap to eliminate any bugs lurking there. Note that microfilters with a carbon element will eliminate most of the chemical taste from chemically treated water, but you must wait the full time before filtering.

Chlorine dioxide. Water treatment using chlorine dioxide (not to be confused with chlorine) is the most effective of the chemical treatments. Chlorine dioxide is available in tablet or two-part liquid formats. The tablets are simply added to the water. Liquid chlorine dioxide is mixed with phosphoric acid 5 minutes before use, turning from clear to bright yellow. The treated water is ready after a wait period.

Electrochlorinators. These battery-driven devices (e.g., MIOX) use a salt solution to create mixed oxidants, primarily chlorine. These systems can purify water with a 15- to 30-minute wait; for crypto, wait four hours. Follow the manufacturer's instructions carefully.

Chlorine and iodine. These two chemicals are equally effective against all bacteria and all viruses but unreliable against parasites and protozoa (see Table 3-7). They are somewhat effective against giardia but not effective against crypto. Both are halogens; another halogen, bromine, is used on navy ships but impractical for backcountry travel. Chlorine (not to be confused with the fundamentally different chlorine dioxide above) is available as household bleach, sodium dichloroisocyanurate, or troclosene sodium tablets. Iodine is available as tablets, drops, or crystals. Adding vitamin C will help eliminate any bad taste, but wait until the disinfection process is complete.

UV Light

Municipal water systems widely use UV light, but backcountry versions are fragile, battery-operated UV lamps. Even clear-looking water can contain enough particles ("turbidity") to shield pathogens from UV light. Users cannot reliably assess turbidity. If water is marginal or dirty, one manufacturer recommends prefiltering with a third-party 0.2-micron filter—not a coarse prefilter with a pore size of well more than 0.2 microns. A microfilter combined with a chemical treatment costs less.

Additional Water Treatment Considerations

For water treatment, consider these conditions.

Cold water, freezing temperatures, snow, and ice. Cold water slows the processes of chemical treatment so longer contact time is needed. Other methods are not affected. Freezing temperatures can destroy water filters in a manner difficult to detect, especially hollow fiber membranes. Pump filters dry and place in a sleeping bag at night. Freshly fallen snow can be considered pure but deciding whether to purify melted snow or ice requires a judgment call, since giardia, crypto, and many bacteria can survive freezing. Avoid drinking the pinkish "watermelon snow" found in older snow banks (from an algae). It can be a laxative.

Turbidity. Organic turbidity (suspended organic solids) creates a "demand," which depletes chemical disinfectants faster than in clear water. Use additional chemical.

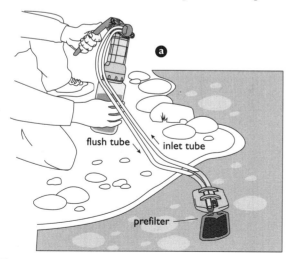
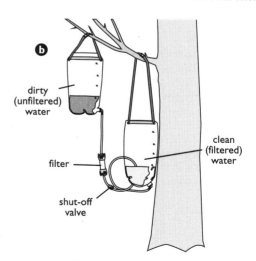

Fig. 3-18. Water filter: a, pump water filter attached directly to water bottle, with prefilter at hose intake end (this particular model offers two-hose continuous self-cleaning); b, gravity-fed water filter hanging from a tree limb. Speed up filtration by keeping the dirty water bag as high as possible and the clean bag as low as possible.

Organic turbidity can also clog filters. Inorganic turbidity (for example, glacial silt) creates "hiding places" for pathogens from UV light. It can also clog filters. If not removed by filtering, glacial silt acts as a laxative. Reduce turbidity significantly by prefiltering with a coffee filter, using a chemical flocculant, or waiting for the solids to settle.

Water storage and dirty hands. Water storage bottles, bags, and hydration devices can easily become contaminated from dirty water or hands. Disinfect with any of the above chemical water treatment methods, bleach, or very hot water. Use only purified water for dishwashing and brushing teeth.

Thoroughly wash hands before handling food. If hand washing is impractical, scrub hand grime with river or lake sand and then clean with hand sanitizer gel or wipes. Backcountry health issues attributed to drinking wilderness water are often caused by fecal-oral contamination from poor hand sanitation.

Chemicals and toxins. None of the treatment methods described above are effective against chemicals or toxins including agricultural runoff (pesticides, herbicides) and industrial runoff (mine tailings, heavy metals). Filters with an activated carbon element offer limited protection. If you're suspicious, move on.

FOOD

Your body needs a variety of foods to tackle a strenuous, demanding activity like mountaineering. With planning, it is possible to choose foods that keep well, are lightweight, and meet all nutritional needs. The longer the trip, the more variable and complex the menu must be. And if the food does not taste good, no one will eat it. If fueling your body quickly and simply is the first aim of alpine cuisine, enjoying your meals is a worthy secondary goal.

Most climbing expeditions plan on providing roughly 4,000 to 5,000 calories a day for each climber. Energy expenditure on a climb can reach as high as 6,000 calories per day, possibly even higher for larger folks. In comparison, most people require only about 1,500 to 2,500 calories per day when living a sedentary life. Adequate caloric intake is essential for climbers. Determine what food intake plan is best, depending on the demands of the trip and your own size, weight, metabolic rate, and level of conditioning. Never engage in calorie restriction (dieting) during a mountaineering trip, for this will interfere with performance and stamina, possibly putting extra demands on others.

COMPOSITION OF FOODS

For the human body to function well, the mountaineer should eat from all three basic food components—carbohydrates (sugars and starch), protein, and fats. The proper proportions are widely debated.

Carbohydrates. The easiest food for the body to convert into energy, carbohydrates should constitute most of the calories. Think of carbohydrates as the main "fuel food" to keep your body functioning most efficiently. Good sources of carbohydrate starch include whole grains, rice, potatoes, cereals, pasta, bread, crackers, and granola bars. Sugars can be supplied not only by honey or granulated sugar but also by fruit (fresh or dried), jam, hot cocoa, energy gels, and drink mixes.

Protein. The daily requirement for proteins is nearly constant regardless of type or level of activity. The body cannot store protein, so once it has met its protein requirement, the excess is either converted to energy or stored as fat. High-protein foods include cheese, peanut butter, nuts, dried meat, canned or vacuum-packed meats and fish, beans, tofu, powdered milk and eggs, and foil-packaged meals containing meat or cheese.

Fats. Because fats pack more than twice as many calories per gram as protein or carbohydrates, they are an important energy source. Fats are digested more slowly than carbohydrates or protein, so they help keep you satisfied longer. This is useful, for example, for staying warm on cold nights. Fats occur naturally in small amounts in vegetables, grains, and beans, and when these are combined with fish, meat, or poultry, the body's requirements for fat are easily met. High-fat foods include butter, margarine, nut butters, nuts, salami, beef jerky, sardines, oils, eggs, seeds, and cheese.

The better a climber's condition, the more efficiently food and water will provide energy during heavy exercise. Many people find that foods high in fat are more difficult to digest during strenuous exercise. One reliable approach is to eat mainly carbohydrates during the day and replenish calorie stores by adding fats and protein to the evening meal. A bedtime snack high in slower-burning food fuel may help keep you warm.

To fuel working muscles, steadily consume carbohydrates and water beginning one to two hours into the climb. The carbohydrate source can be solid food or a prepared beverage. A well-balanced diet replaces most electrolytes that are lost during heavy sweating. Nevertheless, some climbers like to use "high-performance" sports drinks (often diluted) to replace water, carbohydrates, and electrolytes simultaneously. Try these preparations at home, however, before relying on them in the mountains.

FOOD PLANNING AND PACKAGING

As a rough guideline, provide 1.5 to 2.5 pounds (0.7 to 1.1 kilograms) or 2,500 to 4,500 calories of food per person per day. This will vary based on conditions, exertion, and metabolism. Keep in mind that "extra food" is the eighth Ten Essential, but don't get weighed down by excess provisions.

On very short trips, climbers can carry sandwiches, fresh fruit and vegetables, and just about anything else. Taking only cold, ready-to-eat food saves the weight of stove, fuel, and cook pots, a good idea for lightweight bivouacs. In nasty weather, this approach allows you to retreat directly to the tent without the hassle of cooking. Use firm bread, rolls, or bagels for a sandwich that will stand up to packing. Leave out mayonnaise and other ingredients that spoil easily.

For trips of two or three days—or longer, if base camp is close to the road—any food from the grocery store is fair game.For longer trips, food planning becomes more complicated and food weight more critical. Freeze-dried food is compact, lightweight, and easy to prepare but is relatively expensive. Outdoor stores carry a large selection of freeze-dried foods, including main courses, vegetables, soups, breakfasts, and desserts. Some require little or no cooking; just add hot water, let it soak for a while, and eat from the package. Others require cooking in a pot.

With access to a food dehydrator, climbers can enjoy a more varied menu at substantial savings. Simple and nutritious mountaineering foods can be made from dried fruit, vegetables, and meat. Dehydrated produce can be eaten as is or added as an ingredient to a cooked dish. Fruit leather is easy to prepare with a dehydrator. Sauces are too: dry spaghetti sauce to serve with angel-hair pasta (which is thin and cooks quickly). Many dehydrated foods simply require rehydration.

Vacuum sealing provides even more variety. Dehydrate the food first, then seal it. This process removes all air from the food package, reducing spoilage.

A small kitchen scale is useful for precise planning and packaging of food. Transfer food from bulky packaging into resealable plastic bags or other lightweight containers. Enclose identifying labels and cooking instructions, or write this information on the outside of the bag with a permanent marker. Ingredient or meal packages can be placed inside larger bags labeled in broad categories, such as "breakfast," "dinner," or "drinks."

Groups

Because meals are social events, climbing groups often plan food together. A good menu boosts morale. A carefully planned, shared menu can reduce the overall food weight carried by each person. Another common arrangement is to approach only dinner as a group effort.

Group meals can be planned by the group or by a chosen individual. Canvass the group members for food preferences, needs, and allergies; one person may be a vegetarian, another may refuse to eat freeze-dried entrées. Writing down a menu and discussing it with the group can go a long way toward group harmony.

The ideal number of people in a cooking group is two to three per stove, four maximum. Beyond that, group efficiency is outweighed by the complexities of large pots, small stoves, and increased cooking times.

High-Elevation Cooking

Cooking raw foods becomes impractical above about 10,000 feet (3,050 meters). The boiling point of water decreases with altitude as shown in Table 3-8, which increases the time to cook raw food by two to four times at 10,000 feet (3,050 meters) and by four to seven times at 15,000 feet (4,575 meters). The practical answer is to bring foods that require only warming, such as meat or fish in a foil pouch; precooked food that requires only hot water, such as instant rice or quick oats; or simply freeze-dried meals. For the dedicated high-altitude chef, lightweight pressure cookers are available.

The rigors of rapid ascent to higher altitudes also require special attention to the choice of food. Many climbers fall victim to symptoms of mountain sickness, ranging from a slight malaise to vomiting and severe headaches. Under these conditions, food becomes more difficult to digest. Climbers must continue to eat and drink; keeping well hydrated is particularly essential. To cope with this aversion to food, eat light and eat often; also, emphasize

TABLE 3-8. BOILING POINT.

ELEVATION IN FEET (METERS)	TEMPERATURE AT WHICH WATER BOILS °F (°C)
Sea level (0)	212° (100°)
5,000 (1,525)	202° (95°)
10,000 (3,050)	193° (90°)
15,000 (4,575)	184° (85°)
20,000 (6,100)	176° (80°)
25,000 (7,625)	168° (75°)
29,029 (8,848)	162° (72°)

carbohydrate foods, which are easiest to digest. Trial and error will determine what foods your body can tolerate.

MENU SUGGESTIONS
Try out various food combinations before taking them on an extended trip in the mountains.

Breakfasts
For a fast start, prepackage a standard meal before the trip. A single bag can contain oatmeal, cold cereal, or granola with dried or dehydrated fruit, plus powdered milk or sweet spices such as nutmeg or cinnamon. Stir in water—cold or hot—and breakfast is ready. Other quick breakfast options include bakery items; dried fruit and meat; nuts; energy bars; dehydrated applesauce; and freeze-dried breakfasts that combine eggs, meat, and potatoes. Common hot drink choices are instant cocoa, instant cider, coffee, powdered milk, tea, and instant breakfast drinks. To many, caffeine is a civilized way to start the day, and many studies show it brings a measurable increase in endurance and delays exhaustion.

Lunches and Snacks
During a climb, lunch begins shortly after breakfast and continues throughout the day. Eat small amounts, and eat often. At least half of a climber's daily food allotment should be for lunch and snacks. A good munching staple is GORP (originally, "good old raisins and peanuts"), a mixture that can contain nuts, small candies such as chocolate chips, and dried fruit or ginger. One handful makes a snack; several make a meal. Granola is another option, with its mixture of grains, honey or sugar, and bits of fruit and nuts. Other popular snack items are fruit leather, candy bars, energy bars, and dried fruit. A basic lunch can include any of the following:

Protein. Sources include vacuum-sealed meats and fish, beef jerky, salami, powdered hummus, hard cheese, nuts, and seeds.

Starch. Carbohydrates include whole-grain breads, bagels, pita bread, granola, firm crackers, tortillas, rice cakes, chips, pretzels, and energy bars.

Sweets. Some treats are cookies, candy bars, hard candy, muffins, pastries, and jam. Chocolate always gets eaten.

Fruit. Sources include fresh fruit, fruit leather, and dried fruit such as raisins, figs, and apples, or freeze-dried strawberries, blueberries, or mango.

Vegetables. Some vegetables that travel well are fresh carrot or celery sticks, sliced sweet peppers, or dehydrated vegetables.

To encourage rehydration, mix up a flavored beverage such as lemonade or fruit punch at lunch. In cold weather, fill a light thermos with hot water at breakfast, and enjoy a cup of instant soup or miso at lunch.

Dinners
The evening meal should be nourishing and delicious, yet easy and quick to prepare. To supplement liquid intake, include some items that take a lot of water, such as soup, hot cider, herbal tea, fruit drink, or cocoa. A cup of soup makes a quick and satisfying first course. A hearty soup can also serve as the main course. Good choices include miso, minestrone, bean, beef barley, lentil, chili, or chicken. Add to the menu instant potatoes, dehydrated vegetables, rice, crackers, tortilla shells, cheese, or bread, and the meal is complete.

One-pot meals with a carbohydrate base of pasta, rice, beans, potatoes, or grains are easy and nutritious. To ensure that you get adequate protein, fat, and flavor, add other ingredients such as chicken, beef, or fish that has been dried or packaged in a foil pouch; sausage; freeze-dried vegetables or fruit; margarine; or a dehydrated soup or sauce mix. Outdoor retail and online stores carry a variety of freeze-dried entrées that are nutritionally balanced and easy to prepare, though expensive. Prepackaged dishes from the grocery store—such as spaghetti, noodle dishes, and rice mixes—are also good, easy, and less expensive. Freeze-dried or dehydrated vegetables add variety. Prepare them as side dishes, or add to soups or stews. Freeze-dried cooked beans or processed soy products in powdered or textured forms are excellent, low-cost protein additions. Natural-food stores often have a wide selection of these ingredients. Climbers can also prepare and dehydrate sauces and many other ingredients at home.

Margarine, which keeps better than butter, and oils, such as olive oil, improve the flavor of many foods and add significant calories with minimum weight. For seasonings, try salt, pepper, herbs, garlic, chili powder, bacon bits, curry powder, dehydrated onions, grated Parmesan cheese, hot sauce, or soy sauce (just not all together). Dessert choices include dates, cookies, candy, chocolate, no-bake cheesecake, applesauce, cooked dried fruit, instant pudding, and freeze-dried ice cream. Dessert time, accompanied by a cup of hot herbal tea, can provide a pleasant backdrop to group talk about the next day's itinerary and a decision on who will provide the morning wake-up call.

Boiled water cooking. "Cooking" dinner for many alpine chefs simply means boiling water. Packing food that requires no cooking is simple, fast, easy to clean up, and can be delicious. Most freeze-dried entrées are designed

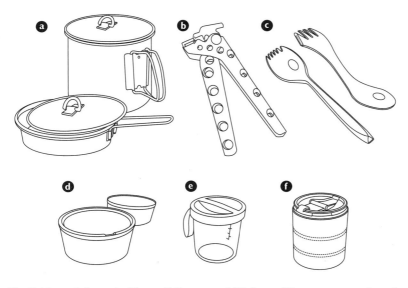

Fig. 3-19. a, alpine pot with small fry pan and lid; b, pot lifter; c, spoon and spork; d, nested bowls; e, cup with lid and measuring marks; f, insulated mug.

and titanium. Aluminum, which is light and inexpensive, is the most common. Stainless steel is strong and easy to clean but heavy. Titanium is light and strong but expensive. A large water pot is useful for melting snow. A wide pot is more stable than a tall, narrow one and more efficient because it catches more of the stove's flame. Be sure all pots have bails or handles, or bring a small metal pot lifter (fig. 3-19b). Tight-fitting pot lids conserve heat. (See "Cooking for a crowd" under "Stoves," above.)

Cups, spoons and forks, and bowls (fig. 3-19c, d, and e) come in the same materials as cook sets and also in strong, light polycarbonate plastic. Insulated mugs (fig. 3-19f) are popular; a sipping lid keeps the contents warm and prevents spills. Some cooking pans have a nonstick coating for easy cleaning but require plastic or silicone utensils to avoid scratches. A coffee press is an accessory for some canister system stoves (see Figure 3-17c). A small silicone spatula is useful for cooking and for efficiently getting food out of the pan, whether for eating or cleaning up. Bring a small plastic scrub pad and a synthetic fabric pack towel for cleaning.

Many specialized pieces of camp kitchenware, such as bake ovens, Dutch ovens, pressure cookers, and espresso makers, are impractical on mountaineering trips.

to be reconstituted in their packaging. Dinner can also be prepared directly in a bowl or cup. Start with some instant soup. The main course could be a starchy food (instant mashed potatoes, instant rice, or couscous) with added protein, vegetables, and condiments. Follow with a dessert of instant applesauce or instant pudding, and end with a rehydrating hot drink of noncaffeinated tea or cider. The only items to wash up are the spoon, cup, and maybe bowl.

COOKWARE AND UTENSILS FOR COOKING AND EATING

On an ultralightweight trip with just cold food, fingers are the only utensils needed. (Wash hands before preparing food or eating, or at least use a hand-sanitizing gel.) Making dinner with the boiled water cooking methods described in "Menu Suggestions," above, requires only a cup and spoon per person, plus one cook pot with a bail or handle for each group of three or four; bowls are convenient but optional.

The popular canister system stoves have a built-in cooking pot or a small set of integrated pots from which to choose. These are optimized for boiled water cooking. For less spartan menus, other stoves accept a variety of cooking pots. Bring one pot for boiling water, another for cooking, and light, unbreakable bowls for eating. Alpine cook sets (fig. 3-19a) come in aluminum, stainless steel,

"IT'S JUST CAMPING"

Pioneer American alpinist Paul Petzoldt said, in an interview about climbing in the Himalaya and Karakoram, "It's just camping." His point was that technical climbing skills are less important than the ability to survive—and even less so than the resourcefulness necessary to be at home and comfortable in the high mountains.

Camping skills are the basis upon which all the more technical mountaineering skills rely. Once climbers develop and hone the skills to stay in the mountains, they will have the confidence to venture further. They will begin to understand what it means to have the freedom of the hills.

CHAPTER 4
PHYSICAL CONDITIONING

An appropriate mountaineering conditioning program includes a proper blend of aerobic and anaerobic cardiovascular training, strength training, flexibility training, skill development, cross training, proper fueling, and adequate rest and recovery based on the fundamental training concepts described in this chapter.

Many mountaineers dedicate an hour or two several days a week to sport-specific conditioning, reserving weekends for longer outings in the mountains. The best way to train for a certain activity is to do that specific activity. However, in situations when that isn't possible, numerous training options help climbers prepare for their sport. This chapter provides guidelines for developing a personal systematic conditioning program to optimize each climber's training time.

GOAL SETTING

In order to begin the journey toward mountaineering fitness, the first requirement is to understand what that means for each climber. *Fitness* is defined here as the full-body conditioning needed to easily perform movements that may be encountered in the mountains while maintaining a reserve of strength and stamina for unforeseen challenges. Before designing a suitable training program, each climber needs to set a personal end goal and the steps needed to get there.

SMART goals. First, set goals that are Specific, Measurable, Action-oriented, Realistic, and Time-stamped: SMART. For example, a goal to "climb Mount X by Y route in three days by the end of the coming summer, through a workout program that includes five weekly workouts and a 6- to 8-mile hike gaining 3,000 feet of elevation every other week, gradually increasing pack weight by 3 to 5 pounds per outing" has all the elements of a SMART goal and will be more motivating than a vague goal to "get fit for mountaineering."

MOUNTAINEERING FITNESS COMPONENTS

The level of fitness required for a beginning-level one-day rock climb differs from that needed for an advanced two-day ice climb; both fitness programs will look different compared with that of someone training for a three-week trek. With an end goal in mind, each climber can plan individualized training.

CARDIOVASCULAR TRAINING

Cardiovascular endurance is the body's ability to perform a repetitive activity for an extended length of time. During cardiovascular work, the body uses large muscle groups simultaneously, either aerobically or anaerobically. A strong cardiovascular base is mandatory for all aspects of mountaineering.

Aerobic exercise is any cardiovascular activity that requires a significant amount of oxygen for sustained effort; it can be categorized as being short (2 to 8 minutes), medium (8 to 30 minutes), or long (more than 30 minutes). When compared with anaerobic activities, aerobic activities are performed for longer durations and at lower intensities.

To start preparing for mountaineering, a climber should be able to complete a 5-mile (8-kilometer) round-trip hike with roughly a 13-pound (5.9-kilogram) pack, ascending and descending 2,000 feet (610 meters) in less than two and a half hours. In addition to having such baseline hiking capability, climbers should build to four or more cardiovascular workouts per week (depending on the objective) as they approach their targeted goal.

While some of these workouts should be in the mountains or at least have an uphill emphasis, most can be done close to home. Cardiovascular training options for mountaineering should include activities that load the spine in an upright position. Suitable examples are using inclined treadmills, elliptical cross-training machines, stair machines, or revolving stair climbers; hiking, hill walking, snowshoeing, or cross-country skiing; doing step aerobics; and trail running. Biking, paddling, and swimming can be included in the off-season, as rehabilitative alternatives as needed to enable continued training or as supplemental cross-training alternatives (see "Cross Training" below).

Anaerobic exercise is near-maximal cardiovascular training that takes climbers to the upper levels of their aerobic training zone and beyond. Such training involves working at heart rates that are higher than those that can be sustained during aerobic sessions. Anaerobic exercise helps climbers when they need a sudden burst of energy to respond to emergencies in the mountains or to link a series of powerful moves together on a climbing wall. Anaerobic training helps climbers increase their leg turnover rate, or how quickly they can move across varied terrain, in order to increase speed. It boosts climbers' entire aerobic zone so that activities that once made them breathless will feel more comfortable. Examples include pack-loaded stair climbing, walking quickly uphill while wearing a pack, or sprinting uphill without a pack.

To periodically assess your personal cardiovascular fitness level, choose a favorite nearby hiking route that is snow-free year-round and use it as a test piece every few weeks. Each time you hike it, challenge yourself in some way: add weight to your pack—no more than 10 percent per week, or 3 to 5 pounds (1 to 2 kilograms) per outing—and go as fast as you have on a previous hike with less weight; or complete the hike in a shorter amount of time. Meeting either of these challenges indicates increased cardiovascular fitness.

An easy way to add pack weight is to fill several 2-quart bottles with water. In early season, to save wear and tear on your joints if necessary, dump the water before descending. As you near your training goal, however, be sure that you can also carry down the weight that you carry up. If you struggle with breathlessness while carrying a light pack, concentrate on developing endurance during weekly training sessions. If your legs feel heavy when you start to increase pack weight, focus on building more strength.

STRENGTH TRAINING

Strength training is crucial to success in mountaineering, because it gives climbers the power and force to withstand challenges, whether predictable or unforeseen, in the mountains. Strength training prevents injuries by helping the body adapt to overloading, provides muscle balance, improves performance, boosts metabolism, and increases lean muscle mass, which in turn can help reduce overall body fat. Climbers should strive to be stronger than they think they will need to be. When the endurance aspect of mountaineering is factored in, the conflicting demands on a climber's body will result in a loss of strength, and that extra training will end up being just enough.

Mountaineers benefit from strong upper-back, core, and leg muscles; solid balance and agility; and flexibility in the calves, knees, torso, and ankles. Rock and ice climbers benefit from strong and balanced upper-body muscles as well. Include full-body strength training year-round to maintain a baseline level of strength, and then build as needed at appropriate times. During the preseason, use single-limb (unilateral) free-weight exercises to correct any weaknesses in legs and hips, particularly in the full range of motion that may be encountered on alpine outings.

Exercises such as static lunges, one-legged dead lifts (see Figure 4-1), step-ups, and step-downs (see Figure 4-2) ensure that legs and hips do equal work. Many of these exercises can be performed at home using body weight, initially, then a loaded pack as balance improves and strength increases. Since the calves will take the brunt of the load whenever a climber is on steep terrain, include straight-leg variations of calf exercises (see Resources for this chapter).

One-legged dead lift. This excellent, sport-specific, unilateral mountaineering exercise develops stability in the ankles, hips, and feet as well as strength in the entire leg, including gluteals and lower back. Stand balancing on one foot while holding a dumbbell in one or two hands (fig. 4-1a). Keep the other foot lifted but near the floor in case it is needed to touch down for balance. Hinge forward at the hips with as much or as little knee bend as desired

4

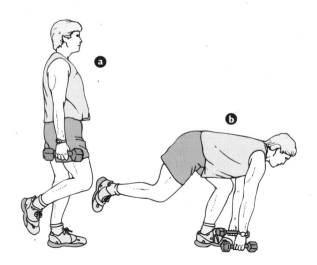

Fig. 4-1. One-legged dead lift: a, stand balanced on one leg, holding dumbbells; b, hinge forward at the hips, reaching dumbbells to the floor, then exhale and return to upright position.

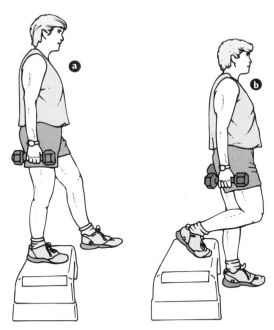

Fig. 4-2. Step-down: a, slowly step off the step as if walking downstairs; b, slowly reverse the movement, starting on toes and using the leg still on the step to lift yourself back up. Keep the knee tracking directly over the middle toe.

and reach the dumbbell(s) to the floor (fig. 4-1b). Exhale and return to a fully upright position with each repetition. Complete two to three sets of 6 to 15 repetitions per leg (depending on the phase of training you are in) and repeat with the other leg.

Step-down. This is one of the most effective and specific unilateral mountaineering exercises to strengthen the quadriceps for downhill travel. Use a 6- to 12-inch (15- to 31-centimeter) step whose height allows you to do the exercise under control without any lateral (side-to-side) knee movement. Start on top of the step, with toes pointing forward and a light dumbbell in each hand (fig. 4-2a). Slowly step off the front of the step as if walking downstairs, controlling the downward movement as though you are stepping onto eggshells. The leg on the step is the working leg, so keep your focus on it. When your foot reaches the floor (fig. 4-2b), reverse the movement, starting on your toes and using the leg that's still on the bench to lift yourself back up. Keep your working knee tracking over your middle toe rather than collapsing toward the midline of the body. Control both the lifting and lowering portions of this exercise. Complete two or three sets of 6 to 15 repetitions per leg (depending on the phase of training you are in) and repeat with the other leg.

Snow shoveler. This functional movement integrates the upper and lower body with torso rotation and prepares

climbers for lifting a heavy pack onto their back, digging snow pits or latrines, or carving ice blocks for wind breaks and snow shelters. Replace floor crunches with exercises like this to optimize training time. Hold a sizable dumbbell in both hands. Stand with your feet wider than shoulder width apart. Squat toward the floor, maintaining a neutral spine (fig. 4-3a). The weight will be directly below your chin.

As you rise to a standing position, pivot to one side as though completing a golf swing, keeping the dumbbell's weight close to your shoulder (fig. 4-3b). Your eyes should follow the dumbbell as you move it to the top of the arc, ending near your shoulder, not overhead. Squat again, then lift to the other side, alternating sides with each repetition. Keep your abdominals tight to avoid overextending your back. Complete two to three sets of 6 to 15 repetitions per side (depending on the phase of training you are in).

During the middle of the preseason, once you have developed good muscle balance and core strength, incorporate full-body, full-range-of-motion exercises, including variations on the squat, dead lift, bench press, pull-up, and

81

Fig. 4-3. Snow shoveler: a, holding dumbbell in both hands, squat with a neutral spine; b, stand up, pivoting to one side and swinging dumbbell up to shoulder, following it with your eyes and keeping abdominals tight. Repeat, pivoting to the other side.

row, among others. Because of the dynamic and unpredictable nature of performing self-arrests with an ice axe, be sure to have full range of motion in your shoulders as well as good strength and joint integrity throughout your chest, shoulders, and torso. Pull-ups, push-ups, and core exercises will enable climbers to get into position rapidly and hold the ice axe in place on icy slopes while stopping themselves from sliding. Options that help increase strength and stamina include lifting free weights, walking uphill, dragging a sled, carrying a weighted pack, training with body-weight exercises (in other words, using your own body for resistance, as in push-ups or pull-ups), and using bands, bouldering, and hang boards developed specifically for climbers.

Consider which muscles your upcoming activities will involve and match your training exercises to the movements that will be required for those activities. For example, if you will be snowshoeing on an approach for a winter mountaineering outing, develop strength endurance in the hip flexors for repeated high-steps. Add ankle weights or ski boots to short anaerobic uphill or strength workouts. Do not, however, add ankle weights to long endurance

workouts, as they can alter a climber's natural stride, not to mention cause an overuse injury. If you are weak on overhanging movements, develop your core and grip by training the abdominals, obliques (the side abdominal muscles involved in rotating the torso), forearms, and fingers, in addition to the larger muscle groups in the upper body.

Use the hiking test piece as a guideline for refining the strength training program. If your ankles fatigue when you hike on uneven terrain, add unilateral balance exercises or incorporate short weekly training sessions walking on gravel or sand or traversing slopes to help them adapt to such terrain. If your quadriceps muscles are sore following steep hikes, increase the number of sets of step-downs, front squats, or lunges and focus on strengthening the front of the thighs. As you add pack weight, if your shoulders and neck get tired, add exercises such as upright rows or shrugs. By tracking such challenges on those training hikes, climbers can determine what body areas need additional strengthening.

FLEXIBILITY TRAINING

Flexibility refers to the active range of motion of muscles around a particular joint. Stretching muscles can help prevent discomfort after strenuous workouts, but it can also help with changes in body alignment (such as during weight gain or loss), with injury recovery, and with correcting faulty biomechanics. While experiencing minor stiffness when starting a new training routine is normal and expected, climbers may help prevent delayed-onset muscle soreness (DOMS) by stretching. DOMS occurs most often after workouts that stress the body with the eccentric, or lowering phase, of an exercise, such as extended downward travel with a heavy pack, downhill trail running, or bouldering that requires dropping from height onto your feet. When returning to training following time off, ease back into the routine with lower intensity, weight, duration, and volume (that is, fewer sets and repetitions) to prevent experiencing mild pain, soreness, stiffness, and joint aches.

Frog stretch. This is a great lower-body stretch to open the hips for vertical rock climbing. Stand with the feet slightly wider than shoulder width apart and sink into a full squat, keeping heels flat on the floor and allowing your torso to lean forward slightly but not collapse over your knees (fig. 4-4). Press your elbows against the inside of your knees to increase the stretch in your hips and inner thighs. Hold for 30 to 60 seconds.

Seated gluteal stretch. This stretch aids the glutes and lower back (fig. 4-5). Sit on a bench, armless chair, or car

Fig. 4-4. Frog stretch: keeping heels on the floor and leaning torso slightly forward, squat down as low as comfortable and press elbows against knees to open up hips.

Fig. 4-5. Seated gluteal stretch: sitting with shins perpendicular to the ground and thighs parallel to each other, cross right ankle over left knee, press chest forward with a straight spine, and hold. Repeat with left ankle over right knee.

bumper so that both shins are perpendicular to the ground and both thighs are parallel to the ground (in other words, knees at right angles). To stretch the right hip, cross the right ankle over the left knee. Press your chest forward with a straight spine (avoid collapsing the chest toward the knee) until you feel a deep stretch in the outer right hip. Hold for 30 to 60 seconds, then repeat with the left ankle over the right knee. Note which hip is tighter (if either),

and in future stretching sessions start by stretching that hip first. Do this stretch while standing on the trail for an additional balance challenge.

SKILL DEVELOPMENT

Skill refers to technique and mastery of coordination. Skilled mountaineers are precise with their movements and use less energy in completing an activity as compared to novices. A beginner climbing four days a week may risk overtraining, whereas a highly conditioned climber can perform the movements with less exertion and strain and may be able to climb at higher frequency without overdoing it. Experienced mountaineers have a sense of when to back off of the intensity or volume of their training sessions and work on less taxing but equally important skills.

Skilled mountaineers also are more comfortable and confident in situations that could cause novice climbers to panic, make mistakes, have poor judgment, or experience accidents that might lead to injury. Develop skill by putting into practice all the techniques discussed in this book and getting appropriate training where needed.

CROSS TRAINING

The final component to consider when preparing for mountaineering is cross training. Cross training simply means doing supplemental physical activities not directly related to your sport. At higher skill levels, cross training recruits muscle groups in different patterns and provides psychological and physiological breaks from excessive repetition. Cross training provides body and muscle balance for sports such as rock and ice climbing that involve high repetition from small muscle groups.

While cross training may not relate directly to sport performance, keeping the joints healthy and preventing overtraining *does* relate to long-term performance. Cross training for the climber may involve horizontal pulling movements or rowing training to balance out the vertical component that dominates the sport. A cross-training sport commonly included in many mountaineering programs is cycling; this seated activity does not load the spine as mountaineering does, but it provides a nonimpact outdoor training mode that is gentler on the legs than the high-impact activity of running.

FUNDAMENTAL TRAINING CONCEPTS

Once you understand what training components are involved in mountaineering conditioning, you can start to manipulate them to create a customized training program.

TABLE 4-1. SAMPLE YEAR-ROUND STRENGTH TRAINING PROGRAM					
PRESEASON			IN-SEASON	POSTSEASON	OFF-SEASON
Early	Middle	Late			
Fewer sets with moderate number of repetitions	Moderate number of sets with fewer repetitions, focusing on strength	Moderate number of sets with high number of repetitions, focusing on strength, endurance	Maintenance, with moderate number of sets and repetitions	Focus on imbalanced areas developed from sport-specific activities	Training of weak points

Source: Courtenay W. Schurman and Doug G. Schurman, *The Outdoor Athlete* (see Resources).

FITT PARAMETERS

The four FITT parameters—frequency (how often you exercise), intensity (how hard you exercise), time (how long you exercise), and type (what exercise modes you do)—together constitute the training load, or stress. A person who trains for a one-day beginner rock climb has a low workload: low frequency, low intensity, low time (duration). An advanced high-altitude mountaineer getting ready for an expedition has a high workload: high frequency, low to high intensity, high time (duration). The greater the workload, the more carefully designed the training program needs to be, with sufficient rest and recovery days, in order to prevent physical and psychological burnout.

Frequency. How often climbers train depends on their current fitness level, their end goal, and their desired level of achievement. According to the American College of Sports Medicine and the American Heart Association, a suitable fitness program for average healthy adults includes three to five aerobic workouts per week of 20 or more minutes each *and* activities that maintain or increase muscular strength and endurance a minimum of two nonconsecutive days a week. Mountaineering is a strenuous activity that requires far more training than what an average healthy adult needs on a daily basis. As climbers progress to more demanding alpine goals, the frequency of their cardiovascular, sport-specific, and strength training workouts will increase, and their workouts will vary in intensity and time (duration).

Intensity. How hard a workout is determines its intensity. The optimal cardiovascular intensity for fitness improvement is 65 to 95 percent of a person's maximum heart rate. Most early preseason workouts should be at a low intensity. Gradually build cardiovascular endurance before adding high-intensity anaerobic workouts in late preseason.

Strength training should also start with low-intensity workouts. Work with lighter weights for a moderate number of repetitions (for example, sets of 8 to 10 repetitions), especially if you are relatively new to strength training. Next, progress to a phase emphasizing gaining strength by performing more sets with heavier weight and fewer reps. As you peak for reaching your training goal, focus on increasing strength endurance by using lighter weights than in the strength phase but completing more repetitions. Table 4-1 indicates how strength sets and repetitions will vary according to the phase of training you are in.

Time. Cardiovascular and strength workouts range in length, also known as duration, according to the end goals, training cycle, and exercise type. Aerobic exercise in a climber's training zone should be done for at least 15 to 20 minutes per session in order to see improvements. A strength workout as short as 8 to 10 minutes can provide some benefits, although a typical strength workout ranges from 20 to 60 minutes, depending on the frequency of the strength training.

Type. Workouts vary according to the specific cardiovascular exercises and strength exercises they encompass. Exercise selection depends on individual preference, location (climate and terrain), season, and sport discipline. Choices will vary from one athlete to the next: a rock or ice climber may spend more time at indoor climbing gyms and focus on upper-body and core training in the off-season, while a high-altitude alpine climber may opt for backpacking trips year-round and focus on core and lower-body conditioning exercises in the off-season. Supplemental cross training outside of the chosen sport provides rest and recovery as well as additional training stimulus for the cardiovascular and musculoskeletal systems.

TRAINING GUIDELINES

In addition to properly manipulating the four FITT parameters, climbers should also adhere to the following training guidelines.

Train specifically. Match the cardiovascular modes and intensities of a training program to the primary movements of the intended sport. Sometimes it is difficult to practice a sport—ice climbing is challenging in a warm winter, rock climbing is difficult in the middle of a city, and high-altitude trekking may be impossible for those who live at sea level. And sometimes it is beneficial to include cross training for rehabilitation or injury prevention.

For most of a training program, however, choose comparable activities that work the muscle groups in the same ways the intended sport works them. In a well-rounded program for mountaineering, spinal-loading choices, such as hill climbing, stair climbing, and using inclined cardiovascular machines (for example, an elliptical trainer, treadmill, stair climber, or stepmill)—all with or without a pack—as well as trail running without a pack, should be the dominant cardiovascular choices. Non-spinal-loading cardiovascular activities such as biking, rowing, and swimming may be included for cross-training purposes.

Train functionally. Keep the exercise selection functional, choosing exercises that integrate as many muscle groups as possible rather than train the body in isolation. Training with free weights provides far greater benefits compared with using weight machines, because training with free weights requires you to balance weight and exercise coordination in all three dimensions, which loads the spine the same way it is loaded when climbers are on a hiking trail, snowshoes, a pair of skis, a slope, or a rock ledge.

Increase gradually. Increase training volume by no more than 5 to 15 percent at any given time. If a training program starts with 20-minute workouts, add 2 minutes to subsequent cardiovascular sessions. This suggested progression is based on the amount of musculature used, impact on joints, and relative support provided for the body. Activities that rely heavily on smaller upper-body musculature or rigorous full-body movements (for example, cross-country skiing or technical climbing) should increase by no more than 5 percent at a time; high-impact activities that use large muscles (such as trail running or telemark skiing) should increase by no more than 10 percent at a time; and low-impact activities (for instance, hiking or scrambling) or seated, supported activities (such as biking) should increase by under 15 percent at a time.

Include adequate recovery time. The impact of high-intensity workouts requires more recovery time. Endurance days may be done at low intensities; but if pack weight or hilly terrain is added, follow them with a recovery day. Low-intensity recovery cross-training exercises may include walking, swimming, dancing, easy flat biking, yoga, or yard work. Such light days help prevent overtraining by allowing tired muscles to rest before they perform again. As climbers grow older, they may need additional recovery time as well as training time to reach their training goals.

NUTRITION HABITS

Comprehensive nutrition guidelines are beyond the scope of this chapter, but no discussion of conditioning is complete without addressing basic nutrition needs (see Chapter 3, Camping, Food, and Water, for other considerations regarding food and water). Six basic habits for good nutrition that do not require calorie counting, measuring food, or giving up favorites are recommended here. They focus on healthy choices and are as applicable to the occasional weekend sport-climbing vegan mountaineer as they are to the die-hard steak-consuming mountaineer who wants to climb the Seven Summits. All that these habits require for performance and measurement are each climber's own hands.

Habit 1. Eat *slowly*, and try to stop eating when you reach 80 percent full (that is, still slightly hungry), to teach yourself what your level of "comfortably full" feels like. After eating slowly for 20 minutes (the approximate amount of time it takes for satiety signals to reach the brain), if you are still hungry, have more.

Habit 2. Include vegetables with each meal. A cup of leafy greens or a half cup of other vegetables qualifies as one serving; try to include one to two servings every meal for women, two to four for men. Eat from every color of the rainbow for maximum phytonutrient benefits.

Habit 3. Include protein with each meal. Think "palm-sized" according to the size of your own hand—one palm for women per meal, two palms for men. Good sources of protein include whole eggs; lean beef, pork, or lamb; poultry or seafood; and lentils or beans.

Habit 4. Make sure to get healthy fats with each meal—fats that are rich in omega-3 fatty acids and low in omega-6 fatty acids. Nuts, seeds, nut butters, extra-virgin olive oil, avocados, and fish oils are all excellent choices. Women should include one thumb-sized portion each meal, men should include two.

Habit 5. Eliminate or reduce starchy carbohydrates on days you don't exercise, replacing them instead with added

TABLE 4-2. SAMPLE TRAINING BLOCKS AND GOALS FOR ONE YEAR					
PRESEASON			IN-SEASON	POSTSEASON	OFF-SEASON
Early	Middle	Late			
Establish baseline.	Increase cardiovascular endurance and build strength.	Enhance mental toughness and stamina; peak and taper.	Maintain performance level.	Focus on imbalances developed from sport-specific activities.	Prioritize training of weak points.

Source: Courtenay W. Schurman and Doug G. Schurman, *The Outdoor Athlete* (see Resources).

servings of fruits or vegetables. If you *have* exercised that day, include one fist-sized (cooked) portion of starchy carbohydrate for women, two for men, choosing from such foods as wild rice, quinoa, sprouted grains, squash, pasta, or other whole grains with little to no added sugar. If you must have a sweet snack like a doughnut, make sure to include veggies, protein, and some healthy fat with it, and sit down and treat it like a full meal. In most cases, by going through the extra effort, you'll decide it's not worth it or wait until you're legitimately hungry for a complete meal.

Habit 6. Drink plenty of plain potable water, especially if you consume any soda, alcohol, caffeinated beverages, or juices. It's best to eliminate those beverages entirely, but if that's not possible, increase your water intake to 60 or more ounces per day—more on days when you are training longer than an hour, enough to keep your output clear.

FITNESS PROGRAM TRAINING BLOCKS

In order to develop a suitable program, start by noting the date you want to attain your end goal. In many cases, registering for a climb or making a deposit on a trip provides a deadline that is hard to change. There may also be a short window of opportunity for a given climb, for example for ice climbs in most parts of the world. Once a firm date is set, break the time between that end goal and the training program starting point into six distinct training blocks; each block of time will have a different objective. Table 4-2 illustrates how an entire year may be divided into training blocks.

Preseason. In the *early phase* of preseason training, the goal is to establish a solid foundation, or baseline, on which the rest of the training builds. Frequency, intensity, and time for both cardiovascular training and strength training will probably be fairly low. In the *middle phase*, as the focus of preseason training shifts to increasing cardiovascular endurance, frequency and time of cardiovascular exercise will gradually increase while intensity remains low. Focus on building strength specific to the chosen activity with increased intensity (more weight, fewer repetitions, more sets) for strength exercises. In the *late stages* of preseason training, the focus will shift to enhancing mental toughness and increasing stamina, adding intensity to one or two weekly anaerobic sessions, adding pack weight and distance to long weekend conditioners, and training for more strength endurance (lighter weight, higher repetitions) as the in-season approaches. The late phase of the preseason will be devoted to peaking and tapering for a climb or for the start of the season for the intended sport. Preseason can last as long as one to six months.

In-season. A sport's in-season might mean getting out to the mountains as frequently as several times a month or more. In-season encompasses a series of climbs or trips, generally in summer (ice climbing would be winter). The training goal in-season is to maintain performance level during the intended activity.

Postseason. After the completion of in-season activities, the training focus is on addressing any imbalances that arose from the in-season activities. Common to climbing is the need to balance a season of horizontal and vertical pulling by adding horizontal and vertical pressing movements, thus improving shoulder stability. The postseason lasts two to four weeks, immediately following the completion of the in-season events.

Off-season. During the off-season, training prioritizes any weak points that have emerged such as quadriceps that fatigued on steep downhills, hips that got tight on longer trips, or a low back that fatigued with heavier pack weight. The length of the off-season is the time that remains between postseason and the next preseason—generally several months, unless a climber participates in multiple sports.

A sample year. If a novice climber is training for a first, very easy mountaineering outing, the early phase of the training program may last only one to two weeks, with two or three weeks for each of the other five training blocks. A more experienced mountaineer, or a climber who is working toward complex goals that require more than half a year of training, might spend a month in each training block and cycle several times through the middle phase of preseason training, alternating between a strength-building phase and an endurance building phase, separating each ramp-up with a week of active recovery. Each block in a training program has a different focus, so the daily workouts should reflect that focus.

BUILDING AN ANNUAL TRAINING PROGRAM

This section provides details on how to set up an annual training program, with a sample calendar based on a northern-hemisphere mountaineer who typically climbs most during the late spring and summer. This calendar would vary depending on where climbers do most of their mountaineering.

Postseason. After an intense season of mountaineering, the body needs a break. The postseason includes shorter aerobic workouts, reduced pack weights, and cross-training workouts unrelated to the in-season activity. The goal in this training block is to rest, both physically and mentally. For the example northern-hemisphere climber, postseason would generally encompass the month of October; many of these climbers shift to training for winter activities after several weeks of reduced intensity, to get ready for snow sports such as snowshoeing, cross-country skiing, downhill skiing, or winter ice climbing.

Off-season. This is the ideal time to evaluate what worked well in the training program from the previous season. Include strength training sessions that address any muscle imbalances that may have developed or been identified during the in-season activities. Add flexibility training if there is any residual stiffness that might have stemmed from a season of repetitive movement or overuse. Intensity and time remain low, but frequency of training may increase once a climber is fully recovered from in-season activities. For the example northern-hemisphere climber, off-season would be November and December. But if that climber is participating in winter ice climbing during the off-season, adding a focus on calf, core, and forearm training would be appropriate to swinging ice axes overhead for longer periods of time.

Preseason. This is the time to include unilateral strength exercises for balance and agility to address any problems detected in the off-season. Introduce pack carrying and other sport-specific training for the intended activity at somewhat reduced intensities from those of the previous postseason, and gradually build back up to weight-carrying and distance-traveling goals. Increase training volume by 15 percent or less per week. For the example northern-hemisphere climber, preseason would be January to April.

In-season. Participate in as many trips, climbs, or events as desired, and schedule suitable recovery time following outings. Shift the training focus to maintenance. Do full-body strength training twice a week and weekly anaerobic training when appropriate. For the example northern-hemisphere climber, in-season would incorporate the months of May to September.

Training for two in-seasons. A mountaineer who climbs in two seasons—for example, both summer rock and winter ice—can take one to two weeks of "off-season" for evaluation and flexibility training between the end of one in-season activity (summer rock climbing or winter climbing) and the beginning of the next. In such cases, climbers will have two seasons to prepare for and smaller lead-in times for each sport. The advantage is that participating in two sports helps a climber maintain a baseline of climbing strength and flexibility so that preseason training does not have to be as extensive.

Training for year-round climbing readiness. The climber who is outdoors year-round—for example, climbing alpine ice in the summer, climbing rock in spring and fall, and traveling over glaciers in austral summer—may need a program with four seasonal cycles leading up to specific high-priority climbing objectives. "Off-season" might refer to any one of the seasons that is lower priority, and training frequency, intensity, time, and type will vary according to what is the highest-priority goal.

SAMPLE TRAINING PROGRAM

When climbers assemble their goals and exercise preferences, evaluate their skill level, and combine all the fitness components and training parameters together, they have a personalized training program that will work uniquely for them. Each climber's program will look different from anyone else's, based on individual body type and size, goals, age, and social environment. A single program *cannot possibly* work for every mountaineer.

The template shown in Table 4-3 illustrates just one example of how all the program variables might fit together into a complete six-week preseason training program suitable for a goal such as a 7-mile (11.3-kilometer) outing

TABLE 4-3. SAMPLE SIX-WEEK PREPARATION FOR STRENUOUS DAY HIKES

WEEK	DAY 1	DAY 2	DAY 3	DAY 4	DAY 5	WEEKEND (1 DAY)
BUILD STRENGTH						
1	40 minutes aerobic 75% to 85% MHR; 30 minutes strength	60 minutes aerobic 65% to 75% MHR, 15-pound (6.8 kg) pack	Off	60 minutes aerobic 65% to 75% MHR, no pack	30 minutes full-body, sport-specific strength	2,300 feet (701 m) gain, 5 to 6 miles (8 to 9.7 km) round-trip, 13-pound (5.9 kg) pack
2	40 minutes aerobic 75% to 85% MHR; 30 minutes strength	60 minutes aerobic 65% to 75% MHR, 17-pound (7.7 kg) pack	Off	65 minutes aerobic 65% to 75% MHR, no pack	30 minutes full-body, sport-specific strength	2,600 feet (792 m) gain, 5 to 6 miles (8 to 9.7 km) round-trip, 16-pound (7.3 kg) pack
3	45 minutes aerobic 75% to 85% MHR; 40 minutes strength	30 minutes uphill or stair intervals, 20-pound (9.1 kg) pack	Off	70 minutes aerobic 65% to 75% MHR, no pack	45 minutes full-body, sport-specific strength	2,600 feet (792 m) gain, 5 to 6 miles (8 to 9.7 km) round-trip, 19-pound (8.6 kg) pack
BUILD STAMINA						
4	45 minutes aerobic 75% to 85% MHR; 45 minutes strength	35 minutes uphill or stair intervals, 22-pound (10 kg) pack	Off	60 minutes aerobic 70% to 75% MHR, no pack	45 minutes full-body, sport-specific strength	2,900 feet (884 m) gain, 6 to 8 miles (9.7 to 12.9 km) round-trip, 19-pound (8.6 kg) pack
5	45 minutes aerobic 75% to 85% MHR; 45 minutes strength	40 minutes uphill or stair intervals, 25 pound (11.3 kg) pack	Off	65 minutes aerobic 70% to 75% MHR, no pack	45 minutes full-body, sport-specific strength	2,900 feet (884 m) gain, 6 to 8 miles (9.7 to 12.9 km) round-trip, 23-pound (10.4 kg) pack
6	60 minutes recovery (easy) cardio 65% MHR	30 minutes 75% to 85% MHR cardio; 45 minutes strength	Off	45 minutes aerobic 65% MHR, no pack	Off	3,200 feet (975 m) gain, 7 miles (11.3 km) round-trip, 20-pound (9.1 kg) pack

Note: MHR stands for maximum heart rate.
Source: Courtenay W. Schurman and Doug G. Schurman, *The Outdoor Athlete* (see Resources).

with a 20-pound (9.1-kilogram) pack covering an elevation gain and loss of 3,200 feet (975 meters). The progression begins with baseline hiking of 5 miles (8 kilometers) round-trip with 2,300 feet (700 meters) of elevation gain while carrying a 13-pound (5.9-kilogram) pack and gradually transitions to steeper terrain by increasing elevation gain by 300 to 500 feet (91 to 152 meters) per outing and gradually increasing pack weight to 20 pounds (9.1 kilograms). At each step along the way climbers then choose types of cardiovascular exercise and specific strength movements to fit personal preferences, lifestyle factors, and individual body needs.

BEYOND TRAINING: RECOVERY

All the hard training in the world will mean nothing unless you give your body the recovery time it needs to repair damage, replenish muscle glycogen stores, and prepare to work hard again. High-intensity cardiovascular and strength workouts require more recovery time than do endurance or recovery workouts. While endurance days (for example, aerobic workouts lasting over an hour) are done at lower intensities, as soon as pack weight or hilly terrain is added, also insert a rest day, unless the program calls for back-to-back training in preparation for a multiday trip. Recovery days at lower intensity (less than 65 percent of maximum heart rate) may include cross-training exercises such as walking, swimming, dancing, easy flat biking, yoga, or yard work. Such easy days help avoid strain by allowing tired muscles to rest before they perform again. Mountaineers over the age of 50 may need to plan on even more recovery time and training time to reach their fitness goals.

Pay close attention to your body. When warming up for workouts, if you still feel tired or sore from a previous workout or climb, reduce the intensity or complete a shorter workout than scheduled. If your finger or elbow tendons are tender to the touch following a hard climb or workout, insert cross training to allow for adequate recovery. Place strength training sessions or highly demanding rock or ice climbs at least 48 hours apart so that the targeted muscles, tendons, and ligaments can recover before they are stressed again. If multiple days of climbing are anticipated, try to alternate days of higher-intensity workloads (or carries, in the case of expeditions) with those of lower-intensity workloads (or "climb high, sleep low," in the case of high-altitude expeditions). Tendons and ligaments take longer than muscles to adjust to increased workloads. They also take a frustrating amount of time to heal once they are injured.

Although it is difficult for most mountaineers to take time off from a favorite activity, it is better to let the body heal completely before resuming; otherwise, an acute irritation may turn into a chronic injury that requires a much longer time away from the sport. Knowing that you have done the physical training necessary to succeed will empower you to face challenges or worst-case scenarios not only in the chosen activity but also in daily life. The first step toward achieving mountaineering goals is acquiring the knowledge needed to get there; the rest is up to you.

CHAPTER 5

NAVIGATION

"Where am I now, and how can I find my way to the summit—and back? What if I need help in an emergency?" These are the most frequently asked questions in mountaineering. This chapter shows how to find the answers with the first of the Ten Essentials: navigation.

Modern mountaineers have a broad set of tools to accomplish the two key objectives of navigation: First, they need to know where they are and how to get to their objective and back safely. Second, they need to be able to communicate with emergency responders should the need arise. The modern tools of navigation allow the mountaineer to accomplish both objectives with far more confidence than in the past. Today there are five essential tools for navigating the backcountry: map, altimeter, compass, GPS device, and a personal locator beacon (PLB) or other device to contact emergency first responders. Using multiple tools increases mountaineers' confidence in their location and route, provides backup when tools fail, and increases situational awareness (see "Mountaineering with a GPS Device" later in this chapter).

TRIP PREPARATION

First, a few definitions concerning navigation are in order. *Orientation* is determining your exact position on the earth. *Navigation* is guiding yourself to a destination. *Routefinding* is selecting and following the best path to that destination. Routefinding is covered in more detail in Chapter 6, Wilderness Travel, but understanding it requires a solid foundation in the tools and skills described in this chapter.

Routefinding begins at home. Consult guidebooks and internet sources for critical information. Seek out other climbers who have done the climb who can perhaps provide a GPS track or critical waypoints (see "GPS" later in this chapter). Useful details are also packed into various types of maps and satellite images. Maps must be downloaded or installed onto GPS devices at home prior to the climb. See "Gather Route Information" in Chapter 6, Wilderness Travel, for suggestions on researching a route.

Before starting any trip into the wilderness, be sure to have a mental image of the route to the planned climb. Using the information gained from guidebooks or other climbers, plot the route on the topographic map. Based upon your experience, and from all the sources of information about the climb, make the terrain work in your favor.

To avoid brush, keep the route out of watercourses and drainages; select ridges rather than hillsides and gullies. Clear-cuts are also often full of logging slash or second-growth trees. A rock slide area can be a feasible route—providing the party avoids generating new rockfall. One problem in planning the route is that a rock slide area may look the same on a map as an avalanche gully, which can be an avalanche hazard in winter and spring and choked with brush in summer and fall. If sources are not helpful, only a firsthand look can clear up this question.

The most straightforward return route is usually the same as the route going in. If the plan is to come back a different way, careful advance preparation for that route is also necessary. And before leaving on the trip, give the trip itinerary—members of the party, trailhead, vehicle description and license plate number, and expected return date—to a responsible person (see "Organizing and Leading a Climb" in Chapter 22, Leadership, for more details).

MAP

Every mountaineer should travel with a map. There are several types.

Relief maps. Terrain is shown in three dimensions with various hues of green, gray, and brown, plus terrain shading, on relief maps. These maps help in visualizing the ups and downs of the landscape and have some value in trip planning.

Land management and recreation maps. Because recreation maps are updated frequently, they are useful for current details on roads, trails, ranger stations, and other human constructions. They usually show only a two-dimensional (flat) relationship of natural features, without contour lines that indicate the shape of the land (see "Topographic maps" below). These recreation maps, published by the US Forest Service and other government agencies, are suitable for trip planning.

Climbers' sketch maps. Often called climbers' topos, climbers' sketch maps are not topographic maps but are generally crudely drawn, two-dimensional sketches that usually make up in specialized route detail what they lack in draftsmanship. Such drawings can be effective supplements to other map and guidebook information.

Guidebook maps. Some guidebook maps are merely sketches, whereas others are accurate interpretations of topographic maps. They vary greatly in quality but generally contain useful details on roads, trails, and climbing routes.

Topographic maps. Essential to off-trail travel, topographic maps (or *topos*) are the best of all for climbers. They depict topography—the shape of the earth's surface—by showing contour lines that represent constant elevations above sea level. These maps are produced in many countries. Some are produced by government agencies; others are printed by private companies, with special emphasis on trails and other recreational features.

The most familiar topographic maps in the United States are those produced by the US Geological Survey (USGS). Up to about the year 2006, the USGS produced a series of topographic maps using aerial photographs, with trails and structures added manually based on field observations; these maps are now referred to as "Historical." Since then, the USGS has produced a new series referred to as "US Topo," dated 2011 and beyond. These maps contain more "layers" of data (such as aerial and satellite photos and terrain features), which users can select online. All of the older "Historical" topographic maps have been digitized and are still available from the USGS digital map database.

In some areas of the United States, private companies produce maps based on USGS topographic maps, but that are updated with more recent trail and road details, and sometimes these commercially produced maps combine sections of USGS maps. These maps are often useful supplements to standard topographic maps.

Digital maps. A variety of sources exist from which digital maps can be created, installed, and used with home computers, phones, some watches, and dedicated GPS receivers. GPS manufacturers (such as Garmin) sell or provide free a variety of map packages to install onto their devices, and some devices come with topographic maps already installed. Some GPS devices also allow users to install maps obtained from third parties (see Resources for examples). A variety of phone apps (such as Gaia GPS and BackCountry Navigator) allow users to seamlessly download a wide variety of map types, typically free, for viewing on phones and tablets. These sources include all of the USGS maps ("Historical" and "US Topo"); US National Park Service and Forest Service maps; Canadian topographic maps from Natural Resources Canada (NRCan); road, nautical, and cycling maps; overlays for shaded relief, slope, and contours; satellite photographs; and Open-StreetMap (OSM) maps. OpenStreetMap, a collaborative project inspired by Wikipedia to create a free map of the world, often has the most up-to-date information on trails and roads worldwide. (For map sources, see Resources.)

Digital maps, when displayed on GPS devices, hold one overwhelmingly compelling advantage over their paper progenitors: they show a "you are here" arrow that renders orientation trivial. Other advantages include the ability to record a GPS track of the exact route traveled, to mark waypoints of critical locations, and to follow a planned route or track of previous climbers. With so many freely available map sources, climbers can afford to download multiple map types for a single trip, as well as a much larger seamless map area than will likely be needed to allow for unexpected changes in plans.

Though these digital maps are valuable when loaded onto GPS devices, they disappear when the device's batteries die. For this reason, physical (paper or plastic) maps should also be printed and carried along with the digital maps, to ensure that climbers always have a map of the climbing area. When printing maps, it is preferable to use a laser jet printer if possible, since maps printed on cheaper inkjet printers can smear if they get wet.

Satellite photographs. Though not maps, satellite photographs can be of significant help in researching wilderness routes. With some GPS devices, satellite photographs can be downloaded like any other map type.

HANDLING AND CARRYING MAPS

Sometimes a trip travels through an area covered by portions of two or more maps. Either fold adjoining maps at the edges and bring them together, or create a customized map by cutting out the pertinent areas and splicing them with tape. Include plenty of territory so that there is an overview of the trip area, including the surrounding terrain. Computer programs can create customized maps, though these maps are limited by printer quality and paper size.

Maps—precious objects that they are—deserve tender care in the wild. Some custom maps can be obtained or printed on waterproof paper that makes it easier to care for them under wet conditions that can destroy ordinary paper maps. A physical map can also be kept in a protective map case or resealable plastic bag. Some maps are printed on plastic rather than paper, which makes them easier to protect. On the climb, carry the map in a pocket or other easily accessible place where you can keep it relatively flat and you do not have to take off your pack to reach it.

READING A TOPOGRAPHIC MAP

Topographic maps are essential to wilderness travel, and mountaineers must be able to glean as much information from them as possible. Understanding topographic features such as coordinate systems, datums, scale, and contour lines is a crucial navigation skill.

All topographic maps are prepared according to a legend of symbols and colors used for the map's features. For example, in a "Historical" USGS map (see "Topographic maps" above), contour lines are brown except on permanent snowfields or glaciers, where they are blue. Blue is also used for water features such as lakes and rivers. Multiple methods and colors are used to show roads, trails, vegetation, and other features. Be sure that digital maps have legends, too, in order to know what the mapmaker intends you to learn from the map.

Coordinate Systems

Maps use three principal coordinate systems to describe a location on the earth: latitude and longitude, UTM, and MGRS (see below for more on these last two).

Latitude and longitude coordinates divide the earth into the 360 degrees of a circle. A measurement east or west around the globe is called *longitude*; a measurement north or south is called *latitude*. Longitude is measured 180 degrees east and 180 degrees west, starting at the north-south line (*meridian*) that goes through the Royal Observatory, Greenwich, near London, England. Latitude is measured 0 to 90 degrees north and 0 to 90 degrees south, starting from the equator. This system allows each place on the planet to have a unique set of coordinates. For example, New York City is situated near 74 degrees west longitude and 41 degrees north latitude.

Each degree of latitude or longitude is divided into 60 minutes, and each minute is further subdivided into 60 seconds—just as for units of time. On a map, a latitude of 47 degrees, 41 minutes, 7 seconds north is written like this: 47°41'7"N. Search and rescue organizations, as well as cell phones, tend to use decimal degrees; the latitude in the previous example would be written in decimal degrees as 47.6853°, with the positive number indicating north (a negative number would indicate south). Longitudes east of Greenwich to 180 degrees east are written as positive numbers, while those west of Greenwich to 180 degrees west and throughout the western hemisphere are written as negative numbers.

The most common type of USGS topographic map used by mountaineers in the United States covers an area of 7.5 minutes (that is, 1/8 degree) of latitude by 7.5 minutes of longitude. These maps are known as the "7.5-minute series." An older type of USGS map covers an area of 15 minutes (that is, 1/4 degree) of latitude by 15 minutes of longitude. These maps are part of what is called the "15-minute series."

The Universal Transverse Mercator (UTM) coordinate system is another method for identifying a point on a map. Because the UTM system is metric-based, it allows easy computation of distances between points and is often used with GPS (see "Orientation Using GPS" near the end of this chapter).

The UTM system evolved into the Military Grid Reference System (MGRS), used today by the United States Department of Defense and the militaries of other nations in the North Atlantic Treaty Organization (NATO).

5

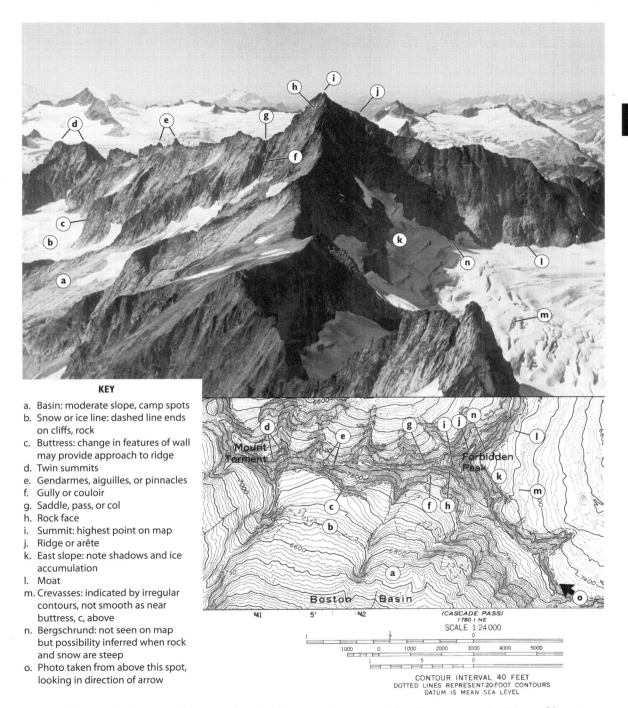

KEY

a. Basin: moderate slope, camp spots
b. Snow or ice line: dashed line ends on cliffs, rock
c. Buttress: change in features of wall may provide approach to ridge
d. Twin summits
e. Gendarmes, aiguilles, or pinnacles
f. Gully or couloir
g. Saddle, pass, or col
h. Rock face
i. Summit: highest point on map
j. Ridge or arête
k. East slope: note shadows and ice accumulation
l. Moat
m. Crevasses: indicated by irregular contours, not smooth as near buttress, c, above
n. Bergschrund: not seen on map but possibility inferred when rock and snow are steep
o. Photo taken from above this spot, looking in direction of arrow

Fig. 5-1. Photograph of a mountainous area; keyed features are also represented on the accompanying topographic map.

93

Datums

The coordinate systems described in the preceding section must be anchored to actual points on the earth, similar to surveyors' benchmarks. These anchoring points are referred to as a *datum*, and maps are made using many datums. Datums are important because a single set of coordinates (for instance, a latitude and longitude or UTM coordinates) will yield different points on the earth depending on the datum used.

The two datums currently used on USGS topos are North American Datum 1927 (NAD27) and World Geodetic System 1984 (WGS84). The difference in position between these two datums can be as much as about 500 feet (160 meters), which is important to know when using topographical maps in conjunction with GPS devices (see "GPS" later in this chapter). NAD27 is used on "Historical" USGS topos, whereas WGS84 is used on the new "US Topo" series, and is the default system for most GPS devices.

Scale

The scale of a map is a ratio between measurements on the map and measurements in the real world. A common way to state the scale is to compare a map measurement with a ground measurement—for example, 1 inch equals 1 mile—or to give a specific mathematical ratio of map inches to real-world inches: for example, 1:63,360, which means that 1 map inch is equal to 63,360 real-world inches—exactly 1 mile. The scale is usually shown graphically at the bottom of a map (fig. 5-1).

Metric maps are used in Canada and most other countries of the world outside of the United States. The scales of such maps are often 1:25,000 (1 centimeter on the map equals 250 meters or 0.25 kilometer in the field) or 1:50,000.

In the USGS 7.5-minute series, the scale is 1:24,000, which means that 1 map inch is equal to 24,000 real-world inches—about 0.38 mile—or, inversely, roughly 2.5 inches to 1 mile (4.2 centimeters to 1 kilometer). The map's north-south extent is about 9 miles (14 kilometers), while its east-west extent varies from about 6 miles (10 kilometers) in the north to about 8 miles (13 kilometers) in the south. (The east-west span of maps decreases as one moves north, due to the fact that the lines of longitude converge as they get closer to the North and South poles.) In the older 15-minute series, the scale is usually 1:62,500, or about 1 inch to 1 mile (1.6 centimeters to 1 kilometer), and each map covers four times the area of the 7.5-minute maps. Mountaineers prefer the 7.5-minute maps because of their greater detail. The scale of 1:24,000 is used for all US states except Alaska, where the scale is 1:63,360.

The 7.5-minute map is now the standard for the United States, except for Alaska. The 15-minute maps have been phased out by the USGS for the other 49 states, though some private companies still produce them (such as Green Trails Maps for selected regions of Washington, Oregon, California, Nevada, Arizona, and British Columbia).

Each topographic map is referred to as a quadrangle (or *quad*) and covers an area bounded on the north and south by latitude lines that differ by an amount equal to the map series (such as 7.5 minutes or 15 minutes) and on the east and west by longitude lines that differ by the same amount. Each quadrangle is given the name of a prominent topographic or human feature of the area: for example, USGS Mount Rainier West.

Contour Lines

The distinctive feature of a topographic map that provides the heart of its useful information is its overlay of contour lines, each line indicating a constant elevation as it follows the shape of the actual landscape. A map's contour interval is the difference in elevation between two adjacent contour lines. In mountainous areas, this interval is often 40 or 50 feet (12 or 15 meters) on 7.5-minute maps, and 80 or 100 feet (24 or 30 meters) on 15-minute maps. To make contour lines easier to use, every fifth contour line is printed darker than the other lines and is labeled periodically with the elevation. On metric maps, a contour interval of 5, 10, or 20 meters (16, 33, or 66 feet) is usually used.

A topographic map shows whether a route travels uphill or downhill. If the route crosses contour lines of increasingly higher elevation, it is going uphill; if it crosses contour lines of increasingly lower elevation, it is going downhill. Flat or sidehill travel is indicated by a route that crosses no contour lines. The direction perpendicular to contour lines is the *fall line*, that is, the direction of the slope. Contours also indicate cliffs, summits, passes, and other terrain features (see Figure 5-2). Climbers can improve their interpretation of these lines by comparing actual terrain with the map (see Figure 5-1). The goal is to be able to glance at a topographic map and have a clear mental image of the actual lay of the land. Following are the main features depicted by contour lines:

Flat areas have no contour lines at all, or contour lines very far apart (fig. 5-2a).

Gentle slopes have widely spaced contour lines (fig. 5-2b; see also Figure 5-1a).

Steep slopes have closely spaced contour lines (fig. 5-2c; see also Figure 5-1k).

5

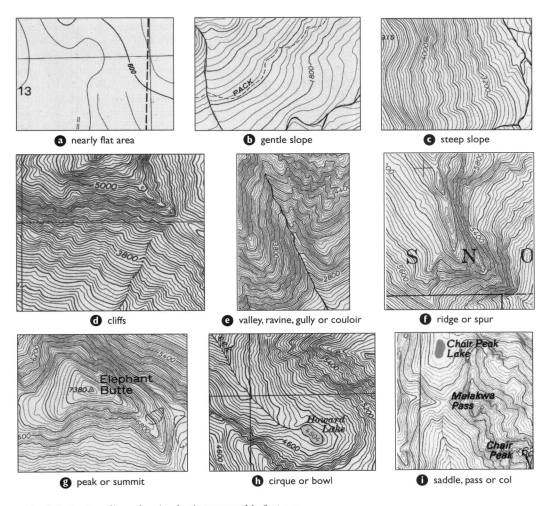

a nearly flat area

b gentle slope

c steep slope

d cliffs

e valley, ravine, gully or couloir

f ridge or spur

g peak or summit

h cirque or bowl

i saddle, pass or col

Fig. 5-2. Contour lines showing basic topographic features.

Cliffs have contour lines extremely close together or touching (fig. 5-2d; see also Figure 5-1h).

Valleys, ravines, gullies, and couloirs have contour lines in a U or V pattern pointing uphill. An uphill-pointing U pattern shows a gentle, rounded valley or gully; an uphill-pointing V pattern shows a sharp valley or gully (fig. 5-2e; see also Figure 5-1f). The U and V patterns point in the direction of higher elevation.

Ridges or spurs have contour lines in a U or V pattern pointing downhill. A downhill-pointing U pattern shows a gentle, rounded ridge; a downhill-pointing V shows a sharp ridge (fig. 5-2f; see also Figure 5-1j). The U and V patterns point in the direction of lower elevation.

Peaks or summits have concentric patterns of contour lines, with the summit the innermost and highest ring (fig. 5-2g; see also Figure 5-1d and i). A peak may also be indicated by an "x," an elevation number, a benchmark (BM), or a triangle symbol.

Cirques or bowls have patterns of contour lines forming a semicircle, rising from a low spot in the center of the partial circle, showing a natural amphitheater at the head of a valley (fig. 5-2h).

Saddles, passes, or cols have an hourglass shape, with higher contour lines on each side, indicating a low point on a ridge (fig. 5-2i; see also Figure 5-1g). The closer the contour lines, the steeper the terrain.

Other Information on Topographic Maps

The margin of a USGS topographic map holds important information, such as date of publication and revision, names of maps of adjacent areas, the contour interval, and the map scale. The margin also gives the area's magnetic declination (discussed later in this chapter), which is the difference between true north and magnetic north.

Topographic maps have certain limitations. They do not show all the terrain features that can actually be seen on a route because there is a limit to what can be jammed onto a map without reducing it to an unreadable clutter. If a feature is not at least as high as the contour interval, it may not be shown, so if climbers are navigating with a map that has a 40-foot contour interval, a 30-foot cliff may come as a surprise to them.

All USGS topos have their dates printed upon them. Be sure to check the date of the map, because topographic maps are not revised very often—so information on forests, magnetic declination, roads, streams and rivers, and other changeable features could be out of date. A forest may have been logged or a road either extended or closed since the last map revision. Although topographic maps are essential to wilderness travel, climbers may need to supplement them with information from visitors to the area, Forest Service or Park Service rangers, guidebooks, and other maps. Note changes on the map as they are encountered.

Choosing a Topographic Map

The new "US Topo" series maps are, at present, a work in progress. They are totally digital, with clear, sharp, and accurate representations of topography, and can be viewed and downloaded free on the USGS.gov website. However, they currently do not contain certain features commonly found on the "Historical" topographic maps: trails, printed elevations (other than for index contours), structures such as buildings and shelters, and edges of glaciers and permanent snowfields. The USGS plans to add some of these features over time. Accordingly, these maps are, at least for now, less useful to the mountaineer than the "Historical" map series.

When using the "Historical" topo maps, it is important to recognize their temporal nature, especially for older maps. For example, glaciers are shrinking around the world, so an older "Historical" map may show a glacier covering an area where it does not exist today. Some other features of the "US Topo" series maps also differ from those of the "Historical" maps, such as the representation of contour lines on glaciers as solid blue lines on "Historical" maps but as brown contour lines on the "US Topo" maps.

Table 5-1 provides a summary of different types of topographic maps for mountaineering use. Printed topo maps are available from a variety of sources, including brick-and-mortar stores such as Recreational Equipment, Inc. and Canadian Map Distribution Centres, as well as by mail order from the USGS and from online retailers (see Resources).

ROUTEFINDING WITH A MAP

Most routefinding with a map is done by simply looking at the surroundings and comparing them with the map before, during, and after a trip.

Before the Trip

Before the trip, make some navigational preparations with the map, such as identifying handrails and baselines (see below), as well as possible routefinding problems. Prepare a route plan: a well-thought-out description of how the party plans on navigating to its objective and getting back.

Identify handrails and baselines. Any linear feature on a map that parallels the direction of travel is called a *handrail*: a feature that helps a party to stay on route. The handrail should be within frequent sight of the route, so it can serve as an aid to navigation. Roads, trails, powerlines, railroad tracks, fences, borders of meadows, valleys, streams, cliff bands, ridges, and lakeshores could all serve as useful handrails.

A long, unmistakable line that always lies in the same direction from the party, no matter where the party is during a trip, is called a *baseline*; it provides another map technique that can help the party find its way home if they have gone offtrack. A baseline (or *catch line*) can be a road, the shore of a large lake, a river, a trail, a powerline, or any other feature that is at least as long as the area the party will be traveling in. During trip planning, pick out a baseline. If the party knows the shore of a large lake always lies west of the trip area, heading west at any time will get the party to this identifiable landmark and may save the group from being truly lost.

Anticipate routefinding problems. Before the trip, anticipate specific routefinding problems. For example, if the route traverses a glacier or any large, featureless area such as a snowfield, consider carrying route-marking wands (see Chapter 16, Snow Travel and Climbing). Identify any escape routes that can be used in case of sudden bad weather, loss of visibility, or other setbacks.

TABLE 5-1. COMPARISON OF TOPOGRAPHIC MAPS

MAP TYPE	SOURCES	SIZE IN INCHES (CM)	COST AND AVAILABILITY	ADVANTAGES	DISADVANTAGES
USGS "Historical" topos (standard scale is 1:24,000)	USGS.gov or via mail order, plus other sources	26 in. (66 cm) long by variable width	$8 USD; Up to 2 weeks by mail	All features shown, including trails and elevations; professional print quality	May not be up to date: some created 40 years ago, others as recently as 10 years ago
USGS "US Topo" maps (standard scale is 1:24,000)	USGS.gov or via mail order, plus other sources	26 in. (66 cm) long by variable width	$15 USD; Up to 1 week by mail	Custom features, such as grids; professional print quality; more current than "Historical" topos	Do not contain trails or some other features, such as printed elevations of some locations shown on USGS "Historical" topos
Canadian topo maps (standard scale is 1:50,000)	Canadian Map Distribution Centres and online sources	Typically 24 in. x 36 in. (61 x 91 cm); varies with location	$15 USD, typically	More area shown than USGS 1:24,000 maps	Less detail than USGS 1:24,000 maps
Digital topo maps printed on paper	Phone apps, USGS.gov, CalTopo, Gmap4	Limited by printer	Cost of paper and ink	Instant availability; customized map location and format; can share and customize	Print quality depends on size and resolution of map image and type of printer and paper
Digital topo maps used on a GPS device	Phone apps, dedicated GPS unit, watch device manufacturers, and other sources	Equal to screen size	Free for phone apps and bundled with some dedicated GPS units	Instant availability; most current; can typically share and customize; multiple types can be easily downloaded for field use	Small screen size; device is battery dependent

Obtain maps and route descriptions. Obtain a topographical map or maps of the area covering the entire route. Allow up to two weeks for postal delivery of physical topographic maps from the USGS (see Resources at the back of the book). If the party is doing a spur-of-the-moment trip, go to the USGS website or a number of others to view, download, and print portions of the USGS map. Using a color printer provides the most descriptive maps. Once you have the physical topographic map, read a route description of the trip in a guidebook or online, if available, then trace the route description onto the map.

Prepare GPS. See Table 5-5, "Navigation Workflow with GPS Devices," later in this chapter.

Set the compass. Always confirm that your compass is set for the amount and direction of magnetic declination at the site of the trip (see "Compass," below). If the trip is to a location far from home, remember to reset declination.

During the Trip

Get off on the right foot by making sure that everyone in the party understands the route and the route plan. At the trailhead, gather the party around the map, taking time to discuss the route and make contingency plans in case the party gets separated. On the map, point out where the party is and correlate the surroundings with what is shown on the physical map in front of everyone.

Monitor the rate of travel. Part of navigation is having a sense of the party's speed; estimating the rate of travel along with elapsed time helps to maintain orientation. Given all the variables, will it take the party one hour to travel 2 miles (3.2 kilometers), or will it take two hours to travel 1 mile (1.6 kilometers)? The answer is rather important if it is 3:00 p.m. and base camp is still 5 miles (8 kilometers) away. After enough trips into the wilds, climbers are good at estimating their speed (see the "Typical Speeds for Average Party" sidebar). There will be much variation; for example, in heavy brush the rate of travel can drop to a third or even a quarter of what it would be on a good trail. At high altitudes, the rate of travel will also greatly decrease, perhaps down to as little as 100 feet (30 meters) of elevation gain per hour.

With a watch and a notebook (or a good memory), monitor the rate of progress on any outing. Always make sure to note the time of starting from the trailhead. Also note the times at which important identifiable streams, ridges, trail junctions, and other points along the route are reached; this helps you for the return trip.

Experienced climbers regularly assess their party's progress and compare it with trip plans. Make estimates—and reestimates—of what time the party will reach the summit or other destination, as well as what time the party will get back to base camp or the trailhead. If it begins to look as

though the party could become trapped in tricky terrain after dark, the group may decide to change its plans and bivouac in a safe place or call it a day and return home.

Relate surroundings to the map. Along the way, everyone should keep relating the terrain to the map. Ignorance is definitely not bliss for any daydreaming climber who does not pay attention to the territory and then gets separated from the party. Whenever a new landmark appears, connect it with the map. At every chance—at a pass, a clearing, or a break in the clouds—update your fix on the group's exact position. Keeping track of your position this way makes it easy to plan each succeeding leg of the trip, and it will help to prevent climbers from getting lost. It also may turn them into expert map interpreters, because they will know what a specific valley or ridge looks like compared with its representation on the map.

Look ahead to the return trip. The route always looks amazingly different on the way back. Avoid surprises and confusion by glancing back over your shoulder from time to time on the way in to see what the route should look like on the return. If you cannot keep track of it all, jot down times, elevations, landmarks, and so on in a notebook. A few cryptic words—"7,600, intersect ridge"—can save a lot of grief on the descent. It will remind you that when the party has dropped to 7,600 feet, it is time to leave the ridge and start down the slope. If using a GPS device, you should mark waypoints at crucial points along the way; also see Table 5-5, "Navigation Workflow with GPS Devices," later in this chapter.

Think about the route. Your brain is your most valuable navigational tool; be sure to use it. As the party heads upward, ask questions: "How will we recognize this important spot on our return?" "What will we do if the climb leader is injured?" "Would we be able to find our way out in a whiteout or if snow covered our tracks?" "Should we be using wands or other route-marking methods right now?" "Should I mark and save a waypoint here?" Ask the questions as you go, and act on the answers. Each person in the party should know the route, the route plan, and how to get back.

Mark the route if necessary. At times, it may be best to mark the route going in so that it can be found again on the way out. This situation can arise when the route is over snowfields or glaciers during changeable weather, when the route is in heavy forest, or when fog or nightfall threatens to hide landmarks. On snow, climbers sometimes use wands to mark the path. In the forest, plastic surveyors' tape is sometimes tied to branches to show the

---

TYPICAL SPEEDS FOR AVERAGE PARTY

- **Hiking on a gentle trail, with a light day pack:** 2 to 3 miles per hour (3 to 5 kilometers per hour)
- **Hiking up a steep trail, with a heavy full-size pack:** 1 to 2 miles per hour (2 to 3 kilometers per hour)
- **Traveling cross-country up a moderate slope, with a light day pack:** 1,000 feet (300 meters) of elevation gain per hour
- **Traveling cross-country up a moderate slope, with a heavy full-size pack:** 500 feet (150 meters) of elevation gain per hour

route, but its use is discouraged due to its blight and permanence. From an ecological standpoint, a short length of unbleached toilet paper is the best marker, because it will usually disintegrate during the next rainfall. Use toilet paper if you are certain of dry weather. If not, use white crepe paper in thin rolls. It will survive an approaching storm but will disintegrate over the winter.

One commandment is needed here: Remove route markers. Markers are litter, and mountaineers never, ever litter. If there is any chance the party will not come back the same way and will not be able to remove the markers, be especially sure to use degradable paper markers.

Piles of rocks used as markers—*cairns*—appear here and there, sometimes dotting an entire route and at other times signaling the point where a route changes direction. These heaps of rock are another imposition on the landscape, and they can create confusion for any traveler but the one who put them together—so do not build them. If there comes a time when a cairn must be built, then do so, but tear it down on the way out. The rule is different for existing cairns: let them be, on the assumption that someone, perhaps even land managers, may depend on them.

Keep oriented. As the trip goes on, it may be helpful to mark the party's progress on the map. Keep oriented so that at any time you can point out your actual position to within roughly a half mile (about a kilometer) on the map.

On Technical Portions of a Climb

When the going gets tough, it is easy to forget about navigation and start worrying about the next foothold—but climbers should keep the map and other route information handy for use during occasional rests. On rock climbs, do not let the mechanics of technical climbing overwhelm the need to stay on route.

On a Summit

The summit provides a golden opportunity to rest, relax, and enjoy—and to learn more about the area and about map reading by comparing the actual view with the way it looks on the map. The summit is also the place to make final plans for the descent, which often leads to many more routefinding errors than on the ascent. Remind one another that once the party has reached the summit, the climb is only half complete, so avoid letting your guard down with regard to safety and care in navigation. Repeat the trailhead get-together by discussing the route plan and emergency strategies with everyone. Stress the importance of keeping the party together on the descent, when some climbers will

want to race ahead while others lag behind. Give yourselves enough time to return to camp or car in daylight on the way down.

During a Descent

The descent of a climb is a time for extra caution while mountaineers fight to keep fatigue and inattention at bay. As on the ascent, everyone should maintain a good sense of the route and how it relates to the map. Stay together, do not rush, and be even more careful if the party is taking a descent route that is different from the ascent route.

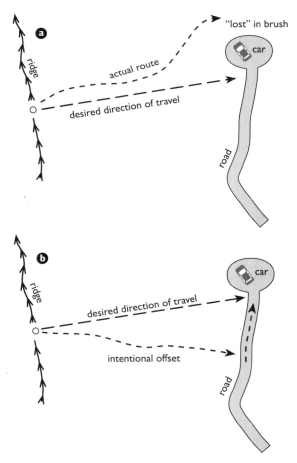

Fig. 5-3. Navigating to a specific point on a line: a, inevitable minor errors can sometimes have disastrous consequences; b, to avoid such problems, follow a course with an intentional offset.

Imagine that the climbing team is almost back to the car after a tough 12-hour climb. The party follows a compass bearing directly back to the logging road but cannot see the car, because the group has gotten off route by a few degrees. The car is on the road to either the left or the right, perhaps around a bend, so the party may have to guess which way to go. It will be a bad ending to a good day if the car is to the right of the route and the party goes left. It will be even worse if the car is parked at the end of the road and a routefinding error takes the party beyond that point and on and on through the forest (fig. 5-3a).

Intentional offset. This situation gave rise to the concept of intentional offset, also called *aiming off* (fig. 5-3b). If the party fears it might get into this kind of trouble, just travel in a direction that is intentionally offset some amount (say, 20 to 30 degrees) to the right or the left of where it really wants to be. When the group intersects the road (or river, ridge, or whatever), there will be less doubt about which way to turn. The correct location can sometimes be confirmed using an altimeter (see below).

After the Trip

Back home, write a description of the route and of any problems, mistakes, or unusual features; do it while the details are fresh in mind. Imagine what you would like to know if you were about to take this trip for the first time, so you will be ready with the right answers when another hiker or climber asks about it. If a guidebook or a map was confusing or wrong, take time to write to the publisher.

ALTIMETER

Mountaineers have long understood the importance of knowing elevation for navigation. An altimeter provides a simple elevation point. With a topographic map and just one more scrap of data—a trail, a stream, a ridge, or a bearing to a known peak—location can often be determined. By monitoring elevation and checking it against the topographic map, mountaineers can keep track of their progress, pinpoint their location, and find the way to critical junctions in the route. Every climber in the party should carry some type of altimeter.

Barometric altimeters. Sometimes called pressure altimeters, these are basically modified barometers. Both instruments measure air pressure (the weight of air), but whereas the barometer is calibrated in inches of mercury, hectopascals, or millibars, the altimeter is calibrated in feet or meters above sea level based on the predictable decrease in air pressure with increasing altitude. Barometric altimeters are available in digital wristwatches and on some GPS devices. They are affected by weather changes and so must be set at a known elevation.

Digital altimeters. Today's digital altimeter is based on a sliver of silicon that can measure air pressure (barometrically) or use GPS satellite signals—or a combination of the two. The most popular digital altimeter is the unit worn on the wrist. Most climbers wear a watch anyway, so this type of altimeter is helpful because it combines two functions in one piece of equipment. The altimeter worn on the wrist is also more convenient to use than one kept in a pocket or pack. Some digital altimeters display additional information, such as the temperature and the rate of change in altitude gain or loss.

Though a digital altimeter requires a battery, these batteries are usually good for years, and climbing parties typically carry more than one altimeter, so if one altimeter's battery dies, another climber's altimeter can be used. Another drawback to digital altimeters is that their liquid-crystal display (LCD) screens usually go blank at temperatures near about 0 degrees Fahrenheit (minus 18 degrees Celsius), though this is usually not a problem if they are worn on the wrist and under a parka. (To keep an altimeter watch from getting banged up on the rock or ice when a climber is starting a technical pitch, it is a good idea to remove it from the wrist and attach it to a pack strap or put it in a pocket or pack.) Inexpensive wristwatch altimeters costing less than $40 are perfectly adequate for mountaineering use. Wristwatch altimeters are instantly available for a quick check of altitude, whereas GPS devices (see below) are frequently turned off to conserve battery power, and after they are turned back on, require a minute or more to acquire satellite signals and display a position and altitude.

Altimeter as a function of GPS devices. GPS devices determine position in three dimensions—horizontal position (from east to west and from north to south) as well as elevation above sea level—and can therefore display a climber's altitude as determined by GPS satellites, rather than by barometric pressure. Some phones, as well as dedicated GPS units, also have an internal altimeter using a barometric pressure sensor and can display altitude derived from multiple sources based on the two types of sensors, or one altitude that uses both sensors. Some GPS apps for phones (see "GPS" later in this chapter) include altitude readouts as well as horizontal position; other apps are available that display altitude only.

TABLE 5-2. COMPARISON OF ALTIMETERS			
ALTIMETER TYPE	COST	ADVANTAGES	DISADVANTAGES
Digital wristwatch	$40 to $600	Convenient to carry; altitude always displayed at a glance; inexpensive unit is adequate; long battery life	Needs recalibration for changes in weather; LCD screen can go blank at subfreezing temperatures; battery occasionally needs replacement (one year or more battery life)
Dedicated GPS unit	Internal barometer adds $50 or more to cost of GPS device	GPS (satellite-derived) altitude reading unaffected by weather; altitude plus position displayed together; may display altitude from GPS or internal barometric altimeter	Needs time to access satellites before displaying altitude; shorter battery life than wrist or pocket units; LCD screen can go blank at subfreezing temperatures
Smartphone with app	Free app	Same as above	Same disadvantages as above; also may need a case to make it rugged enough for mountaineering use

Analog altimeters. Early altimeters were expensive analog devices with Swiss-made gears. They have been almost totally replaced by today's ubiquitous digital wristwatch altimeters.

Altimeter accuracy. The accuracy of a barometric altimeter depends on the weather because a change in weather is generally accompanied by a change in air pressure, which changes the altimeter reading. During periods of unstable weather, the indicated elevation may change by as much as 500 feet (150 meters) in one day even though the actual elevation has remained the same. Even during apparently stable conditions, an erroneously indicated change in elevation of 100 feet (30 meters) per day is not uncommon. Because of the strong influence of weather on a barometric altimeter's accuracy, *do not trust the instrument until it is first set at a location of known elevation*, such as a trailhead or using a GPS device. Then, while traveling, check the reading whenever another point of known elevation is reached (or occasionally using GPS) and reset the altimeter if necessary, or at least be aware of the error. A combined GPS-barometric altimeter can usually do better. Table 5-2 provides a summary of the features of altimeters used for mountaineering.

HOW ALTIMETERS AID MOUNTAINEERS

Altimeters can help mountaineers in several key ways: calculating the party's rate of ascent, determining its position (orientation) and navigating, and predicting the weather.

Calculating Rate of Ascent

The altimeter helps mountaineers decide whether to continue a climb or to turn back, by letting them calculate their rate of ascent. For example, during a climb, a party that checks time and elevation hourly, by taking altimeter readings, sees that they have gained only 500 feet (150 meters) in the past hour. The summit is at an elevation of 8,400 feet (2,560 meters), and an altimeter reading shows the party is now at 6,400 feet (1,950 meters), so they still have 2,000 feet (610 meters) to gain. The climbers can predict that if they maintain their present ascent rate, it will take roughly four more hours to reach the summit. That information, courtesy of the altimeter, combined with a look at the weather, the time of day, and the condition of the party members, gives the group the data on which to base a sound decision about whether to proceed with the climb or turn back.

Determining Position and Navigating

An altimeter also can help determine exactly where a party is (orientation). If they are climbing a ridge or hiking up a trail shown on the map but they do not know their exact position along the ridge or trail, they can check the altimeter for elevation. The likely location is where the ridge or trail reaches the contour line closest to that elevation on the map.

Another way to use an altimeter to determine where a climbing party is located is to start with a compass bearing to a summit or some other known feature (see "Compass" below). Find that peak on the map, and plot the bearing line from the mountain back toward the climbing party. The group now knows it must be somewhere along that line—but where? Take an altimeter reading and find out the elevation. The party's likely location is where the compass bearing line crosses a contour line at that elevation on the map.

The altimeter, map, and compass can be used together to help confirm or reject your assumed location by using the fall line: the direction a falling object travels downhill. Since the direction perpendicular to the contour lines indicates the direction uphill or downhill, a climber can take a bearing in the direction of the fall line and note the elevation using the altimeter. Then a glance at the map for your assumed location should show that the direction perpendicular to the contour lines at that elevation is the same as that measured with your compass. If they match, your assumed position may be correct, though not with absolute certainty. If they do not match, then your assumed position is definitely wrong.

Navigation gets easier with the aid of an altimeter. If climbers find a convenient couloir that gains the summit ridge, they can note the elevation of the top of the couloir. On the way back, they can descend the ridge to that same elevation to easily find the couloir again, to ensure that they descend the correct couloir. Some guidebook descriptions direct climbers to change course at particular elevations; doing so is much easier if an altimeter is used.

Last but not least, an altimeter may reveal whether the party is on the true summit, not a false one, for example, when the visibility is too poor to allow climbers to tell by looking around.

Predicting Weather

The barometric altimeter can help in predicting weather. The readings on a barometric altimeter and on a barometer operate inversely to each other: when one goes up, the other goes down. A barometric altimeter reading showing an increase in elevation when no actual elevation change has taken place (such as at camp overnight) means a falling barometric pressure, which often predicts deteriorating weather. A decreasing barometric altimeter reading, on the other hand, means increasing barometric pressure and improving weather. This is an oversimplification, of course, because weather forecasting is complicated by the wind, local weather peculiarities, and the rate of barometric pressure change. (See "Field Forecasting in the Mountains" in Chapter 28, Mountain Weather, for more information on interpreting barometric changes.)

Some digital wristwatch altimeters can be adjusted to read barometric pressure instead of altitude, but keep in mind that changes in barometric pressure are caused not only by changes in the weather but also by changes in elevation while climbing. This will lead to erroneous conclusions regarding barometric pressure.

GPS devices whose altitude display is derived from GPS satellites only (devices that do not use internal barometric sensors) are not useful by themselves for weather forecasting. To differentiate between changes in air pressure readings caused by changes in elevation while climbing or descending and those caused by changing weather conditions, first calibrate the barometric altimeter to the GPS elevation and then watch to see if they diverge significantly over the next few hours. If the barometric altimeter diverges from the GPS altitude, the cause is likely due to changing weather conditions. See Table 28-2 to determine what action to take.

CAUTIONS REGARDING ALTIMETER USE

Because barometric altimeters are strongly affected by the weather, do not be misled into trusting them to an accuracy greater than is possible. Though a typical high-quality barometric altimeter may have a resolution of 3 feet (1 meter), this does not mean that the altimeter will be that accurate. Changes in weather could easily throw the reading off by hundreds of feet or meters.

An altimeter sensor expands and contracts due to variations in temperature, causing changes in the indicated elevation. All altimeters compensate for temperature changes, but the compensation is not perfect. Try to keep the temperature of an altimeter as constant as possible. Body heat is usually enough to warm a wristwatch altimeter, particularly if it is worn under a parka when the outside temperature is low.

Get to know your own altimeter, use it often, check it at every opportunity, and note differences of information between it and the map. Recalibrate barometric altimeters at known elevations (for instance, saddles or summits). You will soon know just what accuracy to expect, and your altimeter will then be a dependable aid.

COMPASS

A compass is essentially a freely rotating magnetized needle that responds to the earth's magnetic field and is marked on one end to indicate north. Available compasses include the traditional baseplate compass, compass apps for smartphones, and features in some dedicated GPS units

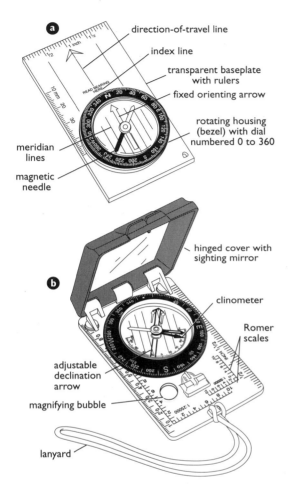

direction-of-travel line
index line
transparent baseplate with rulers
fixed orienting arrow
rotating housing (bezel) with dial numbered 0 to 360
meridian lines
magnetic needle

hinged cover with sighting mirror
clinometer
Romer scales
adjustable declination arrow
magnifying bubble
lanyard

Fig. 5-4. Features of mountaineering compasses: a, essential features; b, useful optional features.

and some watches. The baseplate compass is an essential tool for navigation, not only to determine direction but also to measure and plot bearings on a map. The baseplate compass doesn't require batteries or calibration, and it operates in subzero temperatures. The essential features of a baseplate compass (fig. 5-4a) are as follows:

- **Rotating housing (bezel).** This is sometimes filled with a fluid to dampen (reduce) vibrations of the needle.
- **Dial around the circumference of the housing.** This dial is graduated clockwise in degrees from 0 to 360.
- **Orienting arrow and a set of parallel meridian lines.** These are used for aligning with a map.

- **Transparent baseplate.** This includes a **direction-of-travel line.**
- **Rulers.** These are used for measuring distances on a map.
- **Index line.** Bearings are read and set at the index line, which may be one end of the direction-of-travel line.

Optional features on some compasses (fig. 5-4b) include the following:

- **Adjustable declination arrow.** The adjustable declination arrow is an easy way to correct for magnetic declination. "Gear-driven" adjustability, made with a tiny screwdriver, is easier and more dependable than "tool-free" adjustability.
- **Sighting mirror.** This mirror, with a sighting notch at the top of the housing, improves accuracy (and also permits emergency signaling). The direction-of-travel line may be a line extending from the notch across the center of the mirror.
- **Clinometer.** This is used to measure the angle of a slope and the upward or downward angle to another object (see "Clinometer" later in this chapter).
- **Romer scale.** A Romer (interpolation) scale is used to measure UTM position.
- **Lanyard.** This cord attaches the compass to a belt, jacket, or pack. Putting it around your neck is unsafe, particularly when doing any technical climbing.
- **Magnifying glass.** Use the magnifier to help read closely spaced contour lines.

Some compasses that have an adjustable declination arrow but no mirror offer a good cost compromise. Table 5-3 provides a summary of compass characteristics for mountaineering use.

BEARINGS

A bearing (also known as an *azimuth*) is the direction from one place to another, measured in degrees of angle from true north. The round dial of a compass is divided into 360 degrees (fig. 5-5). The cardinal directions are: north at 0 degrees (the same as 360 degrees), east at 90 degrees, south at 180 degrees, and west at 270 degrees. The *intercardinal* directions are halfway between the cardinal directions: northeast is at 45 degrees; southeast, 135 degrees; southwest, 225 degrees; and northwest, 315 degrees.

The compass is used for two tasks regarding bearings:

1. **Taking bearings,** also known as *measuring bearings*. Taking a bearing means measuring the direction from one point to another, either on a map or on the ground.

TABLE 5-3. COMPARISON OF COMPASS TYPES

COMPASS TYPE	COST	ADVANTAGES	DISADVANTAGES
Full-featured with gear-driven adjustable declination arrow and sighting mirror	$50 to $90	No need to correct for magnetic declination mentally or by modifying compass	Most expensive
Full-featured with tool-free adjustable declination arrow and sighting mirror	$20 to $50	Same as above	Some have difficult-to-use declination adjustment.
Full-featured with gear-driven adjustable declination arrow; no sighting mirror	$20 to $50	Same as above	Slightly less accurate without mirror
Full-featured with tool-free adjustable declination arrow; no sighting mirror	$20 to $30	Same as above	Same as above; some have difficult-to-use declination adjustment.
Basic baseplate compass without adjustable declination arrow; no sighting mirror	$10 to $40	Lowest cost	Must correct declination mentally or by modifying compass (see "Adjusting Bearings for Magnetic Declination" later in this chapter)
Electronic compass on dedicated GPS unit, smartphone, or watch	Often included in these digital items	Convenience of one instrument for several functions	Cannot use to measure or plot bearings on map; may require recalibrations; battery-dependent; may not display at subfreezing temperatures

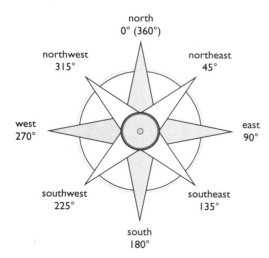

Fig. 5-5. Cardinal and intercardinal directions and corresponding bearings in degrees on the compass.

2. **Plotting bearings,** also known as *following bearings.* Plotting a bearing means setting a specified bearing on the compass and then plotting out, or following, the direction where that bearing points, either on a map or on the ground.

Bearings on a Map

The compass is used as a protractor to both measure and plot bearings on a map. Magnetic north and magnetic declination have nothing to do with these operations. Therefore, never make any use of the magnetic needle when taking or plotting bearings on a map. The only time the magnetic needle is used on the map is whenever you orient the map to true north (see "Orientation by Instrument" later in this chapter), but there is no need to orient the map to measure or plot bearings.

Taking (measuring) a bearing on the map. Place the compass on the map, with one long edge of the baseplate running directly between two points of interest (fig. 5-6).

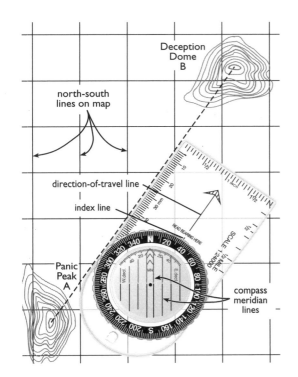

Fig. 5-6. Taking a bearing on a map with the compass as a protractor (magnetic needle omitted for clarity).

While measuring the bearing from point A to point B, make sure that the compass's direction-of-travel line always points in the direction from point A to point B, as shown—don't reverse the compass 180 degrees so the direction-of-travel line points from B to A.

Then turn the rotating housing, or bezel, until its meridian lines are parallel to the north-south lines on the map. If the map does not have north-south lines, draw some in, parallel to the edge of the map and at intervals of 1 to 2 inches (3 to 5 centimeters). Be sure the orienting arrow (not the magnetic needle) that turns with the meridian lines is pointing to the top of the map, to the north. If the orienting arrow is pointed toward the bottom of the map, to the south, the reading will be 180 degrees off. (In Figure 5-6, the magnetic needle has been omitted to provide a better view of the meridian lines and orienting arrow.)

Now read the number on the dial that intersects with the index line. This is the bearing from point A to point B. In the example shown in Figure 5-6, the bearing from point A, Panic Peak, to point B, Deception Dome, is 34 degrees.

Plotting (following) a bearing on the map. To follow a bearing, you must start with a known bearing. Where does that bearing come from? It comes from an actual landscape compass reading. In a hypothetical example, a friend returns from a climb, remorseful for having left his camera somewhere along the trail. During a rest stop, he had taken some pictures of Mount Magnificent, and at the same time, he had taken a compass bearing on Mount Magnificent and found it to be 130 degrees. That is all you need to know. You happen to be heading into that same area next week, so get out the Mount Magnificent quadrangle, and prepare to figure out where your friend left his camera.

First, turn the rotating housing to set the bearing of 130 degrees at the compass index line (fig. 5-7). Next, place the compass on the map, with one long edge of the baseplate touching the summit of Mount Magnificent. Now rotate the entire compass (without further turning the rotating housing) until the compass meridian lines are parallel with the map's north-south lines (again, draw some lines on the map if necessary; see the preceding section), and make sure the edge of the baseplate is still touching the mountain's summit. Ensure that the orienting arrow points to the top of the map, toward north.

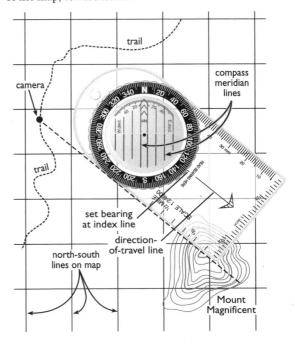

Fig. 5-7. Plotting a bearing on a map with the compass as a protractor (magnetic needle omitted for clarity).

Now follow the edge of the baseplate, heading in the opposite direction from the direction-of-travel line, because the original bearing was measured toward the mountain. Where an imaginary line extending from the edge of the baseplate crosses the trail is where your friend's camera is (or was last week).

Bearings in the Field

All bearings in the field are based on where the magnetic needle points, so now that needle must do its job. The first two examples below, for the sake of simplicity, ignore the effects of magnetic declination (covered in the next section): imagine taking bearings in central Arkansas, where declination is negligible in 2017.

Taking (measuring) a bearing in the field. Holding the compass in front of you, first, point the direction-of-travel line at the object whose bearing you want to find (fig. 5-8). Second, rotate the compass housing until the pointed end of the orienting arrow is aligned with the north-seeking end of the magnetic needle. Last, read the bearing on the dial where it intersects the index line; for example, in Figure 5-8 the bearing is 270 degrees.

If the compass has no sighting mirror, hold the compass at or near arm's length and at or near waist level (fig. 5-9). If the compass has a sighting mirror, fold the mirror back at about a 45-degree angle and hold the compass at eye level, with the sighting notch at the top of the mirror pointing at the object (fig. 5-10). Observe the magnetic needle and the orienting arrow in the mirror while rotating the housing to align the needle and the arrow.

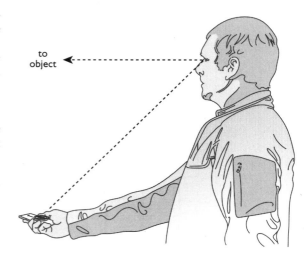

Fig. 5-9. Holding compass with no sighting mirror at arm's length and waist height.

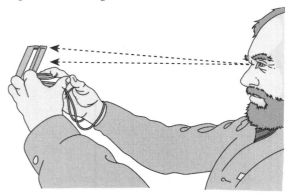

Fig. 5-10. Using a sighting mirror.

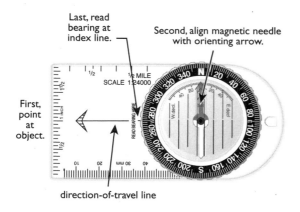

Fig. 5-8. Taking a compass bearing in the field in an area with zero declination.

In either case, hold the compass level. Keep it away from ferrous metal objects, which can easily deflect the magnetic needle (see "Cautions in Using a Compass" below).

Plotting (following) a bearing in the field. Simply reverse the process used to take a bearing in the field. Start by rotating the compass housing until the desired bearing, say 270 degrees (due west), is set at the index line (see Figure 5-8). Hold the compass level in front of you, and then turn your entire body (including your feet) until the north-seeking end of the magnetic needle is aligned with the pointed end of the orienting arrow. The direction-of-travel line is now pointing due west.

106

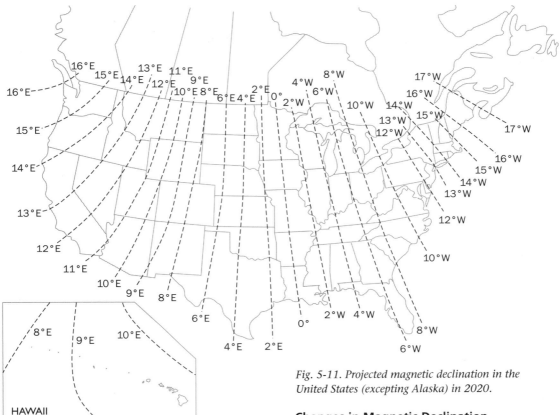

Fig. 5-11. Projected magnetic declination in the United States (excepting Alaska) in 2020.

MAGNETIC DECLINATION

A compass needle is attracted to *magnetic north*, whereas most maps are oriented to a different point on the earth: the geographic North Pole, called *true north*. This difference between the direction to true north and the direction to magnetic north is called *magnetic declination*. It is usually expressed in degrees east or west of true north. A simple compass adjustment or modification is necessary to correct for magnetic declination.

The line connecting all points where true north aligns with magnetic north is called the *line of zero declination*. In the United States, this line now runs from Minnesota to Louisiana (fig. 5-11). In areas west of the line of zero declination, the magnetic needle points somewhere to the east of true north, so these areas are said to have east declination. It works just the opposite east of the line of zero declination, where the magnetic needle points somewhere to the west of true north: these areas have west declination.

Changes in Magnetic Declination

Declination changes with time (hence, figures show projected declination), because the molten magnetic material in the earth's core is continually moving. Declination is shown on all USGS topographic maps, but since these are not updated very frequently, the declination shown on maps may be somewhat out of date. The map in Figure 5-11 shows the declination for the year 2020 for the contiguous 48 states and Hawaii, and it will be accurate to within about half a degree for most such locations from 2017 to about 2023.

The map in Figure 5-12 shows the declination for the year 2018 for the state of Alaska, and it should be accurate to within about 1 degree for the period from 2016 to 2020. Some websites can be used to find the current magnetic declination for any location on the earth (fig. 5-13): the Geological Survey of Canada calculator at the National Resources Canada (NRCan) site, for example, as well as the US National Oceanic and Atmospheric Administration's (NOAA) National Geophysical Data Center site (see Resources).

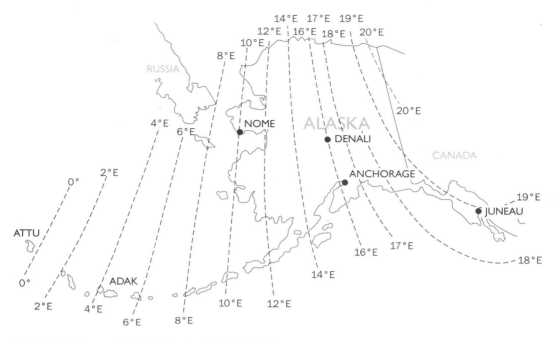

Fig. 5-12. Projected magnetic declination in Alaska in 2018.

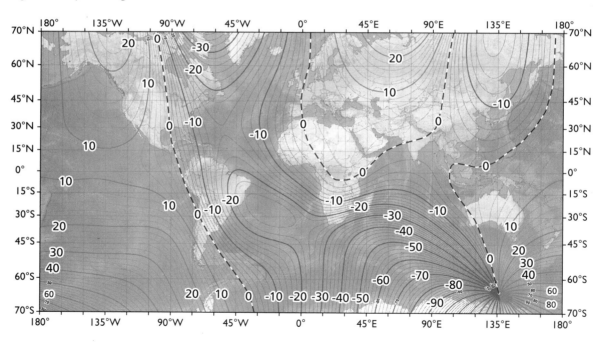

Fig. 5-13. World declination map for the year 2015: lines of constant declination are at 2-degree intervals. Positive numbers indicate east declinations, and negative numbers indicate west declinations.

As an example of declination change, a USGS map of the Snoqualmie Pass area of Washington State dated 1989 stated a declination of 19°30'E (19.5 degrees). Another map of the same area dated 2003 gave a declination of 18°10'E (18.2 degrees).

Declination change varies widely throughout the world. In Washington, DC, declination is barely changing as of 2017. In northeast Alaska, it is changing by as much as 1 degree every three years. In Washington State, the change is about 1 degree every six years. In Colorado, it is about 1 degree every eight years. (These values can be found for any location in the world using either the NOAA or NRCan website; see Resources.) From these examples, it should be clear that the declination on maps more than a few years old should not be trusted; it is important to find the latest declination information to prevent errors in navigation by compass.

Adjusting Bearings for Magnetic Declination

Consider a traveler in eastern Idaho, where the declination is 12 degrees east (fig. 5-14a). The *true bearing* is a measurement of the angle between the line to true north and the line to the objective. The compass's magnetic needle, however, is pulled toward magnetic north, not true north. So instead it measures the angle between the line to magnetic north and the line to the objective. This *magnetic bearing* is 12 degrees less than the true bearing in eastern Idaho. To get the true bearing, it is possible to add 12 degrees to the magnetic bearing, though easier ways are described in the "Adjustable declination arrow" paragraph below.

Travelers in all areas west of the zero declination line, as in the Idaho example above, could add the declination to the magnetic bearing. In the Rocky Mountains of Colorado, for example, about 8 degrees would be added. In central Washington State, it is about 15 degrees.

East of the zero declination line, the declination can be subtracted from the magnetic bearing to get the true bearing. In northern New Hampshire, for example, the magnetic bearing is 15 degrees greater than the true bearing (fig. 5-14b). Subtracting the declination of 15 degrees gives a climber in New Hampshire the true bearing.

Adjustable declination arrow. Adjusting for magnetic declination is very simple in theory but can be confusing in practice, and in the wilderness, errors in mental arithmetic can have potentially serious consequences. A more practical way to handle the minor complication of declination is to pay somewhat more for a compass with an adjustable declination arrow (as shown in Figure 5-4b) instead of buying one with a fixed orienting arrow (as

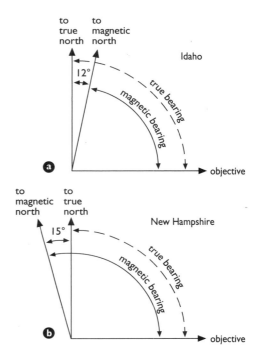

Fig. 5-14. Magnetic and true bearings: a, in Idaho, east declination; b, in New Hampshire, west declination.

shown in Figure 5-4a). The declination arrow can quickly be set for any declination by following the instructions supplied with the compass. Then the bearing at the index line will automatically be the true bearing, and there will be no need for concern about a declination error. If climbers travel to a location with a different declination, they can make a simple adjustment to set the new declination value.

Customized declination arrow. On compasses with fixed, nonadjustable orienting arrows, a similar effect can be achieved by sticking a thin strip of adhesive or masking tape to the bottom of the rotating housing to serve as a customized declination arrow, as shown in Figure 5-15. Trim the tape to a point, with the point aimed directly at the specific declination for the intended climbing area, and use this homemade arrow, not the prepainted original.

In the eastern Idaho example, the taped declination arrow must point at 12 degrees east (clockwise) from the 360-degree point (marked "N" for north) on the rotating compass dial (fig. 5-15a). In the northern New Hampshire example, it must point at 15 degrees west (counterclockwise) from the 360-degree point on the dial, that is,

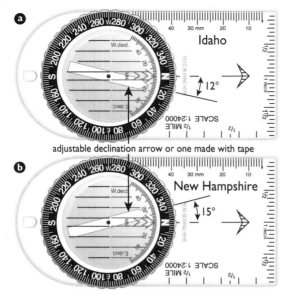

Fig. 5-15. Compass declination corrections (magnetic needle omitted for clarity): a, for an area west of the zero-declination line (Idaho); b, for an area east of the zero-declination line (New Hampshire).

at 345 degrees (fig. 5-15b). In central Washington State, it must point at 15 degrees east (clockwise) from 360 degrees. If you travel to a place with a different declination, peel the tape off and apply a new customized tape arrow for the new declination.

Taking or following bearings in the field. To take or to follow a bearing (that has been adjusted for magnetic declination) in the field, follow exactly the same procedure used in the earlier examples from Arkansas (see "Bearings in the Field" above), where the declination is near zero. The only difference is that you will now align the magnetic needle with the adjustable declination arrow or the taped declination arrow instead of with the orienting arrow.

Note: From here on, this chapter assumes you are using a compass with a declination arrow—either an adjustable arrow or an added tape arrow. For all bearings in the field, align the needle with this declination arrow. Unless otherwise stated, all bearings referred to in this chapter are true bearings, not magnetic.

COMPASS DIP

The magnetic needle of the compass is affected not only by the horizontal direction of the earth's magnetic field but also by its vertical pull. The closer a compass user gets to the magnetic North Pole, the more the north-seeking end of the needle tends to point downward, toward the ground. Near the equator, the needle is level; at the magnetic South Pole, the north-seeking end of the needle tries to point upward. This phenomenon is referred to as *compass dip.*

To compensate for this effect, most compass manufacturers purposely introduce a slight imbalance to the magnetic needles of their compasses, so that their dip is negligible for the geographic area where they will be used. However, if a climber buys a compass in the northern hemisphere—say, in North America or Europe—and then tries to use it in the southern hemisphere—say, in New Zealand or Chile—the difference in dip may be enough to introduce errors in compass readings or even make it impossible to use. For this reason, if climbers bring compasses to a faraway place, as soon as they get to the country they are visiting, they must first try out their compasses in an urban area to make sure they work properly before heading out into the wilderness, and then purchase one balanced for dip in that area if they do not work.

Some compass manufacturers produce compasses that are not affected by dip. Some such compasses have the term "global" in their names or a notation on the package that the compass is corrected for dip anywhere in the world, though these are generally more expensive. Climbers who intend to go on worldwide climbing expeditions might consider such a compass.

COMPASS PRACTICE

Before counting on your compass skills in the wilderness, test them near where you live (see the "Map and Compass Checklist" sidebar). The best place to practice is someplace where you already know all the answers, such as a street intersection where the roads run exactly north-south and east-west. Avoid any location near metallic objects such as fire hydrants.

Take a bearing in a direction you know to be east. When the direction-of-travel line or arrow is pointed at something that you know is due east of you—such as the edge of the sidewalk or a road or a curb that is east of you—and the declination arrow is lined up with the magnetic needle, the number on the dial that intersects with the index line should be within a few degrees of 90. Repeat for the other cardinal directions: south, west, and north.

Then do the reverse: Pretend you do not know which way is west. Set 270 degrees (west) at the index line and hold the compass in front of you as you turn your entire body until the magnetic needle is again aligned with the

MAP AND COMPASS CHECKLIST

Do you understand how to use a map and compass? Run through the whole procedure once more. Check off each step as you do it. And remember the following:

- Never use the magnetic needle or the declination arrow when measuring or plotting bearings on the map.
- When taking or following a bearing in the field, always align the pointed end of the declination arrow with the north-seeking (usually red) end of the magnetic needle.

Taking (Measuring) a Bearing on a Map
1. Place the compass on the map, with the edge of the baseplate joining the two points of interest.
2. Rotate the housing to align the compass meridian lines with the north-south lines on the map.
3. Read the bearing at the compass's index line.

Plotting (Following) a Bearing on a Map
1. Set the desired bearing at the index line by rotating the compass housing.
2. Place the compass on the map, with the edge of the baseplate on the feature from which you wish to plot a bearing.
3. Turn the entire compass to align the meridian lines with the map's north-south lines. The edge of the baseplate is the bearing line.

Taking (Measuring) a Bearing in the Field
1. Hold the compass level in front of you and point the direction-of-travel line at the desired object.
2. Rotate the housing to align the declination arrow with the magnetic needle.
3. Read the bearing at the index line.

Plotting (Following) a Bearing in the Field
1. Set the desired bearing at the index line by rotating the compass housing.
2. Hold the compass level in front of you and turn your entire body until the magnetic needle is aligned with the declination arrow.
3. Travel in the direction shown by the direction-of-travel line.

declination arrow. The direction-of-travel line should now point west. Does it? Repeat for the other cardinal directions. This set of exercises will help develop skill and self-confidence at compass reading and also is a way to check the accuracy of the compass.

Look for chances to practice in the mountains. A good place is any known location—such as a summit or a lakeshore—from which identifiable landmarks can be seen. Take bearings as time permits, plot them on the map, and see how close the result is to the actual location.

CAUTIONS IN USING A COMPASS

It pays to understand some common errors made while using a compass and other factors that may affect its functioning.

Map and compass versus fieldwork. When measuring and plotting bearings on a map, completely ignore the compass needle. The compass is simply being used as a protractor, so just align the meridian lines on the compass housing with the north-south lines on the map. For taking and following bearings in the wilderness, however, the magnetic needle must obviously be used.

Metal interference. The presence of nearby metal can interfere with a compass reading. Ferrous objects—iron, steel, and other materials with magnetic properties—will deflect the magnetic needle and produce false readings. Keep the compass away from watches, belt buckles, ice axes, and other metal objects such as a vehicle. Iron content in nearby rocks can make the bearing information nearly useless. If a compass reading does not seem to make sense, move 10 to 100 feet (3 to 30 meters) and check to see if the bearing changes. If so, it is likely being affected by nearby metal.

Errors of 180 degrees. Keep your wits about you when pointing the declination arrow and the direction-of-travel line. If either is pointed backward—an easy thing to do—the reading will be 180 degrees off. (If outside, note where the sun is in the sky. That can often help jog your directional presence of mind.) If the bearing is north, the compass will say it is south. Remember that the north-seeking end of the magnetic needle must be aligned with the pointed end of the declination arrow and that the direction-of-travel line must point from you to the objective, not the reverse.

There is yet another way to introduce a 180-degree error in a compass reading: by aligning the compass meridian lines with the north-south lines on a map but pointing the rotating housing backward. The way to avoid this is to check that "N" on the compass dial is pointing to north (usually the top) on the map.

Trust the compass. If you are in doubt, trust the compass. The compass, correctly used, is almost always right, whereas a climber's contrary judgment may be clouded by fatigue, confusion, or hurry. If you get a nonsensical reading, check to see that you are not making one of those 180-degree errors. If not, and if there is no metal in sight, verify the reading with other members of the party and other navigation devices: altimeter and GPS. If other navigation devices provide the same answer, trust the tools over hunches and intuition.

CLINOMETER

Clinometers are useful tools for measuring the angle of a slope for orientation and for assessing avalanche risk (see Chapter 17, Avalanche Safety). Clinometers are a feature of some compasses; they are also available as small devices that attach to ski poles and on phones as smartphone apps.

The compass clinometer (see Figure 5-4b) consists of a small nonmagnetic needle that points, due to gravity, downward toward a scale calibrated in degrees. To use the clinometer, first set either 90 or 270 degrees at the index line. Then hold the compass on edge and with the direction-of-travel line level, so that the clinometer needle swings freely and points downward toward the numbered scale.

The needle should then point to 0 degrees. Tilting the compass up or down then causes the needle to point to the number of degrees of inclination.

You can also align the baseplate edge with a distant slope in profile to measure its inclination (fig. 5-16), or set the baseplate edge on a ski pole or ice axe (aligned on the fall line) to measure the local slope. Phone clinometer apps measure slope angle by using the edge of the phone or, for distant points, the camera. The ski-pole clinometer is a small electronic device that attaches to ski and trekking poles with Velcro and measures slope angle when a button is pushed.

GPS

The US Department of Defense and similar agencies in other countries have placed satellites in orbit around the earth for space-based navigation systems. The systems that are most commonly used are the United States', referred to as the Global Positioning System (GPS), and the Russians', referred to as the Global Navigation Satellite System (GLONASS). Other countries have systems in development as well. These systems have revolutionized navigation. This chapter refers to all these systems collectively as GPS.

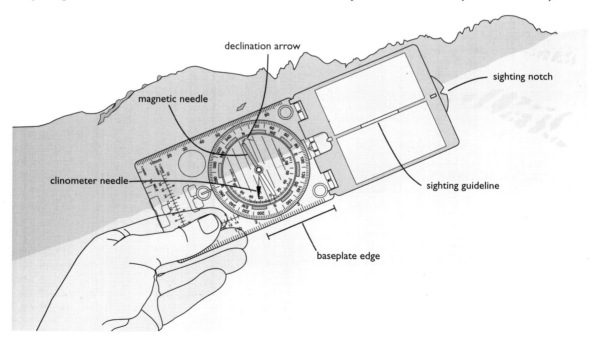

Fig. 5-16. Using a baseplate compass's clinometer to measure slope angle.

GPS DEVICES

This chapter uses "GPS device" to refer to both phones or tablets with GPS apps and dedicated GPS units. These devices can receive and simultaneously use the signals from both the US GPS and GLONASS satellites and give the user's position and altitude to within about 50 feet (15 meters). A GPS device has various features that allow users to display their specific positions (*waypoints*), determine the compass bearing and the distance between waypoints, plot out routes comprising a series of waypoints from one position to another, and record *tracks* (the actual route traveled along a path) as they travel. A party should seriously consider bringing a GPS device for every climb unless they are certain the route is straightforward, even in darkness or storm. GPS devices can cost from as little as $20 (to purchase a smartphone app) to hundreds of dollars for a more durable dedicated GPS unit. (For a device comparison, see Table 5-4 below.)

5

TABLE 5-4. COMPARISON OF GPS DEVICES			
FEATURES	PHONE WITH GPS APP	TABLET WITH GPS APP	DEDICATED GPS UNIT	GPS WRISTWATCH
Screen size (diagonal measurement)	4.7 to 6.2 in. (12 to 16 cm)	Up to 12 in. (30 cm)	2 to 4 in. (5 to 10 cm)	1 to 2 in. (3 to 5 cm)
Weight	4 to 6 oz. (110 to 170 g)	12 to 24 oz. (340 to 680 g)	5 to 8 oz. (140 to 220 g)	Approx. 3 oz. (80 g)
Internal map capability	All	All	Most	Some
Map libraries	Extensive map libraries available; mostly free		Map libraries available; some free	
Touch screen	All	All	Some	Rarely
Electronic compass	Most	Rarely	Some	Some
Barometric altimeter	Most	None	Some	All
Expandable memory	Some use microSD card		Some use microSD card	No
Water resistance	Some phones and cases provide water resistance; screens difficult to use when wet		Yes	Yes
Minimum operating temperature	-4°F to 32°F (-20°C to 0°C)		-4°F to 14°F (-20°C to -10°C)	-5°F to 0°F (-21°C to -18°C)
Maximum operating temperature	95°F to 122°F (35°C to 50°C)		140°F to 158°F (60°C to 70°C)	130°F to 140°F (54°C to 60°C)
Battery type	Mostly nonreplaceable lithium-ion		Mostly replaceable AA	Nonreplaceable
Battery life while using GPS	Variable depending on usage strategy (can help to bring a portable battery pack, but adds weight)		14 to 25 hours	20 to 200 hours
Cost	$20 for app (plus cost of phone)		$100 to $700; no recurring cost, unless more maps needed	$100 to $600; no recurring cost, unless more maps needed

Some special preparations prior to a trip are necessary (see "Tips for Using GPS in the Mountains" later in this chapter). Phones and dedicated GPS units break or are lost, and batteries die, so having two or three GPS devices in the party reduces the risk of depending on any single unit. When trees or mountains block your view of the sky and satellites, adequate satellite signals can sometimes not reach you, resulting in poor GPS accuracy or sometimes even the inability to obtain a position at all. For this reason, always carry a detailed hardcopy topographic map of the travel area, an altimeter, and a baseplate compass.

Phones or Tablets with GPS App

Phones can receive GPS signals from US GPS and Russian GLONASS satellites, even far from cell tower coverage. To navigate by phone or tablet, you must first install a GPS software app and download the required digital maps while the device is still connected to the internet. The mapping app shows climbers where they are on a map within tens of feet or meters. Some programs offer free extensive libraries of maps; be sure to download needed subsets before each trip.

The phone's effectiveness as a GPS navigation device—inside or outside of cell phone range—allows its use for backcountry navigation on all climbs where navigation may take the climber off well-known paths. In more extreme conditions, the ruggedness of dedicated GPS units may be more appropriate.

There are cautions regarding using GPS-enabled phones and tablets. Most are powered by proprietary batteries that are usually not replaceable by users. Thrifty use of the phone battery power (see "Limitations of GPS Devices in the Backcountry" later in this chapter) is therefore necessary on full day trips or longer. However, external battery packs allow continuous use for days, or intermittent use for weeks, although they add to overall pack weight.

Dedicated GPS Units

Most handheld dedicated GPS units also receive GPS signals from both US GPS and GLONASS satellites. Manufactured by Garmin and Magellan, among others (fig. 5-17a and b), they are usually powered by a pair of readily available AA batteries. Dedicated GPS units are usually more rugged and more weatherproof and operable in lower and higher temperatures than phones and tablets, which makes dedicated GPS units a better choice in extreme environments. Detailed topographic maps can be added to most such devices, some by purchasing secure digital (SD) or microSD cards containing maps of specific areas (such as a large state or a number of smaller states), or by downloading maps from the internet or from supplied CDs. Some of the more expensive dedicated GPS units come with topographic maps already installed.

A wristwatch GPS device (fig. 5-17c) generally has similar functionality as other dedicated GPS receivers, though with an altimeter, barometer, compass, GPS, and timekeeping.

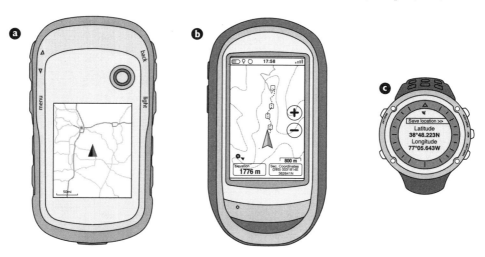

Fig. 5-17. Dedicated GPS units: a, Garmin eTrex series; b, Magellan eXplorist series; c, Suunto Ambit GPS watch.

Wristwatch GPS devices are usually powered by nonre-placeable proprietary batteries that can be charged from a USB port on a home computer or from an AC power adapter. Though wearable and functional, GPS watches have not gained as much popularity as dedicated GPS units and GPS-capable phones due to their small screens and high cost.

The GPS Signal, the Cellular Network, and Wi-Fi

From orbits of about 12,000 miles (20,000 kilometers) above the earth, GPS satellite signals are available any-where on the planet; cellular phone signals have a range of a few miles; and local Wi-Fi networks have a range of several hundred feet. Neither cellular phone signals nor Wi-Fi is dependably available in the wilderness.

For GPS navigation (though not for calls), phones and tablets work effectively even when they are out of range of cell phone towers—a condition frequently encountered in the wilderness. Tablets have some value in trip plan-ning and documentation at home before and after a climb, particularly due to their large screen size, which allows a better view of topographic maps than the small screens of cell phones and other GPS devices. However, outside of expeditions, tablets are impractical to carry on most climbs due to their size, weight, and battery power limitations.

It is easy and inexpensive to find and install one or more GPS apps onto a phone. Access to the internet is needed for downloading apps, maps, routes, tracks, and trails, but cell service is not needed for these downloads. Many forms of maps are free through phone GPS apps, allowing the mountaineer to easily download multiple map types as well as satellite images for a trip. Free map sources can also be downloaded to dedicated GPS units.

To get the most benefit from a GPS device, be sure to read the instruction manual carefully to master all of its features. In addition, several good books and useful web-sites are available that explain GPS in greater detail (see Resources). Table 5-4 provides a snapshot comparison of the different types of GPS devices based on information at time of publication; note, this technology changes rapidly.

Basics of Using GPS

First, select which units to use: miles or kilometers, feet or meters, magnetic or true bearings, et cetera, and enter these preferences in the "settings" screen. Next—very import-ant—select the datum that agrees with the datum for the topographic map you will be using. Many GPS devices use WGS84 as the default datum, which is the same default datum used on the new USGS "US Topo" maps published

as PDF files. The USGS "Historical" topographical maps (more useful for climbers), which were published on paper prior to 2007, use the NAD27 datum. (See "Datums" earlier in this chapter.) The difference in position between these two datums can be as much as 500 feet (160 meters), so it is essential to check the datum and change it, if necessary, prior to using a GPS device with a map.

Try the GPS device out around home, in city parks, and on trail hikes before taking it on a climb. Talk with friends familiar with GPS use. Take a class, if possible, to obtain helpful hints in using GPS.

MOUNTAINEERING WITH A GPS DEVICE

GPS devices are marvelous tools for the mountaineer. Using them can significantly aid in navigation. Keep in mind, however, that they are not foolproof and that topography, forest cover, battery life, electronic failure, extremely high or low temperatures, and inadequate user knowledge can prevent their effective use. The first rule of using a GPS device is to avoid becoming dangerously dependent on this battery-powered electronic apparatus that can fail or whose batteries may become depleted (see "The Importance of Maintaining Situational Awareness" sidebar).

Some GPS devices have built-in electronic compasses, which also depend on battery power. These can lose accu-racy over time or when the batteries are replaced, requir-ing occasional recalibration. GPS devices are not complete substitutes for an ordinary baseplate compass or physi-cal maps. Climbers should always carry a physical topo-graphic map and a nonelectronic baseplate compass (see "Compass," earlier in this chapter), even if the GPS device has a compass and/or topographic map capability.

In addition, for complex routefinding, carry route-marking materials such as flagging and wands, regardless of whether a GPS device is being carried or not. GPS devices display their altitude, in feet or meters above sea level, along with their horizontal position. Since this GPS func-tion is also dependent on limited battery power, and GPS devices can fail, it is recommended that all party members bring separate altimeters (see "Altimeter" earlier in this chapter) so that the party will always know its altitude.

When using a dedicated GPS unit, start each trip with a fresh set of batteries and carry spare batteries. Rechargeable nickel–metal hydride (NiMH) batteries are a good choice for use in a dedicated GPS unit. These batteries, as well as a spare backup pair, should be fully charged prior to a trip. For even better battery performance, use disposable lithium cells. They cost more but last longer, perform

THE IMPORTANCE OF MAINTAINING SITUATIONAL AWARENESS

Experienced navigators both respect and are wary of using a GPS device or app to navigate. Too often they see climbers "heads down" following their tiny screen unaware of their surroundings. When the navigator simply follows the GPS device and ignores cues from the passing terrain, "situational awareness"—and, therefore, safety—is diminished. The climber using GPS must fight this tendency by using the following techniques.

Observe. Start by observing the surroundings and updating your mental map of the landscape. Where have you come from? Where are you now? Where are you going? What are the dangers?

Orient. Correlate the surroundings with the physical map to see if they are in agreement. Study myriad details, including slope, sun position, ridges, and terrain features. Then confirm your understanding using multiple tools from the navigation toolset. Confirm the elevation with an altimeter, the cardinal directions with the compass, and your position with GPS.

Decide. Where do you go from here? Decide on your next steps.

Act. Climb on! And maintain your heightened sense of situational awareness by repeating the observe-orient-decide-act cycle with close observation and by continually updating your mental map while moving through the landscape.

Maintaining situational awareness is not just a topic of navigation but of safety in general: What is happening with the weather? What is the condition of the party? How many hours of daylight remain? Maintaining a high level of situational awareness can help keep climbers on course and safe, thus enabling everyone to fully enjoy the experience.

better at cold temperatures, and weigh considerably less than alkaline or NiMH cells. A pair of lithium AA cells weighs about 1.1 ounces (31 grams), compared with about 1.9 ounces (53 grams) for a pair of alkaline or NiMH cells. When using a phone with GPS app, be sure to fully charge the phone at home prior to the climb. Make sure to conserve valuable power while driving to the climb, and carry a rechargeable battery pack and/or a solar charger for multiday climbs.

Never rely solely on a GPS device for wilderness navigation. Carry a conventional map, compass, and altimeter. And keep your terrain navigation skills sharp so you maintain a high level of situational awareness and can rely on your terrain navigation skills.

Download Maps Before You Go

Most modern phones, when combined with a good app, have the same GPS capability as a dedicated GPS unit. They can display your position on a map, as shown in Figure 5-18. However, as with most dedicated units, the digital maps themselves are not downloadable to phones or tablets through a GPS signal. Maps for the area in which the party will be traveling must first be downloaded from the internet while in range of Wi-Fi or the slower cellular network of land-based towers. Downloading maps to a phone app is usually seamless, simple, and free; be sure to do this in an area with a strong internet signal, since attempting to download data-rich, detailed maps while

driving to remote trailheads can be slow and frustrating, if possible at all. Test this action before depending on it. Map sources allow downloading of several types of maps and satellite-sourced images.

If the party has not previously downloaded a map of the area, the device will show its location as a dot on a blank grid (fig. 5-19). The GPS apps nevertheless allow them to find their location by displaying the latitude and longitude or (preferably) UTM coordinates, even if a map is not displayed. Then the party can find its position on the physical map they are carrying. Alternatively, they can take and save a series of waypoints along the route from the camp to the summit, then follow this "bread crumb trail" back to the starting point.

Tips for Using GPS in the Mountains

GPS devices have a wide variety of features that can be applied in many different ways in the mountains. How a GPS device is used on a climb depends on user knowledge, user navigational preference, terrain, weather, intended destination, type of climb, length of climb, and other factors. This section provides some examples of how using a GPS device can help in mountaineering situations. These examples cover the most commonly used features but are not an all-inclusive list.

Identify a location. The primary feature of a GPS device is to provide its user with a location, usually in latitude-longitude or UTM coordinates or as a symbol on a map on

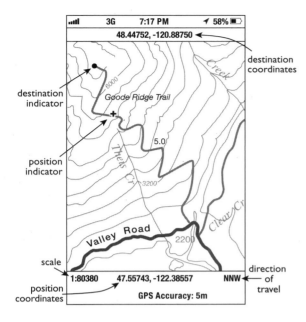

Fig. 5-18. Position and latitude/longitude coordinates shown on a phone within cell range or using a previously downloaded topo map.

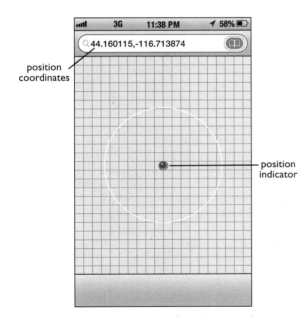

Fig. 5-19. Position and coordinates shown on a phone that is out of cell range and has no downloaded map.

the screen of the GPS device. An example is provided in "Orientation by Instrument" later in this chapter.

Create and follow waypoints. Another basic feature of a GPS device is the ability to create and use waypoints for point-to-point navigation. Waypoints can be locations such as trailheads, trail intersections, summits, campsites, gear stashes, and other locations the user would like to pinpoint or remember. The coordinates for waypoints can be obtained from maps, guidebooks, websites, mapping software, and other sources; waypoints can also be entered into the GPS device during a trip. It is essential to take (or *mark*) a waypoint at any place to which the party will want to return, such as a car, camp, or any crucial point along the route. At any later time, it is then possible to tell the GPS device to "Go" to that waypoint, and the device will display the distance and direction to that waypoint. Climbers can then travel to that destination either by observing the GPS screen or by setting the bearing on a baseplate compass and following its direction of travel while turning the GPS device off to save battery power. An example of this is provided in "Navigation by Instrument" later in this chapter.

Provide trip data. Most GPS devices have a "trip computer" feature that displays data such as the number of satellites in use by the device, its current location, speed of travel, time of day, trip odometer, remaining battery power, and other items. Although this information can be useful, if the device loses satellite reception for part of the trip (which can happen in thick forests, narrow canyons, or when it is turned off to conserve battery power), some items, such as the trip odometer, may not be accurate.

Create a track. Another useful feature of GPS devices is the ability to create a track. If the GPS device is left on continually during an entire climb or during a critical portion of it, another party can later follow the tracks that were created by the device. Or the original party can follow the track back to the trailhead. For example, in Figure 5-20, a track was made from the trailhead to the summit of West Tiger Mountain, and the track was saved. Later, another user can follow the same track from the trailhead to the summit of West Tiger Mountain; see "Use GPS data in mapping software" below for how other users can access the information in these tracks.

If you are making tracks with your GPS device and are leaving the device on, attach the device or its case to a pack strap to avoid having to hold it in your hand. You might need to use that hand for climbing or for holding an ice axe or a trekking pole. A GPS watch can also be used to record a track.

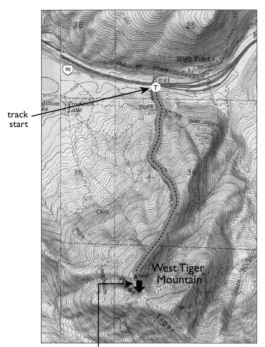

track start

arrow shows current location and direction of travel

Fig. 5-20. GPS tracks: saved sample track, which can be reused and shared with other users later.

Use GPS data in mapping software. The waypoints and tracks can later be downloaded to mapping services such as CalTopo or GaiaGPS or with software that comes with particular GPS device models, such as Garmin's BaseCamp. This allows climbers to see the entire route on the screen of a home computer and to save it for future reference. Using mapping software, tracks can usually be saved in the universal GPX or KML file format. This provides the ability to transfer tracks into another GPS unit so that other users can follow these tracks on their climbs. Additionally, with mapping software, they can view and print a map of the area that will show the route that was taken by the original user. This is useful both while planning a trip and while on the actual climb.

Conserve batteries. Most dedicated GPS receivers operate on a pair of AA batteries that are readily available almost anywhere, so it is easy to buy a few extra batteries and carry them as spares. Phones, on the other hand, often operate on nonreplaceable proprietary batteries, so using a phone's GPS function requires special attention to saving power and prolonging battery life (see the next section).

Carry battery-recharging gear. Fortunately, lightweight battery packs and solar panels are available to recharge cell phones, if you are willing to carry some additional weight and spend time waiting for them to recharge. The most common way of recharging a device on a trip is with external battery packs. Solar panels are awkward when a party is mobile but are common at expedition base camps.

Limitations of GPS Devices in the Backcountry

A GPS device is essential for navigation, but it should be used along with the other four essential tools: map, altimeter, compass, and a PLB (or other device to contact emergency first responders). Some important limitations of GPS devices are described below.

They can be damaged. A GPS device may fail during a climb. Protect the device from impact by using a sturdy case and perhaps a lanyard. Most dedicated units and some phones are waterproof; protect them against water and sweat as necessary. Have the party carry two or more devices in case a single unit fails.

They are not a subsitute for a physical map. GPS devices can plot a route straight from one point to another, but they cannot automatically find a route around rivers, lakes, or cliffs. Such tasks, including large-scale planning, require careful map reading, often best accomplished on a physical map, which allows for a better understanding of surrounding terrain.

They won't work in extreme temperatures. Some GPS devices (mainly phones and tablets) will not work at temperatures much below freezing (see Table 5-4). Lithium batteries are helpful in extending cold-weather battery life for dedicated GPS units. Phones and tablets are more heat sensitive than dedicated GPS units and may not function at temperatures near or above about 95 degrees Fahrenheit (35 degrees Celsius).

They are unreliable if they can't pick up enough signals from satellites. A GPS device must be able to pick up signals from at least four satellites in order to provide an accurate position. Because GPS devices use both US and Russian satellites, this is usually not a problem, but under some conditions, such as in caves or deep canyons or under dense forest cover, a GPS device may not be able to receive signals from enough satellites to accurately determine its position. When this occurs, the device sacrifices altitude information in favor of horizontal position.

They are battery dependent. Battery life is limited to a day or two, depending on the model and how it is used. The best way to conserve power for any GPS device, whether a dedicated device or one enabled by a GPS app, is of course to turn it off completely when it is not needed. When navigation is straightforward, such as on easy trails or roads or at rest stops or camps, turn off the device. Then turn it on only at key locations, obtain an accurate position that makes sense, save the waypoint, and turn it off again. GPS devices connect these waypoints to create tracks spanning time periods while they are switched off. You can also use the GPS device to take a needed travel bearing, shut off the device, and follow the bearing using a baseplate compass. Using the GPS device as little as necessary conserves the battery.

Reducing the track point resolution also saves energy. Disabling the device's compass or barometer also helps extend battery life. Other useful tricks are to turn down the brightness of the display and to decrease the amount of time the auto-lock feature allows before automatically putting the device into sleep mode. The display consumes much energy, and even a slight dimming correlates to increased battery life. (That said, on a bright day above tree line, while wearing sunglasses, climbers will find the dimmed display harder to read.) Experiment with different settings for screen brightness to see just how bright the screen really needs to be in order to be usefully visible outdoors. Viewing the screen in the shade, such as in a shadow, may help.

The GPS function in a phone is a significant battery drain, especially when used continually, as when recording tracks. To extend a phone's battery life while the GPS function is powered up, first disable the cellular communication function by putting the phone into "airplane mode." This action retains GPS and camera functionality. With the cellular communication function disabled, batteries should last longer than during city use. It is also wise to completely turn off any unnecessary apps while using a cell phone's GPS function on a climb, since open apps running in the background consume additional power.

NAVIGATION WORKFLOW USING GPS

When a climbing party is using GPS, they should still perform route planning (see "Trip Preparation") and trip execution (see "Routefinding with a Map") as described earlier in this chapter. With GPS there is now additional work that must be done at home, at the trailhead, and en route, as well as after the trip. For a summary of this additional work, see Table 5-5, "Navigation Workflow with GPS Devices," which provides cross-references to locations in this and other chapters where these tasks are described in detail.

ORIENTATION BY INSTRUMENT

The goal of orientation is to determine the precise point on the earth where you are standing. That position can then be represented by a mere dot on a map, which is known as the point position. There are two less-specific levels of orientation. One is called *line position*: the party knows it is along a certain line on a map—such as a river, a trail, or a bearing or elevation line—but does not know where it is along the line. The least specific is *area position*: the party knows the general area it is in, but that is about it.

POINT POSITION

The primary objective of orientation is to determine an exact point position. First steps are simple: just look around and compare what you see with what is on the map. Sometimes this is not accurate enough, or there is nothing much nearby to identify on the map. The usual solution then is to get out the compass and take bearings on landscape features. This is an example of orientation by instrument. Orientation by GPS, which is different, is described later in this chapter. When point position is known, climbers can proceed to identify on the map any major feature visible on the landscape. They can also identify on the landscape any visible feature shown on the map.

For example, climbers on the summit of Forbidden Peak know that their point position is at the top of Forbidden Peak (see Figure 5-1i on the topographic map). The climbers see an unknown mountain and want to know what it is. They take a bearing on it and get 275 degrees. They plot 275 degrees from Forbidden Peak on their topographic map, and it passes through Mount Torment (see Figure 5-1d). They conclude that the unknown mountain is Mount Torment.

In reverse, if the climbers atop Forbidden Peak want to identify which mountain in the distance is Mount Torment, they must do the map work first. They can measure the bearing on the map from Forbidden Peak to Mount Torment and come up with 275 degrees. Keeping 275 at the index line on the compass, they turn the compass until the magnetic needle is aligned with the declination arrow. The direction-of-travel line then points to Mount Torment, and they can identify it.

Finding Point Position
from a Known Line Position

With line position known, the goal is to determine point position. When climbers know they are on a trail, ridge, or some other identifiable line, they need only one more trustworthy piece of information. For example, a climbing

TABLE 5-5. NAVIGATION WORKFLOW WITH GPS DEVICES

Modern navigation tools offer climbers more certainty, but coordinating map, altimeter, compass, and GPS requires careful work. It is helpful to think of this effort as a workflow that begins at home, continues at the trailhead and en route, and then wraps up after the trip.

AT HOME AND/OR WHILE STILL CONNECTED TO THE INTERNET

1. Research routes from guidebooks and other sources.
2. Purchase relevant topographical maps, if available and time allows. Otherwise, download topographical maps from the internet. Customize them with collected routes, tracks, waypoints, and notes, and then print. Be sure the map includes the data, such as the UTM grid, that you will need.
3. Download helpful maps and satellite images to a GPS device at the appropriate level of detail. Include an area that surrounds the intended travel area in case plans change; the larger map can be at a lower level of detail if storage space is an issue.
4. Research weather trends, road and trail conditions, and avalanche conditions (see Chapters 6, Wilderness Travel, and 17, Avalanche Safety).
5. Confirm that electronics are ready: data downloaded, batteries charged, PLBs registered and the preset ("canned" or user-definable) messages on satellite communicators updated (see "Communication Devices" later in this chapter).
6. Leave the trip itinerary, including trailhead, vehicle description, and license plate, with a responsible person (see "Organizing and Leading a Climb" in Chapter 22, Leadership).

AT THE TRAILHEAD

1. Confirm the party is at the right place to begin the climb: Orient the map to the surroundings—do they correlate? Confirm using GPS.
2. Set a GPS waypoint at the trailhead.
3. Set the GPS device's datum to match that of the physical map.
4. Have the party calibrate all barometric-based altimeters to the trailhead elevation using a map or GPS device.
5. Note magnetic declination, and adjust compasses as needed. (See "Magnetic Declination," earlier.)
6. Turn off electronics or configure them to extend battery life to last the length of the trip.

EN ROUTE

1. Actively engage the entire party in navigation, including assessing whether the current position and planned path through the landscape continue to appear safe and can be correlated to the map using multiple navigation tools. (See "The Importance of Maintaining Situational Awareness" sidebar, earlier.)
2. Familiarize the party with the appearance of the return trip.
3. Occasionally recalibrate barometric-based altimeters at known locations shown on map or a GPS device.
4. Gather GPS waypoints and tracks en route if they may be helpful later, especially if the party may need to renegotiate complex terrain.

AFTER THE TRIP

Gather together and organize all the digital and physical navigation information that will help the party—or the next climbing party—safely navigate the same area on another trip.

party knows it is on Unsavory Ridge—but exactly where? Off in the distance to the southwest is Mount Majestic. A bearing on Majestic reads 220 degrees. Plot 220 degrees from Mount Majestic on the map. Run this line back toward Unsavory Ridge, and where it intersects the ridge is the point position where the climbers are (fig. 5-21).

Finding Point Position from a Known Area Position

Suppose a climbing party knows only its area position: the general area of Fantastic Crags (fig. 5-22). To move from knowing area position to knowing point position, two trustworthy pieces of information are needed. The

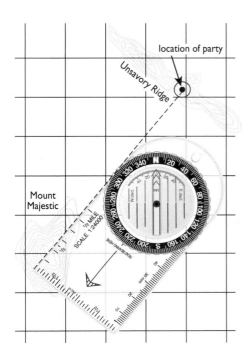

Fig. 5-21. Orientation from a known line position to determine point position (magnetic needle omitted for clarity).

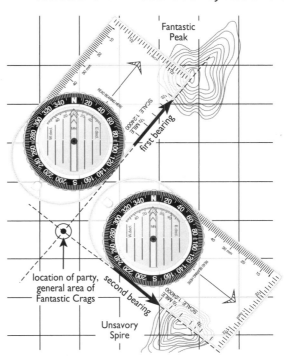

Fig. 5-22. Orientation from a known area position to determine point position (magnetic needle omitted for clarity).

climbers want to determine line position and then, from that, point position.

Climbers may be able to use bearings on two visible features. Suppose they take a bearing on Fantastic Peak and get a reading of 39 degrees. They plot a line on the map, through Fantastic Peak, at 39 degrees. They know they must be somewhere on that bearing line, so they now have their line position.

They can also see Unsavory Spire. A bearing on the spire shows 129 degrees. They plot a second line on the map, through Unsavory Spire, at 129 degrees. The two bearing lines intersect, and that shows their point position. (The closer an angle of intersection is to 90 degrees, the more accurate the point position will be.)

Climbers should use every scrap of information at their disposal, but they must be sure their conclusions agree with common sense. If they take bearings on Fantastic Peak and Unsavory Spire and find that the two lines on the map intersect in a river, but they are on a high point of land, something is wrong. They should try to take a bearing on another landmark and plot it. If the lines intersect at a

map location with no similarity to the terrain where you are, something is wrong. There may have been an error in taking or plotting bearings, there might be some magnetic anomaly in the rocks, or the map may be inaccurate. And who knows? Maybe those peaks are not really Fantastic and Unsavory in the first place.

FINDING LINE POSITION FROM A KNOWN AREA POSITION

When the area position is known and there is just one visible feature to take a bearing on, the compass cannot provide anything more than line position. That can be a big help, though. If the climbers in the preceding example are in the general vicinity of Fantastic River, they can plot a bearing line from the one visible feature to the river and then know they are near where the bearing line intersects the river. Perhaps from a study of the map, the climbers can then figure out their point position. They can also read the altimeter and find the spot on the map where the bearing line intersects the contour line for that elevation, which may provide an unambiguous position.

ORIENTING A MAP

During a climb, it frequently helps to hold the map so that north on the map is pointed in the actual direction of true north. This is known as orienting the map, a good way to gain a better feel of the relationship between the map and the countryside.

It is a simple process. Set 0 or 360 degrees at the index line of the compass, and place the compass on the map near its lower-left corner (fig. 5-23). Put the edge of the compass's baseplate along the left edge of the map, with the direction-of-travel line pointing toward north on the map. Then turn the map and compass together until the north-seeking end of the magnetic needle is aligned with the pointed end of the compass's declination arrow. The map is now oriented to the scene before you. (Map orientation can give a general feel for the area but cannot replace the more precise methods of orientation described above.)

ORIENTATION USING GPS

Suppose a climbing party wants to identify its point position on a topographical map. Take out the GPS device, turn it on, and let it acquire an accurate position. The device is probably reading latitude-longitude, the usual default coordinate system. For mountaineering use, the UTM system is easier and more accurate for manual plotting because the UTM reference lines are much closer together (1,000 meters = 0.62 mile) than the reference lines for latitude-longitude (about every 2.5 minutes—approximately 2 to 3 miles or 3 to 4 kilometers).

Using the GPS device's setup screen, the climbers should be able to change the coordinate system from latitude-longitude to UTM. They can then correlate the UTM numbers on the device's screen with the UTM grid on the map. Without using a scale or a ruler, climbers can usually "eyeball" their position to within about 100 meters (about 300 feet), which is often close enough to get to within sight of an objective. If greater accuracy is desired, use the "meters" scale at the bottom of the map, the Romer (interpolation) scale on some compasses, or a separate plastic Romer scale.

For example, suppose a party is climbing Glacier Peak and clouds obscure all visibility. They reach a summit but are not sure if it is Glacier Peak. They turn on a GPS device and let it acquire a position. The UTM numbers on the screen of the device are as follows: 10 U640612E, 5329491N. (fig. 5-24)

The "10" is the UTM zone number, which can be found in the lower-left corner of the USGS topographic map.

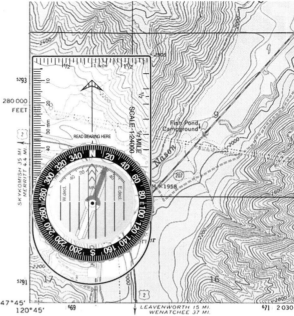

Fig. 5-23. Using a compass to orient a map in an area with 20 degrees east declination.

The "U" is a latitude band, used by most, but not all, GPS devices; each letter indicates a certain range of latitudes. The first long number, 640612E, is called the easting and indicates that the climbers' position is 640,612 meters east of the reference line for their area. Along the top edge of the map, they can find the number $^{6}40^{000m}$E. This is the *full easting* (except for zone number and latitude band). To the right of this on the map is the number $^{6}41$, a *partial easting*, with the "000" meters omitted. The climbers can see that the number 10 U640612E on the screen of the GPS device is approximately six-tenths of the way between 640000 and 641000. Their east-west position is therefore about six-tenths of the way between the $^{6}40^{000}$ and the $^{6}41$ lines.

Along the left edge of the map is the number $^{53}31^{000m}$N. This is the *full northing*, which indicates that this line is 5,331,000 meters north of the equator or South Pole. (Northings being measured from the South Pole are sometimes designated with a minus sign.) Below this is a line labeled [53]30 and another labeled [53]29. These are *partial northings*, with the "000" meters omitted. The second (lower) number displayed on the GPS device screen in this example is 5329491N. This is a horizontal line about halfway between [53]29 and [53]30. The point where the easting and northing lines intersect is the climbers' point position. Finding this point in Figure 5-24 shows that they are on Disappointment Peak, not Glacier Peak.

The internal topographic map capability of some GPS devices can be useful in quickly identifying a location without having to interpolate the UTM position, though the maps can be difficult to interpret because the screens are very small. Zooming in to observe the contour lines causes climbers to lose sight of the surrounding area. Zooming out to observe the surrounding area causes the contour lines to disappear. Electronic maps are therefore useful supplements to conventional physical maps but cannot fully replace physical maps.

NAVIGATION BY INSTRUMENT

Getting from point A to point B is usually just a matter of keeping an eye on the landscape and watching where you are going, helped by an occasional glance at the map. However, if the current objective is out of sight, take compass in hand, set a bearing, and follow the direction-of-travel line as it guides you to the goal. This is navigation by instrument.

Navigation by instrument is sometimes the only practical method for finding the way. It also serves as a supplement to other methods and as a way of verifying that the party is on the right track. Again, use common sense and question a compass bearing that defies reason. (For example, is the declination arrow pointing the wrong way, sending the party 180 degrees off course?)

USING MAP AND COMPASS

The most common situation requiring instrument navigation comes when the route is unclear because the topography is featureless or because landmarks are obscured by forest or fog. In this case, if the climbers know exactly where they are and where they want to go, they can identify on the map both their current position and their destination. They must simply measure the bearing to the objective on the map and then follow that bearing.

Suppose you measure a bearing of 285 degrees on the map (fig. 5-25a). Read this bearing at the index line and leave it set there. Then hold the compass out in front of

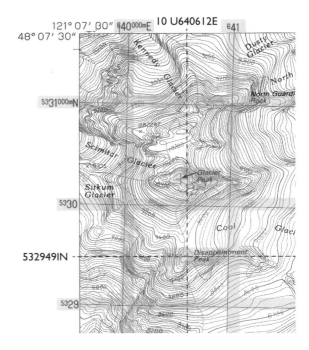

Fig. 5-24. Example of orientation using a GPS receiver and a topo map.

you as you rotate your body until the north-seeking end of the magnetic needle is aligned with the pointed end of the declination arrow. The direction-of-travel line on the compass now points to the objective in the terrain (fig. 5-25b). Start walking in that direction.

USING COMPASS ALONE

Navigators of air and ocean often travel by instrument alone; so can climbers. For example, if a party is approaching a pass and clouds begin to obscure it, they can take a quick compass bearing on the pass. Then they follow the bearing, compass in hand if desired. It is not even necessary to note the numerical bearing; just align the magnetic needle with the declination arrow and keep it aligned, and follow the direction-of-travel line.

Likewise, if climbers are heading into a valley where fog or forest will hide the mountain that is the goal, they can take a bearing on the peak while it is still visible, before dropping into the valley (fig. 5-26). Then they navigate by compass through the valley. This method becomes more accurate if two or more people travel together with compass in hand, checking one another's work.

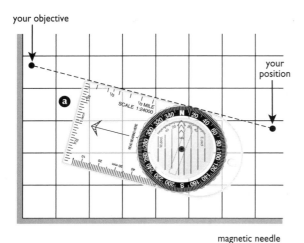

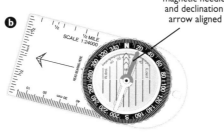

Fig. 5-25. Navigation using the map and compass: a, measure the bearing on the map from your position to your destination and, maintaining the bearing at the index line, pick up the compass (magnetic needle omitted for clarity); b, follow the bearing and direction-of-travel line, lining up the magnetic needle to the declination arrow.

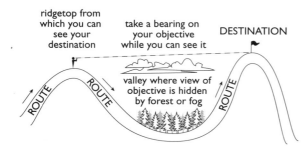

Fig. 5-26. Following a compass bearing when the view of the objective is obscured by forest or fog.

USING INTERMEDIATE OBJECTIVES

The technique of using intermediate objectives is handy for those frustrating times when climbers try to stay exactly on a compass bearing but keep getting diverted by obstructions such as cliffs, dense brush, or crevasses. They can sight past the obstruction to a tree, a rock, or another object that is exactly on the bearing line between their position and the principal objective (fig. 5-27a). This is the intermediate objective. Then they scramble over to the tree or rock by whatever route is easiest. When they get to the intermediate objective, they can be confident that they are still on the correct route. Then they repeat the process toward the next intermediate objective. The technique is useful even when there is no obstruction. Moving from one intermediate objective to another means it is possible to put the compass away for those stretches, rather than having to check it every few steps.

Sometimes on snow, on glaciers, or in fog, there are no natural intermediate objectives, just an undifferentiated white landscape. A similar situation can occur in a forest, where all the trees may look the same. Then another member of the party can serve as the intermediate objective (fig. 5-27b). That person travels out to near the limit of visibility or past the obstruction. The rest of the group waves that party member left or right until the person is directly on the bearing line. That person can then improve the accuracy of the route by taking a back bearing on the rest of the party. (For a back bearing, keep the same bearing set at the index line, but align the south-seeking end of the magnetic needle with the pointed end of the declination arrow.) The combination of a bearing and a back bearing tends to counteract any compass error.

USING GPS

Suppose a climbing party can identify its desired destination on the map but cannot actually see it in the field. They can read the UTM position of the destination off the map and then enter it into the GPS device's memory as a waypoint.

Going back to the Glacier Peak example shown in Figure 5-24, suppose the climbers wish to find a route to the summit of Glacier Peak. They can see that this point is about halfway between the eastings of 640000 and 641000, so they could estimate the easting as 10 U640500E (the zone number is 10 in this example). They can also see that the summit is about three-tenths of the way between the northings of 5330000 and 5331000, so they can estimate the full northing to be 5330300N. They can now enter these coordinates into the GPS device by simply turning it on, activating its "create waypoint" function,

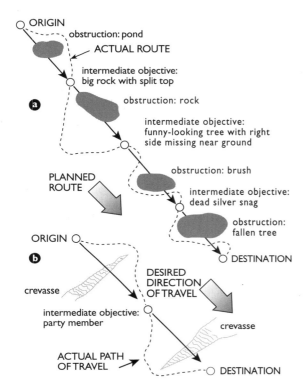

Fig. 5-27. Using intermediate objectives: a, in a forest; b, on a glacier.

and entering the UTM coordinates of 10 U640500E and 5330300N. They can then name the waypoint (for example, "GLPEAK") and save it. When using a phone or dedicated GPS device that displays topographic maps, a climber can simply tap or click on the desired location on the screen to mark and save a waypoint, without having to interpolate the UTM position from the map.

Once they have entered their destination into the GPS device's memory, they let it acquire a position. Then they ask it to "Go" to the name of the new waypoint ("GLPEAK" in this example), and the device will tell them the distance and compass bearing from wherever they are to the summit of Glacier Peak. Then they can set this bearing on their baseplate compasses, turn off the GPS device and put it away, and follow the compass bearing until they arrive at Glacier Peak. Alternatively, some devices have a built-in compass that can be used, but it may need to be calibrated prior to use and may not be as accurate as a baseplate compass.

What if a party gets off route due to a crevasse or other obstruction? After passing the obstruction, turn on the

GPS device, acquire a position, and again ask it to "Go" to the waypoint that is the destination. The device will then display the new distance and compass bearing to the destination. Set the new bearing on the compass and follow it to the destination.

COMMUNICATION DEVICES

Historically, the mountaineer has needed to be completely self-reliant, and that ethic should dominate the thinking of those entering the wilderness (see the "Ethic of Self-Reliance" sidebar). But when, despite good tools, preparation, and training, life becomes threatened, most climbers welcome help from emergency responders. The climbing party in need of outside assistance has several means of requesting help.

Cell phones. As both a navigation and a communication device, phones are the obvious first choice for requesting outside help—*when the climbing party is within cell phone range*, which is the only time they will work for this purpose. In such cases, phones can dramatically shorten the time it takes to summon rescuers. They are also useful for telling people back home that the party will be late but is not in trouble, and thus can forestall unnecessary rescue efforts. However, unless the climbing party is certain to the contrary, they should *assume that phones will not function for making calls from the backcountry.*

Satellite communications. Since the pulse of the original Sputnik satellites suggested early versions of GPS to its

ETHIC OF SELF-RELIANCE

Understanding the limits of PLBs and other communication tools is as important as understanding their usefulness: Batteries deplete; electronics fail; cell phone service is limited in most mountain locations; a rescue may not be possible due to weather conditions or availability of rescuers. A PLB or satellite communicator is not a substitute for self-reliance. No party should set out ill prepared or inadequately equipped, nor should they attempt a route beyond their ability and assume that emergency help can be summoned.

The climbers who wrote the early editions of this book had no easy options for rescue in the mountains. They knew that the freedom of the hills could come at great cost and that a safe return would depend on the party's experience, preparation, skill, and judgment.

inventors, satellites have simplified communications and navigation. In 1982 an international satellite-based search and rescue system came online for aviation and maritime uses, the latter using devices known as EPIRBs (emergency position-indicating radio beacons). Satellite phones have come down in price and weight, and so they have become a reasonable option, although they are expensive per minute of call time.

PLBs and satellite communicators. In 2003, PLBs were introduced using the same government-based system but intended for those away from normal emergency services on land. These PLBs determine a party's coordinates using GPS and transmit them through international satellites to the appropriate emergency responders. Registration is required, but there are no subscription fees for PLBs using the government-based system. Avoid older PLBs that rely on radio homing beacon technology without GPS.

Since 2008, two commercial companies have introduced devices that function similar to PLBs, known as satellite communicators. The ones currently available are: the SPOT Satellite GPS Messenger, which allows one-way messaging, and the Garmin (formerly DeLorme) inReach Satellite Communicators, which allows two-way messaging.

These devices determine the party's position using GPS and then send a message out using commercial satellite networks. Some units allow for short, preset, nonemergency text messages to be sent (for example, "Camping here tonight"); some allow free-form text messages to be sent; and some allow for two-way texting. Satellite communicators require subscriptions for using their systems, and each manufacturer offers plans whose cost varies based on factors such as the number of messages transmitted, tracking, or other services used.

Some users find the distinction between PLBs and satellite communicators important, but both are commonly referred to as PLBs. PLBs are currently more powerful, but satellite communicators have additional functionality; see Table 5-6 for a comparison. PLBs and satellite communicators have saved many lives, and *all climbers should strongly consider carrying one in order to increase the climbing party's margin of safety.*

Other alternatives. Modern handheld amateur radios, also called "ham" radios, are inexpensive, lightweight, and compact in size but cannot be consistently relied upon for emergency communications from the backcountry. These battery-powered amateur radios can communicate either directly from radio to radio or, in many locations worldwide, via "repeaters." Repeaters are electronic devices stationed at high locations that receive the ham radio signal and retransmit it at a higher power level so that communication can occur over longer distances. In some locations, ham radio repeater coverage is equal to or better than cell phone coverage, but, like cell phone coverage, cannot be consistently relied on in the backcountry.

Family radio service (FRS) two-way radios are useful as local communication devices. See "Local Communication Devices" in Chapter 2, Clothing and Equipment.

LOST

Why do people get lost? Some travel without a map because the route seems obvious. Some people trust their own instincts over the compass. Others do not bother with the map homework that can start them off with a good mental picture of the area. Some do not pay enough attention to the route on the way in to be able to find it on the way out. Some rely on the skill of their climbing partner, who may be getting them lost. Some are lost when they become separated from their party. Some do not take the time to think about where they are going, so they miss trail junctions or wander off on game paths, charging ahead despite deteriorating weather and visibility or fatigue. Some are lost due to an overreliance on technology—for example, assuming that their GPS device will somehow keep them from getting lost, without having saved the necessary waypoints and downloaded the appropriate map while connected to the internet.

Groups of two or more rarely become dangerously lost, even if they have no wilderness experience. The real danger is when a single individual is separated from the rest of the party. For this reason, always try to keep everyone together, and assign a sweep (or rear guard) to keep track of stragglers. Good navigators are never truly lost—but, having learned humility through years of experience, they always carry enough food, clothing, and bivouac gear to get them through a few days of temporary confusion.

WHAT IF YOUR PARTY IS LOST?

If your party becomes lost, the first rule is to stop. Avoid the temptation to plunge hopefully on. Try to determine where the party is. If that does not work, figure out the last time the party knew its exact location. If that spot is fairly close, within an hour or so, retrace your steps and get back to that point. But if that spot is hours back, the party might instead decide to head toward the baseline they established when they started out. If darkness falls or your party tires before it has found its way out, safely bivouac for the night.

TABLE 5-6. COMPARISON OF PLBS, SATELLITE COMMUNICATORS, AND SATELLITE PHONES		
	SATELLITE SYSTEM	**FUNCTIONALITY**	**ADVANTAGES AND DISADVANTAGES**
PLBs	Dedicated government search and rescue system	• Sends location to emergency responders	• Requires registration • Somewhat stronger signal than satellite communicators
Satellite Communicators	Commercial systems	• Sends location to emergency responders via private companies • One or two-way messaging options, depending on model • Can send location to friends and family • Some models are also GPS navigation devices. One model, the Garmin inReach Explorer+, includes a digital compass, barometric altimeter, and internal mapping capability, making it suitable as a GPS device too.	• Requires subscription fees (cost varies depending on services) • Some models also function as a full mapping GPS device
Satellite Phones	Commercial systems	• Two-way backcountry telephone communications	• Expensive call time

WHAT IF YOU ARE LOST ALONE?

The first rule if you are lost while alone is, again, to stop. Look for other members of the party, shout or sound a whistle, and listen for a response. If the only answer is silence, sit down, regain your calm, and combat panic with reason.

Once you have calmed down, start doing the right things. Look at the map in an attempt to determine your location, and plan a route home in case you do not connect with the other climbers. Mark your location with a cairn or other objects, and then scout in all directions, each time returning to the marked position. Well before dark, prepare for the night by finding water and shelter. Go to an open area so that you can be seen from the air. Spread out some brightly colored clothing or other material to give searchers something to see. Staying busy will raise your spirits; try singing—it will give you something to do and searchers something to hear.

The odds are that you will be reunited with your group by morning. If not, fight terror. After a night alone, you may decide to hike out to a baseline feature picked out before the trip—a ridge, stream, or highway. If the terrain is too difficult for you to travel alone, or if you are injured or sick, it might be better to concentrate on letting yourself be found. It is easier for rescuers to find a lost climber who stays in one place in the open and shouts periodically than one who thrashes on in hysterical hope, one step ahead of the rescue party.

FINDING THE FREEDOM OF THE HILLS

The mountains await those who have learned the skills of orientation, navigation, and routefinding. In large part, navigation is the subject of this entire book because it is so essential to all off-trail adventure.

In medieval times, the greatest honors a visitor could receive were the rights of a citizen and the freedom of the city, sometimes even today symbolized by presenting a guest with the "keys to the city." For the modern alpine traveler, navigation is the key to wandering at will through valleys and meadows, up cliffs and over glaciers, thereby earning the rights of a citizen in a magical land—a mountaineer with the freedom of the hills.

CHAPTER 6

WILDERNESS TRAVEL

Climbing the mountain is one thing; getting from the trailhead to the mountain is another. Wilderness travel is the art of getting there—along trails, around brush, across rock, over snow, and across streams. If you learn the skills of wilderness travel, you open the gateway to the summits.

WILDERNESS ROUTEFINDING

Wilderness routefinding is the art of working out an efficient route from trailhead to summit that is within the abilities of the climbing party. Intuition and luck play a role, but it takes skill and experience to surmount the hazards and hurdles between the parking lot and the top. Aside from the orientation and navigation skills described in Chapter 5, Navigation, climbers rely on their ability to interpret trail, rock, snow, and weather conditions before and during the climb to skillfully travel over different types of terrain and to comprehend the clues that the wilderness offers.

GATHER ROUTE INFORMATION

The more information you gather ahead of time, the better your ability to make sound decisions later on. Take time to research the geology and climate of the party's selected area, in addition to your specific objective. Each mountain range has its own peculiarities that affect routefinding and travel. For example, mountaineers familiar with the Canadian Rockies, accustomed to broad valleys and open forests, will need to learn new rules to contend with the heavily vegetated, narrow canyons of British Columbia's Coast Range. The Pacific Northwest mountaineer familiar with deep snow at 4,000 feet (1,200 meters) in June will discover drastically different June conditions in the California Sierra.

Guidebooks offer detailed climb descriptions, including information on the climbing route, the estimated time necessary to complete it, elevation gain, distance, and so forth. But be aware that guidebooks become outdated; one bad winter can completely alter an approach. Make sure to consult the latest edition, and take a look at two or three different guidebooks, if available. Publications that cover other aspects of the area—its skiing, hiking, geology, and history—may also have something to offer as the party plans its trip.

Check online resources for weather forecasts, snow conditions, and Forest Service and Park Service information. Check also for information from other climbers, on message boards or in other venues. Climbers who have made the trip can describe landmarks, hazards, and routefinding difficulties, and quite often these descriptions contain helpful photographs. As always, exercise judgment when using online sources.

Useful details are packed into maps of all sorts: Forest Service maps, road maps, aerial maps, climbers' sketch maps, and topographic maps. More and more maps and topographic materials, as with information in general, are becoming available online and are downloadable or printable to take with you.

For a trip into an area that is especially unfamiliar, you will need to prepare in more depth. This might include scouting into the area, making observations from vantage points, or studying oblique (taken at an angle) aerial photos. Forest Service or Park Service rangers can usually provide information on road and trail conditions. The most popular climbing areas may even have designated climbing rangers who are in the mountains regularly and can give informed and current reports. Google Earth (www.google.com/earth) provides invaluable three-dimensional views of maps from any chosen vantage point.

Some of the best route details come out of conversations with locals. The person pouring coffee in the local cafe may be a veteran climber of the area. Ask about trails that do not appear on the maps, current snow conditions, and best places to ford streams.

Always consider the season and the amount of snowfall in a given year when preparing for a climb. Early in the season, avalanche danger may be high on steep slopes, especially if there is a heavy accumulation of snow from the winter before. Late in the season, or following a warm winter with low snowfall, a slope that is usually covered in snow may be exposed talus.

Finally, do not let outdated information ruin a trip. Check beforehand with the appropriate agencies about roads and trails, especially closures, and about climbing routes and regulations, permits, limitations on party size, and camping requirements.

LEARN FROM EXPERIENCE

There is no substitute for firsthand experience. As you learn, climb with seasoned mountaineers, watch their techniques, and ask questions. The more familiar you are with the wilderness, the greater your freedom to find your own way.

BE OBSERVANT ON THE APPROACH

Climb with your eyes. Continually study the mountain for climbing routes. A distant view can reveal patterns of ridges, cliffs, snowfields, and glaciers, as well as the degree of incline. At closer range, details of fault lines, bands of cliffs, and crevasse fields appear. Look for clues of routes: ridges with lower incline than the faces they divide; cracks, ledges, and chimneys leading up or across the faces; snowfields or glaciers offering easy or predictable pitches. Look for climbable sections and link them together visually. With experience comes a good eye for what you know you can climb.

If the approach skirts the base of the mountain, try to view the peak from various perspectives. Even moderate slopes can appear steep when you look at them head on. A system of ledges indistinguishable against background cliffs may show clearly from another angle or as shadows cross the mountain.

The presence of snow sometimes promises a modest angle and easy climbing, because snow does not last long on slopes of greater than 50 degrees. Snow and shrubs that appear on distant rock faces often turn out to be "sidewalks" with smaller ledges between. However, snow can be deceptive. What appear to be snowfields high on the mountain may be ice. Deep, high-angle couloirs often retain snow or ice year-round, or stay icy late in the day, especially when shaded.

WATCH FOR HAZARDS

Stay alert to climbing hazards. Study snowfields and icefalls for avalanche danger and cliffs for signs of possible rockfall. Snowfields reveal recent rockfall by the appearance of dirty snow or rock-filled craters. If the route goes through avalanche and rockfall territory, travel in the cold hours of night or very early morning, before the sun melts the ice that bonds precariously perched boulders and ice towers. Move through such places quickly.

Take rest breaks before or after danger zones, and when you enter them, try not to get caught behind slower parties. If possible, avoid these areas in heavy rain. Also watch for changing weather conditions (see Chapter 28, Mountain Weather). Keep evaluating hazards and looking for the most appropriate route, given the conditions. If the route you initially planned on climbing begins to look questionable, search for alternatives and make decisions as early as possible.

THINK ABOUT THE RETURN

Always consider the descent while you are making the approach. What is easy going up is not necessarily easy going down; nor is it easy to find. Look back frequently, take notes, take GPS and altimeter readings, and, if necessary, mark the route. (For additional information, see Chapters 5, Navigation; 7, Leave No Trace; and 16, Snow Travel and Climbing.)

The approach is also a time to look ahead to the end of the day. Consider where the party has to be by dark and whether the area will be safe to travel through by headlamp, if necessary. Keep an eye out for emergency campsites, water supplies, and anything else that may make the return trip easier and safer. Notice how long it took you to travel in to estimate how long it might take to return. If you have not already done so as you planned the trip, establish a "turnaround time"—that is, the time you will need to begin your return whether or not you have achieved your objective. Share that information with others on the trip so that they can also plan and understand the expectations for the outing.

WALKING

Reaching the summit often involves more walking than climbing. Walking is as important a skill as any other that climbers learn. Before hitting the trail, stretch your legs, hips, back, and shoulders. Drink some water. Consider taping or putting Moleskin on areas prone to blisters. Take time to adjust your pack and boots to avoid aches and pains—and frequent stops—later on.

Prepare for stops before you start out on the approach. Use your pack's outside pockets for items that you will need repeatedly throughout the day, such as snacks, water, jacket, hat, gloves, gaiters, sunglasses, and headlamp. Not only will it be easy for you to reach these items but other members of the party can also reach them for you if necessary, without your needing to remove your pack or even reduce the pace. Strap your ice axe and trekking poles to the outside of your pack so they are readily available for rough terrain. The ice axe will often be very useful even before snow line.

PACE

Setting the right pace from the start ensures a happier, stronger day of climbing. The most common mistake is walking too fast to begin with. This may perhaps be done out of concern for the long miles ahead or from a desire to perform well with companions. But why get worn out on the first mile of a 10-mile (16-kilometer) approach if the whole day is available? You are going too fast if you cannot sustain your pace hour after hour or if you cannot converse without losing your breath. Take your time and enjoy yourself (see the "Hiking with a Group" sidebar).

The other mistake is walking too slowly, which prolongs the hike and leaves less time to negotiate the more technical portions of the trip. If you are walking slowly due to fatigue, remember that the body has considerable reserves. Muscles may ache but still have many miles left in them. A degree of discomfort is inevitable; walking too fast or too slow only creates additional fatigue.

At the start, walk slowly to allow your body to warm up. Before you start to sweat, take a break and remove some clothing. Then increase the pace and accept the pain as your body works harder to experience its second wind.

HIKING WITH A GROUP

Walking with others involves certain considerations that help make travel more efficient and enjoyable:

- **Set a pace that makes good time but does not burn out slower climbers.** Adjust the party's pace so that slower climbers do not fall far behind. Do not allow anyone to travel alone, either last or first. Give the last person time to catch up with the party at rest stops—and time to rest once that person gets there.
- **Try putting the slowest person in front to set the pace.** This helps keep the group together and may motivate a slow hiker to set a faster pace.
- **Redistribute group gear to energetic people.**
- **Stay three to five paces behind the person ahead.** Give the climber—as well as that person's ice axe or trekking poles—some space.
- **Stay close to the group.** Do not lose contact with other hikers or make them continually wait for you or wonder how far ahead you are.
- **Step off the trail when you stop.** Don't block the trail for others.
- **Ask permission to pass,** and pick a good spot to do so.
- **Mind the person behind you when you grab branches.** Before releasing branches, look back and call out "Branch."
- **Be courteous when meeting an oncoming party.** Traditionally, the party heading downhill steps aside to let the ascending climbers continue upward without breaking pace. However, if the terrain is steep or if the descending party is larger, the climbers moving uphill may step aside and take a few breaths. Generally, stand on the uphill side of the trail to let others past. However, when a party meets pack animals, it is often expected that those on foot will move aside and stand on the downhill side of the trail; speak quietly and make no sudden movements. People on mountain bikes should always yield to those on foot.
- **Select gathering points for the party during long approaches and descents where routefinding is not a concern.** This allows party members to find their natural pace within smaller groups. Regroup at trail junctions and difficult stream crossings. Ask the most experienced members to take front and rear positions.
- **Be cheerful and helpful.** Be someone you would want to hike with.

6

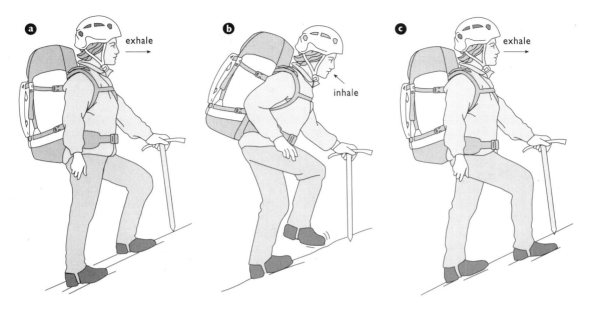

Fig. 6-1. The rest step: a, stand with entire body weight on right leg and exhale, completely relaxing left leg; b, inhale and step forward with right leg, shifting weight to left leg; c, place entire body weight on left leg and exhale, completely relaxing right leg.

Physiologically, your heartbeat and circulation increase and muscles loosen. As endorphins kick in and the feelings of physical stress subside, you feel strong and happy.

Vary the pace depending on the trail. Plod slowly and methodically up steep hills. As the grade lessens, pick up the tempo. Eventually you will find a natural pace that adapts to pack weight, terrain, weather, and other conditions. The pace will inevitably slow late in the day as fatigue sets in. Adrenaline may fuel short bursts of exertion, but there is no "third wind."

THE REST STEP

Slow and steady is a pace that gains the summit. On steep slopes, in snow, and at high altitudes, the rest step controls your pace and reduces fatigue. Use this technique instead of frequent rest stops whenever legs or lungs need to recuperate. The rest step is simple but subtle; practice it.

The essence of the technique is to end every step with a momentary but complete stop, giving your leg muscles a rest. Swing one foot forward for the next step. Stand upright and exhale while letting your rear leg support your entire body weight (fig. 6-1a). Straighten your rear leg so that you are supported by bone, not muscle. Feel the weight sink into your bones and foot. Now completely relax and soften the muscles of your forward leg, especially the thigh. This momentary rest, no matter how brief, refreshes the muscles. The momentary rest also tends to make your foot placement more secure. Then take a breath and swing your rear foot forward for the next step (fig. 6-1b), and repeat the rest step for your other leg (fig. 6-1c).

Synchronize breathing with leg movements. Typically, take a new breath with each step. Inhale and take a step up; exhale while pausing and letting your front leg rest as your rear leg supports your weight. Keep repeating the sequence. Many experienced climbers find a tune they replay in their head to help them keep a comfortable rhythm. The number of breaths per step depends on the difficulty of the work and your level of fatigue. At high altitudes, climbers sometimes take three or four deep breaths before each step up.

The rest step requires patience. For some, the monotony of the pace can undermine morale, especially when you are following another climber up a snowfield and there is no routefinding or step kicking to occupy your thoughts. But focus on the rhythm or hum a tune in your head (settle on an upbeat tune if that helps). Trust the technique to chew up the miles, even though the summit may seem so far away.

131

RESTS

Rests allow your body to recover from strenuous activity and to maintain an efficient pace. Take rests only when necessary; otherwise, keep moving. Numerous unnecessary stops can turn a 10-hour day into a 15-hour day, affecting group morale or even the team's chance of reaching a summit.

During the first half hour, stop to allow the group to readjust bootlaces and pack straps, add or take off layers of clothing, stretch warmed-up muscles, et cetera. Take short breathers—once every one to one and a half hours—during the early part of the day, while bodies are fresh. Rest in a standing or semireclining position, leaning against a tree or hillside to remove pack weight from your shoulders. Take deep breaths, and have a bite to eat and something to drink. Stay hydrated—always drink at every stop.

Remember to declare regular party separations (toilet stops), especially out of courtesy to the person who may be too shy to express the need. However, in order to minimize your impact on the mountains, your first toilet stop should be at the last available restroom facility found at or before the trailhead.

Later in the day, feelings of fatigue may demand more thorough relaxation, and the party can take a full rest every two hours or so. Look for a place with advantages, such as water or convenient slopes for removing packs and enjoying a view. Stretch muscles and put on additional clothing to avoid stiffness and chilling. Remove extra clothing before starting out again in order to prevent another stop a few minutes down the trail.

Also, take care that you do not waste unnecessary time during each stop. To help prevent a stop from taking up too much time, clearly establish how long that stop will last when you begin the break. Then adhere to your plan, unless there's a reason to change.

DOWNHILL

Walking downhill is a mixed blessing. The pace quickens without increasing fatigue; however, climbers may feel pain long after the day is over. When you walk downhill, your body and pack weight drop abruptly on your legs, knees, and feet. Toes jam forward. Jolts travel up your spine and jar your entire body. Avoid a host of injuries—including blisters, knee cartilage damage, sore toes, blackened toenails, headaches, and back pain—just by using a few of the following tricks:

- Trim toenails close before starting out.
- Tighten laces—especially on the upper part of the boots—to reduce foot movement inside the boots and avoid jamming toes.

- Bend the knees with each step to cushion the shock. As dancers like to say, "Remember your plié."
- Place each foot lightly, as if it were already sore.
- Use ski or trekking poles to reduce the load on the knees and to provide additional stability.
- Maintain a measured pace that is slower than the one urged by gravity.
- Use an ice axe for balance or for braking when necessary. The ice axe is not just for snow. It is also helpful in steep meadow, forest, and heather. (To learn ice-axe techniques, see Chapter 16, Snow Travel and Climbing.)
- Find a place to sit briefly every 45 to 60 minutes, to reduce fatigue on the knees if necessary.

SIDEHILL

The ups and downs of climbing are far preferable to the torments of cross-country sidehilling (traversing). Walking across the side of a slope twists your ankles, contorts your hips, and undermines balance. If possible, hike straight up, abandon a sidehill, drop down into a brush-free valley, or go up onto a rounded ridge. If traversing is unavoidable, look for rocks, animal trails, and the ground just above clumps of grass or heather to provide flat spots of relief. Switchback regularly to avoid ankle strain in one leg.

UPHILL

As you climb uphill, in addition to watching for specific hazards, continue to monitor the steepness and general nature of what you are climbing into. Consider whether continuing will lead you into territory so steep and technical that you will have difficulty downclimbing or otherwise retreating. If you begin to notice that you might have difficulty retreating, especially if there is any chance you are not on the trail you intended to follow, take time to confirm that you are on route and that you do not have other options. Otherwise, retreating while you still feel comfortable with the terrain is likely the best option.

TRAIL FINDING

For a wilderness traveler, a "trail" is any visible route—no matter how ragged—that efficiently gets the party where they want to go. The goal is to find the easiest route using the tools at hand: awareness of the terrain, navigational skills, weather conditions, and tips from guidebooks and experts.

Even in popular areas with heavy foot traffic and signage, keep alert to find and stay on the trail. Missing a turnoff is easy if a sign is gone or if logging, erosion, an avalanche, treefall, or rockfall obliterates the trail. On an established forest trail in deep snow or through a lot of woody debris, saw-cut log ends peeking through may be the only indication of a trail's location.

Old blazes cut in tree trunks, or surveyors' ribbon tied to branches, often mark the trail through a forest. Rock cairns (piles of rocks placed along the route as markers where the path is not obvious) may show the way above timberline. These pointers may be unreliable. A tiny cairn or a wisp of ribbon may indicate nothing more than a lost climber, a route to an alternate destination, or an old route since obstructed by rockfall. Navigation tools like the compass may stand you in good stead too (see Chapter 5, Navigation).

The trick, however, is to stay on the trail until the inevitable moment it disappears or until it becomes necessary to head off trail in order to go in the right direction. Choose a course that a trail would follow if there were a trail. Trail builders look for the easiest way to go. Do as they do.

SHARING THE WILDERNESS WITH ANIMALS

Alpine wildlife is fascinating and often charming, but enjoy the birds and animals from a distance and do not disturb them. When you encounter animals on the route, move slowly and allow them plenty of time to drift away. Try to pass on their downhill side; typically they head uphill to escape. Give them plenty of room. An animal rushing from a close encounter with a human is in danger of stress or injury; if it has too many of these encounters, it may feel forced to abandon its home grounds for poorer terrain.

BEARS AND COUGARS

In bear country, stay out of the "personal space" of bears. Try not to surprise them. Whenever possible go around brushy ravines with poor visibility rather than through them, even if it makes the route considerably longer. Make plenty of noise in unavoidable lower-visibility areas to warn animals of your approach.

If the climbing party surprises a bear or cougar, do not turn and run. Running may elicit a chase response in large predators, and bears and cougars are very fast runners. Instead, stand your ground, face the animal, talk, and slowly edge away while still facing the animal. (See Resources for more about handling animal encounters.)

NEGOTIATING DIFFICULT TERRAIN

The biggest barriers on the way to a mountaintop often appear below the snow line.

BRUSH

Brush thrives in younger forests or in low-altitude, wet, subalpine areas that have few trees. A river that frequently changes course prevents large-tree growth and permits brush to thrive. In gullies swept by winter avalanches, the shrubs simply bend undamaged under the snow and flourish in spring and summer.

Brush can be a backcountry horror, and "bushwhacking" makes for difficult, dangerous travel. Downward-slanting vine maple and slide alder are slippery. Brush obscures the peril of cliffs, boulders, and ravines. Brush snares ropes and ice-axe picks. The best policy is to avoid brush, but if that is not possible, try the following techniques (see also the "Tips to Minimize Brush Hassles" sidebar):

- **Use trails as much as possible.** Five miles (8 kilometers) of trail may be less work and take less time than 1 mile (1.6 kilometers) of brush.
- **Travel when snow covers brush.** Some valleys make for easy going in the spring when it is possible to walk on snow, but they are almost impossible in summer when it is necessary to burrow through the brush.
- **Avoid avalanche tracks.** When you are climbing a valley wall, stay in the trees between avalanche tracks to avoid the brush.
- **Aim for the big trees, where brush is thinner.** Mature forests block sunlight and stifle brush growth.
- **Travel on talus, scree, or snow remnants** rather than in adjacent thickets.
- **Look for game trails.** Animals generally follow the path of least resistance. Use these trails but take care not to startle large animals in heavy brush.
- **Travel on ridges and ridge spurs,** which may be dry and brushless, whereas creek bottoms and valley floors are often choked with vegetation.
- **Scout both sides of a stream** for the route with the least amount of bushwhacking.
- **Consider going into the stream channel** if the route parallels a stream. Wading may be necessary, but the streambed can be an easier tunnel through the brush. Dry streambeds are often ideal. Take care in deep canyons, where waterfalls and fallen trees interrupt a stream.

6

- **Take a high route.** Climb directly to timberline or a ridgetop.
- **Go up to the base of side bluffs,** where there is often an open, flattened corridor next to the rock.

TALUS, SCREE, AND BOULDERS

Mountain peaks constantly crumble, dropping rock fragments that pile up below as talus, scree, and boulders. Most of the rubble pours from gullies and spreads out in alluvial fans that often merge into one another, forming a broad band of broken rock between valley greenery and the peaks. These fans can alternate in vertical strips with forest. Talus consists of larger fragments, usually big enough to step on individually. Scree is smaller—from the size of coarse sand up to a couple inches across—and may flow a bit around your feet when you step on it. When even larger rocks fall off cliff faces, they form boulder fields. Slopes of talus, scree, and boulders can either help or hinder a climber. Most offer handy, brush-free pathways to the mountains, but some are loose and dangerous, with sharp-edged rock that can cause injury.

Talus. Talus slopes build gradually over the ages, and on the oldest slopes, soil fills the spaces between the rocks, locking them together to create smooth pathways. But talus can be loose on volcanoes and younger mountains, where vegetation has not filled in the spaces. Even large rocks can roll or teeter. Try for a route where the rock is lichen covered, which indicates that the rock has remained in place for a long time. Move nimbly on talus, ready to leap away if a rock shifts underfoot. Use your eyes and plan four or five steps ahead. Try to set your foot smoothly and flex your foot to accommodate the angle of the surface you are stepping on. That may help the piece remain stable. Take care on wet talus.

TIPS TO MINIMIZE BRUSH HASSLES

Some skirmishes with brush are inevitable; here are some tips for dealing with it:
- Choose the shortest route across the brushy area.
- Look for animal trails through the brush.
- Use fallen trees with long, straight trunks as elevated walkways.
- Push and pull the bushes apart, sometimes by stepping on lower limbs and lifting and clinging to higher ones, to make a passageway.
- Use hardy shrubs as hand- and footholds on steep terrain.

Scree. Loose scree can make going uphill a slow-motion torment, with part of each step lost as your foot settles in. Stepping on or just above a larger rock in scree can pry or wedge it out. However, descents can be fun. It may be possible to move down the scree in a sliding stride—something like cross-country skiing or plunge-stepping down snow. Ice axes are helpful; the technique on scree is similar to that on snow (see Chapter 16, Snow Travel and Climbing). Nonetheless, be aware that scree can sometimes consist of only a thin, ball bearing–sized cover over large rocks. If there is vegetation on the slope, avoid setting off scree slides that can damage the plants. Although riding a scree slope can be fun, bits of rock can work their way into your boots and cause discomfort when you reach talus or a downward trail. You could wear short, lightweight gaiters in the summer if you expect to encounter scree.

Boulders. Boulder fields can be pleasant alternatives to torturous scree slopes, but they have their own dangers. Normally, fallen boulders form a steep slope beneath the cliff they detached from—the steepest slope that such boulders can pile up on is called the *angle of repose*. The boulders landing on even steeper slopes tend to fall off unless stabilized by vegetation. The most commonly traveled routes up boulder fields are usually quite stable, since foot traffic has gradually shifted the riskiest boulders to more stable places. Beware the unfrequented boulder field—where there are no boot marks on the boulder moss, for instance.

Rockfall

Sometimes the route ascends a steep gully filled with a mix of boulders embedded in talus and scree—this is a classic scenario for party-induced rockfall. Disturbing one key stone on a glacial moraine or a talus slope can set off a rock avalanche. Safety dictates traveling outside the fall line of climbers above and below you if possible. If you are in a narrow gully where this is not possible, tread gently and be ready to loudly shout "*Rock! Rock! Rock!*" if a stone dislodges. Keep the party close together so a rock set off by one climber cannot gain dangerous momentum before reaching others (fig. 6-2a). Consider permitting just one climber (or small groups keeping closely together) to move at a time while the rest of the party remains in protected spots (fig. 6-2b).

Party-induced rockfall is by no means the only hazard of loose gullies. Even rainfall can set off rockfall. Other times, rockfall may be set off by another climbing party out of your party's sight. Overall, rockfall is one of the most common causes of mountain accidents, so beware!

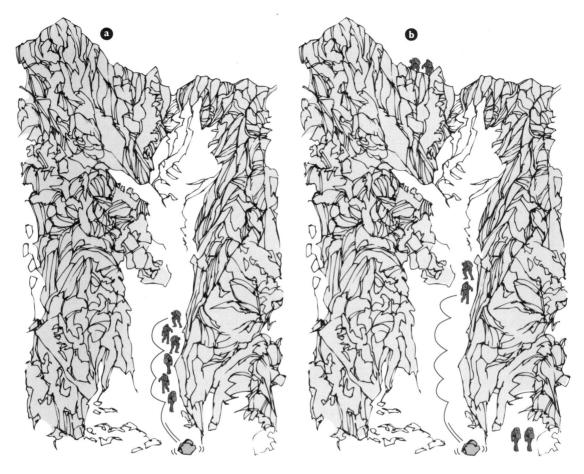

Fig. 6-2. Traveling safely on loose rock: a, climbers stay close together so that a dislodged rock does not gain dangerous momentum before reaching the climbers below; b, climbers ascend in pairs or small groups out of one another's fall line, so a dislodged rock passes the climbers below.

Consider wearing a helmet any time you are traveling over terrain where a climber may be exposed to rockfall from above or could have a serious fall.

Descending

Facing exposure while descending talus, scree, or boulders can be intimidating. Climbers may hesitate or move slowly. This can be dangerous. Move in short, smooth, quick steps, and know where the next step is, so you are ready to quickly get off a moving rock and avoid injury. Trekking poles or an ice axe are helpful; keep your pole or axe in front of you to avoid it becoming caught between rocks or disturbing rocks above you.

SNOW

Snow can be very helpful for wilderness travel. Many peaks are best climbed early in the season when consolidated snow covers talus, brush, and logging slash and when snow bridges provide easy access over streams. However, in a different season or with less-than-ideal snow conditions, snow can be a curse. Trails are lost under snow or are washed out by avalanche or heavy thaw. Thin snow is unstable and may obscure dangerous conditions. Watch for terrain traps if spring avalanches are a possibility (see Chapter 16, Snow Travel and Climbing). A party may encounter different snow conditions on the approach, the climb, and the descent, given the time of day, the pace, or changing weather conditions. Be sure to study weather and snow conditions before the climb.

If traveling on snow, watch for visible terrain features, because they may indicate thin or melting snow. The snow next to logs and boulders often covers holes and soft spots called *moats*, which occur when the snow partially melts away from the wood and the rock. A moat is common around trees where lower limbs keep the snow from filling in next to the trunk (in this situation called a *tree well*). Probe with an ice axe to avoid likely trouble spots, step wide off logs and rocks, and stay away from treetops poking above the snow. If the snow is thin on a talus slope, there can be large voids under the snow that are easy to punch through. Especially if the day is warm, go slow on talus on the return trip if the snow is thin.

Streams will melt the underside of a snow bridge until it can no longer support your weight. To guard against a dunking (or worse), watch for depressions in the snow and variations in color or texture, and listen for sounds of running water. Water emerging at the foot of a snowfield indicates the existence, and perhaps the size, of a cavity beneath the snow. Probe for thin spots with your ice axe.

With experience, you will recognize both the advantages and dangers of snow and learn to use the medium to make wilderness travel easier and more enjoyable. See Chapters 16, Snow Travel and Climbing, and 27, The Cycle of Snow, for more information.

RIVERS AND STREAMS

When your objective lies on the far side of a sizable river or stream, crossing it is a major factor in route selection. Crossings can consume huge amounts of time and energy, and they can be the most dangerous part of the trip.

Finding the Crossing

Try to get a distant, overall view of the river and scope out crossing possibilities. This can be more useful than a hundred close looks from the riverbank. When a distant view is impossible or unhelpful, the party may have to choose between either thrashing through the river-bottom brush to find a way across or traversing the slopes high above the river in hopes of a sure crossing.

The surrounding landscape indicates the options. In a deep forest, there is a good chance of finding easy passage on a large log or logjam, even over wide rivers. Higher in the mountains, foot logs are harder to come by, especially if the river frequently changes course and prevents the growth of large trees near its channel.

If it is necessary to wade across, find the widest part of the river. The narrows may be the shortest way, but they are also the deepest, swiftest, and most dangerous. If snowmelt feeds a river, its flow is at a minimum in the early morning and might be a dangerous raging torrent in the afternoon. Sometimes a party may camp overnight to take advantage of this morning low water.

Making the Crossing

Unfasten the hip belt and sternum straps of your pack before you try any stream crossing that may require swimming in case of a fall. Make sure you will be able to remove your pack in a hurry.

Logs. A foot log is a great way across. If the log is thin, slippery, or steeply inclined, use a trekking pole (or poles), an ice axe, a sturdy stick, crampons, or a tightly stretched hand line (see below) to help with balance, traction, and support. Sit down and scoot across if that helps.

Boulder hopping. Boulders offer another way across. Before you cross, mentally rehearse the entire sequence of leaps. Safety lies in smooth and steady progress over stones that may be too slippery and unsteady for you to stop on for more than an instant. Use an ice axe or trekking pole(s) for additional balance. Avoid mossy or algae-covered stones if you can.

Wading. If you are wading, try to keep your gear, including your boots, dry. If the water is placid and the stones rounded, put your boots and socks in your pack while you wade across barefoot, or in sandals or lightweight tennis shoes brought for that purpose. In tougher conditions, wear your boots but put your socks and insoles in the pack; on the far side, drain your boots and replace the dry insoles and socks. In deeper crossings, consider removing your pants or other clothing: loose clothing increases the drag from the water, but it also reduces chilling and may permit a longer crossing.

If you are trying to cross where the water is deep but not swift, cross with the least force against your body by angling downstream at about the same speed as the current. However, the best way to cross is to face upstream, lean into the current, and firmly plant an ice axe, trekking pole, or stout stick upstream for a third point of support. Use your leading foot to probe for solid placement on the shifting river bottom, advance your following foot, and thrust the axe or pole into a new position.

Swift water is easy to underestimate. With one false step, you can be pushed under and dashed against rocks and logs or sent bouncing along in white water. Water is dangerous whenever it boils above your knee. A swift stream flowing only shin deep can boil up against your knees. Knee-deep water may boil above your waist and give a disconcerting sensation of buoyancy. Frothy water, containing a great deal of air, is wet enough to drown you but may not be dense enough to float a human body. Streams fed by glaciers present an added difficulty because their bottoms are hidden by milky water from glacier-milled rock flour.

Team crossing. Two or more travelers can cross together, each in turn moving to a solid new stance while remaining secured to the other(s) by linked arms or hands. Team crossing with a pole is another method: Team members enter the water, each grasping the pole, which is held horizontal and parallel to the flow of the stream. The upstream member breaks the force of the current. Anyone who slips hangs onto the pole while the others keep the pole steady.

Hand lines. A hand line for small streams can be helpful. Angle the line downstream so that if any climbers lose their footing, they will be swept to shore. If a nylon climbing rope is the only option available, consider the rope stretch. Always use appropriate anchors (see Chapter 10, Belaying).

Using ropes for stream crossings in deep, swift water can be hazardous. If someone is belayed across the river, there is a possibility that the crossing person can be held by the belay but trapped underwater. Consider belaying the pack, however. That way, if a climber falls and sheds the pack, it will not get swept away.

Falling In

If you are swept downstream by a swift current, the safest position is on your back with your feet pointed downstream; use a backstroke to steer. This position vastly improves your chances for survival with minimal injuries. Be alert. If you approach a "strainer" (a small dam or collection of debris), switch quickly to normal headfirst swimming. Swim furiously to stay high in the water and get on top of the debris. The strainer may be your route ashore.

If falling off a log into the water seems imminent, try to fall off on the downstream side to avoid getting swept under the log. If a member of the party falls in, those on shore can try to reach out with a pole, ice axe, or branch. It may be possible to throw out a floating object, such as an inflated water bag. Make a realistic evaluation of the danger to yourself before you decide to go into the stream to attempt a hands-on rescue.

READY FOR THE WILDERNESS

Traveling in the wilderness is like wandering in a foreign country: The unfamiliarity of a place is the attraction, yet it also limits the journey. Preparation is essential, and nothing rivals the knowledge gained from personal experience.

Immerse yourself in the wilderness again and again; study it as if it were a new language. Use all five senses to master the "vocabulary" of the terrain. Some of your best moments will come when you discover your ability to respond well to what it asks of you. With fluency comes the freedom to roam, and with that freedom comes responsibility. The next chapter discusses ways to keep the wild places wild for those who travel after us, so they too can experience the exhilaration of discovery.

CHAPTER 7

LEAVE NO TRACE

Mountaineers seek the uncharted way, the trail less traveled, and a summit to stand on. Climbers recognize that the wilderness they seek is a resource that they must protect.

A skilled mountaineer is courageous, fit, perceptive, and tough—and a great teammate. These traits are discussed in climbing magazines, applauded in first ascents, and even featured in blockbuster movies. Less heralded, but of no less importance, is *conscientiousness*. Conscientious climbers are respectful of their surroundings and implement low-impact recreation skills as an integral part of their technical pursuits. They leave no trace of their time outdoors because their enthusiasm for exploring the natural environment is matched by their desire to protect it.

Most mountaineers have seen the consequences of overuse, carelessness, and thoughtlessness in the backcountry. In Alaska's Denali National Park, approximately 152,000 pounds of human waste have been thrown into the Kahiltna Glacier. Within the next decade, the waste is expected to "melt out" downstream from base camp, exacerbating an area that already tested positive for fecal coliform in 2010 and 2012. Today, Clean Mountain Cans (portable toilets) are mandatory above the 14,200-foot base camp.

Stewardship advancements in Denali are part of an ethical evolution in climbing, beginning in the 1970s when the first chocks replaced rock-deforming pitons. In 1994, the Leave No Trace Center for Outdoor Ethics was established as a nonprofit educational organization to promote a consistent set of minimum-impact guidelines, now referred to as Leave No Trace.

Leave No Trace is taught with seven easy-to-remember principles (see the "Seven Principles of Leave No Trace" sidebar). This chapter illuminates the skills necessary to execute these principles, with special emphasis placed on the unique techniques required in mountaineering.

To learn more from the Leave No Trace Center for Outdoor Ethics, which partners with US land managers and other organizations to instill responsible recreation, see Resources.

SEVEN PRINCIPLES OF LEAVE NO TRACE

1. Plan ahead and prepare.
2. Travel and camp on durable surfaces.
3. Dispose of waste properly.
4. Leave what you find.
5. Minimize campfire impacts.
6. Respect wildlife.
7. Be considerate of other visitors.

1. PLAN AHEAD AND PREPARE

Planning ahead achieves more than a summit; it is essential to practicing Leave No Trace skills.

PROTECT THE CLIMBING PARTY, PROTECT THE PLACE

A climbing group that stretches itself to the limit, and perhaps gets into trouble, will no longer be able to care about the principles of Leave No Trace. For example, they may grow fatigued and have to set up camp in a sensitive area. They may get cold and have to start a campfire in a fire-ban zone. If rescuers must be called, safety comes first, regardless of environmental damage. However, realistic planning can often prevent these kinds of desperate situations in the first place.

MEAL PLANNING

As with many Leave No Trace skills, meal planning not only protects the environment, it makes for more-efficient mountaineers. Mastering two techniques—repackaging food and preparing one-pot meals—will speed up cooking, lighten loads, and decrease garbage.

The more packaging climbers carry, the greater the chance that something will be left in the backcountry. Plus, excess packaging is a nuisance to fiddle with while attempting a climb. To repackage food, remove wraps, twist ties, and covers; then place food in reusable containers or resealable bags. After food has been used, empty bags can be placed inside one another for packing out.

One-pot meals prepared on a backpacking stove require minimal cooking utensils and cleaning and produce less food waste. Stoves are fast, clean, and convenient to use, and they work in just about any weather. Plan meals so the group takes only the amount of food necessary, except for emergency rations; if there are leftovers after a meal, they should be eaten later or packed out (not buried, burned, or dumped in a stream).

CONSIDER CONDITIONS AND LAND MANAGEMENT NORMS

A little research goes a long way. Know the required permits and other possible regulations ahead of time—every place is different. For example, permits aren't required to climb mountains in Europe, but places like the Matterhorn do restrict the number people who can stay in huts. In the United States, there are numerous land management norms, which vary among land management agencies and among specific locations.

These management norms, which help mitigate the impact of visitors' time in the outdoors, can include seasonal closures for wildlife, restoration and revegetation, or other conservation efforts. Likewise, frequency of use, required waste-disposal systems, fire bans, and ecological

sensitivities should all be understood beforehand. Consult land management agency resources and officials wherever you plan to recreate. Inquire about fragile or sensitive areas, including flora, fauna, geology, and soil conditions and moisture level (factors of concern for fire). Be willing to modify your plans or your route if fragile conditions or sensitive circumstances are discovered.

2. TRAVEL AND CAMP ON DURABLE SURFACES

The size of a climber's footprint or tent tarp may seem infinitesimal amid the vast peaks of Europe's Alps, the western United States' Cascades, or Asia's Himalaya. However, as climbing and mountaineering continue to grow in popularity, these areas host millions of visitors a year. Whenever possible, hike on established trails and camp in established sites. As climbers move off trail into pristine environments, practicing responsible recreating by implementing Leave No Trace skills becomes even more critical.

Fig. 7-1. Actual trailside sign at Mount Rainier National Park.

HIKING

Staying on established trails and following best hiking practices make it possible for wild places to stay wild. For example, Washington's Mount Rainier National Park hosts one to two million visitors a year, which makes managing trails and access to sensitive environments, such as alpine zones, very important.

Think of trails as wilderness highways. Like the roads people drive on, trails that are properly designed can withstand high foot traffic, channel users through fragile areas, manage water flow, and prevent soil erosion. Please stay on trails and obey trailside signs (fig. 7-1).

On-Trail Travel

While mountaineers venture beyond the beaten path, nearly every outing involves some established trails. Observe these practices to help preserve the trails and the areas they pass through and respect other trail users.

- **Always use and stay on trails where they exist.**
- **Stay within the established trail,** even if it is muddy or rutted, to protect trailside vegetation, and hike single file. These practices keep hikers from unintentionally widening trails. Wearing waterproof footwear and gaiters makes it possible to stay on the trail even where it is wet and muddy. Take care along stream banks to avoid erosion.
- **Never cut switchbacks.** Doing so increases your chances of becoming injured on unstable ground, kills plants, and compacts and erodes the soil.
- **Travel on snow when possible.** It is a natural protective layer between boot steps and the ground. Take extra care when traveling through the fragile transition zone between dirt and snow where the soil is saturated with water, especially during spring and late fall.
- **Select resilient areas, such as rocks, sand, or unvegetated areas, for rest breaks.** Move off and away from the trail to remain unobtrusive to fellow hikers. If this is not possible due to fragile or dense vegetation, find a wide spot in the trail.
- **Yield to other hikers by first finding a durable spot to step aside to** rather than trampling vegetation. This sets an even better example than standard trail etiquette, which calls for stepping aside immediately.
- **Pick up scraps of litter** left by others and put them in a plastic bag in your pocket. Carry a large garbage bag to haul out larger materials, especially on the trip back out.

Off-Trail Travel

Often a mountaineering objective lies well off any established trail. Mountaineers traveling off trail can incorporate the following skills into how they climb.

- **Keep a slow enough pace** to be aware of the surroundings and to plan a low-impact route.
- **Spread the party out for off-trail travel,** unlike trail travel, with each member taking a separate path, especially in fragile meadows. Avoid traveling single file, which creates a new trail and leaves a significant "trace." The exception is where there is an established climbers trail to use.
- **Look for durable surfaces** to walk on, such as bare ground (patches between vegetation, wildlife trails), rock (bedrock, talus, scree, stream gravel), and sedge grasses. Avoid tromping on woody or herbaceous vegetation, even if it appears to be hardy. Walking on durable surfaces is especially important as the party transitions into higher elevations, where vegetation experiences shorter growing seasons and more-extreme growing conditions; it is harder for such plants to recover from harm.
- **Take extra care in transition areas** between dirt and snow where the soil is water-saturated during spring and late fall; it is easy to damage soils here.
- **Leave areas free of cairns and flagging,** unless those markers are already there. Never carve trees. If your party needs to mark the route, remove the markers on the way back down. Let the next party have its own routefinding adventure.

CAMPING

Many of the world's most popular summit routes and backcountry trails have a proliferation of established campsites. For example, at the Mount Whitney Trail Camp in California, a number of previous visitors have built rock walls for wind protection. In instances like this, don't further disrupt the natural landscape by setting up new campsites. Look for previously used, established campsites. Resist the temptation to use a less-disturbed site because it has a better view or is closer to a water source. (See Table 7-1 for guidelines in choosing campsites.)

If a pristine location is all that is available, stay only a night or two and then find another location, which allows the area to recover. If a climbing party has a choice between a pristine spot and a new, slightly impacted campsite, the better choice could be the pristine site if the Leave No Trace guidelines are carefully applied. Although this choice may

TABLE 7-1. WILDERNESS CAMPSITE OPTIONS

CAMPSITE OPTIONS FROM OPTIMAL TO LESS OPTIMAL	REASONS TO SELECT OR NOT SELECT THIS CAMPSITE
1. Established, fully impacted campsite	A hardened site cannot be impacted much further, as long as it is not enlarged or manipulated in any way. Use existing rocks and logs instead of moving more in.
2. Snow	Snow will melt and show no sign of use, but avoid the area if vegetation or soil is showing. Before leaving, break down snow structures and make the site as natural looking as possible.
3. Rock slab	Solid rock resists most damaging effects except fire scars.
4. Sand, dirt, or gravelly flat	Most signs of human presence can be swept away, and no vegetation will be impacted.
5. Duff in deep forest	Duff and other decaying matter are only lightly harmed by campers' presence.
6. Grass-covered meadow	A meadow covered by tents for a week can have its entire growing season wiped out. Move a long-term camp every few days to reduce the harm to any one spot. The higher the meadow, the more sensitive it is to trampling.
7. Plant-covered meadow above timberline	Alpine plants grow very slowly, and woody plants are more sensitive to impact than grasses. Heather, for example, has only a couple of months to bloom, seed, and add a fraction of an inch of growth for the year. Alpine plants could take many years to recover from the damage of a brief encampment.
8. Waterfront along lakes and streams	Waterside plant life is delicate, and water pollution is a growing problem as more people head into the backcountry.

be contrary to first instinct, it allows a slightly impacted area to recover from use rather than receive more use.

In pristine sites, observe these recommendations:

- **Avoid grouping tents together.**
- **Disperse toilet sites and vary walkways** so that no single path gets so trampled that the vegetation cannot recover. Carry a pair of sandals or lightweight soft-soled shoes to wear around camp; heavy lug-soled boots are hard on soil and vegetation.
- **Never "landscape" a site** by leveling it, removing vegetation, or digging trenches, for example. Never cut tree boughs or vegetation for bedding; use a sleeping pad. If a campsite has an excessive number of log seats, improvised tables, or fire rings, thoughtfully disperse logs and rocks.
- **Find a spot with a slight natural slope** so that water will not pool beneath a tent and tempt campers to dig a trench.

When selecting a campsite, apply the 200-foot rule (about 75 paces): camp at least 200 feet (60 meters) away from water, trails, and people. Land managers may allow use of already hardened sites even though they are close to water; if so, go ahead and use them, but do not create a new site in the same vicinity. In a pristine area, enhance the sense of solitude for yourself and others by choosing an out-of-the-way site or one with good natural screening.

Try to use established mountaineering bivy sites or high camps. Moving alpine rocks may kill fragile plants that take many years to grow (plants in the alpine are often tiny and you have to look hard to see them; they are often nestled up against rocks and stones). Moving rocks also disturbs habitat for insects and other wildlife. Build new sites or improve existing ones only when absolutely necessary. Then select rocks that disturb the least possible amount of vegetation.

Keep track of gear and maintain a tidy camp so that equipment and food are not lost or forgotten. Leave the site in better condition than you found it. Pristine sites require a little extra effort; cover used areas with native materials, brushing out footprints and fluffing up matted grass.

3. DISPOSE OF WASTE PROPERLY

For decades, climbers practiced a laissez-faire approach to food and human waste as well as wastewater. Mountaineers would defecate in shallow snow holes; big wall climbers would toss their poop off rock faces in paper bags. Personal stories like that of professional climber Cedar Wright, who placed both hands in a pile of feces at the top of a small overhang on El Capitan in California's Yosemite National Park, exemplify the need for change. Globally, from Denali to Everest, watersheds have been contaminated from mountaineers' waste, garbage, and wastewater. With backcountry ventures on the rise, human health and environmental health depend on all climbers using best practices.

MANAGING HUMAN WASTE IN THE MOUNTAINS

The Wild West of waste disposal has come to an end. Always follow these guidelines:

- Whenever possible, use an outhouse.
- If an outhouse is unavailable, the two acceptable and time-tested methods for ethical and safe human feces disposal are cat-hole burial and packing it out. Research ahead of time to know which option is best for the area where your group will be traveling. Be prepared to use the cat-hole burial technique for defecating or to pack it out. (Both are explained in more detail below.)
- If you use toilet paper, use neutral-colored and nonscented and pack it out. Leaving piles of used paper is gross, plus the paper takes a long time to decompose in dry alpine environments. Burying it attracts animals, and burning it is a fire hazard.
- Instead of toilet paper, consider using natural materials such as smooth stones, conifer cones, broad leaves (being careful to recognize and use safe vegetation), or snow.
- Tampons, used diapers, pet waste, and personal hygiene products must be packed out.
- Urinate on bare ground or rocks—not vegetation—because the salt in urine attracts animals that might dig soils and damage plants while trying to eat the salts.
- On snow or ice, concentrate urine at designated locations in camp or at rest stops rather than creating a proliferation of pee holes. Cover yellow snow.
- Use the 200-foot (60-meter) rule for dog waste, too: bury it in a cat hole or pack it out.

- On steep rock or ice faces, wait until you reach a place where urine can be streamed away from the climbing route. In tents or on long routes, some climbers use a pee bottle to collect urine for later disposal.

Digging and Covering a Cat Hole

Using a cat hole to bury feces is most suited to lower elevations where there is a deep layer of organic soil. Find a suitable, thoughtful location away from trails, campsites, gathering areas, or water sources—apply the 200-foot (60-meter) rule. Remember, if it is easy for you to reach, it will be easy for others, too.

When you find a good location, use a small, lightweight trowel, sharp stick, or ice axe to remove a top layer, or divot, about 4 to 6 inches (10 to 15 centimeters) in diameter, and set it aside. Dig the hole no more than 8 inches (20 centimeters) deep—deeper than forest litter and duff, but not deeper than the humus: the dark organic soil containing nutrients and microbes that break down fecal matter (fig. 7-2).

After making your deposit, fill the hole with loose soil. Using a stick or something organic that can be left in the hole, mix the waste with some soil, then replace the divot. Tamp the soil and distribute area vegetation to create a natural appearance. Clean your hands using an alcohol-based hand sanitizer.

In thin mineral soil, high alpine areas, or in desert canyon country—all places where the waste will not readily break down—burying solid waste is not recommended. Although it is possible to hide waste by burying it or covering it with rock, it will take a long time to decompose. The cat hole is not suitable in snow, either, unless organic soil can be found underneath it, possibly in a tree well.

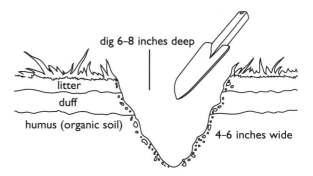

Fig. 7-2. Digging a cat hole.

Packing Out Poop

Mountaineers are already accustomed to packing out used toilet paper and personal hygiene products (used bandages, sanitary napkins, tampons, et cetera). However, climbers must be prepared to pack out feces as well. Packing out waste is the preferred practice on popular glacier routes, in alpine areas with thin mineral soils, in desert country, on steep rock and ice routes including big wall climbs, on arctic tundra, and during winter travel. Below are some methods for packing it out and disposing of it once the party is back at the trailhead.

Double-bag it. Two resealable plastic bags, stored in a stuff sack or a garbage bag, work effectively and safely. Like a dog owner picking up after a pet, invert the inner bag over your hand like a glove and scoop up the solid waste. Then turn the bag inside out to envelop the waste, seal the bag, place it inside the second bag, and seal or tie it as well. You can reduce odor in the first bag by including a 2-inch-square (5-centimeter-square) sponge saturated with ammonia or by adding some chlorinated lime, cat-box filler, or chemical gelling treatments.

Commercially available waste alleviation and gelling kits such as the WAG BAG use a degradable-plastic double-bag system approved for deposit in landfills, with the inner bag containing powder that gels waste and neutralizes odors. In some wilderness areas, land managers hand out ready-made basic double-bag sets, gelling kits, or other supplies, such as a cardboard sheet for initial deposit of waste and a paper bag with cat-box filler inside in which to bag the cardboard sheet. Be aware of the available options and those promoted by the area the group is visiting, especially since land managers may provide collection containers for climbers to deposit their waste in if using the agency's preferred method.

Contain the bags. Most backcountry travelers will want some kind of sturdy container in which to store the double bags used to initially collect waste. This container could be as simple as an old stuff sack, a watertight dry bag (such as those used on river trips), or sturdy commercially available products, all of which can be reused. Commercial containers include products designed for big wall climbers, such as the Metolius Waste Case, which is made out of haul-bag material and has sturdy haul straps to allow for secure hauling of the container below the haul bag. Another sturdy, commercially made product is the Clean Mountain Can, designed for use on Denali, which contains waste in a hard-sided cylinder, has a large capacity, and can be used as a toilet. Climbers can fashion their own container using the many types of light, durable, watertight plastic containers that are available.

Dispose of packed-out poop properly. Waste-disposal options must be thoughtfully implemented. There are no easy answers to the question of proper waste disposal. Increasingly, at popular climbing and mountaineering routes, land managers provide specially marked collection bins for human waste once climbers are out of the backcountry. Usually, however, it will be up to each group to dispose of waste properly after they have finished a trip.

Do not simply put human waste in a garbage can. Waste in paper bags may go into RV dump stations or front-country restrooms of the type that get pumped out. Paper or plastic bags should not go into pit toilets, flush toilets, or composting toilets. Waste in plastic bags should be emptied into a flush toilet, then the bag should be washed out before it is thrown into the garbage. Be sure to wash your hands with soap and water, scrubbing for at least 20 seconds, or use an alcohol-based hand sanitizer after handling fecal waste.

Crevasse Burial in Extremely Remote Areas

For remote expedition glacier travel, waste disposal in crevasses used to be standard practice. However, it is increasingly less so, as it is learned that these places are melting out faster and human waste is ending up downstream. The waste might not be ground up by the moving ice, as once was thought, and may lead to polluted snow that can cause gastrointestinal illnesses in other travelers. Thus, all climbers should research the best option for managing waste on remote objectives. Check with the responsible land management agency. Where crevasse disposal is acceptable, collect solid waste in a biodegradable plastic bag and then throw into a deep crevasse, away from the climbing route, after the party breaks camp. However, this practice could be on the cusp of change as distant routes gain popularity.

HANDLING FOOD AND GARBAGE

Leave No Trace applies to everything people bring into nature. Developing efficient systems for handling food waste and garbage will lighten the load for climbers and for the environment. As discussed in "1. Plan Ahead and Prepare" earlier in this chapter, repackaging food means less garbage to pack out and a little less weight to carry in. Carry out any leftover food. Never bury or burn food waste or garbage or dump it in outhouses.

When eating, be careful not to drop food scraps. Food not native to the environment's habitat can have unintended consequences, such as feeding wildlife who become habituated. Even food that will easily decompose—such as apple cores and banana peels—are not native to the mountain environment and should be packed out.

Keep all aspects of your backcountry kitchen away from water sources—apply the 200-foot (60-meter) rule. After cooking in the backcountry, strain cookwater through a screen to collect food particles, and pack them out with other trash. Clean cook pots by scraping them out with a plastic scrubber rather than sand or grass, and pack out the remaining food particles.

WASHING

Never wash anything directly in a water source. If you have applied sunscreen or insect repellent, wash off before jumping into a lake or stream; these chemicals and oils can cause harm to aquatic plants and wildlife and will leave an oily surface film. Wash your hands or yourself at least 200 feet (75 steps) away from camp and water sources using a biodegradable soap in very small quantities (keep it off plants), or use quick-drying liquid disinfectant. Take a pot of water 200 feet away from water sources, trails, and campsites, then wash, rinse, and dispose of the washwater—known as *graywater*—200 feet away as well. Dig a small cat hole downwind from the campsite for disposing of graywater. Pour the graywater into the hole, so it can be better distributed through the soil. Or disperse wastewater by flinging it out in an arc with a fast sweeping motion, which disperses the water in fine droplets.

4. LEAVE WHAT YOU FIND

Climbers who leave rocks, plants, archaeological artifacts, and other resources as they find them allow others the same sense of discovery and nature that drew them to mountaineering and climbing.

To that end, avoid disturbing vegetation or rocks on a climbing route. Look at, draw, or photograph wilderness flora rather than picking or collecting. Do not touch or remove fossils you may discover. Leave untouched any area with evidence of archaeological or historic artifacts, such as those left by prehistoric or native populations. Report findings to land managers so they can document them. As the adage says, "Take only photos, leave only footprints."

5. MINIMIZE CAMPFIRE IMPACTS

The classic image of camping is of folks gathered around a campfire at night. However, campfires make it difficult to have a low impact, so in most instances campfires should not be a part of the alpine experience. Thoughtful selection of equipment and clothing is an important part of Leave No Trace. Use lightweight stoves rather than campfires; stoves do not consume wild materials, do not fill the mountain air with smoke, and are much less likely to be the source of forest fires—pack in stove fuel rather than despoiling areas in search of firewood. Stoves and adequate, warm clothing eliminate the need for fires.

Since campfires are permitted in some places, identify the conditions for creating a safe permitted campfire. Use existing fire rings at established, front-country sites. Carry a fire pan or learn how to make and break down a Leave No Trace mound fire when in the backcountry (see the Leave No Trace website in Resources). Use only dry sticks found on the ground that can be broken by hand. When collecting wood for a campfire, avoid trampling vegetation, stripping trees and shrubs, even dead trees, which create visual variety and wildlife habitat, and creating unwanted social trails, all of which negatively impact local wildlife as well as other users. Burn wood to ash, and scatter cooled ashes so there is no visual evidence. Campfire rings and blackened rocks and trees are visual impacts that last for decades.

6. RESPECT WILDLIFE

In 2016, visitors in Wyoming's Yellowstone National Park put a newborn bison in the back of their SUV because "it looked cold." Unable to reconnect the calf with its herd, park rangers were forced to euthanize it. While this is an extreme example, this lesson holds true for all situations: animals are part of complex ecosystems, and our responsibility in the backcountry is to let these processes continue unfettered.

- **Never approach or touch wildlife.** Keep safe distances, both for your safety and that of the animals.
- **Never feed wildlife.** It threatens their health and creates dangerous dependence. This is true for all animals, even birds and chipmunks. A fed animal is a dead animal.
- **Clean up** even the smallest specks of food at trail stops and campsites. Microcrumbs are not natural to the environment.
- **Watch for nesting birds,** especially raptors, on rock routes so as not to disturb them. Check with land managers for nesting seasons and closures. If climbers do encounter nesting birds, they should back off or take another route.

■ **Ensure your pet doesn't disturb wildlife.** The mere presence of a dog can cause wild animals to flee, using up energy and exposing themselves to predators. Consider leaving pets at home. If you do bring a pet into the wilderness, do so only where permitted. Educate yourself on best practices for bringing your furry companion with you. In many areas, pets must be leashed at all times.

7. BE CONSIDERATE OF OTHER VISITORS

Most people go into the wilderness to experience untrammeled areas and a level of solitude. Mountaineers can contribute to the wilderness experience of others by camping away from them and using earth tones instead of more visible, "hot" colors for tents, packs, and clothing to reduce the sense of overcrowding. Respect the privacy of others, traveling through their space only if necessary, and keep voices and other sounds to a minimum.

Enjoy the sounds of the wilderness. Soon enough, climbers will return to their daily routine and urban sounds. Climbers may want to listen to music on long expeditions, but for most backcountry trips, audio devices can be distracting to you, and worse to others. Check with trip companions before taking any of these along. If you do, wear earphones. If you must make a summit call, find a space away from others.

THINK SMALL

Limit the size of the group. Outdoor trips are often social events, but keeping groups smaller enhances the sense of solitude for the party and other visitors. If local land managers have a party size limit, consider making your group even smaller. Climbers should ask themselves, "What is the minimum group size needed for safety?"

MINIMIZE CLIMBING IMPACTS

Climbers have a special obligation beyond the seven Leave No Trace principles. Simply put, implement anchoring fundamentals (see "Anchors" in Chapter 10, Belaying). Additional fixed-anchor best practices include these:

■ **Use natural-colored webbing at rappel points.**
■ **Don't leave webbing if it is not needed.** Remove excess, unsafe webbing left by other climbers when possible.

■ **Avoid setting up new, permanent fixed anchors and rappel points** or reinforcing existing ones, unless it is necessary for safety.

Leave the climbing environment as the party found it, as much as possible:

■ **Never chip holds or alter the rock structure** for climbing purposes. Rather than pushing loose rocks off on an alpine climb, try adjusting them to make them stable (except at popular sport-climbing crags, however, where it may be better to remove loose rocks because of the danger they pose in crowded areas).
■ **Leave plants on route whenever possible.** Clean new routes of vegetation only for safety, not aesthetics.
■ **Use as little chalk as possible.**
■ **Modern climbing ethics dictate limited use of pitons.** Use them only when modern clean climbing gear cannot be used, such as in certain winter conditions and on challenging aid-climbing objectives.
■ **Break down snow shelters** before you leave, to reduce visual impact and inadvertent safety hazards.

Learn about and respect the customs and culture of the area in which you are adventuring. Do not climb, and never bolt, near indigenous rock artwork. Here are some additional considerations regarding bolting:

■ **Bolts should be considered only when no other protection is possible** and when they are needed to provide a margin of safety. Consult local climbing norms and the local climbing community before deciding to place bolts.
■ **Follow the local practices and rules for bolting** at climbing crags. In one area, local climbers may use only camouflaged bolt hangers (painted so that they are not shiny); in another area, the bolting of new routes may be illegal.

RESPECT THE FREEDOM OF THE HILLS

Mountaineers do their part to protect and preserve the wild country they explore by applying Leave No Trace principles, using good judgment, and educating others. There is no more positive way to help ensure continued access, unfettered by restrictions and excessive rules and regulations. When climbers enter the backcountry, they are active stewards and contribute to the lasting protection of wild resources for themselves and future generations.

CHAPTER 8

ACCESS AND STEWARDSHIP

Perhaps because of their unique relationship with the mountains, climbers have long been at the forefront of protecting wild places around the globe. John Muir, a leading conservationist of the nineteenth century, was a climber, as was David Brower, a leading conservationist of the twentieth century. Nearly every powerful advocate and conservationist of the last century first connected with the outdoors through recreation.

The tradition of climbers working to protect wild places continues today. On every continent, climbers act as stewards of the mountains, taking on actions as small as packing out their own refuse and as large as fighting large-scale development that threatens the places mountaineers love.

Access and stewardship are intertwined. Access to outdoor experiences and places to climb, hike, and explore is the foundation of a stewardship ethic. Having meaningful outdoor experiences nurtures an inclination to protect these places as stewards, advocates, and conservationists. As more and more people turn to the mountains, stewardship becomes even more important for protecting these places, both today and into the future.

Stewardship, especially work to minimize the impact of recreation, ensures that climbers can continue to have access to the outdoors. Maintaining access to wild places depends on minimizing the actual and potential conflicts between mountaineers, other users, and the interests of those who manage the land. On public and private lands, recreation is often just one of many activities that take place. Land managers, who are often responsible for balancing the multiple uses and activities on public lands, sometimes must place restriction on outdoor exploration on the land where mountaineers climb. Although

practicing good stewardship should rightfully be considered the moral obligation of every climber, it is also the key to minimizing access conflicts.

LESS IMPACT, MORE ACCESS

Being aware of potential conditions that can affect access to climbing areas allows climbers to protect and enjoy recreational resources. Climbers are responsible for educating themselves about local customs, land rules and regulations, and any access restrictions where they wish to climb.

ENVIRONMENTAL IMPACTS

Stewardship starts with the natural environments that attract mountaineers in the first place. Alpine ecosystems are typically fragile and highly affected by humans. Vegetation is delicate and shallow-rooted. Human waste is particularly slow to decompose in the ice and rock zone, and it can become a problem on popular routes and at bivouac or camping areas. If a single climber fails to utilize Leave No Trace principles (see Chapter 7, Leave No Trace), the damage may be visible for months or years.

Cliff environments often have their own unique features. Cliffs may host nesting raptors, serve as home to bat

146

colonies, and support highly specialized (and sometimes very rare) plant communities. Because cliffs may create their own microclimates and provide conditions that are either drier or wetter than the surrounding area, the tops and bases of cliffs may feature plant and wildlife concentrations unique to an area. Climber impacts can occur both on the cliff faces themselves (through wildlife disturbance and passive or active devegetation) and at cliff tops and bottoms (often in the form of erosion and ground-cover loss associated with concentrated foot travel and group gatherings).

In addition to affecting the environment, these impacts can also lead to access restrictions. Recreation impacts can create conflicts with regulations that are intended to protect places, including laws to protect habitat for endangered species and rules about other user groups. Most land managers have acceptable levels of impacts, which can vary greatly depending on who manages the land. The same impacts that are acceptable in a park that is being managed for recreation may be unacceptable in an area managed specifically for habitat preservation.

To avoid such access problems, every climber should adhere to the principles discussed in Chapter 7, Leave No Trace. In practical terms, this means adjusting climbing practices in relation to whatever constitutes a "trace" where you are climbing. What constitutes a "trace" may be different at a popular roadside crag than at a remote alpine area. Climbers should strive to minimize their impacts everywhere, and go to even greater lengths in wilderness and environmentally sensitive areas. Become familiar with who or what agency manages chosen climbing destinations, and learn the rules that govern use of those areas.

CULTURAL IMPACTS

Local populations, including indigenous peoples and religious groups, often work to protect places based on the religious or historical significance attached to natural features. Oftentimes, tribes or local groups work together with recreation groups to protect an important place for its cultural and recreational value. At other times, the need to protect cultural values has conflicted with access for climbing.

The issues are complex when climbing intersects with religious beliefs that attach significance to a climbing objective. At a minimum, become knowledgeable of the local customs that may be harmed or affected when you are climbing at a new area, and make decisions based on cultural sensitivities and local land management practices and norms. For instance, good stewardship requires leaving artifacts and rock art (petroglyphs and pictographs) undisturbed.

I felt then that [this] was another special place. A place where climbers lived who cared for it, and knew it well enough to say that the yellow rock was more brittle than the red, or that there are hidden holds inside that crack, or that the number of condors is on the up, that the boulder in the next valley gives good shelter, or at what time exactly does the sun shine on that face of the mountain. Simple shared knowledge. That which we have of our home rocks.
—Paul Pritchard, *Deep Play*

AESTHETIC IMPACTS

The use of fixed gear such as bolts, in situ pitons, and rappel slings has been at the center of a number of access issues because of its aesthetic impact on natural places. When climbing has a visual impact on the outdoors, such as a high density of bolts on a cliff or rappel anchors that stand out at a distance, it can diminish the outdoor experience of climbers and nonclimbers alike. Another aesthetic impact to consider is the use of chalk by rock climbers where chalk residue on holds visually contrasts sharply with the surrounding rock or is not removed by weathering. Climbers can turn to the Access Fund, a nonprofit organization focused on climbing access and stewardship (see Resources for this chapter), for more information, background, and climbing-specific low-impact recreation skills.

We are entering a new era of climbing, an era that may well be characterized by incredible advances in equipment, by the overcoming of great difficulties, with even greater technological wizardry, and by the rendering of the mountains to a low, though democratic, mean.

Or it could be the start of more spiritual climbing, where we assault the mountains with less equipment and with more awareness, more experience and more courage.

—Yvon Chouinard, "Coonyard Mouths Off," *Ascent*

ACCESS FEES

Fees that apply to all recreational users can also affect climbing access. Access fees, climbing fees, and permit fees can create an economic barrier for some mountaineers. These fees, particularly in Asia, are sometimes used for stewardship by land management agencies, and sometimes they are chiefly governmental revenue devices.

HAVING A SAY IN ACCESS

As people who enjoy the outdoors, climbers and mountaineers have a responsibility to protect outdoor places and a stake in preserving access to them. There are a few important ways you can act to protect your outdoor experiences.

SPEAK UP AS A STAKEHOLDER

If climbers want to have a say about how to protect the places where they love to climb, one place to start is with federal land management agencies. Land management agencies—for example, the US National Park Service, Forest Service, and Bureau of Land Management—manage millions of acres of public lands on behalf of all citizens. On these lands, all citizens are stakeholders. These agencies employ public processes to gather input about management decisions. These public processes solicit feedback from stakeholders, including advocacy groups such as The Mountaineers, environmental organizations, local businesses, developers, and the wider public.

For instance, if climbers love visiting a local national forest, they can get involved in protecting their access to climbing there by participating in ongoing public processes or by contacting their local land managers. Since these agencies can be huge (sometimes with hundreds or thousands of employees that take care of millions of acres of land), it can sometimes be overwhelming to get involved. Many times, a local advocacy organization that works with these agencies can help climbers figure out the most effective way to share their voices.

SPEAK UP THROUGH A MEMBERSHIP GROUP

Membership organizations such as The Mountaineers, the Access Fund, the Alpine Club of Canada, the American Alpine Club, and the Outdoor Alliance are active in access issues, stewardship projects, and advocating for wild places. These membership organizations work hard to protect climbing access and can also introduce climbers to opportunities for sharing their voices with local and federal land managers. Membership in these organizations is important not just as a symbolic contribution to climbing access, but also because a membership organization is only as strong politically as the size of its membership. An organization with one hundred thousand members has more political weight than one with only several hundred members. When climbers join one of these groups, they are not just contributing financially to the organization's work; they are also loaning their voices so that this advocacy group has more power to protect the places and the climbing that matters to them.

These membership organizations influence policy in a number of ways and often share with members multiple opportunities to contribute to those efforts. They work with agencies that develop management plans for climbing and assist in tailoring site-specific closures to protect critical resources, such as seasonal restrictions for nesting raptors. They provide grants for land acquisition, trail building, trailhead maintenance, and other conservation projects, as well as scientific studies related to climbing impacts. Some local and regional climbing organizations have been formed at a number of climbing areas to address access issues close to home.

EXERT INFLUENCE AS A STEWARD

Small acts of stewardship matter greatly for protecting places and a climber's access to them. All climbers have the responsibility to minimize their impact on the natural environment and to practice Leave No Trace principles (see Chapter 7, Leave No Trace). If climbers love a place, they treat it with care and encourage others to do the same. Stewardship can be as simple as picking up someone else's litter, decaying slings, and abandoned fixed lines. For climbers with more time to dedicate, stewardship can also involve weekends spent on trail-building and revegetation projects. Membership organizations often offer opportunities for trail and site stewardship, as well as advocacy.

THE FUTURE OF MOUNTAINEERING

Mountaineers pursue unconfined exploration. And yet the future of mountaineering relies on all climbers taking care to mitigate their impacts and think of themselves as stewards of wild places. As more people continue to join the ranks of climbers, it is incumbent on all climbers to minimize their impacts and maximize their stewardship of shared lands and waters. By doing so, they and the generations of mountaineers who follow can continue to enjoy the experience of a new trail, a challenging climb, or a mountain summit—the freedom of the hills.

PART II

CLIMBING FUNDAMENTALS

CHAPTER 9

BASIC SAFETY SYSTEM

The climbing safety system protects you when the difficulty of a pitch or an unexpected occurrence—a slip or a collapsing snow bridge—causes you to fall.

The safety system is more than just a rope. It also includes the harness that attaches you to the rope, the knots and carabiners that join the various parts of the climbing system, and the loops of webbing (known as runners) used to connect the rope to rock, snow, or ice. This chapter provides an understanding of the mechanical components of the safety system and how to use them effectively and safely. Avoid using any critical climbing equipment if you are unfamiliar with its history. Secondhand equipment, whether found or passed along without an account of its use, increases the possibility of a weak link in the chain protecting the lives of you and your climbing partners.

ROPES

Nylon climbing ropes are lightweight and very strong, capable of bearing a load of more than two tons. They also have the remarkable quality of elasticity, which is the critical component in the rope's ability to protect a climber in a fall. Rather than bringing a falling climber to an abrupt, jolting stop, nylon ropes stretch and dynamically dissipate much of the energy generated by the fall, thereby reducing the forces associated with the fall.

Early nylon ropes were of "laid" or "twisted" construction. They were composed of many tiny nylon filaments bunched into three or four major strands that were then twisted together to form the rope. Gradually, twisted nylon ropes were replaced by kernmantle ropes designed specifically for climbing. Today's kernmantle ropes (fig. 9-1) are composed of a core of braided or parallel nylon filaments encased in a smooth, woven sheath of nylon. Kernmantle rope maintains the advantages of nylon but minimizes the problems associated with ropes constructed by twisting: stiffness, friction, and excessive elasticity. Kernmantle ropes are now the only climbing ropes approved by the International Climbing and Mountaineering Federation (Union Internationale des Associations d'Alpinisme, UIAA), the internationally recognized authority in setting standards for climbing equipment, and the European Committee on Standardization (Comité Européen de Normalisation, CEN, listed as "CE" on equipment labels), the European group responsible for creating and maintaining standards for all equipment, including climbing gear (fig. 9-2).

VARIETIES OF CLIMBING ROPE

Climbing ropes are available in a great variety of diameters, lengths, and characteristics. Any rope used for climbing should have the manufacturer's label, a UIAA or CEN rating, and specifications such as length, diameter, elongation or impact force, and fall rating. Rope measurements universally use the metric system; in this book, imperial units of measurement (inches, feet, and so on) are occasionally given in parentheses as well.

Dynamic. Kernmantle ropes designed for climbing are termed "dynamic" ropes. Dynamic ropes achieve low impact forces by stretching under the force of a fall. One of the most important considerations when looking at rope

DIAMETER	TYPE	COMMON USE
TABLE 9-1. SOME TYPICAL ROPES AND THEIR COMMON USES		
10.1–11 mm	Dynamic	Most durable single rope for rock and ice climbing (the workhorse)
9.5–10 mm	Dynamic	Moderate-weight single rope for rock and ice climbing (versatile)
8.9–9.4 mm	Dynamic	Lightweight single rope for rock and ice climbing and glacier travel
8–9 mm	Dynamic	Part of a double-rope system for rock and ice climbing or a lightweight single rope for simple glacier travel
7–8 mm	Dynamic	Part of a twin-rope system for rock and ice climbing
9–13 mm	Static	Fixed lines on expedition-style climbs, caving, or rescue and haul lines on big walls (not for lead climbing)

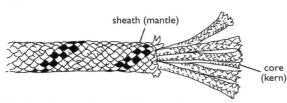

Fig. 9-1. Construction of a kernmantle rope.

Fig. 9-2. The logos of the two organizations that approve kernmantle ropes.

specifications is the impact force—generally, lower is better. Using a rope with a lower impact force means that a climber's fall will be stopped less abruptly (a "softer catch") and less force will be imparted onto the fallen climber, the belayer, and the anchor system.

Dynamic ropes come in a variety of diameters that are acceptable for technical climbing. Table 9-1 illustrates some typical ropes and their common uses. Smaller-diameter dynamic ropes (down to about 7 millimeters) are typically used in pairs as part of either a twin- or double-rope system (see Chapter 14, Leading on Rock). These small-diameter rope systems rely on the elastic properties of both ropes to protect the climber and must be used as a pair. The current trend in rope manufacturing—and, therefore, in rope use—is toward thinner and lighter ropes, but it is important to keep in mind that every rope is rated for certain intended uses, as indicated on the rope's label.

Dynamic ropes also come in a variety of lengths. Useful lengths range from 30 meters to 70 meters. Although 60 meters (200 feet) is the most common length for all-around

recreational climbing, a climber might want to choose a rope that is either shorter or longer, for a variety of reasons. Rope weight, the nature and length of the route, and the ability to rappel safely are some things to consider when selecting a rope's length.

Static. In contrast to dynamic ropes, static ropes, nylon slings, and cord stretch very little, and a fall of even a few feet on nondynamic materials such as these can generate impact forces severe enough to cause failure of the anchor system or severe injury to the climber.

Climbers use no-stretch or very low-stretch ropes for purposes other than protecting the lead climber, including cave exploring or rescue work, as fixed line on expedition-style climbs, or sometimes as the haul line, jug line, and rappel line during aid climbing. Although static ropes often are sold at climbing stores, these ropes should never be used for lead climbing, which requires the impact-absorbing qualities of a dynamic rope.

Colors of Ropes

Ropes are manufactured with different patterns and colors woven into the sheath. Some ropes have a few inches of contrasting color at the midpoint; bicolor ropes have a change in color or pattern at the midpoint to make it easy to find the middle of the rope and differentiate the ends. Others have distinctively colored ends so that it is easier for climbers to visually determine that the end of the rope is being reached while they are belaying or rappelling. If a climb calls for two ropes, it is useful to use different colors to assist climbers in distinguishing between the ropes. The UIAA warns against marking a rope with any substance that has not been specifically approved by the rope manufacturer.

Water-Repellent Ropes

Wet ropes, in addition to being unpleasant to handle and heavy to carry, can freeze and become very difficult to manage. Equally important, studies show that wet ropes hold fewer falls and have about 30 percent less strength than the same ropes when they are dry.

Rope manufacturers treat some of their ropes with either a silicone-based coating or a synthetic fluorine-containing resin coating (such as Teflon) to make them more water-repellent and therefore stronger in wet conditions. The "dry rope" treatment improves the abrasion resistance of the rope and also reduces friction of the rope as it runs through carabiners. Dry ropes usually cost about 15 percent more than untreated ropes.

PERFORMANCE TESTS

The UIAA and CEN test equipment to determine which gear meets their standards. Because climbing is a sport in which equipment failure can be fatal, it is wise to purchase equipment that has earned UIAA and/or CEN approval.

In its rope tests, the UIAA checks the strength of the single ropes used in most climbing—which generally measure between 8.9 and 11 millimeters in diameter—and also the thinner ropes used in double-rope climbing. To receive UIAA approval, a rope must survive a required minimum number of falls. The tests measure the impact force of the rope, which determines the stress of the fall on the climber's body and on the pieces of protection.

The UIAA also applies static tension tests to determine how much the ropes elongate under load. Approved ropes do not stretch by more than a specified percentage.

ROPE CARE

A rope protects your life and must be treated with care.

Preventing Damage to the Rope

Stepping on a rope can grind sharp particles into and through the sheath. Over time, the particles act like tiny knives that slice the rope's nylon filaments. Climbers wearing crampons must be doubly careful about keeping off the rope, because a misstep could damage the rope. Crampons may damage the core of a rope without leaving any visible gash on the sheath.

Protect the rope from contact with corrosive chemicals (especially acids) that might damage the rope. For example, parking lot surfaces or a car trunk or basement may harbor substances that could damage a rope.

Washing and Drying

Follow the manufacturer's recommendations for care. Most ropes should be washed frequently with tepid water and mild soap, although some manufacturers recommend

THE LIFE OF A ROPE

Following are some general guidelines to help climbers decide when to retire their ropes:

- A rope used daily should be retired within a year.
- A rope used on most weekends should give about two years of service.
- An occasionally used rope should be retired after about four years (nylon deteriorates over time).

against using petroleum-based or other detergents on water-repellent ropes. The rope's water-repellent finish can also be renewed with aftermarket products made for that purpose. A rope can be washed by hand in a bathtub or in a front-loading washing machine (ropes can get caught under the agitator in a top-loading machine). Rinse the rope several times in clean water and then hang it to dry, out of direct sunlight.

Storing

Before storing any rope, be sure it is completely dry. Remove all knots, coil the rope loosely (see "Coiling the Rope," below), and store it in a cool, dry area away from sunlight, heat, petroleum products, and corrosive chemicals such as acids.

Retiring a Rope

Examine a rope's sheath to get the best picture of the rope's overall condition. Inspect ropes frequently, particularly after a fall, to ensure that the sheath is clean, that there are no abraded or soft spots in the rope, and that the ends are properly fused and not fraying or unraveling. If a crampon wound, excessive abrasion, rockfall, or a sharp edge leaves the sheath looking tattered, the rope's integrity should be seriously questioned. If the core of the rope is visible, it is time to retire the rope.

It is harder to decide when to retire the rope if it does not contain any obvious soft spots or scars in the sheath. The rope's actual condition depends on many factors, including frequency of use, the care it has received, the number of falls it has endured, and how old it is.

After a severe fall, it may be wise to replace a rope, particularly if any segment of the rope feels mushy or flat. In deciding whether to retire the rope, consider the rope's history and other factors affecting its condition. The guidelines for rope replacement (see "The Life of a Rope" sidebar) assume that the rope is kept properly cleaned and stored.

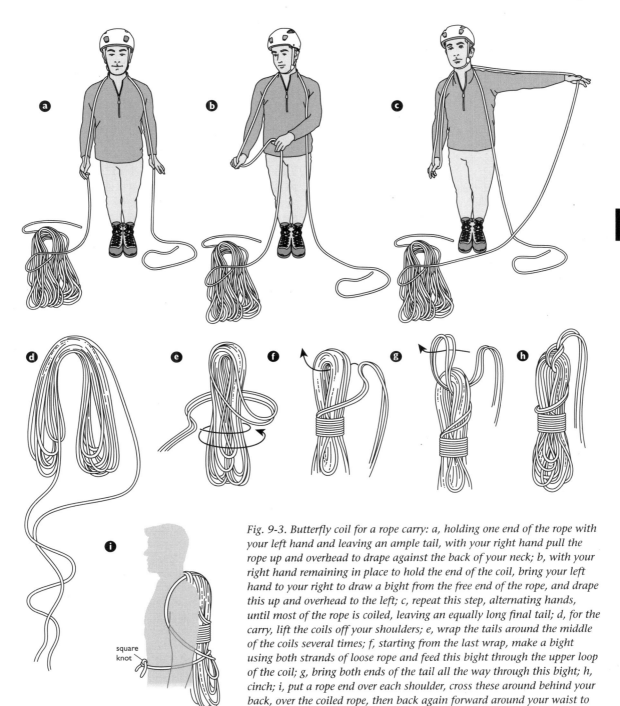

Fig. 9-3. Butterfly coil for a rope carry: a, holding one end of the rope with your left hand and leaving an ample tail, with your right hand pull the rope up and overhead to drape against the back of your neck; b, with your right hand remaining in place to hold the end of the coil, bring your left hand to your right to draw a bight from the free end of the rope, and drape this up and overhead to the left; c, repeat this step, alternating hands, until most of the rope is coiled, leaving an equally long final tail; d, for the carry, lift the coils off your shoulders; e, wrap the tails around the middle of the coils several times; f, starting from the last wrap, make a bight using both strands of loose rope and feed this bight through the upper loop of the coil; g, bring both ends of the tail all the way through this bight; h, cinch; i, put a rope end over each shoulder, cross these around behind your back, over the coiled rope, then back again forward around your waist to secure the load with a square knot.

square knot

COILING THE ROPE

For carrying or storing, the rope is normally coiled, most commonly in the butterfly coil. Once it is coiled, the rope can be tied snugly to your body if you are not wearing a pack. Below are steps to create a single butterfly coil using your arms as a measure and your neck and shoulders to rest the coils. The rope can also be coiled starting from the middle, coiling two strands at a time to form a double coil. While somewhat faster, this double coil is much more likely to tangle than the single butterfly coil, and is therefore not recommended.

Butterfly coil. Fast to create and easy to undo, a single butterfly coil does not kink the rope. To coil the rope, hold one end of the rope with your left hand, leaving an ample tail (two "wingspans" is a good guideline), and slide your right hand out along the rope, then lift the rope length created up and over your head and drape it against the back of your neck (fig. 9-3a). Next, bring your left hand to your right hand (fig. 9-3b) and use your free left thumb to pull a bight of the free end of the rope up and over your head while your right hand remains in place and holds the end of the coil (fig. 9-3c). Hold this coil in place while using your right hand this time to pull a new bight of rope to drape up and over your head. Continue alternating these moves from left to right, making and placing new coils until you reach the end of the rope, leaving a tail equal in length to the other tail. Shorten the last coil if necessary to adjust the tail. This will result in multiple coils in the shape of a horseshoe (fig. 9-3d).

To secure the horseshoe of coils, gather the two loose tail ends together and wrap them tightly and neatly around the middle of the coil several times (fig. 9-3e), avoiding twists. Bring a bight of the two loose ends through the loop at the top of the coil that is created by wrapping the coil's middle (fig. 9-3f), pulling enough of the tails through to form a good-sized loop. Then bring the rest of the loose tail ends through this good-sized loop (fig. 9-3g), drawing the loose ends all the way through (fig. 9-3h). To tie the butterfly coil to your body, place the coil against your back and draw one of the loose ends over each shoulder and around your back, crossing them over the coil and bringing them around your waist; tie them together in front (fig. 9-3i).

Flaking out the rope. It is important to uncoil the rope carefully before you use it, to minimize the chance of coils balling up into a tangle. Do not just drop the coils and start pulling on one end, which will create a tangled mess. Untie the cinch knot and then uncoil the rope, one loop at a time, into a pile, a procedure known as "flaking out the rope." Always flake out the rope before each belay to avoid twisting, knots, and tangles.

Rope bags or tarps. Alternatives to coiling the rope include using rope bags or tarps. Either can be used to protect a rope during transport. The unfolded rope bag or tarp also protects a rope from sand and grit on the ground. The bags and tarps add weight and cost, but for certain situations, such as cragging, they are worth it.

KNOTS, BENDS, AND HITCHES

Knots allow you to use the rope for many special purposes. Knots let you tie in to the rope, anchor to the mountain, tie two ropes together for long rappels, use slings to climb the rope itself, and much more. In common usage, the word "knot" is often used generically to refer to either a knot, a bend, or a hitch. But, properly speaking, they are different from each other. A *knot* refers to material tied on itself; a *bend* refers to a joining of material ends; a *hitch* refers to material tied around a solid object. In this book, the word "knot" is often used in its all-inclusive sense.

Climbers rely most heavily on a dozen or so basic knots, bends, and hitches. Practice these knots until tying them is second nature. Online sources such as the Animated Knots website and app (see Resources for this chapter) can be valuable resources for learning to tie these knots. Know that all knots weaken the rope, some more than others. In drop tests and pull tests, when a rope does break, it typically breaks at the knot. Table 9-2 shows the typical strength reduction of some knots. Some knots may be preferred over others because of their strength. Others may be chosen because they are easier to tie or are less likely to come apart in use.

Some terms and techniques are common to all knot tying, regardless of which knot is used. The end of the rope that is not being actively used is called the *standing end*; the other end is called the *loose end*. A 180-degree bend in the rope is called a *bight*; a *loop* is formed when the rope is curled around in 360 degrees so that both ends of the loop join or overlap. A *double knot* is a knot tied in a pair of ropes or in a doubled portion of one rope.

Regardless of what type of knot you tie, tie it neatly, keeping the separate strands of the knot parallel and free of twists. Tightly cinch every knot by pulling on each loose strand, and tie off loose ends with an overhand knot (see below). Always tie knots in perfect form so it becomes easy to recognize a properly tied knot. In the words of Colorado mountain guide and climber Michael Covington, "A good knot is a pretty knot." Develop the habit of routinely

KNOT	REDUCTION IN BREAKING STRENGTH	KNOT	REDUCTION IN BREAKING STRENGTH
TABLE 9-2. REDUCTION IN BREAKING STRENGTH OF A SINGLE KERNMANTLE ROPE AT THE KNOT (relative to an unknotted kernmantle rope)			
Bowline	26–45 %	Figure eight on a bight	23–34 %
Butterfly knot	28–39 %	Girth hitch	25–40 %
Clove hitch	25–40 %	Overhand loop	32–42 %
Double fisherman's bend	20–35 %	Square knot	53–57 %
Figure-eight bend	25–30 %	Water knot (ring bend)	30–40 %

Source: Clyde Soles, *The Outdoor Knots Book* (see Resources).

inspecting your own knots and those of your climbing partners, particularly before beginning a pitch or a rappel. As a general rule, keep knots away from points of greatest stress, sharp edges and corners, friction, and abrasion.

BASIC KNOTS

Basic knots are used for tying in to harnesses, for tying ropes together for rappel, for tying slings, and for anchoring and rescue procedures.

Overhand Knot

To tie an overhand knot, pass the loose end of the rope through a bight of rope (fig. 9-4a). The overhand knot is frequently used to secure loose rope ends after another knot has been tied. For instance, the overhand knot can be used to secure rope ends after tying a square knot (fig. 9-4b) or a rewoven figure eight (fig. 9-4c).

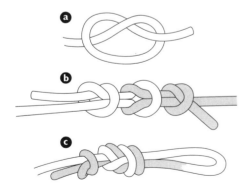

Fig. 9-4. Overhand knot: a, tying an overhand knot; b, overhand knots backing up both sides of a square knot; c, overhand knot backing up a rewoven figure eight.

Flat Overhand Bend (a.k.a. Offset Overhand Bend)

The flat overhand bend is tied using the loose ends of two ropes to set up a double-rope rappel (fig. 9-5a). Be sure to leave at least 12 to 18 inches of tail (fig. 9-5b) to prevent the knot from working itself loose. Compared with the double fisherman's bend (see below), this knot has a lower profile, and thus is less likely to be caught on edges, stuck in cracks, and tangled on trees when the rappel rope is retrieved.

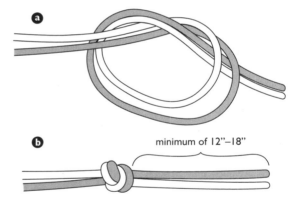

minimum of 12"–18"

Fig. 9-5. Flat overhand bend: a, tie an overhand knot in two strands of rope; b, pull all four strands tight.

Overhand Loop

The basic overhand loop is tied using a bight in the rope rather than a loose end (fig. 9-6). The overhand loop is often used for creating leg loops in accessory cord as part of the Texas prusik system (described in Chapter 18, Glacier Travel and Crevasse Rescue) or to make a loop in a doubled rope or a length of webbing.

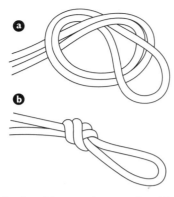

Fig. 9-6. Overhand loop: a, tie an overhand knot in a bight of rope or cord; b, dress and pull all strands tight.

Water Knot (Ring Bend)

The water knot, also known as the ring bend, is frequently used to tie the two ends of a length of tubular webbing (fig. 9-7a, b, and c) into a runner (see "Runners" later in this chapter). A water knot can work loose over time, so it is important to cinch the knot by pulling each of the four strands tight and to make the tails of the knot at least 2 to 3 inches (5 to 7.5 centimeters) long (fig. 9-7d). Check water knots often and retie any that have worked loose or that have short tails.

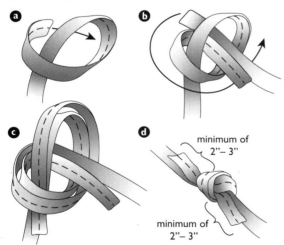

Fig. 9-7. Water knot (ring bend): a, draw a loose end through a bight of webbing; b, bring other loose end through the bight, around the first end, and under itself; c, draw ends well through knot so 2- to 3-inch tails extend; d, pull all four strands tight.

Square Knot

The square knot (fig. 9-8) can be used to join two ends of a rope together—for example, to secure the ends of the butterfly coil when it is carried on a climber's back (see Figure 9-3i).

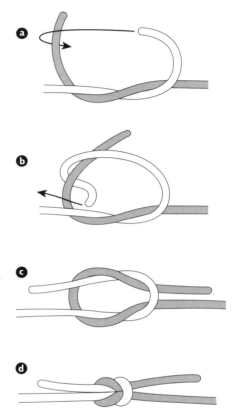

Fig. 9-8. Square knot: a, cross two loose ends over each other and bring one end up and around the other; b, bring end through the loop; c, dress all four strands; d, pull all four strands tight.

Fisherman's Bend

The fisherman's bend is used to join two ropes together. To tie it, overlap a loose end of each rope and tie each end in an overhand knot around the other rope's standing end (fig. 9-9). While no longer used for climbing, the single fisherman's bend is shown here to provide a clearer understanding of the double fisherman's bend. Note that the barrel knot is the fisherman's tied on a single strand; see Figure 11-13 in Chapter 11, Rappelling.

Fig. 9-9. Fisherman's bend: a, overlap a loose end of each rope, and tie each end in an overhand knot around other rope's standing end; b, pull all four strands tight.

Double Fisherman's Bend

The double fisherman's bend, also known as the grapevine knot, is used to join two ropes or both ends of a rope together. To tie it, overlap a loose end of each rope and pass each loose end twice around the other rope's standing end before pulling each end through both its two loops (fig. 9-10a) and then pulling both knots tight (fig. 9-10b). This is a very secure knot for tying the ends of two ropes together for a rappel or for tying secure loops in round cords. It is important to ensure that the two parts of this knot are symmetrical. This can be tested by checking that one side of the knot has four neat parallel strands of rope (fig. 9-10c) and that the other side has two Xs (the knot itself, see Figure 9-10b) neatly nested together.

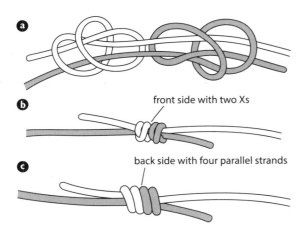

front side with two Xs

back side with four parallel strands

Fig. 9-10. Double fisherman's bend: a, pass each loose end twice around the other rope's standing end and then tie an overhand knot; b, pull all four strands tight; c, back side of correctly tied double fisherman's.

Triple Fisherman's Bend

This knot is similar to the double fisherman's bend (see Figure 9-10), but the loose end goes around the other rope's standing end three times instead of twice. The triple fisherman's bend is preferred when low-friction materials such as Spectra cord are joined together.

Figure Eight on a Bight

The figure eight on a bight (fig. 9-11) is a strong knot that can be tied rapidly. It is commonly used to back up a clove hitch attachment to an anchor in multipitch rock climbing or to tie in to the middle of a rope in glacier climbing.

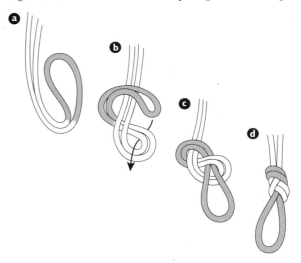

Fig. 9-11. Figure eight on a bight: a, bring a bight back parallel to the standing ends; b, bring bight under and then over the ends, forming an eight, then bring the bight down through the bottom loop of the eight; c, dress the strands; d, pull all four strands tight.

Rewoven Figure Eight

The rewoven figure eight is an excellent knot for tying the end of the rope in to a seat harness. The loose end of a figure eight (fig. 9-12a) is passed around the padded waist belt and leg loops and above the keeper strap, then rewoven (fig. 9-12b and c). The harness's keeper strap "keeps" the rope from slipping around or down a leg loop strap. Finish off the knot by tying an overhand knot in the loose end of the rope. Note that the overhand knot is just a way to keep the tail in place. It does not add security or safety to the knot. The tail of the knot needs to be about the same length as the knot itself to ensure the security of the knot.

9

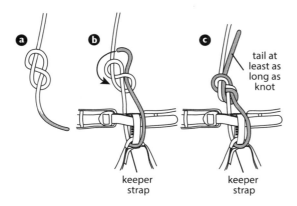

Fig. 9-12. Rewoven figure eight: a, tie a figure eight; b, double the loose end back and retrace the eight so the loose end is parallel to the standing end; c, pull both the ends of the loop and the end loop tight.

Figure-Eight Bend

The figure-eight bend may be used to join two ropes together for rappelling or to create a cordelette or equalette for building anchors (see Chapter 10, Belaying). Tie a figure eight in the loose end of one rope (fig. 9-13a). Use the loose end of the other rope to retrace the figure eight, going toward the standing end of the first rope (fig. 9-13b, c, and d). *Caution: Do not accidentally tie an offset figure-eight bend by matching the two loose ends side by side and tying a figure eight with the two strands; this is very dangerous to use for a rappel.* After being weighted, the figure-eight bend is easier to untie than the double fisherman's bend.

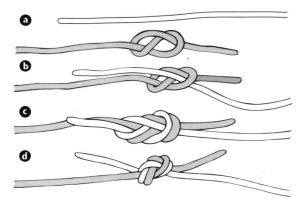

Fig. 9-13. Figure eight bend: a, tie a figure eight in the loose end of one rope; b and c, retrace the eight using the other rope's loose end; d, tighten all four strands.

Single Bowline

The single bowline makes a loop at the end of the climbing rope that will not slip, and it can secure the rope around a tree or other anchor. The loose end of the rope should come out on the inside of the bowline's loop (the rabbit goes up around the tree and back down the hole, fig. 9-14a and b). Tie off the loose end with an overhand knot (fig. 9-14c and d). This knot is easy to untie after it has been loaded, making it a good choice for a top-rope tie-in. Be aware that the bowline knot is not a secure knot. It tends to loosen when not under constant load; so make sure to leave a long tail when you tie the knot and frequently inspect it.

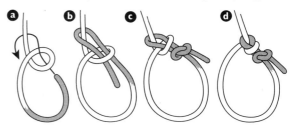

Fig. 9-14. Single bowline: a, make a loop and pass the loose end of the rope under and through it, then around the back of the standing end; b, bring the loose end back down through the loop; c, pull ends tight and tie an overhand knot; d, dressed and backed-up knot.

Single Bowline with a Yosemite Finish

The single bowline with a Yosemite finish, as popularized by Yosemite climbers, is started (fig. 9-15a) the same as a single bowline, but the loose end retraces the rope until it is parallel with the standing end (fig. 9-15b), avoiding the need to tie off the single bowline with an overhand knot (fig. 9-15c).

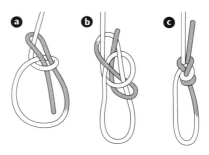

Fig. 9-15. Single bowline with a Yosemite finish: a, tie a single bowline, keeping the knot loose; b, bring the loose end under and over the rope and under the entire knot, then up through the bowline's topmost loop; c, pull all four strands tight.

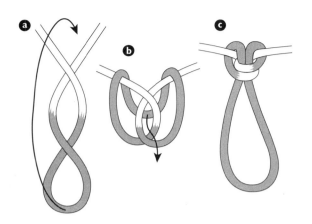

Fig. 9-16. *Butterfly knot: a, form a double loop; b, pull the lower loop over and then back down through upper loop; c, pull loop and both strands tight.*

Butterfly Knot

The butterfly knot is formed in the middle of a rope by making two loops (fig. 9-16a) and then pulling the endmost loop over and through the other loop (fig. 9-16b). The useful characteristic of the butterfly knot is that it can sustain a pull on either end of the rope or the loop (fig. 9-16c) and not come undone. A connection to this knot is made with a locking carabiner through the loop. It is commonly used to tie in to the middle of a rope for glacier climbing. The American Mountain Guides Association (AMGA) recommends using two locking carabiners, opposite and opposed, when using this knot to tie in to the middle of a rope.

Clove Hitch

The clove hitch, formed by making two loops side by side (fig. 9-17a) and then stacking one loop behind the other

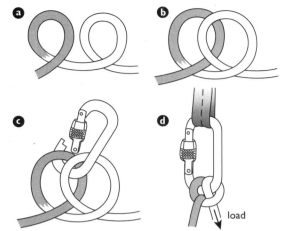

Fig. 9-17. *Clove hitch: a, form two identical loops, side by side; b, bring left-hand loop behind the other; c, clip a locking carabiner through both loops; d, pull both ends tight.*

(fig. 9-17b), is a quick knot for clipping in to a locking carabiner (fig. 9-17c) attached to an anchor (fig. 9-17d). The main advantage of the clove hitch is that the knot makes it easy to adjust the length of the rope between the belayer and the anchor without unclipping the rope from the carabiner. *Make sure to dress this knot by tightening both strands firmly. If the knot is correctly tied, it will stop the pull when loaded.*

Girth Hitch

The girth hitch (fig. 9-18a) is a simple knot that can serve a variety of purposes, such as attaching webbing or cord to a natural anchor or to a pack's haul loop (fig. 9-18b). It can also be used to tie off a short-driven piton (see Figure 13-9 in Chapter 13, Rock Protection).

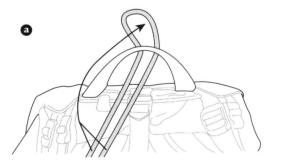

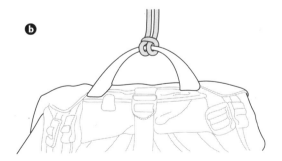

Fig. 9-18. *Girth-hitch: a, reach a bight behind or around an object and pull both ends of webbing or cord through the bight; b, dressed webbing or cord girth-hitched around a pack's haul loop.*

Overhand Slipknot

The overhand slipknot is another simple knot, formed by making a loop (fig. 9-19a), then bringing a bight up through the loop and drawing it closed to tie off the bight (fig. 9-19b). This knot may be used to attach a tie-off loop (see "Runners" below) or one end of a personal anchor (see "Personal Anchors" below) to a carabiner. The overhand slipknot has the added benefit of immobilizing a runner's knot or sewn bar tacks on the carabiner (fig. 9-19c). Like the girth hitch, it can also be used to cinch a runner to a rock feature or to tie off a short-driven piton.

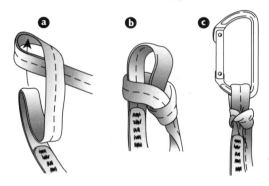

Fig. 9-19. Overhand slipknot: a, make a loop, then bring a bight up through the loop; b, draw loop closed to tie off bight; c, clip bight into a carabiner and pull both ends tight.

Mule Knot

The mule knot is used to temporarily free the belayer's hand and also is a useful temporary tie-off when stopping during a rappel. In an emergency, it can be used to tie off a belay to a fallen climber so that both hands may be safely used to set up an anchor and/or free the belayer from the climbing rope (see "Escaping the Belay" in Chapter 10, Belaying).

When used with a belay device, this knot is called a *device-mule*. While holding your braking hand back in the brake position, start by pulling a bight of rope through the locking carabiner on your harness using your free hand (fig. 9-20a); continue to hold the brake with your other hand. Pull the bight behind the loaded strand of rope going to the fallen climber and twist it to form a loop, then fold another bight of rope over the loaded strand and push it through the loop (fig. 9-20b). Remove any slack and pull the knot tight by pulling on the upper strand (fig. 9-20c); back up the device-mule with an overhand knot tied around the loaded strand (fig. 9-20d).

When using a munter hitch belay (this hitch is described below), the mule knot is called a *munter-mule*. Hold the fallen climber with your braking hand and make a loop in the rope on the same side as your braking hand. With your free hand, pull some slack rope behind the loaded strand of rope going to the climber and make a bight (fig. 9-21a). Fold the bight over the rope and push it through the loop, then

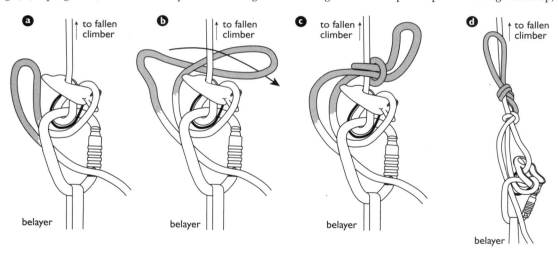

Fig. 9-20. Mule knot with belay device (device-mule): a, pull a bight of rope through the locking carabiner; b, pull the bight behind the loaded strand and form a loop, then fold another bight over the front of the loaded strand and push it through the loop; c, remove slack and tighten knot by pulling on the upper strand; d, back up with an overhand knot tied around the loaded strand, pulling on the lower strand if more rope is needed.

tighten the knot by pulling on the upper strand (fig. 9-21b). Pull additional slack through the mule knot as needed by pulling on the lower strand; back up the munter-mule with an overhand knot around the climbing rope (fig. 9-21c).

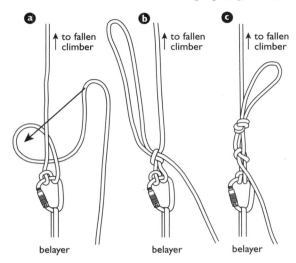

Fig. 9-21. Mule knot with munter hitch (munter-mule): a, make a loop under the loaded strand, then take a bight and fold it around the loaded strand and through the loop; b, tighten the knot by pulling on the upper strand; c, back up with an overhand knot around the loaded strand, pulling on the lower strand if more rope is needed.

FRICTION HITCHES

Friction hitches are a quick and simple way to set up a system for ascending or descending a climbing rope without the use of mechanical ascenders or for backing up a rappel. Hitches grip the climbing rope when weight is placed on them but are free to move when the weight is released. The best-known friction hitch is the prusik, but others, such as the bachmann, the klemheist, and the autoblock, are also useful.

Prusik Hitch

For the prusik hitch, an accessory cord loop is attached to the climbing rope via a girth hitch (fig. 9-22a), followed by a few additional wraps around the climbing rope (fig. 9-22b and c). For use on a climbing rope, a tie-off loop of 5- to 7-millimeter accessory cord, for example, is wrapped twice (fig. 9-22d) or three times (fig. 9-22e) around the rope. Icy ropes, thinner-diameter ropes, or heavy loads require more wraps of the hitch to ensure sufficient friction to hold the load.

To create the necessary friction, the cord must be smaller in diameter than the climbing rope; the greater the difference in diameter, the better the hitch grips. However, very small-diameter cords make the prusik hitch more difficult to manipulate than do cords of larger diameter. Experiment to see which diameter of cord works best. Webbing is not usually used for prusik hitches because it provides less friction than cord.

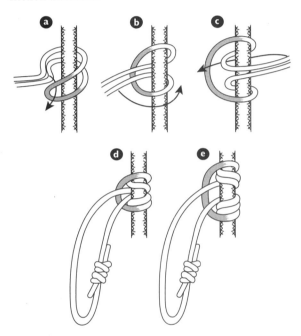

Fig. 9-22. Prusik hitch: a, girth-hitch cord around rope; b, bring loose ends of cord around rope and under cord; c, wrap loose ends around rope again; d, two-wrap prusik hitch; e, three-wrap prusik hitch.

By attaching two cords to a climbing rope with prusik hitches, you can ascend or descend the climbing rope. Chapter 18, Glacier Travel and Crevasse Rescue, explains the Texas prusik method of ascending the rope using prusiks. The prusik hitch is also used as part of the rescue systems needed to raise and lower people and equipment during rescues, and to pass safety knots in the rope. These systems are also described in Chapters 18 and 25, Alpine Rescue.

Bachmann Hitch

The bachmann hitch is used for the same purposes as a prusik hitch. The bachmann hitch is tied around a carabiner and the climbing rope (fig. 9-23), which makes the bachmann much easier to loosen and slide than a prusik. The bachmann hitch has the virtue of sometimes being "self-tending" (it will feed rope in the non-load-bearing direction without requiring you to actively manipulate it).

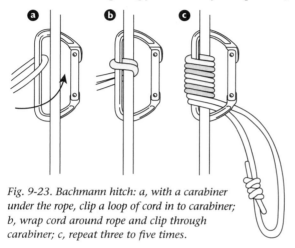

Fig. 9-23. Bachmann hitch: a, with a carabiner under the rope, clip a loop of cord in to carabiner; b, wrap cord around rope and clip through carabiner; c, repeat three to five times.

Klemheist Hitch

The klemheist hitch is another alternative to the prusik, with the advantage that it can be made from either accessory cord or webbing, which may become important if you are caught with an ample supply of webbing but little cord. A tied loop of cord or webbing is wound around the main rope in a spiral and then threaded through the loop created by the top wrap of the cord or webbing (fig. 9-24a). Pull down to create the basic klemheist (fig. 9-24b), which can be clipped to a carabiner (fig. 9-24c). The tied-off klemheist (fig. 9-24d) is less likely to jam and easier to loosen and slide than the basic klemheist. The klemheist can also be tied around a carabiner (fig. 9-24e), which provides a good handhold for sliding the knot along the rope.

Autoblock Hitch

The autoblock hitch is similar to the klemheist. In general, the autoblock is easier than the prusik to release once it has been loaded, but it doesn't provide as much friction. It is meant to simulate the grip of a hand rather than support full body weight. The autoblock hitch is tied using a short loop of cord or webbing. When using it for self-belay when rappelling with extension, wrap the cord three or more times around the rope to provide friction (fig. 9-25a–c), and then clip both ends into a carabiner attached to the belay

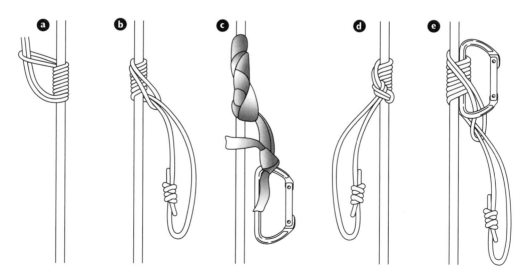

Fig. 9-24. Klemheist hitch: a, wrap a loop of cord around the rope five times and draw loose ends through the end loop; b, pull ends down; c, klemheist hitch tied using webbing and clipped to a carabiner; d, klemheist hitch tied off—bring ends up, then under and over the loop, forming a new loop, and then down through this loop, pulling the ends tight; e, klemheist tied around a carabiner.

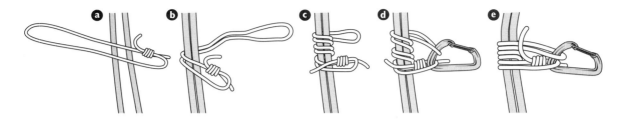

Fig. 9-25. Autoblock hitch: a, lay a loop of cord, tied with a double fisherman's bend near one end, perpendicular to the climbing rope; b, wrap the cord around the rope; c, wrap three times; d, clip both ends of the cord to a carabiner; e, dress the knot, making sure there are no twists or overlapping strands and that the double fisherman's bend is neither in the wrap nor squarely on the carabiner.

9

loop of the harness (fig. 9-25d and e). For rappelling without extension, the carabiner should be attached to a leg loop instead. If using the rappel extension, then both ends of the autoblock would be clipped directly in to the harness carabiner (see Figure 11-21 in Chapter 11, Rappelling).

Munter Hitch

The munter hitch (originally dubbed the *halbmastwurf sicherung*, meaning "half clove-hitch belay," abbreviated as HMS) is very easy to set up and use, but it feeds rope effectively only if used on a "pear-shaped" HMS locking carabiner (pearabiner)—that is, a carabiner large enough at its wider end to accommodate multiple turns of the rope. The munter is a simple hitch in the rope that is clipped in to an HMS carabiner (fig. 9-26a and b) to create friction (fig. 9-26c).

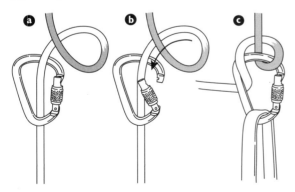

Fig. 9-26. Munter hitch: a, draw rope up through carabiner and form a loop; b, clip carabiner through loop; c, pull ends in opposite directions.

The munter hitch is an excellent method of belaying a leader or lowering a climber, because the hitch is reversible (the rope can be fed out of the carabiner, or the rope can be pulled back in through the carabiner) and the knot provides sufficient friction for the belayer to stop a falling or lowering climber by holding the braking end of the rope. The munter hitch can also be used for rappelling, though it puts more twist in the rope than other rappel methods. Even if you prefer to use a specialized belay device, this hitch is worth knowing as a backup if you lose or forget your belay device.

HELMETS

Climbing helmets help protect your head from rockfall and from gear dropped by climbers above you. Helmets also protect you from the many ways in which you can suddenly hit hard surfaces such as rock or ice: a fall to the ground, a leader fall that swings you into a wall, or a quick move upward against a sharp outcropping. However, keep in mind that no helmet can protect you from all possible impacts.

Modern climbing helmets are lightweight, ventilated, and available in many designs. Buy a climbing helmet with UIAA and/or CEN certification, which ensures minimum standards of impact resistance.

Hardshell helmets. Also called suspension or hybrid helmets, hardshell helmets (fig. 9-27a) have a thick, hard outer shell, usually ABS plastic, covering a small bit of polystyrene foam combined with a suspension system. The ABS shell is very durable and resistant to dings. Hardshell helmets are suitable for all styles of climbing, including ice, alpine rock, and aid climbing.

Lightweight foam helmets. Constructed primarily of polystyrene covered in a thin polycarbonate shell (or in rare cases, foam covered with no shell at all), lightweight foam helmets (fig. 9-27b) dissipate impact forces via deformation. These helmets are typically lighter and more ventilated than hardshell helmets. Because they lack an outer shell, lightweight foam helmets are not as long lasting, need to be handled more carefully, and may need to be replaced more often. For these reasons, they are probably better suited for experienced climbers.

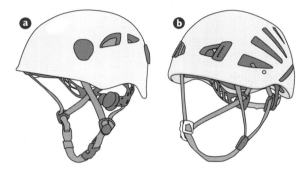

Fig. 9-27. Climbing helmets: a, hardshell helmet; b, lightweight foam helmet.

How to choose a helmet. Before picking out a helmet, consider the type of climbing you plan to do. For example, helmets with large air vents add comfort on hot days but do not protect as well against smaller rocks or other projectiles. Most helmets have clips for headlamps (fig. 9-27b), but check for this feature. Because normal skull shapes and sizes vary, fit is individual. Try on many different styles and brands. Choose a helmet that fits well and that can be adjusted to fit whether you are bareheaded or wearing a hat or balaclava. To protect your forehead and frontal lobe, make sure to wear the helmet so it is riding forward (fig. 9-28a), not tipping back (fig. 9-28b).

When to replace a helmet. Climbing helmets have a limited life span. Even with minimal use, they should be retired no later than 10 years after the date of manufacture (stamped on some brands), and frequent climbers may want to cut this time in half. Even with ultraviolet radiation inhibitors, the plastics in helmets are vulnerable to sunlight and weaken with exposure; helmets can be damaged and not show obvious wear and tear. Retire a helmet when it is obviously dented, cracked, or damaged or the straps are worn or torn. It is recommended that a helmet be replaced as soon as possible after a significant impact: any

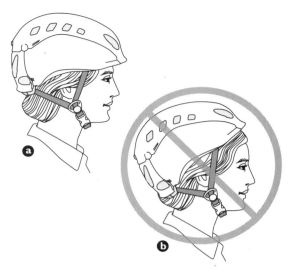

Fig. 9-28. Wearing a helmet: a, properly adjusted; b, adjusted incorrectly, leaving forehead exposed to rockfall and icefall.

time you take a hard hit and think to yourself, "I would have been seriously hurt if not for my helmet," the helmet has done its job and it is time to get a new one.

To maximize the life of your helmet, protect it from banging against hard surfaces when not on your head, which makes it vulnerable to chipping and cracking. Follow manufacturers' recommendations for storage, which for helmets includes avoiding leaving them under a window or in the trunk of a car. Follow these steps each time before storing your helmet:

- Test to see that the chin buckle and adjustment hardware are in good working order.
- Check whether the suspension or other webbing is in good shape and free of frays and tears.
- Make sure any foam casing is secure, and that all components are free of cracks and dents. Minor dings are okay; major dents are not.

HARNESSES

In the early days of climbing, the climbing rope was looped around a climber's waist several times and then the waist loop was tied in to the rope with a bowline on a coil. That practice is no longer considered safe because long falls onto waist loops can severely injure a climber's back and ribs. Additionally, falls that leave the climber hanging, such as a fall into a crevasse or over the lip of an overhang, could cause the rope to ride up and constrict the climber's diaphragm, leading to suffocation. Improvising leg loops and attaching them to the whole coil can help prevent injury, but the bowline on a coil is best avoided except for emergencies.

Today, climbers connect to the rope using a harness designed to distribute the force of a fall over a larger percentage of the climber's body. A climber at either end of a climbing rope ties in to the harness with a knot such as the rewoven figure eight (see Figure 9-12) or a single bowline with a Yosemite finish (see Figure 9-15). A climber in the middle of a rope usually ties in to the harness with a butterfly knot (see Figure 9-16) or a figure eight on a bight (see Figure 9-11).

Harnesses deteriorate over time; they should be inspected often and replaced with the same frequency as a climbing rope. The bowline on a coil remains an option for emergency use if no harness or harness material is available, but an improvised diaper sling (see below) would be a better choice.

SEAT HARNESSES

With properly fitted leg loops, a seat harness rides snugly above your hip bones yet transfers the force of a fall over your entire pelvis. It also provides a comfortable seat during rappelling. Throughout this book, when not otherwise specified, "harness" refers to a seat harness.

Manufactured Seat Harness

Several features are particularly desirable in a mountaineering seat harness (fig. 9-29). Adjustable leg loops maintain a snug fit no matter how few or how many layers of clothing you are wearing. Padding on the waist belt and leg loops can provide additional comfort, particularly if you will be hanging for any length of time, although padding adds to the bulk and weight of the harness. Leg loops that can be unbuckled or unclipped from the backside of the harness permit toilet calls without your having to remove the harness or untie from the rope. A belay loop can make it easier to attach a belay device for belaying or rappelling, while having the waist buckle located toward one side helps avoid conflict with the rope tie-in or with the locking carabiner that you attach to the harness for use in belaying and rappelling in the absence of a belay loop. Gear loops are desirable for carrying carabiners and other pieces of climbing gear.

Before buying a harness, try it on to be sure the harness fits properly over your climbing clothes. With the profusion of harness styles on the market, you must consult

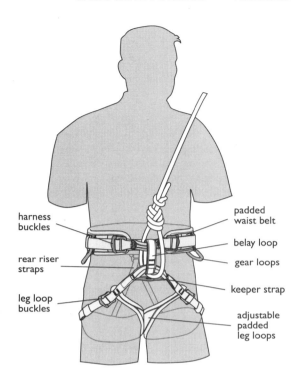

Fig. 9-29. Seat harness with common features.

each manufacturer's instructions to learn how to safely wear and tie in to that particular harness. Printed instructions accompany any new harness, and they also are usually sewn inside the waist belt. For some harnesses, you must pass the waist strap back over and through the main buckle a second time for safety (on these models, you must usually do the same for the leg loop straps and buckles). Be sure at least 2 to 3 inches (about 5 centimeters) of strap extends beyond the buckle after you reweave the strap.

Diaper Sling

In an emergency, a diaper sling may be improvised as a seat harness. The diaper sling takes about 10 feet (3 meters) of webbing tied in a large loop. With the loop behind your back, pull each end around your sides to your stomach (fig. 9-30a). Bring one piece of the webbing loop down from behind your back and between your legs, then up to your stomach to meet the other two loop ends (fig. 9-30b). Clip them together in front with two opposite and opposed carabiners (see Figure 9-37a) or a locking carabiner (fig. 9-30c). The diaper sling may also be clipped to a safety loop made of webbing tied around your waist.

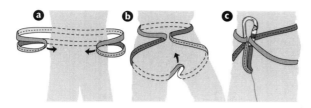

Fig. 9-30. Diaper sling: a, bring large loop around waist from the back; b, bring one piece of loop behind back down through the legs and up; c, clip all three parts together with a locking carabiner (shown here) or two opposite and opposed carabiners.

A description of how to build a homemade seat harness can be found in a book for professional rescuers: *Technical Rescue Riggers Guide*, by Rick Lipke (see Resources). The homemade seat harness is not a substitute for the effective reliability of a modern commercial seat harness, but the knowledge of how to build one could be useful in an emergency if the requisite amount of tubular webbing is available.

Personal Anchors

On multipitch alpine rock climbs, most climbers use the climbing rope itself to tie in to the anchor (see "Tying In to the Anchor" in Chapter 10, Belaying). Nevertheless, it is sometimes necessary to use a personal anchor or leash to attach yourself to belay and rappel anchors while you set up and tear down the belay, the rappel, and/or the anchor. Use a runner, usually double-length (see "Runners" below), and girth-hitch one end to the seat harness, following the same path with the runner as you would to tie the climbing rope to your harness. Add a locking carabiner to the other end of the runner for connecting to the anchor.

When not in use, the personal anchor can be wrapped around your waist and clipped to the seat harness or otherwise neatly stowed on the seat harness. Commercial personal anchors are available that are made of a series of full-strength loops, so the system can be shortened and lengthened.

Daisy chains are sometimes used as personal anchors, but they are dangerous if used incorrectly. They are made for aid climbing (see Chapter 15, Aid and Big Wall Climbing), and the stitches of the sewn links are rated for body weight only. If a climber cross-clips only a sewn link (that is, clips in to the anchor through two loops of the daisy chain), a fall can break the relatively weak bar tacks separating the loops and completely detach the climber from the anchor. The result can be catastrophic failure.

CHEST HARNESS

A chest harness helps keep a climber upright after a fall or while ascending a rope using prusiks or mechanical ascenders. Following a fall, simply clip the climbing rope through the carabiner of the chest harness, which provides stability and assists you in staying upright. The chest harness will deliver some of the force of a fall to your chest, which is more easily injured than your pelvis (where the force is directed by a seat harness). Thus, a rope is not usually clipped in to the chest harness during rock climbing or general mountaineering. Some snow or glacier climbers travel with the rope passing up through a carabiner on the chest harness, but this is not recommended, because if the climber must arrest and hold a fall, the force will come high on the body and could spin the climber out of arrest position. It is therefore preferable to leave the rope unclipped until a crevasse fall actually occurs (see Chapter 18, Glacier Travel and Crevasse Rescue). The chest harness is also useful when rappelling with a heavy backpack to help the climber stay upright.

A chest harness may be purchased or is readily improvised with a long loop of webbing (a long runner). One popular design depends on a carabiner to bring the ends of the harness together at your chest. To make a carabiner chest harness, start with 9.5 feet (2.9 meters) of $9/16$-inch or 1-inch tubular webbing. Use a distinctive color of webbing to distinguish the chest harness from other double-length runners (see "Runners" below). Tie the webbing into a loop with a water knot; adjust the size of the webbing loop to fit comfortably. Give the loop a half twist to create two temporary loops, and push one arm all the way

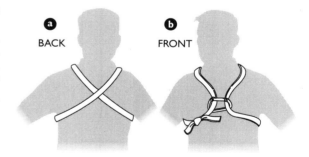

Fig. 9-31. Carabiner chest harness: Using a loop of webbing made with a water knot, twist the loop and put your arms in the two new loops; a, lift the runner over your head and let the crossed portion drop against your back; b, clip a carabiner through the two front sides.

through each loop. Lift the runner over your head and let it drop against your back, with the crossed portion at your back (fig. 9-31a); then pull the two sides together in front and clip with a carabiner at your chest (fig. 9-31b). Keep the knot in front of you and out of the way of the carabiner.

FULL-BODY HARNESS

Full-body harnesses, which incorporate both a seat harness and a chest harness, have a higher tie-in point (fig. 9-32). This reduces the chance of your flipping over backward during a fall. Because a body harness distributes the force of a fall throughout the trunk of your body, there may be less danger of lower-back injury.

Although in some circumstances body harnesses may be safer, they have not found popular favor in mountaineering. They are not recommended for glacier travel for the reason mentioned above: if a climber must arrest to hold a fall, the force will come high on the body and could spin the climber out of arrest position. Body harnesses are more expensive, more restrictive of movement, and make it hard to add or remove clothing. Instead, most climbers use a

Fig. 9-32. Full-body harness.

seat harness and then improvise a chest harness when one is warranted, such as when climbing with a heavy pack, crossing glaciers, or aid climbing under large overhangs. However, full-body harnesses are necessary for children whose hips are not yet fully developed, because they could slide out of the seat harness if they become inverted. Full-body harnesses are also recommended for pregnant women, a decision which a climber should make in consultation with her physician.

RUNNERS

Loops of tubular webbing or round accessory cord, called *runners* or *slings*, are among the simplest pieces of climbing equipment and among the most useful. (Note that flat webbing differs from tubular webbing: flat webbing is used for things like pack straps, while tubular webbing—so-called even though it lies flat—is used in climbing-specific applications.) Runners are a critical link in climbing systems. Standard single runners require 5 feet (1.5 meters) of webbing or cord. Double-length runners require 9 feet (2.7 meters) of webbing or cord. Triple-length runners require 13 feet (3.9 meters) of webbing or cord. After being sewn or tied into loops, the standard lengths become 2 feet (0.6 meter), 4 feet (1.2 meters), and 6 feet (1.8 meters) for single-, double-, and triple-length runners, respectively. A beginning climber should own many single runners and a few doubles.

To help you quickly identify the different lengths, it is useful to use single runners of one color of webbing, double runners of another color, and triple runners of a third color. For a tied webbing runner, it is useful to write your initials and the date the runner was made on one of the tails of the water knot. Identifying the runner and its age helps in deciding when to retire it. Runners should be retired regularly, using the same considerations as for retiring a rope or harness (see those sections above).

It is very important to remember that webbing and accessory cord do not have dynamic characteristics. If they are used without a dynamic rope, a fall of even a few feet can impart catastrophic force onto the anchor system and climber (see "Limiting Impact Force with Dynamic Rope" in Chapter 10, Belaying).

Sewn. High-strength, presewn runners (fig. 9-33a) can be purchased at climbing stores. Sewn runners come in various lengths: 4-inch (10-centimeter), 6-inch (15-centimeter), 12-inch (30-centimeter, called half-length), 2-foot (0.6-meter, called single-length), 4-foot (1.2-meter, called double-length), and 6-foot (1.8-meter, called triple-length), as well

9

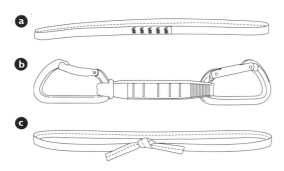

Fig. 9-33. Runners made of webbing: a, sewn runner; b, sewn quickdraw; c, tied runner.

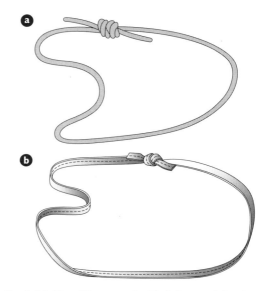

Fig. 9-34. Tie-off loops: a, double fisherman's bend in cord; b, water knot in webbing.

as in sizes between the standard half-, single-, double-, and triple-length runners. Some runners are specially sewn into preformed *quickdraws*, which are typically 4 to 8 inches (10 to 20 centimeters) long, and have carabiners attached at each end (fig. 9-33b). Sewn runners also come in a variety of widths, with $^5/_{16}$-, $^3/_8$-, $^9/_{16}$-, $^{11}/_{16}$-, and 1-inch (8-, 10-, 14-, 17-, and 25-millimeter) widths the most common.

Runners are often made from Dyneema and Spectra, high-performance polyethylene fibers that are stronger, more durable, and less susceptible to ultraviolet deterioration than nylon. However, these materials have a lower melting temperature and provide less friction than nylon, which can affect their use in friction hitches. Sewn runners are generally stronger, usually lighter, and less bulky than tied runners. Using a sewn runner also eliminates the possibility of the knot coming untied, a concern with tied runners.

Tied. Runners can be made by tying a loop in $^9/_{16}$- to 1-inch tubular webbing or in 7- to 9-millimeter Perlon accessory cord. A webbing runner is usually tied with a water knot (see Figure 9-7) to make the loop (fig. 9-33c). Avoid putting twists into the runner while tying it. A cord runner is typically tied with either a double fisherman's bend (see Figure 9-10) or a triple fisherman's bend, required for Spectra or aramid fiber (Kevlar) cord. Tails on tied runners should be 2 to 3 inches (5 to 7.5 centimeters) long. If the webbing or cord is cut to make the runner, the ends must be melted with a small flame to keep the ends from unraveling.

While bulkier and heavier, tied runners do have several advantages over commercially sewn runners. Tied runners are inexpensive to make, can be untied and threaded around trees and natural chockstones (rocks firmly lodged in cracks), and can be untied and retied with another runner to create longer runners.

Tie-off loops. Also called *hero loops*, tie-off loops are short runners usually made of 5- to 8-millimeter cord tied into a loop (fig. 9-34a), although a loop of webbing can be used in a pinch (fig. 9-34b). The length of the loop depends on its intended use. They are commonly used for escaping belays (see Chapter 10, Belaying), for self-belay during a rappel (see Chapter 11, Rappelling), for aid climbing (see Chapter 15, Aid and Big Wall Climbing), and for attaching the anchor to the rope in crevasse rescue (see "Crevasse Rescue Response" in Chapter 18, Glacier Travel and Crevasse Rescue).

Load-limiting runners. A climber can effectively limit the maximum impact on individual protection placements by using a load-limiting device (such as the Yates Gear Screamer). A load-limiting runner consists of a sewn runner with a series of weaker bar tacks (fig. 9-35a), usually encased in a sheath (fig. 9-35b); the bar tacks fail at a specific impact force, which reduces high loads, while the runner retains full strength if fully extended (fig. 9-35c shows the runner partially extended).

CARABINERS

Carabiners are another versatile and indispensable climbing tool used for belaying, rappelling, prusiking, clipping in to anchors, securing the rope to points of protection, and numerous other tasks. All modern carabiners are

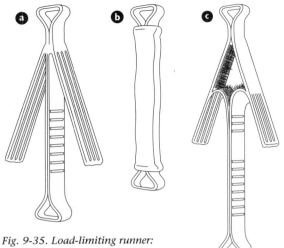

Fig. 9-35. Load-limiting runner:
a, constructed with a sewn loop on both ends for clipping to protection; b, usually enclosed in a sheath that reduces abrasion and makes the unit more compact; c, when partially deployed, and even if all the load-limiting bar tacks fail, the runner still retains its full strength and integrity as a closed loop.

marked with the "working load limit," that is, the force at which the carabiner will fail. At a minimum, a CEN-certified carabiner should have a working load limit of 20 kilonewtons closed gate strength and 7 kilonewtons open gate and minor axis strength. This means that the carabiner should be able to withstand the force of up to a 20-kilonewton pull when its gate is closed—a substantial safety margin over the forces generated by a fallen climber (see "Understanding Fall Factors" in Chapter 10, Belaying).

SHAPES AND STYLES

Carabiners come in many sizes and shapes. Ovals (fig. 9-36a) were once very popular for general mountaineering because their symmetry makes them good for many purposes. D carabiners (fig. 9-36b) also offer a good general-purpose shape, plus they are stronger than ovals with the same amount of metal because more of the load is transferred to the long axis and away from the gate, the typical point of failure for a carabiner. Offset Ds (fig. 9-36c) have the strength advantage of standard Ds, but the offset D's gate opens wider, making it easier to clip in awkward situations. Bent-gate carabiners (fig. 9-36d) facilitate clipping and allow climbers to quickly clip and unclip the

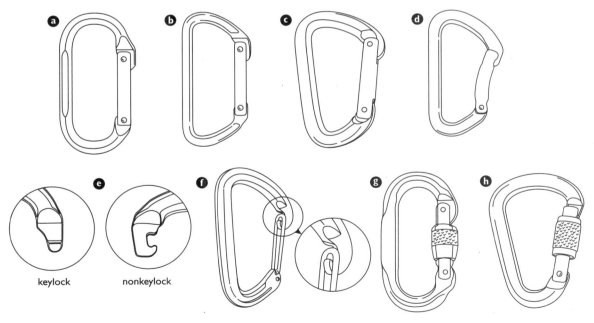

Fig. 9-36. Carabiners: *a, oval carabiner; b, standard D carabiner; c, offset D carabiner; d, bent-gate carabiner; e, detail of a keylock latch; f, wire-gate carabiner with detail of nonkeylock latch; g, standard locking carabiner; h, pear-shaped HMS locking carabiner (pearabiner).*

carabiners by the feel of the gates alone; bent-gate carabiners are often used in quickdraws to attach to the rope and bolt hangers for sport climbing.

Traditionally, the gate of a carabiner connects to the rest of the frame through a latch that creates a hook toward the inside of the carabiner. Because this latch's hook can interfere with unclipping ropes or slings, several models of carabiner now use a keylock connection that doesn't use a hook (fig. 9-36e).

With a trend toward lighter and stronger gear, wire-gate carabiners have become very common (fig. 9-36f). They provide a strong gate at a reduced weight, and they are less prone to freezing shut or having their clipping action become sticky. Some studies also indicate that wire-gate carabiners are less prone to gate fluttering, which can occur when a rope passes quickly through a carabiner during a leader fall.

Some carabiners are made from metal bars with cross sections that are oval, T-shaped or cross-shaped, or wedge-shaped—as opposed to round—in order to save weight. Note that "regular" carabiner refers to carabiners of whatever shape that do not lock.

Locking carabiners. With a sleeve that covers one end of the gate to minimize accidental opening, locking carabiners (fig. 9-36g) provide a wider margin of safety for rappelling, belaying, or clipping in to anchors. Most locking carabiners have a sleeve that screws over one end of the gate. Others have a spring that automatically rotates the sleeve into place whenever the gate is closed, rather than the climber having to screw it down. Regardless of the carabiner's particular locking mechanism, always check to make sure that the carabiner is properly locked. Test it manually before relying on it.

Pear-shaped locking carabiners, also called HMS carabiners (fig. 9-36h), are much larger at the gate-opening end than at the hinge end; they are ideal for belaying with the munter hitch (see Figure 9-26). They are also a good choice for use in conjunction with the seat harness. The extra cost and weight of pear-shaped locking carabiners is justified by the increased ease they provide in loading and managing all the ropes, knots, cords, and runners that are used at the seat harness's anchor point.

Two regular carabiners can be substituted for a locking carabiner, but only if they are joined correctly. Align the gate side of each carabiner with the spine side of the other, so their gates are on opposite sides. The gate-opening ends should face the same direction, so the two gates open toward—or opposed to—each other (fig. 9-37a). This

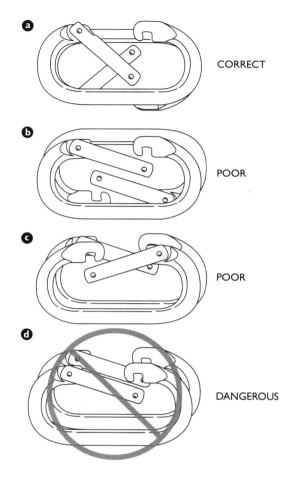

Fig. 9-37. Substituting double oval carabiners for a locking carabiner: a, gates are on opposite sides and the same ends, so they are opposite and opposed (correct); b, gates are on opposite sides and ends, so they are opposite and parallel (poor); c, gates are on same sides and opposite ends, so they are parallel and opposed (poor); d, gates are on the same sides and ends, so they are doubly parallel (dangerous).

opposite and opposed configuration helps prevent the carabiners from being forced open and accidentally unclipping (as they could if configured as in fig. 9-37b, c, or d). You can check that the carabiners are in the proper configuration by opening both gates at the same time; in profile, the gates should appear to cross, forming an X.

USE AND CARE

A few basic rules apply to the use and care of all carabiners. Always make sure the force on a carabiner falls along the long axis and closer to the spine side; be especially careful that the gate does not receive the load. For example, see Figure 14-9 on clipping technique in Chapter 14, Leading on Rock.

Check the carabiner gates occasionally. A gate should open easily, even when the carabiner is loaded, and the gate should have good side-to-side rigidity when open.

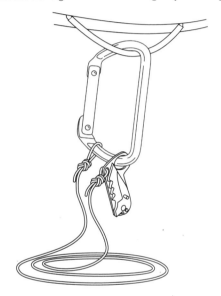

Fig. 9-38. Knife attached to carabiner with a lanyard.

A dirty gate can be cleaned by applying a solvent or lubricant (lightweight oil, citrus solvent, or products such as WD-40) to the hinge, working the hinge until it operates smoothly again, and then dipping the carabiner in boiling water for about 20 seconds to remove the cleaning agent.

Also, avoid bringing carabiners into contact with corrosive chemicals, especially acids, and avoid storing metals in damp and acidic environments.

KNIFE

A knife is an essential climbing tool that should always be kept within easy reach. It should be attached to the harness with a carabiner, and secured with an arm's length lanyard to avoid dropping it when unclipped for use (fig. 9-38). A knife could prove invaluable if an item becomes caught in the rappel device, for example. Always use caution when wielding a knife to avoid nicking the rope, especially when the rope is weighted. Ropes under tension can be easily nicked or worse.

KEEPING THE SAFETY NET STRONG

Ropes, harnesses, runners, and carabiners, as well as protection pieces (see Chapter 13, Rock Protection) and belay devices (see Chapter 10, Belaying), are all vital links in your chain of protection. Knowing your equipment and knowing how to use it is essential for safe climbing. But the most important part of the basic safety system is you. Your safety net, and the common sense, judgment, and awareness to use it properly, will keep you safe in a climbing environment.

9

CHAPTER 10
BELAYING

A fundamental technique for climbing safely, belaying is a system of using a rope to stop a fall if one should occur. This system can safely control the enormous energy that a falling climber generates, but belaying well takes practice and requires an understanding of its underlying principles.

In its simplest form, a belay consists of nothing more than a rope that runs from a climber to another person—the belayer—who is ready to stop a fall. Three things are necessary to make the system work: a method of applying and amplifying a stopping force to the rope, an anchor strong enough to resist the pull of the fall, and a skilled belayer. There are different ways to apply this stopping force and many methods of setting up and tying in to a *belay anchor*—a secure point to which the rest of the system is attached. This chapter introduces the principal techniques and major options of belaying so that climbers can choose the methods that work best in their own climbing.

HOW BELAYS ARE USED IN CLIMBING

On a climb, belay setups are usually established on the ground or on a ledge that provides reasonable comfort and the possibility of solid anchors. A long climb is divided into sections, with one climber taking the lead and, belayed from below, moving up the route to the next desirable stopping spot and setting up a new belay. The distance between belays is known as a *pitch* or a *lead*. Rope length and the location of a convenient spot to establish the next belay usually determine the length of each pitch. A short climb can be climbed in a single pitch; longer climbs are called *multipitch*.

THREE BELAY SCENARIOS
This section discusses how the mechanics work in each of three types of belay scenarios.

Slingshot top-rope belay. In this scenario, the anchor is on the top of the route and the belayer belays at the bottom of the route. The rope has already been set up, running from the bottom of the route to the top anchor and back to the ground (fig. 10-1). This scenario, which usually only applies to single-pitch routes, is typical at a climbing gym or a cragging area.

In the slingshot top-rope belay, the rope always runs down toward the belayer, who takes rope in as the climber heads up. The direction of rope travel never changes. As long as the belayer keeps the slack out of the rope, the force of a fall is similar to the weight of the climber.

The belayer is not always connected to a ground anchor, and instead often uses his or her weight as the counterforce for the climber. However, certain factors may demand an anchor—for example, if the weight difference between the climber and the belayer is significant or if they are starting the climb (or pitch) from an exposed ledge.

10

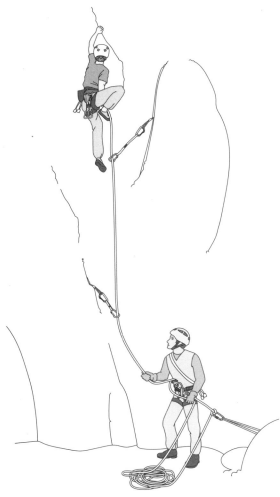

Fig. 10-2. Lead belay.

Fig. 10-1. Slingshot top-rope belay.

Lead belay. In a lead belay, the climber is leading the route, placing protection while climbing up. This scenario applies to both single-pitch and multipitch climbs. When the top of a route is not accessible by other means, a slingshot top rope has to be set up this way.

In a lead belay, most of the time the rope moves up and away from the belayer. The exception is that after the leader has clipped the rope to a piece of protection above waist height, as the leader resumes climbing the rope will drop down before going up again. The belayer should be vigilant and move the rope to keep slack at a minimum, without pulling down on the leader. In Figure 10-2, the leader has climbed above the last piece of protection.

In a lead belay, the force of a fall depends on how far the climber is above the last piece of protection—and the fall force could potentially be much greater than the climber's body weight. Thus, in belaying a leader, especially when a long fall could happen, the belayer is typically tied to a ground anchor to avoid being yanked off the ground in the case of a fall. This is extremely important if the belay is on an exposed ledge or under a roof. Exceptions can be made if there is no risk of falling off exposed ledges, if the

173

Fig. 10-3. Belaying a follower.

belayer outweighs the climber significantly, or if the falls are expected to be short—for instance, in a climbing gym.

Belaying a follower. After a lead climber has finished leading a pitch, he or she can belay the other climber (who has finished belaying the leader) from the top of the pitch (fig. 10-3). Belaying the follower from the top is done for numerous reasons: it could be a multipitch route on which they both will continue climbing; the route could

be too long for slingshot top roping; *rope drag* (friction that impedes the rope's travel) or traverses could make this scenario safer than slingshot top roping. In any case, the climber being belayed from above is known as a *follower* or a *second*; these terms are used interchangeably throughout this chapter.

In this scenario, the rope always moves up and toward the anchor. As in a slingshot top-rope belay, the force of a fall in this scenario should be similar to the follower's body weight as long as the belayer always keeps the slack in the rope at a minimum. The belayer is usually anchored to the belay anchor unless the belayer is belaying directly off the belay anchor and the belay is located on a sizable ledge where falls are not a concern.

CHOOSING A BELAY SPOT

Belaying is a demanding and important task that is often awkward, of long duration, and boring—yet it also requires constant vigilance for the safety of the climber. The belayer's job is much easier if the belayer is able to find a comfortable spot on which to establish a secure position. A good belay location should have three attributes:

1. Good placement for anchors (when an anchor is warranted)
2. Safe position
3. Reasonable comfort

Good placement for anchors. When choosing a belay position, always look for solid anchor placements. Critical to a safe belay, solid anchors are of paramount concern.

Safe position. When selecting a belay location, be aware of the possibility of rockfall or icefall, and pick a stance that will provide some shelter if they seem a likely hazard. If a belay location is exposed to imminent danger from rockfall or icefall, safety may require moving the belay to a location with less-desirable anchors. Additionally, it is useful, though not always possible, to find a position where climbing partners can see and/or communicate with each other.

Reasonable comfort. A leader may shorten a pitch because a comfortable stance at a partial rope length is of greater advantage than pushing the lead as far as possible.

Many factors ultimately determine the best choice for a belay spot. Longer leads are more efficient, so if several good belay ledges are available, climbers generally pick the highest one. However, the leader may decide to stop and set up the next belay early to mitigate rope drag. Belay spots can also be limited by the protection options on the leader's rack for building an anchor.

HOLDING A FALL

A belay serves two equally important purposes: to catch a fall so the climber doesn't hit the ground and to limit the impact force exerted on the climber so that the climber isn't injured.

Understanding Impact Force

The basic concepts of climbing physics discussed here provide an understanding of impact force.

Mass. The first concept climbers need to understand is mass. In simple terms, mass is the amount of material an object has. The bigger and the denser an object, the more mass it has.

Gravity is the downward force exerted by the earth. Gravity gives weight to objects that have mass. The direction of gravity is always downward, and the magnitude of gravity's pull is proportional to the mass of the object.

Acceleration is the rate at which the velocity of an object changes. *Velocity* is the speed and direction in which an object travels. If the speed and direction of travel don't change, the acceleration is zero. Note that deceleration is also acceleration, but in the opposite direction of the velocity. For example, if it takes 5 seconds for a car to reach the speed of 60 miles per hour and it also takes 5 seconds for it to come to a full stop, the average acceleration during the two events is of the same magnitude but in opposite directions.

Now, with an understanding of these three concepts, it is possible to explore how Newton's laws of motion are applied in climbing.

Newton's first law of motion states that an object at rest stays at rest, or an object in motion travels at the same velocity unless acted upon by a force or by forces that don't completely cancel each other (an unbalanced force). In other words, the acceleration of an object is zero unless there is an unbalanced force on it. Acceleration is not zero for the falling climber because of the force of gravity. And because any object on the earth that has mass is acted upon by the planet's gravity, for an object to stay at rest, there must be another force or forces to counter the pull of gravity. When a climber hangs on a rope, the rope provides that *counterforce* by holding the climber in the air against gravity's pull.

In a somewhat simplified model in which rope stretch and slippage are ignored, when someone is climbing or following on a top rope and the belayer always holds the rope tight, the climber's velocity is zero before and after a fall—therefore the acceleration is also zero during the fall. The rope only needs to provide enough force to counter the climber's weight.

However, when a climber is leading, the scenario becomes rather complicated. The lead climber places intermediate pieces of protection and clips the rope in to these pieces, then climbs past them until placing another piece. If the climber falls when he or she is above the last piece of protection, the climber will experience a free fall for double the distance from the last piece of protection (the climber falls to the last piece of protection, and then that much again beyond it). To better understand this scenario, consider Newton's second law of motion, in which unbalanced forces that don't cancel each other are called the *net force*.

Newton's second law of motion states that the net force on an object is equal to the mass of the object multiplied by the acceleration of the object. This relationship is expressed mathematically as $F = m \times a$, or force equals mass times acceleration. In intuitive terms, the more mass an object has, the more force it exerts; the more acceleration an object has, the more force it exerts.

What this means for climbers is, due to gravity (an unbalanced force), a falling climber's velocity will increase as he or she free-falls. This acceleration will remain constant because the earth's gravity does not change. The longer the climber free-falls, the faster he or she will fall. The purpose of belaying is to use the rope to catch the climber, reducing the velocity of the climber's fall to zero. During the catch, an unbalanced net force must act upon the climber to cause that deceleration, and in a belay that force is upward, coming from the rope—this is called *impact force*.

Limiting Impact Force with Dynamic Rope

During the belayer's catch of a climber's fall, if the rope is allowed to slip or stretch more, stopping the fall will take longer—that is, the magnitude of the deceleration is reduced. Thus, according to Newton's second law, less force will be needed to stop the climber—but then the fall will last longer. Stopping a fall as quickly as possible may prevent the falling climber from hitting something, such as a ledge; however, stopping a fall too suddenly would subject every component of the system—including the falling climber—to dangerously high impact forces. Thus there is a trade-off to be made between minimizing the length of the fall and minimizing the fall's impact force. Climbers say a catch is "soft," or a belay is "dynamic," when the rope slips or stretches to limit the impact force to a comfortable range.

Because modern belay devices limit rope slippage, something else in the belay system must provide a soft catch

10

for a falling climber. That something is rope stretch, and often movement of the belayer as well. In many situations, the belayer is confined in a small space and rope stretch is the only means of limiting impact force. Modern dynamic climbing ropes are designed to prevent dangerously high impact forces by elongating under load to absorb energy.

In the days of hemp ropes, the golden rule of belaying was "the rope must run." That was because the rope had neither the strength to withstand high impact forces nor the shock absorption to avoid injuring the climber. The only safe way to stop a fall was by making the belay dynamic, allowing some rope to slip through the belay to make a soft catch. This worked, but not without problems: it was difficult to learn, and the friction of the running rope could badly burn a belayer's hands.

For a rope to be safe for leading—an activity in which falls must be anticipated—it must be an approved dynamic climbing rope. The International Climbing and Mountaineering Federation (UIAA) and European Committee on Standardization (CEN) are two equipment safety organizations that test the designs of new climbing gear prior to production and help set safety ratings. All safe and tested climbing equipment will depict the UIAA safety label and/or the CEN mark (see Figure 9-2 in Chapter 9, Basic Safety System). For detailed information on how ropes are tested, see "The Standard Drop-Test Fall for Dynamic Ropes" sidebar.

Static ropes, webbing slings, and accessory cord, while fine for rappelling, constructing anchors, or other uses, do not stretch enough to safely catch a dynamic fall. Look at the manufacturer's specifications for climbing ropes. They are rated not by tensile strength but by impact force. This is because the rope does more than simply not break under the impact of a falling climber; it also stretches to absorb the energy of multiple falls. These two criteria align with the two purposes of the belay: to catch a fall and to limit the impact force.

The beauty of dynamic climbing ropes is that, because they limit the impact force of a fall, less force is exerted throughout the system. As a result, the anchor is subjected to lower stresses, the falling leader receives a softer catch, and the belayer has an easier task holding the fall.

Understanding Fall Factors

Impact forces generated by falls onto dynamic ropes are determined by both the length of the fall and how much dynamic rope is available to absorb the energy of that fall. Together, these determine the fall factor: the length of the fall divided by the length of rope fallen on. It may not seem intuitive, but fall factor, not length of fall, determines

THE STANDARD DROP-TEST FALL FOR DYNAMIC ROPES

In the standard UIAA-CEN single dynamic-rope drop-test fall, an 80-kilogram (176-pound) mass affixed to a solid fixed anchor is dropped 5 meters (16 feet 5 inches) on a 2.8-meter (9-foot and 2-inch) section of rope running over a 1-centimeter ($\frac{3}{8}$-inch) steel bar. To pass the test, a rope must withstand at least five standard drops and not exceed a 12 kilonewton (kN) impact force on the first drop.

This maximum 12 kN figure is derived from studies showing that the human body could briefly withstand 15 times its weight when dropped. Maximum impact forces for current single ropes usually range between 8.5 and 10.5 kN. Be aware that as a rope ages it loses some of its ability to absorb energy. A frequently used rope may generate considerably higher forces than the figures for new test ropes (see "Rope Care" in Chapter 9, Basic Safety System).

By design, the standard drop test produces a fall that would be considered severe in normal climbing situations. First, in most real-life situations any belay is, to a certain extent, a dynamic belay. Rope slippage, belayer movement, and rope friction against rock and through carabiners all dissipate impact force. The standard drop test is not a dynamic belay; the rope absorbs virtually all of the impact force of the fall.

Additionally, the standard drop-test fall is set up with a high *fall factor*: the length of the fall divided by the length of rope fallen on. In the UIAA-CEN standard drop test, the fall factor is calculated like this: fall factor = 5 m ÷ 2.8 m = 1.78, where 5 m is the fall length and 2.8 m is the rope length, as mentioned above.

This test gauges the rope's properties to ensure that it will absorb the impact force generated by a severe fall without subjecting the system to excessively high loads. While the maximum fall factor of 2.0 could be encountered under normal climbing circumstances, such high-factor falls are uncommon enough that 1.78 is an acceptable and more realistic fall factor.

the impact force that is generated in a fall. This is written mathematically as follows: fall factor = length of fall ÷ length of rope fallen on.

The longer the fall, the bigger the fall factor; the more rope to fall on, the smaller the fall factor. Therefore, lower fall factors always mean lower impact forces because there is more rope relative to the length of fall, hence more rope to stretch and absorb impact.

In any normal climbing situation, a fall factor of 2.0 is the highest a climber could ever encounter, because this would mean falling exactly twice the length of the rope that the climber has run out. For example, assume that two climbers are on a smooth vertical face with no ledges or other hazards to hit in a fall. If the leader falls from 10 feet (3 meters) above the belay without any protection, there would have been 10 feet of rope played out. That climber would end up 10 feet below the belay stance (the point of protection), having fallen 20 feet (6 meters) on 10 feet (3 meters) of rope. Applying this example to the fall factor formula looks like this: fall factor = 20 feet ÷ 10 feet = 2.0.

This would be a fall factor of 2.0, also stated as a factor 2 fall. Such a fall would generate the maximum impact on anchors and climbers, creating a hazardous situation. If there is any slack in the rope, intermediate points of protection, rope slippage, or movement of the belayer, the fall factor would always be less than 2.0. When more rope is played out, falls of a similar length will generate much lower impact forces, putting less stress on the system. That same 20-foot fall on a 100-foot section of rope would still involve an exciting bit of air time, but the catch would be quite gentle by comparison: fall factor = 20 feet ÷ 100 feet = 0.2.

It is important to realize that any fall of the same factor will generate the same impact force, although this is not immediately obvious. An intuitive explanation without involving math is, the length of the fall determines the maximum speed the fallen climber reaches before being caught by the rope and starting to decelerate. Obviously, the longer the fall, the greater the speed. On the other hand, the length of rope catching the fall determines how fast the fall is stopped. The more rope, the more it stretches, and the longer it takes to stop the fall. So although a longer fall involves higher speed, if the fall factor is constant, reducing that speed to zero also takes longer. The deceleration rate remains the same.

Take the 5-meter UIAA-CEN drop-test fall described in the sidebar "The Standard Drop-Test Fall for Dynamic Ropes" and multiply it by 5; now it is a 25-meter (82-foot) fall on 14 meters (46 feet) of rope, but the fall factor remains the same: 1.78. The fall is much longer (and clearly riskier for the falling climber), but because the amount of rope available to absorb shock is also greater, the amount of impact force that the belay system is subjected to remains the same.

PROTECTING THE LEADER

Understanding fall factor and how it determines impact forces is fundamental to safe leading. As described in "Lead belay" above, the leader places intermediate points of protection to reduce potential fall length, and a leader fall is at least twice the distance between the climber and the last placement of protection. As described in "Understanding Fall Factors" above, the impact forces are highest when a fall occurs when the fall factor is 2.0. This would happen when the leader starts up a pitch and falls before any intermediate protection has been placed to limit the distance of that fall.

Therefore, climbers should always establish a solid first placement as soon as possible after starting a new lead. This will not only reduce the chance for a high-factor fall, but will also establish the direction from which the force of a leader fall will come (see "Judging the Direction of Fall Forces" in Chapter 14, Leading on Rock). Understanding the dynamics involved will help climbers make more sense of how belaying protects the leader.

APPLYING BRAKING FORCE TO THE ROPE

Climbing belays must be able to resist the large forces generated in a fall. With the dynamic climbing rope acting as the shock absorber in the system, the belayer's job is to quickly stop the rope from running. Any additional rope that runs through the belay system as the fall is caught has two related effects: reducing the impact forces and lengthening the distance fallen. Occasionally the belayer may want to deliberately provide a more dynamic belay—for instance, if protection is suspected to be weak. But there is always the trade-off of a longer fall, with increased possibility of the lead climber hitting a ledge or other hazard.

Because everything starts with the braking force applied by the belayer's grip, it is important to consider the factors that affect the generation of this force. Grip strength varies considerably from one person to another, with the average being somewhere around 50 pounds (about 0.2 kilonewton). This likely becomes reduced when the belayer is substantially fatigued or awkwardly positioned. Ropes that are thinner, as is the current trend, are more difficult to grip, and reduced rope friction, as occurs with wet, icy, or (possibly) dry-treated ropes, will lower braking force to some degree. Conversely, as ropes age they develop a rougher sheath with higher friction and therefore can be easier to grip.

10

However, in all cases, grip strength alone is not sufficient to stop a fall. Instead, climbers rely on a mechanical means of amplifying the force of their grip strength. This arresting force is greatly enhanced by the use of some friction-producing element, commonly a belay device, to stop the falling climber.

The belayer's hand that holds the rope coming from the climber is known as the *feeling hand* and is used to pay the rope in and out. The other hand, known as the *braking hand*, must never let go of its grip on the rope, remaining ready to catch a fall at any time. In any belay method, the rope from the climber goes around or through the friction-producing element—a belay device, the camming action of an assisted-braking belay device, a munter hitch on a carabiner, or the belayer's hips—and then to the belayer's braking hand. The braking hand gripping the rope produces the initial force. The braking method or belay device is the essential means by which the limited force of the belayer's grip strength can control the large impact forces generated in a fall.

Stopping a fall is accomplished when a belayer assumes the braking position, gripping the rope tightly with the braking hand, then pulls back on the free end of the rope (see Figure 10-10 as an example). This action must be practiced and learned well so that it becomes automatic; immediately going into braking position as soon as a fall is sensed is the best way to stop a fall.

Wearing gloves while belaying is an option some belayers consider for safety and comfort. Gloves protect the belayer's hands from friction burns in the case of rope slippage. The material of the gloves should be rough enough to add some friction to the system, essentially increasing the belayer's grip strength. Gloves should fit well enough that there are no wrinkles or folds of fabric. Some climbers dislike the fact that gloves may interfere with dexterity and tend to leave their hands damp and soft, which is undesirable for climbing rock; some wear fingerless gloves to mitigate the reduction of dexterity while still protecting the palm.

The most important thing for all belayers to do is to perfect whichever belay method they use. Having one method that you can absolutely count on is the first priority; after that, learning other methods for versatility is valuable.

USING BELAY DEVICES

When properly used, belay devices multiply the rope friction and the grip strength of the belayer's braking hand by passing the rope through an aperture, wrapping it around a post in the device, and passing the rope back out through

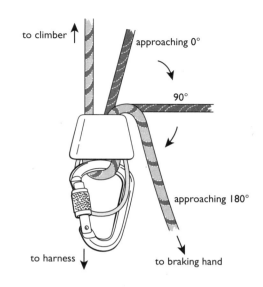

Fig. 10-4. Angle of separation between the two rope strands.

the aperture. This configuration provides a wrap, or bend, in the rope to assist in producing a stopping force. The post is usually a locking carabiner or a part of the belay device itself. The belayer's braking hand is the initial, and critical, source of friction; without the braking hand on the rope, there is no belay.

The total braking force exerted on the rope during the arrest of a fall depends on three things: (1) the total degree of bend that the belay device produces in the rope, as well as the rope's inherent resistance to bending and deforming; (2) the friction generated as the rope runs over the surfaces of the belay device; and (3) the force exerted by the belayer's grip. Fortunately, despite the variations in the strength of belayers' grips, modern belay devices work well enough that when they are properly used, adequate stopping force can be generated with even modest grip strength.

To stop a fall, the belayer pulls back on the free end of the rope with the braking hand to create a difference in angle of at least 90 degrees between the rope from the climber entering the belay device and the rope leaving the device to the braking hand. This angle of separation between the two strands of the rope (fig. 10-4) is critical to the strength of the belay. Figure 10-4 shows how the braking force is increased as the braking hand pulls the rope farther back to increase the angle of separation from 90 degrees toward 180 degrees. Nothing must be in the way

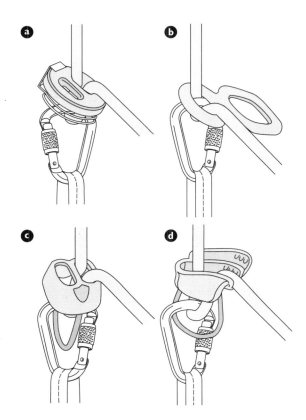

Fig. 10-5. Belay devices: a, Sticht plate; b, figure eight; c, tubular device; d, tubular device with friction grooves.

the advanced dynamic-rope technologies and mechanical belay devices, climbers should seldom rely on their body as a belay device, though the hip belay may be useful in some situations (see "Using the Hip Belay" later in this chapter).

There are many popular belay devices; this section describes some of them. When using any belay device, always read and follow the manufacturer's instructions carefully; be certain that you fully understand these instructions and that the device is properly rigged each time you use it. Note that each belay device works with only a certain range of rope diameters.

Aperture belay devices include Sticht plates (fig. 10-5a), figure eights (fig. 10-5b), and tubular devices (fig. 10-5c). These devices all work in a similar fashion: they simply provide an opening through which a bight of rope is pushed and then clipped in to the locking carabiner on the belay loop of the seat harness, as shown in Figure 10-10. The Sticht plate was the first mechanical belay and rappel device, created in the 1960s and named after its designer, Fritz Sticht. Sticht plates have become less popular now that more-modern tubular designs provide smoother control over the rope and are less prone to jamming. Figure-eight devices were originally designed for rappelling, not belaying, but some figure-eight devices can serve both functions. Make certain that the figure-eight device is intended for belaying use by the manufacturer; many are not. Although figure-eight devices are not used as much these days as a belay and rappel device because of their lack of versatility and because they tend to twist the rope, some climbers still prefer them for their smoothness, especially when the load is heavy.

Most current belay devices are a cone-shaped or somewhat square tube, as shown in Figure 10-5c; the Black Diamond ATC (air traffic controller), DMM Bug, and Trango Pyramid are examples of such devices. Plates and tubes must be kept from sliding down the rope and out of reach, so most of these devices include a wire loop that is clipped in to the locking carabiner on the seat harness, as shown in Figure 10-4. The connection to the harness must be long enough so that it does not interfere with belaying in any direction.

Many current tubular devices have a high- and a regular-friction mode, usually achieved by adding V-shaped slots and/or ridges to one side of the aperture: Figure 10-6a shows the regular-friction mode. In high-friction mode (fig. 10-6b), the device is rigged so that the rope going to the braking hand is pulled into the narrower V slot or over the ridges to increase the braking force. This is useful when extra friction is desirable for belaying and rappelling.

10

of the braking hand or elbow (such as a rock wall behind the belayer's arm) when the belayer goes into the braking position; also, this critical task must not require an unnatural body twist or motion.

One of the simplest and most convenient belay methods is to clip a belay device in to a locking carabiner on the harness, which is typically clipped through a sewn belay loop, as shown in Figure 10-10. It is important to follow the manufacturer's instructions for clipping in properly, as to do otherwise loads the harness in ways it was not designed for and may lead to failure. Many harnesses have a sewn-in label showing the proper way to wear the harness and clip in to it.

Types of Belay Devices

Before mechanical belay devices were invented, climbers ran ropes around their hips and relied on the friction of the rope around their body to arrest a fall. Nowadays, with

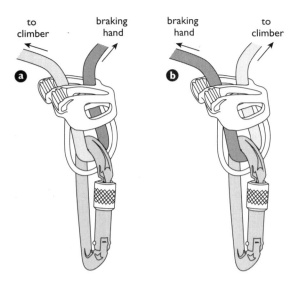

Fig. 10-6. Aperture belay device: a, in regular-friction mode; b, in high-friction mode.

Auto-locking belay devices are designed to function in the same way as a standard aperture device, but they also have an alternative rigging mode that provides a secure means of belaying one or two followers directly off an anchor. Typical examples include the Petzl Reverso 4 and Black Diamond ATC Guide, but many climbing equipment manufacturers have their own versions of auto-locking belay devices. Most work in a similar way. Most of these devices can be used to belay two followers at the same time. Follow the manufacturer's instructions to safely use these devices. Note that auto-locking belay devices are not hands-free devices: they still require the belayer's braking hand to provide the initial force. The braking hand must never lose its grip on the rope.

These devices look similar to other aperture devices and may be used off the harness in the same way as a standard aperture device; but in auto-locking mode, the device is connected directly to the anchor with a locking carabiner while the rope runs through the device and through a second locking carabiner (fig. 10-7). When the device is rigged this way, the belayer can easily pull the rope in, but if the climber's strand is loaded, as in a fall, the rope locks down on itself. When the climber falls, the climber's strand of the rope is loaded with the climber's weight, and that loaded strand presses on the braking strand, preventing it from moving, similar to trying to pull a rug out from under someone who is standing on it.

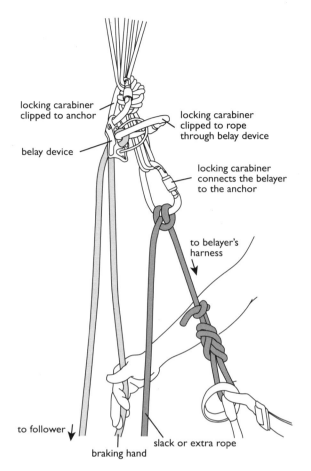

Fig. 10-7. Auto-locking belay device rigged in auto-locking mode.

If the belayed climber falls and is unable to unload the device, the belayer must have a way to unlock the device. To release the device, the belayer needs to find a way to lift the loaded climber's strand off the braking strand. A climber's fingers do not have enough strength to do that, so the belayer can use a carabiner (or any rod that is strong enough) as a lever—or, alternatively, the belayer can attach a cord and redirect his or her body weight to pull against the load. Many newer auto-locking devices have a hole specifically designed for attaching a cord or carabiner (fig. 10-8) to release a locked device in order to lower the fallen climber. Otherwise, it would be necessary to attach a raising system to the rope to take the fallen climber's weight off the device so it can be unlocked.

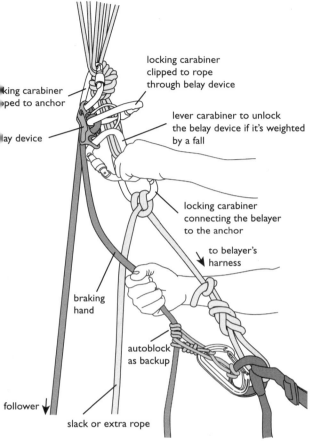

locking carabiner clipped to rope through belay device

king carabiner ped to anchor

ay device

lever carabiner to unlock the belay device if it's weighted by a fall

locking carabiner connecting the belayer to the anchor

to belayer's harness

braking hand

autoblock as backup

follower

slack or extra rope

Fig. 10-8. Releasing a loaded auto-locking belay device.

Assisted-braking belay devices are specialized devices with an internal cam that locks down on the rope when the rope suddenly accelerates in a fall; this locking action creates a braking force that is not dependent on resistance from the belayer's grip (fig. 10-9b). Models include the Petzl Grigri+ (fig. 10-9a), Trango Vergo (fig. 10-9c), and Edelrid Eddy. Popular for gym, sport, and aid climbing, they have definite advantages when used properly. For example, they enable a smaller, lighter belayer to confidently arrest and hold even heavy partners or to stop long falls. All current models have a release mechanism, a lever, that allows controlled rappelling or lowering of a climber on top-rope (fig. 10-9d).

These devices have a tendency to lock up when the lead climber makes a sudden move up or when the belayer feeds the rope too quickly. It is extremely important to carefully follow manufacturer's instructions and test proper setup each time the device is rigged. Disadvantages include their greater weight and bulk. It is also harder to give a soft and dynamic belay with an assisted-braking belay device, compared with tubular belay devices, because the former catches the rope much more quickly. With assisted-braking belay devices, the belayer often must resort to body movement to soften the catch. These devices also cannot be used to rappel on two strands, hence they are not suitable for alpine climbing. Note that assisted-braking belay devices are not hands-free devices: they still require the belayer's braking hand to provide the initial force. The braking hand must never lose its grip on the rope.

Belaying Technique When Using a Belay Device

This section describes the technique of belaying a climber off the harness using a belay device. To assume the belay

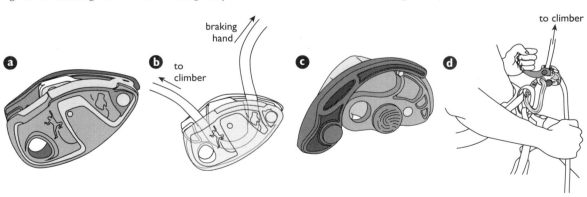

braking hand

to climber

a

b to climber

c

d to climber

Fig. 10-9. Assisted-braking belay devices: a, Petzl Grigri+; b, Grigri+ in belaying mode; c, Trango Vergo; d, Vergo in lowering mode.

Fig. 10-10. Hand motions for taking in rope from a standing belay, with the braking hand never leaving the rope: a, start with both hands on the rope with the feeling hand extended and the braking hand close to the body; b, pull the feeling hand toward your body and the braking hand away from your body; c, drop the braking hand into the braking position and move the feeling hand to grasp the rope under the braking hand; d, slide the braking hand back toward your body while maintaining the braking position.

position, grab the rope with the braking hand, with the thumb pointing upward and the palm facing yourself or the ground. This is a natural position in which your hand has the greatest strength. Make sure the belay device, the rope, and the harness's belay loop are not twisted. Grip the rope with the feeling hand at your eye level, feeling the slack of the rope, but not pulling it, as shown in Figure 10-10a.

Taking in the rope. Known as **PBUS** (pull, brake, under, slide), this current standard technique is taught at most rock gyms and by most climbing guides. With both hands on the rope, start with the braking hand close to the body and the feeling hand extended to eye level (fig. 10-10a). First, **pull** down the climber's strand of the rope with the feeling hand; at the same time, pull the braking hand away from your body to pull the rope through the belay device (fig. 10-10b). Then without losing the grip, **brake** by dropping the braking hand down to the braking position. Place the feeling hand **under** the braking hand and grasp the rope (fig. 10-10c). Without removing the braking hand from the rope, **slide** it up until it's close to the belay device and grasp the rope again (fig. 10-10d). Then move the feeling hand back up on the climber's strand of the rope. Repeat the sequence as often as needed to take in the appropriate

amount of rope. Remember that the braking hand must never leave the rope.

Letting out the rope. It is easy and intuitive to let out the rope. With the feeling hand, pull the rope away from your body while using the braking hand to feed the rope toward the climber. Again, the braking hand must never leave the rope. If you are letting out a lot of rope quickly, slide your braking hand away from your body until it is fully extended, so you can maximize the amount of rope you can feed to the feeling hand in one motion.

USING THE MUNTER HITCH

The munter hitch is an effective alternative to using a belay device. It uses only the rope, a specialized carabiner, and a hitch to provide the friction necessary to stop a fall. Efficient belaying with a munter hitch requires an HMS-type (pear-shaped) carabiner with an opening large enough to allow the hitch to feed through smoothly. As a result of its configuration, the hitch multiplies the effect of the braking hand with friction created by the rope being wrapped on itself and around the HMS carabiner.

The munter hitch is unique in that it provides sufficient friction regardless of the angle at which the braking end of the rope is held. With regular aperture belay devices, maximum friction is generated when the braking hand strand of the rope is held at an angle of 180 degrees from the strand of rope attached to the climber, as shown in Figure 10-4. These devices are useless when both strands are aligned. In contrast, the munter hitch, because of the way it wraps around the HMS carabiner, actually generates *more* friction when both strands of the rope are aligned (see Figure 9-26 in Chapter 9, Basic Safety System). At an angle of 180 degrees, it still provides about 85 percent of the maximum friction. In other words, you can hold the munter hitch at any position and still have sufficient friction.

Because no special braking position is required, the munter hitch has an advantage over most belay devices in that if a climber fall takes a belayer by surprise, the hitch will function even if the belayer does no more than firmly grip the rope. With the munter hitch, rope handling is quick and easy, making the munter hitch an ideal method when climbers are moving rapidly over easy ground. Because no specialized equipment other than an HMS carabiner is required, the munter hitch provides a ready backup belay method if a belay device is lost.

The munter hitch has some drawbacks as well as advantages. It can kink the rope more than other belay methods, but this can be minimized by allowing the rope to feed freely unless needed to arrest a fall. To unkink the rope, shake it out while it is hanging free. The munter hitch can also unscrew the lock on a carabiner gate as the rope runs across the gate. Pay attention to the carabiner gate when using a munter hitch. After a big fall, the outermost layer of the rope's sheath may be glazed—which is only cosmetic; this glazing, which also occurs to some degree with mechanical belay devices, wears off with use.

USING THE HIP BELAY

The hip belay—also called the body belay—is a belay method in which the rope is wrapped around the belayer's body to generate enough friction to stop a climber's fall. The belayer clips in to a solid anchor and assumes a stable stance facing the direction of an anticipated pull on the rope. The rope from the climber passes around the belayer's back and rides just below the top of the hips (fig. 10-11a). To arrest a fall, grip the rope tightly with the

10

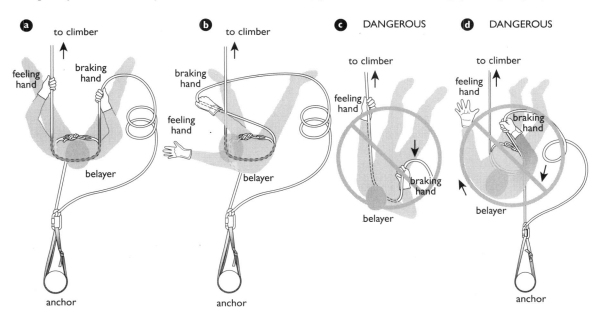

Fig. 10-11. The hip or body belay: a, the belayer is anchored and ready to arrest a fall—the rope goes from the braking hand around the back (to produce friction) and to the climber; b, the braking position—with the braking arm extended across the stomach to create additional friction; c, if the elbow of the braking hand is not straightened before braking begins, then the braking arm may be pulled into a helpless position (dangerous); d, having the anchor attachment on the same side as the braking hand can allow the hip belay to unwrap (dangerous).

braking hand and pull the braking arm across the stomach into the braking, or arrest, position (fig. 10-11b). The braking action must be practiced and learned well so that it becomes automatic; immediately going into arrest position as soon as a fall is sensed is the best way to stop a fall using the hip belay. The braking position increases the amount of friction-producing wrap of the rope around the body, thereby increasing the stopping force.

Because the force of a fall is dissipated as friction against the belayer's body, a belayer stopping a severe fall can suffer serious rope burns. Protective clothes are required to prevent this. Even fairly minor leader falls can melt and severely damage expensive synthetic garments. If a belayer is burned badly enough, the belayer could drop a falling climber. Because the belayer's hands provide a greater proportion of friction in the hip belay than in other methods, gloves are essential to protect the hands from burns. A tighter grip causes less-severe burns because faster stops and less rope slippage generate less heat. Another problem with the hip belay is that if the climbing rope runs over the anchor attachment during a fall, the anchor attachment may be burned.

Because the hip belay requires more time for the belayer to attain braking position and generates less braking force than any other method, more rope slippage generally occurs and the climber usually falls farther. If the belay stance fails, it is much more likely that the belayer will lose control of the rope than with other methods. In summary, all elements of the hip belay must come together to make it work effectively during a long, hard fall.

Despite its drawbacks as a general-purpose belay method, the hip belay does have advantages that make it worth learning, if only for special purposes. With the hip belay, the belayer can take in rope much faster than with other methods, and the hip belay can be set up quickly with a minimum of equipment. It is probably most useful when belaying a fast-moving partner over moderate terrain. A common and efficient practice is to use a simple hip belay to bring a following climber up a relatively easy pitch and then switch to another method when this climber leads the next pitch.

The hip belay can also be useful for belaying on snow, where it may be desirable to have a more dynamic belay because anchors are absent or suspect (see Chapters 16, Snow Travel and Climbing, and 19, Alpine Ice Climbing). Also, if climbers have lost or forgotten their belay device and do not have the right kind of carabiner (pear-shaped carabiner is recommended) for a munter hitch, there may be no choice but to use the hip belay.

Special Considerations in Using the Hip Belay

When using the hip belay, climbers must keep a number of special considerations in mind. To catch a fall with this method, straighten the elbow of the braking arm before beginning to grip hard. Then bring the braking arm across in front of your body to increase the amount of wrap for maximum friction. The natural reaction is to grip the rope first, but this may pull the braking arm into a helpless position (fig. 10-11c), requiring the belayer to let go and grasp the rope again. An optimal braking position can be learned only with practice, ideally with actual weights being dropped and held.

When the belayer attaches to the anchor, rig the connection to the side opposite the braking hand. Note that this is different from tying in for belaying with a mechanical device. If the braking hand and anchor rope are on the same side of your body, the force of a fall can partly unwrap the rope from around your body (fig. 10-11d), decreasing both friction and stability.

Another precaution is to clip a control carabiner on your seat harness (fig. 10-12). The carabiner goes in front, or on the same side as the rope coming from the climber, but well forward of your hip bone. Clipping the rope in to this carabiner keeps the rope where it is needed (at your hip), counteracts body rotation, and adds friction to the system.

Be aware of any potential direction of pull from a fallen climber, and take advantage of a stable stance and the anchor attachment to keep you and the climbing rope from being pulled out of position, causing loss of control of the belay. Wrapping the rope around your back and

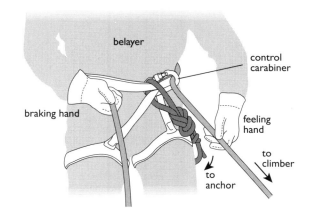

Fig. 10-12. Control carabiner added to a hip belay.

above the anchor attachment will prevent the rope from being pulled below your seat. If the pull will come from above with no possibility of a downward pull, wrap the rope around your back and below the anchor attachment to prevent the rope from being pulled over your head.

CHOOSING A BELAY METHOD

It might seem that the choice of a general-purpose belay method would be a simple matter of choosing the method that exerts the most stopping force. However, even if two belay methods differ significantly in the maximum stopping force they can exert, there may be little practical difference between them. For most falls, the belayer can exert sufficient force regardless of the method.

However, the choice of belay methods does matter in the case of a high-factor fall on steep terrain, with little or nothing to produce friction other than the belay; in this situation, the belay method can mean the difference between the rope running and not running. These types of falls are the critical ones, wherein there is little margin for error.

If the rope starts to run while the belayer is holding a fall, the climber will fall that much farther than if the fall were held with no run-through. A longer fall is generally undesirable and potentially dangerous. However, in any protected leader fall, it is important to consider that the force acts on the protection as well as the climber: the maximum force on the top piece of protection is one and a half to two times as high as the maximum force on the climber—in a high-factor fall on vertical rock, the maximum force on the climber can easily reach 7 kilonewtons (more than 1,500 pounds). If the protection fails under this force, the climber will definitely fall farther. To reduce this force on the protection, some belayers choose a relatively weak method of belaying, one that will let the rope start to run at a lower force to lessen the likelihood of the protection failing.

The leader can also effectively limit the maximum impact on individual protection placements by using a load-limiting runner (see "Runners" in Chapter 9, Basic Safety System). The leader may clip in to a suspect placement with one of these devices without compromising overall belay strength. During a fall, a force greater than the runner's activation point (usually 2 kilonewtons) will start to tear the load-limiting runner's weak bar tacks. As the total energy of the fall increases, more of the weak bar tacks on the load-limiting runner will fail and can reduce by 3 to 8 kilonewtons the peak load that the fall imposes on the placement.

ANCHORS

Secure anchors are vital. Climbers should remind themselves that they cannot anticipate the moment when they will have to stop an extreme leader fall. And when it happens, the anchor must hold, or the climbers—leader and belayer both—will suffer a catastrophic fall.

The word "anchor" refers to a whole system. An anchor can be composed of many components and one or more anchor points: it may include natural features, fixed protection pieces, removable protection pieces, runners, carabiners, and the climbing rope itself.

SELECTING AN ANCHOR

This section gives a few tips on selecting good anchors for belays, but for full details on finding and using natural features and on setting artificial anchors on rock, snow, and ice, study Chapters 13, Rock Protection; 14, Leading on Rock; 16, Snow Travel and Climbing; and 19, Alpine Ice Climbing. Also see Resources for all these chapters.

When selecting belay anchors, always consider every possible direction from which a force may load the anchors. Ideally, the anchor should be directly above the last piece of protection, or as close to it as possible. If a follower falls, the direction of the pull is from the last piece of protection below the belay anchor (fig. 10-13). Once that piece is removed or fails, then the follower pendulums to and past the fall line (fig. 10-14). In a free-hanging situation without friction, the follower can pendulum past the fall line to the same angle as the initial angle between the rope and the fall line. The leader should pay attention to the angle and distance between the anchor and the last piece of protection for the sake of the follower. A big angle puts the follower at a higher risk if he or she falls. A belay anchor directly above the last piece minimizes such a pendulum.

If a leader falls, the *belayer* is pulled toward the first piece of protection, which is usually upward. This is a good reminder to make sure the belay anchors will withstand a pull from any conceivable fall.

Natural Anchors

A large natural feature, such as a good-sized, well-rooted live tree or a pillar of sound rock, can make an ideal anchor. Climbers can also build and remove an anchor very quickly on such features.

Trees and large bushes provide the most obvious anchors, but do not trust a tree or shrub that is loose or appears weak or brittle. Carefully evaluate tree anchors near or on cliff faces; these trees may be shallow-rooted

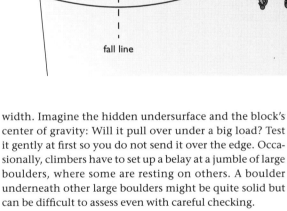

Fig. 10-13. (above) When a follower falls, the direction of pull on the belayer is from the last piece of protection.

Fig. 10-14. (right) If the last piece of protection is removed or fails, then the follower pendulums to and past the fall line.

and not as solid as they appear. Test all trees by pushing against them with one foot. Attaching to an unquestionably stout tree branch rather than low on the trunk helps limit the rope's contact with the ground, reducing abrasion on the rope and reducing the risk of falling rock. However, connecting to a branch rather than the trunk puts more leverage on the tree, increasing the danger that the tree could be uprooted. Be cautious about using a bush as an anchor. If you use one, consider placing an additional anchor or two for safety. Also be careful about using trees and bushes in very cold weather, when their wood can become brittle.

Rock features—horns, columns, rock tunnels such as those formed by the contact point between two boulders, large and flat-bottomed boulders—are commonly used as anchors. Note that it is easy to overestimate the stability of large boulders. As important as size are the shape of the boulder's bottom, the shape of the socket it is sitting in or the angle of the slope it is on, and the ratio of its height to width. Imagine the hidden undersurface and the block's center of gravity: Will it pull over under a big load? Test it gently at first so you do not send it over the edge. Occasionally, climbers have to set up a belay at a jumble of large boulders, where some are resting on others. A boulder underneath other large boulders might be quite solid but can be difficult to assess even with careful checking.

Check any rock feature used as an anchor for fracture lines, which may be subtle and difficult to judge, such as at the base of a rock horn or near the edge of a crack. When using protection in a crack for an anchor, check to see whether one side of the crack may actually be a detachable block or movable flake; a crack has to widen only a fraction of an inch under the force of a fall for the protection to pull out.

Always evaluate the probable strength and stability of a rock feature or chockstone prior to using it as an anchor. Place a sling on a rock feature well below the feature's center of gravity to reduce the chance of it tipping or dislodging. If there is any question about a natural anchor, test it before gear is attached, never after the rope or the belayer is clipped in. (See also "Natural Protection" in Chapter 13, Rock Protection.)

Fixed Anchors

Artificial (manufactured) anchors include bolts and pitons that, once set, are usually left "fixed" permanently in place. On established routes, climbers may encounter previously placed bolts and pitons; in unknown alpine terrain, some climbers carry pitons and a hammer to set anchors.

Bolts are permanent pieces of artificial protection that are driven into a hole that has been drilled into the rock. Bolt hangers, which may or may not be permanent, allow carabiners to be attached to bolts (see Figure 13-6 in Chapter 13, Rock Protection). *Pitons* are metal spikes pounded into cracks. The blade of the piton is driven into the crack; the eye is the point of attachment for a carabiner (see Figure 13-8 in Chapter 13, Rock Protection). On rock climbing topo maps, bolts and fixed pitons are often shown as "x" and "fp" (for "fixed protection"), respectively (see Figure 14-3 in Chapter 14, Leading on Rock).

Climbers may also encounter other fixed pieces—hardware such as nuts, hexes, and so forth—which are normally removable protection that became fixed when someone could not remove them. Fixed pieces left in place by previous climbers must be evaluated for safety. Bolts and fixed pitons are often solid if of recent vintage, but older placements are notoriously difficult to assess (see "Fixed Protection" in Chapter 13, Rock Protection). Old ¼-inch bolts are no longer the accepted standard and should not be trusted.

Many popular routes now feature fixed anchors at belay stations; commonly these consist of two or more bolts, sometimes connected with a short section or sections of chain.

Removable Anchors

Where natural features or fixed protection are not available, climbers build anchors and remove them as they complete a pitch (see Chapters 13, Rock Protection, and 14, Leading on Rock, for rock anchors; Chapter 16, Snow Travel and Climbing, for snow anchors; and Chapter 19, Alpine Ice Climbing, for ice anchors).

EQUALIZING THE ANCHOR

Commonly, belays use two or three anchor placements, so the anchor system has redundancy and is not dependent on any single anchor placement: if one anchor placement fails, one or both of the two other anchor placements may still hold. The reliability of multiple anchor placements is further increased by distributing the load among the placements, a technique called *equalization*.

Most ways of equalizing the load on multiple anchor points make use of runners or loops of accessory cord (both of which are called *legs*) to connect the anchor points into a single *power point*, or *master point*. These equalization methods can be roughly divided into two types: static equalization and self-equalization. *Static equalization* distributes the load in only one direction. *Self-equalization* distributes the load in a range of directions. Various commonly used equalization methods have advantages and disadvantages, and no one choice is preferable across all scenarios. It is important to understand the variables involved, to know how anchors function in different situations, and to make informed decisions about how best to construct anchors in various configurations. Ultimately, any multipart anchor is only as good as its individual components, and safety depends on skillful placement of individual pieces.

In building a multipoint anchor, the first question to ask is, how many anchor points are needed? There is no universal answer to this question. It depends on lots of factors: the maximum possible force, the quality of rock or natural protection, et cetera. But the general rule of thumb is, to build two bombproof pieces or three good pieces. As your confidence in pieces lowers, add more pieces and do a better job of equalizing them.

The next factor to consider is the angle formed by all the legs at the power point: the main connection point of the anchor system. This angle is sometimes called the *V-angle* because the legs form the shape of a V. Figure 10-15 shows a two-point anchor, in which the two legs are symmetric. According to rules of basic physics, the bigger the angle, the more force is delivered to each anchor point and the less effective the equalization is.

At a V-angle approaching 0 degrees, or when the two anchor points are perfectly aligned, each anchor point receives half the load (fig. 10-15a). Strive to keep the V-angle of a belay anchor system less than 60 degrees (fig. 10-15b). With a V-angle greater than 60 degrees, the load on each anchor point increases significantly (fig. 10-15c). When the V-angle is 120 degrees, the force on either anchor point is the same as the load itself (fig. 10-15d). In this case, the force is not reduced at all—the equalization serves no purpose other than providing redundancy (if one anchor point fails, the other takes over). When the V-angle exceeds 120 degrees, the force is amplified, and it grows rapidly as the V-angle increases (fig. 10-16). An anchor system with

10

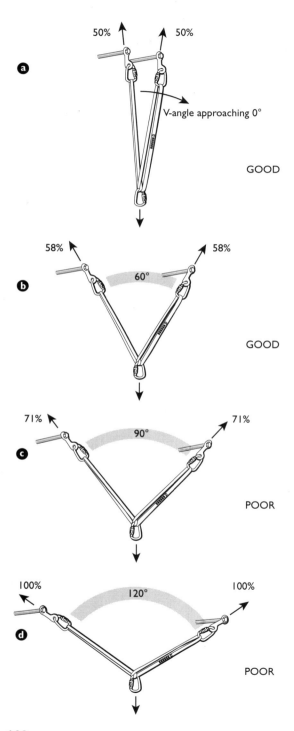

Fig. 10-15. (left) V-angle effect on percent load or force in a two-point anchor system equalized with sewn runners: a, at a V-angle approaching 0 degrees the load is shared equally; b and c, as the V-angle increases, the load on each anchor point increases; d, at angles greater than 120 degrees, the load exceeds 100 percent on each anchor point. Strive to keep the V-angle of a belay anchor system less than 60 degrees.

Fig. 10-15. (left) V-angle effect on percent load or force in a two-point anchor system equalized with sewn runners: a, at a V-angle approaching 0 degrees the load is shared equally; b and c, as the V-angle increases, the load on each anchor point increases; d, at angles greater than 120 degrees, the load exceeds 100 percent on each anchor point. Strive to keep the V-angle of a belay anchor system less than 60 degrees.

more than two anchor points is a little harder to analyze, but the principles remain the same: keep the overall V-angle relatively small.

Static Equalization

With static equalization, the anchor takes the load in only one direction.

Two anchor points. To statically equalize two anchor points, a common method is to clip a double-length (48-inch/120-centimeter) runner in to the two anchor points—one end of the runner to one anchor point, the other end of the runner to the other anchor point—then gather the resulting four strands of the runner, tie them in an overhand or figure-eight knot, and clip a locking carabiner to the resulting loop (power point) that is on the opposite side of the knot from the anchor points (fig. 10-17).

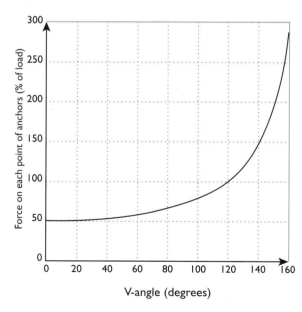

Fig. 10-16. V-angle effect on force multiplication.

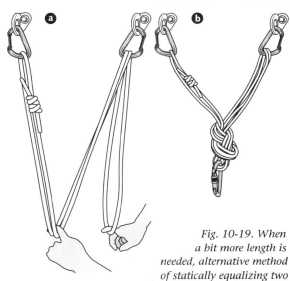

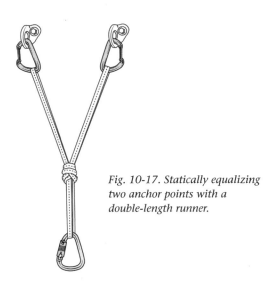

Fig. 10-17. Statically equalizing two anchor points with a double-length runner.

Fig. 10-19. When a bit more length is needed, alternative method of statically equalizing two anchor points with cordelette: a, clip one bight of the cordelette into one anchor point and clip both strands of the cordelette to the other anchor point; b, knot the resulting six strands together to create a power point.

The drawback of this method is that the overhand or figure-eight knot is hard to untie after it has been heavily loaded. Also, the knot is usually very small if the runner is skinny, and a small knot on a skinny runner significantly weakens the strength of the runner. To mitigate this problem, climbers can use a *cordelette*, a long runner of about 20 feet (about 6 meters) usually made of 7- to 8-millimeter nylon accessory cord or a small-diameter, high-strength cord of a material such as Spectra or Dyneema. First, double the cordelette to half its length, then create a power point with the loop (fig. 10-18) as for a double-length runner. Alternatively, if the power point must be extended a little

farther from the anchor points, clip one bight of the cordelette in to one anchor point and clip both strands of the cordelette to the other anchor point (fig. 10-19a), then tie a figure eight or overhand knot with the resulting six strands to create the power point (fig. 10-19b).

Three anchor points. To equalize three anchor points, clip the cordelette in to each anchor point's carabiner and pull down the top segments between the anchor points (fig. 10-20a). Join these segments with the bottom part of the cordelette by gripping the resulting three loops and connecting a locking carabiner to all three loops (fig. 10-20b). Shift the carabiner around while you gather the strands together to even out the tension in all strands as best you can. Then, while pulling in the anticipated direction of force, tie all three segments together into an overhand or figure eight (fig. 10-20c). Either knot is acceptable; the overhand requires less cord than the figure eight, but it will be much harder to untie if it is heavily loaded. Pull on the carabiner at the end loop (power point) to make sure all three legs are weighted. Static equalization with a cordelette can also be done with more than three anchor points.

The shelf. In either a two-point or three-point anchor, the end loop (power point) created by the overhand or figure-eight knot is the main attachment point to the belay anchor. Additional connection points, such as a second climber clipping in on arrival at the belay station,

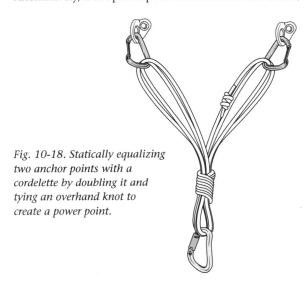

Fig. 10-18. Statically equalizing two anchor points with a cordelette by doubling it and tying an overhand knot to create a power point.

189

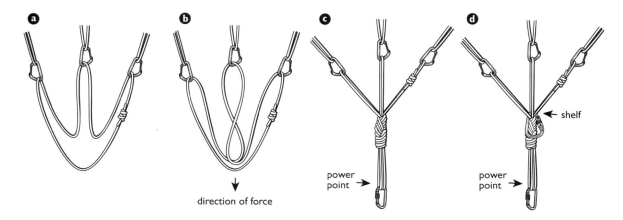

Fig. 10-20. Static equalization of three anchor points with cordelette: a, clip in to each of three anchor point carabiners and pull down the top segments between the anchor points; b, gather the strands together at an even length; c, knot the resulting six strands together to create a power point with a locking carabiner; d, clip another locker into the shelf.

can be made by creating a "shelf" consisting of all anchor placements above the power point: clip a carabiner to one strand coming from each of the anchor points (fig. 10-20d). It is very important that only one strand from each anchor point is clipped. A shelf does not exist in an anchor system unless each anchor point has two strands. This shelf can simplify clipping in to or unclipping from a loaded anchor and can avoid much clutter and confusion.

Uneven distribution of forces in static equalization. Load-testing of cordelettes shows that the ideal, even distribution of forces is not usually achieved using three anchor points: even under ideal circumstances—with three anchor placements symmetrically arranged—the middle leg may be subjected to twice the load of the two side legs (fig. 10-21a). Asymmetrical configurations tend to primarily load the two legs closest to the direction of pull. As the lengths of the different legs become more uneven, as is common when an anchor is rigged in a vertical crack, the lowest leg is subjected to much higher loads than the longer legs (fig. 10-21b). These differences are due to greater elongation that occurs with longer sections of cord. The effects of unevenly rigged configurations can be reduced by extending the individual placements with low-stretch runners to equalize the length of the elastic cordelette legs. Any slack in a leg of the cordelette means that it supports negligible weight and is not equalized.

Self-Equalization

Self-equalization is intended to react to changing load direction and to distribute any force equally among all the

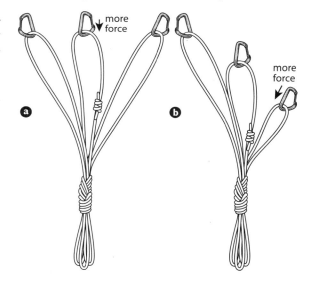

Fig. 10-21. Uneven distribution of forces in static equalization: a, in a symmetrical anchor, pull appears equal on both side strands, but the middle strand may be subjected to twice their load; b, in an asymmetrical anchor, the load is shifted to one side—now the lowest anchor point is subjected to higher loads than the other two longer legs.

anchor components. There are two primary methods of self-equalization.

Sliding X. Two-point equalizing is the simplest example of self-equalization. Clip a runner in to the two anchor

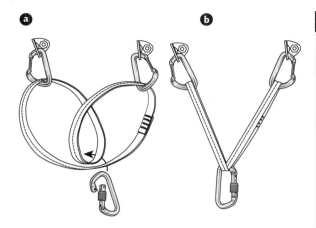

Fig. 10-22. Sliding X self-equalizing anchor: a, grasp the top part of the runner between the two anchor points and put a half twist in it, making an X and forming a loop; b, clip the loop and the bottom part of the runner together with a locking carabiner and tie the rope to this carabiner.

carabiners; grasp the top part of the runner between the two anchor points and put a half twist in it, making an X and forming a loop (fig. 10-22a); then clip the loop and the bottom part of the runner together with a locking carabiner. Tie the rope to this carabiner (fig. 10-22b). It is essential to put the loop in the runner rather than just clipping the top and bottom of the runner. Otherwise, if one anchor point fails, the runner will simply slip through this carabiner, leaving the rope completely unanchored. With a longer runner, the sliding X can work well to equalize more than two anchor points.

The sliding X method depends on the carabiner attachment sliding freely to self-equalize as the direction of pull changes. Take care in rigging this system to minimize friction between the sliding carabiner and the X. New, thinner sewn runners work better with this method than bulky ⁹⁄₁₆-inch or wider webbing. Using larger-diameter carabiners also reduces friction.

Equalization always conflicts with the "No Extension" principle described in the "SERENE Anchor Systems" sidebar. To mitigate, you can use shorter slings or tie limiter knots (usually overhand knots) in the runner (fig. 10-23). Limiter knots minimize the length the anchor can extend as well as limit the extent to which the anchor is equalized. Without such limiter knots, if one anchor point fails, it shock-loads the remaining anchor points, creating a risk of failure.

SERENE ANCHOR SYSTEMS

A simple yet highly effective set of principles to follow when evaluating anchor systems goes by the acronym SERENE. Strive to fulfill these requirements, but note that the principles of "Equalized" and "No Extension" are inherently in conflict with each other. Climbers must make conscious compromises.

- **Solid.** Each individual component should be solid to the greatest extent feasible.
- **Efficient.** An anchor system should be efficiently built and dismantled.
- **Redundant.** Always use redundant components in setting up an anchor; this applies not only to anchor points but to all elements in an anchor system.
- **Equalized.** Use a rigging method that tries to equally distribute the load among the various individual anchor points, which greatly increases the reliability of each part of the system.
- **No Extension.** Minimize the possibility that failure of one component in the anchor system will cause the anchor to suddenly extend, which would cause subsequent shock loading and generate dangerously high impact forces on the remaining components.

10

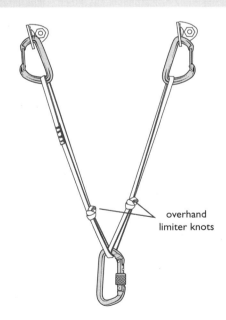

overhand
limiter knots

Fig. 10-23. Sliding X with limiter knots.

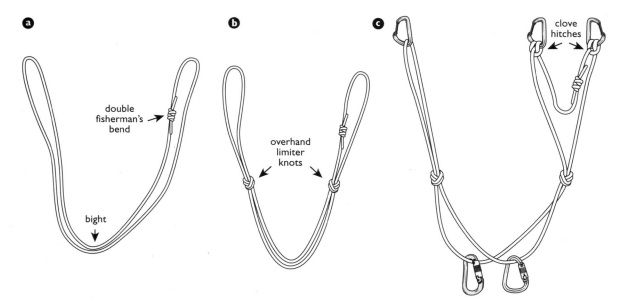

Figure 10-24. Self-equalizing with an equalette: a, grab a bight to form a double-stranded U, with the fisherman's bend slightly offset from one end of the loop; b, tie overhand limiter knots on both sides, creating an isolated center section with two longer side loops; c, connect the side loops to one or more anchor components, and clip in to the central section with two carabiners, one per strand. Here, the right-hand loop is connected to two anchors and equalized with clove hitches.

Equalettes. The equalette was developed to overcome the disadvantages of friction and elongation associated with the sliding X and the potentially poor equalization of a cordelette. It combines elements from both the sliding X and the cordelette.

Equalettes are normally constructed from 20 feet (6 meters) of 7-millimeter nylon or smaller-diameter, high-strength cord. Tie the cord into a loop with a double or triple fisherman's bend, as appropriate to the material. Grab a bight to form a double-stranded U, with the fisherman's bend slightly offset from one end of the loop (fig. 10-24a), then tie overhand limiter knots on both sides of the U to create a section about 10 inches (25 centimeters) long. You now have a loop about 8 feet (2.5 meters) long consisting of an isolated center section and two longer side loops (fig. 10-24b). To build a multipoint anchor using the equalette, estimate the most likely direction that the force of a fall will come from, and orient the central section toward that pull, just as is done when tying a power point in a cordelette anchor system.

Now connect both of the side loops to one or more anchor components. Various configurations are possible using one or more anchor elements per side, equal-ized with combinations of clove hitches, sliding Xs, and so on. Once the anchor is constructed, clip in to the bottom center section of the equalette, preferably using one locking carabiner for each of the two central strands (fig. 10-24c). If using one carabiner to clip in, instead of two, be sure to put a half twist and loop in one of the strands, just as with the sliding X, to prevent complete disconnection if one side of the equalette were to fail.

In action, this method is designed to self-equalize; the tie-in can redirect itself and maintain load distribution to both sides if the direction of pull changes. If one leg were to completely fail, the limiter knots would keep extension to a reasonable minimum. Though it might seem rather complicated at first, the equalette addresses the criticisms of static and self-equalized systems, and it does not add too much complexity or time to anchor setups.

TYING IN TO THE ANCHOR

The connection between the harness and the anchor, whether the belayer uses a tie-in or a clip-in, should be made with a separate carabiner. The best way for the belayer to connect to the anchor is to tie in with the climbing rope itself, using the first few feet of rope as it comes from its tie-in at the belayer's harness. This ensures that there will be a dynamic link between the belayer and anchor because the rope itself is dynamic.

Climbers often connect to the anchor using runners or their personal anchors. Although this may save time and keeps the maximum amount of rope available for climbing longer pitches, there are hazards associated with this practice. Runners and personal anchors usually have low stretch and do not react dynamically under load. If a climber is any distance above the anchor and falls, the climber may experience a high-factor fall, and even short falls on these low-stretch materials can generate extremely high impact forces. Despite their high strength, such runners, as well as carabiners, have failed under these circumstances. An even bigger risk is the high impact force on the climber in the case of a high-factor fall. Human bodies can usually tolerate 12 kilonewtons without serious or fatal injuries. If using a personal anchor, keep the slack minimal, and do not climb above the anchor.

BELAY POSITION AND STANCE

In deciding on a belay position in relation to the belay anchor, think through the possibilities of what could go wrong given varying positions and potential falls. Try to plan for worst-case scenarios and make sure that a bad fall would be caught by the belay anchor before the belayer would be pulled off the belay stance, which entails the very real possibility of losing control of the belay.

BELAYING A LEADER OR TOP-ROPE CLIMBER

When belaying a leader or a top-rope climber, belay directly off the seat harness. This position puts the belayer's hands and arms in the correct position to manage the rope and to apply braking force the instant a fall occurs.

Anticipate the direction of pull in case of a fall. That force tends to pull the belayer upward and into the rock. If you are not anchored (often the case in single-pitch cragging), you could be slammed into any object in the way. Therefore, it's best to stand close to the rock, with a stable bent-knee athletic stance. No matter which direction you are facing—in toward the mountain or out—keep in line with the anchor and the direction of pull. Otherwise the fall will spin you into an awkward position.

If the belay is anchored, tie in to the anchor no more than an arm's length away, so that you can still reach the anchor if your tie-in is pulled tight by a fall. At the same time, don't tie in awkwardly close to the anchor. Leave a little room for the braking hand, as well as a little slack in the rope should you need to move your body to give the climber a soft catch if a fall occurs.

When belaying a leader, there are many advantages to facing in toward the mountain. Facing in usually allows you to watch your partner climb, enabling you to anticipate movements and to pay out or take in rope more efficiently (see "Rope Handling" below). You may also be able to figure out how to get past some of the difficult sections when it is time for you to climb if you have seen where your partner had difficulty and how your partner negotiated these cruxes. You are better able to see rockfall early and take cover. And you are in the best position to see a leader fall start, so you can quickly brace and go into the braking position. Being able to see a leader's fall begin is a particular advantage when the first piece of protection is low and the force of the fall would tend to pull you into the rock.

These advantages of facing in are lost when belaying in an alcove with a roof or bulge overhead that prevents you from watching your partner. In this situation, you are no worse off facing out when it comes to holding a protected leader fall, and you are probably in a much better position to hold an unprotected leader fall because you are not in danger of being spun around.

When belaying a leader, the most likely direction of pull in the case of a leader fall is upward. But in the severe situation in which the leader falls past the anchor before placing the first piece of protection (factor 2 fall), the force is downward. A belayer with a fairly long attachment to an anchor at about waist height or lower—very commonly seen—is not prepared to stop an unprotected leader fall. If the belayer is standing on a ledge and the partner falls past the belayer, the downward force builds quickly beyond the point that the belay stance can hold. The belayer would then be pulled violently off the ledge or driven sharply down onto it, with almost certain loss of control of the belay and probable injuries. To prevent this possibility, attach tightly to an anchor above waist level so that you cannot be pulled down more than a few inches.

BELAYING A FOLLOWER

When belaying a follower, choose between belaying off the anchor or the harness.

Belay Off the Harness

The traditional way to belay a second is off the harness—that is, the belay device is clipped directly to the belay loop on the harness (fig. 10-25). The advantage is that you can

10

Fig. 10-25. Belaying a follower off the harness.

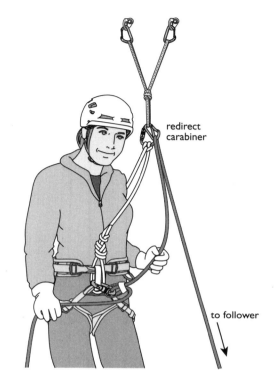

Fig. 10-26. Belaying a follower off the harness with a redirect.

use your body movement to provide a soft belay, which is useful when the anchor is less than bombproof. However, this method doesn't work very well if the terrain below is vertical, because the follower's weight will pull the belayer to the fall line. When that happens, the belayer could be pulled out of the belay stance and end up suspended awkwardly, unable to get the braking hand back into the brake position. Most belay device manufacturers also don't recommend belaying the second off the harness.

Belay Off the Harness with a Redirect

An improvement over belaying off the harness is to redirect the rope through a carabiner above the belayer's harness, as shown in Figure 10-26. This way, the fall force would come from above instead of below, and the belayer is in a more comfortable position when holding a fall. However, when the belayer catches the fall, the force on the redirect carabiner is twice the body weight of the follower (not considering friction) due to the pulley effect. Be aware of the multiplied force when choosing this method. Also consider using the strongest point in the anchor system

for redirection, which is usually the power point or shelf. However, the force multiplication is irrelevant in a hanging belay, wherein the weight of the belayer is already on the anchor.

Belay Off the Anchor

The preferred method of belaying a follower is directly off the anchor (from a belay device or munter hitch on the anchor), sometimes also called a "direct belay." One big advantage is that the belayer is out of the system, hence not subject to the forces created by a fall and therefore less likely to be injured or lose control of the belay. When something goes wrong, it's easy for the belayer to "escape" (see "Escaping the Belay" below). This is also very useful if the follower is less experienced and needs to be coached from above.

A common method for a direct belay is to use an assisted-braking belay device or an auto-locking belay device in its auto-locking mode clipped directly in to the anchor, as shown in Figure 10-7. An alternative method is to belay with a munter hitch on the anchor (fig. 10-27). Different

Fig. 10-27. Belaying off the anchor using a munter hitch.

manufacturers use different terminologies for auto-locking mode. For instance, Black Diamond calls it "guide mode"; consult the manufacturer's instructions.

A regular non-auto-locking belay device should not be used for a belay directly off the anchor. To arrest a fall, the belayer would have to push the braking hand away from the body and back behind the device in order to separate the rope strands by the minimum of 90 degrees. This can be awkward, perhaps impossible, and the braking hand grip will be comparatively weak. In fact, most manufacturers do not allow a regular aperture belay device to be used directly off the anchor at all. When an auto-locking belay device is not used in the auto-locking mode, it should be treated like a regular belay device.

Regardless of the belay device or method used to belay off the anchor, position the tie-in so that the anchor's power point is at roughly shoulder level when the belayer is leaning on the anchor. This way, the belayer has enough work space between the tie-in and the anchor to make pulling and coiling the rope easier. If the power point is too low, consider using the anchor shelf if there is one.

ROPE HANDLING

In addition to stopping a fall if one should occur, it is important for the belayer to maintain the correct tension on the rope: prevent excess slack, anticipate the climber's movements and rope needs, let out rope as the climber moves up or clips in to protection, take rope in as needed, and manage the accumulating rope. The techniques below are described in the stance for belaying the leader off the harness, but the techniques can easily be modified for other belay methods. Practice until you learn to quickly take in or let out rope with the feeling hand as needed while never removing the braking hand from the rope.

Maintaining the right amount of slack. Keeping just enough but not too much slack in the rope during a belay is a skill that requires practice. Obviously, too much slack will lengthen a fall and hence increase the impact force and the risk of the climber getting injured (fig. 10-28). Too much slack also makes it hard for the belayer to "feel" the rope movement and needs of the climber. Too little slack, on the other hand, can impede the climber's movement and balance. A good belayer uses the feeling hand and is always aware of how much slack is in the rope. Ideally, when belaying a follower, there is almost no slack in the rope (fig. 10-29), but at the same time, the rope should not be taut, especially on a traverse when balance is crucial.

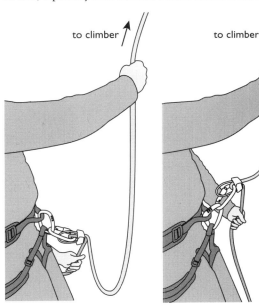

Fig. 10-28. Too much rope slack.

Fig. 10-29. Right amount of rope slack.

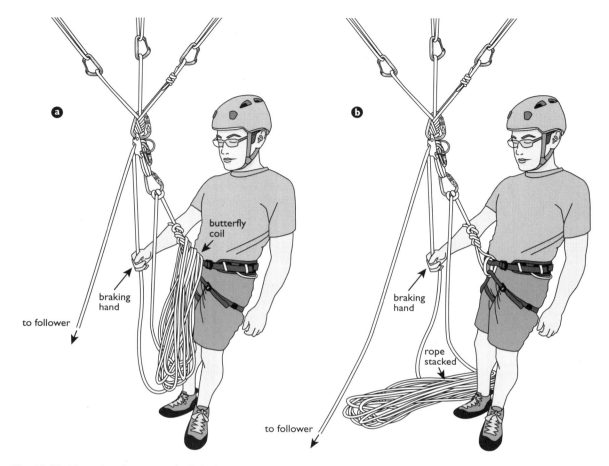

Fig. 10-30. Managing the rope at the belay: a, a butterfly coil laid across the belayer's anchor tie-in; b, stacking the rope on the ground.

Anticipating the leader's rope needs. To minimize falling distance, leaders preparing to make difficult moves often place protection well above their harness tie-in and clip in to that protection before moving up. In these cases, the leader needs some additional slack, and the direction of rope movement will reverse twice. After letting out rope for the leader to make a clip, the belayer will need to take in slack as the climber moves up to the protection. The belayer will then pay out rope again once the climber moves past the protection and uses up most of the slack in the rope. These switches call for extra attention, especially because this tends to happen at the most difficult spots on a route. It's worth noting, however, that when the leader clips above waist level and pulls extra rope to clip in, he or she is momentarily subject to a longer fall, so the leader

should do this only from a comfortable and safe stance.

When belaying the leader, an alert belayer keeps just a hint of slack and responds immediately to the leader's advance by paying out more rope. The belayer is also always ready to transition between paying out rope and pulling in slack when the leader clips in to protection. Any friction applied by the belayer is multiplied, so if the leader says that rope drag is a problem, keep about a foot or so of slack in the rope and do everything possible to eliminate any pull. If the climber falls when there is a lot of friction in the system, the belayer may actually be unsure whether a fall even took place. If it is impossible to communicate with the climber, the belayer can find out by letting out a few inches of rope. If the same tension remains, then the belayer is probably holding the climber's weight.

Managing the rope. Proper rope management is essential so that the belayer may keep the right amount of slack at all times. The belayer does not want to be distracted by knots and tangles in the rope when belaying. Before belaying a leader, neatly pile or coil the rope with the climber's end on top. Do this by carefully flaking out the rope, shaking it out as needed to avoid unwanted twists, and stacking the rope on the ground before starting to belay.

When belaying a follower up to the belay station, either stack the rope on the ground if the belay station is big enough or coil it using the butterfly coil. For the butterfly coil, coil the rope back and forth across the belayer's anchor tie-in (fig. 10-30a); it helps to keep the tie-in under a little tension even if it's not a hanging belay. If the belayer stacks the rope on the ground, make sure the rope pile has a small footprint and is not tangled with rock flakes and tree branches (fig. 10-30b).

If the climbing team is swapping leads—that is, the follower will become the new leader on the next pitch—the belayer doesn't need to do anything with the rope because the leader's end is already on the top and the rope should be nicely piled or coiled for the next pitch. However, if the climbing team is leading in blocks—that is, the climber who led the last pitch is going to lead the next—the belayer must reverse the rope. If the rope is butterfly-coiled, grab the middle of the coil and flip it onto the follower's anchor tie-in. Reversing the rope is a little more difficult if the rope is stacked in a pile: the belayer can carefully flip the whole pile like a pancake, but if that fails, the whole rope must be reflaked, which is time-consuming.

COMMUNICATION

Effective and efficient communication between members of a climbing party is key to safe and speedy ascents. A set of standardized and concise commands understood by all climbers can tremendously reduce confusion and save time and hassle. Make sure everyone in the climbing party agrees upon the commands before they start climbing, especially if they are breaking in a new climbing partner. The commands in Table 10-1 have been developed to produce a distinctive pattern, and they are used universally, even among non-English-speaking climbers.

As climber and belayer get farther apart, they begin to have difficulty hearing each other. It is impossible to communicate in full sentences, and often the first syllable is not heard. When the belayer is a long way from the climbing partner, shout as loudly as possible and space out each syllable, using very big spaces if there are echoes. In a crowded area, clearly preface commands with your partner's name to avoid confusion about who is being safely belayed or lowered, who is off belay, et cetera. Prefixing commands with climbers' names also has the advantage that climbers will pause upon hearing their name as the first word and thus have a better chance of understanding the remainder of the command. Sometimes climbers may rely on a third party to relay their commands.

Verbal communication often becomes impossible because of wind or obstructions. In such cases, people have suggested using rope pulls. However, there is no universal protocol for rope signals. Also, if there is enough wind or obstructions to impede verbal communication, rope tugs usually cannot be easily or reliably felt.

Some climbers use two-way radios for communication. If you do, check local radio frequency regulations and make sure your radios conform. Also be aware of the limitations of radios. Battery life is shorter in cold conditions. When the batteries run out, make sure you have alternative means of communication. A useful tip for radios is to not start talking at the same time you press the "talk" button because the first couple of words will be lost. Instead, press the button, wait for a second or two, and then start talking.

Always use positive commands instead of negative ones. For example, when there is too much slack in the rope, use "Up rope" instead of "Too much slack," because the latter can be misheard or mistakenly interpreted as "Slack," which is the exact opposite of what you mean. Always try to stick to the standard commands listed in Table 10-1 instead of creating your own commands, because standard commands can be understood by everyone.

The rule of thumb in communication is to keep it simple. Here are the recommended commands in Table 10-1 configured for exchanges between the climber and the belayer in two different scenarios.

SINGLE-PITCH CLIMB

In this scenario, the belayer is belaying a climber who is either leading or top-roping on a slingshot setup. The command exchange takes place after both parties have done the safety check.

> *Climber: "On belay?"*
> *Belayer: "Belay on."*
> *Climber: "Climbing."*
> *Belayer: "Climb on."*

The climber climbs to the top. If the climber is leading, he or she sets up the top anchor and clips the rope in to the anchor. Now the climber is ready to put the weight on the rope and be lowered.

	TABLE 10-1. COMMONLY USED CLIMBING COMMANDS	
COMMAND	SAID BY	MEANING
"On belay?"	Climber	Do you have me on belay? Are you ready to brake my fall?
"Belay on."	Belayer	Yes, I have you on belay. Can be a response to "On belay?"
"Climbing."	Climber	I'm about to climb.
"Climb on/climb away."	Belayer	Go ahead and climb. Response to "Climbing."
"Off belay."	Climber	I'm safe, either on the ground or attached to an anchor. Please take the rope out of the belay device.
"Belay off."	Belayer	You are no longer on belay. Response to "Off belay."
"Take."	Climber	Pull all the slack in the rope and I'm going to put my weight on it.
"Got you."	Belayer	All slack has been pulled out. Go ahead and lean on the rope. Response to "Take."
"Lower me/lower."	Climber	I have finished climbing. Please lower me to the ground.
"Lowering."	Belayer	I'm starting to lower you. Response to "Lower me."
"That's me."	Follower	You have taken in all the slack in the rope. The resistance to your pull is my body.
"Slack."	Climber	Give me some slack. The rope is too tight.
"Up rope."	Climber	Pull up some slack. The rope has too much slack.
"Watch me."	Climber	Give me an attentive belay. I may fall.
"Falling!"	Climber	I'm falling. Brake my fall.
"Rock/ice!"	Anyone	Falling rock, ice, or other objects. Take cover, everyone!
"Clipping."	Leader	I'm about to clip the rope into a piece of protection.
"Half rope."	Belayer	You have led half the length of the rope.
"X feet/X meters."	Belayer	You have X feet (meters) of rope left.

Climber: "Take."
Belayer: "Got you."
Climber: "Lower me."
Belayer: "Lowering."
The belayer lowers the climber to the ground.
Climber: "Off belay."
Belayer: "Belay off."
If the leader is cleaning the protection on the way down, he or she may also ask the belayer to pause at each protection point so he or she can remove them. The commands are "Stop" for pausing and "Lower" for resuming.

MULTIPITCH CLIMB

In this scenario, the follower belays the leader. When the leader gets to the top of a pitch, he or she sets up an anchor and belays the follower to the top. When they continue climbing the next pitch, they may or may not exchange roles as belayer and leader for the next pitch.
Leader: "On belay?"
Belayer: "Belay on."
Leader: "Climbing."
Belayer: "Climb away."

The leader arrives at the top of the first pitch, sets up an anchor, and secures him- or herself to the anchor.
Leader: "Off belay."
Follower: "Belay off."
The leader pulls the rope and the follower gets ready to follow the pitch. As the rope gets taut, they communicate:
Follower: "That's me!"
Leader: "Belay on."
The follower removes the previous anchor, then starts ascending.
Follower: "Climbing."
Leader: "Climb on."
The follower arrives at the belay station and secures him- or herself to the anchor.
Follower: "Off belay."
Leader: "Belay off."

ACTIONS BASED ON THE COMMANDS

Specific actions are associated with particular commands that the belayer and follower use.

Slack is especially useful to a climber who is leading or traversing.

Up rope is used when there is too much slack in the system and the belayer should take up the slack.

Watch me is used when the climber is about to make some difficult moves and needs an especially attentive belay.

Clipping is used to indicate that the belayer should pay attention to the direction of the rope travel, and to warn of a possible pull on the rope made by the leader. If the protection is above the leader's waist, the rope will travel away from the belayer, then toward him or her before traveling away again.

Half rope gives the leader a sense of the length of the route.

X feet (X meters) is used in a multipitch scenario to help the leader decide when and where to build an anchor. Outside of the United States, people usually use meters (a meter is roughly 3 feet).

ESCAPING THE BELAY

One aspect of belaying that most climbers hope they will never have to use is tying off and escaping the belay in order to help an injured partner. If a climbing partner is seriously injured and other climbers are nearby, it is usually best to let them help while you continue to belay. By staying in place, you could also help in raising or lowering the victim if needed. But if two climbers are alone, it may be necessary to tie off the climbing rope to remove yourself from the belay system, so you can investigate, help your partner, or go for help. Escaping the belay is the first step of many rescue scenarios. The goal of belay escape is to have the load connected directly to the anchor and the belayer out of the system.

When belaying off the anchor. When you are belaying off the anchor using a munter hitch or auto-locking device, the fallen climber's weight is already on the anchor, and the only thing the belayer needs to do is to free the braking hand (remember, an auto-locking device is not a hands-free device). To do so, you simply need to tie a mule knot with the braking strand while still holding on to the braking strand, backing it up with an overhand knot (fig. 10-31; see also Figures 9-20 and 9-21 in Chapter 9, Basic Safety System).

When belaying using a belay device attached to the seat harness. If belaying from the harness, more steps are involved to escape the belay because the fallen climber's weight is on the belayer. The first step is to free the belayer's hands. With the braking hand still holding the rope, stick a couple fingers of your other hand through the belay carabiner and pull a bight of rope over so that now

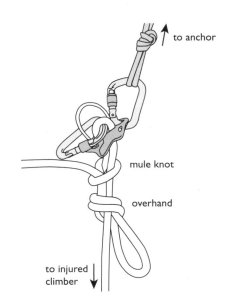

Fig. 10-31. Tying off a direct belay.

your other hand becomes the braking hand. The braking strand is now in line with the load. Use your free hand to tie a device-mule knot with an overhand backup knot (fig. 10-32a). Both hands of the belayer are now free.

The next steps are to transfer the weight to the anchor so that the belayer can get out of the system. To achieve this, attach a cord tie-off loop to the climber's end of the rope with a prusik hitch and connect this loop to a locking carabiner. Attach this locking carabiner to the loose rope coming from the belayer tie-in at the anchor, using a munter hitch with a mule knot to connect the carabiner and rope, then back it up with an overhand knot; the entire knot is called a munter-mule-overhand, or MMO (fig. 10-32b; see also Figure 9-21 in Chapter 9, Basic Safety System). Now, put a braking hand back on the braking strand to backup the connection to the anchor as you follow the next step. Untie the first overhand knot backup and device-mule knot (from the belay setup on the harness), and slowly transfer the load to the tie-off loop using the belay device (fig. 10-32c).

Now the fallen climber's weight is secured to the anchor but on a potentially weak tie-off cord. Connect the rope from the fallen climber to the anchor with another MMO as a backup leaving just enough slack to disassemble the belay (fig. 10-32d). Now disassemble the belay, disconnect the belay device from the system, and untie from the anchor (fig. 10-32e).

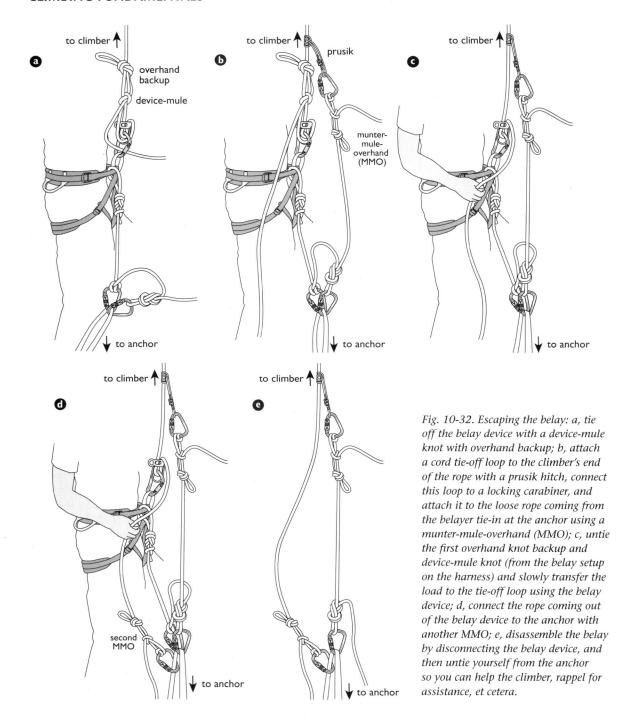

Fig. 10-32. Escaping the belay: a, tie off the belay device with a device-mule knot with overhand backup; b, attach a cord tie-off loop to the climber's end of the rope with a prusik hitch, connect this loop to a locking carabiner, and attach it to the loose rope coming from the belayer tie-in at the anchor using a munter-mule-overhand (MMO); c, untie the first overhand knot backup and device-mule knot (from the belay setup on the harness) and slowly transfer the load to the tie-off loop using the belay device; d, connect the rope coming out of the belay device to the anchor with another MMO; e, disassemble the belay by disconnecting the belay device, and then untie yourself from the anchor so you can help the climber, rappel for assistance, et cetera.

When belaying using a munter hitch attached to the seat harness. The steps involved are very similar except the first step. To free your hands, tie an MMO (see Figure 9-21). The rest of the steps to escape the belay are exactly the same.

As the above steps illustrate, an MMO knot or a device-mule knot with an overhand backup is used in transferring a live load. Such a knot is also called a *releasable knot*. Releasable knots are extremely helpful in a rescue scenario because it should always be assumed that the fallen climber is incapacitated and cannot release the load from the rope, even momentarily. That's the reason a second MMO is used to hold the fallen climber's weight and a third MMO is used as the backup. This provides the flexibility needed later to either lower the fallen climber using the belay device or munter hitch or to rig a raising system.

SECURING THE FREEDOM OF THE HILLS

Belaying and anchor setup are the fundamental skills of technical climbing. Practice belaying often, alternating between using your right hand and left hand as the braking hand. Study and practice anchor techniques. There are many different ways of anchoring yourself. Always use the SERENE principles to evaluate your anchors.

Being proficient with belay technique and anchor setup helps climbers become good team partners. These methods are also related to skills required for rappelling; once climbers become proficient in belay skills, they will have more confidence when it comes to rappel. Overall, solid skills in belaying and anchor setup will help climbers secure the freedom of the hills.

10

CHAPTER 11

RAPPELLING

Indispensable to technical climbing in the mountains, rappelling is the technique of descending an anchored rope by using friction to safely control the rate of descent. Unfortunately, because rappelling is often so easy and routine, climbers may forget or ignore its inherent risks, making it one of the more dangerous techniques they employ. Proper rappelling technique is vital to a safe descent of many climbs.

In the words of climber Ed Viesturs, "Getting to the top is optional; getting down is mandatory." Safe rappelling can be achieved only by using a trustworthy anchor and rope and proper technique. If any element of the rappel system fails, the result will likely be catastrophic. Unlike the belay system, which is a secondary safety system—it is called upon only *if* a fall occurs—the rappel system is the primary fall restraint system, necessarily called upon to absorb the forces exerted by the rappel the entire time it is in use. Consequently, there is no room for error in the setup or use of the rappel system. The 2011 edition of *Accidents in North American Mountaineering* notes most rappelling accidents are preventable: the top three causes are (1) uneven rope lengths, (2) an inadequate anchor system, and (3) an inadequate rappel backup.

When descending a climb, a team may have the choice to down-climb instead of rappel. Party size and experience, timing, weather, terrain, and available equipment should be factored into the decision regarding how to descend. When down-climbing is within the capability of the climbing party, it can be preferable because it can be faster and pose a lower risk than rappelling. Down-climbing is particularly attractive in terrain rated Class 4 and below, where the slope angle and presence of loose rocks increase the likelihood of getting a rappel rope stuck or of pulling rocks down on climbers while rappelling or retrieving the rope. When there are varying skill levels within a climbing team, it may be appropriate to set up a fixed rope for less-experienced climbers to use as a hand line or to connect to with a prusik while down-climbing (see "Fixed Lines" in Chapter 21, Expedition Climbing). If the team chooses to rappel, safety and efficiency are imperative; this chapter describes best practices to ensure safe and efficient rappels.

THE RAPPEL SYSTEM

A rappel system has four basic elements: an anchor, a rope, a rappel method for applying friction to the rope, and the person rappelling (fig. 11-1). Each element is equally and vitally important. Always remember all four of the rappel elements—especially when you are cold, tired, hungry, or racing to beat the darkness—and double-check that every element is in place, functioning properly, and connected together to make an integrated system.

It is common practice for climbing partners to check each other's equipment setup at the start of a climb; partner checks during descent are equally important and

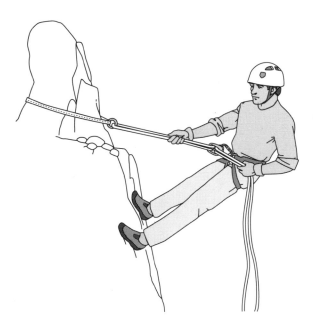

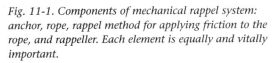

Fig. 11-1. Components of mechanical rappel system: anchor, rope, rappel method for applying friction to the rope, and rappeller. Each element is equally and vitally important.

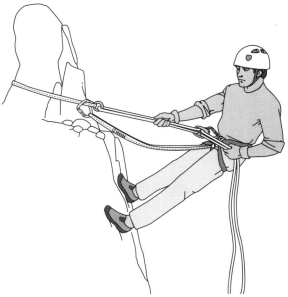

Fig. 11-2. Weighting a rappel setup to test it while attached to anchor with a personal anchor.

should be routine. The last person to rappel may be able to set up his or her rappel before the second-to-last person leaves the anchor (see "Finishing the Rappel" later in this chapter), but if this is not possible, the last climber should consider him- or herself at elevated risk for mistakes and take extra measures to check, recheck, and test his or her own setup. Another important measure to confirm correct setup of a rappel before heading down is to weight the rappel while maintaining security through use of a personal anchor (fig. 11-2).

Following a routine checklist before every rappel can help ensure nothing is missed. One example of a routine that ensures a coherent system involves starting with the rock or mountain and working outward toward the climber: check the anchor attached to the rock, then the rope attached to the anchor, then the rope properly threaded through the rappel device (assuming a mechanical system is being used—see "Rappel Method" below), then the device properly attached to the rappeller's harness, and finally the harness properly fastened to the rappeller. Each of these elements is briefly described below, followed by expanded sections in the rest of this chapter.

RAPPEL ANCHOR

The first element of the rappel system is the anchor: the point on the rock or mountain to which the rest of the system is attached. The anchor must be carefully selected for strength and reliability. Once the rappel has begun, a safe descent depends on the integrity of the anchor, and returning to the anchor to make adjustments can be problematic, if not impossible.

ROPE

The second element is the rope. Typically, the midpoint of the rope is looped through a metal ring (called a *rappel ring*) at the anchor, with the two ends of the rope hanging down the descent route. The rappeller descends both halves of the doubled rope and then retrieves it from below by pulling on one end.

Rappels shorter than half a rope length can be made with just one rope. Longer rappels need the extra length of two ropes tied together. It is necessary to research a route beforehand to determine whether the rappels will require one or two ropes. If two ropes are required (often called a *double-rope rappel*), the knot joining the ropes should be placed near the anchor, with the two equal-length ends hanging down the route. Using two ropes of different

203

colors can help you remember which rope to pull when retrieving the ropes, for example, "pull on blue."

RAPPEL METHOD

The third element is the method used to apply friction to the rope to control the rate of descent while the rappeller remains firmly attached to the rope. There are two types of systems for applying friction:

Mechanical systems. The rope passes through a friction device attached to the harness.

Nonmechanical systems. The rope is wrapped around the rappeller's body to provide the necessary friction.

In either case, the braking hand grasps the rope to control the amount of friction and the rate of descent. Be aware of atypical circumstances that could reduce the friction in the system, such as a new, small-diameter, stiff, or icy rope, a heavier pack, and so forth.

RAPPELLER

The final and most variable element in the rappel system is the rappeller, who must use proper technique both to attach into the rappel system and to descend safely. Transient circumstances such as the rappeller's attitude, level of fatigue and anxiety, level of attentiveness, level of skill and training, poor weather, impending darkness, and presence of rockfall or icefall can affect the safety of the rappel.

SETTING UP RAPPEL ANCHORS

A rappel anchor attaches the rappel system to the rock, snow, or ice that will be descended. The rappel anchor must be strong enough to support one or more climbers' full weight as well as any additional forces that may occur, such as the dynamic force of bouncing or a sudden stop during the rappel.

Set up the anchor as near to the edge of the rappel route as possible while ensuring a solid and safe anchor. This affords the longest possible rappel and minimizes risks of getting the rope stuck or inducing rockfall during retrieval of the rope. When looking for an anchor, think about how the rope will route from the anchor location to the ground. Consider any sharp edges that might damage the rope as it is loaded. Choose an anchor location that minimizes chances of the rope being pulled into a crack or otherwise hanging up on horns or features when it is retrieved from below. Consider these risks when setting up the anchor and then double-check the rappel route after the first rappeller is down. In winter conditions, be aware that if the rope cuts into snow or ice, it can freeze in place.

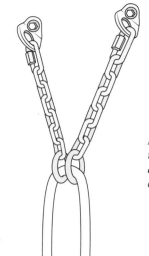

Fig. 11-3. Rope threaded through rappel rings at the ends of bolted chains.

Natural anchors or artificial (manufactured) anchors serve as suitable rappel anchors (see "Selecting an Anchor" in Chapter 10, Belaying). For details on placing removable protection in rock, using natural features, and clipping bolted anchors, see Chapter 13, Rock Protection. For information on anchors for use in snow and ice, see the sections on anchors in Chapters 16, Snow Travel and Climbing; 19, Alpine Ice Climbing; and 20, Waterfall Ice and Mixed Climbing.

A commonly found anchor used for rappelling consists of bolts with chains (fig. 11-3). The rope can be routed directly through the circular rings at the end of the chains for rappelling only—do *not* top-rope this way, it wears out and weakens the rings quickly. If chains and rings are not secured to the bolts at the anchor, add webbing and rappel rings.

On popular climbs, established rappel anchors will have slings (fig. 11-4) and perhaps rappel rings left behind from prior parties, with some parties adding a newer sling to back up the rappel station; these remnants need to be closely scrutinized for wear and damage:

- Slings with significant wear, damage, nicks, et cetera, should be considered unsafe and removed.
- Slings that are bleached or washed-out in color and have a dry, stiff feel exhibit evidence of damage from ultraviolet light (new slings have saturated color and are supple). However, nylon may be weakened by ultraviolet exposure without visible effects.

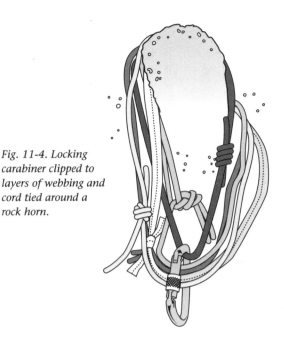

Fig. 11-4. Locking carabiner clipped to layers of webbing and cord tied around a rock horn.

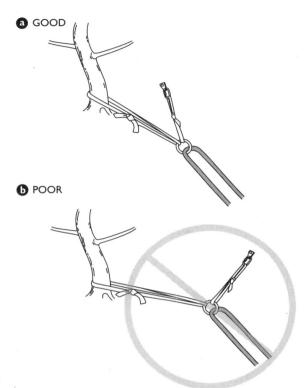

Fig. 11-5. The most common method of attaching the rope to multiple anchors uses a separate sling attached to each of two anchors meeting at the rappel ring; a, a narrow angle between slings provides a stronger overall anchor; b, when the angle between slings is too wide, the load on each anchor point increases significantly.

- Inspecting the entire length of slings routed around large boulders may often be difficult since sections of the slings may be hidden. Do not trust existing slings unless the entire length can be inspected.
- Slings not equipped with a rappel ring or carabiner may no longer be safe because rappel ropes have been pulled through them on previous rappels, which generates friction capable of melting and weakening the sling.
- Sometimes so many slings compose an anchor that total failure of every sling is unlikely. Still, a prudent rappeller might cut out a few of the oldest slings and add a new one before attaching the rope.
- If using more than one sling, make them of equal length to help distribute the load and avoid shock-loading the rappel system should one fail.

When two anchor points are used, it is common to run a separate sling from each point, with the slings meeting at the rappel ring. Try to adjust the slings so the force is the same on each anchor point. Keep the V-angle between the two slings narrow (fig. 11-5). See Chapter 10, Belaying, for methods of equalizing anchor points and Figure 10-15 for an explanation of forces at work.

When climbing and belaying, climbers build strong and redundant anchors in case of a fall. But when climbers

rappel, their life hangs on the loaded anchor from start to finish. It is essential to build rappel anchors that are SERENE: Solid, Efficient, Redundant, Equalized, and with No Extension (see the "SERENE Anchor Systems" sidebar in Chapter 10, Belaying).

NATURAL ANCHORS

Often the best natural anchor is a healthy, live, large, well-rooted tree (see "Natural Anchors" in Chapter 10, Belaying). The rope usually goes through a rappel ring attached to a runner (or sling) that is attached to the tree (fig. 11-6a). The rope could be looped directly around a tree without the use of a sling (fig. 11-6b), but this abrades the rope, soils the rope with tree resins, makes it harder to retrieve the rope, and causes unnecessary damage to the tree. Attaching

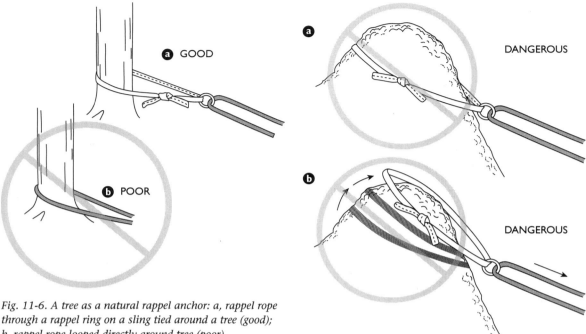

Fig. 11-6. A tree as a natural rappel anchor: a, rappel rope through a rappel ring on a sling tied around a tree (good); b, rappel rope looped directly around tree (poor).

Fig. 11-7. Poor use of a rock horn as a natural rappel anchor: a, dangerous runner placement; b, runner can ride up and slip off rock horn.

a runner to an unquestionably stout tree branch rather than low on the trunk often helps make it easier to retrieve the rope (the rope runs more directly to the person retrieving it) and reduces the risk of rockfall. However, connecting to a branch rather than the trunk puts more leverage on the tree and should not be practiced unless the trade-offs have been considered.

A single anchor point might be used if it is an unquestionably solid, dependable natural anchor. But if there are any doubts, add another equalizing feature or two to the anchor (see "Equalizing the Anchor" in Chapter 10, Belaying). If there are no other natural options for creating a multipoint anchor, the team will gain additional confidence by backing up the anchor with cams or nuts, allowing the heaviest climbers to rappel first, and then removing the backup for the last rappeller if the natural anchor performed well on the first rappels. Note that the natural anchor must carry all the weight under this test scenario, and thus the backup protection should be extremely robust to handle the excess force should the natural anchor fail and the weight suddenly shift to the backup.

Another useful natural anchor is a rock horn slung with a runner. Never run the rope directly around a rock horn. Always inspect and test the horn carefully to be sure it is

not in fact a loose rock masquerading as a solid feature. Guard against the dire possibility that the runner could slide up and come off the horn during a rappel (fig. 11-7).

Single natural anchors are not recommended if multiple people need to rappel simultaneously, such as in a rescue situation.

ARTIFICIAL ANCHORS

As a rule, when using artificial (manufactured) fixed or removable protection for an anchor, use two or more anchor points and equalize the load between them. The most common artificial rappel anchors are bolts or pitons in the rock that have been left in place by previous climbers. These must be evaluated for damage, corrosion, and improper installation just as they would if they were being used for belaying or for protection while climbing. Never put the rope directly through the eye of the bolt hanger or piton, because friction may make it impossible to pull the rope back down from below, and the hanger's or piton's sharp edges might damage the rope.

Removable protection such as nuts and hexes are usually used only if no good alternative is available, because it requires leaving behind gear; but it is better to use and leave behind some equipment for added safety than to rely upon a dubious natural anchor. Be suspicious of removable protection found already in place, perhaps left behind by climbers who were unable to remove the pieces. Also be wary of slings attached to such protection, because they may be old, damaged, and unsafe. If fully set and immovable in the rock, an abandoned nut or hex may be used like a natural chockstone by looping a runner directly around it, ignoring the original sling.

SETTING UP THE ROPE

Before setting up the rappel, run through the entire length of the rope to check that no cuts, fraying, or other damage occurred during the climb or on a previous rappel.

ATTACHING THE ROPE TO THE ANCHOR

To prepare the rope for rappelling, attach it to the anchor, in the simplest case suspending the midpoint of the rope from one or more runners or slings that have been attached to the anchor (as shown in Figures 11-1, 11-3, and 11-5a). Some rappellers prefer to use two slings instead of one, for added security. Keep the point of connection between the rappel anchor sling and the rope away from the edge of the rock, snow, or ice of the rappel route (fig. 11-8a) to help prevent abrasion (fig. 11-8b) and binding (fig. 11-8c).

Rappel Rings

Best practice is to use a rappel ring instead of looping the rope directly through the slings; because if the rope rubs significantly on the slings, the friction will create heat that may weaken or melt the slings. Rappel rings (also known as "descending rings" or "rap rings") are simply continuous aluminum, steel, or titanium rings about 1.5 inches (3 centimeters) in diameter, made for rappelling. Note that instead of rappel rings, quick links—metal ovals with threaded sleeves for opening and closing the link (fig. 11-9)—may be used, but only those that are made specifically for climbing.

The rappel ring (fig. 11-10a) does add another possible point of failure, and some climbers insist on using two rings for redundancy. An alternative is a single ring backed up by a non-weight-bearing sling from the anchor through the rope, ready to hold the rope if the ring fails (fig. 11-10b). Carabiners can be used in place of rappel rings, but as part of the anchor they also must then be left behind.

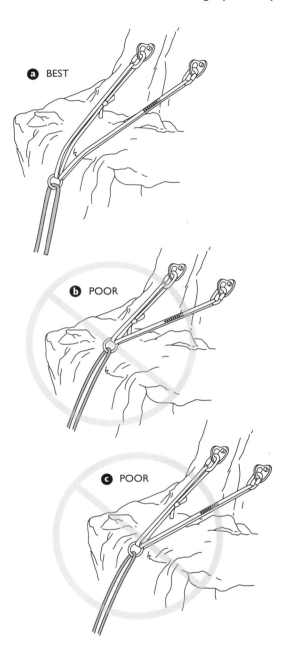

a BEST

b POOR

c POOR

Fig. 11-8. The point of connection between rappel slings with attached ring and rappel rope: a, rope clear of the rock and free to move (good); b, rope will not bind but will still abrade (poor); c, rope, placed at a rock lip or edge, will bind and abrade (dangerous).

11

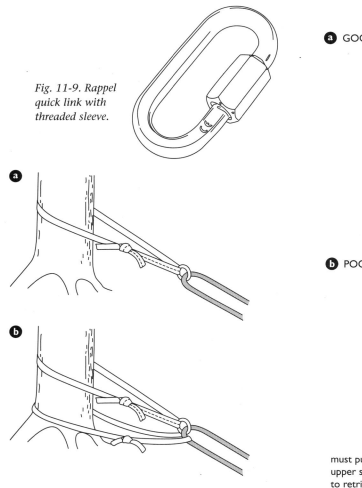

Fig. 11-9. Rappel quick link with threaded sleeve.

Fig. 11-10. Rappel rope attached to anchor through a rappel ring: a, single ring; b, single ring with loose backup sling.

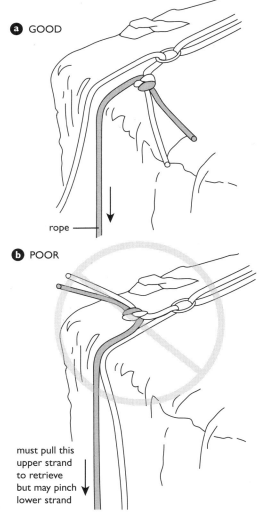

Fig. 11-11. Knot placement with two-rope rappel: a, with the knot on the side of the lower rope, the rope can be retrieved without getting stuck; b, with the knot on the side of the upper rope, the lower rope can be pinched tight (between rock and upper rope) when you try to retrieve the rope by pulling on the top strand.

One Rope

If the rappel is shorter than half a rope length, put one end of the rope through the rappel ring and pull it through until the rope's midpoint is reached and the ends are even.

Two Ropes

For longer rappels, join two ropes together. If the rope lies with one strand against the rock and the other strand on top of the first, friction will impede retrieval, and it may be possible to pull only the strand closest to the rock. When using two ropes, place the knot joining them below the anchor, on the side of the strand to be pulled, which is also the lower of the two strands (fig. 11-11a)—otherwise, the rope may pinch between the rock and the end of the rope being pulled, and retrieval may not be possible (fig. 11-11b).

There are multiple ways to tie the rappel ropes together, each having benefits and drawbacks; "Knots, Bends, and Hitches" in Chapter 9, Basic Safety System, describes all of these knots. Here we highlight knots for joining rappel ropes; these knots are easy to untie following tension.

Flat overhand bend. This knot is also called an offset overhand bend or "European Death Knot" even though it is very safe when tied properly. To tie this knot, hold the tails of the two ropes together and tie an overhand knot. Dress the knot carefully, taking care to tighten it by pulling on each of the four strands (fig. 11-12a). It is extremely important for the tails to be 12 to 18 inches (30 to 46 centimeters) long, because the knot has been known to roll (or "capsize") under load. When the knot rolls, one side of the knot flips over the other side (toward the tail), shortening the tails. If rolled enough times, the knot will roll off the ends of the rope. The rolled knot is identical to the original knot, but has shorter tails.

Because the flat overhand bend's knot lies offset from the axis of the direction of force, it is less likely than other knots to get stuck in cracks (fig. 11-12b). It is a good idea to use a second overhand as a backup knot (see the next section), which could optionally be removed before the last climber rappels to reduce the chance of the rope getting stuck in a crack when it is retrieved. Note that it is important that this is an overhand, not a figure eight.

Double fisherman's bend. This is a very secure knot, so if more than one person must rappel at the same time, it is the preferred knot. It must be tied with long tails. However, it is bulkier and more likely to become stuck in cracks.

USING BACKUP KNOTS

Even very experienced rappellers have inadvertently rappelled off the end of their ropes, with tragic results. When using a rappel device, put a large knot, such as a double or triple barrel (fig. 11-13), or a figure eight, in the ends of the rope to reduce this danger. If you add knots, do not rely blindly on them; knots might come untied, and in any case, you must keep an eye on the ends of the rope to plan where to stop. Knots also may jam in the rappel device or become lodged in a crack. To prevent the knots from becoming lodged in a crack below the next belay station, knot the ends of the rope and then secure them to the harness while you descend.

11

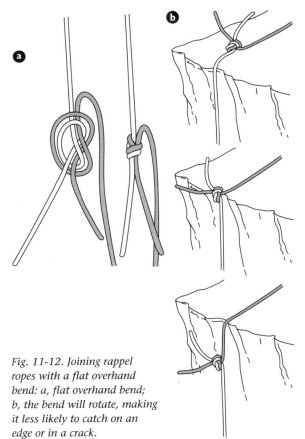

Fig. 11-12. Joining rappel ropes with a flat overhand bend: a, flat overhand bend; b, the bend will rotate, making it less likely to catch on an edge or in a crack.

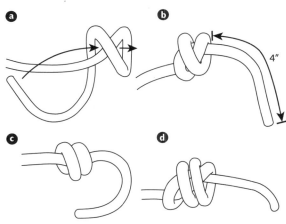

Fig. 11-13. Barrel knot: a, wrap the end of the rope around itself twice, pulling the end through the loops; b, cinch down the loose end and make sure the tail is at least 4 inches long; c, back side of the resulting barrel knot; d, add another wrap for a triple barrel knot.

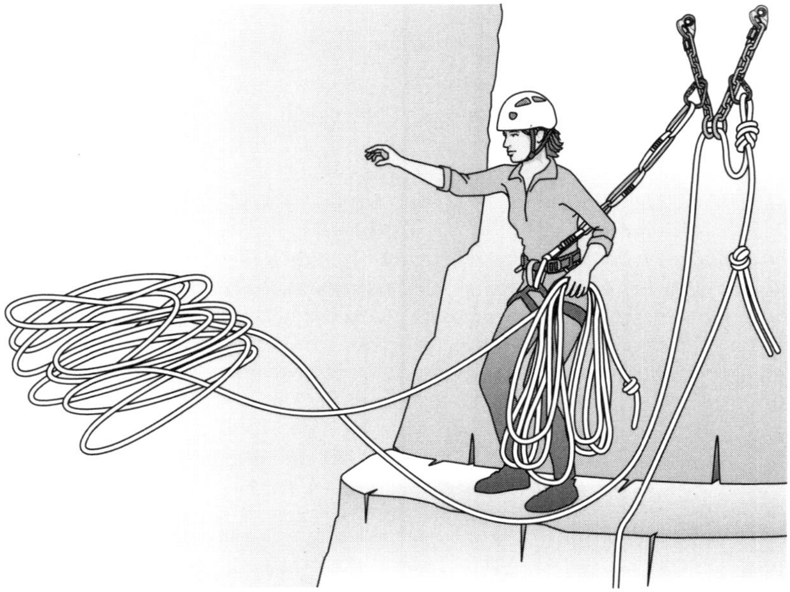

Fig. 11-14. *Throwing down the rope: Climber is connected to the anchor for safety while working near the edge; rope (in this case two tied together) is clipped to the anchor with a bight near the middle to prevent losing it and has been threaded through the rappel rings then coiled. Toss the coil nearest the anchor first, then the rope-end coil.*

THROWING DOWN THE ROPE

After threading the rappel rope through an anchor and equalizing the ends, prepare the rope for the rappel. There are several methods for tossing, or lowering, the rope down the rappel route. With any method, the goal is to reduce rope snags and tangling, as well as move the rope toward the bottom.

1. Attach yourself to an anchor using a personal anchor to secure yourself, preferably with a locking carabiner (see "Personal Anchors" in Chapter 9, Basic Safety System). Make sure your waist is not above the anchor: a slip could apply significant load to the anchor because the personal anchor system is static (fig. 11-14).
2. Tie an overhand knot on a bight of rope near its midpoint and clip it to the rappel anchor with a carabiner to prevent the disaster of losing the rope when the coils are tossed.
3. Tie backup knots at the ends of the rope (see "Using Backup Knots" above).
4. Beginning from the middle of the rope, coil each half of the rope separately into two butterfly coils, creating a total of four butterfly coils, two on each side of the anchor.
5. Evaluate the wind and terrain before throwing the coils out. Be sure to compensate for any significant wind. Avoid throwing the coils onto snags, pinch points, or sharp edges below.
6. Before making the toss, alert others below by shouting "Rope!" It is a good idea to shout the word two

times and/or wait a moment after the warning before throwing the rope, to give anyone below time to respond.

7. Start on one side of the anchor, tossing the coil nearest the anchor out and down the route, then the rope-end coil. Repeat for the other half of the rope (in Figure 11-14, one half of the rope has already been dropped below).
8. After all the coils have been tossed, remove the carabiner and bight, leaving the rope running free in the rappel rings.

If the rope tangles or hangs up on the rappel route below, it is usually best to pull it back up, recoil it, and toss it again. Sometimes, however, it is possible to free the rope during the rappel.

Instead of throwing the rope, an alternative is to secure the coiled rope to your harness and feed it out as you rappel. This works better than tossing the rope in windy conditions. One method is to simply feed the rope out of a pack or rope bag during the descent.

Another option is to fashion the rope coil into "saddlebags": girth-hitch a single-length runner to the harness wherever it is convenient. Cradle the butterfly coils in the runner next to the harness, and clip the other end of the runner to the harness with a carabiner (fig. 11-15). The butterfly coil should be oriented so that it feeds freely as the climber rappels.

When either feeding rope out of a rope bag or using this saddlebag method, the rappeller may need to actively tend the rope to get it to feed out properly during the rappel.

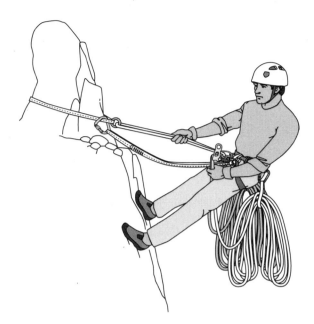

Fig. 11-15. Setting up the rappel with "saddlebags" of rope.

KEEPING ROPE LENGTHS EQUAL

As noted at the start of this chapter, rappelling with ropes of unequal length was found to be the top cause of accidents reported in *Accidents in North American Mountaineering*. Both strands of the rappel rope must either touch the next stance or hang equally. If not, one end may pull through the rappel device before the rappeller reaches a stance at the end of the rappel. Should this occur, the rappeller would lose the ability to control the descent and would free-fall. Watch for the potential problems discussed below. Backup knots at the ends of the rope are strongly recommended (see "Using Backup Knots" above). These stopper knots keep you from rappelling off the ends of the rope should the rope be too short. The correct stopper knot prevents the end of the rope from passing through your rappel device.

When using two ropes of unequal diameters, take extra care to monitor the length of each strand during the rappel. The differing diameters and elastic characteristics of the ropes may cause one rope to advance through the rappel device more quickly than the other, thereby altering the relative lengths of the rope strands. Place the knot on the side of the anchor with the rope that is most likely to slide; usually this is the smaller-diameter rope.

Also, be aware that ropes that are nominally equal in length, even from the same manufacturer, are often actually somewhat different lengths.

RAPPEL METHOD

Once the rappel anchor and the rope are set up, the climber needs a method of connecting to the rope and applying friction to it to control the rappel. Typically, a mechanical device provides a secure means of attachment, but methods of wrapping the rope around the body may also be used. If climbers rely on a mechanical rappel device, it is imperative that they be skilled in a secondary rappel method such as carabiner brake or munter rappel in case they drop their rappel device midclimb.

MECHANICAL RAPPEL SYSTEMS

Most rappellers use a system consisting of their climbing harness and a belay-rappel device as their principal rappelling method. All of the devices operate in essentially the same manner: by applying varying degrees of friction to the rope. With some belay devices, the rope does not feed through the device smoothly on rappel. Some devices may also easily heat up from rope friction. Before using any new device, closely read and follow the manufacturer's instructions.

The two strands of rope at the rappel anchor are inserted into the rappel device, which is then clipped with a locking carabiner to the climber's harness, in much the same way as for belaying. During the rappel, the bends in the rope that pass through the device and around the locking carabiner apply friction, magnifying the force exerted by the climber's braking hand (fig. 11-16). The position of the braking hand, which holds both strands of rope below the device (see Figure 11-15), provides a controlled descent. The rappel device and the braking hand together control the speed of descent and allow the rappeller to halt the descent at any time.

At the top of the rappel, the weight of the rope hanging below the device adds friction, making it easier to control the rate of descent near the top of a rappel than at the bottom. This is especially so on very steep or overhanging rappels where most of the rope hangs free. But no matter how little grip strength may be required to control the descent, the braking hand must never leave the rope. The other hand—the guiding, or uphill, hand—may slide freely along the rope to help maintain balance. With some setups, wrapping the rope partly around your back further increases friction. A leather glove is recommended to

11

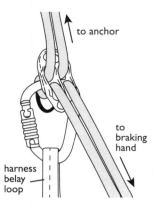

Fig. 11-16. An aperture-style device set up for rappelling.

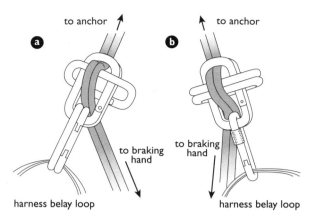

Fig. 11-17. Carabiner brake system: a, with two opposite and opposed carabiners at the harness and one braking carabiner clipped across the outer (opposite and opposed) carabiner pair; b, with one locking carabiner at the harness and two braking carabiners clipped across the outer (opposite and opposed) carabiner pair in order to provide greater friction.

protect the braking hand, which is important when a rappel exceeds the desired speed and would otherwise burn a bare hand.

Rappelling with a mechanical system requires a harness (see Chapter 9, Basic Safety System). Never rappel with just a waist loop (a simple loop of webbing tied around your waist); it can constrict your diaphragm enough to cause you to lose consciousness. In an emergency, an improvised diaper sling may be used for rappelling, even though it would not ordinarily be used for climbing (see "Diaper Sling" in Chapter 9, Basic Safety System).

Carabiner Brake Method

The carabiner brake method for rappelling is somewhat complex to set up but has the virtue of not requiring any special equipment—just carabiners. The carabiner brake system works best with oval carabiners but can also be managed with D-shaped carabiners (see "Carabiners" in Chapter 9, Basic Safety System).

To create the carabiner brake setup, start by attaching one locking or two regular carabiners to the seat harness. Because a harness carabiner could be subjected to a twisting or side load, two carabiners or a locking carabiner should be used. When using two nonlocking carabiners, position the gates to keep them from being forced open and accidentally unclipping. The correct position (called "opposite and opposed") is with the gates on opposing sides, forming an X when they are opened at the same time (see Figure 9-37a in Chapter 9, Basic Safety System).

Next, clip a pair of carabiners—here, a pair is required: a single locking carabiner will not suffice—to the harness belay loop carabiner(s), also with the gates opposite and opposed. Lift a bight of the rappel ropes through the outer carabiner pair, from the bottom—do this facing the anchor to ensure the system is oriented properly for descent. Take

yet another carabiner and clip it across the outer carabiner pair, beneath the bight of rope, so its gate is facing away from the rope loop. The rope then runs across the spine (not the gate!) of this final carabiner, known as the braking carabiner (fig. 11-17a).

One braking carabiner provides enough friction for most rappels on ropes that are 10 to 11 millimeters in diameter. A second (or even third) braking carabiner will add friction to the system (fig. 11-17b) and might be used for thinner ropes, heavy climbers, heavy packs, or steep or overhanging rappels. The ropes must always run over the solid side of the braking carabiner(s), never across the gate.

The weight of the rope hanging down the cliff may make it very difficult to pull the bight of rope up through the outer pair of carabiners and hold it while you clip in the braking carabiner. It helps to get that weight off the system. Pull up some slack rope and throw a couple of wraps around your leg to take the weight in order to solve this problem. Alternatively, set up an autoblock first (see "Safety Backups" later in this chapter) and pull up the rope, allowing the autoblock to hold the rope's weight.

Improvised Carabiner Brake

A second carabiner brake method, an improvised carabiner brake, is simpler than the carabiner brake method and requires only three locking carabiners. The steps to

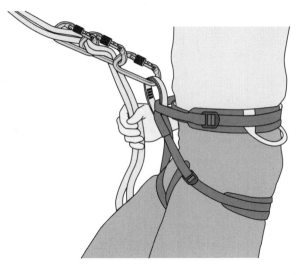

Fig. 11-18. Improvised carabiner brake system.

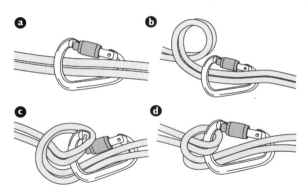

Fig. 11-19. To rappel using a munter hitch: a, clip locking carabiner around rope; b, create loop using both strands of rope above carabiner, with anchor strand of rope behind the climber strand; c, hook carabiner into loop; d, lock carabiner gate.

11

setting up this method are outlined below and shown in Figure 11-18.

1. Clip and lock one locking carabiner to the harness belay loop.
2. Clip and lock a second locking carabiner to the first.
3. Pull a bight of rope through the second carabiner.
4. Clip and lock a third locking carabiner to this bight and the rope strand running to the anchor.
5. Ensure all carabiners are locked, and take care that the rope does not run against the screw gates of any of the carabiners.

This approach generally provides less friction than other methods of rappelling but has the advantages of using fewer carabiners than the carabiner brake method and not adding twists to the rope, which is common with the munter hitch shown below.

Munter Hitch

The same hitch that is used for belaying can also be used for rappelling (see Chapter 10, Belaying). It is worthwhile to learn this method as insurance because it requires only one locking carabiner and no other equipment. Though it is easy to set up and very safe, it puts significantly more twists in the rope than other rappel methods do. You must be very sure to keep the brake rope on the spine side of the carabiner (fig. 11-19), because if the rope runs over the gate, it may unlock the carabiner while you are rappelling. For additional security, a backup is recommended, such as an autoblock or a fireman's belay (see "Safety Backups" later in this chapter).

Rappel Extension

Many climbers extend the rappel device connection to their harness with a personal anchor so that the rappel device rides higher on the rappel rope and in front of their chest (fig. 11-20). Rappel extension is recommended for its advantages:

- The rappeller can comfortably use either hand (or both hands) to brake the rappel and can add—and manage—a superior autoblock (see "Safety Backups" later in this chapter).
- Both ends of the autoblock can be clipped in to the belay loop of the harness, which is better than using the leg loop attachment.
- That way, the autoblock cannot run against the rappel device, which can cause the autoblock to fail.
- The personal anchor is readily available for clipping to anchors.

The disadvantages of rappel extension are that this technique introduces one more piece into the rappel system—the runner used for the extension—and it brings the rappel device closer to long hair, which may get caught in the device; it is essential to have a knife handy to remedy this situation.

Here is how to create the extension with double-length runner, although a personal anchor can be used as well. Tie an overhand knot in the middle of the runner to create two loops of equal length. Girth-hitch the runner to the harness tie-in points, not to the belay loop, keeping its knot or stitching points clear of the girth hitch or carabiner clipping points. A locking carabiner at the far end of the two-

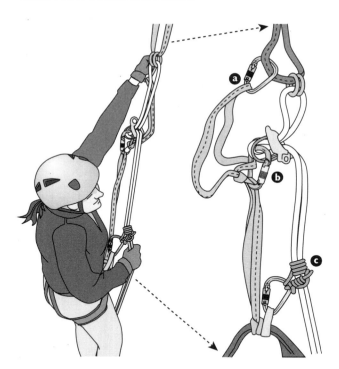

Fig. 11-20. Rappel extension (double-length runner clipped in the middle to the rappel device) with: a, integrated personal anchor (carabiner in climber's left hand, the outer half of the rappel extension); b, carabiner below knot, clipped in to runner and both rope strands; c, autoblock, wrapped around the rappel rope and both ends clipped to the belay loop with a locking carabiner.

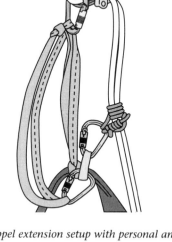

Fig. 11-21. Rappel extension setup with personal anchor stowed on harness belay loop.

loop runner (fig. 11-20a) serves as the personal anchor (a slipknot at the end keeps the carabiner in place); a locking carabiner attached to both loops of the runner (fig. 11-20b) serves as the attachment for the rappel device. To add an autoblock, attach both of its ends directly to the carabiner on the harness belay loop instead of to the harness leg loop (fig. 11-20c), and loop the cord around the rope below the rappel connection. When the personal-anchor component is not in use, simply "stow it" by clipping and locking the carabiner to the harness belay loop (fig. 11-21).

NONMECHANICAL METHODS

Two traditional rappel methods use no hardware whatsoever to create friction on the rope. Instead, the rope is simply wrapped around parts of the climber's body. These methods can be especially helpful if climbers find themselves without a harness.

Dulfersitz

A simple, all-purpose method, the *dulfersitz* (fig. 11-22) should be mastered by every climber in the event that a harness or carabiners are not available. To set up, face the anchor and straddle the rope. Bring it from behind you and around one hip, up across your chest, over the opposite shoulder, and then down your back to be held by the braking hand (the downhill hand) on the same side as your wrapped hip. Your other hand is the guiding hand, which holds the rope above and keeps you upright. Add padding if possible between your body and the rope.

The *dulfersitz* has a number of drawbacks compared with mechanical rappel systems. It can unwrap from your leg, especially on high-angle rappels; this risk can be mitigated by keeping your wrapped leg slightly lower than your other leg. As with all rappel methods, stay under careful control. If you are wearing a pack, the *dulfersitz* is even more awkward. The *dulfersitz* is used in modern climbing only when there is no reasonable alternative or for short and easy, low-angle rappels to save the trouble of putting a harness back on (though down-climbing should be considered as an alternative in this case).

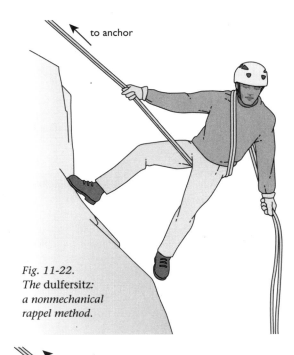

Fig. 11-22. *The* dulfersitz: *a nonmechanical rappel method.*

Arm Rappel

Though the arm rappel is not used much, it is occasionally helpful for quick descent of a low-angle slope. Lay the rappel rope behind your back, bring it under your armpits, and wrap it once around each arm (fig. 11-23). Be sure the rope does not run over any exposed flesh, which can cause rope burns. Control the rate of descent with your hand grip. For an arm rappel with a pack, be sure the rope goes around your pack rather than on top of or underneath it.

RAPPEL TECHNIQUE

Typically the first rappeller is one of the more experienced members of the group. On the rappel, this first rappeller usually fixes any tangles or problems with the rope and clears the anchor area and route of debris that might be dislodged during rappels.

GETTING STARTED

Just before descending, shout "On rappel!" to warn others that a rappel has begun. Now comes the most nerve-wracking part of many rappels. To gain stability, your legs must be nearly perpendicular to the rock, which means you must lean backward, out over the edge of the cliff (fig. 11-24), and commit to weighting the rope for rappel. If the terrain allows it, ease the transition by down-climbing several feet before leaning out and weighting the rope to start the

11

Fig. 11-23. *The arm rappel: another nonmechanical rappel method.*

Fig. 11-24. *Starting to rappel from a high anchor.*

Fig. 11-25. Down-climbing to get below a low anchor before starting to rappel.

rappel (fig. 11-25). Take up any slack between you and the anchor before leaning out or weighting the rope.

You may be able to sit or crouch on the edge of the rappel ledge (fig. 11-26a) and wiggle gently off (fig. 11-26b), simultaneously turning inward to face the slope (fig. 11-26c). This technique is referred to as a "sit-and-spin." It is particularly useful when you are starting the rappel above an overhang or when the anchor is located lower than your harness when you are standing on the rappel edge.

MAKING THE RAPPEL

Three things that must be considered during the rappel are position, speed, and movement.

Position

While descending, seek a stable body position: feet shoulder-width apart, knees flexed, body at a comfortable angle to the slope and facing a little toward the braking hand for a view of the route (see Figure 11-26c). Common beginners' mistakes include keeping the feet too close together and not leaning back far enough, which can cause feet to slip off the rock. Some go to the other extreme and lean too far back, increasing their chance of flipping over. If anything should happen, such as tipping over or losing your footing, it is absolutely critical to remember to hold on to the rope with the braking hand.

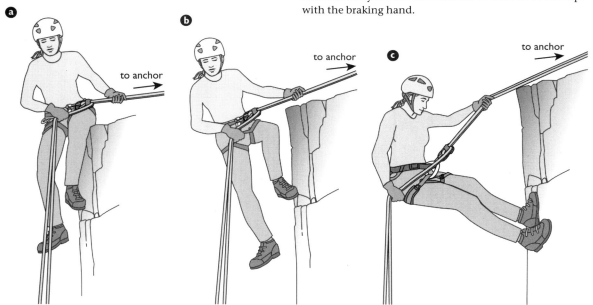

Fig. 11-26. Starting to rappel from a steep ledge and a low anchor: a, sitting down on the ledge; b, squirming off to get started; c, turning inward to face the slope.

POTENTIAL PROBLEMS WHEN RAPPELLING

Climbers have to be aware of the many problems they may encounter when rappelling, especially because climbers are often tired when setting up to rappel. These tips will help you troubleshoot.

Loose rock. Use extreme caution when rappelling a face with loose or rotten rock. Rock may be knocked loose either by you as you descend, or by the rope as it rubs against the rock above you. The loose rock could injure you or damage the rope. Another danger is that the next rappeller could knock rocks down on you. Take care to position yourself in a safe area (out of the fall line or under a rock outcropping) before calling "Off rappel!," and stay there until the entire party has rappelled. Rocks are also often knocked loose when the rope is pulled at the end of the rappel. Keep an eye above you while pulling the rope and make sure no party members remove their helmets until the rope has been safely retrieved after the final rappel.

Overhangs. It is easy to swing into the face below an overhang, smashing your hands and feet. There is also the risk of jamming the brake system on the lip of the overhang. A couple of methods assist in making the difficult transition from above the lip of an overhang to below it.

One method is to bend deeply at your knees with your feet at the uppermost edge of the overhang, then release enough braking tension to slip down 3 or 4 feet (about 1 meter) at once, and then lock off the rappel with sudden braking action, which halts further acceleration once you are past the lip of the overhang. The abrupt halt and resulting bounce stress the rappel system, but this method helps reduce both the chance of a swing into the face below and of jamming the brake system on the lip.

Another method is to place your feet on the lip of the overhang and then lower your waist down below your feet. Then "walk" your feet down the underside of the overhang until the rope above makes contact with the rock face above.

Below an overhang, you will dangle free on the rope. Assume a sitting position, use the guiding hand on the rope above to remain upright, and continue steadily downward. Often you will slowly spin as twists in the rope unwind.

Pendulums. Sometimes reaching the next rappel stance requires you to move to the right or left of the fall line, walking down the face diagonally instead of moving straight down. If a slip occurs, you will pendulum back toward the fall line. After such a fall, it may be difficult to get reestablished on the proper rappel course without climbing back up the rope with prusik slings or mechanical devices. To avoid this potentially dangerous situation, try to set up rappel routes so that you are rappelling down the fall line as much as possible. A pendulum fall presents a risk of injury and possibly letting go of the brake rope—making a backup method imperative when a diagonal rappel is unavoidable.

Loose ends. Clothing, long hair, pack straps, chin straps from a helmet, and just about anything with a loose end all have the potential to get pulled into the braking system. Keep a knife handy to cut foreign material out of the system, but be extremely careful with a sharp knife around rope, especially a rope under tension, which cuts easily.

Rope tangles. If the rope gets tangled or jammed during your descent, the problem must be corrected before you rappel past it. Stop at the last convenient ledge above the area, or stop with a leg wrap (see "Stopping Midrappel" below). Pull the rope up, correct the problem, then throw it down again. Sometimes there is a simple solution; for instance, when you are rappelling down blank slabs, tangles often may be shaken out as they are encountered. Keep an eye out for tangles or other possible problems below you.

Jammed rappel device. If the rappel brake system jams on something (such as a shirt) despite your precautions, it can most likely be freed by unweighting it. First, free your hands by using a leg wrap or a backup mule knot (see "Stopping Midrappel" below). Next, unweight the brake system by either standing on a ledge or tying a prusik hitch above your brake system and chaining slings together until they are long enough to stand in. In the worst case, you might even Texas-prusik some distance up the rappel ropes (see "Prusik System" in Chapter 18, Glacier Travel and Crevasse Rescue, for information on the Texas prusik) or climb the wall. Then, if you are unable to free the jammed material, cut it away from the brake system, taking care not to nick the rope. A prusik loop, three or four slings, and a knife should always be on hand.

11

Some climbers prefer to brake with both hands. With two hands, use an alternating, hand-over-hand, shuffle-brake motion to feed the rope through the rappel device. Others feel more secure with a nonbraking hand high on the rope, to help keep them upright and to fend off any hazards (see the "Potential Problems When Rappelling" sidebar). Either way, what is imperative is that one hand remains on the brake rope at all times.

Speed and Movement

As you rappel, move slowly and steadily, with no bounces or leaps. Feed the rope slowly and steadily into the rappel system, avoiding fast stops and jerks, which shock-load the anchor. A sudden stop during a rapid descent subjects the anchor to additional force. Higher rappel speeds put more heat and stress on the rappel system; very fast rappels can damage a rope. You could also lose control of the rope.

STOPPING MIDRAPPEL

If you need to stop partway down a rappel, you can secure the rope in a couple of ways, described below. Some rappel or belay devices have other ways to stop the rope in the device; consult the manufacturer's instructions or obtain reliable instruction on their use.

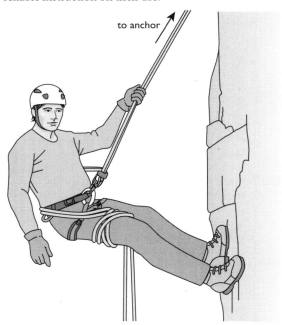

to anchor

Fig. 11-27. Leg wrap: stopping "hands free" midrappel with the rope wrapped around one leg.

Leg Wrap

One method for securing the rope midrappel is to wrap the rope two or three times around one leg. The friction of the wrap, increased by the weight of the rope hanging below the wrap, is usually enough to halt further descent. Keep the braking hand on the rope while passing the rope behind your back, and use the guiding hand to assist with wrapping the rope around your leg (fig. 11-27). Keep the braking hand in position until the wraps are completed and tested. For even more friction, tuck a bight of the loose end of the rope under all the leg wraps.

To continue the descent, be sure to reestablish the braking hand before releasing the leg wraps. On steep rappels, simply remove your foot and leg from contact with the rock and shake the wraps off while holding the rope with the braking hand.

Mule Knot

Another method for securing the rope midrappel is to use a mule knot to tie off the rappel, just like tying off a belay; see "Mule Knot" and Figures 9-20 and 9-21 in Chapter 9, Basic Safety System. The mule knot is a load-releasing knot; other knots may be difficult to remove once they are loaded.

SAFETY BACKUPS

Belay methods and backup knots at the end of rappel ropes can enhance the safety of a rappel. In addition, they add security to particularly risky or unnerving rappels and may save the life of a rappeller hit by rockfall. They also help beginners gain confidence in rappelling.

SELF-BELAY WITH AN AUTOBLOCK OR PRUSIK

Tying a friction hitch (such as an autoblock or a prusik) on to the rope below the rappel device, clipped to a harness belay loop or leg loop, enables you to stop without gripping the ropes. If tied properly, these self-belay hitches will grip the rope and halt your descent any time you do not actively tend them.

To make a self-belay autoblock, use a sewn runner or accessory cord tied in a loop (see "Runners" in Chapter 9, Basic Safety System); the appropriate size of the runner or cord varies with rope diameter—always test compatibility before you use the hitch by making sure the hitch will grab the rope. Attach the runner or loop to the seat-harness leg loop with a carabiner or a girth hitch; wrap the

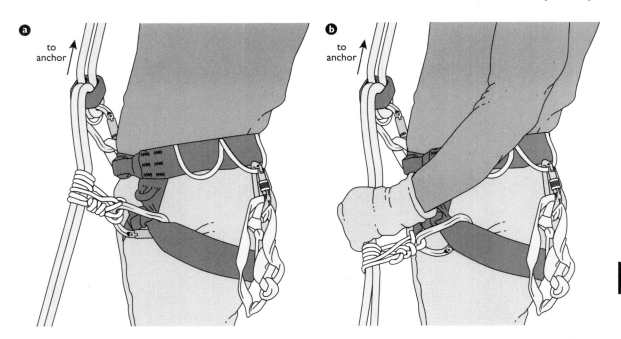

Fig. 11-28. Self-belay autoblock on rappel: a, with an aperture-style device setup; b, tend the friction hitch by manually sliding it down along the rope.

loop around both strands of the rappel rope(s) below the rappel device—typically, three wraps provide enough (but not too much) friction; then clip the end of the runner or loop to the seat-harness leg loop with the same carabiner (fig. 11-28a). Alternatively, tie the tie-off loop to both strands of the rappel rope(s) with a prusik hitch below the rappel device and clip the free end of the loop to the harness leg loop. The autoblock can be connected to the belay loop on the harness in the case of an extended rappel (see "Rappel Extension" above). If the rappel is not extended, the leg loop must be used to avoid having the cord pulled into the rappel device.

In general, the autoblock is easier than the prusik to release once it has been loaded. For both the autoblock and the prusik, the runner or loop must be short enough that the hitch cannot either jam the rappel device or be tended by the rappel device (which could result in failure of the hitch to hold).

If the braking hand releases the rope—for instance, as the result of rockfall—a self-belay friction hitch can prevent a rappeller from accelerating out of control. Reestablish the braking hand and tend the self-belay hitch by manually sliding it down along the rope to allow the descent to resume (fig. 11-28b).

These hitches require some testing and adjustment before each rappel in order to establish the runner or loop's proper length (so the hitch does not hang up in the rappel device) and the proper amount of friction (adjusted by the number of wraps) to accommodate the climber's weight, rappel device, comfort, and any other individual considerations.

FIREMAN'S BELAY

A person standing below a rappeller can easily control the rappeller's movement or stop it altogether—thus providing an effective backup—simply by pulling down on the rappel rope(s), which puts friction on the brake system (fig. 11-29). To safeguard the rappeller with this method, the person at the bottom simply holds the rope strands loosely, ready to pull them tight the instant the rappeller has difficulty.

TOP BELAY

A rappeller can also be protected by a belay from above with a separate rope. If the belayer uses a separate anchor, there is redundancy for the entire system, even the rappel anchor. A top belay may be chosen for use with beginners, climbers with minor injuries, and the first person descending on a suspect anchor. Top belays are too time-consuming for routine use.

Fig. 11-29. Fireman's belay: rappel halted by a climber below, who is pulling down on the ends of the rope.

FINISHING THE RAPPEL

Near the end of the rappel, it becomes much easier to feed rope through the rappel device because the extra friction caused by the weight of the rope below the rappeller is now considerably less. The amount of rope stretch, particularly on a two-rope rappel, may be surprising. Be aware of this stretch factor as the rope is cleared from the rappel device after the rappel is completed. If you let go of the rappel

rope, it could contract to its normal length and suddenly be up out of reach. It's better to end the rappel *near* the end of the rope rather than at the very end of it.

As you near the end of the rope, look for a good place to finish the rappel. Establish a good stance and anchor yourself in before clearing the rope from the rappel device. In establishing a secure stance, consider the possibility of rockfall and icefall, and attempt to be out of the way of the next person coming down.

Shout "Off rappel!" only after you are detached from the rope and safely away from the fall line, to avoid rock or ice the next rappeller might dislodge. If you are the first person down a double-rope rappel, test the pull on the rope with the knot to make sure it is running smoothly. Recenter the knot before the second person descends.

THE LAST RAPPELLER

With a double-rope rappel, it is critical to know which rope to pull on from below when the rappel is completed. Pull the wrong one, and the knot will jam in the rappel ring (see Figure 11-11b).

The last rappeller should take a good final look at the rope(s) and the rappel sling to see that everything is in order and that the rope(s) will not catch on the sling or the rock, snow, or ice. Before the last person starts down, a person at the bottom should pull on the proper strand to check that it pulls freely. The rappeller above should confirm that the connecting knot in a double-rope rappel can be pulled free of the edge and that the rope does not bind on itself when pulled (see Figures 11-11b and 11-12).

On a double-rope rappel, the last person who starts down may want to stop at the first convenient ledge and pull enough of the rope down so that the connecting knot is clear of the edge. However, this practice also shortens one rope end, so be sure there is still enough rope to reach the next rappel stance safely and that there are knots in the ends of both ropes.

PULLING THE ROPE(S) DOWN

Once everyone has made the rappel, take out any visible twists in the rope and remove any safety knots in the ends of the strands. Stand away from the rock, if possible, then give the proper strand a slow, steady pull. Before the pulled strand starts to travel freely, yell "Rope!" to warn of falling rope. Others should take shelter to stay out of the way of falling rope, rocks, or other debris. Until all climbers and ropes are on the ground, everyone should keep their helmets on.

Rope Jams

A jammed rappel rope may be a serious problem, perhaps even stranding a party on a descent that requires further rappels. If the rope hangs up, either before or after the end clears the anchor, try flipping the rope with whipping and circular motions before attempting any extreme pulling. Often a change in angle, back from the face or to the right or left, can free the rope. Sometimes pulling on the other end of the rope (if it is still in reach) or using a seesaw motion to pull on each end alternately can free the rope. Be alert and cautious when pulling a stuck rope; as it springs free, it may be accompanied by rock- or icefall.

If the rope gets stuck and cannot be pulled free, below are some options, in descending order of preference:

1. **Climb with a secured prusik.** If both ends of the rope(s) are still in reach when the hangup occurs, it is possible to safely prusik up both strands (see "The Texas Prusik" in Chapter 18, Glacier Travel and Crevasse Rescue, for one ascending method on a free-hanging rope), clear the jam, and rappel back down. Tie in to the rope at frequent intervals to back up the prusiks.

2. **Climb with a belay.** If only one rope end can be reached, it may be necessary to climb up and free the rope(s). If enough rope is available from the pulled strand, lead climb with a belay to reach the knot. There is a risk you may end up stuck, unable to be lowered or to rappel if you cannot reach the hangup, so don't attempt this if you are unsure whether the available rope will reach.

3. **Climb self-belayed.** If not enough rope is available from the pulled strand, lead climb with a self-belay by attaching to the available rope with a prusik. Anchor the end of the rope at the belay ledge and then further secure it to the mountain with conventional protection as you climb. If the rope suddenly pulls free from above, hopefully the combination of the prusik attachment, the periodic protection, and the anchor will limit the length of the fall.

4. **Climb with an unsecured prusik.** If no belay is possible, and if the party cannot proceed without the rope, a final resort is to attempt the desperate and very dangerous tactic of ascending the stuck rope with a prusik or mechanical ascenders. The extreme danger of climbing an unsecured rope must be weighed against the consequences of remaining stranded until another rope is available. If it is possible to place protection during the ascent, tie in to the loose end and attach the rope to protection with clove hitches; the consequences of the rope pulling free from above might be mitigated. If the stuck rope is not necessary to complete the descent and cannot be freed, consider leaving it rather than undertaking risky maneuvers to free it.

If the rope available from the pulled strand is not enough, there are some alternative approaches appropriate for advanced climbers, but these alternatives are not described here. Note that climbing up to free a stuck rope may require building a new anchor for the climber to rappel from after freeing the rope. He or she should bring up enough gear to build a new solid anchor.

MULTIPLE RAPPELS

A descent route often involves a series of rappels. These multiple rappels, especially in alpine terrain, present special problems and require maximum efficiency to keep the party moving.

As a party moves through a series of rappels, the first person down each pitch usually carries gear for setting up the next rappel—after finding a secure stance, establishing an anchor, and attaching to it out of the path of icefall and rockfall. More experienced climbers in a party can take turns being first and last. It is best for beginners to be in the middle of the rotation so that assistance is available at the start and end of each rappel.

UNKNOWN TERRAIN

The trickiest multiple rappel is one down an unfamiliar route. Avoid this if possible. If an unfamiliar rappel is necessary, take time to check out the possible rappel lines as carefully as time and terrain permit. If a photo of the rappel route can be found, bring it along for reference. Keep in mind that the first few rappels down an unfamiliar route may, for better or worse, commit the party to that route.

If the bottom of an unfamiliar rappel pitch cannot be seen, the first person down must be prepared to climb back up in case the rappel hangs free at the end of the rope before there is a good stance or anchor. This rappeller should carry prusik slings or mechanical ascenders for ascending the rope if necessary.

Rappelling down unfamiliar terrain brings an increased risk of getting the rope hung up. Minimize the problem

11

by down-climbing as much as possible instead of rappelling. Also, consider rappels using just one rope, even if two ropes are available. Although this increases the number of rappels and the time spent descending, one rope is less likely to hang up than two. If one rope does get stuck, the second rope is available to protect a climb back up to free the stuck rope. You may then carefully climb back down or establish an intermediate rappel where the hangup occurred.

Although it is efficient to gain the maximum distance from each rappel, do not bypass a good rappel anchor spot—even well before the end of the rope—if there are doubts about finding a good place farther down.

EXPERIENCING THE FREEDOM OF THE HILLS

Rappelling is one of the activities central to climbing; learn it thoroughly and employ it carefully, so that it is safe and works well. Take care to avoid complacency. Rappelling is an essential, specialized technique that enables climbers to experience the freedom of the hills.

PART III

ROCK CLIMBING

CHAPTER 12
ALPINE ROCK CLIMBING

Alpine rock climbing can range from moderate routes only a few hours from the trailhead to multiday climbs in remote settings. Rock climbing provides the kinesthetic pleasure of movement combined with the challenge of solving a three-dimensional puzzle on intriguing landforms.

This chapter focuses on the basic and intermediate-level rock climbing skills needed in the mountains. For those interested in a sport-climbing emphasis, see Resources for several excellent texts on techniques more suited to that environment.

Note: When rock climbing on technical terrain, you should always be on belay. However, to more clearly show body positions involved in different climbing techniques, the illustrations in this chapter omit components of the basic safety system such as ropes, harnesses, and protection.

TYPES OF ROCK CLIMBING

Technical climbing begins when the party's safety requires the use of anchored belays. *Free climbing* is simply climbing using your own physical ability to move over the rock via handholds and footholds, with the rope and protection used only for safety. This is in contrast with *aid climbing*, which involves the use of artificial aids to make upward progress, such as protection placed in the rock for use as hand- and footholds. Climbers use aid technique (see Chapter 15, Aid and Big Wall Climbing) if the rock does not offer enough natural features or if the route is too hard for their skill level. *Big wall climbing* means climbing on—what else?—a large, sheer wall, which usually requires extensive aid, but frequently these wall routes include

sections of free climbing. Ascents of big walls typically take longer than one day, usually including either a hanging bivouac or ledge bivouac as well as bag hauling. *Solo climbing* is, of course, climbing alone, but it usually refers to unroped climbing (called *free soloing*); a climber can also *rope-solo* a route, using gear, and so self-belay on a solo free or aid climb.

A climb is rated by its most difficult portion. Nontechnical climbs, or *scrambles*, occur on second-, third-, or even fourth-class terrain (see Appendix: Rating Systems). Note that "third-classing" a climb also means to do it unroped. Portions of a long route may be considerably easier than the route's overall rating, perhaps even second class. Depending on the skills and experience of the climbers and the condition of the routes, some easier sections may be climbed unroped, walked while the rope is coiled short (see "Climbing in Coils" in Chapter 14, Leading on Rock), or climbed with a running belay (using a technique called *simul-climbing*; again, see Chapter 14). This compromise of safety is often made to gain the speed necessary to climb a longer route in a shorter period of time with less gear. For experts, these easier sections may be as hard as midfifth class, despite the potential for fatal consequences should a climber fall.

Although experienced climbers occasionally free-solo a route, all unroped climbing is risky. The risk depends on not only how likely a climber is to fall but what the consequences of a fall would be. Is the rock loose? Is it raining, which makes the rock slippery? Could a climber be hit by rockfall—or by a climber falling from above—and thereby be knocked off the holds? Is the ground 10 feet (3 meters) below or several hundred feet? Fatal falls have occurred on third-class terrain as well as on 5.12 routes.

Sport climbing and crag climbing are two types of free climbing that refer to technical rock climbs close to roads and civilization that do not require alpine skills. To the mountaineer who climbs distant peaks in the wilderness, sport and crag climbing might be viewed as ways to practice the technical, physical, and mental aspects of rock climbing in a less remote, relatively lower-risk environment—for example, where help is usually more accessible in the event of an accident.

In contrast to a traditional climb, or *trad climb*, in which climbers place and remove rock protection, *sport climbing* involves routes where bolts have been previously drilled into the rock face for protection. The emphasis is on each climber pushing personal physical limits in terms of gymnastic ability, physical strength, and endurance. For more information on sport climbing, refer to books in Resources, and seek out instruction in the proper techniques for falling while on lead, belaying a climber on lead who is expected to fall, and assessing the safety of falling on a given route.

Crag climbs generally require placement of traditional rock protection in cracks in the rock face. However, entire routes or sections of routes with extensive face climbing and little opportunity for traditional protection placements may be bolted. Lead falls taken on bolts or traditional rock gear while crag climbing are not necessarily safe; carefully assess each route's risk compared with the level of risk you are willing to accept and the likelihood of falling, compounded by the consequences of such a fall. Crag routes vary widely in length, ranging from one to more than 15 pitches. Some have bolts for belay and rappel anchors, whereas others require that climbers build an anchor for belaying or that they walk or scramble down for the descent.

Alpine rock climbing refers to routes farther from civilization that require many of the technical, physical, and mental aspects of rock climbing involved in sport and crag climbing, in addition to alpine routefinding or glacier climbing skills and equipment. Alpine routes are almost never bolted.

Of course, all these categories have some overlap. For example, some multipitch bolted climbs are in somewhat remote areas.

GEAR

Ropes and harnesses are covered in Chapter 9, Basic Safety System; protection hardware is covered in Chapter 13, Rock Protection.

FOOTWEAR

On rock climbs of easy difficulty, the same boots climbers wear on the approach generally work well for the actual climbing. (For more information on mountaineering boots, see Chapter 2, Clothing and Equipment.) When the climbing is more difficult, specialized footwear—rock shoes (fig. 12-1a, b, and c)—give a significant advantage. Most rock shoes have flexible uppers, plus smooth, flexible soles and rands of sticky rubber. These soles create excellent friction when weighted on rock, allowing purchase on angles and nubbins that can amaze the beginning climber.

On a climb that is a carryover—climbers do not go back to their starting point or base camp on the way down—using rock shoes on the route means climbing with the weight and bulk of boots in their pack. If the climbing includes

12

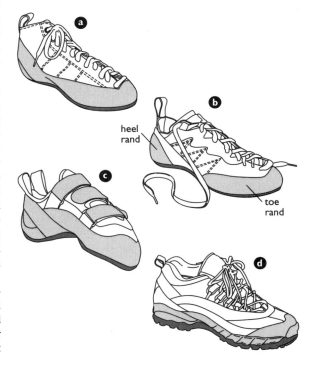

heel rand

toe rand

Fig. 12-1. Rock shoes: a, all-around shoe (flat last); b, more specialized edging shoe; c, Velcro-closure slipper (cambered last); d, combined approach and climbing shoe.

patches of snow or ice between the rock sections, wearing boots for the entire route avoids time-consuming breaks for changing footwear. Some advanced climbers climb through short sections of snow with rock shoes, or one climber leads the rock pitches in rock shoes and the other climber leads the mixed pitches of rock, snow, and ice in boots. For difficult rock climbing, especially narrow cracks, the better purchase and thinner profile afforded by rock shoes may make for safer and faster climbing. The choice of footwear and pack is personal and depends on the route. Climbing in mountaineering boots is more common on alpine rock routes without technically difficult rock sections. Rock shoes are used on more technical rock terrain, usually rated 5.6 or harder, when crack climbing is required.

Approach shoes (fig. 12-1d) are a compromise between mountaineering boots and rock shoes. These are useful when the approach is snow free, and they can be worn on the climb itself if the route is of moderate difficulty. To avoid the burden of carrying boots on a sustained rock climb, some experienced climbers strap crampons onto running shoes for short snow crossings, such as a small pocket glacier.

When choosing an appropriate pair of rock shoes, climbers can find the confusing array at outdoor stores daunting. Remember that climbing technique is far more important than the shoes! Specifically, until you have mastered the techniques necessary to climb at the 5.10 or 5.11 level and beyond, your choice of rock shoe will likely not make a significant difference. That said, below are some useful guidelines on rock-shoe selection.

Stiff-soled, more cambered shoes are better at edging (see Figure 12-1b); flexible shoes are better at frictioning or smearing (see "Footholds" later in this chapter). Shoes with laces, such as in Figure 12-1a and b (as opposed to laceless "slippers" in Figure 12-1c), and higher tops that cover the anklebones (as in Figure 12-1a) offer protection when climbers jam their feet in cracks. If a climber is restricted to owning only one pair of rock shoes, a pair with all-around characteristics is best.

Good fit is paramount. Rock shoes should fit snugly, to allow dexterity and a good sense of the rock's features, yet not so tightly as to cause pain. Rock shoes should be comfortable enough to wear for an all-day climb. Unlike sport climbers at local crags, crag and alpine rock climbers do not have the luxury of taking their shoes off after each 40-foot (12-meter) pitch. Some makes of rock shoes are sized for wider or narrower feet than others; try on different styles to find what fits. A thin pair of liner socks add comfort and a little warmth, a bonus when climbing in chilly conditions. Some climbers have a pair of "alpine rock shoes" sized to fit over their mountain-boot socks. All rock shoes stretch somewhat, usually only a quarter to a half size in width and much less in length. Leather shoes stretch more than synthetic shoes. Lined shoes stretch the least.

Rock-shoe rubber oxidizes and hardens over time; try a brisk scrubbing with a wire brush to expose a new, stickier layer. Rock shoes can often be resoled when their rubber wears down but usually only if a hole has not yet been worn through. Resoling is significantly less expensive than buying a new pair.

CLOTHING

Alpine rock climbing clothing must be comfortable, allow free range of movement, and handle changing weather conditions. For details on fabrics and general information on alpine clothing, see Chapter 2, Clothing and Equipment.

Remove rings, bracelets, and watches before climbing rock, because they will probably get scratched at the very least; much worse, they may catch in a crack and damage your hands. A stuck ring can cause serious injury, even amputation of the finger.

TAPE

Athletic tape can be used to protect hands from abrasive rock when you are crack climbing. Tape is advisable for those learning crack techniques, for those climbing more difficult cracks (especially on rock that has many sharp crystals), or for those who have occupations where raw hands could be a hazard (such as health care or food service). Some climbers feel that tape around their fingers helps support and protect finger tendons.

Taping methods vary; see Figure 12-2 for a method that leaves the palm untaped, to ensure sensitivity while face climbing. When taping your hands, flex them so that when you later make a fist or hand jam, the tape will not be too tight. After climbing, you can often cut off your tape "gloves" and save them for later use.

CHALK

Climbers chalk can improve a climber's grip, especially in hot weather, by absorbing sweat. Chalk is available as loose powder and as a crushable block, either of which climbers usually carry in a chalk bag. Chalk is also available contained inside mesh balls (refillable) that allow smaller amounts of chalk to sift out into the chalk bag and minimize spillage.

Chalk marks tend to identify the holds that are used, thus making a climber's moves obvious and minimizing

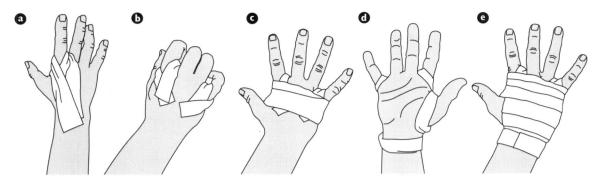

Fig. 12-2. Hand taped for climbing: a, wrap tape around first finger; b, wrap tape around pinky; c, cover back of hand with overlapping tape strips; d, palm is left mostly open; e, add wraps down to wrist to protect entire back of hand.

the adventure for the next climber. Excess chalk on holds makes them slippery and leaves residue on the rock, which affects other users. Use chalk sparingly, especially in sensitive or heavily used areas.

CLIMBING EFFICIENTLY

Efficient technique makes alpine rock climbing more enjoyable. It enables climbers to ascend with as much speed as is reasonable, without exhaustion. Climbers must have enough strength for the approach and the climb itself, as well as the descent and the hike back out. Good technique combines balance, footwork, and handwork with the minimum expenditure of strength. Climbing efficiently also requires proficiency with technical gear by both the leader and follower (described in Chapters 13, Rock Protection, and 14, Leading on Rock). All of this comes with time and practice.

Rock climbing may appear to require great arm strength. It is true that strength may get climbers up certain rock sections if they have no technique, but they will also burn out quickly. On some rock features, strength alone will not work; technique is necessary. The best of both worlds combines technique with good physical training in strength, power, and endurance (see Chapter 4, Physical Conditioning; Eric Hörst's *How to Climb 5.12* is also a good resource for physical training, listed in Resources). Following are some general guidelines about technique that apply to climbing any type of rock, whether a face or a crack.

FOCUS ON SPEED AND SAFETY

Speed is often an important part of safety on an alpine rock climb. Less time climbing means less time exposed to rockfall and changing weather, as well as more time to solve

routefinding problems, deal with injury, get off the mountain before dark, or handle any number of possible risks inherent in the alpine environment. However, reasonable caution must not be sacrificed to speed. Practice on shorter, easier routes and move to longer, more difficult routes as your efficiency improves.

Aim to move smoothly over the rock and set up belays, exchange gear, and manage the rope with a minimum of wasted time. Alpine rock climbing often necessitates carrying a pack, and choices regarding packs depend on the route and personal preference. Pack enough gear to do the climb and survive unexpected situations, but be spartan. Depending on the situation, for speed and safety, both climbers in a climbing team may choose to carry similar packs, or the follower might carry either the only pack or the larger one.

Keep small snacks and water readily accessible for nibbling or sipping in a few seconds at a belay station. Many a climber has "bonked" while up high: gotten dangerously tired and slow from inadequate nutrition or hydration during the day. Be aware of your own—as well as your partner's—food and water intake and energy levels.

The size of the climbing party and the number of rope teams affect overall trip speed. The more rope teams there are, the longer it will take for the entire party to finish, all else being equal.

CLIMB WITH YOUR EYES

Observe the rock. See where the holds are—the edges, the cracks—before even setting foot on the rock. Obviously, specifics of the entire pitch cannot be visually memorized beforehand, but it is possible to get an overall idea. Look off to the side as well as up and down while climbing, to continually check where the holds are and will be in relation

12

to your hands and feet. Many choices of holds are available on easy to moderate routes; look around and do not let tunnel vision stop you from seeing them.

Because the number of available holds decreases as the route's difficulty increases, a calm attitude helps on more difficult terrain. (Arno Ilgner's book *The Rock Warrior's Way: Mental Training for Climbers* discusses the mental aspects of climbing in detail; see Resources.) Tune in to how your balance feels as you move deliberately, smoothly, and fluidly. Much of successful climbing results from a relaxed yet alert mind.

USE FOOTWORK

Footwork and balance are the foundations of rock climbing. Good footwork gives a climber good balance and requires less exertion than handwork does. Leg muscles are larger and stronger than arm muscles, and therefore they provide the most efficient use of muscle power. That is why climbers are frequently told to climb with their feet.

Look for footholds that are comfortably spaced. Shorter steps take less energy than longer, higher steps, and you will stay in balance more easily. However, steps too close together take up more time per foot of upward progress.

Stand erect over your feet—this keeps your body weight centered over your feet, and the resulting down-pressure helps keep your feet on the holds. Anxious climbers tend to hug or lean into the rock, but this just tends to push their feet off the rock because the pressure is out, not down.

Try to walk up the rock from foothold to foothold, as if you were going up a ladder—use your hands merely for balance. When you raise a foot toward the next foothold, eye the hold and aim precisely for it. Once your foot is set in place, commit to the hold and leave your foot there. Adjust your balance to the new position by shifting your hips over the new hold. Continue transferring your weight through your leg down to that foot. Complete the move: stand up by using your leg muscles to push your body up.

MAINTAIN THREE POINTS OF CONTACT

When you begin to learn rock climbing, keep three body points—any combination of hands and feet—weighted on the rock at all times. This can be two hands and one foot (fig. 12-3) or one hand and two feet. Keep your balance over your feet until you release a hold to move for the next one. This is an especially useful approach when testing a hold for looseness without weighting it because it allows you to balance securely on three holds while testing the new one.

Fig. 12-3. Three-point suspension: Keep three body points weighted on rock at all times; here, the climber's hands and right foot provide a secure stance while she moves her left foot higher.

Be aware of where your center of gravity is—directly over your feet is usually the most stable stance. Moving your center of gravity over a new foot- or handhold causes your weight to shift to that new hold.

On more difficult climbs, it is not always possible to keep three body points in contact with the rock. There may be only one or two sound holds, so use your body position to maintain a delicate balance over those holds. Regardless of the number of points you have in contact, however, the same principle of balance applies: keep your weight over your holds.

CHECK FOR LOOSE HOLDS

Loose rock can be all too common in the mountains. Many loose holds are obvious, but be alert for those that are not. Look for fracture lines and loose rocks (fig. 12-4a). Gently nudge any suspect hold, or give it a push with the heel of your hand (fig. 12-4b). A hollow-sounding rock is usually loose. Make sure your testing does not actually dislodge the rock! If loose rock cannot be avoided, move with extra care and deliberation. Sometimes a loose hand- or foothold can be used if you carefully push downward and in on it while weighting it—but be careful.

BASIC TECHNIQUES

This section covers concepts, rather than specific types of moves, that can be used in all kinds of climbing.

DOWNWARD-PRESSURE

For the downward-pressure technique, place fingertips or the palm, side, or heel of the hand on the hold and press down (fig. 12-5). Pressing down with the thumb can be useful on very small holds. A common technique is to pull down on a hold from above and then put downward-pressure on it after you move above it. Downward-pressure may be used alone or in combination with other techniques, such as in counterforce with a lieback hold or as part of a stemming move (see "Crack Climbing" later in this chapter). With arm extended and elbow locked, climbers can balance one-handed by pressing down on a hold as they move the other hand to the next hold.

COUNTERFORCE

Counterforce plays a part in many of the climbing maneuvers described in this chapter. It is the use of pressure in opposing directions to help keep the climber in place. Specific counterforce techniques can be used in face climbing or crack climbing.

12

Fig. 12-4. Looking for loose holds: a, visually inspect the route for loose rocks (circled); b, if loose rock cannot be avoided, use extra caution in that area and test holds before using them.

Fig. 12-5. Using left hand to exert downward-pressure.

COUNTERBALANCE

Counterbalance, or *flagging*, is the principle of distributing your body weight in a way that maintains your balance. This means selecting holds that do the best job of keeping your body in balance. But it also sometimes means putting a hand or foot in a particular location, even if no obvious hold is available, in order to provide counterbalance to the rest of your body (fig. 12-6). Your hips and shoulders also come into play as you move them to provide counterbalance. Flagging is useful because it enables climbers to extend their reach.

LONG REACHES

Several techniques can be used when the next available handhold is a long reach away or even out of reach. First, make the most of available holds. Move as high as possible on existing holds. Stand on your toes, but remember that this is strenuous and can contribute to muscle fatigue if you continue too long. Sometimes a longer reach is possible by standing on the outside edge of a climbing shoe, which tends to turn the body somewhat sideways to the rock. The longest reach possible is with the hand on the same side of your body as the foot you are standing on.

DYNAMIC MOVES

Another option for overcoming a long reach is to make quick intermediate moves, using holds that are marginal but can be used just long enough to allow the climber to scamper up to the next good hold. This leads to using a dynamic move (or *dyno*): a lunge or simply a quick move before you lose your balance. The time to grab the next higher handhold while making a dynamic move is at the "dead point": the apex of the arc of movement when your body is weightless for a fraction of a second before it begins to fall. Movement is most efficient at that point.

Make a dynamic move only after calculating and accepting the consequences of failure. If a dynamic move fails, a fall is likely. Do not make a dynamic move out of desperation. Ensure beforehand that the protection is secure and that a fall onto the protection will not result in hitting a ledge or the ground.

PLACEMENT EXCHANGES

Sometimes a climber needs to move one foot onto a small hold already occupied by the other foot or one hand onto a hold being used by the other hand. Either move can be made several different ways.

Fig. 12-6. Two examples of counterbalance, which enables an extended reach: a, the left foot is flagged to the side to provide counterbalance; b, the left foot is flagged behind the right for counterbalance.

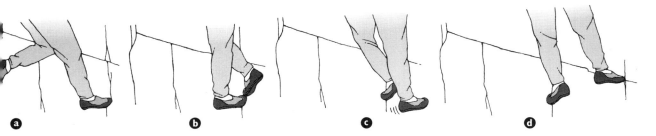

Fig. 12-7. Using a crossover to exchange foot placements on a small hold: a, right foot is on a hold; b, left foot crosses in front of the right and presses down; c, left foot presses on the hold while right foot readies for next hold; d, right foot shifts to next hold.

To exchange a foot placement, make an intermediate move using a poorer, even marginal, hold to get the one foot off the good hold long enough for the other one to take it over. Or hop off the hold while replacing one foot with the other. Or try sharing the hold by matching feet (this is known as *matching*), moving one foot to the very edge of the hold to make enough room for the other.

The crossover is another technique: one foot crosses in front of the other (fig. 12-7a and b) to occupy a small spot on the hold while the first foot moves off that hold (fig. 12-7c) to another (fig. 12-7d).

An intermediate move can be made to trade hands, much as might be done in exchanging feet. Place both hands on the same hold, one on top of the other, or if space is limited, try picking up the fingers of one hand, one finger at a time, and replacing them with the fingers of the other hand. The crossover technique also is occasionally useful.

FACE CLIMBING

Face climbing is simply climbing by using the various features on the surface of a rock face, as contrasted with climbing the cracks that may split a face. A particular hold may be used in a variety of ways by feet and hands as the climber moves up the rock. Face climbing also includes the ascent of nearly featureless slabs, using friction and balance (fig. 12-8).

HANDHOLDS

Handholds can be used for balance, for helping climbers raise themselves by pulling up on the hold, or for providing various forms of counterpressure. Handholds that are at about head height are best because they do not demand a tiring overreach.

Fig. 12-8. Face climbing uses friction and balance when holds are minimal.

Handholds offer maximum security when all the fingers are used. Keeping fingers close together provides a stronger grip on the hold. A large hold, commonly known as a *jug*, allows the entire hand to be cupped over the hold (fig. 12-9a). A smaller open grip hold (fig. 12-9b) may allow room only for fingertips. If the hold is not large enough for all the fingers to be placed on it, "crimp" it by curling the other fingers and placing the thumb over the index finger, which permits the fingers in use to get the most force from

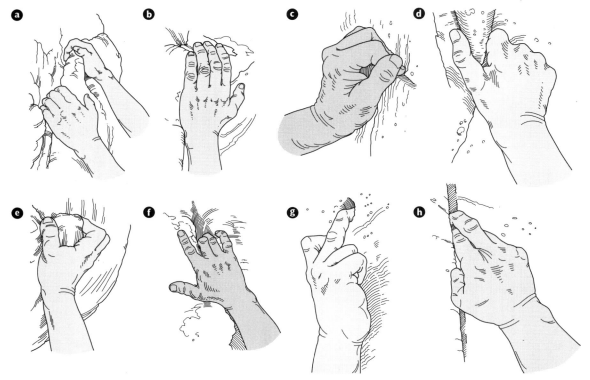

Fig. 12-9. Handholds: a, hands on a jug with fingers close together; b, smaller open grip hold; c, crimping on a smaller hold (more stressful on finger joints); d, finger pinch; e, thumb pinch; f, two-finger pocket; g, mono pocket; h, stacked fingers.

the muscle and tendon system (fig. 12-9c); this type of hold is called a *crimp*. Be careful not to overstress fingers and cause injury by using holds that are too difficult or small for your technique or conditioning level.

Because climbers depend mainly on their legs for upward progress, handholds are sometimes used only for balance. The finger pinch (fig. 12-9d) is a handhold that may allow climbers to maintain a balanced stance on good footholds long enough to shake out their free arm and to reach for a higher, more secure handhold or to place protection.

Smaller holds require different techniques. For example, with fingers holding onto a tiny ledge, for additional strength climbers may use the thumb in opposition on a minor wrinkle, as in a thumb pinch (fig. 12-9e), or in small holes, they may use more than one finger, as in a two-pocket (fig. 12-9f). On a narrow hold or a small pocket in the rock, climbers can use one or two fingers in a mono pocket (fig. 12-9g). On a very narrow hold, climbers can stack fingers on top of each other to increase pressure on the hold (fig. 12-9h).

Handholds that are at about head height are ideal if it is necessary to hang straight-armed for a rest (fig. 12-10), which is less tiring than hanging from bent arms. Climbers can lower their center of gravity by bending their knees or leaning out away from the rock. When it is possible, hang an arm down and shake it out for a brief recovery before climbing again.

Some other types of handholds include slopers and side pulls. *Slopers* require an open hand and skin friction, and the holds, true to their name, slope downward. A *side pull* is a vertically oriented hold off to one side. Lean away from it as you pull on it.

Other techniques can also be useful on friction slabs. Face holds and cracks may be intermittently available for hands or feet. On small edges or irregularities, use down-pressure (see above) with fingertips, thumb, or heel of the hand. A lieback (see later in this chapter) with one hand might be possible using tiny edges. Look for an opportunity for stemming (see later in this chapter), which could mean a chance to rest.

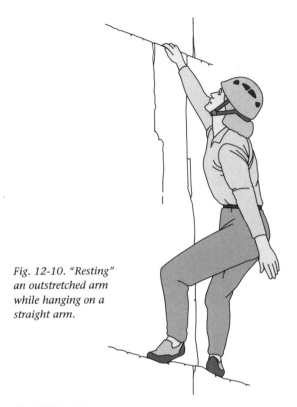

Fig. 12-10. "Resting" an outstretched arm while hanging on a straight arm.

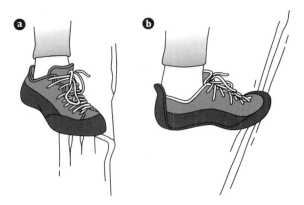

Fig. 12-11. Footholds: a, edging; b, smearing.

FOOTHOLDS

Climbers use most footholds by employing one of two techniques: edging and smearing. On many holds, either technique will work, and the one to use depends on personal preference and the stiffness of the climber's footwear. A third technique, foot jamming, is covered in "Crack Climbing" later in this chapter.

When *edging*, the climber weights the edge of the shoe sole over the hold (fig. 12-11a). Climbers use either the inside or outside edge, but they usually prefer the inside for greater ease and security. The ideal point of contact may vary, but generally it is between the ball of the foot and the end of the big toe. Keeping the heel higher than the toes provides greater precision but is more tiring. Using the toe of a boot or rock shoe on a hold (*toeing in*) is also very tiring. With practice, climbers become proficient using progressively smaller footholds.

In *smearing*, the foot points uphill, with the sole of the shoe "smeared" over the hold (fig. 12-11b). Smearing works best with rock shoes or flexible boots. On lower-angle rock, climbers may not need to use an actual hold but only to achieve enough friction between sole and rock. On steeper terrain, smearing the front of the foot over a hold allows even tiny irregularities in the rock to provide significant friction and security. Slab or friction climbing requires liberal use of smearing (also called *frictioning*) moves. Balance and footwork are the keys to success, and the primary technique is smearing with the feet. In using footholds, make the best use of the direction of force on the hold. Flexing the ankle may increase the surface area of contact between sole and rock, giving maximum holding power. Leaning away from the rock creates inward as well as downward force on the hold, increasing security.

When using large footholds, called *buckets*, place only as much of the foot as necessary on the hold (fig. 12-12a). Putting a foot too far into the bucket can sometimes force the lower leg outward, making for an out-of-balance stance (fig. 12-12b).

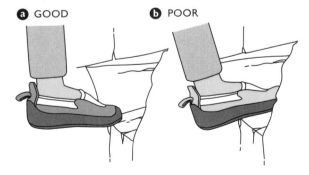

Fig. 12-12. Bucket hold: a, use only as much of the hold as is needed (good); b, a foot too far into a bucket can force lower leg outward (poor).

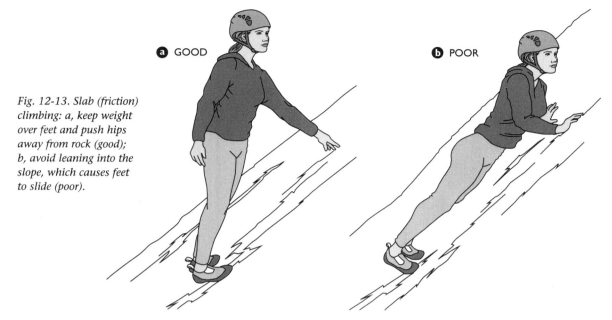

Fig. 12-13. Slab (friction) climbing: a, keep weight over feet and push hips away from rock (good); b, avoid leaning into the slope, which causes feet to slide (poor).

Avoid placing knees on a hold, because knees are susceptible to injury and offer little stability. Nevertheless, even experienced climbers may on rare occasions use a knee hold to avoid an especially high or awkward step. The main considerations are to avoid injury from pebbles and sharp crystals and to avoid becoming trapped on your knees, unable to rise beneath a bulge or roof.

Fatigue, often aggravated by anxiety, can lead to troublesome spastic contractions of the leg muscles, jocularly known among climbers as "sewing-machine" or "Elvis" leg. The best way to stop it is to relax your mind, remember to breathe, and change your leg position somehow, by moving on to the next hold, lowering your heel, or straightening your leg.

When smearing, remember to flex the ankle (lowering the heel) and to keep weight directly over the ball of the foot for maximum friction between rock and sole (fig. 12-13a). Avoid leaning into the slope with your body, which causes the feet to slide down and out from under you (fig. 12-13b). Instead, keep your weight over the feet, bending at the waist to allow the hands to touch the rock and pushing the hips and buttocks away.

Take short steps to maintain balance with your weight over your feet. Look for the small edges, rough spots, or changes in angle that provide the best foot placements. Sometimes climbers actually have to feel with their hands or feet to find the irregularities.

MANTEL

The mantel is a specific use of the down-pressure technique. It lets climbers use hand down-pressure to get their feet up onto the same hold that their hands are using when no useful handholds are available higher.

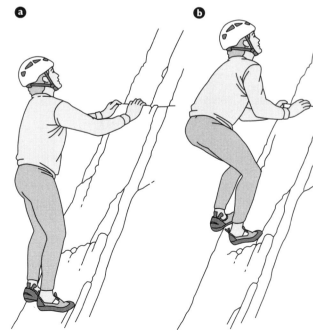

The classic mantel is easiest if the ledge is at about chest height (fig. 12-14a). As you grip the ledge, walk your feet up the rock (fig. 12-14b) until you can place both hands flat on the ledge, palms down, with the fingers of each hand pointing toward the other hand. Then raise your body up onto stiffened arms (fig. 12-14c). Continue to walk your feet up the rock or, if you can, spring up from a good foothold, lifting one foot up onto the ledge (fig. 12-14d), and stand up, reaching for the next handholds for balance (fig. 12-14e).

This basic mantel, however, is not always possible, because a ledge is often higher, smaller, or steeper than a climber might wish. If the ledge is narrow, it may be possible to use the heel of the hand, with the fingers pointed down. If the ledge is over your head, pull down on it first and then use downward-pressure as you move upward. If the ledge is not big enough for both hands, mantel on just one arm while the other hand makes use of any available hold or perhaps just balances against the rock. Do not forget to leave room for your foot.

Avoid using knees on a mantel because it may be difficult to get off them and back on your feet, especially if the rock above is steep or overhanging. Sometimes in mid-mantel it is possible to reach up to a handhold to help as you begin standing up.

COUNTERFORCE IN FACE CLIMBING

Counterforce can be used to pull in on widely spaced holds—a pulling-together action (fig. 12-15a)—or to press in on both sides of a sharp ridge (fig. 12-15b) to create inward pressure. The hands can also be used in counterforce to the feet, as in the undercling (see below).

Stemming on a Face

Stemming is a valuable counterforce technique that lets climbers support themselves between two spots on the rock that might be of little or no use alone. It often

Fig. 12-14. Mantel: (facing page) a, with a ledge at about chest height; b, walk feet up; (above) c, place both hands flat on ledge, palms down and fingers of each hand pointing toward the other hand; d, place one foot on the ledge; e, stand up and reach for the next handholds.

235

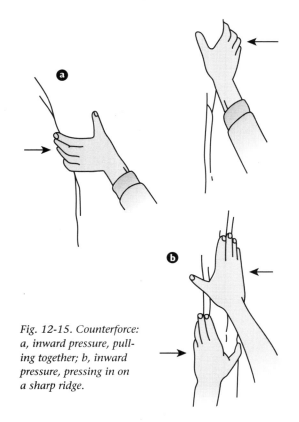

Fig. 12-15. Counterforce:
a, inward pressure, pull-
ing together; b, inward
pressure, pressing in on
a sharp ridge.

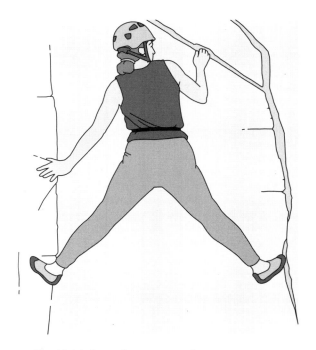

Fig. 12-16. Stemming on a steep face.

provides a method of climbing steep rock where no holds are apparent, simply by pressing in opposing directions with the feet or with a hand and a foot.

Stemming may open an avenue of ascent on a steep face, where climbers can press one foot against a slight protrusion while the other foot or a hand gives opposing pressure against another wrinkle (also known as a "rugosity") in the rock (fig. 12-16).

Undercling

To undercling, your hands (palms up) pull outward beneath a flake or lip of rock while your body leans out and your feet push against rock (fig. 12-17). Your arms pull while your feet push, creating a counterforce. Try to keep your arms extended. Both hands can undercling at the same time, or one hand can undercling while the other uses a different type of hold.

An undercling hold may have multiple uses. For example, from below a rock flake, climbers can hold its bottom edge in a finger pinch or thumb pinch and then convert to an undercling as they move up to the flake.

Fig. 12-17. Undercling: arrows show direction of pressure—hands pull out, feet push in.

CRACK CLIMBING

Many climbing routes follow the natural lines of cracks in the rock. Cracks have the advantage of offering handholds and footholds virtually anywhere along their length, as well as protection opportunities (see Chapter 13, Rock Protection). Some climbers seem to find crack-climbing technique more difficult to develop than face-climbing technique. Perhaps this is because even easy crack climbs demand a higher proportion of technique to strength than do face climbs. Crack climbing is also very individualized, based on the size of each climber's hands and fingers. A crack climb that is easy for one climber may be more difficult for others with smaller hands, for example, or vice versa. Because of the individualized nature of crack climbing, experiment with what works for you; as with face climbing, balance and continued practice are the keys to success. That said, the following crack-climbing techniques are essential tools.

JAMMING

Jamming is the basic technique of crack climbing. To jam, place a hand or foot into a crack, then turn the foot or flex the hand so that it is snugly in contact with both sides of the crack. This wedging must be secure enough that the hand or foot will not come out when weighted. Look for constrictions in the crack, and place hand and foot jams just above these constrictions. When learning to crack climb, it is a good idea to try weighting jams as a test—while remaining balanced on the other points of contact—before actually trying to move up on the jams.

Cracks may be climbed with a pure jamming technique, with both feet and hands using jams, or in combination with other types of holds. While moving up on a jam, maintain the jammed position by using down-pressure (see above). Of course, there is nothing to stop a climber from also using any nearby face holds (fig. 12-18).

The following technique descriptions are basic guidelines that may be adapted to the varying size and configuration of the particular crack a climber is on. With practice, climbers become more adept at selecting the appropriate technique to apply in a given situation.

Hand-Sized Cracks

The easiest crack to master is the hand-sized crack. As the name implies, climbers insert their entire hand into the crack—relax the hand when you insert it, and then expand it so that it becomes wedged in the crack. Different ways to increase hand width include flexing the thumb toward the palm so that the lower "meaty" part of the hand firmly

Fig. 12-18. Combining jamming with face climbing.

contacts the walls of the crack, as well as cupping the hand for full contact (fig. 12-19a). To increase pressure against the walls, climbers sometimes tuck their thumb below their fingers and across the palm, especially in wider cracks (fig. 12-19b). The hold can often be improved by bending the wrist so the hand points into the crack rather than straight up and down.

The hand jam is done either thumb up or thumb down. The thumb-up technique often is easiest and most comfortable for a vertical crack (see Figure 12-19a and b; see also bottom hand in Figure 12-19d), and it allows climbers to reach higher in vertical cracks. The thumb-up configuration is most secure when the climber's body leans to the same side as the hand that is jammed.

The thumb-down technique (fig. 12-19c; see also top hand in Figure 12-19d) may allow for a more secure jam when the thumbs-up technique feels insecure. However, it is not possible to reach as high with this jam in a vertical crack, resulting in more hand jams and more energy expended. Because the hand can be twisted for better adhesion, climbers can lean in any direction off this jam.

12

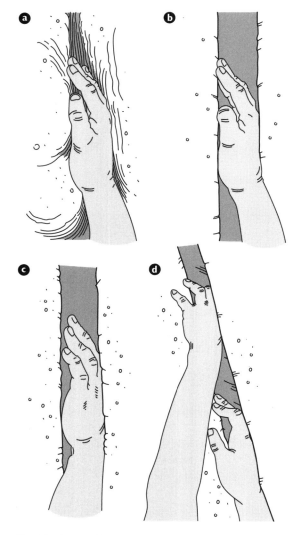

Fig. 12-19. Hand jams: a, thumb-up jam; b, with thumb tucked across palm; c, thumb-down jam; d, combining thumb-down and thumb-up jams in a diagonal crack.

Climbers use a combination of thumbs up and thumbs down, especially in diagonal cracks, where it is often useful to jam the upper hand thumb down and the lower hand thumb up (fig. 12-19d).

With hand jams, climbers must keep alert to the effect of their elbow and body position on the security of the hold. As they move up, they may have to rotate their shoulder or trunk to keep sufficient torque and downward pressure to maintain the jam. Direction of force should be pulling down, not out of the crack. In general, keep the forearm parallel to the crack while climbing.

In dealing with hand jams, climbers encounter variants at both ends of the size scale: thinner cracks that will not admit an entire hand but are larger than finger cracks, up to wider cracks that are not quite large enough for a fist jam but require extra hand twisting to create enough expansion for a secure hand jam. The size of a climber's hand is a major factor in determining the appropriate technique and the degree of difficulty of any particular crack.

Hand-sized cracks are good for foot jamming too, and it is generally possible to wedge a shoe in as far as the ball of the foot. Insert a foot sideways (fig. 12-20a), with the sole facing the side of the crack (big toe facing up), and then twist it sole-down to jam (fig. 12-20b). Avoid twisting the foot so securely that it gets stuck.

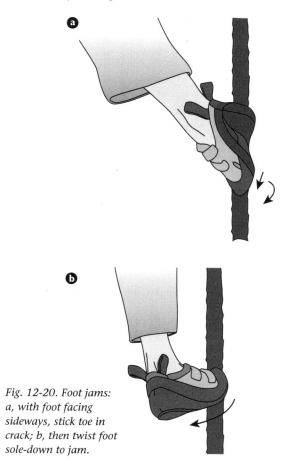

Fig. 12-20. Foot jams: a, with foot facing sideways, stick toe in crack; b, then twist foot sole-down to jam.

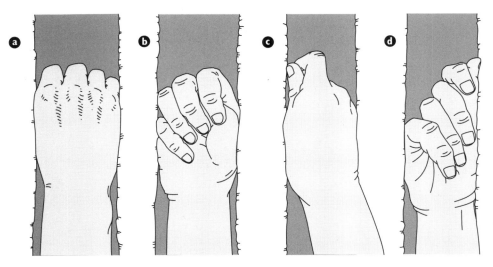

Fig. 12-21. Fist jams: a, palm facing in; b, palm facing out; c, oblique facing in; d, oblique facing out.

Fist-Sized Cracks

In a crack that is too wide for a hand jam, climbers can insert a fist. The thumb may be inside or outside the fist, depending on which provides the best fit. The palm may face either the back of the crack (fig. 12-21a) or the front (fig. 12-21b); if a full fist jam cannot be done, try turning the hand slightly to the side to do an oblique fist jam (fig. 12-21c and d). Flexing the muscles in the fist can expand it slightly to help fit the crack. Fist jams are often painful, but they can be very useful. For the most secure hold, try to find a constriction in the crack and jam the fist above it. If the crack is too wide for a hand but too small for a fist, it is often possible to shove an entire forearm into the crack and flex it for purchase.

Fist-sized cracks can generally accept an entire foot. As with hand-sized cracks, insert a foot sideways, sole facing the side of the crack, and rotate the foot to jam it securely in place. In even wider cracks, it is possible to jam a foot diagonally or heel to toe (fig. 12-22).

Finger-Sized Cracks

Finger jams make it possible to climb some of the narrowest cracks, where a climber may be able to insert only one or more fingers or perhaps just the fingertips. Finger jams are commonly done with the thumb down. Slip the fingers into the crack and twist the hand to lock the fingers in place (fig. 12-23a). Climbers get added strength by stacking fingers and also by pressing their thumb against their index finger in a ring jam (fig. 12-23b and c).

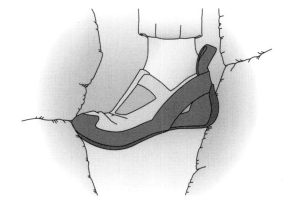

Fig. 12-22. Heel-toe foot jam.

In slightly wider cracks, try a thumb lock, also called a *thumb cam* (fig. 12-23d). Place an upward-pointing thumb in the crack, the thumb pad against one side of the crack and a knuckle against the other. Slide the tip of the index finger tightly down over the first joint of the thumb to create the lock.

The pinkie jam is done with a thumb up (fig. 12-23e and f). Put the little finger in a crack and stack the other fingers on top—fingertips down, nails up. In slightly larger cracks, it may be possible to wedge the heel of a hand and its smaller fingers into a crack that is not quite wide enough for a full hand jam. The weight here is borne by the heel of the hand.

12

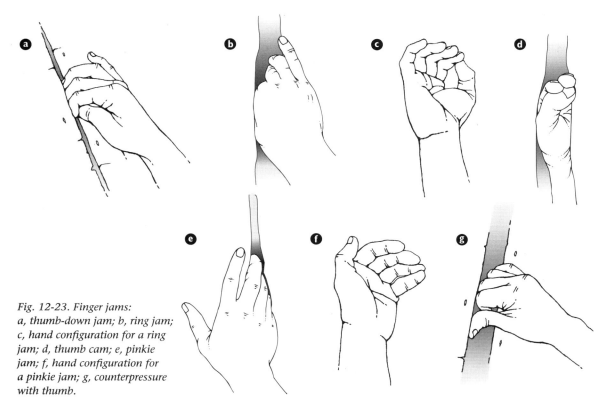

Fig. 12-23. Finger jams:
a, thumb-down jam; b, ring jam;
c, hand configuration for a ring
jam; d, thumb cam; e, pinkie
jam; f, hand configuration for
a pinkie jam; g, counterpressure
with thumb.

For another variation done with thumb down, use the counterpressure of a thumb pushing against one side of the crack and the fingers pushing against the other (fig. 12-23g).

Finger-sized cracks are not big enough to accept a climber's foot, but there is often room for toes. Wedge toes into a crack by turning the foot sideways—usually with the inside of the ankle up—and inserting toes in the crack (see Figure 12-20a), then twist the foot to jam it (fig. 12-24a). Climbers also wedge their toes into a steep inside corner with a smearing technique, keeping their heel lower than their toes and putting pressure down and in to keep their toes in place (fig. 12-24b). Using smearing and friction for the feet also works well when climbing a finger-sized crack.

COUNTERFORCE IN CRACK CLIMBING

Counterforce can be used in a vertical crack by placing both hands in the crack and pulling in opposite directions on the sides of the crack—a pulling-apart action (fig. 12-25)—to create outward pressure. Two other types of counterforce are described below.

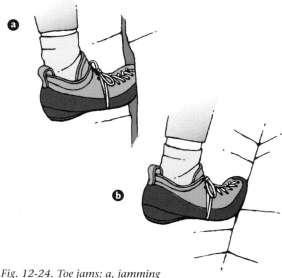

Fig. 12-24. Toe jams: a, jamming in a crack; b, smearing in a corner.

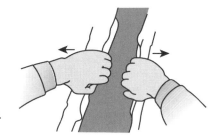

Fig. 12-25. Counterforce in a vertical crack: outward pressure.

Classic Stemming

The classic use of stemming is in climbing a rock chimney. It also comes into play in climbing a dihedral (also called an *open book*), where two walls meet in an approximately right-angled inside corner. One foot presses against one wall of the chimney or dihedral, while the other foot or an opposing hand pushes against the other wall (fig. 12-26).

Liebacking

The classic lieback technique, another form of counterforce, uses hands pulling and feet pushing in opposition as the climber moves upward in shuffling movements (fig. 12-27a). It is used to climb a crack in a corner, a crack with one edge offset beyond the other, or along the edge of a flake. Grasp one edge of the crack with both hands

Fig. 12-26. Stemming across a chimney.

12

Fig. 12-27. Lieback: a, classic lieback; b, combining a lieback (right hand and foot) with face holds (left hand and foot). Arrows show direction of pressure.

and lean back and to the side, away from the crack, on straightened arms. At the same time, push your feet against the opposite wall of the crack. Keep your arms extended to minimize muscle stress. Keep your feet high enough to maintain friction on the rock, but not so high that it is too strenuous. As always, feel for your body's balance and adjust accordingly. This is a strenuous technique, and it is difficult to place protection when liebacking.

The lieback can be used along with other holds as the rock allows. Climbers can lieback on a single handhold in combination with other holds or use one hand and foot in a lieback while using face holds for the opposite hand and foot (fig. 12-27b).

When using the lieback technique, a climber's body may have a tendency to swing sideways out of balance toward the crack, in what is known as the "barn-door" effect, which usually results in a fall. To avoid the barn-door effect, do not apply too much pressure with the leg closest to the rock.

CHIMNEYS

A chimney is any crack big enough to climb inside, ranging in size from those that will barely admit a climber's body (called *squeeze chimneys*) to those that a climber's body can barely span.

The basic principle is to span the chimney with the body, using counterforce to keep from falling. Depending on the width of the crack, either face one side of the chimney or face directly into or out of the chimney. The best body position and technique to use depend on the situation, the climber's size, and whether the climber is wearing a pack. Which direction to face may depend on what holds are available outside the chimney and what the best way will be to climb out of it.

In squeeze chimneys, wedge the body in whatever way works best (fig. 12-28a) and squirm upward (fig. 12-28b). Look for handholds on the outside edge or inside the chimney. Arm bars and chicken wings (see "Off-Width Cracks" below) may be useful. It is helpful, sometimes, to press a foot and knee of one or both legs, for example, against opposite sides of the chimney (fig. 12-28c and d). Try stacking both feet in a T configuration, with one foot placed parallel to one side of the rock and the other placed perpendicular to it, jammed between the first foot and the opposite wall (fig. 12-28e). Climbing squeeze chimneys can be very strenuous.

A crack that is somewhat wider than a squeeze chimney offers more room to maneuver. Press the back and feet against one side of the chimney as the knees and hands push against the other side (fig. 12-29a). Move upward by

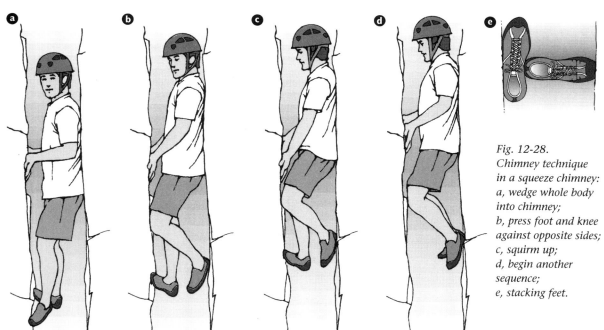

Fig. 12-28. Chimney technique in a squeeze chimney: a, wedge whole body into chimney; b, press foot and knee against opposite sides; c, squirm up; d, begin another sequence; e, stacking feet.

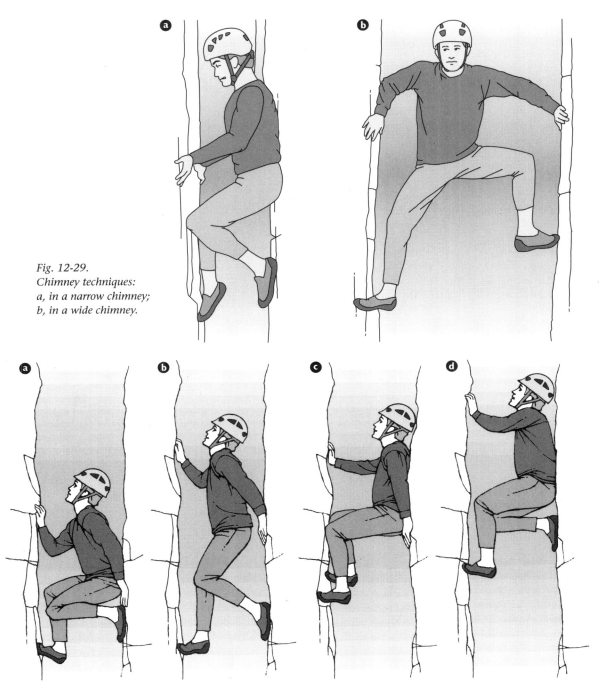

Fig. 12-29.
Chimney techniques:
a, in a narrow chimney;
b, in a wide chimney.

12

Fig. 12-30. Chimney techniques in a moderate-width chimney: a, using counterforce between hands and between feet; b, moving up; c, using counterforce between buttocks and feet; d, beginning the sequence again.

squirming. Or try a sequence of wedging the upper body while raising feet and knees and then wedging them and raising the upper body.

A wide chimney calls for stemming technique, in which a climber faces directly into or out of the chimney (fig. 12-29b). Counterforce is applied between the right hand and foot on one side of the chimney and the left hand and foot on the other side. Press down as well as against the sides, especially if there are holds on the sides of the chimney. Ascend either by alternately moving arms and legs or by moving each leg and then each arm.

A moderate-width chimney is perhaps 3 feet (1 meter) wide. To climb a moderate-width chimney, start by facing one wall of the chimney with your back toward the other one wall. Press one foot against each wall and one hand against each wall (fig. 12-30a). Move upward by straightening your legs and then reestablishing hand positions (fig. 12-30b). Immediately bring your back-wall leg across to the same side as the forward leg (fig. 12-30c). Then swing your forward leg across to the back-wall position (fig. 12-30d). Now move upward again by straightening your legs. Alternatively, your hands may push against one wall in counterforce to your back pressed against the other, or your feet may push against one wall in counterforce to your buttocks against the other (see Figure 12-30c).

Beware of getting too far inside a chimney: though it may feel more secure psychologically, it can leave you lodged deep inside and make it difficult to move back out. There is a better chance of finding useful handholds and footholds near the outside of the chimney. Climbing deep inside the chimney also can make it harder to exit at the top. The transition from the top of the chimney to other types of climbing is often a challenge that may require extra thought and creativity.

Chimney technique may be useful in places that do not look like classic chimneys. It can be used to climb dihedrals (fig. 12-31) or short, wide sections of otherwise narrower cracks. Knee pads can be very useful when climbing routes with extensive chimney sections.

OFF-WIDTH CRACKS

Climbers have figured out ways to jam their arms, shoulders, hips, knees, and just about anything else into the difficult and awkward features known as off-width cracks. They are "off-width" because they are too wide for hand or fist jams but too narrow to admit the entire body for chimneying.

The basic off-width technique calls for standing sideways to the crack and inserting one full side of the body

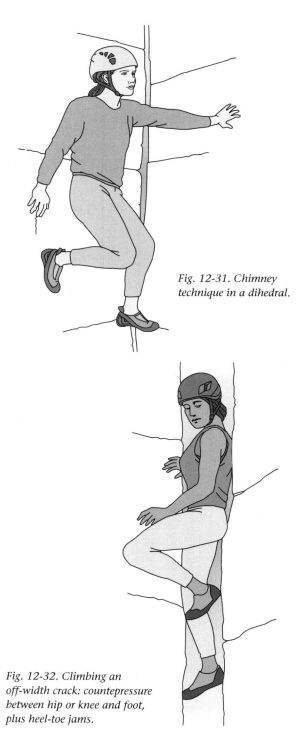

Fig. 12-31. Chimney technique in a dihedral.

Fig. 12-32. Climbing an off-width crack: countepressure between hip or knee and foot, plus heel-toe jams.

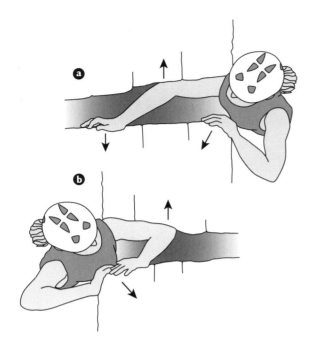

Fig. 12-33. Off-width climbing techniques: a, arm bar; b, chicken wing.

into it (fig. 12-32). When confronted with an off-width crack, first decide which side of the body to put inside the crack. This depends on several things, such as holds in the crack or on the face, the direction in which the crack leans, and whether it flares larger in places.

After settling on which side to use, put the inside leg inside the crack to form a leg bar, usually with counterpressure between foot and knee or foot and hip. This foot is often placed in a heel-toe jam (see Figure 12-22). The outside foot also is inside the crack in a heel-toe jam. Try to keep heels above toes (for better friction) and turned into the crack (to allow the outside knee to turn out).

A primary body-jam technique is the arm bar. With your body sideways to the crack, insert one arm fully into the crack, with the elbow and the back of the upper arm on one side of the crack giving counterpressure to the heel of the hand on the other side (fig. 12-33a). Get the shoulder in as far as possible, and have the arm bar extend diagonally down from the shoulder.

For chicken-winging, a variation of the arm bar, fold an arm back at the elbow before inserting it in the crack, and press the palm against the opposite side in counterforce to the shoulder (fig. 12-33b).

In either the arm bar or the chicken wing, use the outside arm to provide down-pressure to help hold you in the crack, or bring it across the front of your chest and push it against the opposite side of the crack, elbow out.

You are now wedged securely in the crack. To climb, move the outside leg upward to establish a higher heel-toe jam. When this jam is set, stand up on it. Then reestablish the inside leg bar and arm bar (or chicken wing), and reposition the outside arm. This again wedges your body in the crack. You are now ready to move the outside leg upward again to establish a yet higher heel-toe jam. Continue repeating this procedure.

Climbers may use their outside foot occasionally on face holds, but watch out for the tendency for these outside footholds to pull you out of the crack.

For especially awkward crack sizes, climbers may have to stack hand jams (the "butterfly technique") or fist jams in the crack, or jam with the knee. A specialized technique, Leavittation (named after Yosemite climber Randy Leavitt), is used to climb an overhanging off-width.

Many alpine climbs have short sections of off-width cracks, but some climbs with long, strenuous off-widths have a cultlike following. For these, specialized rock protection (such as Big Bros; see Chapter 13, Rock Protection) and extra clothing and padding to protect the skin are a must. Online resources go into detail about specialized crack climbing (see Resources).

COMBINING CRACK- AND FACE-CLIMBING TECHNIQUES

Cracks also may be climbed with a pure lieback technique (see Figure 12-27a), by liebacking with one hand and foot (see Figure 12-27b), or by liebacking with one arm in combination with face holds for the other hand (fig. 12-34). This may result in a kind of stemming action.

Dihedrals may be climbed by using various combinations, such as hands jammed in a crack splitting the dihedral, combined with feet stemming on opposite sides of the dihedral (fig. 12-35).

Climbers may find useful edges or other holds hidden within cracks—on the sides or even at the back of wide cracks. It is also possible to pull down on a horizontal crack like a regular hold or ledge.

OTHER CLIMBING TECHNIQUES

Features such as overhangs, roofs, horizontal or diagonal sequences, and ledges challenge climbers to employ a variety of techniques, tactics, and body positions.

12

245

NEGOTIATING OVERHANGS AND ROOFS

To climb overhangs and roofs, remember the main points for any style of climbing: stay in balance and conserve strength. Identify handholds for moving up and over the bulge. Make the most of footholds by keeping feet high and hips low to help press weight against the footholds (fig. 12-36). In some situations, it means pressing hips into the rock, with the back arched, to keep weight over feet while poised under an overhang.

To conserve strength, weight the feet as much as possible, even when negotiating a roof (fig. 12-37a). Keep arms straight while raising the feet (fig. 12-37b). Avoid hanging on bent arms, because this position will quickly exhaust arm strength. Push your body up with your legs rather than pulling with your arms (fig. 12-37c). Move quickly to minimize the time spent in these strenuous positions. Occasionally it may be necessary to rise up on the feet while making a dynamic reach to a handhold. Another trick is to throw one foot up onto a ledge while pushing with the other foot and pulling with the arms to swing up onto the top foot (fig. 12-37d).

Fig. 12-34. Liebacking combined with face holds.

Fig. 12-35. Climbing a dihedral using stemming and hand jams.

Fig. 12-36. Climbing an overhanging route: keep feet high and hips low.

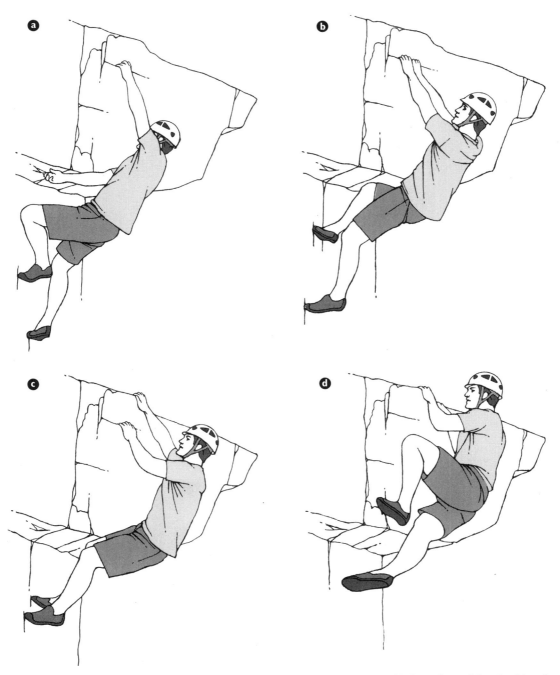

Fig. 12-37. Climbing over a roof: a, lean out with an outstretched arm to locate a hold above the roof, keeping hips close to the rock and feet weighted; b, move other hand up above roof, keeping arms straight; c, move feet up higher and push them against the rock; d, bring one foot up and begin to pull over the roof.

Fig. 12-38. Traversing a steep face (an advanced technique): a, start with right foot on a hold in the direction of the traverse; b, twisting the body, reach through with left hand and shift weight over right foot; c, move right hand to new hold, while shifting both feet to right.

TRAVERSING

Traversing—going sideways across a section of rock—calls for a wide variety of climbing techniques. The main ones are side-pulling, liebacking, and stemming. Good balance and being aware of your center of gravity are especially important during traverses.

Usually climbers face into the rock when traversing, their feet pointed away from each other (fig. 12-38a). Commonly climbers shuffle their hands and feet sideways, although it can be very useful to exchange one hand for the other (see "Placement Exchanges" above), or one foot for the other, on a single hold. Climbers may occasionally

Fig. 12-39. Hand traverse: a, push feet against rock, providing counterforce; b, cross one hand over the other.

cross one foot behind the other or one hand over the other to reach the next hold (fig. 12-38b and c).

A hand traverse is necessary when footholds are marginal or nonexistent. The hands grip a series of holds or shuffle along an edge, while the feet provide a counterforce by pushing against the rock, as in a lieback or undercling (fig. 12-39a). Keep feet high and the center of gravity low so feet are pushed into the rock. Cross one hand over the other (fig. 12-39b). Again, keep arms straight to conserve arm strength and to let the legs do as much of the work as possible.

EXITING ONTO LEDGES

When approaching a ledge, continue to walk the feet up the rock, and then use down-pressure with hands near the edge of the ledge. A classic mantel (see Figure 12-14) is often an excellent exit move onto a ledge (fig. 12-40a). Avoid the temptation to simply lean forward and pull your torso onto the ledge; shifting your weight like that may throw you off balance and also make it impossible to keep an eye on the footholds (fig. 12-40b).

DOWN-CLIMBING

Efficient down-climbing is useful on many alpine climbs. Down-climbing is sometimes faster, safer, or easier than rappelling, and it may provide another retreat option when necessary.

Holds are harder to see when down-climbing than when climbing upward. The steeper the face, the harder the holds are to see. It is difficult to test holds without committing to them. On low-angle rock, face outward for the best ability to see the route when down-climbing (fig. 12-41a). Keep hands low and use down-pressure holds whenever possible. Keep your weight over your feet to maximize friction, especially when going down slabs. It may help to keep your center of gravity low, with knees well bent

12

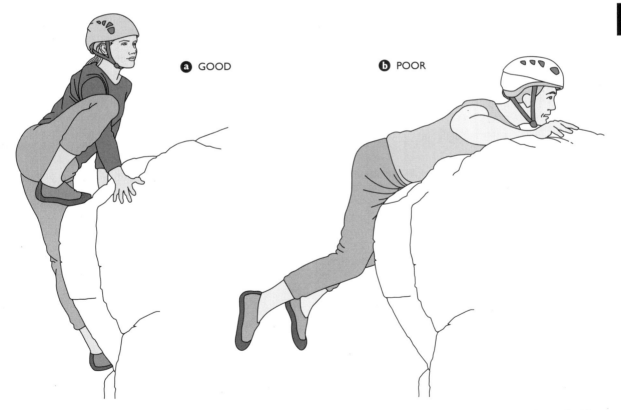

Fig. 12-40. Exiting onto a ledge: a, keep hands close to lip of ledge and mantel up (good); b, reaching too far forward with hands causes feet to lose their purchase (poor).

Fig. 12-41. Down-climbing techniques: a, facing out on low-angle rock; b, going down a friction slab; c, facing sideways on steeper rock; d, facing in on steep rock.

(fig. 12-41b). As the rock steepens, turn sideways, leaning away from the rock for better ability to see the route (fig. 12-41c). If the angle gets even steeper, face into the rock and look down and around behind you (fig. 12-41d).

STYLE AND ETHICS

Climbers debate endlessly over which styles are fair and which are less than sporting and over which practices are harmful to the environment and which are not. Climbers soon discover that getting to the end of the pitch or the top of the peak is not the only goal—another is getting there in a way that feels right, respects the rock, and tests a climber's skill and resolve. These are matters of style and ethics.

The terms "style" and "ethics" are sometimes used interchangeably by climbers, but *style* is generally an individual attribute, while *ethics* pertains to overall application of the pursuit. In other words, style refers to each climber's personal mode of climbing; for example, is it fair to say you have led a first ascent if you first climbed the route on a top rope? Ethics pertain to issues concerning preservation of the rock and the environment itself.

DIVERSITY OF STYLES

Styles change and attitudes evolve, but the core of the debate on climbing styles is about how to maintain the challenge of climber against rock and how to play the game in a way that fairly tests the climber.

Climbers adhering to *traditional style* prefer to climb each route strictly from the ground up, with no help from such aids as top ropes or preplaced protection such as bolts. New routes are explored and protected only on lead. This type of climbing characterizes rock climbing in the alpine setting, but it is also found at many popular crags.

Climbers following the *sport-climbing style* influenced by Europeans are more likely to find other techniques acceptable as well. This can include inspecting the route on rappel before trying to lead it from below. It can also mean cleaning the route (removing protection placed by the lead climber or by another climber) and perhaps preplacing protection on rappel. Routes may be climbed with multiple falls, by resting on the rope while checking out the next move (*hangdogging*), or by rehearsing moves with the help of a top rope. These techniques have made it possible to climb harder and harder routes with the climber assuming less risk.

Often, due to the commitment and remoteness of alpine ascents, climbers will pull on gear or stand in a sling to climb through a hard section with greater speed and safety. Just as alpine climbers can improve their technique by cross training with sport climbing, they will also benefit from a knowledge of aid climbing (see Chapter 15, Aid and Big Wall Climbing).

A particular climbing area may lend itself more to one style than another because of the type of rock, the difficulty of the routes, or the prevailing style among the local climbers. In the world of climbing, there is room for a diversity of styles, and most climbers experience a variety of them.

ETHICS AND THE ROCK

The subject of ethics has to do with respecting the rock and every person's chance to use it. Unlike climbing style, ethics involves personal decisions that do affect others' experience and enjoyment. This includes the sticky question of the manner in which bolts are placed on a route. Are bolts that are placed on rappel different from—less "ethical" than—bolts placed on the lead? Some climbers may argue that bolts placed while on rappel rob others of the chance to try the route from the ground up, and such bolts are often placed at less-convenient places than they would be if they were placed on a ground-up ascent. But other climbers may say that placing the bolts on rappel gives them a chance at an otherwise unclimbable route.

Each area has its own tradition of what styles and ethics are acceptable. Visiting climbers should observe the local standards, which are usually described in local guidebooks, as well as any land management regulations, since some areas prohibit any bolting or placing of permanent anchors. Sometimes locals may disagree among themselves. This book does not try to resolve issues of style and ethics, but there is general agreement on a couple of principles.

Preservation of the rock is paramount. Chipping the rock to create new holds is unacceptable and destroys a natural feature—and who knows? It may be climbed someday as it is. Although bolt-protected routes are common in many areas, bolting should not be indiscriminate. In the mountains or other wilderness areas, away from concen-trated centers of rock climbing, it is particularly important to preserve the environment for those who follow. If possible, stick to clean climbing, using only removable gear for protection (see Chapter 13, Rock Protection).

It is almost never justifiable to add a bolt to an existing route (*retro-bolting*). If you feel you cannot safely climb the route as it is, do not try it. Retro-bolting usually occurs when a consensus of local climbers agree that more bolts should be placed to promote safety and enjoyment and the first ascensionists concur.

There should be no objection to replacement of an old bolt with a newer, stronger one at an established belay or rappel point, provided you have the necessary skills and experience to replace it.

COURTESY

Climbers should keep others in mind when they are out climbing. If a climbing party is moving up a multipitch route at a much slower pace than that of the people behind them, the first group should let the following party pass at a safe spot, such as a belay ledge. Passing can be awkward or dangerous on some longer, harder routes so a party traveling more slowly than the norm for such a route may leave many frustrated climbers waiting for several hours or having to retreat.

BEING PREPARED

Beware of tackling climbs that are beyond your personal abilities. Try climbs at your limit on the crags rather than in the mountains. If inexperience gets a climbing party in trouble in the mountains, they may involve other climbers in a time-consuming and dangerous rescue of their party. Come prepared to handle the possibilities inherent in the chosen climb. Aim to be self-reliant within your climbing party and capable of self-rescue. This competence will add to climbers' confidence and enjoyment of the alpine environment.

12

CHAPTER 13

ROCK PROTECTION

The "rack and rope" are, collectively, the rock climber's protection. The rope connects two climbers—one leading a pitch while the other belays. Protection, or "pro," connects them both to the rock face. The belayer is connected to an anchor that can be natural, such as a live tree, or formed from several pieces of protection. To limit a fall, the climber on lead periodically places protection from the rack (the collection of gear used for protection) while climbing.

The quality and location of the protection that the lead climber places largely determine the consequences of a potential fall. If a climber falls while leading, the length of the fall will be about twice the distance between the climber and the last point of protection, plus rope stretch (fig. 13-1). If the last piece placed pulls out, the fall increases in length by double the distance to the next piece that holds the fall (see "Understanding Impact Force" and "Understanding Fall Factors" in Chapter 10, Belaying). Climbers need to be skilled at both selecting solid locations for protection and in making the placement.

CONNECTING THE ROPE TO PROTECTION

Carabiners and runners are the tools climbers use to connect the climbing rope to protection (fig. 13-2a). One carabiner is attached to the protection, the other is attached to the rope. The carabiner should almost always be used in the down-and-out position: the gate should point down and away from the rock surface (fig. 13-2b). This position lessens the chance that the carabiner gate will accidentally open during a fall—potentially disastrous. The rope itself should be clipped in so that it runs freely through the carabiner in the direction of travel (fig. 13-2c): the rope should

travel from the rock surface upward through the carabiner and then out toward the climber. If the climbing route does not take the climber straight upward, the rope exits the carabiner on one side or the other; it should exit on the side opposite from the gate. This minimizes the chance that the rope will twist across the gate and open it during a fall (see Figure 14-9 in Chapter 14, Leading on Rock).

Runners, slings, and cordelette serve to lengthen the distance between the point of protection and the rope. This helps to isolate rope movement from the protection, keeping protection from wiggling or "walking" from its intended placement or dislodging completely, and also helps to minimize friction or rope drag on the climbing rope by allowing it to run in more of a straight line. Runners, slings, and cordelette can connect directly to natural protection (see Figures 13-3 and 13-4) or, rarely, to preexisting fixed protection without the use of an intervening carabiner. Carabiners should be placed so they are not at risk of being cross-loaded across the rock in the event of a fall.

NATURAL PROTECTION

Trees and rock features can provide excellent protection, conserve gear, and offer a quicker alternative than placing gear, but carefully evaluate them for stability and strength.

252

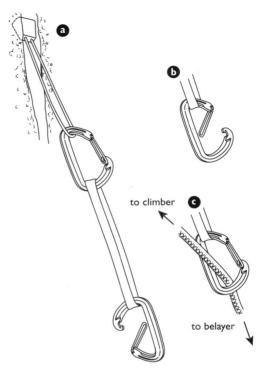

Fig. 13-1. Leader fall with intermediate points of protection in place.

Fig. 13-2. Correct down-and-out positioning of a carabiner: a, clip the carabiner into the pro's runner in a downward direction; b, then rotate it out and away from the rock (gate opening is now down and facing out from rock); c, rope clipped through carabiner in direction of travel.

"Test before you trust" is a good rule. Be wary of rock that is brittle, vegetation that is poorly rooted, and other suggestions of weakness. (See "Natural Anchors" in Chapter 10, Belaying.) An error in judgment could result not only in failed protection but also in a rock or tree crashing down upon the climber, the belayer, or other parties on the route.

Trees and large bushes provide the most obvious points of attachment, but do not trust a dead, brittle, weak, or loose tree or shrub. Look for a healthy trunk with live branches and a solid root system. If there is any question, test smaller trees by pushing against them with one foot. For using natural protection midpitch, single or double runners are commonly looped around the base of the trunk, with the ends clipped together with a carabiner (fig. 13-3a). You can also untie a knotted sling and retie it around the trunk. A third method is to use a girth hitch (fig. 13-3b). If using the natural protection point as an anchor, a cordelette is commonly looped around the base of the trunk and tied with a figure eight, with the resulting power point of all strands clipped to a locking carabiner (fig. 13-3c). The cordelette usually should be as close to the tree roots as possible, although with a strong tree the cordelette may be placed higher if necessary. Often a 20-foot (6 meters) or longer cordelette is needed.

13

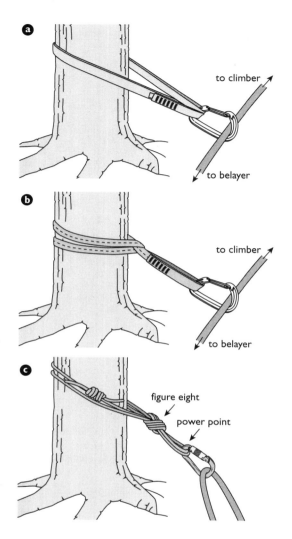

Fig. 13-3. Using a tree trunk as a protection point: a, sewn sling wrapped around trunk; b, sewn sling girth hitched around trunk; c, anchor setup with a cordelette tied around trunk using a figure eight.

Rock features—horns, columns, rock tunnels, chockstones, large and flat-bottomed boulders—are other common forms of natural protection. In evaluating a rock feature, consider its relative hardness, how crumbly it is, and whether it is firmly attached to the rock around it. Attempt to move the rock, being careful not to pull it loose. Whack it a few times with a hand or fist. Beware of hollow sounds or brittleness.

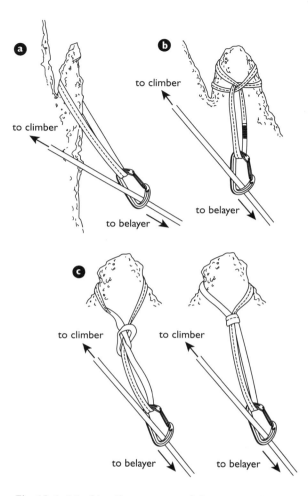

Fig. 13-4. Attaching the rope to a rock feature: a, using one runner and one carabiner to link a point of natural protection with the rope; b, securing a runner to a rock horn with a clove hitch; c, slinging a horn with a slipknot on a runner, with the dressed slipknot shown at right.

Horns (also called knobs or chicken heads, depending on their shape and size) are the most common type of natural rock protection. If there is any question about rock horns, test them by pushing against them with one foot. To attach to a rock horn, a runner can be looped over the horn and clipped in to the rope (fig. 13-4a), but it may be pulled off the horn by rope movement. Use a clove hitch (fig. 13-4b) or slipknot (fig. 13-4c) to tighten the runner around the horn to help prevent it from slipping off. The slipknot can be tied easily with one hand and requires less sling material

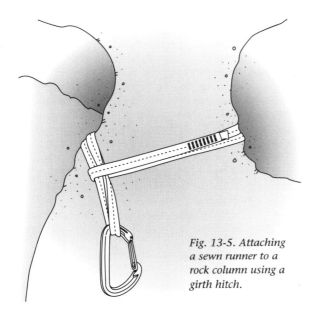

Fig. 13-5. Attaching a sewn runner to a rock column using a girth hitch.

than a girth hitch or clove hitch. (See "Knots, Bends, and Hitches" in Chapter 9, Basic Safety System.)

To attach to a rock column or chockstone or through a rock tunnel, first thread a sewn runner around the feature, then clip both ends of the loop with a carabiner. Alternatively, thread the runner around the rock feature and then secure it with a girth hitch (fig. 13-5) or untie a knotted runner and retie it after threading it through the point of protection.

Take extra care when using freestanding boulders. They should not move or rock when tested. Consider not just the size but the shape of the boulder, what it rests on, and how it is affected by changing conditions such as snow or ice. Avoid any feature with a rounded bottom or a narrowed base, as well as features that rest on gravel, sand, or downsloping ledges. Sling a boulder around its base. Keep the pulling point low to minimize leverage on the boulder.

Natural protection used for anchors on popular routes often accumulates slings as each party rappels from a route and leaves yet another sling behind. Do not trust these slings with your life without inspecting and testing their strength. Sunlight, weather, and age can degrade them.

FIXED PROTECTION

On established routes, climbers may encounter previously placed bolts and pitons (see also "Fixed Anchors" in Chapter 10, Belaying). Climbers also may encounter removable

protection that became fixed when someone could not remove it. On rock climbing topo maps (see Figure 14-3 in Chapter 14, Leading on Rock), bolts and fixed pitons are often shown as "x" and "fp," respectively.

BOLTS

Bolts are most commonly seen in sport-climbing areas, but they may also be found on traditional or aid-climbing routes. Bolt hangers allow carabiners to be attached to bolts (fig. 13-6a and b). Chains are sometimes found at sport-climbing anchors (fig. 13-6c) to facilitate rappelling (see Figure 11-3 for a bolted rappel anchor setup).

A well-placed bolt will last for years, but age and weather can compromise it. Be especially wary of ¼-inch bolts, which were placed primarily in the 1960s and 1970s. Bolts measuring ³⁄₁₆ to ½ inch in diameter have been used since the mid-1980s and are now the standard. Standard metric bolts are 10, 12, and 14 millimeters in diameter.

Visually check both the bolt and its hanger for signs of weakness, especially for cracks, excessive corrosion, or brittleness. A rust streak below the bolt indicates metal wear. Do not trust an old sheet-metal-style hanger with heavy rust. Test whether the bolt is securely anchored into the

13

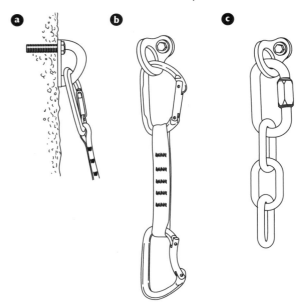

Fig. 13-6. Bolt and bolt hanger: a, from the side with a carabiner clipped to hanger; b, from the front with a quickdraw clipped to hanger; c, with quick link and chains attached.

rock by clipping in to the bolt hanger with a carabiner and trying to pull the bolt around or out. Any bolt that can be moved in any direction, however slightly, is probably not trustworthy. Avoid banging on the bolt, which weakens it. Back up any suspect bolt with another point of protection wherever possible.

If the bolt and its placement seem solid, use a carabiner to clip a runner to the bolt hanger. At a fixed anchor with chains hanging from the bolt hangers (see Figure 13-6c), clip the bolt hangers if at all possible, to free up the quick links, chain links, or rap rings for rappels. Some carabiners may not fit through the chains' upper links.

Bolts without hangers can be reliable protection if a hanger is added. If you anticipate hangerless bolts, carry extra hangers and nuts. If a bolt has no hanger, a last-resort solution is to slide a wired nut down its wires (fig. 13-7a), slip the upper wire loop around the bolt stud, and snug the nut up again against the bolt (fig. 13-7b). Attach a runner to the lower end of the nut wire.

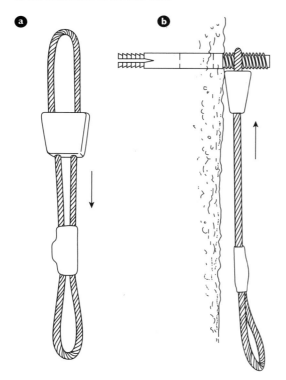

Fig. 13-7. Placing a wired nut on a hangerless bolt: a, create a loop by sliding the nut down its wires; b, slide the nut up its wires to form a noose around the bolt.

PITONS

Pitons were commonly used in mountaineering through the 1970s but are rarely used today, because placing and removing them scars the rock. However, many pitons remain as fixed placements on various routes. While it is better to rely on your own protection, these fixed pitons may be clipped as protection and might be helpful at times in retreating, when attempting to minimize gear left behind.

Pitons, even more than bolts, are vulnerable to weathering. Years of melt-freeze cycles widen cracks in the rock and loosen pitons. Examine pitons closely for signs of corrosion or weakness, and examine the cracks they are in for deterioration. Heavy use, failed attempts at removal, and falls on a piton can lead to cracks in the metal around the eye or other damage.

Ideally the piton was driven in all the way, with its eye close to the rock and the piton perpendicular to the likely direction of pull. If the piton appears secure, and in good condition, clip a carabiner (with runner attached) through the eye of the piton (fig. 13-8). Place the carabiner so that under a load it will not be levered against the rock.

If a piton is driven in only partially but otherwise is secure, or if the eye is damaged and can't accept a carabiner, use a runner to tie the piton off next to the rock with a girth hitch, clove hitch, or slipknot (fig. 13-9) to reduce the leverage on the piton under the impact of a fall. If the eye is usable, you may want to girth hitch a keeper sling to the eye and clip the carabiner in to it to catch the piton if it falls. Do not rely on this setup if there is better protection available.

Fig. 13-8. Piton driven into rock: carabiner (with runner attached) clipped through piton's eye.

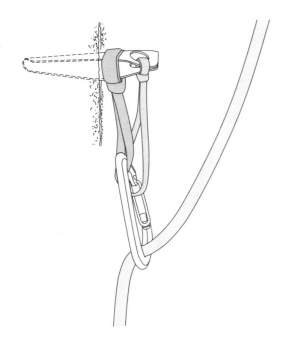

Fig. 13-9. Partially driven piton, with a runner girth-hitched to it close to the rock to reduce leverage and a keeper sling added to catch the piton if it pulls out.

OTHER FIXED PIECES

Removable protection may be abandoned when a party is unable to remove it. Do not trust removable gear that someone else placed. When these "fixed" pieces are encountered, examine them carefully and consider that the party may have abandoned it as the oldest piece on the rack that they were retiring anyway.

In addition to examining the gear and the rock where the piece is placed, note whether the sling attached to the fixed gear appears to be worn or damaged. Because of fixed gear's questionable integrity, consider it primarily backup protection.

REMOVABLE PROTECTION

Removable protection includes the various types of artificial protection other than bolts and pitons. Removable protection generally consists of a metal device that can be secured into the rock, with a sling for use in linking the metal piece to the rope. Removable protection must be placed in high-quality rock to maximize strength. For environmental reasons, using removable protection is preferred to placing new pitons or bolts because it leaves no scars on the rock. Removable protection generally falls into one of two categories: without moving parts (*passive*) or with moving parts (*active*).

Passive removable protection pieces, also known as *chocks*, are made from a single piece of metal and a connecting sling or cable. A typical placement is into a constriction in a crack. Shapes can vary from a tapered wedge, often called a *nut* or *stopper* (see Figure 13-10), to a deformed hexagonal tube, often called a *hex* (see Figure 13-11a, b, c, and d), to the more unusually shaped passive camming pieces such as the Tricam (see Figure 13-11e) that can be used in a torquing orientation, with counterforce exerted between the piece's point and its curved side. Tube chocks, often called *Big Bros* (see Figure 13-13), do have movable parts—they telescope out to a desired size—but they are passively placed much like a hex or a Tricam.

Spring-loaded camming devices (SLCDs), which are commonly called *cams*, are active devices that use spring mechanisms to allow portions of the device to cam against opposite walls of a crack (see Figure 13-14). Loading the device increases the pressure against the rock. Triggers on the device retract the parts, allowing insertion and removal.

PASSIVE REMOVABLE PROTECTION

Multiple chock shapes fit multiple rock cracks, but chocks are strongest when the most metal is in contact with the rock. Chocks have a primary placement direction, but many chocks also are designed for multiple placement options to maximize adaptability. Manufacturers rate the breaking strength of gear, and in general bigger chocks have higher breaking strength.

Passive wedging chocks come in a wide variety of shapes and sizes, but most have a generally wedge-shaped appearance (see Figure 13-10). They are called by many names, from brand names such as Stoppers to simply "wired nuts" or "nuts." Nuts are narrower at the base than at the top (fig. 13-10a), which lets them slip down into a constriction. Variations of nuts include flat faces, curved faces (fig. 13-10b), more-curved faces (fig. 13-10c), faces with notches or grooves (fig. 13-10d), and sides that may be parallel or offset, with both horizontal and vertical tapers.

Some of the smallest nuts, referred to as *micronuts*, are designed for very thin cracks and for aid climbing (fig. 13-10e). Manufacturers construct the nuts with softer metals so that the rock bites into them better than it does into standard aluminum nuts, but this also makes

13

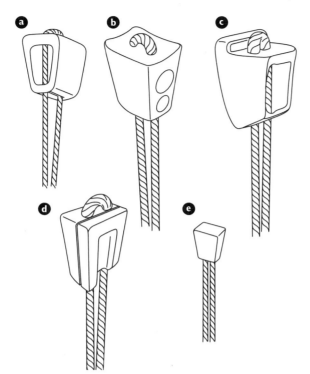

Fig. 13-10. Nuts: a, Stopper; b, curved nut; c, Wallnut; d, offset nut with grooves; e, micronut.

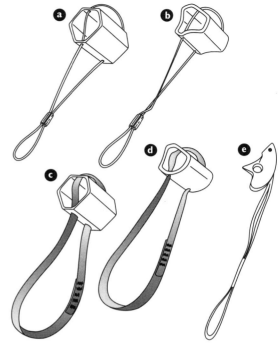

Fig. 13-11. Passive camming chocks: a, wired hex; b, wired curved hex; c, hex slung with high-strength webbing; d, curved hex slung with high-strength webbing; e, Tricam.

micronuts less durable. The thinness of the micronut's cable makes it more prone to damage from normal use. Inspect micronuts and their cables often for nicks and other signs of wear, and retire them if the cable is damaged.

Hexentrics and other similar chocks take their name from their hexagonal shape (fig. 13-11a through d). Each pair of opposing sides on a hex is a different distance apart, permitting three different placement options per piece. The off-center sling creates the camming action (fig. 13-12a), or the piece can be wedged in a constriction. More-rounded versions of the hex work on the same principles.

Tricams have curved rails along one side opposite from a point, or "stinger," on the other side (fig. 13-11e). Camming action is produced by running the sling between the curved side rails and setting the stinger in a small depression or irregularity in the crack (fig. 13-12b); the load on the sling rotates the device into the rock with a camlike action. Tricams also can be used as passive devices simply set into a constriction (see Figure 13-20b), particularly those that narrow sharply.

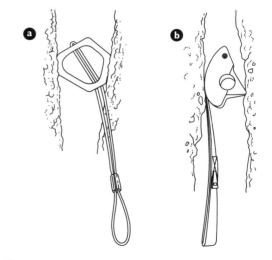

Fig. 13-12. Passive camming chocks in a vertical crack: a, Hexentric; b, Tricam.

Another device that acts as a passive cam (even though it is spring loaded) is the Big Bro, a tube chock with a spring-loaded inner sleeve that telescopes out to bridge a crack when a release button is pressed (fig. 13-13a). The extended sleeve is then locked into place by spinning the collar down snugly against the outer tube. The sling is attached at one end so a torquing action adds to stability when loaded (fig. 13-13b). Tube chocks are specialized for wide parallel cracks known as off-widths.

Most nuts and some hexes are slung with wire cable, which is much stronger than cord or webbing of the same size. The stiffness of the wire cable sometimes aids in placing the chock. Other chocks have sewn slings of cord, nylon webbing, or high-strength materials such as Spectra. A few are available without slings, and the climber must tie them. The sling material should be rated for climbing forces and should be twice as long as the desired sling length, plus about 12 inches (30 centimeters) for the

knot and 1-inch-long (2.5-centimeter-long) tails—or 28 to 32 inches (71 to 81 centimeters) of material to make a loop 8 to 10 inches (20 to 25 centimeters) long. Due to the greater stiffness and lower friction of Spectra and other high-strength materials, a triple fisherman's bend is recommended for tying the sling (see Figure 13-13b). Inspect cables and slings regularly for damage, and follow manufacturer's instructions for replacing or repairing them.

ACTIVE REMOVABLE PROTECTION

Spring-loaded protection devices expand the limits of free climbing by providing protection that can be placed easily with one hand and that can adapt to a variety of cracks.

Spring-Loaded Camming Devices

The first spring-loaded cams, called Friends, were introduced in the mid-1970s. Now spring-loaded camming devices (SLCDs or "cams") are manufactured in a wide size range and with multiple designs (see Figure 13-15). The basic design has four lobes—called a four-cam unit—that rotate from one or two axles, connected to a trigger mechanism on a stem. When the trigger is pulled, the lobes retract (fig. 13-14a), narrowing the profile of the device for placement in a crack or pocket. When the trigger is released, the lobes open up against the sides of the rock (fig. 13-14b). The cams move independently of each other, permitting each to rotate to the point needed for maximum contact

13

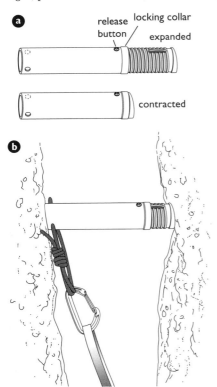

Fig. 13-13. Spring-loaded tube chock: a, contracted and expanded; b, correctly placed in a vertical crack, where it acts as a passive cam.

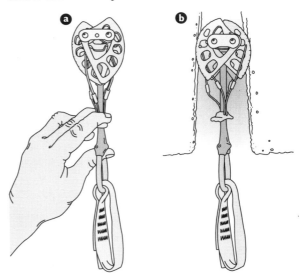

Fig. 13-14. SLCD or cam: a, retracted; b, correctly placed in a vertically oriented crack.

259

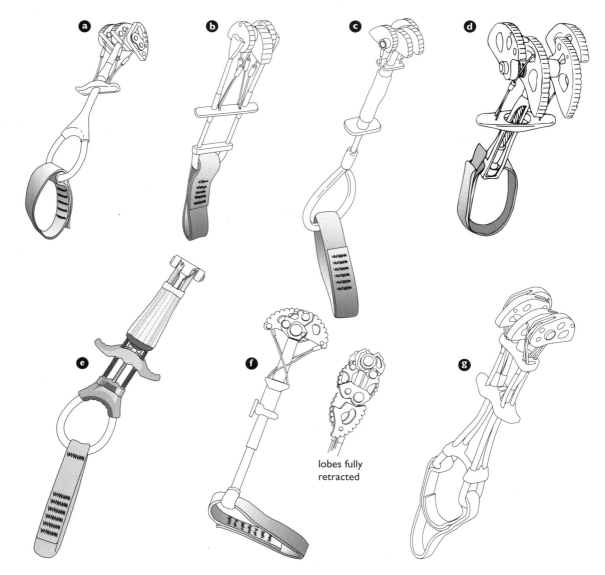

lobes fully
retracted

Fig. 13-15. SLCDs: a, Black Diamond Camalot C4; b, Metolius three-cam unit (TCU); c, CCH Alien; d, Wild Country Technical Friend; e, Black Diamond Camalot C3; f, Omega Pacific Link Cam, g, Totem Cam.

with the rock. This movement sets the device in place. If you fall, the stem is pulled downward or outward, increasing both the camming action and the outward pressure of the cams on the rock.

Variations of SLCDs include double-axle cams that can be used in the totally open position—called Camalots (figure 13-15a is a C4)—and those that cannot; specialized cams that fit into narrower placements (side to side) such as three-cam units (fig. 13-15b), called TCUs, and Aliens (fig. 13-15c), as well as two-cam units; cams with rigid stems or flexible stems; specialized cams designed to hold better in sandstone—called Fat Cams; cams with different trigger designs; specialized cams designed for flaring cracks, such as the Hybrid Alien; lightweight cams that cover wide ranges (figure 13-15d is a Technical Friend); cams for small cracks (figure 13-15e is a C3); extended-range cams (fig. 13-15f) that maximize the range of a single piece of gear; and flexible-body cams (figure 13-15g is a Totem Cam) with a wide expansion range. Some manufacturers, such as Metolius, indicate the optimal camming range with colored dots on the sides of the camming units.

Spring-Loaded Nuts

Spring-loaded nuts (fig. 13-16a) use a small sliding piece to expand the profile of the nut after it is placed in a crack. To place one, first retract the smaller piece by pulling back on the spring-loaded trigger, thereby narrowing the profile of the nut so it can be inserted into a thin crack (fig. 13-16b). Then release the trigger, permitting the smaller piece to press up between the larger piece and the rock, filling in the gap and increasing the area of the nut that is in contact with the rock (fig. 13-16c).

Spring-loaded nuts work particularly well in small, parallel-sided cracks where other devices may be difficult or impossible to place. But like micronuts, these nuts have less holding power than larger nuts with no moving parts because of the smaller surface area gripping the rock and because the spring may allow some movement—or "walking"—within the crack after placement.

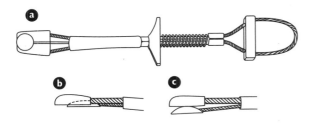

Fig. 13-16. Spring-loaded nuts: a, C.A.M.P. USA Ball Nut; b, contracted; c, expanded.

PLACING REMOVABLE PROTECTION

Placing solid protection is both art and science. Developing an eye for good placement sites and then placing the right piece into the right place securely and efficiently require practice to perfect (see the "General Considerations in Placing Removable Protection" sidebar).

Good placements start with good rock; in poor rock, even apparently good placements may not hold a fall at all. In good rock, look for constrictions in a crack, irregularities

---

GENERAL CONSIDERATIONS IN PLACING REMOVABLE PROTECTION

To climb confidently and safely, climbers must know how to place protection efficiently. Consider these guidelines when selecting where to place protection on difficult terrain.

- **Select high-quality rock** and avoid rock that crumbles or flakes.
- **Learn to estimate the right chock size and shape** for a particular placement. Use your hands to size the crack to the equipment. The better your estimate, the more efficient the placement.
- **Cams or hexes are often best in parallel cracks,** while offset cams or Tricams are best in flaring cracks. Chocks with slings or flexible stems are best in horizontal cracks.
- **Use your fingers to place the piece** just where you want it. Avoid dragging the chock blindly through a crack and hoping it catches.
- **Reinforce doubtful placements** with another chock, use a load-limiting runner to decrease forces on the piece, or find a better placement.
- **Remember the climber who will be following** behind you and removing the protection. Make your placements secure, but also try to make them reasonably easy to remove and within reach of a shorter follower if necessary.
- **Let your follower know (if possible) if an intricate series of moves was necessary** to place the piece, so your follower can reverse the moves and return your gear.
- **Avoid shallow placements** where chocks can easily pull out of the crack, but avoid very deep placements that are hard for the follower to retrieve.
- **Recheck the chock after it is placed.** Look to see that it is in good contact with the rock. Give the piece a strong tug in the direction of pull to set the piece and test the reliability of the placement.
- **Clip a runner between the chock and the rope** to minimize the effect of rope movement on the piece. An adequate length of runner not only prevents pulling on the piece but also helps prevent rope drag (see Chapter 14, Leading on Rock).
- **Use a cam or oppositional chocks as the first placement** to avoid the zipper effect caused by an outward or upward pull in a fall (see "Using Opposition Placement," later in this chapter).

13

in crack surfaces, and prominences behind a flake. A good site for protection placement has solid rock sides—free of vegetation, dirt, or deteriorating rock. Avoid crystals or irregularities that may not be bonded strongly to the surrounding rock. Check for loose blocks or flakes by shaking or hitting the rock with your fist; if the rock moves or sounds hollow, look for a better spot.

The next consideration is the type of protection to use. Wedges work best when placed behind constrictions in a vertically oriented crack. Hexes or Tricams work well in horizontal cracks and behind small irregularities in cracks or flakes where it may be difficult or impossible to position wedges. Tricams often are the only pieces that will work in shallow, flaring pockets. SLCDs are easier to place, but they are relatively heavy and expensive, and placement integrity can be more difficult to evaluate. However, SLCDs often work in parallel-sided or slightly flaring cracks where it is difficult or impossible to get anything else to hold.

More than one type of device may work in a given spot. Make a choice based on ease of placement and what may be needed later on the pitch. Ration the pieces that will be needed higher up.

Placing Nuts

The basic procedure for placing nuts (passive wedging chocks) is quite simple: find a crack with a constriction at some point, place an appropriate piece of protection above the constriction (fig. 13-17a), slide it into place (fig. 13-17b), and pull down on the sling to set the nut firmly in position (fig. 13-17c). Slot the nut completely into the crack, with as much of the metal surface as possible con-

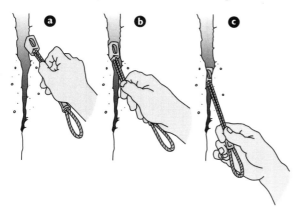

Fig. 13-17. Placing a nut: a, place nut into crack above constriction; b, slide it into place; c, tug on nut wire to set it.

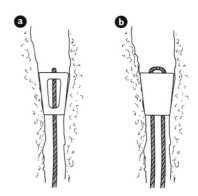

Fig. 13-18. Placement of nuts: a, stronger placement with wide sides in contact with rock; b, weaker placement with ends in contact with rock.

tacting the rock. Use your fingers to set the piece in the best spot, although sometimes threading the cable behind a protrusion is the best option.

The best choice of nut for any given placement is whichever size and shape offers the best fit. As a general rule, greater contact between nut and rock means a stronger placement. Therefore, larger nuts generally are stronger than smaller ones, and wide-side placements (fig. 13-18a; presenting more surface area) generally are stronger than end placements (13-18b); however, the fit is most important. Micronuts must be placed especially carefully and have excellent contact with the rock, given their lower strength.

Evaluate nut placements from multiple directions if possible. Even if the front looks good, the back may not be in contact with the rock. If it looks doubtful from other angles, find a better placement or piece. Carefully evaluate the potential effects of rope drag and the direction of loading in the event of a fall. In vertical cracks, setting a nut with a downward pull usually keeps the chock in place, although the rope may pull sideways or upward. In horizontal cracks, nuts will be pulled outward. Climbers can also place two nuts to equalize or oppose for greater security (techniques discussed in "Using Opposition Placement" and "Equalizing Protection" later in this chapter).

Placing Hexes and Tricams

In addition to being used as a chock in a constriction, a hex or a Tricam also is designed to cam under load. In parallel-sided cracks, this feature must be used for the placement to work. A good placement is tight enough to have good contact with the rock and to avoid being displaced by the rope, yet positioned to allow camming action under load.

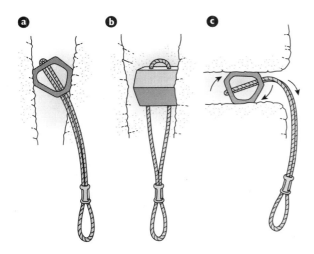

Fig. 13-19. *Placements of a hex: a, in a vertical crack as a passive cam; b, sideways in a vertical crack as a passive wedging chock; c, facing out in a horizontal crack as a passive cam.*

In vertical cracks, the piece will be more secure if it is placed just above a constriction or irregularity in the crack and if it is oriented so that the camming action pulls it more tightly against any irregularity (figs. 13-19a and 13-20a and b). Placed as a passive wedging chock, a hex's camming surfaces face out (fig. 13-19b).

In horizontal cracks, the piece should be placed so that the downward or outward pull of a fall would maximize camming action. Hexes should be positioned so that the sling exits the crack closer to the roof than to the floor (fig. 13-19c) to maximize camming action. Tricams should be

placed to optimize overall fit, and the sling and rails can be either down or up (Figure 13-20c shows rails and sling up).

Placing Spring-Loaded Camming Devices

An SLCD can be placed very quickly. It is the device of choice for parallel-sided cracks that lack the constrictions or irregularities needed for passive chocks. It also can be used in slightly flaring cracks and in cracks under roofs where other chocks may be slow or difficult to place or questionable to use.

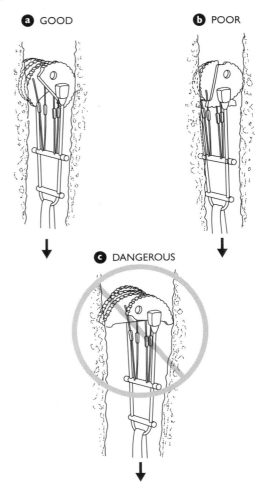

Fig. 13-21. *Placement of SLCDs: a, cams expanded to mid-point—stem in likely direction of pull (good); b, cams are over-retracted—hard to remove (poor); c, cams are overexpanded—failure likely (dangerous).*

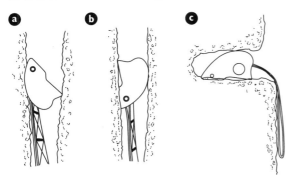

Fig. 13-20. *Placements of the Tricam: a, as a passive cam in a vertical crack; b, as a passive wedging chock in a vertical crack; c, as a passive cam in a horizontal crack.*

TIPS FOR PLACING SLCDS

- **Be certain all cams contact the rock** so the placement is stable (see Figure 13-21a).
- **Be aware that the device may become jammed** in the crack and impossible to remove if the cams are fully retracted in the placement (see Figure 13-21b).
- **Do not overexpand the cams,** since little camming action can then occur (see Figure 13-21c), making the device more likely to pull loose during a fall.
- **Remember that SLCDs placed in soft rock can be pulled out by a hard fall,** even when they are placed properly. This is true of sandstone and limestone.
- **Place SLCDs with their stems pointing in the direction of pull from a fall.**
- **Make a careful placement and use a suitable runner** to minimize "walking": rope movement can cause the entire piece to "walk," moving it either deeper into or out of the crack, jeopardizing stability of the placement.
- **In a horizontal crack,** place a three-cam unit's side with two cams on the bottom for best stability. **In vertical cracks,** place the two cams on whichever side provides the best fit in the crack.

Within their given range, the three or four individual cams in the device will adjust to the width and irregularities of the crack as the trigger is released. The stem of the device must be pointed in the likely direction of pull during a fall to provide maximum strength and to help keep it from being pulled out of position. SLCDs work best in harder rock such as granite rather than sandstone and in cracks with relatively even sides.

When placed well (see the "Tips for Placing SLCDs" sidebar and Figure 13-21), SLCDs can protect against somewhat multidirectional loads, and climbers may use these to decrease chances of the zipper effect (see Chapter 14, Leading on Rock). After clipping a runner to the SLCD and rope, wiggle the rope and make sure the SLCD does not walk back in the crack. SLCDs have a flexible stem that will hang out over the edge of the crack in horizontal or near-horizontal cracks (fig. 13-22).

Placing Spring-Loaded Nuts

Spring-loaded nuts can be used almost anywhere a passive nut would be used, but they really come into their own in thin cracks, including parallel-sided cracks (fig. 13-23). When placing spring-loaded nuts, select just the right size for the crack, because the placement size range for any one of these devices is quite narrow. They are susceptible to being pulled out of place by rope movement, so attach a

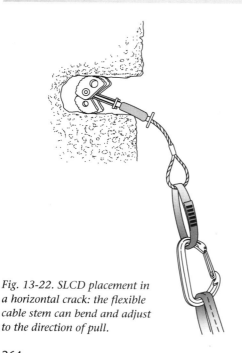

Fig. 13-22. SLCD placement in a horizontal crack: the flexible cable stem can bend and adjust to the direction of pull.

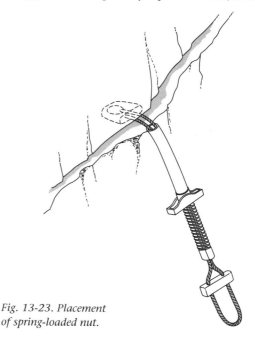

Fig. 13-23. Placement of spring-loaded nut.

runner to the piece. As with any piece of protection, place the device so it is strongest in the direction of the force of a potential fall.

USING OPPOSITION PLACEMENT

Sometimes a second chock must be placed in order to keep the initial one in position, such as the first placement on a pitch to avoid the zipper effect (see Chapter 14, Leading on Rock). Single placements can sometimes be dislodged by sideways or upward pulls on the rope as the lead climber advances, because of changes in the direction of the route (see Figure 14-10 in Chapter 14, Leading on Rock).

To form an opposition placement, place two pieces that will pull toward each other when linked. Use carabiners with slings to link the chocks. Ideally the chocks should be held together under a slight tension. Use clove hitches to tie a runner between the carabiners on the chock slings, then cinch up the runner; the climbing rope may then be clipped to the long loop of the runner (fig. 13-24a). Or just clove-hitch the runner to the upper carabiner, which tensions the lower carabiner, and clip the climbing rope to the runner (fig. 13-24b).

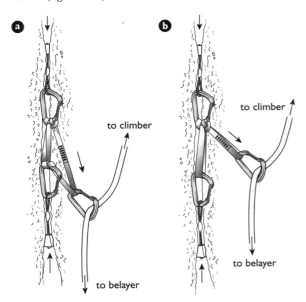

Fig. 13-24. Opposing chocks in a vertically oriented crack: a, connected by a runner secured with clove hitches to each chock's carabiner; b, connected by a runner clove-hitched to the upper chock's carabiner, which tensions the lower carabiner.

EQUALIZING PROTECTION

A leader who is faced with a hard move or questionable protection may decide to place two pieces of protection close together. If one piece fails, the other remains as a backup. Another option is to equalize the load over two protection points, subjecting each to only a portion of the total force. (For equalizing protection to establish an anchor, see "Equalizing the Anchor" in Chapter 10, Belaying.)

It is possible to equalize the forces between two points of protection with one hand and only one runner. First clip the runner in to both chocks. Next put a half twist in the middle of one length of the runner and pull the resulting loop down to meet the other side of the runner (see Figure 10-22, the sliding X, in Chapter 10, Belaying). Then simply clip an extra carabiner through both runner strands, with the rope attached to this carabiner. If one chock later pulls out, the twist in the runner will slide down and catch around the carabiner, but some extension will occur. Clipping in to the twist is essential because without it the entire setup will fail if one chock comes loose.

STACKING

If nothing on a rack will accommodate the crack in which protection must be placed, the advanced technique called stacking can sometimes help. Place two passive wedges in opposition, with the larger one on top (fig. 13-25).

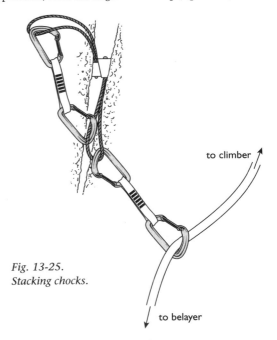

Fig. 13-25.
Stacking chocks.

13

265

A downward pull on the larger chock causes it to wedge between one side of the crack and one side of the other chock. Seat the larger chock with a firm tug before using it, and connect it to the rope in the usual way. Use a runner to clip the smaller chock in to the wire of the larger chock or another runner to keep the smaller chock from becoming a flying missile when it is removed by the follower or if it comes loose in a fall. Use only chocks that seat well against one another; otherwise, stacking is not effective.

REMOVING PROTECTION

Removable pro can be easy to place but sometimes difficult to remove, whether for the leader who wants to choose a different piece for a crack other than the one just placed or for the follower cleaning the pitch. A nut tool (also known as a *cleaning tool* or *chock pick*) is a specialized tool to assist in removing protection (see Figure 14-4 in Chapter 14, Leading on Rock). Nut tools often are racked separately on the harness, sometimes with retractable cord to avoid losing them if dropped. Nut tools can be used to apply force underneath a stubborn piece to push it up and to reverse how it was placed. In a narrow crack, the tool can be used to grab the cable at the top of a wedge and pull it out from above.

ROCK PROTECTION ETIQUETTE

Chapter 12, Alpine Rock Climbing, discusses the issue of ethics in placing protection. Specifically, many climbing areas expressly forbid placing or even replacing bolts, and it is each climber's responsibility to understand the rules before installing a bolt. Some land managers request that climbers receive permission before placing or replacing bolts. Common practice for sport-climbing routes is for the first ascensionist to place the only bolts.

Popular routes where natural features such as trees and horns are common rappel stations often collect slings from various parties over time. If climbers find damaged slings, they should cut the slings off and remove them from the route. Many climbing areas encourage the use of natural-colored bolts and slings for those that are left on routes, to address aesthetic concerns of nonclimbing visitors.

BUILDING SKILLS

The way to become proficient at placing protection is very simple: practice. First, practice by placing protection while standing on the ground. When following as a second, observe closely how the leader places protection. Practice placing pieces while climbing on a top rope. When you believe you are ready to try leading, start on an easy pitch that you have already climbed as a second or while on top-rope. Place more pieces than are needed, just for the practice. Do not be discouraged if the first time turns out to be harder than it looks. Bring along a knowledgeable, experienced climber as your second—it is a great way to get valuable feedback. Just keep at it, and soon you will be the one giving advice.

CHAPTER 14
LEADING ON ROCK

Leading on rock requires the complementary skills of both the leader and the belayer. The lead climber determines the route ahead, places protection for the pitch, and sets up the next belay station. The belayer monitors the leader, feeds out rope, anticipates the leader's need for tension or slack, and comunicates with the leader about remaining rope length, route descriptions, and more. Although the leader incurs additional risk while on the "sharp end of the rope," the belayer and leader both play a critical role in making each pitch safe and successful.

Imagine two climbers high on a rock face. One is on lead, climbing up a crack, belayed by rope through numerous points of protection by a partner anchored to a ledge below. The leader gives a sharp yank to the stopper he just placed in the crack. Grasping the rope tied to his harness, he pulls it up and clips it in to the protection. His belayer yells up to him "Halfway!" to indicate that he has reached the midpoint on the rope. He exhales deeply, switches hands in the crack, and shakes out his arm before raising his eyes to study the route ahead. He sees that the thin splitter crack continues up steeply, with a few uneven pockets where a hand jam appears solid. From his rack, he readies a cam he feels would be ideal for placement when he reaches the most promising pocket several moves up. He mentally rehearses his moves, then resumes climbing.

Leading on rock requires merging climbing skill and psychological readiness. How do climbers decide whether they are ready? Others, especially more experienced climbers, can help assess someone's skills. However, only the individual climber can assess personal mental preparation, so each must search deeply within. Prepare by practicing and gaining confidence with placing rock protection, building anchors, belaying, learning how to manage the

rope, and understanding fall forces (see Chapter 9, Basic Safety System). Work on rock technique, a methodology of gear selection and placement, and routefinding. Use every pitch you follow as an opportunity to observe and learn. Experience helps refine judgment.

LEADING ON NONTECHNICAL TERRAIN

A climbing party may travel unroped or unbelayed over second-class and third-class rock, each person climbing in balance and maintaining three points of contact with the rock. If the risks of the climb escalate beyond the party's comfort level, the leader has several options for using a rope to help minimize danger, short of full belayed climbing.

HAND LINE

A fixed hand line can be set up for members of an unroped party on less technical but exposed terrain to save the time it would take to belay multiple party members. The leader can either be belayed up or can scramble up this section, bringing along the loose end of the rope and placing

267

Fig. 14-1. A hand line offers limited protection for an unroped party.

protection along the way, if warranted. At the top, the leader anchors the rope, taking care not to place the rope under tension over sharp edges. The other climbers then move through this section, either holding on to this hand line or preparing to grab it if needed. Alternatively, if they are wearing harnesses, they can clip in to the line with a carabiner attached to a runner from their harness (fig. 14-1), or they can clip a carabiner directly from their harness in to a sling attached to the line with a prusik hitch. The rope may also be anchored at the start of this section to make it easier to prusik—that is, to move along the rope using the climbers' prusik slings tied to the rope or to safeguard a traverse. The last climber removes the protection and breaks down the hand line while ascending, possibly on belay or while prusiking up the hand line.

RUNNING BELAY

The running belay, also known as *simul-climbing*, is another useful option when a team is climbing together over relatively easy terrain but is still roped together (fig. 14-2). Roped climbing teams normally consist of only two people. To establish a running belay, the lead climber simply clips the rope in to some rock protection that she places at appropriate intervals. At least two pieces of protection should be in place, clipped in to the rope between the leader and the follower at all times. The follower climbs simultaneously with the leader (hence the term "simul-climbing"), removing any protection that he passes. If one climber takes a fall, the rope will remain linked to the protection—and the weight of the other climber will naturally arrest the fall at some point.

If a party decides to use a running belay, the climbers must decide how much rope to leave between the leader and follower. Having more rope out has the advantage of absorbing more force should a fall occur, but it also increases the potential for the rope to snag on blocky or bushy terrain, introduces rope drag, and can make communication between the leader and follower more difficult. When the situation calls for it, coils (see below) can be used to shorten the rope to the appropriate length.

The running belay is less secure than belayed climbing but considerably safer than no protection at all. Given the advantages and disadvantages of this technique, the decision to simul-climb should be made carefully, weighing the potential risks and benefits for the given party and the specific situation. Important factors to consider include both the skill and comfort level of the climbing party, the degree of time pressure experienced during the climb, the likelihood of falling, and the degree of runout and exposure or the consequences of falling in the given situation. The lead climber needs to be sensitive to the skill level of the follower and should be ready to set up an anchored belay if the follower needs that degree of security. Communication is imperative between the climbing team. An anchored belay would also need to be set up if the lead climber runs out of protection while simul-climbing, so that the follower can either transfer gear back to the leader or can switch leads and continue the running belay.

CLIMBING IN COILS

Sometimes, between sections of more technical terrain where running or fixed belays are used, climbers coil most of the rope between them, leaving themselves tied in and with about 10–16 feet (3–5 meters) of climbing rope separating them. This is called "climbing in coils." (See more about "Shortening the Rope with Coils" in Chapter 18, Glacier Travel and Crevasse Rescue.) Climbers coil the extra rope over their shoulders and tie in short to a locking carabiner attached to their harness. This method can increase efficiency, saving time because climbers can forgo untying from the rope and packing it up in between more technical pitches. Also, by climbing closely together, climbers can minimize rope-induced rockfall.

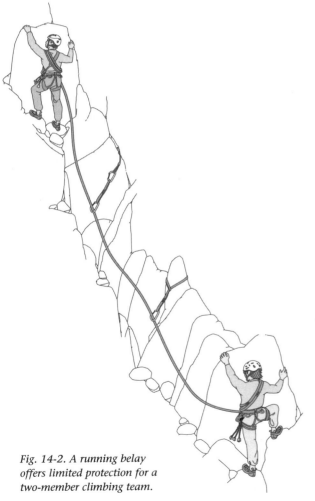

Fig. 14-2. A running belay offers limited protection for a two-member climbing team.

LEADING TECHNICAL CLIMBS

Technical rock climbing begins when anchored belays are needed for the party's safety, and deciding when to choose this option is subjective. In this scenario, each pitch is led and belayed. The leader accepts more risk than the second, who is belayed from above. An aspiring leader should learn the mechanics of leading while climbing well below his or her actual climbing ability. It may sound obvious, but always be sure your climbing ability is consistent with the route you decide to lead. For example, you may be good at face climbing but have trouble with cracks; in that case, if a route requires crack climbing, make sure that it is within your crack-climbing ability.

Steep, bolt-protected sport-climbing routes can be relatively safe places to attempt leading hard moves. An overhanging 5.11 route can be safer to lead than a 5.7 climb with ledges if the only risk in a fall off the former is hitting air. When transitioning from sport climbing to alpine rock climbing, be conservative in estimating your climbing abilities. The extra time and additional skills required for setting protection can substantially increase the difficulty of a traditional climb compared with a bolted sport climb of the same rating. In addition, trad climbing difficulty is increased by carrying a pack and wearing or carrying mountaineering boots. On a long, remote alpine climb, even if the actual rating of the climb is relatively easy, the consequences of a fall can be great. Evaluate routes in terms of potential risk and your ability to manage the consequences of a fall, and be conservative in choosing an alpine route and gear.

CHOOSING THE RACK

The collection of gear used for protection is called the *rack*. Each climbing team prepares just one rack, which is carried by the leader. While climbing each pitch, the leader places individual pieces of protection from the rack; the follower removes the equipment and carries the pieces up while climbing. At the top of the pitch, the rack is reorganized, and the leader takes the gear needed for protecting the next pitch.

The decision about what to bring is determined by the climb and each climber's comfort level. If the selected climb is in an area covered by a guidebook, check the book for general information such as the type of rock and what a "standard rack" for that area contains. The climbing route sketch map (fig. 14-3) for the selected climb, called a *topo*, may show the width of cracks, the amount of natural protection or fixed protection (labeled as "fp"), the length and direction of each pitch, the difficulty of each section and

14

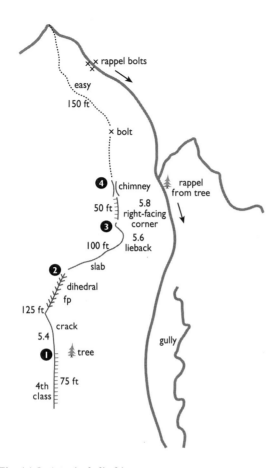

Fig. 14-3. A typical climbing route topo.

the overall climb, and perhaps even the precise sizes of the pieces of protection needed. Particularly on commonly climbed routes, more detailed information regarding the specific protection needed can sometimes be found online in climbing trip reports or climbing community blogs or websites.

If the selected climb is in a remote area, usually less information is available. Take too big a rack, and the extra weight and equipment can impede the climbing. Take too little protection or the wrong pieces, and the team may not have what it needs to safely climb the route. Research the climb by consulting several guidebooks or talking with other climbers who have done the route, as well as by checking any relevant resources on the internet.

A typical rack includes a selection of passive chocks (nuts and hexes, for example), spring-loaded camming

devices (SLCDs or cams), carabiners, and runners. The specific selection of protection varies with each route. A long, thin crack might dictate small wired nuts and some small cams. A wide crack may require the largest cams, hexes, or tube chocks. A long, parallel hand crack may require multiple 2-inch (5-centimeter) cams. Many cases are less clearcut, requiring a full range of sizes. The "standard rack" is difficult to define narrowly, since different climbs call for different types and sizes of protection; in addition, individual climbers often have their own preferences for gear that they never leave home without. However, as an example, a rack that will accommodate a large number of traditional alpine climbs in Washington State's Cascade Mountains and beyond is generally defined as one that includes gear up to 2 or 3 inches (5 to 7.6 centimeters), consisting of at least a full set of nuts, some additional chocks (such as hexes and Tricams), and a set of cams ranging from small to medium-sized.

Each piece of protection typically connects to the rope with two nonlocking carabiners and a runner or quickdraw. Locking carabiners can be used instead if the gate is in a position where it could be forced open during a fall (by striking the rock). Carry a few extra carabiners as insurance against running short of them. The ideal runner at any protection point will be just long enough to help the rope stay in as straight a line as possible. A runner that is longer than necessary lengthens a fall, and one that is shorter than necessary causes rope drag. Quickdraws may work well for a straight-up climb. A zigzag route line, roofs, or turns on the pitch require longer runners. Additional runners may be needed for belay anchors, unanticipated protection placements, and rappel slings. Especially on alpine climbs and any routes that deviate from a direct vertical line, it is recommended to bring several longer slings (multiple singles and at least a few doubles), as quickdraws will be insufficient. Slings are inexpensive and light, and they can be shortened and used as quickdraws for straight pitches (see Figure 14-7). The importance of bringing and using sufficiently long runners for reducing or preventing rope drag cannot be overemphasized (see Figure 14-10), yet failing to do so is a common mistake made by novice leaders.

The nut tool, a thin metal device designed to help extract pieces of protection (fig. 14-4), is carried by each climber to use when following a pitch; if a team is swinging leads, both climbers will take turns following. Also known as a *cleaning tool* or *chock pick*, the nut tool can help the follower retrieve pieces of protection that do not come out easily. It is also recommended that climbers carry this device when leading, since occasionally the leader may need it to reset

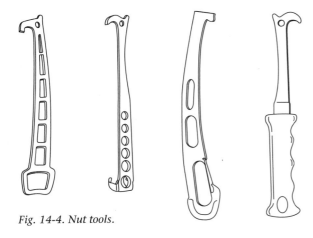

Fig. 14-4. Nut tools.

or replace a piece of protection in order to take advantage of a more secure placement.

In addition to carrying gear for protection, carabiners, runners, and a nut tool, a rock climber also carries a few other important pieces of equipment. These include a belay device, material for building belay anchors (in other words, a cordelette, equalette, and/or webbing for equalizing anchor points—see Chapter 10, Belaying), a tie-off loop (a short loop of accessory cord for emergency techniques, tying off a climber after a fall, or backing up a rappel—see Chapters 9, Basic Safety System; 10, Belaying; and 11, Rappelling), at least one rappel ring, a knife for removing old slings (or for emergencies), and perhaps chalk for keeping hands dry. Overall equipment choices, which are influenced by the setting and the type and length of the rock climb, warrant careful consideration and planning.

OTHER IMPORTANT ITEMS

Particularly for multipitch routes that the climbing party is not intimately familiar with, it is also a good idea for the party to bring along a route description, route topo, and/or notes to help with routefinding. Packs (of varying sizes, depending on the route and the speed of the climbing party) are often carried by at least one member of the climbing team for many alpine climbs or for traditional crag climbs in which the party does not plan to return to the base of the climb. Depending on conditions and the comfort level and skill of the individual climbers, various types of footwear may be chosen for the approach and the climb itself. Mountaineering boots (from very lightweight to heavyweight) or lightweight approach shoes are typically used for the approach (and sometimes on the climb itself as well). Rock shoes (see Figure 12-1 in Chapter 12,

Alpine Rock Climbing) are generally the preferred choice for climbers leading technical routes, especially on climbs of higher relative difficulty and on virtually all cragging and sport climbs.

HOW TO RACK

The ideal racking method permits the leader to place protection efficiently and to climb smoothly despite carrying the gear; it also allows easy transfers between climbers for swinging leads. Keeping the hardware away from the rock makes the gear more readily available. For instance, when you are climbing an inside corner with your left side in, it is easier to have the rack hang from your left shoulder and under your right arm, using a sling to carry the equipment (see "Where to Rack Gear," below). No racking method is perfect, but several are commonly used, alone or in combination.

Group passive pieces or small cams together on a single carabiner. When you are organizing gear for the rack, it generally works best to group several pieces of passive protection (nuts, hexes, or Tricams) on a single carabiner (see Figure 14-6a). For example, most climbers group a partial or full set of nuts together on a single carabiner. If a large number of nuts are included on the rack, or if there are doubles in certain sizes, sometimes climbers will divide the set of nuts into smaller and larger sizes, and use a couple of carabiners. Climbers often use the same method for small cams as well.

This strategy reduces the number of carabiners needed for carrying these pieces, and this method can make climbing easier because it results in a less bulky rack with better weight distribution. This technique also facilitates more efficient gear placement for these types of pieces. To choose the best piece for a placement, unclip the carabiner of gear for that size range and hold the whole batch of pieces up to the placement, eyeing each piece for fit. Then unclip the carabiner from the chosen piece, place the chock or cam, and return the carabiner and unused pieces to the gear sling.

With this method, climbers usually have two carabiners pre-attached to several runners or quickdraws because the placed protection lacks a carabiner (remember that one carabiner attaches to the protection and the other carabiner attaches to the rope; see Figure 13-2 in Chapter 13, Rock Protection). Although this method of racking may somewhat increase the risk of dropping gear, since more gear is handled every time a piece is placed, many climbers feel that the increased ease of climbing this method offers far outweighs this disadvantage.

14

Place other pieces of protection on separate carabiners. In contrast to passive pieces and small cams, most climbers prefer racking medium-sized to large cams and other active pieces such as tube chocks on separate carabiners (see Figure 14-6). By design, active pieces of protection like cams (at least medium-sized to large units) cover a wider range of sizes than passive pieces such as nuts or hexes. With experience, it is easier to select the single right cam for a given placement than it is to identify a single nut that is the right size in a given situation. Arranging medium-sized to large cams on separate carabiners results in faster placement and less awkward juggling of multiple large pieces of protection on the same carabiner. After placing the appropriate cam in the rock, the leader can simply clip the cam's pre-attached carabiner to a runner, then the runner's carabiner to the rope.

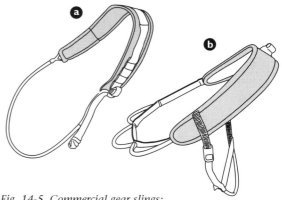

Fig. 14-5. Commercial gear slings: a, basic padded gear sling; b, partitioned gear sling.

WHERE TO RACK GEAR

After deciding how many pieces to place on the carabiners on the rack, the next question to answer is where a climber will rack the gear. The three most common options are on a gear sling, on the climbing harness, or on a combination of the two. A padded gear sling from a climbing shop may be the most comfortable choice, but a single-length runner can also be used. Commercial gear slings (fig. 14-5a) are also available with partitions (fig. 14-5b).

Rack gear on a sling. Climbers racking protection on a gear sling (fig. 14-6a) place the sling over one shoulder and under the opposite arm (see Figure 14-6c). This method of

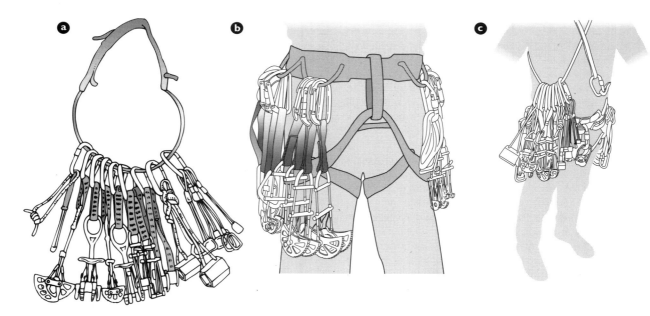

Fig. 14-6. Examples of racking methods: a, pieces of protection racked on a gear sling; b, pieces of protection attached to gear loops on the seat harness; c, hybrid method in which gear is racked on both a gear sling and the harness, and one or more double-length runners are also looped over one shoulder.

racking has the advantage of smooth gear transfers when switching leads, since the entire rack can be passed from the belayer to the leader at once. The primary disadvantage of this method is that having the entire rack over the shoulder can make the climber feel a bit top-heavy, and, at least with nonpartitioned slings, the weight of the rack can shift quite a bit when the leader is climbing.

Rack gear on the climbing harness gear loops. Using the gear loops on the climbing harness to rack gear (fig. 14-6b) evenly distributes the weight of the rack on the climber's waist, and the different types of protection can be separated (although the latter can also be done with a partitioned gear sling; see Figure 14-5b).

Transfer of gear at belays can take longer with this method of racking, since gear must be transferred from multiple gear loops rather than a single gear sling. However, for experienced climbers, this time difference is likely to be nominal. Besides the time needed for reracking, the primary disadvantage of this system is that some equipment will be inaccessible when you wedge your body into larger cracks. When using this racking method, be sure the gear does not hang down so far that it interferes with climbing footwork. Also, on many climbs, it is a good idea to rack runners and/or quickdraws and carabiners on both sides of the harness for easy access when clipping the rope in to protection.

Rack gear on both the harness and a gear sling. Perhaps the most common method of racking is a hybrid of these two systems (fig. 14-6c). For example, a climber could place all the pieces of protection on a sling over the shoulder but place runners and carabiners on the harness. Conversely, a climber could place the protection on the harness, with runners and carabiners on a sling. Or a climber could place some gear on a sling and some on the harness.

Whatever method is used, rack the protection in a systematic order so that a particular piece can be found in a hurry. The usual order is to start at the front with the smallest wired chocks and work back with larger pieces. For each carabiner clipped to the rack, use the same orientation so that each one unclips in exactly the same way. For example, all the gates of the carabiners should be facing the same way—either in or out, but not both. This allows you to unclip by feel rather than having to look at the gear.

Particularly for climbers who are relatively inexperienced at swinging leads or transferring gear at belays, it is recommended that climbing partners agree beforehand on using one racking technique; otherwise, much precious time may be lost in reracking at each belay when climbers are swinging leads.

OTHER RACKING CONSIDERATIONS

Runners need to be racked as well. Quickdraws can be racked on the harness or on a sling. Climbers can carry single-length runners over one shoulder, but if a number of them are carried, it can be difficult to retrieve just one

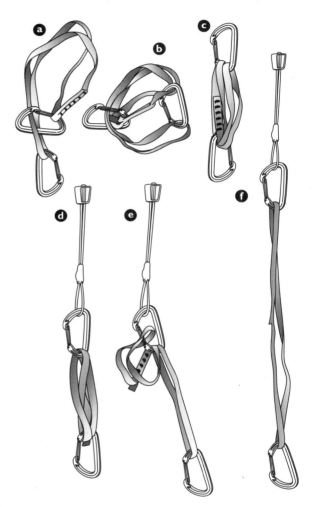

Fig. 14-7. Racking and extending a single-length runner quickdraw-style (also known as an alpine draw): a, clip two carabiners to a single-length runner and pass one carabiner through the other; b, clip the first carabiner back in to the newly formed loop; c, straighten the loops; d, clip the protection to one carabiner; e, unclip the other carabiner from all but one loop of the runner; f, straighten and extend the runner.

273

from the tangle. Climbers can carry a single-length runner quickdraw-style by attaching two carabiners to it and threading one carabiner through the other (fig. 14-7a), then clipping the resulting loop (fig. 14-7b) and straightening it (fig. 14-7c). This style is also called an *alpine draw*; clip one carabiner to protection (fig. 14-7d). Such runners can be quickly extended by unclipping all but a single strand from one carabiner (fig. 14-7e) and then pulling this carabiner until the runner is fully extended (fig. 14-7f). Climbers can carry double-length runners looped over a shoulder and connected with a carabiner (see Figure 14-6c). Alternatively, climbers can chain the runner (fig. 14-8) before attaching it to the harness; when it is needed, pull or shake it out to remove the loops. Climbers can also fold a double- or triple-length runner several times and tie it in an overhand or figure-eight knot, then clip it to the harness.

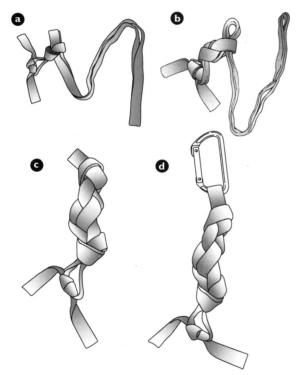

Fig. 14-8. Chaining a long runner: a, form a slipknot; b, pull runner through the loop formed by the slipknot; c, repeat this process until the runner is chained; d, attach the final loop to a carabiner to carry it and to ensure that it does not unravel.

When climbing with a pack, put it on first, then the rack. When carrying double-length and single-length runners over one shoulder (or both shoulders), put the single-length runners on top so that the singles come off without tangles and the doubles can be removed without displacing the singles.

Carry cordelette (or other anchor-equalizing cord or webbing), nut tool, and belay device on the harness gear loops so that they are easily accessible. Other gear such as a knife and tie-off loop can be clipped to the harness or carried around the neck so they are out of the way but accessible.

LEADING ON ROCK, STEP BY STEP

Whether you are leading the next pitch or the next climb, it is imperative to plan the route, evaluate rope and rack requirements, and know the descent. Leading is a complex business. Beginners usually need an apprenticeship, moving behind seasoned climbers before they can safely "take the sharp end of the rope" (lead). Never take the lead if you do not feel ready, and do not pressure others into leading. Keep the art of leading exciting, challenging, satisfying, and safe—as it ought to be.

PLANNING THE ROUTE

Planning a route begins with background research at home. Look for climb descriptions in printed guidebooks and online climbers' blogs. Talk to others who have climbed the route before. For alpine climbs, obtain needed maps for the approach, and check weather and avalanche conditions for the dates being considered (see Chapters 5, Navigation, and 28, Mountain Weather). The skill required depends on the location and nature of the climb as well as potential difficulties that might be encountered on the approach and descent.

Routefinding can be as easy as following a guidebook picture with a climbing route topo or simply following a line of bolts on a crag, but it can also be as difficult as an off-trail multiday approach and ambiguous technical climb with a vague route description. Routefinding on alpine climbs or some long crag routes can be complex. Longer routes often are less clearly defined. The guidebook description may be sketchy: "Ascend northeast buttress for several hundred feet of moderate climbing." The descent may be complicated and vaguely described.

For any climb, confirm the descent and—if it is not obvious—perhaps check with others who have done the route. Decide whether boots are needed for the descent in addition to rock shoes for the climb. Make sure the rope is long enough for rappels.

ON THE WAY IN

Once the climbing party is on the way, study the route on the approach if possible; often the best view of a climbing route is at a distance from the start of the climb. Look for major features that the line of ascent might follow, such as crack systems, dihedrals, chimneys, or areas of broken rock. Note areas of small trees or bushes that could indicate belay ledges or rappel anchors. Identify landmarks that, when reached, will help determine the party's position on the route. For this kind of planning, the climbers' eyes will tell them what the topographical map cannot.

Watch out for deceptively tempting lines leading to poor-quality rock, broad roofs, blank walls, or false summits. These may not be visible once the party is on the climb, and if they climb these features in error, they may dead-end after several pitches.

Develop a plan for the line of ascent, but keep likely alternatives in mind. Continue planning the routefinding as the actual climb begins, looking for more local features and landmarks. Seek out natural lines to follow when leading the route. Form a tentative plan for each pitch, perhaps including a place for the first piece of protection and a spot for the next belay station. Do not hesitate to look around the corner for easier route alternatives that may not be visible from below.

When faced with a choice between pitches of varying difficulty, consider the rest of the climb. Two moderate pitches are better than an easy pitch followed by one beyond the party's ability (see the "Questions to Ask Before Leading a Pitch" sidebar).

On the way up, keep track of retreat possibilities in case the climb is aborted, and study—to the extent possible—the party's planned descent route. Rain, lightning, unexpected wind or cold, injury, or illness may make it prudent to retreat from the route. As the climb progresses, evaluate changing route conditions, the weather, and the climbing party. Know the party's alternative responses to any changes, weighing all resources. Consider whether the party is equipped to deal with an unplanned bivy while on the climb. Know descent or escape routes in case they are needed. See Part V, Emergency Prevention and Response, for more about dealing with uexpected or emergency situations.

QUESTIONS TO ASK BEFORE LEADING A PITCH

- **How long and hard is the pitch?**
- **Can the leader see the general path of the pitch** and where the next anchor will be?
- **What is the nature and location of the crux** (most difficult move of the pitch)?
- **What sizes, types, and amount of protection** will be needed?
- **How much other gear,** including carabiners and runners, will be needed to protect the lead?
- **What gear will be needed to build the anchor at the end of the pitch?**
- **What climbing techniques will be used?** Liebacking? Chimneying? Jamming? As a result, on what side should the climber rack?
- **Does the leader want the belayer to shout out how much rope is left while climbing,** calling out "halfway," "20 feet," or "3 feet . . . 2 feet . . . 0"?
- **Will the belayer and leader be able to hear each other throughout the climb?** If not, do they have rope signals? Radios?
- **How will a fall affect the belay?** Could the leader drop past the belayer in a fall? Is the belayer well secured for any pull from a potential leader fall?
- **Where and how will the first piece of protection be placed?** Will it minimize the fall factor and the chance of setting off the zipper effect? (See "The Zipper Effect" later in this chapter.)

PROTECTING THE LEAD

Placing protection every few feet requires a big rack and eats up time. Placing very little protection at all greatly increases the risk of a long leader fall and potential injury. Learning the appropriate balance requires practice and sound judgment. Climbers certainly should protect moves they expect to be hard. Always space the protection to avoid potential falls that are excessively long or dangerous. Protection above a move provides the safety of a top rope. In deciding when to place another piece of protection, keep in mind the quality of the placements already made. Consider how to minimize dangerous rope drag—which is exacerbated by changing rope angles through protection and around rock corners, and which is eased by keeping the rope running straight on route—and how to take the fall factor into account (see Chapter 10, Belaying).

14

SELECTING AND MAKING A PLACEMENT

The perfect placement is a combination of a crack sized and shaped ideally for placing protection with a comfortable stance from which to place it, located right at the next hard move—but two out of three is not bad either. When on the sharp end of the rope, avoid making difficult moves far away from the last protection. Place protection right before and after a hard move.

Chapter 13, Rock Protection, details types of protection and good placements. Consider the stability of the rock

when placing protection. Look, listen, and feel for the soundness of the rock by hitting suspect rock with the heel of a hand. Beware of expanding flakes and hollow-sounding or crumbling rock. Remember that a protection placement is only as solid as the rock into which it is placed.

To place protection, find a stance that is secure enough that you can release one hand, because you must be able to make the placement and then clip in to it without falling or seriously tiring. When possible, take advantage of natural protection—a tree, bush, rock tunnel, or horn—

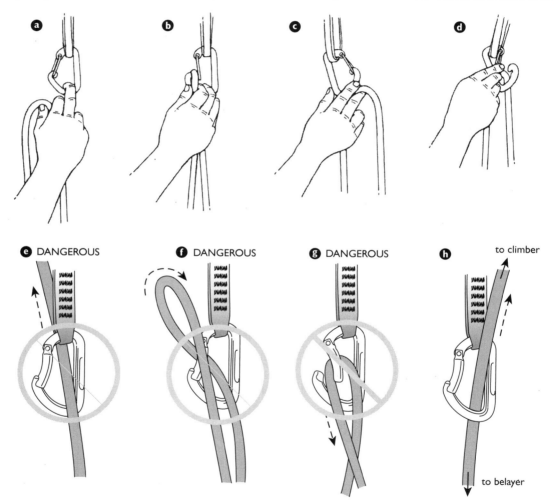

Fig. 14-9. Clipping technique: a and b, gate facing left, right hand; c and d, gate facing right, right hand; e, rope is back-clipped (dangerous); f and g, back-clipped rope causes carabiner gate to open in a fall; h, correctly clipped carabiner.

because it can be easy to use and is often multidirectional, and doing so can save on gear. The leader must be able to quickly place and clip sound protection (see "Connecting the Rope to Protection" in Chapter 13, Rock Protection) with either hand, whether the carabiner gate faces left (fig. 14-9a and b) or right (fig. 14-9c and d), to make the lead safer. Reverse these techniques when using your left hand.

Clipping inefficiently and incorrectly is a common and potentially dangerous mistake made by new leaders. An especially common mistake among novice leaders is *back-clipping*: that is, the leader's end of the rope is clipped so that it travels *behind*—rather than in front of—the carabiner to which it is clipped (fig. 14-9e) as the leader ascends above this piece of protection. A consequence of back-clipping is the rope accidentally opening the carabiner gate (fig. 14-9f and g) during a leader fall. In a correct clip the leader's end of the rope travels out the front of the carabiner to which it is clipped and up to the lead climber (fig. 14-9h). (See "Clipping Bolts and Other Protection," later in this chapter.) Study diagrams on correct clipping technique, and then practice clipping with either hand until the process is fluid and fast.

Suppose that as a leader you are faced with a choice between two or more possible placements. Ask these questions:

- Which placement combines the best fit with stability in the direction(s) of pull?
- Which placement will be stronger?
- What size chocks or cams should be conserved for use higher on the pitch or at the anchor?
- Which placement will be easier for the second to remove?
- Will one placement interfere with a needed foothold or handhold?
- Which placement will minimize rope drag?

If the unfortunate choice is between questionable protection and none at all, by all means place something, but also plan to place additional protection as soon as possible. Placing and equalizing two pieces can also help (see Chapter 13, Rock Protection). Do not let such placement give a sense of false security, however. Do not trust obviously bad protection.

Suppose the leader faces a hard move without any apparent protection. Restudy the rock for some less obvious way of protecting the move. Evaluate whether there is a movement sequence or rock feature not seen at the outset. The options are these:

- Protect the move after all, and then resume climbing.
- Go ahead and attempt the move without good protection.
- Down-climb and see if the belayer will lead the pitch.
- Find an easier line to climb.
- Consider retreating from the climb.

After studying the situation and evaluating the consequences of a fall, carefully and calmly weigh the options, and then decide on the course of action that seems best.

DETERMINING THE LENGTH OF THE PITCH

The length of a given pitch is dictated by several factors. On most sport climbs and many single-pitch traditional crag climbs, the end of a pitch is clearly indicated by the presence of bolt anchors and/or chains, and the pitch is often short enough that the leader can be lowered back to the ground by the belayer. On other traditional crag climbs and most alpine rock climbs, the pitches are more variable in length and may be considerably more ambiguous, since they are often not marked with bolted belay anchors but instead utilize natural anchors or require the leader to construct gear anchors. This latter type of route requires more routefinding and discretion by the leader.

The maximum length of a pitch can never exceed the length of the rope, which typically ranges from 50 to 70 meters (164 to 230 feet), with 60 meters (197 feet) being the most commonly used rope length for most rock climbs. However, in many cases, the ideal pitch length will be less than the full length of the rope, often considerably less. The key point is that the leader should be prepared to do pitches of varying lengths, depending on the circumstances. Avoid the temptation to make every pitch a full rope length, which can result in slower, rather than faster, climbing, especially when it causes rope drag or the need to down-climb to a more secure belay location that a leader passed up.

When determining pitch length, use any available information from route descriptions and topos. Beyond this, seek out and use good belay spots (when in doubt about the best pitch length, do not pass up a great location to set up a belay anchor), try to maintain communication (particularly in windy conditions, long pitches can significantly compromise communication with a climbing partner), and work to prevent or minimize rope drag. If rope drag becomes a problem, seek out a good belay spot sooner rather than later.

14

JUDGING THE DIRECTION OF FALL FORCES

The leader must anticipate the direction of forces on the protection in order to make placements, but this judgment must take into account the entire climbing system. A protection point may seem solid for a fall when it is placed, but later it could pop out when the system causes pulls in directions not initially anticipated.

A zigzagging climbing rope causes severe directional forces as well as rope drag that, at its worst, can immobilize the leader (fig. 14-10a). Pieces of protection that may have been placed to hold only a downward pull may now be in danger of taking sharp pulls from quite different directions in case of a fall. In catching a fall, the rope loads and straightens from the belayer up to the highest protection

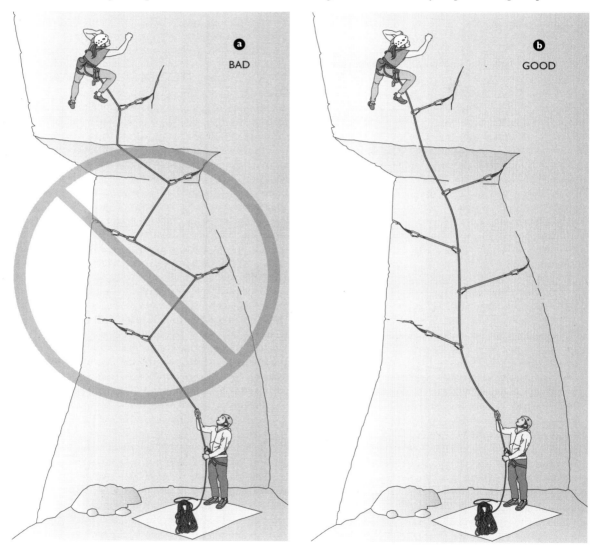

Fig. 14-10. Avoid rope drag: a, zigzagging rope can result in severe rope drag, which can impede the leader's ability to move upward; b, use runners to extend the connection to the pieces of protection and keep the line of the rope more vertical, reducing drag and keeping the pieces from being loaded from the side.

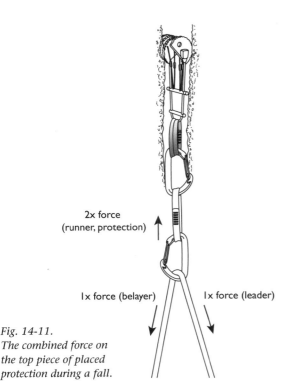

2x force
(runner, protection)

1x force (belayer)   1x force (leader)

Fig. 14-11.
The combined force on
the top piece of placed
protection during a fall.

point and then back down to the falling climber. When the protection has been placed in a zigzag, pieces can be pulled sideways or upward by the tightening rope. If protection is placed for only a downward pull, it can be pulled out by falls higher up the pitch. Instead, extend the runner from protection to the rope, so the line of the rope from belayer to leader is more vertical than zigzagging (fig. 14-10b).

During a fall, the top piece of protection is loaded with high forces: the force of the falling climber, plus the force of the belayer holding the fallen climber, potentially increased by other factors such as distance of fall, amount of rope out, diameter of rope, and how the belayer is anchored, minus friction forces in the system between the fallen climber and belayer. Typically a piece of protection would see at least two times the forces exerted below it when arresting a fall (fig. 14-11). All protection placements should be solid, but consider backing up protection before hard moves if the placements afforded are less than ideal. Protection that allows the rope to follow in a straight line helps preserve the integrity of the system and minimizes rope drag; extend protection by using longer runners to connect it to the rope where needed (see Figure 14-10b). Rope drag not only makes climbing harder for the leader,

but it also decreases the rope's ability to absorb forces in case of a fall by effectively increasing the fall factor (see Chapter 10, Belaying). Make placements multidirectional when a bend in the climbing line must be made—use natural protection, opposing chocks, or cams that can safely rotate with minimal walking (see "Using Opposition Placement" in Chapter 13, Rock Protection). Or consider placing the belay on the other side of the bend.

The Zipper Effect

The full-scale zipper effect is a dramatic demonstration of the importance of anticipating force directions. The zipper effect occurs most readily where the belay is established away from the base of the pitch (fig. 14-12a) or where the rope zigzags up the route (see Figure 14-10a). Again, as the rope loads during a leader fall, the bottom chock can have a tremendous outward pull placed on it. If it pulls out, the next piece becomes subject to the outward pull. Each in turn could fail, causing the line of chocks to be yanked out one by one as the "zipper" opens from the bottom up (as in Figure 14-12a). Overhangs and sharp traverses also have the potential to zipper.

Prevent the zipper effect by making the suspect placements multidirectional through the use of multidirectional cams (fig. 14-12b) and by eliminating the potential for outward pull by extending pieces with runners. The belayer could also reduce outward pull by belaying closer to the base of the route (see Figure 14-12b).

14

PROTECTING SPECIAL SITUATIONS

Leading on overhangs or traverses requires special considerations to keep climbers safe.

Overhangs

Keep the rope running as free of an overhang as possible. Extend the rope with runners in order to reduce rope drag (fig. 14-13a), prevent dangerous fall forces such as the zipper effect, and keep the rope from being cut by the edge of the overhang (fig. 14-13b). On small overhangs, leaning out and placing protection above it may be the most effective strategy.

Traverses

When leading a traverse, be sure to place protection both before and after a hard move (fig. 14-14a). This guards not only the leader but also the follower from the possibility of a long pendulum fall (fig. 14-14b). In addition to the danger of injury, that kind of fall could leave the second in a tough spot, off route and with no easy way back.

Fig. 14-12. The zipper effect: a, the zipper effect in action; b, a well-placed cam (or opposing chocks) placed at the bottom of a pitch provides multidirectional protection against the zipper effect.

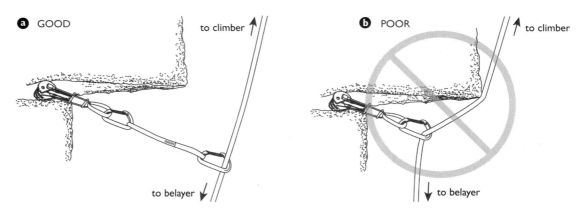

Fig. 14-13. Placements under overhangs: a, rope running free of the overhang (good); b, bends cause rope drag, and rope could be cut by rock edge during a fall (poor).

When leading a diagonal or traversing section, keep in mind the effect each placement could have on the second climber. Put yourself in the second's shoes and ask, "Would I like some protection here?" If so, place it. Asking this question will help climbers avoid a common and potentially dangerous mistake made by beginning leaders: neglecting to adequately protect the follower on a traverse.

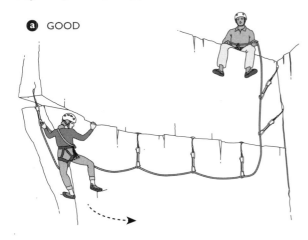

Fig. 14-14. Protecting a traverse: a, placing a piece of protection both before and after a hard move on a traverse reduces potential for a long pendulum fall (good); b, the second climber faces a long pendulum in case of a fall because of inadequate protection (poor).

If the party has the necessary equipment and it seems prudent, consider belaying the second with an extra rope, which may help protect against a long pendulum fall and provide better protection than using the leader's rope. If the party is using the double-rope technique (see "Double- and Twin-Rope Techniques" later in this chapter), do not clip in both ropes during the traverse, so that the follower can receive a belay from above on the free rope.

CLIPPING BOLTS AND OTHER PROTECTION

A carabiner clipped to a bolt hanger should normally have its gate facing away from the leader's subsequent direction of travel (fig. 14-15a and b). Otherwise, the carabiner may rotate or slide in such a way that the gate makes direct contact with the bolt hanger (fig. 14-15c). In the case of a sudden fall, the gate can then open and potentially unclip by striking the bolt hanger. However, not all carabiners and bolt hangers are alike, so the leader should evaluate each circumstance with that in mind, with the goal of trying to safeguard against situations in which the gate of a carabiner could unclip when sudden force is applied.

The same basic principle applies when clipping in to pieces of protection other than bolts. Avoid placing a carabiner in a position wherein the gate could open if it strikes the rock or any other contact point.

14

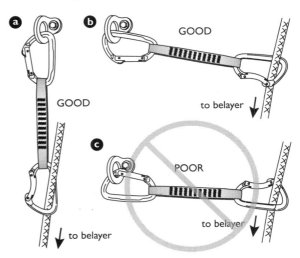

Fig. 14-15. Clipping a carabiner in to a bolt hanger: a and b, gates face opposite direction of climb that goes up and right and are not in danger of unclipping (good); c, gates face wrong direction and are in danger of unclipping (poor).

Similarly, the gate of the carabiner clipped in to the rope should always face the opposite direction that the rope is traveling. If the climb proceeds to the right after a protection point, the gate of the lower carabiner clipped to the rope should face left (as in Figure 14-15a). If the climb proceeds to the left, the gate should face right. If this principle is not followed, there is an increased risk that the rope could travel over the gate if a fall occurs and open up the carabiner, causing the rope to become unclipped. When the climb travels straight up from the last protection point, the gate can be facing either left or right.

ARRIVING AT THE NEXT BELAY

At the top of the pitch, clip in to a solid anchor before signaling "Off belay!" Add additional pieces as needed to form a multidirectional belay anchor (see Chapter 10, Belaying). Make sure the anchor secures the leader against being pulled from the stance by the second.

Think through the belay sequence before settling in so that it is clear which hand to use for the braking hand and where to flake the rope while belaying up the second. Keep the belay system simple. Strive for straight, easily traceable lines from the anchor points to you. Effective rope management techniques are critical to a safe belay, especially when at a hanging or sloping belay stance (fig. 14-16). The most common method is for the belayer to flake or stack the rope neatly on the rope or runner that connects him or her to the belay anchor; alternatively, devices such as rope hooks or rope buckets specifically made for this purpose can be used.

Never lay belay devices, gloves, carabiners, or other items on the ground. If an item is not in use, keep it attached to your harness or a sling or to an anchor. Have only one item, such as the rope, a chock, or a carabiner, in hand at a time. The moment an item is no longer needed for whatever you are doing, reattach it to your harness or a sling or the anchor. Unattached objects are easily knocked or blown off the belay ledge. Take off your pack and rack and attach them to the anchor, but keep them within easy reach. That way, you will be more comfortable while belaying the second.

When the belayer is settled in, haul up the slack rope until it is taut. The second should yell, "That's me." After placing the second on belay, yell, "On belay." See Chapter 10, Belaying, for a full set of climbing commands.

CLEANING A PITCH

The climber who follows the leader should climb as quickly and efficiently as possible after being put on belay

Fig. 14-16. Multidirectional belay anchor at top of a pitch: careful and clean rope management, shown here at a sloping belay stance, is a critical skill for leaders.

(see the "Tips to Save Time and Energy as the Second" sidebar). While ascending, the second climber cleans the pitch: removes the protection from the rock in an orderly way, organizes it, and efficiently transfers it to the belayer at the end of the pitch.

The second can minimize the risk of dropping gear by using a careful cleaning procedure, which may depend on the method used to rack the hardware. Consider a typical placement consisting of chock-carabiner-runner-carabiner-rope. The following procedure is an efficient way to clean gear that minimizes the risk of dropping gear:

1. First remove the chock from the rock.
2. Holding the carabiner that is clipped to the chock, clip the carabiner-chock combination directly to the gear sling or harness gear loop.
3. Then unclip the carabiner-chock combination from the runner.

4. Next, loop the runner over your head, unclip the runner-carabiner combination from the rope, and rotate the runner-carabiner combination so that it is under one arm.

5. Continue climbing to the next piece of protection, then repeat.

If the placement uses a quickdraw instead of a runner, follow this procedure:

1. First remove the chock from the rock.

2. Next, clip the carabiner that connects the chock and quickdraw in to the racking sling.

3. Last, unclip the quickdraw's other carabiner from the rope.

In general, cleaning from rock to the rope is best. This keeps the pieces clipped to something at all times, and there is little possibility of dropping any gear. In any racking procedure, minimize the handling of unattached gear to also lessen the risk of dropping it.

TRANSFERRING EQUIPMENT AT THE TOP OF A PITCH

The first thing the second climber needs to do when arriving at a belay station—before being taken off belay—is to clip in to the belay anchor. If the climbers are swinging leads, then the belayer need not remove the rope from the belay device but can back it up with an overhand or figure eight on a bight. If they are not swinging leads, the climbers have to trade places, with the follower taking over the belay to free up the leader to lead the next pitch. In either case, if the second is neat, organized, and efficient in cleaning the pitch, the transfer of gear at the belay station should go quickly, whether the original leader transfers the rest of the rack to the second, who will now lead, or the second transfers the cleaned pieces back to the leader's rack. Follow this sequence, remembering that both climbers always stay anchored to the rock:

1. First, reconstruct the rack. Clip the cleaned pieces to the rack, whether the original leader or the new leader has it. Be careful not to drop any gear.

2. Then hand the removed runners and/or quickdraws over to whoever will lead.

3. If either climber is wearing a pack, it can be removed and clipped in to the anchor.

4. If the original leader plans to lead the next pitch, reflake the rope so that the second's end of the rope is on the bottom and the leader's end is on top; the second should then settle into the belay position.

Swinging leads is more efficient but requires both climbers to be competent at leading. The new leader shoulders

TIPS TO SAVE TIME AND ENERGY AS THE SECOND

- **Start preparing to climb as soon as the leader is off belay.** When it is safe to do so, begin breaking down the belay station (but always stay clipped in to at least one anchor until the leader has you on belay).

- **Put the pack on before anything else.** If you are already carrying climbing hardware on a gear sling, put it on next. Plan where to put the gear that you clean, whether on the gear sling, the harness, or another sling.

- **Give the area a last look to make sure nothing is left behind.** Then, once you are on belay, yell, "Climbing!" and start out.

- **Remove each chock by reversing the way it was placed.** A stopper slotted down and behind a constriction should be removed by pushing it back away from the constriction and up.

- **Be persistent but careful.** Use the nut tool to tap on a stubborn wedge or hex-shaped chock to loosen it, taking care to avoid hitting the piece's wires; then lift the chock out gently. Prying and tugging often only tightens or wedges the chock more and can damage its wires. Use a loose rock or other object, if available, to tap on the end of the nut tool.

- **Sometimes nut tools can retract the triggers of cams** that have "walked" back into a crack; if their trigger cannot be retracted with your fingers, try the nut tool. Or use the wires of two stoppers to snare the trigger device so you can retract the cams.

- **Consider asking your belayer for tension** and put your weight on the rope, freeing your hands to work on removing a chock that refuses to budge.

- **As a final option, simply abandon protection if necessary.** Too much time and effort can be wasted on a piece of protection that is not going to come out.

the reconstructed rack and then racks the runners according to the climbers' chosen system. The new leader rechecks and adjusts the rack to ensure that everything is ready for the next pitch. A look at the route description may be in order. At the very least, the leader should examine the next pitch and have a sense for the general line to be traveled. The leader is placed on belay and then unclips from the anchor, and the climbing resumes.

14

CLIMBING WITH A PARTY OF THREE

Most rock climbing is done in pairs, but occasionally a party has three climbers. A three-person team generally is more awkward and less efficient than a two-person team. However, it has an advantage of an extra person available for hauling, rescue, et cetera, and a team of three is faster than two teams of two. Two ropes are required unless the pitches are extremely short. Each of the three climbers must remain securely anchored when not climbing.

Using two ropes sequentially, also known as *caterpillar technique:* In a team of three, the leader climbs with one rope while the second belays and the third remains anchored at the belay station. At the top of the pitch, the leader sets up a belay and brings up the second, who is belayed on the first rope and has the second rope either clipped with a locking carabiner to the harness's back haul loop or tied in at the front of the harness; the second rope will be used by the third climber.

If the pitch follows a straight line up, the second can clean the pitch; remember, a top belay is very safe, and if a fall occurs, the climber falls only a very short distance. If the pitch includes some traversing, some or all of the protection should stay in place for the third climber to help prevent a pendulum fall. In this situation, the second climber unclips each piece of protection from the first rope and clips the protection to the second rope. Once the second climber is at the top of the pitch, the first rope is now completely at the top belay, and the second rope is put on belay to bring up the third climber. When the third climber reaches the top of the pitch, the climbers then may decide to swing leads, with the third climber leading the next pitch using the second rope. For the second to lead, the ropes may need to be retied and perhaps restacked.

Using two ropes simultaneously, also known as *parallel technique:* Another way to climb with three is for the leader to tie in to both ropes while the second and third climbers each tie in to one of the ropes. Double ropes can be used for this method instead of two larger-diameter single ropes (see the next section), if desired. The leader then climbs the pitch, belayed on both ropes. The belay can be provided by one belayer with two ropes in one device (preferable) or by two belayers with one rope per belayer. At the top of the pitch, the leader sets up a belay station. Then the leader can either belay one follower at a time or bring both up together, one slightly ahead of the other, making sure to leave sufficient space between the climbers so that they will not collide if the higher climber falls.

Several belay devices available on the market work well for belaying two climbers at a time (see "Auto-locking belay devices" in Chapter 10, Belaying). This technique takes more rope management, but this way three climbers can ascend nearly as fast as two. When using this strategy, it is simplest for the original leader to remain on lead throughout the climb, because with the additional rope and climber involved in a three-person team, belay stations can be more confusing and messy.

DOUBLE- AND TWIN-ROPE TECHNIQUES

Most of this book describes climbing situations in which a single rope is usually used. However, climbers can opt for one of the methods that use two smaller-diameter ropes: double-rope technique or twin-rope technique. For both techniques, an advantage is that two ropes are available for rappels.

Double-Rope Technique

The double-rope technique uses two ropes that serve as independent belay lines. Each rope is referred to as a "half rope," is approved by the UIAA and/or CEN for such use, and is marked by a "½" on the end of the rope. Half ropes are usually 8 to 9 millimeters in diameter. The leader clips each rope in to its own protection on the way up, and the belayer manages the ropes separately. Most belay devices with two slots can be used, but some are specially designed for use with double ropes. See the manufacturer's guidelines for more details on the approved use of different devices.

Although the double-rope technique is more complicated than using a single rope, it does offer some advantages. Rope friction can be greatly reduced, falls can be shorter, two ropes are less likely than one to be severed by rockfall or sharp edges, and two ropes are available for rappel. The technique is widely used by European climbers, by ice climbers, and by an increasing number of climbers everywhere to increase protection on highly technical routes. The ropes should be different colors to allow for clear communication about which rope needs slack or tension.

The double-rope technique offers great advantages when the route meanders. With a series of zigzag placements, one rope can be clipped in to the pieces on the left and one rope in to those on the right, allowing the ropes to remain relatively straight, in roughly parallel lines that do not cross (fig. 14-17a). Be careful to keep each rope on the same side so that rope drag does not become a serious

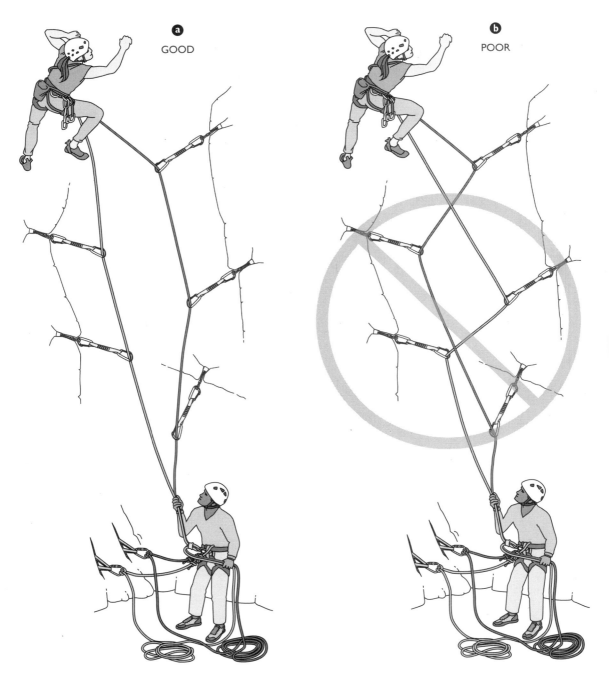

14

Fig. 14-17. Double-rope technique: a, two ropes do not cross but run reasonably straight to reduce rope drag (good); b, two ropes cross and run in a zigzag, increasing rope drag and sideways stress on the protection (poor).

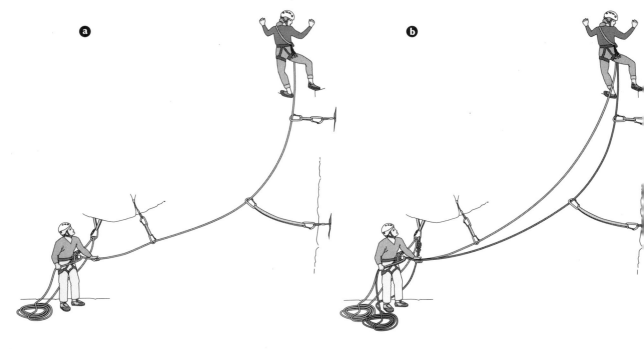

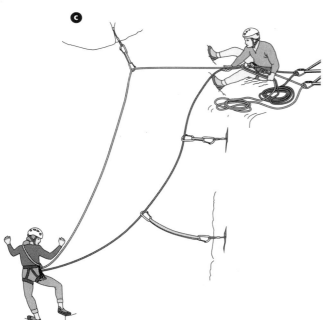

Fig. 14-18. Advantages of double-rope technique: a, using a single rope, the second climber will be exposed to a longer pendulum fall after traversing beyond the first piece of protection; b, one rope through the first piece of protection can safeguard the second climber on the traverse, while the second rope protects the leader on the direct ascent; c, off-line protection (placed off the route line) can be used to minimize or eliminate the pendulum risk.

problem (fig. 14-17b). When both ropes are clipped to the same protection placement, each rope is attached using a separate carabiner.

Traverses can be better protected with the double-rope technique, especially when the route traverses at the start of a pitch and then heads straight up. The leader can use one rope for protection on the traverse and leave the other free to belay the second climber from above. If the climbers are using only a single rope, the second climber could risk a long pendulum fall (fig. 14-18a). But with double ropes, the belay on the free rope can minimize or prevent a long pendulum (fig. 14-18b and c).

Another major advantage of the double-rope technique is that it reduces the worries of the leader who is straining to clip in to the next piece of protection. In single-rope

One disadvantage is that the belayer's job is more complex, handling the movements of two ropes at the same time—often letting out slack on one rope while taking it in on the other. Also, the two ropes weigh and cost more than a single rope or twin ropes. Another drawback is that the technique requires more practice for both leader and belayer than does single-rope technique. However, many climbers find that on long, challenging, and complex rock pitches, the advantages of double ropes greatly outweigh the disadvantages.

Twin-Rope Technique

UIAA- and/or CEN-approved twin ropes are generally 7.5 to 8.5 millimeters in diameter, **and they are not rated for use as single ropes.** The ends of the rope are marked with a symbol of two overlapping circles.

The twin-rope technique shares some characteristics with the single-rope technique and some with the double-rope technique. Two ropes are used, but they are each clipped in to the same pieces of protection, as a single larger-diameter rope would be (fig. 14-19). Twin ropes are commonly used when climbing a route that requires a double-rope rappel. This allows a team of two to climb the route without having to carry an extra rope to rappel at the end.

The twin ropes together absorb more energy and can withstand more falls than a single rope. Though twin ropes are smaller-diameter, the likelihood of severing both at one time is less likely than that of severing one larger-diameter rope.

A disadvantage is that the thinner the rope, the more likely it is to tangle. Also, together, twin ropes weigh and cost more than a single rope. Another disadvantage is that the technique lacks the specific advantages of the double-rope system on meandering routes, traverses, and shorter falls. As with double-rope technique, the belayer has to deal with two ropes, but separate management of each rope is greatly lessened.

Fig. 14-19. Twin-rope technique: two small-diameter ropes are used as one, with both attached to each piece of protection.

climbing, the rope is slack as the leader pulls up a big length to clip in to the next placement, but with a double rope, the slack for clipping is provided on one rope, and the other rope is held snug by the belayer. Thus, when the leader is clipping in to a newly placed piece of protection, a potential fall is shorter.

PERSONAL RESPONSIBILITY

Leading on rock is a serious commitment. Climbers face decisions in which a poor choice may be fatal. It is impossible to have a rule for every possible situation. Memorized dogma will not ensure safety. Accurately evaluating the risks of climbing requires instead a fundamental understanding of the risks of the environment and the consequences of each climber's own actions. Base your decisions and actions not on superficial rules but, rather, on the knowledge gained through study and experience.

CHAPTER 15
AID AND BIG WALL CLIMBING

Aid climbing is the technique of using gear to support your weight as you climb. It can be as simple as pulling on a quickdraw or as complex as climbing an entire multiday route on big walls with your weight suspended from gear you have placed. Aid climbing is an intricate and personal art, and each climber approaches it somewhat differently.

Historically, nearly all rock climbs included piton placements and aid climbing, and many classic free climbs enjoyed today were first established as aid climbs. Pioneers such as Fred Beckey, Royal Robbins, Allen Steck, and Layton Kor relied heavily on aid climbing to achieve historic first ascents.

As free-climbing skills continue to rise, climbers are freeing many routes originally climbed with aid. But despite the rise in free-climbing standards, there will always be tempting routes that are more difficult still—and so devoid of natural features—that a climber will need some of the aid-climbing skills described in this chapter. And whereas today's elite climbers may be able to free an aid route at a high standard of free climbing, the average climber will likely still perform aid climbing to complete these routes in the historical style.

Skills in aid climbing can also help overcome unexpected difficulties during normal free climbing. Aid techniques can provide a way to move safely up or down when bad weather or an accident jeopardizes a climbing party. Many routes have short sections of very difficult climbing or poor rock that may be negotiated by aid climbing to reach excellent free climbing or a summit. Finally, aid-climbing techniques give climbers access to the vertical world of the big walls, such as El Capitan in Yosemite

National Park, California, that inspire the dreams of so many climbers around the world.

Aid climbing requires skill, judgment, and a lot of practice. To learn both the basics and the many tricks of aid climbing, work with an experienced partner, and climb often.

CLEAN AID CLIMBING

Aid climbing takes a lot of gear, but it does not need to damage the rock. Traditionally, aid climbing involved hammering in pitons of various sizes, and in the early development of climbing, the entire rack for a climb consisted exclusively of pitons. Both placing and removing pitons permanently damages the rock and over time creates scars and ever-widening placements. On popular routes, tiny cracks sometimes evolve into finger or hand cracks after generations of climbers force them to accept pitons. Today, with chocks, spring-loaded camming devices, hooks, and other gear available, climbers have a better chance of climbing aid routes "clean."

A clean placement is one made without using a hammer. Gear placed cleanly can almost always be removed without defacing the rock, leaving no trace of the party's ascent. Nailing in gear with a hammer is more time-consuming for both leader and follower than making clean placements, so climbing clean not only benefits the rock and the state of the route for future parties, but can also speed the ascent.

Because the first-ascent party may have left fixed protection (see "Fixed Protection," in Chapter 13, Rock Protection) such as bolts, pitons, or copperheads, a clean ascent of an aid route often entails using fixed gear while also carrying some pitons, copperheads, and other nailing hardware in case fixed gear has been removed or is no longer usable. Thus, most clean ascents rely on some protection that earlier parties placed with a hammer and left in place.

Aid and big wall climbers almost always bring a hammer, even if they intend to make only clean placements, as it is a critical tool used for a wide range of functions in aid climbing. Route conditions may require unexpected hammered placements, the hammer may be needed to extend the climber's reach, or it can be essential in removing gear needed to continue the route. Some experienced aid climbers enjoy the added challenge of "hammerless" climbing—climbing with no hammer available on the route—on established aid routes with known fixed gear or even on new routes. Both the clean and hammerless styles of climbing present increasing levels of commitment; climbers choosing these styles should accept the possibility of retreat.

USES OF AID CLIMBING

Aid climbing can be roughly categorized based on the extent of its use on a particular climb. See Appendix: Rating Systems, for information on the various grades of difficulty in aid climbing.

Alpine climbing. When ascending a route in the alpine environment, climbing without weighting any gear is usually the climber's goal. However, climbers may use aid techniques and equipment to overcome short, blank, or extremely difficult sections of a route that otherwise can be free-climbed. This type of climbing often requires little or no specialized aid equipment; usually climbers just use the free-climbing gear they have along. Techniques could include pulling on gear, stepping in a sling, or even creating a makeshift aider or two from slings to get through a section. Sometimes climbers pull on gear to speed progress and minimize exposure to objective hazards or other risks in the mountains. Some routes have one pitch of aid climbing (or a relatively small number of aid pitches on the overall route), allowing an otherwise free line to be ascended. Packs may be hauled on a difficult pitch, or climbers may perform a pendulum swing to reach the next section of free climbing.

Aid may also be used on alpine climbs for extended distances and with aid-specific equipment, although aid- and free-climbing techniques may be interspersed. Long one-day climbs may involve fixing the initial pitches on a preceding day—putting up ropes and leaving them in place so they can be climbed with mechanical ascenders (a technique called *jugging*) to reach the previous day's high point—and completing the route on a second day.

Big wall aid climbing. Ascents of big walls typically take longer than one day to complete, even if the initial pitches are fixed. These climbs usually involve a bivouac and require hauling techniques. With the proliferation of speed-climbing techniques, some big walls that originally took many days to ascend can now be climbed in a day by expert climbers. Many big wall climbs require aid on every pitch, and wall climbers typically have many items of aid-specific equipment.

AID-CLIMBING EQUIPMENT

The range of equipment used in aid climbing builds on all the gear and techniques described in Chapters 13, Rock Protection, and 14, Leading on Rock. Unique to aid climbing is the use of gear that is designed only for the body weight of the climber. All technical equipment for free climbing is designed to protect climbers in the event of a fall and to withstand the high fall forces generated. In aid climbing, certain equipment is used that is designed only for upward progress on the climb, and this equipment is not expected or rated to catch a fall.

BASIC EQUIPMENT FOR AID CLIMBING

Aid climbing relies heavily on standard free-climbing equipment—aid climbers may simply need more of it. The following gear used in free climbing is also used in aid climbing, with some differences in how it is used at times discussed below.

Chocks and Camming Devices

The same chocks and spring-loaded camming devices (SLCDs, or cams) used in free climbing are used on aid climbs. Units that feature shorter clip-in points are preferred to help gain the maximum elevation out of each placement. Some SLCDs, such as the Camalot and the Alien, feature a large clip-in point on the unit itself in addition to the sling sewn onto the SLCD (see Figure 13-15a and c in Chapter 13, Rock Protection). This feature makes it possible to clip an *aider* (a webbing ladder used in aid climbing, also called an *etrier*) directly to the piece of

15

protection, which is a higher and more convenient clip-in point than the SLCD's sewn sling (see also "Racking" under "Basic Aid Techniques" later in this chapter). This technique allows the climber to make fewer placements overall by getting as high as possible in aiders on each SLCD placement.

SLCDs specifically designed for tricky placements, such as Totem Cams (see Figure 13-15g in Chapter 13, Rock Protection), feature clip-in points that weight only some of the SLCD lobes, instead of all lobes, to use when it is not possible to place the SLCD with all lobes contacting the rock. Extremely small SLCDs with a traditional design but a small size and low load rating are also helpful on aid climbs to make upward progress. These various specialty cams can be useful in passing difficult moves or sections, but due to their narrow application of use, they usually do not make up the bulk of the gear selected for the climb.

Some SLCDs fit better than others into flaring *pin scars* (rock that has been damaged by placement and removal of pitons). Many aid climbers prefer Aliens for pin scar placements. Alien Hybrids, also called offset Aliens, with cams of different sizes on each side of the unit, eliminate the need to hammer piton placements on many pitches. Similarly, some chocks fit better into pin scars, such as offset nuts (discussed below).

It is often helpful to mix many brands and styles of chocks and SLCDs on the rack when aid climbing, because sometimes the perfect piece for a particular crack will be in between the sizes made by one manufacturer. In that case, a different brand of chock or SLCD that is slightly different in size may fit the crack better.

Small and Offset Nuts

Aid racks include small micronuts that are even more specialized than those for typical free-climbing racks. These very small nuts are often used instead of thin pitons or in pin scars, but they may not be as strong. The smallest sizes are not rated to catch a fall and serve only for upward progress.

Two general styles of micronuts are available. The first is a smaller version of the classic tapered Stopper. The other style, which has both horizontal and vertical tapers, is referred to as an *offset nut*. More secure in flaring cracks and pin scars, offset nuts come in larger sizes than micronuts, usually aluminum in the larger sizes, and are very useful, possibly indispensable, for climbing walls with pin scars. (See Figure 13-10d in Chapter 13, Rock Protection.)

The heads of small nuts are usually made from softer metals, such as brass or copper/iron mixtures. The rock bites into these softer materials, and so these nuts tend to hold better in marginal placements. The very smallest of micronuts by most manufacturers are not rated to take falls; they are used just for upward progress in direct aid. Small and offset nuts can be difficult or impossible to remove after they have been weighted by the aid climber. The heads of the smallest nuts are very small, and the nut's cable blocks the area that a climber would normally hit with a nut tool (see Chapter 14, Leading on Rock). Using a hammer and funkness device (see "Universal Aid-Specific Equipment" below) is often the only way to remove micronuts once they have been weighted.

Carabiners

Aid climbing employs many carabiners. Carabiners are used to rack protection, to sling protection (see "Slings" below), to build anchors, to clip the haul bag to the haul line, to clip critical gear to gear loops inside the haul bag, to attach aiders, daisy chains, and ascenders—and for many other purposes. The more organized and efficient the climbers are, especially at building anchors and packing gear inside the haul bag, the fewer carabiners they will need.

Traditionally, aid climbers preferred oval carabiners for the entire rack because of the *carabiner shift* phenomenon. Carabiner shift occurs after a climber clips one carabiner to another so that a piece of protection can be weighted while the climber stands in aiders, and then a carabiner shifts, making a sound like gear popping. In the context of aid climbing, this can be a terrifying false alarm of an imminent fall. However, the modern techniques of clipping directly in to the aid protection with the aider and using oval keylock carabiners on both aiders eliminate carabiner shift most of the time. As there is no longer a special emphasis on oval carabiners, most aid climbers now carry lighter wire-gate carabiners as much as possible to reduce the overall weight of the aid rack. One common method is to use wire-gate carabiners for protection and slings and to carry conventional-gate carabiners, including many locking carabiners, for anchors. Aid racks are especially heavy on the climb's descent, so saving weight using modern lightweight and wire-gate carabiners pays off.

Ropes

The tough duty of aid climbing usually requires a 10- to 11-millimeter kernmantle lead rope, 60 meters (approximately 200 feet) long. The haul line is typically a second lead rope or a 10-millimeter static line. If the route entails long pendulum swings or other unusual problems, a third rope may be needed—either another kernmantle rope or another static line. When selecting a rope, keep in mind its resistance to abrasion and edge cutting, because of the typically rough terrain and demands associated with aid climbing. See "Ropes" in Chapter 9, Basic Safety System.

Examine ropes often, and consider retiring aid ropes earlier than a free-climbing rope might be retired. Jugging, rappelling, and hauling put extreme wear on ropes. Climbers trust their life to the rope when using ascenders to jug a fixed line, so they do not want to worry about whether they waited too long before retiring it.

Slings

Carry single-length slings for establishing anchors, extending placements to reduce rope drag, and other normal rock climbing uses. Single-length slings are the most useful because they can easily be carried over the shoulder; they can also be carried like quickdraws and easily extended to full length after the first half is clipped to the placement (referred to as "alpine draws"; see Figure 14-7 in Chapter 14, Leading on Rock).

Load-limiting runners, such as the Yates Screamer, are sometimes used to climb above placements of questionable strength. In a fall, the slings limit the shock delivered to the protection (see Figure 9-35 in Chapter 9, Basic Safety System).

Cordelettes and other sling materials used to create anchors for free climbing are equally useful for aid climbing. Cordelettes are popular for anchors on big walls, because multiple anchor points are usually employed. See Chapters 9, Basic Safety System, and 10, Belaying, for more information on slings and cordelettes.

Assisted-Braking Belay Device

Certain assisted-braking belay devices, such as the Petzl Grigri, have special uses in aid climbing. While aid routes can be climbed without these devices, these multipurpose tools (see Figure 10-9 in Chapter 10, Belaying) are helpful in many tricky situations encountered in aid climbing. During long belays, for example, a Grigri can help climbers manage the rope while accomplishing other tasks such as managing the haul line, eating, drinking, and even relieving themselves. The Grigri is also helpful as a backup when a climber is following; it can be used during hauling; it can substitute as a mechanical ascender if one is dropped; it allows superior control during rappels on a single line—and it serves many other helpful purposes on an aid climb. Be sure to select a Grigri that functions properly on the 10- to 11-millimeter ropes used in aid climbing, as some units are designed for smaller-diameter free-climbing ropes.

Helmet

A helmet is absolutely essential for aid climbing (see Chapter 9, Basic Safety System). Steep terrain, large racks (which make the climber top-heavy), and the dynamics of a popped placement tend to send aid climbers into headfirst falls. Other hazards include rockfall, dropped gear, roofs, and other climbers. If used properly, a chest harness may keep the climber upright if the rope draws taut prior to the climber contacting the rock, but this in no way replaces the need for head protection. Within the range of weight and materials that modern helmets offer, all-purpose hardshell helmets better withstand the rigors and length of aid and big wall climbs.

Gloves

Over and above their value for belaying and rappelling, leather gloves are critical for hauling. Gloves protect the climber's hands during jugging and removing protection. Aid climbing is very hard on gloves, and they need to be replaced often. Leather gardening gloves can be used, with the fingertips just slightly cut off. Tape makes a great reinforcement on the cut edge to keep cut fingertips from unraveling (fig. 15-1).

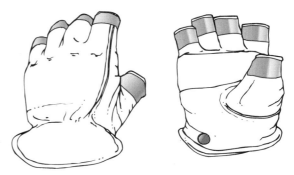

Fig. 15-1. Leather gloves with cutoff fingers, reinforced with tape, and with holes cut as a clip-in point.

Shoes

If the route involves only a small amount of aid, normal rock shoes perform best. If sustained aid climbing is anticipated, shoes or boots with greater sole rigidity provide a better working platform and more comfort. Sticky rubber approach shoes are very popular for aid climbing, including on big walls. They provide arch support and good torsional rigidity for aid climbing yet have a flexible toe and a soft friction-rubber sole for good free-climbing capabilities.

15

Eye Protection

It is important both for leaders and followers to protect their eyes from debris when cleaning out cracks, from equipment, especially the hammer, and other hazards that could contact the face. Sunglasses typically provide adequate protection; however, leaders may not able to remove sunglasses midlead, and lead times can be many hours. Therefore, consider photochromic or changeable lenses so that eye protection can still be worn comfortably when the weather is not sunny or when the climbing route is in the shade.

Knife

Just as in free climbing, a sharp knife is required equipment on the harness. Climbers often must remove webbing or cord in order to be able to clip a carabiner to a piece of fixed protection, to replace the worn webbing with new webbing, or simply to remove unnecessary old fixed slings from the rock to help keep the climb pristine for other climbers. Given the heavy loads involved in aid climbing, unexpected situations can occur wherein a sling or cord has to be cut in order to free a load or fix an error. For example, if a climber accidentally ties in a haul bag on a docking cord with a non-releasable knot, the only way to free the bag might be to cut that docking cord (see "Big Wall Multiday Techniques" later in this chapter). A knife comes in handy for repairing or making homemade gear during a multiday climb and for many other purposes.

UNIVERSAL AID-SPECIFIC EQUIPMENT

In addition to equipment normally used in free climbing, aid climbers need a selection of gear that is used both for clean aid climbing and for aid that may involve placing pitons.

Aiders (*Etriers*)

Webbing ladders, called *aiders* or *etriers*, allow the climber to step up from one placement to the next when the aiders are clipped to a piece of protection. When making or buying aiders, consider their intended use. For alpine climbs, minimize weight by using a single lightweight pair of aiders. For most aid climbing, offset-step or ladder-style five- or six-step aiders sewn from 1-inch (2.5-centimeter) webbing are standard (fig. 15-2a and b). They are used, usually in pairs, in leapfrog fashion as the climber ascends. Aiders should be long enough to allow the climber to reach the bottom step of the higher ladder when testing aid placements from a comfortable stance on the lower ladder. More difficult aid routes usually require six-step ladders,

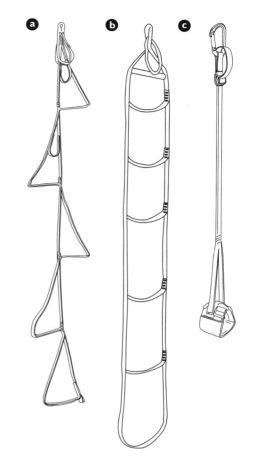

Fig. 15-2. Types of aiders: a, offset-step style; b, ladder style; c, adjustable.

because there may be longer distances between placement options and because down-climbing to the lower piece is more common.

The basic aid sequence (see "The Basic Aid Sequence" later in this chapter) uses two aiders. However, some aid climbers use four aiders, permanently set up in pairs. A third method is to use two aiders but to have a spare third aider available, possibly loose on the harness, for occasional tricky sequences. The use of more than two aiders is popular on more difficult aid routes, but ultimately, the number of aiders used depends on personal preference.

An adjustable type of aider (fig. 15-2c) tends to be lighter and is especially well suited for quick adjustment for optimal jugging. Most climbers use adjustable aiders as follower gear only. Other different aider systems include the

"Russian aider" system, which completely diverges from the ladder design: it instead uses a system of slings with small metal rings and a knee strap, which is equipped with hooks that allow the climber to "hook" the aider and stand suspended in the rings. However, the ladder-type system remains the most commonly used and most commercially available.

Daisy Chains

Traditional daisy chains are sewn slings with multiple loops (fig. 15-3a)—formed by stitching—every 3 to 6 inches (8 to 15 centimeters). Daisy chains are used as tethers to keep new placements and aiders attached to the lead climber; they are an integral part of the jugging setup. A daisy chain should, when attached to the harness, reach at least as far as the climber's raised hand. Typical daisy chains are 45 to 55 inches (115 to 140 centimeters) long. Longer daisy chains are helpful for difficult aid routes, because they permit the climber to down-climb longer distances below a piece of protection, which allows for adequate testing

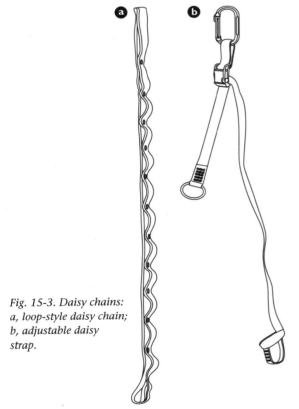

Fig. 15-3. Daisy chains: a, loop-style daisy chain; b, adjustable daisy strap.

(see the "The Basic Aid Sequence" later in this chapter). The sewn loops are used to shorten the daisy chain when it is used in the jugging mode. This shortening must be done in accordance with the manufacturer's guidelines.

Usually two daisy chains are carried, one for the left-side aider and one for the right-side aider. One end of each daisy chain is girth-hitched to the climbing harness through the tie-in points. The other end is attached to the appropriate aider with a carabiner, preferably a dedicated oval keylock carabiner. Connecting the aider to the daisy chain prevents the loss of an aider if it is dropped or if a placement fails, and the daisy chain also provides a convenient method for resting on a placement by using a fifi hook (see below). Adjustable daisy straps (fig. 15-3b) are an alternative to the classic daisy chain, and they have special features outside of their use as a tether (see below). Adjustable daisy straps must also be used in accordance with the manufacturer's guidelines. Some designs are sturdier and more reliable than others.

Fifi Hooks

The classic fifi hook (fig. 15-4a) is girth-hitched to the harness with a sling that reaches 2 to 4 inches (5 to 10 centimeters) away from the harness after the girth hitch is tied. An adjustable fifi hook (fig. 15-4b) is rigged with slippery 6-millimeter accessory cord and is tied in to the harness with one end of this cord, typically with a rewoven figure-eight knot. The adjustable fifi hook can be placed higher away from the harness initially than the classic fifi hook, and then the distance can be shortened as needed by pulling on the cord.

A fifi hook can be a critical part of the basic aid sequence, especially on steep terrain. It is used to hook in to a placement and to hold the climber's body weight. Using a fifi hook or an adjustable daisy strap helps conserve energy when aid climbing steep routes, including roofs. A fifi hook allows climbers to rest on placements, which is more efficient than holding their weight with body tension or with their arms and legs. The fifi hook also provides helpful countertension when used to hook a piece at waist level, after which the climber stands up above it to top-step (see Figure 15-21) or to make difficult reaches above protection, such as on overhangs.

An adjustable daisy strap (see "Daisy Chains" above) can be used in place of an adjustable fifi hook. Some climbers use two traditional daisy chains as tethers to attach their aiders to their harness and one adjustable daisy strap to rest on pieces.

15

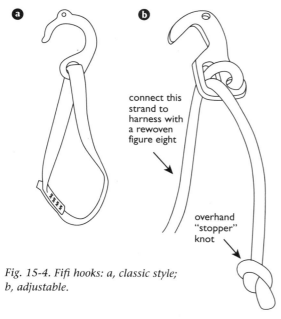

connect this strand to harness with a rewoven figure eight

overhand "stopper" knot

Fig. 15-4. Fifi hooks: a, classic style; b, adjustable.

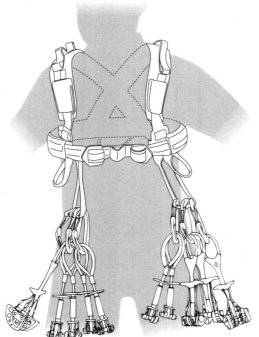

Fig. 15-5. Double gear sling with racked SLCDs (SLCD slings omitted for clarity).

Double Gear Sling

A double gear sling distributes the weight of the hardware, utilizing equipment slings on both sides of the climber's body (fig. 15-5). It improves balance and comfort, and it reduces neck strain caused by the single bearing point of a traditional free-climbing gear sling. A double gear sling can also serve as a chest harness, if it is designed for this use, assisting the climber when jugging up a rope through a steep section, or helping to keep the climber upright during a fall. Racking methods vary widely, but given the weight and volume of gear carried on aid climbs, double gear slings are standard equipment.

Aid-Specific Seat Harness

Harnesses made specifically for aid climbing are not required, but they typically feature an extra-wide belt and larger leg loops, and on some harnesses, both belt and leg loops have padding. Most such harnesses also feature a hammer holster. Some have other special features, including wider, extra-strong belay loops. All these features help ease the pain of continuous days in the harness during big wall climbs.

Knee Pads

A climber's knees are regularly in contact with the rock during low-angle aid climbing and during hauling, so wearing knee pads protects them. Knee pads should be comfortable. To avoid hot and sweaty knees, choose knee pads with good ventilation.

Belay Seat

A belay seat is a great creature comfort during hanging belays. *Warning:* Never let the belay seat be the sole means of attaching to an anchor. Clip in from the harness to the anchor with the climbing rope as usual, and attach the belay seat to any secure point with its own carabiner. Belay seats can be purchased, or climbers can make their own out of wood, a little padding, and some slings.

Mechanical Ascenders

When aid climbing was pioneered, ascending fixed ropes was always done with prusik hitches. Mechanical ascenders—often referred to as *jugs* or *jumars* (fig. 15-6)—are stronger, safer, faster, and less tiring; they have generally replaced the prusik hitch for ascending a fixed line. The devices are also very helpful for hauling bags up big walls.

All ascenders employ a cam, allowing them to slide freely in one direction on a rope but to grip tightly when pulled in the opposite direction. Ascenders also have

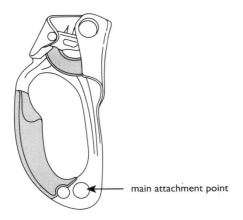

main attachment point

Fig. 15-6. Handled mechanical ascender for left hand (right-hand ascender is a mirror image): the rope passes through the vertical passage near the top; carabiner holes at top and bottom are used for a number of purposes.

a trigger or locking mechanism to keep them from accidentally coming off the rope. Some triggers are difficult to release, decreasing the chance of accidental removal but making it harder to get them off the rope when the climber wants to remove them. They are designed for use by a specific hand, either left or right, and when using two, climbers carry one for each hand. (See "Using Ascenders" later in this chapter.)

In addition to the main opening at the bottom of the ascender, which is used as the primary attachment point, additional carabiner holes at the top and the bottom of the ascender come in handy for a number of purposes.

Big Wall Hammers

The big wall hammer (see Figure 15-7) is a basic aid tool that has a flat striking surface for cleaning and driving pitons and a blunt pick for prying out protection, cleaning dirty cracks, and placing malleable pieces. A carabiner hole in the head is useful for cleaning pieces (see "Cleaning" later in this chapter).

A sling attached to the hammer handle helps prevent the hammer from being lost if dropped. Hammer slings can be clipped to the harness, worn across the body, or even clipped to an aider or piece of gear when the hammer is in use. The sling length should allow a climber to have full arm extension when using the hammer. Be sure to check the sling regularly for wear. It is a good idea to holster the hammer whenever it is not in use, to keep it secure and to allow quick access; a commercial holster can be added to the harness.

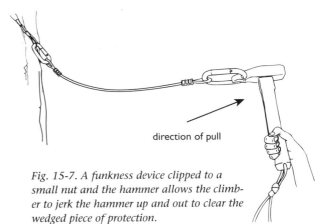

direction of pull

Fig. 15-7. A funkness device clipped to a small nut and the hammer allows the climber to jerk the hammer up and out to clear the wedged piece of protection.

Funkness Device

A funkness device (fig. 15-7), also called simply a *funkness*, is a metal sling made from cable, with loops on each end for clipping carabiners. The device is used as a static sling to assist in cleaning pieces; it is helpful for removing pins as well as nuts that have been weighted by the leader. A climber clips one of the funkness's carabiners to the piece that needs to be removed and connects the other carabiner to the hammer; then the climber jerks upward and outward with the hammer to remove the wedged piece. To remove pins, multiple directions of pull may be needed. A climbing team shares one funkness, which is passed between climbers as they change leads, so the device must work with all the climbers' hammers. In order to withstand the inevitable beating they take, carabiners used with a funkness should be conventional (not wire-gate) and should fit comfortably in the holes of all hammers used on the climb so that the funkness can be easily clipped in and also have adequate range of movement while in use.

Tie-Off Loops

Tie-off loops are carried in a variety of sizes and strengths. Sizes range from 4 to 8 inches (10 to 20 centimeters) long when tied. The loops are made either of full-strength webbing—meaning the webbing has a strength rating expected to arrest a fall—or of thinner ½-inch webbing that is meant for body weight only. Climbers often purchase sewn full-strength tie-off loops to avoid having a knot on these small slings, but they typically tie their own body-weight tie-off loops (see Figure 9-34b).

Body-weight tie-off loops are very inexpensive to create, which makes them attractive for leaving behind on a route—for example, girth-hitched to fixed gear, often for

15

the purpose of lowering off of a fixed piece when following a pitch. Body-weight tie-off loops are also used to prevent the loss of stacked pieces (see "Piton Placement" later in this chapter).

Full-strength tie-off loops are used on a placement expected to hold a fall. These loops might be used for threading through the head of a fixed piton if the eye would not accommodate a carabiner, for tying off partially driven pins (see Figure 13-9 in Chapter 13, Rock Protection), or for improvising a quickdraw if the leader runs out of gear.

Hooks

Hooks (sometimes called *standard hooks,* with the advent of camming hooks—see below) come in many shapes; they are commonly used to grip ledges or small holes. Hooks are typically made of chromium molybdenum steel for strength and curved for stability. Hooks are used for body weight only and, by their nature, are almost never left behind as protection (see "Hook Placement and Use" later in this chapter).

Attach a sling, usually ½-inch tie-off webbing, to a hook by feeding a tie-off loop through from the front until the knot jams (see Figure 15-8b). The sling should hang from the rock side of the hook, with the knot on the other side. This puts the line of force next to the rock, eliminates rotation of the tip of the hook off the rock feature, and keeps the knot out of the way, allowing the hook to rest against the wall.

Many different sizes and types of hooks can be useful on a big wall. Some popular models no longer commercially available are still considered critical gear for certain types of ascents and popular routes. (This creates a sourcing challenge for aspiring aid climbers.) In general, for most routes consider carrying at least one basic hook (fig. 15-8a), one bat hook (fig. 15-8b), and one large hook (fig. 15-8c). One

model, the Talon, features three differently shaped hooks (fig. 15-8d). Because the Talon's two extra hooks can serve as "legs," this hook can be the best fit for some features. It is a good idea to carry two of each type of hook on longer aid routes, in case the same type of hook is needed two times in a row or in case a hook is dropped.

Greater stability can be achieved on some placements if the tip of the hook is filed to a point that can be set into small holes drilled at the back of tiny ledges. Bat hooks are used almost exclusively in shallow, ¼-inch-diameter (6-millimeter-diameter) holes that have been drilled for their use.

There are additional variations on the hooks shown here, as well as many more shapes and sizes not shown.

Camming Hooks

Camming hooks (also called *cam hooks*) are simple, hard-steel levers that can be used in any crack that is at least as wide as the thickness of the metal and no wider than the width across the hook's tip. Often, a cam hook can be used to avoid placing a pin, especially in scars made by wedge pitons (Lost Arrows, for instance). While all about the same thickness of metal, cam hooks have different tip widths and "arm" lengths (fig. 15-9a), which produce different leverage on the rock features (fig. 15-9b and c). Too much leverage may bite into the rock or expand a flake, whereas too little leverage may make the placement insecure. Narrow cam hooks tend to have higher leverage;

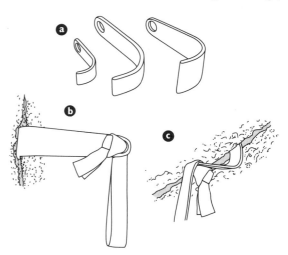

Fig. 15-9. Cam hooks: a, typical cam hook sizes—small, medium, large; b, cam hook placement in vertical crack; c, cam hook upside down under a roof.

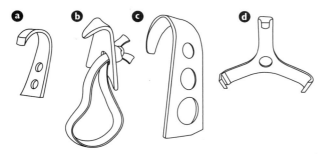

Fig. 15-8. Standard hook types: a, basic; b, bat hook; c, large hook; d, Talon.

wider cam hooks tend to have lower leverage. Cam hooks can be used in leapfrog style to advance quickly on relatively easy terrain.

Rivet Hangers

Rivet hangers are used to attach to bolt studs and rivets, which are basically shallowly driven ¼-inch bolts with a wide head.

Wire rivet hangers are loops of wire ⅛ inch or ³⁄₃₂ inch (3 or 2 millimeters) in diameter, with a slider to cinch the wire tight (fig. 15-10a and b). Small nuts with wire slings can be used in a similar manner, with the nut itself acting as the slider to tighten the wire against the bolt stud (see Figure 13-7 in Chapter 13, Rock Protection); however, because nuts have a longer wire loop than wire rivet hangers do, and therefore hang lower, they do not provide as much elevation gain. Wire rivet hangers primarily assist with upward progress and may not catch a fall, and rivets are generally considered body-weight protection only, so use careful judgment when relying on them as protection.

Regular and keyhole hangers are rivet hangers made from shaped pieces of metal (fig. 15-10c). They are especially useful for belay anchors and for fixed bolts that have no hangers. On a keyhole hanger, the metal between the bolt hole and the carabiner hole is filed out to allow placement over rivets and buttonhead bolts. When a regular or keyhole hanger is placed over a good bolt, it is considered

Fig. 15-10. Rivet hangers:
a, basic wire;
b, self-cinching wire;
c, keyhole.

protection that would arrest a fall. It is also wise to carry a few loose ¼-inch and ⅜-inch nuts in your pocket to screw onto bolts and rivets without hangers.

IRON HARDWARE AND BOLTS

The full range of aid-climbing techniques can be mastered only with knowledge of pitons, malleable hardware, and bolts.

Pitons

Modern pitons—also called *pins*—are made of hardened chromium molybdenum steel or other suitable alloys such as titanium alloys. Rather than molding to cracks the way the older, first-generation malleable pitons did, modern pitons made of harder materials are more unyielding and force the crack to their form. The key to effective piton placement is choosing the piton that is the best size for the crack. To fit the diverse cracks climbers encounter on rock walls, pitons vary tremendously in size and shape.

Realized Ultimate Reality Piton. The RURP is the smallest piton—a postage-stamp-sized, hatchet-shaped pin (fig. 15-11a) used in incipient cracks. It will usually support only body weight.

Birdbeaks. Also called *beaks* and commonly known by the brand name Peckers, birdbeaks (fig. 15-11b) range from those close in size to RURPs to larger units that fit in placements similar to those in which knifeblades or even wedge pitons (see below) fit. Beaks are particularly strong when they can be placed so that the long nose of the beak creates camming action inside the crack, which often makes them a more secure choice than knifeblades. In an excellent beak placement, the nose of the beak goes back into the crack away from the climber and also angles down into the crack toward the ground, so that when removing the beak, the follower must nail it not only up and down, as with a typical piton (see "Seconding" below), but also outward toward the follower. Thus, beaks can be especially difficult to clean. It is common to damage the cable on the beak when cleaning, so take care and consider backing up the cable with webbing.

Knifeblades. Also called *blades*, knifeblades are long and thin and have two eyes: one at the end of the blade and a second in the offset portion of the pin (fig. 15-11c). They come in different lengths and in thicknesses ranging from ⅛ to ³⁄₁₆ inch (3 to 4 millimeters). They are commonly used to fit cracks that are too thin for tiny nuts. Many routes have plenty of fixed blades in place, but their use has become less common because beaks tend to be more secure in cracks of the same size.

15

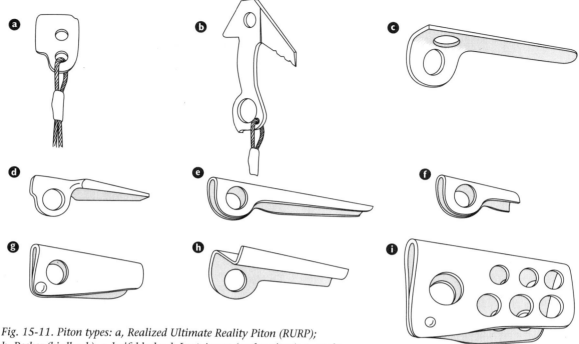

*Fig. 15-11. Piton types: a, Realized Ultimate Reality Piton (RURP);
b, Pecker (birdbeak); c, knifeblade; d, Lost Arrow (wedge piton); e, angle;
f, sawed-off angle; g, large sawed-off angle; h, Leeper Z; i, bong.*

Wedge pitons. Known commonly by the brand name Lost Arrows or just *arrows*, wedge pitons are one of the more commonly used versatile pins. They have a single eye centered and set perpendicular to the end of the pin (fig. 15-11d) and come in several lengths, in thicknesses ranging from ⁵⁄₃₂ to ⁹⁄₃₂ inch (4 to 8 millimeters). Among other uses, arrows are very good in horizontal cracks.

Angles. Pitons formed into a V shape are called angles (fig. 15-11e, f, and g). The V varies in height from ½ to 1½ inches (12 to 38 millimeters). The strength of these pitons is derived from the metal's resistance to bending and spreading. Angles are commonly used in angle pin scars, since oftentimes nothing else will fit in a pin scar except a pin. Otherwise, a crack large enough to accept an angle will normally accept clean climbing equipment if the crack has never been used for pin placements.

Leeper Z pitons. The Leeper Z piton has a Z-shaped profile (fig. 15-11h), as opposed to the V profile of an angle. These pitons often make very solid placements and work well for pin stacking (see "Stacking" later in this chapter). Sawed-off Leeper Z pins (see below) can work well in angle scars.

Bongs. Bongs are large angle pitons, varying from 2 to 6 inches (5 to 15 centimeters) wide (fig. 15-11i). SLCDs and other large gear options have generally replaced the need for bongs.

Sawed-off pitons. Angles and Leeper Z pitons with a few inches cut off the end (see Figure 15-11f and g) are useful for shallow placements. These sawed-off pitons are handy for protection on routes that have been heavily climbed using pitons, which leave shallow pin scars. Pins with the proportions of sawed-off angles are sometimes available commercially; otherwise, climbers saw their own pitons using a vise and a hacksaw. Angles of widths from ¾ to 1½ inches (19 to 38 millimeters) are the most common size of angle to saw off.

Malleable Hardware

Generally called *copperheads* (even when not made of copper), or just *heads*, malleable hardware is designed to hold weight by melding the soft head of the piece to the irregularities of the rock, such as a small constriction or corner. The security of heads varies greatly, and it is difficult to gauge the strength of a copperhead when placed, making them last-resort equipment, generally capable of holding only body weight, although they may hold falls.

Copperheads. Copperheads have a sleeve, called a *ferrule*, of copper or aluminum, the "head," swaged to one end of a short cable that has a clip loop swaged at the other end (fig. 15-12a). They are placed by pounding the relatively soft metal head end into an irregularity in the rock. Copper forms well and is more durable than aluminum; aluminum copperheads (made of softer aluminum than that used in carabiners, et cetera) are not as strong but are more malleable, and because of that, they are generally easier to place correctly. Aluminum is the best choice for most placements; copper is generally used for only the smallest copperheads.

Circleheads. Circleheads consist of a wire loop with one or more copper or aluminum ferrules swaged on the loop (fig. 15-12b), one of which is pounded into the rock in the same manner as a copperhead. They are used in horizontal cracks, overhead placements, and other applications wherein the symmetry of the wire loop's attachment point is preferable to a regular head because of the anticipated direction of pull.

Bolts

Chapter 13, Rock Protection, includes a section on the use of existing bolts found on climbing routes. Proper bolt placement, including rivet placement, is a special skill beyond the scope of this book; bolt placement is best left to the judgment and skill of very experienced climbers. (See "Rock Protection Etiquette" in Chapter 13, Rock Protection.)

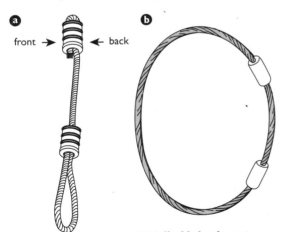

Fig. 15-12. Malleable hardware types: a, copperhead; b, circlehead.

BIG WALL EQUIPMENT

Climbers undertaking a big wall have other specialized equipment needs to consider. Safeguard important equipment taken on a big wall climb by using tie-in loops or lanyards to attach anything that might be dropped. Bring gear that will get the party through the worst possible weather, because there is not likely to be any easy way to retreat. Be sure all equipment is durable, and consider reinforcing equipment—with duct tape, when applicable—such as water bottles, portaledges, haul bags, and other items that can be protected from failure with some preventive maintenance.

Pulleys and Hauling Devices

Pulleys are necessary to ease the chore of hauling. They receive much abuse, so they must be durable. Pulleys with bearings and larger wheels operate more smoothly. Commercially offered hauling devices (which are pulleys with self-locking cams), also called *haulers*, are especially useful for extensive hauling and are used by most climbers (fig. 15-13a, b, and c). A large pulley combined with a locking carabiner, two slings, and one ascender—all gear that is usually carried on an aid climb—can be assembled to form a basic hauling system (fig. 15-13d) if the

15

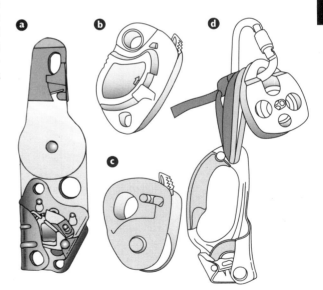

Fig. 15-13. Hauling devices (or haulers): a, Kong Block Roll; b, Petzl Pro Traxion; c, Petzl Micro Traxion; d, basic hauling system composed of an ascender, pulley, locking carabiner, and two slings.

hauling device is dropped. Some climbers prefer this type of noncommercial basic hauling system for heavy loads, since they can select larger pulleys and this type of system has fewer specialized parts that are subject to breaking (see "Hauling" later in this chapter for additional discussion on rigging this setup). It is a good idea to also carry simple pulleys for setting up mechanical advantage during a haul or for rescue situations (see Chapter 25, Alpine Rescue).

Haul Bags

Haul bags carry clothing, water, food, sleeping bags, and other climbing and nonclimbing paraphernalia (fig. 15-14a). A good haul bag has adequate cargo capacity, a solid haul suspension, durable fabric, no snag points, and a removable backpacking harness system. A knot protector covers the knot connecting the haul bag to the haul line to protect the knot, and may reduce snagging problems during hauling. An effective knot protector can be fashioned from the top of a 2-liter plastic bottle and some cord (fig. 15-14b). Before leaving the ground, equip the haul bag with a docking cord, typically 20 feet (7 meters) of 8-millimeter cord. Attach the cord directly to the primary haul strap of the haul bag with a rewoven figure eight (see also "Hauling" under "Big Wall Multiday Techniques" later in this chapter).

Cheater Sticks

Cheater sticks allow climbers to clip the rope or an aider in to a piece of hardware beyond their reach. The most important reason to carry some kind of cheater stick on a big wall is for use in down-aiding (making placements and clipping the rope in to them while rappelling) in the event of a retreat through steep terrain. If a fixed placement is missing or broken, using a cheater stick to reach another placement might provide an alternative to placing new pitons, copperheads, or bolts.

A tent pole or hiking pole can be fashioned into a cheater stick in an emergency by taping on a carabiner with duct tape or climbing tape. Cheater sticks as simple as a quickdraw reinforced and taped to be rigid may be mandatory for shorter climbers, especially when the gear is fixed and intermediate placements are not available.

Duct Tape

On big walls, duct tape is indispensable for repairing equipment, protecting gear, and climbing. Duct tape is used to tape down hooks, to tape the edges of hangerless bolts to prevent rivet hangers from sliding off, to attach rivet hangers to the aider carabiner to extend the climber's reach to a

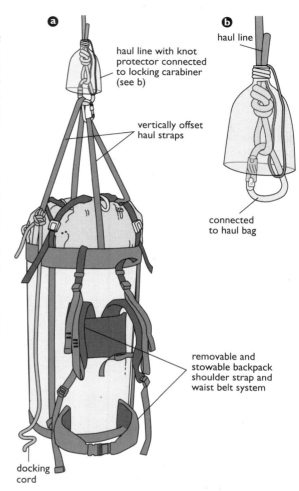

a haul line with knot protector connected to locking carabiner (see b)

vertically offset haul straps

b haul line

connected to haul bag

removable and stowable backpack shoulder strap and waist belt system

docking cord

Fig. 15-14. Haul bag: a, features include solid haul suspension and removable backpacking harness system; b, protecting the knot.

rivet, or to tape the nut tool or hammer (or both) to aiders, hooks, or protection to reach an especially high placement. Duct tape can be stuck to the rock to pad sharp edges in order to protect the rope. Duct tape is also commonly used to repair gear and to fashion homemade aid-specific equipment. Small-diameter rolls can be slung with cord and carried on the harness.

Portaledges

A climber's sleeping platform, also called a portaledge (fig. 15-15), is a lightweight cot that provides a place for climbers to sleep reasonably well on a big wall without

Fig. 15-15. Portaledge anchored to a wall (climbers' individual anchors to wall and helmets not shown, for clarity).

having to reach a natural ledge. Portaledges can be folded up and hauled with the haul bag. They can also be equipped with a rain fly to provide protection in a storm. Portaledges and rain-fly styles vary, and some rain flies are more suitable for big storms than others. An alternative to a portaledge is a hammock, which is significantly lighter and more uncomfortable. As with belay seats (see "Universal Aid-Specific Equipment" earlier in this chapter), when using portaledges or hammocks, climbers must always be anchored directly to the rock, not to the portaledge or hammock.

Waste Containers

On big wall ascents, waste containers must be carried to haul and pack out human waste, and these containers are typically attached to and hauled below the haul bag. It is very important that the haul straps on the container are reliable and attached securely, so the container will not detach during the ascent. Such detachments not only leave the team without an appropriate waste container but they leave waste on the rock or at the base and can injure parties below. While homemade containers may survive the rigors of a big wall, commercial containers specifically designed for big wall climbing, such as the Metolius Waste Case,

tend to be more reliable. Outer containers are usually used in combination with internal packaging of the waste. (See Chapter 7, Leave No Trace.) It should go without saying that it is never appropriate to toss waste off the cliff during an ascent.

AID PLACEMENTS

The general rule for aid climbing is to place each aid piece as high as possible. For example, making most placements at 4-foot (1.2-meter) intervals rather than at 3-foot (0.9-meter) intervals over the course of a 160-foot (approximately 50-meter) pitch saves more than 10 placements and much time.

Most of the techniques for placing free-climbing protection apply to aid climbing; however, unlike in free climbing, some aid-climbing placements are generally suitable to hold only body weight, not fall forces. Also more often used in aid climbing than free climbing is the practice of back-cleaning. *Back-cleaning* is when a leader climbs past a piece onto a new piece of protection and decides to remove the previous piece, in order to use it again higher on the climb (see the "Tips for Leading Aid Pitches" sidebar later in this chapter). It is important to keep in mind good basic protection skills and free-climbing concepts when back-cleaning and to leave quality protection at adequate intervals. Also, always keep in mind that if the follower will be jugging (climbing the rope using mechanical ascenders), the leader needs to leave protection close enough together that the follower will be able to clean the placements. When there is a change in direction or angle of the climb, removing too many pieces can create a problem for the follower jugging a rope under tension.

Using a solid cam hook placement rather than a nut or piton placement can save considerable time for both leader (placement is much simpler) and follower (because there is nothing to clean), but this provides no protection against the consequences of a fall.

Placing nuts during an aid climb is similar to placing them on a free climb, but because aid nuts take the weight of the lead climber, and because they may be smaller than the nut tool, they can be difficult to remove. Consider using nuts only for protection and not weighting nuts for upward progress if possible.

Evaluate fixed pins, bolts, and other fixed gear before using them (see Chapter 13, Rock Protection). Clip a carabiner directly to fixed gear left as protection whenever possible rather than clipping in to old fixed slings that might be attached to the fixed gear. For example, cut old slings

15

from piton eyes when necessary so that the piton eye can accept a carabiner. If for some reason a carabiner will not fit in the eye—because the pin is bent or is too close to an obstruction, or because fixed webbing cannot be removed from the eye—thread a full-strength tie-off loop through the eye and then either girth-hitch it or clip the two ends of the tie-off loop with a carabiner.

PITON PLACEMENT

A properly sized pin can be placed one-half to two-thirds of the way by hand; the remainder of the pin is then hammered into place. Select the correct pin to fit the crack. A pin that inserts smoothly, with good contact between the pin and rock and reasonably matches the shape of the crack, will do less damage to the rock when hammered in than a pin that is too large or the wrong shape. Using an ill-fitting pin causes more destruction to the rock. A sound piton rings with a higher-pitched ping with each strike of the hammer. After the pin is driven, bounce-test the piece (see "The Basic Aid Sequence" later in this chapter). Well-placed pins or fixed pins can flex when weighted, but they should not shift. Knowing just how much to hammer a piton is a matter of touch and experience. Excessive hammering wastes energy, makes it harder for the second to remove the piton, and needlessly damages the rock. Under-driving a piton, however, increases the risk of its pulling out. If several pins are underdriven, the failure of one could result in a long fall as the series of pins zippers out. Here are additional guidelines for the sound placement of pitons:

- **Hand-place pitons, without any driving by the hammer,** if possible, to eliminate damage to the rock; use an existing scar and do not hammer the pin. Hand-placed pitons may be less secure for upward progress and are less likely to catch a fall than hammered pitons, but with practice some placements can be accomplished this way.
- **Try to determine what type of pin was previously placed** and how it was placed, since most piton placements now occur in pin scars, in order to use the scar in the same manner it was created.
- **Place pins in wider portions of a crack,** in the way nuts are placed. If the crack is thinner below and above the pin, the pin will be supported when it has to take your weight (fig. 15-16a).
- **Add a full-strength tie-off loop** to the piton if the piton's position causes the connecting carabiner to extend over an edge, to prevent cross-loading the carabiner across its sides (fig. 15-16b).

- **Keep the three points of the V in contact with the rock** when placing angles (fig. 15-16c). The back (the point of the V) must always be in contact with one wall, while the edges (the two tips of the V) are in contact with the opposing wall. In a horizontal crack, put the back of the angle up and the edges down.
- **Stop hammering when a pin bottoms out in a crack**—that is, cannot be driven in all the way. The piton must be tied off around the shaft at the point where it emerges from the rock. A tie-off loop connected with an overhand slipknot, girth-hitched or clove-hitched to the pin, supports the climber's weight and reduces levering action (see Figure 13-9 in Chapter 13, Rock Protection). Loop a longer sling (or a second carabiner) through the eye of the pin and clip it in to the tie-off loop or its carabiner. This "keeper sling" does not bear weight but will catch the pin if it pops out.

STACKING

When no single pin, chock, or SLCD fits the crack at hand, aid climbers get very creative. Whether a climber has run out of proper-sized pieces or is facing a beat-out, pod-shaped pin scar, it is time to improvise by driving in two or more pins together, known as *stacking*. This can be done many different ways, depending on the size of the crack and the pins available, as shown in Figure 15-17.

Blades are stacked back to back and are usually driven together. If a third blade is necessary, the first two are inserted by hand, and then the third is driven in between them. Leeper Z pitons are especially useful for stacking, and Lost Arrows can also be stacked, either back to back or with a shorter arrow on top of a longer arrow. You can mix any pins together in a stack that nicely fill the crack and with good contact between the individual pins in the stack. Creativity is the key.

There is some disagreement about the best way to stack angles. Some climbers stack them by keeping the spines of both angles against each other and the edges of each piton into the rock, but any combination will work. Try to avoid stacking angles by simply placing one over the other, because these may be very hard to separate once they are removed.

When pins are stacked, girth-hitch the pins together with a tie-off loop (fig. 15-17a and c). It is typical to clip in to only one pin directly (fig. 15-17b), or if the eyes of the stacked pins are blocked (as in Figure 15-17a), it may be necessary to clip directly to the tie-off loop. In either case,

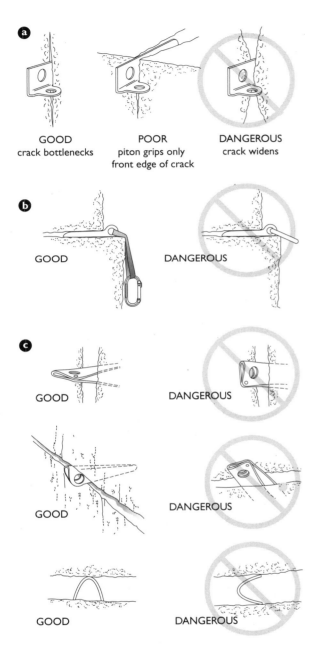

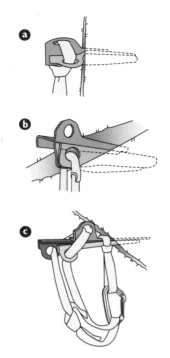

Fig. 15-17. Examples of pitons and angles stacked and nested (some keeper slings omitted for clarity): a, arrow and knifeblade stacked back-to-back; b, Leeper Z and angle, nested; c, two arrows and knifeblade, stacked.

15

using a tie-off loop ensures that if the stacked pins fail, you will not lose the pins that have not been clipped directly in to the rope.

HOOK PLACEMENT AND USE

To place a hook, set the hook on the ledge, flake, or hole where it will be used. When learning, try several hooks to see which one sits most securely in the feature. Move the hook around to try to find the most secure positioning by feel, and if the hooked feature can be seen, visually inspect the quality of the placement as well. Hooks can sometimes be placed on top of a fixed copperhead that has lost its wire (called a "dead head").

After selecting the hook and placement position, clip an aider and daisy chain to the hook. Test all hooks before applying full body weight (or gently "ooze" body weight onto the hook if it is off to the side or otherwise cannot be tested). Climbers usually start very low in their aiders so that their weight and stance are well below the hook before they move up the aiders one step at a time.

Fig. 15-16. Piton placements: a, placements are best if crack constricts above and below piton; b, safely extending a piton to avoid cross-loading the carabiner; c, angle piton placements should have all three points in contact with the rock.

Climbers should avoid standing with their face directly in front of the hook because it could pop out with a good deal of force. Once your weight is on the hook in one aider (or one pair), it can be helpful to "fifi in"—to hook in to the aider's carabiner and hang your body weight—just as with other pieces of protection. Always keep constant downward pressure on the hook when standing in the aiders, especially when moving up in the aiders and switching weight from one foot to the other.

Cam hooks should be placed in the crack or pocket in a fashion that will make the hook bind up and rotate to cause a camming force on the rock. These placements rely on the force created by the torque (camming action) of the hook into the rock. With practice, cam hooks can be placed in many seemingly unlikely positions and orientations. The tighter the cam hook fits into the crack (in other words, the closer the width of the metal sheet is to the width of the crack), the more secure the placement and the less potential there is to do any damage to the rock. A cam hook can be hit once with a hammer to increase the placement's security when needed. Sometimes a hammer is needed to remove a cam hook, even when it has supported only body weight. Climbers generally agree that cam hooks should not be used in certain rock, such as sandstone, because they may damage the rock with their camming action.

MALLEABLE PLACEMENTS

Because climbers often cannot tell how secure the placements of malleable heads are, and because such heads damage the rock, do not use them except where other protection will not work. Heads are used like any other aid piece but have an inescapable weakness: inspection cannot guarantee that the head has been molded to the rock. Some heads may hold a short fall, others will support body weight only, and others might fail. All malleable head placements are suspect, and accepting this fact is inherent in their use.

Assuming that an adequate selection of heads is available, use the largest head the rock feature will best accommodate. Gently bounce-test all head placements (see "The Basic Aid Sequence" below), whether placed by you or a previous party. Do not get impatient when placing heads—spend as much time as needed to make the placement as good as possible. Consider using load-limiting runners on heads, since a well-placed head may arrest a fall.

Copperheads and circleheads take more practice to place than other types of aid gear, and placing them requires

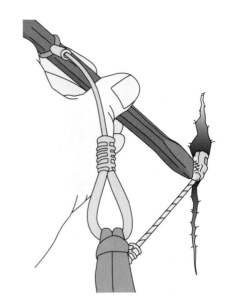

Fig. 15-18. Placing a copperhead by hammering directly on a chisel, rather than on the copperhead itself.

specialized tools. The hammer pick works for setting ("pasting") large heads, but small heads require hammering a striking tool such as a blunt chisel (fig. 15-18) or a punch—or, in a pinch, a Lost Arrow or nut tool. Hammering a striking tool rather than the piece itself reduces the likelihood of a missed hit, which causes undue damage to the rock.

Before placing a head, examine it carefully. Note that, starting with the clip-in loop, the cable comes up through the "back" of the head, does a 180-degree turn, and ends at the bottom of the "front" of the head (see Figure 15-12a). Make sure the back of the head is placed against the rock and the frayed ends of the cut cable at the front of the head are visible, in order to minimize the cable's outward bending movement (or torque) on the head itself and to protect the cable when the head is being pasted.

Look for a placement option like a downward-tapered groove or crack that at least has parallel sides, similar to a nut placement, but that can't take a nut, possibly because it is too shallow. Practice head placement on the ground, perhaps in some boulders or other nonclimbable rock, to gain experience before placing heads on an established climbing route. Follow these steps when placing a head:

1. **Warm up the head** by hitting it on every surface with the hammer a few times. If needed, carefully shape the head slightly to match the intended

placement by rotating the head while hitting it gently, approximately 10 to 20 times.

2. **Place the head** by positioning it similarly to a nut—in a narrowing portion of a flare or seam, making sure to orient the head correctly: with the back of the head placed against the rock.

3. **Seat the head** into the rock, preferably using a punch to hit it perhaps four to five times, over the entire head. If no punch is available, at this stage use the narrow tip of the wall hammer. At this point, the goal is simply for the head to stay in place in the constriction during additional pasting without the climber having to hold on to it.

4. **Pound the head in,** using a chisel to make many angled strokes that form an X pattern on the head, or simply hit the head repeatedly enough times to weld the head into the placement. Take care not to hit and damage the rock or the cable of the head. Hit the head all over—top, middle, and bottom. If the head rocks while being hit on its top or bottom, go back to hitting the middle of the head. If the metal starts separating from the cable, stop hitting, to avoid overpasting the head.

5. **Paste the head** on its edges by setting the chisel right on the edge of the head and pounding both sides to past the edges of the head.

6. **"Pin" the head** on the top and bottom with special care; this is the area of the head that often gets the best "bite" in the rock.

7. **Gently bounce-test the head** before committing your weight to ensure that it will hold. However, overaggressive bounce-testing can pull a good head placement, so try to generate only about twice the force of the body weight to be held (see "The Basic Aid Sequence" below).

BASIC AID TECHNIQUES

Before starting to lead any aid pitch, study the terrain and make a plan. Decide what gear the leader will need and what the second can carry. Generally, the leader should carry personal ascenders, belay device(s) including an assisted-braking belay device, and a nut tool, among other gear, as this gear—normally considered follower gear—may be needed when leading aid climbs. Figure out how to minimize rope drag. Spot any obstructions that might create hauling problems. Decide whether to save aid pieces of certain sizes for the end of the pitch.

RACKING

Racking varies greatly with personal style. It is common on aid routes to have more than one SLCD on each racking carabiner. Racking SLCDs on wire-gate carabiners is preferred because these carabiners are lighter.

A recommended racking system is to attach the SLCD's clip-in loop to the carabiner instead of clipping the SLCD in with its sewn sling as is done in free climbing. Face the gate of the carabiner out and away from the harness, with the opening of the gate at the bottom of the carabiner. This allows the climber to open the carabiner by flicking the rigid loop of the SLCD against the carabiner gate, removing just one SLCD from the carabiner with one hand. When racking multiple SLCDs on one carabiner, consider mixing sizes so that if one carabiner full of SLCDs is dropped, all of the pieces of that size are not lost. (Figure 15-5 shows how SLCDs are typically racked for aid climbing.)

Consider racking half of the SLCDs, nuts, pins, and slings of each size on each side of your body so that all sizes of gear are available from both sides. Typically, gear is racked from small to large or large to small. Some climbers rack all their slings on their seat harness and all their protection on their chest harness. Making "two-packs" of slings reduces the amount of space the slings take up on the harness (fig. 15-19a). Or rack single slings over a shoulder.

It is helpful to rack pitons on oval carabiners, because they allow pieces to rotate on and off the carabiner smoothly in either direction (fig. 15-19b); specialized oval wire-gate carabiners weigh less. Do not overload a carabiner to the point that gear is lost because the equipment cannot be accessed easily enough. Alternate the direction of angles and Lost Arrows for better nesting on the carabiner, which allows more pins per carabiner. Consider racking nuts and hooks onto traditional latch-style (nonkeylock) carabiners (see Figure 9-36e), which have a hook that makes it that much harder for the nuts or hooks to accidentally come off of the carabiner. Free carabiners are often racked as "footballs" in groups of five or seven carabiners, depending on the climber's preference, to make them easy to organize and to use minimal space on the rack (fig. 15-19c).

Often it is useful for the leader to have a nut tool for removing unsettled placements and for cleaning grass, dirt, and other debris out of cracks as necessary. Finally, check that the hammer, if one is being carried, is accessible, with its sling untangled.

15

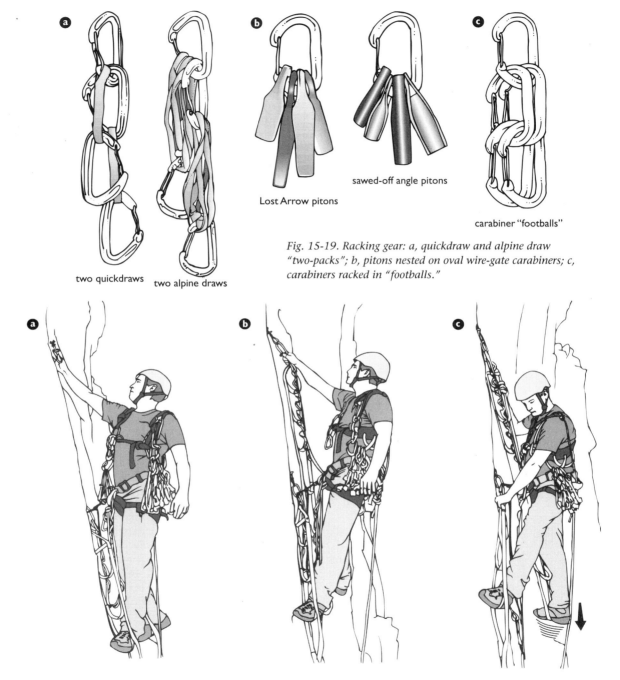

two quickdraws   two alpine draws

Lost Arrow pitons

sawed-off angle pitons

carabiner "footballs"

Fig. 15-19. Racking gear: a, quickdraw and alpine draw "two-packs"; b, pitons nested on oval wire-gate carabiners; c, carabiners racked in "footballs."

Fig. 15-20. The basic aid sequence (some equipment omitted for clarity): a, select and place piece of protection; b, clip aider-daisy to the protection; c, bounce-test the protection (continued on facing page);

THE BASIC AID SEQUENCE

The basic aid sequence is the same no matter where the leader starts: from the ground, a comfortable free stance, or the top step of the aiders. The following basic sequence assumes that the climber is using two aiders (see also the "Tips for Leading Aid Pitches" sidebar):

1. Look at and feel the terrain above, and select an aid piece to place at the highest suitable spot within reach (fig. 15-20a).
2. Place the piece and visually inspect it if possible. Clip the free aider and daisy chain combination in to the new piece with its dedicated oval keylock carabiner (fig. 15-20b).
3. Bounce-test the new piece in the typical sequence: (a) Tug down firmly one or more times on the aider with a hand; (b) step one foot into the aider and give a few solid, down-forcing "kicks" with that foot (keep all your weight supported on the previous piece during this first leg test); (c) transfer about

half of your weight to the new piece and give a few more vigorous hops (keep a hand on the aider of the previous piece and the other foot in that aider so that you can hold yourself upright and on the previous piece should the new piece fail during this step; if possible, stay fified in to the previous piece); and (d) transfer all of your weight to the new piece and give more vigorous bounces (fig. 15-20c).

If the new piece is questionable, is not intended for more than body weight, or is behind an expanding feature, some climbers may decide to avoid aggressive bounce-testing. Instead, (a) hand-set the placement (if appropriate) with a firm tug, and (b) simply "ooze" onto the new placement, applying your weight as gradually and smoothly as possible.

Some climbers rely on their experience and knowledge of the specific rock type to set good placements and forgo anything more than hand-setting the placement. Others believe that the only safe

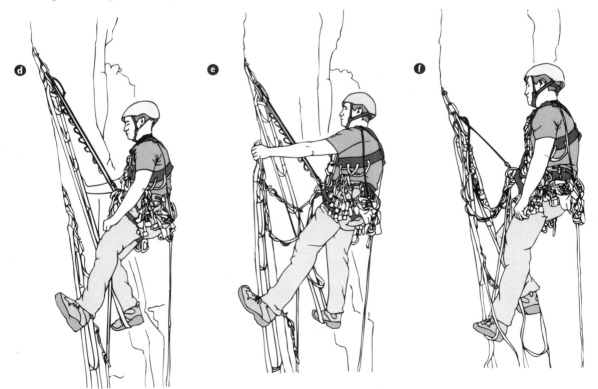

Fig. 15-20. *(continued from facing page) d, shift weight to newly placed aider and protection and rest on fifi hook; e, clip rope to previous piece of protection and remove lower aider-daisy; f, clip lower aider-daisy to higher aider-daisy and prepare to climb high in aiders and repeat the sequence.*

climbing method is vigorous bounce-testing. Warn the belayer when you are about to test or move onto a dubious placement.

4. Once your weight is committed to the new placement, fifi in to the piece with the fifi hook, or clip in the adjustable daisy strap, and rest (fig. 15-20d). If not using an adjustable fifi hook or an adjustable daisy, climb up to the second or third steps in the aiders at this point in order to fifi in to the new piece. With a classic fifi hook, it is also possible to fifi in to one of the traditional daisy-chain loops.

5. While resting on the new piece, reach back to the previous piece. If clipping this piece for protection, add a carabiner, quickdraw, or sling and clip in the rope, then remove the aider and daisy chain combination (fig. 15-20e) and clip the oval keylock carabiner of this aider and daisy chain combination in to the oval keylock carabiner of the higher aider (fig. 15-20f). If removing this lower piece, rerack the piece.

6. Climb as high as possible in the aiders, possibly to the second or top steps, moving or adjusting the fifi or adjustable daisy while advancing higher (as shown in Figure 15-20f). Resist the temptation to look for placements until you have climbed as high as you plan to climb in the aiders. This helps ensure that you do not get distracted by lower placement possibilities and increases efficiency of piece selection.

7. Repeat the process starting with step 1.

TOP-STEPPING

Moving onto the top step of the aiders can be unnerving, but being able to do so greatly improves the efficiency of aid climbing. The process is simple on low-angle rock, where the top steps are used like any other foothold and the climber's hands provide balance. Sometimes it is faster and less fatiguing to make multiple placements from steps lower than the top step, such as on very steep terrain or when aiding deep inside awkward cracks and corners. On such terrain, climbers may find that they can move faster by always placing from the second step. However, the ideal is to top-step as much as possible.

Vertical and overhanging rock can make top-stepping difficult because the climber's center of gravity moves away from the rock and above the point where the aiders are clipped to the aid placement. If the rock offers any features, use hands or an intermediate placement as a handhold to provide balance. If the rock is blank and the placement suitable, keep your weight on your feet while standing up

TIPS FOR LEADING AID PITCHES

- **Minimize rope drag,** as in free climbing. Consider each placement carefully, and extend slings when necessary to keep the rope running straight. If the follower will ascend using ascenders, pay attention to how the rope runs over edges, and set protection and slings so that the rope does not rub over sharp edges. If necessary, pad edges, usually with duct tape.

- **Think strategically while climbing** about what pieces can be left and what pieces should be removed as you go, known as back-cleaning, for reuse later on the pitch. Some pitches will require a large number of pieces of the same size, or the leader may have only one or two of certain critical pieces, so these pieces will have to be back-cleaned often. Avoid back-cleaning low on the start of a pitch, and leave protection at close-enough intervals often enough to prevent serious falls.

- **Consider when to clip the rope,** which depends on personal preference and on the quality of the lower and higher pieces of protection. Some climbers prefer to clip the rope in to the lower placement before completing the final bounce-testing or before committing full weight to the new placement, so that if the new placement fails, the leader will not take a fall onto the lower piece caught only by the daisy chain and not the rope. Other climbers rely on bounce-testing to ensure that the new higher piece will hold their weight long enough for them to reach down and clip the rope to the lower piece. Generally, climbers do not want to pull up rope in order to clip to the highest piece before moving past it, as this increases the length of a potential fall. However, the more suspect the new higher piece, the more likely that the climber will clip the current piece as protection prior to moving onto the higher piece, rather than after moving onto the higher piece, as in the basic sequence. On pitches rated A1 or C1, where all placements should be secure, generally follow the basic sequence.

and applying tension to the fifi hook or adjustable daisy strap between the harness and the aid placement. That tension provides the means of balancing yourself (fig. 15-21). If using a classic fifi, an alternative method is to clip a quickdraw in to the piece and use it as a handhold, pulling

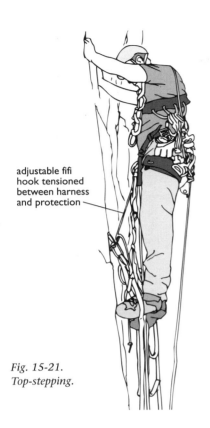

adjustable fifi hook tensioned between harness and protection —

Fig. 15-21.
Top-stepping.

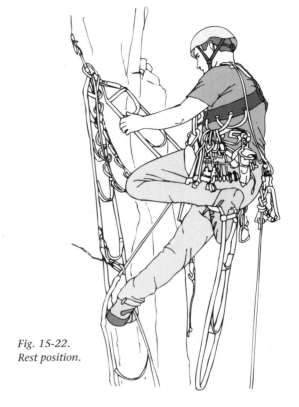

Fig. 15-22.
Rest position.

15

upward on the quickdraw with one hand and making the next placement with the other hand.

RESTING

Do not wear yourself out. Climb in a relaxed fashion, taking rests as often as necessary to conserve strength or to plot the next series of moves. The best way to rest is to immediately clip in to a new tested piece with a fifi hook or adjustable daisy strap. Rest by fully weighting the fifi or adjustable daisy, freeing your feet completely before using the aiders to move up on the piece. This also allows you to switch feet between aiders as needed, to reach sideways to attach aiders to a new piece, or to execute whatever change of direction the next move may require. As you advance upward on pieces, move your classic fifi up or pull in your adjustable fifi or adjustable daisy, resting on this equipment as much as possible.

If not using a fifi hook or adjustable daisy, or if on lower-angle terrain, try this rest technique: With each foot in separate aiders and one foot one step below the other, bend the knee of the higher leg and bring that foot under you.

Most of your weight now rests over the bent leg. The outstretched leg takes minimal weight but maintains balance (fig. 15-22).

Another way to rest is to ask the belayer for tension and then rest on the climbing rope once it has been clipped in to the supporting piece. This is not an efficient method, however, due to stretch in the rope and the need for verbal communication.

Finally, relaxing stances can often be found in the aiders. Generally, the greatest stability is obtained by standing with heels together and toes spread apart against the rock. The heels-together position can be very helpful when standing high in the aiders and stretching up to make a difficult placement.

SWITCHING BETWEEN AID AND FREE CLIMBING

Stowing and deploying aiders as well as free climbing with aid gear, a large rack, and a haul line are some of the difficulties in switching between aid and free climbing during a big wall climb. For free climbers, reorienting to a totally

309

different style and repurposing free gear into aid gear is the challenge. Weighting the first piece on aid after free climbing can be scary when the last piece of protection is far away or untested. Communicate clearly with your partner on transitions between aid and free.

From Free to Aid

Switching from free climbing to aid climbing is the easier transition, if the climb accepts rock protection, as the climber can simply call for tension or clip the belay loop directly in to a piece. If the climber has been free climbing because the rock did not accept protection, the last piece may be far below and the transition can be trickier. Whenever possible, start the transition at a piece of reliable protection and consider placing two pieces. Either way, test the first piece of aid protection carefully, especially with the first visual inspection and tests prior to weighting the piece. If using aiders to aid climb the section, release the aiders and daisy chains (see "Daisy Chains," earlier in the chapter), which could already be rigged on the harness, and move into the basic aid sequence (see "The Basic Aid Sequence"). This is easy if the climber has anticipated changing to aid, but if the climber is not expecting to use aid and suddenly needs it, problems arise. When in this bind, prepare slings or quickdraws for improvised aiders by interconnecting several slings, and then use the improvised aiders to move through the aid section over the blank area. If not using daisy chains on a short section of aid, take great care not to drop the improvised aiders.

From Aid to Free

A climber may wish to transition from aid to free climbing when encountering a section that cannot be aided (such as face climbing terrain where no rock protection is available) or when the climbing becomes easy enough that free climbing is faster and more efficient than aid climbing. Make sure your belayer knows you will be moving faster as you transition to free climbing. Two methods are commonly used to switch to free climbing:

1. **On easier or low-angle terrain,** it is often possible to move out of the aiders and onto the rock with all your weight on your hands and feet and still reach back to unclip the aiders to bring them along. If the transition occurs at a ledge or stance, simply clip aiders and daisy chains to the harness gear loops and start free climbing. Make sure that the aid equipment will not hinder your movement when free climbing.

2. **When the aid climbing is steep just before the transition to free climbing,** the preferred technique is to clip a single or double runner to the last piece of aid protection. Then stand in the runner, using this sling as an improvised aider. Remove the aiders and stow them on the harness. This enables the climber to make free-climbing moves and not have to reach down to retrieve the aiders. When possible, clip the rope to the sling before stepping in the sling and free climbing away—otherwise, the piece will not assist in catching a fall, and if it is not connected to the rope, the piece and sling might be out of reach for the follower to clean. If moving from a hook to free climbing, simply pull up on the aider or aiders from the first free moves, and the hook and the aider should release.

TENSION TRAVERSES AND PENDULUM SWINGS

Tension traverses and pendulum swings are used to move horizontally across unaidable territory into a new crack system. First ascensionists use these techniques to avoid placing bolt ladders to reach the new system.

The main difference between a tension traverse and a pendulum is that a pendulum requires the climber to run across the face in order to reach the new system, while during a tension traverse the climber does not run but uses friction on small holds to work hands and feet sideways. Both pendulums and tension traverses can be difficult, and they pose special problems for the second climber, who must both follow and clean protection.

For both methods, the leader starts by placing a solid piece of protection at the top of the planned traverse and clipping the rope in to this protection or clipping in to fixed gear at this point. Usually the equipment used for the tension or pendulum point cannot be retrieved, unless it is possible to come back to it from above, so these points on most routes are equipped with fixed gear. Climbers might use a locking carabiner on a tension or pendulum point for extra security.

During a tension traverse, after clipping in the rope, the leader takes tension from the belayer, lowers some amount, and starts to move toward the new crack system, using hands and feet to move across the rock (fig. 15-23a). Some tension traverses require climbers to achieve a sideways or even nearly upside-down position as they move. Often during tension traverses, leaders will call for more slack as they make progress. Keep good communication with the belayer, with clear "Lower me," "Stop," or

Fig. 15-23. Leading horizontally: a, tension traverse; b, pendulum.

"Hold" commands. Once the final destination is reached, the leader may need to call for slack so that the tension ceases and climbing can continue in the new crack.

For a pendulum, the leader clips in to the pendulum point with the rope and has the belayer take tension. Then the leader calls for a lower. The belayer lowers the leader until there is enough rope out for the leader to run back and forth across the rock and swing into the new crack system (fig. 15-23b). When being lowered by the belayer, it is better to be lowered too little than too much, because if you are too low, it may be very difficult to correct the error. Stop early and try the pendulum. If necessary, lower again until the best position is reached. While running back and forth across the rock, start slow and increase speed on each back and forth. Stay in control to avoid spinning and hitting the rock.

Some pendulums and traverses are difficult due to length, angle of the face, or other factors. Climbers may want to attach an SLCD to their aider so that they can jam this piece into the new crack very quickly (see Figure 5-23b). If a climber has barely reached the new crack but has managed to bury the right piece into it, the piece and the daisy chain will catch the climber's weight before he or she swings back into the old plumb line. Once in the new crack system, climb as high as safety allows before clipping the rope in to aid pieces for protection. The higher a climber gets before placing protection, the easier it is for the belayer, who will second the pendulum (see "Seconding Tension Traverses and Pendulum Swings" later in this chapter).

A Grigri is helpful for the belayer to use for tension traverses and pendulums. In a tension traverse, it allows for a precise belay and perfect amount of tension as called for by the leader. In a pendulum, it allows the belayer to hold the leader in the exact position required.

OVERHANGS AND ROOFS

Overhangs and roofs can appear intimidating but often are easier than they look to aid through, especially because fixed gear tends to be prevalent in roofs. Keep ascenders handy, because if a piece pulls out and you end up hanging, you may need ascenders to climb back up to the last secure piece.

Under a steep overhanging wall or a roof, it may not be possible to place your feet against the rock. In this situation, start by hanging as far below the piece as possible and in the low steps on the aiders. To move up and reach the next placement, use the fifi hook or adjustable daisy strap to hang from the harness rather than trying to stand with your full weight in the aiders. After making the new placement, test it and clip in an aider, then step into the lowest possible step and fifi in.

When climbing very steep overhangs, placements will probably be made close together. Be careful not to remove gear during these sections, because the follower will need more gear left in place in order to successfully clean the pitch. Or consider back-cleaning the entire section to allow the second to simply ascend the fixed line. As an overhang becomes horizontal, it will actually become easier to aid

15

because the climber can stand fully erect in the aiders under the roof, possibly in the bottom steps, and aid sideways through the horizontal crack system.

Despite the difference in balance, for aiding over a roof climbers use the same basic aid sequence described earlier in this chapter. Reach up and over the roof to find the next placement. It may be necessary to feel the placement without getting a good visual inspection. When first moving onto the aider clipped to the piece above the roof, it may be difficult to pull yourself up to the piece and over the roof. Stepping into the lowest step on the aider and standing up in that aider can help you get started. Then, with an adjustable fifi or an adjustable daisy, it should be possible to fifi in to the piece above the roof.

Rope drag is a common side effect of overhangs. Try not to give in to the temptation to put long slings on these placements, because it will make cleaning very difficult for the follower. Some climbers pull along a second belay rope and start climbing on it after clearing the lip of the overhang, although this technique is not common.

Finally, try to relax when working out moves over a big roof. Have confidence in your pieces. Clutching at them will not keep them in place but will drain your strength.

ESTABLISHING BELAYS

Upon reaching the end of a pitch, the leader must establish an anchor. Many routes have bolts at the end of the pitches, but climbers may have to place their own gear. If hauling, the leader will typically set up an anchor with two main power points (see "Equalizing the Anchor" in Chapter 10, Belaying): one for fixing the lead line and supporting the weight and safety of the climbers, and one for the haul system. Carefully consider which side to put the lead line on versus the haul system. Generally, try to keep the haul system in a straight line, and position the haul anchor out of the path of the route so that the follower does not have to push past the haul bag(s). Other considerations in selecting the location of the lead-line and haul-system anchors are the quality of the protection and the weight of the haul bag(s). With these considerations in mind, the leader sets up an anchor upon completing the pitch (fig. 15-24a).

Lead-line anchor. Attach the lead line to the lead-line anchor first (fig. 15-24b). To do this, call for slack, pull up several armfuls of rope, and fix the line for the follower. Typically the rope is fixed by clove-hitching it to a carabiner that is clipped to a solid piece of protection already used in the anchor, preferably a bolt. Use a clove hitch so that it can be easily untied after being weighted. Then

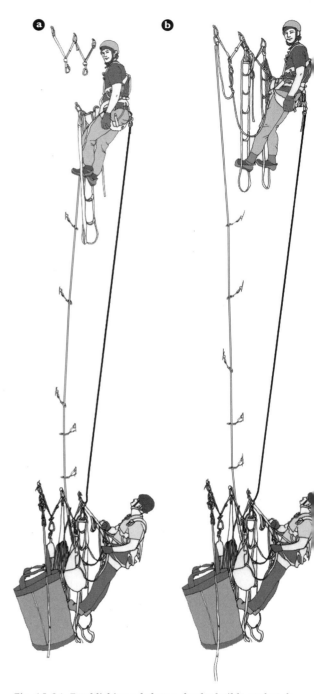

Fig. 15-24. Establishing a belay: a, leader builds anchor; b, leader fixes lead line; (continued on facing page)

15

Fig. 15-24. (continued from facing page) c, second attaches to lead line and begins dismantling lower anchor; d, leader sets up the hauling system while second prepares to jug and clean; e, second releases haul bag; f, leader hauls while second jugs and cleans.

back up this clove hitch with a figure eight on a bight. Clip this figure eight to the power point of the lead-line anchor. Make sure that there is enough rope between this figure eight and the leader building the anchor to allow the leader to perform the haul. As soon as the lead line is fixed with the clove hitch and backed up, the leader calls down to the follower that the lead line is fixed. This also tells the follower that the leader is off belay (or "Off belay" may be called separately).

The follower immediately attaches to the lead line with ascenders and a backup, removes most of the anchor from the belay station, and unties the backup knot in the haul line (fig. 15-24c). The only pieces that the follower leaves in place until the haul starts are those directly weighted by the haul-bag docking cord. This ensures that the follower will be ready to ascend as soon as the haul bag leaves the belay station.

Haul-system anchor. After fixing the lead line and while the second is preparing to jug and clean, the leader sets up the haul system (fig. 15-24d; see also "Hauling" under "Big Wall Multiday Techniques," later in this chapter). When setting up the haul-system anchor, the leader may use one of the points in the lead-line anchor as part of the haul anchor. This creates a backup for both of the anchors. As part of the hauling sequence, the follower releases the haul bag from the belay anchor so that the leader can haul (fig. 15-24e), then removes any pieces that the haul bag was directly weighting, and finally ascends the fixed lead line.

As the leader hauls, the haul line is stacked neatly so that it is ready to go for the next lead (fig. 15-24f). After the hauling is completed (or after the climbing rope is fixed, if the leader is not hauling), the leader sets up a belay seat, gets comfortable, and prepares to exchange leads by sorting the rack, organizing the ropes, preparing the belay system, and so forth.

TYROLEAN TRAVERSES

Tyrolean traverses may be used to move between two rock features, such as a main wall and a detached pinnacle. They are also useful for crossing rivers and other spans. Ropes are strung between points on each side of the span, allowing climbers to traverse through the air, attached to the rope. As an example, the instructions that follow are for a Tyrolean traverse between a main wall and a detached pinnacle, such as the Lost Arrow Spire in Yosemite National Park, California.

1. After setting up a bombproof anchor on the main wall—one that can take both a horizontal and a vertical pull—**connect one end of a single-strand rappel line to this anchor**. Rappel this rope to the saddle between the main wall and the detached pinnacle. Note the rappel line must be greater than two times the distance of the span between the main wall and the detached pinnacle, with the extra length more than two times what is needed for tying two knots.

2. **Climb the pinnacle using an additional climbing rope** if needed. Build an anchor at the top for a horizontal pull (or, as in many cases—including this example of Lost Arrow Spire—use the fixed anchors that are provided). Note that after the traverse, the equipment used for the pinnacle anchor cannot be recovered. The follower brings up the free end of the rappel line if it was not used as the climbing rope (consider tying in to this line to avoid dropping it).

3. Once both climbers are atop the pinnacle and attached to the pinnacle anchor, **pull the rappel line** (which becomes the traverse line) **tight against the anchor on the main wall** and fix this rope to the pinnacle anchor. Feed the free end of the traverse line through the anchor just as would be done to set up a rappel (if using two ropes, untying and retying is best). If using the free end of the rappel line to initiate the traverse (see step 5 below), consider fixing the second rope to the pinnacle anchor for redundancy and to avoid passing a knot on the rappel.

4. **Select the gear to attach to the traverse line and use for crossing.** If the traverse line is mostly horizontal or if the destination is higher than the starting point, many methods can be used to cross the span on the traverse line: using a Micro Traxion clipped to the harness and one ascender, perhaps with an aider or foot sling attached to the ascender (fig. 15-25a); using two ascenders, with one ascender clipped to the harness, and again with perhaps an aider or foot sling clipped to the other ascender (fig. 15-25b); or using a combination of pulleys, carabiners, and prusik hitches. In addition to the two primary devices used for connecting to the traverse line, always rig a backup, such as a double runner girth-hitched to the harness tie-in point and clipped around the traverse line with a locked carabiner.

5. **The first climber connects to the tensioned traverse rope** and takes the free end of the traverse line with him or her (consider tying in to the end to ensure that it is not dropped). Depending on the terrain,

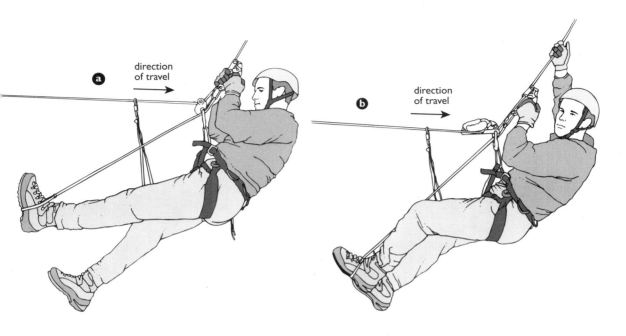

Fig. 15-25. Tyrolean traverse setups: a, using Petzl Micro Traxion and one ascender; b, using two ascenders.

15

span distance, elevation difference, rope stretch, and tension in the traverse line, a short lower-out, rappel, down-jugging, or down-prusiking may be necessary to start the traverse and prevent the climber from careening away from the detached pillar at an uncontrolled speed. Often, the first climber may rappel on the free, nontensioned end of the traverse line to initiate the traverse. Do not attach a rappel device to the tensioned traverse rope, because this device will likely become tensioned and stuck near the midpoint of the traverse. In this case of the Lost Arrow Spire where the destination is higher than the starting point, only a short rappel or lower-out is required before ascending comes into play.

However, if the destination is lower than the starting point, a rappel will likely be required for the entire traverse for all climbers, and ascending equipment would be needed only for the final few feet and could be attached when needed. In this case, climbers attach themselves to the traverse line with a locking carabiner or a pulley and locking carabiner. They rappel on a separate line while suspended from the traverse line. Plan ahead to ensure

that adequate equipment and lines are available to safely perform the traverse.

6. After the first climber traverses from the pinnacle back to a new location on the main wall, **the second climber unfixes the first rope from the pinnacle anchor,** ensuring that the rope is threaded through the anchor; if two ropes are used, the second takes note of the correct rope to pull when the traverse is complete, just as when preparing a double-rope rappel. Then the first climber tightens and fixes the free end of the traverse line in to the new anchor at the new location on the main wall, which retensions the original line and tensions the free end for the first time so that now two tensioned lines cross the span.

7. **The second climber sets up for the traverse using the system of choice** (see steps 4 and 5 above); if two ropes are used, the second selects the strand of traverse rope without a knot so that no knot pass is required on the traverse.

8. Once both climbers are at the new location on the main wall, **they untie the ends of the traverse line** from the main wall anchor and pull the rope, taking care that the ends of the lines do not tangle.

SECONDING

On short sections of aid, the second climber usually follows the same sequence as the leader, except that the second is belayed from above. The second might use aiders for following a short section of aid, clipping these aiders to the protection left by the leader, or the second might just pull on the protection left by the leader and use the rock for counterpressure or stances. The follower's technique depends on how steep and smooth the short section of aid is that is being followed.

Long sections of aid and big walls call for a different strategy. The leader fixes the lead line to the anchor, and the second uses mechanical ascenders to ascend the fixed climbing rope and also cleans the protection left by the leader. If the team is hauling a bag, the second must release the bag for hauling before leaving the lower anchor (see Figure 15-24e). If the bag hangs up along the way, the follower can help to free it.

USING ASCENDERS

Each ascender (left and right) should have a dedicated locking carabiner. Smaller oval or D-shaped carabiners with a regular locking gate (not an auto-locking gate) are usually most convenient. When ascenders are not in use, they reside on the harness or gear sling on their dedicated locking carabiner.

When preparing to follow a pitch, attach the locking carabiner to each aider and daisy chain combination. The ascender is always clipped in to the end of the daisy chain rather than in to one of its loops. Lock the carabiner to ensure that the ascender will stay attached to the daisy chain and aider, primarily to ensure that the attachment to the daisy chain is secure before weighting it. Place the ascender for your dominant hand above the other ascender on the rope (fig. 15-26a).

For most ascending, shorten the overall length of the daisy chain for the upper ascender. The amount that this daisy chain is shortened varies based on the steepness of the pitch and may change many times during an individual pitch. In general, the upper daisy chain should be adjusted so that it draws tight prior to or exactly at full arm extension.

To shorten the daisy chain, first place the ascender at approximately full arm extension. Pull up the daisy chain from the harness and find the loop that touches the locking carabiner attached to the ascender. Use a free carabiner (usually the dedicated oval keylock carabiner belonging to the aider and daisy chain combination) to attach this loop of the daisy chain directly to the locking carabiner. This

method of shortening the daisy chain allows the climber to change the length of the daisy during the pitch without opening the locking carabiner (fig. 15-26b). Experiment with jugging with the daisy chain shortened to different lengths to find what is most comfortable and efficient. It is not necessary to shorten the daisy chain for the non-dominant hand. Another option is to use an adjustable daisy strap.

When jugging, offset your feet in the aider steps: If the left hand is dominant and that ascender is higher, and if the left foot is in the fifth step from the top, the right foot

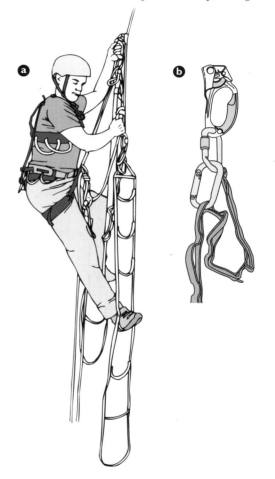

Fig. 15-26. Using ascenders: a, efficient jugging technique, with dominant left hand's ascender higher and right foot higher in its aider's ladder; b, proper method to shorten daisy chain for attaching to ascender.

would typically be in the fourth step from the top. This way, your feet are at roughly the same height, which is an efficient jugging technique.

When you move the ascenders up, the upper ascender will move easily while you stand with your weight on the lower ascender and aider, but the lower ascender may be more difficult to advance because there is no weight below that ascender. Resist the temptation to hold or pull down on the rope below the lower ascender in order to be able to move it up. Although this works, it is an inefficient and inadequate technique for covering long distances. Instead, practice "thumbing"—using your thumb to slightly open the cam on the lower ascender so that it will move upward. Most ascenders will open with thumbing without risk of opening fully and detaching from the fixed line. Thumbing is very efficient, and it may be necessary to do it on every stroke.

Ascending Steep Terrain

When ascending very steep terrain, rather than fully weighting the aiders during the entire ascending process, the climber should drastically shorten the upper daisy chain, probably to about the third loop from the harness, and rest body weight directly on the upper ascender after moving it up. In this sequence, move up the upper ascender and then rest with all your weight by hanging in the harness from the ascender. Move up the lower ascender, stand up, and push up the upper ascender a few feet and hang again. Other variations of this technique exist, so climbers should experiment to find out what works best for them.

Backing Up Ascenders

As a rule, do not untie from the end of the climbing rope while ascending. Remaining tied in serves as a backup in case both ascenders fail. To further decrease the likelihood of a long fall, periodically "tie in short," using the climbing rope as the backup (as discussed below), or otherwise provide a backup on the rope below the ascenders. Tying in short or providing a backup below the ascenders is an easy precaution that has saved lives. Conversely, mistakes in attaching and backing up ascenders have led to many deaths.

As the second ascends, an ever-lengthening loop of climbing rope forms below the lower ascender, making for a long fall if the ascenders fail. A backup shortens this potential fall. One way to achieve this backup is to attach the Grigri directly below the ascenders. This not only provides a backup but also allows the Grigri to be employed in other simple and extremely efficient techniques for following pitches and cleaning gear (for example, the Grigri lower-out method, described later in this chapter).

To use the climbing rope as the backup, stop periodically and tie any knot, such as an overhand on a bight, just below the ascenders, and clip the loop in to your harness with a locking carabiner. This "ties you in short" to the climbing rope. Repeat this procedure as often as necessary, clipping new knots to the same one locking carabiner, to shorten the fall potential. Keep in mind that the ascenders are most likely to come off on a traverse and less likely to come off on simple jugging up a straight line. Most climbers using this method keep all the loops clipped in to their harness until they reach the anchor.

Often while jugging, the climber may choose to remove the upper ascender from the rope and place it above a piece of protection that is under tension as the climber ascends. It is prudent to tie in short or make sure to use a backup method before removing the upper ascender from the rope.

Other Precautions While Ascending

Other precautions should be taken while ascending. First, carry a spare prusik sling just in case an ascender fails or is dropped. A Grigri is a much more effective and efficient lower ascender than a prusik, so this is the first backup to an ascender. And, as in all climbing, beware of sharp edges. Jugging places the rope under tension, and sharp edges can cut it. Ascend as smoothly as possible to minimize any sawing action on the rope running over an edge.

ROPE MANAGEMENT

Rope management while following is critical, especially when high winds or "rope-eating" cracks may foul or snag the rope. Popular methods of managing the rope include clipping a rope bag to some part of the harness, such as a leg loop, and stuffing the rope hanging below the ascenders into the rope bag while the climber is ascending; clipping in backup loops (see "Backing Up Ascenders" above); or making coils of the rope and clipping them to the harness. Leaving the rope hanging for the entire pitch is not recommended, but it can work when the pitch is overhanging or there is otherwise little risk of the rope hanging up. When the rope is hanging, eventually this weight makes moving the lower ascender easier as the climber ascends, and thumbing is not required (see "Using Ascenders").

CLEANING

Efficiency in aid climbing is directly linked to organization. While ascending and cleaning a pitch, the follower should take the extra time to rerack the equipment for

15

TIPS FOR CLEANING PINS

- **First, tap the pin lightly** to get an idea of how much it moves initially. While pins may need to be hit many times to remove them, attaching a carabiner to the pin too early makes it harder to hit and slows the cleaning. For all pins except sawed-off angles, it should be possible to move the pin before the sling is attached. But be careful! If the pin flies out with no sling attached, the pin will probably be lost forever.

- **Attach either a carabiner with a sling or the funkness device** once the pin is loosened—or, for sawed-off angles, before hitting at all. Clip one end to the pin and one end to yourself, possibly to the aider or daisy chain. Continue to hit the pin back and forth until it comes out. Try not to hit the funkness carabiner, because it can break. Use one hand to hold the carabiner to the side while you make blows. It might be a good idea to use the pick side of the hammer when the funkness is attached. For sawed-off angles, err on the side of putting the sling on early. They do not visibly move much, and it is hard to know when they will come out.

- **Try clipping the free end of the funkness to the hammer** if the pin does not come out with back-and-forth hits. Then "funk" on the pin by making a big jerk out and up with the hammer (see Figure 15-7) and then another separate "funk" with a jerk out and down. "Funk" the pin multiple times, as needed, up and down to loosen it. Sometimes jerking straight out away from the rock is helpful, especially with angles. Protect your face when using the funkness.

leading, including reracking single slings into quickdraws. This makes belay transitions go faster. Keep specialized cleaning gear handy, including the nut tool and funkness.

When cleaning a pin, first hit it back and forth or up and down, along the axis of the crack. For pins placed in vertical cracks, try to favor the upward hits, which can create future nut placements. (See the "Tips for Cleaning Pins" sidebar.)

SECONDING TRAVERSES AND OVERHANGS

Seconding traverses when aid climbing can be both strenuous and technical. Some of the most common and useful methods are described below. These basic methods can often be applied to overhangs as well.

Re-aiding

When traversing horizontally, it may be more efficient to aid climb across the traverse, using aiders, as if leading (called re-aiding). Aiding in this fashion, the second can self-belay by using a Grigri as an attachment point to the rope to keep the rope tight from above or by attaching ascenders to the harness with slings and sliding the ascenders along the climbing rope. Make sure to back yourself up to the lead rope or tie in short from time to time, while of course always staying tied in to the end of the rope.

Seconding Short and/or Diagonal Traverses

The second can cross short traverses and sections of pitches that are more diagonal than horizontal by using normal jugging techniques. Two main techniques can be used to second a short diagonal traverse with normal jugging techniques, rather than re-aiding as described above:

Grigri lower-out method. The first technique is very easy and requires a Grigri. Jug up to the piece you plan to pass, moving both ascenders as close to the piece as possible (fig. 15-27a). Then bring the Grigri up under the lower ascender and rest all weight onto the Grigri (fig. 15-27b). Remove the top ascender and place it above the piece, and then repeat with the lower ascender (fig. 15-27c). Then open the handle of the Grigri and feed out rope, lowering yourself onto the ascenders and daisy chains (fig. 15-27d). Reestablish your weight in the aiders and reach back to clean the piece (fig. 15-27e).

Alternate method without a Grigri. Although the alternate method is a little trickier, it works if the climber does not have a Grigri. When approaching a piece of protection, leave the lower ascender some distance below the piece, about an arm's length or so, depending on the steepness of the terrain and the distance to and position of the next piece. With your weight on the lower ascender, remove the upper ascender and attach it as far as possible above the currently weighted piece. Then transfer your weight to the upper ascender; this will pull the lower ascender up toward the piece. If you have allowed enough space, the lower ascender will not jam into the carabiner of the piece, and it will be possible to remove the piece and move up the lower ascender.

Seconding Longer and/or Horizontal Traverses

The best way to follow longer traverses, tension traverses, and horizontal traverses is often to do a "lower-out," using the methods described below. If the leader has left some kind of piece that is suitable to lower off of and then cleans all of the traversing pieces, the second can lower from

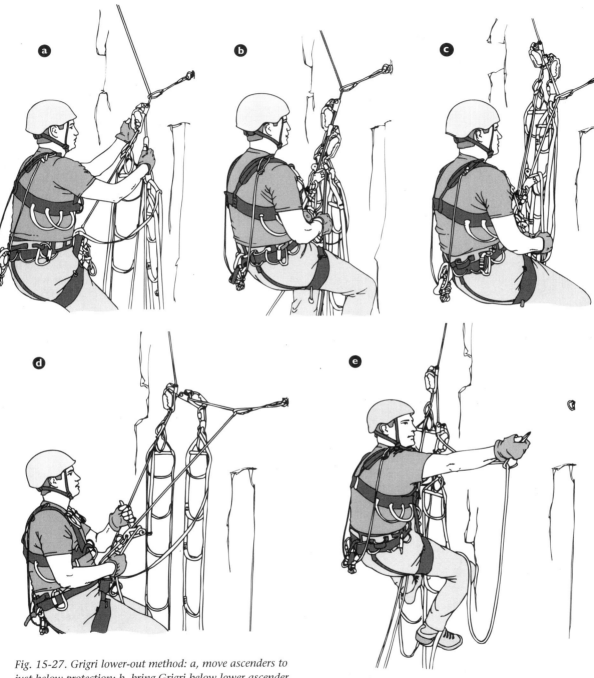

15

Fig. 15-27. Grigri lower-out method: a, move ascenders to just below protection; b, bring Grigri below lower ascender and transfer weight to it; c, remove ascenders—upper first, then lower—and reinstall above protection; d, lower with Grigri until weight is transferred to ascenders in new plumb line; e, clean the piece.

the beginning of the traverse to the next piece left by the leader. This method is often faster than other methods of following a traverse, but whether or not to use this method is largely up to the leader, who has to decide whether a piece of gear can be left fixed while he or she is protecting the pitch.

SECONDING TENSION TRAVERSES AND PENDULUM SWINGS

The best method for seconding a long, mostly horizontal span between gear, including spans resulting from the leader performing a tension traverse or a pendulum swing, depends on the distance to be traveled and the ropes available. As described in "Tension Traverses and Pendulum Swings" earlier in this chapter, the lower-off point is usually fixed and is often a carabiner, a rappel ring, or a piece (or pieces) of webbing. If the leader climbs a long distance without leaving gear, expecting the second to lower out to reach the new plumb line, the leader should ensure that there is adequate fixed gear left for the second to lower out from. The term *lower-out* is used to describe a variety of methods of lowering into a new plumb line, including the two techniques discussed below for following shorter and longer distances.

Short Pendulum Swings and Tension Traverses ("Stay Tied In" Method)

One clever and useful method of accomplishing a shorter lower-out is shown in Figure 15-28. The follower stays tied in to the climbing rope during the entire sequence, making this a safe and preferable method. This method requires the available rope to be four times as long as the distance to be traveled.

1. **Jug up to the fixed point.** If possible, fifi in to something without blocking the opening of the lower-out point (fig. 15-28a). Often, the leader will place protection near but separate from the lower-out point itself. Or, if using a Grigri as a backup, hold your weight on the Grigri.
2. **Clip a carabiner to the belay loop on your harness.** Then find the end of the rope that is tied in to the harness. Take this rope out to about arm's length from the harness tie-in knot and make a bend in it. Push this bight of rope through the lower-out point, and then bring the bight back toward the harness (fig. 15-28b).
3. **Clip the bight in to the carabiner attached to the belay loop.** Pulling on the free end that comes out of the lower-out point, cinch yourself up and hold

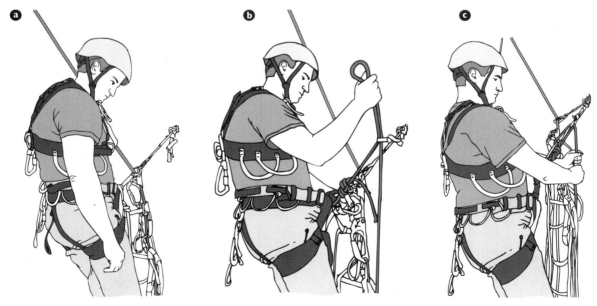

Fig. 15-28. Lower-out method for seconding short pendulum or traverse: a, jug until ascenders are just below protection at lower-out point, then fifi to protection (here, a quickdraw); b, clip a carabiner to harness belay loop, then pull a bight of rope through lower-out point; c, clip bight to harness belay loop and transfer weight to rope; (continued on facing page)

your weight on the climbing rope through the lower-out point (fig. 15-28c). Retrieve all of the team gear before lowering out. Two additional optional steps are (1) clipping a carabiner as a backup around the rope and through the top hole of either (or both) ascender(s), to ensure that the ascender stays on the rope (see Figure 15-29), and (2) shortening the daisy chain on the upper ascender to reduce the overall lower-out distance.

4. **To lower out, let the rope feed through your hand** (fig. 15-28d). At first, there will be considerable friction, but be diligent as you lower yourself to avoid dropping the rope and lowering too fast. As your weight comes onto the ascenders in the new plumb line, continue to feed rope through the lower-out system.

5. **Unclip the bight of rope from the carabiner on the harness belay loop** once you have all your weight on the ascenders in the new plumb line. Pull the ends of the rope so that the bight of rope that was clipped to the harness gets pulled through the lower-out point (fig. 15-28e). The rope has now been freed.

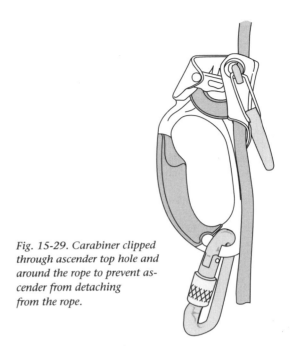

Fig. 15-29. Carabiner clipped through ascender top hole and around the rope to prevent ascender from detaching from the rope.

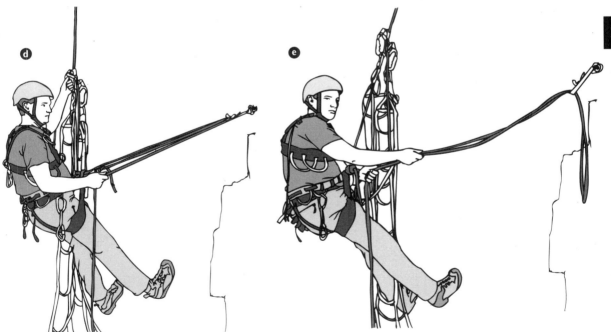

Fig. 15-28. (continued from facing page) d, feed the rope through the harness carabiner until ascenders are weighted; e, unclip the bight of rope from harness and pull it through the lower-out point.

Sometimes distances can be seconded without actually lowering out, especially when the terrain is not steep. The follower moves up to the piece and finds a stance or a nearby crack or feature to hold on to, which takes the climber's weight off of the piece to be cleaned. Then the follower removes the piece and, with anticipation of a swing, lets go without lowering out, swinging into the new plumb line while hanging from the ascenders and daisy chains. When used with good judgment, this technique, sometimes called the "Rudy," can be a safe and fast way of following a short, low-angle pendulum swing.

Long Pendulum Swings and Tension Traverses ("Untie" Method)

The lower-out method discussed above requires the available rope to be four times as long as the distance the follower must span, so it works well for seconding short pendulum swings and tension traverses. For longer lower-outs, or when this length of rope is not available to the follower, a different method that involves untying from the climbing rope must be used. Since it is preferable to stay tied in to the climbing rope, this technique is used only when the above technique suggested for shorter distances is not possible. For this alternative method, the available rope must be twice as long as the distance the follower needs to span.

1. After the leader indicates that the lead line is fixed, the follower prepares to untie from the climbing rope. Before untying, the follower makes sure their harness is attached to the anchor with at least two points of protection, such as the daisy chains. Pull up a bight of rope and tie in short to the harness. Check and double-check the attachment points, then untie from the lead line (fig. 15-30a).

2. Thread the end of the lead line through the lower-out point. For large lower-outs on established routes, the lower-out point should be fixed and is likely to be a sturdy metal rappel ring. Feed the entire length of the rope through the ring (fig. 15-30b).

Fig. 15-30. Seconding a long pendulum: a, tie in short, attach daisy chains to two points of protection, then untie from the rope; b, feed the free end of the rope through the lower-out point (here, a metal rappel ring on fixed protection); c, rig rappel device, then attach both ascenders to rope; (continued on facing page)

3. Put yourself on rappel on the tail of the rope, in the manner of a single-rope rappel. Clip both of the ascenders to the lead line, above the rappel setup (fig. 15-30c), and shorten the daisy chains (optional). It is possible to make the lower-out much shorter by pushing the ascenders up the rope as high as possible. If desired, use a Grigri below the ascenders on the end of the rope that goes to the leader, for another backup. Consider clipping a carabiner through the hole of the ascender and around the rope, for one or both ascenders (fig. 15-29).

4. Rappel the pendulum (fig. 15-30d).

5. Once all weight is on the ascenders in the new plumb line, remove the rappel device and pull the end of the rope through the lower-out point (fig. 15-30e). The rope has now been freed. Tie back in to the end of the rope before continuing to follow the pitch.

CHANGING LEADS

Unorganized belay stations can become a rat's nest of tangled ropes, twisted slings, and jumbled hardware. Basic organization keeps the belay station manageable and the team functioning efficiently. The following methods improve organization of the belay station:

- **Use ropes of a different color** when possible, to easily differentiate them.
- **Always stack the haul line** while hauling the bag, using rest intervals to stack the haul line in a rope bag or on a sling. After hauling, organize what remains of the rack and put it all on one side of your body or on a sling on the anchor so that the second can rerack for the next pitch without the leader's help, freeing the leader for other chores after the second arrives.
- **Plan where the second will come up,** and have a locking carabiner ready to clip the second in to the anchor, or ask the second for one as soon as he or she arrives. This allows the second to safely and quickly anchor in.

Fig. 15-30. (continued from facing page) d, rappel the pendulum; e, remove rappel device, pull rope through the lower-out point and tie back into the rope.

- **Focus on the needs of the new leader** when the second arrives. Get the weight of the lead rope off of the second as soon as possible. While the second reracks, pull up the lead line and restack it if necessary. Put the new leader on belay immediately, even if that climber is not ready to lead. Find out what the new leader needs in order to leave, and facilitate that. Accept from the new leader any gear not wanted for the next pitch, and offer food or water.

- **For a smooth belay transition,** all team members should at all times be doing some chore to advance the team, until the leader starts out on the next pitch. If you are the next belayer, try not to eat, drink, adjust your clothing, or take care of yourself when the new leader is still at the belay. These needs should be taken care of after you finish hauling and before the follower arrives, or while the new leader heads out on the next pitch. Watch the new leader attentively until he or she places protection on the new pitch. Then consider your needs while belaying the leader farther up the pitch.

BIG WALL MULTIDAY TECHNIQUES

For some climbers, only the reward of a big Grade VI wall could entice them to pick up ascenders and aiders and undertake the process of aid climbing. Big wall climbing is sometimes referred to as vertical backpacking, because the big wall climber hauls heavy bags with water, food, and camping supplies and typically covers ground very slowly, compared with free climbing. Climbing big walls is hard work, with endless chores of rope stacking, bag hauling, and ascending. Efficiency, organization, and proper conditioning are critical to success.

Big walls also call for a high degree of mental composure. Inexperienced wall climbers easily find themselves the victim of heightened fears brought on by prolonged and severe exposure. Climbers who are new to the game can perhaps soothe their fears by realizing that techniques for dealing with major walls are much the same as those needed for smaller climbs. Concentrate on the problem at hand, and work away at the objective one move at a time.

Guidebooks and other climbers are helpful sources of information in preparing for a big wall. Beware, however, of overdependence on climbing route topos and equipment lists. Routes do change over time, especially if pins are used regularly.

Solid, efficient aid technique is a prerequisite for completing a major wall within the time constraints dictated by reasonable food and water supplies. For success on big walls, develop competence in hoisting heavy haul bags up a route and in living comfortably in the vertical world for days at a time. Amazing journeys to seldom-visited places amid a sweeping sea of granite await those who accept this adventure.

Note: The anchor setup and hauling diagrams in this chapter assume anchors that include one or more bolts properly installed in good rock, which is the situation most likely encountered on well-traveled aid routes. In the event that climbers must construct their own anchors, they should carefully evaluate the strength of each piece of protection used in the anchor and consider fixing the lead line or attaching the haul device to the power point of the anchor rather than directly to one point of protection.

HAULING

The leader anchors in and fixes the climbing rope for the second, then begins hauling, using one or more of the techniques described below. Regardless of which methods the team uses, the climbers should always connect themselves to the anchor with the climbing rope.

1. **Load the hauling device with the haul line.** Tie an overhand knot on a bight in the end of the haul line and attach this to the locking carabiner on the hauling device. Clip this hauling device to the haul anchor. Prepare a sling or rope bag to stack the haul line into while hauling (fig. 15-31a). Pull up all the slack in the haul line, through the device, until the line comes tight. Your follower should then call out "That's the bag."

   If not using a hauling device, set up a haul system with a pulley and one ascender (see Figure 15-13d). Run the haul line through a regular pulley and clip the end of the haul line to the locking carabiner on this pulley. Clip this pulley to the haul anchor. Attach an upside-down ascender to the haul line on the haul-bag side of the pulley. Clip the upside-down ascender in to the anchor, near the pulley. It may be helpful to use a short sling, such as a full-strength tie-off loop, to connect the ascender to the pulley's locking carabiner so that it is positioned directly below the pulley on the anchor system. Consider using two slings for redundancy.

2. **Connect one ascender to the belay loop on the harness and lock the carabiner.** Attach this ascender to the haul line on the slack side of the rope coming out of the hauling device or pulley. Do a small amount of hauling, just a few inches at a time, as

described in step 3 below, to unweight the bags off of the lower anchor (fig. 15-31b). Then the follower can free the haul bag from the anchor and call out, "Bags are free, haul away."

3. **Begin the regular hauling process.** Push back from the wall using legs and palms to raise the haul bag (fig. 15-31c). As the bag comes up, the climber's body lowers until the rope between harness and anchor tightens. Then stop, stand up (maybe in the aiders), move the ascender back up the rope toward the hauling device, and reset. Repeat. For heavy bags, it may be necessary to also pull up with one hand on the weighted haul line while pushing back with the legs. When you stop hauling, the cam in the hauling device or upside-down ascender acts as a brake to prevent the haul bag from slipping backward. Slack is needed in the climbing rope between yourself and the anchor to allow hauling movement—usually a few feet.

You can also haul by allowing greater slack of 6 to 8 feet (2 to 3 meters) between the tie-in knot and attachment point to the anchor. Then walk down the wall 6 to 8 feet until the anchor rope tightens. Climb back to your original position by jugging, possibly with one aider and daisy chain on an ascender and with one Grigri. Repeat the process. This method works best with lighter bags.

Counterweight hauling. A counterweight method can be used if two people are needed to lift a very heavy bag. The leader can stay at the anchor station and haul the bag normally, while the follower can attach his or her ascenders on the pulling side of the haul rope, about 6 to 8 feet (2 to 3 meters) below the leader. As the leader hauls, the follower hangs on the haul line to provide counterweight and walks down the wall while the leader hauls. The follower must use a longer tie-in to the anchor, about 12 to 16 feet (4 to 6 meters). To prevent the follower's tie-in to the anchor from becoming tight, the follower must jug periodically.

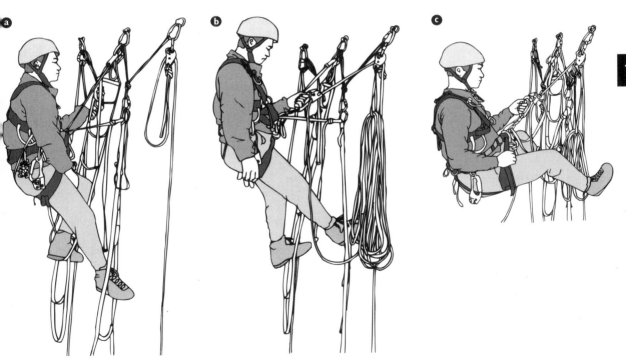

Fig. 15-31. Hauling: a, install haul rope in hauling device, then pull up and stack rope until rope is taut; b, use one ascender (clipped to harness belay loop) to haul rope until haul bag is lifted from lower anchor; c, haul away after the second releases the haul bag from the lower anchor.

Docking the bag. Once the leader has completed the haul, the haul bag must be "docked" in order to attach it to the wall and free the haul line for the next pitch. First, always be sure to stop hauling before the knot in the haul line that attaches the haul rope to the top of the haul bag reaches the haul device's pulley. This is critical—if the knot gets too close, it will be sucked into the hauling device, jamming it. Then select a spot in the anchor to dock the bag, and attach a carabiner to this location. Pull the docking cord up from the top of the haul bag and tie the cord to the carabiner as close to the haul bag as possible, using a load-releasing hitch such as a munter-mule (see Figure 9-21 in Chapter 9, Basic Safety System). Back up the hitch with another knot in the docking cord (fig. 15-32a).

Then do a minihaul on the hauling system, raising the bag just an inch or so, to allow the cam of the hauling device or the upside-down ascender to be disengaged. Unlock the hauling device or upside-down ascender, then carefully lower the bag, using your weight and the ascender clipped to the harness belay loop, so that the bag's weight rests on the docking cord (fig. 15-32b).

It may be necessary to reengage the cam on the hauling device or upside-down ascender and repeat this minihaul process one or more additional times before the bag's weight completely rests on the docking cord, allowing the leader to fully disengage the hauling device or upside-down ascender from the haul line and remove it. With the bag free from the hauling system, also tie the haul line from the bag in to the anchor with a figure eight on a bight as a backup (fig. 15-32c) in case the docking cord should fail.

Dock the bag as high as possible on the anchor, so that less bag height is lost during the dock and so the bag can be accessed during the belay. If there is time, the leader can restack the haul line so the free end of the haul line is stacked on top. Or, more efficiently, just feed the haul line as it is while the leader is aiding the next pitch.

FIXING PITCHES

On long aid climbs, climbers often "*fix*" pitches: put up ropes and leave them in place so they can be climbed quickly with mechanical ascenders later to reach the previous high point. Climbers frequently fix one or two pitches above the ground or beyond the bivouac site, and at the high point they leave gear not needed for the bivouac. The lower end of each fixed rope is attached to the anchor of the previous pitch.

When fixing pitches, take care to protect the rope from sharp edges or abrupt contours by using duct tape or other material to cover the sharp feature. Intermediate anchor points, if available, should be used; they reduce rope stretch, contour the rope toward the direction of travel, and are useful in avoiding abrasion points. Leave enough slack in the rope when fixing it to the lower anchor to allow for reversal of rope stretch after rappelling, but not so much that loops of rope can blow around when unattended. Make a tidy coil of any rope left on the ground.

Never ascend someone else's fixed rope without knowledge of its rigging and permission of the rope's owner. Close calls have occurred in ascending unknown "fixed ropes" not actually rigged for ascending.

RETREATING

Before a major aid climb, plan retreat lines in case of bad weather, an accident, or another emergency. Locate other easily reached routes that offer a speedier descent or fixed retreat lines.

If there is no retreat route, consider carrying a bolt kit for emergencies, to allow placement of rappel anchors. Also, as each pitch is climbed, consider how to descend it. On major walls, rescues may be slow and difficult, if they are possible at all. It may be up to the climbing team to get back down in an emergency. Rappelling the route for retreat with haul bags can be difficult, so practice this skill.

LIVING IN THE VERTICAL WORLD

Living for days on a vertical wall of rock brings some intriguing problems. Once gear is dropped, for instance, it is gone for good. All vital items must have clip-in loops and should be clipped in when not in use or not in the haul bag. Handoffs of gear between partners must be done with care, and "Got it" is a phrase used frequently so that both partners are sure when gear is secure during a handoff. Consider bringing duplicates of key items, such as knives for opening canned food, communication devices, an extra aider or two for the team, et cetera.

Learn about the gear so that it can be used confidently. Get acquainted with unfamiliar items, such as portaledges or hammocks, beforehand, preferably by testing them out in a hanging environment.

Big wall climbers must carry all their water with them. Each climber generally needs a minimum of 1 gallon (almost 4 liters) per day. For hot weather, especially if the route gets a lot of sun, carry even more. Often, climbers choose to bring food, such as canned food, with high water content; since water must be hauled anyway, the weight of this food is not a consideration. Canned soups, stews, fish, and fruit are favorite big wall fare. Bringing food that requires water to prepare demands accurate planning, since running out of water is bad, but running out of water when it is needed in order to eat is even worse. Some climbers boil water on the wall, especially those who enjoy daily hot drinks. Stoves and cooking accessories must be usable in a hanging environment, and they add weight to the haul bag.

Waste disposal poses another challenge. Do not toss garbage down the wall. Haul it up and off the climb. Keep all bivouac sites clean and sanitary, with no sign of your passing. Use a waste container to pack out human waste. Whenever feasible, pack out garbage left behind by others, to leave the wall in better condition than you found it.

Generally, synthetic sleeping bags and clothing are the best choices for a big wall climb because they retain their insulating properties when wet. Inflatable pads are more compact and, thus, easier to pack in the haul bag, and they are warmer to sleep on in the portaledge. Just as in camping on the ground, consider backing up an inflatable pad with a closed-cell foam pad, in case the inflatable pad fails. Some climbers use foam pads to help pad the haul bag, but

on the first days of a climb these are all but impossible to remove from the haul bag and then repack. The best plan is to always bring a bivy sack, no matter the weather forecast. Your sleeping bag can be stored in its bivy sack, and neither needs to be stuffed into stuff sacks—they provide great padding in the haul bag.

Consider that the air temperature, both day and night, may cool significantly during the ascent of a big wall, so bring extra clothing. Some clothing can be shared, such as a large insulated belay jacket (see Chapter 2, Clothing and Equipment). When selecting layers, consider the chore of hauling and try to wear clothing that will protect the skin from being rubbed by the harness.

Organization on the wall goes beyond climbing gear to include the items in the haul bag. Knowing the location of every item and having it accessible when needed will speed the climb and ensure that climbers can address their needs and any emergencies in a timely manner. Stuff sacks, often of different colors and sizes for identification, help greatly with organization inside the haul bag. Break up

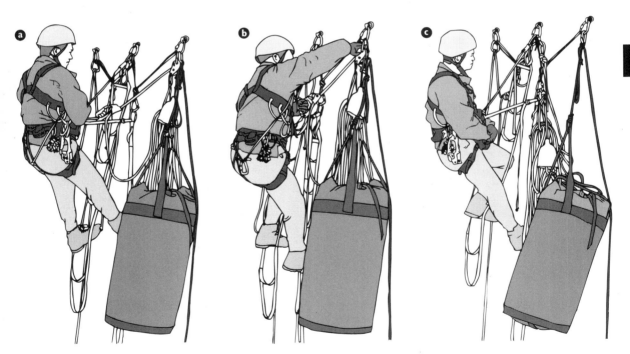

Fig. 15-32. Docking the haul bag: a, attach the haul bag's docking cord to the anchor with a munter-mule and an overhand backup; b, haul enough to release the hauling device and lower the haul bag onto its docking cord; c, remove the rope from the hauling device and back up the docking cord by tying a figure eight on a bight into the haul rope.

critical items, such as food for a long wall, into multiple bags to reduce the impact on the team if a bag is dropped. Use bags strong enough to stand up to wear and tear on the wall, and consider using bags with sewn-on full-strength webbing for clipping in to the wall. It is smart to know where storm gear, the first-aid kit, and human waste kits are located and to pack these items where they can be accessed quickly.

DESCENDING

After completing a major wall, climbers need to get their gear back down. Usually, they must hike or rappel off of the route with all their gear packed in haul bags. Before packing the haul bag, consider whether ropes need to be left accessible for rappelling; if rappelling, set aside all personal gear needed on the rappels before packing the bags.

Haul bags can be tossed off of walls and packed in such a way that all gear arrives intact, but this technique requires special training from an experienced tosser, as well as an improvised parachute for the haul bag. There are no guarantees that the bags will land where intended, and in some places this practice is illegal. Furthermore, many climbers have discovered that their gear has been stolen by the time they get back down. The safest, least stressful bet is to do the hard work of humping out all the gear.

Before packing the haul bag, make sure that the backpack harness is attached, or it will be necessary to unload the bag and pack it again to get the harness system in place. Pack haul bags with the heaviest items on the bottom for the hike out. Attempt to fill all the small spaces in the bag while packing it from the bottom up so that the bag is packed compactly. Sleeping bags, bivy sacks, and clothing make good space fillers. Consider loading climbing gear into the haul bag loose, unclipping carabiners from protection and unclipping all gear from gear slings, to allow the bag to be packed much more compactly. A compact, tightly packed haul bag can be safely carried off a difficult descent much easier than a tall, floppy, top-heavy haul bag. If the team has to carry multiple bags, consider packing the smaller bag(s) with the heavier items and making any larger haul bags a little lighter to compensate for carrying a tall, bulky load.

As is true for all long climbs, the hike out can be a dangerous time, because the climbers are exhausted from the effort expended on the climb. Take your time, watch your step, and double-check your systems when rappelling or performing other technical maneuvers.

THE SPIRIT OF AID CLIMBING

Aid climbing offers high adventure in exchange for perseverance and hard work. The pioneers of rock climbing developed aid climbing to open up the vertical world and its fabulous summits, including legendary walls such as El Capitan and Half Dome in Yosemite National Park, California. In following the path of aid climbing's pioneers, you will reach locations visited by relatively few climbers and can imagine the great vision and dedication required by the first ascensionists to establish these routes.

Aid routes require technical skill in placing gear and boldness to climb thin cracks and steep walls while relying on the proper use of equipment. Keep aid climbing adventurous by resisting the temptation to alter established routes by adding bolts, drilling holes of any kind, nailing pitons, and even leaving behind excess fixed gear. Clean up routes when climbing them by removing old and tired fixed slings, and in general try to leave the route in better condition than you found it. Always practice Leave No Trace ethics on the wall. The rewards of all alpine trips are great, but most likely, your memories of long, multiday wall routes will stand out in a lifetime of climbing as unique and special experiences.

PART IV

SNOW, ICE, AND ALPINE CLIMBING

CHAPTER 16

SNOW TRAVEL AND CLIMBING

Climbing in snow is fundamental to mountaineering. Snow is magical stuff, cloaking the landscape in a sparkling mantle. Gently falling snowflakes can be a balm to the human spirit, an aesthetic delight. But technically, snow is rather dryly defined as "a consolidated mass of water crystals." It is the degree of consolidation that is significant to the climber.

Snow falls in a variety of forms ranging from tiny crystals to coarse pellets. Initially the snowpack can consist of up to 90 percent air by volume. Once the snow is on the ground, a cyclic process of melting and freezing begins. Even though a snow climber might be literally walking on air, climbing on snow is not to be taken lightly. Snow becomes increasingly dense as the air is displaced, and ultimately, it will become a glacier. The density of glacial ice can be the same as that of ice formed directly from water. See Chapter 27, The Cycle of Snow, for more about snow.

Snow displays a broad spectrum of physical characteristics, and the distinction between hard snow and ice is rather arbitrary. Snow climbing is described in this chapter, whereas ice climbing techniques are discussed in Chapters 19, Alpine Ice Climbing, and 20, Waterfall Ice and Mixed Climbing, but note that the techniques overlap with no distinct separation.

Climbers travel in a world that is affected by snow on two very different scales. On a rather grand scale, snow—in the form of glaciers—sculpts the terrain. On a more human scale, snow often is the climbers' landscape, largely determining how and where they can travel.

Traveling on snow is trickier than hiking a trail or climbing a rock wall. A rock face is essentially unchanging, whereas the snowpack undergoes rapid changes. Depending on the degree of consolidation, snow can present a widely variable surface: seemingly insubstantial and bottomless unconsolidated powder, a consistently firm and resilient snow surface, or rock-hard alpine ice. A snowpack that appears to be firm can under certain conditions suddenly collapse and flow (avalanche) and then quickly set up as hard as concrete. Safe snow travel requires judgment based on experience.

During a single season, a snowfield may start as a dusting of snow over a brushy slope, progress to a bowlful of powder ready to avalanche, then change to a solid surface offering firm footing, and finally revert back to scattered snow patches. In the course of a day, snow can change from a firm surface in the morning to slush in the afternoon.

Snow can facilitate travel, making climbs easier by providing a pathway over brush and other obstacles on the approach hike and reducing the danger of loose rock on the ascent. But snow conditions also affect decisions on routefinding and climbing technique. Should the climbing party hike up the more easily traversed, snow-covered valley slopes or on the ridge crest away from avalanche hazard? Should climbers go for easy step-kicking up the sunny slope or the more labor-intensive climb on the firmer, more stable snow of the shaded hillside? Is it safer to travel roped or unroped? The changeable nature of snow requires climbers to be flexible in choosing their mode of travel and to be ready to use snowshoes, skis, or crampons.

EQUIPMENT

Ice axes and crampons are at the top of the list of basic snow climbing equipment. Snowshoes, skis, ski poles, and shovels are other important snow travel aids. Climbers must also sometimes construct anchors in snow (snow protection equipment is discussed in "Snow Anchors" later in this chapter).

ICE AXE

The ice axe, or *piolet*, and skill in its use allow climbers to venture onto all forms of snow and ice, enjoying a greater variety of mountain terrain during all seasons of the year. Selecting an ice axe means choosing between features designed for specific uses. A long axe is suitable for cross-country travel and scrambling, in which it is used as a cane and to provide security in low-angle climbing. However, on steeper slopes, a shorter axe is better. Axes designed for ice climbing (typically called ice tools) have even shorter shafts and specialized features including the shape of pick and adze and the placement of teeth. (Ice tools are discussed in Chapter 19, Alpine Ice Climbing.)

Weight is another consideration. The adage "light is right" should not be taken too far. Be sure to select an axe that is designed for the intended use. Some very light axes are meant for only light use—that is, ski mountaineering or trekking. Ice axes that meet the European Committee on Standardization (CEN) standards for general mountaineering (see Chapter 9, Basic Safety System) are designated by a "B," generally tamped on the ice axe. At the other extreme, technical ice axes tend to be heavier (and more expensive) than general mountaineering axes. Tools that meet the CEN standards for technical mountaineering are designated by a "T." Ice axes designated with a "T" rating meet higher strength requirements than "B"-rated axes.

Parts of the Ice Axe

The main parts of an ice axe include: the head, pick, adze, shaft, and spike.

Head. The head of an ice axe—the pick and the adze (fig. 16-1)—is typically made of steel alloy or aluminum. The hole in the axe head, the carabiner hole, is used by most climbers to attach the ice-axe leash.

Pick. The pick is curved or drooped (fig. 16-2a), a design that provides better hooking action in snow or ice, enabling the axe to dig in when climbers are seeking purchase or trying to stop themselves (self-arrest) after a fall. A moderate hooking angle of 65 to 70 degrees relative to the shaft is typical of general mountaineering axes (fig. 16-2b). A sharper angle of 55 to 60 degrees is better for technical

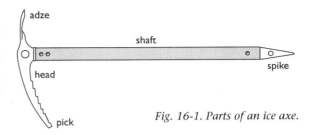

Fig. 16-1. Parts of an ice axe.

ice climbing (fig. 16-2c); the more acutely angled pick holds better in ice and snow and it coincides with the arc of the tool head as it is swung.

The pick teeth provide grip in ice and hard snow. Ice axes designed for general mountaineering typically have aggressive teeth only at the end of the pick, as shown in Figure 16-2a and b. Picks of ice axes and tools designed for technical climbing typically have aggressive teeth along the entire length, as shown in Figure 16-2c.

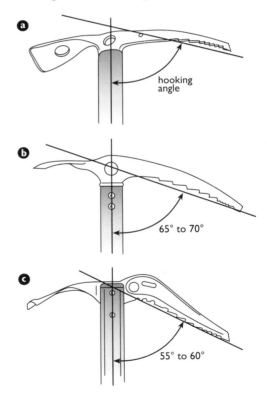

Fig. 16-2. Ice-axe pick shapes and teeth patterns: a and b, for general mountaineering; c, for technical ice climbing.

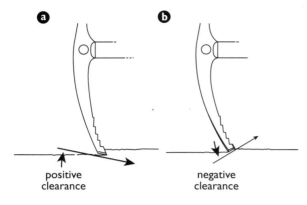

Fig. 16-3. Ice-axe clearance: a, positive; b, negative.

The end of the pick may have clearance that is termed positive (fig. 16-3a), neutral, or negative (fig. 16-3b). The clearance is determined by comparing the angle of the pick tip relative to the axis of the shaft; positive clearance means the pick tip's angle is greater than 90 degrees relative to the shaft, and negative clearance means the pick tip's angle is less than 90 degrees relative to the shaft. In theory, the degree of clearance affects how the axe performs in self-arrest. A pick with positive clearance should penetrate more readily; a pick with negative clearance would tend to skate across and lose purchase on ice or hard snow. However, the clearance actually makes little difference: self-arrest is almost impossible on ice, and in softer snow the pick will dig in regardless of what type of clearance it has. Positive clearance is important for technical use in ice climbing. (Ice tools are discussed in Chapter 19, Alpine Ice Climbing.)

Adze. The adze is used mainly to cut steps in hard snow or ice. The flat top of the adze also provides a firm, comfortable platform for a hand when the climber is using the self-belay grasp (see "Basic Techniques of Snow Climbing" later in this chapter). Most adzes for general mountaineering are relatively flat and straight-edged with sharp corners (see Figure 16-2a). This is the best all-around design for cutting steps.

Shaft. Ice-axe shafts (see Figure 16-1) are made of aluminum or a composite material such as fiberglass, Kevlar, or carbon fiber—or a combination of these. A typical ice-axe shaft for general mountaineering is straight. Ice axes with a shaped shaft are designed for more technical use such as swinging the ice axe for ice climbing.

Some shafts are covered at least partly by a rubber material, which gives climbers a better grip and, hence, better control of the axe, and it also dampens vibrations and increases a climber's control in planting the pick. If the axe shaft lacks a rubber grip, wrap the shaft with athletic grip tape (for example, bicycle handlebar tape) or wear gloves with leather or rubberized palms. However, the friction of any shaft covering may impede the axe from readily penetrating the snow when it is being used for a boot-axe belay, for probing, or for self-belay.

Spike. The spike—the metal tip of the axe (see Figure 16-1)—should be sharp enough to readily penetrate snow and ice. Using the ice axe for balance on rocky trails and talus slopes dulls the spike (see "Ice-Axe Maintenance and Safety" below).

Ice-Axe Length

Ice axes are described only in metric units; they range in length from 40 to 90 centimeters (16 to 35 inches). The shortest axes are for technical ice climbing; the longest ones are for tall mountaineers using the axe as a cane on easy terrain.

The optimal length for an ice axe depends upon both the intended use and the height of the climber. A common rule of thumb is for an ice-axe spike to barely reach the ground when you hold the head loosely at your side. This length offers the best compromise of balance and appropriate length for use on steep snow slopes. For climbers who are mostly traveling across glaciers and lower angle snow, a longer axe will give a nice length for balance and safety. For climbers who are on steeper snow, a shorter axe, with a spike that reaches the ankle when the axe is loosely held at your side, may be easier to place for balance and protection.

Axes shorter than 50 centimeters are technical ice climbing tools, excellent for placements on very steep slopes. However, these ice tools are not as good for self-arrest; the shorter shafts offer less leverage, and many of the technical pick designs do not lend themselves to the self-arrest technique. A 70-centimeter axe is the longest that is generally useful for technical ice climbing. Thus, a length of 50 to 70 centimeters works well in most alpine situations, wherein climbing is on moderately steep snow slopes and the axe is being used for self-belay and self-arrest. Longer axes are better for cross-country travel and scrambling, for snow anchors, and for probing for cornices and crevasses.

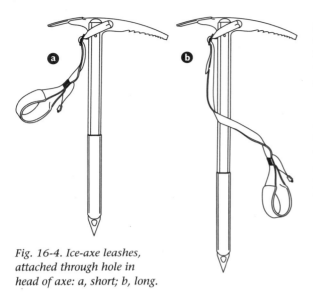

Fig. 16-4. Ice-axe leashes, attached through hole in head of axe: a, short; b, long.

Ice-Axe Leash

The ice-axe leash provides a sure way to attach the ice axe to the climber's wrist or harness. A leash is valuable insurance on crevassed glaciers or long, steep slopes where losing an axe would leave a climber without a principal safety tool and put climbers below in danger from the runaway axe. A leash also allows climbers to let the ice axe hang free while they make a move or two on the occasional rock they encounter during a snow climb.

There are two schools of thought regarding the use of an ice-axe leash during snow travel that requires using self-belay technique. Most climbers use a leash to keep from losing the ice axe. Others, however, believe that a flailing ice axe, hanging by the leash from the wrist of a climber who is no longer gripping the shaft, poses danger during a fall. Ultimately, choosing whether to use a leash is a personal judgment call.

The leash typically consists of a piece of accessory cord or webbing attached to the carabiner hole in the ice-axe head. A vast array of commercially manufactured leashes are available, or a leash can be made using either 5- or 6-millimeter Perlon accessory cord or ½- to 1-inch tubular webbing. Tie the ends of the material together with a suitable knot to create a sling, girth-hitch the sling through the carabiner hole, then tie an overhand knot to form a wrist loop.

The length of a leash can vary. Short leashes (fig. 16-4a) are favored by those using ice axes for basic snow and glacier travel. The short leash is easy to use and allows climbers to regain control of the ice axe quickly during a fall. During an uncontrolled fall in which a climber loses the grip on the ice axe, an axe on a short leash will not flail around as much as one on a longer leash.

However, the majority of climbers prefer a longer leash (fig. 16-4b). When shifting the axe from one hand to the other while changing direction up a snow slope, a climber with a long leash does not need to switch the leash from wrist to wrist. A long leash can be chained to a runner clipped to the harness, so that the axe can be used as a personal anchor. The long leash also makes the axe more versatile for climbing steep snow or ice. A long leash is usually about as long as the axe shaft, and if it is adjusted correctly, it will reduce arm fatigue during step-cutting and ice climbing. The climber should be able to grasp the end of the shaft near the spike when that hand is placed through the wrist loop.

Ice-Axe Maintenance and Safety

Ice axes require very little special care. Before each use, inspect the shaft for deep dents that might weaken it to the point of failure under load (but do not worry about minor nicks and scratches). After each climb, clean mud and dirt off the axe. Use a combination of solvents (such as a lubricating and penetrating oil) and abrasives (scouring pads or a soft ski hone—a soft synthetic block with embedded abrasive) to remove any rust.

Check the pick, adze, and spike regularly for sharpness. To sharpen, use a hand file, not a power-driven grinding wheel. High-speed grinding can overheat the metal and change the temper, diminishing the strength of the metal.

Guards are available to cover the sharp edges and points of the pick, adze, and spike if the ice axe is not in use. Some people leave the guards on when carrying the ice axe on their pack. (See also "How to Carry an Ice Axe," later in this chapter.) For storage following a climb, dry the ice axe and store without the guards on to protect the pick from rusting.

CRAMPONS

Crampons are a set of metal spikes that strap on over boots to penetrate hard snow and ice where boot soles cannot gain sufficient traction (see the "History of Crampons" sidebar). Crampons are useful for both ascending and descending steep snow and ice. The choice to wear crampons depends upon a variety of factors, including snow conditions and the confidence and experience of the climber.

16

HISTORY OF CRAMPONS

Crampons are an ancient tool, invented more than 2,000 years ago. Early inhabitants of the Caucasus region wore leather sandals soled with spiked iron plates to travel on snow and ice. Celtic miners used iron foot spikes as early as 2,700 years ago. Medieval alpine shepherds wore three-point crampons—horseshoe-shaped frames bearing three sharp spikes.

At the end of the 19th century, the four-point crampon was state of the art. Then in 1908 Oscar Eckenstein created the 10-point crampon. Many alpinists thought the gadgets were an unsporting advantage. However, these crampons relieved climbers of the tremendous tedium of cutting steps and opened up a vast array of unclimbed snow and ice faces. In 1932 Laurent Grivel added two front points, creating the 12-point crampon, which was specifically designed for climbing steep hard snow and ice. This design has evolved into the crampons that are essential for mountaineering today.

In harder, icy conditions where a dangerous fall is possible, crampons are likely a good choice. For an inexperienced climber on softer snow with a steep angle, crampons can provide an additional sense of confidence to complete the climb. Make this decision based on individual skill and experience, as well as personal assessment of conditions as described below in "Basic Techniques of Snow Climbing." Choosing among the different crampon designs involves a trade-off between features that are essential for general alpine use and those designed for technical ice climbing (see the "Questions to Consider When Selecting Crampons" sidebar).

Crampon Points

The early-model 10-point crampon was eclipsed in the 1930s by the 12-point crampon, with two forward-slanting or "front" points, which reduced the need for step-cutting and permitted front-pointing up steep snow and ice (see Chapter 19, Alpine Ice Climbing). Currently, crampons designed for general mountaineering include both 12-point and lighter 10-point models, but all have front points.

Most crampons are made from chromium molybdenum steel, an extremely strong, lightweight alloy. However, some models are fabricated from aircraft-grade aluminum alloys, which are about 50 percent lighter than steel but also much softer. Aluminum crampons are mainly used for glacier travel or early-season climbs with snow but not hard ice. Snow and ice routes often include short sections of rock that are climbed wearing crampons. Most crampons are able to take the punishment, but extended travel on rock will dull the points.

The relative angles and orientation of the first two rows of points determine the best use for a set of crampons. When the first row (front points) is drooped and the second row (secondary points) is angled toward the front of the crampon (fig. 16-5a), the crampons are better suited for ice climbing than for general mountaineering. This configuration allows easier engagement of the secondary points when front-pointing, which greatly reduces calf strain (see Chapter 19, Alpine Ice Climbing). In contrast, downward-angled secondary points (fig. 16-5b) facilitate a more ergonomic walking motion on moderate terrain.

Front points can be either horizontally (the point is wide side to side but thin, fig. 16-5c) or vertically (the point is narrow side to side but "tall" top to bottom, fig. 16-5d) oriented. Vertically oriented front points, with height that is greater than their width, are designed for technical ice climbing. Their shape mimics that of an ice-axe pick. They are well suited for penetration into hard water ice, but in softer alpine ice and snow, they are prone to shearing through unless they are deeply set. In contrast, horizontally oriented front points, with width that is greater than their height, are designed for the alpine ice and snow conditions encountered in most general mountaineering situations. They provide a larger surface area and, therefore, are more stable in softer snow.

Hinged and Semirigid Crampons

Mountaineering crampons are generally categorized into two types—hinged and semirigid—based on the connection between the forward and rear units.

QUESTIONS TO CONSIDER WHEN SELECTING CRAMPONS

When shopping for crampons, ask the following questions:

- What type of crampon is appropriate for your intended activity?
- What terrain is the crampon designed for?
- How will you know when the crampons fit your boots?
- Which attachment system is best for your needs?

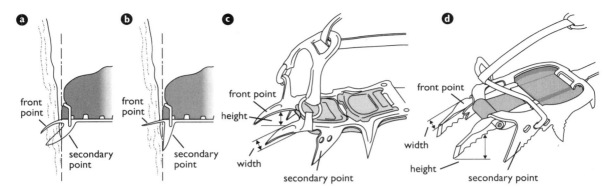

Fig. 16-5. Angle of first two rows of points: a, out from toe of boot suited for front-pointing; b, downward-angled secondary points best suited for general mountaineering; c, horizontal front points best suited for general mountaineering; d, vertical front points best suited for technical ice climbing.

Hinged. Crampons designed for general mountaineering can be hinged (fig. 16-6a), with forward and rear units connected by a flexible bar. They fit a wide variety of mountaineering boots, are light, and flex with the natural rocking action of walking. Hinged crampons work well on low-angle snowfields and glaciers.

Semirigid. Crampons designed for both general mountaineering and technical ice climbing (fig. 16-6b) have forward and rear units connected by a more rigid bar. They have some flex, which creates some give with a fairly stiff-soled boot. Semirigid crampons are designed with either horizontally or vertically oriented front points. This type of crampon works well on a variety of alpine snow and ice routes.

Crampon Attachment

There are three main crampon attachment systems: strap, clip-on, and hybrid. In general, hinged crampons work best with strap systems and flexible boots. Semirigid crampons work best with hybrid attachment systems—a combination of a rear clip and straps over the front of the boot—and fairly stiff boots. Ultimately, the choice of crampon attachment system is largely dictated by the attachment platform that the boot provides as well as the intended use.

Straps. Modern strap, or universal, bindings (fig. 16-7a) are much easier and faster to use than earlier strap systems. If climbers plan to do a wide variety of climbing and scrambling over a range of terrain (trail, rock, and snow), this binding type will provide secure and fast attachment with the widest selection of footwear. These are excellent bindings for use with a mountaineering boot covered by an insulating overboot.

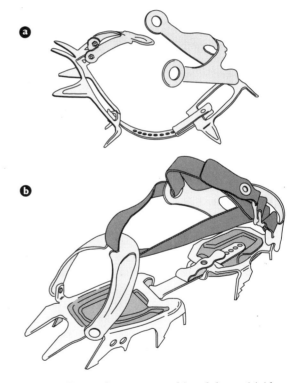

Fig. 16-6. Types of crampons: a, hinged; b, semirigid.

Clip-ons. With clip-on bindings, the crampons attach to the boot with a wire toe bail and a heel clip or lever (fig. 16-7b). These systems are fast and easy to use. With clip-on bindings, the fit of the crampon to the boot is

335

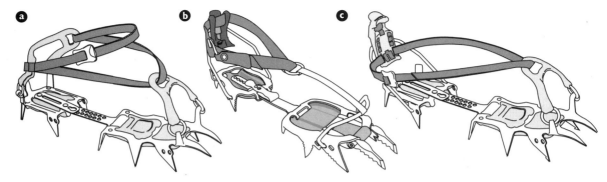

Fig. 16-7. Systems for attaching crampons to boots: a, strap or universal; b, clip-on; c, hybrid.

much more critical than with crampons that strap on. In order to fit securely, the boot must have pronounced grooves at both the heel and toe. When the crampon is sized correctly, the heel clip should decisively "snap" into place, forcing the wire toe bail firmly into the boot toe groove. Clip-on bindings typically include a safety strap wrapped around the ankle to secure the crampon if it pops off the boot. Some clip-on bindings also include a metal strap attached to the toe bail; the ankle safety strap is threaded through the metal toe-bail strap to prevent the crampon from popping off the boot.

Hybrid. Hybrid bindings feature toe straps combined with a heel clip (fig. 16-7c). These bindings are popular because they work well on boots that have a pronounced heel groove but may lack a toe groove. As with clip-on bindings, the hybrid's heel clip should decisively "snap" into place, forcing the boot into the front posts attached to the toe strap. Hybrid bindings also include a safety strap connecting the heel bail to the toe strap.

TIPS FOR FITTING CRAMPONS

- Clip-on bindings grip the boot at toe and heel, so the boot's welt is especially important. Clip-on bindings require well-defined grooves at the toe and heel on plastic and very stiff leather boots.
- The front crampon points should protrude ¾ to 1 inch (2 to 2.5 centimeters) beyond the toe of the boot.
- Crampons must be fitted to overboots or expedition gaiters if either will be worn to help insulate feet from the cold and snow in very cold conditions. Make sure any attachment straps are long enough.

Crampon Fit

It is critical that crampons fit boots perfectly. When purchasing crampons, bring the boots to the shop for a proper crampon fitting (see the "Tips for Fitting Crampons" sidebar). If the crampons will be used on more than one pair of boots, check the fit on all pairs. Be sure to purchase crampons that match the intended usage.

Practice putting on the crampons while in the comfort of home. There will be plenty of opportunity to put them on under less-ideal conditions: by feel in dim light or in the limited illumination of a headlamp, fumbling with cold, numbed fingers.

Crampon Maintenance and Safety

Regular simple maintenance keeps crampons safe and dependable (see the "Crampon Safety Rules" sidebar). After every climb, clean and dry the crampons and inspect them for wear. Repair or replace worn straps, nuts, bolts, and screws. Check the points: For ice climbing, maintaining sharp points is essential, but for most snow climbing and classic mountaineering, it is best not to have sharp points. New crampons frequently come with razor-sharp points (fig. 16-8a) and will almost always require a bit of maintenance or tuning before use (fig. 16-8b); file down burrs, rough edges, and very sharp points with a small file. If crampon points are overly dull, a file can also be used to sharpen them. Also check alignment of the points: splayed points make the crampons less efficient at penetrating snow and ice and more likely to slash pants, gaiters, and legs. It is probably best to retire a pair of crampons when points have been badly bent or overly filed.

In soft, sticky snow, crampons can accumulate a growing buildup of snow. This ball of snow can interfere with the crampon points' penetration and be dangerous, particularly where sticky snow overlays an icy base. To minimize

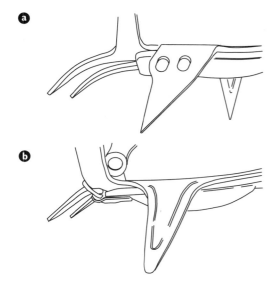

Fig. 16-8. How to finish crampon points: a, very sharp (new); b, rounded off (after filing).

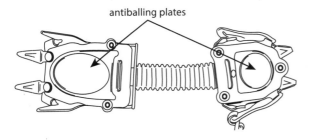

antiballing plates

Fig. 16-9. Crampons with antiballing plates.

this hazard, climbers can use manufactured antiballing plates: plastic, rubber, or vinyl sheets that can be slid into rubber-fitted metal stays on the bottom of the disassembled crampon (fig. 16-9). Alternatively, climbers can wrap the bottom of the crampon with duct tape. When soft, sticky snow is encountered, consider whether crampons are really needed. It may be safer to proceed without them.

Instep and Approach Crampons

Small instep crampons with four or six points are designed for crossing an occasional short snowfield. Because these crampons have no points at the heel or toe, they are not suitable for mountaineering and can be dangerous on steep snow or ice. Approach crampons are flexible, full-length

---

CRAMPON SAFETY RULES

In the mountains, climbers can follow a few rules to protect themselves, their gear, and their climbing companions from sharp crampon points:

- Use a crampon pouch or a set of rubber point protectors when carrying crampons.
- Always bring the tools needed to adjust the crampons, as well as any necessary spare parts.
- While climbing with crampons on, step deliberately to avoid snagging pants or gaiters, gashing a leg, or stepping on the rope.
- Be careful not to snag gear that is hanging low from gear loops on the climbing harness; avoid letting slings hang below the thigh.

---

plates that typically have eight points. Approach crampons are designed for use on moderate terrain, and they also are not suitable for mountaineering. Instep and approach crampons are not a substitute for 10- or 12-point mountaineering crampons.

SKI POLES

Ski poles are used not only for skiing; ski or trekking poles can be used whether climbers are traveling on foot, snowshoes, or skis. Poles are better than an ice axe for balance when climbers are carrying heavy packs over level or low-angle snow, slippery ground, or scree or when they are crossing a stream or boulder field. Poles also can take some of the weight off the lower body, and the basket at the bottom of the poles keeps them from penetrating too deeply into soft snow.

Some ski and trekking poles have features helpful to the mountaineer. Adjustable poles enable climbers to set the length to suit the conditions or the terrain; on a traverse, the uphill pole can be set to a length shorter than the downhill pole. These poles can be fully compressed for easy packing. Adjustable poles require more maintenance; after each trip, disassemble, clean, and dry them.

Poles with removable baskets can serve as probes for crevasses when their baskets are removed. Some poles are made so that a pair can be fastened together to form a serviceable avalanche probe. However, they are a poor substitute for a commercial avalanche probe.

Some ski poles can be fitted with a special self-arrest grip that has a plastic or metal-tipped pick, but on technical terrain this option is *not* a substitute for an ice axe.

16

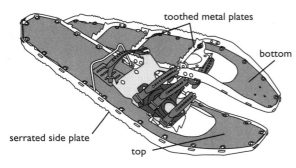

Fig. 16-10. Snowshoes for winter mountaineering.

SNOWSHOES

Snowshoes, a traditional aid for snow travel, have been updated recently to be smaller and lighter. Modern designs include models consisting of tubular metal frames with lightweight, durable decking materials (fig. 16-10), as well as plastic-composite models. Modern bindings are easy to use and more stable than older models. Snowshoes include crampon-like, toothed metal plates designed to improve traction on hard snow; many models also include serrated heel and/or side plates that decrease side-to-side slippage.

Snowshoes permit efficient travel in soft snow, where hikers otherwise laboriously posthole, sinking deeply with each step. Snowshoes can be used to kick steps uphill. Although travel on snowshoes may be slower than travel on skis, snowshoes can be used in brushy or rocky terrain where skis would be awkward, and snowshoes are often more practical than skis when climbers are carrying heavy packs. If the climbing party includes some people who are not very good on skis, it is much less frustrating and more efficient for the group to travel on snowshoes. Snowshoe bindings can be used with almost any footwear, whereas most ski bindings require specialized boots.

SKIS

Mountaineering skis fitted with climbing skins provide a convenient mode of travel in the mountains. The two styles of mountaineering skiing, telemark and alpine touring (AT or randonée), require specialized boots (some bindings can accommodate mountaineering boots, but there is a significant loss of skiing performance). Telemark and AT or randonée bindings allow the skier's boot heel to hinge upward for easy uphill touring as if cross-country skiing. But whereas the traditional telemark ski binding (fig. 16-11a) has a "free heel" for telemark turns down the slope, the randonée or AT binding locks the boot down for parallel turns and standard downhill technique (fig. 16-11b).

The past two decades have seen a marked evolution and rapid development of both AT and telemark ski gear for ski mountaineering in terms of weight, shape, and size. In fact, skis used for AT and telemark are now often the same make and model, differing only in the types of bindings used. Both modern types of skis are quite wide compared to the older alpine gear. And both modern types are highly shaped, often with modified tips and tails for ease and stability of turning during the descent. Telemark and randonée skis permit climbers to travel the backcountry through the use of climbing skins attached temporarily to ski bottoms to provide traction for uphill travel (fig. 16-11c). Climbing skins, originally made of seal fur and now of a napped synthetic material, allow skis to slide forward over snow while gripping and holding the skis from sliding backward.

Climbers who are not accomplished skiers may find that the disadvantages of using skis in the backcountry outweigh the advantages. When the skis must be carried, they can be awkward in some terrain—catching on rocks and trees—and add weight to a pack already laden with technical gear. Wearing skis complicates self-arrest, and skiing can be difficult when climbers are carrying heavy packs. Every party member must have similar skiing ability for the group to keep a steady pace. This is especially true for roped glacier travel.

Skis can be faster for basic snow travel, and they can provide a way to reach areas that are otherwise inaccessible. Skis offer a bonus for glacier travel: they distribute the climber's weight over a larger area and may decrease the chance of breaking through snow bridges. Skis can also come in handy for rescue work, because they can be converted into a makeshift stretcher or sled.

Backcountry skiing is a complex activity, utilizing special techniques and equipment. For detailed information, see Resources.

SHOVEL

A broad-bladed shovel is both a tool and a safety device for the snow traveler. A shovel is a necessity for uncovering an avalanche victim. Shovels are also used for constructing snow shelters and tent platforms, and they have even been used as climbing tools to ascend particularly snowy routes.

A good shovel (see Figure 3-11a, b, and c in Chapter 3, Camping, Food, and Water) has a blade large enough to move snow efficiently and a handle long enough for good leverage but short enough for use in a confined area: 2 to 3 feet (60 to 90 centimeters) long. Some shovels have extendable and/or detachable handles. Another desirable feature is

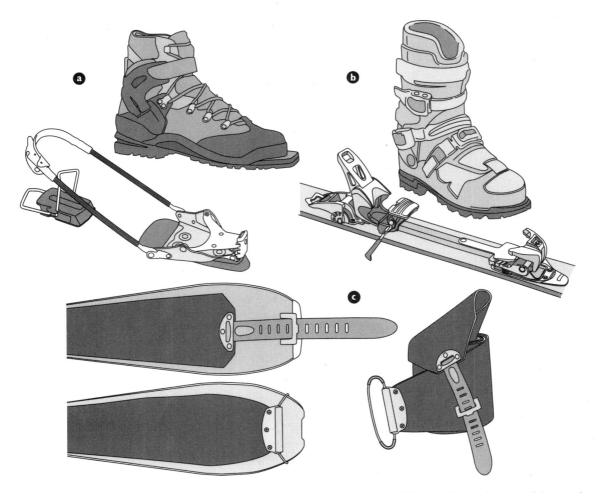

Fig. 16-11. Ski equipment for mountaineering: a, traditional telemark boot and binding; b, randonée or alpine touring (AT) boot and binding; c, climbing skins for skis.

a blade that can be rotated perpendicular to the handle and locked so that the shovel can be used as a trenching tool. A D-shaped grip on the handle can make shoveling more comfortable. Some models have a hollow handle, inside which climbers can carry a snow saw or avalanche probe.

In dry, powdery snow, a plastic-bladed shovel provides a good compromise of weight to strength. However, metal-bladed shovels are much stiffer and therefore better for chopping through hard snow or avalanche debris. The edge of a shovel blade (whether metal or plastic) can be sharpened with a file for better cutting of hard snow. Shovels are also used in various snow stability tests (see Chapter 17, Avalanche Safety).

BASIC TECHNIQUES OF SNOW CLIMBING

The first priority of snow travel is to avoid a slip or fall, but if climbers do slip on snow, they must know how to regain control as quickly as possible. Travel on steep alpine snow slopes is dangerous unless climbers have an ice axe and crampons—and the skill to use them.

To determine the route, terrain, and equipment choices for traveling on steep alpine snow safely, ask the following questions: Is the snow good for self-belay, or is it too hard for the ice-axe shaft to be placed securely? If someone were to fall, what does the runout look like? Will crampons be helpful or a hindrance? What are the climbers' levels of experience and skill? Is everyone comfortable with the particular situation? Are climbers wearing heavy overnight packs?

Relying on self-belay or self-arrest (see "Stopping a Fall" later in this section) should be considered adequate only for very experienced climbers. Understanding the limits of self-belay and self-arrest, combined with assessing the runout, are crucial considerations.

ASSESSING RUNOUT

Because a falling climber's acceleration rate on a 30-degree snow slope can approach that of free-falling, it is important to always be aware of a snow slope's runout. Are there rocks, crevasses, a moat, a bergschrund, or cliffs below

Fig. 16-12. Assessing runout: rocks below a snow slope make for a dangerous runout.

you (fig. 16-12)? Constantly assessing and being aware of runout is the first thing to consider when deciding what techniques and equipment to use for travel on snow slopes.

If the runout is dangerous or unknown, always carefully consider how to proceed. Is a belay with anchor and rope required? If a belay is deemed necessary and there is not time, skill, or equipment for a solid belay, the climbing party will probably be safer turning around.

USING THE ICE AXE

The ice axe, an inherently simple tool, has many uses. Below the snow line, it can serve as a walking cane or be used to help climbers brake when they are going downhill. But its main role is in snow and ice travel, wherein it is a balance aid, a tool to prevent a fall, and a tool to stop a fall. The ice axe is also used in a variety of ways to make a snow anchor.

How to Carry an Ice Axe

Always carry an ice axe carefully. Be aware of what its sharp points and edges can do to you and others in the climbing party.

When the axe is not needed, carry it on your pack. Slip it down through the pack ice-axe loop, flip the shaft up, and strap it to the pack (fig. 16-13a). Keep guards on the pick, adze, and spike. To carry the axe in one hand, grasp the shaft with the spike forward and the pick down to avoid jabbing the person behind you (fig. 16-13b).

When travel on snow alternates briefly with areas of rocks or steep brush, where both hands need to be free, slide the axe diagonally between your back and the pack (fig. 16-13c). Place the spike down and the pick between the pack's two shoulder straps, so the axe head is clear of your neck and pointing in the same general direction as the angle of the shaft. In this position, the axe can be stowed and retrieved quickly.

How to Grasp an Ice Axe

There are two ways to grasp an ice axe. Conditions determine which grasp is best at any moment.

Self-arrest grasp. Place your thumb under the adze and your palm and fingers over the pick, near the top of the shaft (fig. 16-14a). While climbing, point the adze forward. The self-arrest grasp puts climbers in position to go directly into arrest in case of a fall (see "Self-Arrest" later in this section).

Self-belay grasp. Rest your palm on top of the adze and wrap your thumb and index finger under the pick (fig. 16-14b). While climbing, point the pick forward. The

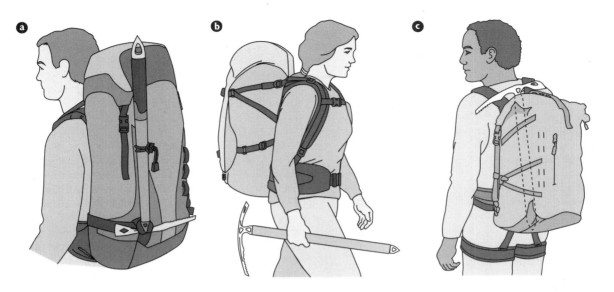

Fig. 16-13. Carrying an ice axe, when not in use: a, attached to pack by ice-axe loop and straps; b, in hand while walking, with spike forward and pick down; c, temporarily between back and pack.

self-belay grasp can be more comfortable and is appropriate when the consequences of an unchecked slide are not a concern (see "Self-Belay" later in this section).

It is generally easier to start out holding the axe in the self-arrest grasp when practicing with an ice axe. Most climbers simply choose to use the self-arrest grasp at all times. Some prefer the comfort of the self-belay grasp but shift to the self-arrest grasp whenever they feel the runout is a concern or there is a significant danger of slipping.

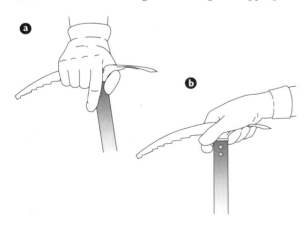

Fig. 16-14. Grasping an ice axe: a, self-arrest grasp; b, self-belay grasp.

USING CRAMPONS

Crampons are generally considered essential when conditions are icy, but they can also be useful on snow, even soft snow. For ice, a bit of crampon technique is usually necessary (see "Climbing with Crampons" in Chapter 19, Alpine Ice Climbing). For snow, simply use the same techniques you would without crampons: step-kicking, combined with balance and use of an ice axe (all described in this section); the crampon points will improve traction and security.

Learn how and when to use crampons. Ask these questions: Are crampons helpful? Do they make walking on snow easier and more efficient? Does the slope have a dangerous or unknown runout? (If yes, then crampons should always be considered.) What footwear is being worn? (Rigid-soled boots kick steps much better than softer, more flexible boots; crampons should be considered more often with softer, more flexible footwear because many crampon designs will add stiffness to the boots.)

One reason for not wearing crampons is the increased potential for tripping in them or even being injured by their sharp points. Learning to walk in crampons without tripping takes practice, and injury from sharp points can be reduced with proper crampon maintenance (see "Crampon Maintenance and Safety" above).

Another reason not to use crampons is if snow is balling up underfoot. Snow can stick to the underside of the metal crampon frame, packing into a ball that interferes with the

16

effectiveness of the crampon points. Fresh snow combined with warm temperatures can create conditions that even antiballing plates cannot overcome. Such conditions can be particularly challenging. Sometimes the snow may be hard under the softer fresh snow, requiring crampon use even when the snow sticks to them. These conditions with or without crampons require great care, and they will certainly slow progress. If the decision is made to wear crampons, then knocking the stuck snow free with an ice axe may be necessary, sometimes with every step.

ASCENDING SNOW

Climbing up snow slopes takes a set of special skills. Different techniques come into play, depending on the slope's hardness or steepness. The direction of ascent can be either direct or diagonal.

Climbing in Balance

Although climbers need to be proficient at ice-axe self-arrest, this skill is a last resort and every effort should be made to avoid arresting. Climb in balance to avoid falling. Climbing in balance means moving from one position of balance to another, avoiding any prolonged stance in an out-of-balance position.

On a diagonal uphill route, a climber is in a position of balance when the inside (uphill side) foot is in front of and above the outside (downhill side) foot, because body weight is evenly distributed between both feet (see Figure 16-15a). When the outside foot is forward, the climber is out of balance because the trailing inside leg, which is not fully extended and therefore cannot make use of the skeletal structure to minimize muscular effort, is nonetheless bearing most of the body's weight (see Figure 16-15b).

The diagonal ascent is a two-step sequence: from a position of balance through an out-of-balance position and back to a position of balance. From the position of balance, place the axe above and ahead of you into the snow in the self-belay position (fig. 16-15a). Move up one step, bringing your outside (downhill) foot in front of your inside (uphill) foot, which puts you out of balance (fig. 16-15b). Then move up another step, putting your inside foot in front of your outside foot, which puts you back in a position of balance (fig. 16-15c). Then reposition the ice axe. Keep your weight over your feet and avoid leaning into the slope. Keep the axe on your uphill side.

If a climber is heading straight up the fall line, there is no longer an uphill or downhill reference for positioning arms and legs. Just carry the axe in whichever hand feels comfortable, and climb in a steady, controlled manner. Regardless of the direction of travel, firmly place the axe before each move to provide self-belay protection.

Fig. 16-15. Ascending a snow slope, diagonally, in balance: a, placing the ice axe from a position of balance; b, advancing one step into an out-of-balance position; c, advancing another step back into a position of balance.

Using the Rest Step

Climbing a long, featureless snow slope can give a frustrating sensation of getting nowhere. Few landmarks help measure progress. Novice climbers try a dash-and-gasp pace in an attempt to rush the objective. But the only way to the top of the slope is to find a pace that can be maintained—and then maintain it. The solution is the rest step, a technique that conserves energy as it moves the climber methodically forward. Use the rest step whenever legs or lungs need a bit of recuperation between steps. At lower elevations, it is usually leg muscles that require a break; at higher elevations, lungs need the pause. See "The Rest Step" in Chapter 6, Wilderness Travel.

Step-Kicking

Step-kicking creates a path of upward steps with the best possible footing and the least expenditure of energy. Climbers move in single file up the steps, improving them as they go. The head of the line has the hardest job: kicking fresh steps and looking for the safest route up the slope.

The most efficient kick to use for creating snow steps is to swing your leg and allow its own weight and momentum to provide the impact, with little muscular effort. This works well in soft snow. Harder snow requires more effort, and the steps may be smaller and less secure.

An average climber needs steps deep enough to place the ball of the foot when going straight up and at least half of the boot on a diagonal ascent. Steps that are kicked level or tilted slightly into the slope are more secure. The less space there is on a step, the more important it is that the step be angled into the slope.

When kicking steps, keep other climbers in the party in mind. They can follow up your staircase if the steps are spaced evenly and somewhat close together. Make allowance for climbers with shorter legs.

Followers improve the steps as they climb. The follower must kick into the step, because simply walking onto the existing platform is not secure. In compact snow, drive your toe in and deepen the step. In soft snow, bring your boot down onto the step, compacting the snow and making the step stronger.

Switch leads occasionally to share the heavy work. The leader can step aside and fall in at the end of the line. (The related skills of step-cutting and cramponing are discussed in Chapter 19, Alpine Ice Climbing.)

Fig. 16-16. Direct ascent with ice axe in cane position.

Fig. 16-17. Direct ascent with ice axe in stake position.

Making a Direct Ascent

Speed is a consideration on a long snow climb, and a direct ascent is a good choice if climbers face bad weather, avalanche or rockfall danger, poor bivouac conditions, or a difficult descent. Ice-axe technique varies according to snow conditions and steepness.

Cane position. On a slope of a low or moderate angle, climb with the axe in the cane position: holding it in one hand by the head and using it for balance (fig. 16-16). Continue in the cane position as the snow gets steeper, as long as it feels secure. Setting the axe firmly before each move provides a self-belay.

Stake position. As the snow gets steeper, climbers may choose to switch to the two-handed stake position (fig. 16-17). Before moving upward, use both hands to plant the axe as far as it will go into the snow. Then continue to grasp it with both hands on the head or with one hand on the head and one on the shaft. This position is useful on steeper soft snow.

Horizontal position. On steep, hard snow covered with a soft layer, climb with the axe in the horizontal position. Hold the axe with both hands, one in the self-arrest grasp on the head and the other near the spike end of the shaft. Jab the axe horizontally into the snow above you, the pick down and the shaft at a right angle to your body (fig. 16-18). This jabs the pick into the harder base while the shaft gets some purchase in the softer surface snow.

Making a Diagonal Ascent

When time and weather conditions permit, climbers may prefer a longer diagonal ascent, switchbacking up moderately angled slopes. In marginal conditions, a diagonal route may be more difficult because of the work of kicking numerous edged, traversing steps in hard snow. Again, ice-axe technique varies according to snow conditions and steepness.

Cane position. The axe works fine in the cane position on moderate slopes (see Figure 16-16). As the slope gets steeper, this position becomes awkward.

Cross-body position. Hold the axe perpendicular to the angle of the slope, one hand grasping the head and the other holding the spike end of the shaft, and jab the spike into the snow (fig. 16-19). The axe crosses diagonally in front of you, the pick pointing away from your body. The shaft should bear your weight, while the hand on the head of the axe stabilizes the axe.

Fig. 16-18. Direct ascent with ice axe in horizontal position.

Fig. 16-19. Diagonal ascent with ice axe in cross-body position.

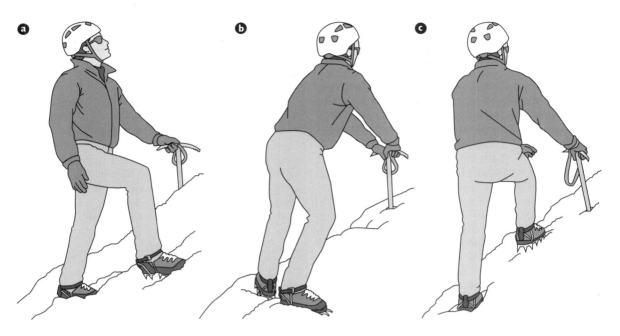

Fig. 16-20. Changing direction on a diagonal ascent: a, jab ice-axe shaft straight down and step forward with outside (downhill) foot; b, move into a stance facing uphill with feet splayed; c, turn in new direction of travel and step forward with new inside (uphill) foot.

Changing directions. Diagonal ascents often mean changing direction, or switchbacking. The sequence of steps to change direction safely on a diagonal route, whether the axe is in the cane position or the cross-body position, is this:

1. Start from a position of balance, with your inside (uphill) foot in front of and above your outside (downhill) foot. Jab the axe shaft straight down into the snow at a spot directly above your location.
2. Move your outside (downhill) foot forward, bringing you into an out-of-balance position (fig. 16-20a).
3. Grasp the head of the axe with both hands. Continue holding onto the head with both hands while moving into a stance facing uphill, turning your inside foot toward the new direction of travel and ending with your feet in a splayed position (fig. 16-20b). Kick steps into the slope if your splayed feet feel unstable.
4. Turn your body toward the new direction of travel, returning to a position of balance by placing your new uphill foot in front of and above your new outside (downhill) foot (fig. 16-20c).

In the cane position, your new uphill hand now grasps the axe head (as in Figure 16-20c). In the cross-body

position, the hands holding the head and the shaft are now reversed.

Traversing

Long horizontal traverses that neither gain nor lose elevation are best avoided. This "sidehill gouging" is fine on soft snow at low and moderate angles, although it is not as comfortable or as efficient as a diagonal route. If it is necessary to traverse over hard or steep snow, face directly into the slope and kick straight into it for the most secure steps.

DESCENDING SNOW

One mark of a skillful snow climber is the ability to go downhill efficiently and confidently. Descending snow is frequently more challenging than ascending the same slope. Due to gravity and momentum, it is easier to slip while descending than while ascending. Many otherwise competent and aggressive climbers blanch at the prospect of going forward down a steep, exposed snow gully. To move down, place the axe down low, which provides a less-comfortable stance and handhold than on the way up. Master the following descent techniques to help conquer any uneasiness about downhill travel.

16

345

Facing Out (Plunge-Stepping)

When descending, determine technique mainly by the same factors as when ascending: the hardness and angle of the snow. In soft snow on a moderate slope, simply face outward and walk down. With harder snow or a steeper angle, use the plunge step.

The plunge step is a confident, aggressive move. Face outward, step assertively away from the slope, and land solidly on your heel with your straightened leg vertical, transferring weight solidly to the new position (fig. 16-21a). Avoid leaning back into the slope, which can result in less secure steps or perhaps an unplanned glissade. Keep knees slightly bent, not locked, and lean forward to maintain balance. How much the knees are bent depends on the angle of the slope (the steeper the slope, the greater the bend) and the firmness of the surface (the harder the snow, the greater the bend). Plunge-stepping can be secure with steps that hold only the heel of the boot, but most climbers do not trust steps shallower than that.

When plunge-stepping, maintain a steady rhythm, almost like marching. This helps maintain balance. Once a comfortable rhythm is found, do not stop. Plunge-stepping in a stop-and-start fashion can cause climbers to lose their balance.

When plunge-stepping, hold the ice axe in one hand in either the self-arrest or self-belay grasp, with the spike close to the surface of the snow, well forward and ready to be planted in the snow (see Figure 16-21a). Spread out your other arm and move it for balance. Some climbers hold the axe in both hands in the full self-arrest position—one hand on the head, the other near the end of the shaft—but this allows less arm movement for maintaining balance.

An aggressive stride creates a deep step. Take care in deep, soft snow not to plunge so deeply that your legs get stuck and you fall forward, injuring yourself. If the snow is too hard or steep for plunge-stepping, descend in a crouched position, planting the axe as low as possible in a self-belay with each step (fig. 16-21b). Typically it is easier to plunge-step by picking your own line rather than following others' footsteps down.

Fig. 16-21. Facing out (plunge-stepping): a, on moderate slope; b, with self-belay on steeper slope.

Facing In (Backing Down)

While generally slower than facing out, backing down is usually more comfortable and secure. Try to plunge the shaft of the ice axe as low on the slope as is comfortable before stepping down (fig. 16-22). If the snow is too firm for a solid shaft placement, the pick of the axe (placed low) can be used for support while the climber steps down. Remember that leaning into the slope does not put your body in a good position of balance. Try to keep your weight centered over your feet as much as possible.

Fig. 16-22. Facing in (backing down): place axe low on the slope and don't lean in toward the slope.

Glissading

Glissading is the fastest, easiest, and most exhilarating way down many snow slopes if climbers are on foot. On slopes where speed can be controlled, it is an efficient alternative to walking or plunge-stepping.

Glissading can be hazardous. Do not glissade in crevassed terrain. Glissade only when a safe runout is close enough that if a slide goes out of control, the climber will not be injured before reaching it. Unless the climbing party can see the entire descent route, the first person down must use extreme caution and stop frequently to look ahead. The biggest risk is losing control at such a high speed that self-arrest is impossible. This is most likely to happen on the best glissading slope: one with firm snow.

Before glissading, remove crampons and stow them and other hardware inside the pack; crampon points can catch in the snow and send climbers tumbling. Wear waterproof breathable hardshell pants to keep dry (see Chapter 2, Clothing and Equipment). Wear gloves to protect hands from the abrasive snow.

Always maintain control of the ice axe. If an ice-axe leash is worn, climbers risk injury from a flailing axe if it is knocked loose from their grip. If a leash is not used, climbers risk losing their axe.

Effective glissading requires a smooth blend of several techniques. Climbers who lack finesse in the standing glissade (see below) often use a combination: breaking into a plunge step to control speed, stepping off in a new direction rather than making a ski-style turn, and skating to maintain momentum as the slope angle lessens.

Sometimes in soft snow, a glissader accidentally sets off a mass of surface snow, which slides down the slope with the glissader aboard. These are small avalanches, known as "avalanche cushions." The trick is to decide whether the avalanche cushion is safe to ride or is about to become a serious avalanche. If the moving snow is more than a few inches deep, self-arrest will not work because the ice-axe pick cannot penetrate to the stable layer below. Sometimes climbers can drive the spike deep enough to slow the glissade, although probably not deep enough to stop themselves. Unless you are sure the cushion is safe and the glissade speed is under control, get off. Roll sideways out of the path of the moving snow and then self-arrest.

Of the three methods of glissading—the sitting glissade, the standing glissade, and the crouching glissade—the one to use depends on snow and slope conditions, the appearance of the runout, and the climber's mastery of the techniques.

Sitting glissade. On soft snow on which climbers would bog down if they tried a standing glissade, the sitting glissade works. Sit erect in the snow, bend the knees, and plant boot soles flat along the snow surface (fig. 16-23a). Hold the ice axe in self-arrest position while glissading downhill. To maintain control, run the spike of the axe like a rudder along the snow on one side of you. Keep both hands on the axe. Put pressure on the spike to reduce speed and to thwart any tendency of the ice-axe head to pivot downward.

16

Fig. 16-23. Glissade positions: a, sitting; b, standing; c, crouching.

The standard posture, with knees bent and feet flat, also reduces speed. This posture is good when the snow is crusted or firmly consolidated, pitted with icy ruts or small suncups (hollows melted by the sun), or dotted with rocks or shrubs. It provides more stability and control than having legs straight out in front and helps minimize wear and tear on a climber's bottom.

To stop, use the spike to slow down, then dig in your heels—but not at high speed, or a somersault may be the result. For an emergency stop, roll over and self-arrest.

Turns are almost impossible to make in a sitting glissade. The best way to get around an obstruction is to stop, walk sideways to a point that is not directly above the obstacle, and glissade again.

Standing glissade. The most maneuverable technique is the standing glissade, and it saves clothes from getting wet and abraded. This glissade is similar to downhill skiing. Crouch slightly over your feet, bend the knees, and spread out your arms (fig. 16-23b). Feet, which provide stability, can be spread out or placed together, with one foot slightly forward to improve stability and prevent nosedives. Bring the feet closer together and lean forward over them to increase speed.

To slow down and stop, stand up and dig in your heels, turn feet sideways and dig their edges into the slope, or crouch and drag the ice-axe spike as in the crouching glissade (see below).

It is also possible to perform a turn similar to skiing by rotating your shoulders, upper body, and knees in the direction you want to turn and rolling your knees and ankles in the same direction to rock your feet onto boot edges.

The standing glissade is most effective on a firm base with a softer layer on top. The softer the snow, the steeper the slope needs to be to maintain speed. It is possible to do a standing glissade down slopes of harder snow, but these are usually slopes of lower angles with a safe runout. It is possible to skate slopes of very low angles if the snow is firm.

Responding to changes in the snow texture is tricky. If you hit softer, slower snow, your head and torso will suddenly outpace your legs, so move one boot forward for stability. If you hit harder, faster snow or ice below the surface, lean well forward to prevent a slip. Keep the glissade speed under control by regularly braking and traversing.

Crouching glissade. The crouching glissade is slower than a standing glissade and easier to learn. From the standing glissade position, simply lean back, hold the ice axe in the self-arrest position to one side of your body, and drag the spike in the snow (fig. 16-23c). Because it uses three points of contact, the crouching glissade is also more stable. However, turning and controlling speed when crouching are more difficult.

Fig. 16-24. The self-belay:
a, climbing; b, falling; c, recovering.

STOPPING A FALL

To prevent a fall, climbers need to know how to self-belay, and to stop a fall, they must be prepared to self-arrest. Always wear gloves on snow slopes; snow is quite abrasive, and sliding unprotected over its surface can cause hands to lose their grip on the ice axe.

Self-Belay

Self-belay can keep a simple slip or misstep on a snow slope from turning into a serious fall. To self-belay, be sure both feet are secure, then jam the spike and shaft of the ice axe straight down into the snow (fig. 16-24a). Continue to grip the head of the axe with your uphill hand while moving forward. (Use either the self-belay grasp or the self-arrest grasp to perform self-belay.) Take a step or two, pull out the axe, and replant it. For self-belay to work, the shaft must be placed deep enough in firm snow to hold your full weight.

If you slip, keep one hand on the head of the axe and grab the shaft at the surface of the snow with your other hand (fig. 16-24b). The key to successful self-belay is to grab the shaft right next to the surface, so that you pull against the buried shaft. Your hand on the head of the axe minimizes the risk of levering the axe out (fig. 16-24c).

If self-belay fails and you begin an uncontrolled slide down the slope, you must immediately self-arrest.

Self-Arrest

Preventing a fall is a primary goal while climbing, but if climbers do fall, their life may depend on self-arrest skills and stopping the fall as quickly as possible. Self-arrest technique holds a climber's fall or the fall of a rope mate. During glacier travel, self-arrest stops the rest of the team from sliding into a crevasse (discussed in Chapter 18, Glacier Travel and Crevasse Rescue). For climbers who master self-arrest, steep snow slopes become highways to the summit.

The primary goal of self-arrest is to stop a fall, ideally in a safe, secure, and stable position. Figures 16-25c, 16-27e, and 16-28d illustrate the completion of a successful self-arrest: lying facedown in the snow with the ice axe beneath you. Here is how to do it:

- **Hold the axe in a solid grip.** Place one hand in the self-arrest grasp, with your thumb under the adze and fingers over the pick (see Figure 16-14a), and your other hand on the shaft just above the spike.
- **Press the pick into the snow above your shoulder.** Place the adze near the angle formed by your neck and shoulder. This is crucial. Sufficient force cannot be exerted on the pick if the adze is not in the proper position.

16

349

- **Place the shaft across your chest diagonally.** Hold the spike end close to the hip that is opposite the axe head. Grip the shaft near the spike end to prevent that hand from acting as a pivot point around which the spike can swing to jab your thigh. (A short axe is held the same way, although the spike will not reach the opposite hip.)
- **Press your chest and shoulder down on the ice-axe shaft.** Successful self-arrest relies on your body weight falling and pressing on the axe, rather than arm strength alone driving the axe into the snow.
- **Keep your head facedown.** Place the brim of your helmet in contact with the slope. This position prevents your shoulders and chest from lifting up and keeps weight over the adze.
- **Place your face in the snow.** Your nose should be touching the snow.
- **Arch your spine slightly away from the snow.** This places the bulk of your weight on the axe head and on your toes or knees, which are the points that dig into the snow to force a stop. Pull up on the spike end of the shaft, which starts the arch and rolls your weight toward your shoulder by the axe head.
- **Bend your knees slightly.** Place them against the surface to slow the fall in soft snow. On harder surfaces, where knees have little stopping power, they help stabilize your body position.
- **Keep your legs stiff and spread apart, toes digging in.** If wearing crampons, dig in with knees and keep toes off the snow. If it's a life-or-death situation, dig in with whatever you can.

Self-arrest technique depends on the position the climber is in after a fall. A fallen climber will be sliding in one of four positions: head uphill or head downhill and, in either case, facedown or on the back.

If a climber is falling, the immediate goal is to get the body into the only effective self-arrest position: head uphill, feet downhill, and face pressed into the snow. The first move toward that goal is to grasp the axe with both hands, one hand on the axe head in the self-arrest grasp and the other hand at the base of the shaft. The next moves depend on what position the climber is in while falling.

Head uphill, facedown. All the climber has to do is get the pick pressed into the snow and body over the axe shaft, ending in a secure self-arrest.

Head uphill, on your back. Falling with your head uphill, on your back (fig. 16-25a), is not much more difficult to self-arrest than falling with your head uphill, facedown. Roll toward the head of the axe and aggressively plant the pick into the snow at your side while rolling over onto your stomach (fig. 16-25b). Roll in the direction of the axe head (fig. 16-25c). When you fall (fig. 16-26a), beware of rolling toward the spike, which can jam the spike in the snow before the pick (fig. 16-26b) and wrench the axe from your hands (fig. 16-26c).

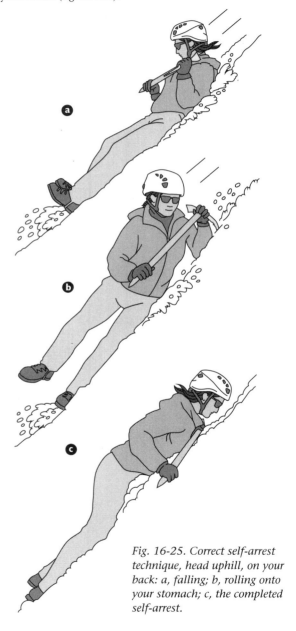

Fig. 16-25. Correct self-arrest technique, head uphill, on your back: a, falling; b, rolling onto your stomach; c, the completed self-arrest.

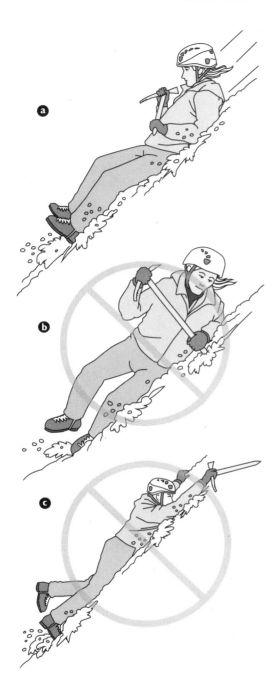

Head downhill, facedown. Self-arrest from a headfirst fall is more difficult because you must first swing your feet downhill. In this facedown predicament, reach downhill and off to the axe-head side (fig. 16-27a) and get the pick into the snow (fig. 16-27b) to serve as a pivot to swing your body around (fig. 16-27c). Work to swing your legs around (fig. 16-27d) so they are pointing downhill (fig. 16-27e). Never jab the spike into the snow and pivot on that end of the axe. That will bring the pick and adze of the axe across your slide path and on a collision course with your chest and face.

Head downhill, on your back. Again, self-arrest from a headfirst fall is more difficult because you must first swing your feet downhill. In this faceup predicament, hold the axe across your torso and aggressively jab the pick into the snow (fig. 16-28a), then twist and roll toward it (fig. 16-28b). Once again, the pick placed to the side serves as a pivot point. Planting the pick will not bring you around to the final self-arrest position. Work at rolling your chest toward the axe head (fig. 16-28c) while swinging your legs around to point downhill (fig. 16-28d). A sitting-up motion using body core strength helps the roll.

Practice self-arrest in all positions on increasingly steeper slopes and hard snow above a safe runout. Practice with a full pack. The key to success is to get quickly into the arrest position and dig in. During practice, leave the ice-axe leash off your wrist so there is less chance of the axe striking you if you lose control of it. Cover or pad the adze and spike to minimize chances of injury. Although crampons are often worn on snow slopes where self-arrest may be necessary, crampons should never be worn when practicing self-arrest.

The effectiveness of the self-arrest depends on the climber's reaction time, the steepness and length of the slope, and snow conditions.

On steep or slippery slopes. When the slope is too steep or slippery, even the best technique will not stop a slide. Acceleration on hard snow, on even a modest snow slope, can be so rapid that the first instant of the fall is the whole story: the climber rockets into the air and crashes back to the unyielding surface with stunning impact, losing uphill-downhill orientation.

On hard or loose snow. Arresting on hard snow is difficult, if not impossible, but always give it a try, even if on belay. In loose snow, the pick may not be able to reach compact snow, making the usual self-arrest useless. The best brakes in this case are feet and knees and elbows, widely spaced and deeply pressed into the snow. If the initial efforts at self-arrest are unsuccessful, do not give up.

Fig. 16-26. Incorrect self-arrest technique, head uphill, on your back: a, falling; b, rolling toward spike; c, axe is wrenched out of your hands.

16

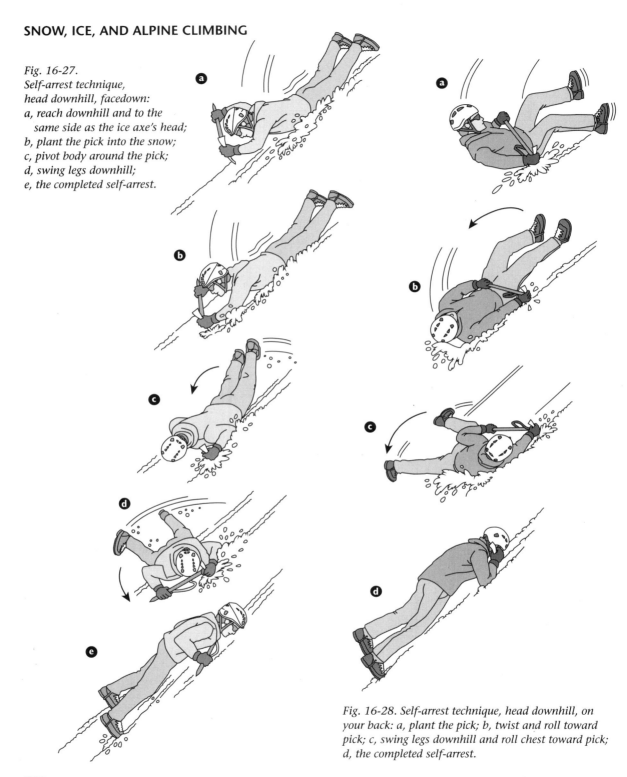

Fig. 16-27.
Self-arrest technique,
head downhill, facedown:
a, reach downhill and to the
  same side as the ice axe's head;
b, plant the pick into the snow;
c, pivot body around the pick;
d, swing legs downhill;
e, the completed self-arrest.

Fig. 16-28. Self-arrest technique, head downhill, on
your back: a, plant the pick; b, twist and roll toward
pick; c, swing legs downhill and roll chest toward pick;
d, the completed self-arrest.

Keep fighting. Even if you do not stop, the attempt itself may slow the fall and help prevent rolling, tumbling, and bouncing. It may also help keep you sliding feetfirst, the best position if you end up hitting rocks or trees. If a falling climber is roped to other climbers, anything the falling climber can do to slow the fall increases the chance that self-arrests or belays will hold.

Without an axe. If you lose your ice axe in a fall, use hands, elbows, knees, and boots to dig into the snow slope, using positioning similar to what you would use if you still had the axe. Try to clasp hands together against the slope so that snow is accumulated in them and creates more friction.

Trekking poles provide minimal capability to arrest and are not advised. Trekking pole tips are not sharp like that of an ice axe for penetrating harder snow, nor do poles have the density and strength of an ice-axe shaft to aid in arresting. Trekking poles may be an aid on lower-angle slopes, used for balance, but they are ineffective in firmer snow or at steeper angles and should not be used with dangerous runouts.

Times when self-arrest should not be trusted include when a slope seems too fast or the runout too dangerous, or when members of the climbing party doubt their strength or skill. If this is the case, back off, look for another route, or rope up and put in protection. (See "Roped Snow Climbing Techniques" below.)

Crampons and Self-Arrest

It has traditionally been taught that wearing crampons when trying to self-arrest may not be a good idea, because they can catch and flip a climber over backward or even break an ankle. This may be especially true if the snow is hard or icy. Unfortunately, if climbers are on a slope where self-arrest may be necessary, there is a good chance they will want to be wearing crampons. This is also especially true if the snow is hard or icy.

The most important thing is to take action immediately and stop yourself. Crampons may actually help in executing a self-arrest in many snow conditions by providing more traction than boots alone, possibly stopping the fall before a person has achieved any speed. On an icy slope with a dangerous runout, a belay of some type is generally recommended instead of relying on self-arrest, but climbing parties have to assess the terrain and decide for themselves.

ROPED SNOW CLIMBING TECHNIQUES

On a glacier, teams rope up for protection from hidden crevasses. On a nonglaciated snow slope, the decision is not so clear-cut, and climbers have to weigh several options.

The party can climb unroped, relying on each individual to stop a personal fall. They may decide to travel roped together but unbelayed, which offers some security for a weaker climber and gets the rope set up in case no convenient rope-up place exists later. Or they may decide to travel roped together and to use belays, because route conditions or the climbers' abilities dictate this level of protection.

The risks of roping up are not trivial. One climber can fall and pull the entire rope team off the mountain. Risk of avalanche and rockfall exposure is also higher, and the party will move more slowly.

OPTIONS FOR ROPED TEAM PROTECTION

If the climbing party decides it is safer overall to rope up, several different methods allow a party to match the type of rope protection to climbing conditions and climbers' strengths.

Team Arrest (Roped But Unbelayed)

Team arrest depends on individual climbers to stop their own falls and to provide backup in case someone else falls. Relying on team arrest as the ultimate team security makes sense only in certain situations, such as on a low- or moderate-angle glacier or snow slope. The proficient members of the rope team can save a less skilled climber from a dangerous slide.

On steeper, harder slopes, the party has to decide which option is safest: continuing to rely on team arrest, using anchors for protection, or unroping and letting each climber go it alone. To increase the odds that team arrest will work on a snow slope, use the following procedures:

Carry a few feet of slack rope coiled in your hand if any climbers are below you. If a climber falls, drop the loose rope, which allows an extra instant before the rope is loaded; use this moment to get the ice axe into self-arrest position and to brace before the falling climber's weight impacts the rope. However, if too much slack is carried, the distance that your rope mates will slide before you stop them is increased, heightening the danger to your teammates and you due to momentum, dangerous runouts, or objective hazards close by.

16

Put the weakest climber on the downhill end of the rope. As a rule, the least skilled climber should be last on the rope while ascending and first on the rope while descending. This puts the climber most likely to fall in a position where a fall will be less serious: below the other climbers, where the impact will be felt quickly along the rope.

Climb on a shortened rope. This technique is best for a two-person rope team. A climbing pair that uses only a portion of the rope reduces the sliding distance and the tug from the fall if one partner falls. To shorten the rope, wind as many coils as necessary until the desired length remains. Then use a loop of the climbing rope to tie an overhand knot through the coils, and clip the loop in to your harness with a locking carabiner. Carry the coils over one shoulder and under the opposite arm. If more than two climbers are on the rope, the middle climber or climbers should take coils in the direction of the leader. (See "Special Rescue Situations" in Chapter 18, Glacier Travel and Crevasse Rescue, for a description and illustration, Figure 18-24, of a similar technique, called "climbing in coils.")

Climb in separate parallel tracks. This is another option that is best for a two-person rope team. The climbers are abreast of each other, separated by the rope. A falling climber will pendulum down, putting force on the rope to the side of and below the partner. The tug on the rope will be less than if the climber fell from high above. Also, the friction of the rope as it pendulums across the snow will absorb some of the force. On ascents where kicking two sets of steps would be a waste of time and energy, this style may be impractical, but on ascents of harder snow and on descents, it can be good.

Handle the rope properly. Keep the rope on the downhill side of the team so that there is less chance of stepping on it. Hold the rope in your downhill hand, in a short loop. You can then take in or let out the rope, adjusting to the pace of the person ahead of you or the person behind you, rather than getting into a tug-of-war.

Observe your rope mates' pace and position and adjust and prepare accordingly. When the rope goes taut, it may be hung up on the snow, or your rope mates may be in a delicate situation in which any additional tug on the rope could yank them off their feet.

Yell "Falling!" whenever any climber falls. This alerts all rope partners to self-arrest and avoid getting pulled off their feet.

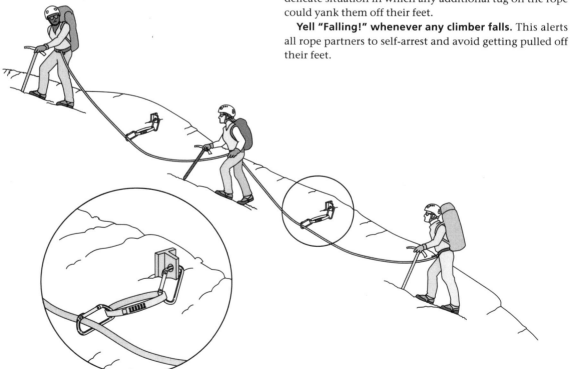

Fig. 16-29. A running belay setup; detail shows anchor attachment.

Running Belays

Roped climbers can move together on snow with the help of running belays. The running belay offers an intermediate level of protection, somewhere between team arrest and fixed belays. This technique saves time over regular belayed climbing but still allows for protection. Running belays, which are also useful in rock climbing, ice climbing, and alpine climbing, are discussed in Chapters 14, Leading on Rock, and 19, Alpine Ice Climbing. The running belay helps when a successful team arrest is improbable but fixed belays are impractical. For example, running protection may do the job on long snow faces and couloirs.

To place running belays, the leader puts in pieces of snow protection when necessary and uses carabiners and a runner to clip the rope in to each one. (For more information on snow anchors, see the next section.) All members of the rope team continue to climb at the same time, just as in unbelayed travel, except that now there is protection in the snow that will likely stop a fall (fig. 16-29). To pass each running belay point, when the middle climbers reach an anchor, they unclip the rope that is in front of them from the carabiner attached to the protection, then clip the rope that is behind them to the carabiner. The last climber on the rope removes each piece of protection.

Combination Protection Techniques

Long snow routes usually demand fast travel to reach the summit. Climbers often use a combination of roped and unroped travel, mostly unbelayed. They rely primarily on team arrest or running belays, and some sections of the climb will warrant unroped travel. Belays are typically used on steeper, harder snow or when climbers are tired or hurt. The option of turning around is always worth considering (see the "Decision Making for Roped Snow Travel" sidebar). The party can select a new route, choose another destination, or just head home.

SNOW ANCHORS

Snow anchors provide protection and secure rappels and belays. The strength of a snow anchor placement depends on the strength of the snow. The greater the area of snow the anchor pulls against and the firmer the snow, the stronger the anchor. Ultimately, the strength of snow anchors depends greatly on proper placement and snow conditions. Common snow anchors are pickets, deadman anchors, and bollards.

Picket

A picket is a stake driven into the snow as an anchor. Aluminum pickets are available in lengths ranging from 18 to 36 inches (46 to 91 centimeters) and in different styles, including V- or T-profile stakes (Figure 16-30 shows a T-profile stake), with carabiner attachment holes at the end and (in many models) along the length of the picket.

The angle for placing a picket depends on the angle of the snow slope. The picket should be placed so that it can withstand the direction of pull while having the greatest possible area of snow to pull against. On a gentler slope, the placement should be vertical or at an angle of a few degrees toward the top of the slope. On a steeper slope, the placement should be at an angle of about 45 degrees from the direction of pull (fig. 16-30a). Drive the picket as far into the snow as possible with a rock, the side of an ice axe, or an ice tool hammer. Attach a runner to the picket at the level of the snow surface—not higher on the picket, or a pull may lever it out of the snow. A fully sunk ice axe or ice tool can also serve as a makeshift picket.

A picket works best in firm, hard snow. If the snow is too soft for a vertical top-clip attachment, place the picket with a vertical midclip attachment (fig. 16-30b). Clip the webbing to the middle of the picket and lean the picket upslope 45 degrees from perpendicular to the snow. Drive the picket down in the snow as far as possible and clear a trench just wide enough for long webbing and a carabiner to reach above the snow. The runner should be twice the length of the picket. The picket should compact the snow and dive down if stressed; but be aware that the angle could flatten out if it hits a hard layer, which would weaken the anchor.

16

DECISION MAKING FOR ROPED SNOW TRAVEL

A team always ropes up on glaciers, but on snow or mixed terrain the climbing team has a few considerations:

1. Is each member of the party able to use self-belay or self-arrest? If the answer is yes, the party can continue unroped.
2. Can the team stop all falls by roping up and relying on team arrest? If so, rope up and continue climbing unbelayed.
3. Can the team use some form of belay (running or fixed) that will provide adequate protection? If so, begin belaying.
4. Should the team turn around, or should the team either rope up or proceed unroped?

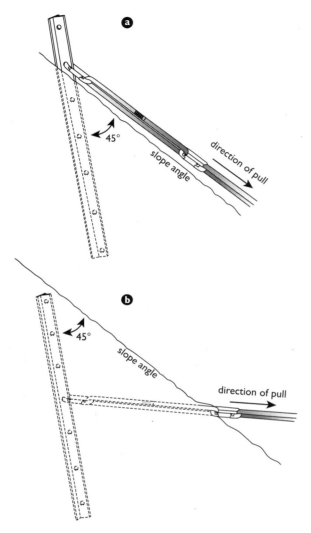

Deadman

A deadman anchor is any object buried in the snow as a point of attachment for the rope. Ice axes, ice tools, and pickets can be used as deadman anchors. Here are the steps to build a deadman:

1. Dig a trench as long as the item being used and perpendicular to the load.
2. Girth-hitch a runner to the item at its midpoint and place the item in the trench. To prevent the runner from sliding off the ends, use a carabiner. For a picket, clip a carabiner to the picket's midpoint and to the runner (fig. 16-31a). For an ice axe or ice tool, clip a carabiner to the hole at the spike end (fig. 16-31b).
3. Cut a slot in the snow that is as deep as the trench, to allow the runner to lie in the direction of pull. If this slot is shallower than the trench, there will be an upward pull on the anchor.

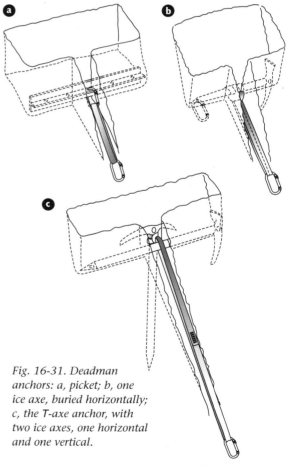

Fig. 16-30. The angle of picket placement varies with the steepness of the slope: a, in firm snow on a steep slope; b, in softer snow with attachment clipped to middle of picket. Note: Runner is not to scale—should be twice the length of the picket.

Another option is to use the picket as a deadman (see Figure 16-31a). Make sure the picket is not pulling out of the snow and that there are no visible cracks in the snow in the area against which the picket exerts force. Every member of a rope team using a running belay should check the picket as they pass it.

Fig. 16-31. Deadman anchors: a, picket; b, one ice axe, buried horizontally; c, the T-axe anchor, with two ice axes, one horizontal and one vertical.

4. Cover everything with snow except the tail of the runner. Stamp down on everything to compact and strengthen the snow.

5. Clip in to the end of the runner.

If the snow is soft, increase the strength of the deadman placement by increasing the area of snow it pulls against; do this by using a larger object. Try using a pack, a pair of skis, or a long, large stuff sack tightly filled with snow. Do not use ski or trekking poles—they are not strong enough.

In a variation of the buried-axe deadman anchor, place a second axe vertically behind the horizontal axe (fig. 16-31c). In this variation, called the T-axe anchor, girth-hitch a runner to the vertical axe and run the shaft of the horizontal axe through the runner's loop.

As with all snow anchors, inspect a deadman after every use. Look for cracks and bulges in the snow above the buried item.

Snow Bollard

A snow bollard is a mound carved out of snow. When rigged with rope or webbing, bollards can provide strong, reliable snow anchors. However, building bollards can be time consuming.

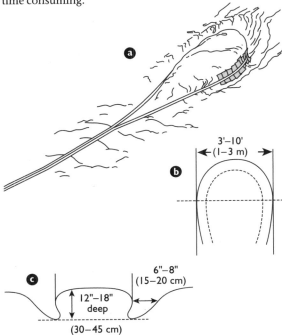

Fig. 16-32. Snow bollard: a, in a rappel setup; b, viewed from above; c, cross section.

Create the mound by making a horseshoe-shaped trench in the snow, with the open end of the horseshoe pointing downhill (fig. 16-32a). In hard snow, chop out the trench using the adze of an ice axe; in soft snow, stamp out a trench or dig one. In hard snow, the mound should be at least 3 feet (1 meter) in diameter (fig. 16-32b), and in soft snow it should be up to 10 feet (3 meters). The trench should be 6 to 8 inches (15 to 20 centimeters) wide and 12 to 18 inches (30 to 45 centimeters) deep (fig. 16-32c).

The bollard should not be in an oval teardrop shape in which the legs of the trench come together. This configuration results in a weaker anchor by not taking advantage of the entire snow slope in front of the mound.

During construction, assess the snow in the trench for changes in consistency or weak layers that could allow the rope or webbing to cut through the mound. Webbing is less likely than rope to saw into the mound. Avoid pulling on the rope or webbing after it is placed. Ice axes planted vertically at the shoulders of the trench prevent rope or webbing from cutting in. Pad the rear and sides of the mound with packs, clothing, or foam pads (as shown in Figure 16-32a). Inspect the bollard for damage after each use.

Multiple Anchors

Multiple anchors are safest. They can be placed one behind the other to provide backup and absorb any remaining force (fig. 16-33a), or they can be placed independently and connected to share the load (fig. 16-33b). Keep the anchors several feet apart so they do not share any localized weaknesses in the snow. Inspect every anchor after each use. (More details and illustrations on joining multiple anchors are found in "Equalizing the Anchor" in Chapter 10, Belaying, and in "Equalizing Protection" in Chapter 13, Rock Protection.)

BELAYING ON SNOW

When ascending on snow, climbers give quicker and less formal belays using an ice axe, or they set up belays using established snow anchors. No matter what the belaying technique, every snow belay should be as secure and dynamic as possible to help limit the force on the anchor. The hip belay can provide a more gradual, dynamic belay than a belay using a belay device, but it takes more practice to execute correctly (see "Using the Hip Belay" in Chapter 10, Belaying). Plan your stance so your body takes the force, which is dissipated as much as possible by the belay. The dynamic, shock-absorbing quality of climbing rope also helps to minimize chances of an abrupt stop to a fall.

16

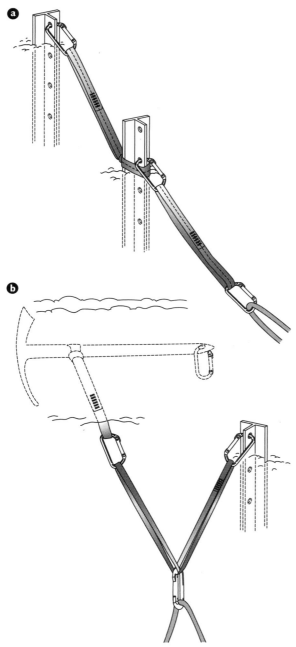

Set up a belay close to the climbing difficulties. To belay the lead climber, get out of the line of fire by setting up the belay stance to one side of the fall line. If the leader is heading up on a diagonal, get outside any point where that climber's route can cross directly above you. On a ridge crest, it is not always possible to predict a fall line and plan a belay in advance. If a rope mate slips off one side of the ridge, the best tactic may actually be to jump off the opposite side, with the rope running over the ridge and thus saving both climbers.

Carabiner–ice axe belay. The carabiner–ice axe belay provides better security than a boot-axe belay (see below), with easier rope handling. One good thing about the carabiner–ice axe belay is that the force of a fall pulls the belayer more firmly into the stance.

To set it up, plant the axe as deeply as possible, the pick perpendicular to the fall line. Girth-hitch a very short sling to the axe shaft at the surface of the snow, and clip a carabiner to the sling (fig. 16-34a). Stand at a right angle to the fall line, facing the same side as the climber's route,

Fig. 16-33. Two methods of connecting multiple snow anchors: a, two pickets linked serially, with top anchor supporting lower anchor; b, two independent anchors with self-equalized connecting runner (sliding X).

Fig. 16-34. Carabiner–ice axe belay: a, girth-hitch a short runner to axe and clip carabiner to it; b, plant axe, stand on runner, and run rope up through carabiner and around waist.

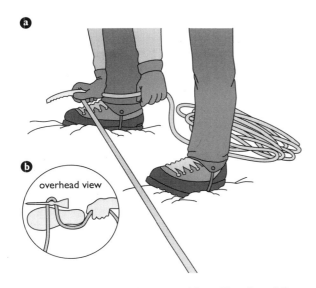

Fig. 16-35. Boot-axe belay: a, position of hands and feet; b, rope configuration.

with a control carabiner on your harness. Brace the axe with your uphill boot, standing atop the sling but leaving the carabiner exposed (fig. 16-34b). Keep crampons off the sling. The rope runs from the potential direction of pull up

through the carabiner at snow level, through the control carabiner on your harness, and then around the back of your waist and into your uphill (braking) hand.

Boot-axe belay. The boot-axe belay is a fast and easy way to provide protection as a rope team moves up together. The boot-axe belay, a form of dynamic belay, cannot hold the force of a high fall from above the belay, and because of the belayer's hunched-over stance, rope management is difficult. The boot-axe belay may be used to protect a rope mate who is probing a cornice or crevasse edge or to provide a top belay. With practice, this belay can be set up in a matter of seconds with a jab of the ice axe into the snow and a quick sweep of the rope around the shaft near the head, then in front of your ankle (fig. 16-35a and b).

Belay devices and munter hitch. Belay devices and the munter hitch used in conjunction with a snow anchor provide a very secure belay on snow. The belayer may be standing, sitting, or belaying directly off of the anchor, depending on a number of factors (see "Belay Position and Stance" in Chapter 10, Belaying). Consider belaying directly off of the anchor only when multiple anchor points are used. Standing and belaying from the harness or belaying directly from the anchor permits the belayer to get into a drier, more comfortable position. These belays are easy to set up and operate even with wet or icy ropes.

Fig. 16-36. Sitting hip belay.

16

359

Sitting hip belay. Used with a snow anchor, the sitting hip belay is dynamic and secure on snow. It does have its drawbacks. The sitting belayer may face the prospect of a cold, wet assignment, and the belay can be difficult to work if the rope is frozen.

To set up the belay, stamp or chop a seat in the snow as well as a platform to brace each boot against. Put down a pack, foam pad, or other material as insulation from the snow, and then settle into a standard hip belay, with legs outstretched and stiffened (fig. 16-36). (See "Using the Hip Belay" in Chapter 10, Belaying.)

ROUTEFINDING ON SNOW

Snow can provide passage over some frustrating obstacles, including tundra, talus, brush, streams, and logging debris. At its best it provides a smooth, uniform surface and a straight shot up the mountain.

At its worst, snow can be too soft to support your weight, or it can be hard and dangerously slick. It can obscure trails, cairns, ridge crests, and other guideposts to the route, especially above tree line. Dangers often lie beneath the surface: moats, creeks, or glacier crevasses hidden by a thin snow cover. Unstable snow slopes may avalanche.

Minimize the frustrations and dangers of snow travel by studying the medium. See Chapter 27, The Cycle of Snow, for information on snow formation, types of snow, and the creation of glaciers. Learn how seasonal weather patterns affect snow accumulation and avalanche conditions. Hone your navigation skills. Make the snow work for you: read the snow surface and terrain features to determine a safe, efficient route. If the terrain involves both snow and rock, leaving some tracks in the snow may help the party on the return trip.

ROUTEFINDING AIDS

A good routefinder uses a variety of tools, including map, compass, altimeter, GPS devices (see Chapter 5, Navigation), wands, the sun, and other visual landmarks.

SURFACE CONSIDERATIONS

The best snow to travel on is snow that will support climbers' weight and provide easy step-kicking, as well as being stable enough not to avalanche. The location of the best snow varies from day to day, even from hour to hour. If the snow in one spot is slushy, too hard, or too crusty, look around: there may be better snow a few feet away. Here are some tips for making the best use of the snow surface:

- **On a slushy slope,** walk in shade or use suncups as stairs to find patches of firmer snow.
- **On a slope that is too firm for good step-kicking,** try to find patches of softer snow.
- **When the going is difficult,** detour toward any surface that has a different appearance.
- **To find the best snow on a descent,** use a different route if necessary.
- **To find a firmer surface,** look for dirty snow. It absorbs more heat and therefore consolidates more quickly than clean snow does.
- **South- and west-facing slopes in the northern hemisphere** catch the heat of afternoon sun and consolidate earlier in the season and more quickly after storms. They offer hard surfaces when east- and north-facing slopes are still soft and unstable.
- **Take advantage of strong crusts on open slopes** before they melt. Get an early start after a clear, cold night that follows a hot day.
- **Beware of hidden holes** next to logs, trees, and rocks, where the snow has melted away from these warmer surfaces.
- **If the conditions are unfavorable on one side** of a ridge, gully, clump of trees, or large boulder, try the other side. The difference may be considerable.

VISIBILITY CONSIDERATIONS

The creative use of several routefinding methods becomes especially important when visibility is poor. In a whiteout, it is possible to lose all orientation. Distinguishing between uphill and downhill is difficult, as is distinguishing between solid snow and dense clouds. A whiteout can be caused by temporary cloud cover or blowing snow that limits visibility and makes navigation difficult and hazardous.

A GPS device can keep a party on track even when visibility is poor. Without GPS, care must be taken to avoid going off route. If a whiteout seems to be approaching, get out map, compass, and altimeter to navigate. Other options include placing wands, waiting it out a while before proceeding, or turning back.

TERRAIN CONSIDERATIONS AND FEATURES

Major terrain features present obstacles as well as opportunities (fig. 16-37). Know which ones to use and which ones to avoid.

Ridges

A ridge (fig. 16-37b) may be the route of choice if it is not too steep or craggy. Ridges are generally free of rockfall and avalanche hazard. However, ridge routes take the full brunt of wind and bad weather, and climbers must be alert to the hazard of cornices (see below), which form on ridge crests.

Cornices

Cornices form when windblown snow accumulates horizontally on ridge crests and the sides of gullies, hanging suspended out past the supporting rock (fig. 16-37d). The shape of a ridge determines the extent of the cornice that can develop. A ridge that slopes on one side and breaks into an abrupt cliff on the other is a good candidate for a gigantic cornice. A knife-edge ridge (where snow cannot accumulate) or a ridge that is gentle on both sides (where snow can disperse) typically has only a small cornice, if any at all—although exceptions do exist.

When the physical features are right for building cornices, wind direction decides the exact location of the cornice. Because storm winds have definite patterns in each mountain range, most cornices in the same area face the same way. In the Pacific Northwest region of the United States, for example, most snowstorms come from the west or southwest, so the majority of cornices form on the north and east sides. These same northern and eastern exposures were made steep by past glaciation, creating ridges ideally shaped for cornice formation.

There are exceptions. Temporary or local wind deflection can contradict the general pattern. In rare instances, cornices are even built one atop the other, facing opposite directions, the lower one partially destroyed and hidden by later formations.

Cornices are a hazard. If climbers are traveling on a cornice, it could collapse spontaneously or under the added load of their weight, or the climbers could break through the cornice. Collapsing cornices can trigger avalanches. Cornices can fracture, falling into gullies or along the slopes below, or they can separate slightly from their host ridge, forming a crack or cornice crevasse. (See Figure 17-5 in Chapter 17, Avalanche Safety.)

The safest course along a corniced crest is well behind the probable fracture line. Do not be misled by appearances. On a mature cornice, the probable line of fracture could be 30 feet (9 meters) or more back from the lip—farther back than might be expected upon examination. Usually the fracture line is not visible. Look for any crack or indentation in the snow, which might indicate a cornice that has partially collapsed and recently been covered with new snow.

The colder the weather, the more secure the cornice. A late-season cornice that is almost completely broken down also is not a problem. The safest strategy with cornices is to avoid them. Do not travel on them, under them, or through them.

Approaching from windward. The back side of a cornice appears to be a smooth snow slope that runs out to meet the sky.

Look at nearby ridges for an idea of the frequency, size, and location of cornices in the area. Try to view the lee side of the ridge from a safe vantage point, such as a rock or tree jutting through the crest.

Although rocks and trees projecting from the snow are safe, they do not indicate a stable route across the entire ridge. These can easily be on the tops of buttresses that randomly jut out perpendicularly to the ridge. The area directly in front of and behind these outcroppings may be all cornice. Many climbers have had the enlightening experience of looking back along a ridge only to discover that their tracks pass above a chasm.

When approaching from windward, stay well back from the crest if a cornice is suspected. If the crest must be approached, consider belaying the lead climber, who should probe carefully while advancing. The belayer also assumes a risk. If the cornice collapses, the belayer may have to bear the weight of the falling snow in addition to that of the climber.

Approaching from leeward. A cornice cannot be missed from the leeward side. Resembling a wave frozen as it is breaking, a large cornice close above a climber is an awesome sight. If a cornice's stability is doubtful, stay among trees or on the crest of a spur ridge while traveling below it.

Occasionally it may be necessary to climb directly through a cornice to force a way to a ridge crest or pass. Penetrate at an overhang, a rock spur, or a point where the cornice has partially collapsed. The lead climber cuts straight uphill at the point of least overhang, carefully tunneling and upsetting as little of the mass as possible.

Couloirs

Couloirs—steeply angled gullies (fig. 16-37t)—can provide a main avenue to the summit. Their overall angle is often less than that of the cliffs they breach, offering technically easier climbing. Couloirs are also the deadly debris chutes of mountains: snow, rocks, and ice blocks that are loosened by the sun often pour down couloirs (fig. 16-37ee). Here are some tips for using couloirs:

- **Try to be out of couloirs before the sun hits them.** They can be safer in early morning when the snow is solid and when rocks and ice are frozen in place.

Fig. 16-37. Alpine terrain features.

a. Horn or aiguille
b. Ridge
c. Rock arête
d. Cornice
e. Glacier basin
f. Seracs
g. Fallen seracs
h. Icefall
i. Glacier
j. Crevasses
k. Lateral moraine
l. Snout
m. Moraine lake
n. Terminal moraine
o. Glacial runoff
p. Erratic blocks
q. Rock band
r. Shoulder
s. Col
t. Couloir or gully
u. Hanging glacier
v. Bergschrund
w. Buttress
x. Cirque or bowl
y. Headwall
z. Flutings
aa. Ice wall
bb. Summit
cc. Ice arête
dd. Towers or gendarmes
ee. Avalanche chute
ff. Avalanche debris
gg. Snowfield

16

- **Keep to the sides, because most of the debris comes down the center.**
- **Listen for suspicious sounds from above;** keep an eye out for quiet slides and silently falling rock.
- **Examine a gully carefully before ascending it.** Couloirs can become increasingly nasty higher up, with extreme steepness, moats (see below), rubble strewn loosely over smooth rock slabs, thin layers of ice over rock, and cornices.
- **Bring crampons.** Deeply shaded couloirs may retain a layer of ice year-round. Early in the season, they are covered by hard snow and ice caused by freezing or avalanche scouring. Later in the season, climbers encounter the remaining hard snow and ice, sometimes with steep moats lining its edges.
- **Observe snow and avalanche conditions above steep gullies and on their floors.** Avalanches scour deep ruts in the floors of many steep couloirs. Cornices can hang above. Early in the year, the floors of the ruts offer the soundest snow available, and in cold weather they may be quite safe, particularly for a fast descent. If these conditions do not exist, cross the ruts rapidly or avoid them altogether.
- **During the ascent, look for alternative descent routes,** just in case time or changing snow conditions prevent descending the couloir on the return.
- **Research the area beforehand.** Finding the correct couloir on a particular route can be challenging. They often look alike, and there may be several in the area. Rely on route information and knowledge of the terrain in order to choose the couloir that gives access to the summit rather than leading to a dead end.
- **Beware of meltwater streams running above or underneath the snow.** Listen for water. Look for sagging or holes in the snow where the stream may be. Walk on the sides of the gully and avoid any water; it may be slick with ice.

Bergschrunds

A bergschrund is the giant crevasse found at the upper limit of glacier movement, formed where the moving glacier breaks away from the permanent snow or ice cap above (fig. 16-37v). The downhill lip of the bergschrund can be considerably lower than the uphill edge, which may be overhanging. Sometimes the bergschrund is the final problem of the ascent. (See Chapter 18, Glacier Travel and Crevasse Rescue, for more information.)

Moats

Moats occur when snow partially melts and settles away from warmer rocks or trees. Moats are encountered on snowfields, around rock outcroppings and trees on ridges and along slopes, and in couloirs. Crossing a moat at the top of a snowfield where it separates from its rocky border can be as tough as getting past a bergschrund, with the main difference being that the uphill wall of a moat is rock, whereas the uphill wall of a bergschrund is ice.

Moats around trees and rocks may not be visible, appearing as merely an unstable layer of snow but actually covering an unseen large hole underneath. Stay away from treetops poking through the snow, and probe uncertain areas with an ice axe before stepping onto them. If a wide moat borders both sides of a slope along a steep couloir, it may indicate an equally wide moat at the head of the gully. Climbers may have to cross it or, worse yet, retreat and find an alternate ascent.

Rockfall

Snowfields and glaciers are subject to rockfall from bordering walls and ridges. Wear helmets in hazardous areas. Try to schedule climbs for less-dangerous periods. Early-season outings face less rockfall than summer climbs because snow still cements loose rock in place. In the northern hemisphere, southern and eastern slopes get the sun first, so climb these slopes early. The shaded northern exposures offer less rockfall danger.

SAFE SNOW TRAVEL

Snow is a constantly changing medium. Safe snow travel requires alertness, preparation, and a constant reassessment of conditions. Here are some points to remember:

- **Continually assess the runout and snow conditions.**
- **Do not rely on self-arrest if the runout is dangerous or unknown.** If climbers are uncomfortable using a self-belay, use a running belay or an anchored belay, or turn back and find another route.
- **Bring crampons on snow climbs,** even in warm weather. Crampons are not just for glacier travel.

Climbers may encounter a shady couloir or slope with ice or hard snow.

- **Anchor the climbing party** if it has to adjust equipment, such as crampons, on an exposed slope.
- **Wear gloves whenever on snow,** even when the weather is warm and it would be more comfortable to take them off. A climber can fall at any time.
- **Yell "Falling!" whenever anyone, including you, falls.** Follow up with "Arrest! Arrest!" until the fallen climber has safely come to a stop.
- **Continually observe the party's overall condition and climbing ability.** Late in the day, exhaustion may diminish reaction time in the event of a fall.

GAINING FREEDOM OF THE SNOWY HILLS

Traveling across snow to reach a climbing objective is one of the most rewarding experiences in the backcountry. In summer, the excitement of encountering snow can be a delight, while winter snow creates a wonderland-like experience during pursuit of an objective. The basic techniques discussed here can help increase efficiency, safety, and enjoyment while traveling over snow. One additional factor is taking care in avalanche terrain. The next chapter provides some basic ideas on how to avoid avalanches when traveling or climbing under snowy conditions and on snowy terrain.

16

CHAPTER 17

AVALANCHE SAFETY

Mountaineers seek the freedom of the hills, and no freedom is harder to earn than that of the snowy hills. In North America, according to the Colorado Avalanche Information Center, avalanches kill more winter recreationists than any other natural hazard: 34 in 2012, 24 in 2013, 35 in 2014, 11 in 2015, and 29 in 2016. Nearly all avalanches that involve people are triggered either by the victims themselves or by a member of their party. According to avalanche expert Bruce Tremper, about 90 percent of avalanche victims trigger their own slide.

Climbers, backcountry skiers, snowmobilers, and snow-shoers are prime victims of avalanches. Better mountain gear and changing trends in backcountry recreation are leading more and more people to have fun where there are avalanche-prone slopes. The high level of risk to climbers and backcountry skiers can be explained by two factors:

1. Climbers' and backcountry skiers' destinations are often in avalanche terrain; therefore they spend more time exposed to risk of involvement in an avalanche.
2. Climbers' and backcountry skiers' routes to their destinations often cross avalanche-prone areas where human triggering is possible or even likely.

Reaching a climbing objective often involves traveling on steep and exposed avalanche start zones (see "Understanding Avalanches" below). When choosing route options, climbers must contend with the challenges of evaluating avalanche hazard. Early start times, really fast travel, and brute ambition are not enough to evade all avalanches. Avalanche hazard, unlike high-mountain exposure and severe weather, is not always obvious.

However, avalanches are not a mysterious phenomenon.

Avalanche education can help backcountry travelers make better decisions about safe snow travel. This chapter introduces the subject of avalanches, reviews some of the ways that snow travelers can evaluate hazards and minimize risk, and explains methods of searching for avalanche victims. This material is not intended to be comprehensive. For a more complete understanding of the subject, consult specialized publications (see Resources) and take a level 1 course offered by the American Institute for Avalanche Research and Education (AIARE), or equivalent, to learn how to make informed decisions in avalanche terrain. For an explanation of the formation of avalanches and an assessment of dangers associated with various forms of snow, see Chapter 27, The Cycle of Snow.

UNDERSTANDING AVALANCHES

Most avalanche victims are involved in small to medium-sized slides. Imagine a snowfield the size of a couple of tennis courts; it is poised on a slope, with weak layers hidden beneath the surface. A climber or skier enters the scene, and the additional load causes a failure: *crack!* The slab is off and away. The snow breaks and shears along the bed surface (the ground, ice, or hard snow layer that forms the sliding surface) between the weak layers, and across the top of the snowfield a fracture line marks the point where the tension holding the snow failed. Below the avalanche start zone (typically a 25- to 50-degree slope), the slab breaks up, and the churning snow accelerates down the avalanche track and into the runout zone, where a change in the terrain stops the moving snow and the dense deposit accumulates and buries victims, on average, 3 to 4 feet (about 1 to 1.3 meters) deep. Because the motion is sudden, it has an unbalancing effect; the suddenness, speed, and power of the avalanche typically sweep victims off their feet or skis, sometimes hurtling them into bad terrain or forcing them through confined tracks and burying them deeply in a cement-like medium tightly packed in a terrain trap.

Many avalanches create a destructive force capable of breaking trees, crushing a car, or wiping out a small cluster of buildings. Avalanche movement is varied; imagine slow lava, flowing white water, or 220-mile-per-hour (350-kilometer-per-hour) airborne turbulent masses.

When the following three elements coincide, an avalanche can occur:

1. **Unstable snow.** The snow is loose (for example, powder, which is part of the allure of a climbing, snowshoeing, or skiing trip) or the snow layers are poorly bonded.
2. **Steep terrain.** The slope angle is steep enough to produce a slide.
3. **Trigger.** Something initiates the failure of the bonds holding the snowpack in place.

Natural avalanches may occur when new snow deposited by storms loads the previous layers of snowpack, adding more stress and triggering an avalanche. A skier or climber may add sufficient stress to trigger a slide, as can falling chunks of snow, ice, or rock. The two principal types of avalanches that climbers encounter in a typical spring and summer climbing season are slab avalanches and loose-snow avalanches. (See "The Formation of Snow Avalanches" in Chapter 27, The Cycle of Snow.)

SLAB AVALANCHES

Slab avalanches are very dangerous to skiers, snowshoers, and winter climbers and scramblers. They are formed by a cohesive stronger snowpack layer forming over a weaker layer (see "Terrain" in the next section). A slab avalanche occurs when the slope fails first in compression (the *whumph* sound that climbers sometimes hear) and then

in tension (the breaking of the slab that allows the slab to begin moving). A large area of snow (the slab) begins to move simultaneously and often breaks up into large plates and blocks of snow. Slab avalanches can strip snow all the way to the ground or can involve only the top layer(s) of poorly bonded snow. Wet springtime slab avalanches occur when the intense warming of long spring days and higher sun angles softens layers in the existing snowpack that formed during the winter; wet slab avalanche conditions are very sensitive to the slope aspect, time of day, and temperature.

LOOSE-SNOW AVALANCHES

Loose-snow avalanches, which can consist of wet or dry snow, originate from a single point of release. They often look like an inverted V as they spread out and move downslope. They often move relatively slowly compared with slab avalanches. Wet loose-snow avalanches (common in spring) can overload a slope and cause failure in an underlying slab, resulting in a large and dangerous slab avalanche.

EVALUATING AVALANCHE HAZARD

The interaction of three crucial variables—unstable snow, terrain, and a trigger—determines whether or not an avalanche is possible (fig. 17-1). What is the layering of the snow? Is the terrain capable of producing an avalanche? Could I or one of my party be the trigger? Could a change in the weather trigger an avalanche? (See "Avalanche Triggers" in Chapter 27, The Cycle of Snow.)

Evaluating avalanche hazard is both an art and a science. It takes years of experience to become good at evaluating hazard. Local knowledge and experience reading the weather and snowpack typical of each of the world's mountain ranges is vital to achieving a high degree of competence at predicting when and where avalanches are likely to occur. Many regions offer detailed avalanche and mountain weather forecasts, explaining what (if any) weak layers exist, what the current avalanche problems are, and what terrain to avoid (see www.avalanche.org to find forecast websites near your objective).

Forecasting is not an exact science and weather does not always unfold as predicted, so it is vital to understand the logic behind the forecast and to confirm that the conditions in the field match the conditions predicted by the forecast. In addition, forecasts are often generalized to cover large geographical areas, so it is also vital to confirm that local conditions on your route match the forecast.

17

Fig. 17-1. Avalanche hazard triangle: terrain, snowpack, and weather—with the added variable of backcountry travelers.

The composition of the current snowpack can to a large extent be inferred based on the weather history. Online spreadsheets that provide hourly snapshots of data such as wind speed, wind direction, temperature, rates of precipitation, and so on can give a very good idea of whether the snowpack in a particular area is likely to be stable or not. If this data is no longer available once climbers are out in the field, they need to observe and record their observations in order to form their own accurate forecasts.

Climbers in an unfamiliar area need to make conservative decisions about where to travel. When climbing in remote areas, where professional forecasts are unavailable, climbers need to become their own forecasters, which requires a high degree of competence at evaluating the snowpack and analyzing the available weather data. Even when professional avalanche forecasts are available and you are climbing in familiar mountains, it is important to make these same weather observations, as well as to continually study and test the snowpack, in order to confirm that the forecast you are depending on really corresponds to the conditions you are encountering.

TERRAIN

Understanding avalanche terrain is the key to safe travel in snowy mountains. Of the three variables in Figure 17-1, the weather cannot be controlled, and an unstable

snowpack can persist over large areas for long periods, but climbers can always choose to travel in terrain that will not generate an avalanche. Choosing safe terrain based on an understanding of the local conditions is the central concept of safe travel in avalanche country.

Learning to recognize avalanche terrain is the first step in the process of evaluating avalanche hazard. The steepness of a slope, its aspect (which direction it faces), and the slope's shape and natural features (its configuration) are all important factors in determining whether a slide can occur on a particular slope.

Slope Angle

Of all of the terrain factors, the steepness, or slope angle, is the most important. Slab avalanches commonly occur on slopes with starting-zone angles between about 30 and 45 degrees, but slab avalanches occasionally occur on slopes of less than 30 and greater than 45 to 55 degrees (fig. 17-2). Slopes steeper than about 50 to 60 degrees tend to sluff snow constantly, and slopes of about 25 degrees or less are generally not steep enough or require highly unstable snow before they can slide.

It is difficult to estimate the angle of a slope just by looking at it. Use a clinometer to measure slope angles in the field. Simple plastic models are available, and many compasses have clinometers built into them (see Chapter 5, Navigation, for a discussion of clinometers and how to measure slope angle). Learn to measure slope angle accurately on topographical maps; special scales make it easy to measure slope angle directly from the map based on the spacing of contour lines (fig. 17-3).

The angle of the slope the climbers are on is not the only concern, because an avalanche could start from an adjacent slope. A party does not have to be climbing or skiing on a slope for it to avalanche. This is a very important concept: All of the snow is connected. Climbers can be traveling on a gentle slope or a snow-covered road, and if the snowpack is unstable enough, they can trigger a slide on the steeper slope above them, even though they are not on a steep slope. All of the snow is connected, remember? It is critical to know what is above you as you travel. Because adjacent terrain is often out of view or obscured by the weather, study a topographical map to identify sources of hazard that may lie above or below your route.

Slope Aspect

The direction a slope faces—its slope aspect—determines how much sun and wind the slope gets, which indicates a great deal about its avalanche potential. Here is how it

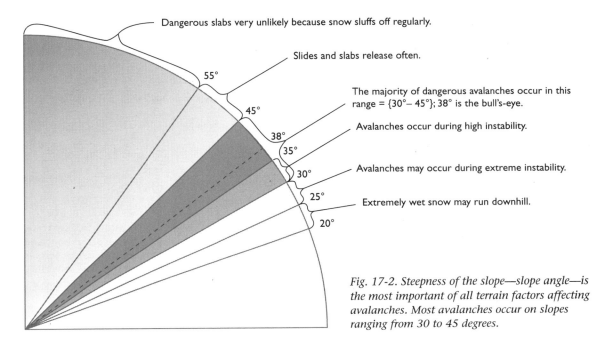

Dangerous slabs very unlikely because snow sluffs off regularly.

Slides and slabs release often.

55°

45°

The majority of dangerous avalanches occur in this range = {30°– 45°}; 38° is the bull's-eye.

38°

Avalanches occur during high instability.

35°

30°

Avalanches may occur during extreme instability.

25°

Extremely wet snow may run downhill.

20°

Fig. 17-2. Steepness of the slope—slope angle—is the most important of all terrain factors affecting avalanches. Most avalanches occur on slopes ranging from 30 to 45 degrees.

works in the northern hemisphere (it is the opposite on mountains south of the equator).

South-facing slopes. Snow settles and stabilizes faster on slopes that receive more sun than it does on north-facing slopes. In general (with plenty of local exceptions), this may

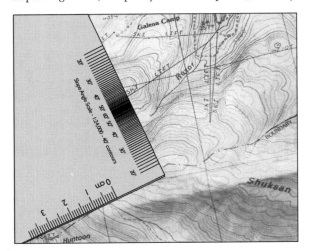

Fig. 17-3. Measuring slope angle based on contour lines using the 1:24,000 scale in the American Institute for Avalanche Research and Education (AIARE) Field Book.

make south-facing slopes somewhat safer in winter. They tend to release avalanches sooner after a storm, so if they are avalanching, it is an indication that slopes facing in other directions may soon follow their lead. As warmer spring and summer days arrive, south slopes become prone to wet-snow avalanches, and north-facing slopes may be safer.

North-facing slopes. On slopes that receive little or no sun in the winter, consolidation of the snowpack takes longer. Colder temperatures within the snowpack create weak layers. Therefore, in general (again, with local exceptions), north slopes are more likely to slide in midwinter. In spring and summer, as south slopes become dangerously wet, look to the north side for firmer, safer snow.

Windward slopes. Slopes that face into the wind tend to be safer than leeward slopes. Windward slopes may be blown clear of snow, or the remaining snow may be compacted by the force of the wind.

Leeward slopes. Slopes that face away from the wind are particularly dangerous because of windloading, which happens when the wind transports snow rapidly from a wind-exposed area of the slope to a less wind-exposed leeward area of the slope. A slope can become "top-loaded" by wind blowing snow over the top of a ridge crest and depositing it on the lee side, or it can become "cross-loaded" by the wind blowing across the slope and depositing the snow in gullies between ridges. Leeward slopes collect

17

snow rapidly when even moderate winds move snow from windward slopes onto the leeward side. The results are the formation of cornices on the lee side of ridges, snow that is deeper and less consolidated, and the formation of wind slabs ready to avalanche.

Be especially aware that in some areas, such as the passes in Washington State's North Cascades, the wind very often shifts direction with the onset of a storm, and what a climber thought was the windward slope may then become the leeward slope. It is quite common to have the wind blow the snow that was deposited by the last storm on the north and east aspects onto the south and west aspects as a storm approaches these mountains from the southwest. This makes the west and southwest aspects temporarily the leeward slopes, and avalanche conditions become dangerous on those slopes. As the storm moves onshore from the Pacific Ocean and into the Cascades, the wind then shifts to blowing from the west and southwest and begins to redeposit the snow on the now leeward north and northeast aspects, the "traditional" dangerous leeward slopes.

Slope Configuration

Smooth slopes—those that, beneath the snow, are covered with grass or smooth rock slabs—generally do not anchor the snow well, and thus provide a good bed surface for a slide. Trees and rocks may serve as anchors that tend to stabilize the snow—at least until the snow covers them. But, in general, to act as effective anchors, the trees and rocks need to be so close together that it can be difficult or impossible for a climbing party to move through them. After these trees and rocks are buried by snowfall, they can actually become a source of weakness in the snowpack: as foreign bodies, the trees and rocks can inhibit or interfere with the bonding of the snow layers. Slides are less likely to originate in a dense forest, but they can run through dense forest from above. Forested slopes avalanche less often, not because the trees hold the snow in place, but because snow falling from treetops will often speed up the stabilization of fresh snow after a storm or because tree cover may inhibit the formation of surface hoar (a potential cause of weak layers in the snowpack). In addition, an established forest provides historical evidence that very large slides do not often occur in the forested terrain.

The shape of a slope also affects the hazard level. Snow on a slope that is straight, open, and moderately steep presents the most obvious danger. Snow on a convex slope, under tension as it stretches tightly over the bulge in the terrain, is more prone to avalanche than snow on a

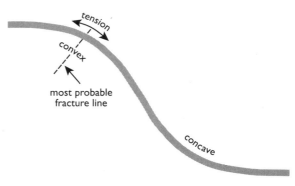

Fig. 17-4. Convex and concave slope configurations.

concave slope (fig. 17-4). Fracture lines frequently occur at or just below a convex area. Ridges are often the safest route up a mountain where avalanches may be a problem, because they present a lower-angle path and keep climbers off open slopes; however, on ridges be wary of overhanging cornices or adjacent wind slabs.

Terrain Traps

The term "terrain trap" describes hazardous terrain that increases the consequences of being buried or injured if a climber is caught in an avalanche. These traps can be found in a wide variety of terrain, including cliffs below the route that a snowslide might carry you over or a grove of trees that might injure you if a slide sweeps you into them. It is particularly important to be aware of terrain configurations that will concentrate or funnel an avalanche into a smaller runout zone so that a person caught in the slide is buried very deeply. Even a relatively small and shallow snowslide that might be harmless on an open slope can bury and kill a climber if it flows into a narrow gully. Many ice climbing routes follow gullies that, though they may be too steep to be a source of avalanches, are routinely swept by powerful avalanches generated higher on the mountain. Other examples of deadly terrain traps include buried streams, glacier crevasses, valleys, and flat roadways cutting across a slope.

SNOWPACK

The typical snowpack is composed of a series of distinct layers deposited by each storm and characterized by relative strength, hardness, and thickness. The depth and distribution of weak layers within the snowpack are significant factors in determining the stability of the snowpack. Climbers must determine the composition of the snowpack—its configuration.

Bonding Ability

Throughout the winter, the snowpack accumulates layer by layer with each new precipitation, temperature, and wind event. A snowpack has both strong and weak layers. Strong layers tend to be cohesive—denser layers composed of small, round snow grains packed closely together and well bonded to each other. Weak layers tend to be less dense, composed of poorly bonded grains. These weak layers often appear loose or "sugary." Because weak layers prevent strong layers from bonding with one another, it is important for the backcountry traveler to know the relationship of these layers. Remember, the snow slab that becomes a slab avalanche is a stronger layer of snow on top of a weaker layer of snow; where slab avalanches are suspected, the backcountry traveler may dig snow pits and probe the snow looking for strong-over-weak layers in the snowpack.

Sensitivity to Stress

The snowpack exists in a balance between its strength and the stresses placed upon it. When the snow's strength is greater than the stresses, the snow is stable. Fortunately, this is most often the case; otherwise, snow would never stay on a hillside. But sometimes the balance between strength and stress is almost equal, and then the snowpack is unstable. Avalanches occur only when and if the snowpack is unstable. For an avalanche to occur, something must disturb the balance so that the stress on or within the snowpack exceeds its strength. The snowpack can adjust to only a limited amount of stress and only at a certain rate of speed. Add another stress such as a rapid load of precipitation, a sudden increase in temperature, windblown snow, or the weight of a climber or skier, and an avalanche could be triggered.

WEATHER

Before and during any backcountry trip, study the weather closely. Heavy precipitation, high winds, or extreme temperatures mean changes in the snowpack. Be prepared to look critically at the snow to see how the snowpack has been affected by recent weather. The snowpack adapts poorly to sudden changes, so rapid turns in the weather contribute to instability of the snowpack. The snowpack can bend and adapt when forces are applied slowly, but sudden stress can cause it to break (see "The Formation of Snow Avalanches" in Chapter 27, The Cycle of Snow).

In some climates, such as maritime areas, the storm snow typically stabilizes within 72 hours, so climbers may need to look at weather data for a week or two prior to their trip,

in order to determine how the snowpack has evolved since the last time it was stable. Even in a maritime mountain range, persistent weak layers do sometimes occur, however, requiring climbers to consider a hazard caused by weather events from much earlier in the season. In colder mountain climates with shallower snowpacks, persistent weak layers are the norm and climbers almost always need to consider the weather history and snowpack evolution through the entire avalanche season. It is especially important when climbers are in an unfamiliar part of the world to study the ways that weather and snowpack interact; the typical avalanche problems can be very different from place to place. Weather and snow pack formation is covered in greater depth in Chapter 28, Mountain Weather.

Precipitation

Both forms of precipitation—either solid (snow and hail) or liquid (rain)—add to stress on the snowpack. Avalanche danger increases rapidly with snowfall of 1 inch (2.5 centimeters) or more per hour. The threshold of 12 inches (30 centimeters) or more in a day is critical. If a heavy load of new snow accumulates too quickly for the strength of the existing snowpack, an avalanche may result.

Rain can percolate into the snow, weakening bonds between layers. Rain tends to lubricate the layers, making it easier for a slide to start. Rain adds significant weight, and it may also rapidly warm the snowpack. Avalanches can be triggered very quickly after rainfall begins.

With either rain or new snow, consider these questions: How well does new snow bond with the snowpack? How big a load does it represent? The weight of the water in rain or new snow is the primary contributor of stress on the snowpack.

17

Wind

The high winds that transport snow from windward slopes and deposit it on leeward slopes break the interlocking bonds between snow crystals. These particles, once they are made smaller, pack closely together, forming firm cohesive slabs that fracture efficiently, resulting in avalanches. A wind slab is a typical strong layer, ready to slide as a unit when it breaks free of a weaker underlying layer. High winds also shape the cornices that overhang lee slopes (fig. 17-5a and b). Cornices can break and fall, sometimes triggering an avalanche (fig. 17-5c). Be aware that when winds blow from one direction and then later from another direction, it is sometimes possible for wind slabs to form on both sides of a ridge. Local terrain features can force prevailing winds to blow in atypical directions as

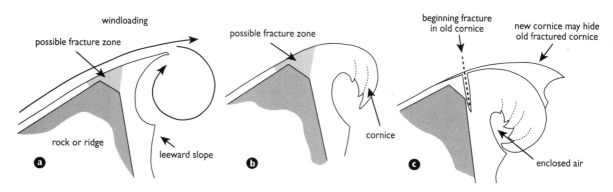

Fig. 17-5. How cornices form: a, wind blows snow beyond the edge of a ridge; b, successive storms build up layers and extend snow farther away from ridge; c, original cornice becomes fully enclosed and a new cornice begins on top of it.

well. Always study weather over a sufficient span of time and make observations in the field rather than going by simple assumptions.

Temperature

Significant differences in temperature between the ground and the snow surface promote growth of highly faceted snow crystals (depth hoar, or "sugar snow") that cannot support much load. This temperature differential and the resulting sugar snow are especially common early in the season, notably in interior, snowy climates such as that of the Rocky Mountains or in the drier and colder parts of the North Cascades like the Washington Pass area. Less severe temperature gradients and a deeper snowpack act as insulation that may allow this snow to stabilize. But highly faceted snow can persist as a dangerous underlying layer well into the snow season or until avalanches release it.

Another persistent weak layer, similar to dew, is surface hoar. It is found in all mountain ranges. The conditions that encourage its growth are cold, clear nights with little to no wind at the snow surface and a source of moisture nearby such as a stream or lake. When the thin, feathered crystals of surface hoar are covered by subsequent snowfall, they can form weak layers that—like sugar snow—increase avalanche hazard.

Melt-freeze crusts form from sun or rain on snow followed by rapid cooling, resulting in a dense icy layer with poor bonding characteristics. These crusts may persist for a long time before they break down, leaving a smooth, hard bed surface ready to be reloaded by the next storm.

Temperature affects snow stability, especially that of new snow, in complicated ways. Warm temperatures accelerate settling, causing the snowpack to become denser and

stronger and, thus, over the long term, more stable. But rapid, prolonged warming, particularly after a cold spell, initially weakens the snow cover, making it less stable and more susceptible to human-triggered failure. The snowpack remains unstable until temperatures cool down. Cold temperatures make dense snow layers stronger but are unlikely to strengthen weak layers of new, low-density snow. Cold temperatures also tend to preserve such weak layers, extending the time that they may remain a hazard.

KNOW BEFORE YOU GO: PLANNING A TRIP

It is up to all climbers to gather important data before they head into avalanche terrain. There are many ways to minimize the risk of avalanches and to increase the chances of survival if one hits. In addition to evaluating avalanche hazard during a trip, climbers can also reduce avalanche risk by the things they do before they head into the mountains. See "Organizing and Leading a Climb" in Chapter 22, Leadership.

Take a class: a level 1 avalanche course is critical to climbers' learning how to make good decisions about safe travel in avalanche terrain. Reading this chapter provides an introduction to decision making in avalanche terrain. After taking an avalanche course, climbers should be able to identify avalanche terrain; identify basic snow grain types, weak layers, and strong layers; perform field tests to look for instability in the snowpack; recognize weather and terrain factors contributing to instability; perform rescue through fast and efficient transceiver use; and apply safe travel techniques. There is no such thing as too much avalanche education.

CHECK WEATHER AND AVALANCHE FORECASTS

It is obvious advice, but check the weather and avalanche forecasts before a trip. Most local avalanche centers, such as the Northwest Avalanche Center (see Resources), issue avalanche warnings throughout the winter. Before heading out, check the avalanche bulletin for the area the party plans to visit, and use this forecast to make decisions about where it might be safe to travel. If possible, study the weather trends and snowfall history of the area, which provide information about the snowpack. Talk to people with local knowledge of the intended route, including any ranger who may be responsible for that area. Often,

---

TIPS FOR SELECTING A SAFE ROUTE

Travel safely in the backcountry by seeking routes that limit the party's exposure to danger. The following guidelines are based on some of the important considerations discussed in this chapter:

- **Favor windward slopes,** which tend to be more stable.
- **Avoid leeward slopes** where winds have deposited snow slabs.
- **Choose the lowest-angle slopes** that avoid 30 to 45 degrees and will get the party to its objective.
- **Favor the edges of slopes,** where avalanches are less likely and safer terrain is closer in case one does occur.
- **Be particularly cautious of slopes of 30 to 45 degrees;** use a clinometer to identify them. The majority of avalanches occur on slopes close to 38 degrees.
- **Be suspicious of convex rollovers;** they are likely trigger points for avalanches.
- **Be careful of shaded slopes** in winter and the very warm, sunny slopes of spring.
- **Avoid gullies and other terrain traps,** which can be chutes for large quantities of snow that can deeply bury climbers or sweep them away.
- **Keep aware of the runout zone** below snow slopes and gullies, especially avoiding areas with cliffs below.
- **Avoid camping in valleys** or any other place that can be exposed to avalanche danger from above (fig. 17-6).
- **Develop "avalanche eyeballs"** by continually evaluating avalanche danger and its potential consequences.

---

detailed trip reports can be found on websites that post beta gathered by climbers, skiers, and others. Do not be afraid to rethink well-laid plans if crucial new pretrip information is uncovered.

Climbers can also improve their safety margin by taking the normal precautions called for on any climbing trip or ski tour: studying maps, Google Earth, and photos of the area; researching alternative routes; preparing for an emergency bivouac; and identifying possible retreat routes. Determine the route—including its slope aspects, elevations, slope sizes and shapes, and exposure—and identify the probable locations of hazards. See the "Tips for Selecting a Safe Route" sidebar.

It is an excellent idea to include a safe alternate destination in every trip plan. Having a safe option already picked out and planned for helps defeat the momentum that so often leads people to plunge ahead in dangerous conditions, instead of making a rational decision to go elsewhere.

Trip planning is much more effective if all climbers in a party use a small field book to note weather and snowpack data and forecasts, route plans, emergency contact information, and so forth. The same book can be used to note snowpack and weather observations in the field, which is a huge help in tracking how well the conditions encountered support the avalanche forecast upon which the initial trip plan was based. The *AIARE Field Book* provides a standardized format for this purpose, with a "Trip Plan" form on one page and a "Field Observations" form on the adjacent facing page (fig. 17-7). This useful little book also provides basic reference tables and checklists for travel in

17

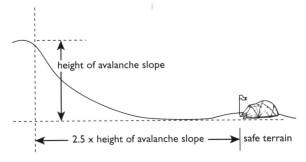

height of avalanche slope

2.5 x height of avalanche slope ────▶ safe terrain

Fig. 17-6. Calculation to arrive at a safe camping zone: the formula requires that the climber accurately determine the full extent of the applicable avalanche slope, but it gives a good idea of where safe terrain can be found below avalanche-prone slopes. Narrow valleys may not have a safe zone.

TRIP PLAN

DATE:	TIME:	FIELD LOCATION:

AVALANCHE DANGER: AVALANCHE ACTIVITY? • BULLETIN DANGER RATINGS?
"Where are avalanches likely to occur?" "Describe the problem?" "Specifically, which slopes will we avoid?"

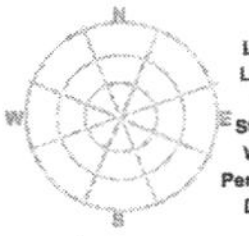

Loose Dry ☐
Loose Wet ☐
Wet Slab ☐
Storm Slab ☐
Wind Slab ☐
Persist. Slab ☐
Deep Slab ☐
Cornice ☐

SNOWPACK DISCUSSION: NEW / STORM SNOW? • WARMING? • WEAKLAYER(S) TYPE / DEPTH / PERSISTENCE?
"Where is the best snow?" "What field observations needed?" "Do we have experience w/ these conditions?"

WEATHER FORECAST: SKY / VISIBILITY • PRECIPITATION • WINDS / BLOWING SNOW • TEMPERATURES • TRENDS
"How will forecast affect snow conditions?" "...affect our observations? communication? decision-making?"

TRAVEL PLAN: OBJECTIVE • OPTIONS • ANTICIPATED HAZARDS • OBSERVATION PTS • DECISION PTS • GROUP MGMT
"Is plan appropriate for our goals, experience, abilities?" "Everyone included in discussion, w/ consensus?"

EMERGENCY RESPONSE: LEADERSHIP • GEAR ASSIGNMENTS • COMM. PLAN • EVAC ROUTE • EMERGENCY #'s
"Are we prepared & practiced?" "Outside help realistic?" "All concerns voiced re: dangers, risk, response?"

FIELD OBSERVATIONS

NAMES:				
Location •Time •Elevation •Aspect				
Sky •Cloud cover •Precipitation				
Temperature •Air •Surface & 20cm↓				
Wind •Speed / direction •Blowing snow				
Snow •Surf form / size •New snow •Snow height •Pen boot / ski				

TERRAIN USE • SIGNS OF UNSTABLE SNOW • PATTERNS
Red Flags • Avalanches • Snowpack Tests • Other Observations • Comments

REVIEW THE DAY: *"Were our choices in line w/ our forecast / plan?" "When were we most at risk?" "Where could we have triggered a slide?" "What would we do differently next time?"*

Fig. 17-7. "Trip Plan" and "Field Observations" forms, reproduced from the AIARE Field Book.

avalanche terrain. (For more information or to contact AIARE, see Resources.)

In areas where professional avalanche forecasting is available, climbers should take forecast warnings very seriously. It is never a good idea to enter terrain the forecast declares to be unsafe. In addition, it is important that climbers keep a sharp eye out for unsafe conditions even in areas the forecast has not singled out for extra caution.

The trend in avalanche forecasting is to present the forecast hazards in terms of one or more "avalanche problems," as shown in Table 17-1, excerpted from the *AIARE Field Book.*

For each of the typical "avalanche problems" listed in Table 17-1, there are lists of red-flag observations as well as specific tests and other practical considerations that can

AVALANCHE EDUCATION

The American Institute for Avalanche Research and Education (AIARE) is a nationally recognized curriculum for avalanche educators in the United States, South America, and Europe. The mission is to "save lives through avalanche education" with avalanche training courses reflecting the latest knowledge, research, and ideas in avalanche safety for backcountry travelers. AIARE's goals include increasing public awareness of avalanches and avalanche safety; providing high-quality avalanche education to enhance public awareness and safety; and developing an international network of professional avalanche educators.

TABLE 17-1. AVALANCHES AND OBSERVATIONS REFERENCE

CRITICAL (RED-FLAG) OBSERVATIONS	FIELD TESTS & RELEVANT OBSERVATIONS	IMPORTANT CONSIDERATIONS
THE PROBLEM: LOOSE DRY SNOW		
▪ Fan-shaped avalanches: fine debris ▪ Loose surface snow ≥12 inches (30 cm) deep	▪ Boots or skis penetrate ≥12 inches (30 cm). ▪ Slope tests and cuts result in sluffs. ▪ Snow surface texture is loose (as opposed to wind-affected, refrozen, or other stiff snow textures).	▪ Loose-snow avalanche can be triggered by falling snow, cornice fall, rockfall, brief periods of sun, wind, or a rider. ▪ Sluffs can run fast and far. ▪ Small slides are dangerous with terrain traps and/or cliffs. ▪ Sluffs can trigger slabs in certain conditions.
THE PROBLEM: LOOSE WET SNOW		
▪ Rain and/or rapid warming ▪ Air temperature >32°F (>0°C) for longer than 24 hours (cloud cover may prevent nighttime cooling) ▪ Pinwheels or roller balls ▪ Fan-shaped avalanches: debris lumpy and chunky	▪ Compare observed and forecasted temperature trend. ▪ Temperatures (air, surface, 20 cm deep) and freezing level indicate near-surface snow temperatures at 32°F (0°C). ▪ Note slopes receiving or that will receive intense radiation. ▪ Snow surface is wet: water visible between the grains with a loupe; may be able to squeeze water out with hands.	▪ Timing is critical: danger can increase quickly (minutes to hours). ▪ No freeze for multiple nights worsens conditions; however, nighttime freeze can stabilize conditions. ▪ Gullies and cirques receive more radiation and retain more heat than open slopes. ▪ Shallow snow areas become unstable first—may slide to ground in terrain with shallower, less-dense snowpack. ▪ Loose-snow avalanche may initiate from rocks or vegetation. ▪ Loose-snow avalanche can occur on all aspects on cloudy days and nights. ▪ Conditions may also include cornice fall, rockfall, or increased icefall hazards.
THE PROBLEM: WET SLAB		
▪ Rain on snow, especially dry snow ▪ Current or recent wet slab avalanches: debris has channels and/or ridges, high water content; may entrain rocks and vegetation ▪ Prolonged warming trend, especially the first melt on dry snow	▪ Consider loose wet snow observations. ▪ Melting snow surface (rain or strong radiation) of a slab is observed over weak layer. ▪ Tests show change in strength of weak layer due to water and/or water lubrication above crust or ground layer. ▪ Identify depth at which snow is 32°F (0°C).	▪ Snow temperature of slab is at or near 32°F (0°C). ▪ Loose wet snow slides can occur just prior to wet slab activity. ▪ Possible lag can occur between melt event and wet slab activity.

17

continued

TABLE 17-1. AVALANCHES AND OBSERVATIONS REFERENCE *continued*

CRITICAL (RED-FLAG) OBSERVATIONS	FIELD TESTS & RELEVANT OBSERVATIONS	IMPORTANT CONSIDERATIONS
THE PROBLEM: WET SLAB *cont.*		
	■ Monitor liquid water content and deteriorating snow strength using hardness and penetration tests. ■ Nearby glide cracks may be widening during rapid warming.	
THE PROBLEM: STORM SLAB		
■ Natural avalanches in steep terrain with little or no wind ■ At least 12 inches (30 cm) snowfall in last 24 hours or less with warmer, heavier snow ■ Poor bond to old snow: slab cracks or avalanches under a rider's weight	■ Observe storm snow depth, accumulation rate, and water equivalent. ■ Observe settlement trend: settlement cones, boot or ski penetration, measured change in storm snow (more than 25% in 24 hours is rapid). ■ Tests show poor bond with underlying layer (tilt and ski tests). ■ Identify weak layer character. ■ Denser storm snow is observed over less-dense snow (boot or ski penetration, hand hardness).	■ Rapid settlement may strengthen the snowpack or form a slab over weak snow. ■ When storm slabs exist in sheltered areas, wind slabs may also be present in exposed terrain. ■ Storm slab may strengthen and stabilize in hours or days depending on weak layer character. ■ Potential for slab fracturing across terrain can be underestimated.
THE PROBLEM: WIND SLAB		
■ Recent slab avalanches below ridgetop and/or on cross-loaded features ■ Blowing snow at ridgetop combined with significant snow available for transport ■ Blowing snow combined with snowfall: deposition zones may accumulate three to five times more than sheltered areas	■ Evidence of wind-transported snow (drifts, plumes, cornice growth, variable snow surface penetration with cracking) is observed. ■ Evidence of recent wind (dense surface snow or crust; snow blown off trees) is observed. ■ Moderate (or stronger) wind speeds for significant duration are observed (reports, weather stations, field observations).	■ Often it is hard to determine where the slab lies and how unstable and dangerous the situation remains. ■ Slope-specific observations, including watching wind slabs form, are often the best tool. ■ Strong winds may result in deposition lower on slopes. ■ Avalanches are commonly triggered from thin areas (edges) of the slab. ■ Wind transport and subsequent avalanching can occur days after last snowfall.

TABLE 17-1. AVALANCHES AND OBSERVATIONS REFERENCE *continued*

CRITICAL (RED-FLAG) OBSERVATIONS	FIELD TESTS & RELEVANT OBSERVATIONS	IMPORTANT CONSIDERATIONS
THE PROBLEM: PERSISTENT SLAB		
■ Bulletins or experts warn of persistent weak layer: surface hoar, facet and crust, depth hoar. ■ Cracking and/or whumping	■ Profiles reveal a slab over a persistent weak layer. ■ Use multiple tests that will verify location of this condition in terrain. ■ Small column tests (compression test) indicate sudden results; large column tests (extended column test, propagation saw test, Rutschblock test) show tendency for propagating cracks.	■ Instability may be localized to specific slopes (often more common on cooler north and northeast aspects) and hard to forecast. ■ Despite no natural occurrences, slopes may trigger with small loads—more likely when weak layer is 8–36 inches (20–85 cm) deep. ■ Human-triggered avalanches are still possible long after slab formed.
THE PROBLEM: DEEP SLAB		
■ Remotely triggered slabs ■ Recent and possibly large isolated avalanches with deep, clean crown face	■ Profiles indicate well preserved but deep (≥3 feet [1 m]), persistent weak layer. ■ Column tests may not indicate propagating cracks; propagation saw test can provide more-consistent results. ■ Heavy loads (cornice drops or explosives test) may be needed to release the slope—large and destructive avalanches result.	■ Avalanches may be aspect or elevation specific: it is very important to track a weak layer over terrain. ■ Slight changes, including moderate snowfall and warming, can reactivate deeper layers. ■ Terrain may be dangerous after nearby activity has ceased. ■ Tests with no results are not conclusive. ■ Avalanches may be remotely triggered from shallower, weaker areas; it is difficult to forecast and manage terrain choices.
THE PROBLEM: CORNICES		
■ Recent cornice growth ■ Recent cornice fall ■ Warming: solar, rain at ridgetops	■ Note rate, extent, location, and pattern of cornice growth and erosion. ■ Observe photos tracking change over time.	■ Cornices often break farther back onto ridgetop than expected. ■ Sun's effect on back of cornice can be underestimated during travel on cool, shaded aspects.

Source: AIARE.

17

help in choosing safe terrain. Note that several of these avalanche problems may exist in the same area and/or at the same time. It is also possible for changing conditions to cause one avalanche problem to morph into another, as when a wind slab warms up and becomes a wet wind slab.

Focusing on the relevant avalanche problems makes it easier for a team to concentrate on avoiding the most dangerous terrain, as well as on making more relevant observations; however, the potential for discovering additional avalanche problems should never be ignored. Choosing safe terrain based on an understanding of specific avalanche problems can also help prevent a tendency to rely too much on the generalized "Danger Level" categories used by forecasters. In North America the North American Public Avalanche Danger Scale (fig. 17-8) provides an overall rating of avalanche danger levels;

North American Public Avalanche Danger Scale

Avalanche danger is determined by the likelihood, size and distribution of avalanches.

Danger Level		Travel Advice	Likelihood of Avalanches	Avalanche Size and Distribution
5 Extreme	 4 5 ✕	Avoid all avalanche terrain.	Natural and human-triggered avalanches certain.	Large to very large avalanches in many areas.
4 High	 4 5 ✕	Very dangerous avalanche conditions. Travel in avalanche terrain not recommended.	Natural avalanches likely; human-triggered avalanches very likely.	Large avalanches in many areas; or very large avalanches in specific areas.
3 Considerable	 3 ‼	Dangerous avalanche conditions. Careful snowpack evaluation, cautious route-finding and conservative decision-making essential.	Natural avalanches possible; human-triggered avalanches likely.	Small avalanches in many areas; or large avalanches in specific areas; or very large avalanches in isolated areas.
2 Moderate	 2 !	Heightened avalanche conditions on specific terrain features. Evaluate snow and terrain carefully; identify features of concern.	Natural avalanches unlikely; human-triggered avalanches possible.	Small avalanches in specific areas; or large avalanches in isolated areas.
1 Low	 1 ✓	Generally safe avalanche conditions. Watch for unstable snow on isolated terrain features.	Natural and human-triggered avalanches unlikely.	Small avalanches in isolated areas or extreme terrain.

Safe backcountry travel requires training and experience. You control your own risk by choosing where, when and how you travel.

Fig. 17-8. North American Public Avalanche Danger Scale.

similar danger scales are used in other parts of the world. It is crucial to realize that even when the overall danger is moderate or even low, potentially deadly avalanches can occur in specific terrain and conditions. Studying the relevant avalanche problems is one way to stay focused on avoiding these specific danger areas.

CONSIDER HUMAN FACTORS

In evaluating avalanche hazard, a prime component is the human factor. The judgments that mountaineers make affect the level of risk they face. In terms of avalanche safety, the term "human factors" has come to represent the whole constellation of psychological foibles and mental shortcuts that lead people to make poor decisions when they encounter hazardous conditions. In hindsight, most avalanche survivors can point to various human factors that were the pivotal causes in the chain of events leading up to the mishap. It is worth studying troublesome human factors in more detail than is covered here (see Chapters 22, Leadership, and 23, Safety). A few of the more common human factors include these:

- **Peer pressure:** Feeling that you must do the same things as others so that they will like you.

- **Overconfidence:** Having too much confidence in your ability or assessment of a situation.
- **Familiarity:** The tendency to assume that familiar places are safe places.
- **Rule-following:** Using rules of thumb instead of careful thought.
- **Momentum:** The tendency to just keep going rather than considering alternatives.
- **Euphoria or hypoxia:** The heightened state of physical excitement that comes with strenuous exercise in a thrilling environment, which can have an insidious negative impact on clear thinking.
- **Large group size:** The tendency for large groups to inhibit communication and thus replace good decision-making processes with the herd mentality.
- **"Expert halo":** The tendency for people to blindly follow a leader or, even worse, to blindly follow tracks left in the snow by a group of strangers.

Communication

Good communication—and participation by all members in the group—is the most effective way to promote good decision making and to reduce the bad effects of those

Fig. 17-9: Good communication keeps the group focused on important observations and evaluations of avalanche hazards, terrain, snowpack, and weather.

unavoidable human factors. Before setting off into the backcountry, a party should agree on a process for making decisions as a group. The party should agree on its goals, acceptable level of risk, and understanding of the hazard data each member has been collecting. Consider and discuss the party's tolerance for risk and its degree of commitment to a climbing objective even in the face of hazard. Determine how willing the group is to look objectively at information on terrain, the snowpack, and weather.

Many parties allow their desires to cloud the hard facts. Most avalanche victims were aware of the hazard but chose to interpret the information in such a way that an accident occurred. An unsafe attitude can be fatal. Good communication defeats human-factor trouble by keeping the group focused on important observations and evaluations, by providing a valve to release social pressures and by recruiting all the eyes and minds in a group instead of depending on one person to think of everything. For instance, sharing the tasks of making observations can allow a group to gather more data while also moving faster.

Parties make the best decisions when they work together to make a travel plan and gather data, then reevaluate the plan as a group once they are in the field (fig. 17-9). Groups that take each person's thinking into account usually make better decisions than individuals. All climbers in the party have an obligation to express their concerns clearly and freely, even in the face of differing opinions. When the party faces the risk of fatalities, it is essential that every climber be ready and able to communicate prudent reservations with the rest of the group.

It is particularly important to avoid the powder fever that so often takes over on the first blue-sky day after several days of storm and a couple of feet of new snow. Each person must understand the possible consequences of decisions and any alternatives. Everyone should understand any assumptions underlying the decision to enter avalanche terrain, including assessments of the party's risk tolerance and its ability to deal with an avalanche.

The decision-making process should be based on group discussion and should cover these areas:

1. Identify potential hazards.
2. Collect, evaluate, and integrate information continuously during trip.
3. Consciously explore assumptions, the consequences of a particular decision, and all alternatives to that decision.
4. Make a decision—but be willing to reevaluate based on new information.

17

It can be very useful to formalize this decision-making process by identifying one or more places along a route where decisions may need to be made and marking these down in the trip plan or on a map, to ensure that the group takes time to reevaluate conditions and discuss options as a team.

Technical Skill Level

How skilled are members of the party at snow travel and at evaluating avalanche hazard? Are the party's overall mountaineering skills high? Just average? Low? In theory, a balanced party of able, experienced mountaineers can be expected to do well at avoiding avalanches and at responding efficiently if one strikes. In fact, experienced and knowledgeable climbers are caught by avalanches every year, and this is nearly always largely due to errors of judgment because of human factors and not because the party was unaware of the hazard. A relatively untested party, or one whose members have a great difference in experience and skill levels, must be extra conservative in its decisions.

Strength and Equipment

What shape is the party in? Decide whether members of the group are strong and healthy enough to go on a demanding and possibly hazardous trip. How well equipped is the party to deal with an avalanche? Determine whether the party is adequately prepared, with shovels, rescue transceivers, avalanche probes, first-aid supplies, and other gear that would be needed in case all precautions fail and the party is involved in an avalanche.

USING THESE SKILLS IN THE FIELD

Once climbers have learned (and practiced) the fundamentals of avalanche safety, they must use these skills in the backcountry. Identifying avalanche terrain or suspect weather patterns is not enough; climbers must know how to put it all together. This section helps prepare climbers for making decisions and taking action in the backcountry. As with other aspects of avalanche safety, practice the techniques before you end up in hazardous terrain or are involved in an avalanche rescue.

OBSERVING SNOW CONDITIONS

Climbers should understand the terrain they are heading into before they get there and include in the trip plan where and when the most relevant observations might be made. Look at conditions on similar terrain as soon and as often as possible. Observe the big picture first: on the road,

up the trail, at camp, out on the terrain. Then fit the party's plans and situation into that picture. Use this perspective to decide where the party might test the snow for its stability and what tests will be used, and also use this perspective to aid the party in avoiding avalanche hazard.

There is often tremendous variability in the snowpack from place to place. This means that testing the snow in one place does not mean the snow is stable anywhere else. For this reason, snow stability tests should be used to gain a general understanding of local conditions and to look for any unexpected signs of danger—but snow stability tests should *not* be used to predict the stability of adjacent slopes. In other words, if the overall conditions lead a party to conclude that a slope may be dangerous, then the climbers should never change that forecast based on field tests that happen to show a stable result. On the other hand, if the party's forecast was for good stability and a local test of the snowpack uncovers unstable conditions, the climbers should assume that other unstable areas may exist on similar slopes.

To travel safely in the backcountry, climbers must be able to recognize unstable conditions. Generally, when unstable snow conditions exist, the majority of results from observations and tests will confirm that conditions are unstable on certain slope aspects, at certain elevations, and within a certain range of slope angles. Because there will be some uncertainty, particularly when the weather is changing, an extra margin of safety is required. Always make observations, looking for obvious signs of instability. Use the major clues shown in Table 17-1 in the preceding section.

Snowpack Observation Techniques

It is often more practical to make many quick tests and observations of the snowpack as a climbing party maintains steady forward progress than it is to stop and carry out scientific snow stability tests or dig full-scale snow pits (fig. 17-10) to gather detailed observations from a single location. Nevertheless, it is a very good idea for those who travel in avalanche terrain to familiarize themselves with the range of stability tests and snow observation techniques that professional forecasters use to understand the snowpack.

Full descriptions of these tests are beyond the scope of this text, and they are much better learned in the snow by taking an avalanche course. Learning how to carry out these tests provides the backcountry traveler with tools for looking deeper into the snowpack and understanding how weather affects the snow. Knowing how to conduct these tests will also help climbers understand the basis for avalanche forecasting. It is a very good idea to practice these tests and

Fig. 17-10. Evaluating layers in a correctly constructed snow pit.

dig snow study pits, when time allows, for the knowledge you can gain. Comparing what you actually find in the snow to the data and discussion gleaned from avalanche forecast reports can yield a much deeper understanding of avalanche hazard. Stability tests can also be a useful way to look for unexpected danger in the snowpack, but they have limited value in decision making since one or more tests that indicate a stable snowpack can never be used as a basis for entering avalanche terrain in questionable conditions.

A well-equipped climbing party may carry tools to evaluate the snowpack. A snow study kit with a snow crystal card, a clinometer, and a snow saw help in analysis of slopes and the snowpack. Climbers well-educated in avalanche safety should understand the procedures and terminology used in the extended column test (ECT; fig. 17-11), Rutschblock test (RB), compression test (CT), propagation saw test (PST), and any other tests commonly performed by professional forecasters in their part of the world. It also pays to learn the correct methods used in making snowpack observations, as well as the standardized ways of noting the data from these tests and observations. Full profiles are dug in the snow to allow a close inspection of the layers in the upper 3 feet (1 meter) of the snow. They allow a detailed look at the snowpack, but they are time-consuming to do properly and represent only a single sample in a vast landscape. In the United States, level 2 avalanche courses cover this material and introduce people to the basics of snow science and forecasting.

17

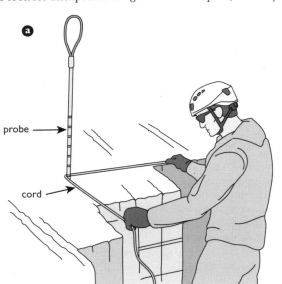

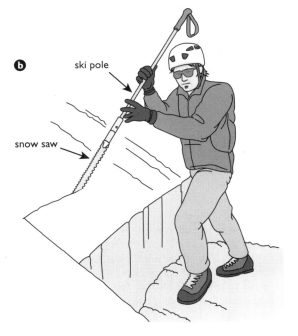

Fig. 17-11. Isolating the snowpack column for an extended column test: a, using a probe and cord to cut a column; b, a snow saw on a ski pole to cut a column.

Test profiles, quickly scooped in the snow by hand or shovel, can give an idea of what is going on in the near-surface layers of the snowpack. It is a good idea to regularly push your ski pole or ice-axe spike into the snow as you travel along to feel for weaker and stronger layers. If the snow is very soft, push the basket end of a ski pole smoothly into the snow; then pull it slowly out, trying to feel any hard or soft layers. It may be possible to reach down into the ski-pole hole and feel the snow layers with your fingers. In most other snow, remove the basket or use the handle end of the ski pole to penetrate the snow. Usually only the top 39 to 48 inches (100 to 120 centimeters) of snow needs to be observed in assessing snow-pack stability because the stresses generated by a climber or skier generally will not penetrate more than about 33 or 34 inches (85 centimeters) into the snow.

Regularly making these test-profile observations and discussing them with party members reinforces an awareness of avalanche hazard and preparedness. These informal tests will not give information on the bonding of snow layers and they will miss thin shear planes, but they can reveal gross discontinuities in the snowpack structure that suggest instability.

MAKING DECISIONS IN THE FIELD

Making a decision about whether or not to enter avalanche terrain can be a vexing problem. The variables that go into the decision can be complex and often seem contradictory. Add to this that social and time pressures can make it hard to think calmly, and it is easy to see how people often make the wrong decision and enter unsafe terrain when they shouldn't.

It is often best to think in terms of the party's levels of certainty, instead of agonizing over the particulars in an attempt to come up with a simple decision of "go" or "no go." Take a hard look at the information available and then determine whether or not there is enough information to make a safe decision *based on the available data and the skill and experience of the party.* If you look at the information available to you and cannot decide whether the terrain is safe, then there is simply too much uncertainty to proceed safely. In this situation, it is best to choose to travel on alternative terrain that you are certain will be safe for your party in the conditions. Be sure that every trip plan includes a safe alternate destination.

When a party encounters potential hazard along the way, ask these questions:

1. Do current observations still support the assumptions behind the trip plan?
2. Is the snow unstable?
3. Could I be a trigger?
4. Is the weather contributing to instability?
5. What are the alternatives and their possible consequences?

To respond effectively to these overall questions, the party should come up with answers to a series of secondary queries about the big picture—terrain, snowpack, weather, the climbing party itself—thinking holistically and applying concrete observations and information.

USING SAFE TRAVEL TECHNIQUES

Even after a party has made every effort to choose terrain that is safe in the existing conditions, it can be a good idea to use travel techniques designed to add a layer of safety when crossing a potential avalanche slope. The task is to travel with the least danger of disturbing the slope and to minimize the consequences of a possible avalanche.

Prepare Clothing and Gear

Just as during travel on a crevassed glacier, it may make sense to put on a hat, mittens, and warm clothing and to zip up clothing. Undo ski-pole straps. Use releasable bindings on skis or snowshoes, and remove the safety straps that connect boots to the bindings. (Skis and snowshoes spread a person's weight over a relatively large area, putting less strain on the slope than boots do.) Stow all essential gear securely inside packs, including vital avalanche rescue tools such as shovel and probe; if these are strapped to the outside of the pack, they will likely be torn away and lost in an avalanche, just when they are needed most. If you are using an airbag, such as an AvaLung, make sure it's ready to deploy.

Choose a Safe Line of Travel

When the route lies up a slope (and the party is walking, not skiing), head straight up the fall line instead of switchbacking, which can undercut the snow. However, a straight line up the mountainside may not be as safe as a more meandering route that seeks out lower-angle terrain and avoids convex rollovers and exposure to terrain traps. Always look ahead and make use of topographical maps to avoid routes that dead-end in unsafe terrain. The route should follow a line as high on the slope as practical. It may be possible to hug cliff bands at the top of the slope. Choosing the most efficient and safe line up a mountainside while setting a skin track is an advanced skill in which experienced ski mountaineers take great pride. The fastest line is never the steepest one.

Stay Together

On a tricky traverse, only one person moves at a time, and everyone else watches from safe places, ready to shout if a slide starts. (Alternatively, the group may spread out and travel far apart simultaneously, but within view of each other.) Cross with long, smooth strides, being careful not to cut a trench across the slope. Each climber follows in turn, stepping in the leader's footprints or skiing in the same track. Everyone listens and watches for an avalanche. It is not always best practice to spread out or travel one at a time: in very low visibility it is often safer to stay close together. Never let any member of a group out of sight of others. The best way to ensure this is to pair people up to look after each other; using the buddy system can prevent an individual from getting separated from the group, or buried, without anyone noticing. Move from one position of safety to another, minimizing the potential exposure period. Do not fall; falling puts a sudden load on the snowpack. On an avalanche-ready slope, the impact of a falling body can be like the detonation of a little bomb. Be aware of other parties; try not to travel or ski above others moving up the slope.

Rope Up or Not?

Think twice before roping up on questionable slopes. Decide whether the risk of the slope avalanching is greater than the risk of a climber falling, because roping up can risk the belayer being pulled into an avalanche. If the party chooses to use a rope, belay directly off the anchor; the belayer should not tie in to the rope, to avoid being pulled into an avalanche. If there are no solid anchors from which to belay, it may be better to go unroped.

SURVIVING AN AVALANCHE

Climbers must think ahead about what they would do in the event of an avalanche, because after one starts, there is no time. While traveling, keep an eye out for escape paths.

If you are caught in an avalanche, do not give up. Fight to survive. Try to get off the moving snow. Yell to your climbing partners. Jettison any gear you want to get rid of, including skis and ski poles. It is a good idea to keep your pack on to protect your back and neck. Larger objects tend to be transported to the surface of avalanche debris; the pack may help keep you near the surface, and it may help protect you from trauma. If you survive the traumatic forces of the avalanche, you will need the clothing and equipment in the pack.

At the start of an avalanche, try to stop before being swept away. Grab a rock or tree, or dig your ice axe or a ski pole into the snow, and hold on. If that does not work, try to stay on the surface by using swimming motions, flailing your arms and legs, or by rolling. Try to move to the side of the slide.

If your head goes below the surface, close your mouth to avoid being suffocated by snow. As the avalanche slows, thrust upward. If you are buried, try to make a breathing space by putting an elbow or hand in front of your face. Inhale deeply before the snow stops, in order to expand your ribs; as the snow closes around you, you won't be able to move. Do not shout or struggle. Relax. Try to conserve oxygen and energy. Your climbing partners should know what to do, and they will begin rescue efforts immediately.

RESCUING A COMPANION IN AN AVALANCHE

The mountaineer's primary emphasis should be on avalanche evaluation and safe travel. Rescue skills are very important, but it is vital to keep in mind that they cannot keep you safe; self-rescue is the last resort, to be used when you have failed to stay safe. Every party needs avalanche rescue skills and equipment, but these are no substitute for the ability to make sound judgments that promote safe travel in avalanche terrain. If an avalanche does occur, this section covers what to do. Also, Resources, at the back of the book, lists several widely available books about avalanche rescue, as well as online resources such as www .avalanche.org, a comprehensive website run by several avalanche research organizations that provides international statistics, links to avalanche courses, and links to avalanche information centers.

When buried in a snow avalanche, people very seldom live long enough to be rescued by people who are not close by when the accident occurs. It can often take hours, or even days, to bring in rescuers from outside to the scene of an avalanche. A victim who survives the physical trauma of an avalanche almost always depends on companions to dig him or her up quickly, before the victim suffocates or dies of hypothermia.

THE WELL-PREPARED PARTY

A climbing party's level of preparedness is an important factor in minimizing avalanche hazard. A well-prepared party has the training and practice, conditioning, equipment, and critical judgment to evaluate avalanche hazard and to respond effectively to an avalanche if one occurs. Each climber should carry a digital triple-antenna avalanche rescue transceiver, shovel, and commercial

17

avalanche probe 104 inches (265 centimeters) or longer to perform a rescue, and they must have developed the skills to use them. They know that seconds—not minutes—count should an avalanche occur.

The well-equipped party may carry new products to help avalanche victims survive, including the Black Diamond AvaLung II and avalanche air bags. Research and try out any avalanche safety item before relying on it in the backcountry.

AVALANCHE RESCUE TRANSCEIVERS

The digital avalanche rescue transceiver, often called an *avalanche beacon*, is the principal tool for finding buried victims. Rescue depends on each member of the party carrying a transceiver. A rescue transceiver can be switched to either transmit or receive signals. Digital transceivers convert the analog signal to a digital readout, and they typically provide both audible and visible signals in the receive (search) mode. The international standard frequency for avalanche transceivers is 457 kilohertz; transceivers that work at 2,275 hertz are obsolete and should not be used.

Continued progress in the avalanche safety field has produced transceivers with increasingly sophisticated digital processor capabilities. Older analog and newer digital transceivers are compatible, and both types use the 457-kilohertz standard frequency. But modern digital transceivers are much more effective than the old analog versions. Use a modern digital transceiver with three or four antennas. The recommended transceivers for backcountry travelers and climbers operate exclusively at 457 kilohertz and use three or more antennas for the most accurate readings and fastest search. It is not necessarily an advantage to use the models with the most features, which can be confusing in an emergency; the current simple transceiver models can be excellent.

A valuable feature of newer digital transceivers is their ability to quickly separate and isolate signals in a multiple-burial scenario in which two or more victims have been buried. Some people argue that multiple-burial scenarios are rare; however, they do occur, and even in a single-victim burial if a searcher inadvertently reverts to transmit, it is very useful to have a transceiver that can let searchers know whether multiple transceivers are in transmit mode.

The various models do not have consistent features or controls, so it is important to study the instructions that come with the receiver, and it is not a bad idea to learn something about how your companions' transceivers work in case you need to use one in an emergency. All members

of a party must know how to use the transceivers correctly. This skill requires regular practice, so practice before and during every season. The same thinking applies to phones or other communication devices: all team members should know how to turn on all devices and call for help.

Preparing to Travel

At the trailhead and at the beginning of each day, the group should verify that all transceivers can transmit and receive signals properly. Fresh batteries usually last for about 300 hours (a lot less time when used in search mode), but carry extras in case the signal from any transceiver weakens. Test the battery life of your transceiver while practicing search methods. Always check the charge level before you head out and try to determine where on the battery-level-indicator scale you need to change the batteries in order to ensure that there will always be enough power left to carry out a search in an emergency.

Strap the transceiver around your neck and torso. Carry it under clothing, just outside your innermost garment, to keep it from being lost in an avalanche. Do not carry it in your pack. Carrying the transceiver inside a secure zipped front pants pocket has also been determined to be safe, but use a leash to secure the device to you as well. During the climb, leave transceivers on, set to the transmit mode. When you are staying overnight in a snow cave or in an avalanche-prone area, consider leaving the transceiver on, set to transmit, even at night.

Cellular phones, radios, GPS devices, MP3 players, and other electronics have been shown to interfere with the function of avalanche transceivers. Consider turning such devices off (or putting them in "airplane mode") if they are not needed for travel or communication; if they are turned on, keep them 12 to 20 inches (30 to 50 centimeters) away from where the transceiver is stowed on your body. For instance, you might carry a radio in the top pocket of your pack if the transceiver is low on your torso.

FIRST STEPS IN A RESCUE

Climbers may need to consciously control their feelings of shock and anxiety in order to be effective at trying to find the missing person(s).

Identify the Area Where the Victim Was Seen Last

The rescue effort starts even before the avalanche has stopped. In the shock of the moment, the first step in a successful rescue is a tough one: pay attention to the point where a victim is last seen. Identify the area to be searched based on this last seen area. Do a head count to make sure you know how many are missing.

Select a Search Leader

Choose a search leader to direct a thorough and methodical rescue effort. Before entering the search area, the leader considers the safety of the search party: evaluate the potential for other slides in the area, choose a safe approach to the search area, and designate an escape path in case of another avalanche. It is usually easier to move downhill while searching. The leader assigns tasks to make the best use of the available people. If the search party is large enough, the leader should stand back and avoid hands-on participation in the rescue process, which can narrow the leader's focus and prevent effective leadership. Only enough people to cover the search area are needed to proceed with the initial transceiver search.

If someone is available, it is often a good idea to have that person make an initial call to alert outside rescuers to the situation, even to simply report the ongoing search and the party's location and arrange to call back. It can take a long time to mount a search by outside search and rescue organizations, and in the event that a trauma victim needs evacuation, the leader should start this process right away. Sometimes, with a long downhill search zone, there may not be a signal at the bottom of the slope, so it might be a long time before the call can be made if it is postponed too long. On the other hand, if everyone is needed to carry out an effective companion rescue, it may be best to postpone the call for help until after the victim is recovered.

Do Not Go for Help

A critical principle of avalanche rescue is this: Do not send anyone for help. Stay and search. Survival depends on locating the victim quickly. A person located in the first 15 minutes has an approximately 90 percent chance of survival if he or she survived the avalanche and did not hit rocks or trees or suffer trauma. The probability of survival drops off rapidly after that time. After 90 minutes, the probability of survival is approximately 25 percent. Wait until after the victim is unburied or after search efforts turn out to be futile to send someone for help.

Prepare to Search

Once a search begins, unstrap the transceiver and bring it out for rescue work; all rescuers must switch their transceivers to the receive mode to locate the transmission from a victim. It is critically important that every searcher switch to receive; if a searcher's transceiver is left in the transmit mode, searchers will waste valuable time receiving this signal rather than the victim's signal.

Each searcher listens for beeps and watches an optical display to detect the buried victim. A rescuer should be able to locate the buried victim in less than 5 minutes once a signal has been acquired. It is essential to practice using rescue transceivers to ensure that searchers have the best chance of locating victims before they suffocate.

Commence Searching

Work rapidly but efficiently. Don't forget to search with your eyes. Try to determine if anyone can point out the last place the victim was seen, then move quickly into the transceiver search. Searchers should remember to look for items of clothing or other clues and consider the location of terrain traps where a person might be lodged. Searchers not needed for the transceiver search should quickly follow the transceiver searchers while deploying their probes in readiness. All searchers should keep their packs and all emergency gear with them if they can.

THREE PHASES OF A SEARCH WITH A MODERN DIGITAL TRANSCEIVER

The digital transceiver search for an avalanche victim or victims occurs in three phases: coarse, fine, and pinpoint.

Phase 1: Coarse Search

In the coarse search phase, a signal has not yet been detected. The searchers start from the victim's last-seen point and fan out no more than 65 feet (20 meters) apart—about the effective range of a modern digital transceiver (with an overlap for an extra margin of safety)—across the slope, each moving straight down the fall line with their transceivers in receive mode until a signal is picked up (fig. 17-12a). If there is no clear last-seen point, then the searchers much check the entire slope. *Note:* A lone searcher must switchback down the slope with no more than 65 feet (20 meters), the effective range of the transceiver, between switchbacks (fig. 17-12b).

Once a signal is detected, some searchers can move to the fine search while other rescuers prepare to dig out the victim. If there is more than one victim, the rest of the rescuers continue the coarse search until all are found. Modern transceivers should allow a continued search without any need to turn off the recovered victim's transceiver. Try to avoid turning anyone's transceiver off if at all possible, in case another avalanche comes along.

17

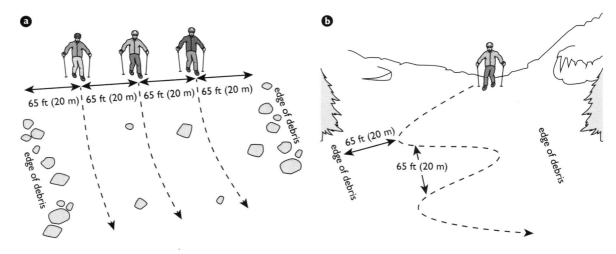

Fig. 17-12. Paths taken during a coarse search phase: a, multiple searchers; b, single searcher. Space the search paths closely enough to stay in range of the victim's transceiver.

Phase 2: Fine Search

The fine search phase begins when the searchers detect a signal. Use the directional lights and distance meter on the transceiver to follow the signal to roughly where the victim is buried. This will often be a curved path, as the transceiver is following the induction line. The induction line follows a curved path because the radio signal transmissions from the victim's transceiver are propagated outward in a curved shape.

Move as quickly as is practical during this phase. The digital distance readout on a transceiver is not ultraprecise, but it gives a good idea of the distance to the victim's transceiver beneath the snow. After practicing searches with your transceiver, you will begin to get a good idea what the distance readings mean and you will become familiar with the range of curves that search lines may follow. This experience will greatly improve your search times, and such practice can teach you how best to pace yourself to get through the search quickly but without moving so fast that you outpace the transceiver's processor or make mistakes that waste time.

Phase 3: Pinpoint Search

Once a searcher is within roughly 10 feet (3 meters) of the victim, the pinpoint search begins, and the searcher slows down even more, and moves the transceiver as close as practical to the surface of the snow. At this point it is usually best to remove skis to make it easier to get right down

on the snow and move with precision. You will need to take skis off in order to dig, in any case.

Search along a straight line to try to pinpoint the victim more closely (fig. 17-13a). Ignore the transceiver's directional arrows and audible signals from this point on (some beacons switch them off automatically at this stage) and use only the distance indicator numbers to find the point along this straight line that is closest to the victim. As you move along the line, maintain a steady speed, not too fast, and keep the transceiver oriented exactly the same way—do not swing it back and forth or orient it at different angles, which will reduce the precision of the distance readout. It is critically important to practice with your transceiver, since there are subtle differences in operation and sensitivity between the various models.

At some point along the line, you will see the distance numbers dip to a low point and then start to climb again. Make a mark in the snow at the first point where the distance number went up again and then move back along the line (without changing the transceiver orientation) at the same steady pace until the number dips low and rises to the same higher number again, then mark this point. Now you have two marks along your straight line. Precisely mark the midpoint of the span between the marks. This is the point along your first line where you are closest to the victim, but you may not yet be directly above the victim.

Now strike a line exactly perpendicular to your original line that crosses it at this close-to-the-victim point (fig. 17-13b). Follow along this second line in either direction (again, with the transceiver in the same orientation it has been in all along) until you again find the lowest distance reading by marking the two points where the reading first rises above the low and then marking their midpoint. The victim should be below this mark.

Probe at this point and *be sure to probe perpendicular to the snow surface* instead of straight up and down (fig. 17-14). The shortest distance from the closest point detected by a transceiver will be along a line perpendicular to the snow surface; probing on a plumb line from this point can easily miss a buried person.

Commercial avalanche probes work far better than any other alternative. However, to find a buried victim, use whatever is at hand as a probe, including commercial avalanche probes, ski poles, ice axes, or wands. Carry a real avalanche probe and a sturdy metal shovel. Ski-pole probes and plastic shovels have a reputation for failing.

If you have done a good job, you will often strike the victim with this first probe, even with a deep burial. Less-proficient searchers may have to continue probing in a spiral pattern outward from this point, moving in 10-inch (25-centimeter) increments out from the closest point found in the transceiver search. Take care to keep the angle of your probe very consistently parallel to previous probes so as not to miss the victim due to sloppy probing. Probe down to a depth of 6½ feet (2 meters). People are sometimes buried more deeply but in these cases they are less likely to survive long enough to be dug out. As soon as the person is located, leave the probe in place, touching the victim, and begin digging.

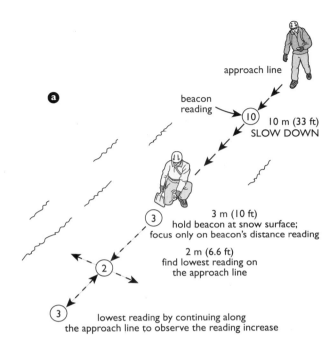

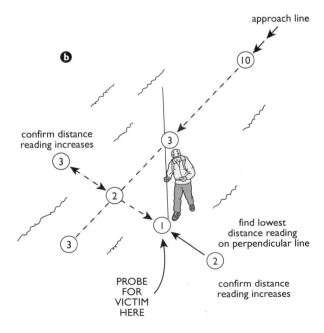

Fig. 17-13. Steps of a pinpoint search: a, When beacon reads 33 feet (10 meters), slow down. Continue until the beacon displays a higher distance reading. Mark this point, then return along the line past the lowest reading and back until the reading rises again, and mark this point; b, Now strike a new line perpendicular to the approach line at the midpoint between these marks. Repeat the process to find the closest point to the victim along this second line, and probe for the victim here.

17

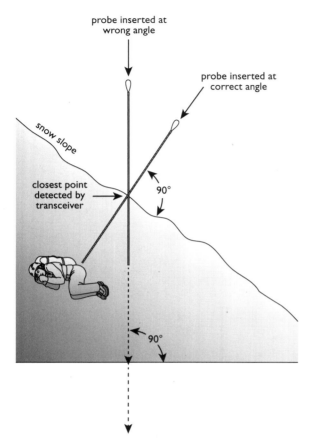

Fig. 17-14. After locating victim with a beacon, insert probe perpendicular to the slope. Inserting probe on a plumb line may easily miss the victim.

PROBE SEARCHES

Probing is a slow and uncertain mechanical process, but it may be the only alternative if rescue transceivers fail to locate a victim or if the party is traveling without transceivers. Probe first at likely areas: near pieces of the victim's equipment, at the points of disappearance, and around trees and rocks. Probing in a group is a skill that must be practiced before it is needed. It is hard work involving discipline and concentration. In the backcountry, there may not be enough people to carry out formal probe procedures. Systematic probing involves a group of people working in a line, with probes always held plumb and probing in unison in a grid pattern so as not to miss the victim.

EFFICIENT SHOVELING AND RECOVERY

After locating the victim using the pinpoint search, take care to avoid injuring the victim with probes or shovels or otherwise endangering the person being rescued. Some victims report that the most terrifying part of their avalanche experience was having their air space trampled on as they were being rescued. Nevertheless, don't hold back: dig as fast as you can while following a systematic and efficient process and working as an organized team. Practicing efficient shoveling methods with your climbing team is a very valuable exercise that has certainly saved lives.

Expect to work very hard: snow in an avalanche undergoes a transition as it slides, and it sets up like concrete when it finally comes to a stop and settles. Digging out the victim is the hardest and most time-consuming part of companion rescue. The goal in any recovery effort is to first uncover the victim's face and chest to get an airway established.

Start shoveling on the downhill side, away from the victim at a distance of approximately one and a half times the estimated depth of the probe to the victim. Move snow downhill. Excavate either in steps or at an angle to the victim, rather than straight down (fig. 17-15). The search leader should organize the shovelers so that one person at a time spearheads the shoveling; the others should hang back and extend the digging area while also sweeping the lead digger's snow piles and chunks out of the way. Diggers should take turns in the lead position, rotating very frequently to avoid slowing due to fatigue. The goal is to keep a wide area open behind the lead digger where snow can rapidly be cleared away. This method is much faster than tunneling straight down, even though it moves more snow, plus an open and relatively level area may be very important if the rescuers need to extract and treat a trauma victim.

As the victim is uncovered, check to see that the person's mouth is not filled with snow and that there are no other obvious obstructions to breathing. Clear snow away from the victim's chest to allow room for it to expand and take in air. Be prepared to start cardiopulmonary resuscitation (CPR); the person need not be fully extracted from the snow before CPR begins. Be aware that suddenly moving a burial victim may cause cardiac failure as cold blood from the extremities moves to the heart (read more about "afterdrop" in "Hypothermia" in Chapter 24, First Aid). Make the person as warm and comfortable as possible, and be prepared to treat for hypothermia and injuries (see Chapter 24, First Aid).

Once it is determined that the rescued individual does not need urgent care, continue to search for any other buried victims.

Fig. 17-15. Digging out a fully buried avalanche victim, shoveling at an angle on the downhill side from victim's estimated location.

17

TRAVELING SAFELY IN AVALANCHE TERRAIN

Snow is a constantly changing medium. Safe travel in avalanche terrain requires preparation, constant reassessment of conditions, and alertness. Here are some points to remember:

- **Continually assess the stability of the snow.** What is the relative level of avalanche hazard? Start with pretrip research and continually reassess throughout the climb.
- **Practice safe travel techniques in avalanche-prone areas.** Always choose the safest path of travel and consider crossing avalanche-prone slopes one person at a time.
- **Carry the necessary rescue gear in avalanche terrain.** Carry avalanche transceivers, probes, shovels, and a first-aid kit, and be trained in their proper use.

Unfortunately, many climbers consider avalanche safety an abstruse specialty of more concern to skiers and winter mountaineers than to the average climber, so they may not bother to make a thorough study of the subject. Yet avalanches can and do occur year-round in many mountain ranges. There is no question that anyone who travels on steep snow, at any time of year, will benefit greatly from avalanche safety training. The study of snow and avalanches is fascinating, as well as useful; the more you learn the more interesting the topic becomes. The knowledge gained turns out to overlap with many other topics in mountaineering. In particular, the emphasis modern avalanche training puts on planning and decision making is valuable and directly applicable to all backcountry travel. The cycle of snow is both an art and a science that you can study for a lifetime. Avoiding avalanches is only one of many benefits of such study. Understanding snow and mountain weather is vital—even outside avalanche terrain—to truly gaining the freedom of the hills.

CHAPTER 18

GLACIER TRAVEL AND CREVASSE RESCUE

Glaciers can offer a convenient route to alpine summits, but they hold many hazards—namely crevasses, the chasms that split a glacier as its great mass of consolidated snow flows slowly downhill. Although glacier travel is a specialized skill, it is very necessary to mountaineering; therefore, climbers must learn how to contend with crevasses.

To travel safely on a glacier, climbers first need all the basic snow travel skills outlined in Chapter 16, Snow Travel and Climbing. To that must be added the ability to detect and avoid crevasses and other glacier hazards. If climbers regard crevasses with a healthy respect, they may never fall into one. If a fall does occur, it is imperative that climbers know the techniques that provide the best chance of safe recovery and escape from a crevasse. Before stepping onto a glacier, climbers must have a clear appreciation of the dangers as well as confidence in their ability to deal with those dangers.

GLACIERS AND CREVASSES

Glaciers constantly change as snow supply and temperature influence their advance and retreat. In classic form, glaciers are like a frozen river creeping down a mountain (as shown in Figure 18-1), yet they differ from a river in many ways. Some glaciers are small, relatively stagnant pockets of frozen snow. Others are icefields of immense proportions, full of teetering forms and dramatic releases of ice. (See Chapter 27, The Cycle of Snow, for information on the formation of glaciers.)

Glacial flow patterns can be very complex, but a typical mountain glacier may flow between 150 and 1,300 feet (roughly 45 to 400 meters) per year. Most glaciers flow faster in the warmth of summer than in winter because they are lubricated by increased meltwater. Glacial flow breaks the surface of the ice into those elemental mountaineering obstacles known as crevasses.

Crevasses often form where the angle of the slope increases significantly, putting tension on the snow and ice, which then split open (fig. 18-1e). Crevasses also commonly form where a glacier makes a turn, with the outside edge usually crevassing more (fig. 18-1f); where the distance between valley walls either narrows or expands; or where two glaciers meet. Crevasses may also develop around a bedrock feature that obstructs the glacial flow, such as a rock formation protruding through the ice—a *nunatak* (fig. 18-1d). At the point where a moving glacier breaks away from the permanent snowcap or ice cap above, the large crevasse called a bergschrund is formed (fig. 18-1b). The middle of a glacier tends to have fewer crevasses than the sides, and a gently sloping glacier usually has fewer crevasses than a steep, fast-moving one.

Crevasses are most dangerous in the accumulation zone (fig. 18-1h), that portion of a glacier that receives more snow every year than it loses to melting. Here, crevasses (fig. 18-2a and b) are frequently covered with snow bridges that may be too weak to support a climber. Below the

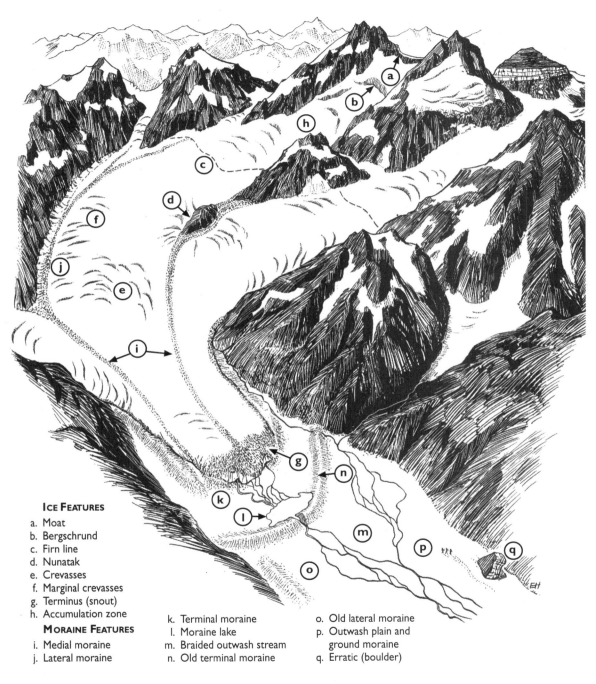

ICE FEATURES

a. Moat
b. Bergschrund
c. Firn line
d. Nunatak
e. Crevasses
f. Marginal crevasses
g. Terminus (snout)
h. Accumulation zone

MORAINE FEATURES

i. Medial moraine
j. Lateral moraine
k. Terminal moraine
l. Moraine lake
m. Braided outwash stream
n. Old terminal moraine
o. Old lateral moraine
p. Outwash plain and ground moraine
q. Erratic (boulder)

Fig. 18-1. Aerial view of a glacier showing principal features.

18

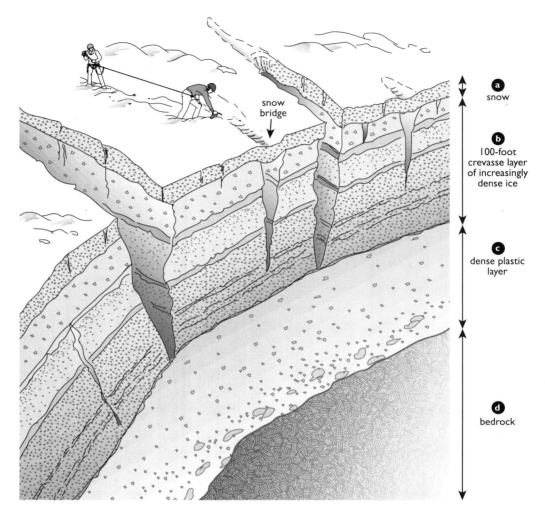

Fig. 18-2. Crevasse formation: a and b, crevasses open up in the upper snow and ice layers as glacier angle increases; c, denser lower area moves without splitting; d, bedrock.

accumulation zone is the area of the glacier where annual melting matches or exceeds the yearly snowfall. Between the two zones is the *firn* line, also known as the *névé* line (fig. 18-1c), both words for "old snow."

The deeper layers of a glacier, denser and more plastic than the upper section, can move and deform without cracking (fig. 18-2c). If this deeper, older ice becomes exposed, the glacier takes on a folded, seamless appearance, often without any true open crevasses. Travel on such a glacier can be relatively simple and safe. These glaciers are usually fairly flat, with narrow, shallow crevasses that are not difficult to cross. Below it all is bedrock (fig. 18-2d).

OTHER COMMON GLACIER HAZARDS

Common hazards on glaciers beyond crevasses include: ice avalanches, moats, glacial moraines, meltwater, whiteouts, and rockfall.

Ice avalanches. Ice avalanches can pour from the steep, jumbled glacial sections known as icefalls (see Figure 16-37h in Chapter 16, Snow Travel and Climbing) when seracs (towers of ice) come crashing down (see Figure 16-37f and g). The inexorable movement of a glacier means that ice avalanches can occur anytime; their activity is only partly related to season, temperature, or snowfall. Serac collapse does seem to happen frequently during the day when the temperature rises above freezing and at night when it drops below freezing. Travel through these areas should be prudently swift if it cannot be avoided.

Moats. Big gaps that appear when winter snows melt back from a rock face, called moats (fig. 18-1a), can present major barriers to glacier travelers who need to regain the rock in order to stay on route. Belayed mountaineers may be able to cross a snow bridge over a moat or climb into the moat and back up onto the rock on the other side.

Glacial moraines. Mounds of rocky debris carried and then deposited by the glacier, called glacial moraines (fig. 18-1i, j, k, n, and o), make rugged venues indeed for mountain travel, impeding efficient movement by a climbing party. Moraines are typically steep-sided, narrow ridges with partly buried boulders ready to dislodge at the slightest touch. The moraine surface is often as hard as cement. As climbers approach the fringe where the glacier begins, there may be a soupy mix of ice and moraine gravel, or rocks skating around like ball bearings on hard ice.

Meltwater. The runoff flowing from a glacier (fig. 18-1m) can be a chilling challenge to cross. During warm weather, consider waiting to cross until the cooler hours of the next morning, when flow should be at its lowest. (See "Rivers and Streams" in Chapter 6, Wilderness Travel, for more advice on crossing rivers.)

Whiteouts. In a whiteout on a glacier, sky and snow merge into a seamless blend of white—with no apparent up or down, east or west—taxing routefinding skills to the utmost. Climbers can defend against a whiteout by taking such precautions as placing route-marking wands, noting compass bearings and altimeter readings, or recording GPS waypoints during the ascent—even when it looks as though clear weather will prevail. If snow or clouds close in and leave the climbing party in a whiteout, these simple precautions will pay off on the descent.

Rockfall. Glaciers are subject to rockfall from bordering walls and ridges. For glacier climbs, whatever the season, the general rule is "early on and early off." The nighttime cold freezes rock in place and prevents most rockfall, whereas direct sun melts the bonds. The greatest hazard comes in the late morning, when sun melts the ice, and in the evening, when meltwater expands as it refreezes, breaking rocks loose.

EQUIPMENT FOR GLACIER TRAVEL

Take a look at climbing gear with glaciers and crevasses in mind. Here are some considerations in getting ready for glacier travel.

ROPES

Ropes with "dry" treatment, although more expensive, absorb much less water from melting snow and pick up less grit from a glacier. This makes them lighter and easier to work with following an overnight freeze. The type of rope needed depends on the glacier.

Shorter 30- to 50-meter (121- to 164-foot) half and twin ropes are generally adequate for most glacier travel. The lighter, thinner rope is more than adequate for general glacier use, because crevasse falls put a relatively gradual impact on the rope due to rope friction on the snow and over the lip of the crevasse. An added advantage is the lighter pack weight.

Steep technical climbing, however, which has the possibility of severe leader falls, requires a 50- to 60-meter (164- to 196-foot) single climbing rope or two half or twin ropes used in the double-rope or twin-rope technique (see Chapter 14, Leading on Rock).

HARNESSES

For glacier travel, be sure the waist belt and leg loops of the harness can adjust to fit over several layers of cold-weather clothing. Glacier travelers also wear a chest harness, which can be made from a piece of webbing. (See "Harnesses" in Chapter 9, Basic Safety System.)

ICE AXE AND CRAMPONS

An ice axe and crampons are as important for safe glacier travel as they are for travel on any firm, sloped surface of snow or ice. The ice axe aids with balance and provides a means for self-belay and self-arrest. If a rope mate drops into a crevasse, other climbers on the rope use their ice axes to go into self-arrest, controlling and stopping the fall. Choose an ice axe with a uniform taper from the spike to the shaft, because a blunt spike, curved shaft, and grip enhancements make it hard to sink the axe into the snow when probing for crevasses.

When walking roped on a glacier, climbers may consider tethering their ice axe to the harness. The benefit is that in the event climbers lose their grip on the ice axe, it will not get lost. The downside is that in case of a fall, climbers may get injured by the ice axe. (See "Ice-Axe Leash" in Chapter 16, Snow Travel and Climbing.)

18

TABLE 18-1. SIZING PRUSIK SLINGS		
CLIMBER'S HEIGHT	FOOT SLING LENGTH	WAIST SLING LENGTH
5 feet (1.5 meters)	11 feet (3.4 meters)	5 feet (1.5 meters)
5 feet 6 inches (1.7 meters)	11 feet 6 inches (3.5 meters)	5 feet 6 inches (1.7 meters)
6 feet (1.8 meters)	12 feet (3.6 meters)	6 feet (1.8 meters)
6 feet 6 inches (2 meters)	13 feet (3.9 meters)	6 feet 6 inches (2 meters)

Crampons provide secure footing and enable efficient travel on refrozen snow, which is typically very hard in the early morning. A word of warning about using crampons for descending steep glacial terrain: A number of accidents and falls have resulted from crampon points getting caught on climbers' clothing or gear hanging low from gear loops. It is important to develop good habits of foot placement and gear management (see the "Crampon Safety Rules" sidebar in Chapter 16, Snow Travel and Climbing). Wearing crampons in soft snow—often encountered on descent later in the day during warmer months—can also be dangerous, so weigh the benefits and risks of keeping crampons on as you travel.

ASCENDERS

Climbers traveling on glaciers also carry prusik slings and/or ascenders, depending on the route.

Prusik System

For personal safety, one of the most important pieces of gear a glacier traveler can carry is a set of prusik slings for ascending the rope after a crevasse fall. The slings are two loops of 5- to 7-millimeter Perlon accessory cord attached to the climbing rope with friction hitches. When a climber puts weight on a prusik sling, the hitch grips the rope firmly; when the climber's weight is removed, the hitch can be loosened and moved up or down the rope.

Though there are many ways to configure a prusik setup for glacier travel, the Texas prusik system is the focus here. Figure 18-3 shows details on how to make Texas prusik slings for the feet (fig. 18-3a) and waist (fig. 18-3b) using 6-millimeter accessory cord. As with all prusik systems, it is critical to size the slings correctly for each individual's height (see Table 18-1). Figure 18-4 shows a way to approximately gauge the correct sizing. When a climber is standing in the sling (as shown in Figure 18-20c), the top of the foot sling (fig. 18-4a) should be at about waist level and the top of the waist sling (fig. 18-4b) should be at about eye level.

Before taking the slings out onto a glacier, check their sizing at home. Dangle in the slings from a rope thrown over a garage rafter or a tree limb to find out if or whether they need to be adjusted.

The two slings are commonly attached to the rope with prusik hitches. Some climbers prefer the bachmann friction hitch because it incorporates a carabiner, which makes a good handle to use while loosening and sliding the slings because it can be gripped easily with a gloved hand. If webbing must be used rather than accessory cord, the klemheist is the best friction hitch to use. (See "Knots, Bends, and Hitches" in Chapter 9, Basic Safety System.)

Mechanical Ascenders

Some glacier travelers carry mechanical ascenders, which attach to the rope more easily than friction knots do. On icy ropes, the ascenders work better and can be operated more readily with gloved hands. A disadvantage is that ascenders traditionally have been heavy and expensive, though a number of cheaper, lightweight devices are now available. Some models have smooth, rather than toothed, cams. These ascenders grip the rope by pure camming action, so they may be safer to use in situations where high fall forces may occur, such as in a crevasse fall. (See "Mechanical Ascenders" in Chapter 15, Aid and Big Wall Climbing.)

OTHER STANDARD GLACIER GEAR

Often each climbing party carries a shovel, which is useful in flattening campsites and in rescue situations. Each party member should also carry the following gear:

Rescue pulley. Many models of pulley have been designed for use in climbing. Pulleys for use in rescue hauling systems should be compatible with a friction hitch (that is, the pulley should not get jammed when used with a prusik or bachmann hitch). If no pulley is available, a carabiner can be used in the rescue hauling system, but it adds considerable friction.

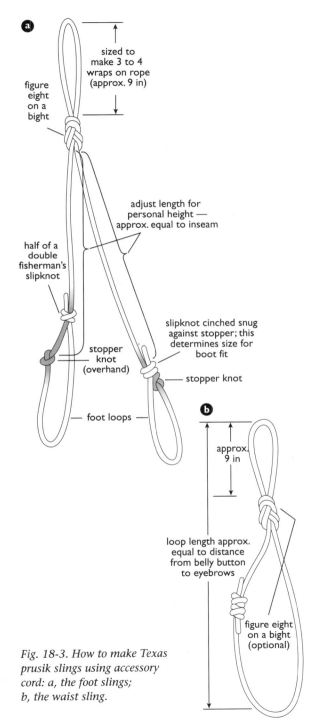

sized to
make 3 to 4
wraps on rope
(approx. 9 in)

figure
eight
on a
bight

adjust length for
personal height —
approx. equal to inseam

half of a
double
fisherman's
slipknot

slipknot cinched snug
against stopper; this
determines size for
boot fit

stopper
knot
(overhand)

stopper knot

foot loops

approx.
9 in

loop length approx.
equal to distance
from belly button
to eyebrows

figure eight
on a bight
(optional)

Fig. 18-3. How to make Texas
prusik slings using accessory
cord: a, the foot slings;
b, the waist sling.

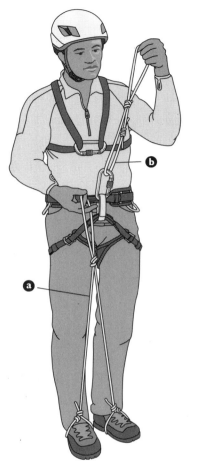

Fig. 18-4. Texas prusik dimensions: a, foot sling should
extend from boots to belly button; b, waist sling should
extend from belly button to eyebrows.

Anchor. If conditions warrant, carry a snow or ice anchor
such as a snow picket or an ice screw. (See "Snow Anchors"
in Chapter 16, Snow Travel and Climbing, and "Ice Screws"
in Chapter 19, Alpine Ice Climbing.)

Runners. Bring at least one double-length and two single-
length runners for attaching to anchors. Tied runners,
rather than sewn runners, work better for crevasse rescue,
because their length can be more easily adjusted.

Belay device. See "Using Belay Devices" in Chapter 10,
Belaying.

Carabiners. Carry at least two locking carabiners and
three regular carabiners.

18

CLOTHING

To be ready for a fall into a crevasse, climbers need to dress for the frigid interior of the glacier even when it is a hot day on top. Priorities collide here, because climbers are preparing for the cold but at the same time trying to minimize sweating.

Select outer garments that can easily be ventilated, such as pants with side zippers and a jacket with armpit zippers. Zip these closed if you end up in a crevasse. Consider strapping an insulated jacket, if you are not wearing it, to the outside of the pack, where it can easily be reached. Stash a warm hat and gloves in the jacket pockets.

For the base layer, wear a long-sleeved light-colored top that reflects the sun's heat but still provides warmth if you end up inside a crevasse. A lightweight wind jacket can take the edge off breezy conditions and serve as a valuable midlayer without taking up much space or weight in the pack. Another useful item is a lightweight neck gaiter that can be pulled up over the face or converted to a head covering for sun and wind protection. Wear liner gloves, at a minimum, to protect hands in the event of self-arrest.

SKIS AND SNOWSHOES

Skis or snowshoes are essential for winter or arctic mountaineering because they distribute climbers' weight over a larger area, thus keeping them from sinking too deeply into the snow. Skis or snowshoes also reduce the chance of a climber breaking through snow bridges over hidden crevasses, which is helpful on some glacier climbs. Snowshoes are usually more practical than skis for roped glacier travel unless all members of the rope team are highly skilled skiers (for further information on ski mountaineering, see Resources).

WANDS

Wands can be used to mark the location of crevasses, identify turning points, and show the climbing route in case a whiteout occurs on the return and the climbing team is not using a GPS device. Space between wands should be a distance equal to the total length of the climbing party when roped and moving in single file. For example, a party of nine (three rope teams on 50- or 60-meter ropes) will use 10 to 12 wands for each mile (1.6 kilometers) of glacier walking; smaller teams or climbers on shorter ropes will need more.

Wands can also be used to indicate potential danger. Two wands forming an X indicate a known danger, such as a weak snow bridge over a crevasse. Wands can also be used when setting up camp on a glacier to mark the boundaries of the safe areas for unroped walking and the location of buried supplies (caches).

Climbers usually make their own wands using 30- to 48-inch (76- to 122-centimeter) green-stained bamboo garden stakes topped with a colored duct tape flag. Write the party's initials on the flags (and consider numbering them) to be certain the team is retracing the correct route. On ascent, insert the wands so they indicate the direction of travel, deeply enough to compensate for melting snow or high winds. Make sure to remove your wands on descent, but do not remove other parties' wands.

FUNDAMENTALS OF GLACIER TRAVEL

Climbers should be moving well before the sun rises and begins weakening snow bridges and loosening avalanche slopes. On glacier climbs, parties grow to appreciate alpine starts: the brilliance of stars at higher altitudes, perhaps the glow of moonlight on snow, the distinctive sounds of crampons on ice, the tinkling of carabiners in the still night. Sometimes the climbing party is alone on the glacier; other times, distant trains of lights show that other parties are also on the route. The magic of watching a sunrise from high on a mountain above a sea of clouds remains with a climber long after memories of the trip's exertion have faded.

Climbers should head out on the glacier with prevention in mind, practicing effective risk management strategies to avoid a crevasse rescue scenario. See the "Crevasse Risk Management" sidebar.

USING THE ROPE

When and where to rope up for glacier travel is a major decision that requires considerable experience and expertise. However, the general rule of safe glacier travel is to rope up. This holds whether or not climbers are familiar with the glacier and whether or not they believe they can see and avoid all of its crevasses. Roping up is especially important in areas above the firn line, where snow accumulates and conceals some crevasses.

It is tempting to walk unroped onto a glacier that looks like a benign snowfield, especially if climbers have gone up similar routes time after time without mishap. Avoid the temptation. Taking the extra time to deal with the rope, like wearing a seat belt in a car, greatly increases a climber's chances of surviving the most likely accident on a glacier: falling into a crevasse. Some climbers travel unroped on certain glaciers in the area below the firn line if crevasses

CREVASSE RISK MANAGEMENT

Defending against a crevasse fall
- First line of defense: reliable footwork, good routefinding, vigilance
- Second line of defense: good rope management and glacier travel skills
- Third line of defense: adequate power to stop a fall

Rescuing after a crevasse fall
- Preclimb assignment of a crevasse rescue incident commander and backup commander
- Formulation of a simple, effective rescue plan tailored to the circumstances
- Timely, accurate assessment of a fall and its consequences
- Quick appraisal of available rescue personnel and gear resources
- Competent deployment of the rescue plan

are stable and easily seen, but this kind of unroped travel is best left to climbers with a great deal of glacier travel experience.

On bare ice, which is often encountered in the late season, it is dangerous to rope up, because crevasse falls are almost impossible to arrest on hard ice. Under these circumstances, consider the conditions and determine if using a running belay would be prudent (see "Running Belays" in Chapter 16, Snow Travel and Climbing).

Rope Teams

Rope team size is a complex decision that must take into account the need for speed and efficiency, the experience of the team members, and the conditions. Generally, smaller teams are better coordinated, more efficient, and faster than larger teams. On the other hand, larger teams are better able to arrest a fall and have more haulers available for crevasse rescue. Like many climbing decisions, there are unavoidable trade-offs that are best made on the basis of skill and experience.

Rope teams of three or four climbers each are ideal for travel on glaciers where no technical climbing will be encountered. With a rope team of three or four, more people are available to arrest a rope mate's fall or aid a climber who has fallen into a crevasse. A minimum party size of two rope teams is recommended so a team involved in an accident will have backup help.

Glacier travelers usually put three people on a 37-meter (121-foot) rope and three or four people on a 50- or 60-meter (164- or 196-foot) rope. These configurations space the climbers far enough apart so that as the rope team crosses a typical crevasse, only one person at a time is at risk. Where there are truly humongous crevasses—in the Himalaya or the Alaska Range, for example—climbers may need to space themselves farther apart. Keep in mind that under more typical glacier travel conditions, closer spacing allows for better communication and more rapid response to falls.

On technical glacier terrain—with slopes steeper than 40 degrees or with severe crevassing—belaying may be necessary, making it more efficient to travel in two-person rope teams. In this situation, having a second rope team as rescue backup becomes even more important. While the person who is on the same rope as the fallen climber holds the rope fast, the second team can set up a snow anchor and initiate the rescue (see "Crevasse Rescue Response," later in this chapter).

Tying In

It is best to tie the rope directly in to the tie-in loops on the harness—rather than tying a butterfly knot or a figure eight on a bight in the rope and clipping the loop in to two locking carabiners at the harness—because the direct tie-in does not require a carabiner (a potential weak link) to connect climber and rope. Of course, a clip-in connection makes it easy to disconnect and reconnect to the rope, but this is not normally done repeatedly over the course of a day on a glacier. Following are some general glacier tie-in procedures, depending on the size of the rope team.

Two-person rope. The most convenient procedure is to have only a portion of the rope stretched between the climbers, because a full rope length can have too much slack as the climbers weave through a maze of crevasses. Using only part of the rope also leaves some rope free for rescue use. Shortening the rope with coils is the preferred method for tying in to a shortened rope, although the remaining rope may also be stored in the climber's pack. This is illustrated and explained in "Special Rescue Situations" later in this chapter.

Three-person rope. Two of the climbers tie in at the very ends of the rope, usually with a rewoven figure eight through the tie-in loops of their harnesses (fig. 18-5). The middle climber ties in to the center of the rope, most commonly with a butterfly knot (fig. 18-6). It has the advantage of being easier to untie after having been weighted, but as noted above, it adds two carabiners to the tie-in. Use two dedicated locking carabiners opposite and opposed to clip it to the harness belay loop, separate from the carabiner

18

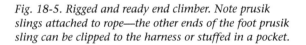

Fig. 18-5. Rigged and ready end climber. Note prusik slings attached to rope—the other ends of the foot prusik sling can be clipped to the harness or stuffed in a pocket.

Fig. 18-6. Rigged and ready middle climber: butterfly knot and three locking carabiners (two for the butterfly knot, the other for the waist prusik sling).

for the waist prusik sling. If the waist prusik sling is on the same carabiner, it could be difficult to remove the sling should it need to be moved to the other strand of rope because the butterfly knot would be loaded with the fallen climber's weight.

Four-person rope. Divide the rope into thirds. Two climbers tie in at the ends, as just described above; the other two tie in at the one-third points, as described above.

Chest Harness

The purpose of the chest harness is to keep the climber upright in case of a crevasse fall. A chest harness can easily be created from a length of tied webbing (see "Chest Harness" in Chapter 9, Basic Safety System). Put the chest harness on over your base layer, or any layers you will not be removing, before heading out onto the glacier. Adjust the size of the harness to fit snugly yet comfortably.

In most cases on nontechnical glacier climbs with lighter packs, the chest harness is not clipped in to the rope during travel. In expedition travel or when climbers are carrying heavy packs, clipping the chest harness will help them stay upright in case of a fall; not clipping the chest harness may

make it very difficult to regain an upright stance inside a crevasse. Traveling with the chest harness clipped to the rope hampers the ability to perform self-arrest in case of a teammate's fall, though, because the tension on the rope comes high on a climber's body. A good compromise is to unzip outer layers enough to clip the climbing rope in to the chest-harness carabiner when crossing a snow bridge or otherwise facing immediate danger of a crevasse fall; otherwise, travel with the chest harness unclipped.

Prusik Slings

Attach prusik slings to the climbing rope immediately after roping up to begin glacier travel, so that the slings are ready for use in an emergency (see Figure 18-5). The middle person on the rope will not know which end of the rope might have to be climbed after a fall; therefore, the middle climber should attach one prusik to the section of rope that goes to the climber in front and the other prusik to the section that goes to the climber behind (see Figure 18-6). After any fall, only one of the prusik slings will have to be moved to the side of the rope that must be climbed. Regardless of how the prusik slings are attached, stuff both foot loops into pockets, so they are ready to be pulled out and slipped onto the feet when needed, or clip them to the harness.

Rigging for glacier travel with a cordelette in place of the Texas foot prusik may be preferable. A single foot loop system allows the other foot freedom to balance against the crevasse wall, which can aid ascent if the unhindered crampon can make adequate purchase on the wall. This may be especially useful at the crevasse lip.

If using mechanical ascenders, do not attach them to the rope until after a crevasse fall; if an ascender receives a shock load, it can damage the rope.

Some climbers girth-hitch a sling to their pack haul loop and clip it to a shoulder strap with a carabiner, so that if they fall into a crevasse, the pack is easier to secure and take off. This also makes it easier to anchor a pack on steep sections of the glacier.

Rope Management

Following a couple of rules will help keep a roped party safe on a glacier.

No slack. The first rule of rope management on a glacier is to keep the rope extended—not taut, but without undue slack. A rope that is fully extended between climbers is insurance against a long plunge into a hidden crevasse. Increasing slack in the climbing rope puts additional force on the next climber in case of a fall (because the first climber is falling deeper into the crevasse), making it more and more difficult to arrest promptly. The falling climber therefore drops farther, increasing the chance of hitting something or becoming wedged if the crevasse narrows. For the climbers holding the fall, a slack rope can also pose the danger of causing them to be dragged into the hole too.

The rope leader should set a pace the others can follow for a long time. Consider the type of terrain the team is moving through and adjust the pace accordingly. The second, third, or fourth climbers must try to closely match the pace of the leader so the rope stays extended. Followers should be alert going downhill, when it becomes easy to walk too fast and create slack.

At sharp turns, the rope tends to go slack when the climber in front of you heads in the new direction and then tightens when you near the turn yourself. Throughout the turn, adjust your pace to keep the slack out of the rope. At sharp turns, it is usually necessary to make new tracks, outside the leader's footsteps, in order to keep the rope fully extended—though at other times, following climbers would normally stay in the leader's path for safety and ease of travel.

To keep the right amount of tension in the rope, travel with a small loop of the climbing rope, 6 to 12 inches (15 to 30 centimeters) long, held in the downhill hand. Gripping this makes it easier to feel the progress of rope mates and adjust your pace as needed. Keeping the rope on the downhill side of a glacier keeps the rope out from under your feet and helps avoid entangling the rope in crampons.

Do not forget safety when the party reaches a rest stop or campsite. Always belay climbers into and out of a gathering place. The rope must stay extended and slack-free until the area has been thoroughly probed for crevasses. Once a safe area for the team has been established, the climber in front belays the next climber into the safe area by pulling the rope through his or her prusik, with ice axe in hand. In case of a fall, the belayer releases the rope and drops into the arrest position; the prusik hitch will hold the rope. When leaving the safe area to resume climbing, belay the climbers out using the prusik as well.

Right angle to crevasses. The second important rule of rope management on a glacier is to run the rope at right angles to a crevasse whenever possible. A rope team that travels more or less parallel to a crevasse is risking a lengthy pendulum fall for a climber who falls in (fig. 18-7). Although it is not always possible to keep the rope at right angles to a crevasse, keeping this goal in mind helps climbers choose the best possible route (fig. 18-8).

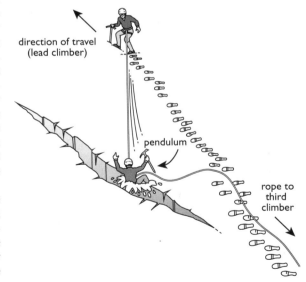

direction of travel
(lead climber)

pendulum

rope to third climber

Fig. 18-7. Where the rope runs more or less parallel to a crevasse, a fall would be made worse by a pendulum.

18

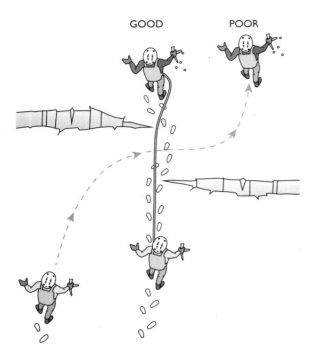

GOOD   POOR

Fig. 18-8. Be aware of your rope partner's position in order to keep the rope as perpendicular to crevasses as possible.

DETECTING CREVASSES

Figuring out where the crevasses are and picking a route through them is fundamental to safe glacier travel. On many glaciers, routefinding is part planning, part experience, and part luck. See the "Tips for Detecting Crevasses" sidebar below.

Sometimes climbers can get a head start on planning by studying photographs of the glacier before the trip, because some crevasse patterns remain fairly constant from year to year. Online mapping resources provide overhead views of the glacier that can be helpful in identifying these patterns. Seek out recent reports from parties who have visited the area, though in summer, reports older than a week are generally not too helpful, due to melting. On the approach hike, try to get a good up-valley or cross-valley look at the glacier before reaching it. Climbers may see an obvious route that would be impossible to discover once they are on the glacier. Take photos and make notes to help remember major crevasses, landmarks, and route options.

Though looking at guidebook photographs and getting distant views of a glacier are useful, prepare to be surprised

---

TIPS FOR DETECTING CREVASSES

- **Keep an eye out for sagging trenches in the snow** that mark where gravity has pulled down on snow over a crevasse's opening. This is a prime characteristic of a hidden crevasse. The sags are visible by their slight difference in sheen, texture, or color. The low-angle light of early morning and late afternoon tends to accentuate this feature. (The sags may be impossible to detect in the flat light of a fog or in the glare of the midafternoon sun, and it takes additional information to distinguish them from certain wind-created forms.)
- **Be wary after storms.** New snow can fill a sagging trench and make it blend into the surrounding surface. (At other times, however, the new snow can actually make the sagging trench more apparent by creating a hollow of new snow that contrasts with surrounding areas of old snow.)
- **Be especially alert in areas where crevasses are known to form**—for example, where a glacier makes an outside turn or where slope angle increases.
- **Regularly sweep your eyes to the sides of the route to check for open cracks to the left or right.** Cracks could hint at crevasses that extend beneath your path.
- **Remember that where there is one crevasse, there are often many.**

---

when you actually get there. What appeared to be small cracks may be gaping chasms. Also, just because a crevasse cannot be seen does not mean it is not there; it may be covered by a thin layer of snow or may not be visible from your angle of view. Stay alert and be prepared to backtrack and take an alternate route.

After setting up base camp, have an advance party scout out the first portion of the route in daylight; this can sometimes save many hours of predawn routefinding, resulting in a more efficient and safer climb.

Snow Probing

Snow probing is the technique to use if a suspicious-looking area has been found and the party wants to search it for crevasses. If a probe locates a crevasse, continue probing in all directions around this area to find the crevasse's true lip. Probe with the ice axe, thrusting the shaft into the snow a couple of feet ahead. Keep the axe perpendicular to the slope and thrust it in with a smooth motion. If resistance to the thrust is uniform, the snow is consistent to at least the depth of the axe. If resistance lessens abruptly, you have probably found a hole. If the route must continue in the direction of this hole, use further axe thrusts to establish the extent of the hole. The leader should open up the hole so it is obvious to followers.

The value of probing depends on climbers' skill and experience at interpreting the changes they feel in the snow layers. An inexperienced prober may think the shaft has broken through into a hole when all it has done is hit a softer layer of snow. The ice axe is a limited probe because it is relatively short. The lead climber can also use a ski pole (with the basket removed), which is lighter, longer, and thinner than an axe, for easier, deeper probes.

CROSSING A CREVASSE FIELD

Climbers have a number of ways to safely cross a field of crevasses. The techniques described below are typical, but they will have to be adapted as needed in the field. Route-finding on a glacier involves finding a path around or over all the visible crevasses, guarding all the time against hidden crevasses. The crossing is seldom without its detours as climbers carefully pick their way over the glacier.

Make an End Run

Crossing directly over a crevasse is rarely a preferred choice. Where a crevasse narrows in width, often near its end, the safest and most dependable technique is to go around it, in an end run. A 0.25-mile (400-meter) detour may gain the rope team only 20 or 30 feet (7 to 10 meters) of forward progress, but it is often better than a direct confrontation with the crevasse. In late summer, when the winter snow has melted down to the ice, it may be possible to see the true end of the crevasse, but if seasonal snows still blanket the glacier, the visible end of the crack may not be its true end. Make a wide swing around the corner, probing carefully (fig. 18-9). Look closely at adjacent crevasses to judge whether one of them could be an extension of your crevasse; you might actually be crossing a snow bridge.

Use a Snow Bridge

If an end run is impractical, the next choice is to cross a crevasse on a snow bridge. Deep winter snow hardened by wind can create a crevasse bridge that lasts into the summer climbing season. Other, sturdier bridges are actually thin isthmuses between two crevasses, with foundations that extend deep into the body of the glacier.

Study a snow bridge carefully—try for a side view—before putting any faith in it. If in doubt, the leader can

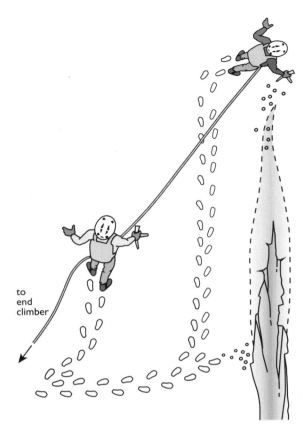

Fig. 18-9. End run around a crevasse, keeping the rope fully extended by not following in the leader's footsteps.

18

approach it to probe and get a close-up look while the second climber stays braced against the taut rope, prepared in case the leader possibly breaks through and ready to drop into self-arrest if needed (fig. 18-10). After the leader gets across, the rest of the party follows exactly in the leader's steps, also receiving a degree of protection from a taut rope held by a braced climber.

A snow bridge's strength varies tremendously with temperature. A bridge that might support a truck in the cold of winter or early morning may collapse under its own weight during an afternoon thaw. Use caution every time you cross a snow bridge. Do not assume that a bridge that held in the morning during the ascent will still be safe during the descent in the afternoon. In cases of dubious snow bridges, setting up a belay may save the party from having to execute a time-consuming crevasse rescue.

Fig. 18-10. Crossing a snow bridge with caution.

Jump

Jumping is one of the least common tactics for crossing a crevasse (fig. 18-11). Most jumps across crevasses are short, simple leaps. Before planning a desperate lunge, be sure you have ruled out all the alternatives and see that you are well belayed.

While well supported by a taut rope or by a belay, probe to find the true edge of the crevasse. If a running start is needed for the jump, tramp down the snow for better footing. Put on a jacket and gloves (you should already be wearing a helmet); check prusiks and harness; and spool out the amount of rope slack needed from the belayer. Then jump with your ice axe in the self-arrest position, ready to help you claw over the lip if you fall shy of a clean landing on the other side.

Once the leader is safely on the other side, the rope is now linked to the landing side, so the other climbers have a less-dangerous jump ahead: the belay rope can help pull up any jumper who falls just short of the target.

Use caution and common sense if the leap is from the high lip of a crevasse over to a lower side. (Bergschrunds, for example, often have an overhanging high wall on the uphill side.) Injuries are possible in a long, hard leap. If such a leap must be made, keep feet slightly apart for balance, knees bent to absorb shock, and ice axe held ready for a quick self-arrest. Beware of getting crampons caught on clothing.

Go into the Crevasse

On rare occasions, it may be practical to get to the other side of a shallow crevasse by climbing down into the crevasse, crossing it at the bottom or at a narrow point, and climbing up on the other side. This tactic should be attempted only by a strong, highly trained, well-equipped party that is ready to provide a good belay. One further caution: often what appears to be a solid bottom is not; if the crevasse bottom collapses and leaves a climber hanging, the party must be able to provide assistance.

Fig. 18-11. Jumping a crevasse (tie-in knot and belayer not shown).

Use the Echelon Formation

Certain crevasse patterns preclude the rule of keeping the rope at right angles to crevasses. If the route demands travel that is parallel to crevasses, it sometimes helps to use the echelon formation: climbers somewhat to the side of and behind the leader, as in a series of stair steps (fig. 18-12). This formation is safest on stable, heavily crevassed glaciers on which the location of crevasses is known and the risk of hidden holes is small. The formation offers an alternative to following in the leader's footsteps through a maze of crevasses where single-file travel is impractical. Avoid moving in echelon formation where hidden crevasses are likely.

CREVASSE RESCUE RESPONSE

The depths of a great crevasse are awe-inspiring. On a fine day, the walls are a sheen of soft blue ice in the filtered light from high above, and the cavern is cool, still, and quiet. It is a place every climber should visit occasionally—for crevasse rescue practice. But if you end up in a crevasse at another time, you may be relying on your climbing teammates to get you out safely (see the "Crevasse Rescue Safety Precautions" sidebar).

Fig. 18-12. Echelon formation, with a rope team in a stair-step-like position.

It is typically the first person on the rope—often one of the more experienced members of the team—who falls in when a rope team crosses a hidden crevasse. Here is the scenario: You are the middle person on a three-person rope team traveling up a moderately angled glacier. The leader walking 50 feet (15 meters) in front of you suddenly disappears beneath the snow. What do you do? (A middle-climber fall is discussed in "Special Rescue Situations," later in this chapter.)

Stop the fall immediately! Drop into self-arrest (facing away from the direction of pull) and hold the fall. The other rope partner (the end climber) will do the same thing. (Chapter 16, Snow Travel and Climbing, has details on ice-axe self-arrest.)

Once the fall is stopped (fig. 18-13), the critical steps in crevasse rescue begin. Learning these procedures well

18

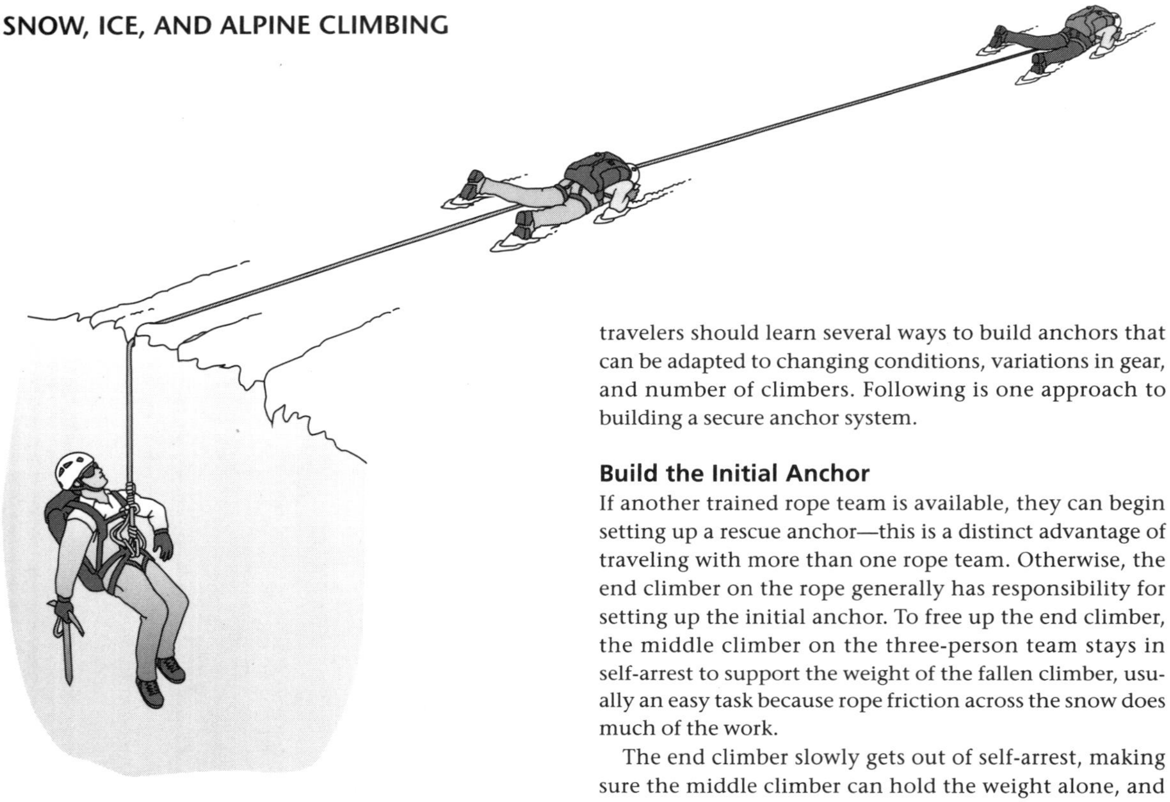

Fig. 18-13. Stop and hold a fall into a crevasse.

requires training in the field, augmented with annual practice. The principal steps in a successful crevasse rescue, beginning the instant the fall is stopped, are listed briefly here and discussed in detail in the sections that follow. (The more involved seven steps in accident response are discussed in Chapters 24, First Aid, and 25, Alpine Rescue.)

Step 1. Set up a secure anchor system.

Step 2. Communicate with the fallen climber.

Step 3. Devise a rescue plan. There are two basic choices: **Option 1.** Self-rescue—the fallen climber ascends the rope with prusik slings. **Option 2.** Team rescue—team members use a hauling system to pull the climber out.

Step 4. Carry out the plan: **Option 1.** For a self-rescue, assist the fallen climber as needed. **Option 2.** For a team rescue, set up the chosen hauling system, then haul the climber out.

STEP 1. SET UP A SECURE ANCHOR SYSTEM

The goal in the first step of crevasse rescue is to anchor the climber in the crevasse and allow the rescuers safe access to communicate with the fallen climber. There are many ways to build a bomber crevasse rescue anchor. Glacier travelers should learn several ways to build anchors that can be adapted to changing conditions, variations in gear, and number of climbers. Following is one approach to building a secure anchor system.

Build the Initial Anchor

If another trained rope team is available, they can begin setting up a rescue anchor—this is a distinct advantage of traveling with more than one rope team. Otherwise, the end climber on the rope generally has responsibility for setting up the initial anchor. To free up the end climber, the middle climber on the three-person team stays in self-arrest to support the weight of the fallen climber, usually an easy task because rope friction across the snow does much of the work.

The end climber slowly gets out of self-arrest, making sure the middle climber can hold the weight alone, and then sets to work establishing an anchor (fig. 18-14). In snow, a picket is often a good choice for the initial anchor because it can be placed quickly in a vertical position, with either a top-clip or midclip attachment, depending on the consolidation of the snow. An ice axe may also be used (see "Snow Anchors" in Chapter 16, Snow Travel and Climbing). If there is ice present, an ice-screw anchor will be needed (see "Ice Screws" and "Setting Up Ice Anchors" in Chapter 19, Alpine Ice Climbing). Place the anchor 5 to 10 feet (1.5 to 3 meters) down-rope from the middle climber, toward the lip of the crevasse.

CREVASSE RESCUE SAFETY PRECAUTIONS

While working to rescue a fallen climber, observe these primary safety considerations:

- All anchor systems must be absolutely reliable, with backup anchors to guard against failure.
- All rescuers must be connected to anchors at all times.
- The rescue must proceed as quickly as possible using efficient, thorough execution of every essential step.

Fig. 18-14. End climber sets up the initial anchor, while middle climber holds fallen climber.

Attach the Rope to the Anchor

The person who has set up the anchor now attaches a short sling to the climbing rope with a prusik hitch; a bachmann or klemheist friction hitch may also be used (see "Knots, Bends, and Hitches" in Chapter 9, Basic Safety System). This person then attaches a runner to the sling with a carabiner and then clips the other end of the runner to the anchor with a locking carabiner (as shown in Figure 18-14).

The next move is to slide the friction hitch down the rope, toward the crevasse, until the sling assembly is tight, ready to take a load. Now anyone who is still in self-arrest can ease the load onto the anchor (but still remains in self-arrest, to back up the initial anchor). Confirm that the anchor is solid and that the hitch is gripping the climbing rope tightly. (Keep in mind that if a prusik hitch is used, one rescuer will have to tend the hitch later, whenever the fallen climber is being pulled up. The bachmann friction hitch, on the other hand, usually requires less tending.)

As soon as the load is transferred to the initial anchor, back up the friction hitch. Tie a figure eight on a bight in the climbing rope 12 inches or so (about 30 centimeters) up-rope from the friction hitch. At the same time, use a locking carabiner to clip a rescue pulley to the carabiner already on the sling, running the climbing rope through the pulley. Clip the figure-eight loop in to this new carabiner (fig. 18-15). With the pulley in place, the beginnings of a 3:1 (Z) pulley hauling system are now created (see "Step 3. Devise a Rescue Plan" below), saving time later if such a system needs to be set up to haul the climber from the crevasse.

Build the Second Anchor

Never trust a single anchor that is certain to be fully weighted. Back it up with a second anchor. While the end climber is building the second anchor, the middle climber remains in the self-arrest position as a temporary backup to the initial anchor.

The second anchor makes the system as fail-safe as possible. This anchor needs to be bomber, so take the time to do it right. As with the initial anchor, use a picket or a deadman for snow or an ice screw for ice. In snow, a good

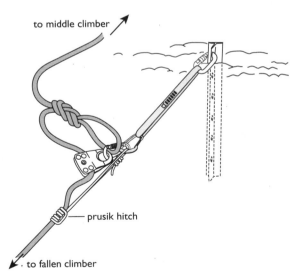

to middle climber

prusik hitch

to fallen climber

Fig. 18-15. Pulley and figure eight on a bight installed in the initial anchor.

18

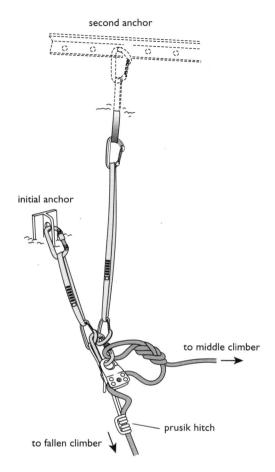

Fig. 18-16. Install a second anchor to make a tight and well-aligned connection.

combination is a picket for the first anchor and a deadman (such as a buried picket) for the second anchor (fig. 18-16).

Link the second anchor to the sling that is tied to the climbing rope with a prusik hitch in the same way that the initial anchor was linked to the sling. Attach a runner to the sling with a carabiner (also clipping through the pulley carabiner at the same time), and then clip the other end of the runner to the second anchor with a carabiner. Try to make a taut connection from anchor to sling, and remember the principles of equalization: keep the angle between the two anchor slings small (see "Equalizing the Anchor" in Chapter 10, Belaying).

With a secure anchor system in place, the team members are free to proceed to the next steps in the crevasse rescue

response. It is important for climbers to remain attached to the main anchor at all times during the rescue, using a personal anchor clipped directly in to the main anchor, using a waist prusik or other sling friction-hitched to the climbing rope, or by staying tied in to the climbing rope and requesting a belay.

STEP 2. COMMUNICATE WITH THE FALLEN CLIMBER

To develop a complete understanding of the fallen climber's situation so the party can devise a rescue plan, someone now needs to assess the fallen climber's situation.

A rescuer can be belayed from the anchor by a teammate or, better yet, a rescuer can move to the lip of the crevasse with a self-belay. Use a prusik hitch to connect a sling to a rope that is attached to the anchor (this can be the climbing rope or a separate rope that is anchored), then clip the sling to the harness with a locking carabiner. By sliding this prusik hitch along the rope, a rescuer can move toward the crevasse edge on an anchored self-belay (fig. 18-17).

Probe with the ice axe when approaching the crevasse lip to discover where the snow surface may be undercut. Approach the lip to the side of where the fall occurred so you do not knock snow and ice down onto the fallen climber.

Try to talk with the fallen climber. If there is no answer, the fallen climber may simply be out of earshot, or noisy wind on the glacier may be masking the response. If further attempts still bring no response, the rescuer needs to rappel or be lowered on belay into the crevasse to further assess the situation and perform urgent first aid if needed. If the climber is seriously injured or unconscious, the rescue method must take into account that the climber cannot actively participate in the rescue. Some crevasse rescue systems are better for dealing with this situation than others. (See the information on an unconscious fallen climber in "Special Rescue Situations" later in this chapter.)

If there is voice contact with the fallen climber, ask questions to find out the full situation. Is the climber wedged in? Injured? In need of more clothing? Is the climber now standing in prusik slings? Most importantly, assure the climber that things are progressing topside but that the rescuers need more information to determine the best way to carry out the rescue.

The fallen climber should be able to tell the rescuer whether self-rescue—by climbing up the side of the crevasse or by prusiking out—is a possibility or whether a hoist from above will be needed. There may even be the option of lowering the climber farther down, to a ramp or

Fig. 18-17. *Anchor system complete; self-belayed rescuer communicating with fallen climber. Note anchored ice axe protecting rope from entrenchment at lip of crevasse.*

ledge from where self-rescue or hauling might be easier. The rescuer appointed to make assessments at the lip of the crevasse has a great deal of responsibility, so this person should be skilled in rescue techniques and first aid and be prepared to provide important input on the rescue plan.

Minimize Entrenching of the Rope

Regardless of the rescue method, it is essential to pad the lip of the crevasse to minimize further entrenching of the rope. The entrenched rope adds a lot of friction to the raising system, which exerts tremendous force on the anchors if enough mechanical advantage or pulling power is used. An entrenched rope will also hinder the rescuers' efforts to hoist the climber up over the lip and will confound a fallen climber's own attempts to prusik over it. Properly prepping the lip may take some careful excavation.

For padding, slide the shaft of an ice axe, a ski, a foam pad, or even a pack under the rescue rope as close to the edge of the crevasse as can safely be reached. Be careful when working with sharp objects (ice-axe picks, ski edges) around the entrenched rope since a tensioned line is more easily cut. Anchor the padding items so they cannot fall into the crevasse (see Figure 18-17).

STEP 3. DEVISE A RESCUE PLAN

Now it is time to choose a method for getting the fallen climber safely out of the crevasse. Will the climber attempt self-rescue? Or will the team members topside set up a hauling system to pull the climber out? After choosing between self-rescue or team rescue, the party must choose among the various methods of either self-rescue or team rescue. Factors that affect these decisions include the condition of the climber, the number of rescuers, the equipment available (ice climbing tools, additional ropes, pulleys, and so forth), weather conditions, topography of the crevasse area, and any other variables that will affect the safety of victim and rescuers.

Option 1. Self-Rescue

Self-rescue is often the easiest and fastest form of crevasse rescue, regardless of party size. It has the added advantage of keeping the fallen climber active and warm. Of course, it requires that the fallen climber be basically uninjured and able to maneuver in the crevasse. For small parties that lack the muscle power to hoist the fallen climber or that are pinned down holding the rope, self-rescue may be the only practical option. This is especially true for a two-person party traveling alone. A good self-rescue method for ascending the rope is the Texas prusik (see "Rescue Methods" later in this chapter).

Option 2. Team Rescue

Climbers have several choices among team-rescue methods, each with its own particular advantages. Described and illustrated in "Rescue Methods" later in this chapter, they are summarized here as part of the decision-making process.

Direct haul. For a large party with an unentrenched rope, direct pull using brute force works very well. It is fast and uncomplicated, uses minimal equipment, and requires little or no help from the fallen climber. It works best when perhaps a half dozen strong rescuers can haul on the rope and when the pullers are on flat ground or downhill from the fallen climber.

2:1 (single) pulley method. When the rope is badly entrenched or when there are sufficient haulers, the 2:1

18

pulley method may be best. An entrenched rope will not matter because this method requires a separate length of rope—either the unused end of the accident rope or another rope entirely. The length of available rope must be at least twice as long as the distance from the initial anchor to the fallen climber. The mechanical advantage of the pulley makes hoisting this way a lot easier than by using brute force alone, though it still usually takes a minimum of three or four people to do the pulling. The fallen climber must be able to contribute to the rescue, with at least one good hand for clipping in to the rescue pulley and for maintaining balance.

3:1 (Z) pulley method. When a fallen climber is unable to help in the rescue or when few haulers are available, the 3:1 pulley may be the best method. The pull force is on the accident rope, which may be partially entrenched in the snow, but the high mechanical advantage of the system gives haulers the power to overcome some entrenchment.

Other rescue methods. Though the crevasse rescue systems mentioned above are among the most common, there are other team-rescue methods worth considering. Piggybacking two systems together, such as a single-pulley setup hauling on a 3:1 pulley system, creates a higher mechanical advantage and, thus, even more hauling power. Other notable options include the Double Mariner 5:1 haul, the 6:1 drop loop method, and the Spanish Burton 5:1 system—all worth exploring further.

Alternatives

A climber who falls into a crevasse does not necessarily have to come back out at the same spot. Check the possibility of lowering or swinging the fallen climber to a ledge. It might be a good spot for the victim to rest, as well as perhaps a gateway to a different part of the crevasse where rescue will be easier. Consider whether the bottom of the crevasse looks solid. This could offer another resting spot and a possible path to a climbing route or a snow ramp back to the surface.

STEP 4. CARRY OUT THE PLAN

Now the fallen climber must be safely removed from the crevasse. If self-rescue is the chosen plan, the climbers topside assist as needed. If it will be a team rescue, the climbers topside set up the selected hauling system and pull the fallen climber out. See "Rescue Methods" later in this chapter.

A party with enough people or a second rope team should assign one climber as the communicator at the lip of the crevasse throughout the rescue. Be careful near unstable crevasse edges so as not to dislodge debris onto the climber

below. Good communication is especially important as the fallen climber approaches the lip to ensure that the climber is not getting pulled into the crevasse wall.

In cases where the fallen climber has trouble climbing out over the crevasse lip due to an entrenched rope, consider lowering gear (ideally, linked to a different anchor) such as slings tied together, carabiner chains, et cetera, to provide additional support points or an alternate exit.

INSIDE THE CREVASSE

While the climbers on top are preparing for rescue, the fallen climber has work to do down in the crevasse, beginning with the moment of recovery from the fall. The fallen climber should do the following.

Get Pack and Ice Axe Out of the Way

If possible, send your pack and ice axe up on a rope lowered by the rescuers. If this is not possible, clip the axe to your harness, letting it hang so it does not interfere with your movement (see Figures 18-14 and 18-17). If at the beginning of the climb you did not rig a runner to the pack's haul loop (see "Using the Rope" earlier in this chapter), do this now: Girth-hitch a short sling through the pack's haul loop, then clip the sling with a carabiner in to the climbing rope between your harness and prusik attachments. The pack will then hang below you; as you prusik up the rope, the hanging pack will slide freely along the bottom of the loop of climbing rope and weight the rope, making it easier for you to climb (fig. 18-18).

Attain an Upright Position

If you did not land upright or already shift your body, work yourself into an upright position. Normally you do this by clipping the climbing rope through the carabiner at your chest harness. (This may be difficult or impossible to do until you have hung your pack, as described above.)

Get into Prusik Slings

Remove the prusik slings' foot loops from your pocket and slip one of the two adjustable loops over each boot (see "Using the Rope" earlier in this chapter). If you are wearing crampons, it will not be easy. Cinch the slipknot to tighten the slings around your boots. Getting into your prusik slings that are attached to the climbing rope permits you to alternate between standing in the foot sling and sitting from the waist sling as you dangle (fig. 18-19). You will be a lot more comfortable and will be ready to climb up the rope using the slings.

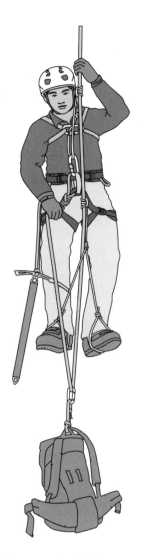

Fig. 18-19. Resting while using the Texas prusik system.

Fig. 18-18. Self-rescue using the Texas prusik system with the pack out of the way.

As soon as you have clipped in to your chest harness, moved your pack and ice axe out of the way, and caught your breath, it is usually advisable to begin prusiking partway to the top if you are just dangling free in the crevasse (see "Rescue Methods" below for a description of the Texas prusik). If possible, let the other climbers know what you are doing. Move carefully and deliberately so that you do not put sharp or sudden tugs on the rope that could interfere with their work holding your weight and setting up

an anchor. Normally, though, the snow provides enough friction to help hold the rope, especially if it is entrenched at the lip of the crevasse, so your prusiking will not hamper your rescuers.

This preliminary prusiking gets you closer to the glacier surface, where it is easier to communicate with rescuers. You and the other climbers can then decide together on the best rescue plan. If the final plan is to use a hauling system, your initial prusiking will have helped by making the haul shorter. Even if the final plan is self-rescue by prusiking, you will probably need their help in getting over the crevasse lip.

If the fall did not leave you dangling free but, instead, dropped you onto a ledge, where most of your weight is off the rope, a different approach to prusiking is required. In this case, go ahead and get into the prusik slings, but wait

18

to begin prusiking until you have talked it over with your rescuers. If you were to start prusiking without an OK from topside, your full weight coming suddenly onto the rope could unbalance and endanger the whole team.

Keep Warm

Zip up your jacket, put on the hat and gloves you stuffed in its pockets earlier, and try to put on additional layers of outerwear if possible.

RESCUE METHODS

This section describes the principal prusiking method for self-rescue and the hauling methods for team rescue.

OPTION 1. SELF-RESCUE

The Texas prusik is a simple system that permits more progress per cycle and more comfortable rests than other methods such as the stair-step prusik. A climber with an injured leg can still ascend the rope with the Texas prusik by using just one of the foot loops. Unlike the stair-step prusik, the

Texas prusik is easy to learn and execute. It will keep the climber upright without having to be connected to a chest harness. In fact, it may be easier to move the upper prusik when the climber is unclipped from the chest harness.

The Texas Prusik

This method of ascending the rope, developed by spelunkers (cavers), uses one prusik sling for the feet and a separate sling for the waist (which is clipped with a locking carabiner to your harness). The foot sling has two loops, one for each foot, tied so that they will adjust and cinch down on the boots. These are the steps for using the Texas prusik after recovering from a fall into a crevasse:

1. Stand up in the foot loops. You are now ready to move upward.
2. Unclip from the chest harness.
3. Loosen the friction hitch attached to the waist sling and slide it up the rope until it is taut.
4. Sit down in the harness, putting all your weight on the waist sling, which releases your weight from the foot sling.

Fig. 18-20. Ascending a rope using the Texas prusik system (pack and ice axe omitted for clarity): a, sitting or resting and moving foot prusik sling up; b, sitting on heels, ready to stand; c, standing and moving waist sling up.

5. Loosen the friction hitch attached to the foot sling and slide it up the rope—18 to 24 inches (50 to 75 centimeters), if the sling is properly adjusted. Raise your feet with it (fig. 18-20a).
6. Stand up again in the foot loops (fig. 18-20b and c).
7. Keep repeating steps 3 through 6.

OPTION 2. TEAM RESCUE

All rescues are team rescues to some degree, because even in a self-rescue, the fallen climber usually needs some help getting over the crevasse lip. A full team rescue usually involves hauling the fallen climber to safety. The principal hauling methods—direct haul, 2:1 (single) pulley, 3:1 (Z) pulley, and piggyback systems—are described in the sections that follow. In any rescue system calling for pulleys, carabiners can be substituted if necessary. However, carabiners create far more friction and make the rope harder to pull, and the load on the anchor system is correspondingly increased.

Direct Haul

A half dozen or so strong haulers line up along the accident rope and grasp it. They position themselves up-rope beyond the point where the initial anchor is attached to the climbing rope with a prusik hitch or bachmann friction hitch. The hitch is then in the right place to hold the rope if the haulers slip or need a rest. Before hauling begins, unclip the backup figure-eight loop (shown in Figures 18-15, 18-16, and 18-17) from the anchor system. Then the haulers go to work, pulling hand over hand on the rope or moving step by step away from the crevasse.

One rescuer tends the hitch, making sure the rope moves smoothly through it, and also keeps an eye on the anchor system. If there are enough people, another person can be stationed at the lip of the crevasse to stay in communication with the fallen climber.

The haulers should pull the rope at a slow, steady pace, especially when the fallen climber reaches the crevasse lip. If the rope has cut into the lip, the fallen climber could be injured by being pulled into the crevasse wall. At this point, rescuers may ask the fallen climber to scramble over the lip (with the help of an ice axe) while they hoist.

2:1 (Single) Pulley System

The 2:1 pulley system theoretically doubles the amount of weight that each hauler could raise without a pulley, though friction lowers this ratio somewhat. Because this method uses a length of rope that is separate from the rope going to the fallen climber, this is the method of choice if the accident rope is entrenched into the edge of the crevasse. However, it also requires the assistance of the fallen climber, so it cannot be performed when the fallen climber is unconscious. To carry out a rescue using the 2:1 pulley system, follow these steps:

1. Use a rescue rope (the unused end of the accident rope or a separate rope altogether) that is at least twice as long as the distance from the initial anchor down to the fallen climber. Attach the rope to either the existing anchor system or a new rescue anchor.
2. At the point where the rescue rope will go over the lip of the crevasse, prepare the lip with padding, such as an ice axe or pack, to prevent the rescue rope from entrenching itself in the snow.
3. Double the rescue rope into a big loop. Affix a pulley to the loop and attach a locking carabiner to the pulley. Leave the carabiner unlocked.
4. Lower the pulley and carabiner dangling from the loop down to the fallen climber (fig. 18-21a). Have the climber clip and lock the carabiner in to the belay loop on the harness. Confirm that this has been done. Check that all the climber's equipment is secure and ready for hauling to begin. Have the climber clip the rescue rope—the portion that is between the pulley and the pulling rescuers above (not the portion that is between the pulley and the anchors above)—in to the chest harness, to help the climber stay upright.
5. Assign a rescuer to attend to the slack that will develop in the original accident rope as the fallen climber is raised. It is critically important that this person pull slack through the friction hitch so that the rope is always ready to accept the fallen climber's weight, in case the pullers slip or need a rest. If the fallen climber's pack is clipped to the accident rope, there will be considerable weight on the rope, and it may require two people to take in the slack. Keep the existing backup figure eight on a bight tied to the initial anchor in the system while the slack is taken in; do not remove the knot.
6. With everything ready, the haulers start pulling on the unanchored end of the rescue rope (fig. 18-21b). To ease their task somewhat, the fallen climber can pull up on the anchored side of the rescue rope while the hauling proceeds; this unweights the unanchored end of the rescue rope somewhat.

18

Fig. 18-21. Setting up and raising a climber with the 2:1 (single) pulley system on a new rope (rescuers' personal anchors omitted for clarity): a, lowering the pulley to the fallen climber; b, raising the fallen climber.

3:1 (Z) Pulley System

The 3:1 pulley system magnifies the muscle power of small climbing parties by offering a three-to-one theoretical mechanical advantage through the use of two pulleys. It can be set up and operated with no help from the fallen climber, making it valuable for rescuing an unconscious person. The 3:1 pulley system normally uses the accident rope. It requires more equipment and is more complicated than the other hauling methods described above.

First, confirm the solidity of the initial anchor system, because the 3:1 pulley system puts considerable stress on

it. Take the loose end of the climbing rope attached to the fallen climber—the end that extends unweighted beyond the anchor—and lay out a long loop on the snow. This loop and the rest of the rope going from the anchor to the fallen climber should form a giant flat S in the snow, somewhat like a Z or a backward Z with the sharp edges worn off.

At the first bend in the Z (by the initial anchor system), the first pulley for hauling is already in place; this is the pulley attached to the initial anchor system with a locking carabiner when the system was first set up. Also clipped in to the locking carabiner are the prusik sling (also called the

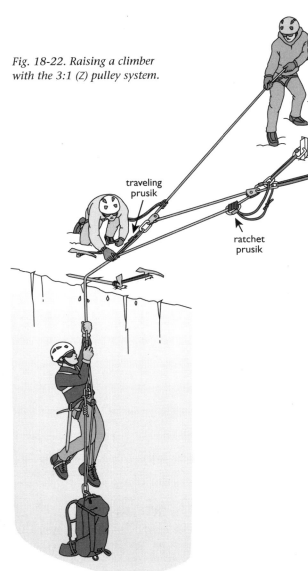

Fig. 18-22. Raising a climber with the 3:1 (Z) pulley system.

traveling prusik

ratchet prusik

ratchet prusik) and the backup figure-eight loop (see Figures 18-15, 18-16, and 18-17).

At the second bend in the Z (the slack bend, closer to the crevasse lip), install a second pulley on the rope. Use a friction hitch to attach a short sling to the taut section of rope going from the anchor's first pulley to the fallen climber, and clip this sling with a carabiner in to the second pulley (this is called the *traveling sling* or *traveling prusik*). Drag the friction hitch (traveling prusik) and traveling pulley as far down the taut rope as possible toward the crevasse (fig. 18-22). It may have to be seen to be believed, but this is

now a 3:1 pulley system, ready for use. Here's how to haul using the 3:1 pulley system:

1. Unclip the backup figure-eight loop from the initial anchor system and untie the knot as soon as the haulers and fallen climber are ready for pulling.
2. If the ratchet or keeper sling used a prusik hitch to attach the accident rope to the initial anchor system, assign a rescuer to tend the hitch so that the rope slips freely through it as the rope is pulled in. If a bachmann friction hitch was used instead, the attachment should tend itself, and the front hauler can simply keep an eye on it to see that all is well.
3. Start pulling at a steady rate, either hand over hand or by holding tight and walking backward.
4. The hauling will soon bring the second (traveling) pulley in close to the first (stationary or ratchet) pulley at the initial anchor. Stop hauling when the pulleys are about 2 feet (0.5 meter) apart. If they are pulled too close, the figure Z is collapsed and the mechanical advantage is lost.
5. Once hauling has stopped, relax the pull on the rope enough to transfer the fallen climber's weight back onto the ratchet or keeper sling at the initial anchor.
6. Reset the traveling pulley by loosening the traveling sling that is linked to the traveling pulley and sliding it back down the taut accident rope toward the crevasse lip once again.
7. Keep repeating steps 3 through 6.

Beware of the pulling power of the 3:1 (Z) pulley system. If care is not used, the climber can be injured by being pulled forcefully up into the lip. As the fallen climber nears the lip of the crevasse, use a friction hitch (for example, a prusik hitch) to attach a webbing chain to the taut accident rope and lower the webbing chain to the fallen climber (fig. 18-23a), who can use it like an aider (*etrier*) to step up and pull up over the lip of the crevasse (fig. 18-23b). See "Aiders (*Etriers*)" in Chapter 15, Aid and Big Wall Climbing.

18

Fig. 18-23. Helping fallen climber over the lip of a crevasse (foot prusiks omitted for clarity): a, rescuer lowers webbing chain attached to taut accident line so climber can put right foot into it; b, as climber steps up in webbing, rescuer helps the fallen climber scramble over the lip.

Piggyback Pulleys

To get even more mechanical advantage out of a rescue hauling setup, combine or "piggyback" two systems. For example, establish a separate 2:1 pulley setup to haul on the rope coming from a 3:1 pulley system. This gives a six-to-one theoretical mechanical advantage. One note of caution: beware of using piggyback systems to overcome the resistance of pulling the victim over the crevasse lip; serious injuries have resulted.

A 5:1 pulley system can be constructed in different ways. One method is to clip a carabiner and a triple runner or cordelette 15 to 25 feet (5 to 8 meters) long to the traveling prusik. Another method is to add a second traveling prusik and pulley (or carabiner) to a 3:1 pulley system (see Figure 25-6c in Chapter 25, Alpine Rescue). For a 4:1 advantage, set up a 2:1 single-pulley system to haul on another 2:1 pulley system.

SPECIAL RESCUE SITUATIONS

A crevasse rescue can be complicated by any number of unusual twists. This section describes some special situations that could be encountered and ideas on how to deal with them. The situations can become complicated, and the rescuers' response will have to be adapted to the conditions of the moment. Anything that works safely is fine. (See Chapter 25, Alpine Rescue, for more details on accident response and additional rescue techniques.)

WHEN THE MIDDLE PERSON FALLS IN

It is awkward at best when the middle person on a three-person rope team falls into a crevasse, especially if no other climbers are around to set up the rescue anchor. With no second team, the only two people who can help are separated by a crevasse, each in self-arrest. Here is a general procedure for getting out of this fix.

The climbers begin by deciding which side of the crevasse will be the rescue side—that is, which side the fallen climber should come out on. Usually, one of the two rescuers in self-arrest is holding more weight than the other. The one holding the least weight usually has the best chance to get up and establish an anchor—this climber's side will be the rescue side—while the rescuer on the other side stays in self-arrest to hold the fall.

After the climber on the rescue side sets up the rescue anchor (see "Step 1. Set Up a Secure Anchor System" above), the climber in self-arrest on the other side of the crevasse can slowly release tension on the climbing rope and ease the fallen climber's weight onto the anchor.

If the climber who was in self-arrest is needed to help in the rescue operation, the climber on the rescue side now tries to belay the climber on the self-arrest side over to the rescue side. The rope on the rescue side can be used for belaying, if it is long enough, or a second rope—carrying a second rope is a good precaution for a rope team traveling alone—can provide the belay. If no belay or safe route across the crevasse is available, however, the climber on the self-arrest side could be stuck there. This climber would then set up an anchor and stay put.

The most advantageous rescue plan now is for the fallen climber to self-rescue by ascending the rope on prusik slings, coming out on the rescue side, where the anchor has been placed. If a self-rescue by prusiking is not possible, then a 3:1 pulley or a piggyback system could be tried. This all takes plenty of time, competence, equipment, and resourcefulness. Learn to use the bachmann friction hitch (see "Friction Hitches" in Chapter 9, Basic Safety System) for times when you might have to haul alone, because the hitch requires less tending than a standard prusik hitch in a hauling system.

In the case of a four-person rope team, the situation is a little simpler in the event that one of the two middle members falls into a crevasse. Conduct the rescue in a routine manner from the side that has two climbers topside.

WHEN A TWO-PERSON TEAM IS ALONE

For a party of two people with no other rope team nearby, glacier travel is risky and discouraged. Both climbers absolutely need to know their rescue techniques, period. The climber who stops a fall must set up an anchor alone while in self-arrest and then create a hauling system appropriate for a single person (such as a 6:1 drop loop system) if one is needed. Therefore, each climber must carry at least two pieces of snow or ice protection for an anchor appropriate to the conditions, plus the equipment (pulleys, carabiners, slings) to set up a hauling system. And all of this must be readily at hand on harnesses or pack straps.

Rope teams of two should shorten their rope by taking in coils (see below), which automatically makes available an extra length of rope for rescue use. Packing along a second rope is also a good precaution. The climbers should not have the rope clipped in to their chest harnesses, because this makes rescue very difficult. And with only two people, it is even more important than usual to travel with a personal prusik system ready for use.

If you end up as the sole rescuer in a two-person rope team, holding your partner's fall with your self-arrest, begin your rescue efforts by augmenting the security of your arrest position by digging in your feet and pressing the ice axe more firmly into the snow. Imagine that you are establishing a belay stance while lying down.

Try to free one hand by rotating the upper half of your body—but keep leaning on the axe and bracing yourself with at least one stiff leg. If the rope is clipped in to your chest harness, unclip it now. At this point, you will see the value of keeping the appropriate anchors easily accessible.

When you get one hand free, place a picket, ice screw, or second ice tool—anything secure enough to hold the fallen climber and allow you to get up and create a main anchor. Once the initial protection is in place, clip the loose end of your foot prusiks to this protection with a carabiner. Slowly transfer the weight of the fallen climber to the initial protection. Now follow the steps described in "Crevasse Rescue Response" earlier in this chapter, though you will probably experience more difficulty than would a larger rope team or group of teams: set up a secure main anchor, communicate with your fallen partner, settle on a rescue plan, and carry it out. Ideally, your partner will be able to handle self-rescue, prusiking out. If not, try a 3:1 pulley or piggyback hauling system. Of course, if you are unable to make an initial placement of protection in the first place, the climber in the crevasse has no choice but to try self-rescue while you remain in self-arrest.

Traveling on a glacier alone as a party of two requires a high degree of competency with crevasse rescue systems. Study and practice plenty before attempting it.

Shortening the Rope with Coils

Shortening the rope by coiling it over the shoulder—"climbing in coils"—is the preferred method of travel for two-person glacier teams. The technique results in closer spacing between rope partners for more efficient, comfortable travel, and it provides some free rope for a hauling system or other rescue use.

18

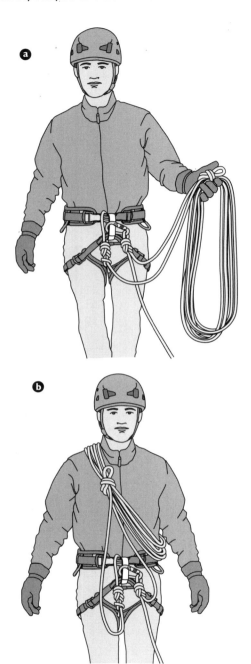

Fig. 18-24. Shortening the rope with a coil: a, tying in and creating the coil; b, draping the coil out of the way (prusik slings omitted for clarity).

The coil also provides a means of quick transition between the closer spacing of roped glacier travel and the full rope-length requirements of belayed climbing. This transition is important on an alpine climb where a glacier approach is followed by belayed rock or ice climbing. To create the coil, take these steps:

1. Tie in to the rope at your harness, as you would normally.
2. Take a series of coils of rope into your hand (usually five, but no more than nine) until you have the desired spacing between you and your rope partner. Secure the coils together by tying an overhand knot around them, using a loop of the rope (fig. 18-24a).
3. Get the coils out of the way for travel, stowing them securely anywhere, such as in the top of your pack or over one shoulder and under the opposite arm, where they are easily accessible (fig. 18-24b).
4. Attach the shortened length of climbing rope to your harness with a figure eight on a bight clipped to the belay loop with a locking carabiner so that any force coming onto the rope will be taken by this knot.

A variation of the coil is often used in Europe; climbers put six butterfly knots on a bight in the rope, three at each end near each of the two climbers. Research by Ecole Nationale de Ski et d'Alpinisme (ENSA) Chamonix recommends an initial 10-foot (3-meter) space between the climber and the first knot, a second knot 6 feet (2 meters) beyond the first knot, and a third knot 6 feet (2 meters) beyond the second knot (fig. 18-25). This method works on the principle that in the event of a fall into a crevasse, the rope will entrench and the knots will catch in the crevasse lip. This takes most of the weight off the arresting climber, which makes it considerably easier to set up the initial rescue anchor.

To use this rope to extract the fallen climber from the crevasse, the other climber must untie the knots in the rope before hauling. This may be possible because most of the load should be taken by the knot wedged in the lip of the crevasse. If the rescuer cannot do this, then rescue may be performed using a 2:1 pulley system with the loose end of the rope or using another rope if there are sufficient people to haul and the fallen climber is uninjured. For a single hauler, the best approach is a 6:1 drop loop on the accident rope. Since more complex systems are beyond the scope of this book, take time to research this method online or through information listed in Resources.

When self-rescuing, one disadvantage of tying knots in the rope is that the fallen climber must pass them when ascending out of the crevasse. This is a bit awkward and

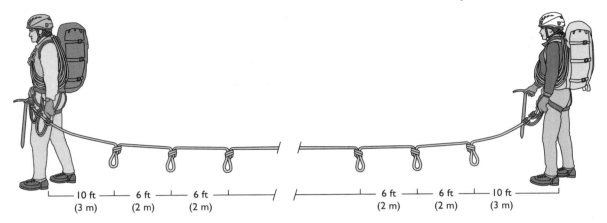

Fig. 18-25. Two-person glacier travel team with knots in rope, which aid in arresting a fall into a crevasse by catching in crevasse lip.

slow but doable: the fallen climber ties their prusik onto the rope above the loaded knot, transfers weight to the prusik to unweight the loaded knot, unties the butterfly knot in the rope below, and continues prusiking, repeating this process for each knot that needs to be passed.

WHEN THE FALLEN CLIMBER IS UNCONSCIOUS

To help an unconscious climber, a rescuer must descend immediately by rappelling or being lowered on belay. This rescuer must descend with enough clothing and equipment to avoid hypothermia, ascend independently if needed, and provide proper first aid. Major crevasse falls are likely to cause injuries. The rescuer can administer urgent first aid and also get the fallen climber right-side up if necessary. Time is critical because there may also be an increased risk of suspension trauma, asphyxiation, and/or hypothermia—and possibly cardiac arrest when moving a hypothermic crevasse rescue victim. The rescuers must then consider which of the hauling methods they will use, keeping in mind that the fallen climber is unable to participate in the rescue. Helping an unconscious climber over the lip of the crevasse will require a rescuer to work right at the edge of or from inside the crevasse. Monitor the condition of the unconscious person, taking care to cause no further injury.

WHEN THERE IS MORE THAN ONE VICTIM

If more than one person has fallen into a crevasse, assess each person's condition and the best method for getting each one out, and then decide the order of rescue. Practicality usually determines the order of rescue, unless there is ample backup for rescuers and equipment. Be sure that each fallen climber is given warm clothing, if needed, and keep everyone informed of rescue plans as they develop.

WHEN THE WORKING SPACE IS CRAMPED

The climber who drops into self-arrest position to stop a rope mate's fall could be lying so close to the lip of the crevasse that there is very little room to place an anchor or pulley system. A solution to this situation is to set up the main anchor where there is enough room—on the up-rope side of the climber in self-arrest (instead of the usual place, between the rescuer and the crevasse). Leave 24 inches or so (60 centimeters) of slack between the main anchor and this rescuer, so that this person is not trapped in the system by tension on the rope.

Then set up a temporary anchor, between the rescuer in self-arrest and the crevasse, that will take the weight of the fallen climber long enough to enable the rescuer to get up from self-arrest position and untie from the rope. Once hauling begins, untie the prusik sling attached to the temporary anchor.

WHEN THE WORKING SPACE IS BETWEEN TWO CREVASSES

Rescuers trying to work in a very narrow area between two crevasses can consider moving the operation. The rescue might proceed better if it is run from the opposite side of the crevasse that holds the fallen climber.

Another option is to change the direction of pull on a 3:1 pulley system. Hook a third pulley to the anchor and run the hauling end of the rope through it (fig. 18-26). Now the rescuers can pull in a direction more parallel to the crevasses.

18

417

Fig. 18-26. Adding another pulley to the 3:1 (Z) pulley system for a change of direction in a tight space, such as between two crevasses.

WHEN THE ROPES ARE ENTRENCHED

The upward progress of a person climbing out or being pulled out of a crevasse can be stopped cold by a rope that has dug itself into the lip. This situation calls for some improvisation. For instance, a rescuer can attach prusik slings or aiders (*etriers*) above the entrenched portion of the rope and drop them down for the climber to step into. See "Aiders (*Etriers*)" in Chapter 15, Aid and Big Wall Climbing.

Another option is to switch to a new rescue rope. A rescuer can lower a new rope to the fallen climber (as shown in Figure 18-21). Or the fallen climber can, in effect, provide a new rope by tossing the loose end of the climbing rope up to the rescuers. This is done by prusiking up to the lip, tying in higher up on the climbing rope, untying from the loose end of the climbing rope, and throwing the loose end up to the rescuers.

A new rescue rope, carefully padded at the lip of the crevasse so it does not also get entrenched, opens up several rescue possibilities. The fallen climber can switch prusik slings from the original climbing rope to the new free rope. Or the rescuers can haul the fallen climber up and out on the new rope. Or the fallen climber can merely transfer all weight to the new rope to give rescuers a much better chance of freeing the entrenched line.

PATHS TO THE SUMMIT

Glaciers can appear to be obvious, rather convenient routes to alpine summits, but in reality they are massive, dynamic systems that hold many hazards—especially with climate change reshaping the glacial landscape. Climbers who seek the freedom of the glaciated peaks must learn how to safely negotiate crevasses and other dangers. Clearly, the best strategy for travel on a glacier is to minimize risk by defending against a crevasse fall. Even when precautions are taken, however, falls and other accidents can occur. Anyone planning to travel on a glacier must master the techniques for dealing with the hazards and effecting a successful rescue if necessary. With these skills, climbers can safely take advantage of these glacial paths up to alpine summits.

CHAPTER 19

ALPINE ICE CLIMBING

Ice is found on or around the summits of many alpine peaks, and developing ice climbing skills increases climbers' opportunities for safe exploration of those summits. With proper skills, they will be able to use ice as yet another avenue to the alpine realm.

To climb ice, mountaineers use much of what they have learned about rock and snow climbing, adding the special tools and techniques needed for climbing ice. Ice climbers experience the same joys as snow climbers do and face the same perils: avalanches, hazardous couloirs and unstable cornices, ice blocks, and icefalls. Ice climbing opportunities can be found year-round, from climbing waterfall ice on the short, dark days of winter to ascending alpine ice on long, warm summer days.

Ice can appear in a variety of forms. Under the combined effects of pressure, heat, and time, snow and other forms of frozen precipitation metamorphose into the alpine ice of glaciers, icefields, and couloirs. There is no clear distinction between alpine ice and hard snow. Alpine ice sometimes appears as blue ice; this hue means that the ice is relatively pure. Black alpine ice—old, hard ice mixed with dirt, pebbles, or other debris—is another common variation. Liquid water freezes to form water ice. Water-ice formations can be as dramatic as a frozen waterfall or as common as *verglas*, the thin, clear coating of ice that forms when rainfall or melting snow freezes on a surface, such as rock. Verglas is difficult to climb because the thin, weak layer provides scant purchase for crampons and ice tools. Old alpine hard water ice is usually the most compact and difficult-to-penetrate form of ice when compared with alpine névé or more recently frozen alpine ice.

The next chapter, Chapter 20, Waterfall Ice and Mixed Climbing, hones in on very steep ice and mixed ice and rock. This chapter covers the rest.

Ice is as changeable and ephemeral as snow. A rock route is likely to be there unchanged for years or decades, but what was a water-ice route in the morning may be, by afternoon, nothing but a jumbled pile of ice blocks or a wet spot on the rock. Similarly, with glacial alpine ice a single route may morph throughout the year: in early season the climb may be a straightforward jaunt up perfect névé, but by August or September (in the northern hemisphere) it becomes a jumble of crevasses and seracs requiring as much routefinding ability as it does technical climbing skills.

Climbers must learn to anticipate the changeability of ice. Ice can exhibit a wide range of characteristics. At one extreme, it can seem as hard as steel; ice tools bounce off it, barely scratching the surface. Hard ice can also be as brittle as glass, requiring climbers to expend time and energy chopping away at the surface until they can plant an ice tool without the placement shattering. At other times, ice can be soft and plastic, allowing climbers to make secure placements effortlessly with a single swing—an ice climber's dream. Ice can also be too soft and weak to provide good protection placements or to support a climber's weight. It takes experience to assess the relative condition of ice.

419

TABLE 19-1. STEEPNESS OF SLOPES	
DESCRIPTION	**APPROXIMATE ANGLE OF STEEPNESS**
Gentle	0° to 30°
Moderate	30° to 45°
Steep	45° to 60°
Extremely steep	60° to 80°
Vertical	80° to 90°
Overhanging	Greater than 90°

As is true of all types of climbing, the steepness of the slope greatly affects which ice climbing technique is appropriate. On flat névé—or on relatively level areas of rock-impregnated ice such as a glacier below the firn line—it is usually possible to walk without crampons. But on flat ice that is hard and smooth, crampons might be needed to avoid falling. Modern crampons are relatively quick and easy to put on and take off, but this can use up precious time. Occasionally, for one or two moves on a short slope where there is limited exposure, an ice axe can be used to chop steps. However, in almost every instance where the snow or ice is too firm to kick a trustworthy step, especially if it is exposed, crampons should be used.

As the slope angle increases, climbers can use French technique, also called *flat-footing*, but only up to a point. The steepest routes require front-pointing, also called *German technique*. Chapter 20, Waterfall Ice and Mixed Climbing, covers steep ice techniques in more depth.

This chapter uses the descriptive terms in Table 19-1 in referring to the approximate steepness of slopes.

EQUIPMENT

Continuing refinements in equipment have helped ice climbers improve and expand their techniques and use them to undertake greater climbing challenges. Manufacturers are producing a steady stream of specialized and innovative clothing, boots, crampons, ice tools, and ice protection. (See Chapter 16, Snow Travel and Climbing, for a general description of gear such as crampons and ice axes.) This section describes the equipment that is specific to alpine ice climbing.

CLOTHING

Clothes for ice climbing should offer a combination of comfort and function. Employ a layered system, with layers appropriate to the conditions. Whatever system you choose, ensure the components work together and use either specialized fabrics or openings to regulate your body temperature. Clothing manufacturers are constantly bringing forward new fabrics that dissipate excess heat while still providing warmth, water repellency, and wind protection. Pants with side zippers ventilate the lower body without exposing your boot tops. Jackets with armpit zippers also allow you to regulate your temperature. It is important to choose unrestrictive clothing that stretches as you move and is designed to stay put when you lift up your arms. See Chapter 2, Clothing and Equipment, to learn more about technical climbing clothes for various conditions.

Handwear

Ice climbers' hands need protection from dampness, cold, and abrasion. The type of handwear you choose and use depends on the difficulty, steepness, and conditions of the ice or snow. Your choices always strike a balance between dexterity, strength, and warmth. Walking or climbing low-angle alpine snow or ice on a summer day with an ice axe in hand may require nothing more than a pair of lightweight gloves. Climbing steep, deep snow on a cold day and plunging your ice tools and hands well under the surface calls for a well-insulated pair of bulky gloves or mitts with waterproof taped shells. When ascending steep to overhanging snow and ice, the best choice is gloves with a snug fit and enough friction on the palms to allow a good grip on your tools. Thin gloves provide dexterity to place screws or manipulate gear.

Some climbs may demand several different pairs of gloves or mitts. For example, on long, cold technical routes you may want to use a lightweight pair of gloves or liners for the nontechnical approach, a pair of thin, snug gloves for climbing—plus a spare in case they get wet or lost—along with a thick, warm pair of gloves or mittens to keep your hands warm at belays or rests.

BOOTS

When you select boots, it is essential to get a precise fit: room for the toes to wiggle a little but snug in the instep and heel. There should be minimal lift at the heel to prevent stress on the calves when front-pointing or walking, yet not so snug over the top of the foot that circulation to the toes is impeded. Be sure to fit boots to accommodate the sock system you will wear. Most modern mountaineering boots have molded toe and heel grooves to accommodate clip-on crampons.

Leather and synthetic. For alpine ice climbing in moderate to cold conditions, modern leather or high-performance synthetic mountaineering boots are the best choice. Boots used for extensive front-pointing must have very stiff soles to prevent overstressing the crampon frame or letting the foot twist out of a clip-on crampon binding. In French technique (flat-footing), ankle rotation is critical; boots must permit good range of motion, and leather boots are better in this regard. For extreme cold, or at high altitude, double boots, with a removable insulated liner, provide extra warmth. The outer and inner boot materials on modern double boots are an ever-changing combination of fabrics and foam materials and even carbon fiber insoles. Boots keep getting lighter and better.

GAITERS

Today, few alpine and waterfall ice climbers use full-length gaiters. Some alpine ice climbing boots now come with built-in gaiters to repel snow, ice, and moisture. Modern climbing pants feature either an integrated gaiter, hooks or straps that go under the boot (so the pant leg acts as a gaiter), or pant cuffs fit close enough to the boot that gaiters are not needed. Hardshell pants are another common alternative. Sometimes a climber opts for short gaiters that cover only the boot top and are worn underneath pants. However, there are conditions in which full-length gaiters may be useful, such as deep snow or very cold temperatures. When using full-length gaiters, make sure they fit your boots securely, can accommodate any additional layers of insulation you wear on your legs, and can accommodate your specific crampon attachment method. Gaiters or pants with reinforced leg bottoms can help prevent abrasions and snags from crampon points.

CRAMPONS

A variety of modern crampons are available for different types of snow and ice climbing, including technical crampons designed for better performance on steep ice and for mixed climbing. (See "Crampons" in Chapter 16, Snow Travel and Climbing.) Regardless of the type of crampons selected, points must be sharp; the harder the ice, the sharper the points need to be. Check the points before each climb and sharpen them if necessary before setting out.

Front and Secondary Points

The front points on nearly all crampons, whether intended for use on alpine climbing or waterfall ice, are angled downward. The front points on crampons designed for snow and alpine ice are often oriented horizontally to give

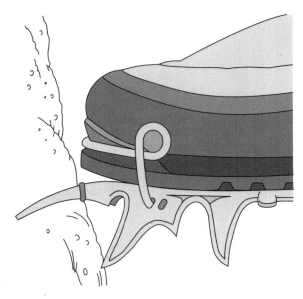

Fig. 19-1. Side view showing how front points and secondary points on crampons engage in near vertical ice.

them more purchase in snow. Waterfall ice crampons, on the other hand, often have front points oriented vertically to give better penetration in hard ice (fig. 19-1). The secondary points immediately behind the front points are angled forward on most modern crampons to provide added stability.

ICE TOOLS

Ice tools come in three basic styles. For steep ice (greater than 45 degrees), it is advantageous to have a hybrid ice axe similar to a general mountaineering axe but with a slightly bent shaft. Hybrid ice axes come in various lengths. They generally have an integrated pick and adze or hammer, but they are also available with a modular head to accommodate replacement picks.

For extremely steep terrain (greater than 60 degrees) it is better to have a bent-grip shaft ice tool with teeth with a grip rest at the base of the shaft. For extremely steep and vertical ice and mixed climbing, many climbers prefer an ice tool with an ergonomic handle and bent shaft. These tools come in fixed lengths (commonly 50 centimeters) and have a modular head to accommodate different types of picks, with a choice of hammerhead or adze (see Chapter 16, Snow Travel and Climbing, for a description of ice axes versus ice tools). Some ice tools have removable head weights that allow climbers to fine-tune the tool's "swing weight."

19

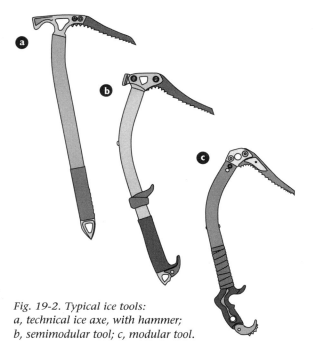

Fig. 19-2. Typical ice tools:
a, technical ice axe, with hammer;
b, semimodular tool; c, modular tool.

Ice tools are usually equipped with a hammer opposite the pick rather than an adze (fig. 19-2a). However, for alpine routes where excavating snow or digging a tent platform in dirt or gravel might be required, some climbers prefer to equip one ice tool with an adze. Having a sharp adze when ice climbing deserves caution. If a tool with an adze suddenly pops out of the ice or slips off a hold, it can cause a nasty gash on a climber's face.

Modern ice tools feature modular and semimodular designs. With semimodular tools, only the pick is interchangeable (fig. 19-2b). Fully modular tools provide the option of interchangeable picks and adzes or hammers (fig. 19-2c). Being able to replace picks, adzes, and hammers as the need arises provides added flexibility because the tool can be assembled to accommodate prevailing conditions, or a broken pick can be replaced in the field.

There is no standard fastening system for interchangeable parts on modular ice tools. Components of one manufacturer's system are not compatible with those from another company, and some systems are easier to use than others. The trend has been to design fastening systems that require a minimum of tools. The components of some ice tools are designed to be changed by using a simple wrench, or the pick or spike of another ice tool made by the same manufacturer.

What is the "perfect" ice tool? It is whatever works best for you. Try to demo a variety of tools on ice to determine which work best for you in terms of weight, technical features, and how they handle. See the "Questions to Consider When Selecting Ice Tools" sidebar.

The styles of ice tools vary greatly. The following sections describe the principal design variations of the parts of the ice tool: shaft, pick, adze or hammer, spike/teeth, and tether.

Shafts

Ice-tool shafts are mostly manufactured from aluminum alloy, carbon fiber composites, and steel. Only general mountaineering ice axes now come with straight shafts. Ice tools intended for steep terrain (greater than 45 degrees) all come with bent shafts that enable the tool to reach around bulges in the ice and keep the climber's fingers from hitting the ice when swinging. The angles of bent shafts can vary (figs. 19-3a, b, and c) depending on the purpose of the tool. The sharper the bend, the steeper the terrain it is intended for. Check to see that the curve of the bend and the swing weight complement your natural swing.

Shafts on modern ice tools to facilitate grip are usually covered partially in rubber. Although modern bent-grip tools make it easier to climb steep ice and mixed terrain, the ergonomic handle and the grip rest may impede plunging the shaft into snow. Some technical ice tools come without a grip rest, which might be a better choice for situations where there will be a lot of steep snow. The bent shaft also makes hammering pitons awkward; if a lot of piton work is anticipated, some climbers carry a light piton hammer to make that job easier.

The circumference and cross-sectional shape of the shaft affect your grip. A particular shaft might be too large or too small for your hand. A shaft that is too large in circumference

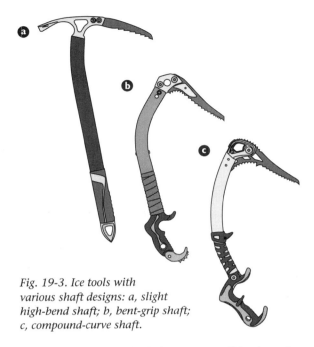

Fig. 19-3. Ice tools with
various shaft designs: a, slight
high-bend shaft; b, bent-grip shaft;
c, compound-curve shaft.

is fatiguing to grip. A shaft that is too small in circumference is hard to control. A climber's choice of handwear also affects the grip (see "Handwear" above).

Picks

The ice tool's pick must penetrate the ice, hold against a downward pull, and release easily when its grip is no longer needed. The holding and releasing characteristics of a pick are determined by its geometry, thickness, and tooth configuration. The teeth should be shaped to bite into the ice when pulling down on the shaft of the ice tool. In most cases, only the first few teeth provide any useful bite into the ice.

Ice-tool picks are made for the type of tool that you purchase and often come in multiple thicknesses. The thinner pick is meant primarily for pure ice with penetration. The thicker pick is a bit more likely to shatter the ice, but it is stronger and meant to be used for mixed climbing and dry tooling where torquing it in cracks and other abuse might break a thinner pick.

Technically curved. The pick of a general mountaineering ice axe curves slightly downward, whereas the technically curved pick of an ice tool (fig. 19-4a) curves down more sharply and thus holds better in ice. It is most often used on alpine ice and glacial ice climbs. It is the most effective technical pick for self-arrest.

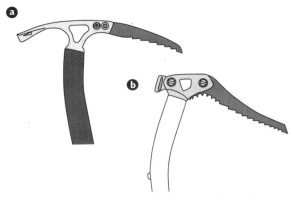

Fig. 19-4. Picks: a, technically curved; b, reverse curved.

Reverse curved. The reverse-curved pick (fig. 19-4b) is both secure and easy to remove from the ice, making it the most popular choice for extremely steep ice routes. During self-arrest, this pick grabs so well that climbers may not be able to hold on to the tool.

Picks are easily dulled when swinging into thin ice and hitting the rock underneath. Picks also get worn from climbing on rock while used when mixed climbing and dry tooling. A dull pick can be sharpened with a good file; but after being filed multiple times, the pick can get filed back to the first tooth. Once this has happened, it is time to replace the pick. A pick will last longer if it is sharpened only enough to reestablish its original shape and edge (fig. 19-5). Using a grinder may remove more metal than is necessary; take care not to weaken the pick by overheating it.

Adzes and Hammers

As with picks, ice-tool adzes come in an array of shapes and sizes. The most common adze is straight, extending more or less perpendicular to the shaft or drooping slightly downward (see Figure 19-4a). Modular ice tools provide the option of installing either an adze or a hammer.

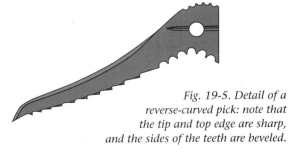

Fig. 19-5. Detail of a
reverse-curved pick: note that
the tip and top edge are sharp,
and the sides of the teeth are beveled.

19

Spikes or Teeth

To penetrate ice, the spike or teeth on the bottom of an ice tool's shaft must be reasonably sharp. Most spikes have carabiner holes (see Figures 19-2 and 19-3), to which a climber can clip a tether to keep from losing the tool if dropped.

Tethers

For the most part, leashes attaching the wrist to the ice tool are no longer used when alpine ice climbing, waterfall ice climbing, and mixed climbing. To prevent the loss of a dropped tool, tethers (also called *umbilicals*) are often used. A tether is usually made of an elastic cord with a clip on one end (for attaching to the spike of the ice tool) and a loop on the other (for girth-hitching to the harness; fig. 19-6). Tethers made for two tools feature two cords and clips coming together in a single loop. Some manufacturers still provide a removable wrist leash for climbers who prefer them, but the flexibility of climbing leashless has made the use of wrist leashes almost obsolete.

Maintenance

Inspect ice tools before each outing, checking for rust, cracks, and other signs of wear or damage. Be sure that adzes, picks, and spikes are sharp. If the tools are a modular design, also check to see that all fastening systems are secure.

ICE SCREWS

Modern ice screws are made from steel, aluminum, or titanium alloy. Ice screws come in a variety of lengths ranging from 10 to 22 centimeters (ice screws are commonly measured in metric units). The length of an ice screw has a great bearing on its strength. A longer screw is stronger but only when the ice is thicker than the length of the screw. Modern screws include hangers with knobs (fig. 19-7), which make placement, clipping, and removal almost effortless compared with older screws (see the "History of Ice Screws" sidebar).

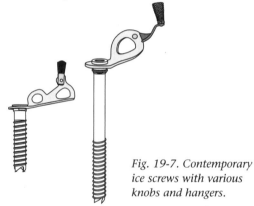

Fig. 19-7. Contemporary ice screws with various knobs and hangers.

OTHER GEAR

Ice climbers use other gear adapted specifically for ice, including racking devices, eye protection, and V-thread tools.

Racking Devices

Personal preference and compatibility with a particular harness influence how a climber chooses to rack ice screws. Most commonly, climbers use a specialized plastic carabiner that attaches directly to the harness waist belt (fig. 19-8). These devices allow ice screws to be racked conveniently and provide easy, one-handed unclipping when the gear is needed. These clips can also be used for temporarily securing ice tools. The downside of a plastic device is that it can break if pressed against a hard surface: for example, in a rock chimney on a mixed climb.

Fig. 19-6. Tethers, or umbilical leashes, attached to harness.

HISTORY OF ICE SCREWS

Until the mid-twentieth century, ice pitons were extra long, blade-type rock pitons with holes, notches, or bulges to increase their grip in ice. After World War II, climbers experimented with new designs that featured a greater surface area (to decrease the load per square inch on the ice) and more holes (to help the shaft freeze into the slope). In the early 1960s, when ice pitons evolved into ice screws, enthusiasts claimed that they would revolutionize ice climbing, bringing security to the slopes. Critics countered that the screws were not much better than the older ice pitons. This was true of the lightweight, relatively weak "coat hanger" ice screws, which are no longer in use. Ice screws have continued to improve and now provide reliable protection when placed in good ice.

Ropes

Standard 60- or 70-meter double ropes (see "Double- and Twin-Rope Techinques" in Chapter 14, Leading on Rock) are most commonly used for alpine ice climbing, though this depends on the type of climb and the climbers' preferences (see also Table 9-1 in Chapter 9, Basic Safety System). Double ropes are each individually lighter than a single rope. Double ropes are safe to use on ice (on rock a larger-diameter rope may provide greater resistance to abrasion and cuts from sharp edges), and they allow for full-length rappels on the descent.

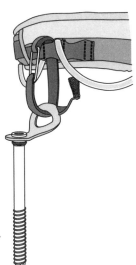

Fig. 19-8. Ice screw on a specialized racking device.

Manufacturers of all ropes, both single and double, are continuing to develop ropes of increasingly smaller diameter that satisfy international testing standards. These smaller-diameter ropes are an advantage to alpinists because they are much lighter. The trade-off is the smallest-diameter ropes may not be as durable as a larger-diameter rope.

Because ice climbing can be wet, water-repellent ("dry") ropes are worth the extra cost. In comparison with untreated ropes, dry ropes retain more strength and are less likely to freeze—though a dry rope can still become coated in ice, and the water repellency may not last the lifetime of the rope.

Head and Eye Protection

All ice climbers should wear helmets. Most helmets have an adjustable band around the head that accommodates a lightweight hat or balaclava. Safety glasses or sunglasses are recommended to keep eyes safe from flying debris.

V-Thread Tools

The V-thread tool is a hooking or snaring device used to pull cord or webbing through the drilled tunnel of V-thread anchors (see "Setting Up Ice Anchors" later in this

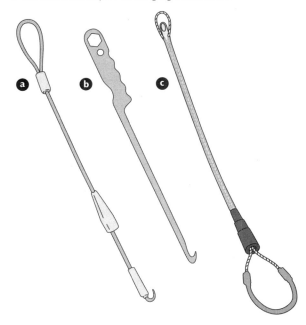

Fig. 19-9. V-thread tools. a, fish-hook cable with hook guard; b, pick-type multipurpose tool; c, snare, no hook.

19

chapter). Several styles of V-thread tools are available commercially. They can consist of a piece of wire cable with a hook swaged to one end (fig. 19-9a), a piece of stamped metal or plastic with a hook on one end (fig. 19-9b), or a simple snare to capture the end of a rope without damaging it (fig. 19-9c). Some budget-conscious climbers make V-thread tools from a piece of wire hanger. For tools with hooks, remember to keep the hook sharp, and protect it from catching on clothing or gear.

TECHNIQUES OF ALPINE ICE CLIMBING

Climbing the perennially shaded side of a mountain can be an exhilarating passage over an ever-changing medium in a steep and cold environment, all of which challenges both mind and body. An alpine ice climber must move quickly and efficiently up long and sometimes sparsely protected faces to reach the summit, then safely descend within the allotted time.

On alpine ice, climbers use surface features, seeking out depressions, pockets, and ledges for tool placements, crampon purchase, and belay points. Unlike rock climbers, and unless they are climbing mixed rock and ice (see Chapter 20, Waterfall Ice and Mixed Climbing), ice climbers are not in direct contact with the surface of the mountain. The ice climber must rely on ice tools, axes, and crampons. They make do with anchors and protection placements that can be uncertain. Note that many of the techniques described here are also used to climb waterfall ice.

CLIMBING WITHOUT CRAMPONS

Alpine climbers often encounter short sections of ice or frozen snow. Sometimes they are not carrying crampons, or they may face short ice problems that do not merit taking the time to put on crampons. Negotiating these sections without crampons requires climbing in balance with caution and skill, moving up from one position of balance to the next. At each position of balance, the inside (uphill) foot is in front of and above the trailing outside (downhill) foot. The axe, in the uphill hand, moves only after body and feet are in balance, and the feet move only after the axe has been moved forward. Shift weight from one foot to the other smoothly as though friction climbing on rock. While climbing, look for irregularities in the surface of the ice such as *suncups* (small hollows that have been melted by the sun) or embedded rocks to use as footholds.

If the slope is too steep for secure balance, consider taking another route, or returning with crampons.

Step-Cutting

For the earliest alpinists, chopping or cutting steps was the only technique available for climbing steep ice and hard snow. While the invention of crampons reduced the need for step-cutting, there are some good reasons for understanding the technique of cutting steps with the ice axe. A lost or broken crampon, or an injured or inexperienced climber, may be reason enough to cut steps. Climbers should also be able to chop out a comfortable belay platform.

The adze of the ice axe can be used for cutting steps in two ways. It can be used to slash the ice by swinging the tool in a motion nearly parallel to the surface of the ice to create a slash step (fig. 19-10), or it can be swung perpendicular to the ice to chop out a pigeonhole step (see below).

Slash steps. The most frequently used step-cutting technique is cutting slash steps, for traversing up or down gentle to moderate slopes. To cut ascending slash steps, stand in a position of balance, holding the axe in the inside (uphill) hand (fig. 19-11a). To cut two steps in sequence, swing the adze parallel to the uphill foot and away from the body. Swing the axe from the shoulder, cutting with the adze and letting the weight of the axe do most of the work. With successive swings, slice ice out of the step, starting at the heel end of the new step and working toward the toe. Scoop out chunks of ice with the adze, and use the adze and pick to finish the step. The climber proceeds up the slope, moving in and out of a position of balance on the steps (fig. 19-11b).

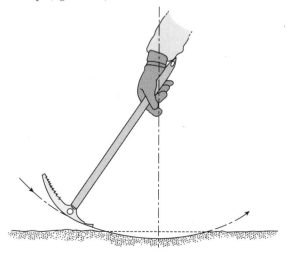

Fig. 19-10. The motion of the ice axe in cutting a slash step.

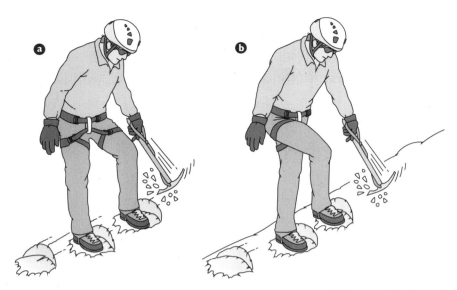

Fig. 19-11. Cutting slash steps on a diagonal ascent: a, working from a position of balance, with the axe in the inside (uphill) hand; b, working from an out-of-balance position.

Pigeonhole steps. For negotiating steeper slopes, cut pigeonhole steps. This is done by swinging the axe perpendicular to the ice and chopping out a hole with the adze. Each step should slope slightly inward to help keep boots from slipping out of the step. On gentler slopes, it is acceptable if the step holds only a small part of a boot, but the steps on steeper slopes should be large enough for the front half of a boot. Space the steps so they are convenient for all members of the party to use. Pigeonhole steps for the direct ascent of steep ice are placed about shoulder width apart and within easy stepping distance of each other. Each step functions as both a handhold and foothold, so each should have a small lip to serve as a handhold.

Ladder steps. To chop steps down an ice slope, the easiest method is to cut a "ladder" of pigeonhole steps that descend almost straight down the hill. To cut two steps in sequence, start in a position of balance, facing down the slope. Chop two pigeonhole steps directly below. When the new steps are ready, step down with the outside (downhill) foot and then the inside (uphill) foot. To cut just one step at a time, again start in a position of balance. Cut the step for the outside (downhill) foot and move that foot down into the step. Then cut the step for the inside (uphill) foot and move that foot down into it. Some climbers may opt to rappel rather than cut steps down an icy incline. Note that climbers usually rope up on ice; see "Roped Ice Climbing Techniques" later in this chapter.

CLIMBING WITH CRAMPONS

Ice climbers usually employ two basic techniques, depending on steepness of the slope, conditions of the ice, and their ability and confidence level: French technique and German technique. Although each technique has its own distinct benefits, modern ice climbing melds the two. Mastery of both French and German techniques is essential for climbing in the changeable alpine environment. Below are brief descriptions of these methods, followed by sections that apply them to specific types of terrain.

French Technique (Flat-Footing)

French technique, also called flat-footing, is the easiest and most efficient method of climbing on gentle to steep ice and hard snow (see Figure 19-13). Good French technique demands balance, rhythm, joint flexibility, and the confident use of crampons and ice axe. Specifics of this technique are described in the sections that follow.

Front-Pointing (German Technique)

Developed by Germans and Austrians for climbing the harder snow and ice of the eastern Alps, German technique, better known as front-pointing, allows an experienced ice climber to go up the steepest and most difficult ice slopes. With this technique, even average climbers can quickly overcome sections that would be difficult or impossible with French technique. The German technique

19

427

TABLE 19-2. TECHNIQUES FOR CRAMPONS, ICE AXES, AND ICE TOOLS

TECHNIQUE	APPROXIMATE STEEPNESS OF SLOPE
CRAMPONS	
Walking (French technique; *pied marche*)	Gentle, 0° to 15°
Duckwalk (French technique; *pied en canard*)	Gentle, 15° to 30°
Flat-footing (French technique; *pied à plat*)	Moderate to steep, 30° to 60°
Rest position (French technique; *pied assis*)	Extremely steep, 60° and higher
Three o'clock position (American technique; *pied troisième*)	Extremely steep, 60° and higher
Front-pointing (German technique)	Steep through vertical and overhanging, 45° and higher
ICE AXES AND ICE TOOLS (FRENCH AND GERMAN TECHNIQUE)	
Cane position (*piolet canne*)	Gentle to moderate, 0° to 45°
Cross-body position (*piolet ramasse*)	Moderate, 30° to 45°
Anchor position (*piolet ancre*)	Steep to extremely steep, 45° and higher
Low-dagger position (*piolet panne*)	Steep, 45° to 55°
High-dagger position (*piolet poignard*)	Steep, 50° to 60°
Traction position (*piolet traction*)	Extremely steep through vertical and overhanging, 60° and higher

is much like kicking steps straight up a snow slope, but instead of kicking a boot into the snow, kick that boot's front crampon points into the ice; then step up with the other foot, directly supported by the placed boot's front points. Just as in French technique, good front-pointing is efficient, rhythmic, and balanced, with the weight of the body balanced over the crampons.

Combination Technique (American Technique)

Modern crampon technique evolved from the French and German styles. As on rock, climbing on ice involves the efficient and confident use of footwork to maintain balance and minimize fatigue. Flat-footing is generally used on lower-angle slopes and where crampon point penetration is easy. Front-pointing is most commonly used on slopes steeper than 45 degrees and on very hard ice. In practice, most climbers blend these two techniques into a combination approach, sometimes called American technique.

In any technique, the most important element is confident use of the crampons. Practice on gentle and moderate slopes (see Chapter 16, Snow Travel and Climbing) to develop the skill, confidence, and the aggressive approach needed at steeper angles. On alpine ice, a skilled ice climber, whether flat-footing or front-pointing, displays the same deliberate movement as a skilled rock climber. The crampon points must be carefully and deliberately placed into the ice and the climber's weight smoothly and decisively transferred from one foot to the other. Boldness is essential to skillful crampon technique. Exposure must be disregarded and concentration focused solely on the climbing. But boldness is not blind bravado. It is confidence and skill born of experience and enthusiasm, nurtured in many practice sessions on glacial seracs and on ice bulges in frozen gullies, then matured through ascents of increasing length and difficulty.

ICE CLIMBING TERMS

Table 19-2 lists ice climbing techniques for crampons, ice axe, and ice tools, along with the approximate steepness of the slope on which each technique is used. (A clinometer helps determine slope angle if you are unsure; see "Slope Angle" in Chapter 17, Avalanche Safety.) French terms are sometimes used, given in parentheses. The French word *pied* (pronounced "pee-EY") means "foot"; the French word *piolet* (pronounced "pee-oh-LAY") means "ice axe." Terms including the word *pied* refer to footwork; terms including the word *piolet* refer to ice-axe positions.

None of these techniques are restricted to any particular set of conditions, and all can be useful in a wide range of snow and ice situations. When practicing these techniques, keep in mind that a "sharp crampon is a happy crampon," requiring only body weight to set it securely in place.

CLIMBING ON GENTLE TO MODERATE SLOPES

On gently to moderately sloped ice, French technique (flat-footing) dominates. An essential alpine ice climbing technique, flat-footing means firmly setting all bottom points of the crampon into the ice. Keep boot soles parallel to the ice surface and feet slightly farther apart than normal to avoid snagging a crampon point on clothing or on a crampon strap on the other foot. Use the ice axe in the cane position (see Figures 19-12 and 19-13), holding the axe in the self-belay grasp (for ice axe positions and grasps, see Chapter 16, Snow Travel and Climbing).

On gentle slopes, begin by simply walking. Flexible ankles are sometimes necessary in order to keep boot soles parallel to the surface. Boots that are flexible at the ankle facilitate flat-footing. Climbers with rigid boots can loosen

their bootlaces at the cuff for more comfortable flat-footing. As the gentle slope steepens slightly, splay feet outward in duckwalk fashion (fig. 19-12), easing ankle strain. Keep knees bent and weight balanced over the feet. Continue to use the axe as a cane.

As the slope gets steeper still, no longer gentle but moderate, duckwalking straight upward causes severe ankle strain. Instead, turn sideways to the slope and ascend diagonally for a more relaxed, comfortable step. Be sure to use flat-footing, with all crampon points weighted into the ice (fig. 19-13). When using this technique for the first time, people have a tendency to edge with their crampons. The crampon points can skate off the ice, throwing the climber off balance. Fight this tendency, and keep the crampon points flat against the ice at all times. Start with feet pointed in the direction of travel. As the slope steepens, rotate both feet more and more downward in order to keep them flat. As the slope angle increases, ease ankle strain by pointing both boots downhill more and more, so

Fig. 19-12. French technique on an ascent of a gentle slope: duckwalk combined with ice axe in cane position.

Fig. 19-13. French technique on a diagonal ascent of a moderate slope: flat-footing combined with ice axe in cane position.

19

Fig. 19-14. French technique on a diagonal ascent of a moderate slope—flat-footing combined with ice axe in cross-body position (pick forward): a, in-balance position; b, out-of-balance position; c, back to in-balance position.

that the flex needed to keep both feet flat comes from the more normal forward flex of the ankle and from the knees, which are bent away from the slope and spread well apart (see Figure 19-14). On the steepest slopes, both knees may be pointing straight downhill.

As the slope angle changes from gentle to moderate, using the axe in the cane position becomes awkward. Greater security can now be achieved by holding the axe in the cross-body position. Grip the shaft just above the spike with the inside (uphill) hand and hold the head of the axe in the self-belay grasp, pick pointing forward, with the outside (downhill) hand. Drive the spike into the ice, the shaft perpendicular to the slope. In the cross-body position, most of the force on the axe should be from the hand on the shaft. The hand on the head stabilizes the axe and is a reminder not to lean into the slope. To keep from leaning into the ice, a full-length ice axe is needed, rather than a shorter ice tool. Even experienced ice climbers have difficulty maintaining proper French technique with a short axe.

Move diagonally upward in a two-step sequence, much the same as ascending a snow slope without crampons. Remember to keep feet flat at all times. Start from a position of balance, with the inside (uphill) foot in front of and above the trailing outside (downhill) leg (fig. 19-14a). From this in-balance position, bring the outside foot in front of and above the inside foot, into the out-of-balance

position (fig. 19-14b). Cross the outside leg over the knee of the inside leg; crossing at the ankle compromises stability and makes the next step difficult to accomplish. To return to a position of balance, bring the inside foot up from behind and place it again in front of the outside foot (fig. 19-14c). Keep the body centered over the crampons. Avoid leaning into the slope and creating the danger of crampon points twisting out of the ice. Step on lower-angle spots and natural irregularities in the ice to ease ankle strain and conserve energy.

During this diagonal ascent, plant the axe about an arm's length ahead (as shown in Figure 19-14a) each time before moving another two steps. Whether using the axe in the cane or the cross-body position, plant it far enough forward so that it will be near the hip after you move up to the next in-balance position (as shown in Figure 19-14c).

To change direction (switchback) on a diagonal ascent of a moderate ice slope, use the same technique as on a snow slope where crampons would not be used, but keep both feet flat. From a position of balance, place the axe directly above this location. Move the outside (downhill) foot forward, into the out-of-balance position, to about the same elevation as the other foot and pointing slightly uphill (fig. 19-15a). Grasping the axe with both hands, turn into the slope, moving the inside (uphill) foot to point in the new direction and slightly uphill. You are now facing into the slope, standing with feet splayed outward in opposite

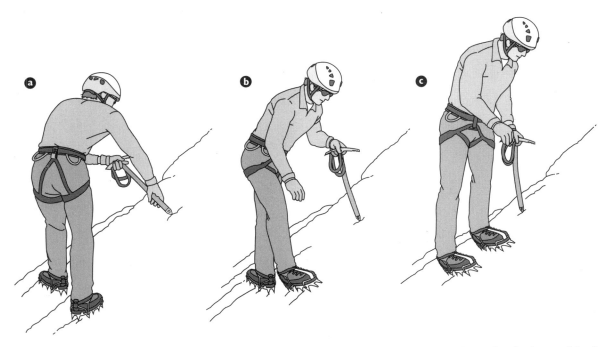

Fig. 19-15. French technique while changing direction on a diagonal ascent of a moderate slope—flat-footing combined with ice axe in cross-body position: a, out-of-balance position; b, turning; c, in-balance position in new direction.

directions (fig. 19-15b). If the splayed-foot position feels unstable, front-point. Return to the in-balance position by moving the foot that is still pointing in the original direction to above and in front of the other foot. Reposition your grasp on the ice axe, for either the cane or cross-body position. You are now back in balance and facing the new direction of travel (fig. 19-15c).

CLIMBING ON MODERATE TO STEEP SLOPES

Steeper ice calls for other variations of flat-footing. At some point, the German technique of front-pointing comes into play.

Using French Technique

For more security on moderate to steep slopes, switch the ice axe from the cross-body position to what is known as the anchor position. Your feet remain flat, with all bottom crampon points weighted into the ice at each step.

To place the axe in the anchor position, begin in a position of balance. Grip the ice axe shaft just above the spike with the outside (downhill) hand (fig. 19-16a). Swing the axe so that the pick sticks into the ice in front of and above your head, with the shaft parallel to the slope; with

the other hand, take hold of the axe head in the self-arrest grasp (fig. 19-16b). Now pull out on the spike end of the axe with the outside (downhill) hand while moving two steps forward, as described for Figure 19-14 to a new position of balance (fig. 19-16c). Use a gentle and constant outward pull on the ice axe to set its teeth and keep it locked into the ice. When it is time to release it, push the bottom of the shaft toward the ice and lift the pick up and out.

To keep feet flat at these angles, you must lean your body farther away from the slope, with knees and ankles flexed and the toes of your boots increasingly pointing downhill. Try to continue advancing upward in the standard sequence, moving two steps at a time. At the steepest angles, however, your feet point downhill and you must take increasingly smaller steps, essentially moving backward up the slope. But continue to plant and remove the pick from a position of balance. The foot that is on the same side as the direction of travel should be at least slightly higher than the other foot, allowing your upper body to rotate for a smooth, strong swing of the axe.

To change diagonal direction when the ice axe is in the anchor position, use the same sequence as with the cane or cross-body position, as in Figure 19-15. However, on the

19

431

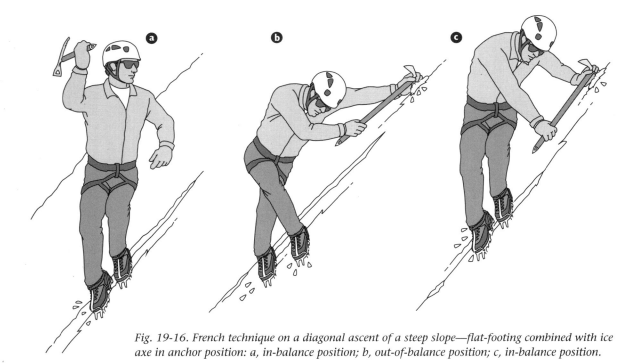

Fig. 19-16. French technique on a diagonal ascent of a steep slope—flat-footing combined with ice axe in anchor position: a, in-balance position; b, out-of-balance position; c, in-balance position.

Fig. 19-17. French technique of pied assis for a balanced rest while climbing a steep slope.

steepest slopes, where you are stepping backward, change direction simply by switching hands on the axe and planting it on the other side. There is not much diagonal movement at this point, because you are mainly moving backward straight up the slope.

The French also devised a rest position—called *pied assis*—that gives leg muscles a rest and provides more security for replanting the axe. From a position of balance, bring the outside (downhill) foot up and beneath your buttocks, with the boot—flat, as always—pointing straight downhill. Then sit down on the heel of that foot (fig. 19-17). This is a balanced position, and a relatively comfortable one.

The invaluable technique of flat-footing, used with the ice axe in the cane or cross-body position, will serve an experienced climber for many alpine routes. For short stretches of steeper ice, flat-footing combined with the ice axe in anchor position will often work, but this marks the upper limit of French technique.

Using German Technique (Front-Pointing)

On steep ice slopes, use of French technique and front-pointing begins to overlap. They both have a place on these slopes. Most people pick up front-pointing quickly because

Fig. 19-18. Soft-soled boots flex too much for front-pointing with crampons.

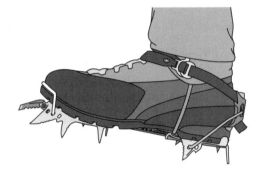

Fig. 19-19. To front-point effectively, toes should be straight in with heels slightly down.

it feels natural and secure. Unfortunately, this encourages its use on moderate slopes where flat-footing would be just as secure and more efficient. In flat-footing, most of the strain is on the large, powerful thigh muscles. Front-pointing, however, depends almost solely on the smaller calf muscles, which burn out much faster. Even climbers who strongly prefer front-pointing would benefit from alternating the techniques to give their calf muscles a rest.

Well-fitting, very stiff-soled boots provide a firm base for crampons and make front-pointing easiest. Less-stiff-soled boots can be used in some cases but require more muscular effort. However, flexible-soled boots just do not provide the necessary support for front-pointing (fig. 19-18). Pioneer ice climber Yvon Chouinard said it well in *Climbing Ice*: "You can't dance on hard ice with soft-soled shoes" (see Resources).

Front-pointing uses not only the primary points of the crampons but also the secondary points immediately behind them. These points, attached to a rigid boot and properly placed in the ice, provide a stable platform that can be stood upon. The most stable placement of the boot is straight into the ice, perpendicular to the surface. Avoid splayed feet, which tend to rotate the outside front points out of the ice; the boot soles should be perpendicular to the ice surface, with heels slightly down in order to engage the secondary points in the ice and complete the four-point platform for standing (fig. 19-19). Slightly bend at the knee to reduce the strain on calf muscles.

Resist the temptation to raise your heels. This pulls the secondary points from the ice, endangering placement of the front points, and accelerates calf muscle fatigue. Your heels will normally feel lower than they really are, so if it feels as though your heels are too low, the odds are that they are in the correct position: slightly lower than horizontal. This is especially important when a climber is coming over the top of steep ice onto a gentler slope, where the natural tendency is to raise the heels, relax the level of concentration, and hurry. This is a formula for trouble because it could cause the crampon points to shear from the ice. A good way to become comfortable with the essential skills of crampon placement and foot positioning is to practice on a top rope with an experienced ice climber who can critique your style.

In the initial crampon placements on a route, concentrate on determining the amount of force required to secure a foothold. After that, a single confident leg swing should be all you need. Watch out for two common mistakes: kicking too hard (which is fatiguing) and kicking too often in one place (which fractures the ice and makes it harder to get a good foothold). As with climbing rock, make your foot placement and keep to it. After making a crampon placement, avoid foot movement because it can make the points rotate out of the ice.

Front-pointing uses a variety of ice-axe positions. Dagger positions (see below) are useful in hard snow and relatively soft ice. They do not work well in hard ice. The jabbing and stabbing motions of placing the pick are not very powerful, and poor pick penetration into the hard ice could mean an insecure placement. Attempts to force a deeper placement may result in nothing more than a bruised hand. For harder ice or a steeper slope, abandon the dagger positions for the anchor and traction positions.

Low-dagger position. Hold the axe by the adze in the self-belay grasp and push the pick into the ice near waist level, to aid balance (fig. 19-20). This position is helpful in tackling a short, relatively steep section that requires only a few quick front-pointing moves. It tends to hold you away from the slope and out over your feet, the correct stance for front-pointing.

19

433

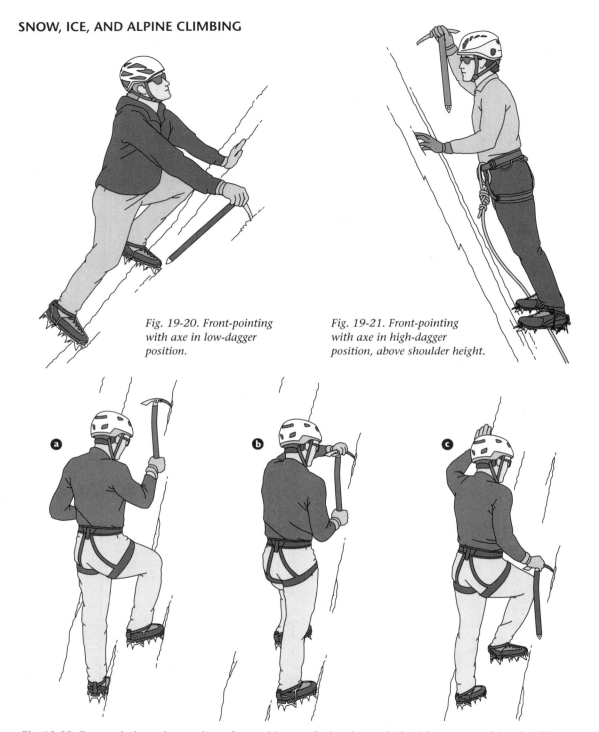

Fig. 19-20. Front-pointing with axe in low-dagger position.

Fig. 19-21. Front-pointing with axe in high-dagger position, above shoulder height.

Fig. 19-22. Front-pointing using axe in anchor position: a, placing the axe high without overreaching; b, adding a self-arrest grasp on the axe while moving up; c, holding the axe in the low-dagger position before moving it up again.

Fig. 19-23. *Front-pointing with axe overhead in* piolet traction, *pulling straight down on axe without moving the hand on the shaft.*

Fig. 19-24. *Front-pointing using two tools, both in low-dagger position.*

High-dagger position. Hold the axe head in the self-arrest grasp and jab the pick into the ice above shoulder height (fig. 19-21). Use this position if the slope is a bit too steep to insert the pick effectively into the ice at waist level in the low-dagger position.

Anchor position. While standing on front points, hold the axe shaft near the spike and swing the pick in as high as possible without overreaching (fig. 19-22a). Front-point upward, moving your hand higher and higher on the shaft while you progress, adding a self-arrest grasp on the adze with your other hand when you are high enough (fig. 19-22b). Finally, switch hands on the adze, converting the anchor position to the low-dagger position (fig. 19-22c); when the adze is at waist level, remove it from the ice and replant it higher, again in the anchor position. Use the anchor position on harder ice or a steeper slope.

Piolet traction. Hold the axe near the spike and plant it high; then climb the ice by pulling straight down on the axe while front-pointing up (fig. 19-23). Do not move your hand on the shaft. Use *piolet traction* on the steepest and hardest ice.

On very hard or extremely steep ice, when it becomes too difficult to balance on front points while replanting

the axe, it is necessary to use a second ice tool. You can use two tools at the same time because, except for the anchor position, all ice-axe techniques used with front-pointing require only one hand.

Using two tools provides three points of support—for example, two crampons and one ice tool while you replant the second tool. The placements must be secure enough so that if one point of support fails, the other two will hold you until you replace the third point. Your legs carry most of the weight, but your arms help with both weight bearing and balance.

In double-tool technique, you can use the same ice-axe method for both hands or a different method for each. For instance, climb with both tools in low-dagger position (fig. 19-24), or place one tool in high-dagger position and the other in *piolet traction* (fig. 19-25). (See "Climbing on Vertical Ice" later in this chapter for details of double-tool technique using *piolet traction* with both tools.)

Using Combination Technique

One fast and powerful technique combines flat-footing and front-pointing. This is called the three o'clock position, *pied troisième* (fig. 19-26), because as one foot is front-pointing, the other is flat and points to the side (to three o'clock if it is the right foot or to nine o'clock if it is the left). This combination is an example of American technique.

The three o'clock position is a potent resource for a direct line of ascent, much less tiring than front-pointing

19

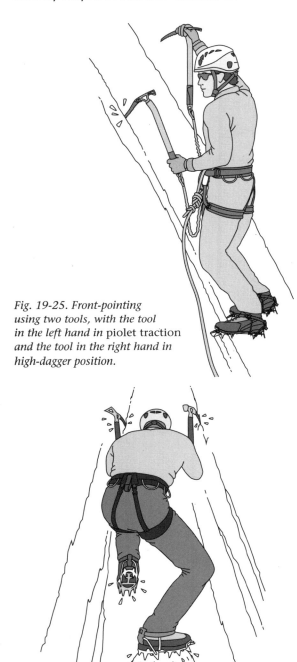

Fig. 19-25. Front-pointing using two tools, with the tool in the left hand in piolet traction and the tool in the right hand in high-dagger position.

Fig. 19-26. Three o'clock position for the feet, combining flat-footing (right foot) and front-pointing (left foot).

alone. The position lets climbers distribute the work over more muscle groups by alternating techniques with each leg. When climbing, seek out irregular flatter spots and any pockets or ledges for flat-footing, allowing calf muscles to rest. Use whatever ice-tool positions are appropriate for the situation.

Climbers alternate crampon techniques depending on ice conditions. Flat-footing is usually more secure on frozen snow, ice crust over snow, and soft or rotten ice, because more crampon points dig into the surface than the four points of front-pointing. When soft snow covers ice or hard snow, using front-pointing technique (or the three o'clock position) lets the four front points blast through the surface to get into the firmer layer beneath. Front-pointing is often the most secure technique for the average climber to use on very hard ice on all but gentle slopes. If you are having serious problems on a climb with flat-footing—perhaps due to fatigue, winds, high altitude, or fear—switch to front-pointing or the three o'clock position.

ICE-TOOL PLACEMENTS

The objective of placing any ice tool is to establish a solid placement with one swing. Each swing saved during a pitch means that much less fatigue at the top. It takes a lot of practice to learn pinpoint placement, especially when swinging the tool with the nondominant arm. But with a combination of proper technique and equipment, it should be possible to place a tool swiftly and precisely so that it is both secure and easy to remove.

At the base of the route, try a few tool placements to get a feel for the plasticity of the ice. Plasticity—which determines the ability of the ice to hold and release a tool—varies tremendously with temperature and age of the ice. Study the ice for good placements. Ice holds the pick better in depressions than in bulges, which shatter or break off under the impact of an ice tool due to radiating fracture lines. Try to make placements in opaque ice, which is less brittle than clear ice because it has more air trapped inside. Minimize the number of placements needed by planting the pick as high as possible and by moving upward as far as possible with each placement. Placement techniques vary, depending on the type of pick.

Technically curved. Also known as alpine picks, technically curved picks are most like the pick of a standard ice axe (see Figure 19-4a). However, the picks are more acutely curved than that of a regular axe, so they hold better in ice. A tool with a technically curved pick is placed with a natural swing from the shoulder. This pick is used in conditions

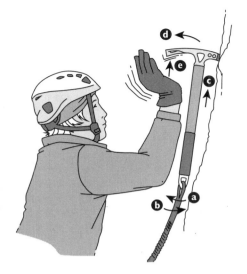

Fig. 19-27. How to remove an ice tool: a and b, rock the shaft back and forth in the same plane as the pick; c and d, push up with the shaft and then pull the shaft out; e, strike up on the adze (or hammerhead).

ranging from soft serac ice to hard water ice, though a harder swing is needed for good penetration in hard ice.

Reverse curved. The more acute angles of reverse-curved picks (see Figure 19-4b) require a somewhat different swing, with a definite wrist snap just prior to connecting. To plant the pick, bring your arm back, with your elbow bent about 90 degrees, then swing at the desired spot. At the end of the swing, snap your wrist toward the ice. The steeper the droop of the pick, the more wrist action is needed to set the pick. The reverse-curved pick also works well for hooking holes in the ice. Large icicles often form in clusters on vertical sections, creating slots or gaps that are ideal for secure hooking placements.

Removing the Tool

In addition to learning the proper force to use in placing a tool, climbers must also learn the best way to remove it. Unless it is done correctly, removing a tool can be more tiring than placing it. Try to remove the tool in reverse of the motion used to set it. First, loosen the placement by rocking the spike end of the shaft of the tool up and down in the same plane as the pick (fig. 19-27a and b): away from and back toward the ice. Then try to remove the tool by pushing the shaft up toward the pick and then pulling the shaft out from up near the pick (fig. 19-27c and d). If this fails, release your grip on the tool and try to knock it loose by hitting up against the adze with the palm

of your hand (fig. 19-27e). Then grab the head and pull up and out. Never remove a tool by torquing it from side to side because the pick may break.

CLIMBING ON VERTICAL ICE

The most efficient and secure method of climbing vertical ice is front-pointing combined with use of two ice tools, vertically staggered, in *piolet traction*. This method of climbing ice is called *tracking*. The standard position for the feet is about shoulder width apart and level with each other, a stable and relatively comfortable stance. One tool is planted above your head so that your arm is straight. The other tool is planted and weighted, at shoulder height. At this point your feet and upper tool form a triangle against the ice. Pull down and slightly outward on the spike ends of the tools' shafts to keep the picks' teeth set in the ice, and apply inward pressure on the crampon points.

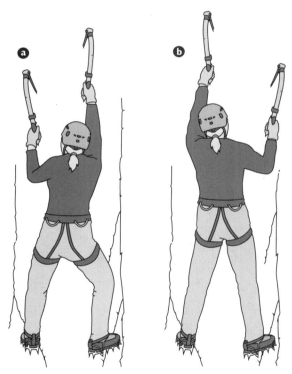

19

Fig. 19-28. Staying in balance on vertical ice: a, center body weight on the right-hand tool and remove the left-hand tool for higher placement; b, after moving the feet up, center body weight on the replanted left-hand tool and remove the right-hand tool for the higher placement.

To ascend, grasp the tools, walk both feet up taking small steps, then remove the lower tool (fig. 19-28a) and replant it above your head. Maintain three points of contact at all times. Let your legs do most of the work; do not burn out your arms by doing pull-ups while climbing. Now repeat the sequence: place one tool, move both feet, place the other tool (fig. 19-28b), move both feet, and so on. Be careful not to overreach for a tool placement because that motion may cause your front points to dislodge from the ice. Concentrate on efficient, methodical placement of crampon points and ice tools. Rhythm is as important as balance.

Climbers sometimes find themselves "barn-dooring"— their body swinging sideways away from ice, out of balance—as they remove one tool in order to place it higher. Avoid this by shifting your center of balance toward the tool that will remain in the ice, as shown in Figure 19-28a. Once that new, higher placement is made, shift your center of balance to the higher tool (as shown in Figure 19-28b) and then remove the lower tool.

Tracking, also referred to as the "tripod" or the "A-frame," is a good technique to use for ascending ice bulges, small overhangs, and longer vertical sections (see Chapter 20, Waterfall Ice and Mixed Climbing).

From Vertical to a Horizontal Stretch

Oddly enough, one of the most challenging sequences involves climbing from a vertical face up onto a horizontal step or ledge. With a secure horizontal section of ice ahead, climbers may relax concentration and forget about good foot placement. At the same time, they face the problem that it is virtually impossible to obtain a confident tool placement by blindly swinging over a ledge. They must move high enough to see onto the ledge.

To do this, make shorter tool and foot placements when approaching the lip of the ledge, then step up to a high-dagger position so you can see onto the ledge and look for a good spot to place an ice tool. You may need to remove snow or rotten ice, which often accumulates on ledges and moderate ice slopes. Place an ice tool securely into the ledge, well back from the lip, and then place the second ice tool (fig. 19-29a); move your feet up until they are safely over the lip (fig. 19-29b). Remember that it is especially important to keep the heels low.

TRAVERSING STEEP TO VERTICAL ICE

The principles for traversing are much the same as for front-pointing up steep ice. However, because the climber is moving to the side instead of straight up, it is more

Fig. 19-29. Pulling onto a ledge: a, plant tools on ledge; b, move feet up and over the lip.

Fig. 19-30. Traversing to the right on vertical ice: a, planting the leading tool to the side to begin the traverse; b, shifting the right foot under it; c, shifting the left foot closer to the right; d, shifting trailing tool closer to leading tool.

difficult to keep one foot perpendicular to the ice while replacing the front points of the other foot. If your heel rotates, the front points will also rotate and come out of the ice. Ice tools also tend to rotate out during sideways travel.

Start from a secure position with both feet at the same level. Lean in the direction of travel and plant the leading tool in the ice (fig. 19-30a). This places the leading tool lower than it would be if you were ascending, but not so far to the side that it causes your body to rotate out from the wall (barn-door) when the trailing tool is removed. This also puts the trailing tool in a position so that it can be pulled on in a modified lieback while you are traversing, without twisting the tool out of the ice.

Now shuffle sideways on front points (fig. 19-30b and c). Move the trailing tool closer to the lead tool (fig. 19-30d). It is also possible to make a two-step move, crossing the trailing foot over the leading foot and then bringing the other foot back into the lead. Most climbers prefer the shuffle, which is less awkward and feels more secure. After moving your feet, replant the trailing tool closer to your body at a 45-degree angle (as in Figure 19-30a), lean in the direction of travel and replant the leading tool, and repeat the process.

DESCENDING ON ICE

Depending on the angle of the ice, a climber may use French, German, or American technique while descending.

Using French Technique

Once mastered, French technique is the most efficient means of descending gentle to moderate icy terrain.

Cane position. To descend gently sloping ice, simply face directly downhill, bend your knees slightly, and walk firmly downward. Plant all bottom crampon points into the ice with each step. Hold the axe in the cane position. As the descent angle steepens, bend your knees more and spread them apart, with your body weight over your feet so that all crampon points bite securely (fig. 19-31). Thigh muscles do the bulk of the work.

Cross-body position. For greater security, plant the axe perpendicular to the slope in the cross-body position (fig. 19-32).

Support position. For the next level of security, use the axe in the support position (fig. 19-33). Grasp the axe near the middle of the shaft and hold it beside you while descending, with the axe head pointing uphill, pick down, and the spike pointing downhill. This position is more secure because the pick and axe are in contact with the surface and the axe is set up for self-arresting.

Banister position. As the slope steepens, use the axe in the banister position. Grasp the axe near the spike and plant the pick as far below you as possible (fig. 19-34a). Walk downward, sliding your hand along the shaft toward the head of the axe (fig. 19-34b). Maintain a slight outward pull (away from the ice) on the end of the shaft to keep

19

Fig. 19-31. Flat-footing on descent with ice axe in cane position.

Fig. 19-32. Flat-footing on descent with ice axe in cross-body position.

Fig. 19-33. Flat-footing on descent with ice axe in support position.

Fig. 19-34. Flat-footing on descent with ice axe in banister position: a, plant the axe; b, slide hand along the shaft like you would a banister; c, pull outward slightly to keep axe locked in ice; (continued on facing page)

the pick locked in the ice (fig. 19-34c). With a reverse-curved pick, this is less secure; you must pull parallel to the ice. Keep moving down until you are below the axe head (fig. 19-34d), then release the pick (fig. 19-34e) and replant the axe farther down.

Anchor position. On a slope too steep to safely descend facing outward, turn sideways and descend diagonally. Your footwork changes to the same flat-footing technique used to ascend diagonally. Use the axe in the anchor position (fig. 19-35). With your outside arm, swing the axe out in front and plant the pick in the ice; take hold of the head with the other hand in the self-arrest grasp; and then flat-foot diagonally down below the axe. The shaft rotates as you pass below it.

Using Front-Point Technique

On steeper slopes, front-point and ice-tool techniques are generally the same for going down as they are for going up. But, just as on rock, down-climbing is more difficult. The tendency is to step too low, which keeps your heels too high, so front points may fail to penetrate in the first place or may shear out. A good view of the route is not possible on a descent (although descending on a slight diagonal helps). It is awkward to plant the ice tools because they must be placed closer to your body, so the power of a good full swing is lost. On a descent, the only feasible way to get

Fig. 19-35. Flat-footing on descent with ice axe in the anchor position.

Fig. 19-34. (continued from facing page) d, ready to replant the axe; e, remove to replant it.

19

secure placements may be to plant the tools back in the holes that were made on the ascent.

Climbers do not often front-point to descend, but it is still a valuable skill for some occasions, such as retreating from a route. Down-climbing ability also builds confidence in ascending. Ice climbers usually rappel down steeper routes (see "Rappelling on Ice" later in this chapter).

ROPED ICE CLIMBING TECHNIQUES

Climbers usually rope up on ice. Ice pitches can be climbed using a standard single rope or by using two ropes (see "Double- and Twin-Rope Techniques" in Chapter 14, Leading on Rock). The principal exception comes when overall team safety is served best by climbing unroped. Late on a stormy day or while ascending a couloir threatened by rockfall, a climbing party might find that unroped travel offers relatively more safety with its greater speed than would continuing on the rope. It may be sensible to travel unroped through a section so difficult to protect that a fall by one roped climber would sweep away the whole team. However, make no mistake: unroped ice climbing is serious business.

PLACING PROTECTION ON ICE

Modern ice screws offer reliable protection in good ice. However, some safety is sacrificed because of the time and energy it takes to place them. Therefore leaders commonly place fewer points of protection on an ice pitch than they typically would on a rock pitch of the same length. Ice climbers also make some use of natural protection. Practice so that you are able to use either hand to place protection.

Natural Protection

Natural protection is often hard to come by on an alpine ice route. Good natural protection may be available not on the ice itself but in rock bordering the route or protruding through the ice. Shrubs and trees may provide protection opportunities as well.

Protection with Ice Screws

For any given ice-screw placement, there are dozens of variations. And climbers must ask some very serious questions: What is the quality of the ice? What is the depth of the ice? What is the projected amount of force on the piece? What is the projected direction of force? Which screws are still left on the rack? Which will be needed later? Observations, calculations, estimates, and experience will help climbers answer these questions and place gear accordingly.

Each screw placement is different, which is one of the great things about climbing ice. It is an ever-changing medium. In solid ice and under ideal conditions, ice screw placements are actually stronger if the screw is placed in the projected direction of force. In other cases, placements are stronger if the screws are oriented away from the direction of force. But the decision must be made at the time the placement is made.

A favorable location for an ice-screw placement is the same as that for an ice tool. A good choice is a natural depression, where fracture lines caused by the screw are not as likely to reach the surface. A screw placed in a bulge in the ice, on the other hand, can cause serious fracturing that weakens the placement or makes it useless. In general, keep screw placements at least 2 feet (60 centimeters) apart to reduce danger that fracture lines from one placement will reach the other, weakening both. Avoid the temptation to reuse a previous screw placement, unless it has refrozen.

The procedures for placing a screw vary somewhat with ice conditions, but the basic routine is much the same in any case:

1. For maximum leverage during placement, keep the screw placement at about waist level. If the ice screw doesn't "bite" into the ice right away, the climber can punch out a small starting hole with the pick or spike of the ice tool, to give the starting threads or teeth of the screw a good grip. Make the hole gently, with light taps, to avoid fracturing the ice. The starting hole can also be an old pick hole.

2. Start the screw in the hole by setting it at the selected angle; in solid ice, for example, place the screw at a right angle to the ice surface, with the screw head angled downward about 5 to 15 degrees off perpendicular. This takes advantage of the holding power of the screw threads in the ice in the event of a downward load (see Figure 20-6 in Chapter 20, Waterfall Ice and Mixed Climbing). Press the screw firmly with one hand and twist it into the ice at the same time. Drive the screw in until the hanger is flush with the ice surface and pointed in the direction of load. In poor-quality or rapidly deteriorating ice (rotten, slushy, sun-exposed, et cetera) where there is no better protection option, place the screw at a right angle to the ice surface with the screw head angled uphill 15 degrees to take advantage of the levering action of the screw.

3. Clip a quickdraw or runner in to the eye of the screw hanger, with the carabiner gate down and out. Clip the rope.

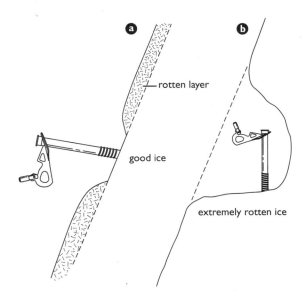

Fig. 19-36. Ice-screw placements: a, with soft or rotten surface layer; b, in extremely rotten ice.

On ice topped with a layer of soft snow or rotten ice, use the adze or pick to scrape down to a hard, trustworthy surface before you make the starting hole (fig. 19-36a). In extremely rotten ice, make a large horizontal step with an ice tool and place the screw vertically at the back of the step (fig. 19-36b). If the ice fractures and shatters at the surface, you may still get a secure placement by continuing to drive the screw and gently chopping out the shattered ice with sideways strokes of the pick.

Climbing extremely steep ice is fatiguing, both physically and mentally, so minimize the number of screw placements when it is safe to do so. Unless the ice is rotten, only one screw is placed at each protection point. Relying mainly on your tool and crampon placements and skills for safety (a concept known as "self-belayed" climbing) also affects the number of ice screws that need to be placed.

With practice, it should be possible to place an ice screw with either hand. On a moderate to steep slope, it may help to chop a step to stand in while placing the screw. On extremely steep ice, however, chopping steps is too difficult, so save your energy. Try to place screws from natural resting spots on the route. Maintain your body weight on your feet, using a tool placement for balance only. Do not wear yourself out by overgripping the tool while placing screws. On extremely steep ice, placing ice screws is exact-ing business. When it is time to place an ice screw, do it efficiently and confidently from your front points, and then continue climbing.

After you remove a screw, ice inside its core must be cleaned out immediately or it may freeze in place, rendering the screw useless until it is cleared. The interiors of some screws are slightly tapered, facilitating ice removal. Shake the screw to remove the ice core; if this does not work, then tap the hanger end of the screw against the ice or the shaft of an ice tool. Do not bang the teeth or threads of the screw against anything hard. This will only pit the teeth and screw threads and make the screw harder to place, especially in cold conditions. If ice does freeze to the inside of the screw, try to melt it with your breath, with the warmth of your hand, or inside a jacket pocket. Be careful about cleaning out a screw with your pick or a metal V-thread tool; this can damage the inner surface of the screw, making ice more likely to stick in the future. If this continues to be a problem, try squirting a lubricating and penetrating oil inside the screw before climbs.

SETTING UP ICE ANCHORS

For belaying or rappelling, ice climbers have several options for anchors, including the V-thread, an ice bollard, and ice screws. This section discusses the V-thread and ice bollard, which are used mainly in rappelling. The next section, "Belaying on Ice," explains the standard anchor setup using two ice screws.

The V-Thread

The V-thread anchor (see Figure 19-37) is popular because it is simple and easy to construct. Devised by Vitaly Abalakov, a premier Soviet alpinist in the 1930s, the V-thread anchor (also known as the Abalakov) is nothing more than a V-shaped tunnel bored into the ice, with accessory cord or webbing threaded through the tunnel and tied to form a sling. The V-thread anchor has held up well in testing and in use, but remember that it is only as strong as the ice in which it is constructed. Multiple V-thread placements can be constructed and rigged together to create an equalized anchor point. Here are the steps to construct a V-thread anchor:

1. Screw a 22-centimeter ice screw into the slope. Angle the screw uphill 10 degrees against the anticipated direction of pull; also tilt it about 60 degrees to one side of perpendicular to the slope (fig. 19-37a).
2. Back this screw out about halfway, but keep it there as a guide. Insert a second screw into the slope 6 to 8 inches (about 20 centimeters) from the first,

19

443

angling it about 60 degrees to the other side of perpendicular so it will intersect the first hole at its bottom (fig. 19-37b). In other words, the angle between the two screws is about 120 degrees, with an imaginary line perpendicular to the slope being at the midpoint (60 degrees from either screw). Remove both screws.

3. Thread a length of 6- to 8-millimeter accessory cord into one side of the V-shaped tunnel. Use a V-thread tool to fish the end of the cord out through the other side of the tunnel (fig. 19-37c).

4. Holding both ends of the cord, saw it back and forth in the tunnel in order to smooth the sharp edge of the ice where the two screw holes intersect. Otherwise, the edge might cut the cord in a fall. Tie the cord so that it forms a sling (fig. 19-37d).

5. Place an ice screw 2 to 3 feet (0.6 to 1 meter) above the V-thread anchor. Clip this screw to the V-thread sling as a backup. The anchor is now complete.

For a rappel, the rope is threaded directly through the loop of cord or webbing and then pulled free when the rappel is completed. Alternatively, if no accessory cord is available, the rappel rope itself can be threaded through the tunnel (sometimes referred to as a "zero-thread"). But be aware that ropes have been known to freeze in the V-thread tunnel.

Many abandoned V-threads are found on popular ice climbs at rappel and/or belay stations. As with any other fixed anchor, check it carefully before committing your life to it. Inspect the sling material for burn marks, wear, or other damage, and check that the knot is secure. Sometimes the free tails of the knot may be frozen in place, resembling a secure portion of the sling. Take care! Be sure that the rope is rigged through the sling and not through these frozen tails. Do not make that fatal error. Inspect the integrity of the V-shaped tunnel. See if it has melted out to an extent that it is too shallow for safety. If you have any doubt about the anchor, back it up or replace it.

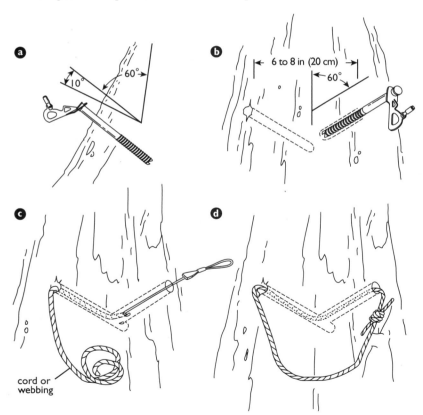

Fig. 19-37. The Abalakov, or V-thread anchor: a, bore first hole with ice screw tilted up 10 degrees and tilted out to the side 60 degrees; b, bore an intersecting hole with another ice screw; c, thread a piece of accessory cord through the V-shaped tunnel, using a V-thread tool; d, tie cord to form a sling and complete the anchor.

Ice Bollard

A bollard can be among an ice climber's most useful natural anchors. While they take time to create, it is a technique worth knowing. The strength of a bollard is proportional to its size and the quality of the ice. Made in hard, solid ice, a bollard can be stronger than the rope. The single largest disadvantage to a bollard is the long time it takes to construct one. A completed ice bollard is teardrop-shaped when viewed from above (as in Figure 19-38a and c) and mushroom-shaped when viewed from the side (as in Figure 19-38b). All that is needed for an ice bollard is an ice axe and good ice, uniform and without cracks or holes.

Cut the outline of the bollard with the axe pick. In hard ice, give it a diameter of 12 to 18 inches (30 to 45 centimeters) across the wide end of the teardrop, and make it 24 inches (61 centimeters) long (fig. 19-38a). Cut a trench around the bollard at least 6 inches (15 centimeters) deep (fig. 19-38b), working outward from the outline with both the pick and the adze. Undercut the sides and top half of the bollard to form a horn that prevents the rope from popping off over the top (fig. 19-38c). This is the most sensitive part of the construction because the bollard is easily fractured or broken if you do not take care. Bollards are also used as anchors in snow (see Chapter 16, Snow Travel and Climbing).

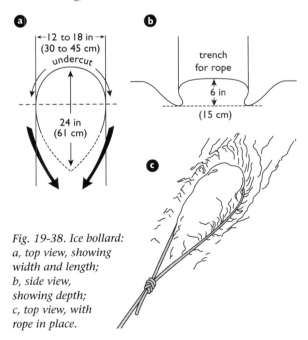

Fig. 19-38. Ice bollard: a, top view, showing width and length; b, side view, showing depth; c, top view, with rope in place.

BELAYING ON ICE

Ice climbers have the options of using running belays or fixed belays, as in other types of roped climbing.

Running Belays

By setting up a running belay, ice climbers can get a measure of protection that is somewhere between climbing on belay and climbing unroped. A running belay is another way for a team to move faster when storms or avalanches threaten—circumstances under which, more than ever, speed means safety. It can also be useful on gentle to moderate terrain where danger of falling is minimal and fixed belays would be too time-consuming.

A running belay on ice is created in very much the same way as a running belay on rock (see Chapter 14, Leading on Rock) or snow (see Chapter 16, Snow Travel and Climbing). The team members, usually just two climbers, move simultaneously. The leader places protection as they climb and clips the rope through it; the follower removes the protection. The idea is to keep at least two points of protection between them at all times to hold the rope in case of a fall. The protection is usually spaced so that as the leader makes each new placement, the follower is removing the bottom one.

Because the technique of running belays sacrifices much of the safety of true belaying, the decision to use it takes fine judgment, based on extensive experience. As the difficulty of the route changes, the team can easily shift between running belays and pitched climbing.

Fixed Belays

Fixed belays (pitches) on ice require a belayer, a belay anchor, and intermediate points of protection, just as they do on rock or snow. A belay anchor is set up; the leader climbs the pitch on belay, sets up another anchor, and then belays the follower (also called the second) up the route. The climbers can either swing leads, or one climber can continue as the leader.

The leader should, when near the end of a pitch, keep an eye out for a good belay spot, perhaps at a slight depression, at a place where the ice is not so steep, or in an area where a platform can be chopped out quickly. If you choose to chop out a stance, place an ice tool off to one side for balance while chopping a step large enough for you to stand facing the ice with both feet flat and splayed. On steep ice, it may be possible to chop only a simple ledge the width of your foot.

19

Belay Anchor

A standard anchor setup for an ice belay must meet the same SERENE (Solid, Efficient, Redundant, Equalized, and No Extension; see Chapter 10, Belaying) standards as a rock anchor; it takes two ice screws (a third can be added if conditions are less than optimal), preferably screws with either two clipping eyes or a single oversized eye that will accommodate two carabiners. (Ice bollards and V-threads also can serve as belay anchors, but they are more time-consuming to set up and are used primarily for rappelling.)

Place the first screw in the ice directly in front of you at about waist to chest level. Clip in a locking carabiner, then clip yourself in independently using a personal anchor or the rope. Now place the second ice screw, 18 to 24 inches (46 to 61 centimeters) to the side of and slightly above the first screw, so the small fractures created by any screw placement don't intersect, which would weaken the entire section of ice. Clip a runner or cordelette to each screw and create an equalized anchor (see "Equalizing the Anchor" in Chapter 10, Belaying). This completes the anchor setup (shaded rope and the runner in fig. 19-39).

Belay Methods

Choose between belaying off the anchor using a belay device or a munter hitch, or belaying using a hip belay. The anchor setup is the same in any case. The choice probably depends on what the climbers are accustomed to and on the degree of their confidence in the anchor. The hip belay (see below) tends to be somewhat dynamic, with a bit of movement at the belay—resulting in a slower stop to a fall but less force on the anchor and intermediate protection points—yet may be the only option if the rope is iced up and will not work in a belay device. Belay devices and the munter hitch, on the other hand, tend to be less dynamic, stopping a fall faster but putting more force on the anchor and intermediate protection points. For a detailed description of belaying indirectly off the harness, see Chapter 10, Belaying; the mechanics for belaying on ice are essentially the same. For more, see "Choosing a Belay Method" in Chapter 10, Belaying.

Regardless of the belay method employed, rope management remains the same. As the belayer brings rope in while the second ascends, "butterfly" it in coils draped across the rope tethering the belayer to the master point of the anchor. Do not let it fall loosely below, as the dangling loops of rope can impede the second's ascent and subsequently get hooked on small ice features as the next climber leads out above.

Belaying directly off the anchor. Belaying with an auto-locking belay device or a munter hitch directly off the anchor is easy and efficient (as shown in Figure 19-39), and many ice climbers use this method as standard procedure. Attach the belay device or a munter-capable (pear-shaped) locking carabiner to the shelf of the equalized anchor just above the figure-eight knot of the master point (see Figure 10-20 and "Static Equalization" in Chapter 10, Belaying) or to a second locking carabiner attached to the master point, then rig the device (per manufacturer's instructions) or munter hitch properly (see "Belaying a Follower" in Chapter 10, Belaying) and announce to the second that he or she is on belay.

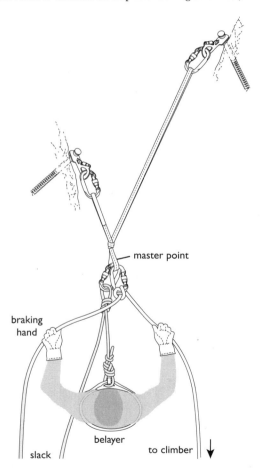

Fig. 19-39. Anchor setup for belaying the second directly off the ice anchor, using two ice screws 18 to 24 inches apart. Second climber is on belay using a munter hitch.

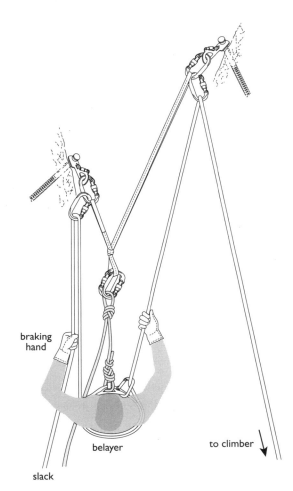

braking
hand

belayer

to climber

slack

Fig. 19-40. Ice belay setup for a hip belay.

Hip belay. The hip belay is favored when the rope is stiff and frozen and could jam in belay devices. To establish a hip belay, stand facing the ice belay anchor, run the belay rope through an extra carabiner or quickdraw on the second screw, then through a control carabiner at your waist, around your back, through an extra carabiner on the first screw, and into your braking hand (fig. 19-40).

Swapping Leads on Ice

Once the following climber has reached the anchor, both climbers should secure themselves to the anchor using a personal anchor or the rope attached to either screw or to the shelf of the equalized runner, then exchange gear as needed. If the belayer has been belaying directly off the anchor, move the device and its carabiner from the anchor to the belay loop on the belayer's harness and clip the rope leading from the device to the second climber through the quickdraw attached to the upper screw.

The leader now becomes the second, placing the second climber—the new leader—on belay; the new leader detaches his or her personal anchor and begins climbing. The quickdraw attached to the upper anchor screw temporarily becomes the new leader's first piece of protection. Once the new leader has placed the first piece of protection above the anchor, the belayer detaches the quickdraw on the upper anchor screw from the lead rope. Repeat this changeover sequence at the top of each pitch to the end of the climb.

RAPPELLING ON ICE

For descending steep ice, rappelling is usually the method of choice. The principal considerations for rappelling on ice are the same as for rappelling on rock (see Chapter 11, Rappelling), but there is a big difference in anchor options. On rock, a natural anchor such as a rock horn or a tree can often be used. On ice, climbers frequently have to make their own anchors. The most popular rappel anchor for ice is the V-thread, with the ice bollard as an alternative if conditions and available equipment dictate (see "Setting Up Ice Anchors" above). An ice screw is commonly used to back up an ice anchor until the last member of the party descends. The last person removes the screw and rappels on the anchor with no backup.

PRACTICING FOR THE FREEDOM OF THE HILLS

Skill and confidence in alpine ice climbing come with long practice. The ability to assess or read the ice comes with years of experience. Link up with a steady ice climbing partner if possible. Practice together often. Work on pinpoint ice-tool and crampon placement, which conserves energy. Also work to increase the speed and efficiency of your climbing, gearing it to the conditions of the ice and your body's strength. It is up to each climber to decide when to rope up for protection—and when it is safer not to. Experienced ice climbers learn these skills, continue to hone them, and apply them with confidence and good judgment so they can meet the rigors of their chosen routes.

19

CHAPTER 20

WATERFALL ICE AND MIXED CLIMBING

As the temperature falls below the freezing point, liquid water changes to a solid. Even raging torrents can become spectacular, massive hanging waterfall ice formations. Water ice is formed by gradual buildup. The usual formation is not a single monolithic crystalline structure. Typically, ice formations are the result of a series of freezes, and they have a laminated, or layered, structure. Water ice can take many forms: smooth, broad slabs; flat runnels; cauliflower-textured walls; latticed sheets; chandeliered curtains; massive ice pillars; fantastic, free-hanging icicles.

Compared with the life cycle of glacial ice, the life spans of winter waterfall ice formations are all too brief. During a single winter season's freeze-thaw cycles, waterfall ice can form, collapse, then re-form, only to collapse again when the spring thaw arrives. When climbers visit the sites of winter ice climbs in warmer seasons, they may not be able to picture what is there in winter. Summer tourists traveling in Alberta, Canada, along the Icefields Parkway in Jasper National Park can easily miss the wet spot that marks the location that attracts waterfall ice climbers from around the world in winter: the Weeping Wall's spectacular ice curtain, an acre of vertical ice.

The technical difficulty of waterfall ice climbing continues to rise. The sport has transcended the traditional style—simple ascension of ice formations—and now includes dry tooling (climbing on technical rock with ice tools and crampons to link formations of ice separated by rock). Climbing on mixed terrain (rock, thin ice, and ice) is not a new concept: it has long been part of ascending Scottish gullies in winter and climbing technical routes in the Alps. In the classic sense, mixed climbing meant having one foot on rock and the other on ice—usually thin ice. However, the focus of the sport has shifted. On a modern mixed route, climbers may spend as much or more time on

rock as on ice. Often the crux of a route consists of making an athletic transition from rock to an overhanging curtain or spear of ice.

Waterfall ice and mixed-route climbers must exercise caution on terrain that changes abruptly from ice to rock and back, but they must also act with concern for the environment. The hard steel of ice tools and crampons does scratch and can break the rock surface and harm lichens or plants. When dry tooling, exercise care to minimize damage. When establishing mixed routes, give major consideration to the local ethics: avoid climbing in culturally sensitive areas (for example, cliffs with pictographs) and popular rock climbing areas.

Since much waterfall ice climbing occurs during the winter months and requires travel up steep slopes, in gullies, or below basins, snow conditions are a big concern. It is important to assess avalanche risk and exercise prudence any time you are venturing into the backcountry; see Chapter 17, Avalanche Safety.

EQUIPMENT

This section includes a few considerations specific to waterfall ice and mixed climbing. For discussions of snow

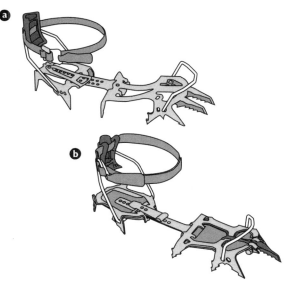

Fig. 20-1. Semirigid crampons with interchangeable front points: a, dual; b, mono.

and alpine ice climbing equipment, see Chapters 16, Snow Travel and Climbing, and 19, Alpine Ice Climbing.

CRAMPONS

For waterfall ice, the front points are more aggressively curved or angled downward than those used in general alpine ice climbing; the secondary points are angled more forward. On extremely steep to overhanging waterfall ice or mixed terrain, the crampons of choice are semirigid or rigid with vertical dual (fig. 20-1a) or mono (fig. 20-1b) front points. Monopoints are better for dry tooling and delicate ice. Some crampon front points are interchangeable, allowing worn front points to be replaced (rather than replacing the entire crampon) or to be switched from mono to dual front points or vice versa.

ICE TOOLS

While a straighter-shafted tool is a more versatile option for alpine ice climbing, a curved technical tool with ergonomic grip and reverse-curved pick (see Figure 19-4b in Chapter 19, Alpine Ice Climbing) is the standard choice for waterfall ice and mixed climbing. There are a variety of technical ice tools on the market (fig. 20-2). Each type has different characteristics (including grip, weight, and balance), so demo several models and choose the one that best fits your needs.

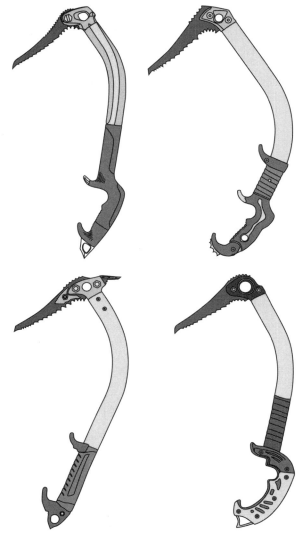

Fig. 20-2. Modern technical ice tools.

WATERFALL ICE CLIMBING

Using crampons and ice tools, ice climbers move vertically on the varied ice found in frozen waterfalls.

CRAMPON TECHNIQUES

Footwork is the foundation of climbing techniques for steep waterfall ice. Good footwork allows climbers to keep most of their weight on their feet and the strong musculature

20

Fig. 20-3. A pigeon-toed stance is sometimes needed to plant front points squarely.

no more than one or two kicks should be necessary. Make sure that your feet are perpendicular to the ice surface in both planes: keep heels low so that the secondary points engage the surface, making for a more stable placement, and make sure the toe of each boot is squarely facing the surface at that particular spot. A pigeon-toed stance (or its opposite, a duck-footed stance) may be necessary to plant the front points squarely (fig. 20-3). Monopoints can be slotted in old pick placements. Once your feet are placed, try to keep them steady until you are ready to move again. Nervous feet weaken the placement.

Keep feet shoulder width, or slightly less, apart to reduce the tendency to "barn-door" to one side. Use several short steps, rather than high-stepping, to reduce the stress on your quadriceps—although high-stepping can be necessary occasionally to get past bulges.

Beyond straight-in front-pointing, footwork that is much more akin to rock climbing techniques is very useful for the variety of features found on many waterfall ice climbs. Stemming and flagging for counterbalance, matching feet (see Chapter 12, Alpine Rock Climbing Technique), and heel hooking (see Figure 20-10) are very useful on waterfall ice.

ICE-TOOL TECHNIQUES

Just as the mainstay of footwork on waterfall ice is front-pointing, the most frequent tool placement is *piolet traction* or "tracking" (see Figure 19-23 in Chapter 19, Alpine Ice Climbing). Because it becomes very tiring to swing tools overhead, do everything possible to reduce the number of swings and placements you make.

When tracking, think of it as climbing on self-belay. Before trusting the integrity of each placement, test it by loading it with partial body weight. Do this test from the relative safety of a stable stance on the ice. This is a key concept: the goal is to create a position of strength and then to climb from that position. If each position is stable, you will climb with comfort and confidence. Do not fall into the trap of relying on a shaky placement, because this robs you of confidence and can lead to increasingly weak and unstable stances.

Selecting a placement and making the placement accurately are the keys to placing ice tools securely and quickly; strive to gain a solid placement with just one swing. One technique for hitting a precise spot is to tap the desired spot with the pick, then swing at that spot with force. The swing is more akin to a racquetball swing, with its wrist snap just prior to connecting with the ball, than to a

of their legs, rather than on their arms, saving precious arm strength. See figures in Chapter 19, Alpine Ice Climbing, for examples of good footwork. Good footwork ensures smooth weight changes and greater efficiency. Poor footwork causes climbers to flail, burn out rapidly, and fall.

Front-pointing is the mainstay of footwork on vertical ice (see Chapter 19, Alpine Ice Climbing, for details on front-pointing). A good ice climber not only looks up for good tool-placement opportunities but also continually looks down for front-point placements that ease the strain on the calves. As is true for tool placements, slight depressions make for ideal front-point placements. Similarly, a spot just above a small bulge can also be a nice placement.

After finding a likely spot, use a firm kick to set the front points in place. Except in rotten, chandelier, or extremely brittle ice (see "Unusual Conditions" later in this chapter), straight-wristed tennis swing. The steeper the droop of the pick, the more wrist action is needed to set the pick at the proper angle. (See "Ice-Tool Placements" in Chapter 19, Alpine Ice Climbing.) Many beginning waterfall ice climbers tend to drive their tools in too hard; take care to avoid this, because sinking a tool makes it much more difficult and tiring to remove it as you continue on. (See "Removing the Tool" in Chapter 19.)

While climbing, conserve energy by looking for secure placements that do not require you to swing the ice tool. Some old tool or monopoint placements may be deep enough that you can simply slot the pick in. Hooking opportunities abound on water ice. Large icicles often form in clusters on vertical sections, creating slots or gaps that are ideal for hooking placements. Larger columns can be hooked horizontally. Reverse-curved picks (see "Ice-Tool Placements" in Chapter 19, Alpine Ice Climbing) are best for hooking placements. Many ice-tool picks have teeth where the pick attaches to the shaft, which provide more secure hooking.

In good ice, vertically stagger the tool placements using the tracking technique (see "Climbing on Vertical Ice" in Chapter 19, Alpine Ice Climbing). By staggering the tools (rather than planting them side by side) and by relying on a single tool at a time, climbers reduce the number of tool placements, thus decreasing the workload on the swinging and gripping muscles of their arms and hands. If the ice is suspect (meaning the placement is too), plant both tools side by side, about 2 feet (0.6 meter) apart, before moving your feet up. This decreases the load on each placement and reduces the chance that a tool will shear out under the load.

Leashed Versus Leashless Tools

Leashes are generally no longer used on water ice tools. They have been replaced in recent years by a variety of grip-aiding devices on the shafts of the tools (see Figure 20-2). Freedom from leashes unexpectedly led to the development of a variety of new techniques and helped to raise standards of both ice and mixed climbing. Leashless tools make it easy for climbers to change tools from hand to hand, regrip the tool at the midshaft grip (which allows for upward movement without a new placement), and release the tool for a shake-out rest or to place a screw.

Climbing leashless requires the climber to adapt techniques to maintain arm and hand strength. Avoid overgripping the tool, which is a waste of energy. When standing in place, relax your grip slightly, taking advantage of the grips and rests inherent in the tool.

Climbers who wish to use leashes to keep from dropping tools may choose to use "umbilicals." Umbilicals are tethers, usually of an elastic material, that connect the tool (usually by being clipped to a hole in the tool's spike) to the climber's harness (see Figure 19-6). Note that neither the umbilical nor its attachment point are belay strength and should never be used as part of a belay or personal anchor. They are solely to prevent the loss of a tool. Another consideration: if a climber is leading with gear racked to the harness, the umbilicals can become entangled in the hanging gear.

VERTICAL PROGRESSION

Just as in climbing on rock, climbing on waterfall ice involves a coordinated combination of climbing techniques used by a leader and a belayer, who are connected by the rope, anchors, and protection points.

Tracking

Follow these steps to combine crampon and ice-tool techniques to "track" your way upward:

1. While standing on front points and with one ice tool in *piolet traction*, place the other ice tool high, at full arm's length; immediately relax, weighting that tool (fig. 20-4a).
2. With the upper tool still weighted (your arm fully extended), move your feet up, using small steps, to stances between ankle and knee height. Ideally, your body position should form a triangle with the apex at the high tool placement (fig. 20-4b). If your feet are too far to one side or the other, you will tend to "barn-door," swinging out of balance to that side.
3. Loosen, but do not yet remove, the lower of the two tools, and look above for the next placement for it.
4. In one motion, stand upright by pushing with your feet and pulling on the upper tool, remove the lower tool, and place it in the chosen spot, again preferably at full arm's length (fig. 20-4c).
5. Relax, weight that tool, then loosen your grip on it, and move your feet up. Once you are certain this new placement is secure, you can remove the lower tool (fig. 20-4d).
6. Repeat these steps. As you repeatedly move through the sequence, you will be "tracking" the tool placements with your feet, moving a little laterally with each move to maintain that triangular position and keeping your feet centered on the tools.

20

Fig. 20-4. Proper tracking technique: a, place one tool at arm's length and weight it; b, move feet up in small steps; c, stand up and place the other tool at arm's length; d, weight the tool and move the feet up.

Belaying

Setting up belay anchors and belaying on waterfall ice uses the same procedures as those discussed in "Belaying on Ice" in Chapter 19, Alpine Ice Climbing. Take extra care in locating belays away from the fall line to avoid being showered with debris from the leader. In gullies, site the belay to one side of the route, seeking protection from the sidewall. On pillars or curtains, try placing the belay behind or to the side of the formation, but be aware that although this position provides greater protection from falling ice, it will make communication more difficult and rope drag a possibility. Look for a compromise between protection and convenience in belay stances.

Leading

Most waterfall ice climbs are led and followed in pitches, though many long climbs offer sections suitable for running belays. Ice pitches may be climbed with a single rope or with two ropes using either double-rope or twin-rope technique (see "Double- and Twin-Rope Techniques" in Chapter 14, Leading on Rock).

PROTECTION

Waterfall ice routes can be protected using both rock and ice gear, which affects racking and placements.

Rock Gear

Some waterfall ice climbs have options for using rock gear. On gully climbs, the rock sidewalls can provide protection opportunities. On freestanding columns or curtains, look behind the ice for placements in the back wall; these most likely will need to be extended by slings to prevent rope drag. In the winter, cracks tend to be filled by ice; as a result, pitons are used more frequently than on summer climbs, though the full variety of clean protection can be used as well.

Natural Protection

Waterfall ice offers more opportunities for natural protection than do the flows and steps of alpine ice, and many natural placements are quicker to set up than ice screws. Runners can be placed around small ice columns (fig. 20-5). A long ice screw tied off with webbing can be

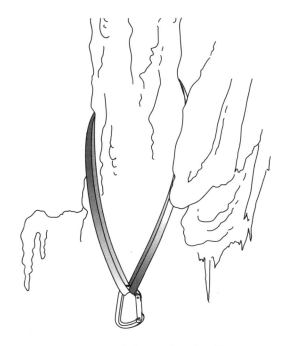

Fig. 20-5. Runner threaded around an ice pillar.

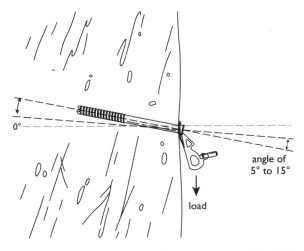

Fig. 20-6. Ice-screw placement is strongest angled 5 to 15 degrees downward in cold, solid ice.

inserted between two columns or through a slot in an ice curtain, then rotated sideways and used as a sort of deadman for temporary protection (for a description of deadman anchors in snow, see Chapter 16, Snow Travel and Climbing). In thin curtains, two holes can be punched in the curtain and then threaded with webbing or accessory cord as for a V-thread anchor. (See "Setting Up Ice Anchors" in Chapter 19, Alpine Ice Climbing.)

Ice Screws and Ice Pitons

Ice screws remain the most common type of protection used on waterfall ice (see Figures 19-7 and 19-8), but ice pitons, pound-in protection designed for thin ice and mixed climbing, may also be part of the rack.

Ice screws. Placing ice screws is described in "Protection with Ice Screws" in Chapter 19, Alpine Ice Climbing. Significant testing has been done to determine the strength of ice-screw placements in solid water ice at cold temperatures. Surprisingly, under those conditions the strongest screw placements are those with the screw head angled downward 5 to 15 degrees off perpendicular, pointing toward the direction of pull (fig. 20-6). This configuration can reduce fracturing of the ice when loaded by a leader fall.

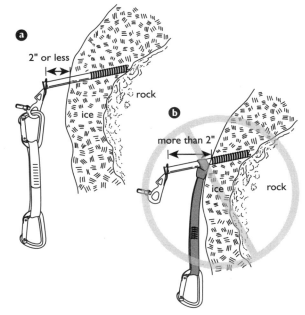

Fig. 20-7. Ice-screw placement in thin ice over rock: a, screw protrudes 2 inches (5 centimeters) or less, clip hanger as normal; b, screw extends more than 2 inches (5 centimeters), tie screw off close to the ice. Note that this second, highly suspect placement is not recommended and should be followed by a stronger placement as soon as possible.

453

It is best to use a screw of a length that can be sunk to the hilt. If the ice is too shallow for a screw to be placed all the way in to its hanger, remove that screw and use a shorter one in a new spot; never reuse an existing screw hole unless it has had a chance to melt and refreeze—much of the strength of the placement is due to the frozen core of ice inside the screw. Carry a variety of screw lengths to decrease the chances of needing to tie off a screw. If the screw protrudes no more than 2 inches (5 centimeters) from the surface of the ice, clip the hanger as you normally would (fig. 20-7a). If the screw protrudes more than 2 inches from the surface, the placement is highly suspect. Tie off the protruding screw with a runner next to the ice (fig. 20-7b). Tie off a screw only as a last resort. When screws fail under loading, they do so by fracturing the ice below them and bending toward the direction of load. In the case of a tied-off screw, the webbing then slides to the hanger and is cut by its sharp edges.

Ice pitons. Another type of protection is the ice piton. Ice pitons are removable protection used to hook features in either ice or rock (fig. 20-8). They can be slotted into holes in ice curtains or between the laced-together icicles in chandelier ice and then set with a light tap. Ice pitons can also be driven into iced-up cracks, hence their name.

Protecting the Leader

Many more options for protecting the leader can be found on waterfall ice than on alpine ice. Alpine ice is limited to using ice screws, with occasional rock protection to the side or in rock "islands." On waterfall ice, rock gear can often be placed to the side of or even behind an ice column, or natural protection can be creatively used in the ice itself, in addition to ice-screw and ice-piton placements.

Fig. 20-8. Ice piton.

THE RACK FOR WATERFALL ICE CLIMBING

A typical ice climbing rack for a multipitch, pure ice climb might contain some or all of the following gear:

- Four long (19- or 22-centimeter) screws for anchors and/or constructing V-thread anchors
- Six to 12 ice screws of varying lengths appropriate for the thickness of the ice
- Eight to 14 quickdraws and/or alpine draws (see Figure 14-7 in Chapter 14, Leading on Rock)
- Two long runners or cordelettes for equalizing belay anchors
- An ice piton (as shown in Figure 20-8) for quick pound-in protection
- A V-thread tool (as shown in Figure 19-9 in Chapter 19, Alpine Ice Climbing)
- A few pieces of 6- to 8-millimeter accessory cord for constructing V-thread anchors
- A knife for cutting webbing and cord

Racking

Most ice climbers rack ice screws and other ice gear on their harness (see Chapter 19, Alpine Ice Climbing). Here is one suggested harness arrangement for racked gear (see also "The Rack for Waterfall Ice Climbing" sidebar):

- **Rack most of the gear needed on lead on the same side as your dominant hand.** Place ice screws in front, arranged front to back by length, short to long, with teeth pointed to the rear. Next, rack quickdraws behind the screws. Rack a few screws and quickdraws on your nondominant side in the event you need to place a screw with that hand.
- **Use the rear gear loops on both sides to rack gear that will not be needed immediately.** This includes longer screws for belay anchors or for creating V-threads, a belay device, free carabiners, a pulley, a V-thread tool, and a cordelette.

Placing Gear on Lead

Placing ice screws while leading on steep ice can be very physically demanding. To conserve energy, minimize the number of screw placements; typically, on a waterfall ice pitch, far fewer protection placements are made than would be placed on a rock pitch of similar length. Similarly, climbers develop techniques for placing screws that minimize the effort expended.

For example, avoid the temptation to place a screw high (above shoulder height) to gain that momentary top-rope

Fig. 20-9. Placing an ice screw on lead.

protection (having the rope above you). In this position, it is very difficult to put enough pressure on the screw so that its threads will bite into the ice. The most efficient placement is right at waist level. You have better leverage and can use your whole body weight to push the screw into the ice. Also, your arm remains below the level of your heart so blood flow remains constant.

Here is one technique for placing screws on lead:

1. Get a good stance for both feet and (if you are right-handed) plant the left tool high (at arm's length); weight the tool, hanging straight-armed. Use the tool placement for balance only; maintain your weight on your feet, as shown in Figure 20-9.

2. At waist level, use the right tool to chip away any rotten or soft ice at the desired placement and make a starter hole for the screw if needed. Secure that tool—clip it to your harness, or place it solidly in the ice out of the way.

3. Place the screw with your right hand (fig. 20-9); attach a quickdraw or runner to the screw hanger; clip in the rope.

4. Retrieve the right tool; place the tool high and weight it; shake the left arm out as needed and continue climbing.

Occasionally body position, ice quality, or solid tool placements may dictate that a screw be placed with your nondominant hand. Practice placing screws with that hand and always rack a few screws on the nondominant side of your harness.

UNUSUAL CONDITIONS

Unlike the more homogeneous ice of most alpine ice climbs, waterfall ice comes in an amazing and beautiful (and, many times, terrifying) array of formations, shapes, textures, features, and quality. These characteristics can make for difficult climbing with little opportunity for protection.

Pillars. Pillars are formed when meltwater drips off a free-hanging icicle until the resulting ice stalactite and stalagmite join. Climbable pillars can range in size from less than a body's width to many feet across. Although big pillars are climbed using the tracking technique (see "Tracking" earlier in this chapter), small pillars require much more varied techniques. The tools must be vertically staggered so as not to weaken the pillar by having the two tools too close together. If placing screws in the pillar might weaken it, place protection in the adjacent rock. Both the tools and the front points might need to be placed in a pigeon-toed angle to keep the points and picks going straight into the ice, perpendicular to the ice in both planes. On really narrow pillars, a combination of front-pointing with one foot and flagging or heel hooking is effective (fig. 20-10). Assess pillars carefully before climbing them. Abnormally warm or cold temperatures can weaken them, as can sudden temperature swings, especially from warm to cold.

Free-hanging ice. Free-hanging ice is formed when a pillar or curtain has not touched down onto ice or the ground or has broken off. Most of the techniques for climbing free-hanging ice are the same as for climbing pillars, as are the stability concerns. Use delicate tool and crampon placements. Place protection in the adjacent rock walls. Place screws in the ice only above its point of attachment to the rock. If screws are placed low in the formation and the formation fails, the climber, connected to the falling block, will be dragged down.

20

Fig. 20-10. Combination footwork: front-pointing and heel hooking.

Chandelier ice. When thousands of small icicles melt and become laced together into a dense latticework, it is called chandelier ice. This ice formation is fairly common, beautiful to see, hard to climb, and difficult to protect. Belays must be situated to avoid the constant rain of debris from the leader. Most of the time, there is little delicacy to climbing a chandelier. Kick your feet deep into the ice structure in hopes of finding secure purchase. Place the tools similarly, although you can be more creative with them. You might hook the slots between two larger icicles, stab the entire head of the tool directly into the ice and then rotate the tool 90 degrees so the hammer or adze and pick straddle the newly created slot, or thrust the entire tool (and your arm) through the lattice and grasp the tool midshaft, using it as a deadman-style placement. You may not be able to place a solid screw, but natural protection may exist.

Cauliflower ice. Cauliflower ice forms at the "drip zone" of ice climbs, usually near the ground or above large ledges where spraying or splashing water has frozen into unusual shapes resembling everything from cauliflowers to open artichokes. The formations can range in size from several inches to several feet wide and deep. Cauliflower ice offers many opportunities for hooking tools. Formations with solid domes can often be flat-footed (see Chapter 19, Alpine Ice Climbing), but use caution climbing the "petals" of ice that resemble more of an open artichoke; they can break easily. Cauliflower ice is best protected by screws set in larger bulges or in the solid center ice of these formations.

Onion skin ice. Another type of spray ice, onion skin ice forms when water sprays onto a layer of fresh snow and freezes, forming a crust of ice over the snow, sometimes several inches thick. These are notoriously unstable formations, however, since the ice is not attached to a solid surface. When climbing through onion skin ice, make sure to place a screw before moving onto it: but do not place a screw in an onion skin.

Brittle ice. The result of very cold temperatures, brittle ice usually appears only on the surface layers of ice formations. Work through the hard, brittle layers to get to the more plastic ice below, and in the process a cascade of falling ice will result, ranging in size from small chips to very large dinner plates. Be sure to stagger the placements of the tools far enough apart that the fracturing created by one tool does not reach the other, causing both placements to fail. Also, beware of falling dinner plates, which can dislodge front points. Place ice screws in the better ice found beneath the brittle layers.

Rotten ice. Often the result of being baked by the sun or weakened by percolating water, rotten ice can run much deeper than brittle ice, even through an entire formation. Rotten ice is difficult to climb and harder to protect; a lengthy section of rotten ice may be all but unclimbable.

Thin ice. Thin ice ranges from just a glaze of ice over the rock to ice a few inches thick. Thin ice can be very exciting and fun to climb. The thinnest ice is *verglas*: thick enough to obscure the underlying rock but not thick enough to gain purchase in with picks or points. Thicker ice is easier to climb, as long as temperatures are cold enough for cohesion to be maintained between the ice and the underlying rock. Make both tool and crampon placements with the gentlest of taps, swinging tools just from the wrist; sometimes placements must be scratched into place by chipping and hooking. Protection is usually found in the rock surrounding the ice. Extremely short screws may offer only psychological protection at best.

Bulges and ledges. These formations (discussed fully in Chapter 19, Alpine Ice Climbing) in water ice entail the same concerns that exist in climbing alpine ice.

DESCENDING

Some waterfall ice climbs, especially gully routes, allow walk-off descents to one side or the other. Most, however, are descended by a combination of down-climbing and rappelling. The techniques of down-climbing ice are discussed fully in Chapter 19, Alpine Ice Climbing; please review them there.

Rappelling

The principal techniques for rappelling on ice are the same as for rappelling on rock. Many rappels on popular waterfall ice climbs are done from fixed anchors, usually a combination of bolts and/or chains, slings on trees, or abandoned V-thread anchors. As with any fixed anchor, inspect these thoroughly before trusting them. Make sure the bolts are secure. Check the slings or accessory cord on the tree or the V-thread anchor for damage, wear, or burn marks, and check all knots. When in doubt, remove and replace the material. Check found V-threads to ensure that they are still solid. If any found anchor is suspect in any way, or if there are none, place your own. The technique for building a V-thread is fully discussed in Chapter 19, Alpine Ice Climbing. Any V-thread should be backed up with a screw until the last climber removes the backup screw, then rappels. Before the last climber rappels, ensure that the rappel lines are not frozen into place or jammed, so they can be pulled free from below.

MIXED CLIMBING

Mixed climbing combines climbing on rock, snow, and ice—and sometimes on frozen mud and moss as well. Mixed climbing might mean climbing a rock route in the winter, with ice-filled cracks and snow-covered ledges. Or it may involve making an alpine ascent up an icy face broken by a rock band. Or it may be climbing with one crampon on rock and the other on ice, one hand inserted into a crack and one ice tool placed in a frozen smear. Modern "sport" mixed climbing has come to mean climbing sections of rock between discontinuous sections of ice, often with preplaced bolted rock protection.

EQUIPMENT AND TECHNIQUES

The equipment used for mixed climbing most likely is whatever the climber was using right before the ice ran out. On a glacier climb, this means mountaineering crampons and a mountaineering ice axe. On a harder alpine ice climb, it most likely means a mountaineering ice axe with a technically curved pick used in combination with a shorter ice tool, likely a hammer, and semirigid crampons. On a frozen waterfall with a mixed section, it is likely to be technical ice climbing tools and crampons.

Crampons

When climbing a mixed route, climbers are usually wearing crampons. Although considerable rock may be showing, it may be impractical to remove crampons only to put them back on when the route returns to the ice. Whichever crampons you choose, be sure that they are fully compatible with your boots. They must fit well to enable the delicate and precise movements required to climb rock while in crampons.

Vertical front points. Many mixed climbers prefer technical crampons with vertical front points (see Figure 20-1a). Monopoint crampons (see Figure 20-1b) are particularly handy for precision accuracy on minuscule ledges, vertical seams, and other subtle features. Monopoints are also advantageous because the point mimics the pick of an ice tool. On ice a monopoint can be placed in the pick hole made just a few moves previously.

Horizontal front points. Some mixed climbers prefer crampons with horizontal front points (see Figure 16-5c in Chapter 16, Snow Travel and Climbing). Such crampons have greater stability because their horizontal alignment matches the features found in the sedimentary strata of many mountain ranges. They also are less prone to shearing away because of their greater surface area.

Crampon Technique

Ultimately, crampon choice is secondary to proper technique. A good mixed climber selects a foothold and delicately places a crampon point or points in the spot. Smooth weight transfer is critical while gradually testing the foothold until it is completely weighted. Once that foot is weighted, it is important to keep it still, to prevent the points from rotating out of a crack or off a ledge. Careful footwork is the key to mixed climbing. With proper technique, climbers will not scratch the rock and their crampon points will remain sharp for any difficult ice climbing lying ahead.

Hands on Rock

Although it may be impractical to remove crampons for a rock section, it often makes sense to secure ice tools and grasp the rock directly with your hands. It may be next to impossible to find a pick placement on a downsloping rock ledge or fist-sized crack, but that same ledge or crack may easily yield a workable handhold.

20

For extensive climbing using your hands on rock, it may be necessary to clip the tool to your harness or otherwise secure it. This can be accomplished either by using a specialized carabiner designed for this purpose (see "Racking Devices" in Chapter 19, Alpine Ice Climbing) or by sliding the shaft of the ice tool into a spare carabiner. Be sure there is no possibility of the ice tool coming out accidentally. Dropping a tool on a one-pitch sport-style mixed route may be annoying and embarrassing, but dropping a tool on a committing alpine route could have devastating consequences.

The surest method of securing an ice tool is to clip the axe-head hole in to a spare carabiner or gear racking device on the harness. To remove the tool, grasp the head of the tool and open the carabiner gate with a thumb.

Once one or both hands are free, use them as on any rock climb. Fist jams, handholds, liebacks, and down-pressure can all be used to give your body the proper balance and positioning to support delicate footwork. Chapter 12, "Alpine Rock Climbing Technique," covers the variety of rock climbing holds and techniques.

Keep in mind that while climbing with your hands on rock, you most likely will be wearing gloves. Technical mixed climbing, like technical rock climbing, requires dexterity. Handholds, carabiners, and protection must all be manipulated efficiently. It is therefore impractical to climb mixed terrain with a bulky glove system. Most mixed climbers wear one pair of low-profile, close-fitting gloves while climbing; keep a second pair warming in a jacket pocket; and stash a third, warmer pair in the top lid of their pack for belays.

Ice Tools on Rock

When the holds become too small for your hands or the cracks are filled with too much ice, it is time to use ice tools. When using an ice axe or ice tools on rock, consider how to employ every part of the tool creatively.

Hooking. The straightforward technique of hooking is the most common method for using the pick of the ice tool to climb rock. However, it is critical that, while pulling through the move, you hold the shaft of the tool steady against the rock (fig. 20-11a). If you pull outward on the spike end of the shaft, the pick will skate off the hold

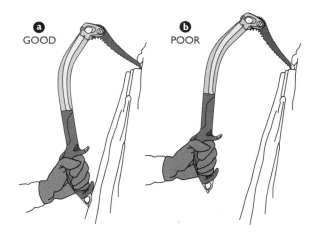

Fig. 20-11. Hooking technique: a, with downward force (good); b, with outward force (poor).

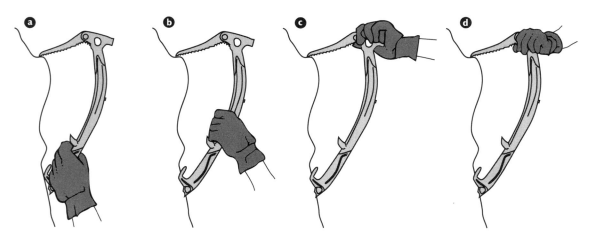

Fig. 20-12. Turning a hooked hold into a mantel move: a, hook the ledge; b, work your hand up the shaft; c, climb up, grasping the head of the tool; d, work your feet higher and mantel.

(fig. 20-11b). You can also use the hammer or adze of the ice tool to hook rock holds, although you must exercise caution, because the pick will be pointing toward you. To find a hook placement in a crack, look for constrictions just as you would look for a small stopper placement.

While moving up, it is sometimes advantageous to turn a hook placement (fig. 20-12a) into a mantel by sliding your hand up the shaft (fig. 20-12b) and grasping the head of the tool (fig. 20-12c and d). This technique is especially handy if the next tool placement is far above you.

Torquing. Slide the pick into a crack that is a little too wide to be secure, and twist the shaft of the tool until the pick is securely wedged (fig. 20-13). As long as you maintain adequate pressure, the placement will be secure. Or torque by using the hammer, adze, or even the shaft of the tool.

The stein puller. A very stable technique, the stein puller is most often performed by inserting the pick upsidedown into a downward-facing seam or flake (fig. 20-14). Then, just as a bartender would pull down on a bar tap handle, pull down on the shaft of the tool, engaging the pick into the hold and forcing the head of the tool against the rock, creating opposing force. The harder you pull down, the stronger the tool placement becomes.

A great advantage of the stein puller is that a hold above your head can be hooked (fig. 20-15a); then you can climb up (fig. 20-15b), turning the stein puller into a mantel without removing the tool from the rock (fig. 20-15c and d).

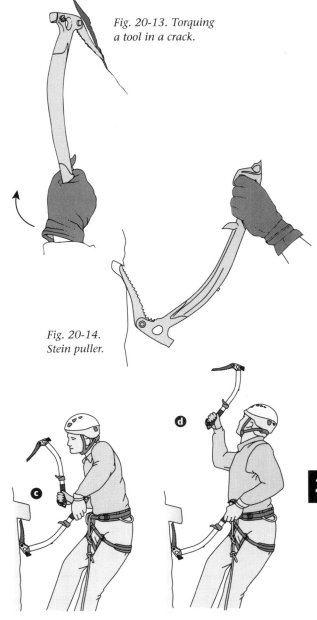

Fig. 20-13. Torquing a tool in a crack.

Fig. 20-14. Stein puller.

Fig. 20-15. Using a stein puller to mantel:
a, place the stein puller;
b, pull on it to work your feet higher;
c, mantel on the tool;
d, reach up and place the other tool.

20

Fig. 20-16. Stacking.

Matching. Another technique that is particularly useful while dry tooling is called matching. Just as on a rock climb when you place both hands on one hold, one hand on top of the other, one hold is used for both ice tools. One of the great things about the pick of the ice tool is that it is so narrow. Both tool picks can easily fit side by side on the same hold, as long as the hold is wider than about ¼ inch (6 to 7 millimeters). When matching, be sure that the hold is strong enough to withstand the force that can be generated by the two ice tools.

Stacking. Another technique used frequently in dry tooling is stacking. If there is one very good tool placement surrounded by bad ones, try hooking the pick of the well-placed tool with the other tool (fig. 20-16). When stacking, make sure once again that the hold is strong enough to withstand the force of two ice tools.

Body Positioning

In order to ascend mixed terrain well, climbers must combine precision crampon and tool placements with calculated body positioning. Rarely do they simply pull down on hooked placements and walk their feet up the wall.

For instance, picture a ledge that slopes down to the right. In order to hook this ledge and keep the tool placements stable through a series of foot placements, pull down and to the left (fig. 20-17). Conversely, a right-leaning lieback is futile unless your crampons are in a position to allow you to push your body sideways to the right (fig. 20-18).

With a lot of practice on mixed terrain, climbers gain confidence in their crampon and tool technique. Climb as many mixed routes on top-rope as possible, no matter how hard the routes may look. If a certain move is elusive, examine your body positioning. A slight change in the way you are leaning may be the difference between frustration and exuberance.

Protection

Previous chapters contain detailed discussions of various types of protection used on rock (Chapter 13, Rock Protection), snow (Chapter 16, Snow Travel and Climbing),

*Fig. 20-17.
Lieback to the left.*

and ice (Chapter 19, Alpine Ice Climbing). Also see "Protection" under "Waterfall Ice Climbing" earlier in this chapter and "The Rack for Mixed Climbing" sidebar. Here is an additional consideration when climbers are combining the various types of protection for mixed climbing.

If there is a choice between a rock anchor and a snow or ice anchor, use the rock anchor. It is relatively easy to evaluate the soundness of rock anchors, but this is not so with most snow or ice anchors. It might be necessary to do some digging and grooming to clear away snow, ice, and debris in order to place a piece of protection in the rock. Powdery snow can be knocked off with your hands, but an ice tool will probably be needed to clear hard snow or ice. If a crack is filled with ice, a piton or ice piton may be useful. Wired nuts can be pounded into cracks with the pick of the ice tool to create solid placements.

Fig. 20-18. Lieback to the right, pushing with feet.

Belaying and Reducing Forces on the Climbing System

Because of the possibly dubious nature of mixed protection, a dynamic belay is required. As always, use a strong multipoint multidirectional belay anchor with well-placed screws or pitons. (See Chapter 10, Belaying, and "Belaying on Ice" in Chapter 19, Alpine Ice Climbing.)

A dynamic belay may be partially obtained by using a rope that has a relatively low impact force (4 to 7 kilonewtons), which means it is stretchier and provides a softer catch. (See Chapter 9, Basic Safety System, for more on dynamic ropes and their specifications.) Most half-rope systems offer lower impact forces. Keep in mind that because low-impact-force ropes are stretchier than larger-diameter climbing ropes, a climber will fall a greater distance and so must watch out for ledges.

Minimizing rope drag is also important (see more in Chapter 14, Leading on Rock) when leading on shaky protection. If the rope zigzags up the route between points of protection and a fall occurs, the friction generated at the bends in the rope will prevent the rope from elongating

THE RACK FOR MIXED CLIMBING

A mixed climbing rack contains gear that is appropriate for the climb. Some modern, sport mixed climbs are fully bolted, requiring only a set of quickdraws for protection. Longer classic mixed climbs require a full rock rack combined with a full ice rack. A typical mixed climbing rack might contain some or all of the following gear:

- Six to 12 ice screws of varying lengths appropriate for the thickness of the ice
- An assortment of nuts and Tricams that can be slotted or pounded into cracks
- Spring-loaded camming devices (SLCDs)
- An assortment of pitons for ice-filled cracks
- Several runners, alpine draws, or quickdraws
- A few long runners or cordelettes for threading gaps between the rock and the ice or ice columns
- An ice piton for quick protection, icy seams, and frozen moss
- A V-thread tool
- A few pieces of 6- to 8-millimeter accessory cord for constructing rappel anchors
- A knife for cutting webbing and accessory cord

20

as it should by design. If this occurs, a disproportionate amount of force will be applied to the protection nearest to the fallen climber. Keep the rope running as straight as possible, using double-rope technique and long runners for protection located off to the side.

Leading

Leading on mixed terrain can be an exhilarating experience, but it is not for everyone. By its very nature, mixed leads tend to be bold and committing. Taking a leader fall while wearing crampons and holding ice tools is serious business. Before you decide to lead a mixed pitch on ice gear, be honest about your ability to climb it responsibly. If you decide that you can indeed climb and protect the pitch safely, here are a few tips to keep in mind:

- **Examine the crux(es) carefully.** Figure out the moves before you get there. Devise a plan and a backup plan for protecting and climbing through the crux.
- **Once on route, place gear at rests,** before the hard parts, instead of halfway through a crux sequence.
- **Calculate your moves and climb with confidence.**
- **Relax and breathe deeply;** this will calm stressed nerves.
- **If you are stumped by a sequence of moves, down-climb to the last rest spot, reevaluate, and try again,** perhaps using a slightly different technique. If the sequence remains elusive, down-climb or lower off.
- **Be prepared to leave some gear behind.**

- **If a fall is imminent, check the landing zone.** Be sure that you will fall away from the trailing rope, which your crampons or tools could damage. Disengage your tools, then your crampons, and push away from the wall. Aim picks on ice tools away from you and to the sides. Direct crampons toward the wall and keep your knees slightly bent to absorb the impact.

CLIMBING IN THE WINTER ENVIRONMENT

The extreme conditions of winter can create fantastic, almost surreal landscapes. On clear winter days, the bright blue sky is a perfect backdrop for the vivid blues of water ice formations. The ice glistening in the sunlight leads skyward.

Waterfall ice and mixed climbing build on the skills of alpine mountaineering and can involve severe conditions that require specialized equipment, a high level of skill, and a tremendous will to succeed. Equipped for the winter environment, the waterfall ice and mixed climber combines the disciplines of rock climbing and ice climbing with snow travel and backcountry risk management. But more importantly, waterfall ice and mixed climbers have an excellent understanding of their own abilities; they climb not for glory or recognition, but to fully experience the freedom of the hills.

CHAPTER 21

EXPEDITION CLIMBING

Expeditions give climbers the opportunity to dream big as they explore the highest and most remote peaks in the world. When climbers immerse themselves in the mountain experience, they test themselves both physically and mentally. In the words of expedition climber Mike Libecki, "The time is now. Why ration passion? Dream big . . . and climb those dreams."

What makes a climb an expedition? Expedition climbing requires significant time, commitment, planning, and preparation. An expedition may involve two or three days of air travel, followed by a day or two of land travel, and then a 10-day trek just to get to base camp. On an expedition, rest breaks may take several days as climbers acclimatize. Some expeditions can involve significant differences in climbing techniques such as ascending fixed lines, hauling sleds, performing crevasse rescues while tied to a sled, and preparing caches. Add to this the challenge of dealing with local languages and customs, climbing etiquette, and the red tape that larger objectives often entail. Successfully executing an expedition will teach you a great deal about your destination, your climbing partners, and yourself.

PLANNING AND PREPARATION

Planning an expedition involves selecting a destination, choosing the climbing party, making sure the team members are prepared, determining a climbing schedule, considering emergency preparedness and guiding services, and preparing supplies. Sometimes the objective is based around a particular team, and sometimes the team is chosen based on the objective. Larger objectives around the world, including in the United States, often entail permits and applications that may take months or years of advance notice and a significant fee to obtain.

CHOOSING AN OBJECTIVE

In deciding what peak to try and which route to climb, choose a destination that excites you. Ask yourself whether you are committed to the substantial effort involved in planning and preparing for an expedition.

Difficulty of the Route

Whatever route is chosen must be well within the climbing ability of the party because the added challenges of remoteness, altitude, changeable weather, and routefinding will compound the route's difficulties. Climbers who are considering an objective for their first few expeditions should think of those trips as opportunities to apply well-practiced climbing skills in a new environment rather than to push the limits of their technical ability.

Choosing a Climbing Style

Most modern expeditions involve a mix of alpine and expedition styles. The choice of which style of climbing to do during what part of the trip greatly influences planning

463

and, thus, is an important decision to be made early in the planning process. The choice will affect the length of trip, amount of risk, equipment and technical gear needed, and physical training goals and conditioning for the trip.

Expedition style. Expedition-style climbing involves multiple trips between camps, during which loads (food, fuel, and supplies needed later in the expedition) are carried to higher camps and buried in clearly marked, animal-proof locations. Technically difficult sections of the route are often protected with fixed lines—ropes anchored in place to minimize danger during repeated trips up and down the route. For these reasons, expedition-style climbing takes longer. This can be an advantage because climbers have more time to acclimatize to high altitude when they are ascending slowly in stages. Expedition-style climbing is often employed in the approach portion of the climb as the party slowly makes its way to a base camp.

Alpine style. Alpine-style climbing means moving up the mountain in a continuous push, so that the party ascends the route only once. The team carries all equipment and supplies needed for the summit with them. There is less margin of safety on alpine-style trips because climbers cannot bring as much equipment and supplies on the alpine-style portion of the climb. However, because the team moves faster, there is also less exposure to objective hazards such as storms, avalanches, or other longer-term changes in conditions. Climbers must climb "fast and light." This is often employed in the technical summit portion of an expedition as climbers climb above a base camp.

Duration of the Climb

In the world's higher regions, the duration of the climb may need to be longer than mileage and elevation gain might suggest. Climbers should not underestimate the time constraints that acclimatization requires (see the "Suggested Acclimatization Schedule" sidebar). The length of the climb may be determined more by how many "rest" days are needed at each camp to safely ascend to higher elevations.

Time of Year

Study information on seasonal temperatures, winds, storms, precipitation, and amount of daylight in the area the party is considering for its expedition. These will affect the expedition's duration and needed gear.

Costs

Expeditions can be costly because of the large amounts of time, equipment, and food required. Major costs include

---

SUGGESTED ACCLIMATIZATION SCHEDULE

If the objective is at 8,000 feet or below, the party can follow a normal ascent time; if the objective is at 8,000 feet or above, they should plan on a slow ascent: 1,000 feet of daily altitude gain above 8,000 feet, with a rest day after every 3,000 feet of elevation gained or at 2- to 4-day intervals. Here are some suggested ascent times, according to the US Army Research Institute of Environmental Medicine:

- 10,000 feet: 3 days
- 14,000 feet: 8 days
- 20,000 feet: 16 days

---

purchased and/or rented specialty equipment for the climb, transportation to the peak, permits and fees related to the climb, and hired porters, support staff, or pack animals. It is best not to scrimp on gear, guide services, or support services: in the big scheme of things, a slightly higher fee or slightly more expensive sleeping bag could make or break your only chance at a trip of a lifetime.

Be sure to budget adequate compensation for porters and other support staff, as well as supplies they will need for their own safety and comfort. The climbing party should be prepared to provide essential equipment, such as sunglasses and extra stove fuel, which many porters may not have. Know the going rates for support staff services, and be sure to pay and tip them accordingly. It is always best to set rates for their services before you head out on the expedition.

Location

There are so many choices for an expedition. Africa, Alaska, China, Europe, India, Kyrgyzstan, Greenland, Mexico, Nepal, New Zealand, Pakistan, Russia, and South America all boast difficult, remote peaks. After you choose a peak, research the mountain and its routes, as well as objective hazards on the mountain. Talk to climbers who have been there; look for descriptions in the journals of the Alpine Club (UK), American Alpine Club, the Alpine Club of Canada, and other climbing organizations. Seek out guidebooks, videos, and articles in climbing magazines, and research online sources. Note that in some countries, maps are considered restricted military information and may be available only once you are in the country and, even then, may not label significant mountain peaks. Select and research a backup route in case the original objective must be scratched because of avalanche hazard, bad weather, inability of some party members to continue, or any other reason. If a highly technical route up the mountain has been chosen, consider acclimatizing by climbing the standard route first and then taking on the tougher challenge.

Find out what travel visas and communication-device and climbing permits are necessary, and determine how long in advance an application must be made. Research vaccines and potential health problems for your specific travel location well in advance so that preparations can be made and vaccine series can be completed. It helps to have copies of itineraries, climbing résumés of party members, equipment lists, and medical information prepared ahead of time and available while traveling to the peak. Evidence of good organization impresses bureaucrats around the world. Consider whether anyone in the party speaks the local language. Get all possible details on logistics, monetary customs, potential problems, what types of fuel are available and where to buy it, what foods are available, whether the water is safe or if bottled water or purification is necessary, and so forth.

CHOOSING THE TEAM

Choosing a compatible climbing team is the most essential step toward an enjoyable experience. Expedition climbing is full of stress, and climbers can be taxed to their physical and mental limits. Make it a goal to head out as friends and return as even better friends.

The skill of the team must be equal to the demands of the climb, personalities need to be compatible, and team members must be able to live harmoniously with others in close quarters under stressful conditions. The climbers should agree on the philosophy of the trip in terms of climbing style, communication style, climbing goals, environmental impact, and degree of acceptable risk.

It is important to agree on how decisions will be made before the trip gets under way. Leadership should be parsed out to various members of the team to distribute the workload and to keep everyone involved. Team members can take the lead on areas such as finances, food, medicine, and equipment. A primary team leader who will step in when necessary, especially in urgent situations, should be designated.

The number of climbers in the expedition depends on the chosen route and climbing style. There are trade-offs that should be considered. A party of two or four climbers may be best in some circumstances because of the speed and efficiency of smaller rope teams and the limited space at bivouac sites. However, climbing with a very small team means that if one person becomes ill or cannot continue, the entire team may have to abandon the climb. Climbing parties of six or eight have the advantage of strength and reserve capacity: if one climber is unable to continue, some of the rest of the party still has a chance to go on with the expedition. Larger parties are also better able to carry out self-rescue than smaller teams. As the number of climbers increases, issues of transportation, food, lodging, equipment, and environmental impact can become more complicated.

PHYSICAL AND MENTAL CONDITIONING

Because expedition climbing requires significant commitment, it is important for each climber to start physical, mental, and technical conditioning many months before the trip. Remember that this may be the trip of a lifetime. You don't want to travel to the peak only to have your ability to reach the top cut short because you didn't prepare well enough for your climb.

Be in the best physical shape of your life. Emphasize both cardiovascular and strength training (see "Mountaineering Fitness Components" in Chapter 4, Physical Conditioning). Plans can be found online, and many guide companies will provide guidelines for physical conditioning. Work with an individualized training plan or personal trainer to complement your preparation for the climb. Conditioning for a major climb can be time consuming, requiring months of daily or twice daily sessions. Train for what the planned climb will require. Will you be hauling a sled? Will you be carrying heavy loads? Will you need excellent endurance as you move to high altitude? Make sure your conditioning plan prepares you for the type and style of climbing you will be doing. Climbers on a typical high-altitude expedition, for example, may need to be able to carry 40 to 100 pounds (18 to 45 kilograms)—sometimes in addition to pulling a sled—for an elevation gain of 2,000 to 3,000 feet (600 to 900 meters) every day, day after day.

"Soft skills" such as your ability to handle decision making under stress, your comfort with uncertainty, and your ability to communicate risk to climbing partners are also essential, and they need to be practiced and mastered. Have you met with and worked with your teammates? Have you learned to communicate effectively and work together as a team? It takes more than physical strength to deal with extreme cold, sickness, cramped quarters, poor food, conflict with teammates, the stress of technical climbing, and the lethargy brought on by high altitude. Preparing your attitude by practicing your flexibility and sense of humor is important. Do not underestimate the mental component of conditioning.

21

Additionally, dialing in your technical skills is essential to a successful climb. Are there techniques such as crevasse rescue with a sled that you need to master or practice more? Do you need to develop skills with fixed lines or technical ice?

Work on physical, mental, and technical conditioning by seeking out experiences that come as close as possible to what can be expected on the expedition. Prepare for the expedition by going on longer trips. If possible, do these as a team so you can learn to work together under physically and mentally stressful situations.

THE CLIMBING ITINERARY

Once climbers have researched their mountain, assembled a team, and begun their conditioning and training program, they must set up an itinerary that includes a good estimate of the number of days needed for the journey. Allow for the approach to the peak, carrying loads up the mountain, climbing, sitting out storms, and resting. An average elevation gain of 1,000 feet (300 meters) per day allows for acclimatization to high altitude, and this figure should be correlated, where possible, with good campsites. Rest days built into the schedule provide time for mental and physical recuperation, equipment sorting, and a time buffer for unplanned delays caused by storms, illness, or other problems. If a storm hits, try to adjust the itinerary to allow a rest period for the same time, making the best of a bad day. Many teams plan an estimated window for arriving at each camp, showing the first possible date of arrival at each camp and a last possible date of arrival at each camp. This allows for a flexible itinerary.

EMERGENCY PREPAREDNESS FOR EXPEDITIONS AND MULTIWEEK CLIMBS

Because expedition and multiweek climbs are more committing and often more remote, the team should consider taking additional measures to prepare themselves for emergencies. They should make a comprehensive emergency response plan that includes a list of emergency contacts for each team member, each team member's medical and insurance plan information, and relevant phone numbers for local contacts, rescue services, embassies, et cetera. The emergency response plan should be detailed, with clear objectives and information for each team member, as well as agency and contact information for the location.

Will the team carry a personal locator beacon (PLB) or other device to contact emergency help as recommended by the Ten Essentials? What will happen if the device is deployed? (For more about these devices and self-reliance, see Chapter 5, Navigation.) Do team members have insurance that covers travel abroad, helicopter evacuation, body recovery, and mountaineering and/or climbing accidents? In some countries, climbers must carry proof of insurance coverage or ability to pay before rescue services are deployed. Research the rescue services available and rescue protocol in the region or country you will be visiting.

A photocopy or scanned electronic copy of the team's emergency response plan should be left with a trusted individual at home. This person should understand the nature of the climb and have a clear directive from the team on when and how to engage in organizing rescue efforts. That individual will then have the information for all individuals on the team and be able to coordinate communication for the entire team.

GUIDED EXPEDITIONS

Guided climbs to just about any expedition destination are available. Climbers should consider hiring a guide if this is their first expedition, if they lack capable partners, or if the prospect of organizing such a major adventure is overwhelming. Using a guide on an expedition allows climbers to spend more time enjoying the experience and less time organizing it. They will be able to concentrate on mental and physical preparation. See the "Questions to Consider When Selecting a Guide Service" sidebar. Conversely, a guided climb costs more than a privately organized venture. Climbers lose control over the selection of party members and other decisions that may affect individual safety or prospects for the summit. Also, there may not be the same unity of purpose and team spirit that characterize the best expedition experiences.

QUESTIONS TO CONSIDER WHEN SELECTING A GUIDE SERVICE

- Is the guide service permitted, licensed, and insured as required by the governing authority of the destination?
- What is the safety record of the guide service?
- What are the qualifications of the guide and the other party members?
- What reputation does the guide service have among climbers? Personal references are very helpful.
- Does the guide service engage in socially responsible environmental, economic, and employment practices?

SUPPLIES

On expeditions to the remote mountains of the world, climbers either bring it with them or they do without it. Having the necessary equipment—and having it in working order—is critical. An expedition needs a complete equipment list, agreed upon by all team members, that includes both group and personal gear. See Table 21-1 later in this section.

Food

Food is the heaviest and arguably the most important supply carried on an expedition. Food provides the necessary fuel for your body to carry loads and climb the route. It can also serve as one of the great pleasures of the trip. Every climber has food preferences, so conduct a team survey of strong food likes and dislikes, as well as allergies, before planning menus.

Will you package and bring your food with you from home, will you buy food and supplies from local markets when you get to your climbing destination, or will you use a combination of these methods? Will you prepare and cook the food yourself, or will you work with a guide, cook, or other support staff? Will you eat all meals as a group or only some meals together, or will members of the team be responsible for all their own meals? Will you cook in a pot, or will all your meals be "boil in a bag"?

If you are working with a guide or cook, be sure to communicate dietary restrictions clearly. Find out what foods will be provided so that you know what foods you will need to bring to supplement the menu. Freeze-dried and other instant foods may not be available at local markets. The foods that you expect and enjoy may not be available in remote locations and other countries. Plan accordingly by being sure to bring these items with you, if needed.

When planning food weight for packing purposes, plan on roughly at least 35 ounces—about 2.5 pounds (1 kilogram)—of food per person per day, although this will vary depending on each climber's metabolism and body type. With no waste, 35 ounces of food would provide more than 5,000 calories. In reality—because of packaging, nonnutritive fiber, caloric density, and the food's irreducible water content—35 ounces of food will provide only about 3,900 calories per day. Most expedition climbers plan to provide roughly 4,000 to 5,000 calories of food per person per day. Experience will tell climbers whether this is just right, too much, or not enough. Too much food means carrying extra heavy loads between camps and possibly a slower trip. Too little means climbers will begin losing weight or have to abandon the climb. For advice on specific menus, see Chapter 3, Camping, Food, and Water; for a description of nutrition habits for climbers, whether in training or on the mountain, see "Fundamental Training Concepts" in Chapter 4, Physical Conditioning.

A condiment and seasoning kit with hot sauce, spices, soy sauce, butter, and mustard adds interest to bland packaged foods and perhaps will salvage inedible foods. As much as possible, try out foods ahead of time, preferably on training climbs with the team.

Early in the trip, foods can differ from those that will be eaten later. Foods for lower elevations and warmer climates during the approach can include those that are more time-consuming to prepare, such as pancakes; items that cannot withstand freezing, such as cheese and peanut butter; and some fresh items such as cabbage or carrots. Foods carried to higher altitudes should be very light and tasty and require minimum preparation, such as freeze-dried items, instant noodles, instant rice, and instant potatoes.

Packaging and organizing food is an important element of expedition planning. Measure and repackage food in appropriately sized portions—either each individual portion in a resealable plastic bag, or each meal-sized portion for the entire group (so much per person per day times the number of people) in a large resealable plastic bag—to get rid of unnecessary packaging. Label everything and keep the preparation instructions with the repackaged foods. Clear plastic bags help organize the food while keeping the contents visible.

Water

Contaminated water plagues nearly every part of the world. The expedition kitchen must be able to furnish adequate potable water for everyone through chemical decontamination, filtering, or boiling (see "Water Treatment" in Chapter 3, Camping, Food, and Water). Research your climbing destination's safe water practices to ascertain how safe the local water is in that area, and when in doubt, treat your water. Keep in mind that in some countries, water may need to be treated in cities and towns as well as in the backcountry and that viruses can be a much bigger concern outside North America and Europe.

Stove and Fuel

In places where you will be melting snow for water, your stove and fuel choices are a matter of life and death. In high-altitude regions, choose a stove that will work efficiently in that environment. (See "Stoves" in Chapter 3, Camping, Food, and Water.) Canister stoves, while lightweight, may not function as well in high-altitude regions.

21

TABLE 21-1. SAMPLE EXPEDITION EQUIPMENT LIST

This checklist includes the Ten Essentials, although they are not called out as such. Refer to Table 2-4 and Table 2-7 in Chapter 2, Clothing and Equipment for more information.

GROUP GEAR

SHELTER
- Expedition-quality tent(s)
- Snow stakes and/or tent flukes
- Sponge for tent condensation
- Snow shelter construction tools: large snow shovel (for moving a lot of snow), small snow shovel (for delicate trimming), snow saw (for cutting blocks)

KITCHEN
- Cook tent
- Stove gear: stove, windscreen and stove platform, fuel containers and fuel, matches and/or butane lighters
- Cooking gear: pots, pot cozy, pot gripper, sponge or scrubber, dipping cup, cooking spoon
- Snow sack (for collecting clean snow to melt for water)
- Spices and condiments
- Water treatment: filter, chemicals

GROUP MEALS
- Food

GROUP CLIMBING GEAR
- Ropes
- Hardware: snow and ice gear (pickets, ice screws), rock gear (pitons, cams, chocks), carabiners, runners, fixed line, extra climbing equipment (spare ice axe or tool, spare crampons, spare rescue pulleys)

REPAIR KIT
- Tent repair kit: pole splices, adhesive-backed repair cloth, seam repair compound
- Stove repair kit
- Crampon and ski repair kit: extra screws, connecting bars, straps

- Duct tape
- Multitool (with slotted and Phillips screwdrivers, small pliers, small wire cutter, shears, file)
- Sewing kit: assorted needles and thread, buckles, safety pins
- Flat webbing
- Other: wire, accessory cord, extra ski-pole basket, patch kit for inflatable foam pads

FIRST-AID KIT
Most expeditions carry a comprehensive group first-aid kit. In addition to normal first-aid items, the kit may include the following drugs, plus others recommended by a physician:
- Prescription drugs vary with the destination, but should include antibiotics, strong analgesics, antidiarrhetics, laxatives, and altitude medications (acetazolamide, dexamethasone)
- Nonprescription drugs vary with the destination, but should include cough suppressants, decongestants, and mild analgesics (aspirin, ibuprofen, acetaminophen)

OTHER GROUP GEAR
- Weather radio
- Altimeter, map, compass
- GPS device
- Whichever communication devices the expedition team prefers: Satellite phone, personal locator beacon (PLB), satellite communicator, two-way radios
- Battery packs
- Solar charger with appropriate cords
- Wands
- Latrine equipment

Multifuel stoves are good in regions where white gas is not readily available and function better at high altitudes. Even with a multifuel stove, check the fuel's compatibility with the stove before heading into the mountains. The cleanliness of fuel in some areas is questionable. If you are using liquid fuel, bring a fuel filter to filter all fuel before it is used, and bring a repair kit and tools for stove repair. Learn to take apart, clean, and troubleshoot repairs on your stove before the trip.

Typically, transporting any type of fuel on airplanes, trains, and buses is prohibited. Research the regulations for the party's specific transportation needs and destination well ahead of time. Make sure the needed fuel is available at the destination and bring the stove that works with that fuel.

If you are using liquid fuel, carry empty fuel containers compatible with your stove and fuel type. Fuel containers must be new or thoroughly cleaned and aired out before transporting, as airlines will object to containers with residual vapors. Consider the environmental impact of empty fuel container disposal and plan accordingly.

Bring sufficient stoves and fuel for any porters or other local individuals who will be part of the expedition.

PERSONAL GEAR

FOOD
- Personal dinners, lunches, snacks, etc.

CLOTHING
- Base layers (long underwear)
- Midlayers (down or synthetic)
- Shell layers: waterproof-breathable wind gear and raingear (top and bottom)
- Belay jacket
- Extremities: hands (liner gloves, insulating gloves, mittens), feet (liner socks, insulating socks), head (balaclava face mask, neck buff, sun hat, insulating hat)
- Double plastic or synthetic mountaineering boots
- Expedition gaiters and/or overboots
- Other: bandannas, sun shirt, synthetic fill or down booties

SLEEP SYSTEM
- Sleeping bag
- Bivy sack
- Inflatable foam pad, insulating air mattress, and/or closed-cell foam pad
- Earplugs

CLIMBING GEAR
- Helmet
- Ice axe
- Second ice tool
- Harness with personal anchor
- Chest harness
- Belay device
- Rescue pulley
- Ascenders and/or prusiks
- Nut tool
- Personal carabiners and slings
- Large-volume pack
- Crampons
- Snowshoes or skis with skins
- Sled with associated hardware for pulling and duffel bag

OTHER GEAR
- Ski poles and trekking poles
- Headlamp, extra batteries
- Avalanche transceiver
- Avalanche probe
- Watch with alarm
- Wide-mouth water bottles
- Sunglasses, spare sunglasses, goggles
- Insulated mug, bowl, spoon
- Spare prescription glasses
- Passport
- Personal hygiene: toilet paper, pee bottle, pee funnel, blue bags, toothbrush, toothpaste, floss, comb, chemical wipes and/or waterless skin cleanser, sunscreen, lip balm, foot powder, soap leaves
- Personal electronics: camera, e-reader, MP3 player and headphones, mini projector, phone

---

Adequate cooking equipment will help reduce the entire team's impact on the environment.

Calculate fuel needs before you go. Note that adverse factors such as wind, cold air, and altitude greatly increase boiling times and fuel needs. (For formulas and factors, see "How Much Fuel?" in Chapter 3, Camping, Food, and Water.) Clean the stove often while in the mountains, especially when using questionable fuel.

Group Gear

Some gear must be decided upon as a group.

Shelter. Decide beforehand as a team how many and what kinds of tents are best. If necessary, also decide ahead of time who will stay in what tent.

Kitchen. For communal cooking, take pots large enough for group meals and for melting large amounts of snow. Water bottles must be filled daily, so pots should be easy to pour from. Bring one cook pot per stove. Bring a metal gripper to use on pots that lack handles or bails, or use wool gloves as pot holders. Be careful using synthetic gloves, which will melt if they get too hot. Consider a stove platform or board, a heat exchanger, a windscreen, and/or pot cozies in cold climates to make your kitchen more efficient. Serving spoons and "dipping" cups may also be needed. Consider what type of lighters and stormproof matches are needed.

Repair kit. Be prepared for critical equipment failure under the prolonged and rugged demands of an expedition. Put together a comprehensive repair kit, keeping in mind the relative importance of each piece of equipment to the progress of the group (see Table 21-1).

First-aid kit. An expedition should assemble a comprehensive first-aid kit. Consider how isolated the peak is and the specifics of medical issues and diseases in that particular region or country. It is a good idea to make a pretrip appointment with a doctor who is a travel specialist or

21

familiar with mountaineering. Discuss the vaccinations and preventive care needed in the destination country and ask specifically for prescriptions for medications needed for your first-aid kit.

The first-aid kit may include such specialized or prescription items as altitude medications, strong painkillers, antibiotics, a dental repair kit, and a suture kit. (See "The Ten Essentials" in Chapter 2, Clothes and Equipment, as well as Chapter 24, First Aid.) Check on any restrictions or cautions regarding transporting drugs and medical equipment to a particular destination. Find out whether different climates or altitudes adversely affect medications that will be taken on the expedition.

Know the specific medical conditions of team members and their medical knowledge. Party members should prepare by obtaining wilderness first-aid training and understanding how the contents of a first-aid kit can be used.

Electronic and communication devices. Electronic gadgets can make expedition climbing safer and more enjoyable. Devices can be used to get weather information, call for emergency help, allow communication between climbers at different locations, and communicate with family and friends back home. They can also provide a welcome distraction when the weather keeps you trapped in a tent.

Technological devices are constantly changing, getting lighter, faster, and more versatile. Some of the current useful devices include: altimeter watches, GPS units, PLBs, et cetera. Every expedition team should strongly consider carrying devices that will allow them to ask emergency responders for help, should they need it. (See more on these tools in Chapters 2, Clothing and Equipment, and 5, Navigation.) Some devices combine features, acting as a two-way communication device, sending text messages and/or emails to friends and family, acting as GPS units, and/or posting GPS coordinates automatically to a blog or website. Investigate these options to determine both the technical feasibility of using them where the party will be traveling and whether local authorities require you to secure their permission. Many excellent choices in solar chargers and battery packs are available for charging various group and personal electronic gear.

Wands. Wands, which are used to mark routes, camp perimeters, gear caches, and snow shelters, are another group gear item. The number of wands needed varies according to the specifics of the climb, such as length, terrain, and route. (See "Wands" in Chapter 18, Glacier Travel and Crevasse Rescue.)

Climbing Gear

The route and the chosen climbing style determine what climbing gear is needed. A route that involves only glacier travel may require just the basics: rope, ice axe, crampons, and crevasse rescue gear. Technical routes can require the whole gamut of equipment, from ice screws and pickets to cams, nuts, and pitons. Depending on the climbing style and organization of the trip, climbing gear can be personal or communal—or a combination. Certain pieces of climbing gear, such as crampons and ice axes, are indispensable personal gear and a large party may want to carry spares.

Ropes. Deciding the type, length, and diameter of the ropes depends on the route and its difficulty. In addition, carefully consider the length and style of rope needed for self-rescue situations. Keep in mind that an expedition can put extraordinary wear and tear on ropes with daily use in bright sunlight and that it may be necessary to inspect and even retire these ropes. The team may need to decide how much static rope to bring for fixed lines along the route.

Ascenders. The cam of a mechanical ascender permits one-way movement, gripping or squeezing the rope when the ascender is pulled downward but freely sliding upward. Ascenders make it easier to ascend fixed lines, handle crevasse rescues, and haul heavy, bulky expedition loads. Expedition climbers may prefer ascenders over prusik slings, both for crevasse rescue and for self-belay while climbing with a fixed line—the extra weight may be justified by the greater utility. A climber may choose a pair of handled ascenders or one ascender (typically the nondominant-hand ascender) plus a prusik sling or a mini-ascender. Regardless of the choice, practice operating the system while wearing bulky gloves or mittens.

Personal Gear

Clothing. Expedition climbers need clothing that can stand up to prolonged use under severe conditions. The suggestions on clothing and equipment in the preceding chapters of this book (see Chapters 2, Clothing and Equipment; 16, Snow Travel and Climbing; and 19, Alpine Ice Climbing) are generally applicable to expeditions.

Sleeping bag. Take into account each sleeping system's comfort rating based on the anticipated climate, season, and altitude of the area the party will be visiting.

Other personal gear. Each climber will likely want some or all of the following:

- **Contact lenses.** Climbers who wear contact lenses should carry an extra set.

- **Prescription sunglasses.** Climbers who require prescription glasses should carry an extra set of prescription sunglasses as well.
- **Journal.** An expedition can make climbers introspective. A field journal made of waterproof paper, plus some pencils, helps pass the time.
- **E-readers.** Catch up on reading while waiting for flights or during rest days and storm days in the field. E Ink–style e-readers can perform better in cold conditions and are generally lighter than tablet e-readers.
- **Personal hygiene items.** During cold-weather trips where water is at a premium, chemical wipes and/or waterless skin cleansers can provide a refreshing sponge bath, and talcum powder can take the edge off the often strong odors that develop over the course of an expedition.
- **Pee bottle and pee funnel.** The pee bottle eliminates those unpleasant trips to the latrine during storms and cold nights. Be sure the bottle has a secure top, is clearly labeled, and is sturdy enough to withstand freezing and thawing. Women can use pee funnels in conjunction with a pee bottle. Practice in the shower at home before the expedition.

EXPEDITIONARY AND MULTIWEEK CLIMBING TECHNIQUES

Expedition mountaineering calls for the rock, snow, ice, alpine, and winter climbing techniques covered throughout this book. An expedition may also add some new techniques to the climber's repertoire: hauling sleds and using fixed lines.

SLED HAULING

To move loads of gear and supplies on long approaches, expedition members often pull sleds behind them (fig. 21-1). Climbers may carry a normal load in a backpack and pull a sled with another pack's worth of gear. Before the expedition, practice on various types of terrain.

A commercial haul sled features zippered covers to hold the load, a waist harness, and semirigid aluminum poles connecting the sled and harness. Commercial haul sleds are typically expensive and sometimes difficult to get, as few companies make them.

A cheaper and more common alternative to a commercial haul sled is a self-made haul sled using a children's plastic sled (fig. 21-2). Drill holes in the sides and attach grommets to the holes to protect the cord. Thread the holes with 4- to 5-millimeter accessory cord for use as rope attachment points and to secure loads. Since there is no zippered cover on a self-made sled, load gear into a duffel bag or haul bag and tie it to the sled. Use accessory cord to attach the front of the sled to a haul line and as an attachment for the back of the sled to the rope. A locking carabiner or pulley helps the sled to move over the snow better. Use 5- to 7-millimeter accessory cord or create poles from common materials (such as PVC pipe) to pull the sled. Most climbers find it more comfortable to attach the haul line or poles to their pack rather than to their climbing harness using two nonlocking carabiners. If using poles, the pole material should be flexible and climbers should consider adding a shock system to the pack or harness pole attachment with dynamic material. Finally, attach a locking carabiner to the back of the sled to use as a tie in for the rope as shown in Figure 21-1.

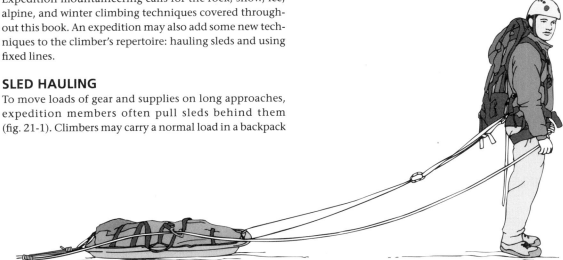

Fig. 21-1. Sled and climber rigged for glacier travel.

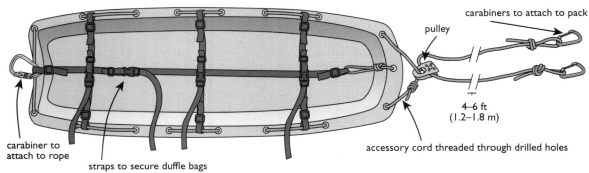

carabiners to attach to pack

pulley

4–6 ft
(1.2–1.8 m)

carabiner to
attach to rope

straps to secure duffle bags

accessory cord threaded through drilled holes

Fig. 21-2. Self-made haul sled and its components.

As the route steepens, the amount of weight that can be pulled in a sled decreases. Sleds cannot be used at all on steep, technical climbing terrain. Haul bags may then be what is needed (see "Hauling" in Chapter 15, Aid and Big Wall Climbing).

Hauling a sled can get complicated during roped travel on glaciers. A fall into a crevasse is more treacherous with a sled plunging down behind the fallen climber. Even if the plummeting sled does not injure the fallen climber, the sled's presence and added weight make rescue more difficult. Minimize the danger of getting hit by the sled during a crevasse fall by using this simple preventive technique: Where the climbing rope runs past the sled, tie it snugly with a clove hitch or prusik hitch to a carabiner attached to the rear of the sled (see Figure 21-2). If a duffel bag is strapped to the sled, be sure to clip the duffel bag to the rope as well.

In a crevasse fall, first the climber will drop into the crevasse, followed by the sled. The sled, however, will be stopped above the climber by the tie-in to the climbing rope (fig. 21-3). If the climber is using a hauling tether attached to the sled instead of semirigid poles, be sure the tether is long enough so that in case of a crevasse fall the climber will be well below the sled as it hangs from the climbing rope. If the climber is using semirigid poles to haul the sled, in a crevasse fall, the hauling poles may pull the climber toward the sled, so the climber may want to have a way to detach the sled from him- or herself while still having the sled tied in to the rope.

This technique depends on having a team member on the rope behind the fallen climber, to arrest the fall of both the climber and the sled. Therefore, it will not work for the

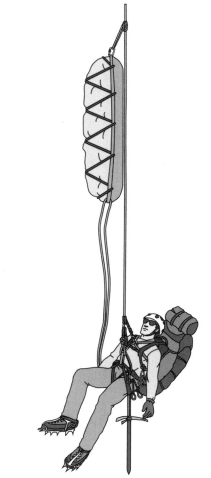

Fig. 21-3. A climber who has fallen into a crevasse, with a sled hanging overhead.

last climber on a rope. The last person either assumes the extra risk, or the team can decide to haul only two sleds for every three climbers on a three-person rope team.

Crevasse Rescue with a Sled

Crevasse rescue with a sled requires improvisation and problem solving beyond the techniques discussed in Chapter 18, Glacier Travel and Crevasse Rescue. It is not only essential that a climber completely understand standard crevasse rescue practices, it is also helpful to practice sled-hauling and sled-falling scenarios by dangling with a loaded sled off a rooftop or tree. As you dangle in the crevasse, your weight may be on the sled haul line, or the sled weight may be completely on you. This complicates crevasse rescue greatly.

First, attach yourself to the climbing rope with your ascending system (either mechanical ascenders or the Texas prusik system; see "Ascenders" in Chapter 18, Glacier Travel and Crevasse Rescue) if you are not already attached. Make sure you are attached and backed up by the climbing rope and that you stay attached to the system at all times.

Now you must get out of the pack-and-sled system. If a sled haul line is attached to your pack, carefully attach the pack to the climbing rope. If possible, take off the pack and let it hang below you from the climbing rope. If you are using a commercial haul sled with a waist harness, carefully tie the sled to the climbing rope and then get out of the waist-harness system, transferring the sled load onto the climbing rope. Take extreme caution in this step, as losing a pack or sled full of gear and supplies could be a serious matter.

Depending on the position of the sled, you may need to ascend around it. In this case, remove your ascenders, one at a time, and reattach them to the climbing rope above the knot securing the sled to the climbing rope. You may also need to untie from the climbing rope in order to move past the sled, as well as to reach the lip of the crevasse. To make it easier to disconnect from the climbing rope, some climbers travel with the rope clipped to two opposite and opposed locking carabiners on their harness, rather than tying the rope directly to the harness itself. If you need to untie from the climbing rope, use extreme caution to ensure that you are attached to the system and backed up at all times.

A fall into a crevasse with a sled can also mean extra effort for topside teammates if they must pull out the fallen climber and the sled. If the fallen climber cannot disconnect from the sled, or if no extra rescue rope is available, topside teammates must haul both climber and sled at the same time (see "Rescue Methods" in Chapter 18, Glacier Travel and Crevasse Rescue).

FIXED LINES

A fixed line is a rope that is anchored and left in place on the climbing route. It allows safe, quick travel up and down a difficult stretch. Climbers protect themselves by tying in to a mechanical ascender on the fixed line, eliminating the need for time-consuming belays. If a climber falls while climbing next to the fixed line, the ascender cam locks onto the fixed line to hold that person (see "Using Ascenders" and "Fixing Pitches" in Chapter 15, Aid and Big Wall Climbing).

The fixed line simplifies the movement of people and equipment, especially when numerous trips up and down the route are required. Fixed lines are common on large expeditions to major peaks in order to provide protection on long stretches of exposed climbing or to protect porters while they make carries from camp to camp. The lines make it possible for climbers and porters to carry heavier loads than they could safely carry without them. Fixed lines are sometimes used as a siege tactic on difficult rock and ice faces, with climbers retreating down the lines each night to a base camp and then ascending again the next day to push the route a little farther.

Fixed lines are often set by guiding companies for their clients to use. There is an unofficial agreement that all climbers can use all fixed lines set by any climbing party or guiding service. Exercise caution in deciding whether to make use of a fixed line already in place on a route. Elapsed time, exposure to weather, and the ice tools or crampons of climbers who used the line before your party may have damaged the rope. Fixed lines should not be used to supplement the climbing ability of an expedition team. Fixed lines should not be added on popular routes or in violation of the local climbing ethic.

Equipment for Fixed Lines

To set up and use fixed lines, the party needs rope, anchors, and ascenders. A static rope—that is, one with low elongation under load—is best because static ropes are designed to stretch less when weighted. The diameter of fixed lines usually varies between 7 and 10 millimeters. The ideal size depends on the terrain and the amount of use the line is expected to get. Fixed lines are usually longer than a normal climbing rope. They are usually manufactured in lengths ranging from 90 to 300 meters (300 to 1,000 feet), depending on diameter.

21

Setting Up Fixed Lines

A variety of methods can be used to set a fixed line, each appropriate for certain conditions, climber preferences, and types of line. The key is to think through the chosen system prior to starting out and, if possible, to test and refine it before it is actually needed. Here are three possible approaches:

- **The most common way** is for two or three climbers to ascend the route, using a standard climbing rope to belay one another or to establish a running belay, and to use a second static rope to set a fixed line as they climb. The climbers carry the entire spool of fixed line with them, letting it out as they ascend and tying it off at each intermediate anchor along the way.
- **Another option** is like the first, but rather than tying the rope off at each anchor along the way, climbers just clip the fixed line in to each intermediate anchor with carabiners instead. In this method, the climbers do not have to carry the spool but can trail just the end of the fixed line with them. At the top of the route, after anchoring the top of the fixed line, the climbers descend, tying off the fixed line at each intermediate anchor on the descent. It can be difficult to pull up on the end of the fixed line and overcome the tremendous friction that develops as the line travels through the carabiners and over the route.
- **A third method** is to set the fixed line entirely on the descent. This means, of course, that all of the material for the fixed line first must be carried to the top of the route. Tie the line in to a bombproof anchor at the top, then rappel or down-climb to tie the line off at intermediate anchors.

Anchoring Fixed Lines

Every fixed line must have an anchor at the bottom and a secure anchor at the top. To anchor the fixed line to the mountain, employ attachment points that are normally used in belaying and climbing on rock, snow, or ice: pitons, nuts, natural outcrops, ice screws, pickets, or deadman anchors. (See "Snow Anchors," in Chapter 16, Snow Travel and Climbing.) Mark the location of the bottom and top anchors with wands, making it easier to find them during or after a snowstorm.

Place a series of intermediate anchors between the bottom and top of the fixed line. These can be anchors that were placed on the earlier ascent of the route, although new ones may be added just for the fixed line. Tie off the fixed line at each anchor (intermediate as well as top and

bottom) so that every section of line is independent of the others. This permits more than one climber at a time on the line. Be sure that a fall by any climber would not cause rope movement, rockfall, or anything else that could endanger a team member.

To tie off the fixed line at each intermediate anchor, use a figure eight on a bight or clove hitch in the fixed line. Tie a sling directly to the anchor, and clip the figure-eight loop or clove hitch in to a carabiner attached to that sling (fig. 21-4a). To minimize the use of carabiners and have one less link in the system, tie the sling directly through the figure-eight loop or clove hitch (fig. 21-4b).

There are several considerations when deciding where to place anchors: Place them to change the direction of the line where necessary or to prevent pendulum falls. Placing an anchor at the top of a difficult section of the route is helpful. If possible, place the intermediate anchors at natural resting spots, making it easier for climbers to stand and move their ascenders past the anchors.

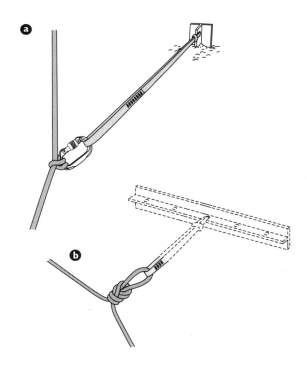

Fig. 21-4. Intermediate anchors on a fixed line: a, anchor with carabiner clove-hitched to fixed line; b, anchor without carabiner, using a sling tied through a figure eight on a bight of a fixed line.

Always bury or cover snow and ice anchors, and inspect them regularly for possible failure due to melting or moving out of place. Keep a close eye on any rock anchors capable of moving out of place or loosening. Place anchors at locations that will keep the line from rubbing on rough or sharp surfaces, or pad the line at points of abrasion. Even small amounts of wear can multiply into dangerous weak spots on fixed lines. Falls will also damage the line. After any fall on the line, inspect it for damage and check the anchors for indications of possible failure.

Ascending Fixed Lines

When ascending a fixed line, attach a sling to a mechanical ascender and place the ascender on the fixed line. Ascenders are camming units that slide freely in one direction and clamp down to hold in the other. Climbers typically use an ascender for their nondominant hand. Tie the sling to the harness where you normally tie in with the climbing rope, or clip the sling in to a locking carabiner attached to the harness. Make the sling long enough so that the ascender will not be out of reach if you fall. If you are climbing a near-vertical section or climbing with a heavy pack, you may choose to pass the sling through your chest harness as well to prevent tipping upside down in a fall.

Follow the specific directions for the brand of ascender you carry. The ascender should be oriented so that a fall will cause it to clamp the rope. It should slide easily up the line but lock tight when pulled down the line. Test it, and check the fittings on your harness, before starting upward.

Use a personal anchor (see "Personal Anchors" in Chapter 9, Basic Safety System), or a carabiner and sling attached to your harness, as a backup safety (fig. 21-5a). It might be preferable for the personal anchor to be above the ascender on upward travel so that the ascender will "push" the personal anchor along. If you fall and the ascender fails, your personal anchor will slide down the fixed line to the next anchor below and arrest the fall.

At each intermediate anchor, the climber must pass the knot or hitch in the fixed line. This is the most dangerous moment in fixed-line travel, particularly if conditions are severe and you are exhausted. It is best to move the safety carabiner first (fig. 21-5b). Unclip the carabiner, then reclip it above the intermediate anchor. Then move the ascender (fig. 21-5c). Another option is to briefly clip your personal anchor in to the intermediate anchor while relocating the ascender. Be sure that your personal anchor stays on the line when the ascender is detached. Think the procedure through in advance and practice it often so you can perform it reliably under the worst possible conditions.

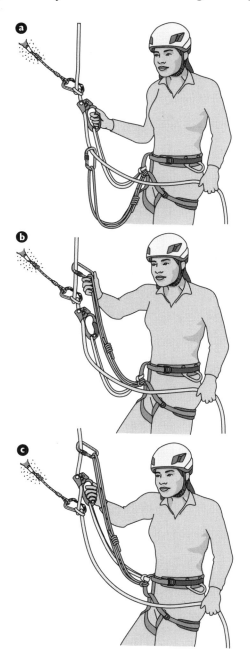

Fig. 21-5. Passing anchors while ascending a fixed line: a, set up for ascending, with carabiner-sling backup; b, move the safety carabiner above the knot first; c, then, move the ascender above the knot, but below the carabiner.

21

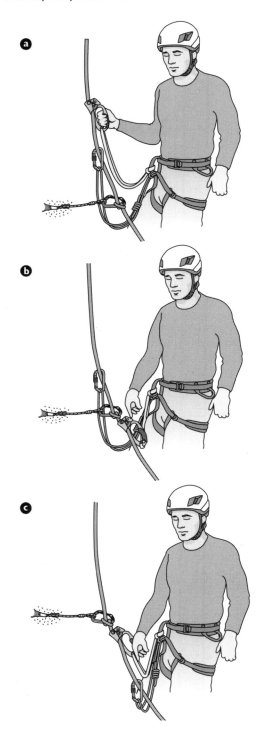

Descending Fixed Lines

Climbing down a fixed line is similar to climbing up. Attach the ascender sling to your harness. Attach the ascender to the fixed line in the same way as on the ascent. Double-check that the ascender locks onto the rope when you pull down on it and that it will be within reach if you end up hanging from it after a fall. Attach your personal anchor as a backup (fig. 21-6a).

Begin the descent using the fixed line as a hand line (see Figure 14-1 in Chapter 14, Leading on Rock) or an arm rappel (see Figure 11-23 in Chapter 11, Rappelling). While moving downward, slide the ascender down the rope by using a light grip on the ascender release. Let go of it instantly in a fall so the ascender will grab the rope. It is natural to try to hang on to something if you lose your balance, but be careful not to grab the ascender release.

As in the ascent, the most difficult part is moving past the intermediate anchors. Move the ascender (fig. 21-6b), then move the personal anchor (fig. 21-6c)—the opposite order from ascending a fixed line. Remember: Never detach the ascender and the personal anchor at the same time. Keep in mind that you can temporarily clip your personal anchor in to the intermediate anchor while relocating the ascender. On steep sections of fixed line, rappelling the fixed line may be a good alternative to down-climbing.

Passing on Fixed Lines

It can be dangerous for climbers to pass one another on a fixed line. However, if passing is necessary, it should be clearly communicated by the team passing to the team being passed, and it should be done at an anchor point. On popular routes with a fixed line intended for descent, ascending the descent line as a means of passing another ascending party should be considered only when the descent line is not currently being used by a descending party—and it should be considered as a means of passing only by small parties that can easily move aside if a team decides to use the fixed descent line to descend.

Removing Fixed Lines

Climbing rope and gear and anchor material of any type are not natural or biodegradable materials. They must be packed out. Teams are responsible for removing any fixed lines, gear, and anchor material that they have placed and

Fig. 21-6. Passing anchors while descending a fixed line: a, set up for descending, with carabiner-sling backup; b, move the ascender below the knot first; c, then, move the safety carabiner below the ascender.

then hauling them out. When setting them up, always bear in mind that they will need to be removed.

EXPEDITION WEATHER

On an expedition, climbers need to become talented amateur weather forecasters because their safety and success are so closely bound to nature's moods. When the party reaches the climbing area, talk to other climbers and to people who live there about local weather patterns. Find out the direction of the prevailing winds. Ask about rain and storms. On the mountain, make note of weather patterns.

The altimeter can serve as a barometer to signal weather changes. Take clues from the clouds. Cirrus clouds warn of a front bringing precipitation within the next 24 hours. Lenticular clouds (cloud caps) mean high winds. A rapidly descending cloud cap is a sign that bad weather is coming. If the party climbs into a cloud cap, expect high winds and poor visibility. (See Chapter 28, Mountain Weather, for more about weather.) Be prepared for the fact that big mountains typically have big storms, strong winds, and rapidly changing weather.

Wait out a storm, if possible, or consider descending before the weather gets too severe. There is risk inherent in descending under bad conditions. If the party expects to be stuck for some time, consider food and fuel cache locations and whether a storm would affect your access to them.

Fair weather poses problems too. If it is hot and sunny, glaciers intensify solar radiation. The result can be collapsing snow bridges, moving crevasses, and increased icefall. In such conditions, it is best to climb at night, when temperatures are lowest and snow and ice are most stable.

HIGH-ALTITUDE HEALTH HAZARDS

Inadequate levels of oxygen, extreme cold, and dehydration, among other things, are all potential health hazards that are intensified by high-altitude conditions. Learn to recognize, prevent, and treat potential health hazards when they occur (see "High-Altitude Conditions" in Chapter 24, First Aid). Consult a physician familiar with mountaineering for detailed information and prescriptions for preventive altitude medications.

On high peaks, temperatures drop well below zero. Although this is good for keeping snow stable, it can have a detrimental effect on a climber's body. Everyone in the expedition party must be aware of the dangers of frostbite, as well as windburn and sunburn.

Expedition climbing, like any mountaineering, takes climbers to altitudes where the human body no longer feels at home. Every climber is affected to varying degrees by reduced oxygen at higher elevations, sometimes leading to acute mountain sickness (AMS; altitude sickness). This can lead to the life-threatening conditions of high-altitude pulmonary edema (HAPE) and high-altitude cerebral edema (HACE). These illnesses are generally avoidable, through proper acclimatization and hydration.

ACCLIMATIZATION

The best way to combat altitude illness is to prevent it in the first place. The best way to do this is to ascend slowly. The human body needs time to acclimatize to higher altitude. (See Chapter 24, First Aid and "Planning and Preparation," earlier in this chapter.)

In high-altitude expedition-style climbing, carry loads to a highcamp and return to lower altitude to recover. Then ascend again the following day. Ascend at a moderate rate, averaging 1,000 feet (300 meters) a day in net elevation gain. For example, if suitable campsites are 3,000 feet (900 meters) apart, carry loads to the next campsite (a 3,000-foot gain) on one day. Descend back to camp for the night, carry the rest of your gear and tents up to the next site the next day, and rest at the new camp the third day, for a net gain of 3,000 feet every three days. Try not to push your limits until you have become well acclimatized. Schedule rest days after big pushes.

High-altitude alpine-style climbers may spend time at a base camp, ascending the intended route farther and farther each day before returning to base camp each night.

Above 18,000 feet (5,400 meters), most people begin to deteriorate physically regardless of acclimatization. Minimize time at high altitudes, and periodically return to lower altitudes to recover. The old advice is still good: climb high, sleep low. The body recovers more quickly at a lower altitude and acclimatizes faster during exertion than during rest. Active rest days when climbers build snow walls, hike to lookouts, or practice skills can help with acclimatization.

HYDRATION

Hydration is critical in avoiding altitude illness (see "Dehydration" in Chapter 24, First Aid). Everyone should drink 5 to 7 quarts or liters of water a day and avoid alcohol and caffeine, which have a dehydrating effect. On many routes, this may mean that several hours each day must be dedicated to melting snow. This is time well spent, however, because adequate hydration is important to the success of an expedition.

21

In addition to using the above recommendations for daily liquid intake, monitor urine output and color. Urine should be copious and clear. Dark urine indicates that a climber is not drinking enough water.

Climbers usually lose their appetite at high altitudes. Everyone tends to eat and drink less than they should. Consider various hot drinks—teas, hot cocoa, hot electrolyte drinks—to supplement water and calorie intake.

UPHOLDING AN EXPEDITION PHILOSOPHY

Members of an expedition need a common code to live by during their weeks of traveling and climbing together. One reliable code can be summed up in three promises that you and your teammates can make to one another: respect the land, take care of yourselves, and come home again.

Respect the land. Every day, the expedition party has the chance to put the health and beauty of the land ahead of its own immediate comfort. The easy way out might be to burn wood fires, set up camp in a virgin meadow, or leave garbage and human waste on the ground. But if all the climbers have promised to respect the land, they will be aware of their impact and be responsible. Leave no trace.

Those who follow your trail will not want to see the wrappers from your snacks or other signs that your group passed through the area. If you pack it in, pack it out. Be sensitive to local customs. Local land managers may have specific wishes about the treatment of their areas. Learn what their expectations are ahead of time and be respectful. If local practices are more relaxed than Leave No Trace techniques, however, do not follow local customs; instead, follow Leave No Trace practices.

Take care of yourselves. If you and your climbing partners have promised to take care of yourselves, you have made a commitment to group self-reliance. There may be no choice in the matter, because the party will likely be a long way from rescuers, helicopters, hospitals, or even other climbers. Prepare by thinking through the possible emergencies that the party could face and by making plans for responding to those. You will feel reassured that plans are ready if you have to use them and grateful if you do not.

In addition, foster team spirit by checking on one another throughout the day regarding adequate fluid intake, use of sunscreen, and other necessities that will keep team members healthy and in good spirits. After all, as the late renowned climber Alex Lowe said, "The best climber in the world is the one having the most fun!"

Come home again. The third promise might be the hardest to keep, because it can conflict with that burning desire for the summit. It is really a promise to climb safely and to be willing to sacrifice dreams of the summit in favor of survival. Expedition climbing is, all things considered, about pushing limits and testing yourself both physically and mentally.

Each person and each team must decide what level of risk they are willing to accept. Keep the third promise by being sure that the team agrees upon what is safe and what is unsafe. Out of that discussion, decisions flow daily regarding how fast to ascend, what gear to carry, when to change routes, and when to retreat.

Most climbers would rather return home safely than push for the summit under unsafe conditions. Having the freedom of the hills does not just mean reaching the summit; the success of an expedition can be measured in many ways.

PART V

LEADERSHIP, SAFETY, AND RESCUE

CHAPTER 22
LEADERSHIP

Just as every climbing party needs steadfast navigation tools, every climb needs good leadership—but the style and form of that guidance varies with the venture. It is one thing to head out with some longtime climbing companions for a sunny weekend of peak bagging, but it is entirely another to mount an extended technical climb with mountaineers who do not know one another to a peak none of them has ever seen.

Climbers who know each other well achieve good leadership very informally, probably without even knowing it. Climbers less familiar with one another require a more formal, structured organization. In both cases, leadership provides the same things: a way to put a climb together and make it a safe and enjoyable experience. As Chinese philosopher Lao-tzu wrote, "Fail to honor people, they fail to honor you. But of a good leader, who talks little, when his work is done, his aim fulfilled, they will say, 'We did this ourselves.'"

THE CLIMB LEADER

A climb leader is someone who has special responsibility for organizing the climb and for making decisions en route. Depending on the nature of the party, the degree of formal organization may vary from highly structured to virtually nonexistent. Nevertheless, certain necessary functions of the group are performed one way or another.

Small, informal parties made up of friends often do not select a leader. Everyone feels responsible for organizing, sharing work, and team building. Communication is good enough that each member knows what the others are doing, so coordination is not much of an issue. The climb organizer or most experienced party member may be tacitly recognized as leader of such a group.

Large groups do better with a designated leader. Members of the climbing party cannot know what every other person is doing, so someone needs to be chief organizer if only to make sure no critical details are overlooked. Large groups may also need more focus on team building, because it is likely that the members will not all know one another.

The leadership structure of most climbing parties tends to fit into one of the following categories.

Peers. A group of acquaintances that decide to go climbing together are peers. Usually there is no designated leader, but members informally allocate key functions. Most decisions are made by consensus. Even in this least formal type of organization, one member will usually emerge as "first among equals" and be regarded as leader. It will be the person who displays initiative, good judgment, and concern for the group and who generally inspires the most confidence.

Climb organizer. The person who organizes the climb is the one who has the original idea for the venture and then recruits others. The organizer is usually recognized as the de facto leader, even if the position is never formalized.

Most experienced. A group tends to bestow leadership upon, and to defer to the judgment of, a climber who is clearly the most experienced in the party.

Climbing clubs and schools. Leadership is formally conferred by the sponsoring group when a climb is part of an organized program. Often, leaders must go through an accreditation process to ensure a certain level of experience and competence. There may even be a hierarchy among the leadership, with an overall leader and assistant instructors to help. There is no doubt who is the leader, and it is not up to the party to select one. The leader is expected to organize the climb and to take charge of equipment, transportation, and other logistical matters. Such climbs are often teaching situations; students are expected to follow the leader's guidance, but they are also supposed to be learning and gaining self-sufficiency.

Guided climbs. Climbers pay guide services to provide competent leadership. Professional guides are often outstanding climbers and are completely in charge of their groups. Guides make the decisions for their clients and assume responsibility for their safety.

ROLES OF THE LEADER

The leader's role is to help the party achieve the team's objectives in a safe, enjoyable manner, with minimum impact on the alpine environment. A leader must be experienced, with technical skills appropriate for the climb, but is not necessarily the most experienced in the group or the best climber. A leader should be in good enough shape to keep up, but need not be the strongest in the party. A leader does need an abundance of good judgment, common sense, and a sincere interest in the welfare of the entire party. Along the way, a leader simultaneously adopts many roles, such as the following:

Guardian of safety. The paramount concern of any party is safety. Starting in the planning stage, a leader should ensure that everyone has appropriate equipment, experience, and stamina and that the route chosen is reasonable for the party and in safe condition. En route, when climbers become tired, impatient, or excited, they get careless. A leader learns to see these conditions as warnings and becomes more alert, watching, gently reminding, and even nagging when necessary. When tough decisions have to be made, such as turning back due to weather changes or time constraints, it is often up to the leader to initiate the unpleasant discussion before the situation becomes critical. (See Chapter 23, Safety.)

Anticipator. Leaders avoid trouble by anticipating it. Leaders should always be thinking ahead. In camp, they think of the climb; on the ascent, of the descent; on the descent, of the trip out. They look for early signs of fatigue in companions; mentally catalog bivouac sites and water sources; keep track of the time and progress; and note any changes in weather. By staying a step ahead they avoid problems or catch burgeoning ones before they become crises.

Planner. Many details need attention if a group of people is to be at the right place at the right time with the right equipment to mount a successful summit attempt. A leader does not have to do all the planning personally, but he or she does bear responsibility for seeing that all necessary preparations are being attended to by someone in the group.

Expert. Giving advice when asked or when needed is an important leadership role. Training, experience, and judgment are the prerequisites for this role. A person does not have to be the party's best climber to be an effective leader but certainly needs enough experience to have developed "mountain sense." A range of skills is needed in addition to technical climbing knowledge. Leaders should know a lot about equipment, navigation, first aid, rescue techniques, weather—in fact, all the topics addressed in the various chapters of this book.

Teacher. When less-experienced climbers are along, teaching becomes part of the leadership role. Usually this involves nothing more than occasional advice and demonstrations. However, if some members lack techniques required for safe progress, it may be wise to halt and conduct a little hands-on learning right then and there, a teaching moment. Many seasoned mountaineers find that passing along their hard-won knowledge is a fulfilling experience—but it should be done with a careful touch. Novices may be embarrassed by their relative lack of skill or intimidated by the physical danger. There is no justification for browbeating. Instead of using the approach that says someone else is wrong, try saying, "Let me show you what works for me." The exception is when a student is doing something dangerous; then a more direct approach is needed.

Coach. This is a little different from the role of teacher. The coach helps people get past difficulties by adding encouragement and support to a base of knowledge. Often the real obstacle is lack of self-confidence. Assisting a companion through some difficulty helps that person and also keeps the entire party moving forward. Coaching effectively, helping people do their best and emerge smiling, can be one of the particular delights of leadership.

Initiator. A climb progresses by the party making a series of decisions: Where shall we make camp? Which route should we take? What time should we get up? When should we rope up? Often the decisions themselves are not hard to make, but they need to be made in a timely fashion. The function of leadership is not necessarily to

22

dictate answers but to get the right issues on the table at the appropriate time.

Arbiter. Once a discussion is under way, differences of opinion will arise. It is good to collect opinions and get all viewpoints out into the open, but this can lead to indecision ("Which course do we select?") or argument ("You are wrong!"). Anyone in a position of leadership, whether or not it was formally conferred, has some leverage that can be used to advantage in these instances. If the party seems to be making a technically incorrect or dangerous decision, if tempers are rising, or if the discussion is aimlessly wandering, the weight of the leader's opinion will often settle matters and get the climb moving again.

Guardian of the environment. Climbers must do their best to leave the alpine environment undisturbed so that future generations may sample the same pleasures. Leaders should set the example by always practicing minimum-impact techniques (see Chapters 3, Camping, Food, and Water and 7, Leave No Trace). If others fail to follow this example, they should be reminded, gently at first, insistently if necessary.

Delegator. A leader's responsibility is to get things done, but not necessarily to do them. Delegating tasks has a host of benefits. It allows the leader to maintain an overview of the entire trip, rather than being tied down by every little problem and decision. It builds team spirit by giving people a chance to get involved and be useful. Also, delegation fosters individual responsibility by clearly demonstrating that doing and deciding are not the tasks of the leader alone. If someone is having difficulty and needs special help, a strong, experienced climber might be delegated the role of personal coach. In a larger group, especially in a teaching situation, the leader should appoint an assistant who can help keep things moving and who can take over if the leader is incapacitated.

STYLES OF LEADERSHIP

Two broad categories characterize the style in which leaders perform their roles. Also see the "Tips for Becoming a Leader" sidebar.

Authoritative style. A goal-oriented leadership style has to do with process and structure—what to do, who will do it, and how they will do it. Goal-oriented leaders concentrate on making decisions and directing others.

Relationship-oriented style. A relationship-oriented leadership style has to do with showing consideration and helping a group of people become a supportive, cooperative team. Relationship-oriented leaders take a personal interest in people and their views, consulting with

them on decisions and thereby building group cohesion and morale.

Most people lean toward one style or the other, but it is not an either-or choice. Neither style should be neglected, and effective leaders balance both styles. The proper balance depends on the nature of the party and the needs of the moment.

Each leader must develop a personal style through the process of learning the craft of mountaineering and discovering effective ways of relating to climbing companions to help them become a happy, effective team. Beyond that, leaders should be themselves. Some people are jolly and talkative; some are more reserved. Successful leaders are found among all types of people. It is more important to be genuine than to try copying some idealized style.

LEADING IN A CRISIS

Everyone hopes it will never happen, but sometimes things go wrong. Perhaps conditions turn dangerous or someone is injured. Then the group focus shifts from recreation to safety and survival. The leader's role also changes. If the group has a designated leader, this is the time for that person to switch to an authoritative style. A small, informal group may find that a leader emerges. When a clear need for coordination arises, people tend to look to the most experienced person or the one who, for whatever reason, inspires the most confidence.

When an accident occurs, there may not be time for lengthy debate. Prompt, effective action is needed, and it should be directed by someone with training and experience. Nevertheless, the leader should stay hands-off as much as possible, instead directing others, maintaining an overview, and thinking ahead to the next steps. The safety of the rescuers comes first—even before that of the victim. Act promptly, but deliberately and calmly. Use procedures that have been learned and practiced; this is no time to experiment.

The outcome of an accident is usually determined by factors beyond the climbers' control. The climb leader will draw upon training and experience to devise an appropriate plan and then carry it out as safely and effectively as conditions permit.

Accidents are unexpected, but climbers can prepare for them by taking courses, reading on the subject, and mentally rehearsing accident scenarios. Take note of the information in Chapters 23, Safety, and 25, Alpine Rescue. First-aid training is a must. Chapter 24, First Aid, describes the prevention and treatment of medical conditions commonly experienced by mountaineers, but it is not a substitute for hands-on training. Public and private agencies offer wilderness-oriented first-aid courses, and some climbing clubs offer mountain-oriented rescue training.

ORGANIZING AND LEADING A CLIMB

Even a simple climb can be a complex undertaking. Once an objective is chosen, the leader has many tasks to complete before the climb. On the way to the trailhead and at the trailhead, last-minute checks and updates keep the outing organized. During the approach, the climb, the descent, and the way out, the leader helps keep the party organized until the outing is over. The checklist in Table 22-1 is a useful guide to this process.

The Ten Essentials are described in detail in Chapter 2, Clothing and Equipment. This section introduces two additional systems approaches for leaders: Nine Planning and Preparing Steps and Eleven Trip Checks. Using the 9-10-11 systems together helps improve the odds for a successful trip (Table 22-1).

BEFORE THE CLIMB: NINE PLANNING AND PREPARING STEPS

Once an objective is chosen, the leader needs to gather information on the approach and the climbing route itself. The leader must also select the party, decide what equipment is needed and who will bring it, make a schedule that includes enough time to complete the climb with a safety margin for contingencies, and coordinate transportation to the trailhead. And in the days leading up to the climb,

---

NINE PLANNING AND PREPARING STEPS

Before the climb:

1. Leadership
2. Research
3. Planning
4. Safety Margin
5. Equipment
6. Party
7. Weather
8. Communications
9. Evaluation

---

the leader will be monitoring weather trends (and snow conditions, if applicable). The Nine Planning and Preparing Steps help guide a leader through the process (see the sidebar).

Leadership

A leader must be capable and qualified. There may be a need for a competent assistant (or two) to whom tasks can be delegated and with whom the leader can consult on key decisions. Each rope team with inexperienced climbers needs a rope leader.

Research

Typically, climbers research the trip so they will know what to expect and can prepare accordingly. Guidebooks are available covering most popular climbing areas with written descriptions of approaches and routes, maps, drawings, and sometimes photos. Topographic maps are invaluable. Check road and trail conditions for the approach as well.

Some climbing clubs keep files of trip reports from their outings; these can be valuable both in themselves and because they often give the names of those who went on the climb. Firsthand experience from someone who has recently done the route can add significantly to data found in guidebooks. For peaks on public land, government agencies such as the National Park Service and US Forest Service can be good sources of information. For a full discussion of researching a route, see "Gather Route Information" in Chapter 6, Wilderness Travel.

Permit, registration, and recreational fee requirements vary greatly from region to region. Many publicly owned parks, forests, and wilderness areas have some form of governmental regulation. Some may limit where the party can camp, which can affect the logistics of a climb. Typically,

22

TABLE 22-1. CHECKLISTS FOR ORGANIZING AND LEADING A CLIMB

BEFORE THE CLIMB: NINE PLANNING AND PREPARING STEPS

1. Leadership
- Choose a leader.

2. Research
- Driving route: check to be sure backcountry roads are open.
- Hiking route: check trail conditions.
- Climbing route: review guidebooks and maps.
- Study trip reports.
- Determine the technical level and any special problems of the route.
- Determine whether wilderness permits or reservations are required.

3. Planning
- Estimate miles and/or hours of driving.
- Estimate miles and/or hours of hiking to high camp or start of climb.
- Estimate hours to summit.
- Estimate hours back to cars.
- Select maps.
- Set compass declination.
- Set GPS datum to match maps.
- Download any waypoints or route information to GPS device, tablet, or phone, as applicable.
- Leave trip itinerary with a responsible person.

4. Safety Margin
- Develop contingency options.
- Have "a little extra" for the unexpected.

5. Equipment
- Determine equipment needs and make arrangements for sharing equipment as needed.
- Personal equipment: Ten Essentials, food, camping equipment, and climbing gear.
- Group equipment: tents, stoves, cookware, ropes, water treatment, and climbing hardware.

6. Party
- Estimate the levels of climbing skill and physical condition required.
- Determine party size.

7. Weather
- Look into current route conditions, the weather forecast, and shifts in the weather window.
- Understand how a change in weather will affect the route and the party's objectives.
- Look into a poor-weather-alternative trip.
- Consider a NOAA weather radio or other means for updated forecasts.

8. Communications
- Bring a PLB or other emergency communication device.
- Consider walkie-talkie two-way radioes.

9. Evaluation
- Critique the entirety of the planning effort.
- Does the plan add up favorably?
- Are there areas of weakness in the trip plan?
- Can the plan be improved?

UNDER WAY: ELEVEN TRIP CHECKS

1. Trailhead
- Register with park or forest agencies if required.
- Make sure everyone has enough food and equipment.
- Take an inventory of group equipment, including tents, stoves, water treatment, ropes, and hardware.
- Distribute group equipment to equalize loads.
- Share an overview of the plan: route, campsite, day's schedule, hazards.

2. Navigation
- Orient early to the map rather than waiting until there is a concern. Set altimeters at a place where you are certain of your elevation, often at trailhead but perhaps at a junction.
- Check occasionally to ensure the party is on route.
- Note important route decision points.
- Create GPS waypoints and tracks helpful for returning in the dark or if visibility declines.

3. People
- Monitor party members for problems.
- Make sure that everyone is eating and drinking.
- Avoid letting anyone lag.

4. Time
- Start early—daylight is invaluable when dealing with the unexpected.
- Optimize the location, timing, and duration of breaks.
- Monitor progress to turnaround time.

5. Hazards
- Watch for anticipated hazards.
- Stay alert for unexpected hazards.
- Where hazards cannot be avoided, find a safe alternative, mitigate their outcome, or turn around.

6. Weather and Environment
- Watch for, and adjust to, adverse changes in weather and route hazards.

7. Perspective
- Stay alert to the big picture. Avoid fixating on a particular aspect of the trip to the detriment of others.
- Think ahead; anticipate.
- Try to catch problems early, when options for dealing with them are most numerous.
- Use the traffic-stoplight analogy to summarize concerns: green (OK), yellow (caution), red (danger; changes are mandatory).

8. Decisions
- Make clear-headed decisions.
- Guard against risk assessment and decision-making biases.
- Make decisions that maintain safety margins.
- Never let judgment be overruled by desire when you are choosing the route or deciding whether to turn back.
- Consider several solutions to a problem, and then choose the best alternative.
- Obey the leader or decisions made by majority rule.

9. Safety
- A leader's primary goal for any outing is to have the whole party return home safely.
- Practice well-reputed climbing techniques.
- Never climb beyond the party's ability and knowledge.

- Rope up on exposed places and glaciers. Have at least two rope teams on a glacier.
- Anchor all belays.
- Redundancy increases the safety of belay and rappel anchors as well as other important systems.
- Where hazards cannot be avoided or mitigated: consider an alternative, or turn around.

10. Team
- On the approach and on the climb, set a pace that is steady and maintainable, not necessarily fast.
- Take rest stops for the whole party.
- Keep the party reasonably together. Agree to regroup at specified times or places—especially at trail junctions.
- Keep rope teams close enough to be in communication with each other.
- Assign a responsible person to "trail sweep" and bring up the rear.
- Be sure that no one leaves the trailhead until everyone is back and all cars have been started.
- Consider a group meal on the trip home as an opportunity to review the trip.

11. Leadership
- Practice sound leadership techniques.
- Look for teaching moments: opportunities that impart knowledge, involve the party, and continue climbers' development.

regulations are designed to preserve the ecology of an area or to increase the value of the wilderness experience. Some are created for the safety of visitors; others are in place to gather fees to maintain an area's infrastructure and support recreation.

Planning

Develop a trip itinerary and manage time spent en route with a trip plan. Time has to be carefully rationed on a climb, and the important thing is not how fast to go but how wisely to use the time the party has.

Establish a schedule before the climb. Estimate the length of each segment—driving time, approach time, ascent time, descent and/or return time—and allow some extra time for the unexpected. A typical estimate might be what is shown in Table 22-2.

In the estimate shown in Table 22-2, if it gets dark at 9:00 p.m. and the climbers want to be back at the trailhead by then, they must start at 6:30 a.m.

Setting a turnaround time is a good practice. In the example just given, the party estimates four and a half hours from summit to trailhead for the descent, with no margin for the unexpected. With an hour for unexpected delays, they might decide it is reasonable to allow five and a half hours. This means they must start descending by 3:30 p.m. or risk walking out in the dark. If the party is moving slowly, another good practice is to start a candid assessment of progress hours before the turnaround time.

Most guidebooks give times for popular climbs and sometimes for the approaches as well. Keep in mind, though, that times vary greatly from party to party. Also, the times may not include breaks. Experience with a particular guidebook will indicate whether its estimates tend to be faster or slower than your personal times; adjust accordingly. Another good source for time estimates is someone who has done the climb.

If no information is available, use rules of thumb based on experience. For example, many climbers have found

22

TABLE 22-2. ESTIMATING TRIP TIME

TRIP SEGMENT	ESTIMATED TIME
Drive to trailhead	2.0 hours
Hike up the trail	2.0 hours
Cross-country approach	1.0 hour
The climb itself	4.0 hours
Descent	2.0 hours
Return to the trail	1.0 hour
Hike out	1.5 hours
Total time estimate	**13.5 hours**
Contingencies	1.0 hour
Total time allowance	**14.5 hours**

that they can average 2 miles (3-plus kilometers) per hour on an easy trail and 1,000 vertical feet (300 vertical meters) per hour on a nontechnical approach with light packs. Be realistic when estimating how long the climb will take.

Prepare and share with party members the overall trip plan, route, participants, equipment, assignments, meeting times, and other pertinent information to ensure all have the same expectations and understandings.

When developing a trip plan, include the following for each party member: name, emergency contact, and contact information. Leave a copy of the trip plan with a responsible person at home, specifying when the party expects to return and how long the person should wait before notifying authorities if the party is overdue. Specify which authorities are to be notified if the party is overdue. For example, in the United States, the National Park Service has responsibility for mountain rescue in national parks; in most other areas of the western United States, it is the county sheriff.

Avoid scheduling important business meetings, airplane flights, or social events for several hours after the scheduled end of a trip. Climbs frequently take significantly longer than expected.

Safety Margin

Plan for self-reliance and develop contingency options. When should climb organizers allow themselves to feel that their preparation is adequate? When is it enough? A good way to gauge is to ask whether the party has the people, proficiency, and equipment it needs to be self-reliant under normal circumstances.

Have "a little extra." It is common for climbs to run over their prescribed schedule. Any climbing party should be prepared to take care of itself in case of slowness, navigation errors, route conditions, a mishap, or a downturn in the weather. In practice, this means having "a little extra" to provide a margin of safety: extra time, extra clothing, extra food, extra flashlight batteries, extra climbing hardware, and, above all, extra reserves of strength. As a general rule, climbers should plan to be self-sufficient for several hours in excess of the planned trip and understand that it may take that long to return to the trailhead. Balancing the benefit of extra supplies against the drag of their weight is an art every mountaineer must develop.

Equipment

The party needs to make decisions about equipment, both personal and shared. Personal equipment is what each climber must bring: ice axe, helmet, and harness, for example, in addition to the Ten Essentials (see "The Ten Essentials" in Chapter 2, Clothing and Equipment). Many personal items, such as harnesses, ice axes, crampons, and avalanche transceivers, are useful only if everybody brings them, so coordination is essential.

Group equipment is shared: tents, stoves and pots, food, ropes, rock and snow protection, snow shovels, some navigation and communication tools, GPS devices, and personal locator beacons (PLBs) are examples. Someone should determine what is needed, survey the climbers to see who owns what, and then decide who will bring which items. (See Chapter 21, Expedition Climbing, for more on personal and group gear.)

The party can give itself a margin of safety by planning to arrive at the trailhead with a little extra equipment for conditions more severe than anticipated during planning or in case someone forgets an item or fails to show up. If the party does not need the surplus gear, stash it out of view in vehicles.

Party

A climbing party must have adequate strength in order to have a safe, enjoyable, and successful trip. Strength refers to the group's ability to accomplish the climb and to cope with situations that may arise. The party's strength is determined by the mountaineering proficiency of the members, their physical condition, the size of the party, and their equipment. Intangibles such as morale, the members' degree of commitment to the climb, and the quality of leadership also affect party strength.

A strong party consists of several experienced, proficient climbers who are in good condition and well equipped. What constitutes weakness is not as easy to define because a party is strong or weak only in relation to its goals. On a very challenging climb, the addition of a single ineffective member would make a party too weak. On easier trips, a party may be strong enough if it has only two strong climbers and several weaker ones; in fact, this is common on guided climbs. A party with no experienced members is weak in any situation.

Researching the route helps determine what party strength is needed for a particular climb. Is the route or the approach physically arduous? What level of technical challenge, routefinding, or decision making does it pose? Is the place so remote that the party will be completely reliant on its own resources, or are there likely to be other people in the vicinity?

Who should go? Every member of a climbing party must be up to the challenge, both physically and technically. Some climbers will go with only proven companions when they are attempting routes near the limit of their abilities. When a leader is considering inclusion of a climber whom the leader does not know, some questions should be asked.

Experience is the surest indicator of ability; someone who has climbed several times at a given level is probably capable of doing so again. Climbing skills should match the chosen route's requirements. For instance, experience gained from an indoor climbing gym will not translate to an alpine environment. Expedition leaders sometimes even request written résumés, but for a weekend climb, a bit of probing conversation is probably enough to ascertain a person's fitness. However, leaders should be aware that inexperienced people probably do not realize they are unprepared for the planned climb.

A party that includes novices, or even experienced people who have never before climbed at the route's required level of skill, will need to include veteran climbers who are willing and able to rope lead and coach. The climb almost surely will take longer, and the chance of success will be reduced. Be sure everyone in the party understands this situation and accepts it.

A leader must also consider *compatibility* when forming a climbing party, especially for a long or arduous trip. Fortunately, most people seem to be on good behavior while they are on climbs. The unspoken knowledge that climbing companions will soon be literally holding one another's lives in their hands does much to promote accommodation. Nevertheless, expedition literature is filled with engaging tales of squabbling parties. To say the least, dissension in a climbing party is no fun. It may reduce the party's chance of success; it is guaranteed to eliminate much of the enjoyment; and it can even compromise safety.

People who are known to dislike each other should not be on the same climb. The tensions and close proximity of the climb situation will only exacerbate any animosity. If two people are not getting along during the climb, other party members should do their best to keep the situation from erupting into open conflict, which might possibly threaten the safety and well-being of the group.

How many should go? The size of the party must be appropriate to the objective. Both strength and speed should be considered—and sometimes these two factors are at odds.

The Climbing Code given in Chapter 1, First Steps, recommends that the *minimum party size* for safety is three climbers: if one climber is hurt, the second can go for help while the third stays with the injured person. The Climbing Code also recommends at least two rope teams for safe travel on a glacier: if one team is pinned down holding a colleague who has fallen into a crevasse, the second team is there to effect the rescue.

These rules are general guidelines for minimum party size, but the specifics of the proposed trip may introduce other considerations. A prolonged wilderness venture may require a larger group to carry equipment and supplies, as well as to provide better backup in case of emergency. Some rock climbs require double-rope rappels on the descent; this lends itself to a second team unless a single team is willing to carry two ropes. Technical rock and ice climbs are best done with just two climbers on each rope; for these climbs, whatever the size of the party, there should ideally be an even number of climbers so that the group is efficient.

Maximum party size is also determined by considerations of speed and efficiency, as well as by concerns about environmental impact and by land-use regulations. A large group can carry more gear and offer more helpers in case of emergency, but a bigger party is not necessarily a safer one. Sometimes speed is safety, and experienced alpinists know that a larger group always moves more slowly. On certain routes, for example, climbers must move quickly to ensure finishing before dark. A larger party tends to get more spread out and may kick down more loose rock.

As a general rule, the more difficult the route, the smaller the group should be. In the extreme case, some

22

long technical climbs are done by parties of just two fast, experienced people, despite the general recommendation that three is the minimum safe party size. With a party of two, carry an emergency communication device or make other arrangements for emergencies.

Large groups have the potential of damaging the fragile alpine environment. They also erode the wilderness experience. Park and wilderness areas typically have party size limits (often 12 people maximum) to reduce impact and preserve aesthetic values. At the very least, these limits must be respected. Responsible mountaineers may even choose to impose tighter restrictions on themselves in particularly fragile places.

Weather

The understanding of current and anticipated route conditions and weather remains as much an art as it is a science. However, mountaineers have ever-increasing access to weather and current route conditions, primarily via the internet. The amount of information available for a given area, mountain, or specific route will vary greatly, and for many ranges and mountains, little or no current information is readily available.

Useful internet sites include those of local and regional governments, national or regional parks, and private recreation areas, as well as those sites that detail weather and road conditions. Some of these sites include real-time weather and web cams for an up-to-the-minute view of conditions. Local climbing sites can also be useful for current route conditions, or the leader may be able to post a question.

However, the best source of information concerning current route conditions will be from a reliable individual who has recently been on the mountain and route the party is considering; a phone call to a park office, climbing shop, bush pilot, or friend in the area is a good idea. This is especially true if the climb involves a long drive or approach.

The "art" portion of understanding conditions and weather forecasting involves knowing how a change in weather will affect the route and the party's climbing objectives. Forecasting is based on inexact models that may vary widely from actual conditions. Relying heavily on the forecast timing is risky. Note how the closing of a favorable weather window might impact the trip if it should run longer than expected. How will specific changes in temperature, wind, humidity, and precipitation affect the climb? Having alternate trips (in separated areas) in mind is a good idea that will help a party avoid "forcing" a climb—nearly always a bad decision.

Communications

Bringing emergency communication devices, such as radios, phones, satellite communicators, and PLBs, dramatically shortens the time it takes to summon rescuers. The devices are also useful for telling people back home that the party will be late but is not in trouble and, thus, can be used to avoid unnecessary rescue efforts. The devices may also be able to supply current weather or avalanche hazard updates. Inexpensive handheld radios may be useful to communicate between rope teams or the front and rear of the party on a trail when sorting out navigation options, to check in with an ill climber who stays at camp rather than head for the summit, to obtain current weather forecasts, and to coordinate during emergencies. Such devices may also allow communication with responding search and rescue authorities.

Understanding the limits of the devices is as important as understanding their usefulness. Phone batteries can be depleted, and in many mountain locations phones (other than satellite phones) are unable to transmit or receive. They should be viewed as an adjunct to, not a substitute for, self-reliance.

Evaluation

Seasoned climb leaders know that taking the time and effort to plan and prepare for the trip is the best practice for positioning the party for success. This step looks at the entirety of that effort. Does it add up favorably? Are there good safety margins? Are there areas of weakness? Can the trip plan be improved? Unfavorable elements foretell of problems that could occur later on, may suggest a hazard, could jeopardize the trip, or might increase the probability of an injury.

No party should set out ill prepared or inadequately equipped or attempt a route beyond the ability of its members; doing so imperils both the climbing party and the rescuers who may have to help them out.

UNDER WAY: ELEVEN TRIP CHECKS

How do you know a trip is on course for a successful summit or headed for a disaster? Careful planning and preparation go a long way in making sure the trip goes favorably; but once the trip gets under way, monitoring ongoing progress provides either further assurance or illuminates issues that may threaten safety or success. Even with the best-prepared plan and thorough preparation, the unexpected can occur. The Eleven Trip Checks help the party stay on track and spot potential pitfalls.

Trailhead

Before the party leaves the trailhead, take a few minutes to check that all necessary equipment and supplies are in the climbers' packs. Pay particular attention to the packs of less experienced climbers. Anyone who has been a climber for very long has had a weekend ruined by a missing critical item. Distribute group equipment. Are pack weights appropriate, and is group gear fairly distributed?

Go over the itinerary one last time to make sure everyone is on the same timetable. Is there new information? Is there a need to make any changes to the plan? Are there any cautionary "yellow" flags? The leader should discuss the planned pace, breaks, hazards, and water sources with the party.

Navigation

Most experienced leaders can share several amusing (in hindsight) stories of navigation misadventures. Orient early to the map rather than waiting until there is a concern. Check now and then to ensure the party is on route. Involve the party; the more people actively navigating, the better to avoid costly mistakes. When you are unsure, take time and effort to regain confidence. Sometimes it may prove easier to eliminate a choice than to confirm which is the correct one. Photograph, make notes, or create a GPS waypoint of key junctions. Record a GPS track if there is concern about routefinding on the return at night or in a storm or whiteout.

ELEVEN TRIP CHECKS

At the trailhead and on the approach, the climb, and the descent:

1. Trailhead
2. Navigation
3. People
4. Time
5. Hazards
6. Weather and Environment
7. Perspective
8. Decisions
9. Safety
10. Team
11. Leadership

People

Team member skills and fitness may vary considerably. Monitor party members for problems. On the approach and on the climb, set a pace that is steady, not necessarily fast. In the long run, the party cannot move faster than its slowest member; progress may even be slower if that person is reduced to exhaustion. The important thing is to keep moving steadily. Watch newer climbers who may have less stamina or are carrying too much weight.

Take rest stops for the whole party, at specific intervals, rather than halting randomly whenever someone decides to stop, which is inefficient. Make sure that everyone is eating and drinking. Is anyone lagging? Lagging will worsen unless the pace, eating, hydration, or other problems are rectified. Try to catch potential problems early, when options for preventing the problem or dealing with it are most numerous.

Time

Manage time and progress. Optimize breaks, taking into account their location, timing, and duration, as well as the party's fatigue, water supplies, et cetera. Daylight can be priceless if the unexpected occurs—start early. Consider adjusting the campsite location to fit the party's progress and schedule. Failure to reach an intended camp may suggest the party will be slow the following day too. Choose a turnaround time that will accommodate some unexpected delay.

Hazards

Stay alert for climbing hazards. Some, such as falling, may have been anticipated, with ropes and equipment brought to mitigate any fall. Others, such as a swollen stream, might be unexpected, requiring impromptu measures. Always bear in mind that the outcome of exposure to a hazard is unpredictable. Avoid hazards; find a safer alternative, or mitigate the consequence.

One technique to help guard against bias in decision making about hazards is to come up with three responses to a hazard (see "Recognizing and Identifying Hazards" in Chapter 23, Safety), then choose the best alternative. Thinking up multiple options counters the tendency to go with an impulsive first solution, which may not be the best resolution. Working through the additional solutions forces a degree of objectivity and rational thought.

22

Weather and Environment

Watch for, and adjust to, adverse changes in weather and route hazards. Does the party have the means to obtain updated weather forecasts? See more about weather in Chapter 28, Mountain Weather.

Perspective

Stay alert to the big picture; avoid fixation on a particular aspect of the trip to the detriment of others. Think ahead; anticipate. Is the situation stressful? The more stressed you are, the harder it is to escape tunnel vision, keep your perspective and make clear-headed decisions.

One assessment tool uses a traffic-stoplight analogy (fig. 22-1). If the party is doing well, this signifies a green light ("OK"). If there are some tolerable bumps in the road to the progress or trip plan, this adds a yellow ("caution") light or lights (changes could be needed). When one or more serious impacts arise, or a number of minor things are going wrong, this signifies a red ("danger") light (changes are mandatory). This tool encourages a group to maintain objectivity and "big-picture" awareness, all while its members keep an eye on problems. In addition to assessing the overall trip, this tool can be applied to each element of the trip: weather, pace, route conditions, and the like.

A traffic signal is an easy mental image to conjure. Presented with several yellow lights or a single red signal, the party might decide to turn around. With extra time and a good safety margin, the party might continue with caution, monitoring their progress.

Decisions

Climbers must make decisions with incomplete information and sometimes when saddled with fatigue, hunger, dehydration, discomfort, or injury. Guard against risk assessment and decision-making biases. What are the facts? What are the options? What do others think? Can the party's safety be ensured? Make decisions that maintain safety margins. Never let judgment be overruled by desire, such as the desire to summit, when you are choosing the route or deciding whether to turn back (see "A Climbing Code" in Chapter 1, First Steps). The outcome of exposing the party to a potentially lethal hazard is unpredictable. If the consequences cannot be mitigated, the party should find a safe alternative: that might mean turning around.

Safety

Remain ever vigilant for hazards. Practice well-reputed climbing techniques. Never climb beyond the party's

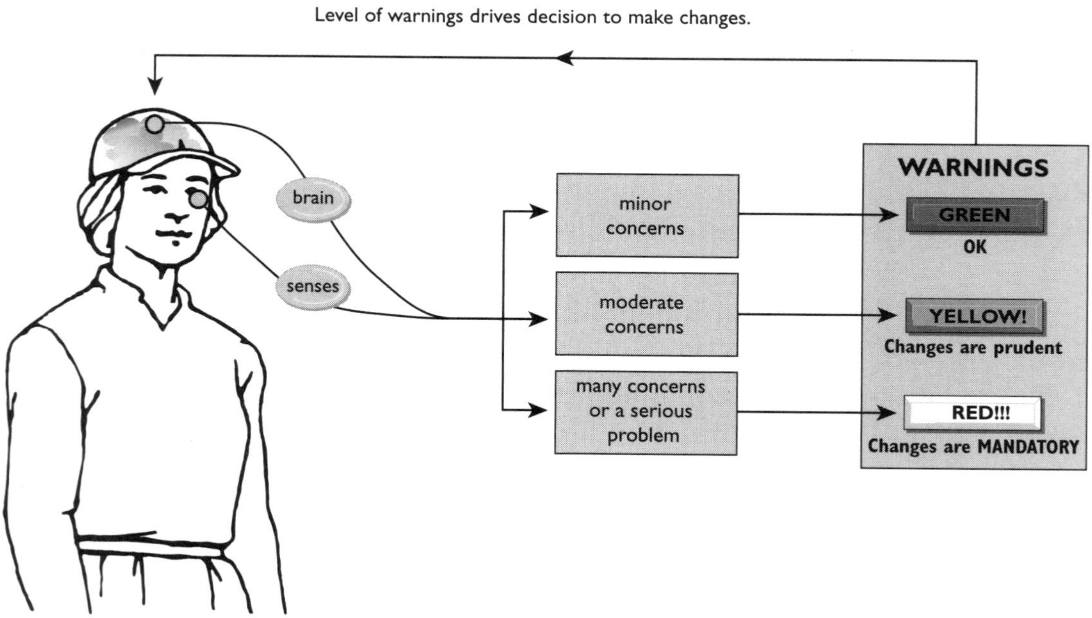

Fig. 22-1. Climbers must keep their senses alert for warnings and then make the necessary changes to stay safe.

ability and knowledge. Rope up on exposed places and glaciers. There should be two rope teams on a glacier. Anchor all belays. (See "A Climbing Code" in Chapter 1, First Steps.) Redundancy greatly increases the safety of belay and rappel anchors as well as many other systems (see "Equalizing the Anchor" in Chapter 10, Belaying). In a questionable situation, can you retreat later if conditions worsen? Sometimes the only safe solution is to withdraw rather than proceed so that you can come back another day when the hazards can be better controlled. Nothing on a climb is worth dying for.

Team

Generally, success reflects the degree to which the members of a party share common values and work cooperatively to reach their goal. A climbing party should stay together—not necessarily in a tight knot, but at least close enough to be in communication with one another. Safety is compromised when the party splits. A party that develops an interest in splitting up indicates serious underlying issues with fitness, speed, or trip objectives.

Typically the stronger members tend to want to forge ahead, leaving those most likely to need help isolated from those best able to give it. The danger of getting separated is greatest on the technical portions of a climb, where the more skilled climbers can move much faster, or on the descent, where some want to sprint while others drag due to fatigue. On a trail where the party becomes spread out, the last two persons should pair up.

A small party of friends will naturally tend to stick together. Problems are more likely with larger groups. A large party benefits from having a designated leader, and the leader should coordinate its movement and keep the party together or in communication. As a leader, give party members some flexibility to hike up the trail at their own pace but have them regroup at designated rendezvous points, especially: trail junctions to make sure everyone goes the right way; danger spots, such as hazardous stream crossings—in case anyone needs help; and bottoms of glissades, which naturally tend to split the party.

Leadership

The leadership needs to be effective at pulling together the many elements of the trip to stay safe and keep on schedule. Other party members then have more freedom to contemplate various facets and possibly suggest actions to improve on the plan.

Party members should obey the leader or decisions made by majority rule (see "A Climbing Code" in Chapter 1, First Steps). A leader need not be at the front of the party. In fact, many prefer to lead from the middle or rear, to better keep an eye on the whole group. However, the leader should be ready to swing into the forefront when a difficulty arises, such as a routefinding puzzle or a patch of demanding technical terrain. It may be wise to appoint a strong member as trail sweep, especially on the descent, to ensure there are no stragglers. Give new climbers the benefit of your experience. Look for teaching moments. A leader's primary goal for any outing is to have the whole party return home safely.

BECOMING A LEADER

The responsibility of leadership is a burden, but the task can have great rewards. It gives the experienced alpinist an opportunity to pass along knowledge gained over the years. Mountaineers do not climb because they must; they climb because they love the mountains. Climb leaders help others enjoy the sport, and that can be deeply satisfying.

Some climbers may never want to take on the role of leader, but they will find that possessing a certain degree of leadership is almost inevitable as they gain experience. A party naturally tends to look to its more seasoned members for guidance, especially in a crisis. Therefore, all climbers should give some forethought to what they would do if they were suddenly called upon to take charge.

Climbers who do aspire to leadership should climb with people they regard as capable leaders. Study them; observe how they organize the trip, make decisions, and work with people. Offer to help in order to participate in some of these activities. Veteran leaders report that they think ahead, anticipating problems that might arise and concocting possible solutions. This type of mental rehearsal is excellent training for future leaders. Climbers should develop the habit of thinking about the entire climb and the whole party, not just their part of it.

Studying respected leaders is always worthwhile, but it may be a mistake to model yourself on anyone too closely. A group must believe that its leader is genuine, and therefore all leaders must develop their own style. Exercising leadership is not always easy, but it should be done in a way that is natural for each person. For example, a reserved person should not strain to act outgoing. Anyone who has technical skill, confidence, and a sincere interest in the party's welfare can succeed as a leader.

On your first time out as a leader, choose a climb comfortably within your abilities. Perhaps invite a proficient friend, someone to rely on. Spend some extra time

22

organizing, and seek input from the more experienced members of the party. Be sure to delegate in order to take advantage of their skills. Do not make an issue of the fact that this is your debut as a leader; that will only undermine the group's confidence.

The Climbing Code in Chapter 1, First Steps, is a time-tested set of guidelines for making leadership decisions. It is deliberately conservative. Following the code may cost you a summit but it is unlikely to cost a life. Seasoned leaders may draw on experience to safely modify some of the rules, but they are not likely to depart from it radically because the code embodies a commonsense approach to safe mountaineering.

EVERYONE A LEADER

Everyone on a climb needs to be a full partner in the twin tasks of moving the group safely toward its goal and of building group cohesion. In other words, each individual must share leadership responsibility. Individual leadership means, for example, being aware of the group and its progress: Is someone lagging behind? Ask whether there is a problem, offer encouragement, and look for ways to help. A group of climbers is weakened whenever the climbers become separated from each other. Work at being aware of where climbing companions are at all times, and help to keep the party together. When you are out front and moving fast, remember to look behind you from time to time. When you are too far ahead, stop and let the group catch up—then let them have a breather before you start off again.

Take part in routefinding. Study guidebooks and maps to become familiar with the approach and the climbing route. The climbing party is much less likely to get lost if everyone is actively involved in navigation. Use the map, compass, and route description frequently so you are always oriented and know where the party is. Everyone should participate in the group's decision making. Each person's experience is a resource for the party, but that resource goes untapped if that person fails to speak up.

Establishing a supportive atmosphere is one very important role of leadership. People need to know that their companions care about them and will help them. Be part of this effort: help set up a tent, fetch water, carry the rope, share a cookie. Morale is intangible, but it makes a party stronger. Morale can be the deciding factor in party success, and it is always the deciding factor in making the climb enjoyable. Morale is everybody's job.

Assume responsibility also for your own knowledge, skill, and preparedness. Research the climb before committing yourself to it; make sure it is within your abilities. Be properly supplied and equipped. If you have questions about whether the climb is appropriate for you, or about what gear to take, ask your companions in advance. If you ever think that you are getting in over your head, speak up. Better to get some help over a rough spot or even quit the climb than to create an emergency. Thinking about the party, its welfare, and how you can contribute is in itself preparation—perhaps the very best preparation—for leadership.

CHAPTER 23
SAFETY

No mountaineer begins a climb intending to become seriously hurt, yet every year climbing accidents injure and kill novice and experienced climbers alike. No climb is worth serious injury or death. Every climber's number-one priority is to return home alive and well.

For an individual climber, serious injury or death is not some esoteric probability; it's as real as it gets. Although climbers universally believe that nothing about a climb is worth their lives, it is surprisingly common to watch climbers gamble with their lives, many unaware that they are doing so. Climbing safely can be contrary to our brains' wiring to discount risk and take shortcuts to save time and effort. In the short term, we usually get away with such shortcuts. Over time, shortcuts and unsafe practices tend to catch up to those who are enchained to these habits, and many of these adventurers eventually succumb to the odds.

Ed Viesturs, the first American to climb the world's 14 highest peaks—whose summits are all above 26,000 feet (8,000 meters)—without supplemental oxygen, has spoken extensively about turning back on many climbs because he insisted on safe conditions. Several of his contemporaries with similar aspirations—but without his safety focus—have perished.

While climbing is less safe than staying home, climbing is not as dangerous as public perception portrays it. Climbing—even difficult, challenging climbing—can be done safely. Nearly all climbing accidents can be avoided with a reasonably straightforward safety focus. Safety-conscious climbers can climb the same peaks or routes as the risk takers. Often, safe practices—which are sound practices—lead to greater successes. In some instances,

climbing safely may take more time, gear, or another attempt to reach the summit. But in the long term, safe climbers can expect to live longer and enjoy more years of climbing, more enjoyable adventures, and more successful summits.

The strategy for safe climbing is pretty simple to state but a bit harder to put into practice. First, climbers need to know what the climb hazards are and address them when planning and preparing for the trip. Then on the climb, it's about spotting and avoiding hazards, or where they can't be avoided, mitigating their consequences.

In *Extreme Alpinism*, Mark Twight shares, "As an alpinist who carries a long list of dead friends and partners, I approach the mountains differently than most. I go to them intending to survive, which I define as a success. A new route or the summit is a bonus."

UNDERSTANDING THE CAUSES OF CLIMBING ACCIDENTS

A common misunderstanding is that climbing is unsafe because of mountain hazards largely out of our control. Shrugged shoulders and comments such as "Stuff happens" are common after climbers learn of an accident.

Yet this view isn't accurate. Accidents don't have to happen. Upon analysis, it turns out we are our own worst enemy; climbers themselves are responsible for nearly all

TABLE 23-1. REPORTED CAUSES OF MOUNTAINEERING ACCIDENTS

MOST FREQUENT *IMMEDIATE* CAUSES
- Fall or slip on rock
- Slip on snow or ice
- Falling rock, ice, or object
- Exceeding abilities

MOST FREQUENT *CONTRIBUTING* CAUSES
- Climbing unroped
- Exceeding abilities
- Placing no or inadequate protection
- Inadequate equipment or clothing
- Weather
- Climbing alone
- No helmet

Source: ANAM (see Resources)

climbing accidents. Due to poor planning and preparation, some parties will even set themselves up for an accident before they leave town for their trip.

There is no official organization responsible for soliciting, collecting, or analyzing information on mountaineering accidents. The best source of mountaineering incident information is *Accidents in North American Mountaineering* (*ANAM*), published annually by the American Alpine Club and the Alpine Club of Canada (see Resources). *ANAM* focuses on injurious and fatal climbing incidents in North America. As the sources of most of this data are voluntary contributions, the number of accidents is underreported. *ANAM*'s cumulative data represents decades of accident reporting and provides historical statistics and trends.

ANAM data shows accidents are generally spread across age groups and experience levels. Many reports are gripping accounts by the victim or party members. In these accounts, it becomes apparent that nearly all accidents could have been prevented by following sound mountaineering practices.

Table 23-1 shows the most common causes of North American mountaineering accidents in descending order of relative frequency. The most likely to occur are first on the list. An *immediate cause* is one that directly precipitates the incident, such as a fall. An immediate cause is generally a surprise, a trigger of the incident. A *contributing cause* is one that sets up the incident and/or increases its harm. Contributing causes often precede an incident, and often the climbing party has missed or dismissed them. According to *ANAM*, falls and slips dominate immediate causes,

while a variety of other dangers, from climbing unroped to weather, are roughly equally likely to be contributing causes.

A typical incident results from one immediate cause and several contributing causes. In one specific example, a novice was on steep snow when she slipped, lost her ice axe, was unable to self-arrest, and broke her leg after sliding 150 feet (45 meters). The slip was the immediate cause; contributing causes were climbing unroped, not having an ice-axe leash, and exceeding one's abilities. An alert climber sees contributing causes as warnings; acting on these warnings may prevent an incident.

Though poor decision making is not included in *ANAM*'s list of accident causes, the analysis of individual reports in *ANAM* discuss poor decisions made, and they are the overwhelming reasons behind injuries, much more so than mountain hazards. The lesson is that climbing is not singularly dangerous—rather, the decisions climbers make are what lead to accidents or bring mountaineers home safely.

DEFINING SAFETY TERMINOLOGY

Learning a number of terms helps a climber understand how and why incidents occur and how to prevent them.

Hazards. Hazards are sources of serious illness, injuries, or death. Such sources may be people or routes themselves, or they can be related to the environment, timing, or weather. (see "Recognizing and Identifying Hazards" later in this chapter). Most serious climbing injuries are *outcomes* (see below) arising from *exposure* (see below) to hazards the victims opened themselves to.

This chapter uses the term "hazard" synonymously with "climbing hazard." Hazards have a recognizable risk for serious injury or death. The definition used herein excludes very low-probability hazards that are not likely to but theoretically could result in serious injury or death, such as tripping while crossing a boulder field, slipping on exposed Class 2 terrain, equipment manufacturing defects, ineffective water treatment, losing footing on a modest snow slope, a car accident while driving to the trailhead, poking an eye with a hiking pole or tree branch, and the like.

Depending upon a climber's experience, skills, equipment, et cetera, what may be hazardous to that climber may not be hazardous for another climber. For example, seasoned climbers ascending or descending steep faces and slopes will have better balance and technique and more-solid foot placements, reducing the hazard of steepness for them compared with people new to climbing.

Exposure. A climber who is subject to the influence of a hazard is "exposed" to that hazard. If there is no exposure to a hazard, there can be no bad outcome, such as injury or death. (Exposure is also used by climbers to denote a place where there is a danger of falling, termed "falling exposure.")

Exposure time. The amount of time a climber is exposed to a hazard increases the *risk* (see below). For example, on a route known to have rockfall, several hours of exposure is riskier than a few minutes. Similarly, quickly crossing a snow slope with suspect stability is less risky than spending more time on that slope.

Outcome. The consequences of exposure to hazards, or outcomes, are unpredictable. Outcomes range from favorable (a climber saves some time by not having donned crampons for a couple of steps across an exposed icy runnel) to lethal (the climber slips during the crossing). Most exposures to hazards will not result in injury—the climber gets away with it. However, any outcome is unpredictable and the full range of consequences exists with every exposure. Repeatedly getting away with hazard exposure leads to an underappreciation of risk, an inflated perception of the *margin of safety* (see below), and a tendency or willingness to be exposed to similar hazards in the future.

Accident. This term is normally not used because it suggests either chance or an unavoidable outcome, which is almost never the case. Terms such as "outcome" and "incident" are better descriptors.

Incident. Any undesirable outcome is called an incident. Incidents are usually grouped as near-miss, non-injurious, injurious, or fatal. In everyday life, injurious incidents would commonly be called accidents.

Risk. Risk is the mathematical probability that a climber's exposure to a hazard will lead to an outcome with serious or lethal injury. A climber's risk for a particular hazard is impossible to accurately calculate. Furthermore, for a particular hazard the risk is unique for each climber and is linked to personal knowledge, skill, experience, fitness, et cetera. Irrespective of statistical probability, the outcome of the next exposure is unforeseeable; it is independent of the probability.

Margin of safety. This term is another way of describing risk—in an inverse fashion. Climbers look to keep risks low and safety margins high. Margin of safety represents how far a climber is from—rather than how close a climber is to—a bad outcome. Each climber's equipment, skills, and knowledge influence that climber's margin of safety, just as risk is unique to each climber.

Here are some illustrations of margin of safety. Crossing a snow bridge has a lower margin of safety than walking around the end of the crevasse: there is greater risk in crossing on the snow bridge; there is a greater margin of safety in circumnavigating it. A climbing move with fall exposure has a lower margin of safety than the same move without such exposure. Crossing a tumultuous stream by walking across a log over it has a lower margin of safety than scooting astride the log on the haunches. An anchored belay has a higher margin of safety than an unanchored one.

Risk perception. How climbers personally perceive their risk for serious injury or death from an exposure to a hazard is their risk perception. Humans have biased risk perception; we overestimate our safety margin and underestimate risk of injury or death outcomes. Also, new climbers have a tendency to overestimate risk, while experienced climbers tend to underestimate risk.

Risk tolerance. Each climber's comfort with their personal perception of risk is called their risk tolerance.

Mitigation. Mitigation is an action that can help avoid, but does not necessarily prevent, injuries. It is an intervention that does not prevent an incident but may prevent an adverse (injurious) outcome. Belays are a good example: If a climber slips while rock climbing where there is considerable falling exposure, the outcome without a belay could be fatal; but with a belay and arrest, the climber may keep climbing (successful mitigation). However, the arrest might fail or the falling climber might pull out the protection and hit the ground or strike a ledge before the belay stops the fall and be injured (unsuccessful mitigation). In another example, if an avalanche buries a climber, his or her beacon (mitigation) might allow other climbers to find and save the climber (successful mitigation), or other climbers might find the buried climber, only to discover the climber has died from trauma (unsuccessful mitigation).

Safe climbing. Climbing that avoids or adequately mitigates climbing hazards is safe climbing.

RECOGNIZING AND IDENTIFYING HAZARDS

Climbing hazards have historically been classified as either objective (mountain-based) or subjective (human-based) hazards. Using driving a car as an analogy, road and driving conditions such as road surface, curves, shoulders, potholes, lane width, lighting, and other traffic are objective hazards. Speeding, tailgating, weaving, diminished alertness, mechanical deficiencies of the vehicle, and distractions such as the radio or conversation are subjective hazards.

23

Mountain hazards. Examples of mountain hazards include steepness, dangerous route conditions, falling distance, duration of exposure, river crossings, bad weather, other environmental considerations, loose rock, rockfall, avalanches, icefall, crevasses, moats, cornices, unstable snow and ice, and many more.

Human hazards. "To err is human"; people make mistakes. Human hazards are underpinned by heuristics. *Heuristics* are mental shortcuts we take to help us agilely draw conclusions and make decisions. Usually they work, but sometimes their oversimplification leads to deficiencies in how we think, termed *biases*. *Cognitive biases* adversely impact memory, team interactions, and decision making. Psychologists have verified dozens of biases that distort a person's thinking and lead to inaccurate conclusions. Unless people are trained to spot these biases, they are unaware of their influence.

For example, a bias leads people to confidently believe they are objective in their assessments and decision making, even when they are not. Another bias leads people to believe they are better at assessments and decision making than others in their group, even when they are not.

Many biases adversely impact decision making. Other examples of how biases manifest include:

- Overconfidence
- Dismissing negative outcomes
- Underestimating the time something takes
- Inaccurate memory
- Favoring statistical outliers
- Relying on bad facts and presumptions
- Faulty analysis and conclusions

Humans are biased toward downplaying risk. The human brain convincingly justifies exposures to hazards. But, always remember: the outcome of an exposure to a hazard is unpredictable no matter what you think, how experienced or skilled you are, or how steadfastly you believe otherwise. Most climbers are unaware of the extent to which cognitive biases distort observations, analyses, and safety decisions.

Besides these biases, climbers can add other human-related "hazards" such as stress, fatigue, dehydration, injury, emotions, adrenaline, and incomplete or poor information, which further corrupt the ability to make safe decisions. As climbers we tend to attribute incidents to mountain hazards alone instead of acknowledging that we should have chosen a safer option or mitigated the outcome of the hazards we took on (fig. 23-1).

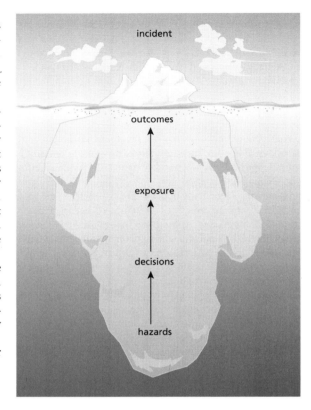

Fig. 23-1. Several underlying hazards and decisions contribute to the causes of an incident.

AVOIDING AND MITIGATING HAZARDS

Some hazards are obvious, but many are not. New climbers often embrace the sport with a narrow focus on climbing technique. As a result, they may get into situations beyond their capabilities and become hurt in the process. Images of leading or soloing sheer rock and ice couloirs are inspiring, but beginning climbers can't appreciate the years of training and experience that prepare climbers for those routes. Nor do sensational pictures reveal the detailed planning and preparations undertaken prior to the photo shoot.

Education, training, practice, and experience all help climbers become better at discovering hazards and recognizing their biases and compensating for them when making decisions. Until climbers gain these, they will not know their personal limits nor will they know all the ways things can go wrong. You don't know what you don't

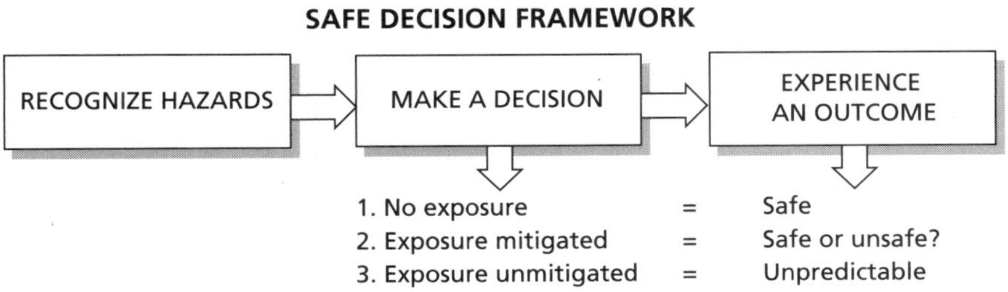

SAFE DECISION FRAMEWORK

Fig. 23-2. *Safe climbers recognize hazards and avoid them. If hazards cannot be avoided, they mitigate to abate or allay those hazards.*

know. It takes time and experience to become an objective and safety-focused decision maker.

One technique to help make decisions less biased and more objective is to think up multiple solutions to a hazard. This forces some objectiveness and analysis into the process. Some suggest coming up with three alternatives, accessing the merits of each, and then picking the best one.

National Park Service search and rescue ranger John Dill gives a sobering overview of Yosemite climbing accidents in an article titled "Climb Safely: Staying Alive." His view is particularly insightful about climbers' states of mind: "It's impossible to know how many climbers were killed by haste or overconfidence, but many survivors will tell you that they somehow lost their good judgment long enough to get hurt. It's a complex subject and sometimes a touchy one. Nevertheless, at least three states of mind frequently contribute to accidents: ignorance, casualness, and distraction."

MAKE SAFE DECISIONS AND RECOGNIZE DISTRACTIONS

Studying the *ANAM* reports helps climbers learn from the misfortunes of others. These reports are poignant reminders that very few of the incidents arise from extraordinary situations. Almost all incidents result from not adhering to well-accepted practices and techniques. Most of the incidents would have been shockingly simple to prevent. Reading the latest *ANAM* every year is a sobering and useful practice to keep this point fresh.

Poorly reined in desire to reach the summit is the most common bias leading to poor decisions: as the Climbing Code (see Chapter 1, First Steps) says, "Never let judgment be overruled by desire when choosing the route or deciding whether to turn back." Sadly, a number of climbers have lost their lives trying to complete a socially designated list

of peaks, when their intense focus on scoring that summit overrode safety. A party motivated by the quality of the trip is less likely to press on into hazards than is a party motivated by the "must-get" summit.

If you are unsure if the hazard is significant or the risk high enough to be dangerous, ponder what would happen if dozens of climbers were exposed to the same situation you face (fig. 23-2). Would it be reasonable to expect some to suffer a mishap resulting in serious injury or death? If so, and recalling that the outcome of a specific exposure is unpredictable, in the scheme of your life, is it worth serious injury or death to go ahead with this exposure to this hazard?

If a climber is "lucky" and a good outcome follows a poor decision, bias can lead to incidents in the future. If you won the roll of the dice this time, a dangerous practice then becomes more tolerable. What about next time? Will you act differently, or will one parameter be slightly different and lead to a devastating outcome? Be sure your biases and decision-making habits are not setting you up for an incident. Do not rely on luck, because when it runs out, the consequences may be serious.

Yosemite ranger John Dill says that "distraction is caused by whatever takes your mind off your work: anxiety, sore feet, skinny-dippers below—the list is endless. Being in a hurry is one of the most common causes." Many experienced climbers, he says, are hurt on easy pitches because they were thinking of a cold beer or a good bivy and made "errors only a beginner would make" by taking shortcuts to get to these goals. One particular climber Dill writes about was distracted by darkness, which led the climber to hurry—he died after rappelling off the end of his rope.

Sometimes many small things, none of which by themselves are significant enough to begin eroding the trip's margin of safety. These changes can involve everything from a little poor weather, some temporary navigation

23

PLAN	PREPARE	CLIMB
Assess leadership. Research area and route. Craft itinerary. Set a safety margin. Assess party members.	Ensure skills. Work on fitness. Prepare equipment. Check weather forecast.	Recognize hazards. Avoid hazards. Mitigate outcome.

Fig. 23-3. Three-part focus for a safe trip: plan, prepare, climb.

confusion, the party moving slowly, or a mildly ill party member (tired, blisters, heavy pack, lack of fitness, leg cramps). At some point, even little things add up to have an impact. Heed Kurt Diemberger's message:

> *It was diabolic machinery, into the cogwheels of which all of us were imperceptibly but irretrievably being sucked—the mechanism being so complicated that it was not recognizable to the individual: every way that might have led us out eventually became blocked by the taking of single decisions, which by themselves would never have been so critical, but in their conjunction opened the death trap for seven people up at 8,000 meters.*
>
> —*Kurt Diemberger,* The Endless Knot

PLAN AND PREPARE FOR THE CLIMB

Discovering and eliminating hazards starts before the party takes the first step on the trail—while the climb is being planned and prepared for. Many hazards can be avoided through preparation and planning (fig. 23-3). Following checklists and acronyms helps guard against forgetfulness and memory errors (see "Organizing and Leading a Climb" in Chapter 22, Leadership).

An oft-quoted climbing adage is "The number-one rule is don't fall." It is smart to learn technical skills in a safe environment such as at a crag or climbing area, where the focus can be on skill development and enhancement, rather than in the backcountry, while also dealing with the myriad trip skills and hazards typical of more-remote venues. In the backcountry, it is best not to climb a route near your maximum skill level. Instead, choose a route that is below your technical best, and focus on the orchestration of all components necessary for a successful trip. The technical portion of a climb may be the highlight, but it is only one of many aspects of a mountaineering trip. There is a tendency to focus too intently on the technical aspects, only to be tripped up by something simple.

When heading to locales subject to adverse weather, plan another trip elsewhere to improve the odds for a successful outing for a given date. Similarly, when a particular peak is the foremost goal, schedule the climb on several calendar dates to improve the odds for acceptable (even stellar) weather.

Once a plan is put together, participants need to prepare for it. For example, if a certain level of fitness is needed for the trip, then all participants must work up to at least that level of fitness.

Careful planning and preparation helps reduce the number of surprises on the trip. However, despite the best possible planning, real-life surprises can arise. With poor planning, the possibility of unexpected hazards rises, and it becomes increasingly challenging to safely avoid or mitigate these hazards.

OVERCOME HAZARDS DURING THE CLIMB

During a trip, climbers should be alert for expected and unexpected hazards. As hazards are identified, the key to safety is to avoid exposure to the hazard or, if the hazard cannot be avoided, to mitigate the possibility of an injurious outcome. If the hazard cannot be avoided or undesirable outcomes mitigated, then the prudent course is to retreat and return when the climb can be done safely.

In another look at the car-driving analogy, maintaining the car, slowing down, selecting a safe route, avoiding congestion, extending vehicle spacing, taking a restful break, being patient, and allowing extra drive time are examples of hazard avoidance. Using shoulder restraints and driving a car with airbags and modern vehicle construction are examples of mitigation: while these factors would not prevent an incident, they will likely mitigate and lessen injury.

On the climb, recognize that safe practices for one type of climbing may not be safe for another type. It may be socially intimidating to use practices contrary to the local norm, and bad habits may develop. For example, at sport climbing areas with bolted anchors and established landings, it may be standard rappel practice to forgo stopper knots in the ends of the rope. A climber habituated to this practice is unlikely to tie stopper knots elsewhere when a safe landing is not ensured.

Redundancy substantially improves safety. Where there are independent backups the probability of all of them failing is the product of the failure rates of each independent part—comparatively, a very low number. For example, lead climbers normally place double or triple pieces of protection when building an anchor—this results in strong redundancy. In contrast, many climbers rappel from a single anchor without a second thought. While frequently used single rappel anchors are "proof tested" by each rappeller and may not benefit from redundancy, temporarily backing up new and infrequently used rappel anchors provides a substantial margin of safety compared with a single anchor.

When considering what to do, decision making requires an objective perspective, which is not easy. You might have a last day of vacation in which to achieve a long-desired summit, but it began to rain during the night and the weather looks unsettled. Do you try for the summit even though you suspect weather and route conditions could be hazardous? Are there safe options for proceeding? How long can you wait for improvements, or can you retreat if hazards arise? Do you decide to go home and come again another time?

CLIMBING SAFELY

Few sports engage us physically and mentally to the extent that climbing does. Perhaps mountaineering exercises us in ways our minds and bodies evolved eons ago. Today, we do not grow up in the wild, so we have to learn safe practices as adults. Safe climbers seek to minimize hazards prior to their trips. While on the climb, they strive to identify hazards and then make decisions to avoid them or mitigate adverse outcomes, so that they return home safely.

23

CHAPTER 24
FIRST AID

First aid is one of the supportive skills of a truly competent self-reliant climber. Most skilled mountaineers grow adept at avoiding and mitigating hazards in the mountains, because it is far preferable to prevent injuries rather than to be experts at treating injuries. Yet accidents and illness can strike mountaineers, just as they can hit anyone at home.

The mountain environment and the physical demands of wilderness travel bring with them new types of injuries and illnesses. Mountaineers may be far away from emergency medical services, so the climbing party must be able to provide first aid. Additionally, mountaineers have a proud history of coming to the aid of injured and ill people in other parties. All climbers should be trained in wilderness first aid.

There are two components to mountaineering accident response: the framework for responding to an accident, and the techniques for treating specific conditions. This chapter begins with planning and preparation, then presents the accident response framework, in the form of seven simple responses appropriate to most backcountry accidents. Following that are medical conditions associated with the backcountry, from mountain-specific maladies to injuries to illnesses. However, many of the essential first-aid skills, such as cardiopulmonary resuscitation (CPR), splinting, and wound care, are limited in scope or omitted here, because this book is not intended to be a comprehensive first-aid text. These skills are best learned by taking first-aid classes focused on outdoor activities and by regularly refereshing your knowledge and practicing your skills.

PLANNING AND PREPARATION

A mountaineering party should determine the general first-aid skills of the party and any relevant personal medical information, such as allergies to bee stings, diabetes, et cetera, while planning the climb. Opinions differ on the best format for gathering this information. Some climb leaders like to ask for medical information individually from each party member in advance of the trip. The information is then shared with any assistant leader and elsewhere as needed. This approach protects individual privacy, but it has the disadvantage of not giving other party members the information they might need to be most helpful to a stricken person. Thus another approach is to ask for this information publically, from the group as a whole, at the trailhead before heading for the climb. Another element of planning for emergency response is making sure that everyone carries a personal first-aid kit.

FIRST-AID KIT

In a mountaineering party, each member carries a basic personal first-aid kit. Table 24-1 lists suggested contents of a personal mountaineering first-aid kit, to which climbers can add as experience, need, and training dictate. Some first-aid items may be found elsewhere in the climber's

TABLE 24-1. BASIC FIRST-AID KIT

Adhesive bandages
Skin closures or cyanoacrylate glue
Hemostatic gauze pad
Nonadherent dressings
Self-adhering roller bandage or wrap
Medical tape
Antiseptic
Blister prevention and treatment supplies
Gloves, nitrile
Tweezers
Needle
Nonprescription pain killer
Nonsteroidal anti-inflammatory
Antidiarrheal
Antihistamine
Topical antibiotic
Accident report form and pencil
Any personal prescriptions (including asthma
    inhalers, epinephrine, etc.)

personal supplies, such as a tweezers on a multitool or tape from a repair kit. Personal emergency medications such as epinephrine for allergies should be well labeled and their location made known to other members of the party. It is wise to put the first-aid kit in a plastic bag to keep the contents dry.

On longer trips or in remote areas, the items and quantities can be adjusted, and a group first-aid kit may make sense. Avoid the temptation to strip a first-aid kit below the bare minimum simply to reduce weight. On most trips, the first-aid kit will not be needed, but that does not make it less essential. An appropriate emergency communication device such as a phone, satellite communicator, or PLB, can expedite medical assistance in a serious situation (see "Requesting Outside Assistance" in Chapter 25, Alpine Rescue).

RESPONDING TO ACCIDENTS

A commonly shared framework for responding to an emergency makes all the difference in how a climbing party translates knowledge and skill into effective action. Without such a framework, accident response will be chaotic and inefficient. The effective response to an accident in the mountains can be simplified into seven steps, as shown in Table 24-2, which are covered below in detail.

STEP 1: TAKE CHARGE OF THE SITUATION

The climb leader is responsible for managing the overall accident response. Safety of survivors is the first priority. Identify, then avoid or mitigate, threatening hazards. Designate a first-aid provider if one has not been established. As appropriate, designate first-aid assistants. Choose a spot for team members to aggregate resources such as first-aid kits, packs, ropes, racks, et cetera, so they are readily

TABLE 24-2. THE SEVEN STEPS IN ACCIDENT RESPONSE

STEP	ACTION TO TAKE
1. Take charge of the situation.	The climb leader is in charge of the party. Safety of the party is the number-one priority. The climb leader designates a first-aid provider to oversee care. The first-aid provider is usually the person with the best medical skills.
2. Approach the patient safely.	There may be dangerous or deadly considerations, such as rockfall, avalanche, steepness, to evaluate. Avoid reckless haste!
3. Perform emergency rescue and urgent first aid.	In a dangerous or unworkable environment, the patient may have to be rescued before treatment can begin. The first-aid provider checks CAB-B—Circulation + Airway + Breathing + deadly Bleeding—and administers urgent first aid.
4. Protect the patient.	Protect the patient from the elements and preemptively treat for shock and hypothermia; provide psychological support.
5. Check for other injuries.	Conduct a thorough secondary examination and record findings on an accident report form (see Figure 24-1).
6. Make a plan.	Decide how best to evacuate the injured person.
7. Carry out the plan.	Implement, monitor, and adapt the plan.

24

accessible. The climb leader maintains the big picture, thinks ahead to the next steps, delegates assignments, and, importantly, avoids being drawn into details that distract from managing the entirety.

If there are several patients, use triage to direct the party's limited resources toward actions likely to have the most benefit and away from actions that can wait or are hopeless.

STEP 2: APPROACH THE PATIENT SAFELY

Gather first-aid supplies, rescue equipment, and other gear and supplies that will be needed. Do not endanger party members in the effort to reach an injured person. Avoid any adrenaline-fueled, tunnel-vision haste to reach the patient. The climb leader selects the best approach strategy. In technical terrain, this could require ropes and rescue techniques. (See Chapter 25, Alpine Rescue.)

STEP 3: PERFORM EMERGENCY RESCUE AND URGENT FIRST AID

Move a patient only if there is imminent danger to the patient or rescuers. Otherwise, do not move the patient until the first-aid provider is satisfied that the move will not aggravate injuries. Patients do not have to be lying on their back to be examined and treated. If the patient must be moved out of danger, do so in such a way as to minimize further injury. Note the patient's body position and mechanism of the injury, and attempt to determine whether it is likely that a back or neck injury has occurred. Attempt to support and immobilize any obvious injured area as well as the neck and spine during emergency extrication.

Protect Rescuers from Bloodborne Pathogens

Protect rescuers from the patient's blood and body fluids that might transmit communicable infectious diseases. Protective measures that create a barrier between the skin and mucous membranes include disposable gloves, eyewear such as sunglasses, or perhaps a bandanna. In situations with considerable bleeding or vomiting, wearing raingear offers additional protection.

Make an Initial Assessment

If the patient is unresponsive, check the patient's CAB-B vital indicators and begin emergency first aid under these circumstances:

Circulation: Is pulse present?
Airway: Is airway clear?
Breathing: Is patient breathing?
Bleeding: Does patient have any heavy bleeding?

SPECIAL CIRCUMSTANCES FOR WITHHOLDING OR TERMINATING CPR

The first-aid provider may withhold or terminate CPR if any of these conditions occur:

- There is unacceptable risk to the rescuer.
- The rescuer is exhausted.
- The environment is one in which CPR is impossible.
- Injuries are incompatible with life.
- The patient's body is frozen solid.
- The avalanche victim is pulseless with obstructed airway and was buried for more than 35 minutes.
- There is no return of a heartbeat after 30 minutes of CPR (except for a hypothermic patient).

Perform Wilderness CPR

If a pulse is absent, you should begin cardiopulmonary resuscitation (CPR) if able. Performing CPR in the wilderness is different from performing CPR minutes away from a hospital; it requires special consideration of injuries and circumstances specific to wilderness settings. See the sidebar "Special Circumstances for Withholding or Terminating CPR"; these are based on recommendations from the International Commission for Alpine Rescue on the termination of CPR in mountain rescue (see Resources). If you do perform CPR, do so in accordance with the training you have received.

Manage Serious Bleeding

If there is deadly bleeding, use direct pressure over a hemostatic dressing or clean clothing. If bleeding persists, apply a pressure dressing. Elevating a limb is not effective. Applying pressure to a pressure point is effective for about

---

MANAGEMENT OF BLEEDING

- Take precautions (gloves, sunglasses, raingear) to protect rescuers from the patient's blood and body fluids.
- Apply a hemostatic dressing.
- Apply direct pressure to control bleeding.
- Use pressure dressings on top of existing ones.
- Apply a tourniquet when all else fails.
- Treat for shock with feet elevated 6 to 12 inches (15 to 30 centimeters).

SYMPTOMS AND SIGNS OF SHOCK

The patient may experience these symptoms:
- Nausea
- Thirst
- Weakness
- Fear and/or restlessness
- Sweating
- Shortness of breath

Observers may note these signs:
- Pulse rapid but weak
- Breathing rapid and shallow
- Skin cool and clammy
- Lips and nail beds blue
- Restlessness
- Face pale
- Eyes dull
- Pupils dilated
- Unresponsiveness (a late sign)

a minute before ancillary circulation is established. If bleeding continues uncontrolled, use a tourniquet 1 inch (2.5 centimeters) wide that incorporates windlass tightening. Place it 2 to 3 inches (5 to 7 centimeters) above the hemorrhage and tighten it until bleeding stops. Using a tourniquet may lead to permanent injury, especially when used longer than about two hours. Before then slowly release the tourniquet to see if the bleeding can be controlled by other means. See the "Management of Bleeding" sidebar.

STEP 4: PROTECT THE PATIENT

The first-aid provider should protect the patient from the environment—heat, cold, precipitation, et cetera—and prevent shock. See the sidebar "Symptoms and Signs of Shock." Make every effort to maintain the patient's body temperature. Initial protection from the elements can be done quickly and usually without moving the patient.

STEP 5: CHECK FOR OTHER INJURIES

Once the patient has been stabilized and treated initially for life-threatening conditions, the first-aid provider checks for other injuries. Conduct a systematic head-to-toe secondary survey, looking for the clues listed in the "Signs of Injury" sidebar. The exam needs to be visual and tactile. For best results, examine bare skin while making thorough observations for possible injuries, unless environmental conditions are prohibitive.

The person conducting the examination should use an accident report form, such as the one in Figure 24-1, to guide the exam. The report provides information in the event of a change in the patient's condition or in case evacuation becomes necessary and the injured person is turned over to outside assistance for treatment. Perform repeated reassessments to detect changes or deterioration in the patient's condition.

STEP 6: MAKE A PLAN

Up until this point, the steps primarily have included urgent first aid and thorough assessment. Additional first aid may be required, such as wound care, splinting an injured limb, hydration, medicating for pain, and preventing shock and hypothermia. The patient may need evacuation, which may be within the resources of the party or may require additional resources from outside organizations. Finally, the needs of the remaining party members have to be considered. All of these are brought together in a plan.

A patient who is not ambulatory nearly always requires additional assistance to evacuate. Carrying a patient by litter requires proper equipment and a large number of people to assist, which is beyond the capabilities of most climbing parties. Self-evacuation should not be attempted if there are any indications of serious head, neck, or back injuries (see "Injuries" later in this chapter). Other factors to consider in deciding whether to attempt a self-evacuation—in addition to the patient's condition—include the terrain, the weather, the time of day, the amount of time a self-evacuation will take, the strength and skills of other party members, and the practicality of stopping en route if an outside evacuation becomes

SIGNS OF INJURY

- Unilateral differences
- Discoloration or bruising
- Disfigurement
- Bleeding or loss of other fluids
- Swelling
- Pain or tenderness
- Limited range of motion
- Guarding of a particular body part
- Numbness

24

FIRST AID/ACCIDENT REPORT FORM (begin here)

FINDINGS
Circulation, Airway, Breathing, Bleeding
Initial Rapid Check
(Chest Wounds, Severe Bleeding)

ASK WHAT HAPPENED:

ASK WHERE IT HURTS:

ALLERGIES		MEDICATIONS	
TAKE PULSE & RESPIRATIONS	PULSE		RESPIRATIONS

SKIN: Color
        Temperature
        Moisture

PUPILS: Regular in size
         Equally reactive

STATE OF CONSCIOUSNESS:

HEAD: Scalp – Wounds
        Ears, Nose – Fluids
        Jaw – Stability
        Mouth – Wounds

NECK: Wounds, Deformity

CHEST: Movement, Symmetry

ABDOMEN: Wounds, Rigidity

PELVIS: Stability

EXTREMETIES: Wounds, Deformity
               Sensations & Movement
Pulses Below Injury

BACK: Wounds, Deformity

PAIN (Location)

MEDICAL PROBLEMS
LOOK FOR MEDICAL ID TAG

VICTIM'S NAME	AGE
COMPLETED BY	DATE TIME

ASSESMENT OF PROBLEMS

PLAN/FIRST AID GIVEN

DETACH HERE – SEND OUT WITH REQUEST FOR FIRST AID — TEAR HERE – KEEP THIS SECTION WITH VICTIM

RESCUE REQUEST
Fill Out One Form Per Victim

TIME OF INCIDENT		
	AM PM	DATE

NATURE OF INCIDENT
EXCESSIVE ☐ HEAT   ☐ COLD
FALL ON   ☐ ROCK   ☐ SNOW   ☐ CREVASSE   ☐ AVALANCHE
           ☐ FALLING ROCK   ☐ ILLNESS
BRIEF DESCRIPTION OF INCIDENT

INJURIES (List Most Severe First)	FIRST AID GIVEN

SKIN TEMP/COLOR:

STATE OF CONSCIOUSNESSS:

PAIN (Location)

RECORD:

Time	Initial			When leave scene
Pulse				
Respiration				

VICTIM'S NAME		AGE

ADDRESS

NOTIFY (Name)

RELATIONSHIP	PHONE

OTHER COMMENTS:

Fig. 24-1. Accident report form and rescue request form.

the preferred option. If self-evacuation is the plan, party members will have to plan and organize the effort.

On the other hand, if the climb leader decides to seek outside help, the party will need a plan for obtaining assistance and taking care of all members remaining in the wilderness. If the party has an emergency communication device such as radio, phone, PLB, or satellite communicator, consider that it is better to request rescue assistance early, rather than the party finding themselves with a deteriorating patient in the middle of the night or a storm and unable to continue self-evacuation. If the plan is to dispatch people to request help, try to send at least two of the party's stronger and more competent members, along with the completed accident report form with information on the patient's condition, the condition of the rest of the party, adequacy of survival supplies, and the party's specific location. Rescue agencies appreciate early notification as well to assist with planning and mobilization. See Chapter 25, Alpine Rescue, for more details.

STEP 7: CARRY OUT THE PLAN

While executing the plan, the party monitors their progress and looks for opportunities to improve the plan. Monitor the patient and provide reassurance and support. Give fluids and carbohydrates if the patient can swallow and tolerate them without nausea. If in doubt, start with occasional sips of water to ensure tolerance without nausea or vomiting, a hardship the patient doesn't need. Remain vigilant because shock may be delayed.

At this stage, psychological support becomes important

SIDE 2 RESCUE REPORT

EXACT LOCATION (Include Marked Map if Possible)

QUADRANGLE: _____ SECTION: _____

GPS Coordinates: _____ DATUM: _____

TERRAIN:
☐ GLACIER ☐ SNOW ☐ ROCK
☐ BRUSH ☐ TIMBER ☐ TRAIL
☐ FLAT ☐ MODERATE ☐ STEEP
☐ OTHER (Describe)

ON-SITE PLANS:
☐ Will Stay Put
☐ Will Evacuate To: _____
Can Stay Overnight Safely ☐ Yes ☐ No
ON-SITE EQUIPMENT: ☐ Tent ☐ Sleeping Bags ☐ Ground Insulation
☐ Flares ☐ Saw ☐ Hardware
☐ Ropes ☐ Stoves ☐ Fuel
☐ Other:

Cell Phone: _____

LOCAL WEATHER

SUGGESTED EVACUATION: ☐ Carry-Out ☐ Helicopter
☐ Lowering ☐ Raising
EQUIPMENT NEEDED: ☐ Rigid Litter ☐ Food ☐ Water
☐ Other: _____

PARTY MEMBERS REMAINING (Indicate Numbers)
_____ Scrambling Students _____ Basic Students _____ Basic Grads
_____ Intermediate Students _____ Intermediate Grads _____ Others

ATTACH THE PRE-TRIP LIST OF PARTY MEMBERS, including names, addresses, and phone numbers. Update the list to accurately reflect party membership and persons to notify in case of delays.
PARTY LEADERS:
NAMES OF MESSENGERS SENT FOR HELP:

WHOM TO NOTIFY TO INITIATE THE RESCUE:
IN NATIONAL PARK: Notify the Park Ranger
OUTSIDE NATIONAL PARK: Sheriff/County Police (Call 911)
IN CANADA: RCMP

VITAL SIGNS RECORD

Record TIME	BREATHS		PULSE		PULSES BELOW INJURY	PUPILS	SKIN	STATE OF CON-SCIOUS-NESS	OTHER
	Rate	Character	Rate	Character					
		Deep Shallow, Noisy, Labored		Strong Weak Regular Irregular	Strong Weak Absent	Equal size React to light Round	Color Temp Moist-ness	Alert Confused Unre-sponsive	Pain Anxiety Thirst Etc.

Other Observations:

Fig. 24-1. (continued) Accident report form and rescue request form.

for the patient and anyone involved in helping the seriously injured. Keep an eye out for anyone behaving irrationally or in an agitated or dazed fashion. Often such individuals can be assigned a simple task that will refocus them.

Party members may need to prepare to spend time where they are: setting up a shelter, rationing food, and perhaps getting ready for a night in the wilderness. See Chapter 25, Alpine Rescue, for details on rescue and evacuation methods.

MOUNTAIN MALADIES

Certain conditions are associated with mountaineering activities. The mountain environment can expose climbers to extremes of heat, cold, sun exposure, and altitude. Field treatment may be challenging since it is rare to be able to remove the ill climber from the causes. Bear in mind if one person is suffering others in the party could be close behind.

DEHYDRATION

Water is the most important nutrient. Maintaining good hydration reduces the risk of heat-related, cold-related, and altitude illnesses. It improves overall physical performance as well.

Individuals vary in the rate at which their bodies lose water. Water loss occurs through sweating, respiration, urination, and diarrhea. Gaining altitude increases urinary and respiratory losses. Various medications can influence

24

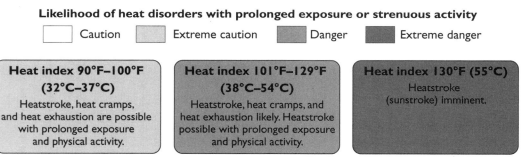

HEAT INDEX
Temperature (°F)

Relative humidity (%)	80	82	84	86	88	90	92	94	96	98	100	102	104	106	108	110
40	80	81	83	85	88	91	94	97	101	105	109	114	119	124	130	136
45	80	82	84	87	89	93	96	100	104	109	114	119	124	130	137	
50	81	83	85	88	91	95	99	103	108	113	118	124	130	137		
55	81	84	86	89	93	97	101	106	112	117	124	130	137			
60	82	84	88	91	95	100	105	110	116	123	129	137				
65	82	85	89	93	98	103	108	114	121	128	136					
70	83	86	90	95	100	105	112	119	126	134						
75	84	88	92	97	103	109	116	124	132							
80	84	89	94	100	106	113	121	129								
85	85	90	96	102	110	117	126	135								
90	86	91	98	105	113	122	131									
95	86	93	100	108	117	127										
100	87	95	103	112	121	132										

Likelihood of heat disorders with prolonged exposure or strenuous activity

Caution	Extreme caution	Danger	Extreme danger

Heat index 90°F–100°F (32°C–37°C)
Heatstroke, heat cramps, and heat exhaustion are possible with prolonged exposure and physical activity.

Heat index 101°F–129°F (38°C–54°C)
Heatstroke, heat cramps, and heat exhaustion likely. Heatstroke possible with prolonged exposure and physical activity.

Heat index 130°F (55°C)
Heatstroke (sunstroke) imminent.

Source: National Weather Service, NOAA

Fig. 24-2. Heat index.

the body's ability to maintain water balance, by changing how much a person sweats or feels thirst or by increasing or decreasing urine output. Conditioning can play a role in the body's efficient maintenance of water balance.

Climbers may not be aware how much water their body is losing. If they do not urinate periodically during the day, or if their urine color becomes darker, they are not drinking enough fluids. Other indications of fluid dehydration are a flushed feeling, headache, or decrease in, or lack of, sweating.

Always begin mountaineering outings well hydrated. Drink a cup (or more) of water 15 minutes before starting out. Once under way, one strategy is to continue drinking fluids at a rate of 1 to 1.5 cups (0.2 to 0.3 liter) every 20 to 30 minutes of intense aerobic activity. This rate of drinking helps maintain hydration without making the stomach distended from the volume taken in. If climbers have been without water for some time and finally get a chance to hydrate, most people can tolerate drinking a pint (0.5 liter), but not two, immediately without stomach distension. Spread the second pint over 15 minutes to avoid that bloated feeling.

Commercial sports and electrolyte drinks are not necessary, but are often useful—especially to make hydration more palatable in warmer climates where more sweating occurs. Electrolytes—body salts—lost through sweating can also be replaced by eating snacks that have some salt content.

EXERCISE-ASSOCIATED HYPONATREMIA

A relatively uncommon fluid-electrolyte disorder called exercise-associated hyponatremia (EAH) is generally caused by drinking too much water, which decreases blood sodium levels for up to 24 hours after prolonged activity. The body has the ability to excrete and sweat about 1–1.5 quarts (1–1.5 liters) of water per hour. Consumption of water in excess of this may eventually result in overhydration, decreasing sodium.

To differentiate between dehydration and overhydration, track the patient's water intake and urination. It may be helpful to determine the capacity of water containers and a timeline of when they have been filled. With heat illnesses, expect increased thirst, rapid heart rate, diminished urination (darker-colored urine), and dizziness, faintness, or lightheadedness only upon standing; these indicators are less likely with EAH.

HEAT-RELATED CONDITIONS

Heat builds up by exertion or by exposure to a hot environment. Humans lose heat largely through their skin. If a person builds up more heat than the body can lose, heat-related illness can result. High humidity impairs heat dissipation because it slows evaporation by perspiration. High temperature combined with high humidity and strenuous exertion *are dangerous conditions for an intense activity to take place*; these can lead to overheating, which can cause a range of problems, from the crippling pain of heat cramps to heat exhaustion or heatstroke. Treatment in the field can be challenging especially when it is hot, sunny, and there is little water, shade, or snow.

Heat Index

The heat index in Figure 24-2 provides a measure of apparent temperature increase due to the effect of increasing humidity. For example, if the ambient air temperature is 90 degrees Fahrenheit (32 degrees Celsius), at a relative humidity of 40 percent, the perceived temperature will be 93 degrees Fahrenheit (33 degrees Celsius); at a relative humidity of 90 percent, the perceived temperature will be 122 degrees Fahrenheit (50 degrees Celsius).

Heat Cramps

Muscle cramps, especially in the legs, can develop if a climber becomes dehydrated or electrolyte-imbalanced during sustained exertion. In general, less-conditioned climbers are more likely to develop heat cramps than climbers who are in better shape. Heat cramps are avoidable if water and electrolytes are replenished throughout

SIGNS AND SYMPTOMS OF HEAT EXHAUSTION

- Headache
- Cool and clammy skin
- Dizziness
- Fatigue
- Nausea
- Thirst
- Rapid pulse and respiratory rate

the climb. Rest, massage, and gentle, slow stretching of the affected muscles usually help. Replacing water and electrolytes is important. Severe leg cramps on an approach or strenuous climb may be a warning sign of pending heat exhaustion.

Heat Exhaustion

Of the two major kinds of heat illness, heat exhaustion is the milder affliction compared with heatstroke (see below). In the effort to reduce body temperature, blood vessels in the skin become so dilated (and sweating-related moisture loss so pronounced) that circulation to the brain and other vital organs becomes inadequate. The result is an effect similar to fainting (see the "Signs and Symptoms of Heat Exhaustion" sidebar). The following people are susceptible to heat exhaustion: the elderly, the poorly conditioned, individuals on medications that interfere with sweating, people inadequately acclimatized to a hot climate, and individuals who are dehydrated or salt-depleted.

Treatment of heat exhaustion consists of resting—reclining with feet up—preferably in the shade, removing excess clothing, and drinking plenty of fluids and electrolytes. Applying water over the head, skin, and clothing can promote evaporative cooling. On average, it takes one hour to get a quart (liter) of fluid into the circulatory system.

Heatstroke

Heatstroke, also called sunstroke, is a life-threatening emergency. In heatstroke, the body's heat gain is so substantial that body core temperature rises to dangerous levels: 105 degrees Fahrenheit (41 degrees Celsius) or more. The most reliable symptom is altered mental state, which might manifest as irritability, combativeness, delusions, or incoherent speech. See the "Signs and Symptoms of Heatstroke" sidebar for others.

24

SIGNS AND SYMPTOMS OF HEATSTROKE

- Altered mental state: confusion or uncooperativeness, advancing toward unconsciousness
- Rapid pulse and respiratory rate
- Headache
- Weakness
- Flushed, hot skin (wet with sweat or sometimes dry)
- Seizures
- Loss of coordination

Treatment of heatstroke must be immediate. Move the patient to the shade. Cool the head and body by packing them in snow or through evaporative cooling by splashing on water and vigorously fanning the person. Remove clothing that retains heat. Add ice packs (snow) to the neck, groin, and armpits, where large blood vessels are located near the body surface. Once body temperature has dropped to 102 degrees Fahrenheit (39 degrees Celsius), the cooling efforts can be stopped. However, continue to monitor the patient's temperature, mental status, and general condition, because temperature instability may continue for some time, and body temperature could climb again, necessitating more cooling. If the patient's gag reflex and swallowing ability are intact, cold drinks may be provided, since rehydration is critical. The ill person may not be able to continue for some hours. A heatstroke patient must be evaluated by competent medical personnel and should not resume activity until after such an evaluation.

COLD-RELATED CONDITIONS

Cold-related illness and injuries can be localized or systemic. With immersion foot, Raynaud's disease, frostnip, and frostbite, the loss is localized, whereas with cold stress and hypothermia, the loss is systemic. Body heat is lost to the environment through evaporation (sweating and breathing), radiation (from uncovered skin), convection (from windy conditions), and conduction (from touching, sitting, or lying on something cold).

Windchill

For a given cool temperature, as wind speed increases it draws away heat by convection. The windchill index, Figure 24-3, provides a mathematical measure of how wind can accelerate the rate of cooling from exposed skin compared with the ambient temperature. For a given temperature, as wind speed increases, it draws more heat from exposed skin. The calculation of windchill is based on heat-transfer theory. For example, if the air temperature is minus 10 degrees Fahrenheit (minus 23 degrees Celsius) and the wind is blowing at 25 miles per hour (40 kilometers per hour), then the windchill temperature is minus 37 degrees Fahrenheit (minus 38 degrees Celsius). At this temperature and at this wind speed, exposed skin can freeze in 10 minutes.

By definition, the windchill index temperature is lower than the air temperature, but loss of heat by windchill cannot cause temperature to drop below the ambient air temperature; it's a measure of cooling and not a measure of ambient temperature. Windchill is of greater significance when the air temperature is relatively cool—that is, when there is risk of frostbite or hypothermia. Keep in mind that windchill cools all warm surfaces while windchill index depicts cooling only on exposed skin; if a climber is properly dressed for the conditions of the mountain environment using windproof materials, the windchill effect can be reduced or eliminated (see "Layering" in Chapter 2, Clothing and Equipment).

Hypothermia

Hypothermia, a cold-related illness that affects the entire body, occurs when cold overcomes the body's ability to maintain a normal temperature. As the body tries to maintain normal core temperature, blood is diverted away from the skin surface and from extremities. Cold stress results when the body's core temperature is between normal and 95 degrees Fahrenheit (35 degrees Celsius). Below this temperature reside the three stages of hypothermia. Unless remedied, hypothermia becomes a life-threatening condition that must be assertively treated to prevent the patient's death. In contrast, other cold-related illnesses—frostbite and immersion foot—are localized in their effects and do not have the same urgency.

A classic example of cold stress occurs when active backcountry winter skiers stop for lunch and wait until they stop sweating and start to feel cool before donning more clothing. The added clothing, at ambient temperature, initially draws even more heat from the skiers. Even within the time frame of a modest lunch break, the skiers progressively feel colder and start shivering; the added clothing doesn't warm them up, and they can't wait to get on the move to warm up.

Usually hypothermia occurs after prolonged exposure to a chilly environment rather than exposure to extreme cold. A drizzly day with the temperature around 25 degrees

WINDCHILL INDEX

Temperature (°F)

Calm	40	35	30	25	20	15	10	5	0	-5	-10	-15	-20	-25	-30	-35	-40	-45
5	36	31	25	19	13	7	1	-5	-11	-16	-22	-28	-34	-40	-46	-52	-57	-63
10	34	27	21	15	9	3	-4	-10	-16	-22	-28	-35	-41	-47	-53	-59	-66	-72
15	32	25	19	13	6	0	-7	-13	-19	-26	-32	-39	-45	-51	-58	-64	-71	-77
20	30	24	17	11	4	-2	-9	-15	-22	-29	-35	-42	-48	-55	-61	-68	-74	-81
25	29	23	16	9	3	-4	-11	-17	-24	-31	-37	-44	-51	-58	-64	-71	-78	-84
30	28	22	15	8	1	-5	-12	-19	-26	-33	-39	-46	-53	-60	-67	-73	-80	-87
35	28	21	14	7	0	-7	-14	-21	-27	-34	-41	-48	-55	-62	-69	-76	-82	-89
40	27	20	13	6	-1	-8	-15	-22	-29	-36	-43	-50	-57	-64	-71	-78	-84	-91
45	26	19	12	5	-2	-9	-16	-23	-30	-37	-44	-51	-58	-65	-72	-79	-86	-93
50	26	19	12	4	-3	-10	-17	-24	-31	-38	-45	-52	-60	-67	-74	-81	-88	-95
55	25	18	11	4	-3	-11	-18	-25	-32	-39	-46	-54	-61	-68	-75	-82	-89	-97
60	25	17	10	3	-4	-11	-19	-26	-33	-40	-48	-55	-62	-69	-76	-84	-91	-98

Wind speed (mph)

Frostbite times

30 minutes   10 minutes   5 minutes

Source: National Weather Service, NOAA

Fig. 24-3. Windchill index.

Fahrenheit (minus 4 degrees Celsius) and a strong breeze is a more typical setting for hypothermia than minus 10 degrees Fahrenheit (minus 23 degrees Celsius) at the ice cliffs. Wet clothing and exposure to wind are major mechanisms for losing body heat. Direct contact with snow or cold rock also robs the body of heat. Dehydration, inadequate food intake, and fatigue are risk factors. An active climber immobilized suddenly by injury in a cool, cold, or windy environment is particularly susceptible.

Hypothermia symptoms vary depending on the individual and the extent to which and the amount of time body core temperature has been reduced (see Table 24-3). Initially, signs and symptoms of cooling lag behind the drop in body core temperature. Typically, the hypothermia patient does not notice the early signs. Shivering is an initial indication of core cooling as the body attempts to rewarm itself through muscular work. As cooling continues, cognitive and physical processes progressively decline.

The distinction between mild and moderate hypothermia is blurry. There is no practical way to accurately measure core temperature in the mountains even with a rectal thermometer. In early hypothermia, symptoms include intense shivering, fumbling hand movements, stumbling, dulling of mental functions, and uncooperative or isolative behavior. The climbing party can evaluate coordination by having the person walk an imaginary tightrope for 15 feet (5 meters), heel to toe. As core temperature slides further, shivering becomes increasingly violent, but at some point it ceases. The patient may not be able to walk but may still be able to maintain posture.

24

TABLE 24-3. STAGES OF CORE COOLING

STAGE	TEMP. (°F)	TEMP. (°C)	SELF-CARE	SHIVERING	MENTAL STATUS
Cold stress	95–98.6	35–37	Yes	Yes	Alert
Mild hypothermia	90–95	32–35	No	May cease	Diminished
Moderate hypothermia	82–90	28–32	No	Will cease	Conscious
Severe to profound hypothermia	<82	<28	No	No	Unconscious

Muscle and nervous system function continue declining. Muscles become stiff and movements uncoordinated. Behavior is confused or irrational.

In severe to profound hypothermia—body core temperatures below 82 degrees Fahrenheit (28 degrees Celsius)—shivering stops and consciousness will gradually be lost. As hypothermia further progresses, it may be extremely difficult to observe a pulse or respiration. The patient's pupils may dilate.

Hypothermia is an emergency condition that will lead to death unless treated. Treat preventively rather than wait until signs and symptoms appear and then be faced with trying to stop, overcome, and reverse the body's inability to generate sufficient heat. The priorities of treatment are to stop heat loss and rewarm (see the "Tips for Preventing Hypothernia" sidebar). Help an ambulatory patient (one who can walk) don clothing, consume food and water, and keep traveling—muscle activity is likely to be the quickest way to warm up.

Treatment of a nonambulatory hypothermic patient (for example, an excavated avalanche victim) begins with ending further heat loss by stopping the person's exposure to the elements. Insulate the patient from the ground, out of the wind and precipitation; remove wet clothing. In mild hypothermia cases, it may suffice to supply dry clothing, add insulation under and around the patient, and shelter the person from the wind and elements. If the patient's gag reflex and swallowing ability are intact, offer liquids, sweet liquids, energy gels, and carbohydrates for food energy for shivering. Use heat packs and hot water bottles. Contrary to mountain lore, supplying warm drinks is not as important as simply replenishing fluids. (Consider this: pouring a teaspoonful of warm water into a cupful of ice water would not be an effective way to warm up the cup.) Treat dehydration until urine output is restored.

Most hypothermia patients with altered consciousness require active rewarming, which can be very challenging for small parties to accomplish in the wilderness. Place hot water bottles wrapped in mittens or socks, to avoid burning, at the patient's chest, neck, armpits, and groin, where large blood vessels are located near the body surface. Enclose the patient in a wrap of clothing, sleeping bags, and sleeping pads to insulate against heat loss. Direct body contact with a (warm) party member is less effective than using heat packs or hot water bottles. While ensuring enough fresh air to prevent carbon monoxide poisoning as well as preventing burns, it may be possible to use a tarp or rain fly set up around the seated patient to capture the heat (sauna-like) from a climbing stove. Allow the recovering

TIPS FOR PREVENTING HYPOTHERMIA

- Avoid sweat wetness.
- Avoid windchill by covering exposed skin.
- Maintain hydration.
- Wear adequate insulation and shells.
- Stay well fed.
- Pace yourself to avoid sweating and fatigue.
- Prior to prolonged stops, don chilled clothing to warm it up.
- If you are starting to feel cool, regardless of moving or stopping, put on more warm clothing.

patient to shiver for at least 30 minutes before exercise to thermally stabilize them.

A profoundly hypothermic patient must be handled gently to avoid inadvertently sending cold blood from the surface circulation back to the heart; this "afterdrop" could cause heart rhythm abnormalities such as ventricular fibrillation. Do not offer oral liquids to a semiconscious patient. Rewarm the patient slowly to minimize afterdrop. Limit limb movement and keep the patient horizontal. Once a patient has adequate energy reserves, the most effective means of heating may be for the patient to walk.

Before starting CPR, feel for a carotid pulse for 1 minute. If there is no detectable pulse, start chest compressions, including rescue breathing. Because a profoundly hypothermic person may appear dead, it is essential not to give up on resuscitation efforts until the patient is warm, has received adequately performed CPR, and still shows no signs of life. Keep in mind the saying that "no one is dead until warm and dead." Severely hypothermic patients have tolerated delayed and interrupted CPR to make full neurologic recovery. As in heatstroke, once the severely hypothermic patient is back to normal body core temperature, the patient must still be monitored because temperature-regulating mechanisms may not be stable for a considerable period.

The party must know when to call off a summit quest. Watch out for each other. When a party member becomes exhausted, that person is often "too tired" to bother adding clothing, to eat, or to drink, making hypothermia more likely to occur. Shivering must never be ignored. Because hypothermia interferes with a mountaineer's judgment and perception, climbing partners must be annoyingly persistent in telling a shivering climber to don warmer gear. (See the "Tips for Preventing Hypothermia" sidebar above.)

Raynaud's Disease

Raynaud's disease is a chronic, temporary, intense vaso-constriction (constriction of blood vessels) of the tissue in which cold is a frequent trigger. A climber with Raynaud's disease may appear to have frostbite. Initially, involved fingers turn white and stiff and feel numb due to diminished blood supply. Later they may turn bluish due to a lack of oxygen. After the blood vessels reopen, the flushing may turn the area red. Those with a history of Raynaud's will be familiar with the course of an episode. These climbers are more susceptible to frostbite or cold injuries and need to use preventive measures—avoid triggers (exposure to cold weather without adequate clothing or touching cold gear, such as an ice axe, for instance) and use good warm gloves or mittens and chemical heat packs—to keep their hands warm and also to treat an episode. Treat as for frostnip (see below).

Frostnip

Frostnip, commonly mistaken for frostbite, is a superficial nonfreezing cold injury associated with intense vaso-constriction (constriction of blood vessels) in exposed skin—usually fingers, cheeks, ears, or nose. It is a common occurrence. Waiting too long to don gloves is a frequent cause. Treat by donning insulated clothing, warming the skin with direct contact with something warm (warm skin or bottles full of hot water), breathing with cupped hands over the nose, and using chemical heat packs in gloves or boots. Exercise increases dilation of blood vessels in limbs, which should help. Rewarming may be painful, but frost-nip does not result in long-term damage. The occurrence of frostnip may signal conditions favorable for frostbite (see below).

Frostbite

Frostbite is true tissue freezing; ice crystals form in the body's internal fluids, leading to tissue dehydration and eventual tissue death. Frostbitten tissue is cold, hard, and pale or darkly discolored and is numb. Frostbite can be classified as superficial (little permanent tissue loss expected) or deep (tissue loss expected). The distinction is usually difficult to make in the wilderness. The affected body part can be severely and permanently damaged, and effects can persist for years. Skin injury is common. Frostbitten tissue is fragile and should never be massaged.

Avoid frostbite by wearing condition-appropriate, non-constrictive clothing in layers, and cover exposed areas. Mittens can be warmer than gloves. Dry feet are important; avoid constricting boots. Chemical hand and toe warmers

are helpful. Wiggle toes and fingers; prompt the party members to check and move theirs. Avoid skin contact with cold metal or stove fuel, which can cause frostbite on contact. Stop and warm fingers and toes before they go numb.

Treatment for frostbite starts with treating for any accompanying hypothermia (see above). Superficial frostbite can be warmed against another warm body—for example, placing a cold finger or foot against a warm belly. In the wilderness, it is undesirable to rewarm a deeply frozen body part, because if the thawed body part is then refrozen, tissue death will be more extensive. Instead, evacuate the patient to a medical facility for rewarming. A frozen foot, once thawed, is impossible to walk on; the patient will have to be carried out. However, do not attempt to retard spontaneous rewarming by deliberately packing the area in snow, keeping it in cold water, or traveling in a chilled vehicle.

In the rare instance in which wilderness rewarming is considered advisable, the frostbitten part should be warmed in a water bath that is 104 to 108 degrees Fahrenheit (40 to 42 degrees Celsius), about the temperature of a hot tub. In the wilderness, it will be challenging to maintain water in this temperature range. Do not use hotter water, as the frostbitten part is extremely susceptible to thermal injury. Rewarming of an extremity will take 30 to 45 minutes and will be painful; pain medication may be necessary. The frostbitten patient should lie down with the injured part elevated. Blisters often emerge during rewarming; do not rupture these blisters. Gently wash any open wounds or already ruptured blisters with a skin antiseptic, and cover them with sterile dressings loose enough to accommodate some swelling. Patients require additional treatment in a hospital setting to minimize secondary effects.

Immersion Foot

Immersion foot, also called trench foot, occurs when a person's feet have been wet and cold for a period ranging from several hours to days. The injury appears to be a kind of trauma to nerves and muscles caused by diminished oxygen distribution (hypoxia), rather than an injury to blood vessels and skin as in frostbite. Immersion foot could occur after a climber wades across a stream and hikes for several hours with wet boots, and soggy feet or on a multiday trip on which the feet never dry out. Immersion foot results in whitish, pulseless, tingling feet; typically, the unhappy mountaineer discovers these symptoms in the tent at night. Prevention consists of assuring the feet are dry for eight hours a day.

24

Treat immersion foot by drying, gently rewarming, and slightly elevating the feet. Following rewarming, the affected feet shift through a painful phase in which they fill with congested blood and other bodily fluids, which may last several days; they become reddened and swollen, with a bounding pulse. It may be necessary to cool the feet in order to tone down the intensity of this phase. After the feet have been rewarmed, the climber may not be able to walk due to pain for 24 to 48 hours. The patient is at risk for recurrence of immersion foot. Infection and gangrene may occur in severe cases.

CONDITIONS RELATED TO ULTRAVIOLET RADIATION

Intense ultraviolet (UV) radiation from the sun, particularly when it is reflected off snow and ice, can burn an unprepared mountaineer at high altitudes. For every 1,000 feet (305 meters) above sea level, UV radiation increases about 5 to 6 percent. Burn injuries from overexposure to UV radiation are potentially serious but preventable.

Sunburn

Cloud cover does not filter out UV radiation effectively, so skin can burn even on an overcast day. Burned skin can range from bright red to blistered. Certain medications such as tetracycline, sulfa drugs, and diuretics can increase the skin's sensitivity to sun and thus to the danger of its burning.

Sunburn should be treated like any other burn: cool the burned area, cover it, and treat for pain. Blistered areas in particular should be covered with sterile dressings to minimize the risk of infection.

The most effective prevention is to cover exposed skin with clothing and use adequate sunscreen. Tightly woven clothing is effective in screening UV radiation; there is no need to use special clothing with an ultraviolet protection factor (UPF) rating. Hats should include a wide brim to protect the back of the neck as well as face and ears. A handkerchief, neck gaiter, or thin balaclava can help cover the face. When skin must be exposed, sunscreen products extend the time that can be spent in the sun without getting burned. (See "Sun Protection" in Chapter 2, Clothing and Equipment.)

Snow Blindness

Snow blindness (ultraviolet keratitis) is a potentially serious problem that results when the outer layers of the eyes are burned by UV radiation. The cornea (the clear layer at the front of the eye) is most easily burned. Its surface can become roughened and blistered. With further radiation, the lenses of the eyes can become burned as well. Snow blindness sets in 6 to 12 hours after the UV radiation exposure. Dry, sandy-feeling eyes become light sensitive, then reddened and teary, and then extremely painful. Recovery takes one or more days.

Prevention of snow blindness is straightforward. In high-UV environs, climbers must wear either goggles or glacier sunglasses with side shields to block UV radiation bouncing off the snow. Choose sunglasses that block 99 to 100 percent of both UVA and UVB rays. Glare can be filtered out with a darkly tinted or polarized lens, but these features do not filter out the burning UV light. If climbers lose their eye protection, emergency goggles can be fashioned out of duct tape or cardboard by cutting narrow horizontal slits for each eye. (See "Sun Protection" in Chapter 2, Clothing and Equipment.)

Treatment of snow blindness includes providing pain relief and preventing further injury. Cool compresses may reduce pain, and sunglasses help with photosensitivity. Remove contact lenses unless the patient can tolerate them and they are needed for evacuation. Advise the snow blindness patient to avoid rubbing the eyes and to rest. There is no evidence to support therapeutic bandaging of the eyes. Topical antibiotic ointments, anti-inflammatories, and systemic pain medications may be used. Recheck for light sensitivity at half-day intervals.

HIGH-ALTITUDE CONDITIONS

With increasing elevation pressure, temperature and humidity decrease while ultraviolet radiation increases. It becomes difficult to climb as efficiently or powerfully as at lower elevations. As elevation increases, the body's organs and tissues struggle to get the oxygen they need for metabolism. Eventually, climbers enter the state of reduced oxygen called hypoxia. Hypoxia is greatest during sleeping.

Physiological Adaptations to Altitude

One adaptation to high-altitude hypoxia is an increase in the rate and depth of breathing. After ascending to high altitude, a climber's respiratory rate continues to increase for several days. The increase in respiratory rate also results in greater expiration of carbon dioxide, which lowers dissolved carbon dioxide in the blood. Another normal adaptation to high-altitude hypoxia is that the kidneys send more water on to the bladder as urine, ridding the body of more fluid. This diuresis makes the blood slightly thicker; the change begins promptly on ascent and continues for several weeks. Eventually the body produces a greater number of red blood cells in an effort to increase oxygen-carrying capacity.

Acclimatization

The body adapts to the environmental change of high altitude, but complete acclimatization takes time. The single most critical reason people get sick at high altitude is that they ascend too high too fast. The single most important way to prevent altitude illness is to undertake a slow ascent to high elevation. On lengthy trips above 10,000 feet (about 3,000 meters), limit increases in sleeping elevation to about 1,000 to 1,500 feet (about 300 to 460 meters) per night. Two or three times a week, allow an additional night at the same elevation as the night before. Be sure to maintain adequate fluid intake.

Insomnia

The ability to sleep soundly deteriorates at high altitude. Most mountaineers have insomnia at altitude, waking up more often during the night and getting less deep sleep. Commonly, an irregular breathing rhythm appears during sleep and sometimes during wakefulness, too. There are periods of apnea (no breathing) interspersed with periods of hyperventilation, an alternating rhythm known as Cheyne-Stokes respiration. The low carbon dioxide content of the blood appears to drive this odd change in breathing. A small dose (one-quarter tablet) of acetazolamide at bedtime decreases Cheyne-Stokes respiration and may aid sleep. New evidence suggests that prescription sleeping pills help with insomnia at altitude; despite concerns that they depress respiration, they have been used at altitude without adverse consequences.

Radial Keratotomy

Hypoxia at altitude causes temporary edema and thickening of the cornea, which may cause increased farsightedness and decreased visual acuity in climbers who have had the radial keratotomy (RK) procedure. One approach is to take along glasses or goggles of different corrective prescriptions. Research is unclear as to altitude effects on laser-assisted in-situ keratomileusis (LASIK) or photorefractive keratectomy (PRK).

Retinal Hemorrhage

At high altitude, an increase in retinal blood flow and subsequent retinal vein dilation can lead to retinal hemorrhages in many climbers. Climbers should be instructed to descend if they develop altered vision. The presence of

SIGNS OF ACUTE MOUNTAIN SICKNESS

People with AMS usually have a headache, plus one of the following:
- Insomnia
- Listlessness and/or lassitude
- Loss of appetite
- Nausea
- Vomiting
- Lightheadedness or dizziness made worse when in an upright position

high-altitude retinal hemorrhage has been associated with altitude illness.

Acute Mountain Sickness

At least half of the sea-level residents who travel rapidly to moderate altitude—8,000 to 14,000 feet (2,400 to 4,300 meters)—experience some degree of acute mountain sickness (AMS). This is a collection of nonspecific symptoms that can resemble a case of flu, a hangover, or carbon monoxide poisoning from stove use inside an inadequately ventilated shelter. Headache is the cardinal symptom, often accompanied by fatigue, loss of appetite, nausea, and, occasionally, vomiting (see the "Signs of Acute Mountain Sickness" sidebar). Headache onset is usually 2 to 12 hours after arrival at a higher altitude and often during or after the first night. Headaches tend to be localized in the occipital or temporal areas. AMS can vary widely in severity but generally resolves with 24 to 72 hours of acclimatization.

AMS can progress in severity. In cases wherein symptoms such as headache and nausea progress, a descent of 2,000 to 3,000 feet (600 to 900 meters) in elevation is the best treatment. The diagnosis of AMS is confirmed if the condition improves upon descent. It is important to differentiate AMS from the more ominous HACE and HAPE (see below).

Some medicines can be used to deal with altitude-related health problems; climbers should ask their physician about the appropriateness of such drugs for their situation. Some mountaineers use acetazolamide (Diamox) the night before or the morning of the ascent and through the first 48 hours at high altitude in order to prevent AMS or block its recurrence. Potential problems caused by this medication are tingling of the extremities, ringing in the ears, nausea, frequent urination, and a change in the sense

24

of taste. It is better to test this possibility at home rather than in the mountains. Acetazolamide does appear to be effective in preventing and treating AMS as well as the breathing changes brought on by high altitude. The steroid dexamethasone is effective in preventing and treating AMS as well as HACE and HAPE; it is usually reserved for treatment or when rapid elevation gain prevents normal acclimatization.

High-Altitude Cerebral Edema

High-altitude cerebral edema (HACE) usually develops in unacclimatized climbers above 10,000 feet (about 3,000 meters), although it can occur as low as 8,500 feet (2,600 meters). HACE may be just the severe manifestation of AMS. HACE rarely occurs out of the blue and more often occurs in people who have had AMS that is worsening. Generally, it takes from one to three days at high altitude for HACE to develop. Vessels in the brain respond to the stress of high altitude by becoming leaky, resulting in the brain swelling with increased fluid. Ultimately, the brain swells inside its rigid container of cranial bones.

Early signs of this deadly condition include deteriorating coordination, headache, loss of energy, and altered mental status, ranging from confusion or signs of not thinking clearly to hallucinating. Use the coordination test: ask the person to walk an imaginary tightrope for 15 feet (5 meters), heel to toe, to check for ataxia. Nausea and forceful vomiting may be present.

Once HACE develops, it may advance rapidly. The patient may become somnolent and lapse into a coma. Descent is critical to survival. On some expeditions, portable hyperbaric chambers (such as the Gamow bag) are used to create an artificial lower elevation in the effort to stabilize the patient for a few hours. Supplemental oxygen can also be helpful. Drugs such as dexamethasone are beneficial; acetazolamide might be an additional part of the treatment.

High-Altitude Pulmonary Edema

In high-altitude pulmonary edema (HAPE), body fluids leak into the lungs to a degree that interferes with respiratory function. HAPE is a potentially fatal condition and survival depends on a rapid response. HAPE is a different disease from AMS or HACE and can occur quite suddenly in climbers who were otherwise performing well. Occasionally, HAPE and HACE do occur together.

Early signs of HAPE may overlap with more benign problems, such as a persistent cough caused by simple bronchial irritation from dry, high-mountain air. Decreasing ability to exercise, needing to take more frequent rest breaks, or falling behind companions might be more subtle signs of HAPE. Breathlessness and a hacking cough appear as HAPE develops. Rates of breathing and pulse increase.

If HAPE is allowed to advance, breathing will require effort and will include bubbling noises. Lips and nail beds may appear dusky or tinged with blue, reflecting the body's inability to transfer oxygen into arterial blood due to the water barrier in the lungs. Some affected people also develop a low-grade fever, making it difficult to distinguish HAPE from pneumonia; one indicator of HAPE is how rapidly it worsens with continued ascent.

The key to treating HAPE is to descend. A descent of 3,000 feet (900 meters) will resolve nearly all HAPE cases that are caught early. If descent is impossible, oxygen and a Gamow bag are useful. Ultimately, however, real descent must occur. Some mountaineers use the drug nifedipine, which widens blood vessels, to help prevent or treat HAPE. Studies suggest that drugs for erectile dysfunction, including tadalafil and sildenafil, also can be used for treatment of HAPE in both men and women, particularly when descent is not feasible.

INJURIES

One study of the National Outdoor Leadership School courses over a five-year period showed that 80 percent of the injuries suffered by course participants were sprains, strains, and soft-tissue injuries. To minimize the extent of injuries from a mountaineering accident, apply skillful and caring first aid. Specific treatments for serious injuries are beyond the scope of this book, so hands-on instruction in mountaineering first aid is essential. (See Resources in the back of the book for detailed first-aid texts.)

BLISTERS

All wilderness travelers dread blisters. These bubbles under the skin, filled with clear or blood-tinged fluid, probably represent the most common health-related reason for ending outings. Small blisters generally are a source of minor irritation and discomfort, but larger blisters can cause significant pain, and if they rupture, they can lead to serious infection and ulceration. Blisters result from the skin rubbing against socks and the inner lining of the boot—often, new or poorly fitting boots. Blisters happen when boots are too large or too loosely laced or when socks are lumpy or wrinkled. Moisture tends to soften the skin, so wet boots or socks promote blister formation.

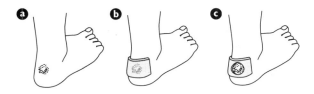

Fig. 24-4. Blisters: a, starting out as a hot spot; b, tape the hot spot to prevent blister formation; c, doughnut-cushion a blister once it forms.

A blister usually becomes noticeable first as a hot spot (fig. 24-4a), a localized sensation of heat that increases in size and intensity over time. Inspect such spots immediately, and take preventive measures. Place a generous strip of waterproof plastic adhesive tape or Moleskin over the spot (fig. 24-4b). Other suitable products include 2nd Skin and Dr. Scholl's Molefoam; some sufferers are successful with duct tape or waterproof first-aid tape. Avoid using adhesive bandage strips (such as Band-Aids) for covering hot spots; these strips seem to promote blister formation when the nonadhesive dressing pad balls up and rubs against the already sensitive skin. Sometimes antichafing products can help as well to prevent hot spots, but these products don't always work in footwear.

Once a blister has formed, avoid opening it unless absolutely necessary; opening a blister may introduce infection to the area. The body will reabsorb the blister fluid after several days, and it will heal. If the hike or whatever activity caused the blister must be continued, pad the blister and protect it from rupture by layering a "doughnut" of padding to a depth that keeps pressure off the blister itself (fig. 24-4c). The padding doughnut must be deeper and wider than the blister. Tape the padding well to prevent it from becoming displaced.

If a blister breaks open, wash and dress it with sterile dressings, as with any open wound. Infection is a concern; avoid further tissue damage if at all possible.

To prevent blisters, fit boots properly. Break them in slowly and thoroughly before launching into any extended hikes. The areas most prone to blistering are over the heel or Achilles tendon at the back of the ankle and on the toes. If you tend to blister easily, pad the blister-prone areas with tape or adhesive foam, but do not pad them so much that a new pressure point is created around the edge of the foam. Keep feet dry, and wear adequate, well-fitting socks. Invest in new socks: threadbare socks can cause blisters.

CHAFING

In addition to foot blisters, friction chafing can occur due to repetitive motion at a number of places on the body, especially between the thighs. Chafing is commonly caused by clothing that doesn't fit, cotton fabrics, dirty clothing, sweat, and sand or dirt. In severe cases it can painfully rub away the skin. For chronic chafing, find and eliminate the source. Lubricating products may help preventively. As for foot blisters, take immediate action after becoming aware of the irritation. It will only get worse without intervention.

BURNS

Burns happen in the wilderness when climbers handle hot cookware and stoves (see also "Sunburn" earlier in this chapter). Burned skin can range from bright red to blistered to charred (first, second, and third degree, respectively). Cool a burn within 30 minutes to reduce pain and depth of injury; use cold water, or snow if available. Filtered or treated water is preferred. Do not drain any blisters and avoid contamination where the skin has been broken. Superficial burns or those with a few blisters can be covered with a topical antimicrobial agent and a nonadherent dressing. More extensive blistering and deeper skin damage, especially to the face and hands, need additional bandaging and urgent medical care.

Burns can also occur from friction against skin. Use of proper gloves when doing certain activities like rappelling will minimize this risk. If these injuries do happen, treat them as you would other burns. Also see "Lightning Strikes" later in this section.

EYE INJURIES

Corneal abrasions are one of the most common eye conditions in the backcountry, and they are usually caused by a foreign body, a blow to the eye, or the extended use of contact lenses. Symptoms include feeling as though there is something caught in the eye even when nothing has been found. Remove any small foreign body from the affected eye. If the eyeball may be ruptured or if deep scratches are apparent in the cornea, then evacuate the affected individual immediately. Treat corneal abrasions with topical antibiotics and frequent use of artificial tears. Sunglasses may help reduce sensitivity to light, but there is no evidence supporting eye patching for corneal abrasions. If the injury is still bothersome after 24 hours, seek further treatment.

24

WOUND CARE

Wounds such as scrapes, cuts, and punctures are common in the wilderness. The goals of wound care are to prevent infection, avoid further trauma, and optimize healing. When providing first aid to someone else, put on protective gloves to prevent exposure to any possible bloodborne pathogens. All grossly contaminated wounds should be thoroughly irrigated with sanitized (filtered, chemically treated, or boiled) water. Pressure irrigation using a syringe or a hydration bladder is more painful but will dislodge dirt and other contaminants more effectively. Gentle scrubbing may be needed to clean the wound. Apply topical antimicrobial agents to reduce the risk of infection before covering the wound with a nonstick dressing and bandage. Lacerations can be closed with skin closures (Steri-Strips) or cyanoacrylate glue if the wound is clean. Use a hemostatic gauze pad where bleeding is persistent.

SPRAINS, STRAINS, AND FRACTURES

Strains are muscle injuries; sprains are injuries to ligaments. The most common type of injury that keeps a party from self-rescue and requires outside assistance is injury to the ankle or foot. While this chapter cannot adequately cover the details of fractures, emergency splinting in the backcountry can be used for severe sprains or fractures until the patient is self-evacuated or rescued. Strains can be quite painful and debilitating. Being well conditioned,

hydrated, and properly warmed up helps prevent strains. Be careful not to push yourself or your party too quickly.

Taping an Ankle Strain or Sprain

The most common ankle sprain results in an injury to the ligaments on the outside of the ankle. Taping a severe ankle sprain or strain, as well as some fractures, may allow a party to self-rescue. Ankle taping is a skill that must be practiced to keep it in a climber's first-aid repertoire. The standard prescription for ankle taping is the "closed basket weave" using 1.5-inch-wide (3.8-centimeter-wide) adhesive tape, as shown in Figure 24-5. Ideally, the skin should be dry, clean, shaven, and free from lotions or oils that keep the tape from sticking to the skin.

To tape an ankle, follow these steps:

1. **Anchor strips.** First place two adjacent anchor strips all the way around the leg just below the calf (fig. 24-5a). Place a third strip all the way around the foot at the arch.

2. **U-shaped strips.** Then with the foot flexed, run a U-shaped arch strip (stirrup strip) from the medial (inner) calf anchor strip, beneath the foot then under tension up to the lateral (outer) calf anchor strip. Place a U-shaped heel strip (horseshoe strips) from the arch anchor strip back around and above the heel and forward to the other side arch anchor, perpendicular to the stirrup strip (fig. 24-5b).

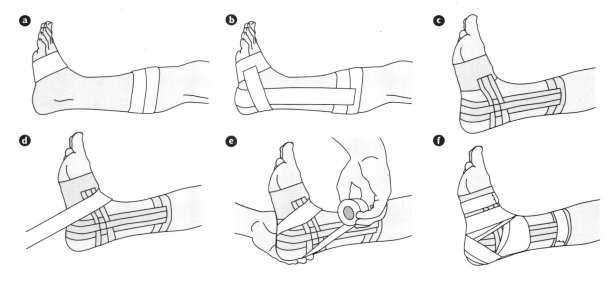

Fig. 24-5. Taping an ankle: a, attach anchor strips; b, add U-shaped strips; c, create the basket weave with layered U-shaped strips; d and e, apply figure-eight heel locks; f, add cover strips.

3. **Basket weave.** Alternate three stirrup strips with three horseshoe strips, with a half strip overlap, working from back to front and bottom to top for a basket-weave appearance. (fig. 24-5c).

4. **End locks.** Apply two figure-eight heel locks: starting from the high lateral (outer) ankle, descend medially across the ankle (to inner ankle), around the heel, under the foot, and medially up the foot, returning to the start (fig. 24-5d and e).

5. **Cover strips.** Add strips to cover ends of stirrups and horseshoe strips (fig. 24-5f).

After taping the ankle, ask about the patient's comfort and check circulation: gently squeeze the toes—the nail bed should turn white, and once the squeeze is released the toes should return to a pink color within a second or two. If the climber develops pain or the skin turns bluish or cold or numb, the tape may need to be loosened or removed.

Splinting a Sprain or Fracture

Several principles apply in backcountry splinting (see the "Fracture Management" sidebar). Splints should be well padded to avoid damage to skin and superficial tissues. This is often accomplished by wrapping elastic bandages around the splint material or by using a soft material to cover the injured limb. A structural aluminum malleable (SAM) splint is highly versatile, lightweight, and reusable. Because it can be rolled, flattened, curved, cut, or folded, a SAM splint is adaptable to many types of injuries.

FRACTURE MANAGEMENT

- Take precautions to protect the first-aid provider from potential contamination from the injured person's blood.
- Assess the limb and/or joint for circulation, sensation, and function.
- Expose the injury site, and control bleeding if present.
- Apply dressings to wounds as needed.
- Prepare a splint.
- Stabilize the injured extremity and apply the splint without excessive movement of the extremity.
- Use padding to fill any large gaps between limb and splint.
- Immobilize the fracture site and joints above and below it.
- Reassess circulation, bleeding, and sensation periodically.

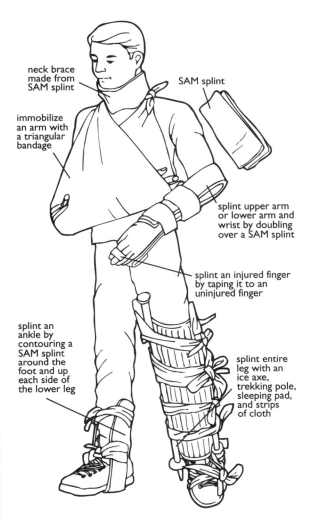

neck brace made from SAM splint

SAM splint

immobilize an arm with a triangular bandage

splint upper arm or lower arm and wrist by doubling over a SAM splint

splint an injured finger by taping it to an uninjured finger

splint an ankle by contouring a SAM splint around the foot and up each side of the lower leg

splint entire leg with an ice axe, trekking pole, sleeping pad, and strips of cloth

Fig. 24-6. Stabilize an injured area with a SAM splint (doubled to brace a neck, doubled over to an appropriate length to splint all of a forearm or wrist, or wrapped around a foot and secured with bandannas to splint an ankle) or improvise with available materials (injured finger taped to adjacent finger, injured hand immobilized with a triangular bandage, entire injured leg splinted with ice axe, trekking pole, and sleeping pad).

For extremity splinting, when possible immobilize the joints above and below the injury with the splint. Splint the injury in a position that is comfortable and natural. For an upper-extremity injury, the patient will generally

24

hold the injured arm in toward the chest, cradling it with the uninjured arm; splint the arm in this position. For a lower-extremity injury, strive to make the splint as comfortable as possible and in line with the patient's body.

Improvising a splint is often necessary (fig. 24-6). For example, if no appropriate material is readily available, a lower-leg injury can often be protected by taping the injured leg to the uninjured leg. Similarly, an injured finger can be secured to the adjacent finger for temporary protection. Splints can be fashioned from a wide variety of materials, including sticks and mountaineering equipment such as a backpack's internal stays, a rolled-up backpack, sleeping pads, trekking poles, or an ice axe. Spare webbing, twisted duct tape, bandannas, or athletic tape can be used to secure an improvised splint.

Swelling can be expected for hours after a fracture or severe sprain. Take care to avoid applying splints too tightly, which can impair circulation to the affected limb. After applying a splint, periodically reassess the patient by checking pulse, skin temperature, and sensation below the injury while awaiting outside care.

To minimize swelling of the injured extremity, a bag of snow or ice can be incorporated into the splint by wrapping the bag in the elastic bandage that secures the splint. Care must be taken to remove the bag periodically to avoid cold injury to soft tissue. In general, the snow or ice should be applied for no more than 20 minutes at a time. The injured extremity should also be elevated to minimize swelling.

HARNESS SUSPENSION TRAUMA

A motionless climber hanging from a harness is facing a life-threatening emergency. Harness leg straps restrict blood flow, which leads to blood pooling in the legs and lowered core blood pressure. The loss of blood pressure may lead to death within minutes.

The priority is to end suspension. If possible, lower the climber to a ledge. If the climber is conscious, he or she should move their legs, transfer weight to any available feature, or stand in improvised aiders made from slings or a prusik. If a climber is unconscious, a rescuer should immediately strive to raise and keep the legs horizontal until the climber can be relocated. The rescued climber can lie flat to help restore normal blood circulation and chemistry. Monitor and treat any secondary effects.

HEAD, NECK, AND BACK INJURIES

Head and spine injuries are common causes of death in alpine wilderness accidents. Blunt force injuries often are caused by falling objects, such as rock or ice, or by a fall

INDICATORS OF POSSIBLE HEAD INJURIES
■ Blunt force to head or neck
■ Unconsciousness
■ Drainage of blood or clear fluid from the ears, nose, or eyes
■ Unequal eye pupil size or unequal constricting response of the pupils to light
■ Black eyes
■ Very slow pulse
■ Fluctuations in respiratory rate
■ Headache
■ Disorientation and confusion
■ Seizure
■ Vomiting

in which the climber's head or back strikes a hard object. For all head injuries, assume that there is a neck (cervical spine) injury until an examination proves otherwise. For all cervical spine injuries, the patient must be monitored for potential head and brain injury. See the "Indicators of Possible Head Injuries" sidebar.

Indicators of possible neck and spine injuries include significant spinal pain or tenderness, numbness, tingling, or paralysis. Some factors that may make it hard to determine if there is a cervical spine injury include head injury, severe or distracting injuries, age greater than 65, and intoxication.

Less-serious injuries may be treatable by the party. A cervical collar is unnecessary with an uninjured spine or stable spine injury, including neck sprains, strains, and even mild fractures (for example, a mild compression fracture). The challenge is to determine if the injury is serious or not. Patients who have had a minor accident, are ambulatory since the injury, are in a sitting position, have delayed onset of neck pain, have an absence of midline cervical spine tenderness, and are able to actively rotate the neck and spine 30 degrees in each plane should not require a cervical collar.

Serious injuries of the head, neck, and spine have the potential to be permanently disabling. With severe injuries, immobilizing the head and spine until rescuers can arrive is the best first-aid treatment. Neutral alignment should be restored and maintained, unless such a maneuver causes the patient to resist, experience increased pain, or exhibit a new or worsening neurologic deficit. Light to moderate traction should be used when returning a cervical

LIGHTNING CAN STRIKE A CLIMBER IN VARIOUS WAYS

- Direct strike of a mountaineer in the open who could not find shelter
- Splash strike, in which the lightning current jumps from an object onto a mountaineer who sought shelter nearby
- Contact injury, from holding an object that lightning hits
- Step voltage, transmitted along the ground or through an object near a climber (even a wet rope)
- Blunt trauma or blast effect, created by the shock wave from a nearby strike

spine to the neutral position. An improvised cervical collar should be used.

If the patient is in significant risk of further injury or death, they may need to be moved. When transferring a patient with possible neck injuries, grab the patient's trapezius muscles (tops of the shoulders between neck and point of the shoulder) and firmly squeeze the patient's head between your forearms, which are placed approximately at the level of the patient's ears. Move the patient as a unit, minimizing movements of the neck and back.

Lightning Strikes

The high-mountain environment receives many more thunderstorms each year than coastal areas do, as the weather systems mass against the mountains before rising over them. Summer afternoons are the most likely time for thunderstorms, and therefore lightning, to endanger the mountaineer. Most lightning ground strikes occur directly below a cloud and hit the nearest high point. But lightning strikes can emanate from several miles away toward high points ahead of (or, less frequently, behind) the main thunderhead cloud formation—"out of a clear blue sky." Therefore, mountaineers can be in danger of a lightning strike at times even when the storm is not directly overhead (see the "Lightning Can Strike a Climber in Various Ways" sidebar).

Lightning-caused injuries include cardiac arrest, burns, and internal injuries. The most immediate danger from being struck by lightning is cardiac arrest. Lightning burns often take several hours to develop after the strike; these burns are usually superficial (similar to first-degree burns) and do not usually require treatment (see "Burns" earlier

in this section), although serious internal injuries can also occur. The patient may be knocked unconscious or have temporary paralysis. The eyes, a vulnerable port of entry for electrical current, can be damaged in a lightning strike. Ear damage also may occur; a patient might not respond to your questions because of a loss of hearing caused by the strike.

After the lightning strike, the patient does not present an electrical hazard to rescuers. Proceed promptly with first aid, assessing CAB-B: Circulation, Airway, Breathing, and deadly Bleeding (see "Responding to Accidents" earlier in this chapter). It is important to get the lightning-strike patient to a medical facility, because vital body functions may remain unstable for a considerable time after resuscitation. For information on how to avoid being struck by lightning, see "Thunder and Lightning" in Chapter 28, Mountain Weather.

ILLNESSES

One study of the National Outdoor Leadership School's courses over a five-year period showed that 60 percent of the illnesses experienced by course participants were non-specific viral illnesses or diarrhea. Hygiene appeared to have a significant impact on these illnesses.

GASTROINTESTINAL DISORDERS

Gastrointestinal (GI) disorders can cause a wide range of symptoms, from a mildly upset stomach to weeks of diarrhea. The onset of any GI disorder will ruin a trip. Understanding, preventing, and treating these disorders is increasingly important to climbers.

Fecal-oral contamination. In mountaineering environments, the most common cause of gastrointestinal infections that entail diarrhea and abdominal cramping is fecal-oral contamination. Most often, the source of the feces is mountaineers themselves. Some rock climbing routes may be contaminated with feces from previous parties. On glacier routes, handling ropes that have dragged through soiled snow and ice can lead to contamination. Water bottles as well as food can become contaminated from soiled hands. Animal waste also presents a risk.

To keep from contaminating your hands, simply wash them with biodegradable soap and water before eating and especially after defecation. This simple step can help a climber avoid many intestinal disorders. Climbers often are gregarious at rest stops—but think twice before offering your snack bag for each person to plunge a hand into; pouring some contents into each person's hands is less risky.

24

Avoid camping near rodent burrows. Cover food and water so that they are secure from rodent invasion at night.

Food poisoning. The symptoms of food poisoning—generally vomiting and diarrhea, but can also be as simple as an upset stomach—arise rapidly following ingestion of food contaminated by pathogenic bacteria, viruses, or parasites as well as chemical or natural toxins. Symptoms tend to subside within 12 hours. Provide water and electrolytes as tolerated, since dehydration is a side effect of vomiting and diarrhea. The patient may need a few hours to regain strength. To prevent food poisoning, use dietary discretion when traveling. Avoid consuming raw fruits or vegetables, raw meat, raw seafood, tap water, and ice made from tap water. Instead, stick to boiled or treated water, properly cooked meat and vegetables, bottled beverages, and reputable eating establishments.

Contaminated water. While the water flowing in the streams and rivers of the backcountry may look pure, it can still be contaminated with bacteria, viruses, parasites, and other contaminants. The incubation period of the pathogens can be a clue to which kind is the source: Bacterial and viral pathogens have an incubation period of 6 to 72 hours. Protozoal pathogens such as *Cryptosporidium*, *Giardia intestinalis*, or *Giardia lamblia* generally have an incubation period of one to three weeks and rarely present symptoms in the first few weeks of travel.

Bacterial and viral illnesses begin with the sudden onset of bothersome symptoms that can range from mild cramps and urgent loose stools to severe abdominal pain, flatulence, fever, vomiting, and bloody diarrhea. Untreated bacterial diarrhea lasts three to seven days. Viral diarrhea generally lasts two to three days. Parasitic diarrhea, such as giardiasis and cryptosporidiosis, generally has a more gradual onset of low-grade symptoms, with two to five loose stools per day. Protozoal diarrhea can persist for weeks to months without treatment. An acute bout of gastroenteritis can lead to persistent gastrointestinal symptoms, even in the absence of continued infection.

For most intestinal infections associated with diarrhea, treatment during a climbing trip consists of adequately replacing fluids and electrolytes. This can be challenging if the climber is also nauseated. Mix a packet of replacement electrolytes into treated drinking water; a packet is generally equal to 1 teaspoon of salt and 8 teaspoons of sugar and is added to 1 quart (liter) of water. If electrolyte replacements are not available, simply replace fluids. Provide palatable foods and broths with a substantial salt content.

If the party is heading into regions with questionable hygiene and water disinfection practices, seek medical advice about antibiotics that can be taken to help ward off infection, and also ask about antimotility (antidiarrheal) drugs. However, taking such drugs is not a substitute for dietary discretion or prudent water treatment practices (see Chapter 3, Camping, Food, and Water).

TICKBORNE DISEASES

Ticks are arachnids that can carry Lyme disease, Rocky Mountain spotted fever, and other infections. Tick bites may appear anywhere on the body. Three to 30 days after a tick bite (7 days on average), disease signs and symptoms can appear, including fever, chills, headache, fatigue, muscle and joint aches, and swollen lymph nodes. A rash at the site of the bite occurs in 70 to 80 percent of infected persons, expanding in area up to 12 inches (30 centimeters) across and sometimes resembling a target or "bull's-eye" appearance. Skin may feel warm but is rarely itchy or painful.

After being in tick habitat, shower as soon as possible to wash ticks off before they attach and to more easily find and remove them. Conduct a full-body tick check using a mirror to view all parts of your body. Examine gear for hitchhiking ticks. Once you are at home, tumble clothes in a dryer on high heat for an hour to kill remaining ticks. If you do find a tick that has attached itself, avoid folklore remedies such as "painting" the tick with nail polish or petroleum jelly or using heat to make the tick detach from the skin. Do not wait for it to detach; follow these steps to remove it:

1. Use fine-tipped tweezers to grasp the tick as close to your skin's surface as possible.
2. Pull outward with steady, even pressure. Don't twist or jerk the tick; this can cause its mouth parts to break off in your skin. If you are unable to easily remove a mouth part, leave it alone.
3. Thoroughly clean the bite area and your hands with soap and water.

Reducing exposure to ticks is the best defense against tickborne infections. Avoid wooded and brushy areas with high grass and leaf litter. Repel ticks by applying 20 percent to 30 percent DEET or 20 percent picaridin on exposed skin and clothing; 0.5 percent permethrin applied to clothing and gear such as boots, pants, socks, and tents remains protective through several washings. (See "Insect Repellent" in Chapter 2, Clothing and Equipment.)

Light-colored clothing helps you spot ticks, which are usually a dark brown.

OTHER ENVIRONMENTAL FACTORS

From centipedes to poison oak, some insects, plants, and animals are poisonous and can cause painful or debilitating conditions. Check with those knowledgeable of local risks and prevention for the area you are visiting.

PANIC AND ANXIETY

Mountaineering outings are usually refreshing and rejuvenating experiences. In extreme situations, such as a serious accident, nearly all climbers have to deal with their own and one another's stress, anxiety, or even panic. Some people also have a tendency toward intense anxiety in response to certain physical situations in climbing, such as exposure to heights or to enclosed spaces. This tendency can erupt in a panic response during a step-across move on a cliff face or while squeezing up a rock chimney. If affected, a climber may freeze and refuse to go on. The climber may hyperventilate (breathe rapidly) or be unable to recognize that there are safe moves available. The person's ability to fully assess the situation will be blocked; physical movements will be clumsy and fearful, raising the risk of a mishap.

If hyperventilation is a problem, breathing into a bag to increase the concentration of carbon dioxide in the inhaled air can slow the breathing rate. Redirecting the climber's focus onto a useful physical task is a strategy for interrupting the snowballing effect of panic. Fellow climbers can help by maintaining an atmosphere of confident acceptance and support, by pointing out an option for retreat if appropriate, and by calmly and matter-of-factly prompting a panicked climber to use these self-calming techniques, which are helpful in such situations:

- Recognize the panic as an adrenaline reaction to perceived risk.
- Focus on slow, steady, deep breathing.
- Run through the options for safe movement.
- Follow them one at a time.

PREPARING FOR THE UNEXPECTED

It is tempting to assume that carefully reading first-aid texts is sufficient training. Unfortunately, first aid is very much like any other skill: people can read, even memorize, all of the greatest texts on skiing, and yet if they do not practice, they simply will not be good skiers. The same is true with first aid: to be truly competent in first aid, climbers must practice and refresh their skills periodically. The best training strategy is to take advantage of courses offered by many respected organizations.

Practicing first aid will help a climber prepare for dealing with the large element of uncertainty that accompanies mountaineering accidents and serious injuries: uncertainty about what happened; uncertainty about the nature, extent, or seriousness of injuries; uncertainty about what should be done; uncertainty about what the outcome will be. An injured person does not wear a big sign saying what is injured and how to best care for it.

Practicing first aid will also help a climber prepare for the alarm and emotion accompanying accidents. Serious accidents are frightening, and they tend to flood people's minds with a spectrum of emotions, which can interfere with a calm, thoughtful, and rational response. Practicing first-aid scenarios in outdoor first-aid classes can help climbers respond well even when the situation is overwhelmingly stressful. Keeping a cool head and having the skills to provide first aid gives mountaineers confidence in facing whatever a climbing expedition might bring.

24

CHAPTER 25
ALPINE RESCUE

Climbing instruction emphasizes strategies for preventing and mitigating accidents, but even the best-prepared climbers may eventually encounter a situation requiring first-aid and rescue skills. With outside assistance often hours or days away, a climbing party must be able to perform first aid, initiate small-party search and rescue (SAR) efforts, and work effectively with SAR authorities.

This chapter introduces some techniques for small-party rescue from high-angle alpine terrain, search strategies, and guidelines for interacting with SAR agencies. In the event of an accident sustained by another party, climbers must prepare to forgo their planned climb. Instead, they should offer assistance and donate gear, time, and expertise to help.

LEARNING RESCUE TECHNIQUES

First aid and alpine rescue are two components of responding to an accident or serious illness. The first-aid skills taught in most urban and workplace classes are designed to help a severely injured patient survive for the short time it takes for emergency medical services to arrive. Wilderness-oriented first aid, in contrast, helps treat and take care of a patient for hours, possibly days, in an outdoor environment. (See Chapter 24, First Aid, for first-aid references throughout this chapter.) Alpine rescue involves actions a party can take to locate a missing climber, rescue an injured climber from steep terrain, and evacuate an ill or injured climber from the wilderness.

As their climbing skills build and broaden, climbers should also add to their knowledge of first-aid and rescue techniques. Due to the wide variety of rescue situations and available techniques, consider taking a course from one of the many organizations that offer classes in self-rescue. Practice setting up and running the systems to keep personal skills fresh.

THE SEVEN STEPS IN ACCIDENT RESPONSE

Accidents are not inevitable. Smart planning and preparing beforehand, practicing sound climbing strategies and techniques, and recognizing, avoiding, and mitigating hazards can all but eliminate accidents (see Chapter 23, Safety).

The challenges of rescue and evacuation of an ill climber can be just as difficult as those for an injured climber. The early identification of a serious illness is the best strategy for treatment or evacuation before it becomes disabling. Share suspicious signs and behaviors with other party members; the discussion of these clues can facilitate a prompt diagnosis and faster response. Many more rescue options are available for the ill climber who can still walk. While this chapter focuses on accidents, many of the techniques are appropriate for rescuing the ill climber.

THE SEVEN STEPS IN ACCIDENT RESPONSE

1. Take charge of the situation.
2. Approach the patient safely.
3. Perform emergency rescue and urgent first aid.
4. Protect the patient.
5. Check for other injuries.
6. Make a plan.
7. Carry out the plan.

When serious accidents do occur, they happen unexpectedly, often stimulating an intense adrenaline response. This evolutionary response of "freeze, fight, or flight" compromises a climber's ability to think clearly while producing a powerful motivation to take immediate action. However, this adrenaline-fueled response can lead to inappropriate action, which is likely to make things worse and lead to more injuries or delays in rescue.

Devastating accidents have the potential to overwhelm and emotionally paralyze people including those not physically harmed. Should this happen to you, acknowledge what occurred, tell yourself to address that aspect later, then focus attention on what needs to be done. Start with something small, something that you have control over. During and immediately after the accident, the smartest course is to focus on personal and team safety until the party is able to take calm, deliberate action.

The seven steps in accident response outlined in Chapter 24, First Aid, serve as guidance for rescue response as well as for first aid. The seven steps help the party focus in an orderly manner on the tasks to be accomplished (see "The Seven Steps in Accident Response" sidebar). This section provides an overview of these steps as they relate to rescue; the section "Putting It All Together" later in this chapter elaborates on how these steps are implemented in an accident scenario.

STEP 1: TAKE CHARGE OF THE SITUATION
The climb leader has overall responsibility for accident response. The immediate priority is to ensure the safety of the remaining climbers. Throughout the situation, the climb leader must keep returning to the big picture, planning ahead, delegating specific tasks, and avoiding being drawn into time- and attention-robbing details. If the climb leader is incapacitated, an experienced party member must step forward to fill that role.

STEP 2: APPROACH THE PATIENT SAFELY
The rescuer and/or first-aid provider needs safe access to the injured climber. In steep or dangerous terrain, this may require climbing, rappelling, or being lowered to the patient. The party members are likely to be desperate to reach their injured team member, but acting hastily only increases the chance of additional injuries and delays. The party must think out its actions and work deliberately rather than reactively, remembering that survivors' safety always comes first. Considering several solutions to reaching the patient fosters objectivity and improves the likelihood of finding the best approach. The time it takes to ensure the party's safety will not make a difference in the outcome of the patient's situation. The adage "half as fast, twice as efficient" is applicable in rescue response.

STEP 3: PERFORM EMERGENCY RESCUE AND URGENT FIRST AID
Provide life-saving circulatory, airway, breathing, and bleeding (CAB-B) treatment, and other crucial first aid. Don't move the patient unless there is a danger at the patient's current location—such as from avalanche, rockfall, icefall, or immersion in water—or unless the patient is in need of urgent first aid that cannot be administered at the current location, such as midpitch on a rock route. See Chapter 24, First Aid, for more on first aid at this stage.

STEP 4: PROTECT THE PATIENT
Be reassuring and communicate to the injured or ill climber what the team is doing to help. Protect the patient from precipitation, wind, heat, cold, and other environmental factors. As early as possible, anticipate and preventively treat the patient for dehydration, shock, and hypothermia, since successful treatment will be much harder if it begins after signs of these have appeared.

STEP 5: CHECK FOR OTHER INJURIES
Make a thorough examination of the patient to determine what injuries, illnesses, or medical conditions exist and their extent (see Chapter 24, First Aid). This may be difficult in steep terrain, so repeat this process as soon as the injured or ill climber can be moved to a more suitable location and after the initial numbing shock of the accident has worn off.

STEP 6: MAKE A PLAN
Input from other party members helps the climb leader take all crucial factors into account, including the following steps, in preparing the rescue plan. WE RAPPED may be a useful acronym:

25

Weather. Take into account anticipated temperature, wind, and precipitation, which may impact both the patient and the rescue team.

Evacuation. In assessing how to evacuate the party, consider these questions: How far is it to the trailhead? Can the patient walk? Can the patient tolerate the rigors of evacuation? If the patient is unable to walk, then outside assistance will be needed. Where is the best place to wait? Where is there helicopter access?

Rope. Is roped climbing required to reach the patient, move rescue personnel, or send a messenger for help? Will a rope system be needed to raise or lower the patient?

Assistance. Are climbing parties nearby who can help? Unless it is obvious that the injured climber can self-evacuate, seek additional assistance. It is better to have outside assistance on the way, even if it turns out later that it might not have been needed, than to delay the request until need is a certainty, because it typically takes several hours for rescuers to mobilize and reach the site. Phones are unreliable in the backcountry, so also carry emergency communication devices—a satellite phone, satellite communicator, or personal locator beacon as appropriate to initiate an official rescue response.

Patient. Is the patient improving, stable, or deteriorating? Is the patient at a good location? Can the patient be moved without significantly aggravating any injuries?

Party. Are other members of the group injured or traumatized? Traumatized survivors may need to be secured to an anchor or relocated to a safe location, to ensure they do not inadvertently endanger themselves or wander off. What are the party's capabilities? Do they need food, water, or rest? Can they remain on-site for several hours or overnight?

Equipment. Was any important equipment lost or damaged in the accident? What equipment is available? What can be done with the available equipment?

Daylight. How much daylight is left? Everything will be much harder after dark. What are the nighttime impacts?

Once the WE RAPPED assessment is complete, the climb leader draws together a plan of action. Initially, it may be more conceptual than detailed. The party should expect the plan to evolve or even radically change as new information becomes available.

STEP 7: CARRY OUT THE PLAN

As the party carries out the plan prepared in step 6, remember to continually assess the team and situation so that the plan may be adjusted or improved upon. With the leader focused on the entirety of the situation, climbers focused on the specific assignments may suggest improvements to the plan.

RESCUE

When an injured climber or stranded hiker is on steep terrain (for example, rock cliffs, ice faces, or steep hillsides), a team may need to use ropes to lower or raise the patient. Figure 25-1 gives an overall picture of what this might look like: a lowering system (fig. 25-1a) with SERENE anchors (fig. 25-1b), backed up by a belayer (fig. 25-1c), and a climber anchored near the edge (fig. 25-1d) to communicate with the rescuer as she stabilizes the patient (fig. 25-1e). (For knots and anchors, see Chapters 9, Basic Safety System, and 10, Belaying.)

Safety. In a stressful rescue situation, ensuring safety is paramount. There is a natural human tendency to fail to appreciate the hazards and take dangerous shortcuts during an emergency. A climbing party must guard against this tunnel-vision urgency, which can make the situation worse.

Everyone contributes to party safety. Everyone must continually observe and analyze the plan, rope systems, activity, and environment for hazards. Before a rope raise or lower, every item in the system must be inspected by more than one person: this redundant check is an important safeguard for catching stress-induced errors.

Redundant components hugely improve the safety of a raising or lowering system. Mathematically, the probability of both components failing is the product of the failure rates of each independent component, comparatively a much smaller number. Independent backups are one way to provide system redundancy. For example, a separate belay rope system provides redundancy to the primary rescue rope system.

EQUIPMENT CONSIDERATIONS

Climbing protection and belay systems are designed to absorb or transfer the forces generated by a one-person, not a two-person, fall; yet rescue situations may necessitate having two people supported by the rope and gear. Because typical climbing gear and protection placements are not strong enough to withstand the fall of two people, to safely use recreational climbing gear in a rescue, the lowering and raising systems must be designed to minimize potential falls and built to withstand higher fall forces. For example, strive to raise and lower from reinforced anchors located above rather than below or off to the side, which must use

Fig. 25-1. Small party rescue: a, lowering system on rescue rope; b, SERENE anchors; c, tandem prusik belay on the belay rope; d, climber anchored near edge communicating; e, rescuer stabilizing patient in front of her.

25

redirection. Redirected components are subject to greater forces than anchors directly in line with the force. Failure of a redirecting component will lead to a drop that will impart large forces on anchors.

Anchors. Strong anchors are the foundation of rescue systems. Due to the probability of two people relying on the anchor, it must be very strong. Follow the principles of building anchors—Solid, Efficient, Redundant, Equalized,

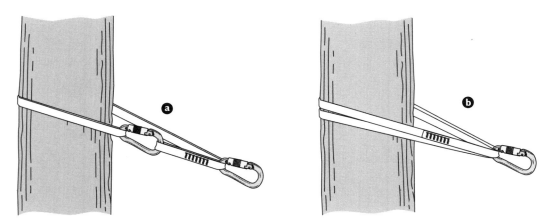

Fig. 25-2. Basket hitch variations around a tree: a, using two carabiners; b, using a single carabiner.

and with No Extension (SERENE)—just as the party would when climbing, until everyone is confident the anchor system will not fail (see "Anchors" in Chapter 10, Belaying). A basket hitch around a tree is a strong anchor that is easy to set up and easy to remove (fig. 25-2).

Because snow and ice anchors are weaker than rock anchors, create snow and ice anchors using several linked pieces of protection. See "Snow Anchors" in Chapter 16, Snow Travel and Climbing, and "Equipment" in Chapter 19, Alpine Ice Climbing.

A prusik hitch may be useful in connecting added pieces of protection to the rope and fine-tuning load distribution within the anchor system. In the event of a fall, an anchor with legs of similar length will better distribute forces among the pieces of protection.

Ropes. Dynamic climbing ropes are designed for a single climber. They typically stretch 6 to 10 percent under the suspended weight of one person; when 100 feet (30 meters) of a dynamic rope is extended, it will stretch nearly 8 feet (2.5 meters). The length of stretch increases with a two-person load. On a steep face, this stretch translates into a rubber-band-like effect. Each time the patient and rescuer hang freely, the rope will stretch. Each time they transfer weight to a feature or ledge, the rope will contract. For example, during a two-person lower, after stepping from a small ledge onto a face, the pair could drop several feet during the rope extension, potentially striking something. The thin mantle (sheath) on climbing ropes is subject to more abrasion with a two-person load than with a one-person load, and the rubber-band-like stretching effect accentuates this abrasion. Pad places where the rope runs over sharp edges.

The original climbing rope may have been damaged in the fall. Prudence calls for transferring the patient to a different rope if available. If a low-stretch or static rope is available, it is better suited for a rescue (see Chapter 9, Basic Safety System). However, this lack of stretch makes such ropes unsuitable for catching any fall, and its anchor system must be built to handle large forces.

When a party is performing a rescue, it is helpful to distinguish ropes by labeling them according to their function. The rope used to raise or lower a patient and/or a rescuer becomes the "rescue rope." A backup rope to the rescue rope, used whenever two people are raised or lowered, becomes the "belay rope."

Double munter hitch. Most belay and rappel devices lack the friction necessary to lower, stop, or hold a two-person load. The double munter hitch (see Figure 25-4b) provides sufficient friction to do this.

Pulleys. In a raising system, even the best pulleys suffer friction losses. Due to frictional losses, a theoretical 3:1 (Z) pulley system may actually have a ratio of 2.7:1 or less; a 9:1 (Z-on-Z) pulley system will have an actual ratio of between 6:1 and 7:1 (see Figure 25-6). Carabiners can be used, at a sufficient friction disadvantage, if no pulleys are available.

Prusiks. Prusiks are useful as rope grabs. Prusiks in combination with a pulley simplify resetting of raising systems by holding the load during resets. They act as an automatic acting belay in the event of a rescue rope failure and provide a hands-free belay if the belayer must temporarily let go of the belay rope to help pull when raising or if forced to let go by rockfall, bees, nearby lightning, et cetera. Prusiks can be used to piggyback supplemental anchor protection and mechanical advantage systems to the rescue rope.

Tension-release hitch. This hitch, known as a TRH, is used to release tension on a weighted rope system. It consists of prusik(s), a locking carabiner, figure eight, and munter (or double munter) hitch around a pearabiner with a mule knot finish.

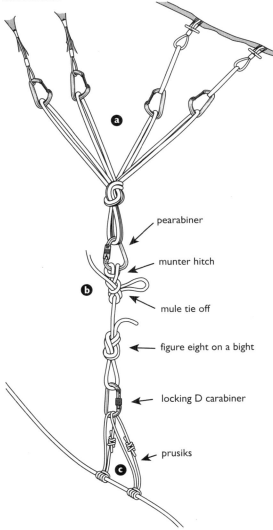

Fig. 25-3. Tandem prusik belay with tension release hitch: a, SERENE anchor; b, munter-mule made from tail of rope; c, tandem prusiks spaced 4 inches apart.

pearabiner

munter hitch

mule tie off

figure eight on a bight

locking D carabiner

prusiks

Belays. The belay rope is an independent rope backup to the rescue rope. The belay system consists of a SERENE anchor (fig. 25-3a); a TRH (fig. 25-3b); and two tandem prusiks around the rescue rope, spaced at least 4 inches (10 centimeters) apart (fig. 25-3c). The belayer pulls rope through the prusiks maintaining a few inches of slack to back up the rescue rope during the raise or lower. The slack will keep the prusiks from inadvertently tightening or grabbing during routine raising or lowering on the rescue rope. If the rescue system fails, the resulting force on the belay rope will cause them to be pulled from the belayer's hands, and the prusiks will automatically grab the rope to catch the load. Although one prusik should work, the second prusik offers redundancy. Once grabbed, the TRH is used to transfer the load from the belay rope back to the rescue rope.

RAISING AND LOWERING SYSTEMS

An injured climber may need to be extricated from steep terrain. If the injuries are not too severe, the party may use a mechanical advantage assist to help raise them or a friction device to lower them as they climb under their own power. For a patient with more severe injuries, a rescuer can help support the patient while the team raises or lowers both of them.

Commands. In addition to the typical climbing commands outlined in Table 10-1 of Chapter 10, Belaying, a couple of additional ones specific to rescues are helpful. At any time, anyone who notices anything appearing unsafe or amiss should shout "Stop!" immediately. Only when the issue is resolved should the rescue resume. Calling out "Stop" a dozen times can be expected. The rescue leader uses "Up" or "Down" to direct those operating the raising or lowering system and "Reset" when the pullers need to reset the traveling pulleys in a raising system. Those to whom the commands are directed should repeat the commands to acknowledge receiving them and help ensure that everyone has heard them.

Unassisted rescue. A single person puts less stress on the rope and anchor system than two people (see "Ropes" in the preceding section), so if the fallen climber is uninjured or has upper-body injuries, the rescuers may decide to raise or lower the patient without an accompanying rescuer. The patient ties in to the rescue rope and is then raised or lowered off the steep terrain by others who do the work.

Assisted rescue. If the fallen climber has more-severe injuries, an accompanying rescuer is required. The rescuer ties in at the end of the rescue rope. Upon reaching

25

the patient, the rescuer clips a double sling between the rescuer's harness and the patient's harness using locking carabiners. The patient and rescuer are now redundantly linked to each other and both ropes.

For assisted raising or lowering, the patient is attached to the rescue rope by a prusik hitch that is girth-hitched to a sling, which is attached by a locking carabiner to the patient's harness belay loop. This can replace the double sling used initially to safeguard the patient. Slide the friction hitch up or down the rescue rope to place the patient alongside the rescuer, in the rescuer's lap, below the rescuer, or on the back of the rescuer with the patient's chest even with the rescuer's upper back (as shown in Figure 25-1e). With an optimal adjustment of the prusik extension, the patient's weight hangs from the rescue rope and not from the rescuer; the rescuer maneuvers and stabilizes the patient as they are being moved. A second rope is used as the belay rope.

As the angle decreases, less weight hangs from the rescue rope and more upon the rescuer. If the rescuer cannot manage the patient's weight on low-angle terrain, such as a wide bench, it may be helpful to have another rescuer rappel from a separate anchor and rope to assist alongside. The rappelling rescuer should use a rappel backup such as the autoblock, as he or she may need both hands to help move the patient (see "Safety Backups" in Chapter 11, Rappelling).

Lowering systems. It is much easier and faster to lower a patient than to raise one, and the double munter hitch is used to lower two people. For instance, a rescuer can be lowered with a munter hitch (fig. 25-4a) to the patient, then the munter hitch can easily be converted to a double munter hitch (fig. 25-4b) to lower both patient and rescuer. The pearabiner must be opened to convert to a double munter. This conversion can be accomplished while the rescuer is hanging on the rope, say, for a mid-face rescue. If the rescuer will be stationary for a while, secure the double munter hitch using a mule hitch tie-off (see Figure 25-3b). Do not lower two people from a harness; lower directly off the anchor.

It is preferable to lower a patient and rescuer than to use an assisted rappel. Tandem rappelling requires the rescuer to do all the work, whereas lowering allows other climbers to control the descent, stops, and raising if needed; the rescuer can focus on controlling the patient. Furthermore, if the patient became unable to continue during a tandem rappel, the rescuer would be in a tough predicament. Also, there may be insufficient friction to safely

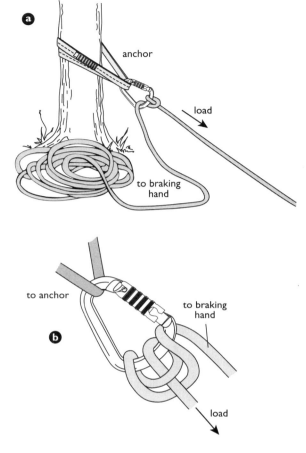

Fig. 25-4. Lowering systems: a, using a munter hitch; b, using a double munter hitch.

control the rappel with some combinations of rope diameter, weight, rappel device, and terrain steepness. In the event that a tandem rappel must be used, two climbers may rappel together by attaching themselves to the same rappel device with a rappel extension made from a double runner (fig. 25-5). The rescuer backs up the rappel with an autoblock.

Raising systems. A raising system leverages the force the puller can pull with. The 3:1 (Z) pulley system is usually the most useful of the simple raising systems (fig. 25-6a). Chapter 18, Glacier Travel and Crevasse Rescue, describes setting up a 3:1 system.

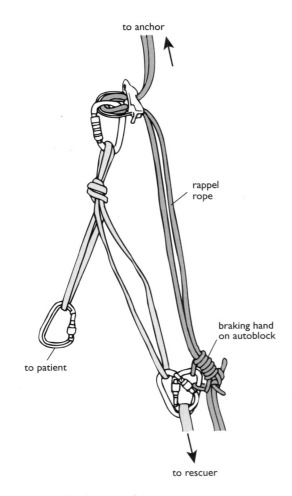

to anchor

rappel rope

braking hand on autoblock

to patient

to rescuer

Fig. 25-5. Tandem rappel setup.

When there is a two-person load or only a few haulers, a second 3:1 system can be added to the pulling end of the first 3:1 system to create a compound 9:1 (Z-on-Z) raising system (fig. 25-6b).

If a 9:1 system provides too much mechanical advantage, it can be easily converted to a 5:1 system by removing the last prusik and connecting that prusik's pulley or carabiner directly to the same carabiner as the second pulley (fig. 25-6c).

A fast, jerky raise makes it difficult for the rescuer and patient to negotiate broken terrain and maintain a stable position. If the rope jams and the haulers keep pulling,

the system then applies its powerful mechanical advantage to the anchors instead of raising the climbers; this may pull out the anchors. During raising, the belayer should take accumulating slack out of the belay system to keep the belay tight by pulling the rope through the tandem prusiks. When practicing rescue techniques, always use a belay rope (see Figure 25-1c).

If a short lower will be followed by a raise, set up a raising system and use it in reverse to lower the rescuer to the patient. Then it is all ready to raise.

Knot passes. If a knot in the rope (such as a butterfly knot used to isolate a damaged section) must pass through a lowering system, use a tension-release hitch (TRH) (see Figure 25-3b).

As a knot approaches the double munter in a lowering system, attach a TRH below the double munter hitch and lower the load onto it. When the rescue rope slackens, relocate the double munter hitch to above the knot. Then loosen the TRH to transfer the load back onto the relocated double munter hitch.

In a raising system, as the knot approaches the traveling pulley prusik, reset and relocate the traveling prusik to below the knot. Continue raising, until the knot is close to the ratchet pulley prusik. Set the ratchet pulley prusik to hold the load and, using slings, extend the ratchet pulley with a new ratchet prusik to below the knot. Continue the raise working the knot through the remainder of the system with resets of different lengths.

PUTTING IT ALL TOGETHER

No definitive step-by-step "recipe" will work for all rescues. There are numerous accident scenarios and possible ways to use rescue techniques to solve the problems that arise. Following the seven steps in accident response and using the party's technical climbing, rescue, and first-aid skills will guide climbers through what needs to be done to respond to an accident in steep terrain.

This section presents possible raising and lowering solutions to a scenario in which a lead climber has fallen on high-angle terrain to illustrate how to use the seven steps, interwoven with many climbing, rescue, and first-aid skills. In this scenario, the climbing party is made up of two rope teams of two climbers each. Each team has a rope, a rack, and a radio. The lead climber has fallen on a steep face more than halfway through a pitch on a multipitch climb and is unconscious and out of sight of the belayer.

25

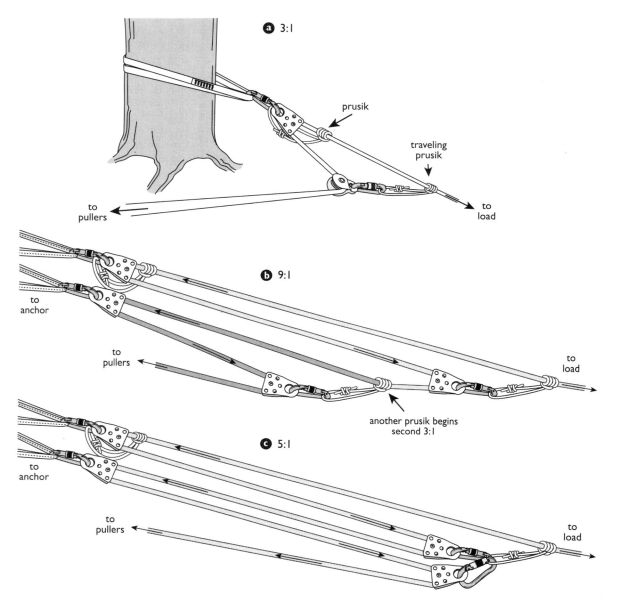

Fig. 25-6. Raising systems: a, 3:1 system; b, 9:1 system; c, 5:1 system.

The climbing rope has been damaged. The other rope team has already completed the climb.

Step 1: Take charge of the situation. The fallen climber's belayer arrests the fall, and after the climber fails to respond or move, the belayer radios to the two other climbers already on the summit. The belayer takes charge. The other team rappels to the top of the pitch, observing the unmoving, hanging climber below. The party contacts emergency first responders by using a phone (unreliable in the backcountry), PLB, satellite communicator, or satellite phone.

Step 2: Approach the patient safely. The top team builds a SERENE anchor system beefed up for a two-person load. One of these two climbers lowers the other, who is now the rescuer, with a munter hitch. The rescuer takes down first-aid supplies, a warm jacket, and the rack. As the rescuer is lowered past the patient's highest remaining protection, from which the patient is hanging, the rescuer notices that the sheath of the patient's rope has been stripped from the core.

Continuing down, the rescuer stops above the patient and builds an anchor in a crack while secured by the rescue rope. Using a TRH, the rescuer attaches the hitch's prusik to the patient's rope below the damaged core. The fallen climber's belayer lowers the patient onto this new anchor. The rescuer is lowered farther down to the patient and attaches a sling between the belay loops of both the patient's and the rescuer's harnesses.

Step 3: Perform emergency rescue and urgent first aid. The rescuer determines that the fallen climber is breathing and is not bleeding profusely but is unconscious. Concerned the patient has sustained spinal injuries in the fall, the rescuer strives to minimize movement of the patient's head, neck, and spine. The rescuer places a sling around the patient's knees and attaches it to the anchor, adjusting it to raise the patient's legs toward a more level orientation to treat possible harness suspension trauma (see Chapter 24, First Aid).

Step 4: Protect the patient. The rescuer zips a warm jacket around the patient's torso and arms to help prevent hypothermia.

Step 5: Check for other injuries. The rescuer examines the patient but can find no obvious injuries.

FIRST SOLUTION: RESCUE BY RAISING

Step 6: Make a plan. The three climbers decide the best course of action is to raise the patient to the top of the pitch and await rescue.

Step 7: Carry out the plan. The patient's belayer unties from the rope; the rescuer pulls the climbing rope through the pieces of protection, isolates the damaged core with a butterfly knot, and tosses the end back down to the patient's belayer (climbing partner).

The rescuer now belays the patient's partner, who climbs and cleans protection up to the rescuer. Here the patient's partner takes both racks, attaches a prusik safety from his or her harness to the rescue rope, and then climbs, sliding the prusik up the rescue rope (self-belaying) while also being belayed by the rescuer, until it's possible to tie in

to the unused end of the rescue rope that has been dropped down. The patient's partner removes the self-belay prusik and continues ascending, top belayed, to the ledge.

The two climbers at the top of the pitch use the damaged climbing rope to set up a tandem prusik belay with a TRH on a new anchor and use the rescue rope to set up a 9:1 (3:1 on 3:1) raising system.

The top climbers maneuver the rescuer with the 9:1 system so that the patient can be secured to the rescuer's back with a nylon webbing carry (see Figure 25-9f). As these two are hoisted and belayed past the mid-face anchor the patient had been suspended from, the rescuer removes the TRH holding the patient. (The tension release feature was not needed.)

Once they are all at the top of the pitch, the party reassesses the patient's injuries, provides more spinal immobilization, and adds clothing and insulation to help prevent hypothermia and shock. They consider their own survival needs and resources, then prepare to wait for outside help from a local search and rescue agency.

Later the three climbers decide it makes little sense for all four to remain at the belay ledge rather than for two of them to leave their extra clothing, food, and water and descend.

SECOND SOLUTION: RESCUE BY LOWERING

Step 6: Make a plan. In this case, when the party makes their plan they decide to lower the patient.

Step 7: Carry out the plan. The patient's belayer unties; the rescuer pulls the climbing rope through the pieces of protection, clips in to it with a butterfly knot beyond the damaged core, threads the rope through the new mid-face anchor, and tosses the free end back down to the patient's belayer, who builds a tandem prusik belay with a TRH.

The rescuer connects a sling from the patient's harness belay loop to a prusik on the rescue rope, then releases the mid-face anchor TRH to transfer the patient onto the rescue rope. The climber at the top lowers the rescuer and patient on a double munter hitch while the patient's partner operates a bottom belay until the rope runs out.

The rescuer takes the belay rope from the bottom belayer and sets up a self-belay with tandem prusiks from the harness belay loop; the rope now runs from the tandem prusiks up through the mid-face anchor and back down to the butterfly tie-in on the rescuer's harness.

The top climber continues the lower of the patient and rescuer to the belay ledge while the rescuer self-belays with the tandem prusiks. The top climber rappels the route, cleaning it.

25

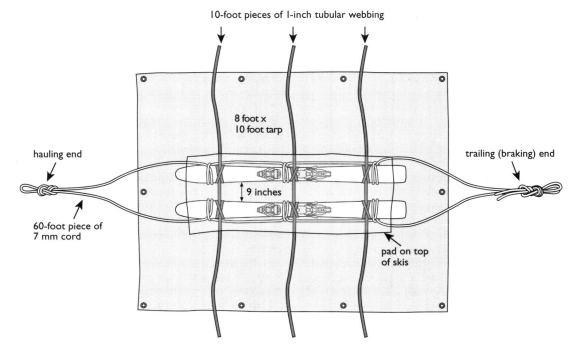

Fig. 25-7. Improvised sled for snow evacuation using a tarp, a pair of skis, and sleeping pads.

EVACUATION

When an injury occurs the party may be miles from the trailhead or even a trail. The patient's condition, the distance to be traveled, and the party's strength determine the feasibility of evacuation to the trailhead. The party may also decide to evacuate the patient to a better location to wait until outside assistance arrives or evacuate to an area suitable for helicopter pickup, or they may remain in place.

For a time after an injury, the patient's pain may be lessened by endorphins in the bloodstream. As time goes on, the endorphin levels drop and swelling tissues may add to pain or limit range of motion. If the patient must be moved or must move under his or her own power, doing this sooner is generally less painful than waiting until later.

Snow evacuations. The party may be able to improvise a sled with typical gear carried by the group (fig. 25-7). Spread out a tarp, bivy sack, tent, or rain fly. Place two skis flat on top of the tarp, with the tips and the tails tied together approximately two to three ski widths apart; the skis provide support for the patient's head, torso, and pelvis, so adjust the final spacing between the skis to

maximize this support. Next, place layers of sleeping pads, packs, clothing, and sleeping bags on the skis to protect the patient from heat loss and bumps by isolating the patient from the ground. Now place the patient on top of the padding. Wrap and secure the tarp around the patient. At the top of the patient's head, gather the tarp material together and tie a rope or sling around this point; an overhand knot in the tarp material is one way of keeping the cord or webbing from slipping off.

Place loops in the hauling rope to go around the pullers' waists. Following the fall line is the easiest path; traversing on a firm slope is difficult. A trailing line, attached to the rear of the sled, may be used as a brake on steeper downhill slopes to keep the sled from overrunning the pulling climbers. On steep slopes, lower the patient with a lowering system rather than pulling the sled.

Cross-country versus trail evacuations. It takes considerable effort to move a nonambulatory patient a short distance on a trail. It is almost impossible without a trail.

Assisted walk. If the patient is able, he or she can walk, with one or more rescuers walking alongside to provide

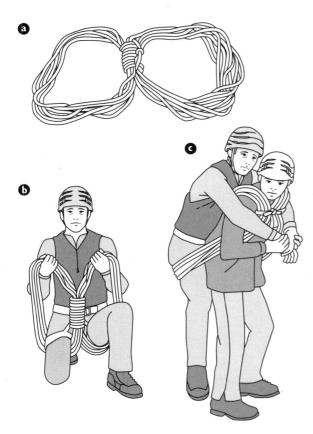

Fig. 25-8. Coil carry: a, coil the rope, sizing the loops to fit from the patient's armpits to crotch, then separate the coil in half to form a pair of loops; b, place patient's legs through loops; c, slip upper part of loops over carrier's shoulders and tie these loops together at the chest with a short piece of webbing.

physical support. A rescuer close behind can help in difficult terrain. Have party members ahead select the easiest route and remove loose branches and other obstacles. Using trekking poles may help. Along some stretches, such as crossing boulder fields or logs, the patient may choose to scoot across on his or her own.

Back carries. A strong climber may be able to carry the patient on his or her back for a short distance if the weight is distributed properly. Either the coil carry (fig. 25-8) or the nylon webbing carry (fig. 25-9) is helpful. For the nylon webbing carry, use 1-inch webbing, and pad pressure points for greater comfort. On a trail, doubling the webbing may

be more comfortable. The rucksack carry is another method of back carry: make slits in the sides of a large backpack so the patient can step into it as though it were a pair of shorts, then the carrier wears the backpack as usual, with the patient as the load. Rescuers should take turns acting as carriers and choose a pace that will not exhaust the party. Using of any of these techniques off trail is difficult.

Stream and obstacle crossings. A rescue party may need to cross slippery streams or jumbled boulders. Loss of footing could prove disastrous to both the patient and a rescuer who is doing a carry. Form two lines of rescuers across the obstacle from one side to the other. These rescuers can act as handholds and supports for the rescuer who is carrying the patient.

With swift water, it is easy to underestimate the water's hydraulic forces. It is dangerous to tie in to a rope; if someone slips, the rope may entrap the person underwater or midstream. Ropes should not cross perpendicular to the banks but at an angle downstream so that the current helps move you across. A Tyrolean traverse may be possible if it can be rigged high enough above the water to ensure that the patient will not sag down into the water. See Chapter 15, Aid and Big Wall Climbing.

RESCUES INVOLVING OUTSIDE RESOURCES

When the party lacks the resources to deal with the search, injuries, rescue, or evacuation, they need outside rescue assistance. Organized search and rescue (SAR) groups bring to the scene the benefits of training and experience, combined with specialized equipment and techniques. When planning a climbing trip, make sure to find out and include in the itinerary what outside agency will be contacted should assistance be required.

Worldwide, there are a variety of approaches to SAR. Many countries may have nationalized SAR services. In urban North America, the local fire department is responsible for rescue. In the backcountry, responsibility most frequently rests with the county sheriff's department. In some parts of the United States, the state, National Park Service, military, or coast guard may be responsible. Most field SAR personnel are volunteers. Mountain rescue teams consist of volunteer climbers who receive training in wilderness-oriented first aid, search, rescue, and helicopter operations.

In North America, it is rare to be charged for SAR costs. In Europe and many other parts of the world, climbers must expect to be charged. Usually, inexpensive insurance policies for climbing can cover these costs.

25

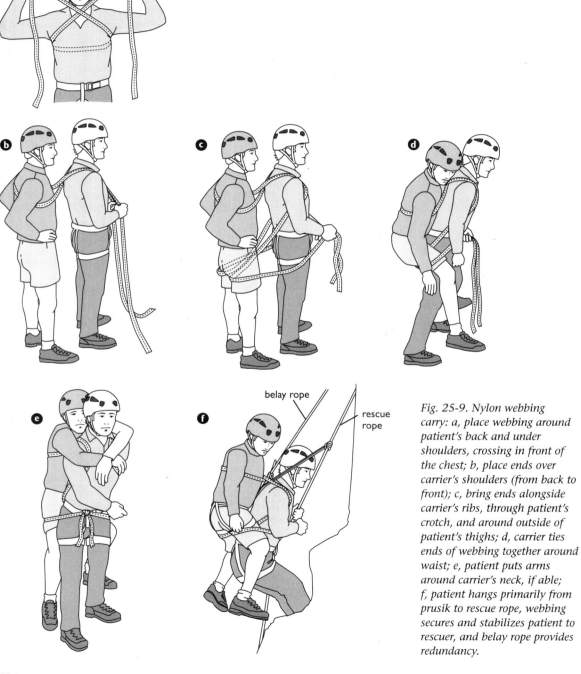

belay rope

rescue rope

Fig. 25-9. Nylon webbing carry: a, place webbing around patient's back and under shoulders, crossing in front of the chest; b, place ends over carrier's shoulders (from back to front); c, bring ends alongside carrier's ribs, through patient's crotch, and around outside of patient's thighs; d, carrier ties ends of webbing together around waist; e, patient puts arms around carrier's neck, if able; f, patient hangs primarily from prusik to rescue rope, webbing secures and stabilizes patient to rescuer, and belay rope provides redundancy.

Requesting Outside Assistance

It is essential to communicate clearly with the SAR agency to avoid miscommunication. From a SAR perspective, location of the patient and whether or not the patient is ambulatory are the most important pieces of information. Next in importance is information on the injury, condition of the patient, and best access to the accident site. The accident report in Figure 24-1, in Chapter 24, First Aid, provides a good format for documenting this crucial information.

Being prepared for the unexpected is a hallmark of competent climbers, and being prepared includes having the ability to summon help in an emergency. Outside rescuers can be contacted using various emergency communication devices such as radios, smartphones (unreliable in the backcountry), PLBs, satellite communicators, or human messengers.

Radios and smartphones. Climbing parties will save hours in obtaining help if they can get through with a radio or smartphone, but in the mountains and wilderness, smartphones and radios tend to be unreliable. Radios require line-of-sight communications with another radio or repeater station. Amateur radios, together with amateur repeaters, are generally the most reliable method of communication from remote locations. These radios are regulated by the federal government; their operation requires a license. Citizens band (CB), family radio service (FRS), and general mobile radio service (GMRS) radios have range and propagation limitations. With all devices, sometimes service can be improved if the caller moves a bit, reorients the antenna, or transmits from a higher elevation. Satellite phones, due to their greater bulk and expense, have not seen widespread acceptance except in remote climbing areas.

Where smartphones have network coverage, they are invaluable for communicating with outside rescuers. During a remote climb, cell phone batteries are likely to be rapidly depleted due to the phones' intensified attempts to stay on the network where coverage is poor. Smartphones should be turned off at the trailhead or, to use the camera or GPS navigation features, place phones in "airplane mode." The display is usually the largest power consumer. Take along an extra battery or power source. When battery life becomes an issue, inform the SAR authorities; it may be best to shut the phone off for an agreed-upon period of time. Texting will help preserve instructions without having to write them down and will save battery life; texting may also be able to access the cellular network when voice will not. Increasingly it is possible to text 9-1-1 call centers.

Personal locator beacons. PLBs are the most reliable means of summoning help; they use technology similar to that used on aircraft and ships for emergencies. The signal's location will be routed to the local government SAR authority. These robust devices—which weigh as little as 4 ounces (112 grams)—will send signals for at least 24 hours in extreme environments.

Satellite communicators. Businesses have developed somewhat similar devices using commercial satellites but they are not as robust. Generally satellite communicators have richer features but require paid subscriptions. Depending on the devices, you can enable ongoing location tracking, send different notifications, summon help, and text message. When a party is running slow, being able to keep friends and family informed provides everyone peace of mind and may head off an unnecessary search and rescue call. (See Chapter 5, Navigation.)

Human messengers. In some situations, sending someone from the climbing party may be the only means of communicating with outside help. If this is the case, try to send two messengers for safety. Resist rushing to send the messengers on their way. Instead, take a few minutes to make sure the messengers have everything they will need such as car keys, the party's plans, emergency contacts, and the like. A messenger should carry a map showing the precise location of the patient. Messengers need to pace themselves and travel safely; they must avoid the natural tendency to rush. It is more important to be certain that the messengers will reach assistance than to worry about the time it will take them to reach assistance.

Interacting with SAR

The initial call for outside assistance should use the normal local procedure for fire, police, or medical emergencies, such as dialing 9-1-1 in the United States. The dispatcher will connect the party to the appropriate SAR authority.

Communicate location. Because emergency dispatch centers rarely handle wilderness emergency requests, there is potential for miscommunication. For example, the jurisdiction where the accident is reported or where the emergency dispatch center is located may be different from where the accident occurred. Geographical names may vary and may even be used for multiple places in the

25

same region. The dispatcher is not likely to be familiar with climbing terminology.

The location of the accident must be communicated unmistakably. Start with simple information such as the state, county, closest city or town, and road names. This may seem too basic, but heartrending stories abound of rescuers being sent to the wrong side of a mountain or of a desperate climbing party watching a helicopter search an adjacent peak. If communicating by radio or phone, give information such as map coordinates; the type of map and its name, along with a description of the location; and the route name, including the guidebook that describes it. Use more than one way to describe the location (redundancy). The party's elevation can be an invaluable piece of information for establishing location. If using a coordinate system, specify the datum and format, especially when using latitude and longitude, since there are several formats. Specify whether any compass bearings are true or magnetic.

Assist the rescuers. Make an effort to speak with the rescue team that will be entering the field. Mountain rescuers will have specific questions about access and route conditions that dispatchers or SAR mission leaders are unlikely to ask. This information will assist the mountain rescuers in formulating the best strategy and selecting the right equipment. Rarely, the party's messengers may be asked to escort rescuers back to the accident scene.

At the scene, do everything possible to help the arriving SAR team. This could range from having drinking water available to setting up fixed lines to help rescuers reach the accident scene. When a mountain rescue team arrives, they will assume responsibility for first-aid treatment and completing the rescue and evacuation. The SAR leader will look to members of the arriving teams to perform most of the vital tasks.

The climbing party can help by cooperating closely with the rescuers. The climb leader remains in charge of the remaining climbing party and is responsible for its safety. The climbing party may be escorted out. However, the climbing party should be prepared to lend a hand in the rescue if requested.

HELICOPTER RESCUE

Helicopters have revolutionized mountain rescue. They can deliver rescue teams to remote areas and pluck injured climbers from cliffs and glaciers. Helicopters can deliver an injured climber to the hospital in hours, whereas ground evacuation can take days. However, do not base rescue plans on an immediate helicopter rescue just because helicopters are used in the area. Bad weather, darkness, hot temperatures, or high altitude may limit helicopter operation. A helicopter also may not be available due to another assignment or maintenance. If a helicopter can rescue an injured climber(s), the remaining party members may or may not be evacuated by helicopter.

Make the party visible. In many types of terrain, it is surprisingly difficult to see people from a helicopter. Help the crew by waving brightly colored items; using mirrors, watch or electronic device display faces, stove windscreens, or shiny pots; making tracks in snow; or moving around on a contrasting background such as snow, forest clearings, ridges, and riverbeds. Effectively sized flares and smoke bombs are too large for climbing parties to carry, but devices similar to laser presentation pointers, intended for signaling helicopters, could be carried. If a helicopter approaches at night, presume the pilot is using night vision goggles. If so, too much light can be disruptive to such vision. A single small light directed at the ground is sufficient once you believe the helicopter is headed toward you. Once the helicopter has positively identified the party, it may fly off to prepare for the rescue or to land rescuers a short distance away.

Prepare the area. A rescue helicopter loads an injured person in one of three ways: it lands (or hovers just above the ground) and takes the patient aboard; it hovers overhead while hoisting the patient aboard; or it hovers overhead to connect the patient to a fixed-length cable. For an anticipated landing, clear a level area for the helicopter. Move all loose objects, such as branches and saplings, well away from a landing site. Fly a brightly-colored wind indicator from a nearby location as high as possible.

Take safety precautions. When dealing with helicopters, safety concerns are of utmost importance. Many things pose a danger, including static electricity buildup on the helicopter, blowing dust and debris, intense windchill, and loss of visibility from blowing rock, dirt, debris, and snow. The downwash and noise of the helicopter are overwhelming; wear eye protection and climbing helmets. Anything not secured will blow away!

Assist the crew. If a radio is lowered to the party, you may need to press a button to talk to the pilot. If the helicopter lands, stay out of the proximate landing area and behind protection from windblown debris. Expect a crew member, upon landing, to come to you; approach *only* when signaled to do so. If you must approach, do so from the front or sides of the helicopter, as long as you can stay well below the main rotor. *Do not approach from behind*, to avoid the low and nearly invisible tail rotor. If a pack must accompany the patient, remove any loose items and place them inside the pack, and be sure to send the written accident report out with the patient. If the helicopter hovers and lowers a crew member to the ground, prepare to assist this crew member in loading the injured climber. This person will not necessarily be a climber and may be unfamiliar with glaciers, steep terrain, and safe climbing practices. Do not touch any cables and baskets from the helicopter until they first touch the ground, which discharges static electricity.

Finally, if the helicopter hovers and lowers a bare hook, allow the helicopter cable's hook to touch the ground to discharge static electricity before touching it! Do not anchor the hook to the ground, and ensure that the hook and cable do not snag on anything. Expect the hook and cable to move about as the helicopter adjusts to hold a stationary hover.

For the patient to remain upright when hoisted, make sure that both a seat harness and a chest harness are on the patient. Girth-hitch a single-length sling to the seat harness belay loop and pass it through the chest harness to create the attachment point. Press the helicopter hook's safety latch to open it, and place the attaching sling in the hook. If a pack is also being hoisted by hook, girth-hitch a double-length sling through both the pack's shoulder straps (the haul loop may not be strong enough) and insert the sling into the same hook with the climber; the pack will hang below the climber.

Once the attaching sling is secured in the hook and the patient is no longer attached to any anchor, make eye contact with the hoist operator and raise your hand overhead, pointing to the sky.

SEARCHES

The Climbing Code described in Chapter 1, First Steps, instructs climbers to stay together. The desire to split the group is an indicator of a worrisome problem within the team; separating sets up the weaker party for a mishap. Generally, the smaller the party, the higher the risk for becoming lost. Solo travelers are at greatest risk. Do not allow a single person to descend on his or her own, and do not spread out the group in unfamiliar terrain and on poorly marked trails. If a climber becomes separated from the climbing party, there is always the risk that an accident might injure that individual, immobilizing him or her.

SEARCHES BY THE CLIMBING PARTY

If a climbing party realizes that a member is missing, it's time to initiate a search.

Prepare a search plan. In preparing to search, examine the topographical map for possible alternate paths the climber may have taken. Try to visualize errors the person might have made. Give consideration to the lost person's skill level, resources, and remaining stamina. Lost people tend to head downhill and to take the path of least resistance. Look at the map for inviting pathways, choke points that focus travel, and barriers that block travel altogether.

Careful strategy saves time. Before sending out party members, the climb leader should set a meeting or return time and place based on a reasonable amount of search time. If radios or cell phones are available, the search teams should agree on a scheduled call-in.

Start the search. If bad weather, difficult terrain, or medical considerations suggest that the missing climber might need help, start the search without delay. The most effective search strategy is to return to the location where the missing person was last seen and retrace the route, looking for places where the climber might have left the path. Use whistles, shouting, or any other noisemaking to extend your reach. Look for clues, especially footprints. Inform any encountered travelers of the search and share instructions to pass on to the lost person. Prominently mark and identify all physical points you want outside searchers to be able to locate.

Request outside help. If, after the designated period of searching, the party members check in and/or meet up only to find that no sign of the missing climber has been seen, it is time to request outside help. The longer a lost person is on the move, the farther he or she can travel and the harder it is to find the person.

SEARCHES INVOLVING OUTSIDE RESOURCES

The science of searching has advanced over the years. Leaders from government agencies responsible for searches have models to help predict the behavior of lost people and determine search segment probabilities. A number of specialized SAR teams may search. Search dogs follow scents and disturbances; human trackers can spot signs of passage; helicopters cover large areas quickly; drones cover smaller parcels; horseback and foot teams search

25

less-difficult terrain; four-wheel-drive and all-terrain vehicles travel rough roads and wait at trailheads; mountain rescue teams cover steep terrain.

Each search has different needs. Once the authorities have been notified, the best action for the original climbing team is to meet with the SAR leader. The SAR leader will want specific information that only the climbing team can provide. The party will be directed where to meet the SAR leader, which usually means waiting at the trailhead. After an initial debriefing, the search leader may ask the climbing team to remain at the SAR base to answer questions that arise. The climb leader should call the emergency contact person for the missing climber. When the climbing party leaves the SAR base, they should always leave their contact information. Friends of the missing person and other untrained volunteers are unlikely to be used during a SAR-organized search.

GOING FORWARD

Planning and preparation identify many hazards before a climb begins, and during the climb, hazard identification and avoidance go a long way in ensuring the party's safety. Still, circumstances do arise, so being prepared to perform rescues is important. Learn leadership, first-aid, and rescue skills, and keep current by regular practice and review. Make sure to *practice* the rescue techniques outlined in this chapter—reading by itself does not provide the necessary skills. Consider contributing your mountaineering skills to the community by joining your local mountain rescue group.

Become one of those climbers—confident in leadership, accident prevention, first-aid, and rescue skills—who has the ability to rescue and evacuate an injured person in treacherous terrain. Then you will be more fully prepared to pursue the freedom of the hills.

CHAPTER 26

MOUNTAIN GEOLOGY

Geology is essential knowledge: climbing success—or even your life—can depend on your understanding the form and substance of mountains. Climbers learn from experience that different types of rock affect what different routes are like, ranging from sheer walls to those having cracks and ledges galore. Climbers also discover that some kinds of rocks are very durable, whereas others crumble under pressure. This knowledge is important for the safe and well-rounded mountaineer.

GEOLOGIC PERSPECTIVES

Climbers can gain a better understanding of mountains by examining them on three scales: as an overall landscape, as a single outcrop, and as a close-up view of a single specimen of rock. Each perspective contributes to a broad comprehension of the mountain environment.

Landscape. The wide-angle landscape view examines the mountain as a whole, sometimes from miles away. Observing geology at this scale helps climbers find a viable route to the summit. Using photos or binoculars, look for routes with strong, supportive rock, or identify areas where rock may be weak and unreliable—in other words, places to trust and places to treat with caution. Ridges may follow a layer of resistant rock. Sets of fractures may offer a zigzag route to the summit. Sudden changes in slope may indicate a *fault* (a fracture along which movement has occurred) or an abrupt change in rock type.

Outcrop. The midrange perspective focuses on specific outcrops from 10 to 100 feet (3 to 30 meters) away. Here climbers can see features that could help—or hinder—an ascent. For example, a regular pattern of cracks is probably a good bet for chock placements, and a reliable avenue

upward may be found in a *resistant dike,* which forms when the intrusive magma that has filled a fracture has cooled to form rock harder than the host rock.

Rock. At arm's length from the outcrop or closer, the details of the rock itself are more apparent. At this scale, climbers can identify rock types and recognize textures that might be difficult to climb or that might provide advantageous holds.

HOW MOUNTAINS ARE FORMED

The ultimate landscape view is the whole earth. When we look at mountain ranges on a global scale, we can see a clear pattern of their occurrence, and this pattern can be explained by plate tectonic processes. According to the theory of plate tectonics, the outermost layer of the earth (the *lithosphere*) is composed of plates that are slowly but constantly moving.

Most mountain ranges are formed by immense forces that squeeze rock masses together or pull them apart. Where tectonic plates move toward each other, their edges (*margins*) are called *convergent*. Where tectonic plates

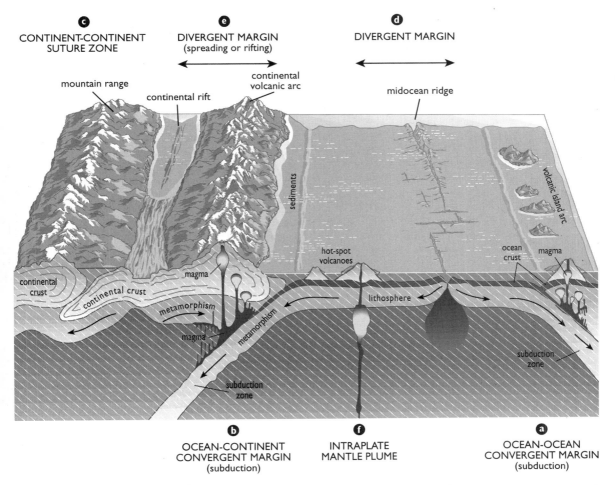

Fig. 26-1. Characteristic features of various types of convergent and divergent plate margins: a, ocean–ocean convergent margin producing a volcanic island arc; b, ocean–continent convergent margin producing a continental volcanic arc; c, continent–continent convergent zone producing a suture zone mountain range; d, oceanic divergent margin producing a midocean ridge; e, continental divergent margin producing a continental rift; f, intraplate mantle plume producing a chain of seafloor hot-spot volcanoes.

pull away from each other, their margins are called *divergent*. Along what are called *transform margins*, blocks of lithosphere move side by side and mountains rarely form. The sections below describe the two types of mountain-forming plate margins.

CONVERGENT PLATE MARGINS

Three varieties of convergent margins each produce a somewhat different type of mountain.

Ocean–Ocean Margins

Where two plates of oceanic lithosphere converge is called an *ocean–ocean margin* (fig. 26-1a). The older, colder slab forms a *subduction zone* by sinking beneath the younger, warmer slab. Deep within the subduction zone, 55 to 60 miles (90 to 100 kilometers) below the earth's surface, abundant *magma* (molten rock beneath the earth's surface) is formed and rises buoyantly. Over time, much of the magma makes its way to the surface, where a chain of

26

541

oceanic island volcanoes grows. The island mountains of the Aleutians and Indonesia are two examples.

Ocean–Continent Margins

Subduction can also occur where oceanic lithosphere is subducted beneath the edge of a continent (fig. 26-1b). This produces a chain of volcanic mountains on land. Three types of volcanoes can be formed.

Shield volcanoes. Great conical stacks of basalt flows with gentle slopes, such as Belknap Crater in the Cascade Range of central Oregon, are shield volcanoes, which are uncommon.

Stratovolcanoes. Most of the climbing destinations along ocean–continent convergent margins are strato-volcanoes (also known as *composite volcanoes*), composed mainly of andesite and having steep slopes, such as Washington State's Mount Rainier and Mount Baker or Japan's Mount Fuji.

Cinder cones. Composed of pyroclastic fragments, cinder cones are generally only a few hundred feet high. Examples include the Black Buttes near Bend, Oregon, and Wizard Island in Oregon's Crater Lake.

As tectonic plates move, they cause various stresses—faulting, folding, and uplift—that create mountain structures (see "Mountain Structures" later in this chapter). These movements, as well as erosion, expose deeper layers of the earth's crust. For example, the schist and gneiss exposed in Washington's North Cascades originated as clay and silt on the seafloor 250 million years ago. During plate convergence, this material was buried as much as 100,000 feet (30,000 meters) beneath the earth's surface, where it was metamorphosed by heat and pressure into schist and gneiss. Continued plate convergence has now moved these rocks back to the surface in the northern part of the North Cascades range. To the south, volcanism has buried the metamorphic basement yet again and has built a chain of large stratovolcanoes that extends from British Columbia to northern California. Mountain ranges of similar origin include the Andes of South America and the Japanese Alps.

Suture Zones

Many of the major mountain ranges of the earth are found where continental plates or island arcs have smashed together as they have converged (fig. 26-1c). For example, the Himalayan range has been uplifted by the collision of India and Asia, Europe's Alps were created by Africa's northward push into Europe, and the Rocky Mountains were uplifted by the collision of numerous microplates that extended the edge of North America hundreds of miles westward over the past 170 million years. In these mountain ranges, faulting may thrust one part of the range over another. These huge thrust-faulted structures are well exposed in the Alps, the Canadian Rockies, and the North Cascades (see Figure 26-3).

DIVERGENT PLATE MARGINS

Where lithospheric plates diverge, the lithosphere is stretched and ultimately breaks apart, as when taffy is pulled too quickly. The most extensive divergent margins are the submarine mountain ranges of the midocean ridges (fig. 26-1d), but these are obviously inaccessible to climbers. Divergent margins also develop within continents (fig. 26-1e), and these definitely produce terrain of interest to mountaineers.

Continental rifts. As the lithospheric plates move apart along continental rifts, vertical faults break the crust into huge block-shaped mountains with nearly vertical faces on one side and gentler slopes on the other. These form great escarpments, such as East Africa's Great Rift Valley. Some mountains of the western United States, including Utah's Wasatch Range and California's Sierra Nevada, are fault-block ranges associated with stretching (extension) within the North American Plate rather than along its margin (see Figure 26-2).

Mountains created by extension generally have less *relief* (contrasting elevations) than those created by convergent margins, but not always. Mount Whitney, part of the Sierra Nevada, is the highest peak in the contiguous United States, at 14,494 feet (4,400 meters); Wheeler Peak of the Snake Range in eastern Nevada rises above 13,000 feet (4,000 meters).

Volcanism also affects the topography of rifted margins. Magma from the upwelling mantle beneath the rift can rise through faults to the surface, where over time it builds up both shield volcanoes and composite volcanoes, such as Africa's Mount Kilimanjaro.

INTRAPLATE HOT-SPOT VOLCANOES

The tallest mountain on Earth is not Mount Everest but, rather, the island of Hawaii, where the summit of Mauna Kea is 30,000 feet (9,000 meters) above the seafloor. Hawaii is part of a chain of volcanic islands and underwater sea-mounts that extend from the mid-Pacific nearly to Japan. These gigantic islands of basalt are the surface expression of thermal plumes, called *hot spots* (fig. 26-1f), that rise from the lower mantle toward the overlying lithosphere like a cumulus cloud building toward the stratosphere on a warm summer day. These plumes burn through the

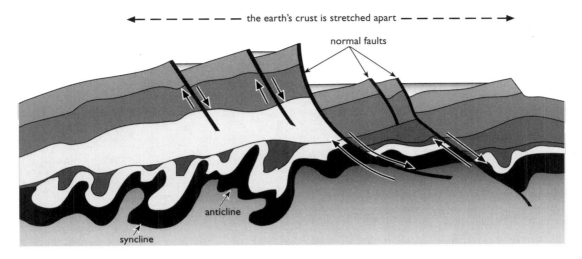

the earth's crust is stretched apart

normal faults

anticline

syncline

Fig. 26-2. Typical structures of a continental divergent plate margin, such as the Basin and Range of the western United States or the East African Great Rift Valley; note steep escarpment formed due to normal faulting.

moving lithosphere, creating a chain of volcanoes built upward from the seafloor.

Hot spots are also located within the continents—an example is the chain of volcanoes and lava flows (*lava* is rock that is molten at the surface of the earth) that extend across the Snake River Plain from near Boise, Idaho, northeast to Yellowstone National Park, where the plume is currently located. Because hot spots produce mainly shield volcanoes with gentle slopes, technical climbing is rarely required to ascend them. However, one of the most interesting traverses in the world is the trail to the summit of Mauna Loa on the island of Hawaii.

MOUNTAIN STRUCTURES

The slowest tectonic plates move at about the same velocity as fingernails grow, and the fastest move at about the same velocity as hair grows: a range of about 2 to 7 inches (5 to 17 centimeters) per year. Such slow movements cannot be seen, but the effect on the earth's surface can be profound. Slow as it is, this movement of the tectonic plates stresses rocks, and the results are the varying structures known as mountains. These stresses move mountains up, down, or from side to side and break them up into pieces. Near the earth's surface the rock layers are brittle, so they fracture into joints or move along faults. At greater depths, where the temperature and pressure are higher, the rocks tend to bend into folds rather than breaking.

FOLDS

Most sedimentary rocks are originally deposited in horizontal layers known as *beds*. However, in mountains such as the Front Range of Colorado, it is common to see beds that dip steeply or are even vertical. These rocks have been compressed into *folds*. This movement can be simulated by laying a napkin flat on a table and pushing its sides together, producing a series of archlike *anticlines* and troughlike *synclines* (fig. 26-2). Folds range in size from microscopic to a mile or more high. In some cases, such as the Ridge and Valley Province of the United States' Appalachians, the shape of the range is dictated by the underlying fold structure. The patterns of folds create ramps, overhangs, and resistant ridges that can be crucial factors in planning a route to a summit.

JOINTS AND VEINS

Joints are cracks that develop when rock masses expand or contract. Contraction joints are formed when hot rock shrinks during cooling. The only common kind of pure contraction jointing is the columnar structure of lava flows. The result is an array of roughly hexagonal columns that are typically 10 feet (3 meters) in height. Exceptionally high columns such as Devils Tower in Wyoming provide spectacular climbing opportunities.

Joints also develop when erosion exposes rocks that were once buried deeply within the earth, and as the overlying rocks are stripped away, fracturing can result from

26

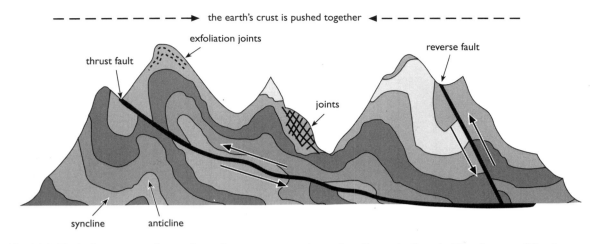

Fig. 26-3. Typical structures of a continental convergent margin, such as Europe's Alps, the Himalaya, and North America's Rocky Mountains.

the once-buried rocks expanding upward. If the expansion joints develop parallel to the exposed surface (as at Half Dome in California's Yosemite National Park), rocks peel off in layers that are called *exfoliation joints* (fig. 26-3). Sets of joints commonly occur at angles of 30, 60, or 90 degrees to each other—and these joint angles tend to be persistent as long as the rock type is the same. Recognition of joint patterns is essential for routefinding, especially on vertical faces in granitic rocks, where joints could be the only path to the summit without aid climbing.

Veins are fractures that have been filled by minerals, most commonly quartz or calcite. Veins can have an important effect on the texture of weathered rock surfaces. Quartz veins tend to project out as resistant ridges, whereas softer calcite veins are recessed. On some sheer faces, these can provide the only holds available, so the pattern of fractures determines where climbers should look for the next hand- or foothold.

FAULTS

Faults are fractures along which movement has occurred. The discernible movement may be only a fraction of an inch, or the movement can uplift a whole mountain range, such as Wyoming's Teton Range. Climbers need to know about faults because they can bring blocks of very different rock together. Fault zones also can consist of very weak, ground-up rock called *gouge* that may present a hazard to climbers.

Faults are classified according to their relative movement. *Normal faults* involve vertical movement that occurs

when the earth's crust is stretched to the point of breaking (see Figure 26-2), as in the Basin and Range region of Nevada, Utah, and California. Vertical movement also occurs along *reverse faults* and along *thrust faults*, which are reverse faults with an angle of less than 20 degrees (as shown in Figure 26-3). Here the fault is caused by compression due to the collision of lithospheric plates; examples are Europe's Alps and the Himalaya.

Strike-slip faults (for example, the San Andreas Fault in California) move the lithosphere in a horizontal plane, rather than up and down. This can move mountains from place to place but generally does not cause uplift.

MOUNTAIN MATERIALS

The rocks that compose mountains are the foundation of the climbing experience. Each type of rock has a different fracture pattern, surface texture, and durability. The strength of rocks, as well as their resistance to erosion and weathering, depends on the minerals of which they are composed. This in turn determines the reliability of holds and the overall climbing strategy for different rock types.

MINERALS

Minerals (crystals that are solid and inorganic) have unique properties by which they can be identified: color, hardness, *cleavage* (the tendency to split along definite crystalline planes), luster, and crystal shape. Only seven minerals compose most rocks of the earth's crust. Six of these are silicate minerals: feldspar, quartz, olivine, pyroxene, amphibole, and biotite. Except for biotite, these silicates are generally hard, durable materials. Only one common mineral, calcite, is soft and soluble. Calcite is composed of calcium carbonate, the major ingredient in many antacid tablets. It is resistant and stable in arid climates but dissolves readily in humid climates—and in acid rain.

Feldspar and quartz are the most resistant to breakdown under the constant assault of weathering. They are also the most abundant rock-forming minerals, composing most granites and sandstones. The other silicates—olivine, pyroxene, amphibole, and biotite—are dark, iron-rich minerals. Pyroxene is commonly found in basalt and gabbro. Amphibole and biotite are familiar as the black crystals in granite, granodiorite, and diorite, as well as in many schists and gneisses.

ROCKS

Rocks are classified into three categories: *igneous* (crystallized from a melt), *sedimentary* (deposited as particles, precipitates, or organic matter), and *metamorphic* (recrystallized by heat and/or pressure). A mountain climber does not need to be an expert in classifying rocks. However, it is very useful to be able to recognize a few general categories, because different rock types call for very different climbing strategies.

The first thing climbers need to know is that rocks are like a box of chocolates: you cannot tell what "flavor" they are until you look inside each one. Weathering, lichens, and biofilms (groups of microorganisms that grow together and stick to a surface) obscure the surface of many rock outcrops. To identify a rock's true color and appearance, look for a fresh surface that has recently broken open. Beneath a brown exterior there may be a black basalt, a white rhyolite, or even a glassy obsidian.

The following sections contain a few generalities about what kinds of climbing are effective on some of the most common rock types.

Igneous Rocks

Igneous rocks (from the Latin *ignis*, meaning "fire") crystallize from magma or lava. They can be either *volcanic* rocks (named for Vulcan, the Roman god of fire), which form from lava that is extruded at the surface, or *plutonic* rocks (named for Pluto, the Roman god of the underworld), which form underground from magma. See Table 26-1.

Volcanic rocks. The two types of volcanic rock are *lava flows* and *pyroclastics*. Most lavas crystallize rapidly under conditions of supercooling, so they commonly consist mainly of very tiny mineral grains that are invisible without magnification. However, they often include large crystals that formed in magma chambers underground before eruption. The composition of lava flows is essentially the same as their plutonic counterparts, the granitoids—in others words, rhyolite has the same chemical composition and minerals as granite, andesite matches diorite, and basalt matches gabbro (see Table 26-1). Most lava flows make very good climbing rock. Exceptions are lavas that are full of small cavities formed by gas bubbles and flows that have been chemically altered (*alteration zones*) by corrosive volcanic gases. This type of lava flow, which is composed of crumbly rock that is hazardous to climb, can be found on most volcanoes.

Pyroclastics are deposits of volcanic rock fragments produced by explosive eruptions. These include outcrops of ash and pumice that tend to fail unpredictably and therefore should be avoided on climbing routes if possible. Many pyroclastics also show some degree of chemical alteration. Anyone climbing stratovolcanoes from

TABLE 26-1. CLASSIFICATION OF IGNEOUS ROCKS

Color and Mineral Content	Volcanic (extrusive): fine-grained rock erupted as lava or ash; cools quickly; may contain small holes or crystals	Plutonic (intrusive): coarse-grained rock that cools and crystallizes slowly underground
Light-colored; very little iron content	Rhyolite or dacite (black, glassy = obsidian)	Granite or granodiorite
Usually gray; moderate iron content	Andesite	Diorite
Dark (black to green-black); high iron content	Basalt	Gabbro or peridotite (rare)

26

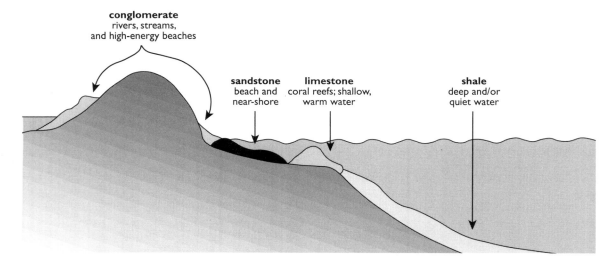

Fig. 26-4. Environments of deposition of various kinds of sedimentary rocks.

the Aleutians to the Andes should be aware of this potential hazard.

Plutonic rocks. The most common plutonic rocks are the coarse-grained granitoids—granite, granodiorite, and diorite. Granitoids are very durable unless highly weathered. They tend to have multiple fracture planes that define crack systems toward the summit or chimneys if accentuated by weathering. A good way to check the reliability of protection in granitoid rock is to hit it with a hammer. If it rings, it is good rock; if it makes a dull thud, be careful.

Sedimentary Rocks

Most sedimentary rocks are made of three types of material: fragments (*clastics*) of preexisting rocks, *precipitates* from solution (chemical), or organic material. Clastic rocks are classified according to the size of fragments in the rock. Fine-grained rocks, including thinly bedded *shales*, are the products of deposition in quiet, low-energy environments such as lakes or the seafloor. Coarse-grained clastic rocks, including *sandstones* and *conglomerates*, are transported and deposited in higher-energy regimes such as stream channels and beaches washed by waves crashing onshore (fig. 26-4).

Sandstone with silica cement (*gritstone*) is, for many, the most desirable rock to climb. It has continuous fracture systems, as do granitoids, coupled with high friction from its sandpapery surface formed of quartz and feldspar grains. Sandstone outcrops are commonly slabby, with many reliable hand- and footholds. Sandstone provides good protection unless it is highly weathered or poorly

cemented. Note that sandstone can be weak when wet.

Shale is also slabby, but because it is composed chiefly of soft clay, it crumbles just as easily as do altered pyroclastics. The best protection is probably a long, thin blade driven between layers, but nothing should be trusted. Avoid shale if possible, but be aware that it is commonly found in layers between sandstones.

Limestones, composed of chemical precipitates or organic material, are deposited in warm equatorial seas. Routefinding on limestone can be challenging because crack systems are far less continuous than on granitoid rocks. Also, limestone is composed of the soft mineral calcite, so if protection points are stressed during an ascent, as in the event of a leader fall, they can degrade and fail. Where limestone has been below the water table before uplift, it can have many solution cavities, caves, and overhangs that make climbing interesting.

Metamorphic Rocks

Metamorphic rocks are igneous or sedimentary rocks that have been recrystallized by heat and pressure. The most distinctive change is *foliation*, wherein minerals are aligned like the grain in wood; foliation is found in slates, phyllites, schists, and gneisses. Foliation is a plane of weakness in the rock, from a rock climber's viewpoint. This weakness dominates in slate, which is fine-grained. If you try to drive a piton parallel to the foliation, a slab of rock will easily split off that looks like a piece of blackboard. *Schist*, which has mineral grains coarse enough to be visible, has more resistance to splitting, but protection is still poor if it is placed parallel to the foliation. Most *gneisses* are similar to granitoids in strength, but climbers should still be aware of the foliation plane.

There are also several nonfoliated metamorphic rock types, including quartzite, marble, and hornfels. *Quartzite*, like sandstone, is a climber's favorite. It is slabby, with long, continuous fractures, and forms very solid outcrops, but it lacks the friction of sandstone, especially when wet. Note that in the alpine zone, where extensive freezing and thawing occur, quartzite slabs can sluff off, but not as easily as sandstone does. *Marble* is similar to limestone in that it is composed of soft calcite that is easily degraded and soluble in humid climates. It tends to have more continuous fractures than limestone, but expect unusual topography. *Hornfels* is a rock formed by heat along the margin of granitoid plutons. It is very hard and brittle. Chocks and cams work well in this rock, but the acts of driving pitons and placing bolts can splinter it.

Climbers should be aware of metamorphic changes along fault zones. In the shallow part of faults, movement shatters or grinds rock into *gouge*. Decomposition can also occur if hot fluids circulate through the fractured rock. Both the gouge and decomposed rock are very weak and are unreliable for protection. Deeper in the fault zone, rocks tend to flow rather than break. This produces *mylonites*, which have an intense foliation and are generally as unreliable as schist for protection points.

WHERE TO GET GEOLOGIC INFORMATION

The primary provider of geologic maps and information in the United States is the US Geological Survey (USGS); its website is the gateway to a cornucopia of geologic data for the entire world (see Resources for all websites mentioned here). Check out links to the USGS map finder—a clickable set of maps showing the name and location of all available 7.5-minute topographic maps. Another useful service of the USGS is the National Geologic Map Database. A new venture of the USGS is the Geology in the Parks program, which provides information via a website and brochures in cooperation with the National Park Service.

Other federal agencies that dispense geologic data are the US Forest Service and the US Bureau of Land Management. Nearly all of the state geological surveys also maintain websites with abundant geologic information; links to state geological surveys are listed online.

Another useful tool for planning climbing trips, Google Earth is a virtual mapping program that displays satellite images. The free program can be downloaded or accessed online. It allows climbers to easily see the terrain and specific features for almost any mountain on Earth, facilitating route planning.

Many mobile applications today provide accessible and useful information via phones and other mobile devices. The caveat to this is not all backcountry areas have data access, so climbers must download this information ahead of time for offline access in the field.

To get a site-specific geologic map or details on the geology of a chosen climbing route, there is no better place than the nearest college geology department. Many have websites with a lot of local geologic information, and all have faculty and students who are avid climbers and know exactly what rocks and structures they have seen on different routes.

Better still, start looking carefully and making detailed notes on the geologic features of the routes that you climb. Climbers are in effect practicing geologists, interpreting rock types and structures as they ascend. Personal observations are the best way to learn how to read the rocks for future climbs.

26

CHAPTER 27
THE CYCLE OF SNOW

Understanding the cycle of snow helps climbers anticipate changing conditions from the bottom of the mountain to the top, from morning to evening, and from day to day. While dramatic changes occur during storms, often subtle changes—caused by different exposures to sun and wind or aging processes—create significant impediments or enhancements to travel.

Snow crystals form in the atmosphere when water vapor condenses at temperatures below freezing. They form around centers of foreign matter, such as microscopic dust particles, and grow as additional atmospheric water vapor condenses onto them. Tiny water droplets also may contribute to snow crystal growth. The crystals generally are hexagonal, but variations in size and shape are almost limitless, including plates (fig. 27-1a), dendrites (fig. 27-1b and e), columns (fig. 27-1c and f), and needles (fig. 27-1d). The particular shape depends on the air temperature and the amount of water vapor available.

When a snow crystal falls through air masses of different temperatures and with different water vapor contents, snow crystals may become more complex or combine. In air that has a temperature near freezing, snow crystals stick together to become snowflakes: aggregates of individual crystals. When snow crystals fall through air that contains water droplets, the droplets freeze to the crystals, forming the rounded snow particles called *graupel* (fig. 27-1g)—soft hail. When snow crystals ascend and descend into alternating layers of above- and below-freezing clouds, layers of glaze and rime build up to form hailstones (fig. 27-1h). Sleet (fig. 27-1i) is a refrozen raindrop or melted snowflakes that have refrozen.

The density of new-fallen snow depends on weather conditions. The general rule is that the higher the temperature, the denser (heavier and wetter) the snow. However, density varies widely in the range of 20 to 32 degrees Fahrenheit (minus 6 to 0 degrees Celsius). Wind affects snow density, because high winds break up falling crystals into fragments that pack together to form dense, fine-grained snow. The stronger the wind, the denser the snow. The lowest-density (lightest and driest) snow falls under moderately cold and

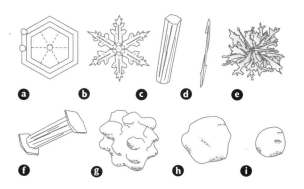

Fig. 27-1. Snow crystal forms: a, plate; b, dendrite (stellar crystal); c, column; d, needle; e, spatial dendrite (combination of feathery crystals); f, capped column; g, graupel (soft hail); h, hail (solid ice); i, sleet (icy shell, inside wet).

very calm conditions. At extremely low temperatures, new snow is fine and granular, with somewhat higher densities. The very highest densities are associated with graupel or needle crystals falling at temperatures near freezing.

The amount of water (solid or liquid) in layers of snow can indicate its density. Higher water content means that more space is occupied by ice or water and less air is present, causing higher density. In new-fallen snow, water content ranges from 1 to 30 percent, sometimes even higher, with the average for mountain snowfall being 7 to 10 percent.

SURFACE FORMS OF SNOW COVER

Snow and ice undergo endless surface changes as they are affected by wind, air temperature, solar radiation, freeze-thaw cycles, and rain. This section describes most of the surface permutations that mountaineers typically encounter. Table 27-1 summarizes the dangers and travel considerations associated with these various forms of snow.

Rime. Formed right at ground level, rime is the dense, dull white deposit formed by water droplets freezing on trees, rocks, and other objects exposed to the wind. Rime deposits build into the oncoming wind. Rime may form large, feathery flakes or a solid incrustation, but it lacks regular crystalline patterns. Typically it is easy to break, forming a weak, crusty surface when it is on top of snow and a poor, unreliable anchor when it is on rock or ice faces.

Hoarfrost. Another type of snow that forms at ground level, hoarfrost forms on solid objects by the process of sublimation: the direct conversion of atmospheric water vapor to a solid. Unlike rime, hoarfrost displays distinct crystalline shapes: blades, cups, and scrolls. The crystals appear fragile and feathery, sparkling brilliantly in sunlight. When deposited on top of snow, hoarfrost is known as *surface hoar*, generally produced during a cold, clear night. A heavy deposit of surface hoar makes for fast, excellent skiing with fun, crinkly sounds. (For depth hoar see "Aging of the Snow Cover" later in this chapter.)

Powder snow. A popular term for light, fluffy new-fallen snow, *powder snow* is more specifically defined as new snow that has lost some of its cohesion because large temperature differences between the pits and peaks of its feathery *dendrite* (branching) crystals have caused recrystallization. The changed snow is loose (uncohesive) and powdery (mostly air). It commonly affords good downhill skiing and may form dry loose-snow avalanches. Climbing or walking through powder is difficult, and any weight on it readily sinks.

Corn snow. After the advent of melting in early spring, a period of fair weather may lead to the formation of coarse, rounded crystals on the snow surface. The crystals, often called *corn snow*, are formed when the same surface layer of snow melts and refreezes for several days. When corn snow thaws each morning after the nighttime freeze, it is great for skiing and step-kicking. Later in the day, after thawing has continued, corn snow can become too thick and gooey for easy travel. During the afternoon, the associated meltwater also may lubricate the underlying snow and promote wet loose-snow avalanches, especially if the snow is stressed by people glissading on it or by the sliding and turning actions of skis, snowboards, and snowmobiles.

Rotten snow. Rotten snow is a spring condition characterized by soft, wet lower layers that offer little support to the firmer layers above. Rotten snow forms when lower layers of depth hoar (see "Aging of the Snow Cover" later in this chapter) become wet and lose what little strength they have. It is a condition that often leads to wet loose-snow or slab avalanches running clear to the bare ground. Continental climates, such as that of the North American Rockies, often produce rotten snow. Maritime climates, such as that of the Pacific coastal ranges, which usually have deep, dense snow covers, are less likely to produce rotten snow conditions. In its worst forms, rotten snow will not support the weight of even a skier. Snow that promises good spring skiing in the morning, when there is some strength in the crust, may deteriorate to rotten snow later in the day.

Meltwater crust. A snow crust that forms when water that melted on the snow's surface refreezes and bonds snow crystals into a cohesive layer is called a *meltwater crust*. Sources of heat that cause meltwater crusts include warm air, condensation at the snow surface, direct sunlight, and rain.

Sun crust. Sun crust is a common variety of meltwater crust that derives its name from the main source of heat for melting. In winter and early spring, the thickness of a sun crust over dry snow usually is determined by the depth of solar heating. Often it is thin enough that skiers and hikers break through, which is very uncomfortable. In later spring and summer, when free water is found throughout the snow cover, the sun crust's thickness—usually less than about 2 inches (5 centimeters)—depends on how cold temperatures become at night.

Rain crust. Another type of meltwater crust, rain crust forms after rainwater has percolated into the surface layers of snow. The rainwater often follows preferred paths as it percolates through the snow, creating fingerlike features

27

TABLE 27-1. SNOW CONDITIONS AND THEIR RELATED TRAVEL CONSIDERATIONS AND DANGERS

SNOW CONDITION	EFFECTS ON TRAVEL	EFFECTS ON PROTECTION	DANGERS
Rime	Breakable; can trap feet or skis		
Hoarfrost	Fun skiing		If hoarfrost is buried, potential avalanche danger
Powder snow	Difficult walking, good skiing	Ropes cut through it; ice axes do not hold in it; clogs crampons; deadmen need reinforcing with buried packs, etc.	Potential avalanche danger
Corn snow	Walking on it best in morning; skiing on it best in afternoon	Bollards must be large to hold	When frozen, avalanche potential low; when melted, stability depends on water content and underlying layer strengths
Rotten snow	Difficult traveling	Ropes cut through it; ice axes do not hold in it; deadmen need reinforcing with buried packs, etc.	Potential avalanche danger
Meltwater crust	Breakable; can trap feet if crust thin; good walking if crust thick; skis require edges	May require crampons	Slippery
Wind slab	Good walking		Potential avalanche danger, especially on leeward slopes
Firnspiegel	Breakable		
Verglas	Breakable; impedes rock travel		Slippery
Suncups	Uneven but solid walking or skiing		Low danger because usually form in old, stable snow
Nieves penitentes	Difficult to negotiate	Ropes catch on them	Low danger because usually form in old, stable snow
Drain channels	Uneven but solid walking or skiing		Low danger because usually form in old, stable snow
Sastrugi and barchans	Uneven but solid walking or skiing	Ropes catch on them	A sign of wind transport and potential slab formation; ski edges may catch on them
Cornices	Difficult to negotiate; best to avoid	Ropes cut through them	Can break away underneath or above traveler
Crevasses	Difficult to negotiate; may be hidden by snow; best to avoid	Require rope protection	Easy to fall into, especially if hidden
Seracs	Difficult to negotiate; best to avoid	Ropes catch on them	Very unstable; can break catastrophically
Avalanche paths	Hard surface, good walking		Slippery; relatively free from avalanche danger unless portion of slab remains or is recharged by new snow
Avalanche debris	Difficult to negotiate		Relatively free from avalanche danger unless portion of slab remains or is recharged by new snow

that act as pinning points, holding the crust to the underlying snow after it refreezes. The pinning action of many rain crusts helps to stabilize the snow against avalanching and makes for strong walking surfaces, especially in the Pacific's coastal ranges where heavy winter rainfall is common, even at high elevations. Glazed rain crusts can be extremely slippery and dangerous. Rain nearly always freezes on top of glacier ice, even during summer. This makes travel on glaciers following a fresh rain particularly hazardous.

Wind slab. After surface snow layers are disturbed by the wind, age hardening takes place to form a wind slab. When fragments of snow crystals broken by the wind come to rest, they are compacted together. Then the wind provides heat, particularly through water vapor condensation, which causes melting. Even when there is not enough heat to cause melting, the disturbed surface layer warms and then cools when the wind dies, providing additional metamorphic hardening. Traveling usually is fast and easy on hard wind slabs, but the slabs can break in long-running fractures, and if they overlie a weak layer or form a cornice, added stress causes avalanching.

Firnspiegel. The thin layer of clear ice sometimes seen on snow surfaces in spring or summer is called *firnspiegel* (a German word meaning "snow mirror," pronounced FEARN-spee-gull). Under the right conditions of sunlight and slope angle, the reflecting of sunlight on firnspiegel produces the brilliant sheen called *glacier fire*. Firnspiegel forms when solar radiation penetrates the snow and causes melting just below the surface at the same time that freezing conditions prevail at the surface. Once firnspiegel is formed, it acts like a greenhouse, allowing snow beneath to melt while the transparent ice layer at the surface remains frozen. Firnspiegel usually is paper thin and quite breakable. Breaking through firnspiegel while traveling causes little discomfort, unlike breaking through sun crusts.

Verglas. A layer of thin, clear ice formed by water (from either rainfall or snowmelt) freezing on rock is called *verglas.* It is most commonly encountered at higher elevations in the spring or summer when a freeze follows a thaw. *Verglas* (a French word meaning "glazed frost" or "glass ice," pronounced vair-GLAH) also may be formed by supercooled raindrops freezing directly as they fall onto exposed objects—a phenomenon known as *freezing rain,* also sometimes inaccurately called *silver thaw.* Verglas forms a very slippery surface, and like black ice on a roadway, it can be difficult to anticipate.

Suncups. Also called *ablation hollows,* suncups can vary in depth from 1 inch to 3 feet (2.5 centimeters to 1 meter)

or more (fig. 27-2a). Where sunshine is intense and the air is relatively dry, suncup depths usually increase with increasing elevation and decreasing latitude. On the ridges of each cup, sun-heated water molecules evaporate from the snow surface. In the hollows, water molecules released by solar heating are trapped near the snow surface, forming a liquid layer that promotes further melt. Because melting can occur with only one-seventh of the heat that is required for evaporation, the hollows melt and deepen faster than the ridges evaporate. The hollows are further deepened by differential melting when dirt in the hollows absorbs solar radiation. The suncups melt faster on the south (sunny) side in the northern hemisphere, so the whole suncup pattern gradually migrates northward across a snowfield.

Warm, moist winds tend to destroy suncups by causing faster melt at the high points and edges. A prolonged summer storm accompanied by fog, wind, and rain often will erase a suncup pattern completely, but the cups start to form again as soon as dry, fair weather returns. While skiing over suncups, it is easy to catch an edge, especially if the cups are hard and frozen from nighttime cooling. The unevenness of suncupped surfaces makes walking uphill tedious, but traveling downhill is made a little easier by "skating" into each hollow.

Nieves penitentes. When suncups grow up, they become *nieves penitentes* (pronounced nee-EH-vays pen-ih-TEN-tays, from the Spanish for "snow penitents," derived from the forms' similarity to the shape of a penitent's cowl). Nieves penitentes are the pillars produced when suncup hollows become very deep, accentuating the ridges into columns of snow that look like praying statues (fig. 27-2b). They are peculiar to snowfields at high altitudes and low latitudes, where solar radiation and atmospheric conditions conducive to suncups are intense. The columns often slant toward the midday sun. Nieves penitentes reach their most striking development among the higher peaks of South America's Andes and the Himalaya, where they may become several feet high and make mountain travel very difficult.

Drain channels. After melting has begun in spring, water runoff forms drainage patterns on snowfields. The actual flow takes place within the snowpack, not on the surface. As snow melts at the surface, the water that is formed percolates downward until it encounters either impervious layers that deflect its course or highly permeable layers that it can easily follow. Much of the water also reaches the ground beneath. Water that flows within the snow often causes a branching pattern of drain channels that appear on

27

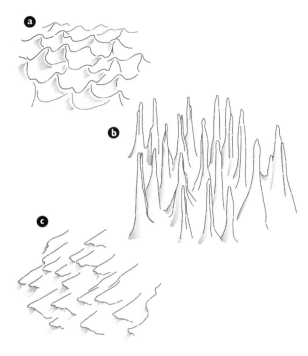

Fig. 27-2. Surface features on snow: a, suncups; b, nieves penitentes; *c,* sastrugi.

the surface. This happens because the flowing water accelerates the snow settlement around its channels, which are soon outlined by depressions at the surface. The dirt that collects in these depressions absorbs solar radiation, causing differential melting that further deepens them.

On a sloping surface, drain channels flow downhill and form a parallel ridge pattern that can make it a little difficult to turn while glissading or skiing. On flat surfaces, drain fields create a dimpled-looking surface, similar to suncups but more rounded. The appearance of dimples or drain channels suggests that a significant amount of water has percolated into the snow cover. If these dimples or channels are frozen, it can be a good sign of stability against avalanches. However, if they are newly formed and still soft with liquid water, snow stability may be compromised by meltwater that has percolated into a susceptible buried layer and weakened it.

***Sastrugi* and barchans.** When it is scoured by wind, the surface of dry snow develops a variety of erosional forms, such as small ripples and irregularities. On flat, treeless territory and high ridges, both of which are under the full sweep of the wind, these features attain considerable size.

Most characteristic are *sastrugi* (pronounced sass-TRUE-gee, a Russian word meaning "grooves"), the wavelike forms with sharp prows directed into the prevailing wind (fig. 27-2c). A field of *sastrugi*—hard, unyielding, and as much as several feet high—can make for tough going.

High winds over featureless snow plains also produce dunes similar to those found in desert sand, with the crescent-shaped dune, or *barchan*, being most common. These stiff, uneven features cause difficult traveling, especially when ice or rocky ground is exposed between each one.

Cornices. Deposits of snow on the lee edge of a ridgetop, pinnacle, or cliff are called *cornices*. Snow that falls during storms furnishes material for cornice formation. Cornices also are formed or enlarged by snow blown from snowfields that lie to the windward side of the ridge or feature (see Figure 17-5a). As a general rule, cornices formed during snowstorms (see Figure 17-5b) are softer than those produced by wind drift alone. Cornices present a particular hazard because they overhang, forming an unsupported, unstable mass (which may not be solid all the way through) that can break off (see Figure 17-5c) due to natural causes or human disturbance. It is dangerous to walk on a cornice. In addition, falling cornices are dangerous to those below and also can set off avalanches.

AGING OF THE SNOW COVER

Snow that remains on the ground changes with time. The crystals undergo a process of change—*metamorphism*—that usually results in smaller, simpler forms and a snowpack that shrinks and settles. Metamorphism begins the moment that snow falls and lasts until it completely melts away. Because the snowpack continually changes over time, mountaineers find it useful to know the recent history of weather and snow conditions in an area, in order to calculate what the snow cover will be like.

Equilibrium growth process. One type of metamorphism, the equilibrium growth process, gradually converts the varied original forms of the snow crystals into old snow: homogeneous, rounded grains of ice (fig. 27-3). Both temperature and pressure affect the rate of change. When temperature within the snow is near the freezing point—32 degrees Fahrenheit (0 degrees Celsius)—change is rapid. The colder it gets, the slower the change; it virtually stops below minus 40 degrees Fahrenheit (minus 40 degrees Celsius). Pressure from the weight of new snowfall speeds changes within older layers. Snow that has reached old age—surviving at least one year and with all original snow crystals now converted into grains of ice—is called

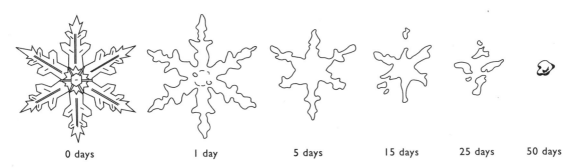

| 0 days | I day | 5 days | I5 days | 25 days | 50 days |

Fig. 27-3. Metamorphism of a snow crystal in the equilibrium growth process; days indicate time required for shapes to change under average temperature and pressure conditions in a typical seasonal snow cover.

firn or *névé*. Any further changes to firn snow lead to formation of glacier ice (see the next section).

Kinetic growth process. Another type of metamorphism, the kinetic growth process, takes place when water vapor moves from one part of the snowpack to another by vapor diffusion, which deposits ice crystals that are different from those of the original snow. This kinetic growth produces faceted crystals (fig. 27-4). When the process is completed, the crystals often have a scroll or cup shape, appear to be layered, and may grow to considerable size—up to 1 inch (2.5 centimeters) or so. They form a fragile structure known as *depth hoar* that loses all strength when crushed and becomes very soft and weak when wet. This weak, unstable snow form is popularly referred to as *sugar snow* when dry and rotten snow when wet. The conditions necessary for its formation are a large difference in temperature at different depths in the snow and sufficient air space so that water vapor can diffuse freely. The conditions are most common early in winter when the snowpack is shallow and unconsolidated.

Age hardening. In addition to undergoing metamorphic changes caused by variations in temperature and pressure, snow can age by mechanical means, such as wind. Snow particles broken by wind or other mechanical disturbances undergo a process known as age hardening for several hours after they are disturbed. This age hardening is the reason why it is easier to travel in snow if you follow tracks previously set by feet, skis, snowshoes, or snowmobiles.

Snow's variations in strength are among the widest strength variations found in nature: New snow is about 90 percent air, and the individual, unconnected grains make it a fluffy, weak material that is easy to break apart. In contrast, wind-packed old snow may contain less than 30 percent air, with the small, broken particles forming strong interconnected bonds that can create layers 50,000 times harder than fluffy new snow. The variations between these two extremes and the continual changes in strength caused by changes in temperature, pressure, and wind make for highly variable conditions from place to place and hour to hour.

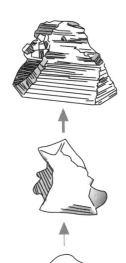

Fig. 27-4. Metamorphism of a snow crystal in the kinetic growth process results in a scroll or cup shape that appears layered and may become relatively large.

THE FORMATION OF GLACIERS

Glaciers form for a rather simple reason: Snow that does not melt or evaporate during the course of a year is carried over to the next winter. If snow continues to accumulate year after year, eventually consolidating and beginning a slow downhill movement, it has become a glacier.

27

553

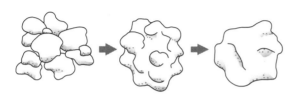

Fig. 27-5. *Rounded snow grains that are pressed and squeezed together form a large glacier ice crystal.*

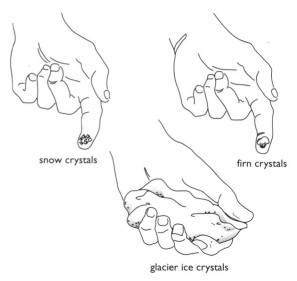

snow crystals

firn crystals

glacier ice crystals

Fig. 27-6. *Ice crystals increase greatly in size as they transform from snowflakes and firn into glacier ice.*

Within the old snow—the firn or névé—the metamorphic conversion of snow crystals into grains of ice has been completed. Now the grains of ice are changed into glacier ice in a process called *firnification*. Firn turns into glacier ice when the air spaces between the grains become sealed off from each other so the mass becomes airtight (fig. 27-5).

Each spring when the lower snow layers are still at temperatures below freezing, percolating meltwater refreezes when it reaches these lower layers. This refrozen meltwater forms ice layers within the firn. Therefore, by the time compaction and metamorphism have prepared an entire area of firn for conversion to glacier ice, the firn may already contain irregular bodies of ice.

Once glacier ice has formed, metamorphism does not cease. Some of the ice grains continue to grow at the expense of their neighbors, and the average size of the ice crystals increases with age (fig. 27-6). Large glaciers, in which the ice takes centuries to reach the glacier's foot, may produce crystals more than 12 inches (30 centimeters) in diameter, gigantic specimens grown from minute snow particles.

To understand how a simple, valley-type alpine glacier is born, picture a mountain in the northern hemisphere that has no glaciers. Now suppose climatic changes occur that cause snow to persist from year to year in a sheltered spot with northern exposure. From the beginning, snow starts to flow toward the valley in the very slow motion called *creep*. New layers are added each year, the patch of firn snow grows deeper and bigger, and the amount of snow in motion increases. The creeping snow, while melting and refreezing, dislodges soil and rock, and the flow of water around and under the snow patch additionally influences the surroundings. This small-scale process of erosion eventually leads to formation of a hollow where the winter snows are deposited in deeper drifts. After the snow deepens beyond 100 feet (30 meters) or so, the increasing pressure of the many upper layers of firn causes the lower layers to begin turning to glacier ice. A glacier is born.

With continued nourishment from heavy winter snows, the glacier flows toward the valley as a stream of ice. At some point in its descent, the glacier reaches an elevation low enough and warm enough that no new snow accumulates. The glacier ice begins to melt. Eventually the glacier reaches a point, even lower and warmer, at which all ice carried down from above melts each year. This is the lower limit of the glacier.

Glaciers vary from stagnant masses with little motion to vigorously flowing rivers of ice that transport large masses each year from higher to lower elevations. Glaciers in relatively temperate climates flow both by internal deformation and by sliding on their beds. Differences in speed within the glacier are somewhat like those in a river: fastest at the center and surface and slower at the sides and bottom where bedrock creates drag. Small polar glaciers present a striking difference in appearance from their temperate cousins, for they are frozen to their beds and can flow only by internal deformation. The polar glaciers look much like flowing molasses, whereas temperate glaciers are rivers of broken ice.

CREVASSES

Crevasses are important features of glaciers. Crevasses are fractures that occur when ice encounters a force greater than it can bear. Near the surface of a glacier, where ice is just beginning to form, the ice is full of tiny flaws and weakly bonded crystals. When it stretches or bends too fast, it can break apart in a brittle manner, like glass. The result is a crevasse.

Crevasses typically are 80 to 100 feet (25 to 30 meters) deep. At depths greater than that, ice layers become stronger, with increasingly large and well-bonded crystals. When stresses try to pull this deeply buried ice apart, overlying pressure further squeezes it together, causing it to flow and deform like thick, gooey honey. In colder glaciers—at high elevations or in polar climates—crevasses can penetrate somewhat deeper because colder ice is more brittle and tends to break more easily.

Temperate glaciers normally have more, and shallower, crevasses than polar glaciers because temperate glaciers usually move faster. When glaciers move very fast, such as over a very precipitous drop, extensive fracturing occurs, which forms an *icefall*. The numerous crevasses link together, isolating columns of ice called *seracs*.

ICE AVALANCHES

Ice avalanches can pour from hanging glaciers, icefalls, and any serac-covered portion of a glacier. Ice avalanches are caused by a combination of glacier movement, temperature, and serac configuration. On warm, low-elevation glaciers, ice avalanches are most common during late summer and early fall when meltwater has accumulated enough to flow underneath the glacier and increase its movement. The avalanche activity of high-elevation glaciers and cold glaciers that are frozen to the bedrock has no such seasonal cycle.

Reports differ on the time of day when ice avalanches are most active. Field observers suggest that they are most common during the afternoon. This may be possible in a snow-covered serac field if daytime heating loosens snow enough to avalanche into seracs and cause them to fall, creating an ice avalanche. However, scientists have discovered an increase in activity during the early morning hours when the ice is cold and most brittle. Ice avalanches can occur any time of year and any time of day or night.

THE FORMATION OF SNOW AVALANCHES

Numerous combinations of snow patterns cause avalanches. Every snowstorm deposits a new layer of snow. Even during the same storm, a different type of layer may be deposited each time the wind shifts or the temperature changes. After snow layers are deposited, their character is continually altered by the forces of wind, temperature, sun, and gravity. Each layer is composed of a set of snow crystals that are similar in shape to each other and that are bonded together in similar ways. Because each layer—each set of crystals—is different, each reacts differently to the various forces. Knowing something about these differences can help climbers understand and avoid avalanches.

Snow avalanches usually are categorized by their release mechanism: *loose-snow avalanches* start at a point; *slab avalanches* begin in blocks. Slab avalanches usually are much larger and involve deeper layers of snow. Loose-snow avalanches can be equally dangerous, however—especially if they are wet and heavy, if they catch victims who are above cliffs or crevasses, or if they trigger slab avalanches or serac falls.

LOOSE-SNOW AVALANCHES

Loose-snow avalanches can occur when new snow builds up on steep slopes and loses its ability to remain on the slope. The snow rolls off the slope, drawing more snow along as it descends. Sun and rain also can weaken the bonds between snow crystals, especially if they are newly deposited, causing individual grains to roll and slide into loose-snow avalanches. Skiing, glissading, and other human activities also can set off loose-snow avalanches by disturbing the snow. Loose-snow avalanches can easily sweep climbers into crevasses and over cliffs, destroy tents, and bury or carry away vital equipment.

SLAB AVALANCHES

Slab avalanches are more difficult to anticipate than loose-snow avalanches because they involve buried layers of snow that often cannot be detected from the surface. Usually a buried weak layer or weak interface is sandwiched between a slab layer and a bed layer or the ground (fig. 27-7). The buried weakness is disturbed in a way that causes it to reduce its frictional hold on the overlying slab.

Slab avalanches create an amount of havoc to climbers that is equal to or greater than that of loose-snow avalanches. Not only can slab avalanches fling people and equipment off slopes or bury them, but the tremendous speed of a slab avalanche and the force of impact have been known to move entire buildings and transport objects and people hundreds of yards downslope. It is difficult to survive an avalanche that is hurtling downslope, and once a person is buried, the snow hardens, rapidly making it difficult to breathe and hampering rescue.

27

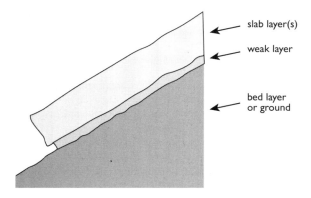

Fig. 27-7. Typical snow layering in a slab avalanche, with a weak layer between the slab and bed layers.

The Buried Weak Layer

Depth hoar and buried surface hoar (hoarfrost) are the most notorious weak layers. They can withstand a significant amount of vertical load but have little or no *shear strength*—that is, they slide easily along their horizontal interface. They may collapse like a house of cards, or their structure may give way like a row of dominoes. In addition, depth hoar and buried surface hoar can survive weeks to months with little change in their fragile structure.

Surface hoar (also known as "frost") can form all across the snow cover, persisting most in shaded places that are protected from wind. Buried by subsequent snowfall, it becomes a weak layer that can promote avalanching. It becomes most dangerous if the first storm following hoarfrost formation begins with cool, calm conditions. This is because it can quickly form a thin layer, even in a matter of hours. This layer is hard to detect, but can still function as a layer for subsequent snow loading.

Depth hoar matures fastest in the shallow snow of early winter, when the ground is still warm and the air is cold (common in continental regions), but it can develop anytime or anyplace where there are large differences in temperature at different depths of snow. Weakness begins as soon as temperature and associated vapor-pressure differences cause molecules of water vapor to move onto facets of individual ice crystals instead of into bonds between crystals. This causes a loose, sugar-like collection of ice grains. Therefore, immature depth hoar (solid, faceted shapes) may be just as weak as mature depth hoar (open, cup, and scroll shapes).

Buried graupel (soft hail; see Figure 27-1g) is another classic weakness within the snowpack because it can act like ball bearings if disrupted. Other weaknesses that can make it easier for slabs to avalanche include plate-shaped crystals (see Figure 27-1a).

Buried weak layers may persist longer over glacier ice than over bare ground. The glacier reduces the amount of geothermal heating available to the snow from the ground, keeping temperatures somewhat cooler and slowing metamorphism. This means that buried weaknesses in seasonal snow underlain by glaciers can persist following storms and well into the summer long after adjacent snowy slopes have stabilized.

The Slab Layer

Once the underpinning of a snowpack is sufficiently weakened, the overlying snow (either a single layer or group of layers) begins to slide. If the overlying snow is cohesive enough to develop some tension as sliding begins—that is, if it sticks together enough to form a slab—it may break in long fractures that propagate across the slope. Lengthy fractures can result in large, heavy blocks that easily pull away from the rest of the slope, such as along the side and bottom of a slope where more-stable snow may exist.

Slabs commonly are formed by brittle, wind-deposited snow layers. Wind often deposits snow in pillow-like patterns on the leeward side of ridges, thickest in the middle of the slope (where most of the weight of the slab, and thus the greatest avalanche danger, exists) and thinner on the edges. Wind slabs can maintain their blocky integrity throughout a slide, thrusting powerful masses downslope.

Slabs also are commonly formed by layers of needle-shaped crystals (see Figure 27-1d) deposited like a pile of pickup sticks and by layers of branching crystals with many interlocking arms (see Figure 27-1b and e), which often pulverize immediately after release to form fast-moving powder avalanches.

Thick rain crusts often bridge over weakened surfaces and are rarely involved in avalanches until they begin to melt in spring. Sun crusts, on the other hand, usually are thinner and weaker than rain crusts and can be incorporated in a group of slab layers.

If the overlying snow is too warm or too wet compared with the underlying weakness, it may not break, instead just deforming slightly in response to the change in basal friction and staying on the slope. However, if the underlying weak layer fails quickly and initial movement is significant, even this wet and pliable slab can avalanche. This scenario occurs commonly during spring when thick layers of old depth hoar are weakened by percolating meltwater. The resulting collapse of the depth hoar can cause a

THE CYCLE OF SNOW ▪ Understanding the Cycle of Snow

bending motion, like a whip, that overstresses the slab and causes it to fracture and slide. This whiplike effect also can occur in dry snow.

If the overlying snow is fragile and noncohesive—technically not a slab—the failure of a weak layer may simply result in snow grains in the overlying snow collapsing over each other but remaining in place. However, if the weak layer is buried surface hoar or slightly rounded branching or plate crystals, the failure can be so rapid that even the most fragile snow layers can turn into slab avalanches.

The Bed Layer
A bed layer provides the initial sliding surface of avalanches. Common bed layers are the smooth surfaces of old snow, meltwater crust, glaciers, bedrock, or grass. The interface of these smooth surfaces and the snow above can be further weakened if temperature changes promote the formation of depth hoar or if the interface is lubricated by meltwater or percolating rainwater. The bed layer also can be the collapsed fragments of old depth hoar.

AVALANCHE TRIGGERS
Humans are efficient trigger mechanisms for avalanches. Descending glissaders, stomping snowshoers, and ascending skiers, especially when executing kick turns, disturb layers of depth hoar or buried surface hoar. The sweeping turns and traversing motions of downhill skiers and snowboarders are effective at releasing loose-snow avalanches and fragile but fast-moving soft-slab avalanches. Snowplow turns, hockey-stops, sideslipping downhill, or falling may release wet loose-snow and wet slab avalanches. It is even possible to initiate an avalanche by traveling below a slope, especially if the buried weakness is surface or depth hoar, because a domino effect can occur as the delicate crystal structure collapses, propagating the failure uphill.

The weight and vibration of snowmobiles can set off avalanches in places where nonmotorized travel would not.

Storms also trigger avalanches. Many types of buried layers (such as thin layers of slightly rounded branches and platelike crystals) fail when a force is applied evenly over a broad surface, as occurs when storms deposit layers of new snow. Earthquakes, cornice and serac falls, and other internal and external effects on the snow can cause avalanches at unpredictable times and places. Loud sounds alone cannot trigger avalanches; for example, it is the concussive impact (not the percussive noise) of bombs set off by ski professionals that triggers a controlled slide. To learn more about avalanches, see Chapter 17, Avalanche Safety.

UNDERSTANDING THE CYCLE OF SNOW
Learning about the terrain and weather preceding a trip can help climbers anticipate snow conditions before leaving home. During a trip, understanding how wind, sun, and precipitation affect snow at different elevations and on different slope aspects will help determine choice of route and use of equipment.

Dense snow can provide good walking surfaces and sound bollards for rope belays, but if the snow is dense enough to have transformed to ice, then the walking can be slippery and carving bollards can be difficult. Fluffy new snow is fun for skiing downhill but makes uphill travel arduous and provides little or no support for belaying. The variety, combination, and timing of snow layering can promote avalanching.

The cycle of snow, from the first falling flake to glacier ice to meltwater, creates a dramatic and ever-evolving environment to challenge and delight climbers.

27

CHAPTER 28

MOUNTAIN WEATHER

It is no accident that many of the world's grandest monuments and temples—the pyramids of Egypt and Mexico, for example—mimic mountains. Mountains exude massive strength and permanence, their summits frequently assailed by storms that the ancients believed were signals of divine presence and power. Approaching the summit of such a peak was an act thought to risk the disfavor of the gods.

Today most climbers believe that a disastrous encounter with severe weather is the result of insufficient respect for the elements or bad luck, rather than the work of an angry god. There is no question that a trip into the mountains can expose people to more dangerous weather than most other environments on earth. Refuge can be harder to find, and major peaks can manufacture their own weather. Despite improvements in weather forecasting, knowledge of exactly how the atmosphere works, particularly in mountainous regions, is still incomplete. The wise climber not only carefully checks weather forecasts and reports before a trip but also develops an ability to assess the weather in the field.

FORCES THAT CREATE WEATHER

Understanding weather forecasts and reports requires a basic grasp of the forces that create weather. Such knowledge will not only help mountaineers better digest such information before leaving home, it will also help climbers detect important changes on the trail or climbing route as the weather changes over time.

THE SUN

The sun does far more than simply illuminate Planet Earth. It is the engine that drives the earth's atmosphere, providing the heat that, along with other factors, creates the temperature variations that are ultimately responsible for wind, rain, snow, thunder, and lightning—everything known as weather.

The key to the sun's impact is that the intensity of the sun's radiation varies across the earth's surface. Closer to the equator, the sun's heat is more intense. The extremes in temperature between the equator and the poles come as little surprise; however, those differences in air temperature also lead to air movement, which moderates those temperature extremes.

AIR MOVEMENT

The horizontal movement of air (what is called *wind*) is all too familiar to anyone who has pitched a tent in the mountains. However, air also rises and descends. When air cools, it becomes denser and sinks; the air pressure increases. But when air warms, it becomes less dense and rises; the air pressure decreases. These pressure differences,

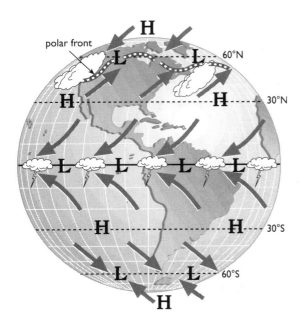

Fig. 28-1. The earth's air circulation patterns: movement from areas of high pressure at the poles toward areas of low pressure at the equator, deflected in the middle latitudes by the earth's rotation.

the result of temperature differences, produce moving air. Air generally moves from an area of high pressure to one of low pressure (fig. 28-1). Remember, wind direction is defined as the direction the wind is coming from, not the direction it is moving toward.

Air moving from high to low pressure carries moisture with it. As that air moves into the zone of lower pressure, then rises and then cools, the moisture may condense into clouds or fog. The reason is that, as the air cools, its capacity to hold water vapor is reduced. This is why you

can "see" your breath when the air temperature becomes cold: the water vapor in your mouth condenses into liquid water droplets as you breathe out. The process of cooling and condensation operates on a large scale in the earth's atmosphere as air moves from high-pressure systems into low-pressure systems, where it rises.

Because Arctic and Antarctic polar air is colder and therefore denser than air closer to the equator, it sinks. The zone where it sinks and piles up is a region of high pressure. As the air sinks and its pressure increases, its temperature warms a bit. The effect is similar to what happens to football or rugby players caught at the bottom of a pile: they get squeezed the most, and their temperature (and possibly temperament) heats up. In the atmosphere, this warming within a high-pressure area tends to evaporate some of the moisture present. That is why the Arctic receives very little precipitation. Although this sinking motion heats the air enough to evaporate much of the moisture in it, the air does not heat up enough to transform the poles into the tropics!

THE EARTH'S ROTATION

If the earth did not rotate, the cold polar air would just continue to slide toward the equator. However, the air sinking and moving from the poles toward the equator and the air rising from the equator do not form a simple loop moving from north to south (or from south to north) and back again. The rotation of the earth around its axis deflects this air. Some of the air rising from the equator descends over the subtropics, creating a region of high pressure. In turn, part of the air moving from these subtropical highs moves north into the air moving south from the north pole (or moves south into the air moving north from the south pole). The boundary between these two very different air masses is called the *polar front* (see Figure 28-1). When this boundary does not move, it is called a *stationary front*. It often serves as a nursery for the development of storms.

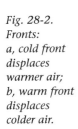

Fig. 28-2. Fronts: a, cold front displaces warmer air; b, warm front displaces colder air.

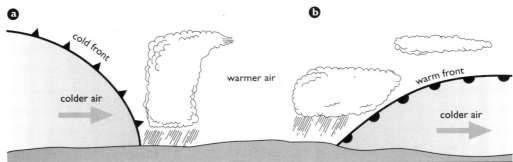

28

COLD FRONTS AND WARM FRONTS

Because of the great contrast in temperatures across the polar front, together with imbalances caused by the rotation of the earth and differing influences of land, sea, ice, and mountains, some of the cold, dry air from the north slides south (or, in the southern hemisphere, air from the south slides north). That forces some of the warm air to rise. The zone where cold air is replacing warm air is referred to as a *cold front* (fig. 28-2a), and the zone where warm air is gradually replacing cooler air is referred to as a *warm front* (fig. 28-2b); both types of fronts appear as a "wave" or bend on the stationary front. An *occluded front* combines characteristics of warm and cold fronts and is typically found near the center of a mature low-pressure system.

Both cold and warm fronts are marked by unique clouds, which help the mountaineer distinguish one type of front from the other. Clouds seen ahead of, along, or just behind a cold front include cumulus (fig. 28-3a), altocumulus (fig. 28-3b), cumulonimbus (fig. 28-3c), and stratocumulus (fig. 28-3d). These clouds are puffy, resembling cotton candy. The name *cumulus* refers to their "pile" or "heap" shape. Stratocumulus clouds are sheetlike layers of cumulus clouds; the name *stratus* refers to the "sheetlike" or "layered" characteristics of these clouds.

Clouds seen ahead of or along a warm front include a halo (fig. 28-3e), lenticular (fig. 28-3f), stratus (fig. 28-3g), cirrocumulus (fig. 28-3h), cirrostratus (fig. 28-3i), altostratus (fig. 28-3j), and nimbostratus (fig. 28-3k). Overall, lowering and thickening clouds signal the approach of precipitation and lowered visibility.

The "wave" or bend that develops along what started out as a stationary front may develop into a low-pressure system, with air circulating counterclockwise around the low (the opposite direction of air moving around a high)—again, a consequence of the earth's rotation and friction.

THUNDER AND LIGHTNING

Thunderstorms can be set off by the collision of different air masses when fronts move through or by the rapid heating of air when it comes in contact with sun-warmed mountain slopes. Once this air is warmed, it becomes buoyant and tends to rise. If the atmosphere above is cold enough, the air tends to keep rising, producing what are called *air-mass thunderstorms*. A single lightning bolt can heat the surrounding air up to 50,000 degrees Fahrenheit (approximately 25,000 degrees Celsius). That heating causes the air to expand explosively, generating earsplitting thunder.

Thunderstorms in the mountains can and do kill (fig. 28-4)—and not just from lightning strikes, although lightning is the biggest killer, claiming an average of 200 lives in the United States alone each year. Lightning can also spark dangerous wildfires, and even a moderate thunderstorm may release up to 125 million gallons (473 million liters) of rainwater. The resulting flash floods can quickly inundate streambeds and small valleys, sweeping away entire campgrounds. The growing popularity of canyoneering, particularly rappelling in deep slot canyons, increases climbers' exposure to flash floods and drowning. Thunderstorms can

TABLE 28-1. CLOUD-COVER CLUES

IF	THEN	CHECK FOR
High cirrus clouds, halo around sun or moon	Precipitation possible within 24–48 hours	Lowering, thickening clouds
High cirrus clouds forming tight ring or corona around sun or moon	Precipitation possible within 24 hours	Lowering, thickening clouds
"Cap" or lenticular clouds forming over peaks	Precipitation possible within 24 to more than 48 hours; strong winds possible near summits or leeward slopes	Lowering, thickening clouds
Thickening, lowering, layered flat clouds	Warm or occluded front likely within 12–24 hours	Shifting wind; dropping pressure
Breaks in cloud cover closing up	Cold front likely within 12 hours	Shifting wind; dropping pressure

a cumulus: with continued upward growth, these suggest showers later in the day

b altocumulus: high-based clouds often indicate potential for thunder and rain showers

c cumulonimbus: cumulus producing rain, snow, or thunder and lightning

d stratocumulus: lumpy, layered clouds often following a cold front suggesting showers

e halo: commonly seen 24 to 48 hours ahead of precipitation

f lenticular: lenslike clouds over mountains often suggesting precipitation within 48 hours

Fig. 28-3. Identifying cloud types: a, b, c, and d, cloud types seen ahead of, along, or just behind a cold front; (continued on next page)

28

g **stratus:** layerlike clouds associated with widespread precipitation or ocean air

h **cirrocumulus:** very high clouds, typically made of ice crystals, a warning of approaching storms

i **cirrostratus:** high, very thin clouds composed of ice crystals

j **altostratus:** when part of an approaching warm front, these clouds follow cirrostratus

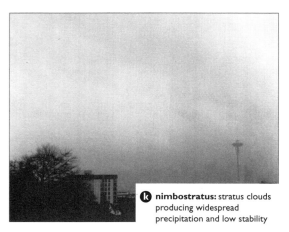

k **nimbostratus:** stratus clouds producing widespread precipitation and low stability

Fig. 28-3. (continued from preceding page) e, f, g, h, i, j, and k, cloud types seen ahead of or along a warm front.

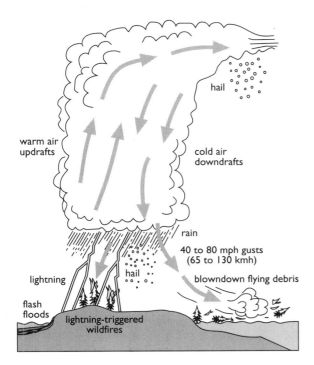

Fig. 28-4. Thunderstorm hazards include lightning, flash floods, and high winds.

also produce winds of lethal intensity, capable of leveling entire stretches of forest.

By taking a few precautions, climbers can avoid most accidents caused by mountain thunderstorms (see the "Tips If Thunderstorms Are Forecast" sidebar). Begin by obtaining updated weather reports and forecasts before hitting the trail.

GAUGE THE MOVEMENT OF A THUNDERSTORM

How is it possible to gauge the movement of a thunderstorm? It is easy with a watch. Use the "flash to bang" principle: The moment lightning flashes, start counting the seconds. Stop timing once the bang of thunder is heard. Divide the number of seconds by five; the result is the thunderstorm's distance away in miles. Continue to time lightning and thunder discharges to judge whether the thunderstorm is approaching, remaining in one place, or receding. If the time interval between the lightning and thunder is decreasing, the thunderstorm is approaching; if the interval is increasing, it is moving away.

This technique works because the light from the lightning moves much faster than the sound from the thunder. Although the thunder occurs at virtually the same instant as the lightning, its sound travels only about 1 mile (1.6 kilometers) every 5 seconds, whereas the lightning flash, traveling at 186,000 miles (300,000 kilometers) per second, arrives essentially instantaneously. That is why the lightning is seen before the thunder is heard, unless the thunderstorm is very close—too close.

IF A THUNDERSTORM APPROACHES

If climbers are caught out in the open during a thunderstorm, they should try to seek shelter. Tents are poor protection: metal tent poles may function as lightning rods; stay away from poles and wet items inside the tent. Take the following precautions to avoid being struck by lightning:

- **Get away from water** because it readily conducts electricity.
- **Seek low ground** if the party is in an open valley or meadow.
- **Move immediately** if your hair stands on end.
- **Avoid standing on ridgetops,** at lookout structures, or near or under lone tall trees, especially isolated or diseased trees, which are more likely to fall in thunderstorm winds.
- **Look for a stand of even-sized trees** if the party is in a wooded area.
- **Do not remain near or on rocky pinnacles or peaks.**
- **Do not remain near, touch, or wear metal or graphite equipment,** such as ice axes, crampons, climbing devices, and frame packs.

28

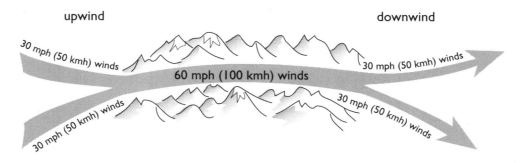

Fig. 28-5. Wind accelerates through gaps and passes.

- **Insulate yourself from the ground** if possible. Place a soft pack or foam pad beneath you to protect against step voltage transfer of the lightning strike through the ground—though ground currents may move through such insulation.
- **Crouch to minimize your profile,** and cover your head and ears.
- **Do not lie down**—lying down puts more of your body in contact with the ground, which can conduct more electrical current.

LOCALIZED WINDS

Understanding large-scale wind patterns, both at the earth's surface and in the upper atmosphere, is important for being able to gauge the weather. However, because mountains, by their very nature, alter wind considerably, understanding localized patterns is crucial to the mountaineer. It can mean the difference between successfully reaching the summit, being tent-bound, or getting blown off the mountain.

GAP WINDS

Winds are often channeled through gaps in the terrain such as major passes or even between two peaks. Wind speeds can easily double as they move through such gaps (fig. 28-5).

Climbers can use this knowledge to their advantage. If possible, gauge the surface wind speeds upwind of a gap or pass before traveling into the vicinity of these terrain features. Knowing the upwind velocities can prepare a climber for gap winds that may be twice as strong. Avoid camping near the downwind portion of the gap, and consider selecting climbing routes not exposed to such winds. A major peak can block or slow winds for a few miles downwind.

VALLEY AND GRAVITY WINDS

Sparsely vegetated ground is typically found closer to ridges. Because it heats more rapidly than forest-covered land near valley floors, and because heated air rises, wind is generated that moves up either side of a valley, spilling over adjoining ridgetops. Such uphill breezes, called valley winds, can reach 10 to 15 miles (16 to 24 kilometers) per

TABLE 28-2. WIND DIRECTION AND SPEED CLUES (NORTHERN HEMISPHERE)

IF	AND IF	THEN
Winds shift to E or SE	Air pressure drops; low-pressure system approaching	Clouds lower, thicken; precipitation possible
Winds shift from SW to NW	Air pressure rises	Drying and clearing likely; showers on windward slopes, especially along US or Canadian west coast
Increasing winds from from E to SE	Continued air pressure drop; low-pressure system approaching	Winds likely to increase
Winds shift from SW to W	Air pressure rises; high-pressure system approaching	Showers possible along windward slopes, especially along US or Canadian west coast

hour, attaining peak speed during the early afternoon and dying out shortly before sunset.

At night the land cools, and the cool air flows downslope in what is called a gravity wind. Such downslope breezes reach their maximum after midnight, dying out just before sunrise. Camping at the base of a cliff may result in an uncomfortably breezy evening. The more open the slopes between a campsite and the ridge above, the faster the winds will be.

FOEHN WINDS (CHINOOKS)

When winds descend a slope, air temperatures may increase dramatically in what is called a *foehn wind* or, in the western United States, a *chinook*. The air heats as it sinks and compresses on the leeward side of the crest (fig. 28-6), sometimes warming 30 degrees Fahrenheit (17 degrees Celsius) in minutes, melting as much as a foot of snow in a few hours. These winds are significant because of their potential speed, the rapid rise in air temperature associated with them, and the potential they create for both rapid melting of snow and flooding. Such winds can increase the risk of avalanches, weaken snow bridges, and lead to sudden rises in stream levels.

Warning signs make it possible to anticipate a potentially dangerous foehn wind or chinook. Expect such a wind with temperatures warming as much as 6 degrees Fahrenheit per 1,000 feet (3 degrees Celsius per 300 meters) of descent, if these three conditions are met:

1. You are downwind of a major ridge or crest, primarily to the east of mountains.
2. Wind speeds across the crest or ridge exceed 30 miles (48 kilometers) per hour.
3. You observe precipitation above the crest.

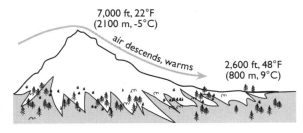

7,000 ft, 22°F
(2100 m, -5°C)

air descends, warms

2,600 ft, 48°F
(800 m, 9°C)

Fig. 28-6. Foehn winds (chinooks) descend and warm quickly.

MAJOR INDICATORS OF AN APPROACHING STORM

- Changes in cloud cover
- Changes in air pressure
- Changes in wind direction
- Changes in wind speed

BORA WINDS

The opposite of a chinook is a *bora* or, as it is called in Greenland, a *piteraq*. A bora is simply wind consisting of air so cold that its sinking, compressing motion as it flows downslope fails to warm it significantly. Such subzero winds are most common downslope of large glaciers. Their speeds can easily exceed 50 miles (80 kilometers) per hour. A bora can blow away tents, throw climbers off balance, lower the windchill to dangerous levels (see "Windchill Index" in Chapter 24, First Aid), and obscure visibility by blowing snow.

FIELD FORECASTING IN THE MOUNTAINS

The process of gathering and evaluating weather data should not end at the trailhead or at the beginning of the climbing route. Changes in weather—which can cause weather-related accidents in the mountains—rarely occur without warning. At times the clues can be subtle, and sometimes they are as broad as daylight (see the "Major Indicators of an Approaching Storm" sidebar).

No single one of the four factors shown in the sidebar will tell you all you need to know; examine each carefully. The rest of this section gives some guidelines for evaluating these elements, which can enhance the weather reports and forecasts climbers obtain before leaving home. Occasionally, such information can also be updated en route via smartphone, although that's subject to coverage and the reliability of the phone app or source. For changes in cloud cover, see Table 28-1; for changes in wind direction and speed, see Table 28-2.

TABLE 28-3. AIR PRESSURE AND/OR ALTIMETER CHANGE OVER 3 HOURS

PRESSURE DECREASE	ALTIMETER INCREASE	ADVISED ACTION
0.02–0.04 inch (0.6–1.2 millibars)	20–40 feet (6–12 meters)	None; continue to monitor
0.04–0.06 inch (1.2–1.8 millibars)	40–60 feet (12–18 meters)	If clouds lowering hourly or thickening, begin checking pressure changes hourly
0.06-0.08 inch (1.8-2.4 millibars)	60–80 feet (18–24 meters)	Winds ranging from 18 to 33 knots (21 to 38 miles per hour) likely—consider less-exposed locations, continue monitoring conditions
More than 0.08 inch (more than 2.4 millibars)	More than 80 feet (more than 24 meters)	Winds of 34 knots (40 miles per hour) or greater likely—move immediately to protected area

AIR PRESSURE CLUES

A barometer or barometric altimeter can give excellent warning of an approaching weather system. A barometer measures air pressure directly; a barometric altimeter measures air pressure and reports elevation. A decrease in air pressure shows on an altimeter as an increase in elevation even when the party has not changed its elevation; an increase in air pressure shows on an altimeter as a decrease in elevation, again, even when the party has not changed its elevation. (See "Altimeter" in Chapter 5, Navigation.)

Table 28-3 evaluates a developing low-pressure system, but rapidly building high pressure also can have its troublesome effects—principally, strong winds.

FREEZING LEVEL AND SNOW LEVEL

It can be useful to estimate the freezing level and snow level. Such estimates are subject to error because they are based on the average decrease in temperature as altitude increases: 3.5 degrees Fahrenheit per 1,000 feet (2 degrees Celsius per 304 meters) of elevation gain (see the

ESTIMATING THE FREEZING LEVEL

To estimate the elevation at which the temperature drops to 32 degrees Fahrenheit, climbers simply need to know their elevation and the temperature in degrees Fahrenheit:

$$\text{your elevation in feet} + \frac{\text{(Fahrenheit temperature} - 32) \times 1000}{3.5} = \text{estimated freezing level}$$

For example:

$$1000 \text{ feet elevation} + \frac{(39 \text{ degrees F} - 32) \times 1000}{3.5} = 1000 \text{ feet} + \frac{7000}{3.5} = 1000 \text{ feet} + 2000 = 3000 \text{ feet}$$

To estimate the elevation at which the temperature drops to 0 degrees Celsius, climbers simply need to know their elevation and the temperature in degrees Celsius:

$$\text{your elevation in meters} + \frac{\text{(camp temperature degrees Celsius)} \times 304}{2} = \text{estimated freezing level}$$

For example:

$$1000 \text{ meters elevation} + \frac{(3 \times 304)}{2} = 1000 \text{ meters} + \frac{912}{2} = 1000 \text{ meters} + 456 = 1456 \text{ meters} (\sim 1500 \text{ meters})$$

TABLE 28-4. ESTIMATING THE SNOW LEVEL		
IF	AND IF	THEN
Stratus clouds or fog present	Steady, widespread precipitation	Expect to find the snow level 1,000 feet (304 meters) below the freezing level
Cumulus clouds present or a cold front approaching	Locally heavy precipitation	Expect to find the snow level as much as 2,000 feet (608 meters) below the freezing level; snow will stick 1,000 feet (304 meters) below the freezing level

"Estimating the Freezing Level" sidebar). Still, such estimates are usually better than the alternative: no estimate. Once the freezing level has been estimated, use the guidelines in Table 28-4 to estimate the snow level.

CREATING CUSTOM WEATHER BRIEFINGS

Consider gathering weather information at least one day, and preferably two to three days, before a planned departure. That gives the party a chance to verify the forecasts by observing conditions. If the forecasts are pretty close to what the party actually sees, climbers can proceed with planning with more confidence than if the forecast and observed weather conditions are 180 degrees apart.

TWO TO THREE DAYS BEFORE THE TRIP

- **Check the overall weather pattern:** the positions of highs, lows, and fronts.
- **Check the projected weather forecast** for the next two days.

ONE DAY BEFORE THE TRIP

- **Check the current weather** to evaluate the accuracy of the previous day's forecasts.
- **Check the overall weather pattern again:** the positions of highs, lows, and fronts.
- **Check the projected weather** for the next two days.

- **Check for updates every six to eight hours** if the possibility of strong winds, thunderstorms, or significant snow or rain is mentioned. The lead time on such forecasts is short because of the rapid changes that sometimes occur.

ON THE DAY OF THE TRIP

- **Check the current weather** to evaluate the accuracy of the previous day's forecasts.
- **Check the projected weather** for the trip's duration.
- **Make decisions** based on current forecasts, the track record of earlier forecasts, personal experience, and the demands of the trip.

APPLYING THE INFORMATION

Mountaineers have a rich supply of weather forecast sources available to them before they depart on a trip. Such information gathered with a purpose is of great value. Begin with the vital step of obtaining current forecasts for the locale of the climb, followed by careful observation during the outing. Analyze changes in cloud cover, pressure, and wind speed and direction. Consider all such weather information thoroughly when selecting approach and climbing routes, camp locations, and start and turn-around times. Constant awareness of the environment and its impact on the party's plans will create a greater margin of safety during your pursuit of the freedom of the hills.

APPENDIX: RATING SYSTEMS

A rating system is a tool that helps a climber choose a climb that is both challenging and within his or her ability. The development of rating systems for climbing began in the late nineteenth and early twentieth centuries in Britain and Germany. In the 1920s, Willo Welzenbach created a rating system, using roman numerals and the British adjectival system, to compare and describe routes in the Alps. This system was used as the basis of the Union Internationale des Associations d'Alpinisme (UIAA, International Climbing and Mountaineering Federation) system of rating. Rating systems have since proliferated. Ratings used internationally today include no fewer than seven systems for rock, four for alpine climbing, four for ice, and two for aid climbing.

Rating climbs is a subjective task, which makes consistency between climbing areas elusive. Climb ratings assume fair weather and availability of the best possible equipment. Variables that affect the rating include the size, strength, and flexibility of the climber, as well as the type of climb (for instance, face, crack, or friction climbing), and the types of holds or features on the climb itself.

Ideally, a route is rated by consensus in order to reduce personal bias, though climbs often are rated by the first-ascent party. A guidebook author typically does not climb every route in the guidebook and therefore has to rely on the opinions of others. In some cases, a route may have been completed only once.

Ratings described as "stiff" indicate that the climb is harder than it is rated, whereas a description of a "soft" rating indicates the climb is easier than it is rated. Of course, evaluation of a rating system is no more precise than the rating system itself. Whenever you climb in an area for the first time, it's a good idea to start out on recommended or "starred" routes at a level lower than your usual ability until you can evaluate the local ratings and the nature of the rock.

ALPINE CLIMBING

The National Climbing Classification System (NCCS), developed in the United States, assigns grades to describe the overall difficulty of a multipitch alpine climb or long rock climb in terms of time and technical rock difficulty. It takes the following factors into account: length of climb, number of difficult pitches, difficulty of hardest pitch, average pitch difficulty, commitment, routefinding problems, and ascent time. The approach and remoteness of a climb might or might not affect the grade given, depending on the guidebook and area. It should be emphasized that with increasing grade, an increasing level of psychological preparation and commitment is necessary. This system assumes a party that is competent for the expected level of climbing.

Grade I. Normally requires several hours; can be of any technical difficulty.

Grade II. Requires half a day; any technical difficulty.

Grade III. Requires a day to do the technical portion; any technical difficulty.

Grade IV. Requires a full day for the technical portion; the hardest pitch is usually no less than 5.7 (in the Yosemite Decimal System for rating rock climbs; see below).

Grade V. Requires a day and a half; the hardest pitch is at least 5.8.

Grade VI. A multiday excursion with difficult free climbing and/or aid climbing.

Grade VII. Requires at least 10 days of suffering on a huge wall, in poor weather, in a remote area. Climbing grades are at least as difficult as those on a Grade VI climb with all other factors increasing in intensity.

Like other rating systems, the grade is subjective. For example, the Nose on El Capitan in California's Yosemite National Park is rated Grade VI. Warren Harding and companions took 45 days for the first ascent, in 1958. John Long,

Billy Westbay, and Jim Bridwell made the first one-day ascent in 1975. Hans Florine and Peter Croft cut the time to under four and a half hours in 1992, and Lynn Hill (accompanied by a belayer) led the first free ascent in 1993 and the first one-day free ascent in 1994. The time needed for a climb is as relative as the abilities and technologies of the climbers. The type of climb affects what factors of the given grade are emphasized. Proper planning, including study of a route description, are more valuable in estimating a party's climbing time than the given grade.

ROCK CLIMBING

Rating systems have been created for free climbing, aid climbing, and bouldering.

FREE CLIMBING

In 1937, a modified Welzenbach rating system was introduced in the United States as the Sierra Club System. In the 1950s, this system was modified to more accurately describe rock climbing being done at Tahquitz Rock in California by adding a decimal to the Class 5 rating. This is now known as the Yosemite Decimal System (YDS). This system categorizes terrain according to the techniques and physical difficulties encountered when rock climbing. Figure A-1 compares the YDS with other international rating systems.

Class 1. Hiking.

Class 2. Simple scrambling, with possible occasional use of the hands.

Class 3. Scrambling; hands are used for balance; a rope might be carried.

Class 4. Simple climbing, often with exposure. A rope is often used. A fall could be fatal. Typically, natural protection can be easily found.

Class 5. Where rock climbing begins in earnest. Climbing involves the use of a rope, belaying, and protection (natural or artificial) to protect the leader from a long fall.

The decimal extension of Class 5 climbing originally was meant to be a closed-end scale—that is, ranging from 5.0 to 5.9. Up until 1960 or so, a climb that was the hardest of that era would be rated 5.9. The rising standards in the 1960s, however, led to a need for an open-ended scale. Strict decimal protocol was abandoned, and 5.10 (pronounced "five-ten") was adopted as the next highest level. As the open-ended system let the decimal numbers go up to 5.11, 5.12, and ever higher, not all climbs were rerated, leaving a disparity between the "old-school ratings" and the new ratings.

The YDS numbers reached 5.15 in the first few years of the twenty-first century. The ratings from 5.10 to 5.15 are subdivided into a, b, c, and d levels to more precisely state the difficulty. The most difficult 5.12 climb, for instance, is rated 5.12d. A plus sign or a minus sign is occasionally used as a more approximate way to refine a classification. Sometimes a plus sign will be added to indicate that the pitch is sustained at its particular rating, while a minus sign might indicate that the pitch has only a single move at that level.

The extended numbers of the fifth-class rating system can't be defined precisely, but the following descriptions offer general guidelines:

5.0–5.7. Easy for experienced climbers; where most novices begin.

5.8–5.9. Where most weekend climbers become comfortable; employs the specific skills of rock climbing, such as jamming, liebacks, and mantels.

5.10–5.11. A committed recreational climber can reach this level.

5.12–5.15. The realm of true experts; demands much training and natural ability, as well as, often, repeated working of a route.

The YDS rates only the hardest move on a pitch and, for multipitch climbs, the hardest pitch on a climb. The YDS gives no indication of overall difficulty, protection, exposure, runouts, or strenuousness. Some guidebooks, however, will rate a pitch higher than the hardest move if the pitch is very sustained at a lower level. A guidebook's introduction should explain any variations on the YDS that may be used.

Because the YDS does not calculate the potential of a fall, but only the difficulty of a move or pitch, a seriousness rating has been developed. This seriousness rating (introduced by James Erickson in 1980) appears in guidebooks in a variety of forms; read the introduction to any guidebook for an explanation of its particular version.

PG-13. Protection is adequate, and if it is properly placed, a fall would not be long.

R. Protection is considered inadequate; there is potential for a long fall, and a falling leader would take a real "whipper," suffering serious injuries.

X. Inadequate or no protection; a fall would be very long with serious, perhaps fatal, consequences.

Ratings of the quality of routes are common in guidebooks. If anything, they are even more subjective than the basic climb ratings because they attempt to indicate aesthetics. The number of stars given for a route indicates the quality of the route in the eyes of the guidebook writer. A standard number of stars for the very best climbs has not

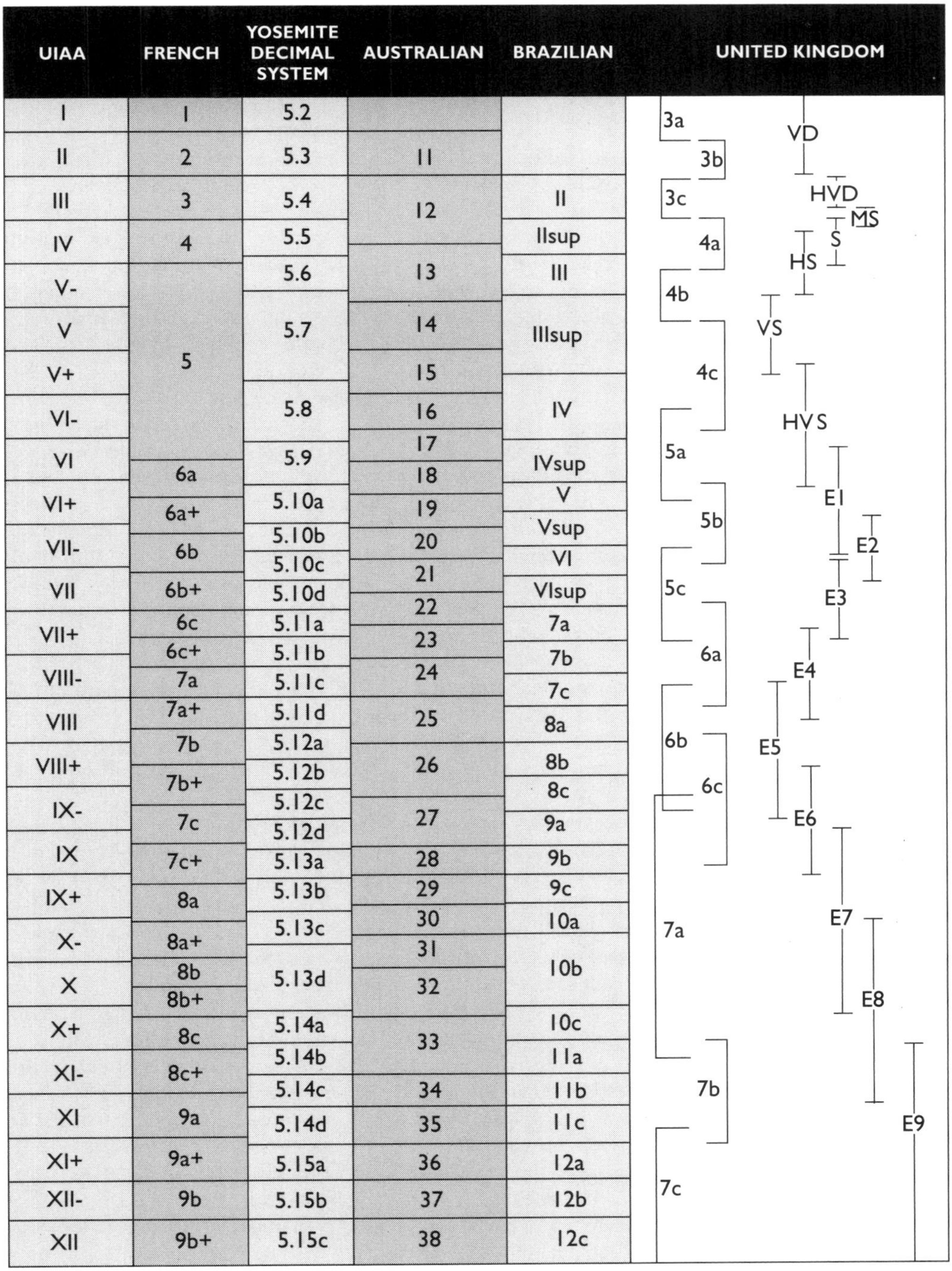

UIAA	FRENCH	YOSEMITE DECIMAL SYSTEM	AUSTRALIAN	BRAZILIAN	UNITED KINGDOM
I	1	5.2			
II	2	5.3	II		
III	3	5.4	12	II	
IV	4	5.5		IIsup	
V−		5.6	13	III	
V	5	5.7	14	IIIsup	
V+			15		
VI−		5.8	16	IV	
VI		5.9	17	IVsup	
	6a		18		
VI+	6a+	5.10a	19	V	
VII−	6b	5.10b	20	Vsup	
		5.10c	21	VI	
VII	6b+	5.10d	22	VIsup	
VII+	6c	5.11a	23	7a	
	6c+	5.11b		7b	
VIII−	7a	5.11c	24	7c	
VIII	7a+	5.11d	25	8a	
	7b	5.12a	26	8b	
VIII+	7b+	5.12b		8c	
IX−	7c	5.12c	27		
		5.12d		9a	
IX	7c+	5.13a	28	9b	
IX+	8a	5.13b	29	9c	
		5.13c	30	10a	
X−	8a+		31		
X	8b	5.13d	32	10b	
	8b+				
X+	8c	5.14a	33	10c	
XI−	8c+	5.14b		11a	
		5.14c	34	11b	
XI	9a	5.14d	35	11c	
XI+	9a+	5.15a	36	12a	
XII−	9b	5.15b	37	12b	
XII	9b+	5.15c	38	12c	

United Kingdom system (technical grades): 3a, 3b, 3c, 4a, 4b, 4c, 5a, 5b, 5c, 6a, 6b, 6c, 7a, 7b, 7c

United Kingdom system (adjectival grades): VD, HVD, MS, S, HS, VS, HVS, E1, E2, E3, E4, E5, E6, E7, E8, E9

Fig. A-1. Six of the world's seventeen climbing rating systems.

571

been established. A climb with no stars does not mean the climb isn't worth doing, nor does a star-spangled listing mean that everyone will like the route.

AID CLIMBING

Rating aid moves or aid climbs is different from rating free climbs in that the rating system is not open-ended like the YDS. An aid climbing rating primarily indicates the severity of a possible fall, based on the quality of protection available. To some extent, an aid rating indicates the difficulty of the climbing, but only in that there is a loose correlation between easy-to-place protection and its ability to arrest a fall. However, following a series of "easy" hook moves for a distance of 40 feet (12 meters) with no protection left to arrest a fall might garner a rating of A3, while conversely some A1 pitches might accommodate high-quality protection at regular intervals but could be extremely difficult to climb if the crack is a deep, awkward flare with protection available only at its very back.

The scale is from A0 to A5 or from C0 to C5. The "A" refers to aid climbs in general, which may utilize pitons, bolts, or chocks. The "C" refers to clean aid climbing, meaning that a hammer is not used to make placements. A rating such as C2F, with the "F" indicating "fixed," indicates that the pitch can be climbed clean only if critical gear normally placed with a hammer has been left in place by other parties. It is sometimes possible to climb a pitch clean that is rated with the A0–A5 system, and some pitches have two ratings, one A rating and one C rating, which indicates the grade with or without a hammer.

The following rating system is used worldwide except in Australia (which uses M0 to M8; the "M" stands for mechanical):

A0 or C0. No aiders are required. Fixed gear such as bolts may be in place, or the climber may be able to simply pull on a piece of gear to get through the section, a technique sometimes called "French free."

A1 or C1. Good aid placements; virtually every placement is capable of holding a fall. Aiders are generally required.

A2 or C2. Placements are fairly good but may be tricky to place. There may be a couple of bad placements between good placements.

A2+ or C2+. Same as A2, though with increased fall potential—perhaps 20 to 30 feet (6 to 10 meters).

A3 or C3. Hard aid. Several hours to lead a pitch, with the potential of 60- to 80-foot (18- to 24-meter) falls, but without danger of grounding (hitting the ground) or serious injury.

A3+ or C3+. Same as A3, but with the potential of serious injury in a fall. Tenuous placements.

A4 or C4. Serious aid. Fall potential of 80 to 100 feet (24 to 30 meters), with very bad landings. Placements hold only body weight.

A4+ or C4+. More serious than A4. More time on the route, with increased danger.

A5 or C5. Placements hold only body weight for an entire pitch, with no solid protection such as bolts. A leader fall at the top of a 150-foot (45-meter) A5 pitch means a 300-foot (90-meter) fall or a fall that would cause a serious impact on a rock feature, the latter of which may be equivalent to hitting the ground.

A5+. A theoretical grade; A5, but with bad belay anchors. A fall means falling to the ground (anchor failure).

Aid ratings are always subject to change. What was once a difficult A4 seam may have been beaten out with pitons to the point that it will accept large chocks, rendering it C1. Camming devices and other examples of newer technology can sometimes turn difficult climbs into easy ones. Some climbs once considered A5 might now be rated A2 or A3 after repeated traffic and with the use of modern equipment.

Big wall climbs are rated like this:

The Nose, El Capitan: VI, 5.8, C2

This means that the Nose route on Yosemite's El Capitan is a Grade VI (a "multiday excursion"); the most difficult moves that you must free-climb (with no option to aid) are YDS 5.8; and the most difficult aid is C2.

BOULDERING

Bouldering—climbing on large rocks, fairly close to the ground—has gained popularity. Though once a game played by alpinists in mountain boots on days too rainy for climbing, bouldering has become an all-out pursuit of its own. John Gill created his B-scale to rate boulder problems:

B1. Requires moves at a high level of skill—moves that would be rated 5.12 or 5.13.

B2. Moves as hard as the hardest climbs being done in standard rock climbing (5.15 currently).

B3. A successful B2 climb that has yet to be repeated. Once repeated, the boulder rating automatically drops to B2.

John Sherman created the open-ended V-scale, which gives permanent ratings to boulder problems (unlike Gill's scale, with its floating ratings). As shown in Figure A-2, Sherman's scale starts at V0- (comparable to 5.8 YDS); it moves up through V0, V0+, V1, V2, and so on, with V16

YOSEMITE DECIMAL SYSTEM	SHERMAN V-SCALE (BOULDERING)
5.8	V0-
5.9	V0
5.10a-b	V0+
5.10c-d	V1
5.11a-b	V2
5.11c-d	V3
5.12-	V4
5.12	V5
5.12+	V6
5.13-	V7
5.13	V8
5.13+	V9
5.14a	V10
5.14b	V11
5.14c	V12
5.14d	V13
5.15a	V14
5.15b	V15
5.15c	V16

Fig. A-2. The Sherman V-scale for rating boulder problems, compared with the Yosemite Decimal System for rating rock climbs.

being comparable to 5.15c YDS. Neither the B- nor V-scale takes into account the consequences of a rough landing on uneven terrain.

ICE CLIMBING

The variable conditions of snow and ice climbing make rating those climbs difficult. The only factors that usually do not vary throughout the season and from year to year are length and steepness. Snow depth, ice thickness, and temperature affect the conditions of the route; these factors plus the nature of the ice and its protection possibilities determine a route's difficulty. These rating systems apply mainly to waterfall ice and other ice formed by meltwater (rather than from consolidating snow, as on glaciers).

COMMITMENT RATING

The important factors in this ice climbing rating system are length of the approach and descent, the length of the climb itself, objective hazards, and the nature of the climbing. (The Roman numeral ratings used in this system have no correlation to the numerals used in the grading system for overall difficulty of alpine climbs; see "Alpine Climbing" earlier.)

I. A short, easy climb near the road, with no avalanche hazard and a straightforward descent.

II. A route of one or two pitches within a short distance of rescue assistance, with very little objective hazard.

III. A multipitch route at low elevation, or a one-pitch climb with an approach that takes an hour or so. The route requires from a few hours to a long day to complete. Descent may require building rappel anchors, and the route might be prone to avalanche.

IV. A multipitch route at higher elevations; may require several hours of approach on skis or foot. Subject to objective hazards; possibly with a hazardous descent.

V. A long climb in a remote setting, requiring all day to complete the climb itself. Requires many rappels off anchors for the descent. Sustained exposure to avalanche or other objective hazard.

VI. A long ice climb in an alpine setting, with sustained technical climbing. Only elite climbers will complete it in a day. A difficult and involved approach and descent, with objective hazards ever-present, all in a remote area far from the road.

VII. Everything a grade VI has, and more of it. Possibly requires days to approach the climb, and objective hazards render survival as certain as a coin toss. Needless to say, difficult physically and mentally.

TECHNICAL RATING

The technical grade rates the single most difficult pitch, taking into account the sustained nature of the climbing, ice thickness, and natural ice features such as chandeliers, mushrooms, or overhanging bulges. These ratings have been further subdivided, with a plus added to grades of 4 and above if the route is usually more difficult than its stated numerical grade.

1. A frozen lake or streambed (the equivalent of an ice rink).
2. A pitch with short sections of ice up to 80 degrees; lots of opportunity for protection and good anchors.
3. Sustained ice up to 80 degrees; the ice is usually good, with places to rest, but it requires skill at placing protection and setting anchors.
4. A sustained pitch that is vertical or slightly less than vertical; may have special features such as chandeliers and runouts between protection.
5. A long, strenuous pitch—possibly 165 feet (50 meters) of 85- to 90-degree ice with few if any rests between anchors. Or the pitch may be shorter but on featureless ice. Good skills at placing protection are required.
6. A full 165-foot pitch of dead-vertical ice, possibly of poor quality; requires efficiency of movement and ability to place protection from awkward stances.
7. A full pitch of thin, vertical or overhanging ice of dubious adhesion. An extremely tough pitch, physically and mentally, requiring agility and creativity.
8. Thin, gymnastic, overhanging, and bold. Pure ice climbs at this level are extremely rare.

These ratings typically describe a route in its first-ascent condition. Therefore a route that was rated a 5 on its first ascent might be a 6- in a lean year for ice, but only a 4+ in a year with thick ice. The numerical ice ratings are often prefaced with WI (water ice, or frozen waterfalls), AI (alpine ice), or M (mixed rock and ice; historically, mixed climbs were described with the YDS).

NEW ENGLAND ICE RATING SYSTEM

A system developed for the water ice found in New England applies to normal winter ascent of a route in moderate weather conditions:

NEI 1. Low-angle water ice of 40 to 50 degrees, or a long, moderate snow climb requiring a basic level of technical expertise for safety.

NEI 2. Low-angle water ice with short bulges up to 60 degrees.

NEI 3. Steeper water ice of 50 to 60 degrees, with bulges of 70 to 90 degrees.

NEI 4. Short vertical columns, interspersed with rests, on 50- to 60-degree ice; fairly sustained climbing.

NEI 5. Generally multipitch ice climbing with sustained difficulties and/or strenuous vertical columns, with little rest possible.

NEI 5+. Multipitch routes with a heightened degree of seriousness, long vertical sections, and extremely sustained difficulties; the hardest ice climbing in New England to date.

MIXED CLIMBING

Jeff Lowe introduced the Modern Mixed Climbing Grade to simplify the rating of the crux on mixed ice and rock routes. It is an open-ended scale with routes rated M1 to M13. A plus sign or a minus sign is added to broaden the range and to prevent grade compression. It is the consensus of top climbers that the M ratings in Europe are inflated by one grade. See Figure A-3 for a comparison of the M grades to YDS ratings.

OTHER MAJOR RATING SYSTEMS

A variety of rating systems are used throughout the world. Figure A-1 compares the principal systems. Apart from the main rating systems described here, other rating systems are used around the world, which are unique to their own treatment of seriousness and local weather and conditional

MODERN MIXED GRADE	YOSEMITE DECIMAL SYSTEM
M4	5.8
M5	5.9
M6	5.10
M7	5.11
M8	5.11+/5.12-
M9	5.12+/5.13-
M10	5.13+/5.14-
M11	5.14+/5.15-
M12	5.15
M13	5.15+

Fig. A-3. The Modern Mixed Climbing Grades for mixed rock and ice climbs, compared with the Yosemite Decimal System for rating rock climbs.

phenomena. The Alaska Grade, for example, is a grading system unique to Alaska that takes into account severe storms, cold, altitude, and cornicing; it extends from Grade 1 to 6 (instead of overall commitment ratings I to VII).

When climbing in a new area, be sure to check with local authorities and/or guidebooks and become knowledgeable about any possible local grading systems and their peculiarities.

ROCK CLIMBING

Australian. The Australian system uses an open-ended number series. The Australian number 38, for example, is equivalent to 5.15c in the YDS.

Brazilian. The rating of climbs in Brazil is composed of two parts. The first part gives the general level of difficulty of the route as a whole, ranging from first to eighth grade (or degree). The second part gives the difficulty of the hardest free move (or sequence of moves without a natural rest). Figure A-1 shows only the second part of the Brazilian system, the part that is most comparable to the other systems shown. The lower range is expressed in roman numerals; the designation "sup" (for superior) is added to refine the accuracy of the rating. The upper range is expressed in Arabic numerals with letter modifiers.

British. The British system is composed of two elements: an adjectival grade and a technical grade.

The adjectival grade—such as Very Difficult (VD) or Hard Severe (HS)—describes the overall difficulty of a route, including such factors as exposure, seriousness, strenuousness, protection, and runouts. The list of adjectives to describe increasingly difficult routes became so cumbersome that the British finally ended it at Extremely Severe (ES) and now simply advance the listing with numbers: E1 for Extremely Severe 1, E2 for Extremely Severe 2, and so forth:

E.	Easy.
M.	Moderate.
D.	Difficult.
VD.	Very difficult.
HVD.	Hard very difficult.
MS.	Mild severe.
S.	Severe.
HS.	Hard severe.
VS.	Very severe.
HVS.	Hard very severe.
ES.	Extremely severe.
E1.	Extremely severe 1.
E2.	Extremely severe 2.
E3.	Extremely severe 3.

The technical grade is defined as the hardest move on a particular route. This numeric component of the British system is also open-ended and is subdivided into a, b, and c.

The two grades are linked to each other. For example, the standard adjectival grade for a well-protected 6a, which is not particularly sustained, is E3 (and the combined rating would be expressed as E3 6a). If the route is a bit run-out, it would be E4; if it is really run-out, it would be E5. See Figure A-1.

French. In the French open-ended system, ratings of 6 and above are subdivided into a, a+, b, b+, c, and c+. The French rating of 9b+ is comparable to 5.15c in the YDS.

UIAA. The UIAA open-ended rating system uses roman numerals. Beginning with the fifth level (V), the ratings also include pluses and minuses. The UIAA rating of XII is comparable to 5.15c in the YDS. German climbers use the UIAA system.

ALPINE CLIMBING AND ICE CLIMBING

The International French Adjectival System (IFAS) is an overall rating of alpine and ice climbs used primarily in the Alps. The system is used by several countries, including France, Britain, Germany, Italy, and Spain. It expresses the seriousness of the route, including factors such as length, objective danger, commitment, altitude, runouts, descent, and technical difficulty in terms of terrain.

The system has six categories that are symbolized by the initials of the French adjectives used. It is further refined with the use of plus or minus signs, or the terms "sup" (superior) or "inf" (inferior). The ratings end with an adjective readily understood in English:

F. *Facile* ("easy"). Steep walking routes, rock scrambling, and easy snow slopes. Crevasses possible on glaciers. Rope not always necessary.

PD. *Peu difficile* ("a little difficult"). Rock climbing with some technical difficulty, snow and ice slopes, serious glaciers, and narrow ridges.

AD. *Assez difficile* ("fairly difficult"). Fairly hard climbs, steep rock climbing, and long snow and/or ice slopes steeper than 50 degrees.

D. *Difficile* ("difficult"). Sustained hard rock and snow and/or ice climbing.

TD. *Très difficile* ("very difficult"). Serious technical climbing on all kinds of terrain.

ED. *Extrêmement difficile* ("extremely difficult"). Extremely serious climbs with long, sustained difficulties of the highest order.

ABO. *Abominable.* Translation—and difficulty—obvious.

GLOSSARY

A

accessory cord Core-and-sheath-constructed cord of diameters ranging from 2 to 8 millimeters, fabricated from aramid (Kevlar), nylon, Perlon, polyester, and polyethylene (Dyneema or Spectra) fibers.

accumulation zone The portion of a glacier that receives more snow every year than it loses to melting.

acute mountain sickness (AMS) An altitude-related illness.

aid climbing Using gear to support a climber's weight while climbing.

aiders Webbing ladders that allow an aid climber to step up. Also called *etriers*.

alpine rock climbing Rock climbing that requires mountaineering skills.

alpine start Starting before daybreak.

alpine touring (AT) *See* randonée skiing.

altimeter Instrument for determining altitude.

American technique Cramponing technique that combines flat-footing (French) and front-pointing (German) techniques on steep snow or ice. Also called *combination technique. See* combination technique.

AMS *See* acute mountain sickness.

anchor The point on the mountain to which the climbing system is securely attached; there are belay anchors, rappel anchors, and protection in rock, snow, and ice.

approach shoes Lightweight, sticky-soled shoes designed for both trails and moderate rock climbing.

ascender Mechanical device used to ascend a rope. Also called *jug, jumar*.

autoblock A hitch that provides modest friction to simulate the grip of a hand. Commonly used while rappelling.

B

back-cleaning A procedure in which the leader cleans some protection while ascending the route.

bearing The direction from one place to another measured in degrees from true north.

belay anchor *See* anchor.

belay device A piece of equipment that applies friction to the rope to arrest a fall.

belaying Fundamental technique of generating friction to stop a rope's movement and the climber attached to that rope.

bergschrund Giant crevasse found at the upper limit of glacier movement, formed where the moving glacier breaks away from the ice cap or snowfield above.

bight A 180-degree bend in a rope.

big wall climbing Climbing on a large, sheer wall, which usually requires bivouacs and extensive aid climbing.

bivy From the French *bivouac*, meaning "temporary encampment."

bivy sack Large fabric envelope that serves as a lightweight alternative to a tent.

body belay *See* hip belay.

bollard A mound carved out of snow or ice and rigged with rope, webbing, or accessory cord to provide an anchor.

bolt Permanent piece of artificial protection consisting of a threaded bolt that is placed into a hole drilled into rock.

braking hand The belayer's hand that secures the belay; must be kept in contact with the rope at all times.

C

cairn A pile of rocks used as a route marker.

cam *See* spring-loaded camming device, Tricam.

camming Application of torquing or counterpressure with climbing gear.

carabiner Metal snap-link that comes in various shapes and sizes; indispensable and versatile tool of climbing used for belaying, rappelling, clipping in to safety anchors, securing the rope to points of protection, and numerous other tasks.

GLOSSARY

CEN European Committee on Standardization, Comité Européen de Normalisation. The European nonprofit organization responsible for creating and maintaining climbing equipment standards. The "CE" mark signifies that a product meets all applicable European legislation. *See also* UIAA.

chimney A crack wide enough to fit a climber's body and narrow enough to allow a climber to apply opposing force to both walls.

chlorine dioxide Chemical water-treatment method (not to be confused with chlorine) for purifying water.

chock Climbers' hardware comprising removable protection. Also called *stopper, wired nut.*

chockstone A rock firmly lodged in a crack or between gully walls.

circlehead *See* copperhead.

clean climbing Climbing without permanently marring the rock.

cleaning Removing protection.

cleaning tool *See* nut tool.

climbing in coils The preferred tie-in method for two-person glacier travel teams—for closer spacing between rope partners and more efficient travel.

combination technique Cramponing technique that combines flat-footing (French) and front-pointing (German) techniques on steep snow or ice. Also called *American technique.*

contour lines Lines on topographic maps that represent constant elevations.

coordinate system A system, such as UTM or latitude and longitude, to describe a location on the earth.

copperhead Malleable hardware used in aid climbing. Also called *head, circlehead.*

cord *See* accessory cord.

cordelette A long runner usually made of 7- to 8-millimeter nylon or small-diameter, high-strength accessory cord.

crag climbing Technical rock climbing in an area close to roads and civilization that does not require alpine skills.

crampons A set of metal spikes that attach to boots in order to penetrate hard snow and ice.

crevasse A crack or chasm in a glacier.

crux The most significant, committing, or difficult section of a pitch or climb.

D

daisy chain Sewn sling with stitched loops.

datum The anchoring points for a coordinate system. Critical when using a map with a GPS device.

deadman Any object buried in the snow to serve as an anchor. Also any piece of hardware such as an ice screw or ice tool used extemporaneously for a protection placement in ice.

declination Compass adjustment needed to correct for local difference between magnetic north and true north.

dihedral Where two walls meet in approximately a right-angled inside corner. Also called *open book.*

dry rope Rope treated to make it more water-repellent.

dry tooling Climbing on rock with ice tools and crampons.

DWR Durable water repellent. A chemical coating applied to fabrics to make them hydrophobic and able to shed water. Currently essential to the functioning of virtually all waterproof-breathable fabrics.

dynamic rope A rope that stretches under loads.

Dyneema Brand name for ultra-high-molecular weight, ultra-strong polyethylene fibers. Material is highly abrasion resistant and very lightweight but has a low melting point and is very slippery, making knots difficult. Commonly used in climbing runners; also called Spectra.

E

edging Climbing technique using either the inside or outside edge of the foot so that the edge of the sole is weighted over the hold.

emergency communication device A device that can be used to summon help in an emergency. Includes radios, smart phones, personal locator beacons (PLBs), satellite phones, and satellite communicators (Garmin InReach and SPOT).

equalette A cordelette with pretied knots used to rig anchors. *See* cordelette.

equalization Equalizing forces on a multipoint anchor.

Esbit fuel Waxy fuel tablets made of hexamine and used in ultralight stoves.

etriers *See* aiders.

F

fall factor The length of a fall divided by the length of the rope between belay device and fallen climber.

fall line The line of travel of a freely falling object.

feeling hand The belayer's hand that pays the rope in and out.

fixed line Rope anchored in place.

fixed pin Permanent piton.

flagging Climbing technique that involves extending a limb for counterbalance, to prevent pivoting or the "barn-door" effect.

flaking Uncoiling the rope, one loop at a time, into a neat pile.

flat-footing *See* French technique.

fluke Metal-plate anchor used in snow and sand.

follower *See* second.

free climbing Using ropes and other means of climbing protection to protect against injury, not assist progress. Originally meant "free from aid."

free solo climbing Climbing without any rope or other means of protection where a fall would result in serious injury or death.

French technique Cramponing technique used on moderately steep snow and ice in which the feet are placed flat against the surface of the snow or ice. Also called *flat-footing*.

friction climbing *See* smearing.

front-pointing Kicking front crampon points into hard snow or ice. Also known as *German technique*.

G

gaiters Article of clothing used to seal boundary between pant legs and boots from water, snow, and debris.

German technique *See* front-pointing.

glissade A controlled slide on snow.

Global Positioning System Collective term for satellite-based navigation system run by US Department of Defense and similar agencies in other countries. Often referred to as GPS.

grade A ranking from I to VII describing the overall difficulty of a multipitch alpine climb or long rock climb in terms of time and technical rock difficulty.

guylines Cords attached to a tent or tarp and staked out to brace it.

H

HACE *See* high-altitude cerebral edema.

halbmastwurf sicherung **(HMS)** German for "half clove-hitch belay"; another term for the munter hitch. Carabiners stamped "HMS" accommodate the munter hitch.

HAPE *See* high-altitude pulmonary edema.

hardshell Typically uninsulated rain parka or pants made from waterproof-breathable fabric. *See also* softshell.

heads *See* copperhead.

hero loop *See* tie-off loop.

hex Hexagonally shaped removable protection.

high-altitude cerebral edema (HACE) An altitude-related illness affecting the brain.

high-altitude pulmonary edema (HAPE) An altitude-related illness affecting the lungs.

hip belay A method of applying friction to the rope with the belayer's body that does not require a mechanical device. Also known as a *body belay*.

HMS *See* halbmastwurf sicherung.

I

ice axe Specialized tool used by climbers, generally for snow and ice travel.

ice screw A tubular, hollow screw used as protection in ice.

ice tool Short ice axe or hammer used for technical ice climbing.

icefall Steep, jumbled section of a glacier.

J

jamming A basic technique of crack climbing in which a hand or foot is jammed into a crack, then turned or flexed so that it is snugly in contact with both sides of the crack and it will not come out when weighted.

jugging Ascending the climbing rope with mechanical ascenders in aid climbing. Also called *jumaring*.

jumaring *See* jugging.

K

kernmantle rope Rope composed of a core of braided or parallel nylon filaments encased in a smooth, woven sheath of nylon; designed specifically for climbing.

Kevlar Aramid synthetic fiber trademarked by DuPont; used in accessory cord, among other things. *See also* accessory cord.

L

leader The climber who takes the lead on a roped pitch.

leashless tool Ice tools specifically designed to be used without leashes.

Leave No Trace Principles of minimum impact developed by the organization of the same name.

lieback To use hands in opposition to feet to create a counterforce.

load-limiting runner A presewn runner with a series of weaker bar tacks that fail at lower impact forces and absorb high loads. Also called *energy-absorbing sling*.

M

mantel To use hand downpressure to permit the raising of the feet.

matching To place both hands or both feet on the same hold.

microfilter Drinking water filter designed to filter parasites, protozoa, and bacteria, but not viruses. *See* purifier-filter.

moat Gap between snow and rock.

moraine Mounds of rock and debris deposited by a glacier.

mountaineering boot Crampon-compatible, stiff-soled footwear.

munter hitch A friction knot used for belaying and rappelling. Also called the *Italian half hitch. See also halbmastwurf sicherung.*

N

nieves penitentes Snow pillars produced when suncup hollows become very deep, accentuating the ridges into columns of snow that look like a person wearing a penitent's cowl.

nut Passive removable protection that is a wedging-type chock.

nut tool Tool used for removing protection. Also known as *cleaning tool* or *chock pick*.

nylon cord *See* accessory cord.

O

objective hazard Physical hazard associated with a climbing route, such as rockfall, exposure, and high altitude.

off-width A crack that is too wide for a hand jam but too narrow for chimney technique.

open book *See* dihedral.

P

pearabiner A carabiner large enough at its wider end to accommodate a munter hitch.

Perlon A brand name for nylon 6. *See* accessory cord.

personal locator beacon Electronic device that broadcasts a user's GPS location to emergency first responders via government-based satellites. Also called PLB; similar to satellite communicators.

picket An aluminum stake used for an anchor in snow.

pitch The distance between belays on a climb.

piton A metal spike used as protection.

plunge-stepping A technique for walking down a snow slope that involves assertively stepping away from the slope and landing solidly on the heel with the leg vertical (but not with the knee locked), transferring weight to the new position.

posthole To sink deeply with each step in snow.

protection Point of attachment that links climbing rope to the terrain. Also known as *pro*.

prusik A friction hitch. Also a technique for ascending a climbing rope using friction hitches.

purifier-filter Drinking water filter designed to filter parasites, protozoa, bacteria, and viruses. *See* microfilter.

Q

quickdraw A presewn runner, typically 4 to 8 inches (10 to 20 centimeters) long, with a carabiner loop sewn into each end through which a carabiner is attached.

R

randonée skiing Ski technique used by climbers that employs hybrid equipment allowing free-heel ascent and alpine descent and that accommodates climbing boots. Also known as *alpine touring*.

rappel anchor *See* anchor.

rappelling Fundamental climbing technique of safely descending a rope using friction to control speed.

rest step Ascent technique that ends every step with a momentary stop relying on skeletal structure to give muscles a rest.

rock shoe Specialized rock climbing footwear with a sticky rubber sole.

rope drag Friction that impedes the rope's travel.

runner Length of webbing or accessory cord used to connect components of the climbing safety system. Also called a *sling*.

running belay Climbing technique in which all members of the rope team climb at the same time, relying on immediate protection rather than a fixed belay. Also called *simul-climbing*.

S

satellite communicator Electronic device that broadcasts a user's GPS location to emergency first responders via commercial satellites. Also called *satellite messengers*. May include texting, location tracking, and other nonemergency communication.

scrambling Unroped, off-trail travel that requires some use of hands.

scree Loose slope of rock fragments smaller than talus.

second The climber who follows the leader on a roped pitch. Also known as a *follower*.

self-arrest Ice-axe technique used to stop a fall on snow.

self-belay Ice-axe technique in which the ice axe is jammed straight down into the snow and held by the head or head and shaft.

serac Tower of ice on a glacier.

simul-climbing *See* running belay.

single-pulley system *See* 2:1 pulley system.

ski mountaineering Involves climbing mountains, either on skis or carrying skis, and skiing down using randonée or telemark gear and style. *See also* alpine touring, randonée skiing.

skins Strips of textured material that attach to the bottom of skis for traction, designed to let the ski slide forward on snow but not backward.

SLCD *See* spring-loaded camming device.

sling *See* runner.

smearing Rock climbing technique in which the foot points uphill and the climber maximizes contact between the rock and the sole of the shoe for friction. Also called *frictioning.*

snow pit Pit dug into snow in order to observe snow conditions.

softshell Article of clothing made from dense, stretchy, woven synthetic fabric.

Spectra *See* Dyneema.

SPF Sun protection factor, the rating system that quantifies the degree of sun protection provided by a sunscreen product.

sport climbing Technical rock climbing that relies on fixed protection (bolts) and does not usually require mountaineering skills; compare trad climbing.

spring-loaded camming device (SLCD) Active removable protection that uses spring-loaded cams to create opposing force in a crack. Also called a *cam.*

spring-loaded nut A chock that uses a small sliding piece to expand the profile of the chock after it is placed in a crack.

static rope A rope that does not stretch; used for fixed lines and hauling.

stemming Climbing technique using counterforce in which one foot presses against one feature while the other foot or an opposing hand pushes against another feature; commonly used to climb chimneys or dihedrals. Also called *bridging.*

step-kicking Climbing technique that creates ascending steps in snow.

stopper *See* wired nut.

suncup Small hollow in snow or ice that is created by melting and evaporation.

T

talus Rock fragments large enough to step on individually. *See also* scree.

team arrest Arrest attempted by several members of a rope team on a snow slope.

technical climbing Climbing in which belays or protection should be used for safety.

Ten Essentials Essential gear that should be carried on all wilderness trips. Developed by The Mountaineers.

3:1 pulley system Raising system that theoretically triples the amount of weight a rescue team could haul without a pulley. Also called *Z-pulley system.*

tie-off loop Short runner commonly used for tying off belays, for self-belay during a rappel, in aid climbing, and in rescue. Also called *hero loop.*

topos Topographic maps or climbers' route sketches.

top roping A sport climbing technique in which the climber is belayed using a rope that runs up from the belayer, through a preplaced top anchor, and back down to the climber.

trad climbing Technical rock climbing in which climbers place and remove protection; compare sport climbing.

Tricam Removable protection with a lobe-shaped camming wedge; can be set actively or passively.

tube chock Telescoping protection used for off-width cracks.

2:1 pulley system Raising system that theoretically doubles the amount of weight that a rescue team could haul without a pulley. Also called *single-pulley system.*

U

UIAA International Climbing and Mountaineering Federation, Union Internationale des Associations d'Alpinisme. The internationally recognized authority in setting standards for climbing equipment. *See also* CEN.

UPF Ultraviolet protection factor, the rating system that quantifies the degree of sun protection provided by a garment.

UTM The Universal Transverse Mercator is one of the principal coordinate systems used to define a location on the earth. *See also* coordinate system *and* datum.

V

verglas The thin, clear coating of ice that forms when rainfall or melting snow freezes on a rock surface.

V-thread anchor A V-shaped tunnel bored into the ice, with accessory cord or webbing threaded through the tunnel and tied to form a sling.

V-thread tool A hooking device used to pull accessory cord or webbing through the drilled tunnel of a V-thread ice anchor.

GLOSSARY

W

webbing *See* runner.

wired nut Passive removable protection. Also known as *chock, stopper.*

Z

Z-pulley system *See* 3:1 pulley system.

RESOURCES

Chapter 1: First Steps

Barcott, Bruce. *The Measure of a Mountain: Beauty and Terror on Mount Rainier*. Seattle: Sasquatch Books, 2007.

Blum, Arlene. *Annapurna: A Woman's Place*. Reprint ed. Berkeley, CA: Counterpoint, 2015.

Bonatti, Walter. *The Mountains of My Life*. Translated and edited by Robert Marshall. London: Penguin Classic, 2010.

Gillman, Peter, and Leni Gillman. *The Wildest Dream: The Biography of George Mallory*. Seattle: Mountaineers Books, 2001.

Herzog, Maurice. *Annapurna: First Conquest of an 8000-Meter Peak*. 2nd ed. Translated by Nea Morin and Janet Adam Smith. Guilford, CT: Lyons Press, 2010.

Krakauer, Jon. *Eiger Dreams: Ventures Among Men and Mountains*. Guilford, CT: Lyons Press, 2009.

Molenaar, Dee. *The Challenge of Rainier: A Record of the Explorations and Ascents, Triumphs and Tragedies on the Northwest's Greatest Mountain*. 40th anniversary ed. Seattle: Mountaineers Books, 2011.

Muir, John. *Nature Writings; The Story of My Boyhood and Youth; My First Summer in the Sierra; The Mountains of California; Stickeen; Essays*. Edited by William Cronon. New York: Library of America, 1997.

———. *Our National Parks*. In *John Muir: The Eight Wilderness-Discovery Books*. Seattle: The Mountaineers; London, Diadem, 1992.

———. *The Wild Muir: Twenty-Two of John Muir's Greatest Adventures*. Selected and introduced by Lee Stetson. Yosemite National Park, CA: Yosemite Conservancy, 1994.

Nash, Roderick Frazier. *Wilderness and the American Mind*. 5th ed. New Haven, CT: Yale University Press, 2014.

Roberts, David. *The Mountain of My Fear and Deborah: Two Mountaineering Classics*. Seattle: Mountaineers Books, 2012.

Simpson, Joe. *Touching the Void: The True Story of One Man's Miraculous Survival*. New York: Perennial, 2004.

Stuck, Hudson. *The Ascent of Denali (Mount McKinley): A Narrative of the First Complete Ascent of the Highest Peak in North America*. New York: Charles Scribner's Sons, 1914 (USA: CreateSpace Independent Publishing Platform, 2015).

Turner, Jack. *Teewinot: Climbing and Contemplating the Teton Range*. New York: St. Martin's Press, 2001.

Washburn, Bradford, and David Roberts. *Mount McKinley: The Conquest of Denali*. New York: Abrams, 2000.

Chapter 2: Clothing and Equipment

Carline, Jan D., Martha J. Lentz, and Steven C. Macdonald. *Mountaineering First Aid: A Guide to Accident Response and First Aid Care*. 5th ed. Seattle: Mountaineers Books, 2004.

"Find the Insect Repellent That Is Right for You." US Environmental Protection Agency (EPA). www.epa.gov/insect-repellents/find-insect-repellent-right-you.

Kirkpatrick, Andy. "Cragmanship: Modern Climbing Gear, Technique, and Theory." http://andy-kirkpatrick.com.

Nasci, Roger, et al. "Protection against Mosquitoes, Ticks, & Other Arthropods." Centers for Disease Control and Prevention (CDC), US Department of Health and Human Services, 2015. https://wwwnc.cdc.gov/travel.

Outdoor Gear Lab, various reviews, www.outdoorgearlab.com.

"Pesticides" US Environmental Protection Agency (EPA). www.epa.gov/pesticides.

Recreational Equipment, Inc. (REI) Expert Advice. www.rei.com/learn/expert-advice.html.

Wilkerson, James A., ed. *Medicine for Mountaineering & Other Wilderness Activities*. 6th ed. Seattle: Mountaineers Books, 2010.

Chapter 3: Camping, Food, and Water

Kirkpatrick, Andy, various articles, www.andy-kirkpatrick.com/writing/gear.

Muir, John. *John of the Mountains: The Unpublished Journals of John Muir.* Edited by Linnie Marsh Wolfe. Madison: University of Wisconsin Press, 1979. First published 1938.

Outdoor Gear Lab, various reviews, www.outdoorgearlab.com.

Recreational Equipment, Inc. (REI) Expert Advice, www.rei.com/learn/expert-advice.html.

Tilton, Buck, and Rick Bennett. *Don't Get Sick: The Hidden Dangers of Camping and Hiking.* Seattle: Mountaineers Books, 2002.

Chapter 4: Physical Conditioning

Berardi, John. "The Five Rules for a High-Performance Body," www.precisionnutrition.com/day-1.

Haskell, W. L., et al. "Physical Activity and Public Health: Updated Recommendation for Adults from the American College of Sports Medicine and the American Heart Association." *Medicine & Science in Sports & Exercise* 39, no. 8 (2007): 1423–1434.

Hörst, Eric J. *How to Climb 5.12.* 3rd ed. Guilford, CT: Globe Pequot/Falcon, 2012.

———. *Maximum Climbing: Mental Training for Peak Performance and Optimal Experience.* Helena, MT: Globe Pequot Press, 2010.

———. *Training for Climbing: The Definitive Guide to Improving Your Performance.* Guilford, CT: Falcon, 2016.

Luebben, Craig. *Rock Climbing: Mastering Basic Skills.* 2nd ed. Seattle: Mountaineers Books, 2014.

Schurman, Courtenay W., and Doug G. Schurman. *The Outdoor Athlete.* Champaign, IL: Human Kinetics, 2009.

———. *Train to Climb Mount Rainier or Any High Peak.* Video. Seattle: Body Results, 2002. www.bodyresults.com.

Soles, Clyde. *Climbing: Training for Peak Performance.* 2nd ed. Seattle: Mountaineers Books, 2008.

Twight, Mark, and James Martin. *Extreme Alpinism: Climbing Light, Fast, and High.* Seattle: Mountaineers Books, 1999.

Chapter 5: Navigation

Burns, Bob, and Mike Burns. *Wilderness Navigation.* 3rd ed. Seattle: Mountaineers Books, 2015.

———. *Wilderness GPS.* Seattle: Mountaineers Books, 2013.

CalTopo, USGS topographic maps, www.caltopo.com.

CanMaps, Canadian topographic maps, www.canmaps.com.

Gaia GPS, topo maps and trails available for Google (Android) and Apple (iOS) phones, www.gaiagps.com.

Geological Survey of Canada, Natural Resources Canada, magnetic declination information, www.geomag.nrcan.gc.ca/calc/mdcal-en.php.

Gmap4, enhanced Google Maps and topo maps, https://mappingsupport.com/p/gmap4-free-online-topo-maps.html.

Google Earth, aerial photographs, www.google.com/earth.

MyTopo, USGS topographic maps, www.mytopo.com.

National Oceanic and Atmospheric Administration (NOAA), National Centers for Environmental Information, magnetic declination information, www.ngdc.noaa.gov/geomag/declination.shtml.

Natural Resources Canada (NRCan), Canadian topographic maps, www.nrcan.gc.ca/earth-sciences/geography/topographic-information/maps/9767.

OpenStreetMap (OSM), a collaborative project to create a free editable map of the world; OSM maps available through apps such as Gaia GPS.

Renner, Jeff. *Mountain Weather: Backcountry Forecasting and Weather Safety for Hikers, Campers, Climbers, Skiers, and Snowboarders.* Seattle: Mountaineers Books, 2005.

Trails.com, topographic maps, www.trails.com.

US Coast Guard, Navigation Center, GPS information, www.gps.gov.

US Geological Survey (USGS), topographic maps, https://store.usgs.gov.

Chapter 6: Wilderness Travel

Allen, Dan. *Don't Die on the Mountain.* 2nd ed. New London, NH: Diapensia Press, 1998.

Anderson, Kristi, ed. *Wilderness Basics.* 4th ed. Seattle: Mountaineers Books, 2013.

Berger, Karen. *Everyday Wisdom: 1001 Expert Tips for Hikers.* Seattle: Mountaineers Books, 1997.

———. *More Everyday Wisdom.* Seattle: Mountaineers Books, 2002.

Cosley, Kathy, and Mark Houston. *Alpine Climbing: Techniques to Take You Higher.* Seattle: Mountaineers Books, 2004.

Fletcher, Colin, and Chip Rawlins. *The Complete Walker IV.* New York: Alfred A. Knopf, 2002.

Herrero, Stephen. *Bear Attacks: Their Causes and Avoidance.* Guilford, CT: Lyons Press, 2002.

Nelson, Dan. *Predators at Risk in the Pacific Northwest.* Seattle: Mountaineers Books, 2000.

Petzoldt, Paul. *The New Wilderness Handbook.* New York: W. W. Norton, 1984.

Smith, Dave. *Backcountry Bear Basics.* 2nd ed. Seattle: Mountaineers Books, 2006.

Zawaski, Mike. *Snow Travel: Skills for Climbing, Hiking, and Moving Across Snow.* Seattle: Mountaineers Books, 2012.

Chapter 7: Leave No Trace

Brame, Rich and David Cole. *NOLS Soft Paths: How to Enjoy the Wilderness Without Harming It.* 4th ed. Mechanicsburg, PA: Stackpole Books, 2011.

Leave No Trace Center for Outdoor Ethics. *Outdoor Skills and Ethics.* Boulder, CO: Leave No Trace Center for Outdoor Ethics, n.d. Booklet series covering regions of the United States and a variety of outdoor activities applicable anywhere. www.lnt.org.

Chapter 8: Access and Stewardship

Access Fund, The. *Climbing Management: A Guide to Climbing Issues and the Development of a Climbing Management Plan.* Boulder, CO: The Access Fund, 2008. www.accessfund.org.

Attarian, Aram, and Kath Pyke, comps. *Climbing and Natural Resources Management: An Annotated Bibliography.* Raleigh: North Carolina State University; Boulder, CO: The Access Fund, 2001.

Chouinard, Yvon. "Coonyard Mouths Off." *Ascent* 1, no. 6: 50–52. San Francisco: Sierra Club, 1972.

Leave No Trace Center for Outdoor Ethics. *Skills and Ethics: Rock Climbing.* Boulder, CO: Leave No Trace Center for Outdoor Ethics, 2001. www.lnt.org.

Pritchard, Paul. *Deep Play: A Climber's Odyssey from Llanberis to the Big Walls.* Seattle: Mountaineers Books, 1998.

Chapter 9: Basic Safety System

Animated Knots by Grog, website and app, www.animatedknots.com.

Lewis, S. Peter, and Dan Cauthorn. *Climbing: From Gym to Crag.* Seattle: Mountaineers Books, 2000.

Lipke, Rick. *Technical Rescue Riggers Guide.* 2nd ed. Bellingham, WA: Conterra, 2009.

Luebben, Craig. *Knots for Climbers.* Guilford, CT: Globe Pequot/Falcon, 2001.

Owen, Peter. *The Book of Climbing Knots.* Guilford, CT: Globe Pequot/Falcon, 2000.

Soles, Clyde. *The Outdoor Knots Book.* Seattle: Mountaineers Books, 2004.

Chapter 10: Belaying

Lewis, S. Peter, and Dan Cauthorn. *Climbing: From Gym to Crag.* Seattle: Mountaineers Books, 2000.

Long, John, and Bob Gaines. *Climbing Anchors.* 3rd ed. Guilford, CT: Globe Pequot/Falcon, 2013.

———. *More Climbing Anchors.* Guilford, CT: Globe Pequot/Falcon, 1998.

Luebben, Craig. *Rock Climbing Anchors: A Comprehensive Guide.* Seattle: Mountaineers Books, 2006.

Samet, Matt. *The Climbing Dictionary: Mountaineering Slang, Terms, Neologisms & Lingo.* Seattle: Mountaineers Books, 2011.

Chapter 11: Rappelling

Lewis, S. Peter, and Dan Cauthorn. *Climbing: From Gym to Crag.* Seattle: Mountaineers Books, 2000.

Luebben, Craig. *How to Rappel!* Guilford, CT: Globe Pequot/Falcon, 2000.

———. *Knots for Climbers.* Guilford, CT: Globe Pequot/Falcon, 2001.

Viesturs, Ed, with David Roberts. *No Shortcuts to the Top: Climbing the World's 14 Highest Peaks.* New York City: Broadway Books, 2006.

Chapter 12: Alpine Rock Climbing

Donahue, Topher. *Advanced Rock Climbing: Expert Skills and Techniques.* Seattle: Mountaineers Books, 2016.

Goddard, Dale, and Udo Neumann. *Performance Rock Climbing.* Mechanicsburg, PA: Stackpole Books, 1993.

Hörst, Eric J. *How to Climb 5.12.* 3rd ed. Guilford, CT: Globe Pequot/Falcon, 2012.

Ilgner, Arno. *The Rock Warrior's Way: Mental Training for Climbers.* 2nd ed. La Vergne, TN: Desiderata Institute, 2006.

Layton, Michael A. *Climbing Stronger, Faster, Healthier: Beyond the Basics.* 2nd ed. Self-published, 2014.

Lewis, S. Peter, and Dan Cauthorn. *Climbing: From Gym to Crag.* Seattle: Mountaineers Books, 2016.

Long, John. *How to Rock Climb!* 5th ed. Guilford, CT: Globe Pequot/Falcon, 2010.

———. *Sport and Face Climbing.* Evergreen, CO: Chockstone Press, 1994.

Loughman, Michael. *Learning to Rock Climb.* San Francisco: Sierra Club Books, 1981.

WideFetish, off-width cracks, www.widefetish.com.

Chapter 13: Rock Protection

Long, John, and Bob Gaines. *Climbing Anchors*. 3rd ed. Guilford, CT: Globe Pequot/Falcon, 2013.

———. *Climbing Anchors Field Guide*. 2nd ed. Guilford, CT: Globe Pequot/Falcon, 2014.

———. *More Climbing Anchors*. Guilford, CT: Globe Pequot/Falcon, 1998.

Long, John, and Craig Luebben. *Advanced Rock Climbing*. Guilford, CT: Globe Pequot/Falcon, 1997.

Luebben, Craig. *Rock Climbing Anchors: A Comprehensive Guide*. Seattle: Mountaineers Books, 2006.

Chapter 14: Leading on Rock

Donahue, Topher. *Advanced Rock Climbing: Expert Skills and Techniques*. Seattle: Mountaineers Books, 2016.

Long, John, and Bob Gaines. *Climbing Anchors*. 3rd ed. Guilford, CT: Globe Pequot/Falcon, 2013.

———. *Climbing Anchors Field Guide*. 2nd ed. Guilford, CT: Globe Pequot/Falcon, 2014.

———. *More Climbing Anchors*. Guilford, CT: Globe Pequot/Falcon, 1998.

Long, John, and Craig Luebben. *Advanced Rock Climbing*. Guilford, CT: Globe Pequot/Falcon, 1997.

Luebben, Craig. *Rock Climbing Anchors: A Comprehensive Guide*. Seattle: Mountaineers Books, 2006.

National Park Service. *Technical Rescue Handbook*. 11th ed. US Department of Interior, 2014.

Chapter 15: Aid and Big Wall Climbing

Long, John, and John Middendorf. *Big Walls*. Guilford, CT: Globe Pequot/Falcon, 1994.

Lowe, Jeff, and Ron Olevsky. *Clean Walls*. Video. Ogden, UT: Adaptable Man Productions, 2004.

McNamara, Chris. *How to Big Wall Climb*. Mill Valley, CA: SuperTopo, 2013.

McNamara, Chris, and Chris Van Leuven. *Yosemite Big Walls*. 3rd ed. San Francisco: SuperTopo, 2011.

Ogden, Jared. *Big Wall Climbing: Elite Technique*. Seattle: Mountaineers Books, 2005.

Robbins, Royal. *Advanced Rockcraft*. Glendale, CA: La Siesta Press, 1973.

Chapter 16: Snow Travel and Climbing

Cliff, Peter. *Ski Mountaineering*. Seattle: Pacific Search Press, 1987.

Fyffe, Allen, and Iain Peter. *The Handbook of Climbing*. London: Pelham Books, 1997.

Parker, Paul. *Free-Heel Skiing: Telemark and Parallel Techniques for All Conditions*. 3rd ed. Seattle: Mountaineers Books, 2001.

Prater, Gene, and Dave Felkley. *Snowshoeing: From Novice to Master*. 5th ed. Seattle: Mountaineers Books, 2002.

Soles, Clyde. *Rock and Ice Gear: Equipment for the Vertical World*. Seattle: Mountaineers Books, 2000.

Twight, Mark, and James Martin. *Extreme Alpinism: Climbing Light, Fast, and High*. Seattle: Mountaineers Books, 1999.

Zawaski, Mike. *Snow Travel: Skills for Climbing, Hiking, and Moving across Snow*. Seattle: Mountaineers Books, 2012.

Chapter 17: Avalanche Safety

American Avalanche Association, www.americanavalancheassociation.org.

American Avalanche Association and USDA Forest Service National Avalanche Center. "Snow, Weather, and Avalanches: Observation Guidelines for Avalanche Programs in the United States." Pagosa Springs, CO: American Avalanche Association, 2010. www.fsavalanche.org/observational-guidelines.

American Institute for Avalanche Research and Education (AIARE), http://avtraining.org.

Avalanche.org, www.avalanche.org.

Avalanche Canada, www.avalanche.ca.

Colorado Avalanche Information Center, US avalanche accident reports, http://avalanche.state.co.us/accidents /statistics-and-reporting/.

Ferguson, Sue A., and Edward R. LaChapelle. *The ABCs of Avalanche Safety*. 3rd ed. Seattle: Mountaineers Books, 2003.

LaChapelle, Edward R. *Secrets of Snow: Visual Clues to Avalanche and Ski Conditions*. Seattle: University of Washington Press, 2001.

McClung, David, and Peter Schaerer. *The Avalanche Handbook*. 3rd ed. Seattle: Mountaineers Books, 2006.

Moynier, John. *Avalanche Aware: The Essential Guide to Avalanche Safety*. Guilford, CT: Falcon, 2006.

Northwest Avalanche Center, www.nwac.us.

O'Bannon, Allen, with illustrations by Mike Clelland. *Allen & Mike's Avalanche Book: A Guide to Staying Safe in Avalanche Terrain*. Guilford, CT: Falcon, 2012.

Tremper, Bruce. *Avalanche Essentials: A Step-by-Step System for Safety and Survival*. Seattle: Mountaineers Books, 2013.

———. *Avalanche Pocket Guide: A Field Reference*. Seattle: Mountaineers Books, 2014.

———. *Staying Alive in Avalanche Terrain*. 2nd ed. Seattle: Mountaineers Books, 2008.

Chapter 18: Glacier Travel and Crevasse Rescue

Cosley, Kathy, and Mark Houston. *Alpine Climbing: Techniques to Take You Higher*. Seattle: Mountaineers Books, 2004.

Selters, Andy. *Glacier Travel and Crevasse Rescue*. 2nd ed. Seattle: Mountaineers Books, 2006.

Tyson, Andy, and Mike Clelland. *Glacier Mountaineering: An Illustrated Guide to Glacier Travel and Crevasse Rescue*. Guilford, CT: Globe Pequot/Falcon, 2009.

Tyson, Andy, and Molly Loomis. *Climbing Self-Rescue: Improvising Solutions for Serious Situations*. Seattle: Mountaineers Books, 2006.

Chapter 19: Alpine Ice Climbing

Barry, John. *Snow and Ice Climbing*. Seattle: Cloudcap Press, 1987.

Chouinard, Yvon. *Climbing Ice*. San Francisco: Sierra Club Books, 1978.

Cosley, Kathy, and Mark Houston. *Alpine Climbing: Techniques to Take You Higher*. Seattle: Mountaineers Books, 2004.

Gadd, Will. *Ice and Mixed Climbing: Modern Technique*. Seattle: Mountaineers Books, 2003.

Harmston, Chris. "Myths, Cautions, and Techniques of Ice Screw Placement." Paper presented at 1999 International Technical Rescue Symposium, Fort Collins, CO, November 5–7, 1999.

Isaac, Sean. *Mixed Climbing*. Guilford, CT: Globe Pequot/Falcon, 2004.

Lowe, Jeff. *The Ice Experience*. Chicago: Contemporary Books, 1979.

———. *Ice World: Techniques and Experiences of Modern Ice Climbing*. Seattle: Mountaineers Books, 1996.

Luebben, Craig. *How to Ice Climb!* Guilford, CT: Globe Pequot/Falcon, 2001.

Raleigh, Duane. *Ice Tools and Techniques*. Carbondale, CO: Primedia, 1995.

Soles, Clyde. *Rock and Ice Gear: Equipment for the Vertical World*. Seattle: Mountaineers Books, 2000.

Twight, Mark, and James Martin. *Extreme Alpinism: Climbing Light, Fast, and High*. Seattle: Mountaineers Books, 1999.

Chapter 20: Waterfall Ice and Mixed Climbing

In addition to this list, the waterfall and mixed ice climbing online community is thriving with information and innovation. Look for instructional videos and materials on AMGA- or IFMGA-certified guide websites.

Chouinard, Yvon. *Climbing Ice*. San Francisco: Sierra Club Books, 1978.

Cosley, Kathy, and Mark Houston. *Alpine Climbing: Techniques to Take You Higher*. Seattle: Mountaineers Books, 2004.

Gadd, Will. *Ice and Mixed Climbing: Modern Technique*. Seattle: Mountaineers Books, 2003.

Harmston, Chris. "Myths, Cautions, and Techniques of Ice Screw Placement." Paper presented at 1999 International Technical Rescue Symposium, Fort Collins, CO, November 5–7, 1999.

Issac, Sean. *Mixed Climbing*. Guilford, CT: Globe Pequot/Falcon, 2004.

Lowe, Jeff. *Ice World: Techniques and Experiences of Modern Ice Climbing*. Seattle: Mountaineers Books, 1996.

Luebben, Craig. *How to Ice Climb!* Guilford, CT: Globe Pequot/Falcon, 2001.

Twight, Mark, and James Martin. *Extreme Alpinism: Climbing Light, Fast, and High*. Seattle: Mountaineers Books, 1999.

Chapter 21: Expedition Climbing

Anderson, Dave, and Molly Absolon. *NOLS Expedition Planning*. Mechanicsburg, PA: Stackpole Books, 2011.

Bezruchka, Stephen. *Altitude Illness: Prevention and Treatment*. 2nd ed. Seattle: Mountaineers Books, 2005.

House, Steve, and Scott Johnston. *Training for the New Alpinism: A Manual for the Climber as Athlete*. Ventura, CA: Patagonia Books, 2014.

Houston, Charles. *Going Higher: Oxygen, Man, and Mountains*. 5th ed. Seattle: Mountaineers Books, 2005.

Powers, Phil, and Clyde Soles. *Climbing: Expedition Planning*. Seattle: Mountaineers Books, 2003.

US Army Research Institute of Environmental Medicine. "Altitude Acclimatization Guide," by Stephen R. Muza, Charles S. Fulco, and Allan Cymerman. USARIEM Technical Note TN04-05. Natick, MA: USARIEM, 2004. http://archive.rubicon-foundation.org/xmlui /bitstream /handle/123456789/7616/ADA423388 .pdf?sequence=1.

Chapter 22: Leadership

American Alpine Club and Alpine Club of Canada. *Accidents in North American Mountaineering*. Annual publication. Distributed by Mountaineers Books, Seattle.

Bass, Bernard M., and Ralph Melvin Stogdill. *Bass and Stogdill's Handbook of Leadership*. 3rd ed. New York: Free Press, 1990.

Chatfield, Rob, and Lewis Glenn, eds. *Leadership the Outward Bound Way: Becoming a Better Leader in the Workplace, in the Wilderness, and in Your Community.* Seattle: Mountaineers Books, 2007.

Graham, John. *Outdoor Leadership: Technique, Common Sense, and Self-Confidence.* Seattle: Mountaineers Books, 1997.

Kosseff, Alex. *AMC Guide to Outdoor Leadership.* Boston: Appalachian Mountain Club Books, 2010.

Martin, Bruce. *Outdoor Leadership: Theory and Practice.* Champaign, IL: Human Kinetics Publishers, 2006.

Petzoldt, Paul. *The New Wilderness Handbook.* New York: W. W. Norton, 1984.

Roskelley, John. *Nanda Devi: The Tragic Expedition.* Seattle: Mountaineers Books, 2000.

Chapter 23: Safety

American Alpine Club and Alpine Club of Canada. *Accidents in North American Mountaineering.* Annual publication. Distributed by Mountaineers Books, Seattle.

Barton, Bob. *Safety, Risk, and Adventure in Outdoor Activities.* London: Paul Chapman Publishing, Ltd., 2007.

Diemberger, Kurt. *The Endless Knot: K2, Mountain of Dreams and Destiny.* Seattle: Mountaineers Books, 1991.

Dill, John. "Climbing Safety: Staying Alive." National Park Service, Yosemite National Park Search and Rescue, 2004. www.friendsof yosar.org/climbing.

Twight, Mark, and James Martin. *Extreme Alpinism: Climbing Light, Fast, and High.* Seattle: Mountaineers Books, 1999.

Viesturs, Ed, with Dave Roberts. *No Shortcuts to the Top: Climbing the World's 14 Highest Peaks.* New York City: Broadway Books, 2006.

Chapter 24: First Aid

"Athletic Taping—Ankle: Closed Basket Weave." Marshfield Clinic, 2011. www.marshfieldclinic.org /mHealthyLiving/Documents/Athletic-Taping-An -Ankle.pdf.

Bennett, Brad, et al. "Wilderness Medical Society Practice Guidelines for Treatment of Exercise-Associated Hyponatremia." *Wilderness and Environmental Medicine* 25. no. 4 (2014): S30–S42. www.wemjournal.org/article /S1080-6032(14)00271-3/fulltext.

Bezruchka, Stephen. *Altitude Illness: Prevention and Treatment.* 2nd ed. Seattle: Mountaineers, 2005.

Bowman, Warren D., American Academy of Orthopaedic Surgeons, and National Ski Patrol. *Outdoor Emergency Care: Comprehensive Prehospital Care for Nonurban Settings.* 4th ed. Boston: Jones and Bartlett, 2003.

Carline, Jan D., Martha J. Lentz, and Steven C. Macdonald. *Mountaineering First Aid: A Guide to Accident Response and First Aid Care.* 5th ed. Seattle: Mountaineers Books, 2004.

Connor, Bradley. "Travelers' Diarrhea." *CDC Health Information for International Travel* (The Yellow Book), 2016. wwwnc.cdc.gov/travel/yellowbook/2016 /the-pre-travel-consultation/travelers-diarrhea.

Davis, Kyle P., and Robert W. Derlet. "Cyanoacrylate Glues for Wilderness and Remote Travel Medical Care." *Wilderness and Environmental Medicine* 24 (2013): 67–74. www.wemjournal.org/article/S1080-6032(12)00266-9 /pdf.

Edlich, Richard. "Cold Injuries." Medscape.com, March 2016. http://emedicine.medscape.com/article /1278523-overview#a5.

Fitch, A. M., B. A. Nicks, et al. "Basic Splinting Techniques." *New England Journal of Medicine* 359 (2008): 26.

Forgey, William W., ed. *Wilderness Medical Society Practice Guidelines for Wilderness Emergency Care.* 5th ed. Guilford, CT: Globe Pequot/Falcon, 2006.

Hackett, Peter H., and David R. Shlim. "Altitude Illness." In *CDC Health Information for International Travel.* (The Yellow Book), 2016. wwwnc.cdc.gov/travel /yellowbook/2016/the-pre-travel-consultation /altitude-illness.

Hackett, Peter H., and Robert C. Roach. "High-Altitude Illness." *New England Journal of Medicine* 345, no. 2 (July 12, 2001): 107–114.

Le Baudour, Chris, and David Bergeron. *Emergency Medical Responder: First on Scene.* 10th ed. New York: Pearson, 2015.

Luks, A. M., and E. R. Swenson. "High-Altitude Pulmonary Edema: Prevention and Treatment." *American College of Chest Physicians* 21 (2007): Lesson 22.

National Weather Service Heat Index, www.nws.noaa .gov/om/heat/heat_index.shtml.

Paal, Peter et al. "Termination of Cardiopulmonary Resuscitation in Mountain Rescue." *High Altitude Medicine and Biology,* 13 #3: 200–208. www.alpine-rescue.org/ikar-cisa/documents/2013 /ikar20131013001086.pdf.

Paterson, Ryan, et al. "Wilderness Medical Society Practice Guidelines for Treatment of Eye Injuries and Illnesses in the Wilderness." *Wilderness and Environmental Medicine*, 25 #4 (2014) S19–S29. www.wemjournal.org /article/S1080-6032(14)00268-3/fulltext#s0025.

Risk Management at NOLS. Available at www.nols.edu. January 2017.

Schimelpfenig, Tod, and Linda Lindsey. *NOLS Wilderness First Aid*. 3rd ed. Mechanicsburg, PA: Stackpole Books, 2002.

Shah, Neeraj, et al. "Wilderness Medicine at High Altitude: Recent Developments in the Field." *Open Access Journal of Sports Medicine* 6 (2015): 319–328. www.ncbi.nlm .nih.gov/pmc/articles/PMC4590685/.

Singer, A. J., and A. B. Dagnum. "Current Management of Acute Cutaneous Wounds." *New England Journal of Medicine* 359 (2008): 10.

Singletary, E. M. et al. "Part 15: First Aid: 2015 American Heart Association and Red Cross Guidelines Update for First Aid." *Circulation* 132, no. 8 (2015): S574–S589. http://circ.ahajournals.org /content/132/18_suppl_2 /S574.full.pdf+html.

"Tactical Combat Casualty Care: Medical Personal Guidelines and Curriculum." National Association of Emergency Medical Technicians, 2016. www.naemt .org/education/TCCC/guidelines_curriculum.

"2015 American Heart Association Guidelines for CPR and ECC." https://eccguidelines.heart.org/index.php /circulation/cpr-ecc-guidelines-2.

Van Tilburg, Christopher, ed. *First Aid: A Pocket Guide: Quick Information for Mountaineering and Backcountry Use*. 4th ed. Seattle: Mountaineers Books, 2001.

Warrell, David, and Sarah Anderson, eds. *Expedition Medicine*. 6th ed. New York: Fitzroy Dearborn Publishers, 2003.

Weiss, Eric A. *Wilderness and Travel Medicine: A Comprehensive Guide*. 4th ed. Seattle: Mountaineers Books, 2011.

———. *Wilderness 911: A Step-by-Step Guide for Medical Emergencies and Improvised Care in the Backcountry*. Seattle: Mountaineers Books, 2007.

West, John, Robert Schoene, Andrew Luks, and James Milledge. *High-Altitude Medicine and Physiology*. 5th ed. Boca Raton, FL: CRC Press, 2012.

Wilkerson, James A., ed. *Medicine for Mountaineering and Other Wilderness Activities*. 6th ed. Seattle: Mountaineers Books, 2009.

Wilkerson, James A., and Gordon Giesbrecht. *Hypothermia, Frostbite, and Other Cold Injuries: Prevention, Recognition, and Prehospital Treatment*. 2nd ed. Seattle: Mountaineers Books, 2006.

Wright, Justin, and Arthur Islas. "Concussion Management in the Wilderness," *Wilderness and Environmental Medicine* 25 (2014): 319–324. www.wemjournal.org /article/S1080-6032(14)00007-6/pdf.

Zafren, Ken, et al. "Wilderness Medical Society Practice Guidelines for the Out-of-Hospital Evaluation and Treatment of Accidental Hypothermia." *Wilderness and Environmental Medicine* 25, #no 4 (2014), S66–S85. www.wemjournal.org/article/S1080-6032(14) /00283=x/pdf.

Chapter 25: Alpine Rescue

Fasulo, David. *Self-Rescue*. 2nd ed. Guilford, CT: Globe Pequot/Chockstone, 2011.

Lipke, Rick. *Technical Rescue Riggers Guide*. 2nd ed. Bellingham, WA: Conterra Technical Systems, 2009.

Long, John, and Bob Gaines. *Climbing Anchors*. 3rd ed. Guilford, CT: Globe Pequot/Falcon, 2013.

———. *More Climbing Anchors*. Guilford, CT: Globe Pequot/Falcon, 1998.

May, W. G. *Mountain Search and Rescue Techniques*. Boulder, CO: Rocky Mountain Rescue Group, 1973.

Tyson, Andy, and Molly Loomis. *Climbing Self-Rescue: Improvising Solutions for Serious Situations*. Seattle: Mountaineers Books, 2006.

Chapter 26: Mountain Geology

Association of American State Geologists, www.stategeologists.org.

Google Earth, www.google.com/earth.

Hiking the Geology series (various states). Seattle: Mountaineers Books, various dates.

McPhee, John. *Assembling California*. New York: Farrar, Straus and Giroux, 1993.

———. *Basin and Range*. New York: Farrar, Straus and Giroux, 1981.

Roadside Geology series (various states). Missoula, MT: Mountain Press, various dates. http://geology.com /store/roadside-geology.shtml.

Tabor, Rowland, and Ralph Haugerud. *Geology of the North Cascades: A Mountain Mosaic*. Seattle: Mountaineers Books, 1999.

US Bureau of Land Management, www.blm.gov.

US Forest Service, www.fs.fed.us.

US Geological Survey, www.usgs.gov.

———. Geology in the Parks program, http://3dparks.wr.usgs.gov.

———. National geologic map database, http://ngmdb.usgs.gov.

Chapter 27: The Cycle of Snow

Benn, Douglas I., and David J. A. Evans. *Glaciers and Glaciation*. 2nd ed. Abingdon, UK: Routledge, 2010.

Colbeck, S., et al. *The International Classification for Seasonal Snow on the Ground*. Cambridge, England: International Glaciological Society and International Association of Scientific Hydrology, 1992.

Cuffey, K. M., and W. S. B, Paterson. *The Physics of Glaciers*. 4th ed. Cambridge, MA: Academic Press, 2010.

Ferguson, Sue A. *Glaciers of North America: A Field Guide*. Golden, CO: Fulcrum Publishing, 1992.

Gray, D. M., and D. H. Male, eds. *Handbook of Snow*. New York: Pergamon Press, 1981.

Hobbs, Peter V. *Ice Physics*. Oxford: Claredon Press, 1974.

LaChapelle, Edward R. *Field Guide to Snow Crystals*. Cambridge, England: International Glaciological Society, 1992.

———. *Secrets of Snow: Visual Clues to Avalanche and Ski Conditions*. Seattle: University of Washington Press; Cambridge, England: International Glaciological Society, 2001.

Post, Austin, and Edward R. LaChapelle. *Glacier Ice*. Seattle: University of Washington Press; Cambridge, England: International Glaciological Society, 2000.

Chapter 28: Mountain Weather

Renner, Jeff. *Lightning Strikes: Staying Safe Under Stormy Skies*. Seattle: Mountaineers Books, 2002.

———. *Mountain Weather: Backcountry Forecasting and Weather for Hikers, Campers, Climbers, Skiers, and Snowboarders*. Seattle: Mountaineers Books, 2005.

———. *Mountain Weather Pocket Guide: A Field Reference*. Seattle: Mountaineers Books, 2017.

Schaefer, Vincent J., and John A. Day. *A Field Guide to the Atmosphere*. Boston: Houghton Mifflin Company, 1991.

Whiteman, C. David. *Mountain Meteorology: Fundamentals and Applications*. New York: Oxford University Press, 2000.

Williams, Jack. *The Weather Book: An Easy-to-Understand Guide to the USA's Weather*. 2nd ed, New York: Vintage, 1997.

INDEX

BRAND NAMES AND TRADEMARKS

The following trademarks and brand names are referenced in this ninth edition: Alien and Alien Hybrids (Fixehardware), Allen wrench, Ambit GPS watch (Suunto), Apex Tool Group, ATC Guide (Black Diamond), AvaLung II (Black Diamond), BackCountry Navigator (Critter Map software), Ball Nut (C.A.M.P. USA), Band-Aid (Johnson & Johnson), BaseCamp (Garmin), Block Roll (Kong), Buff, Bug (DMM), CalTopo, Camalot (Black Diamond), Camalot C3 (Black Diamond), Camalot C4 (Black Diamond), Cinch (Trango), Clean Mountain Can (Paul Becker GTS Inc.), Coleman, Diamox (Lederle Laboratories), Dyneema (DSM), Eddy (Edelrid), E Ink (E Ink Corporation), Esbit (Esbit Compaignie GmbH), Ensolite (Armacell), EpiPen (Dey Laboratories), eTrex series GPS (Garmin), European Committee on Standardization (CE), eXplorist series GPS (Magellan), Fat Cam (Metolius), Friend (Wild Country), FullRange (Patagonia), Gaia GPS, Gamow bag (Chinook Medical Gear), Garmin, GigaPower (Snow Peak), Gmap 4, Google Earth, Gore-Tex, Green Trails Maps, Grigri (Petzl), Hexentric (Black Diamond), Ibex, Icebreaker, inReach Explorer+ and inReach SE+ (both Garmin), Kevlar (DuPont), Leave No Trace, Link Cam (Omega Pacific), Lost Arrow (Black Diamond), Lycra (Invista), MICROspikes (Katoola), Micro Traxion (Petzl), MIOX, Molefoam (Dr. Scholl's), Moleskin (Dr. Scholl's), MSR and NeoAir (Cascade Designs, Inc.), OpenStreetMap (OpenStreetMap Foundation), Parsol 1789 (Givaudan), Pecker (Black Diamond), Perlon (Perlon Monofil GmbH), Phillips screwdriver, Polartec Alpha (Polartec), Primus, Pro Traxion (Petzl), Pyramid (Trango), Recreational Equipment, Inc., Reverso 4 (Petzl), RURP (Black Diamond), Screamer (Yates Gear), 2nd Skin (Spenco), SmartWool, Spectra (Honeywell), SPOT (SPOT, LLC), Stairmaster (Nautilus), Steri-Strip (3M), Stopper (Black Diamond), Svea (Optimus), Talon (Black Diamond), TCU (Metolius), Technical Friend (Wild Country), Teflon (DuPont), Therm-a-Rest (Cascade Designs, Inc.), Totem Cams (Totem Cams), Tricam (C.A.M.P. USA), Trivex (PPG), Tyvek (DuPont), UIAA (International Climbing and Mountaineering Federation), Ursack, Velcro, Vergo (Trango), WAG BAG (Phillips Environmental Products), Waste Case (Metolius), WD-40, Wikipedia, Yates Gear Screamer, and Z piton (Leeper).

MOUNTAINEERS BOOKS is a leading publisher of mountaineering literature and guides, as well as adventure narratives, natural history, and general outdoor recreation. Through our two imprints, Skipstone and Braided River, we also publish titles on sustainability and conservation. We are committed to supporting the environmental and educational goals of our organization by providing expert information on human-powered adventure, sustainable practices at home and on the trail, and preservation of wilderness.

The Mountaineers, founded in 1906, is a 501(c)(3) nonprofit outdoor activity and conservation organization whose mission is to enrich lives and communities by helping people "explore, conserve, learn about, and enjoy the lands and waters of the Pacific Northwest and beyond." One of the largest such organizations in the United States, it sponsors classes and year-round outdoor activities throughout the Pacific Northwest, including climbing, hiking, back-country skiing, snowshoeing, camping, kayaking, sailing, and more. The Mountaineers also supports its mission through its publishing division, Mountaineers Books, and promotes environmental education and citizen engagement. For more information, visit The Mountaineers Program Center, 7700 Sand Point Way NE, Seattle, WA 98115-3996; phone 206-521-6001; www.mountaineers.org; or email info@mountaineers.org.

Our publications are made possible through the generosity of donors and through sales of more than 800 titles on outdoor recreation, sustainable lifestyle, and conservation. To donate, purchase books, or learn more, visit us online:

MOUNTAINEERS BOOKS
1001 SW Klickitat Way, Suite 201 • Seattle, WA 98134
800-553-4453 • mbooks@mountaineersbooks.org • www.mountaineersbooks.org

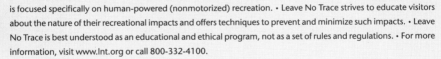
Mountaineers Books is proud to be a corporate sponsor of the Leave No Trace Center for Outdoor Ethics, whose mission is to promote and inspire responsible outdoor recreation through education, research, and partnerships. • The Leave No Trace program is focused specifically on human-powered (nonmotorized) recreation. • Leave No Trace strives to educate visitors about the nature of their recreational impacts and offers techniques to prevent and minimize such impacts. • Leave No Trace is best understood as an educational and ethical program, not as a set of rules and regulations. • For more information, visit www.lnt.org or call 800-332-4100.

OTHER TITLES YOU MIGHT ENJOY FROM MOUNTAINEERS BOOKS

MOUNTAINEERS OUTDOOR EXPERT SERIES
(SELECT TITLES)

AMGA recommended

NOBA winner

AVALANCHE & GLACIER SAFETY

WILDERNESS SKILLS

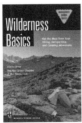
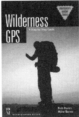
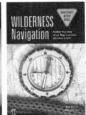

PERSONALITIES & STORIES

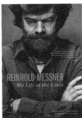

Banff and Boardman–Tasker winner

www.mountaineersbooks.org